PUBLIC INTERNATIONAL LAW

Fifth Edition

Alina Kaczorowska-Ireland

Routledge
Taylor & Francis Group

LONDON AND NEW YORK

Fifth Edition published 2015
by Routledge
2 Park Square, Milton Park, Abingdon, Oxon, OX14 4RN

and by Routledge
711 Third Avenue, New York, NY 10017

Routledge is an imprint of the Taylor & Francis Group, an informa business

First edition published 2002
Fourth edition published 2010

British Library Cataloguing in Publication Data
A catalogue record for this title has been requested

Library of Congress Cataloging-in-Publication Data
Kaczorowska, Alina, author.
  Public international law/ Alina Kaczorowska-Ireland. – Fifth Edition.
  pages cm
  Includes bibliographical references and index.
  ISBN 978–0–415–72235–3 – ISBN 978–0–415–72236–0 – ISBN 978–1–
  315–85833–3 1. International law. I. Title.
  KZ3410.K33 2015
  341–dc23
  2014046927

ISBN: 978-0-415-72235-3 (hbk)
ISBN: 978-0-415-72236-0 (pbk)
ISBN: 978-1-315-85833-3 (ebk)

Typeset in Times New Roman
by Florence Production Ltd, Stoodleigh, Devon, UK
Printed in Great Britain by Ashford Colour Press Ltd.

OUTLINE CONTENTS

DETAILED CONTENTS

PREFACE

In this fifth edition of my book on public international law, I have sought to maintain my 'flagship' style of using a student friendly and simple, but not simplistic, manner of explaining in a comprehendible way those areas of public international law that are usually considered to be complicated. As many will know, part of that style is the insertion into the text of boxes, in which I briefly outline the facts of leading cases, and comment on the content and impact of the judgments on existing law, and its development. In this edition I have occasionally tried to enliven case commentaries by providing details of subsequent events. Additionally, I have chosen to enhance the learning experience of my readers by presenting the end of chapter aides-mémoire in diagrammatic form.

Many readers of previous editions have suggested it might be appropriate for this work to include a chapter on the law of the sea. As my readers will notice I have acted upon that suggestion. In this vein, and bearing in mind that this book has an international audience, I have included additional materials on the way in which international law is interpreted and applied by US courts, and the courts of other jurisdictions. However, I have, as always, paid a lot of attention to new judgments of international courts and tribunals, in particular those of the ICJ.

This edition, as did previous editions, strives to be up to date and of relevance to recent legal and political developments. In this context, it analyses and assesses the work of the International Law Commission on, *inter alia*, the identification of customary international law, reservations to treaties, effects of armed conflicts on treaties, and the expulsion of aliens. At the same time, it examines, among other topics, the controversy concerning the use of force against non-State actors, including targeted killings, the situation in Syria, the progress of Palestine towards statehood, the efforts of the UN to strengthen and enhance the effective functioning of its HRs treaty body system, and the growing importance of non-State actors in the making and breaking of international law.

I am very grateful to many people for their support and encouragement in writing this edition. In particular I would like to express my appreciation to Miss Sumaya Deserai, who assisted me with a lot of research on the law of the sea, my niece Maya Kaczorowski, who was hugely helpful in the preparation of the diagrammatic aides-mémoire, and my very efficient and friendly team of supporters at Routledge, in particular, Fiona Briden and Emma Nugent. I also wish to acknowledge the support received from my faculty and my university.

I hope this edition will inspire readers' enthusiasm for public international law and will, on many pages, be fun to read.

This book is up to date as at 30 November 2014.

Professor Alina Kaczorowska-Ireland,
University of the West Indies, Cave Hill Campus, Barbados.
30 November 2014

TABLE OF CASES

TABLE OF STATUTES

International Statutes

Belgium

Denmark

France

Germany

Hungary

India

Iraq

Israel

USSR

TABLE OF TREATIES

Including Covenants, Treaties, Conventions, ICJ Statute and UN Charter etc.

l

TABLE OF OTHER DOCUMENTS

LIST OF ABBREVIATIONS

AC – Law Reports, Appeal Cases
ACDI – Annuaire Canadien de Droit International
ACHR – American Convention on Human Rights
ACommHPR – African Commission on Human and Peoples' Rights
ACtHPR – African Court of Human and Peoples' Rights
AfrHumRtsLJ – African Human Rights Law journal
AD – Annual Digest and Reports of Public International Law Cases [now International Law Reports]
AEDPA – Effective Death Penalty Act
African Charter – African Charter on Human and Peoples' Rights
AJIL – American Journal of International Law
All ER – All England Law Reports
AMF – Arab Monetary Fund
ANNIDI – Annuaire de l'Institute de Droit International
APCtHPR – Protocol Establsihing the African Court of Human and Peoples' Rights
ASIL – American Society of International Law
AT – Administrative Tribunal of the International Labour Organisation
ATCA – Alien Tort Claims Act
ATS – Antarctic Treaty System
AU – African Union
AUMF – Authorisation for Use of Force Against Terrorists
Australian YIL – Australian Yearbook of International Law
BAD – Banque Africaine de Developpement
BCA – Barbados Court of Appeal
BITs – Bilateral investment treaties
BWC – Convention on the Prohibition of the Development, Production and Stockpiling of Bacteriological (Biological) and Toxin Weapons and in Their Destruction
BYIL – British Yearbook of International Law
CAR – Central African Republic
CAT – Convention against Torture and Other Cruel, Inhuman or Degrading Treatment or Punishment
CCJ – Caribbean Court of Justice
CCM – Convention on Cluster Munitions

CCW – Convention on the Prohibition or Restriction on the Use of Certain Conventional Weapons Which May Be Deemed to be Excessively Injurious or to Have Indiscriminate Effects

CEDAW – Convention on the Elimination of All Forms of Discrimination Against Women

CERD – Convention on the Elimination of All Forms of Racial Discrimination

CFSP – Common Foreign and Security Policy

Ch – English Law Reports, Chancery Division

CIS – Confederation of Independent States

CJA – Criminal Justice Act

CLCS – Commission on the Limits of the Continental Shelf

CMLR – Common Market Law Review

COE – Council of Europe

Colum J Transnatl L – Columbia Journal of Transnational Law

COMECON – Council for Mutual Assistance

CSCE – Conference on Security and Co-operation in Europe

CPIUN – Convention on Privileges and Immunities of the United Nations

CSRT – Combatant Status Review Tribunal

CTA – Central Tracing Agency

CTBT – Comprehensive Nuclear-Test-Ban Treaty

CUP – Cambridge University Press

CWC – Convention on the Prohibition of the Development, Production, Stockpiling and use of Chemical Weapons and on Their Destruction

DA – draft article

DAEA – Draft Articles on the Expulsion of Aliens

DADP – 2006 International Law Commission Draft Articles on Diplomatic Protection

2001 DARSIWA – 2001 International Law Commission Draft Articles on Responsibility of States for Internationally Wrongful Acts

DEA – Drug Enforcement Administration

DPRK – Democratic People's Republic of Korea

DRC – Democratic Republic of Congo

DSST – Designated State Sponsoring Terrorism

DTA – Detainee Treatment Act

Duke J Comp & Int L – Duke Journal of Comparative and International Law

EC – European Community

ECOWAS – Economic Community of West African States

ECHR – European Convention for the Protection of Human Rights and Fundamental Freedoms

ECJ – Court of Justice of the European Union

ECOSOC – United Nations Economic and Social Council

ECR – European Court Reports

ECtHR – European Court of Human Rights

EEC – European Economic Community

EEZ – Exclusive Economic Zone

EHRR – European Human Rights Reports

EJIL – European Journal of International Law

EPC – European Political Co-operation

ERW – Explosive Remnants of War

ETA – Euskadi Ta Askatasuna (Basque Homeland and Freedom Organization)

ETS – European Treaty Series

EU – European Union

EULEX – European Rule of Law Mission

Euratom – European Atomic Energy Community

Fam – Law Reports: Family Division

FAO – Food and Agriculture Organisation of the United Nations

FARC – Revolutionary Armed Forces in Colombia

FLN – Algerian National Liberation Front

FRELIMO – Front for the Liberation of Mozambique

FRETILIN – Revolutionary Front for an Independent East Timor

FRG – Federal Republic of Germany

FSIA – Foreign Sovereign Immunities Act

FRY – Federal Republic of Yugoslavia

Ga J Intl & Comp L – Georgia Journal of International and Comparative Law

GAOR – United Nations General Assembly Official Records

GATT – General Agreement on Tariffs and Trade

GB – Great Britain

GC I-IV – 1949 Geneva Conventions I-IV

GCCS – Geneva Convention on the Continental Shelf

GCHS – Geneva Convention on the High Seas

GCTS – Geneva Convention on the Territorial Sea and Contiguous Zone

GDR – German Democratic Republic

GeoLJ – Georgetown Law Journal

GGE – Groups of Governmental Experts

GPBHR – Guiding Principles on Business and Human Rights

GYIL – German Yearbook of International Law

HarvardILJ – Harvard International law Journal

HowLJ – Howard Law Journal

HRA – Human Rights Act

HRC – Human Rights Committee

HRL – Human Rights Law

HRLRev – Human Rights Law Review

HRs – Human Rights

HumRtsQ – Human Rights Quarterly

IAC – Iraqi Airways Company

IACommHR – Inter-American Commission on Human Rights

IACtHR – Inter-American Court of Human Rights

IAEA – International Atomic Energy Agency

ICC – International Criminal Court

ICCPR – International Covenant on Civil and Political Rights

ICESCR – International Covenant on Economic, Social and Cultural Rights

ICJ – International Court of Justice

ICJ Rep – International Court of Justice, Reports of Judgments, Advisory Opinions and Orders

ICLQ – International and Comparative Law Quarterly
ICRC – International Committee of the Red Cross
ICSID – International Centre for Settlement of Investment Disputes
ICTR – International Criminal Tribunal for Rwanda
ICTY – International Criminal Tribunal for the Former Yugoslavia
IGO – Inter-governmental Organisation
IHL – International Humanitarian Law
IHRR – International Human Rights Reports
IIAs – International Investment Agreements
ILC – International Law Commission
ILM – International Legal Materials
ILO – International Labour Organisation
ILR – International Law Reports
IMF – International Monetary Fund
IMO – International Maritime Organisation
IMT – International Military Tribunal
IMTFE – International Military Tribunal for the Far East
Int Arb – International Arbitration
IRA – Irish Republican Army
IRRC or IntlRevRedCross – International Review of the Red Cross
Israel YBHumRts – Israel Yearbook of Human Rights
ISA – International Seabed Authority
ITC – International Tin Council
ITLOS – International Tribunal for the Law of the Sea
JBioecon – Journal of Bioeconomics
JConflictResol – Journal of Conflict Resolution
J Int Criminal Justice – Journal of International Criminal Justice
JICL – Journal of International and Comparative Law
J Int Disp Settlement – Journal of International Disputes Settlement
JWT – Journal of World Trade
KAC – Kuwait Airways Corporation
KB – English Law Report's, King's Bench
KFOR – Kosovo Force
LJIL – Leiden Journal of International Law
Lloyd's Rep – Lloyd's Law Reports
LNOJ – League of Nations Official Journal
LNTS – League of Nations Treaty Series
LOSC – United Nations Convention on the Law of the Sea
LR – Law Reports: Admiralty and Ecclesiastical
LQR – Law Quarterly Review
Max Planck Yrbk UNL – Max Planck Yearbook of United Nations Law
MLR – Modern Law Review
MNC – Multinational corporation
MOTAPM – Mines Other than Anti-Personnel Mines
MSPA – Maritime Security Patrol Area
NAFTA – North American Free Trade Organisation

NATO – North Atlantic Treaty Organisation
NCT – National Transitional Council
NGO – Non-Governmental Organisation
NILR – Netherlands International Law Review
NM – nautical mile
NPT – Non-Proliferation Treaty
NWFZ – Nuclear-Weapons-Free-Zones
NYR – New York Reports
NYIL or **NILR** – Netherlands Yearbook of International Law
NYU J Int L & Pol – New York University Journal of International Law and Policy
NYS – New York Supplement
OAS – Organisation of the American States
OAU – Organisation of African Union
OCO – Overseas Contingency Operations
OJ – Official Journal of the European Union
ONUC – United Nations Operation in Congo
OPCW – Organisation for the Prohibition of Chemical Weapons
OPT-I – First Optional Protocol
OPT-II – Second Optional Protocol
OR – Ontario Reports
OSCE – Organisation for Security and Co-operation in Europe
OUP – Oxford University Press
P – Law Reports, Probate, Divorce and Admiralty Division, 1891
PAIGC – African Part for the Independence of Guinea and Cape Verde
PCA – Permanent Court of Arbitration
PCIJ – Permanent Court of International Justice
PD – Law Reports, Probate, Divorce and Admiralty Division, 1875–1890
PLO – Palestine Liberation Organisation
POLISARIO – Frente Popular de Liberación de Saguía el Hamra y Río de Oro (Popular Front for the Liberation of Saguía el-Hamra and Río de Oro)
POW – prisoner of war
PRC – People's Republic of China
PSI – Proliferation Security Initiative
QB – Law Reports: Queen's Bench Division
QBD – Law Reports: Queen's Bench Division
RdC or **RCADI** – Recueil des Cours de L'Academie de Droit International de la Haye
RDI – Revue de Droit International
RD McGill – Revue de Droit de McGill
RHDI – Revue Hellénique de Droit International
RIAA – United Nations Reports of International Arbitral Awards
ROC – Republic of China (Taiwan)
RUF – Revolutionary United Front
R2P – Responsibility to Protect
SCR – Supreme Court Reports (Canada)
SCSL – Special Court for Sierra Leone
SEA – Single European Act

SFRY – Socialist Federal Republic of Yugoslavia
SIA – State Immunity Act
SLT – Scots Law Times
SOFAs – Status of Forces Agreements
SOI – statements of interest
S/Res – United Nations Security Council Resolutions
SWAPO – South West Africa People's Organisation
SYBIL – Singapore Year Book of International Law
T&T – Trinidad and Tobago
TEU – Treaty on European Union
TFEU – Treaty on the Functioning of the European Union
Transnatl L & Contemp Probs – Transnational Law and Contemporary Problems
TRNC – Turkish Republic of Northern Cyprus
TVPA – Torture Victim Protection Act
UAE – United Arab Emirates
UCMJ – Uniform Code of Military Justice
UDHR – Universal Declaration of Human Rights
UK – United Kingdom
UKHL – United Kingdom House of Lords
UKHRR – United Kingdom Human Rights Reports
UKMIL – United Kingdom Materials in International Law
UN – United Nations
UN Immunity Convention – United Nations Convention on Jurisdictional Immunities of States and Their Property
UN SCOR – United Nations Security Council Official Records
UNHRC – United Nations Human Rights Council
UNCLOS – United Nations Conference on the Law of the Sea
UNCTAD – United Nations Conference on Trade and Development
UNDC – United Nations Disarmament Commission
UNDOF – United Nations Disengagement Observer Force
UNEF I – United Nations Emergency Force in the Middle East
UNESCO – United Nations Educational, Scientific and Cultural Organisation
UNGA – General Assembly of the United Nations
UNGARs – UN General Assembly Resolutions
UNICITRAL – United Nations Commission on International Trade Law
UNMIK – United Nations Mission in Kosovo
UNMOVIC – United Nations Monitoring, Verification and Inspection Commission
UNPROFOR – United Nations Protective Force
UNSC – United Nations Security Council
UNS-G – Secretary General of the United Nations
UNSCOM – United Nations Special Commission
UNTAET – United Nations Transitional Administration in East Timor
UNTSO – United Nations Truce Supervision Organisation
UNTS – United Nations Treaty Series
UNYB – United Nations Year Book
UPR – Universal Periodic Review

US – United States of America
US – United States Reports (Supreme Court)
VaJIntIL – Virginia Journal of International Law
VandJTransnatL – Vanderbilt Journal of Transnational Law
VCCR – Vienna Convention on Consular Realtions
VCDR – Vienna Convention on Diplomatic Relations
VCLT – Vienna Convention on the Law of Treaties
VDPA – Vienna Declaration and Programme of Action
Ves. Jun – Vesey Junior's Chancery Reports
WEU – Western European Union
WGC – Working Group on Communications
WGS – Working Group on Situations
WHO – World Health Organisation
WIPO – World Intellectual Property Organisation
WLR – Weekly Law Reports
WMD – Weapons of Mass Destruction
WTO – World Trade Organisation
WWI – World War I
WWII – World War II
YaleJIntIL (or **YJIL**) – Yale Journal of International Law
YBILC – Yearbook of the International Law Commission
2001 DARSIWA – Draft Articles on Responsibility of States for Internationally Wrongful
Acts

GLOSSARY OF LATIN
AND FOREIGN WORDS
AND MAXIMS

Á titre de sovereign – as a sovereign

Ab initio – from the beginning

Acta jure imperii – public acts of a State

Acta jure gestionis – private acts of a State, such as trading and commercial activities

Actio in personam – an action against the person, founded on a personal liability

Actio popularis – action by a person or a group in the name of the general public without being a direct victim or being authorised by a victim to represent him

Actio in rem – in admiralty law, an action directed against a specific thing (as a ship or an aircraft) irrespective of the ownership of it, to enforce a claim or lien upon it, or to obtain, out of the thing or out of the proceeds of its sale, satisfaction for an injury alleged by the claimant

AD – Anno Domini. The year of our Lord

Ad hoc – for this, for a particular purpose

Ad litem – for the suit

Alter ego – the other I, a second self

Amicus curiae – friend of the court, a third party allowed to submit a legal opinion to the court

Amparo – protection, refuge. A form of constitutional relief found in the legal systems of various Latin American countries and the Philippines While *habeas corpus* remedies protect physical liberty the *amparo* seeks to protect all rights other than physical liberty.

Animus possidendi – an intention and will to act as sovereign

Aut dedere aut judicare – extradite or prosecute

Bona fides – good faith

Certiorari – to be informed of, to be made certain in regard to

Clausula rebus sic stantibus – at this point of affairs; in these circumstances, things remaining as they are

Comitas – courteousness, comity

Compromis – an agreement between parties to an already existing dispute to submit it to adjudication

Consolato del Mare – Regulation of the Sea, one of the oldest Maritime Code

Contra legem – against the law

Corpus juris gentium – a body of public international law

Coup d'état – sudden takeover of the government of a country by elements from within that country (usually by military) generally carried out by violent or illegal means

Culpa – fault, neglect or negligence, responsibility for wrongdoing

Curia – an association of men, a court of law

Coutume grande-vitesse – high speed customs

Damnum emergens – the loss suffered, as opposed to lucrum cessans (see below)

Debellatio – defeating, the enemy, complete subjection and annexation of a foreign State

De facto – in fact

De jure – by right, by law, according to law

De Jure Belli ac Pacis – the Law of War and Peace

De lega lata – the law as it is

De lege feranda – what the law ought to be rather than what it is

Dies a quo – the day from which

Dies ad quem – the day of the expiry of a time-limit

Dolus malus – an evil intent

Equity intra legem – equity which operates within the boundaries of law

Erga omnes – against everybody

Etc (et cetera) – and others of a like character, and so on, and so forth

Et seq – and the following

Ex aequo et bono – in justice and fairness, according to what is fair and just

Excess de pouvoir – exceeds one's competence

Ex gratia – out of kindness, voluntary

Ex officio – from office, by virtue of the office or position, by right of office

Ex parte – on one side only, done for, on behalf of, or on the application of, one party

Expression unius est exclusio alterius – the expression of one thing is the exclusion of another. This means that express mention of one thing implies the exclusion of another

Fides – faith, honesty

Force majeure – greater force. In law this refers to the occurrence of an irresistible force or of an unforeseen event, beyond one's the control

Forum – a court of justice, a place of jurisdiction, a place of litigation

Forum prorogatum – prorogation of the court jurisdiction based on the consent of the parties

Franc-tireurs – free shooters

Grundnorm – a basic hypothetical norm on which all subsequent norms are based, i.e. every law can be traced back to another law that validates it as a law until the final source can be found in a 'basic norm'

Habeas corpus – to produce the body, a court petition which seeks that a person being detained be produced before a judge for hearing to decide whether the detention is lawful

Hostis humani generis – an enemy of the human race

Ibid – an abbreviated form of 'ibidem' – in the same place, in the same book, on the same page

Id est (ie) – that is

Il principe – the prince

In abstracto – theoretically, reasoning on general terms without taking account of a factual situation, opposed to in concreto

In camera – in private

In lieu – in place

Intra legem – within the boundaries of law

Inter alia – among other things

Interim – in the meantime

Inter pares – between peers, between those who stand on a level of equality

Inter partes – between parties

Inter se – between themselves

Ipso facto – by the fact itself, by the mere fact

Jura novit curia – the court knows the law

Jus ad bellum – law regulating the resort to war

Jus civile – law applicable to relations between citizens of ancient Rome

Jus cogens – compelling law, imperative, peremptory rules of international legal order

Jus dispositivum – legal rules that can be disposed of at convenience of the parties concerned

Jus fetiale – religious rules which governed ancient Rome's external relations and formal declarations of war

Jus gentium also referred as jus volontarium – law of peoples, law of nations

Jus in bello – law regulating the conduct of war

Jus missionis – law regulating diplomatic relations

Jus natural – the law of nature. Law inherent in nature that may be ascertained by reason

Jus strictum – mandatory rules

Jus tractatus – law relating to treaties

Jus voluntarium – see jus gentium

kompetenz kompetenz – competence-competence. The ability of an entity, usually an arbitral tribunal, to rule on the question of whether it has jurisdiction to adjudicate a case

La forme conforme le fond – form must agree with substance

Levée en masse – mass uprising

Lex fori – the law of the place where the court adjudicating the case is located

Lex mercatoria – merchant law

Lex posterior derogat priori – a later statute takes away the effect of a prior one

Lex situs – the law of the State where immovable property is situated

Lex specialis derogat lex generalis – a special statute overrules a general statute

Lex superior derogat lex inferiori – laws of a superior hierarchy prevail over the laws of an inferior hierarchy

Locus standi – recognised position, right to intervene, right to appear in court

Lucrum cessans – the loss of prospective profits

Magna Carta – the great charter. The name of a charter (or constitutional enactment) granted by King John of England to the barons, at Runnymede, on 15 June 1215. It is regarded as the foundation of English constitutional liberty

Male captus bene detentus – wrongly captured, properly detained. This refers to the controversial principle under which a person's unlawful arrested will not affect the jurisdiction of a court to try him

Mare librum – the free sea

Médécins Sans Frontières – medical doctors without borders. An IGO which performs medical and humanitarian tasks whenever and wherever needed

Modus vivendi – the way of living

Ne bis in idem – not twice for the same, this means that no legal action can be instituted twice for the same cause of action

Non liquet – it is not clear

Non ultra petita – not beyond. This refers to powers of an adjudicating body which cannot decide more than it has been asked to

Note Verbale – is a diplomatic communication more formal than an aide-mémoire and less formal than a note. It is unsigned and written in the *third person*

Nulla crimen sine lege – no crime without a pre-existing law making the act a crime

Nulla poena sine lege – no punishment without a pre-existing prohibitary rule of law

Nullum crimen sine poena – no crime without punishment

Nuncius (plural nuncii) – the Pope's legate, the official representative of the Pope at a foreign court or seat of government

Obiter dictum – a remark by the way, any statement of the law made by the court merely by way of illustration, not necessarily concerning the case or essential to its determination

Opinio iuris sive necessitates – of the opinion that it is a necessary law. According to this maxim that a State must perceive a practice as one that it is obliged by international law to observe in order for that practice to become a rule of customary law

Pacta sunt servanda – agreements must be kept

Pacta tertiis nec nocent nec prosun – a treaty applies only between the parties to it

Par in parem non habet imperium – legal persons of equal standing cannot have their disputes settled in the courts of one of them

Par lui-même – by itself

Per se – by himself or itself, in itself, taken alone, inherently, in isolation

Persona non grata – person not wanted. A State is entitled, at any time and without any explanation, to declare a foreign diplomat duly accredited as unwanted on its territory

Piepowder or Pie powder courts – medieval merchant courts which settled disputes at fairs. Piedpowder comes from ancient French ('pied-pouldre' which means 'dusty footed')

Polis – a city-State in ancient Greece

Praetor peregrines – in ancient Rome a judicial magistrate who decided cases between foreigners and between Roman citizens and foreigners. He applied jus gentium (see above) to disputes

Prima facie – at first sight, on the face of it, so far as can be judged from the first disclosure

Proxeny – pro means for and xeny means stranger. This was an arrangement in *ancient Greece* between a citizen chosen by the city and a foreign ambassador whereby the citizen hosted, at his own expense, the ambassador, in return for honorary titles from the State represented by the ambassador

Qua – considered as, in the capacity of

Quorum – a minimum number of members of a *deliberative body* necessary to conduct the business of that group

Raison d'être – reason for being

Ratio decidendi – the reason for deciding. The principle or principles on the basis of which a court decides the case before it

Ratione loci – by reason of location

Ratione materiae – by reason of the matter involved

Ratione personae – by reason of the person concerned

Ratione temporis – by reason of time

Rebus sic stantibus – thing remaining as they are

Refoulment – turn back, push back. In refugee law a principle prohibiting expulsion of a refugee to a country where he may be persecuted

Regime – system, arrangement, order, procedure

Res – a thing

Res communis – a thing which belongs to everybody. In ancient Rome a property that belonged to Rome. In international law a thing which belongs to the community of nations, cannot be acquired by any nation and its use is free of charge

Res derelicta – abandoned property

Res judicata – when a matter has been finally adjudicated upon by a court of competent jurisdiction. It may not be reopened or challenged by the original parties or their successors in interest

Res nullius – a thing that belongs to no one. A property of nobody

Restitutio in integrum – restoration to the original position

Sancta sedes – the Holy See. This refers to the chair of St Peter, i.e. to the Pope

Sine qua non – an indispensable requisite or condition

Stare decisis – old decisions. The doctrine according to which when a court has once laid down a principle of law as applicable to a certain state of facts, it will adhere to that principle, and apply it to all future cases, where the facts are substantially the same

Statu nascendi – in the process of development; in the process of emerging, being born

Status quo ante – the state of things as it used to be

Sui generis – of its own kind, unique

Summa potestas – supreme power of command

Supra – above

Telos – purpose

Terra nullius – a territory which belongs to no one

Troika – a group of three people working together, especially in an administrative or managerial capacity

Travaux preparatoires – preparatory works. They are the official record of a *negotiation* of a treaty

Thalweg – in rivers the deepest channel continuously used for navigation

Tu quoque – you did it too

Ultra vires – beyond the powers. An act which is beyond the powers or authority of the person or organisation which took it

Ut res magis valiat quam pereat – that the matter may have effect rather than fail

Uti possedetis – whatever you possess is yours

Via – by way or by means of

Vice versa – the other way round

Vis-à-vis – in relation to

Volenti non fit injuria – no injury is done to a person who consents

Volte-face – turn the face. This refers to a complete change of opinion or policy

1

HISTORY AND NATURE OF INTERNATIONAL LAW

CHAPTER OUTLINE

1 Definition of international law

There are many definitions of international law. Their content depends on the time and context in which they were formulated, and the perspective from which international law was viewed, e.g. positivist, naturalist, feminist, sociological, or ethical. Nevertheless, Professor Shearer's following definition encompasses the main features of international law:

> International law may be defined as that body of law which is composed for its greater part of the principles and rules of conduct which states feel themselves bound to observe, and therefore, do commonly observe in their relations with each other, and which includes also:
> (a) the rules of law relating to the functioning of international institutions or organisations, their relations with each other, and their relations with states and individuals; and
> (b) certain rules of law relating to individuals and non-states so far as the rights or duties of such individuals and non-state entities are the concern of the international community.

1

2   A brief history of international law

A brief history of international law, beginning with ancient times, is relevant to the understanding of many rules and principles of international law.

A.   From Ancient Times to the Middle Ages

The first recorded treaties concluded around 2100 BC between rulers of ancient Eastern Mediterranean States were based on the principle of *pacta sunt servanda* (i.e. agreements must be kept) and the principle of good faith. Both principles were recognised by the 1969 Vienna Convention of the Law of Treaties (VCLT) as being fundamental principles of the modern law of treaties (see Chapter 3).

Ancient Greece's contribution to the development of international law was the establishment of a highly sophisticated system of international arbitration and the institution of *proxeny* (State hospitality) which is at the root of consular protection of foreigners. Further, certain rules of conduct of wars aimed at restricting the worst atrocities developed between ancient Greek city States, e.g. if a city was captured, those who had taken refuge in a temple were to be spared, and prisoners were to be ransomed or exchanged, or at worst to be enslaved but not killed,

Imperial Rome's contribution was the development of:

■ *jus fetiale*, consisting of religious rules, which governed Rome's external relations and formal declarations of war which, *inter alia*, recognised the inviolability of ambassadors, and was at the origin of the distinction between 'just' and 'unjust' war;

■ *jus gentium*, which governed relations between Roman citizens and foreigners. It became an essential part of Roman law and thus greatly influenced all European legal systems and, through them, public international law;

■ the doctrine of 'just' war by Cicero;

■ the doctrine of the universal law of nature known as 'natural law'.

B.   The Middle Ages

In the Middle Ages two sets of truly international rules developed, one being the *lex mercatoria* which consisted of rules of conduct and fair dealing between merchants and the other being maritime customary law. The doctrine of 'just' and 'unjust' war was further developed by St Augustine of Hippo, and later refined by St Thomas Aquinas (see Chapter 15.2.2), and the first attempts were made at restraining the methods and means of warfare and maintaining peace through the institution of the Peace of God (see Chapters 15.2.2. and 17.3).

C.   From the 1648 Peace Treaty of Westphalia to the 1815 Congress of Vienna

The period from the 1648 Peace Treaty of Westphalia to the 1815 Congress of Vienna is considered as the period of formation of 'classical' international law. The 1648 Treaty of Westphalia, which is often referred to as the constitutional treaty of Europe, recognised the principles of sovereignty, territorial integrity and the equality of States. It legitimised the principle of non-interference in the affairs of a State and recognised that a State was independent of the Church. Further, the Treaty established a system of balance of power, which lasted until the French Revolution and the Napoleonic Wars, and was aimed at preventing wars.

The intellectual support for new ideas was provided by scholars, in particular the Anglo-Dutch School represented by Hugo Grotius and Alberto Gentilli.

At the end of the eighteenth century, the enlightenment ideals supporting the aspirations of the British colonies in North America which were fighting for independence from the British Monarchy, and supporting the French people fighting against France's monarchist tyranny, feudal aristocratic privileges and the Catholic clergy had great influence on the development of human rights (see Chapter 12.1) and the principle of self-determination (see Chapter 13).

D. From the 1815 Congress of Vienna to the outbreak of WWI in 1914

The 1815 Congress of Vienna codified the law on diplomatic agents and missions, prohibited slave trading and laid the foundations for the free navigation of rivers which flow through at least two European States. At the Congress the five powers (The UK, Austria, Prussia and Russia who were joined by France in1818) promised to meet periodically over the next 20 years to discuss common problems and to co-operate on major issues to prevent war. The main objective of the Congress was to achieve a new balance of powers in Europe which would guarantee stability, peace and the status quo in Europe. In order to achieve this, territorial arrangements were made to ensure that no European State would be more powerful than any other and therefore no State would be able to build an empire similar to that built by Napoleon. The restoration of legitimate rulers and the prevention of political revolutions, similar to the 1789 French revolution, supported the new system of balance of powers. The so-called Concert of Europe which developed out of the Congress of Vienna was mostly successful in preserving peace in Europe for almost a century. It constituted the first serious attempt in modern times to establish an international mechanism to maintain peace. The system of periodic meetings also began a new diplomatic era in Europe which was marked by the adoption of numerous multilateral treaties.

The main features of international law during the period 1815–1914 were as follows:

- the unorganised character of the international community, which was composed of a multitude of sovereign States legally equal;

- the acceptance of war as the ultimate instrument of enforcing law and safeguarding national honour and interests;

- the recognition of States as the only subjects of international law.

The nineteenth century was the century of positivism which was enunciated by the French philosopher Auguste Compte. The foundations of positivism in law were laid down by John Austin and Jeremy Bentham.

The second half of the nineteenth century saw the emergence of international organisations, e.g. the International Committee of the Red Cross in the 1860s and the Universal Postal Union in 1874.

3 The nature of international law

The status of international law as 'law' has been challenged at both the theoretical level (by John Austin (1790–1859) and by H.L.A. Hart (1907–1992), and at the practical level. The main argument against the existence of international law as 'law' is that international law does not have any legislature, judiciary or executive within the usual understanding of these terms, responsible for creation, interpretation and enforcement of that law.

The most convincing arguments in favour of the existence of international law as law are that States recognise and observe international law (with the consequence that there is substantial order in international relations) and that international law is practised on a daily basis by international lawyers, intergovernmental organisations (IGOs) and other non-State actors, and applied by domestic and international courts.

4 Enforcement of international law

Methods of enforcement of international law differ from those available under municipal law because international law does not have all the attributes of municipal law i.e. there is no legislature, judiciary or executive. However, the fact that international law has no centralised process of enforcement does not mean that international law is not obeyed. A State obeys international law because:

- the prospective long term advantage of compliance prevails over any short term advantage resulting from violation of international law;

- it wants to maintain its good Reputation; it fears Retaliatory measures or measures based on Reciprocity that may be taken by a victim State ('the three Rs compliance');

- the United Nations Security Council (UNSC) may take various measures, including the use of force, under Chapter VII of the UN Charter to force a State to comply with international law;

- it is bound under many international treaties to accept the compulsory jurisdiction and the judgments of a body established by treaty to deal with disputes arising out of it;

- it fears public opinion both at home and abroad.

Enforcement of international criminal law against individuals is ensured by the International Criminal Court (ICC) which has jurisdiction to prosecute and punish individuals responsible for the most serious violations of human rights law (HRL) and international humanitarian law (IHL) as well as by other international criminal courts, by States, and by individuals who may bring criminal or civil actions in national courts against foreign persons who have violated international law.

5 Situations to which international law is relevant

The situations to which international law is relevant are:

- Co-operation. States are naturally interdependent in many ways and international law facilitates co-operation.

- Co-existence. States have to co-exist with one another and a way of facilitating this is to define their relationships by making treaties and other consensual agreements.

- Conflict. Here, the role of international law is confined to two main functions, i.e. the prescribing of technical rules of conduct and the keeping of any conflict to a minimum.

1.1 Definition of international law

There are many definitions of international law. Their content depends on the time and context in which they were formulated and the perspective from which international law was viewed, e.g. positivist, naturalist, feminist, sociological and ethical.

Some examples of definitions of international law are:

In the *SS Lotus Case* (*France* v *Turkey*)[1] the Permanent Court of International Justice (PCIJ) provided the following definition:

> International law governs relations between independent states. The rules of law binding upon states therefore emanate from their own will as expressed in conventions [treaties] or by usages generally accepted as expressing principles of law established in order to regulate the relations between these co-existing independent communities or with a view to the achievement of common aims.

In *Trendtex Trading Corporation* v *Central Bank of Nigeria*[2] an English judge gave a definition of international law in terms of its impact on English law:

> I know no better definition of it than that it is the sum of rules or usages which civilised states have agreed shall be binding upon them in their dealing with one another.
>
> It is quite true that whatever has received the common consent of civilised nations must have received the assent of our country, and that to which we have assented along with other nations in general may be called international law, and as such will be acknowledged and applied by our municipal tribunals when legitimate occasion arises for those tribunals to decide questions to which doctrines of international law may be relevant.

The Restatement (Third) of Foreign Relations Law of the United States provides the following definition:

> International law, as used in this Restatement, consists of rules and principles of general application dealing with the conduct of states and of international organisations and with their relations inter se, as well as with some of their relations with persons, whether natural or juridical.[3]

The definition formulated by the US Department of State and the American Law Institute emphasises the evolving nature of international law. It states that:

> International law is the standard of conduct, at a given time, for states and other entities thereto. It comprises the rights, privileges, powers, and immunities of states and entities invoking its provisions, as well as the correlative fundamental duties, absence of rights, liabilities, and disabilities. International law is, more or less, in a continual state of change and development. In certain of its aspects the evolution is gradual; in others it is avulsive. International law is based largely on custom, e.g. on practice, and whereas certain customs are recognised as obligatory, others are in retrogression and are recognised as non-obligatory, depending upon the subject matter and its status at a particular time.[4]

---

1   (1927) PCIJ Rep Ser A No 10, 1.
2   [1977] 1 All ER 881, 901 and 902.
3   *Restatement (Third) of Foreign Relations Law of the United States*, §101, 3rd edn, St Paul, MN: American Law Inst Publishers, 1987.
4   I.M. Whiteman, *Digest of International Law*, Washington, DC: US Department of State, 1963.

The definition formulated by Professor Shearer is the most comprehensive. It states that:

> International law may be defined as that body of law which is composed for its greater part of the principles and rules of conduct which states feel themselves bound to observe, and therefore, do commonly observe in their relations with each other, and which includes also:
>
> (a) the rules of law relating to the functioning of international institutions or organisations, their relations with each other, and their relations with states and individuals; and
>
> (b) certain rules of law relating to individuals and non-states so far as the rights or duties of such individuals and non-state entities are the concern of the international community.[5]

Professor Shearer's definition describes the actual practice of States although it may be criticised for lack of flexibility in that it does not put emphasis on the fact that the content of international law is constantly on the move. However, it can be said that some basic general aspects of international law are relatively constant, e.g. diplomatic law and the law of treaties.

1.2 A brief history of international law

The basic structure, and many principles, of international law are deeply rooted in history. Accordingly, a brief history of international law, beginning with ancient times, is relevant to the understanding of international law.

Two points should be noted:

■ Apart from a sketchy reference to ancient Eastern Mediterranean civilisations, it is beyond the scope of this book to examine the development of international law in civilisations other than European.[6]

■ This chapter's historical examination of international law ends at 1919. This is done on purpose. The creation of the League of Nations in 1919, a forerunner of the UN, was a turning point in the shaping of modern international law. Events and developments from 1919 onwards are, where appropriate, dealt with in the main text of this work.

1.2.1 Ancient times

It is impossible to fix a precise date or period in history which marks the beginning of international law as it predates recorded history. It presumably began when a politically organised group came into contact with another group and was prepared to treat that group as equal and, at the same time, felt the need to develop a system of rules to regulate their relations.

One of the first pieces of evidence of international law is a solemn treaty signed around 2100 BC between the rulers of Lagash and Umma (small city States in Mesopotamia) which defined the boundaries between them.

In 1400 BC the Egyptian Pharaoh Rameses II concluded a Treaty of Peace, Alliance and Extradition with the King of Cheta, which recognised the territorial sovereignty over certain areas of each ruler and provided for the extradition of refugees and the exchange of ambassadors.[7]

---

5   In *Starke's International Law*, 11th edn, London: Butterworths, 1994, 3.

6   On this topic see: B. Fassbender and A. Peters (eds), *The Oxford Handbook of History of International Law*, Oxford: Oxford University Press, 2012, and S.C. Neff, *Justice Among Nations, A History of International Law*, Cambridge, MA: Harvard University Press, 2014.

7   C. Fenwick, *International Law*, 4th edn, New York: Appleton-Century Crofts, 1965, 5–6.

The grand empires of Egypt, Mesopotamia, Persia, Assyria and Chaldea, as well as small Hebrew monarchies and the Phoenician city States, concluded treaties based on the equality of signatories, the principle of '*pacta sunt servanda*' (agreements are to be kept) and the principle of good faith.

1.2.1.1   Ancient Greece (1100 BC–146 AD)

Ancient Greece adopted two institutions from oriental civilisations – the technique of treaties and the art of diplomacy – and added two of its own: international arbitration and *proxeny* (State hospitality) which is at the origin of consular protection of foreigners.

Ancient Greece had few relations with its neighbours, but because it consisted of a series of cities independent from one another, certain rules grew up as to how the cities should relate to each other. This was facilitated by their common Greek identity and culture. The rules were:

- war should be avoided;

- war should only be commenced by a declaration;

- heralds were not be harmed;

- soldiers killed in battle were entitled to burial;

- if a city was captured, those who had taken refuge in a temple were to be spared;

- prisoners were to be ransomed or exchanged, or at worst enslaved, but not killed;

- priests and seers were exempt.

Although the Greeks considered the above to be religious obligations and so they are, sometimes, not considered 'law', they were a set of rules for the proper conduct of relations that were generally followed between Greek cities. The Greeks did not have the concept of a State in the modern sense, but their use of the term *polis* to describe the political organisation of cities comes close to the modern understanding of the concept of State.[8]

1.2.1.2   Ancient Rome

The most influential of all ancient civilisations, the Romans, before their period of expansion and conquest, made treaties with Latin cities under which Latins and Romans were given rights in each other's courts and promised mutual co-operation.

Once Rome became an empire the Romans organised their relations with foreigners on the basis of *jus fetiale* and *jus gentium*. *Jus fetiale* consisted of religious rules which governed Rome's external relations and its formal declarations of war which, inter alia, recognised the inviolability of ambassadors and was at the origin of the distinction between just and unjust war. *Jus gentium* was the Roman response (as Rome expanded) to the necessity of regulating legal relations between Roman citizens and foreigners. A special magistrate, the *praetor peregrinus*, was appointed in 242 BC who created law (called *jus gentium*) acceptable to both Roman citizens and foreigners. This law was the first truly international law, although it only regulated relations between private individuals. It was based on the commercial law in use in Mediterranean trade, on *jus civile* (the law applicable to relations between Roman citizens) in its less formalistic version, and on the principles of equity and bona fides (good

---

8   See J. Kelly, *A Short History of Western Legal Theory*, Oxford: Oxford University Press, 1992.

faith). The distinction between *jus civile* and *jus gentium* was obliterated in 212 AD when Roman citizenship was granted to all male inhabitants of the Empire. However, *jus gentium* did not disappear but became an essential part of Roman law and thus greatly influenced all European legal systems and, through them, public international law.

From ancient Rome international law inherited the doctrine of the universal law of nature known as 'natural law', which had initially been developed by Stoic philosophers of ancient Greece, and then adopted by the Romans. This doctrine considered law as the product of 'right reason' emanating from assumptions about the nature of man and society. Because natural law is the expression of 'right reason' inherent in nature and man, and discoverable by reason, it applies universally. Cicero in his *De Republica* gave the following definition of natural law:

> True law is right reason in agreement with Nature; it is of universal application, unchanging and everlasting; it summons to duty by its commands, and averts from wrongdoing by its prohibitions . . . There will not be different laws at Rome and at Athens, or different laws now and in the future, but one eternal and unchangeable law will be valid for all nations and for all times.

The doctrine of natural law is regarded as a precursor to the concept of human rights (See Chapter 12). Cicero had also developed a theory of a just war. He said:

> There is even such a thing as a law of war [*ius bellicum*]; and the terms of an oath must often be observed with an enemy . . . Regulus would have had no right to violate by perjury the terms and agreements made with a foreign enemy: the Romans were dealing with an open and organised enemy, and it is to this category that the whole *ius fetiale* applies, as well as many generally observed rules.[9]

1.2.2 The Middle Ages

There is disagreement as to whether and to what extent the Middle Ages contributed to the development of international law. Some argue that papal leadership in all matters and the voluntarily recognition of feudal suzerainty of the papacy were incompatible with the existence of international law, particularly as at its height in the twelfth and thirteenth centuries the medieval Church was omnipresent and the distinction between Church and 'States' as separate entities had disappeared. Indeed, the basic premise of international law, which requires the co-existence of equal and independent communities, was missing. Others claim that:

> the pyramidal structure of feudalism culminating in Pope and Emperor as spiritual and temporal heads of Western Christendom, was hardly ever fully realised. It left ample scope for relations on a footing of equality between what were often in fact independent states. This applied especially to kingdoms like England and Scotland which existed on the fringe of the Holy Roman Empire. Even within the Empire, relations between the more powerful feudal princes, independent knights and free cities were regulated by rules which in all but form were indistinguishable from those of international law and formed a system of quasi-international law.[10]

There is no doubt that the confrontation between the papacy and German emperors, which lasted for centuries, over the matter of who had ultimate authority in the Christian empire contributed to the revival of legal studies in Italian universities. Indeed, in their confrontation, both sides invoked legal

---

9   Cicero, *De officiis*, 3, 108 (44 BC) cited by Kelly, ibid.
10   G. Schwarzenberger, *A Manual of International Law*, 5th edn, New York: Praeger, 1967, 6.

arguments based on Roman law and canon law, blended with natural law, to bolster their claims. As a result, treaties, principles and standards which were adopted by the medieval Christian world became, at a later stage, the origins of international customary law.

In the Middle Ages two sets of truly international law developed – the *lex mercatoria* and the maritime customary law – to deal with problems that transcended national boundaries:

- *Lex mercatoria*. With the revival of trade in the tenth century merchants started to travel throughout Europe in order to sell, buy and place orders for various goods. These commercial activities required the establishment of a common legal framework. Out of necessity the European merchants created their own rules of conduct and fair dealing which formed the *lex mercatoria*. As royal and feudal courts refused to enforce the newly established rules of conduct invented by merchants, special courts were instituted to deal with litigation involving merchants. They decided cases quickly 'between tides' in ports or in the 'Pie Powder' courts on the last day of a fair. The cases were decided by merchants sitting as judges who relied on business practices, usages of trade, legal principles of Canon law such as *pacta sunt servanda*, and the principle of good faith. Compliance with judgments was ensured because merchants knew each other as they moved together from fair to fair throughout Europe. Thus, an undesirable member of the community could be forced out of business if he refused to comply with a judgment.

- Maritime law. In the Middle Ages maritime customs and usages were formed. The high seas were no-man's land, but with the development of maritime commerce it became necessary to establish some rules and standards. The rules of the sea, based on the Rhodian Sea Law, a codification undertaken by the Byzantine empire, were compiled into widely recognised collections such as the Rolls of Oleron in the 12th century; the English Black Book of the Admiralty; the Maritime Code of Visby established in the 13th century, and the *Consolato del Mare* composed in Barcelona in the mid-fourteenth century. These codifications become accepted throughout Europe.

The Middle Ages saw the rise of nation States. First, there were the microscopic Italian city States which, with increasing wealth and prestige, were searching for legal justifications to accommodate their demands for independence. The Italian School of Law represented by Bartolus (1314–1357), and Baldus (1327–1400) responded to their needs. Although the treatment of international law was fragmentary the Italian School conceived the law of nations as a universal and natural law, applicable between independent princes and free commonwealths.

The works of Niccolò Macchiavelli, a Florentine politician (1469–1527), need to be mentioned. His book, *Il Principe* (The Prince), dedicated to Prince Lorenzo de' Medici, who governed the city of Florence, provided practical advice on how to acquire and keep political power. The most interesting advice concerned a situation where a Prince must choose between law and morals, on the one hand, and his maintenance of power or the preservation of a State against external enemies, on the other. The advice was that if such an irreconcilable conflict exists, then the 'State reason' must prevail over law and morals. The concept of 'State reason' has since been used in international law as a justification for reneging on binding international obligations and nowadays its very restricted version finds its expression in the principle of *clausula rebus sic stantibus* (the termination of a treaty on the basis of fundamental change of circumstances – see Chapter 3.13.2.2.C).

Towards the end of the medieval period the Spanish School of International Law represented by Francesco de Vitoria (*circa* 1486–1546) added its ideas to international law. De Vitoria in his *Reflectiones de Indis Noviter Inventis* confirmed the universal validity of international law and it application in the Americas. He considered that the native Indians were the true owners of the land there, but justified the Spanish colonial expansion on the inferiority of the civilisation of those true owners.

The concept of 'just' and 'unjust' war was developed by St Augustine of Hippo and later refined by St Thomas Aguinas (see Chapter 15.2.2). Also in the Middle Ages the first attempts were made at restraining the methods and means of warfare and maintaining peace through the institution of the Peace of God (see Chapter 15.2.2. and 17.3).

1.2.3 From the 1648 Peace Treaty of Westphalia to the 1815 Congress of Vienna

The period from the 1648 Peace Treaty of Westphalia to the 1815 Congress of Vienna is considered as the period of formation of 'classical' international law. Indeed, international law in its modern version begins with the break-up of the feudal state-system and the formation of society into free nation States. This is commonly traced back to the period leading up to the 1648 Peace Treaty of Westphalia which brought to an end the Thirty Years War in Europe.

The Treaty of Westphalia, which is often referred to as the constitutional treaty of Europe, recognised the principles of sovereignty, territorial integrity and equality of States. From then until the 1945 prohibition of the use of force a State defeated in war could be deprived of some of its territory, but in general was allowed to continue as an independent State. Under the Treaty of Westphalia, European rulers established a system of balance of power aimed at preventing wars. This system lasted until the French Revolution in 1789 and the Napoleonic Wars of 1799–1815 and was then readopted by the 1815 Congress of Vienna to establish a new balance of power in Europe following those wars.

The concept of sovereignty was at the centre of the international system. It justified the authority of kings over their subjects, and placed the supreme power within the State. But since all States are equally sovereign, it also conveyed the idea of independence. The claim of a State to be sovereign does not mean that the power of the State is subject to no limitations. The obvious limitation is territorial: any State is finite and necessarily has boundaries outside which its writ does not run, and other, sovereign States exist. As a result, States had to develop rules governing their relationships with each other which rules became a source of customary international law.

Intellectual support for new ideas was provided by scholars, in particular the Anglo-Dutch School represented by Hugo Grotius and Alberto Gentilli. Alberto Gentilli, an Italian Protestant who fled to England to avoid persecution, was the first to separate international law from theology and ethics.

Grotius, who is considered as the founder of the modern theory of natural law, acknowledged Gentilli's contribution to his work, but further divorced international law from theology by exploring the hypothetical argument that natural law would have validity even if there were no God, or if God was not interested in human affairs. Grotius treated law as deductive, and independent of experience. In respect of international law, in his work *Mare Liberum* (The Free Sea (1609)), he advocated the freedom of the seas. He argued that it would be against natural law to rule over the sea as no country was able to monopolise control over the ocean because of its immensity, lack of stability and lack of fixed limits. His principal work *De Jure Belli ac Pacis* (On the Law of War and Peace (1625)) constituted the first systematic treatment of positive international law. He considered war as violating natural law but accepted its necessity. He supported the idea of a 'just war' which according to him was a war to obtain a right. War was of a punitive character, conducted against State crimes, when conciliation had failed. He considered religious war as unjust because religion was a matter of inner conviction which could not be forced on anyone. He believed that war should be regulated. Consequently he put emphasis on moral conduct during wars. Non-combatants should be protected, hostages and prisoners treated with humanity, and property protected from wanton destruction. The topics of neutrality, treaties and diplomatic practice were examined in his works. He also discussed methods for peaceful settlement of international disputes. He recognised sovereign States as the basic units of international law, and the law of nations as universally accepted, and emphasised that a civil right which derives from the laws of a sovereign State is inferior to a right based on the law of nations because 'the law of nations is more extensive rights, deriving its authority from the consent of all, or at least of many nations'.

Despite Grotius' adherence to the law of nature he also recognised *jus gentium* or *jus voluntarium* comprising customary rules for the conduct of States. The last mentioned did not stem from the law of nature, they were apart. His emphasis on this voluntary law, which is essentially positivist, came to be as influential as his belief in natural law.

Grotius' works were very popular with his contemporaries, and appealed to subsequent generations. His law of nature was further developed by the German jurist Samuel von Pufendorf and the seventeenth century English philosophers, Thomas Hobbes and John Locke. In the nineteenth century the principle of utility – according to which the object of all legislation must be the 'greatest happiness of the greatest number' – developed by Jeremy Bentham, and legal positivism (according to which law is based simply on 'the command of the ruler') formulated by John Austin, rejected the doctrine of natural law as unprovable. However, after WWII the idea that there are some higher standards than positive law revived the interest in natural law.

At the end of the eighteenth century there were two events of great importance to the development of international law. The first was the achievement of independence by the British colonies in North America, which relying on the principle of self-determination, after 7 years of war against the British, were recognised as a new subject of international law even by Great Britain (the 1782 Treaty of Paris). The second was the French revolution which embraced ideas valid for humanity as a whole. In both the US and France, constitutions guaranteed citizens' fundamental rights, and imposed on the State duties with regard to its citizens.

1.2.4 From the 1815 Congress of Vienna to the outbreak of WWI in 1914

From the 1815 Congress of Vienna to WWI international law was based on the following principles: sovereignty, balance of power, legitimacy (in the sense of restoration of 'legitimate' governments to power and of prevention of political revolutions) and equality between nations.

The Congress of Vienna ended 25 years of Napoleonic war in Europe. The Congress was convened by the four European powers which had defeated Napoleon. Its main objective was to establish a new balance of powers of political forces in Europe which would ensure lasting peace and maintain the status quo in Europe by repressing political revolutions. The idea behind the new balance of powers was to make territorial arrangements which would ensure that no European State would be more powerful than any other and therefore no State would be able to build an empire similar to that built by Napoleon.

The Congress codified the law on diplomatic agents and missions, prohibited slave trading and laid the foundations for the free navigation of rivers which flow through at least two European States. At the Congress the five powers, the UK, Austria, Prussia, Russia, and France which joined them in 1818, promised to meet periodically over the next 20 years to discuss common problems and to co-operate on major issues to prevent war. The so-called Concert of Europe which developed out of the Congress of Vienna was largely successful in preserving peace in Europe for almost a century. It constituted the first serious attempt in modern times to establish an international mechanism to maintain peace. The system of periodic meetings also began a new diplomatic era in Europe which was marked by the adoption of numerous treaties, inter alia, establishing the neutrality of Switzerland (1815) and Belgium (1831), laying down general rules for the navigation of rivers (1815), and a number of treaties aimed at establishing rules of conduct of wars and restricting human suffering during international armed conflicts (see Chapter 17.3 and 17.4). During that period State practice produced the framework for modern international law dealing with the recognition of States. This framework achieved prominence in the attitude of the UK and the US to the independence of Greece. Rules governing State responsibility were also developed.

The system which grew up following upon the 1815 Congress of Vienna is referred to as the classical system of international law and was described by Grewe in the following terms:

> the basic and characteristic feature of the classical system was its close commitment to the modern sovereign state as the sole subject of international law. Deriving from this basic structure, two other elements helped to form the shape of the classical system: the unorganised character of the international community, composed of a multitude of sovereign states as legally equal, if *de facto* unequal members; and the acceptance of war as the ultimate instrument of enforcing law and safeguarding national honour and interest.[11]

The nineteenth century was the century of positivism which was introduced by French philosopher Auguste Compte. He posited that humanity had gone through three stages of development: the theological, which focused on religious ideas; the metaphysical, which concentrated on legalistic and jurisprudential ideas, and the 'positive' which rejected the past superstitions, ideas and dogmas to focus on scientific studies of objectively ascertainable facts. In the positivist stage, science could provide answers to all problems including social problems so that individuals and nations could live in harmony and comfort.

In law positivist theories were developed by John Austin (see below) and Jeremy Bentham and came to dominate jurisprudential thinking in general, including with regard to the theory of international law.

1.3 The nature of international law

The question of whether international law is law at all may be examined at two levels.

First, at a practical level, people believe that States have little respect for international law and have no incentive to comply with it in the absence of world government. This belief springs from the common misconception that international law is often breached with impunity. But the same could be said of any legal system in that offenders are not necessarily prosecuted, judged, and punished for crimes committed. Indeed, numerous crimes are never reported and many known to the law enforcement authorities are never solved. Breaches of international law are more spectacular than breaches of national law and therefore the impression is given that because some breaches are never punished there is no effective enforcement of international law, and therefore it cannot exist. In this respect it can be said that, first, enforcement mechanisms of international law are not the same as those available within domestic legal systems because enforcement of international law depends on the will of many sovereign States. Second, in most cases States obey international law, but their compliance is not as highly publicised as is non-compliance. Third, a distinction must be made between the existence of law, and its enforcement (see Chapter 1.4). Enforcement is not essential to its existence because normally rules are obeyed, whether domestic or international, not only out of fear, but because they are perceived to be right, just and appropriate.[12]

Second, at a theoretical level, the existence of international law has been challenged by the positivist theory.

John Austin, the great nineteenth century positivist, argued that international law is not really law because it has no sovereign. He defined laws 'properly so called' as commands of a sovereign. According

---

11   W.G. Grewe in R. Bernhardt, *Encyclopaedia of Public International Law*, Vol. II, 8th edn, North-Holland,1995, 839–840.

12   A. D'Amato, *Is International Law Really 'Law'?* (1985) Northwestern Law Review, 1295.

to him a sovereign is a person who receives obedience of the members of an independent political society and who, in turn, does not owe such obedience to any person. Rules of international law did not qualify as rules of positive law by this test, and, not being commands of any sort, were placed by Austin in the category of laws 'improperly so called'.[13]

The reply to Austin is that no legal system conforms to his theory. In the US the separation of powers does not admit a single sovereign, and in the UK the legislature is not the only source of law-making. Further, Austin's emphasis on the role of habitual obedience to a sovereign does not explain how new sovereign authority emerges. His criticism of international law is largely based on his peculiar conception of law. According to Austin's test the lack of an international sovereign, who commands public international law, deprives international law of its character as law, and places it in the category of a 'positive international morality'. The test for law prescribed by Austin does not reflect the special nature of public international law which derives from the agreement of States rather than from sovereign imposition. Municipal systems, and the international legal system, as they operate at different levels from each other, cannot be compared. Municipal law creates a vertical system, i.e. governs relations between a sovereign and his citizens based on coercion, while international law creates a horizontal system, i.e. regulates relations between equal sovereign, independent States with the consequence that the system is decentralised.

H.L.A. Hart[14] regarded international law as a primitive legal order. According to him, an advanced legal system should be made up of two kinds of rules, i.e. primary rules, which impose duties, and can be found in a primitive legal system, and secondary rules which comprise a 'rule of recognition', 'rules of change', and 'rules of adjudication'. The rule of recognition is fundamental to the system because it allows identification of the primary rules while the rules of change provide a mechanism whereby new rules may be introduced and old rules may be changed or abolished, and the rules of adjudication provide for compulsory adjudication of disputes by courts and other bodies. He posited that international law is a primitive legal system because its institutional limitations have prevented it from developing secondary rules, i.e. there is no legislature and no compulsory jurisdiction of international courts. In response, it can be said that:

■ the rule of recognition exists in that it is incorporated in the Statute of the International Court of Justice (ICJ) (see Chapter 14);

■ rules of change operate, to some extent, through international treaties and customary law;

■ rules of adjudication are, to some extent, present because many international treaties provide for compulsory jurisdiction of international courts, international tribunals, or other international bodies.

Professor Henkin considers[15] that critics of international law ask and answer the wrong questions. He says that what matters is:

■ whether international law is reflected in national policies and in relations between States, rather than whether there is a single legislature in charge of creating international law, judiciary to enforce it and an executive to carry it out;

---

13   J. Austin, *The Province of Jurisprudence Determined*, London: Weidenfeld & Nicolson, 1955.

14   H.L.A. Hart, *The Concept of Law*, Oxford: Clarendon Press, 1961.

15   L. Henkin, *How Nations Behave: Law and Foreign Policy*, 2nd edn, New York: Columbia University Press, 1979, 25–26.

- whether international law deals appropriately with changing needs of the evolving international community, rather than whether there is an effective legislature along a national model;

- whether international disputes are settled in accordance with international law, rather than whether there is an effective judiciary;

- whether States observe international law, rather than whether international law is effectively enforced.

He concludes that States have accepted important limitations imposed on their sovereignty and have observed international rules with the consequence that international relations are conducted in an orderly manner.

Perhaps the best view is that States recognise the existence of international law and feel under an obligation to observe it. As Brierly stated: 'States may often violate international law, just as individuals often violate municipal law, but no more than individuals, do States defend their violations by claiming that they are above the law.'[16] The evidence for the existence of international law is that it is practised on a daily basis by international lawyers who work for governments or private clients, IGOs, and other non-State actors, and is applied by international and domestic courts.

The argument that international law is devoid of proper means of enforcement is dealt with next.

1.4 Enforcement of international law

In municipal systems the machinery for enforcement of national law is centralised in a government authority. In international law it is of necessity decentralised, since the primary subjects of international law are sovereign States.

Professor Kelsen (1881–1973), the Austrian-American legal philosopher who formulated a kind of positivism known as the 'pure theory' of law and was the main representative of the monist school in international law (see Chapter 4.2.2), argued that international law does have machinery for enforcement. Traditionally, in a decentralised society enforcement of laws is accomplished through self-help. The legal order leaves enforcement to the individuals injured by the delict or illegality. He stated that although it may appear that the individuals take law into their own hands, they may nevertheless be considered as acting as organs of the community.[17]

Kelsen's argument is not without historical attraction. Until the 1928 Kellogg-Briand Pact, the use of force did constitute a recognised method of enforcing international law. However, the use of force, except in self-defence, is now illegal (see Chapter 15). The problem therefore arises as to what to put in place of force as a means of enforcement.

In this respect, the system established under the UN Charter was designed to ensure that member States obey and respect international obligations deriving from the Charter. The Cold War and its rigid division of the world distorted the potential of the UN system. However, since the end of the Cold War the enforcement powers of the UN have been invigorated even though the UN is not a law enforcement agency. Indeed, the scope of enforcement actions taken by the UN is steadily growing. Within its function of maintaining international peace and security the UN Security Council (UNSC) has found that it must act in situations involving serious and persistent violations of human rights.

---

16   J.L. Brierly, *The Outlook for International Law*, Oxford: Oxford University Press, 1944, 5.
17   H. Kelsen, *General Theory of Law and State*, transl. A. Wedberg, Cambridge, MA: Harvard University Press, 1949.

In addition the punishment of notorious abusers of human rights has become a concern of the UNSC. The establishment of the two criminal tribunals – the International Criminal Tribunal for the Former Yugoslavia (ICTY) and the International Criminal Tribunal for Rwanda (ICTR) – on the basis of UNSC resolutions illustrates this point (see Chapter 5.12.2.2). In addition to these truly international criminal tribunals, so called hybrid or mixed tribunals (i.e. composed both of national and international judges and prosecutors and having statutes combining rules of international and national criminal law) have been established under the auspices of the UN for Sierra Leone, East Timor, Kosovo, Cambodia and Lebanon. Each mixed tribunal, located in the territory where international crimes have been committed, has *sui generis* jurisdiction, i.e. resulting from the particular historical and political circumstances, but the tribunals' common feature is that the mandate of each is to ensure that perpetrators of crimes falling within its jurisdiction will be brought to justice and punished.

Since the end of the Cold War, the UNSC has been very effective in imposing sanctions, both involving the use of force and not involving the use of force (see Chapter 16.2.3 and 16.2.4).

Outside the framework of the UN, the International Criminal Court (ICC) ensures compliance with international criminal law by prosecuting and punishing individuals responsible for the worst abuses of HRL and IHL. Under Article 13 (b) of the Rome Statute,[18] the UNSC, acting under Chapter VII, may refer to the ICC situations in which crimes within the jurisdiction *ratione materiae* of the ICC appear to have been committed, irrespective of whether the conditions for the exercise of jurisdiction by the ICC contained in Article 12(2) (a) and (b) have been met. In such cases all States of the UN, irrespective of whether they are contacting parties to the Rome Statute, are bound to comply with the UNSC decision to surrender the indicted person or to supply evidence. For the first time, the UNSC used Article 13(b) when referring 'the situation in Darfur since 1 July 2002 to the Prosecutor of the [ICC]'.[19] Article 13(b) of the Rome Statute gives, therefore, the ICC a kind of universal jurisdiction. It should be noted that the UNSC may use its powers under Chapter VII to force compliance with its decisions to refer.

Important to enforcement of international law is the fact that many international treaties provide for compulsory jurisdiction of designated international bodies to settle disputes relating to the relevant treaty. Examples are provided by the European Court of Justice (ECJ) which has jurisdiction to interpret and apply treaties establishing the EU, and the Caribbean Court of Justice which has jurisdiction to apply and interpret the Revised Treaty of Chaguaramas establishing the CARICOM Single Market and Economy.

The existence of international law should not be viewed exclusively in the context of enforcement. Individuals obey municipal law for many reasons, only one of them is the fear of being punished. According to Guzman[20] a State's compliance is based on three factors: reputation, reciprocity and retaliation (the three Rs compliance):

■ Reputation is defined as a judgment about a State's past behaviour which is used to predict its future behaviour. States, like individuals, care about their reputation and thus perform their international obligations and accept the enforcement of judgments against them in order to appear as reliable partners.

---

18   UN Doc A/CONF.183/9.The Rome Statute of the ICC is the treaty that established the ICC. It contains, *inter alia*, provisions on the ICC's jurisdiction, composition and functioning.

19   UNSC Res 1593 (2005) (31 March 2005) SCOR [1 August 2004–31 July 2005] 131.

20   A.T. Guzman, *How International Law Works, A Rational Choice Theory*, Oxford: Oxford University Press, 2008, 33–71.

■ Reciprocity concerns actions taken by a State against another State to respond to a violation by the latter State of an agreement, but without the intent of punishing the offending State. The victim State withdraws its own compliance with the relevant agreement because there is no benefit for the victim State to comply with it. Reciprocal action is not costly so far as the victim State is concerned.However, reciprocity does not make sense in respect of human rights treaties and many multilateral treaties such as the Nuclear Non-Proliferation Treaty (see Chapter 17.3.1.3. A).

■ Retaliation entails the taking of actions by a State to punish the offending State. Such actions are normally costly to the retaliating State, e.g. severance by it of economic relations may harm its own economy.

With regard to reciprocity and retaliation the 2001 Draft Articles on Responsibility of States for Internationally Wrongful Acts (the 2001 DARSIWA) adopted by the International Law Commission (ILC) reinforces the system of remedies available to a State injured by another State's violation of its legal obligations (see Chapter 11). The 2001 DARSIWA legitimated recourse to counter-measures against a delinquent State while strictly defining their scope. The Draft Articles introduce the concept of 'aggravated responsibility' which allows any State to seek compensation on behalf of the victims of serious and widespread human rights violations, and to apply counter-measures when a delinquent State breaches a peremptory norm of international law (see Chapter 11.1).

Another important factor contributing to the enforcement of international law is the growing awareness of ordinary people of their rights under international law, primarily through the growth of HRL, which marks a move away from the traditional view that only States could be subjects of international law. This has two dimensions. On the one hand, people fight for their rights against totalitarian governments and, on the other hand, governments appeal to public opinion for support in the case of breaches of international law by a State. Pressures which are exercised by public opinion on governments should not be underestimated.

Whatever the reason for compliance, according to Professor Henkin 'almost all nations observe almost all principles of international law, and almost all of their obligations, almost all of the time'.[21]

Generally speaking, no country can totally disregard international law, although in more recent times this did occur during the 1966–1976 Cultural Revolution in the People's Republic of China. International law was no longer considered as an academic subject, all law lecturers and professors were dismissed. When the Cultural Revolution ended in 1976 China's leaders, in the light of China's isolation, decided to join the international community in order to conduct better relations with other governments. In 1982 more liberal views were taken and the President of the Chinese Society of International Law in Beijing announced that China had abandoned its parochial view of international law.[22] This indicates that international law is essential for the existence of any State and no State can afford to stand alone.

1.5 Situations to which international law is relevant

International law is relevant at three separate levels in international relations, i.e. those of co-operation, co-existence and conflict.

---

21   Supra note 15, 47.
22   Huan, *Forward to the first edition of the Chinese Yearbook of International Law* (1983).

1.5.1 Co-operation

States are naturally interdependent in many ways and international law facilitates co-operation. When States have a common interest in areas where actions on an international scale are the most effective, they co-operate, e.g. in the creation and maintenance of an international postal system, in eradicating disease by means of common rules as to vaccination, and in combating international terrorism. The most extensive system of co-operation between States has been created by the EU Treaty under which member States have transferred important powers to EU institutions. In some areas, e.g. the Common Commercial Policy and the Common Agricultural Policy, the EU has exclusive powers, i.e. the EU alone is entitled to act at both internal and international level with regard to these areas.

1.5.2 Co-existence

States have to co-exist with one another and a means of doing this is to define their relationship by making treaties and other consensual agreements. At this level, compliance is high and the law is generally effective. Several reasons have been suggested for this fidelity. The concept of reciprocity plays an important part in a State's strategy. Both medium and long-term strategies are involved. The former is illustrated by an example of a State thinking of extending its territorial waters, but not doing so because it may encourage other States to do the same. In the long term all States have an interest in international stability, so there is an incentive not to 'rock the boat' excessively.

1.5.3 Conflict

The role of international law is confined to two main functions i.e. the prescribing of technical rules of conduct and the keeping of any conflict to a minimum. For example, some of the rules of warfare exist in unwritten form but most of them are embodied in international conventions, particularly The Hague Conventions and the 1949 Geneva Conventions and Additional Protocols attached to them (see Chapter 16). All these rules are included in manuals of military law for use by commanders in the field. Breach has important psychological impact. States will try to keep violations of international law to a minimum.

RECOMMENDED READING

Books

Fassbender, B. and Peters, A. (eds), *The Oxford Handbook of History of International Law*, Oxford: Oxford University Press, 2012.

Guzman, A.T., *How International Law Works, A Rational Choice Theory*, Oxford: Oxford University Press, 2008.

Henkin, L., *How Nations Behave: Law and Foreign Policy*, New York: Columbia University Press, 2nd edn, 1979.

Kelly, J., *A Short History of Western Legal Theory*, Oxford: Oxford University Press, 1992.

Neff, S.C., *Justice Among Nations, A History of International Law*, Cambridge, MA: Harvard University Press, 2014.

Articles

D'Amato, A., *Is International Law Really 'Law'?* (1985) Northwestern Law Review, 1295.

Scobbie, I., *Towards the Elimination of International Law: Some Radical Scepticism about Sceptical Radicalism* (1990) BYIL, 339.

AIDE-MÉMOIRE

Key dates in the development of international law

1648	1815	1919	1945	1989–1991

1648

The conclusion of the **Treaty of Westphalia**, often referred to as the constitutional treaty of Europe and generally considered as marking the 'beginning' of international law in the sense that it inaugurated the era of sovereign nation States. The treaty of Westphalia recognised the principle of sovereignty, territorial integrity and the equality of States, established a political balance of power in Europe intended to ensure lasting peace and friendship between States, and recognised that a ruler had the right to impose his chosen religion on his subjects although some protection was guaranteed for religious minorities.

1815

The **Congress of Vienna** which ended the Napoleonic wars established a new political balance of power intended to ensure stability, peace and the *status quo* in Europe. It was based on sovereignty, balance of power, legitimacy (in the sense of restoration of 'legitimate' governments to power and of prevention of political revolutions), and equality between nations. It redrew boundaries in Europe to ensure that no State would be more powerful than any other and therefore no State would be able to build an empire similar to that created by Napoleon. The Congress of Vienna codified the law on diplomatic agents and missions, outlawed the Atlantic slave trade, internationalised major boundary rivers in Europe, created the institution of permanent neutrality (e.g. in respect of Switzerland) and created the Concert of Europe, as a means of enforcing the decisions of the Congress of Vienna.

1919

The **League of Nations** and the **Permanent Court of International Justice** (PCIJ) were established under the auspices of the 1919 Peace Conference, which gathered the Allied victors of WWI to make peace settlements with defeated nations and to put in place a system ensuring lasting peace. The League of Nations was the first universal intergovernmental organisation open to 'any full self-Governing State, Dominion or Colony' (Article 1(2) of the League Covenant). Its main objectives were to maintain peace and security, protect minorities, and supervise the mandate system. The PCIJ, an institution separate from the League of Nations, was the first permanent world court ever created by the international community open to all States with jurisdiction over all international disputes.

1945

The creation of the **United Nations** (UN) after WWII initiated an entirely new approach to international law. The UN, now having the membership of 193 States, was created to pursue the purposes set out in Article 1 of the UN Charter. The UN Charter endows the Security Council (UNSC) with enforcement powers to achieve them. They are set out in Article 1(2) of the UN Charter.

1989–1991

The period from the fall of the Berlin Wall (7 November 1989) to the official dissolution of the Soviet Union (31 December 1991) is considered **the end of the Cold War**. With the collapse of the Soviet Union and the victory of democracy over communism the entire political make-up of the world changed. A new era has commenced for international law and the UN so far as the achievements of the objectives stated in Article 1(2) of the UN Charter are concerned.

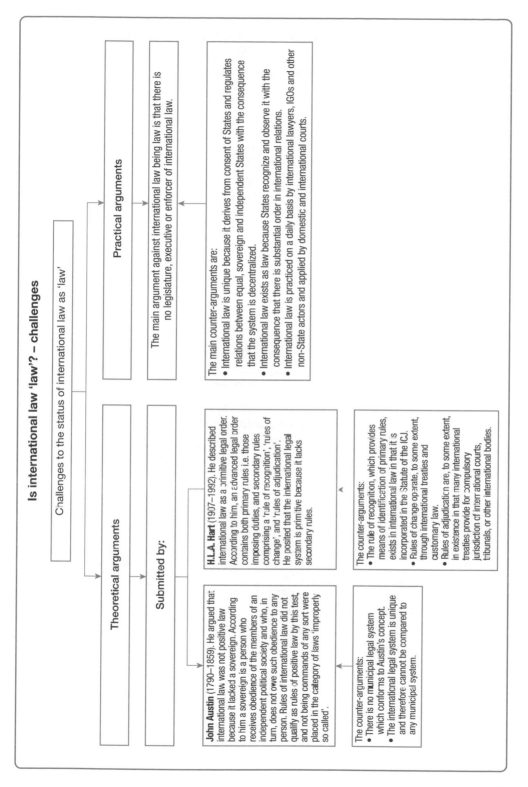

Is international law 'law'? – challenges

Challenges to the status of international law as 'law'

Theoretical arguments

Submitted by:

John Austin (1790–1859). He argued that international law was not positive law because it lacked a sovereign. According to him a sovereign is a person who receives obedience of the members of an independent political society and who, in turn, does not owe such obedience to any person. Rules of international law did not qualify as rules of positive law by this test, and not being commands of any sort were placed in the category of laws 'improperly so called'.

The counter-arguments:
- There is no municipal legal system which conforms to Austin's concept.
- The international legal system is unique and therefore cannot be compared to any municipal system.

H.L.A. Hart (1907–1992). He described international law as a primitive legal order. According to him, an advanced legal order contains both primary rules i.e. those imposing duties, and secondary rules comprising a 'rule of recognition', 'rules of change', and 'rules of adjudication'. He posited that the international legal system is primitive because it lacks secondary rules.

The counter-arguments:
- The rule of recognition, which provides means of identification of primary rules, exists in international law in that it is incorporated in the Statute of the ICJ.
- Rules of change operate, to some extent, through international treaties and customary law.
- Rules of adjudication are, to some extent, in existence in that many international treaties provide for compulsory jurisdiction of international courts, tribunals, or other international bodies.

Practical arguments

The main argument against international law being law is that there is no legislature, executive or enforcer of international law.

The main counter-arguments are:
- International law is unique because it derives from consent of States and regulates relations between equal, sovereign and independent States with the consequence that the system is decentralized.
- International law exists as law because States recognize and observe it with the consequence that there is substantial order in international relations.
- International law is practiced on a daily basis by international lawyers, IGOs and other non-State actors and applied by domestic and international courts.

Compliance with and enforcement of international law

A State usually complies with international law because:

It has consented to international obligations.

The prospective long term advantage of compliance prevails over any short term disadvantage resulting from violation.

It wants to maintain its good reputatioin.

It fears retaliatory measures.

It fears public opinion both at home and abroad.

When international law is made part of national law individuals, by bringing proceedings against a State, force that State to comply.

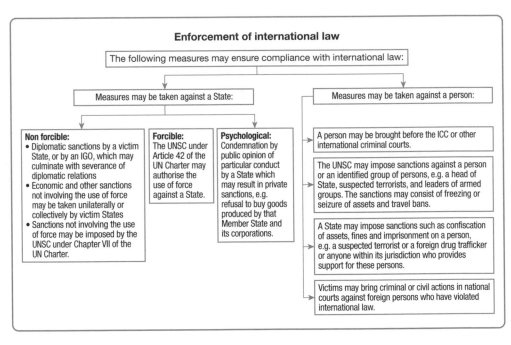

Enforcement of international law

The following measures may ensure compliance with international law:

Measures may be taken against a State:

Non forcible:
- Diplomatic sanctions by a victim State, or by an IGO, which may culminate with severance of diplomatic relations
- Economic and other sanctions not involving the use of force may be taken unilaterally or collectively by victim States
- Sanctions not involving the use of force may be imposed by the UNSC under Chapter VII of the UN Charter.

Forcible:
The UNSC under Article 42 of the UN Charter may authorise the use of force against a State.

Psychological:
Condemnation by public opinion of particular conduct by a State which may result in private sanctions, e.g. refusal to buy goods produced by that Member State and its corporations.

Measures may be taken against a person:

A person may be brought before the ICC or other international criminal courts.

The UNSC may impose sanctions against a person or an identified group of persons, e.g. a head of State, suspected terrorists, and leaders of armed groups. The sanctions may consist of freezing or seizure of assets and travel bans.

A State may impose sanctions such as confiscation of assets, fines and imprisonment on a person, e.g. a suspected terrorist or a foreign drug trafficker or anyone within its jurisdiction who provides support for these persons.

Victims may bring criminal or civil actions in national courts against foreign persons who have violated international law.

2

SOURCES OF INTERNATIONAL LAW

CONTENTS

CHAPTER OUTLINE

1 Introduction

Five distinct sources of international law can be identified from Article 38(1) of the Statute of the ICJ which is generally taken to be the classic statement of the sources of international law. They are:

- treaties;

- international custom;

- general principles of international law;

- judicial decisions;

- the writings of publicists.

Equity, a source additional to the above mentioned, also originates from Article 38. However, the above list, drafted more than 90 years ago (bearing in mind that Article 38 reproduces the same article of the Statute of the Permanent Court of International Justice (PCIJ)), does not take account of the evolution of international law. In particular, secondary legislation of IGOs should be added to the above list. It is debatable whether declarations made by a State or a group of States which produce binding legal effects are to be regarded as a distinct source of international law (though they can be assimilated, as Article 38(1) suggests, under the heading of customary law). Further, in contemporary international law non-binding rules, the so called soft law, which emanate from States and non-State actors, although not a source of law, play an increasingly important role in the international law-making process.

2 Treaties

A treaty can be defined as an agreement (usually written) between two or more States (or a State/group of States and an IGO, or two IGOs), governed by international law and intended to create legal obligations. A distinction is sometimes made between law-making treaties (normative treaties) and treaty contracts. Law-making treaties lay down rules of general or universal application and are intended for future and continuing observance. Treaty contracts resemble contracts in that they are concluded to perform contractual rather than normative functions (e.g. building an aircraft). They are entered into between two, or only a few, States, and deal with a particular matter concerning those States exclusively. Such treaties, like contracts, expire when the parties have performed their obligations (e.g. built the aircraft).

3 International custom

A customary rule requires the presence of two elements:

- a material element consisting of a relatively uniform and constant State practice; and

- a psychological element consisting of the subjective conviction of a State that it is legally bound to behave in a particular way in respect of a particular type of situation, i.e. that it accepts the practice as law. This element is usually referred to as the *opinio juris sive necessitates* or just as *opinion juris*.

A. The material element. This is normally constituted by the repetition of certain behaviour on the part of a State for a certain length of time which manifests a certain attitude, without ambiguity, regarding a particular matter. However, as no particular duration is required for practice to become law, on some occasions, instant customs come into existence. A practice must be constant and uniform, in particular with regard to the affected States, but complete uniformity is not required. It would suffice that conduct is generally consistent with the rule, and that instances of practice inconsistent with the rule are treated as breaches of that rule rather than as recognition of a new rule. So far as generality of the practice is concerned, this will usually mean widespread, but not necessarily universal, adherence to the rule. Indeed, custom may be either general or regional. General customs apply to the international community as a whole. Local or regional customs apply to a group of States or just two States in their relations *inter se*.

B. The psychological element – *opinio juris*. To assume the status of customary international law the rule in question must be accepted as law by States. This is a sort of tautological statement i.e. State practice is not law unless States accept it as law. Nevertheless, the main purpose of *opinio juris* is to distinguish between a customary rule and mere usage followed out of courtesy or habit.

C. The persistent objector rule. If during the formative stage of a rule of customary international law a State persistently objects to that developing rule it will not be bound by it. This rule is known as the persistent objector rule. Once a customary rule has come into existence, it will apply to all States except any persistent objectors. However, an objecting State, in order to rely on the persistent objector rule, must

- raise its objection at the formative stage of the rule in question;

- be consistent in maintaining its objection;

- inform other States of its objection. This is particularly important with regard to a rule which has been almost universally accepted. If a State remains silent, its silence will be interpreted as acquiescence to the new rule.

The burden of proof is on the objecting State.

In 2012 the International Law Commission (ILC) decided to include the topic of identification of customary international law in its work programme and to appoint a Special Rapporteur who so far has submitted two reports, which provide much needed clarifications on how to identify customary rules in concrete cases.

4 The relationship between treaties and international custom

The relationship between customary rules and treaties is complex. They co-exist, develop each other and, sometimes, clash. If there is a clash between a customary rule and a provision of a treaty then, because they are of equal authority (except when the customary rule involved is of a *jus cogens* nature whereupon being superior it will prevail (see point 5)), the one which is identified as being the *lex specialis* will prevail. The *lex specialis* will be determined contextually.

5 Special rules of customary international law: *jus cogens* and rules creating *erga omnes* obligations

Jus cogens rules represent the highest source in the (informal) hierarchy of sources of international law. The main difference between a rule of *jus cogens* and a rule that creates an obligation *erga omnes* is that all *jus cogens* rules create *erga omnes* obligations while only some rules creating *erga omnes* obligations are rules of *jus cogens*. Further, with regard to *jus cogens* obligations the emphasis is on their recognition by the international community 'as a whole' while with regard to obligations *erga omnes* the emphasis is on their nature. The latter mentioned embody moral values which are of universal validity. They are binding because they express moral absolutes from which no State can claim an exemption whatever its political, economic and social organisation. The legal consequences of violations of rules creating *erga omnes* obligations differ from those for breach of the rules of *jus cogens* in that in addition to the consequences deriving from a breach of *erga omnes* obligations further consequences, specified in Article 53 VCLT, follow from violations of the rules of *jus cogens*.

6 General principles of international law

Reference to such principles is to both those which are inferred from municipal laws and those which have no counterparts in municipal law and are inferred from the nature of international community. If there is no treaty relevant to a dispute, or if there is no rule of customary international law that can be applied to it, the ICJ is directed, under Article 38 of its Statute, to apply general principles of international law.

7 Judicial decisions

As there is no binding authority of precedent in international law, international court and tribunal cases do not make law. Judicial decisions are, therefore, strictly speaking not a formal source of law. However, they clarify the existing law on the topic and may, in some circumstances, create a new principle in international law. They can also evidence State practice.

8 The writings of publicists

This source generally only constitutes evidence of customary law. However, learned writings can also play a subsidiary role in developing new rules of law.

9 Equity

This is a complex concept.

A.   Under Article 38(1)(c) of the Statute of the ICJ equity is understood to be:

- a general principle of international law and thus may be considered as a material source of law;

- a way of infusing elements of reasonableness and 'individualised' justice whenever law leaves a margin of discretion to a court in deciding a case. This is equity which operates within the boundaries of law (equity *intra legem*).

B. Under Article 38(2) of the Statute of the ICJ, equity means that a decision may be made *ex aequo et bono*, i.e. the court should decide the case not on legal considerations, but solely on what is fair and reasonable in the circumstances of the case (equity *contra legem*). However, the parties must expressly authorise the court to decide a case *ex aequo et bono*. So far, the ICJ has never delivered any judgment based on Article 38(2) of its Statute.

10 Secondary law of international governmental organisations (IGOs)

There is a disagreement as to whether secondary acts adopted by IGOs constitute a source of law or whether, being a derivative source of law, they do not form part of general international law. In this respect it is important to make a distinction between primary and secondary law of IGOs. Primary law refers to the founding treaties i.e. a treaty establishing the relevant IGO. Secondary law refers to acts adopted by IGOs on the basis of primary law. Under traditional international law, secondary acts cannot be qualified as a separate source of international law as they are neither binding, nor abstract, nor general rules, but derive from the founding treaties, concern a specific area of law and produce legal effects only in respect of member States of the relevant IGO. However, this positivist approach has been challenged by the establishment of IGOs having almost universal membership (e.g. the UN), and by globalisation which entails not only the increasing interdependence of States, but also the need to find swift and appropriate solutions to new problems facing the international community. The better view, therefore, is that secondary law of IGOs constitutes an important source of international law.

11 Declarations – an uncertain source?

Whether a declaration by States is a source of international law depends on the context in which it has been made. It is debatable whether declarations which produce legal effect are a source of international law.

12 Soft law

Non-binding rules of international law are called 'soft law' while binding rules are considered as 'hard law'. Soft law is of relevance and importance to the development of international law because it:

- has the potential of law-making, i.e. it may be a starting point for later 'hardening' of non-binding provisions (e.g. United Nations General Assembly (UNGA) resolutions may be translated into binding treaties);

- may provide evidence of an existing customary rule;

- may be formative of *opinio juris* or of State practice that creates a new customary rule;

- may be helpful as a means of a purposive interpretation of international law;

- may be incorporated within binding treaties, but in provisions which the parties do not intend to be binding;

- may in other ways assist in the development and application of general international law.

The importance of soft law is emphasised by the fact that not only States, but also non-State actors participate in the international law-making process through the creation of soft law.

Nevertheless, soft law is made up of rules lacking binding force, and the general view is that it should not be considered as an independent, formal source of international law despite the fact that it may produce significant legal effects.

13 Codification of international law: the contribution of the International Law Commission (ILC)

The ILC established by the UNGA in 1947, is made up of 34 legal experts representing the world's major legal systems. The two main tasks of the ILC are:

■ the codification of international law, which is defined as the more precise formulation and systematisation of the existing customary rules of international law, and;

■ the progressive development of international law, which involves the creation of new rules of international law either by means of the regulation of a new topic or by means of the revision of the existing rules.

Since its inception the ILC has fulfilled its tasks with great professionalism and dedication producing numerous high quality international treaties, declarations, resolutions and model laws. Its role is highlighted by the facts that it is the only body involved in the progressive development of international law whose recommendations are directly addressed to States and that it has a special relationship with the UNGA.

2.1 Introduction

The question of where to find sources of international law, bearing in mind that the international community has neither a constitution nor legislature, is usually answered by reference to Article 38 of the Statute of the International Court of Justice (ICJ). This provision mirrors Article 38 the Statute of the Permanent Court of International Justice (PCIJ) which operated under the auspices of the League of Nations. It provides:

(1) The Court, whose function is to decide in accordance with international law such disputes as are submitted to it, shall apply:
  (a) international conventions, whether general or particular, establishing rules expressly recognised by the contesting states;
  (b) international custom, as evidence of a general practice accepted as law;
  (c) the general principles of law recognised by civilised nations;
  (d) subject to the provisions of Article 59, judicial decisions and the teaching of the most highly qualified publicists of the various nations, as subsidiary means for the determination of rules of law.

(2) This provision shall not prejudice the power of the Court to decide a case *ex aequo et bono*, if the parties agree thereto.

Five distinct sources can be identified from Article 38 of the Statute of the ICJ:

■ treaties;

■ international custom;

■ general principles of international law;

■ judicial decisions;

■ the writings of publicists.

There is also an incidental source, i.e. equity. While there is little doubt that Article 38 does embody the most important sources of international law, it provides an incomplete list of them. This is because, on the one hand, it envisages sources of international law from a strictly jurisdictional perspective and, on the other hand, being a text adopted more than 90 years ago, it does not take into account the subsequent evolution of international law.

Article 38 has been criticised for a number of reasons:

■ It treats judicial decisions and the writings of publicists as being of equal importance, while in practice judicial decisions have more weight than the writings of publicists.

■ There is a discrepancy between the English and the French texts of Article 38 as to the role of judicial decisions and the writings of publicists which are referred to as 'auxiliary' in the French version, and as 'subsidiary' in the English version. These terms do not have the same meaning.

■ It is worded very generally and thus provides little assistance in resolving the issue of the hierarchy of sources. Notwithstanding this, Article 38 indicates an order of importance, which in practice the Court may be expected to observe although it does not address the issue of a conflict between different sources of law. It operates without any problem when there is, for example, no treaty between the parties to a dispute but there is a customary rule. The situation is more complex where a treaty and a customary rule provide opposite solutions.

■ It does not reflect the evolution of international law. Thus, the reference to international principles 'recognised by civilised nations' appears today as at best archaic, and at worst insulting, implying as it does that some nations may not be civilised. Acts of international organisations which have greatly contributed to the formation of international law are not mentioned in Article 38. Moreover, the concept of *jus cogens*, recognised by the 1969 Vienna Convention on the Law of Treaties (VCLT), endorsed by the ICJ and other international and national courts and tribunals, and which plays a fundamental role in modern international law, is not a part of Article 38.

■ It does not reflect the importance of non-binding sources, in particular the so called soft law, which in many areas have greatly influenced the law-making process.

This chapter examines both the traditional sources as set out in Article 38 and more contemporary sources including soft law. Whatever the shortcomings of Article 38, it certainly provides the starting point for any discussion of sources of international law.

It should be noted that the distinction between formal and material sources appears inappropriate in relation to international law. Salmond explained the distinction between formal and material sources in the following words:

> A formal source is that from which a rule derives its force and validity . . . The material sources, on the other hand, are those from which is derived the matter, not the validity of the law. The material source supplies the substance of the rule to which the formal source gives the force and nature of law.[1]

---

1   *Jurisprudence*, 10th edn, London: Sweet & Maxwell, 1947, 151.

For example, a rule will be binding if it meets the requirements of a custom, which is a formal source of international law, and its substance will be indicated by State practice, which is the material source of the custom. This is comparable to the distinction between primary and secondary rules developed by Hart (see Chapter 1.3).[2]

The peculiarity of international law challenges the distinction between substantive and procedural elements of a rule of international law. As Professor Brownlie stated it is difficult to maintain the distinction between formal and material sources taking into account that the former 'consist simply of quasi-constitutional principles of inevitable but unhelpful generality. What matters is the variety of material sources, the all-important evidence of the existence of consensus among States concerning particular rules of practice'.[3]

2.2 Treaties

Treaties represent a source of international law, the importance of which is ever increasing (see Chapter 3). The effect of a treaty on the formation of rules of international law depends upon the nature of the treaty concerned. A distinction is sometimes made between law-making treaties (normative treaties) and treaty contracts. Law-making treaties lay down rules of general or universal application and are intended for future and continuing observance. Treaty contracts resemble contracts in that they are concluded to perform contractual rather than normative functions (e.g. building an aircraft), are entered into between two or only a few States, and deal with a particular matter concerning those States exclusively. Such treaties, like contracts, expire once the parties have performed their obligations (e.g. built the aircraft). While this distinction may be helpful in distinguishing treaties – usually multilateral – which are general in nature and which establish common principles of law, from those – usually bilateral – which focus more on the regulation of particular conduct (e.g. trade), it is important to bear in mind that:

■ in practice it may be difficult to make a distinction between a law-making treaty and a treaty contract as States may use the same treaty to perform both contractual and normative functions;

■ a treaty, of whatever kind, is a direct source of obligation for the parties. The binding force of a treaty comes from the consent of the parties, not from the subject matter or form of the treaty.

2.2.1 Law-making treaties

Since the middle of the nineteenth century there has been a great increase in the number of law-making treaties primarily due to the inadequacy of custom in meeting the demands of States for rules regulating the industrial and economic changes which have taken place. These treaties deal with a wide range of activities. For example, the protection of submarine cables, the suppression of human trafficking, the regulation of international waterways, the pacific settlement of international disputes, and the protection of refugees, stateless and displaced persons. These are all matters which need to be regulated by treaties and which would not be possible to deal with by relying on the eventual emergence of customary rules.

---

2   *The Concept of Law,* Oxford: Clarendon, 2nd edn, 1994, 80–81.
3   *Principles of Public International Law,* 7th edn, Oxford: Oxford University Press, 2008, 4.

2.2.2   Treaty contracts

Treaty contracts, unlike law-making treaties, usually concern the regulation of a narrow area of practice between two States (e.g. trade agreements). Such treaties may lead to the formation of general international law through the operation of the principles governing the development of customary rules in the following ways:

■ a series of treaties each of which lay down a similar rule may produce a rule of customary international law to the same effect;

■ a rule contained in a treaty originally concluded between a limited number of parties may subsequently be accepted or imitated as a general rule;

■ a treaty may have evidential value as to the existence of a rule which has crystallised into law by an independent process of development.

2.2.3   The essential characteristics of treaties

The essential characteristic of a treaty as a source of law is that it becomes binding on the parties to it by virtue of their consent. While there may be limited circumstances in which a treaty may create rights or duties for third States (see Articles 34–37 VCLT), it remains the case that a treaty, qua treaty, will only be binding as between its parties.

While treaties will, in most cases, be written instruments concluded between States, the term applies equally to unwritten agreements and to agreements between States and international organisations (e.g. the Convention on the Privileges and Immunities of the United Nations 1946), and between international organisations. Agreements between States and private parties, while exhibiting many of the characteristics of treaties, and frequently subject to the same rules of interpretation, are generally described by some other terms, e.g. concessions.[4]

Many treaties, particularly those of a multilateral nature designed to establish general rules of common application, exhibit a mixture of 'legislative' characteristics. A provision of a treaty may:

■ purport to codify existing rules of customary law, e.g. Article 55 of the 1982 Convention on the Law of the Sea which provides for the recognition of the Exclusive Economic Zone;

■ crystallise a developing rule of law, firmly establishing on a legal footing, a situation which has previously been part of the practice of a limited number of States, e.g. the 1958 Geneva Convention on the Continental Shelf which placed on a legal footing the practice that had developed among some States since 1945 to claim an area of sea-bed off their coast;

■ generate rules of law independently of the previous practice of States, e.g. Article 2(4) of the UN Charter which prohibits the threat of, or the use of, force in international relations (see Chapter 15).

2.3   International custom

In 2012 the ILC decided to include the topic of 'Formation and Evidence of Customary International Law' in its work programme, and to appoint Michael Wood as a Special Rapporteur on this topic.[5]

---

4   See *The Anglo-Iranian Oil Company Case* [1952] ICJ Rep 93, 112.
5   See A/CN.4/653, Note on the formation and evidence of customary international law.

The choice of the topic has been widely welcomed bearing in mind that international custom constitutes a very important source of international law, but its identification poses great difficulties for States, international and national courts, as well as for practitioners.

In 2013, upon the presentation by the Special Rapporteur of his first report,[6] the ILC changed the title of the topic to 'Identification of Customary International Law'. The ILC also agreed that the matter of how to identify *jus cogens* rules would not be included in its work, and that the outcome of ILC's work on this topic should be presented as a set of Conclusions with commentaries rather than as Draft Articles. In line with this, the second report presented by the Special Rapporteur in 2014 contains Draft Conclusions (DC) with commentaries.[7] The starting point of the report is the definition of custom. In this respect DC 2 proposes a definition of customary international law as meaning 'those rules of international law that derive from and reflect a general practice accepted as law' i.e. based on two elements:

- a material element: a relatively uniform and constant State practice; and

- a psychological element: the subjective conviction of a State that it is legally bound to behave in a particular way in respect of a particular type of situation, or as the Special Rapporteur suggested, the acceptance of the practice as law by a State. This is referred to as the *opinio juris sive necessitates*, or just *opinio juris*.

The Special Rapporteur noted that the definition of a customary rule based on two elements has been universally accepted and adopted in the practice of States, decisions of international and national courts and endorsed by commentators.[8]

The Special Rapporteur rejected the view that depending on the area of law, e.g. HRL or IHL, only *opinio juris* would suffice. He emphasised that the two elements approach, first ensures that there is no fragmentation of international law, and second is justified by the fact that it is difficult, if not impossible, to separate both elements as they are intrinsically connected and complement one another.[9]

The definition based on two elements has been endorsed by the ICJ. In the *Case Concerning Jurisdictional Immunities of the State (Germany v Italy: Greece intervening)*[10] the Court stated that 'In particular . . . the existence of a rule of customary international law requires that there be "a settled practice" together with *opinio juris*'.

In the *North Sea Continental Shelf Cases (Federal Republic of Germany/Denmark; Federal Republic of Germany/Netherlands) (Merits)*[11] the ICJ noted that States' actions:

> not only must amount to a settled practice, but they must also be such, or to be carried out in such a way, as to be evidence of a belief that this practice is rendered obligatory by the existence of the rule of law requiring it. The need for such belief, i.e. the existence of a subjective element, is implicit in the very notion of the *opinio juris sive necessitates*. The States concerned must therefore feel that they are conforming to what amounts to a legal obligation.

The ICJ in the *Asylum Case (Columbia v Peru)*[12] described custom as a 'constant and uniform usage, accepted as law', i.e. those areas of State practice which arise as a result of a belief by States that they are obliged by law to act in the manner described.

---

6   A/CN.4/663.

7   A/CN.4/672.

8   Ibid, p. 7–10.

9   A/CN.4/672.A/ para 28.

10   [2012] ICJ Rep 99, para 55.

11   [1969] ICJ Rep 4, para 77.

12   [1950] ICJ Rep 266.

Custom may be either general or regional. General customs are binding upon the international community as a whole. Local or regional customs apply to a group of States or just two States in their relations *inter se*.

In the *Right of Passage over Indian Territory Case (Merits) (Portugal v India)*[13] the ICJ accepted the argument that a rule of regional custom existed between India and Portugal. The Court stated:

> With regard to Portugal's claim of a right of passage as formulated by it on the basis of local custom, it is objected on behalf of India that no local custom could be established between only two states. It is difficult to see why the number of states between which a local custom may be established on the basis of long practice must necessarily be larger than two. The Court sees no reason why long continued practice between two states accepted by them as regulating their relations should not form the basis of mutual rights and obligations between the two states.[14]

Local customs may supplement or derogate from general customary international law.

2.3.1 The material element

This is normally constituted by the repetition of certain behaviour on the part of States for a certain length of time which manifests a certain attitude, without ambiguity, to a particular matter.

The Special Rapporteur, in line with the case law of the ICJ, focused on States' conduct as the key element in identifying the material element of a rule of customary law. For the practice to be relevant it must be attributable to the State. Accordingly conduct of all branches of government (executive, legislative, judicial or other) as well as its *de facto* organs, irrespective of whether they are classified as such under municipal law, and irrespective of the position that the relevant organ has in the organisation of the State, are relevant.

Manifestation of a practice may take physical and verbal forms. DC 7 provides the following non exhaustive list of manifestations of practice:

> 2 ... the conduct of States 'on the ground', diplomatic acts and correspondence, legislative acts, judgments of national courts, official publications in the field of international law, statements on behalf of States concerning codification efforts, practice in connection with treaties, and acts in connection with resolutions of organs of international organizations and conferences.
>
> 3 Inaction may also serve as practice.
>
> 4 The acts (including inaction) of international organizations may also serve as practice.

DC 8 emphasises the necessity of assessing various forms of actions (or inaction) in the light of particular circumstances taken as a whole. The last mentioned entails that all available State practice should be taken into consideration and that it is important to determine whether various organs of a State 'speak with one voice'. So if the legislature adopts a position opposite to the judiciary, the practice is ambivalent and its existence may be dubious. The implication of overall assessment of the practice is that 'There is no predetermined hierarchy among the various forms of practice' (DC8), i.e. one manifestation of practice will not be given priority over another as the weight attached to each will depend on the circumstances and on the nature of the rule is question.

As indicated above, the ICJ in the *Asylum Case* described custom as a constant and uniform usage, accepted as law. The Court did not, however, go on to describe what degree of uniformity of practice

---

13 [1960] ICJ Rep 6.
14 Ibid, 37.

and over what duration would be sufficient for the practice to meet the requirement of 'constant and uniform'. Nor did the Court give any indication as to the evidence that would be required before a constant and uniform practice would become a rule of customary law.

Following the *Asylum Case*, three questions remained for consideration:

■ What duration of practice is required?

■ How uniform and consistent must the practice be to give rise to a rule of law?

■ How general must the practice be in order to bind third States?

These matters are examined below.

2.3.1.1 Generality of the practice

In the *North Sea Continental Shelf (Federal Republic of Germany v Denmark and Federal Republic of Germany v Netherlands) (Merits)*,[15] the ICJ said that State practice must be extensive in order to create a customary rule. This means that the actual practice must be widespread, but universality of practice is not required and indeed, is rarely achieved taking into account that any customary rule usually evolves through compromise. If a large number of States representing the major political, legal and socio-economic systems follow a particular practice and expect it to be binding, it will become a customary rule.

As universality of a practice is not necessary, a customary rule may come into existence despite the dissent of some States. In those circumstances a State which has persistently objected to the developing new customary rule from the early stage of its formation will not be bound by it (see Chapter 2.3.3).

International law recognises local and regional custom. Therefore, not only can a widespread practice mature into a binding customary rule but this can also occur with a practice that has been followed by a small number of States, even two States,[16] and has been recognised by them as binding.

In the *Asylum Case*, the ICJ stated:

> The Columbian Government has finally invoked 'American international law in general' . . . it has relied on an alleged regional or local custom particular to Latin American states.
>
> The Party which relies on a custom of this kind must prove that this custom is established in such a manner that it has become binding on the other Party. The Columbian Government must prove that the rule invoked by it is in accordance with a constant and uniform usage practised by the states in question, and that this usage is the expression of a right appertaining to the state granting asylum and a duty incumbent on the territorial state. This follows from Article 38 of the Statute of the Court, which refers to international custom 'as evidence of a general practice accepted as law.[17]

In the *North Sea Continental Shelf Cases*, the ICJ emphasised that in order to rely on a customary rule, a State must show that the relevant practice has been accepted by a State whose interests are particularly affected by it.

---

15   [1969] ICJ Rep 4, para 74.

16   The *Case Concerning Right of Passage over Indian Territory (Portugal v India) (Merits)* [1960] ICJ Rep 6.

17   Supra note 12, 276–277.

The ILC in DC 9 (1) confirmed that:

> To establish a rule of customary international law, the relevant practice must be general, meaning that it must be sufficiently widespread and representative. The practice need not be universal.

Its commentary notes that conduct of specifically affected States bears a great weight as to the establishment of the existence, or otherwise, of a practice

2.3.1.2 Duration of the practice

The jurisprudence of the ICJ indicates that no particular duration is required for practice to become law provided that the consistency and generality of a practice are proved.

In the *North Sea Continental Shelf Cases (Federal Republic of Germany/Denmark; Federal Republic of Germany/The Netherlands)*,[18] it was recognised that there is no precise length of time during which a practice must have existed, simply that it must have been followed long enough to show that the other requirements of a custom are satisfied. The Court stated that:

> Although the passage of only a short period of time is not necessarily, or of itself, a bar to the formation of a new rule of customary international law on the basis of what was originally a purely conventional rule, an indispensable requirement would be that within the period in question, short though it might be, state practice, including that of states whose interests are specially affected, should have been both extensive and virtually uniform in the sense of the provision invoked – and should moreover have occurred in such a way as to show a general recognition that a rule of law or legal obligation is involved.[19]

International law provides examples of customs which were formed in a very short period of time in order to deal with new developments in technology (e.g. the rule on the freedom of extra-atmospheric space) or odious crimes committed in the context of internal conflicts in Rwanda and in the former Yugoslavia. Condorelli calls them the 'coutume grande-vitesse' (high speed customs).[20]

The commentary to DC 9(3) confirms the approach of the ICJ in *North Sea Continental Shelf Cases (Federal Republic of Germany/Denmark; Federal Republic of Germany/The Netherlands)*[21] as to the duration of the practice.

2.3.1.3 Uniformity and consistency of the practice

It is clear that major inconsistencies in practice will prevent the creation of a rule of customary international law. In the *Asylum Case* the ICJ noted that:

> The facts brought to the knowledge of the Court disclose so much uncertainty and contradiction, so much fluctuation and discrepancy in the exercise of diplomatic asylum and in the official views expressed on different occasions; there has been so much inconsistency in the rapid succession of conventions on asylum, ratified by some states and rejected by others, and the practice has been so much influenced by considerations of political expediency in the various cases, that it is not possible to discern in all this any constant and uniform usage, accepted as law . . .[22]

---

18   [1969] ICJ Rep 3.
19   Ibid, para 74.
20   L. Condorelli, 'La Coutume' in M. Bedjaoui (ed.) *Droit International: Bilan et Perspectives*, Paris: Pedone 1991, 187–221.
21   [1969] ICJ Rep 3, 74.
22   Supra note 12, 277.

The ICJ in the *Case Concerning Delimitation of the Maritime Boundary in the Gulf of Maine Area*[23] stated that when the examination of a practice shows 'that each specific case is, in the final analysis, different from all the others . . . [t]his precludes the possibility of those conditions arising which are necessary for the formation of principles and rules of customary law'.

However, complete uniformity is not required and minor inconsistencies will not prevent the creation of a customary rule provided that there is substantial uniformity. In the *North Sea Continental Shelf Cases*, the Court noted that State practice should be 'both extensive and virtually uniform'. This question of uniformity and consistency of practice was returned to by the Court in the *Nicaragua Case (Nicaragua v US) (Merits)*[24] where the ICJ indicated that it was not, in order to establish a rule of custom, necessary that all State practice be rigorously consistent. It would suffice that conduct in general was consistent with the rule and that instances of practice inconsistent with the rule be treated as breaches of that rule rather than as recognition of a new rule. The ICJ added that:

> If a State acts in a way prima facie incompatible with a recognized rule, but defends its conduct by appealing to exceptions or justifications contained within the rule itself, then whether or not the State's conduct is in fact justifiable on that basis, the significance of that attitude is to confirm rather than to weaken the rule.[25]

DR 9(2) confirms the requirement of consistency.[26]

2.3.2 The subjective element – *opinio juris*

To assume the status of customary international law the rule in question must be accepted as law. This is a sort of tautological statement i.e. State practice is not law unless States accept it as law.[27] It is somewhat difficult to see how a State can develop a new custom and at the same time comply with the pre-existing custom. Nevertheless, the main justification for the subjective element is that it allows the making of a distinction between customary rules and rules of international comity. The latter are simply based upon a consistent practice of States not accompanied by any feeling of legal obligation, e.g. the saluting by a ship at sea of another ship flying a different flag.

The distinction between those international rules which create a legal obligation and those which a State follows without being obliged to do so is illustrated in the *SS Lotus Case (France v Turkey)*.[28]

SS LOTUS CASE (FRANCE *V* TURKEY)

The facts were:

The question before the Court was whether Turkey had jurisdiction to try the French officer of a French merchant ship which had, through his alleged negligence, collided with a Turkish merchant ship on the high seas, causing loss of life.

---

23   [1984] ICJ Rep 246, para 81.
24   [1986] ICJ Rep 14.
25   Ibid, para 186.
26   A/CN.4/663. paras 55–56.
27   On the paradox of something becoming a law only at the point at which it is already believed to be the law see: J. Finnis, *Natural Law and Natural Rights*, Oxford: Clarendon, 1980, 238–245.
28   [1927] PCIJ Rep Ser A No 10.

Turkey argued before the Court that in the absence of a rule to the contrary, there was a permissive rule empowering her to try the officer. France, however, argued that there was a customary rule imposing a duty on Turkey not to try the officer as previous practice showed that 'questions of jurisdiction in collision cases . . . are but rarely encountered in the practice of criminal courts . . . in practice prosecutions only occur before the Courts of the state whose flag is flown'.

Held:

The Court rejected the French argument, stating:

> *Even if the rarity of the judicial decisions to be found among the reported cases were sufficient to prove in point of fact the circumstances alleged by the Agent for the French Government, it would merely show that states had often, in practice, abstained from instituting criminal proceedings, and not that they recognised themselves as being obliged to do so; for only if such abstention were based on their being conscious of having a duty to abstain would it be possible to speak of an international custom. The alleged fact does not allow one to infer that states have been conscious of having such a duty . . .*[29]

2.3.2.1 Can opinio juris *be presumed from the general practice of States or must it be strictly proved?*

In the *North Sea Continental Shelf Cases* (see above) the ICJ required that *opinio juris* be strictly proved:

> Not only must the acts concerned amount to a settled practice, but they must also be such, or be carried out in such a way, as to be evidence of a belief that this practice is rendered obligatory by the existence of a rule of law requiring it. The need for such a belief, i.e. the existence of a subjective element, is implicit in the very notion of the *opinio juris sive necessitatis*. The states concerned must therefore feel that they are conforming to what amounts to a legal obligation. The frequency, or even habitual character of the acts is not in itself enough. There are many international acts, e.g. in the field of ceremonial and protocol, which are performed almost invariably, but which are motivated only by considerations of courtesy, convenience or tradition, and not by any sense of legal duty.[30]

A number of the dissenting judges, however, took issue with this strict requirement. Judge Sorenson, echoing comments made years earlier by Sir Hersch Lauterpacht, argued that because of the difficulty in establishing *opinio juris*, uniform conduct should be taken as implying the requisite intention unless the contrary was established. Judge Tanaka, in contrast, proposed that *opinio juris* be inferred from evidence of a need for that rule in the international community. In the *Nicaragua Case*, the majority of the Court accepted that, in cases where a rule of customary law existed alongside a rule of treaty law with similar content, *opinio juris* could be deduced by examining the attitude of the parties to the particular convention. This approach has, however, come in for widespread criticism on the grounds that it confuses two different sources of obligation – a treaty, binding because of the express consent of the parties, and custom, which only becomes law when practice and intention are separately proved.[31]

---

29   Ibid, 158.
30   Supra note 21, para 77.
31   M.H. Mendelson, *The Nicaragua Case and Customary International Law* (1989) 26 Coexistence, 85–99.

Given the practical difficulties in establishing *opinio juris*, however, it seems likely that the Court places increasing emphasis on determining the extent of the practice and is ready to infer *opinio juris* from those examples of practice that confirm that the actions in issue are not merely casual acts or acts dictated by international comity. This is exemplified by the manner in which the ICJ ascertained the existence of a rule of customary international law in the *Case Concerning Jurisdictional Immunities of the State (Germany v Italy: Greece intervening)* [32] (for facts see Chapter 10.3.3.2. B). In this case the ICJ had to decide whether State immunity is a rule of customary international law because neither Italy nor Germany were contracting parties to the UN Convention on the Jurisdictional Immunities of States and their Property (see Chapter 10.6) and only Germany was a contracting party to the European Convention on State Immunity. In order to establish the existence of practice, the ICJ relied on numerous judgments of national courts on immunity, national legislation in this area, work undertaken by the ILC in 1980 in this area which concluded that State immunity was a rule of customary international law, and multinational treaties to establish the existence of the practice. With regard to *opinion juris*, the ICJ held that:

> *Opinio juris* in this context is reflected in particular in the assertion by States claiming immunity that international law accords them a right to such immunity from the jurisdiction of other States; in the acknowledgment, by States granting immunity, that inter-national law imposes upon them an obligation to do so; and, conversely, in the assertion by States in other cases of a right to exercise jurisdiction over foreign States. [33]

The approach of the ILC's Special Rapporteur to the subjective element was that:

First, he suggested that a new formula should be used to describe the subjective element. Instead of referring to 'a feeling of binding obligation' or 'conviction of law' he suggested that the relevant rule must be 'accepted as law' by a State. He justified this suggestion on the ground that 'In general . . . all such references appear to express a common meaning: acceptance by States that their conduct or the conduct of others is in accordance with customary international law.' [34]

Second, acceptance of the practice as law must be evidenced separately from the existence of the practice. He stated that: ' "Acceptance as law" should thus generally not be evidenced by the very practice alleged to be prescribed by customary international law. This provides, moreover, that the same conduct should not serve in a particular case as evidence of both practice and acceptance of that practice as law.' [35] Having said this, the Special Rapportuer examined various forms of manifestations of 'acceptance as law' and while some of them are self evident, e.g. a State makes a declaration that a particular rule is part of customary international law, other manifestations are less convincing. DC 11 provides some examples of such evidence, e.g. diplomatic correspondence, the jurisprudence of national courts, the opinions of government legal advisers, and even inaction of the State.

It is submitted that the Special Rapporteur felt uneasy with the matter of evidence of the subjective element. This can be deduced from DC 11(4) which states: 'The fact that an act (including inaction) by a State establishes practice for the purpose of identifying a rule of customary international law does not preclude the same act from being evidence that the practice in question is accepted as law.'

It is submitted that DC 9(4) clearly allows recycling of the existing evidence, as the same evidence may be used to prove both the existence of the practice, and its 'acceptance as law'. This undermines

---

32   (2012) ICJ Rep 99.
33   Ibid, para 55.
34   A/CN.4/672, para 67.
35   A/CN.4/672, para 74.

the statement that each element must be strictly and separately proved. It is also submitted that, as indicated in dissenting opinions of judges in the *North Sea Continental Shelf Cases*, the matter of evidencing the subjective element is very complex, always depends on the circumstances of the case, and perhaps needs more radical solution than that proposed by the Special Rapporteur. In any event, the ILC does not only codify the existing law but also proposes how it should develop (see Chapter 2.13). It is important to note that the work of the ILC on the topic has not been completed.

2.3.3 The persistent objector rule

When a State persistently objects to a rule of customary international law during the formative stage of that rule it will not be bound by it. This rule is known as the persistent objector rule. Once a customary rule has come into existence it will apply to all States except persistent objectors. Obviously, the greater the number of objecting States the less likely that the rule will acquire the status of customary law. The issue of persistent objectors was dealt with by the ICJ in the *Fisheries Case (UK v Norway)*.[36] In this case the Court rejected the UK argument that the 10-mile closing line for bays was a rule of customary international law, and went on to observe that even if such a rule had acquired the status of a rule of customary international law '[i]n any event the . . . rule would appear to be inapplicable as against Norway, inasmuch as she has always opposed any attempt to apply it to the Norwegian coast'.[37]

A number of conditions must be met by a State in order to rely on the persistent objector rule. These are:

■ The objection must be raised during the formative stage of the rule. The difficulty here is how to identify the relevant time. Unlike treaties, customary rules do not require the express consent of States. The most realistic answer is that a State should raise its objection as early as possible and react to unwelcome developments not only when the subject matter of new developments will affect directly its interest but also when, in the immediate future, those developments have no great relevance to that State. Otherwise, a State may find itself bound by a new customary rule.

■ The objection must be express. The objecting State must inform other States of its objection. This is particularly important with regard to a rule which appears to be becoming universally accepted. If a State remains silent its silence will be interpreted as acquiescence to a new rule.

■ The objection must be maintained consistently. When a State objects to a new rule on some occasions but consents to it on others, it will be unable to benefit from the persistent objector rule.

■ The burden of proof is on the objecting State. This is a great burden. In many cases States prefer to claim that the relevant rule does not exist rather than to prove that they have never accepted it as binding. For example in the *Legality of the Threat or Use of Nuclear Weapons (Advisory Opinion)*,[38] France, the US and the UK argued that the prohibition of the use of nuclear weapons had never acquired the status of a customary rule although the three States had often

---

36   [1951] ICJ Rep 116.
37   Ibid, 131.
38   [1996] ICJ Rep 226.

made declarations objecting to the prohibition.[39] This is evidenced in the 2005 International Committee of the Red Cross (ICRC) Study on customary international humanitarian law which identifies the UK, the US and France as persistent objectors to the prohibition of use of nuclear weapons.[40]

With regard to the persistent objector rule two issues are of interest. First, whether a State can be a persistent objector to a *jus cogens* rule. In this respect, the majority view is that because of the special status of such a rule the persistent objector rule does not apply.[41] The second issue is that of the position of new States which did not participate in the formation of a rule. Can they object? It seems that the answer is that they have to accept customary rules which existed prior to their becoming States. This is justified on the ground that new States, by entering into relations without reservations with other States, show their acceptance of all international law, including its customary rules. Further, to grant them the right to dissent would be highly disruptive to the conduct of international relations.[42]

It is to be noted that the position of the Special Rapporteur on the persistent objector rule will be on the agenda of the ICL in 2015.

2.4 The relationship between treaties and international custom

The relationship between customary rules and treaties is complex. They co-exist, develop each other and, sometimes, clash.

2.4.1 The relation of co-existence and mutual development

As indicated above, treaty provisions will frequently have a close relationship with customary rules. This relationship flows in both directions: treaties may give rise to rules of customary law, and treaties may reflect pre-existing or evolving rules of customary law. In the *North Sea Continental Shelf Cases* the argument advanced on behalf of Denmark and the Netherlands was that, even though Germany was not party to the 1958 Geneva Convention on the Continental Shelf and was not, therefore, bound by Article 6 of that Convention in respect of the delimitation of the shelf, a rule of customary law of similar content had developed since the adoption of the Convention.

The Court accepted that a provision in a treaty could indeed generate a rule of customary law which would become binding on third parties. However, it indicated that this process is not to be lightly inferred. The Court went on to lay down a number of conditions that would have to be satisfied before the process could be accepted:

■ The provision should be of a fundamentally norm-creating character.

■ While a very widespread and representative participation in the Convention would suffice, such participation must include those States whose interests would be specially affected by the

---

39 A. Steinfeld, *Nuclear Objections: The Persistent Objector and the Legality of the Use of Nuclear Weapons* (1996) 62 Brook L Rev 1635–1686.

40 J.M. Henckaerts and L. Doswald-Beck, *Customary International Humanitarian Law*, Cambridge: Cambridge University Press 2005, vol 1, 151–158.

41 This view was expressed by the ICJ in endorsed by the Inter-American Commission on Human Rights in *JT Roach and J Pinkerton v United States* Case 9647 Inter-Am CHR Report No 3/87 OEA/Ser.L/V/II.71 doc 9 rev 1 (1986–87) 147, para 54.

42 S.P. Sinha, *Perspective of the Newly Independent States on the Binding Quality of International Law* (1965) 14 ICLQ, 121 and M. Shaw, *International Law*, 5th edn, 2003, 86.

provision in question. A treaty rule could not become binding on third parties as a rule of customary law if those particular third parties had not shown their consent to the rule. Therefore, a State claiming that a rule has become binding on a third State, not a party to the relevant Convention, must show consent of that third State whereas in other cases, objection to a rule must be shown by the State denying a rule.

■ Within the period of time since the adoption of the Convention, State practice, including that of States whose interests are specifically affected, must have been both extensive and virtually uniform.

In other words, for a treaty provision to become binding as a rule of customary law, the party invoking the rule must be in a position to show that the rule meets all the general requirements for the creation of customary law, and that a third party has consented to it.

In the *North Sea Continental Shelf Cases*, the ICJ stated that a treaty may reflect custom in one of three ways:

■ it may be declarative of custom, i.e. it may codify a pre-existing rule of customary law;

■ it may crystallise a rule of custom in *statu nascendi*, i.e. in the process of emerging;

■ it may serve to generate a rule of customary law in the future; i.e. a treaty rule may come to be accepted as a customary rule.[43]

The process of concluding a treaty may of itself have important consequences for the content of a customary rule. In the first case above, for example, it is likely that the process of codification will alter the content of the customary rule. The very act of putting down in words what had hitherto been a flexible, unwritten rule will almost certainly exert an influence on the content of that rule. Equally, the process of interpreting and amending a rule of treaty law will be different from that relating to a customary rule. The fact that a treaty purports to codify a customary rule does not mean, therefore, that the content of that rule will remain unchanged.

In the second case – that of crystallisation – the act of concluding a treaty may be an important example of State practice. The treaty-making process, with its detailed discussions on the content of the rule and inevitable compromises between parties, may see the content of the nascent rule change. The objective of certainty in the treaty provisions may thus be achieved at the expense of the flexibility of the customary rule.

In the third case – that of generative treaty provisions – the argument in the *North Sea Continental Shelf Cases* discussed above provides an example of treaty provisions which have generated a customary rule.

Further, a customary rule and treaty norms, as the ICJ stated in the *Case Concerning Military and Paramilitary Activities in and against Nicaragua (Nicaragua v United States of America) (Merits),*'retain a separate existence' and exist side by side even if their content is identical.[44] This is because first, a customary rule and a treaty have differing applicability, interpretation and organs competent to verify their implementation and second, a customary rule may change under the influence of practice and thus the content of a treaty norm and a customary rule, identical at the time when a treaty was adopted, may disappear with the passage of time. The latter situation entails that a customary rule, as it evolves, may change an existing treaty. An example of this is the 1958 Convention on the High Seas which

---

43   Supra note 21, para 71.
44   Hereafter referred to as the *Nicaragua Case* [1986] ICJ Rep 14, para 178.

set out the rule that areas outside a State's territorial seas were high seas and thus open to all for fishing. In the *Fisheries Cases*,[45] the ICJ found that this rule was no longer applicable on the ground that customary international law had evolved by 1974 with the consequence that the new customary rule allows a coastal State to establish exclusive rights to a 12-mile fishing zone outside its territorial sea.

2.4.2   A conflict between a rule of a treaty and a rule of customary law

In the event of a conflict between a rule of treaty and a rule of customary law which rule prevails? While it is generally accepted that Article 38(1) of the Statute of the ICJ does not create a strict hierarchy of sources of law, it is possible to discern a number of principles and propositions relating to the hierarchy of sources. These are examined directly below. However, it must be remembered that international law has developed *jus cogens* rules which are regarded as being of superior authority and therefore trump all other rules (see Chapter 2.5).

2.4.2.1   *General rules of interpretation of international law (see Chapter 3.12)*

Of particular relevance are the following three principles:

■ the *lex specialis derogat lex generalis*;

■ the lex superior derogat lex inferiori; and

■ the *lex posteriori derogat lex priori*.

A.   The *lex specialis* principle means that a special rule prevails over a general rule. Ener de Vattel, one of the fathers of modern international law, expressed the rationale for *lex specialis* in this way:

> Of two laws or two conventions, we ought (all other circumstances being equal) to prefer one which is less general, and which approaches nearer to the point in question: because special matter permits of fewer exceptions than that which is general: it is enjoined with greater precision, and appears to have been more pointedly intended.[46]

For the application of the *lex specialis*, it is necessary to identify, in the light of the circumstances of a particular case, which of the two conflicting rules is the most specific. As the ILC in its Conclusion of the Work of the Study Group on the Fragmentation of International law: Difficulties Arising from the Diversification and Expansion of International Law[47] stated, the source of a rule, i.e. whether it is a treaty, a customary rule or general principle of law, is not decisive for the determination of which of them is the *lex specialis*. However, it must be remembered that the *lex specialis* applies in the context of *jus dispositivim*, i.e. rules and principles of international law from which parties may derogate, and not to rules of *jus cogens*, which are non-derogable, and are superior to any other body of law, and thus will always prevail (see Chapter.2.5).

---

45   *The Fisheries Jurisdiction Cases (United Kingdom of Great Britain and Northern Ireland v Iceland) (Merits)* [1974] ICJ Rep 3 and *(Germany v Iceland) (Merits)* [1974] ICJ Rep 175.

46   E. de Vattel, *Les Droits des Gens ou Principes de la Loi Naturelle* (1758), Liv II, Chap VII, para 316. Generally on *lex specialis*, see A. Lindroos, *Addressing Norm Conflicts in a Fragmented Legal System: The Doctrine of Lex Specialis* (2005) 74/1 Nordic Journal of International Law, 27–66.

47   A/61/10, paras 5 and 6.

General law, however, will not always yield to the *lex specialis*. As the ILC in the above conclusions emphasised, there are four situations in which general law will prevail. These are:

1 when the supremacy of general law may be inferred from its form or its nature or from the intent of the parties;

2 when the application of the *lex specialis* might frustrate the purpose of general law;

3 when rights of a third party acquired under general law may be negatively affected by the application of the *lex specialis*; and

4 when 'the balance of rights and obligations established by general law would be negatively affected by the application of the *lex specialis*'.

A special case of the *lex specialis* is that of self-contained regimes. They can be described as a group of rules and principles, concerned with a particular matter, which group comprises both primary rules, i.e. those which lay down rights and obligations on their addressees, and secondary rules, which are those which provide for means of enforcement of compliance with the primary rules. An example of secondary rules is rules which relate to the settlement of disputes, amendments to and modification of existing obligations of the parties and concern measures which may be taken by a State when primary rules are breached.

The ILC in its Conclusions (above) distinguishes three types of self-contained regime:

■ those in which secondary rules are established to deal with breaches and reactions to breaches of primary rules. The ILC regarded diplomatic law as an example of such special regimes (see below) and emphasised that Article 55 of its 2001 Draft Articles on State Responsibility for Internationally Wrongful Acts (the 2001 DARSIWA) covers self-contained regimes so far as the determination of State responsibility is concerned;

■ those which deal with a special subject matter, e.g. rules relating to a specific geographical area such as the protection and navigation of a particular river, or some substantive matter such as a ban on specific weapons;

■ those which regulate a particular area of law, e.g. the law of the sea, human rights law, humanitarian law.[48]

A debate on self-contained regimes was initiated by the ICJ which in the *Case Concerning United States Diplomatic and Consular Staff in Tehran (United States of America v Iran)*[49] stated that diplomatic law is a self-contained regime because it

on the one hand, lays down the receiving State's obligations regarding the facilities, privileges and immunities to be accorded to diplomatic missions and, on the other hand, foresees their possible abuse by members of the mission and specifies the means at the disposal of the receiving State to counter any such abuse. These means are, by their nature, entirely efficacious . . .

Whether diplomatic law is indeed a self contained regime in the sense that it provides effective remedies in all circumstances is debatable.[50] In particular, the Libyan People's Bureau Incident in

---

48 Ibid, para 12.
49 [1980] ICJ Rep 3, para 86.
50 J.S. Beaumont, *Self-Defence as a Justification for Disregarding Diplomatic Immunity* (1991) 29 ACDI, 391 and R. Higgins, *The Abuse of Diplomatic Privileges and Immunities: Recent United Kingdom Experience* (1985) 79 AJIL, 641.

London in 1984 concerning the shooting of a young police woman by a bullet fired from premises occupied by the Libyan embassy (which called itself the Libyan People's Bureau), showed that remedies provided by diplomatic law were ineffective. In this incident, Libya refused to co-operate in the investigation of the fatal shooting and the UK (after many days of siege of the Bureau by the UK police) allowed Libyan diplomats to leave the UK. The UK did not breach the principle of inviolability of diplomatic premises and resorted to the only available remedy under diplomatic law consisting of severance of all diplomatic relations with Libya.

On the assumption that self-contained regimes are those which are sub-systems of international law and that they are autonomous in that they exclude the application of general international law, the fact that under diplomatic law in some situations available remedies are ineffective and thus reference to general international law is required (this being evidenced by the fact that there is no exception to the inviolability of mission premises, whatever the circumstances)[51] excludes diplomatic law from qualifying as a self-contained regime.

The identification of self-contained regimes has been a matter of controversy.[52] Examples such as diplomatic law (see above), the regime of the World Trade Organisation[53] and regimes created by human rights treaties (see Chapter 12) are not convincing in that they cannot be regarded as regimes which are autonomous and exclude the application of general law. To the contrary, it seems that the alleged self-contained regime cannot properly function without resort to general rules. However, it is submitted that the closest to a self-contained regime is the system established by the EU treaty under which member States are prohibited from resorting to countermeasure[54] and are in breach of EU law when they refer a dispute, within the realm of EU law, to bodies or mechanisms other than those established under the EU treaty.[55]

In summary it can be said that with regard to a conflict between a treaty provision and a customary rule, there is no general rule as to which should be applied in any particular case. Whether the Court will apply a rule of customary law or a conflicting rule of treaty law will depend largely on the circumstances of the case. This is exemplified by the approach taken by the ICJ in the *Legality of the Threat or Use of Nuclear Weapons (Advisory Opinion)*[56] where the ICJ did not take any automatic approach based on the superiority of one source of law over another in the application of treaties and customary law relating to the use of force, IHL, HRL and international environmental law. The ICJ examined each aspect of the question of the legality of the threat or use of nuclear weapons in the relevant context. It decided that HRL was applicable in times of war, but IHR, which is designed to regulate the conduct of hostilities, should apply as the *lex specialis* to determine what constitutes 'an arbitrary deprivation of life'[57] in times of armed conflict. With regard to environmental treaties, the ICJ agreed that they continue to apply during an armed conflict and were relevant to assess whether the use of force was proportionate and necessary, but they were not the *lex specialis* because as the ICJ stated they 'could not have been intended to deprive a State of the exercise of its right of self-

---

51   See for example the judgment of the ICJ in *Armed Activities on the Territory of the Congo (Democratic Republic of the Congo v Uganda)* in which it held that the attacks on and occupation of the Ugandan embassy by Congolese forces violated Article 22 VCDR [2005] ICJ Rep, para 337.

52   B. Simma and D. Pulkowski, *Of Planets and the Universe: Self-contained Regimes in International Law* (2006) 17 EJIL, 483–529.

53   A. Lindroos and M. Mehling, *Dispelling the Chimera of 'Self-Contained Regimes' International Law and the WTO* (2005) 16 EJIL, 857.

54   Case 232/78 *Commission v France [Re Restrictions on Imports of Lamb]* [1979] ECR 2729.

55   G. Conway, *Breaches of EC Law and the International Responsibility of Member States* (2002) 13 EJIL, 679–695.

56   [1996] ICJ Rep 226.

57   Ibid, para 25.

defence'.[58] The Court held that the most relevant law to the question of legality of the use of nuclear weapons or otherwise, was the UN Charter together with any specific treaty on nuclear weapons. This reasoning of the ICJ shows that the Court considered all rules as potentially applicable and that the determination of which of them were the *lex specialis* depended on the focus of the question referred to it by the UNGA.

Having said all the above, in practice, when there is a conflict between a provision of a treaty and a rule of customary law, the treaty provision is normally the *lex specialis* and as such prevails over the customary rule, the *lex generalis*. In *the Iran-United States Claims*, the tribunal stated:

> As a *lex specialis* in the relations between the two countries, the Treaty supersedes the *lex generalis*, namely customary international law. This does not mean, however, that the latter is irrelevant. On the contrary, the rules of customary law may be useful in order to fill in possible *lacunae* of the Treaty, to ascertain the meaning of undefined terms in its text or, more generally, to aid interpretation and application of its provisions.[59]

The above judgment emphasises the importance of general law in that it is not dismissed or invalidated by the *lex specialis* but always relevant to fill gaps and to achieve a proper construction of the *lex specialis*.

B. The principle of *lex superior derogat lex inferiori*, i.e. the laws of a superior hierarchy prevail over the laws of an inferior hierarchy is of relevance with regard to rules of *jus cogens*, but not as a conflict-resolving device with regard to a treaty rule and a customary rule. This is because a treaty rule and a rule of customary law are of equal authority.

C. The principle of *lex posteriori derogat lex priori*. According to this principle if laws are of the same hierarchy the most recent law prevails over earlier inconsistent law. This is subject to the usual proviso that a newly developed customary rule should not affect the operation of a treaty unless the conditions identified by the ICJ in the *North Sea Continental Shelf Cases* are met.

2.5 Special rules of customary international law: *jus cogens* and rules creating *erga omnes* obligations

Jus cogens rules have the highest status in the informal hierarchy of sources of international law. The main difference between a rule of *jus cogens* and a rule that creates an obligation *erga omnes* is that all *jus cogens* rules create *erga omnes* obligations, but only some rules creating *erga omnes* obligations are rules of *jus cogens*. Further, with regard to *jus cogens* obligations the emphasis is on their recognition by the international community 'as a whole', while with regard to obligations *erga omnes* the emphasis is on their nature.[60] The latter mentioned embody moral values which are of universal validity. They are binding because they express moral absolutes from which no State can claim an exemption whatever its political, economic and social organisation. Ragazzi explains that the definition of *jus cogens* rules contained in Article 53 VCLT focuses on external tests of identification of *jus cogens* rules (i.e. they must be not only accepted, but also recognised by the international community of States as a 'whole'),

---

58   Ibid, para 30.
59   *Amoco v Islamic Republic of Iran* (1988) 27 II M 1316, para 112.
60   On this topic see M. Ragazzi, *The Concept of International Obligations Erga Omnes*, Oxford: Oxford University Press, 2000.

rather than on the values protected by the norm. Rules of *jus cogens* and rules imposing *erga omnes* obligations, being of a nature different from each other, produce different legal effects. In this respect, only *jus cogens* rules can invalidate treaties in the circumstances described in Articles 53 and 64 VCLT.

2.5.1 *Jus cogens* rules

The introduction of *jus cogens*, or peremptory rules, into international law was inspired by analogy to some national laws which firmly established the hierarchy of legal rules.

Many national laws make a distinction between imperative rules, i.e. rules referring to public order from which no derogation is permitted, and others which parties in their private transactions can ignore and replace according to their wishes (*jus dispositivum*). The consequence of a breach of an imperative rule is nullity of the transaction concerned. In the hierarchy of norms, imperative rules are superior to any other rules. The transposition of this idea into international law entails that some rules of international law are fundamental, or of a higher order, as being rules of international public order. This idea was advanced by Grotius, who made reference to *jus strictum*, and further developed by the modern school of natural law.

When the ILC was preparing the Draft Articles on the Law of Treaties it carefully examined the matter of peremptory rules and decided to introduce them into international law. Article 53 VCLT defines a peremptory norm as:

> a norm accepted and recognised by the international community of states as a whole as a norm from which no derogation is permitted and which can be modified only by a subsequent norm of general international law having the same character.

Article 53 VCLT, therefore, sets out the following test that a rule must satisfy in order to be regarded as being of a *jus cogens* nature:

It must be accepted and recognised by the international community of States as a whole as a rule:

■ from which no derogation is permitted; and

■ which can be modified only by a subsequent norm of general international law having the same character.

Therefore States cannot deviate from a *jus cogens* rule. A new State must accept it and it cannot be changed without the approval of the international community as a whole. Article 53 VCLT provides that a treaty is void if, at the time of its conclusion, it conflicts with a peremptory rule of international law. As to an existing treaty, under Article 64 VCLT if a new rule of *jus cogens* emerges and a treaty conflicts with it, the treaty becomes void and terminates. However, specific procedures set out in Articles 65 and 66 VCLT must be followed if a party to a treaty claims that the existing treaty breaches a new rule of *jus cogens*. Article 69 VCLT provides that a treaty can only be void if its invalidity has been established in accordance with the procedures contained in Articles 65 and 66 VCLT (see Chapter 3.13.2.1. D). Consequently, a party to a treaty must follow these procedures in order to invalidate it, while a State, or an IGO, which is not a party to a treaty, is not required to follow them and therefore may claim that a particular treaty is invalid on the ground that it clashes with a *jus cogens* rule. An example of a situation where a treaty was invalidated on the ground of a violation of *jus cogens* is provided by the Inter-American Court of Human Rights (IACtHR) in *Aloeboetoe Case (Judgment)*.[61]

---

61   IACtHR Series C No 15 (10 September 1993), paras 56–57.

In this case, the Court held that a treaty concluded between the Netherlands and the Saramaka tribe in September 1762 (under which the Saramakas were to sell to the Dutch any captured slaves and other prisoners, as slaves) as well as any similar treaty could not be invoked before any international human rights court as they conflict with *jus cogens* rules. In the *Aloeboetoe Case* the 1762 treaty was in breach of the prohibition of slavery and slave trading, both rules of *jus cogens*. Accordingly, the IACtHR disregarded the 1762 Treaty.

The *jus dispositivum* nature of most rules of international law is based on the fact that a group of States may substitute one conventional rule for another. However, a peremptory rule cannot be derogated from. This prohibition is absolute. The legal consequences of violations of a peremptory rule and other rules of international law were defined by the ILC in its 2001 DARSIWA (see Chapter 11).

The VCLT does not freeze the rules of *jus cogens*. To the contrary, its Article 64 highlights the evolutionary nature of *jus cogens*. It states that 'if a new peremptory norm of general law emerges, any existing treaty which is in conflict with that norm becomes void and terminates'. However, in practice it is difficult to envisage a situation where a new rule of *jus cogens* would overturn an existing rule bearing in mind that by their nature *jus cogens* rules are not only accepted but also recognised by the international community of States as a 'whole'.

The international community has not agreed on any list of peremptory rules (see Chapter 9.6.2.3). However, in the *Case Concerning Questions Relating to the Obligation to Extradite or Prosecute (Belgium v Senegal)*[62] (for facts see Chapter 9.7) the ICJ suggested that in order to identify a rule of *jus cogens*, procedures similar to those relating to the identification of any rule of customary law should be carried out. There must be a widespread practice of States and *opinio juris*. The ICJ referred to the following factors as being relevant: codification of the prohibition in universal treaties, its introduction into domestic law of almost all States, and regular denunciation of acts of torture in national and international *fora*.[63]

2.5.1.1 Assessment of jus cogens

In the light of more recent judgments of the ICJ the role of *jus cogens* seems to be undermined rather than enhanced. In the *Case Concerning Questions Relating to the Obligation to Extradite or Prosecute (Belgium v Senegal)*[64] (for facts and in depth examination of the case see Chapter 9.7) the ICJ found that the prohibition of torture, although a rule of *jus cogens*, did not impose on Senegal the obligation to prosecute the alleged perpetrator of acts of torture which had occurred before the entry into force of the 1984 Convention on the Prohibition of Torture and Other Cruel, Inhuman Treatment or Punishment for Senegal.[65]

In the *Case Concerning Jurisdictional Immunities of the State (Germany v Italy: Greece intervening)*[66] (for facts and in depth examination of the case see Chapter 10.3.3.2. B) the ICJ stated that *jus cogens* rules are rules of substance, while rules relating to State immunity are rules of procedure, and consequently, a conflict between them is conceptually impossible. As Bianchi stated, the distinction between substance and procedure 'enjoys the staunch support of traditional lawyers to whom it speaks volumes for its reproduction of well-known dichotomy, the foundation of which no one would ever

---

62   (2012) ICJ Rep 422.
63   Ibid, para 99.
64   Ibid.
65   Ibid, para 100.
66   (2012) ICJ Rep 99.

dare contest in a legal setting'.[67] In law, this dichotomy between substance and procedure entails that State immunity, as a procedural rule, is not subject to the overriding effect of *jus cogens*.[68] In practice the dichotomy led to astonishing results: Germany was able to, and did, claim immunity for *acte jure imperii* consisting of the commission of international crimes during WWII, the victims of which were left without any remedy. Judge Cançado Trinidade, in his Dissenting Opinion, strongly disagreed with the judgment, and stated: 'To me, the separation between procedural and substantive law is not ontologically nor deontologically viable: *la forme conforme le fond* [French, can be translated as "form must agree with substance"]. Legal procedure is not an end in itself, it is a means to the realization of justice. And the application of substantive law is *finaliste*, it purports to have justice done.'[69] He stated that indeed a conflict existed between the rules of substance and rules of procedure the consequence of which was 'a groundless deconstruction [by the majority of the ICJ] of jus cogens, depriving this latter of its effects and legal consequences'.[70]

In the context of the VCLT the above judgment entails that if States A and B conclude a treaty which contains procedural rules, e.g. providing that State A grants State B immunity from jurisdiction of its courts, and *vice versa*, for various matters including violations of rules of *jus cogens*, such a treaty will not be void under the VCLT because it concerns procedural rules as opposed to substantive *jus cogens* rules. The fact that under such a treaty nationals of State A, who are victims of violations of *jus cogens* rules by State B, will be barred from seeking judicial redress in courts of State B is of no relevance as well as the fact that alleged perpetrators will not be punished.

To conclude it can be said that the concept of *jus cogens* is recognised under public international law, although it raises many controversies taking into account uncertainty surrounding its content, the manner in which new rules of *jus cogens* may be created, and the process of recognition of *jus cogens* by the international community. As Murphy stated it is dazzling in theory, but disappointing in practice.[71] Further, the above judgments of the ICJ make the rules of *jus cogens* irrelevant to major issues confronting international law (see Chapter 10.3.3.1).

2.5.2 *Erga omnes* obligations

In the *Barcelona Traction, Light and Power Co Ltd Case (Second Phase) (Belgium v Spain)*,[72] the ICJ made a distinction between mere bilateral obligations and the obligations of a State 'towards the international community as a whole'. The ICJ making reference to these *erga omnes* obligations stated that:

> Such obligations derive, for example, in contemporary international law, from the outlawing of acts of aggression, and of genocide, and also from the principles and rules concerning the basic rights of the human person, including protection from slavery and racial discrimination.

---

67   A. Bianchi, *Gazing at the Crystal Ball (again): State Immunity and Jus Cogens beyond Germany v Italy* (2013) 4/3 J Int Disp Settlement, 461.

68   For the criticism of this position see A. Orakhelashvili, *The Classification of International Legal Rules: A Reply to Stefan Talmon* (2013) 26 LJIL, 89.

69   Para 295.

70   Para 296.

71   S.D. Murphy, *What a Difference a Year Makes: The International Court of Justice's 2012 Jurisprudence* (2013) 4/3 JInt Dis Settlement, 539.

72   [1970] ICJ Rep 4 at paras 33–34.

It is clear from the judgments of the ICJ that all *jus cogens* rules are, at the same time, rules that create *erga omnes* obligations. However, some rules creating *erga omnes* obligations may not achieve the status of *jus cogens*.

The 2005 Resolution of the Institut de Droit International (the Institute of International Law[73]) examines *erga omnes* obligations. The preamble to the 2005 Resolution specifies that oblgations *erga omnes* are those which refer to fundamental common values, and gives the following examples of *erga omnes* obligations: the prohibition of acts of aggression, the prohibition of genocide, obligations concerning the protection of basic human rights, obligations relating to self-determination and obligations relating to the environment of common space.

The above examples show that most *erga omnes* obligations are of a *jus cogens* nature. However, it is submitted that although some obligations concerning the protection of basic human rights are of a *jus cogens* nature, e.g. the prohibition of torture, others are clearly not, e.g. the right to a fair trial, or the right to respect for private and family life.

Article 1 of the 2005 Resolution provides the following definition of *erga omnes* obligations:

(a) an obligation under general international law that a State owes in any given case to the international community, in view of its common values and its concern for compliance, so that a breach of that obligation enables all States to take action; or

(b) an obligation under a multilateral treaty that a State party to the treaty owes in any given case to all the other States parties to the same treaty, in view of their common values and concern for compliance, so that a breach of that obligation enables all these States to take action.

Under Article 2 of the Resolution a violation of an *erga omnes* obligation entails that all States to which the obligation is owed are entitled, even if they are not specifically affected by the violation, to claim from the responsible State in particular:

(a) cessation of the internationally wrongful act;

(b) performance of the obligation of reparation in the interest of the State, entity or individual which is specially affected by the breach. Restitution should be effected unless materially impossible.

There are many examples of States which have not been directly affected by another State's breach of *erga omnes* obligations having reacted to the breach. For example, when Argentina invaded the Falkland Islands in 1982 the (then) EEC imposed sanctions on Argentina which were considered lawful on the ground that Argentina violated one of the fundamental rules of international law i.e. the prohibition of the use of force.

In the *Legal Consequences of the Construction of a Wall in the Occupied Palestinian Territory (Advisory Opinion),*[74] the ICJ noted that the obligations violated by Israel included certain *erga omnes* obligations. The Court specified those *erga omnes* obligations as being the right of the Palestinian people to self-determination and certain obligations under IHL which are so fundamental that they must be observed by all States, irrespective of whether or not a State is a contracting party to the 1949 Geneva Conventions. Those IHL obligations have, because they constitute intransgressible principles of customary international law, acquired an *erga omnes* character. The ICJ identified the legal consequences for Israel, for other States and for the UN flowing from the violation of the right to self-determination (see Chapter 13.5.2).

---

73   See the official website of the Institut de Droit International: www.idi-iil.org (accessed 13 May 2014).
74   [2004] ICJ Rep 136.

In the *Case Concerning Questions Relating to the Obligation to Extradite or Prosecute (Belgium v Senegal)*[75] the ICJ held that all contracting parties to a treaty which imposes an *erga omnes* obligation can bring proceedings against any party who has breached that obligation, irrespective of whether or not the suing party is affected by the breach, on the ground of the common interest in the protection of the right breached. The Court emphasised that the *erga omnes* obligation is owed by any State party to all other States parties. As a result, the claim of Belgium against Senegal was admissible on this ground.

2.6 General principles of international law

Article 38(1)(c) of the Statute of the ICJ refers to 'the general principles of law recognised by civilised nations'. Sir Hersch Lauterpacht noted that this provision was first introduced into the Statute of the PCIJ by the Commission of Jurists charged with drawing it up in order to avoid the problem of '*non-liquet*' – the argument that a court could not decide a matter because there was no law on the subject.[76] The term '*non-liquet*' derives from Roman law and means 'it is not clear'. The result of a finding of *non-liquet* is that a court cannot decide the case because of the gap in the law. In international law there is a debate as to whether *non-liquet* should be permitted or prohibited. The general view supported by many scholars[77] and international courts[78] is that a *non-liquet* finding should be prohibited although the ICJ in the *Legality of the Threat or Use of Nuclear Weapons (Advisory Opinion)* by refusing to decide whether the threat or use of nuclear weapons would be lawful or unlawful 'in an extreme circumstance of self-defence, in which the very survival of a State would be at stake' gave a *non-liquet* judgment.[79]

2.6.1 The meaning and scope of Article 38(1)(c)

There is little agreement as to the precise meaning of Article 38(1)(c)'s phrase 'the general principles of law recognised by civilised nations'. Neither *travaux preparatoires*[80] nor the Article itself make clear if this provision refers to general principles of international law recognised by civilised nations or general principles of law in the broadest sense, including principles of private law which have their counterpart in most developed legal systems. The case law of the ICJ shows, however, that the Court

---

75   (2012) ICJ Rep 422. See also *Reservations to the Convention on the Prevention and Punishment of the Crime of Genocide*, Advisory Opinion, (1951) ICJ Rep 23.

76   H. Lauterpacht, *International Law*, vol 1, Cambridge: Cambridge University Press, 1970, 69 *et seq*.

77   D. Bodansky, '*Non Liquet* and the Incompleteness of International Law' in L. Boisson de Chazournes and P. Sands (eds), *International Law, the International Court of Justice and Nuclear Weapons*, Cambridge: Cambridge University Press, 1999, 153–170.

78   For example, in *The Mavrommatis Palestine Concessions* Case, the PCIJ stated that in the absence of an applicable legal rule, it was 'at liberty to adopt the principle which it consider[ed] best calculated to ensure the administration of justice, most suited to the procedure before an international tribunal and most in accordance with the fundamental principles of international law' (PCIJ Rep Series A No 2, 16). Under Article 217(2) of the Revised Treaty of Chaguaramas establishing the Caribbean Community including the CARICOM Single Market and Economy, the Caribbean Court of Justice, which has exclusive jurisdiction to interpret and apply this treaty, is prohibited from making a finding of *non-liquet*.

79   [1996] ICJ Rep 226, para 105. The judgment was criticised by dissenting judges including Judges Higgins and Schwebel.

80   Permanent Court of International Justice: Advisory Committee of Jurists *Procès-verbaux of the Proceedings of the Committee, June 16th–July 24th 1920, with Annexes*, The Hague: Van Langhuysen, 1920.

has had recourse to both: those which are inferred from municipal law and those which have no counterparts in municipal law and are therefore inferred from the nature of the international community.

The use of principles recognised by national laws has provided a reserve store of legal principles upon which international law can draw. The inclusion of Article 38(1)(c) can be seen as a rejection of the positivist doctrine, according to which international law consists solely of rules to which States have given their consent, and as affirming the naturalist doctrine whereby if there appeared to be a gap in the rules of international law, recourse could be had to general principles of law, i.e. to natural law. For example, the writers of the seventeenth and eighteenth centuries, when dealing with questions as to the acquisition of territory, turned for assistance to the rules of Roman private law.

2.6.1.1 The principles inferred from municipal laws

It is not necessary for the principles, which originate in municipal laws, to be recognised by all legal systems. It is sufficient that they are common to several national legal systems and that they are appropriate from the point of view of international law.

There remains, however, the question of the manner in which these principles are applied. Are they, for example, imported into international law directly from one or other municipal legal system? This issue was addressed by Lord McNair in his Separate Opinion in the *South West Africa Case*[81] in which South Africa's obligations under the mandate[82] were considered. Drawing analogies with the municipal concept of a trust, McNair, however, indicated that international law would not import 'lock, stock and barrel' principles found in municipal legal systems. It was rather a matter of finding legal principles appropriate to the case in issue and of applying them in a manner consistent with international law.

Apart from the manner of application of general principles, the question also arises as to the ambit of the search for a principle before it can be applied as a general principle of law. Would it be sufficient, for example, that a principle was found in one municipal legal system? If not, how common must be the principle to be accorded the status of a general principle? The better view seems to be that there is no hard and fast rule on the matter. Much will depend on the nature of the case before the Court, the parties to the case and the terms of any special agreement giving the Court jurisdiction.

Some examples of principles inferred from municipal law are examined below.

■ The principle that a breach of an obligation entails an obligation to make reparation

In *the Chorzów Factory Case (Indemnity) (Merits)(Germany* v *Poland)*,[83] the PCIJ stated that 'the Court observes that it is a principle of international law, and even a general concept of law, that any breach of an engagement involves an obligation to make reparation'.

■ The principle of *res judicata*

In the *Effect of Awards of Compensation Made by the United Nations Administrative Tribunal (Advisory Opinion)*[84] the ICJ referred to the 'well established and generally recognised principle of law [that] a judgment rendered by a judicial body is res judicata and has binding force between the parties to the dispute'.

---

81 [1950] ICJ Rep 128.

82 After WWI South Africa was granted a mandate to govern Namibia on behalf of the League of Nations: see Chapter 12.2.1.

83 [1928] PCIJ Rep Ser A, No 17, 29 see also *Case Concerning the Gabčíkovo-Nagymaros Project (Hungary/Slovakia) (Judgment)* [1997] ICJ Rep 7, para 110.

84 [1954] ICJ Rep 47, 53.

■ The principle of estoppel

In the Case Concerning the Temple of Preah Vihear (Cambodia v Thailand) (Merits),[85] the ICJ was asked to rule that Cambodia and not Thailand, had sovereignty over the Temple of Preah Vihear. In 1904 the boundary between Cambodia (then a French protectorate) and Thailand (then Siam) was determined by a treaty between France and Siam under which a map was prepared which placed the Temple in Cambodia. The Siamese received and accepted the map without protest and in 1930 a Siamese prince actually paid a State visit to the disputed area where he was officially received by the French authorities. The Court with reference to these facts stated that:

> Even if there were any doubt as to Siam's acceptance of the map in 1908, and hence of the frontier indicated thereon, the Court would consider, in the light of the subsequent course of events, that Thailand is now precluded by her conduct from asserting that she did not accept it.

■ The principle of the admissibility of circumstantial evidence

In the Corfu Channel Case (United Kingdom of Great Britain and Northern Ireland v Albania (Merits)[86] the ICJ recognised the principle of the admissibility of circumstantial evidence as being a well established and generally accepted principle of law. The ICJ remarked that 'this indirect evidence is admitted in all systems of law, and its use is recognised by international decisions'.

Other examples of municipal principles adopted by international tribunals include the rule that no man may be judge in his own suit,[87] the principle of respect for acquired rights,[88] the principle that 'the parties to a case must abstain from any measure capable of exercising a prejudicial effect in regard to the execution of the decision to be given'[89] and 'general principles of procedural law'.[90]

2.6.1.2 The principles relevant only to international law which derive from the specific nature of international law

These principles have no counterparts in national laws. In order to exist they must be recognised by 'civilized nations'. This entails that they must be recognised by the international community, expressly or by implication, as applicable to inter-State relations. Examples of such principles are: the principle of humanity, the principle of the freedom of maritime navigation,[91] the principle of self-determination[92] and the principle that the ICJ is barred from exercising its contentious jurisdiction without the consent of the parties to a dispute.[93]

---

85   [1962] ICJ Rep 6, 32.

86   [1949] ICJ Rep 4, 18.

87   *The Mosul Boundary Case* [1925] PCIJ Ser B, No12, 32.

88   *The German Interests in Polish Upper Silesia Case* [1925] PCIJ, Rep Ser A, No 6, 22.

89   *The Electricity Company of Sofia and Bulgaria Case* (1939) PCIJ SerA/B, No 77, 199.

90   The *Case Concerning the Land, Island and Maritime Frontier Dispute (El Salvador/Honduras) Application of Nicaragua for Permission to Intervene (Judgment)* [1990] ICJ Rep 92, para102.

91   *The Corfu Channel Case (United Kingdom of Great Britain and Northern Ireland v Albania (Merits)* [1949] ICJ Rep 4, para 22.

92   *The Western Sahara (Advisory Opinion)* [1975] ICJ Rep 12, para 59.

93   The *Case of the Monetary Gold removed from Rome in 1943 (Italy v France, United Kingdom of Great Britain and Northern Ireland and United States of America) (Preliminary Question)* [1954] ICJ Rep 19, para 32.

General principles may become rules of customary law but at the stage where they do not fit into the narrow definition of a customary rule they are just general principles. For example, in the *Case Concerning the Frontier Dispute (Burkina Faso/Republic of Mali)*,[94] the ICJ noted that:

> the fact that the new African States have respected the administrative boundaries and frontiers established by the colonial powers [i.e.the principle of *uti possidetis*] must be seen not as a mere practice contributing to the gradual emergence of a principle of customary international law, limited in its impact to the African continent as it had previously been to Spanish America, but as the application in Africa of a rule of general scope.

This statement implies that the principle of *uti possidetis* (see Chapter 13.7.2) has matured into a binding rule of customary law as both the material and the subjective elements of custom have been fulfilled.

There are a number of general principles which have their origin in the concept of natural justice. They reflect the elementary considerations of humanity and are often embodied in treaties. For example in *the Reservations to the Convention on the Prevention and Punishment of the Crime of Genocide (Advisory Opinion)*,[95] the ICJ stated that 'the principles underlying the Convention are principles which are recognized by civilized nations as binding on States, even without any conventional obligation'.

2.7 Judicial decisions

Article 38(1)(d) of the Statute of the ICJ directs the Court to apply:

> subject to the provisions of Article 59, judicial decisions . . . as subsidiary means for the determination of rules of law.

Article 59 of the Statute of the Court provides that:

> The decision of the Court has no binding force except between the parties and in respect of that particular case.

There is, therefore, no binding authority of precedent in international law, and international court and tribunal cases do not make law. Judicial decisions are not, therefore, strictly speaking a formal source of law.

It can be argued, however, that if an international tribunal is unable to discover an existing treaty or customary rule relevant to a dispute, any rule which the tribunal adopts in deciding the case will, in theory at least, form a new rule of international law. The question is whether the new rule is a rule of customary law or whether the tribunal's decision may itself be regarded as a source of international law.

Several decisions of the ICJ have introduced innovations into international law which have subsequently achieved general acceptance. One of them is examined below.

---

94   [1986] ICJ Rep 554, para 20.
95   [1951] ICJ Rep 15, para 23.

REPARATIONS FOR INJURIES SUFFERED IN THE SERVICE OF THE UNITED NATIONS (ADVISORY OPINION)[96]

Facts:

The ICJ was asked to advise whether the UN had the right to present a claim on the international plane against a State for injuries suffered by UN officials in the performance of their duties.

Held:

The Court decided that the UN could claim damages under international law against a State responsible for injuries suffered by its officials.

Comment:

The Court's decision that such a power could be implied from the express functions entrusted to the Organisation was clearly an extension of the rights of the Organisation as laid down in the UN Charter. The Advisory Opinion either created or confirmed new general principles of international law i.e. the principle of functional protection of an IGO, the principle of implied powers and the principle of the objective legal personality of the UN (see Chapter 5.11.1).

2.7.1 Judicial precedent and the Statute of the ICJ

Article 59 of the Statute was intended to prevent the Court from establishing a system of binding judicial precedent. In the *Certain German Interests in Polish Upper Silesia Case*[97] the Court stated that:

> The object of [Article 59] is simply to prevent legal principles accepted by the Court in a particular case from being binding on other states or in other disputes.

In its practices the Court has, however, of necessity followed previous decisions in the interests of judicial consistency, and has where necessary distinguished its previous decisions from the case actually being heard. This is well illustrated in the *Interpretation of Peace Treaties with Bulgaria, Hungary and Romania (First Phase (Advisory Opinion))*.[98]

INTERPRETATION OF PEACE TREATIES WITH BULGARIA, HUNGARY AND ROMANIA (FIRST PHASE (ADVISORY OPINION))

Facts:

The UNGA requested an advisory opinion regarding the interpretation of the peace treaties concluded between the Allied and Associated Powers after WWII with Bulgaria, Hungary

---

96   [1949] ICJ Rep 174.
97   [1925] PCIJ Rep Ser A No 6, 19.
98   [1950] ICJ Rep 65.

and Romania. These three States, being accused of violation of HRs contained in the Peace Treaties, refused to take part in the proceedings before the Court and argued that, following the Eastern Carelia Case (Advisory Opinion),[99] *the Court should decline to give an advisory opinion. In the Eastern Carelia Case the PCIJ had held it to be a fundamental principle that a State could not, without its consent, be forced to submit its dispute to arbitration or judicial settlement.*

Held:

The Court in rejecting this argument stated:

> *In the opinion of the Court, the circumstances of the present case are profoundly different from those which were before the Permanent Court of International Justice in the Eastern Carelia Case [Advisory Opinion No 5], when that Court declined to give an Opinion because it found the question put to it was directly related to the main point of dispute actually pending between two states, so that answering the question would be substantially equivalent to deciding the dispute between the parties, and that at the same time it raised a question of fact which could not be elucidated without hearing both parties. . . . the present Request for an Opinion is solely concerned with the applicability to certain disputes of the procedure for settlement instituted by the Peace Treaties, and it is justifiable to conclude that it in no way touches the merits of those disputes.*[100]

2.7.2 Decisions of national courts

Article 38(1)(d) of the Statute of the ICJ is not confined to international decisions. Although not in the same category as international courts and tribunals, the decisions of municipal courts do have some evidential value. First, a decision, in particular of a highest court of a particular State expresses the *opinio juris* of that State on a particular matter. Second, a decision of the highest court of one State, although it cannot create or modify international law, may be referred to by municipal courts of other States, not as a binding authority, but as a factor to be considered when they have to decide a similar matter. Third, if many municipal courts have decided the relevant matter in the same way, this may provide evidence that there is an international consensus on that matter.

2.8 The writings of publicists

Article 38(1)(d) directs the Court to apply:

> The teachings of the most highly qualified publicists of the various nations, as subsidiary means for the determination of rules of law.

Although this source only constitutes evidence of customary law, learned writings can also play a subsidiary role in developing new rules of law.

---

99   [1923] PCIJ Rep Ser B No 5.
100   Supra note 98, para 72.

The contributions of writers such as Grotius, Bynkershoek and Vattel were very important to the formulation and development of international law, and writers of general works, such as Oppenheim, Hall, Hyde, Guggenheim and Rousseau, have international reputations. Although it is sometimes argued that some writers reflect national and other prejudices, their opinions are used widely by legal advisers to States, arbitral tribunals and courts. Their value was described by Gray J of the US Supreme Court, in *The Paquete* Habana,[101] as follows:

> International law is part of our law, and must be ascertained and administered by the courts of justice of appropriate jurisdiction, as often as questions of right depending upon it are duly presented for their determination. For this purpose, where there is no treaty, and no controlling executive or legislative act or judicial decision, resort must be had to the customs and usages of civilised nations; and as evidence of these, to the works of jurists and commentators who by years of labour, research, and experience have made themselves peculiarly well acquainted with the subjects of which they treat. Such works are resorted to by judicial tribunals, not for the speculations of their authors concerning what the law ought to be, but for trustworthy evidence of what the law really is.

The ICJ has rarely made reference to the teachings of publicists and on those rare occasions when it did it referred to them in general terms such as 'legal doctrine', 'teachings of publicists', 'the opinions of writers'.[102] Exceptionally, in the *Land, Island and Maritime Frontier Dispute Case (El Salvador/Honduras: Nicaragua Intervening)*, the Chamber of the ICJ referred to the writings of two scholars – Oppenheim's International Law and Gidel's work on the law of the sea.[103] However, the ICJ has quite often cited works prepared by the ILC (see below) which is made up of highly qualified publicists. For example the Draft Articles on State Responsibility (see Chapter 11.1) were referred to by the ICJ in the *Case of Gabčikovo-Nagymaros (Hungary/Slovakia) (Merits)*,[104] in the *Case Concerning Armed Activities on the Territory of the Congo (Democratic Republic of the Congo v Uganda)*[105] and more recently, in the *Case Concerning the Application of the Convention on the Prevention and Punishment of the Crime of Genocide (Bosnia and Herzegovina v Serbia and Montenegro)*.[106] Further, often judges of the ICJ in their separate or dissenting opinions refer to the writing of publicists, e.g. Judges Higgins, Kooijmans, and Buergenthal in their joint Separate Opinion in the *Arrest Warrant of 11 April 2000 (Democratic Republic of the Congo v Belgium) (Judgment)*.[107]

It is submitted that although the ICJ has made scarce reference to the writings of the most highly qualified publicists, either individually or as a group, (e.g. the ILC, the Institut de Droit International, the UN Sixth Committee and the Inter-American Legal Committee) their role in determining the content of international law should not be underestimated. International courts (other than the ICJ) and municipal courts often refer to scholarly works to support their decisions.[108]

---

101   175 US 677 (1900), 700.
102   In the *SS Lotus Case (France v Turkey)*, the PCIJ referred to the 'teachings of publicists', PCIJ Series A No 10, 26.
103   G. Gidel, *Le Droit International Public de la Mer*, Paris: Recueil Sirey, 1932 and 1934.
104   [1997] ICJ Rep 7, para 50.
105   [2006] 45 ILM 271–395, para 160.
106   [2007] ICJ Rep 43, e.g. paras, 398 *et seq*, para 414.
107   [2002] ICJ Rep 3, paras 39, 46, 50, 52.
108   E.g. international criminal tribunals, see M. Bohlander, *The Influence of Academic Research on the Jurisprudence of the International Criminal Tribunal for the Former Yugoslavia: A First Overview* [2003] Yearbook of International Law and Jurisprudence, 195–209.

2.9 Equity

Equity is a complex concept, which, in general, refers to what is fair and reasonable. It has a different meaning under Article 38(1)(c) of the Statute of the ICJ from its meaning under Article 38(2).

2.9.1 Equity under Article 38(1)(c) of the Statute of the ICJ

Under Article 38(1)(c) of the Statute of the ICJ equity is understood as:

■ a general principle of international law;

■ a way of infusing elements of reasonableness and 'individualised' justice whenever law leaves a margin of discretion to a court in deciding a case.

2.9.1.1 *Equity as a general principle of international law.*

Equity is most frequently regarded as being encompassed within the concept of the general principles of law discussed above. In *The Diversion of Water from the Meuse (The Netherlands v Belgium)* Judge Hudson in his dissenting opinion[109] referred to equity as 'general principles of law recognized by civilized nations'.[110] He stated that maxims such as 'equality is equity' and 'he who seeks equity must do equity', would compel a judge to ensure that 'where two parties have assumed an identical or reciprocal obligation, one party which is engaged in a continuing non-performance of that obligation should not be permitted to take advantage of a similar non-performance of that obligation by the other party'. In this case the ICJ rejected the claim of the Netherlands that construction by Belgium of certain canals which would divert water from the river Meuse was in breach of an 1863 agreement in a situation where the Netherlands had, prior to the dispute, constructed a lock affecting the river's water level and flow. Resort to equity in the circumstances of this case may be more easily equated with resort to the principles of fairness and justice. In this respect in the *Case Concerning the Continental Shelf (Tunisia/ Libyan Arab Jamahiriya)*[111] involving the delimitation of the continental shelf, the ICJ held that:

> [Equity] was often contrasted with the rigid rules of positive law, the severity of which had to be mitigated in order to do justice. In general, this contrast has no parallel in the development of international law; the legal concept of equity is a general principle directly applicable as law.[112]

2.9.1.2 *Equity as a way of infusing elements of reasonableness and 'individualised' justice whenever law leaves a margin of discretion to a court in deciding a case*

Equity has also been used indirectly by the ICJ to affect the way in which the substantive law is applied in order to adapt such law to changing circumstances or perhaps to soften the strict law whenever a court has any margin of discretion which would allow this. As Francioni stated: 'In this case equity is not used as a principle endowed with autonomous normativity but rather as a method for infusing elements of reasonableness and "individualised" justice whenever the applicable law leaves a margin

---

109   [1937] PCIJ Rep Ser A/B No 70, 73.
110   Ibid, para 76.
111   [1982] ICJ Rep 18.
112   Ibid, at para 71.

of discretion to the court or tribunal which has to make a decision'.[113] In this context, equity constitutes an element in the making of a legal decision and remains within the confines of law (equity *intra legem*).

2.9.2 Equity under Article 38(2) of the Statute of the ICJ

Article 38(2) of the Statute of the ICJ allows the ICJ, if both parties to a dispute agree, to decide a case *ex aequo et bono*, i.e. the Court should decide the case not on legal considerations, but solely on what is fair and equitable in the circumstances of the case (equity *contra legem*). In the *Gulf of Maine Case (Canada/US)*[114] the Court held that while a decision *ex aeguo et bono* would permit a court or tribunal to examine socio-economic and political considerations, equity within the meaning of Article 38(1)(c) as a component of a legal decision would involve the Court in taking a decision on the basis of legal reasoning.

2.10 Secondary law of international governmental organisations (IGOs)

There is a disagreement as to whether secondary acts adopted by IGOs constitute a source of law or whether, being a derivative source of law, they do not form part of general international law. In this respect it is important to make a distinction between primary and secondary law of IGOs. Primary law refers to the founding treaties i.e. a treaty establishing the relevant IGO. Secondary law refers to acts adopted by IGOs on the basis of primary law. An argument against secondary law being an independent source of international law is that under traditional international law secondary acts cannot be qualified as a separate source of international law, as they are neither binding, nor abstract nor general rules, but derive from the founding treaties, concern a specific area of law and produce legal effects only in respect of member States of the relevant IGO. A further argument in support of this view is that acts of IGOs are not mentioned in Article 38 of the Statute of the ICJ. However, this positivist approach has been challenged by the establishment of IGOs having almost universal membership (e.g. the UN), and by globalisation which entails not only the increasing interdependence of States, but also the need to find swift and appropriate solutions to new problems facing the international community. In particular, while the traditional approach consisting of preparing a treaty to respond to new problems is slow and not very efficient, IGOs, when the relevant matter is within their competence, can quickly and efficiently deal with new challenges. The better view is that, bearing in mind the great importance of the secondary law of IGOs, it does, indeed, constitute an important source of international law.[115] Further, acts of IGOs can have world-wide effect and can directly affect individuals, States which are not members of the relevant IGO and other IGOs. Examples of this are:

- So far as individuals are concerned: The ICTR and the ICTY, as subsidiary organs of the UNSC, directly apply international law to individuals. Another example is provided by some provisions of EU law which are directly applicable to individuals.

- With regard to States which are not members of the relevant IGO: The acts of the International Seabed Authority (ISA) adopted under Part XI of the UN Convention on the Law of the Sea

---

113   F. Francioni, *Equity in International Law*, Max Planck Encyclopedia of Public International Law, can be found at www.mpepil.com (accessed 10 July 2014).

114   [1984] ICJ Rep 246.

115   C. Tomuschat, *Obligations Arising for States Without or Against Their Will* (1993) 241 RdC, 195–374.

and the 1994 Agreement relating to the implementation of Part XI of the UN Convention on the Law of the Sea[116] (see Chapter 8.10.1) concerning resource exploitation and exploitation of the seabed and subsoil beyond the limits of national jurisdiction have *erga omnes* effect as the ISA acts on behalf of 'mankind as a whole'.

■ With regard to other IGOs: Under Article XV(2) of the 1994 GATT,[117] a contracting party to the WTO in all cases where it is called to consider or deal with problems concerning monetary reserves, balances of payments or foreign exchange arrangements, must consult fully with the International Monetary Fund (IMF) and comply with its determination of compatibility of intended action with obligations deriving from membership of both the IMF and WTO.

There are a large number of IGOs. They have varying areas of competence and their binding acts take numerous forms. Only the UNSC has been chosen for examination here on the ground that its resolutions adopted under Chapter VII are binding on all its members, i.e. almost all countries in the world.

2.10.1   The UNSC

Resolutions adopted by the UNSC under Chapter VII of the UN Charter are binding on all members of the UN and create new legal obligations for them (see Chapter 16.2). They are of specific content in that they deal with specific situations which endanger international peace and security. However, in the context of fighting terrorism the UNSC has exercised its legislative powers in a new way. To respond to terrorism, the UNSC has, so far, adopted two new type resolutions which are of a general content. These are:

■ Subsequent to the 9/11 terrorist attacks on the US, the UNSC adopted Resolution 1373 (2001) requiring its members 'to freeze without delay funds and other financial assets or economic resources of persons who commit, or attempt to commit, terrorist acts or participate in or facilitate the commission of terrorist acts'.[118] At the same time the UNSC established a committee to ensure that member States take the appropriate measures to comply with the resolution. The Committee known as the 'Counter-Terrorism Committee' receives reports from members of the UN and assesses whether they have adopted the required executive and legislative measures at the national level to comply with Resolution 1373.

■ The UNSC adopted Resolution 1540 (2004) imposing obligations on its members to prevent non-State actors acquiring weapons of mass destruction. Compliance with this resolution is supervised by a committee known as 'the 1540 Committee'.[119] Under Resolution 1540 member States are required to establish domestic controls to prevent the proliferation of nuclear, chemical and biological weapons, and their means of delivery and establish appropriate controls over related materials.

The content of the above Resolutions 1373 and 1540 is very similar to that of international treaties, which are in existence in the relevant areas, i.e. the 1999 Convention for the Suppression of the Financing of Terrorism and the international conventions on non-proliferation of chemical, biological

---

116   1833 UNTS 396.
117   1867 UNTS 187.
118   S/RES/1373 (2001) point 1(c).
119   See the official webside of the '1540 Committee' at www.un.org/sc/1540 (accessed 9 October14).

or nuclear weapons (see Chapter 17.3.1). On the basis of the above Resolutions, members of the UN are obliged, in fact, to comply with the substance of those conventions, irrespective of whether or not they are contracting parties to them. The exercise by the UNSC of legislative power is very controversial and has been criticised by many in terms of accountability, participation, procedural fairness and transparency. Also, the issues of the extent of the powers of the UNSC under Chapter VII and whether the UNSC is a legitimate *forum* for such legislation are highly controversial.[120]

2.11 Declarations – an uncertain source?

Declarations are of various kinds. They may be made by a group of States, or by a State or by an IGO to express the declarant's intention, position or views on a particular point. Whether a declaration produces legal effects depends on the context in which it has been made. It is debatable whether declarations, which produce legal effect, are a source of international law or whether the fact that they produce legal effects is based on the relevant treaty or customary international law.

In international law some declarations produce legal effect (e.g. when a State issues a protest objecting to an act or action carried out by another State or recognises a particular situation, or renounces a right) and some are sources of obligation (e.g. when a State promises to do something or to abstain from doing something). For example, in *the Nuclear Tests* Case,[121] a unilateral declaration made by France that it would cease conducting atmospheric nuclear tests was considered by the ICJ as giving rise to an obligation, because:

■ it was made publicly and;

■ France had the clear intention to be legally bound by it.

Some declarations have a similar effect to a treaty, e.g. the Joint Declaration of the Government of the United Kingdom of Great Britain and Northern Ireland and the Government of the Peoples' Republic of China on the Question of Hong Kong.[122]

It can be said that most declarations contain political statements only and thus have no binding effect in international law. However, the UNGA has often made declarations (see Chapter 2.12.2) which, although non-binding, have influenced the development of international law e.g. the Universal Declaration of Human Rights (see Chapter 12.2.1); or in some cases have been regarded as reflecting customary law on the relevant topic. For example, in the *Case Concerning Armed Activities on the Territory of the Congo (Democratic Republic of the Congo v Uganda) (Merits)*,[123] the ICJ held that the 1970 UNGA Declaration on Principles of International Law concerning Friendly Relations and Co-operation among States in Accordance with the Charter of the United Nations reflected the rules of customary international law.

2.12 Soft law

It has been submitted that international law consists of rules having varying degrees of force. Some of these rules (e.g. those in international treaties) contain binding obligations while others, such as acts

---

120   S. Talmon, *The Security Council as World Legislature* (2005) 99 AJIL, 175 and I. Johnstone, *Legislation and Adjudication in the UN Security Council: Bringing Down the Deliberative Deficit* (2008) 102 AJIL, 275.
121   The *Nuclear Tests (Australia v France) Case* [1974] ICJ Rep253.
122   (1984) 23 ILM 1366.
123   (2006) 45 ILM 271–395.

adopted by IGOs, are non-binding (e.g. resolutions or declarations of the UNGA, which set out standards of behaviour or ideals which the international community aspires to achieve). The influence of non-binding rules on the development of international law and on State practice is considerable, although these rules cannot be classified as law in positive law. They are called 'soft law' to distinguish them from 'hard law', i.e. binding rules of international law. According to Boyle and Chinkin 'It is certainly a fallacy to dismiss soft law, properly understood, as not law: it can and does contribute to the corpus of international law.'[124] Indeed, soft law has the potential of law-making, i.e. it may be a starting point for later 'hardening' of non-binding provisions (e.g. UNGA resolutions may be translated into binding treaties), may provide evidence of an existing customary rule, may be formative of *opinio juris* or State practice that creates a new customary rule, may be helpful as a means of a purposive interpretation of international law, may be incorporated in binding treaties in provisions which the parties do not intend to be binding, and may in other ways 'assist in the development and application of general international law'.[125] Nevertheless, soft law is made up of rules lacking binding force, and the general view is that it should not be considered as an independent, formal source of international law despite the fact that it may produce significant legal effects.

Soft law has many advantages. It allows States to participate in the creation of new rules without the necessity of implementing them into national law. In many areas, such as the protection of the environment, States are not ready to accept binding obligations at a particular time but are gradually taking measures to conform with international standards. Further non-State actors such as IGOs, NGOs, international private associations and corporations can participate in the elaboration and implementation of soft law. In this respect codes of conduct have become an important part of soft law.

The following can be identified as non binding rules:

- some provisions of international treaties;

- political declarations made by two or more States (see Chapter 2.11);

- recommendations and resolutions of IGOs (see Chapter 2.10 and see below), in particular those adopted by the UNGA;

- codes of conduct.

The growing importance of non-State actors (see Chapter 5.12, 5.13 and 5.14) has relevance to the development of international law. Nowadays, non-State actors actively participate in the negotiation and codification of international law. For example campaigns organised by a coalition of NGOs led to adoption of the Convention on the Prohibition of the Use, Stockpiling, Production and Transfer of Anti-Personal Mines and their Destruction (see Chapter 17.3.1.4.B), and to the creation of the International Criminal Court (ICC). Further, the relevant NGOs are still actively encouraging States to become contracting parties to the above mentioned instruments. Another example is provided by NGOs which participated in the official negotiations at the Earth Summit held in Rio de Janeiro in June 1992 and greatly contributed to its success. There are various forms in which non-State actors, in particular NGOs, initiate and influence the law-making process at the international level.[126]

---

124   A. Boyle and C. Chinkin, *The Making of International Law*, Oxford: Oxford University Press, 2007, 212.

125   The *Case Concerning the Gabčíkovo-Nagymaros Project* (*Hungary/Slovakia*) (*Judgment*) [1997] ICJ Rep 7, para 140.

126   See A. Boyle and Ch. Chinkin, *The Making of International Law*, Oxford: Oxford University Press, 2007, in particular 41–98.

2.12.1 Provisions of treaties

Some provisions of international treaties are part of soft law. These are:

- treaty provisions which do not impose any obligations on the parties, e.g. Article 4(1) and (2) of the 1992 Framework Convention on Climate Changes[127] which is so unclear and obscure with regard to obligations imposed on contracting parties concerning measures to be adopted with a view to tackling greenhouse gas emission, that the US interpreted it as not imposing 'any commitment to any specific level of emissions at any time';[128]

- treaty provisions which provide that the contacting parties should co-operate in a particular area e.g. Article 2 of the 1985 Vienna Convention for the Protection of the Ozone Layer[129] which states that 'Each Contracting Party shall, so far as possible and as appropriate, co-operate with other Contracting Parties directly or, where appropriate through competent international organisations, in respect of areas beyond national jurisdiction and on other matters of mutual interest, for the conservation and sustainable use of biological diversity';

- treaty provisions which state that the contracting parties should reach an agreement on a particular point in the future, e.g. Article 105 of the UN Charter which states that the UN shall enjoy privileges and immunities necessary for fulfilment of its purposes in each member State without further specification. In fact, in order to implement this provision a Convention on the Privileges and Immunities of the United Nations was adopted on 13 February 1946[130] (see Chapter 5.11.1);

- provisions of a treaty not yet in force. These may be persuasive as between those States that have signed and ratified the treaty. It is to be noted that Article 18 VCLT bars a State which has indicated its consent to become a contracting party to a treaty from defeating the object and purposes of that treaty (see Chapter 3.5.4.1).

2.12.2 The UNGA

There is confusion in the approach by many writers as to the question of whether resolutions adopted by the UNGA (UNGARs) constitute a source of international law. Under the provisions of the Charter the majority of such resolutions have no direct legal effect. However, it is clear that some resolutions embody a clear consensus on the part of the international community. Other resolutions may be very significant in influencing the development of international law and practice.

Attempts are often made to fit UNGARs into the parameters of either treaty or custom. Clearly, such resolutions do not conform to the formal requirements of a treaty and it may perhaps be unrealistic to apply treaty rules on interpretation, amendment, etc., to them. Equally, UNGARs do not, on their face, meet the requirements laid down for customary law.

Perhaps, the better view is to regard UNGARs (and resolutions of other international bodies) as evidence of existing customary law, or of *opinio juris*, or of the practice of States, depending on each case. The weight of the evidence would be determined by considering all the relevant factors surrounding the adoption of the resolution in question – the degree of support for the resolution; whether or not

---

127   1771 UNTS 107.
128   See A. Boyle and Ch. Chinkin, *The Making of International Law*, Oxford: Oxford University Press, 2007, 220.
129   1513 UNTS 293.
130   1 UNTS 15.

that support was widespread among ideologically or politically divided groups; the intention of States in voting for the resolution as illustrated by the debates, the form of words used, etc.

The above approach was adopted by arbitrator Dupuy in *Texaco* v *Libya*[131] in which he considered the legal effect of two UNGARs: UNGAR 1803 (XVII) on Permanent Sovereignty over Natural Resources[132] and UNGAR 3281 (XXIX), the Charter of Economic Rights and Duties of States[133] (see Chapter 11.10.1.4.B). Although UNGAR 3281 was adopted 12 years after UNGAR 1803 with very strong support from developing States – 120 votes in favour, six (Belgium, Denmark, the Federal Republic of Germany, Luxembourg, the UK and the US) against and ten abstentions – Dupuy concluded that it was UNGAR 1803 that reflected existing customary law. The reasoning behind this was that UNGAR 1803 had achieved wide support from both the capital-importing (developing) States and capital-exporting (Western) States. UNGAR 1803 was therefore illustrative of a broad consensus between the groups likely to be affected by its provisions. In contrast, UNGAR 3281 had received virtually no support from capital-exporting States. To be regarded as evidencing customary law, a resolution must be seen to have gathered support from a broad cross-section of the international community.

A further example where resolutions of the UNGA were held to be reflective of customary law arose in the *Nicaragua Case (Nicaragua v US) (Merits)*.[134] In that case the majority of the Court considered that UNGAR 2625 (XXV), the Declaration on Principles of International Law Concerning Friendly Relations and Co-operation among States, was illustrative of customary law. While there is little dispute about the relative importance of this resolution, or about the broad measure of support it achieved (it was adopted by consensus), some commentators have voiced concern at the manner in which the Court accepted that the resolution could be evidence of both State practice and *opinio juris* for the purposes of establishing custom. Any acceptance of this dual characteristic of such resolutions would have the effect of elevating UNGARs to a form of 'instant custom'. This approach remains highly controversial.

2.12.3 Codes of conduct

Codes of conduct are often also known as recommendations, resolutions, codes of ethics and guidelines.

There are many different types of code of conduct, but it can be said their common characteristics are that:

- they are non-binding instruments unless otherwise agreed;

- they describe the responsibilities, expected action and expected behaviour of those to whom they are addressed;

- they can be adopted by States, IGOs, NGOs, and other non-State actors; and

- they are addressed mainly to non-State actors although they can also be directed to States.

The objective of codes of conduct is to ensure that their addressees conduct themselves in accordance with the rules and principles set out in the relevant code.

---

131   (1977) 53 ILR 389.

132   (14 December 1962) GAOR seventeenth Session Supp 17, 15.

133   (12 December 1974) GAOR 29th Session Supp 31 vol 1, 50.

134   [1986] ICJ Rep 14.

The earliest modern example of a code of conduct is provided by Lieber's Instructions for the Government of Armies of the United States in the Field, known as the Lieber Code, which was prepared by Professor Lieber during the American Civil War and promulgated by President Lincoln. The Lieber Code was an instruction given by the US President to the Union Forces during the American Civil War on how they should conduct themselves during wartime in terms of treatment of the civil population in the occupied areas, the treatment of captured enemies, etc.

Codes of conduct became popular in the 1970s and 1980s to regulate in an informal way (i.e. through non-binding rules) the conduct of businesses operating in developing countries. This was in response to UNGA's call for the creation of a New International Economic Order.[135] The UNGA itself in 1980 adopted the so called RBA Code which is a Set of Multilaterally Agreed Equitable Principles and Rules for the Control of Restrictive Business Practices. Other IGOs adopted codes of conduct within their areas of competence, e.g. the WHO adopted an International Code of Marketing of Breast-milk Substitutes in 1981[136] and the International Labour Organisation (ILO) adopted the Tripartite Declaration of Principles Concerning Multinational Enterprises and Social Policy in 1977.[137]

From the beginning of the1990s, the manner in which codes of conduct are prepared and implemented has changed in that nowadays all important stakeholders in the relevant sector are usually involved in their preparation. Compliance is now often ensured by follow up procedures consisting of voluntary, or often mandatory, reporting systems. Further, NGOs play an important role in the effective implementation of codes as they, by way of bad publicity, often compel compliance of State and non-State actors with the required standard of behaviour.

IGOs are still the main authors of codes of conduct at the international level. In particular codes of conduct adopted by the UN by way of UNGA resolutions may have worldwide impact. This is exemplified by the UN Global Compact of 2000[138] and the Principles for Responsible Investment of 2006,[139] both of which were prepared by the UN, in co-operation with businesses, to further the objectives of the UN.

It is to be noted that almost all businesses and their trade associations have their codes of conduct. Compliance with codes of conduct by multinational corporations, in particular, may lead to the establishment of new trade usages and culminate with the emergence of new rules of *lex mercatoria*. Additionally, this may contribute to the recognition of corporations as subjects of international law (see Chapter 5.14). Further, businesses have a lot to gain by complying with codes of conduct in that they maintain their reputations, which for any business is a priceless asset, and attract ethically oriented new customers who not only value the quality of a product or service but equally the fact that they deal with a corporation that implements high standards of integrity and professionalism.

It is important to emphasise that although codes of conduct, being non-binding rules, are only a source of soft law their importance in the development of international law should not be underestimated. In particular, with regard to international corporations, codes of conduct often impose on them obligations under international law, and thus provide an argument in favour of their recognition as subjects of international law. So far those obligations have been of a non-binding nature. However, once international

---

135   The Declaration on the Establishment of the New International Economic Order, Res 3201 (S-VI) (1 May 1974) GAOR 6th Spec Session Supp 1, 3.

136   The World Health Organisation 'International Code of Marketing of Breastmilk Substitutes' (adopted 21 May 1981), (1981) 20 ILM 1004.

137   The International Labour Organisation 'Tripartite Declaration of Principles concerning Multinational Enterprises and Social Policy' (adopted 16 November 1977) (1978) 17 ILM 422.

138   United Nations Global Compact available at www.unglobalcompact.org (accessed 10 Septermber 2014).

139   Principles for Responsible Investment (Investor Initiative in Partnership with UNEP Finance Initiative and the UN Global Compact) 'PRI Overview' available at www.unpri.org/files/pri.pdf (accessed 10 September 2014).

law starts to impose binding legal obligations on transnational corporations they will have a good case to claim that their international personality should be acknowledged. In this respect a failed attempt of the UN Commission on Human Rights' Sub-Commission on the Promotion and Protection of Human Rights, which in 2003 adopted the Draft UN Norms on the Responsibility of Transnational Corporations and Other Business Enterprises with regard to Human Rights,[140] is of interest.

The Draft was prepared in consultation with stakeholders including transnational corporations. It imposes binding obligations on transnational corporations concerning the protection of HRs, the protection of the environment, and the protection of consumers. The far reaching HRs obligations which the Draft imposed on the private sector were the main causes of its demise. Many governments and business representatives argued that the protection of HRs is the domain of a State and should not be extended to the private sector. For that reason, the UN Commission on Human Rights failed to adopt it. However, it established the position of the Special Representative of the Secretary General of the United Nations (UNS-G) on the issue of human rights and transnational corporations. In June 2008, the Special Representative, Harvard Professor John Ruggie,[141] submitted his final report to the UN Human Rights Council (UNHRC) (which in 2006 replaced the UN Commission on Human Rights (see Chapter 12.4.1.2)) in which he proposed a policy framework for better managing business and human rights.[142] The Framework rests on three complementary but interdependent pillars:

- the State duty to protect against human rights violations by third parties, including businesses;

- the corporate responsibility to respect human rights; and

- the greater access by victims to effective remedy.

The UNHRC welcomed the report and invited the Special Representative to submit a set of Guiding Principles for the implementation of each pillar of the Framework. In March 2011, the Special Representative submitted to the UNHRC 'Guiding Principles on Business and Human Rights: Implementing the United Nations "Protect, Respect and Remedy" Framework'.[143] The 31 Principles, accompanied by a commentary, provide, for the first time, an authoritative global standard for States and businesses on how to ensure that transnational businesses respect human rights. In July 2011, the UNHRC endorsed by consensus the Guiding Principles on Business and Human Rights (GPBHR) and established a Working Group on the issue of human rights and transnational corporations and other business enterprises, consisting of five independent experts, for a period of 3 years, mandated to promote dissemination and implementation of the principles.[144] The GPBHR have proved popular with businesses (e.g. Coca Cola endorsed them), States, and international organisations. They served as models for elaborating and updating similar standards, e. g. the updated Guidelines for Multinational Enterprises prepared by the OECD, and the 2011 European Commission's Communication on Corporate Social Responsibility,[145] but not with human rights groups which judged them as not sufficient to ensure the appropriate standard of protection.

---

140 UN Sub-Commission on the Promotion and Protection of Human Rights, 'Economic, Social and Cultural Rights: Norms on the Responsibilities of Transnational Corporations and Other Business Enterprises with Regard to Human Rights' (adopted 13 August 2003) UN Doc E/CN.4/Sub.2/2003/12/Rev.2.

141 For the Special Representative's fascinating story regarding the establishment and implementation of the principles see: J.G. Ruggie, *Just Business: Multinational Corporations and Human Rights*, New York: W.W. Norton & Co, 2013.

142 A/HRC/8/5.

143 A/HRC/17/31, annex (2011).

144 Human Rights Council Res 17/4, UN Doc A/HRC/RES/17/4 (6 July 2011), available at http://daccess-dds-ny.un.org/doc/UNDOC/GEN/G11/144/71/PDF/G1114471.pdf?OpenElement. (accessed 26 July 2014).

145 COM(2011) 681final.

In September 2013, Ecuador, acting on behalf of 85 States, expressed the need for establishing a legally binding instrument on business and HRs. This resulted in the adoption in June 2014 by the UNHRC of a resolution entitled 'Elaboration of an International Legally Binding Instrument on Transnational Corporations and other Business Enterprises with Respect to Human Rights' which provides for the establishment of an open-ended intergovernmental working group (IWG) with a view to drafting such an instrument.[146] The resolution was opposed by many developed States, including the UK, US, Japan, Ireland and by the EU which prefer reliance on non-binding GPBHR. However, such States as Russia, China, India, supported the resolution. As evidenced by the GPBHR, a non-binding code of conduct may be the first step towards the adoption of an international treaty in the relevant area.

2.13 Codification of international law: the contribution of the International Law Commission (ILC)

Customary rules lack precision and are difficult to evidence. The idea of codification of customary rules originates from the time of the 1815 Vienna Congress at which the participating States expressed a need for codifying rules in areas of great importance to them, such as the legal regime of international rivers, the prohibition of slavery and the regulation of diplomatic relations. The idea of codification was further developed by private societies and institutions such as the Institut de Droit International and the International Law Association, both founded in 1873. The two Hague Peace Conferences of 1899 and 1907 accomplished an enormous task by codifying the most important customary rules relating to the conduct of war (see Chapter 17.2.6).

After WWI the Assembly of the League of Nations set up the first permanent organ – the Committee of Experts – to examine matters 'sufficiently ripe' for regulation through international conventions. The Committee selected three areas – nationality, the territorial sea and some aspects of State responsibility – as being ready for codification. The League of Nations then convened the Hague Codification Conference in 1930 which produced rather unsatisfactory results as only certain aspects of nationality were agreed by the participating States to be regulated by international conventions.

At the 1945 San Francisco Conference, when the UN Charter was being discussed, the idea of directly investing the UN with full legislative powers was rejected, but the proposal to have a body entrusted with the codification of international law was viewed with favour. The UNGA, therefore, was invited to initiate studies to 'encourage the progressive development of international law and its codification'. The UNGA responded by setting up a Committee entrusted with examining the matter. On the basis of a report from the Committee the UNGA adopted Resolution 174 (II) in November 1947 establishing the ILC. At its first session in 1949 the ILC reviewed topics for possible study and decided to select 14 topics for codification:

1 recognition of States and governments;

2 succession of States and governments;

3 jurisdictional immunities of States and their property;

4 jurisdiction with regard to crimes committed outside national territory;

5 regime of the high seas;

6 regime of territorial waters;

7 nationality and statelessness;

---

146   A/HRC/26/L.22.

8   treatment of aliens;

9   right of asylum;

10   law of treaties;

11   diplomatic intercourse and immunities;

12   consular intercourse and immunities;

13   State responsibility;

14   arbitral procedure.

This list was considered as provisional, but did, in fact, become the ILC's basic long-term programme.

Under the Statute of the ILC the UNGA as well as Members of the UN and other authorised agencies are entitled to refer topics for study to the ILC, although the ILC may also choose topics for codification. However, requests from the UNGA have priority over other proposals.

The ILC is made up of 34 members elected by the UNGA from candidates nominated by the member States of the UN. They serve in their individual capacity and are independent of any government. They are elected on the basis of equitable geographical distribution so as to represent the major legal systems of the world. The ILC holds its sessions in Geneva and meets annually in open session for 10 weeks.

The two main tasks of the ILC are:

■ the codification of international law, which is defined as the more precise formulation and systematisation of the existing customary rules of international law; and

■ the progressive development of international law, which involves the creation of new rules of international law either by means of the regulation of a new topic or by means of the revision of the existing rules.

The above tasks normally require the preparation of international conventions. When a topic for study is selected by the ILC, it appoints a special rapporteur who is entrusted with the task of preparing a report on the subject. At this stage governments may be requested to provide texts of law, statutes, judicial decisions and diplomatic correspondence relevant to the topic under consideration. The special rapporteur submits a report, normally in the form of draft articles with commentaries, which are discussed by the Commission. Once the Commission reaches an agreement on the provisional draft articles it submits the draft articles to the UNGA, and to governments, for their written observations. Under the current procedure governments have about one year to reply. The observations are received by the special rapporteur, who in the light of these, prepares a further report. The ILC, on the basis of that report and observations of governments and the UNGA (Sixth Committee), adopts a final draft which is forwarded to the UNGA and which contains a recommendation regarding further action. Such action may consist of the adoption of the report by resolution, or of the recommendation of the draft for the conclusion of a treaty or the convening of an international conference with a view to the conclusion of a treaty.

The number of international conventions, resolutions and model laws prepared by the ILC is impressive. The ILC itself is unique and has made a unique contribution to the codification and development of international law. It is unique by virtue of:

■ its membership which reflects the main form of civilisation, and the principal legal systems of the world;

■ its special relationship with the UNGA as it is a standing, subsidiary body of the UNGA;

■ its direct contact with members of the UN which are consulted on a regular basis with respect to any topic under examination, and which through the UNGA's Sixth Committee are kept up to date on the ILC's work as they debate and comment on annual reports presented by the ILC.

The ILC fulfils its task of developing and codifying international law with great professionalism and dedication. In effect, the ILC has codified international law and when required has developed it to meet demands of members of the UN.[147] The list of achievements of the ICL is too long to be detailed here. Suffice it to say that there is not one topic in this book which has not been in some way examined, codified or developed by the ILC.

RECOMMENDED READING

Books

Alvarez, J.E., *International Organizations as Law-Makers*, Oxford: Oxford University Press, 2005.

Boyle, A. and Chinkin, C., *The Making of International Law*, Oxford: Oxford University Press, 2007.

Byers, M., Custom, *Power and the Power of Rules: International Relations and Customary International Law*, Cambridge: Cambridge University Press, 1999.

Orakhelashvili,A., *Peremptory Norms in International Law*, Oxford: Oxford University Press, 2006.

Ragazzi, M., *The Concept of International Obligations* Erga Omnes, Oxford: Clarendon Press, 1997.

Ruggie, J.G., *Just Business: Multinational Corporations and Human Rights*, Harvard, MA: Harvard University Press, 2013.

Tams, C.J., *Enforcing Obligations* Erga Omnes *in International Law*, Cambridge: Cambridge University Press, 2005.

Articles

Akehurst, M., *Custom as a Source of International Law* (1974–75) 47 BYIL, 1.

Bianchi, A., *Gazing at the Crystal Ball (again): State Immunity and* Jus Cogens *Beyond Germany v Italy* (2013) 4/3 J Int Disp Settlement, 461.

Bordin, F.L., *Reflections of Customary International Law: The Authority of Codification, Convention and ILC Draft Articles* (2014) 63 ICLQ, 535.

Christenson, G.A., Jus Cogens*: Guarding Interests Fundamental to International Society* (1988) 28 Va J Intl L, 585.

Conway, G., *Breaches of EC Law and the International Responsibility of Member States* (2002) 13 EJIL, 679.

Ford, C.A., *Judicial Discretion in International Jurisprudence: Article 38 (1) (c) and 'General Principles of Law'* (1994–95) 5 Duke J Comp & Intl L, 35.

Johnstone, I., *Legislation and Adjudication in the UN Security Council: Bringing Down the Deliberative Deficit* (2008) 102 AJIL, 275.

Murphy, S.D., *What a Difference a Year Makes: The International Court of Justice's 2012 Jurisprudence* (2013) 4/3 J Int Dis Settlement, 539.

Orakhelashvili, A., *The Classification of International Legal Rules: A Reply to Stefan Talmon* (2013) 26 LJIL, 89.

Simma, B. and Pulkowski, D., *Of Planets and the Universe: Self-contained Regimes in International Law* (2006) 17 EJIL, 483.

Talmon, S. *The Security Council as World Legislature* (2005) 99 AJIL, 175.

Tomuschat, C., *Obligations Arising for States Without or Against Their Will* (1993) 241 RdC 195–374.

---

147   See: G Nolte, 'The International Law Commission Facing the Second Decade of the Twenty- First Century' in U. Fastenrath *et al.* (eds), *From Bilateralism to Community Interest*, Oxford: Oxford University Press, 2011, 781–792 and F.L. Bordin, *Reflections of Customary International Law: The Authority of Codification, Convention and ILC Draft Articles* (2014) 63 ICLQ, 535.

AIDE-MÉMOIRE

Suggested hierarchy of sources of international law and resolution of conflicts between them

Article 38 of the Statute of the ICJ is not intended to set out the hierarchy of sources of international law. However, it indicates the order in which the ICJ will apply, in all cases, where the parties do not decide otherwise, international law. If there is a conflict between sources of international law it is likely to be resolved as follows:

If treaties are in conflict with the rules of *jus cogens* Article 53 VCLT applies. It provides that a treaty is void if, at the time of its conclusion, it conflicts with a "rule of *jus cogens*. As to existing treaties, under Article 64 VCLT if a new rule of *jus cogens* emerges and a treaty conflicts with it, that treaty become void and terminates. However, specific procedures set out in Articles 65 and 66 VCLT must be followed if a party to a treaty claims that an existing treaty breaches a new rule of *jus cogens*. Article 69 VCLT provides that a treaty can only be void if its invalidity is established in accordance with Articles 65 and 66 VCLT. This means that a party to a treaty must follow Articles 65 and 66 VCLT procedures to invalidate it, but a State, which is not a party to a treaty, **or an IGO** does not have to follow Articles 65 and 66 VCLT.

Jus cogens. These are customary rules that have achieved the status of peremptory norms and thus cannot be derogated from or altered except by a norm of comparable strength. They are superior to any other rules and, prevail over any other source of law.

Rules creating *erga omnes* obligations. All *jus cogens* rules create *erga omnes* obligations, but not all rules creating *erga omnes* obligations are *jus cogens* rules.

Treaties.

Treaties, customary rules, and principles of international law.

Equity. This is regarded as a general principle of international law (see above).

Secondary law of IGOs. Its ranking will depend on the IGOs concerned, e.g. resolutions adopted by the UNSC under Chapter VII of the UN Charter prevail over any other sources of international law.

Declarations which produce binding legal effect. Whether these are regarded as a source of international law is debatable. They may have a similar effect to a treaty.

Judicial decisions. Precedent has no binding authority in international law.

The writings of publicists. They constitute evidence of customary law and play a subsidiary role in developing new rules of law.

If there is a conflict between an *erga omnes* rule and a rule of *jus cogens*, the *jus cogens* rule shall prevail.

If there is a conflict between any of these the one which will prevail will be that identified as being the *lex specialis* (i.e. "the special law"). The identification of the *lex specialis* will be determined contextually. However, the *lex specialis* will yield to general law in the following four circumstances:

- When the supremacy of general law may be inferred from its form or its nature or from the intent of the parties
- When the application of the *lex specialis* might frustrate the purpose of general law
- When rights of a third party acquired under general law may be negatively affected by the application of the *lex specialis*
- When the balance of rights and obligations established by general law would be negatively affected by the application of the *lex specialis*.

3

THE LAW OF TREATIES

CONTENTS

CHAPTER OUTLINE

1 Introduction

The law of treaties is a body of rules which provides a definition of a treaty, and deals with matters relating to the conclusion, entry into force, application, validity, amendment, modification, interpretation, suspension and termination of a treaty. Apart from the rules of *jus cogens*, the law of treaties is not concerned with the substance of treaties, i.e. the rights and obligations imposed by treaties.

The expression 'treaty' is used as a generic term to cover a multitude of international agreements and contractual engagements concluded between States. These international agreements are called by various names including treaties, conventions, pacts, declarations, charters, concordats, protocols, covenants, or by even less formal names such as 'exchange of notes' and 'memorandum of agreement'. The confusing nomenclature notwithstanding, what counts is whether the instrument in question shows that the parties have an intent to create a legally binding instrument. If so, then it will be a treaty.

2 The main features of the 1969 Vienna Convention on the Law of Treaties (VCLT)

The VCLT represents both the codification (i.e. of customary law and general principles) and the progressive development of the law of treaties. It came into force on 27 January 1980 and as at 9 November 2014 had been ratified by 114 States. The VCLT applies to treaties which satisfy the conditions set out in Article 2 VCLT (see point 4). It does not have retrospective effect, and only applies to treaties entered into by a State from the time of its entry into force for that State. The VCLT confirms that customary law will apply to issues not regulated by its provisions (Articles 39(a) and 4 and the eight paragraphs of the preamble). In fact, State practice and judgments of the ICJ show that the VCLT, to a great extent, reflects the rules of customary law and therefore, applies whether or not a State has ratified it. There will be no need to reform the VCLT as its built-in safeguards ensure the necessary flexibility to take account of evolving State practice.

3 The fundamental principles of the law of treaties

The three fundamental principles of the law of treaties are: the principle of free consent, the principle of good faith and the principle of *pacta sunt servanda*.

A. The principle of free consent means that a State cannot be bound by a treaty to which it has not consented (Article 34 VCLT). This rule is subject to some exceptions (see point 10C). Further, there is a presumption that a State, not a party to a treaty, consents to a right which that treaty confers on it (Articles 34–36 VCLT).

B. *Pacta sunt servanda*, a latin maxim which literally means that agreements must be kept, is embodied in Article 26 VCLT which states that: 'Every treaty in force is binding upon the parties to it and must be performed by them in good faith.'

C. The principle of good faith is fundamental to the law of treaties. It applies throughout the life of a treaty, from its negotiation, through its performance and up to its termination.

4 The definition of a treaty under the VCLT

Article 2(1) VCLT defines a treaty as any agreement, whatever its appellation or other characteristics, intended to create a legal obligation, concluded in writing between two or more States and governed by international law.

5 Conclusion of treaties

Different stages can be identified in the process of conclusion of a treaty:

A. Negotiations. Representatives of States must have the necessary powers to engage in negotiations. Under Article 7(2) VCLT heads of State or heads of government and Foreign Ministers are *ex officio* empowered to carry out acts necessary for the conclusion of treaties. Accredited representatives are only empowered to represent a State for the purposes of concluding a particular treaty.

B. The adoption of the text. This is a formal act whereby the form and content of the proposed text are settled (Article 9 VCLT).

C. Authentication of the agreed text. During this stage the definitive text of the proposed treaty is established as correct, authentic and not subject to alteration. The method of authentication is usually by signing and initialling the relevant text.

D. Consent to be bound. A State may express its consent to be bound by a treaty by signing it, exchanging instruments constituting the treaty, ratifying, accepting, approving or acceding to it, or by any other means if so agreed (Article 11 VCLT).

6 Reservations to treaties

A. The VCLT provisions on reservations are unclear and contain gaps. In order to elucidate the meaning of six provisions of the VCLT on reservations the ILC spent 18 years of work generating 16 Special Reports. In 2011 The ILC adopted its Guide to Practice on Reservations to Treaties (hereafter referred to as the Guide) together with commentaries, a non-binding document which reflects both customary international law and an attempt at progressive development of the law in this area. It defines both a reservation and an objection to a reservation, and examines legal effects of permissible and non-permissible reservations.

A reservation is defined in Article 2(1)(d) VCLT as a unilateral statement, however phrased or named, made by a State, when signing, ratifying, accepting, approving or acceding to a treaty, whereby it purports to exclude or to modify the legal effect of certain provisions of the treaty in their application to that State. A reservation to a multilateral treaty must:

- be in writing;
- contain, to the extent possible, the reason why it is being made;
- be communicated to the other contracting parties and entities who are entitled to become a party to the treaty, so they can, within 12 months, accept the reservation, or reject it, by formulating an objection.

A reservation may be withdrawn but such withdrawal must be formulated in writing and communicated to the contracting parties.

B. Article 19 VCLT distinguishes between permissible and non-permissible reservations.

Permissible reservations are those which are expressly permitted by the relevant treaty and those which are compatible with the object and purpose of that treaty. Reservations operate on the basis of reciprocity and, if they are permissible, create the following relationships between the reserving State and the other contracting States:

■ Where a contracting State has made no objection to a reservation. The treaty will be modified in that the provision to which the reservation relates will not apply between the contracting State and the reserving State, e.g. if State X made a reservation in respect of provision A and State Y accepted the reservation, the treaty will apply to States X and Y with the exception of provision A.

■ When a contracting party has objected to a reservation and opposed the entry into force of the treaty, the treaty will not enter into force for the reserving State.

■ When a contracting party has objected to a reservation but did not oppose the entry into force of the treaty between itself and the reserving State, the treaty will apply between both parties except for the provisions to which the reservation relates.

Non-permissible reservations are:

■ reservations prohibited by the relevant treaty;

■ reservations which are not included in the list of reservations expressly allowed under the relevant treaty (so applying the latin maxim *expressio unius est exclusio alterius*);

■ reservations which are incompatible with the object and purpose of the relevant treaty.

Non-permissible reservations are invalid, but views differ on whether they are 'totally invalid', which means that the reserving State's ratification is ineffective or whether they are 'partially invalid', which means that they are severed from the reserving State's declaration of consent to be bound by the relevant treaty, with the consequence that the treaty applies to the reserving State and the reservation is disregarded. The ILC Guide takes a middle of the road approach. A reserving State which has made an invalid reservation will be a contracting party to a treaty unless it expresses its intention, at any time, not to be bound by the treaty. If a body monitoring implementation of a particular treaty (a treaty body, see Chapter 12.4.3) decides that a reservation is invalid, the reserving State has 12 months from the date at which the treaty body had made such a decision to express its intention not to be bound by the treaty. If it fails then it will be bound by the treaty without the benefit of the reservation.

7. Interpretative and conditional interpretative declarations and their relationship with reservations

The ICL Guide equates conditional interpretative declarations with reservations.

8. Entry into force, deposit, registration and publication of treaties

A. **Entry into force**. The conditions for the entry into force are normally specified by the treaty. Otherwise, a treaty is presumed to enter into force as soon as all the negotiating States have expressed their consent to be bound by it.

B. **Deposit**. A depository is designated by the contracting parties to a treaty (Article 76(1) VCLT). The depository is the custodian of the treaty and performs administrative tasks relating to it (Articles

76–80 VCLT). However, the depository is not entitled to determine the legal effect of any instrument or communication received from a party. This task is within the competence of the contracting parties.

C. Registration. In order to ensure transparency in the conduct of international relations Article 102 UN Charter requires all treaties and all agreements entered into by any member of the UN to be registered with the UN Secretariat. However, failure to register a treaty has no effect on its validity.

D. Publication. Subsequent to registration, a treaty will be officially published in the UN Treaty Series (UNTS), so that anyone can consult it.

9. Validity of treaties

The VCLT sets out the only grounds on which a State can rely to nullify a treaty (Article 42(1) VCLT). It makes a distinction between grounds of nullity which:

- concern the lack of consent of a party to a treaty with the consequence that a treaty (but not a bilateral treaty) will still be valid for all parties except the State which did not consent to it. The vitiating factors are mentioned in Articles 8, 46–49 VCLT and dealt with in A below;

- lead to nullity of a treaty for all parties on the grounds that it was either concluded in violation of a *jus cogens* rule (Article 53 VCLT) or is in conflict with a *jus cogens* rule which emerged after its conclusion (Article 64 VCLT). These grounds are dealt with in B below.

A. Grounds of nullity which affect the consent of a contracting party and which, if successfully relied upon, may result in the relevant treaty being invalid for the claimant State, are:

- Manifest violation of its internal law (Article 46 VCLT). In order to succeed the alleged violation of domestic law must concern fundamental provisions which relate to the State's treaty-making power and must be evident to any State acting in accordance with normal practice and in good faith.

- Violations of specific restrictions on the competence of the representative of a State (Article 47 VCLT). In order to succeed the restrictions on the competence must have been notified to the other parties.

- Essential error (Article 48 VCLT). In order to succeed, an error, whether unilateral or mutual, must neither concern a question of law nor the wording of the text of a treaty agreed by the parties. It must relate to a fact or a situation which was assumed at the time when a treaty was concluded and formed an essential basis of its consent. Further, a State will not be able to claim error if by its own conduct it contributed to it.

- Fraud (Article 49 VCLT). This is rarely invoked.

- Corruption of a representative (Article 50 VCLT). In order to succeed the 'corruption' must be a 'substantial influence'. A small courtesy or favour shown to a representative will be insufficient.

- Coercion of a representative (Articles 51 VCLT). In order to succeed coercion must be directed at the representative personally (e.g. blackmailing threats or threats against the representative's family) and not consist of a threat of action against his State.

- Coercion of a State (Article 51 VCLT). In order to succeed, it must be shown that the conclusion of a treaty has been procured by the threat or use of force in violation of the principles of international law embodied in the UN Charter.

The doctrine of 'unequal' treaties states that treaties which are 'unequal' either because of their substance (e.g. they impose only obligations on one party and grant only rights to the other, or they impose extreme restrictions on the sovereignty of one party) or because of an unequal procedure (e.g. they are concluded under political, or economic coercion) are not legally binding. This doctrine has been rejected as constituting an independent ground of nullity, but international law addresses the matter of equality by establishing special or differential treatment to ensure that a burden imposed by a treaty is shared equally by contracting States in order to achieve common goals.

B. Grounds of nullity which, if successful, will nullify the treaty as a whole (i.e. for all contracting parties) are based on violations of a *jus cogens* rule. This may occur in two situations:

- under Article 53 VCLT a treaty is void if, at the time of its conclusion, it conflicts with a rule of *jus cogens*;

- under Article 64 VCLT, if a new *jus cogens* rule emerges, any existing treaty which is in conflict with that rule becomes void and terminates.

10. Application of treaties

A. Territorial application. Under Article 29 VCLT, in the absence of any territorial clause or other indication to the contrary, a treaty is presumed to apply to all the territories for which the contracting States are internationally responsible.

B. Conflict between treaties. A conflict between treaties is resolved either on the basis of a conflict clause contained in one or both treaties or upon interpretation, aided by reference to maxims such as the *lex posteriori* and the *lex specialis* (see Chapter 2.4.2.1).

C. Effect of treaties on a third party. The fundamental rule is that a treaty applies only between the parties to it. This is known by the maxim *pacta tertiis nec nocent nec prosunt* and is contained in Article 34 VCLT. There are however some exceptions:

- If a treaty provision imposes an obligation on a third party, that treaty provision may become binding on that party but only if and when it becomes a part of international customary law.

- If a treaty provision confers a right on a third party, and the contracting parties have expressly or by implication intended to create that right for the third party, that third party must, in order to take benefit of the right, consent to it (but this is presumed so long as the contrary is not indicated).

11. Amendment and modification of treaties

A. Amendment. The principle of *pacta sunt servanda* requires the unanimous consent of all parties to the relevant treaty in order to amend it. If this cannot be achieved, Article 40(4) VCLT provides that amendments will not be binding on a party which has not accepted them. However, some treaties provide that amendments adopted by a specified majority will be binding on all contracting States (e.g. the UN Charter).

B. Modification. This occurs when some of the parties to a treaty formally agree to modify the effects of the treaty among themselves, while continuing to be bound by the treaty in their relations with the other parties (Article 41 VCLT). A consistent practice, if it establishes common consent of the parties to be bound by a different rule from that laid down in the treaty, will have the effect of modifying a treaty.

12. Interpretation of treaties

The VCLT endorses the textual, systematic, teleological and historical methods of interpretation (Articles 31 and 32 VCLT). Views differ as to whether the VCLT establishes any hierarchy of these methods.

13. Termination and suspension of treaties

The difference between suspension and termination is that:

- when a treaty is suspended it is still valid but its operation is suspended temporarily, either for all parties or for some of them;

- when a treaty is terminated it is no longer in force as it has ended its existence.

A. Suspension. The circumstances in which a contracting party may suspend the operation of a treaty may be laid down by the relevant treaty, or in the absence of any clause to that effect, are set out in Article 42 VCLT. Article 57(a) VCLT identifies six situations in which suspension of a treaty may take place. Two of these are:

- where all contracting parties agree to suspend its operation, or some of its provisions;

- where two or more parties agree to suspend its operation temporarily between themselves provided that suspension does not impair the enjoyment by other parties of their rights under that treaty, does not affect the performance of their obligations and is compatible with the object and purpose of the relevant treaty.

The remaining grounds are set out in Articles 59–62 VCLT. These are the same as for termination of a treaty. They are examined below:

B. Termination. Articles 65–68 VCLT contain provisions dealing with procedures to be followed with respect to termination or suspension while Articles 70 and 72 set out the consequences of termination or suspension. A treaty may be terminated in the following circumstances:

- when it contains an express provision to this effect and a contracting party acts in conformity with that provision;

- where there is no provision for termination or withdrawal, Article 56(1) VCLT allows it if:

  - it is established that the parties intended to admit the possibility of denunciation or withdrawal, or

  - a right of denunciation or withdrawal can be implied by the nature of the treaty;

- when all contracting parties agree (Article 62(2)(b) VCLT);

- when a new rule of *jus cogens* has emerged and an existing treaty is in conflict with it, that treaty becomes void and is terminated.

Depending upon the circumstances of a particular case, a contracting party may choose either to terminate or to suspend the operation of a treaty. This choice can be exercised in the following situations:

- Subsequent treaty: where all contracting parties to an earlier treaty are also parties to a later treaty and the two treaties relate to the same subject matter (Article 59(1) VCLT).

- Material breach: where another party is in breach of a treaty obligation. However, the breach must be a 'material breach'. Whether a breach is 'material' will depend on the circumstances of each case, but Article 60(3) VCLT defines a material breach as:

  - a repudiation of the treaty not sanctioned by the VCLT;

  - the violation of a provision 'essential to the accomplishment of the object and purpose of the treaty'.

- Impossibility: where it is impossible for a party to perform its obligations, e.g. the object which is indispensable for the existence of a treaty disappears or is destroyed. However, impossibility of performance cannot be relied on by a party if it is a result of breach by that party either of an obligation under the treaty, or of any other international obligation owed to any party to that treaty (Article 61(2) VCLT).

- Fundamental change of circumstances: where there has been a fundamental change of circumstances since the treaty was concluded (this is referred to as the *rebus sic stantibus clause*). Article 62(1) VCLT sets out strict conditions that must be met before a change of circumstances may be claimed. These are:

  - the change must be of circumstances existing at the time of the conclusion of the treaty;

  - the change must be fundamental;

  - the change must have not been foreseen by the parties at the time of conclusion of the treaty;

  - the existence of the original circumstances must have constituted 'an essential basis of the consent of the parties to be bound by the treaty';

  - the change must radically transform the extent of the obligations still to be performed under the treaty.

  The above five conditions are cumulative. A party cannot rely on the *rebus sic stantibus* clause if the change results from its own breach of either an obligation under the treaty or of any other international obligation owed to any other party to the treaty (Article 62(2)(b) VCLT). In order to maintain peace and stability Article 62(2)(a) VCLT excludes treaties fixing boundaries from the operation of the *rebus sic stantibus* clause.

The effects of armed conflicts on the termination of treaties are not within the scope of the VCLT. However, the ILC provides important clarifications on this matter in its Draft Articles on the Effects of Armed Conflicts on Treaties.

14. Settlement of disputes

Articles 65 and 66 VCLT provide the procedure to be followed with respect to invalidity, termination, withdrawal from or suspension of the operation of a treaty when there is a dispute relating to any of those matters.

3.1 Introduction

The law of treaties is a body of rules which provides a definition of a treaty, and deals with matters relating to the conclusion, entry into force, application, validity, amendment, modification, interpretation, suspension and termination of a treaty.

It can be said that the law of treaties plays a role in international law similar to that played by the law of contract in municipal law. The law of treaties does not deal with the substance of a treaty, i.e. the rights and obligations a treaty imposes on the contracting parties – often referred to as treaty law. There is, however, one exception. The law of treaties governs the rights and obligations deriving from the rules of *jus cogens* and thus the VCLT contains specific provisions on this topic (Articles 53 and 64 VCLT).

The VCLT[1] prepared by the ILC represents both the codification and the progressive development of the law of treaties. It came into force on 27 January 1980 and, as at 9 November 2014, had been ratified by 114 States, including the UK, but not the US.

The law of treaties between States and IGOs and between IGOs themselves was codified in the 1986 Vienna Convention on the Law of Treaties between States and International Organisations or between International Organisations (VCLT-IO).[2] The VCLT-IO has not yet come into force and perhaps will never become a binding instrument. However, many provisions of the VCLT apply to treaties covered by the VCLT-IO because:

■ the VCLT represents customary rules on the law of treaties;

■ many of the VCLT-IO provisions are identical to the VCLT, e.g. the first 72 Articles of VCLT-IO closely resemble Articles 1–72 of the VCLT and deal with the same matters;

■ provisions of the VCLT are, in fact, suitable to deal with issues covered by the VCLT-IO.

It is to be noted that the VCLT applies to treaties creating IGOs (since States are contracting parties to such treaties) as well as to treaties concluded by States within the framework of an international organisation: e.g. member States of the EU have amended the original treaty on which it is based many times, *inter alia*, by the Treaty of Maastricht, the Treaty of Amsterdam, the Treaty of Nice, and the Treaty of Lisbon.

This chapter examines rules relating to treaties concluded between States in the light of the VCLT. The VCLT, to a great extent, reflects customary rules on the law of treaties and covers almost all important areas relevant to the law of treaties. For that reason the VCLT is often called the treaty on treaties.

3.2 The main features of the 1969 Vienna Convention on the Law of Treaties (VCLT)

The VCLT is the fruit of 20 years of work by the ILC, which, at its first session held in 1949, selected the law of treaties as a topic for codification (see Chapter 2.13). The VCLT was adopted on 22 May 1969 and entered into force on 27 January 1980, after achieving the required 35 ratifications. The main features of the VCLT are examined below.

---

1   1155 UNTS 331.

2   UN Doc A/CONF.129/16/Add. 1, 93.

3.2.1 The material scope of application of the VCLT

Article 1 VCLT states that the VCLT applies to treaties between States. The meaning of the term 'treaty' is defined in Article 2. The main purpose of Article 1 is to emphasise that the VCLT does not apply to the international agreements listed in Article 3 VCLT, i.e. agreements concluded between subjects of international law other than States, agreements between States and non-State actors, and treaties entered into by States which are not in writing. Article 3 states that the VCLT neither affects the legal force of such agreements nor the application, to any of them, of the customary rules, which are, in any case, embodied in the VCLT.

The following matters are excluded from the VCLT:

■ State succession in respect of treaties. This matter was codified in the 1978 Vienna Convention on Succession of States in respect of Treaties.[3] The Convention entered into force in 1996 after achieving the required 15 ratifications but its popularity has been, and probably will remain, limited because it contains provisions which favour former dependent territories, i.e. States which became independent as a result of decolonisation.

■ The responsibility of a State for breach of a treaty. This matter was dealt with by the ILC in its 2001 Draft Articles on State Responsibility (see Chapter 11.1).

■ The effects of armed conflicts on a treaty. In 2011 the ILC completed its work on the Draft Articles on the Effects of Armed Conflicts on Treaties and submitted them together with Commentaries to the UNGA.[4] On 9 December 2011 UNGA endorsed the Draft Articles and recommended them to member States for attention,[5] but decided to deal with the question of the form that should be given to the Draft Articles at its 69th session in October 2014. No record of any debates taking place at the 69th session of UNGA has been found.

3.2.2 The content of the VCLT

The content of the VCLT is examined in this chapter. It can be said that the VCLT represents both the codification of customary law on treaties and its progressive development as evidenced by Articles 9(2), 19–23, 40–41 and Part V.[6]

3.2.3 No retrospective effect of the VCLT

Article 4 VCLT provides that the VCLT only applies to treaties concluded by a State after the entry into force of the VCLT for that State. This means that if a State concluded a treaty after the entry into force of the VCLT, but before it became a contracting party to the VCLT, the VCLT would not apply to that treaty. In other words, the treaty does not apply to acts or facts which are completed, or to situations which have ceased to exist before the treaty came into force for the State concerned. Obviously,

---

3   1946 UNTS 3.

4   On this topic see: Z.P.B. Tan. *The International Law Commission's Draft Articles on the Effects of Armed Conflicts on Treaties: Evaluating the Applicability of Impossibility of Performance and Fundamental Change* (2013) 3/1 Asian Journal of International Law, 51.

5   A/RES/66/99.

6   I. Sinclair *The Vienna Convention on the Law of Treaties*, 2nd edn, Manchester: University Press Manchester, 1984, 12–18.

a State may always decide to accord retrospective effect to the VCLT or to some of its provisions.

Article 4 VCLT provides that the rule on retrospective effect is, however, without prejudice to the application of any rules in the VCLT to which treaties would be subject under international law independently of those contained in the VCLT. This means that the provisions of the VCLT which embody customary law will apply to treaties concluded before the entry into force of the VCLT, or concluded subsequent to its entry into force but before the VCLT entered into force for parties to those treaties. This raises the issue of the extent to which the VCLT reflects customary law on treaties.

3.2.4 The VCLT and customary law

The VCLT confirms in the eighth paragraph of its preamble and Articles 3(b) and 4 that customary international law will apply to issues not regulated by its provisions.

State practice and judgments of the ICJ show that the VCLT largely mirrors the rules of customary law. So far, only in the *Case Concerning Armed Activities on the Territory of the Congo (Democratic Republic of Congo v Rwanda)*[7] has the ICJ found that the rule embodied in Article 66 VCLT did not represent customary international law. In that case, as the parties did not agree to apply the rule to their dispute, and on the ground of Article 4 VCLT, which excludes retrospective application of the VCLT, Article 66 was not applied by the ICJ. However, in numerous cases, the ICJ has found that provisions of the VCLT contain rules of customary law. For example, in the *Case Concerning Gabčíkovo-Nagymaros Project (Hungary/Slovakia)*,[8] the ICJ applied Articles 60–62 as reflecting customary law, even though previously those provisions had not been generally accepted as representing customary law. Further, the ICJ did not consider the possibility of their being inapplicable despite the fact that neither Slovakia nor Hungary was a contracting party to the VCLT at the relevant time.[9]

It is submitted that the VCLT mirrors, to a great extent, the rules of customary international law and certainly any court or tribunal will consider a rule contained in the VCLT as a starting point when determining whether a disputed rule reflects customary law or whether State practice indicates that the rule should be supplemented or replaced in any given case. In this respect the work of the ILC on how to identify customary law will be of assistance (see Chapter 2.3). It is also submitted that Article 66 VCLT and the provisions of the VCLT relating to reservations and their effects on treaties are not part of customary law.

3.2.5 The need for reform

There will be no need for any reform of the VCLT as its built-in safeguards ensure the necessary flexibility to take account of evolving State practice. Further, many provisions expressly allow a contracting party to depart from the rules established by the VCLT.[10] The only area which required some clarification was that related to reservations and their effects. This matter was placed on the

---

7   *Democratic Republic of the Congo v Rwanda (Jurisdiction and Admissibility)* (2006) 45 ILM 562–620, para 125.
8   [1997] ICJ Rep 7, paras 42–47.
9   For example, the ICJ decided that Article 60 VCLT reflected customary law in the *Legal Consequences for States of the Continued Presence of South Africa in Namibia (South West Africa) Notwithstanding Security Council Resolution 276 (1970) (Advisory Opinion)* [1971] ICJ Rep 16, para 94. Similarly, the ICJ found that Article 52 VCLT in the *Fisheries Jurisdiction Case (Federal Republic of Germany v Iceland)* ([1973] ICJ Rep 49, paras 24 and 36) was a customary rule as were Articles 31 and 32 in the *Case Concerning Kasikili/Sedudu Island (Botswana/Namibia)* [1999] ICJ Rep 1045, para 18.
10   See Articles 9 (2), 10 (a), 11, 12 (1) (b), 13, 14 (1) (b), 15, 16, 17 (1), 20 (1), (3) and (4) (b), 22, 24, 25, 28, 29, 33 (1) and (2), 36 (1), 37 (1), 39, 40, 41, 44 (1), 55–60, 70 (1), 72 (1), 76–78 and 79 (1).

agenda of the ILC which after 18 years of work adopted in 2011 the Guide to Practice on Reservations in Treaties[11] (see Chapter 3.6). The Guide was conceived as a non-binding instrument but there is no doubt that some of its provisions codify customary international law while those that do not are intended to and may shape emerging customary rules.

It can be said that the VCLT has been very successful and is a victim of its own success in that it has not attracted an impressive number of ratifications because whether ratified or not it, in effect, applies anyway given that the vast majority of its provisions reflect customary international law.

3.3 The fundamental principles of the law of treaties

The fundamental principles of the law of treaties are identified in the third paragraph of the preamble to the VCLT as being the principles of free consent, good faith and *pacta sunt servanda*.

3.3.1 The principle of free consent

The principle of free consent means that a State cannot be bound by a treaty to which it has not consented. There are, however, some exceptions to this rule (see Chapter 3.10.3). There is also a presumption that a State, not a party to a treaty, consents to a right which that treaty confers on it (Articles 34–36 VCLT).

A State may express its consent to a treaty in various forms (see Chapter 3.5.4). Further, its consent is required for a reservation to a treaty made by another State to be applicable to it (Articles 19(c) and 20 VCLT) and for amendments to a treaty (Article 39 VCLT) unless the relevant treaty specifies otherwise, e.g. the UN Charter provides that an amendment adopted by a majority of its members is binding on all its members. If a State's consent to a treaty is affected by particular circumstances of error, fraud, corruption, coercion or the threat or use of force (see Chapter 3.9) that treaty will not be binding on it (Articles 48–52 VCLT). Free consent is therefore vital for the initial adoption and subsequent development of a particular treaty as it ensures that a State will be able to refuse changes to which it has not consented.

3.3.2 The principle of *pacta sunt servanda*

The principle of *pacta sunt servanda* is embodied in Article 26 VCLT which states that: 'Every treaty in force is binding upon the parties to it and must be performed by them in good faith.' Article 26 VCLT emphasises the close connection between the principle of good faith and the principle of *pacta sunt servanda*. In the *Case Concerning Gabčíkovo-Nagymaros Project (Judgment) (Hungary/Slovakia)*[12] the ICJ stated: that 'Article 26 [VCLT] combines two elements, which are of equal importance', i.e. the principle of *pacta sunt servanda* and the principle of good faith. Indeed, each time a State is in breach of the principle of *pacta sunt servanda* it also violates the principle of good faith. Thus, if a State does not perform its obligations deriving from a treaty it breaches both principles.

The principle of *pacta sunt servanda* applies only to treaties which are in force, not to invalid, suspended or terminated treaties. In this context, there were contradictory views on whether an outbreak of an armed conflict suspended or terminated a given treaty. This matter has been elucidated by the

---

11   Report of the ILC on the Work of its Sixty-Third Session, UN Doc A/65/10, 36–73.
12   [1997] ICJ Rep 7, para 142.

ILC's Draft Articles on the Effects of Armed Conflicts on Treaties[13] and is examined in Chapter 3.13.2.3.

3.3.3 The principle of good faith

The principle of good faith, a general principle of international law, has been recognised as the foundation of the international legal order. It has many functions. In the *Nuclear Tests Case* (Judgment)*(Australia v France)*[14] the ICJ held that:

> one of the basic principles governing the creation and performance of legal obligations, whatever their source, is the principle of good faith.

Under this principle States and non-State actors are required to comply with binding obligations imposed upon them by international law, irrespective of whether such obligations derive from treaties, customary rules, or any other source of international law.

Contrary to the principle of *pacta sunt servanda*, which applies only to treaties which are in force, the principle of good faith is all encompassing as it even imposes obligations on a State in the pre-ratification stage. In this respect Article 18 VCLT requires a State to refrain from acts which would defeat the object and purpose of a treaty where that State has signed the treaty but not yet ratified it, or when it has ratified the treaty but it has not yet entered into force (but provided that such entry is not unduly delayed). The principle of good faith applies throughout the life of a treaty, from its negotiation, through its performance (Article 26 VCLT) and up to its termination. Treaties must be interpreted in good faith (Article 31(1) VCLT) not only by contracting parties but also by third parties, e.g. arbitrators, international courts, and domestic courts.

3.4 The definition of a treaty under the VCLT

The expression 'treaty' is used as a generic term to cover a multitude of international agreements and contractual engagements concluded between States. These international agreements are called by various names including treaties, conventions, pacts, declarations, charters, concordats, protocols and covenants. They may be quasi-legislative, i.e. setting out general multilateral standards in international law, or purely contractual. They may lay down rules binding upon States concerning new areas into which international law is expanding, or they may codify, clarify and supplement the already existing customary international law on a particular matter. The VCLT provided its own definition of a treaty.

Article 2(1)(a) of the VCLT defines a treaty as:

> an international agreement concluded between states in written form and governed by international law, whether embodied in a single instrument or in two or more related instruments, and whatever its particular designation.

To qualify as a 'treaty' therefore, the agreement must satisfy the following criteria:

- it must be a written instrument or instruments between two or more parties;
- the parties must be States within the meaning of international law;
- it must be governed by international law; and
- the parties must have intended for the agreement to create legal obligations.

---

13   A/RES/66/99.
14   [1974] ICJ Rep 253, para 46.

3.4.1 A written agreement between two or more parties

Although the VCLT does not apply to international agreements which are not made in writing, Article 3 VCLT expressly states that the legal force of such non-written agreements shall not be affected by that fact.

Article 3 of the Vienna Convention provides:

> The fact that the present Convention does not apply to international agreements concluded between states and other subjects of international law or between such other subjects of international law, or to international agreements not in written form, shall not affect:
> (a) the legal force of such agreements;
> (b) the application to them of any of the rules set forth in the present Convention to which they would be subject under international law independently of the Convention;
> (c) the application of the Convention to the relations of states as between themselves under international agreements to which other subjects of international law are also parties.

3.4.2 A treaty must be between States

The VCLT applies only to international agreements concluded between States. Agreements concluded with or between non-State actors are therefore excluded. The reason for limiting the VCLT to treaties entered into between States was the fear that if other agreements were included, in particular treaties to which IGOs are parties, which have their own peculiarities, the differing rules of international law applicable to such agreements would make the VCLT too complicated and delay its drafting.[15]

Article 6 VCLT provides: 'Every state possesses capacity to conclude treaties.' In this respect the VCLT reflects customary international law. According to the ILC commentary, the term 'state' is used in Article 6 VCLT:

> with the same meaning as in the Charter of the United Nations, the Statute of the Court [the ICJ], the [Vienna] Convention on Diplomatic Relations; i.e. it means a state for the purpose of international law.[16]

3.4.3 The agreement must be governed by international law

Simply because two entities endowed with international personality and possessing treaty-making capacity enter into an agreement, it does not follow that the agreement is necessarily a treaty. Certain inter-State agreements can be subject to municipal law, either expressly or by implication.

For example, during the period 1966 to 1968 Denmark entered into a series of loan agreements with other states (e.g. Malawi) which stipulated that, except as otherwise provided therein, 'the Agreement and all rights and obligations deriving from it shall be governed by Danish law'.

There would seem to be no reason why an agreement must be governed exclusively by either international law or by municipal law. Many agreements between States are of a hybrid nature and as such are binding on the international plane as well as being directly governed by municipal law.

---

15   *The Draft Articles on the Law of Treaties with Commentaries 1966*, (1966) Yearbook of the International Law Commission, vol II, 192, 187.

16   Ibid, 192.

The ILC Fourth Special Rapporteur stated in his First Report (1962):

[T]he Commission felt in 1959 that the element of subjection to international law is so essential a part of an international agreement that it should be expressly mentioned in the definition. There may be agreements between states, such as agreements for the acquisition of premises for diplomatic missions or for some purely commercial transaction, the incidents of which are regulated by the local law of one of the parties or by a private law system determined by reference to conflict of law principles. Whether in such cases the two states are internationally accountable to each other at all may be a nice question; but even if that were held to be so, it would not follow that the basis of their international accountability was a treaty obligation. At any rate, the Commission was clear that it ought to confine the notion of an 'international agreement' for the purposes of the law of treaties to one, the whole formation and execution of which (as well as the obligation to execute) is governed by international law.[17]

3.4.4 The agreement should create a legal obligation

The intention to create legal relations is not mentioned in the VCLT. In this respect, the ILC's Rapporteur stated that 'insofar as this [requirement] may be relevant in any case, the element of intention is embraced in the phrase "governed by international law"'.[18]

There are, however, practical reasons for excluding any specific reference to intention. States may wish to reach an agreement as to political intent without going to the extent of making it legally enforceable. Therefore, what may appear to be a treaty may in fact be devoid of any legal content. This is particularly true of the so-called 'joint declaration' by States, examples being the 1941 Atlantic Treaty and the 1943 Cairo Declaration. Such declarations are statements of 'common principles' or 'common purpose' imposing no legal obligation upon the parties to pursue those policies.

Similarly, the 1975 Final Act of the Helsinki Conference on Security and Co-operation in Europe was stated to be: 'not eligible for registration under art 102 of the Charter of the United Nations' and the general understanding expressed at the conference was that the Act would not be binding in law.

However, such agreements, even if not creating rights and obligations directly, may provide the basis for new rights and obligations in the future. So that today, for instance, it is of little practical significance that the Universal Declaration of Human Rights adopted by the UNGA in 1948 was agreed to by member States only on the understanding that it did not create binding obligations upon them (see Chapter 11.2.1).

3.5 Conclusion of treaties

A number of different stages can be identified in the process of concluding a treaty:

3.5.1 Negotiation

This is carried out by the accredited representatives of the State in question. Article 7 VCLT provides that the representative of the State will be someone equipped with an instrument of 'full powers' or a

---

17   Sir Humphrey Waldock, (1962) 2 Yearbook of the International Law Commission, 32.
18   Ibid, 189.

person who, from the normal practice of the State, appears to have such powers. Article 7(2) VCLT then indicates three categories of persons who are deemed to have 'full powers':

■ heads of State, heads of government and ministers of foreign affairs;

■ heads of diplomatic missions, i.e. ambassadors of the State concerned;

■ representatives accredited to international conferences or organisations.

3.5.2 Adoption of the text of a treaty

The adoption of the text is the first stage of the conclusion of a treaty. Article 9 VCLT provides:

1 The adoption of the text of a treaty takes place by the consent of all the states participating in its drawing up except as provided in paragraph 2.
2 The adoption of the text of a treaty at an international conference takes place by the vote of two-thirds of the states present and voting, unless by the same majority they shall decide to apply a different rule.

Therefore, consent remains the general rule for bilateral treaties and for those treaties drawn up between few States. But Article 9(2) recognises that it would be unrealistic to demand unanimity as the general rule for the adoption of treaties drawn up at conferences or within organisations, where the widest possible measure of agreement between the participants is desirable.

The adoption of the text does not by itself create any obligations.

3.5.3 Authentication of the treaty

By authentication parties agree that the finite text of the proposed treaty is correct and authentic and not subject to alteration. The authentication of the text of the treaty may be done in a number of ways. The method of authentication to be adopted is a matter for the parties themselves to agree, but the two usual methods are signing and initialling (Article 10 VCLT). The text may, however, be authenticated in other ways, e.g. by incorporating the text in the final act of the conference.

3.5.4 Consent to be bound

Article 11 VCLT provides: 'The consent of a state to be bound by a treaty may be expressed by signature, exchange of instruments constituting a treaty, ratification, acceptance, approval or accession; or by any other means if so agreed'.

The traditional methods of expressing consent to a treaty are signature, ratification and accession.

3.5.4.1 Signature

The legal effects of signature are as follows:

A. The signing of a treaty may represent simply an authentication of its text.
Where signature is subject to ratification, acceptance or approval, signature does not establish consent to be bound.

B. In the case of a treaty which is only to become binding upon ratification, acceptance or approval that treaty, unless declaratory of customary law, will not be enforceable against a party until one of those steps is taken.

In the *North Sea Continental Shelf (Federal Republic of Germany v Denmark and Federal Republic of Germany v Netherlands) (Merits)*,[19] the Federal Republic of Germany had been a signatory to the 1958 Geneva Convention on the Continental Shelf, but had not ratified it. The Court held that Article 6 of that Convention (together with all other articles) was not binding on Germany because its signature had only been a preliminary step, Germany did not ratify the Convention, was not a party to it and therefore could not be contractually bound by its provisions.[20]

However, under Article 18 VCLT, the act of signing a treaty creates an obligation of good faith on the part of the signatory which is required to refrain from acts calculated to frustrate the objects of the treaty and to submit the treaty to the appropriate constitutional machinery for approval. Signature does not, however, create an obligation to ratify.

An example of a State which wanted to 'unsign' a treaty and thus avoid being in breach of Article 18 VCLT is the US during the presidency of George W. Bush with regard to the Rome Statute. When President Bill Clinton was in power he signed the Rome Statute of the ICC.[21] However, the US government under President George W. Bush decided that the US no longer had any intention of ratifying it. In order to 'unsign' the Rome Statute and thus ensure that the US would not be in breach of Article 18 VCLT, had it decided to take measures which would frustrate the objectives of the Rome Statute, the US Under-Secretary of State for Arms Control and International Security wrote on 27 April 2002 to the UNS-G informing him that the US did not intend to become a contracting party to the Rome Statute and accordingly had no legal obligations arising from its signature.[22] Subsequently, the US relied on Article 98(2) of the Statute of the ICC to make sure that its troops would be immune from prosecution in the ICC. Article 98(2) provides:

> The Court may not proceed with a request for surrender which would require the requested State to act inconsistently with its obligations under international agreements pursuant to which the consent of a sending state is required to surrender a person of that state to the Court, unless the Court can first obtain the cooperation of the sending state for the giving of consent for the surrender.

The Bush administration had entered into many bilateral agreements contemplated under Article 98 of the Statute of the ICC with a view to prohibiting the other parties to the agreements from surrendering US personnel to the ICC without US consent. Had a State refused to enter into such an agreement, under the American Servicemembers' Protection Act (ASPA) passed by Congress in 2002, it would have been deprived of US military assistance. However, the ASPA did not apply to members of NATO and to States expressly indicated by the President. The fierce opposition to the ASPA by the US military, many States and the EU, contributed to the change of attitude of President Bush. Starting from October 2006, restrictions on foreign military assistances had been gradually removed and on 28 January 2008, President Bush signed an amendment to the ASPA removing restrictions on foreign military assistance with regard to States which did not wish to enter into bilateral agreements, mainly Caribbean, African and South American States. Under President Obama the US actively co-operates with the ICC, but the US government has not expressed any intention to ratify the Rome Statute.

C.   Where a treaty is not subject to ratification, acceptance or approval, but a State's signature will signify consent to be bound.

---

19   [1969] ICJ Rep 4.
20   Ibid, para 27.
21   2187 UNTS 90.
22   ASIL, 9 May 2002, 5.

Guidance regarding the above situation is provided by Article 12(1) VCLT which states:

> The consent of a state to be bound by a treaty is expressed by the signature of its representative when:
> (a) the treaty provides that signature shall have that effect;
> (b) it is otherwise established that the negotiating states were agreed that signature should have that effect; or
> (c) the intention of the state to give that effect to the signature appears from the full powers of its representative or was expressed during the negotiations.

3.5.4.2 Ratification

Ratification is the formal act whereby one State declares its acceptance of the terms of the treaty and undertakes to observe them. It should be noted, however, that the word 'ratification' is used to describe two distinct procedural acts, one municipal and one international.

- ■ Municipal law. In municipal law ratification is the formal act of the appropriate organ of the State effected in accordance with national constitutional law. For example, according to English law, ratification is effected in the name of the Crown.

- ■ International law. In international law ratification is a procedure which brings a treaty into force for the State concerned by establishing its definitive consent to be bound by the particular treaty. This can be effected in the various ways specified in Article 14(1) of VCLT. International law is not concerned as to whether a State has complied with the requirements of its constitutional law.

Despite the fact that a treaty may be ratified by nothing more than the signature of the relevant State's representative, many States insist upon a ratification procedure consisting of more formal steps. There are several reasons for this:

- ■ Historically the signing of a treaty followed by its ratification by the sovereign constituted a means by which the sovereign was able to supervise his representatives, i.e. to make sure that diplomats did not exceed their instructions.

- ■ The delay between the time of signature and the completion of the ratification allows a sovereign time to reconsider the matter and, if desired, allows time for the expression of public opinion on the matter.

- ■ It permits the consent of the legislature to be obtained and this may be required as part of the ratification procedure.

Article 14(1) VCLT provides:

> The consent of a state to be bound by a treaty is expressed by ratification when:
> (a) the treaty provides for such consent to be expressed by ratification;
> (b) it is otherwise established that the negotiating states were agreed that ratification should be required;
> (c) the representative of the state has signed the treaty subject to ratification; or
> (d) the intention of the state to sign the treaty subject to ratification appears from the full powers of its representative or was expressed during the negotiations.

Thus, if a treaty should contain no express provision on the subject of ratification Article 14 will regulate the matter by reference to the intention of the parties.

Performance of a treaty may constitute tacit ratification. If a State successfully claims rights under an unratified treaty it will be estopped from alleging that it is not bound by the treaty.

3.5.4.3 Accession

Accession or adherence or adhesion occurs when a State, which did not participate in negotiating and signing of the relevant treaty, formally accepts its provisions. Accession may occur before or after the treaty has entered into force. It is only possible if it is provided for in the treaty, or if all the parties to the treaty agree that the acceding State should be allowed to accede (see Article 15 VCLT). Accession, therefore, has the same effect as signature and ratification combined.

The terms adherence or adhesion have the same meaning as accession.

3.6 Reservations to treaties

A State may be willing to accept most provisions of a treaty, but it may, for various reasons, wish to object to one or more of them. With regard to bilateral treaties reservations pose no problem in that if any party objects, then the matter is discussed and if no agreement can be achieved, the treaty will not be concluded. However, with regard to multilateral treaties, the issue is more complex. The need for a widespread acceptance of the relevant treaty may justify the existence of reservations. It is obviously for the drafters of a treaty to decide whether it is worthwhile to compromise the integrity of a treaty by accepting reservations in exchange for its universal acceptance. For example, the Rome Statute of the International Criminal Court permits no reservations and, despite this, as at 1 September 2014, was ratified by 122 States.

The VCLT contains only six provisions on reservations, including their definition and general guidance as to their legal regime. However, those provisions are unclear and incomplete. Two controversial issues have been of particular importance to States.

The first issue is whether to accept the position of the ICJ in the *Reservations to the Convention on the Prevention and Punishment of the Crime of Genocide (Advisory Opinion)*[23] which stated that if a reservation was incompatible with the object and purpose of the Convention the reserving State could not be regarded as a party to that Convention. Therefore, an inadmissible reservation will render the reserving State's ratification of the relevant treaty ineffective. In fact, the 'total invalidity' position has not been supported by international practice.

The second issue is that the provisions of the VCLT on reservations are inappropriate for HRs treaties seeking to guarantee the minimum standard of inalienable rights for individuals present within the territory of a contracting State. Two main arguments are invoked to show this:

■ to allow reservations to HRs treaties would be tantamount to reducing the standard of protection of HRs which is already very low (i.e. given the multilateral nature of those treaties); and

■ the application of the reciprocity rule relating to reservations (see Chapter 3.6.1) is not appropriate to HRs treaties because they are concluded to benefit individuals, not other contracting States. Therefore, when a State makes a reservation it would be close to preposterous to allow other contracting States to assess whether the reservation is in conformity with the object and purpose

---

23   [1951] ICJ Rep 15.

of the relevant treaty. Further, reciprocity means that when a reservation is accepted, both the reserving State and the accepting State are released from treaty obligations to the extent of the reservation. If this were to apply to HRs treaties, then the accepting State would considerably lower the standard of protection of persons present within its territory (see Chapter 3.6.2.3.B).

HRs courts and other bodies established to monitor HRs treaties have declared themselves competent to decide whether reservations to those treaties are valid, irrespective of whether their decisions are binding or non-binding on the contracting parties. They consider that they are competent to decide whether a reservation in question is permissible. For example, the ECtHR in relation to the European Convention for the Protection of Human Rights and Fundamental Freedoms (ECHR). Under Article 57 ECHR a State is allowed to make reservations when signing, or depositing its instrument of ratification 'in respect of any particular provision of the Convention to the extent that any law then in force in its territory is not in conformity with the provisions' of the ECHR. Further under this Article a reservation which is of a general character or which does not contain a brief statement of the law concerned will be invalid. In *Belios v Switzerland* [24] the ECtHR decided it was competent to determine the validity or otherwise of a reservation. It held that the reservation formulated by Switzerland was invalid because it was too broad and vague and thus it was impossible to determine its exact meaning and scope.

It is important to note that some HRs treaties, e.g. the 1984 Torture Convention[25] and the Rome Statute of the ICC, mentioned above, prohibit reservations.

In the light of the above difficulties, in 1993 the ILC decided to revisit the topic of reservations. It took 18 years to produce the Guide to Practice on Reservations to Treaties together with commentaries, which form an integral part of the Guide, a 630 page document.[26] The Guide was adopted by the ILC on 11 August 2011 as a non-binding document. It will only be binding if its rules become part of the VCLT or customary international law. The Guide is intended to elucidate the VCLT's provisions on reservations by filling gaps, and removing uncertainties while responding to new developments subsequent to the adoption of the VCLT, in particular concerning the effects of impermissible reservations, and thus addresses the controversial issues examined above.[27]

3.6.1 Definitions of a reservation and of an objection to a reservation

Article 2(1)(d) VCLT provides that a reservation is:

> . . . a unilateral statement, however phrased or named, made by a state, when signing, ratifying, accepting, approving or acceding to a treaty, whereby it purports to exclude or to modify the legal effect of certain provisions of the treaty in their application to that state.

The Guide provides the following clarifications of the above definition:

■ It treats reservations to HRs treaties in the same way as reservations to other treaties. As a result, the Guide preserves the unity of treaties in that irrespective of the subject matter of a treaty Article 2(1)(d) applies (see below).

---

24   (1988) 10 EHRR, 466.

25   1465 UNTS 85.

26   Report of the ILC on the work of its 63rd session, GA, Official Records, 66th Session, Supplement No 10, Addendum 1, Doc A/66/10/Add. 1, hereinafter referred to as the 'Guide'.

27   A. Pellet, *The ILC Guide to Practice on Reservations to Treaties: A General Presentation by the Special Rapporteur* (2013) 24/4 EJIL, 1061.

■ It clarifies the meaning of the time factor set out in the definition. Indeed, the literal interpretation of Article 29(1)(d) VCLT entails that reservations made after the conclusion of a treaty, i.e. 'late reservations' are prohibited and thus should be considered as invalid. The Guide provides that late reservations, in accordance with State practice, are within the scope of Article 2(1)(d) VCLT.[28]

■ It clarifies the meaning of 'certain provisions' contained in Article 2(1)(d) VCLT. A narrow interpretation of the term 'certain provisions' appears to exclude reservations that refer to an entire treaty. The Guide makes it clear that the definition includes reservations applying to an entire treaty. These are commonly made without objection.[29] For example, a State may, on ratification, exclude the application of a treaty to its overseas territories or specify that the treaty is not to apply in certain circumstances. The expression 'certain provisions' was included in order to prevent reservations from being too general or imprecise.

A reservation, if accepted by another contacting party, operates on the basis of reciprocity in that it modifies or excludes for both the reserving State and the accepting State provisions of a treaty to which the reservation was made. This works as follows: if State X made a reservation to provision A which reservation was accepted by States Y and Z, Provision A does not apply in relations between States X and Y and States X and Z but it does apply to mutual relations between States Y and Z. A State may indicate its acceptance of a reservation by a unilateral statement to this effect. However, no statement is necessary, and once a State does not make an objection to a reservation, it is taken to have accepted it.

A reservation must be in writing. If it is made orally, it will be invalid.[30] The reservation should, to the extent possible, indicate the reasons why it is being made. Giving a reason is not required under the VCLT but was introduced as a new condition to the validity of a reservation by the ILC in guideline 2.1.1.

A reservation must be communicated to the contracting States or IGOs and other States or IGOs entitled to become parties to the relevant treaty in order to ensure that they can formulate an objection to it within a period of 12 months after being notified of it.

An objection is defined in guideline 2.6.1 of the Guide as:

a unilateral statement, however phrased or named, made by a State or international organization in response to a reservation formulated by another State or international organization, whereby the former State or international organization purports to preclude the reservation from having its intended effect or otherwise opposed the reservation'.

The VCLT requires that an objection, like a reservation, must be made in writing and communicated to all contracting States and States entitled to become party to the treaty. Additionally the Guide indicates that the objection should specify, to the extent possible, the reasons why it is being formulated.

A reservation and an objection to a reservation may be withdrawn or partially withdrawn but such withdrawal or partial withdrawal must be in writing and communicated to the contracting parties. However, the acceptance of a reservation cannot be withdrawn or amended.[31]

---

28 See guidelines 2.3 to 2.3.4, 4.3.2, and 5.1.8. See also guideline 2.4.7 (Late formulation of an interpretative declaration).

29 See guideline 1.2.

30 *Case Concerning Armed Activities on the Territory of the Congo (New Application: 2002) (Democratic Republic of the Congo v Rwanda) (Jurisdiction and Admissibility)* (2006) 45 ILM 562–620, paras 41–44.

31 Guidelines 2.8.7 and 2.8.11.

3.6.2 Permissible and non-permissible reservations and their legal effect in the light of Articles 19 and 20 VCLT

Articles 19 and 20 VCLT deal with reservations and their legal effect on treaties. They are reproduced below.

Article 19 VCLT provides as follows:

A state may, when signing, ratifying, accepting approving or acceding to a treaty, formulate a reservation unless:
(a) the reservation is prohibited by the treaty;
(b) the treaty provides that only specified reservations, which do not include the reservation in question, may be made; or
(c) in cases not falling under sub-paragraphs (a) and (b), the reservation is incompatible with the object and purpose of the treaty.

Article 19 VCLT distinguishes therefore between 'permissible' and 'non-permissible' reservations. This distinction derives from the will of the parties in that they may either prohibit certain reservations or expressly authorise certain reservations.

Article 20 VCLT provides as follows:

1 A reservation expressly authorised by a treaty does not require any subsequent acceptance by the other contracting states unless the treaty so provides.

2 When it appears from the limited number of the negotiating states and the object and purpose of a treaty that the application of the treaty in its entirety between all the parties is an essential condition of the consent of each one to be bound by the treaty, a reservation requires acceptance by all the parties.

3 When a treaty is a constituent instrument of an international organisation and unless it otherwise provides, a reservation requires the acceptance of the competent organ of that organisation.

4 In cases not falling under the preceding paragraphs and unless the treaty otherwise provides:
(a) acceptance by another contracting state of a reservation constitutes the reserving state a party to the treaty in relation to that other state if or when the treaty is in force for those states;
(b) an objection by another contracting state to a reservation does not preclude the entry into force of the treaty as between the objecting and reserving states unless a contrary intention is definitely expressed by the objecting state;
(c) an act expressing a state's consent to be bound by the treaty and containing a reservation is effective as soon as at least one other contracting state has accepted the reservation.

5 For the purpose of paragraphs (2) and (4) and unless the treaty otherwise provides, a reservation is considered to have been accepted by a state if it shall have raised no objection to the reservation by the end of a period of twelve months after it was notified of the reservation or by the date on which it expressed its consent to be bound by the treaty, whichever is later.

3.6.2.1 Permissible reservations and their legal effect

Permissible reservations are those which are not prohibited under Article 19 VCLT, i.e. those which are expressly allowed by the relevant treaty and those which are compatible with the purpose and object of the relevant treaty.

It can be said that a reservation creates a different treaty between a reserving State and other contracting parties that have, expressly or tacitly, accepted it. The regime of reservations is based on reciprocity. Apart from a situation where a reservation is expressly authorised by the relevant treaty, its acceptance or rejection will depend on the reaction of other parties. In accordance with Article 20(4) and (5) VCLT, at least one of them must accept the reservation, either expressly or tacitly, within a period of 12 months from the date of notification of it. A reservation will create the following relationships between the reserving State and other States:

■ Between a reserving State and a contracting State which has made no objection. The treaty will be modified in that the provision to which the reservation relates will not apply between them, e.g. if State X made a reservation to provision A and State Y accepted the reservation, the treaty will apply to States X and Y with the exception of provision A.

■ When a contracting party has objected to the reservation and opposed the entry into force of the treaty, the treaty will not enter into force for the reserving State.

■ When a contracting party has objected to the reservation but did not oppose the entry into force of the treaty between itself and the reserving State. The treaty will apply between both parties except for the provisions to which the reservation relates.

It is to be noted that for contracting parties which made no reservation, irrespective of whether they accepted or objected to a reservation made by another contracting party, all provisions of the relevant treaty will apply to them, e.g. when State X and State Y did not make any reservations but State Z made a reservation to provision A, that provision applies to both X and Y.

3.6.2.2 Non-permissible reservations

Article 19 lists the following reservations as non-permissible:

■ reservations prohibited by the relevant treaty;

■ reservations which are not included in the list of reservations expressly allowed under the relevant treaty;

■ reservations which are incompatible with the object and purpose of the relevant treaty.

It is not difficult to determine whether a reservation falls into the first or second category. However, to decide whether a reservation is incompatible with the object and purpose of the relevant treaty may be more difficult. For that reason the concept of 'object and purpose' which limits the freedom of a State to make reservations needs to be clarified. Certainly, this concept cannot be defined in the abstract. What constitutes the object and purpose must be determined on the basis of the relevant treaty but, it is submitted that the following points will assist in the determining of the object and purpose of the relevant treaty:

■ The concept of 'object and purpose' is a single notion. Otherwise for the same treaty the object could be found as being different from the purpose with the consequence that a reservation could be compatible with the purpose but contrary to its object and *vice versa*. This is intellectually unacceptable.

■ The concept of 'object and purpose' refers to the treaty as a whole. Each provision therefore should be interpreted in the light of the overall purpose and object of the treaty and not with the idea that the provision concerned might have a purpose and object independent of the treaty's 'object and purpose'. Indeed, the object and purpose of the provision concerned, on its own, may be different from the object and purpose of the treaty with the result that different object and purposes could be found for different provisions. This approach would render the entire concept of object and purpose useless.

■ Perhaps, the determination of the 'object and purpose' should be based on textual interpretation of a treaty. This would ensure that the concept of 'object and purpose' will remain the same irrespective of whether one assesses the permissibility of a reservation or the validity of a modification or some other matter. The Special Rapporteur A. Pellet, appointed by the ILC on Reservations to Treaties, suggested, however, that teleological interpretation of the relevant treaty with a view to determining its 'object and purpose' should be preferred[32] (see Chapter 3.12).

The ILC Guide reproduces Article 19 VCLT. It explains in detail how to identify the object and purpose of a treaty.

In addition, the Guide examines the following reservations with a view to clarifying their permissibility or otherwise:

■ Vague or general reservations. In this respect the so called 'Sharia reservation' often formulated by Islamic States stating that their ratification of a treaty is subject to compliance with Sharia law will not be permissible not because of its reference to religious law, but because it is too general (guideline 3.1.5.2).

■ Reservations to a provision of a treaty reflecting a customary rule. In principle a State may make such a reservation, in particular a 'persistent objector' State (see Chapter 2.3.3) or if it has some other valid reason. However, if a customary rule is well established the reserving State remains bound by it independently of the treaty (guideline 3.1.5.3).

■ Reservations to provisions of a treaty concerning rights from which no derogation is permissible under any circumstances (guideline 3.1.5.4).

■ Reservations relating to internal law (including specific rules of an international organisation (guideline 3.1.5.5)). When a State makes a reservation providing that a treaty must comply with its domestic law its reservation will not be permissible unless the contracting State clearly identifies the particular provisions of that law (guideline 3.1.5.5).

■ Reservations to treaties containing numerous interdependent rights and obligations (guideline 3.1.5.6).

■ Reservations to provisions of a treaty concerning dispute settlement or the monitoring of the implementation of the treaty (guideline 3.1.5.7).

The ILC could not agree on whether reservations to provisions of a treaty that reflect a *jus cogens* rule are permissible. This led to a compromise solution. The Guide states that no guideline would be adopted on this topic although guideline 3.1.5.3 seems to suggest that rules relating to reservations concerning provisions of a treaty reflecting a customary rule also apply to *jus cogens* rules. The Guide concludes by stating that:

States and international organizations should refrain from formulating such reservations and, when they deem it indispensable, should instead formulate reservations to the provisions concerning the treaty regime governing the rules in question.[33]

---

32   A. Pellet, Special Rapporteur of the UN ILC 'Tenth Report on Reservations to Treaties', Addendum, 14–15, available at the official website of the ILC.
33   Guideline 3.1.5.3 (22).

3.6.2.3 Legal effect of invalid reservations

The VCLT did not specify the legal effect of invalid reservations. Two contrasting views on the legal effect of these reservations emerged from jurisprudence.

A. Total invalidity

The first position is that taken by the ICJ in its advisory opinion in *Reservations to the Convention on the Prevention and Punishment of the Crime of Genocide*[34] where it stated that if a reservation was incompatible with the object and purpose of the Convention, the reserving State could not be regarded as a party to that Convention. Therefore, an inadmissible reservation will render the reserving State's ratification of the relevant treaty ineffective. This position of 'total invalidity' has not been supported by international practice.

B. Partial invalidity

The practice of bodies which have been established to monitor various treaties shows that such bodies, particularly those which supervise the implementation of HRs treaties, have not adopted the ICJ's approach of total invalidity. Instead, these bodies have adopted the 'partial invalidity' approach.[35] For example, if the Human Rights Committee (HRC) established under the Optional Protocol to the International Covenant on Civil and Political Rights (ICCPR) (see Chapter 12.2.2.2) decides that a reservation is incompatible with the object and purpose of the ICCPR, it declares it inadmissible and severs it from a State's declaration of consent to be bound by the ICCPR. The result is that the ICCPR applies to a reserving State as it is and the reservation is disregarded. Thus, the HRC decided that a reservation made by Trinidad and Tobago (T&T) to Article 6 ICCPR (which article protects the right to life) to exclude its application to prisoners awaiting the execution of a death sentence was incompatible with the object and purpose of the ICCPR.[36] Consequently, an individual communication brought against T&T before the HRC was held admissible and T&T was found in breach of Article 6. In response T&T withdrew from the Optional Protocol to ICCPR under which the HRC has competence to deal with communications submitted by individuals against a contracting party (see Chapter 12.2.2.2).

The 'partial invalidity' or severability approach of the HRC formalised in its General Comment 24(54) was objected to by, *inter alia*, France, the UK and the US.[37] The primary objection to this approach is that it contravenes the fundamental principle that a State is not to be bound by a treaty to which it has not consented as it has the effect of binding a State to a treaty obligation to which it has formulated a reservation. The advantage of this approach, however, is that it maintains the relevant treaty in force for the reserving State by ignoring the incompatible reservation instead of invalidating the treaty with regard to the reserving State (i.e. a reserving State would no longer be a party to the treaty) as is the case under the ICJ's approach. The HRC's approach has also been followed by the ECtHR[38] and the IACtHR.[39] State practice has also favoured the approach, at least in relation to HRs treaties.[40]

---

34   [1951] ICJ Rep 15.
35   K.I. McCall-Smith, *Severing Reservations* (2014) 63 ICLQ, 599.
36   *Kennedy v Trinidad and Tobago (Decision on Admissibility)* UN CCPR/67/D/845/1999.
37   GAOR 59th Session Supp 40, vol 1, 104, 126 and 130.
38   *Belios v Switzerland* (1988) 10 EHRR 466.
39   *Hilaire v Trinidad and Tobago (Preliminary Objection)*, Series C, No 80, para 98.
40   K.I. McCall-Smith, *Severing Reservations* (2014) 63 ICLQ, 599.

C. The ILC Guide

The Guide provides in guideline 4.5.2 that an invalid reservation will be null and void and without any legal effect whether or not an objection has been made to the reservation by any other contracting State.

Guideline 4.5.3 then provides as follows:

1   The status of the author of an invalid reservation in relation to a treaty depends on the intention expressed by the reserving State or international organization on whether it intends to be bound by the treaty without the benefit of the reservation or whether it considers that it is not bound by the treaty.

2   Unless the author of the invalid reservation has expressed a contrary intention or such an intention is otherwise established, it is considered a contracting State or a contracting organization without the benefit of the reservation.

3   Notwithstanding paragraphs 1 and 2, the author of the invalid reservation may express at any time its intention not to be bound by the treaty without the benefit of the reservation.

4   If a treaty monitoring body expresses the view that a reservation is invalid and the reserving State or international organization intends not to be bound by the treaty without the benefit of the reservation, it should express its intention to that effect within a period of twelve months from the date at which the treaty monitoring body made its assessment.

It is clear that guideline 4.5.3 seeks to make 'a middle course solution' between the approach of total invalidity advocated by the ICJ, and the approach of partial invalidity taken by HRs courts and bodies, and provides that the approach to be taken depends upon the author of the invalid reservation. This seems to accord with the fundamental principle of free consent, but may not be welcomed by HRs bodies.[41]

The 'middle course solution' is evidenced by a presumption in guideline 4.5.3(2) that the author of the invalid reservation continues to be party to a treaty without the benefit of its invalid reservation. It is only where a contrary intention is established that the treaty will not continue to apply. Nevertheless, guideline 4.5.3 confers on the author of an invalid reservation an extraordinary right to denounce a treaty that it has otherwise ratified simply because it made a reservation that is invalid. This is problematic as such a ground for withdrawal from a treaty was certainly not contemplated under the VCLT and is unlikely to be a rule of customary international law.

3.7 Interpretative and conditional interpretative declarations and their relationship with reservations

The three concepts: 'interpretative declaration'; 'conditional interpretative declaration'; and 'reservation' have different meanings and effects under the law of treaties.

All three concepts refer to a statement formulated by a State at the time of signing, ratifying, formally confirming, accepting, approving or acceding to a treaty, or when a State gives a notification of succession to a treaty. Each has a different purpose and produces different legal effects:

■   An interpretative declaration, however phrased or named, is made by a State in order to specify or clarify its understanding of the meaning or scope of certain provisions of a treaty, e.g. State X 'understands provision A as meaning . . .'. A declaration of interpretation indicates State X's

---

41   On this topic see: I. Ziemele, *Reservations to Human Rights Treaties: From Draft Guiedlines 3.1.1.2 to Guideline 3.1.5.6* (2013) 24/4 EJIL, 1135.

preference for a particular interpretation of provision A without imposing this interpretation and without ruling out the possibility that provision A may subsequently be interpreted differently. The interpretation suggested by State X is not binding on the parties and does not modify the treaty, although it may influence the subsequent interpretation of provision A (see Chapter 3.12).

- A conditional interpretative declaration, however phrased or named, is made by a State in order to indicate that it does not consent to be bound by the treaty unless a specific interpretation is given to some of its provisions e.g. State X considers that 'provision A means . . . and therefore if provision A is interpreted differently it has no obligation arising from provision A', or State X considers that 'provision A means . . . and therefore if this interpretation is denied, the instrument of ratification will become null and void'. (France attached a similar declaration to its signature of the Treaty for the prohibition of Nuclear Weapons in Latin America.) Accordingly, a conditional declaration seeks to impose on other contracting States the interpretation given by State X to provision A. This modifies relations between the declarant State and the other contracting States under the relevant treaty.

- A reservation, as indicated in Chapter 3.6 excludes or modifies the legal effect of certain provisions of a treaty between the reserving State and other contracting States.

The topic of interpretative declarations was discussed at the time when the VCLT was being prepared. However, as the ILC could not achieve any consensus on how to deal with them, the VCLT does not include any provisions relating to interpretative declarations. When the ILC returned to the topic of reservations in 1993, interpretative declarations became, once again, a controversial issue.

Many delegates were in favour of abolishing conditional interpretative declarations as a separate category and equating them with reservations. Two justifications were advanced:

- their separate existence creates confusion; and

- the equation of a conditional interpretative declaration with a reservation would serve to condone a practice that States have developed to circumvent the rules of the law of treaties. Indeed, it has become increasingly common for States to couch a unilateral statement in the language of an interpretative conditional declaration rather than a reservation. Further, some treaties do not allow reservations and in that circumstance a State by making a conditional interpretative declaration achieves the same result as if it were making a reservation.[42]

On a theoretical level, the distinction between interpretative declarations, conditional interpretative declarations and reservations may not seem to be overly complex but in practice it poses great difficulty. States are using clever words, or confusing terms when making their statements, e.g. when a State declares that it 'considers that its national law is in conformity with Article X of the relevant Treaty' should this statement be qualified as an interpretative declaration, a conditional interpretative declaration or a reservation?

The ILC Guide clarifies the status of conditional interpretative declarations. Guideline 1.4.(2) states that 'conditional interpretative declarations are subject to the rules applicable to reservations'.

---

42   A/CN.4/526/Add.1.

3.8 Entry into force, deposit, registration and publication of treaties

3.8.1 Entry into force

If a treaty does not specify a date, there is a presumption that it is intended to enter into force as soon as all negotiating States have expressed their consent to be bound by it.

In the case of multilateral treaties negotiated by many States it is very unlikely that they will all proceed to ratify it. In such a case the treaty usually provides that it shall enter into force when it has been ratified by a specified number of States. When the minimum number of ratifications is reached the treaty enters into force between those States which have ratified it.

3.8.2 Deposit

Contracting States to a treaty normally agree who will be its depository. The depositary may be a State, international organisation or chief administrative officer of the organisation (Article 77(1)). The depositary's functions and competencies are set out in Articles 76–80 VCLT. The depository is the formal custodian of a treaty and is charged with administrative tasks relating to the relevant treaty. These tasks include:

- receiving instruments of ratifications, notifications and other communications from contracting parties;

- forwarding all relevant information and documents to contracting parties;

- ensuring that the final text of the treaty contains no errors and correcting any errors that may exist;

- preparing certified copies of the treaty; and

- authenticating any translated material.

Following the ICJ's *Advisory Opinion on Reservations to the Convention on the Prevention and Punishment of the Crime of* Genocide,[43] a depository has no power to decide on the compatibility or otherwise of received communications or notifications or reservations. The depository's task is to forward instruments and communications received to the contracting States which will themselves determine the legal effect they produce.

3.8.3 Registration

The reason for registration and publication of a treaty is to ensure transparency in the conduct of international relations.

Article 102 of the UN Charter provides as follows:

1 Every treaty and every international agreement entered into by any Member of the United Nations after the present Charter comes into force shall as soon as possible be registered with the Secretariat and published by it.

2 No party to any such treaty or international agreement which has not been registered in accordance with the provision of paragraph (1) of this article may invoke that treaty or engagement before any organ of the United Nations.

---

43   Supra note 34.

Article 102 was intended to prevent States from entering into secret agreements without the knowledge of their nationals, and without the knowledge of other States, whose interests might be affected by such agreements.

Secret diplomacy was condemned by the League of Nations as it was felt that secret agreements were one of the causes of WWI. Article 18 of the Covenant of the League of Nations imposed an obligation on its members to register with the League's Secretariat 'every treaty of international engagement' entered into by them. Thereafter all such treaties were published. Sanction for non-registration was also provided under Article 18 which stated that international treaties of engagement 'shall not be binding until so registered'. Controversies as to the meaning of those terms were resolved when in the *Case of Pablo Nájera (of the Lebanon) (France v Mexico)*[44] it was decided that Mexico (a non-member of the League) could not avoid the application of a bilateral agreement concluded with France on the ground that France failed to register it with the League. Since that decision it is accepted that a failure to register a treaty has no effect on its validity.

It is to be noted that secret agreements between States are not unlawful and although they are disapproved of and difficult to conceal, they still exist.

3.8.4 Publication

Once a treaty is registered with the UNS-G it will be officially published in the UN Treaty Series 'UNTS', so that anyone can consult it.

3.9 Validity of treaties

Article 42(1) VCLT provides that: 'The validity of a treaty or of the consent of a state to be bound by a treaty may be impeached only through the application of the present Convention.' This is to prevent a State from attempting to evade an inconvenient treaty obligation by alleging spurious grounds of invalidity.

A distinction must be made between grounds of nullity:

- which concern the lack of consent of a party to a treaty with the consequence that the treaty (except if it is a bilateral treaty) will still be valid for all parties except for the State which did not consent to it. The vitiating factors are mentioned in Articles 8, 46–49 VCLT; and the one

- which leads to nullity of a treaty for all parties on the ground that either it was concluded in violation of a *jus cogens* rule (Article 53 VCLT) or it is in conflict with a *jus cogens* rule which has emerged after its conclusion (Article 64 VCLT).

3.9.1 Grounds of nullity affecting the consent of a party to a treaty

These are as follows:

3.9.1.1. Non-compliance with provisions of municipal law

Many States have provisions in their constitutions which prevent their government from entering into treaties, or into certain types of treaty, without the consent of the legislature or some organ of the legislature.

---

44   (1927–28) 4 AnnDig 393.

What is the position if a competent representative, i.e. head of State, foreign secretary, etc disregards the requirements of his State's constitutional law when entering into a treaty? Is the treaty valid or not?

The extent to which constitutional limitations on treaty-making powers can be invoked on the international plane is a matter of controversy and the following views have been put forward:

■ The treaty is void if there is a failure to comply with the requirements of the State's constitutional law.

■ The treaty is only void if the constitutional rule in question is 'notorious', i.e. a well known constitutional limitation.

■ The treaty is valid irrespective of non-compliance with the constitutional law of the State.

■ The treaty is valid except where one party to the treaty knew that the other party was acting in breach of a constitutional requirement.

An additional view, and the one favoured by most States, is reflected in Article 46 VCLT, which provides:

> 1   A state may not invoke the fact that its consent to be bound by a treaty has been expressed in violation of a provision of its internal law regarding competence to conclude treaties as invalidating its consent unless that violation was manifest and concerned a rule of its internal law of fundamental importance.
> 2   A violation is manifest if it would be objectively evident to any state conducting itself in the matter in accordance with normal practice and in good faith.

Accordingly, an alleged violation of a domestic law must concern fundamental provisions which relate to the treaty-making power and must be evident to any State acting in accordance with normal practice and in good faith.

It will be very difficult for a State to nullify a treaty on the basis of Article 46. In the *Case Concerning the Land and Maritime Boundary between Cameroon and Nigeria (Cameroon v Nigeria: Equatorial Guinea Intervening) (Judgment)*,[45] Nigeria argued that the 1975 Maroua Declaration between the two States was not valid on the ground that the then head of State, under the Constitution of Nigeria, lacked capacity to conclude it. The ICJ held that the limitation imposed by constitutional rules on a head of State's capacity to conclude treaties is not manifest within the meaning of Article 46(2) VCLT unless it is at least properly publicised. Additionally, heads of State are considered as having authority to commit the State as they represent their States on the international plane. As to the argument that Cameroon should have known about the constitutional rules, the Court held that:

> There is no general legal obligation for states to keep themselves informed of legislative and constitutional developments in other states which are or may become important for the international relations of these states.[46]

3.9.1.2   Treaties entered into by a representative who lacks authority

The person who is to be regarded as a representative of a State is defined by the VCLT in the following articles:

---

45   [2002] ICJ Rep 303.
46   Ibid, para 266.

Article 7(1) VCLT provides:

> A person is considered as representing a state for the purpose of . . . expressing the consent of the State to be bound by a treaty if: (a) he produces appropriate full powers; or (b) it appears from the practice of the States concerned or from other circumstances that their intention was to consider that person as representing the state for such purposes and to dispense with full powers.

Article 7(2) VCLT provides:

> In virtue of their functions and without having to produce full powers, the following are considered as representing their State: (a) Heads of State, Heads of Government and Ministers for Foreign Affairs . . . (b) heads of diplomatic missions . . . (c) representatives accredited by States.

Article 8 VCLT provides:

> An act relating to the conclusion of a treaty performed by a person who cannot be considered under art 7 as authorised to represent a state for that purpose is without legal effect unless afterwards confirmed by that state.

If the authority of a representative to express the consent of his State to be bound by a particular treaty has been made subject to a specific restriction, then if he fails to observe the restriction, what is the position? In this respect, Article 47 VCLT provides:

> If the authority of a representative to express the consent of a state to be bound by a particular treaty has been made subject to a specific restriction, his omission to observe that restriction may not be invoked as invalidating the consent expressed by him unless the restriction was notified to the other negotiating states prior to his expressing such consent.

Article 47 VCLT confirms that any limitation imposed on a person who has the authority to represent a State, unless notified to other contracting parties, will not constitute a vitiating factor in a situation where such a representative acts *ultra vires*. In particular, if a head of State or a minister of foreign affairs acts within the ostensible authority of his office, the State will be bound by his consent. This issue was examined by the PCIJ in *Legal Status of Eastern Greenland (Denmark v Norway) (Judgment)*.[47]

LEGAL STATUS OF EASTERN GREENLAND (DENMARK *V* NORWAY) (JUDGMENT)

Facts:

In the context of a claim by Denmark to all of Greenland, the Norwegian Minister for Foreign Affairs, Ihlen, in 1919 made the following oral statement in response to a question addressed to him by the Danish diplomatic representatives: 'the Norwegian Government would not make any difficulties in the settlement of this question'. Under the Constitution of Norway, Ihlen was not empowered to make the above statement.

Held:

The Ihlen statement was binding on the government of Norway because it was made on behalf of the Norwegian government and by a representative to whose portfolio the matter belonged.

---

47   PCIJ Ser A/B No 53.

A similar approach was taken by the ICJ in the *Case Concerning the Land and Maritime Boundary between Cameroon and Nigeria (Cameroon v Nigeria: Equatorial Guinea Intervening)*[48] (above).

3.9.1.3 Error

Article 48 VCLT provides:

1   A state may invoke an error in a treaty as invalidating its consent to be bound by the treaty if the error relates to a fact or situation which was assumed by that state to exist at the time when the treaty was concluded and formed an essential basis of its consent to be bound by the treaty.

2   Paragraph (1) shall not apply if the state in question contributed by its own conduct to the error or if the circumstances were such as to put that state on notice of a possible error.

3   An error relating only to the wording of the text of a treaty does not affect its validity.

Only if the error is essential or fundamental to the obligations that a State believed it had undertaken will it be a reason for invalidating a treaty. Thus, to be an invalidating reason, an error, whether unilateral or mutual, must neither concern a question of law nor the wording of text of a treaty agreed by the parties, but relate to a fact or a situation 'which was assumed at the time when a treaty was concluded and formed an essential basis of its [a State's] consent'. Further, a State will not be able to claim error if by its own conduct it contributed to the error. Article 48 VCLT is reflective of current law. As the ILC pointed out, in practice most alleged errors 'concern geographical errors, mostly errors on maps'.

Article 48 VCLT reflects the judgment of the ICJ in the *Case Concerning the Temple of Preah Vihear (Cambodia v Thailand) (Merits)*.[49]

CASE CONCERNING THE TEMPLE OF PREAH VIHEAR (CAMBODIA *V* THAILAND) (MERITS)

Facts:

The ICJ was asked to rule that Cambodia and not Thailand had sovereignty over the Temple of Preah Vihear. In 1904 the boundary between Cambodia (then a French protectorate) and Thailand (then Siam) was determined by a treaty between France and Siam. The treaty stated that it was to follow the watershed line and surveys were conducted by experts on the basis of which a map was prepared. The map placed the Temple in Cambodia and it was this map upon which Cambodia relied for its claim. Thailand argued, inter alia, that the map embodied a material error in that it did not follow the watershed line as required by the treaty. This was argued despite the fact that the map had been received and accepted by the Siamese.

Held:

The Court rejected Thailand's arguments as follows:

It is an established rule of law that the plea of error cannot be allowed as an element vitiating consent if the party advancing it contributed by its own conduct to the error, or could have

---

48   [2002] ICJ Rep 303, para 265.

49   [1962] ICJ Rep 6.

> *avoided it, or if the circumstances were such as to put that party on notice of a possible error. The Court considers that the character and qualifications of the persons who saw the . . . map on the Siamese side would alone make it difficult for Thailand to plead error in law.*[50]

3.9.1.4 Fraud

Article 49 VCLT provides:

> If a state has been induced to conclude a treaty by the fraudulent conduct of another negotiating state, the state may invoke the fraud as invalidating its consent to be bound by the treaty.

There are no recent or significant cases on fraud.

3.9.1.5 Corruption of State representative

Article 50 VCLT provides:

> If the expression of a state's consent to be bound by a treaty has been procured through the corruption of its representative directly or indirectly by another negotiating state, the state may invoke such corruption as invalidating its consent to be bound by the treaty.

The 'corruption' must be a 'substantial influence'. A small courtesy or favour shown to a representative will be insufficient.

3.9.1.6 Coercion of a State's representatives

Article 51 VCLT provides:

> The expression of a state's consent to be bound by a treaty which has been procured by the coercion of its representative through acts or threats directed against him shall be without any legal effect.

Such coercion may include, for example, blackmailing threats or threats against the representative's family. Such coercion must be directed at the representative personally and not coercion of him through a threat of action against his State.

3.9.1.7 Coercion of a State

The traditional doctrine prior to the Covenant of the League of Nations was that the validity of a treaty was not affected by the fact that it had been brought about by the threat of or the use of force. However, Article 2(4) of the UN Charter which prohibits the threat or use of force, together with other developments, now justifies the conclusion that a treaty procured by such coercion will be void.

Article 52 VCLT provides:

> A treaty is void if its conclusion has been procured by the threat or use of force in violation of the principles of international law embodied in the Charter of the United Nations.

---

50   Ibid, 26.

This modern rule against the use of force does not operate retroactively. If a treaty was procured by force before the use of force was made illegal the validity of the treaty is not affected by this subsequent change in the law.

Force, in the context of Article 52, does not include 'economic and political' pressure. A proposed amendment defining force to include these matters was withdrawn (see Chapter 3.9.3).

3.9.2 Grounds of nullity which lead to nullity of a treaty for all contracting parties

A treaty will be invalid if it violates a peremptory norm of international law (see also Chapter 2.5).

Article 53 VCLT deals with the topic of conflict between the rules of *jus cogens* and the provisions of a treaty. It provides:

> A treaty is void if, at the time of its conclusion, it conflicts with a peremptory norm of general international law. For the purposes of the present Convention, a peremptory norm of general international law is a norm accepted and recognised by the international community of states as a whole as a norm from which no derogation is permitted and which can be modified only by a subsequent norm of general international law having the same character.

Article 64 VCLT further provides:

> If a new peremptory norm of general international law emerges, any existing treaty which is in conflict with that norm becomes void and terminates.

3.9.3 Unequal treaties – an additional ground of nullity?

Soviet[51] and Chinese[52] writers have propounded the doctrine of 'unequal treaties', according to which treaties concluded in circumstances where there is inequality of the contracting parties are not legally binding. This doctrine has received substantial support from post-colonial countries.

Unequal treaties were primarily bilateral treaties concluded in the second half of the nineteenth century and the first half of the twentieth century between Western countries, the US and some Latin-American countries, on the one hand, and Asian States and African States, on the other. Having said this, it must be noted that all treaties in which there is substantial or procedural inequality between the parties can be classified as unequal, e.g. the 1938 Munich Agreement and the Soviet Czechoslovak Treaty on the Stationing of Soviet Troops in Czechoslovakia signed after the Soviet military intervention in 1968 in Czechoslovakia.[53]

The doctrine posits that treaties which are 'unequal' either because of their substance (e.g. they impose on one party only obligations and grant to the other only rights, or they impose extreme restrictions on the sovereignty of one party only) or because of the unequal procedure (e.g. they are concluded under political, or economic coercion) are not legally binding.

---

51   I. Tunkin (ed.), *International Law: A Textbook*, Moscow: Progress Publishing, 1986, 48–49.

52   E.S.K. Fung, *The Chinese Nationalists and the Unequal Treaties 1924–1931* (1987) 21 Modern Asian Studies, 793–819.

53   [1968] 7 ILM 1334.

CASE CONCERNING THE TERRITORIAL DISPUTE (LIBYAN ARAB JAMAHIRIYA *V* CHAD)

Facts:

Libya argued that a treaty negotiated in 1955 between itself and France, although valid, should be interpreted favourably towards Libya because, at the time of negotiation, Libya lacked experience in the negotiation of international agreements especially compared to the experience of the French negotiators.

Held:

The Court refused to recognise this factor as a justification for interpreting the treaty in favour of Libya and hence the doctrine of unequal treaties appears to have lost its relevance.

Western jurists oppose the doctrine on the ground of its vagueness and international law does not recognise its existence. The ICJ confirmed this position in the *Case Concerning the Territorial Dispute (Libyan Arab Jamahiriya/Chad)*.[54]

The ILC, when preparing the VCLT, was faced with the matter of unequal treaties when the definition of 'force' under Article 52 VCLT was discussed. Socialist and some African States argued that 'force' means not only military force but also economic and political pressure.[55] However, the ILC rejected this interpretation.[56] During the Conference convened to adopt the VCLT, 19 Asian, African and Latin American countries proposed an amendment to the VCLT aimed at ensuring that treaties concluded through the exercise of economic or political pressure were invalid.[57] This amendment was rejected by Western States and consequently withdrawn in exchange for making the amendment part of an additional declaration to the 1969 *Final Act of the Vienna Conference*. The declaration, as any declaration of this kind, has no binding force. It condemns:

> the threat or use of pressure in any form, whether military, political, or economic, by any State in order to coerce another State to perform any act relating to the conclusion of a treaty in violation of the principles of the sovereign equality of States and freedom of consent.[58]

The problem of unequal treaties has not disappeared but the approach to it has changed. International law addresses it through the principles of special and differential treatment which enhance substantive equality of States and promotes international co-operation to achieve common objectives such as the strengthening of the global response to climate change.[59]

---

54 [1994] ICJ Rep 6.

55 Special Rapporteur M.K. Yasseen, *Report on the Ninth Session of the Asian-African Legal Consultative Committee* (1968) UN Doc A/CN.4/207.

56 UN ILC Special Rapporteur Sir H Waldock, *Fifth Report on the Law of Treaties* (1966) UN Doc A/CN.4/SER A/1966/Add.1, 15–23.

57 United Nations Conference on the Law of Treaties, Summary records of the plenary meetings and of the meetings of the Committee of the Whole, UN Doc A/CONF.39/11, 269–92, 328–29.

58 Ibid, 329.

59 On this topic see: A de Jonge, *From Unequal Treaties to Differential Treatment: Is There a Role for Equality in Treaty Relations* (2014) 4 Asian Journal of International Law, 125.

3.10 Application of treaties

Three topics are examined in this section: the territorial application of treaties; the application of treaties in a situation where they contain overlapping provisions which clash with each other; and the application of treaties to a third party, i.e. a State which is not a contracting party to the relevant treaty.

3.10.1 Territorial application of treaties

Article 29 VCLT provides:

> Unless a different intention appears from the treaty or is otherwise established, a treaty is binding upon each party in respect of its entire territory.

In the absence of any territorial clause or other indication of a contrary intention, a treaty is presumed to apply to all the territories for which the contracting States are internationally responsible. So treaties made by the UK automatically extend to its overseas territories unless the treaty indicates otherwise.

3.10.2 Conflict between treaties

Where a party to a treaty enters into another treaty with overlapping provisions the position is regulated by Article 30 VCLT which provides as follows:

> 1 Subject to art 103 of the Charter of the United Nations, the rights and obligations of states parties to successive treaties relating to the same subject matter shall be determined in accordance with the following paragraphs.
>
> 2 When a treaty specifies that it is subject to, or that it is not to be considered as incompatible with, an earlier or later treaty, the provisions of that other treaty prevail.
>
> 3 When all the parties to the earlier treaty are parties also to the later treaty but the earlier treaty is not terminated or suspended in operation under art 59, the earlier treaty applies only to the extent that its provisions are compatible with those of the later treaty.
>
> 4 When the parties to the later treaty do not include all the parties to the earlier one:
> (a) as between states parties to both treaties the same rule applies as in paragraph (3);
> (b) as between a state party to both treaties and a state party to only one of the treaties, the treaty to which both states are parties governs their mutual rights and obligations.
>
> 5 Paragraph (4) is without prejudice to art 41, or to any question of the termination or suspension of the operation of a treaty under art 60 or to any question of responsibility which may arise for a state from the conclusion or application of a treaty the provisions of which are incompatible with its obligations towards another state under another treaty.

It can be said that a conflict between treaties is resolved in the following manner:

1 If one of the treaties violates a rule of *jus cogens*, the treaty is invalid and therefore not capable of conflicting with another treaty.

2 If a treaty is in conflict with Article 103 of the UN Charter, its provisions which are incompatible with the UN Charter are void.

3 If a treaty contains a conflict clause also known as a saving clause which regulates the relationship between that treaty and other treaties, the conflict clause will indicate which treaty is to be applied if its provisions overlap and are in conflict with another treaty (Article 30(2) VCLT).

4 If two treaties contradict each other and neither contains a saving clause Article 30(3) and (4) applies. This provision endorses the *lex posteriori* maxim, i.e. a later treaty supersedes an earlier treaty. However, the maxim has its limitations, i.e. it applies only where the parties to both treaties are identical and has greater relevance where the conflicting provisions belong to the same 'regime' in the sense that they are institutionally linked or intended to advance the same objectives rather than where they are part of different 'regimes'[60] (see Chapter.2.4.2.1.A). Further, the maxim *lex specialis derogate lex generalis* will be taken into account to give preference to a special or specific provision over a general provision.

3.10.3 Effect of treaties on a third party

The general rule is that a treaty applies only between the parties to it, and this rule is a corollary of the principle of consent and of the sovereignty and independence of States. Article 34 VCLT provides:

> A treaty does not create either obligations or rights for a third state without its consent.

This general rule is known by the maxim *pacta tertiis nec nocent nec prosunt* and Article 34 undoubtedly reflects customary international law in this respect.

Article 2(1)(h) VCLT defines a third State as a State not a party to a treaty. Accordingly, a State may participate in the negotiation of a treaty, have some important connection with the intended contracting States but not become a contracting party unless it ratifies the treaty.

3.10.3.1 Exceptions to the rule that treaties are only binding on contracting parties

Whether any exceptions to the general rule that treaties are only binding on contracting parties exist is a matter of controversy. The ILC was of the firm opinion that a treaty cannot of itself create obligations for non-parties.

Article 35 VCLT provides:

> An obligation arises for a third state from a provision of a treaty if the parties to the treaty intend the provision to be the means of establishing the obligation and the third state expressly accepts that obligation in writing.

The ILC commenting upon this provision acknowledged that the requirements in it are so strict that when they are met:

> there is, in effect, a second collateral agreement between the parties to the treaty, on the one hand and the third state on the other; and that the juridical basis of the latter's obligation is not the treaty itself but the collateral agreement.[61]

A. Recognised exceptions

At least, one exception to the general rule has been recognised. It is accepted that a treaty provision may become binding on non-parties if it becomes a part of international customary law. In the *North*

---

60 Report of the Study Group of the International Law Commission 'Fragmentation of International Law: Difficulties Arising from the Diversification and Expansion of International Law' (Conclusions) (2006) UN Doc A/CN/.4/L.702, Conclusion 26.

61 [1966] Yearbook of the ILC, vol II, 277.

Sea Continental Shelf (Federal Republic of Germany/Denmark and Federal Republic of Germany/ Netherlands) (Merits)[62] the ICJ stated that a provision of a treaty must meet the following stringent requirements before it achieves the status of a customary rule:

- it must be of a norm creating nature;

- the parties to the treaty must agree that the provision is of such a nature; and

- State practice of non-parties to the treaty must indicate that they regard the relevant provision of the treaty as binding.

However, some treaty provisions reflect pre-treaty customary law and some may constitute evidence of the formulation of a new customary rule. In such a situation, the relevant provisions of those treaties apply to third parties.

Views differ as to whether Article 2(6) of the UN Charter imposes obligations on States which are not members of the UN.

Article 2(6) provides:

The Organisation shall ensure that states which are not Members of the United Nations act in accordance with these Principles so far as may be necessary for the maintenance of international peace and security.

It is submitted that Article 2(6) does not create any legal obligations for non-members of the UN as it clearly requires members of the UN to take all appropriate measures to ensure that non-member States will comply with decisions adopted by the UNSC under Chapter VII. However, since 1945, Article 2(6) has acquired the status of customary international law as evidenced by State practice and the almost universal membership of the UN. Therefore, it satisfies the criteria set out by the ICJ in the *North Sea Continental Shelf (Federal Republic of Germany/Denmark and Federal Republic of Germany/ Netherlands) (Merits)* (see above).

B. Conferment of a right on a third party.

Some treaties contain provisions in favour of specified third States or in respect of States generally. Examples of such third party 'rights' are contained for instance in the treaty provisions guaranteeing freedom of passage for ships through the Suez and Kiel Canals. For example, in the 1888 Convention Respecting the Free Navigation of the Suez Maritime Canal[63] Article 1 provides: 'The Suez Maritime Canal shall always be free and open, in time of war as in time of peace, to every vessel of commerce or of war, without distinction of flag'.

When, if at all, does such a 'right' conferred upon a third State become established as a 'right' and enforceable by it?

Two opposing views have been expressed on this point:

- The accepted view is that the third State may only claim the benefit if it assents, either expressly or impliedly, to the creation of the right.

- The right created in favour of the third party is not conditional upon any express act of acceptance by that party.

---

62   [1969] ICJ Rep 4.

63   (Signed 29 October 1888) (1909) 3 AJIL Supp 123.

The ILC adopted the view that in practice the effects of the two opposing views would be substantially the same. The matter was clarified and resolved by Article 36 VCLT which provides:

1 A right arises for a third state from a provision of a treaty if the parties to the treaty intend the provision to accord that right either to the third state, or to a group of states to which it belongs, or to all states, and the third state assents thereto. Its assent shall be presumed so long as the contrary is not indicated, unless the treaty otherwise provides.

2 A state exercising a right in accordance with paragraph (1) shall comply with the conditions for its exercise provided for in the treaty or established in conformity with the treaty.

So this article creates a presumption of assent on the part of the third State. However, a right conferred on the third state may be revoked or modified in the circumstances described in Article 37 VCLT. This article provides:

1 When an obligation has arisen for a third state in conformity with art 35, the obligation may be revoked or modified only with the consent of the parties to the treaty and of the third state, unless it is established that they had otherwise agreed.

2 When a right has arisen for a third state in conformity with art 36, the right may not be revoked or modified by the parties if it is established that the right was intended not to be revocable or subject to modification without the consent of the third state.

3.11 Amendment and modification of treaties

3.11.1 Amendment

The normal method of amending a treaty is by the unanimous agreement of the parties. Indeed, Article 39 VCLT provides that: 'A treaty may be amended by agreement between the parties'.

If all the parties agree to the amendment no difficulty arises. But in a large multilateral convention it may not be possible to obtain unanimous agreement to a proposed amendment.

Many treaties contain provisions for an amendment procedure. For example, Article 109 of the UN Charter provides for the holding of a General Conference of member States 'for the purpose of reviewing the present Charter'.

Other multilateral treaties provide for possible revision at the end of specified periods. For example, Article 312 of the UN Convention on the Law of the Sea 1982 provides that any party, after the expiry of 10 years from the entry into force of the Convention, may request the revision of the Convention by notification in writing to the UNS-G.

In cases where a treaty contains no reference to amendment, Article 40 VCLT is of assistance. It states:

1 Unless the treaty otherwise provides, the amendment of multilateral treaties shall be governed by the following paragraphs.

2 Any proposal to amend a multilateral treaty as between all the parties must be notified to all the contracting states, each one of which shall have the right to take part in:
   (a)   the decision as to the action to be taken in regard to such proposals;
   (b)   the negotiation and conclusion of any agreement for the amendment of the treaty.

3 Every state entitled to become a party to the treaty shall also be entitled to become a party to the treaty as amended.

4 The amending agreement does not bind any state already a party to the treaty which does not become a party to the amending agreement; art 30, paragraph (4(b)) applies in relation to such state.

5 Any state which becomes a party to the treaty after the entry into force of the amending agreement shall, failing an expression of a different intention by that state:

(a) be considered as a party to the treaty as amended; and

(b) be considered as a party to the unamended treaty in relation to any party to the treaty not bound by the amending agreement.

When a treaty establishes a body competent to apply and interpret its provisions (e.g. in particular a judicial body empowered to render binding decisions such as the ECtHR[64] under the ECHR; the Court of Justice of the European Union (ECJ) under the EU Treaty and the Caribbean Court of Justice (CCJ) under the Revised Treaty of Chaguaramas), such body normally adopts an evolutive interpretation of the relevant treaty (see Chapter 3.12.3.) often resulting in *de facto* amendments of that treaty.

3.11.1.1 The legal effect of amendment

The issue of the legal effect of adopted amendments is complex. In principle, an amendment will only bind parties that have agreed to it, and if one State has agreed to the amendment and another State has not, then the terms of the original treaty will remain operative between them. In practice, this rule is not always possible to apply because some multilateral treaties can only work properly if all contracting parties have the same duties and obligations, e.g. treaties creating international organisations, HRs treaties which establish monitoring bodies. One way of pre-empting this problem is to impose on all contracting States amendments when a specified majority of contracting States has approved them. For example, under Article 108 of the UN Charter, once an amendment is accepted by two-thirds of its members, including all permanent members of the UNSC, it enters into force for all member States. A member State which disagrees with the amendment can either resign itself to accepting it, or withdraw from the treaty, although this may not be easy as the UN Charter does not contain a withdrawal clause.

3.11.2 Modification

This occurs where a number of parties to a treaty formally agree to modify the effects of the treaty among themselves, while continuing to be bound by the treaty in their relations with the other parties.

This matter is covered by Article 41 VCLT, which provides:

1 Two or more of the parties to a multilateral treaty may conclude an agreement to modify the treaty as between themselves alone if:

(a) the possibility of such a modification is provided for by the treaty; or

(b) the modification in question is not prohibited by the treaty and

(i) does not affect the enjoyment by the other parties of their rights under the treaty or the performance of their obligations;

(ii) does not relate to a provision, derogation from which is incompatible with the effective execution of the object and purpose of the treaty as a whole.

2 Unless in a case falling under paragraph (1(a)) the treaty otherwise provides, the parties in question shall notify the other parties of their intention to conclude the agreement and of the modification to the treaty for which it provides.

---

64 D. Nicol, *Original Intent and the European Convention on Human Rights* (2005) Public Law, 152–172.

3.11.2.1 Modification by subsequent practice

A consistent practice, if it establishes common consent of the parties to be bound by a different rule from that laid down in the treaty, will have the effect of modifying the treaty. The following is an illustration of the process in operation.

The Italian Peace Treaty of 1947[65] was signed and ratified by nearly 20 States. It provided for the setting up of a Free Territory of Trieste, but this proved impracticable owing to disagreements between the Allied Powers. It was subsequently agreed by four of the signatories that Italy and Yugoslavia should each administer half the territory. This agreement was acted upon by Yugoslavia and Italy and was not objected to by the other States. Thus, the terms of the original Peace Treaty were modified by subsequent practice.

3.12 Interpretation of treaties

Article 31 VCLT states the general rules on interpretation of treaties as follows:

> 1 A treaty shall be interpreted in good faith in accordance with the ordinary meaning to be given to the terms of the treaty in their context and in the light of its object and purpose.
>
> 2 The context for the purpose of the interpretation of a treaty shall comprise, in addition to the text, including its preamble and annexes:
>> (a) any agreement relating to the treaty which was made between all the parties in connection with the conclusion of the treaty;
>> (b) any instrument which was made by one or more parties in connection with the conclusion of the treaty and accepted by the other parties as an instrument related to the treaty.
>
> 3 There shall be taken into account, together with the context:
>> (a) any subsequent agreement between the parties regarding the interpretation of the treaty or the application of its provisions;
>> (b) any subsequent practice in the application of the treaty which establishes the agreement of the parties regarding its interpretation;
>> (c) any relevant rules of international law applicable in the relations between the parties.
>
> 4 A special meaning shall be given to a term if it is established that the parties so intended.

Article 32 VCLT further provides:

> Recourse may be had to supplementary means of interpretation, including the preparatory work of the treaty and the circumstances of its conclusion, in order to confirm the meaning resulting from the application of art 31, or to determine the meaning when the interpretation according to art 31:
>> (a) leaves the meaning ambiguous or obscure; or
>> (b) leads to a result which is manifestly absurd or unreasonable.

It is clear from Articles 31–32 that the VCLT endorses textual, systematic, teleological and historical interpretation. These different methods of interpretation are defined below:

■ The textual approach seeks to ascertain the ordinary meaning of the terms to be interpreted which meaning must be compatible with the text of the relevant treaty.

---

65   49 UNTS 3.

■ The systematic interpretation seeks to ascertain the sense of a wording by the context in which it is used. It includes the surrounding body of law as part of the context and depending on how widely the context or 'system' is understood, tends to work opposite to the principle of *lex specialis* (see Chapter 2.4.2.1).

■ The teleological interpretation searches for the purpose (in Greek *telos* means purpose) of a law. It chooses from among several possible interpretations the one which is most conducive to putting this purpose into practice.

■ Historical interpretation determines the meaning of the legal wording based on historical material such as the preparatory work of the treaty and other documents relevant to its conclusion.

A reference to the principle of effectiveness is present in Article 31 VCLT. Under this principle, which embodies the Latin maxim '*ut res magis valiat quam pereat*' ('that the matter may have effect rather than fail'), provisions of a treaty should be given the 'fullest weight and effect consistent with the language used and with the rest of the text in such a way that every part of it can be given meaning'.[66] Consequently, a provision must be given an interpretation which is 'effective' and 'useful' to produce the appropriate effect.

If it is established that the parties to a treaty intended to give a special meaning to a term, different from its ordinary meaning, the intention of the parties should be given effect.

The problem with the rules on interpretation set out in the VCLT is that it is not clear whether the textual interpretation and the teleological interpretation are intended to be complementary to each other or distinct. If they are distinct then the same terms may be given different interpretations and this then leads to a question of whether there is a hierarchy in the methods of interpretation, e.g. if the textual interpretation fails, then should the teleological interpretation be used. Views differ on this matter (see Chapter 3.12.6). Further, the principle of good faith assumes great importance to the interpretation of treaties. In so far as it relates to the parties to a treaty, who interpret the treaty when performing their obligations flowing from that treaty, the principle of good faith means that they should deal with each other in an honest and fair way. Does the principle of good faith entail that a party should not take advantage of the textual interpretation of the relevant treaty in an unfair and prejudicial way so as to frustrate the legitimate expectations of the other party? It can be said that the teleological interpretation and the reference to the principle of good faith will allow courts to overcome the inconvenience of a textual interpretation, in particular in the light of the fact that the principle of good faith also applies to courts and tribunals when they interpret treaties.

3.12.1 Textual interpretation

The words used should be given their ordinary and natural meaning. If the words used are clear and unambiguous then an international tribunal must give effect to the treaty in the sense required by the clear and unambiguous wording, unless some valid ground can be shown for interpreting the provision otherwise.

In the *Competence of the General Assembly for the Admission of a State to the United Nations Case (Advisory Opinion)*,[67] the ICJ stated the position as follows:

---

66   J. Merrills, *The Development of International Law by the European Court of Human Rights*, Manchester: Manchester University Press, 1988, 98.

67   [1950] ICJ Rep 4, 8.

The Court considers it necessary to say that the first duty of a tribunal which is called upon to interpret and apply the provisions of a treaty, is to endeavour to give effect to them in their natural and ordinary meaning in the context in which they occur. If the relevant words in their natural and ordinary meaning make sense in their context, that is an end of the matter . . . When the Court can give effect to a provision of a treaty by giving to the words used in it their natural and ordinary meaning, it may not interpret the words seeking to give them some other meaning.

The textual approach includes the following principles:

- the words used should be given their ordinary and natural meaning;

- the natural and ordinary meaning must be unambiguous;

- the ordinary and natural meaning must not lead to an absurd or unreasonable result.

3.12.2 Systematic interpretation

Article 31(2) VCLT defines context as the whole text of a treaty including its preamble, annexes, and any agreement relating to the treaty which was made between all the parties in connection with its conclusion and any instrument which was made by one or more parties in connection with the conclusion of the treaty, and accepted by the other parties as an instrument related to the treaty. The context has to be considered together with (i) any subsequent agreement between the parties to the treaty regarding its interpretation or application; (ii) any subsequent practice in the application of the treaty; and (iii) any relevant rules of international law applicable between the parties (Article 31(3) VCLT).[68] Article 31(3) VCLT entails that when relevant, external sources will assist in the interpretation of the relevant provision in various ways, i.e. they may clarify, update and modify the provision of a treaty under consideration (see Chapter 2.4.2.1 on the conflict between rules of international law and Chapter 3.10.2 on the conflict between treaties).

3.12.3 Teleological interpretation

The teleological interpretation requires that the meaning of terms must be ascertained in the light of the object and purpose of the relevant treaty. The 'object and purpose' as mentioned in Chapter 3.6.2.2 is a single notion and refers to the entire treaty. Under the teleological approach, the court will seek the interpretation which is the most appropriate to realise the aim, and achieve the object, of the treaty.

The teleological interpretation allows necessary flexibility with the consequence that the relevant treaty can be interpreted in a 'dynamic' sense, i.e. the interpretation can keep up with and adapt to changing social, political, technological and other circumstances. The teleological interpretation is favoured by bodies interpreting HRs treaties. The ECtHR considers the ECHR as a 'living instrument'. It stated in *Tyrer v UK*[69] that the ECHR is 'a living instrument which . . . must be interpreted in the light of present-day conditions'. As a result, the ECtHR found that lesbians, gay men, bisexuals and

---

68   The Report of the Study Group of the ILC on 'Fragmentation of International Law: Difficulties Arising from the Diversification and Expansion of International Law' (Conclusions) adopted by the ILC and presented to the UNGA, emphasised the importance of Article 31(3) VCLT in the interpretation of treaties because it is in accordance with the idea that treaties whatever their subject matter 'are a creation of the international legal system and their operation is predicated upon that fact' (2006) UN Doc A/CN/.4/L.702, Conclusion 17.

69   (1979–80) 2 EHRR 1,para 31.

transsexuals have rights which must be protected under the ECHR although there is no specific provision in the ECHR to this effect. Similarly in *Öcalan v Turkey*[70] the ECtHR held that the attitude to the death penalty has changed since the adoption of the ECHR. Therefore, the possibility for the applicant to face the death penalty and to be subjected to the agonies of detention on death row was in breach of Article 3 of the ECHR (which prohibits torture and other inhuman, degrading treatment or punishment) as well as Article 2 ECHR (which protects the right to life). With regard to Article 2 ECHR, the ECtHR held that 'capital punishment in peacetime has come to be regarded as an unacceptable, if not inhuman, form of punishment which is no longer acceptable under Article 2'. This interpretation of the ECtHR has judicially revised the ECHR, but is certainly consistent with the object and purpose of the ECHR which requires contracting States to protect individuals not only against threats which existed at the time of its conclusion but also against those not then envisaged.

The Court of Justice of the European Union (ECJ) also favours teleological interpretation and gives special consideration to the principle of effectiveness (see Chapter 3.12.6). In *Case 283/81 Srl CILFIT and Lanificio di Gavardo SpA v Ministry of* Health,[71] the ECJ stated its way of interpreting EU law in the following terms:

> every provision of the Community law [EU law] must be placed in its context and interpreted in the light of the provisions of Community law as a whole, regard being had to the objectives thereof and to its state of evolution at the date on which the provision in question is to be applied.

The ECJ in interpreting EU law takes into consideration the evolving nature of the EU and thus interprets EU law in the light of new needs which did not exist at the time of ratification of the founding Treaty. It has inferred from EU law such fundamental principles as supremacy of EU law, direct applicability, direct effect of EU law, and non-contractual liability of a member State. None of these fundamental principles were contained or provided for in the founding Treaty entered into in 1957 by the six original members of the EU (then the EEC): Belgium, France, Germany, Italy, Luxembourg and the Netherlands, or in the subsequent amendments to that Treaty. They were progressively inferred by the ECJ, and each of them provided an integrationist impetus that appeared, at different times, to be absent on the part of different member States.

3.12.4 The historical interpretation

Article 32 VCLT states that reference to the preparatory work for a treaty and the circumstances of its conclusion can, as a supplementary means of interpretation, be made either to confirm the meaning resulting from the application of Article 31, or to determine the meaning when the interpretation according to Article 31 leaves the meaning ambiguous or obscure or leads to a result which is manifestly absurd or unreasonable.

3.12.5 The principle of effectiveness

In public international law the principle of *effet utile* or effectiveness is applied by a judge when he is confronted with two possible interpretations of the same legal provision, one which confers some meaning on it, and the other which renders it devoid of any significance. In such a situation, he gives priority to the former. The ECJ not only sets aside the interpretation which makes a provision devoid

---

70   (2003) 37 EHRR 10, para 196.
71   [1982] ECR 3415, para 20.

of its *effet utile*, but more importantly rejects any interpretation which results in limiting or weakening the *effet utile* of that provision.[72] It has been submitted by Snyder that in the context of the interpretation of EU law, which in contrast to national law, is 'complex, novel and lacking in legitimacy', the principle of effectiveness has a political and empirical nature i.e. the implementation and enforcement of EU law often requires political decisions in that it requires the exercise of political power and a choice between competing values. As a result, the resort to effectiveness raises the issue of the limits of judicial power of interpretation.[73]

3.12.6 Conclusion

The practice of international courts differs as to whether the VCLT establishes any hierarchy in the different methods of treaty interpretation. The ICJ gives preference to textual and systematic interpretations corroborated by historical interpretation. In the *Case concerning the Territorial Dispute (Libyan Arab Jamahiriya/Chad)* the ICJ stated:

> Interpretation must be based above all upon the text of the treaty. As a supplementary measure recourse may be had to means of interpretation such as the preparatory work of the treaty and the circumstances of its conclusion.[74]

The Appellate Body of the WTO favours the textual interpretation, followed by the systematic interpretation. It rarely uses the teleological interpretation and has no place for historical interpretation, because:

> For the Appellate Body, the low value of the negotiating history results from the secondary rank attributed to this criterion by the Vienna Convention, the lack of reliable records, and the ambiguities resulting from the presence of contradictory statements of the negotiating parties.[75]

The ECtHR's approach to Article 31 was stated in *Golder v UK* in the following words:

> In the way in which it is presented in the 'general rule' in Article 31 of the Vienna Convention, the process of interpretation of a treaty is a unity, a single combined operation; this rule, closely integrated, places on the same footing the various elements enumerated in the four paragraphs of the Article.[76]

Like the ECtHR, the ECJ uses all methods of interpretation, but clearly favours the teleological interpretation and gives great importance to the principle of effectiveness. It rarely relies on the *travaux preparatoires*, i.e. the historical interpretation, mainly because it is of little use in the interpretation of the ever changing objectives of EU law and because of technical difficulties in ascertaining the intention of contracting parties with regard to the text to be interpreted. There are, however, examples of where the ECJ relied on the historical interpretation.[77]

---

72 Case C-437/97 *Evangelischer Krankenhausverein Wien v Abgabenberufungskommission Wien and Wein & Co. HandelsgesmbH v Oberösterreichische Landesregierung* [2000] ECR I-1157.

73 F. Snyder, *The Effectiveness of European Community Law: Institutions, Processes, Tools, and Techniques* (1993) 56(1) MLR, 19–54, 24.

74 [1994] ICJ Rep 6, para 41.

75 C-D. Ehlermann, *Some Personal Experiences as Member of the Appellate Body of the WTO*, Robert Schuman Centre Policy Paper No 02/9 (2002), para 44.

76 [1979–80] 1EHRR 524, para 30.

77 Joined Cases 66, 127, and 128/79, *Amministrazione delle Finanze v. Srl. Meridionale Industria Salumi* [1980] ECR 1237, 1264 and Case C-192/99, *Kaur* [2001] ECR I-1237, paras 23–24.

3.13 Termination and suspension of treaties

The principles of *pacta sunt servanda* and of good faith expressed in Article 26 VCLT entail that a State cannot release itself from its treaty obligations whenever it wishes. If it could do so, treaties would become worthless. However, there are circumstances where suspension or termination of a treaty is justified. The difference between suspension and termination is that:

- when a treaty is suspended it is still valid but its operation is suspended temporarily, either for all parties or for some of them;

- when a treaty is terminated it is no longer in force as it has ended its existence.

It is important to note that the ILC Draft Articles on the Effects of Armed Conflicts on the Termination or Suspension of a Treaty constitute a useful addition to the VCLT in this area (see Chapter 3.13.2.3).

3.13.1 Suspension of a treaty

Contracting parties are allowed, in some circumstances, to suspend the operation of a treaty. During the period of suspension, contracting parties are relieved from carrying out various treaty commitments. The treaty itself remains valid (Article 72 VCLT) but its operation, partial or total, is suspended. However, during the suspension period, the jurisdictional clauses, e.g. giving jurisdiction to the relevant bodies in case of any dispute arising from its application are fully operative. Obviously, when a treaty is suspended, its provisions which reflect customary rules are applicable because customary law cannot be suspended. Suspension can be agreed by all contracting parties, by some of them, or can result from a unilateral act of a contracting party. Often, suspension of the operation of a treaty is a measure taken by a majority of the contracting States to put pressure on a contracting State which has acted in violation of treaty provisions. Under Article 72 VCLT, during the suspension period, contracting parties are required to refrain from any acts tending to obstruct the resumption of the operation of the treaty. A unilateral suspension by a contracting party can be revoked by it.

Probably the most often cited example of suspension of the operation of a treaty is provided by the suspension of air service agreements between several States, on one side, and the USSR, on the other, to respond to the unlawful shooting down by the Soviet forces of a Korean Airlines aircraft on 1 September 1983. Those States, unilaterally, for various periods of time, suspended the relevant agreements with the consequence that the USSR's aircraft belonging to Aeroflot were prevented from landing in their territories.

3.13.1.1 The grounds on which a treaty may be suspended

The circumstances in which a contracting party may suspend the operation of a Treaty may be laid down by the relevant treaty, or in the absence of this, suspension may be able to occur in accord with the principles of international law set out in Article 42 VCLT.

Article 57(a) VCLT identifies six situations in which suspension may take place. The first is described in Article 57(b) VCLT. It relates to a situation where all contracting parties agree to suspend the operation of a treaty, or some of its provisions. The second is described in Article 58 VCLT and concerns a situation where two or more parties agree to suspend the operation of a treaty temporarily between themselves, provided suspension is either allowed under the relevant treaty or not prohibited. However, the suspension is only allowed if it does not impair the enjoyment by other parties of their rights deriving from the relevant treaty, does not affect the performance of their obligations and is compatible with the object and purpose of the treaty.

The remaining grounds, except one, are set out in Articles 59–62 VCLT and are the same as for termination of a treaty. They are examined below. However, it should be noted that an additional ground for suspension exists, not provided for by the VCLT. It occurs when the UNSC takes measures under Chapter VII which may require suspension of the operation of a treaty or some of its provisions, e.g. a bilateral treaty of mutual friendship and assistance will be suspended as a result of the imposition of, let's say, economic and diplomatic sanctions on one of the parties (see Chapter 16.2.3 and 16.2.4).

3.13.2   Termination of a treaty

Few treaties last forever, and in order to prevent the law from becoming too rigid some provision is made for the termination of treaties. But in so doing, the law regarding the termination of treaties tries to steer a middle course between the two extremes of rigidity and insecurity.

Article 42(2) VCLT in seeking to protect the security of legal relations provides:

> The termination of a treaty, its denunciation or the withdrawal of a party, may take place only as a result of the application of the provisions of the treaty or of the present Convention. The same rule applies to suspension of the operation of a treaty.

3.13.2.1   Situations in which a treaty may be terminated

In the following situations a treaty may be terminated:

A.   Termination of a treaty in accordance with the terms of the treaty

Article 54(a) VCLT provides that the termination of a treaty or the withdrawal of a party may take place 'in conformity with the provisions of the treaty'.

The following are examples of the most frequently used provisions for the termination of, or for the withdrawal from, treaty obligations:

- the treaty may be for a specified period and terminate at the end of that period;

- the treaty may be for a minimum period with a right to withdraw at the expiry of that period;

- the treaty may be for a specific purpose and terminate on completion of that purpose;

- the treaty may allow withdrawal at any time;

- the treaty may allow withdrawal in special circumstances.

B.   Termination by agreement

Article 54(b) VCLT provides that the termination of a treaty or withdrawal of a party may take place 'at any time by consent of all the parties after consultation with the other contracting states'.

The agreement of the parties to terminate the treaty may be implied. In this respect Article 56 VCLT provides:

> 1   A treaty which contains no provision regarding its termination and which does not provide for denunciation or withdrawal is not subject to denunciation or withdrawal unless:
>   (a)   it is established that the parties intended to admit the possibility of denunciation or withdrawal; or
>   (b)   a right of denunciation or withdrawal may be implied by the nature of the treaty.
> 2   A party shall give not less than twelve months notice of its intention to denounce or withdraw from a treaty under paragraph (1).

A right of denunciation or withdrawal may therefore be implied in certain types of treaty because of their very nature, for example, treaties of alliance and commercial treaties. However, under Article 56 a right to denounce or withdraw can never be implied if a treaty contains an express provision against denunciation, withdrawal or termination.[78]

C. Implied termination where the parties enter into another treaty on the same subject
Article 59 VCLT provides:

> 1 A treaty shall be considered as terminated if all the parties to it conclude a later treaty relating to the same subject matter and:
>   (a) it appears from the later treaty or is otherwise established that the parties intended that the matter should be governed by that treaty; or
>   (b) the provisions of the later treaty are so far incompatible with those of the earlier one that the two treaties are not capable of being applied at the same time.
> 2 The earlier treaty shall be considered as only suspended in operation if it appears from the later treaty or is otherwise established that such was the intention of the parties.

It is apparent from Article 59 that in the case of multilateral treaties implied termination is less readily established than in the case of bilateral treaties.

D. Termination of a treaty which is in conflict with a *jus cogens* rule
Article 64 VCLT provides:

> If a new peremptory norm of general international law emerges, any existing treaty which is in conflict with that norm becomes void and terminates.

However, Article 64 VCLT does not have retroactive effect on the validity of the treaty. Thus it applies in a situation where there is a conflict between an existing treaty and a new rule of *jus cogens*.

3.13.2.2 Situations where a party may either terminate or suspend a treaty

In the following situations a party may choose either to terminate a treaty or to suspend its operation:

A. Where a party commits a material breach of a treaty
It is recognised that the material breach of a treaty by one party entitles the other party or parties to the treaty to invoke the breach as a ground for termination or suspension. Article 60(1) VCLT provides:

> A material breach of a bilateral treaty by one of the parties entitles the other to invoke the breach as a ground for terminating the treaty or suspending its operation in whole or in part.

This right of termination or suspension has become accepted as being the main sanction for securing the observance of treaties. Obviously, a defaulting State will be held responsible for the breach at the international level.

However, matters are more complex in the case of breach of a multilateral treaty. There are two aspects to such treaties: the rights of the parties to the treaty as a group, and the rights of individual States. In this respect Article 60(2) VCLT provides:

---

78   K. Widdows, *The Unilateral Denunciation of Treaties Containing no Denunciation Clause* (1982) 53 BYIL, 83–114.

A material breach of a multilateral treaty by one of the parties entitles:

(a) the other parties by unanimous agreement to suspend the operation of the treaty in whole or in part or to terminate it either;

    (i)   in the relations between themselves and the defaulting state, or

    (ii)   as between all parties;

(b) a party specially affected by the breach to invoke it as a ground for suspending the operation of the treaty in whole or in part in the relations between itself and the defaulting state;

(c) any party other than the defaulting state to invoke the breach as a ground for suspending the operation of the treaty in whole or in part with respect to itself if the treaty is of such a character that a material breach of its provisions by one party radically changes the position of every party with respect to the further performance of its obligations under the treaty.

Article 60(2)(c) applies in respect of those treaties where a breach by one party tends to undermine the whole regime of the treaty as between all the parties, the best example being disarmament treaties. Article 60(3) VCLT defines 'material breach' as follows:

A material breach of a treaty, for the purposes of this article, consists in: a repudiation of the treaty not sanctioned by the present Convention; or the violation of a provision essential to the accomplishment of the object or purpose of the treaty.

Such a breach does not automatically terminate the treaty; it merely gives the injured party or parties an option to terminate or suspend the treaty. Article 45 VCLT provides that an injured party will lose this right to exercise the option:

if after becoming aware of the facts: it shall have expressly agreed that the treaty . . . remains in force or continues in operation, as the case may be; or it must by reason of its conduct be considered as having acquiesced . . . in its [the treaty] maintenance in force or in operation, as the case may be.

With regard to human rights treaties, however, the contracting parties are not allowed to terminate or suspend the relevant treaty. In this respect Article 60(5) VCLT provides:

Paragraphs 1 to 3 [of art 60] do not apply to provisions relating to the protection of the human person contained in treaties of a humanitarian character, in particular to provisions prohibiting any form of reprisals against persons protected by such treaties.

This provision was adopted with the 1949 Geneva Convention IV in view (see Chapter 17.5.5). Under its provisions reprisals against persons protected by that Convention are prohibited. With the development of HRL, treaties protecting human rights are within the scope of Article 60(5) VCLT. The application of the principle of reciprocity to human rights treaties is inappropriate given that they impose duties on States towards individuals, and thus are not based on the logic of reciprocity that applies to inter-State treaties.

B. Where it is impossible for a party to perform its obligations

There may be circumstances where one of the parties to a treaty may find it literally impossible to perform its obligations. The ILC gave examples of the submergence of an island, the drying up of a river or the destruction of a dam, where these are indispensable to the execution of a treaty.[79] Article 61 therefore provides:

---

79   1966 Draft Articles on Treaties with Commentaries YILC 1966, vol II, 256.

1 A party may invoke the impossibility of performing a treaty as a ground for terminating or withdrawing from it if the impossibility results from the permanent disappearance or destruction of an object indispensable for the execution of the treaty. If the impossibility is temporary, it may be invoked only as a ground for suspending the operation of the treaty.

2. Impossibility of performance may not be invoked by a party as a ground for terminating, withdrawing from or suspending the operation of a treaty if the impossibility is the result of a breach by that party either of an obligation under the treaty or of any other international obligation owed to any other party to the treaty.

C. Where there has been a fundamental change of circumstances since the treaty was concluded
A party is not bound to perform a treaty if there has been a fundamental change of circumstances since the treaty was concluded. The VCLT in Article 62 confines this rule within very narrow limits by providing:

1 A fundamental change of circumstances which has occurred with regard to those existing at the time of the conclusion of a treaty, and which was not foreseen by the parties, may not be invoked as a ground for terminating or withdrawing from the treaty unless:
   (a) the existence of those circumstances constituted an essential basis of the consent of the parties to be bound by the treaty; and
   (b) the effect of the change is radically to transform the extent of obligations still to be performed under the treaty.

2 A fundamental change of circumstances may not be invoked as a ground for terminating or withdrawing from the treaty:
   (a) if the treaty established a boundary; or
   (b) if the fundamental change is the result of a breach by the party invoking it either of an obligation under the treaty or of any other international obligation owed to any other party to the treaty.

3 If, under the foregoing paragraphs, a party may invoke a fundamental change of circumstances as a ground for terminating or withdrawing from a treaty, it may also invoke the change as a ground for suspending the operation of the treaty.

This article reflects the doctrine of *rebus sic stantibus* (things remaining as they are).

Some writers base this doctrine on the fictional rule that every treaty contains an implied term that it shall only remain in force so long as circumstances remain the same. Although State practice supports the doctrine many jurists dislike it and prefer to confine its scope within very narrow limits. They see the doctrine as a considerable threat to the security of treaties and the ILC considered this fictional rule to be undesirable in that it increases the risk of subjective interpretation and abuse. In the *Fisheries Jurisdiction Case (United Kingdom v Iceland)*[80] the ICJ held that Article 62 'may in many respects be considered as a codification of existing customary law on the subject' but held that the dangers to Icelandic interests resulting from new fishing techniques 'cannot constitute a fundamental change with respect to the lapse or subsistence' of the jurisdictional clause in a bilateral agreement.

In the *Case Concerning the Gabčíkovo-Nagymaros Project (Hungary/Slovakia)*[81] Hungary claimed that a fundamental change of circumstances affected a treaty between Hungary and Slovakia concerning

---

80   [1973] ICJ Rep 3, para 36.
81   [1997] ICJ Rep 7.

the construction and operation of the Gabčíkovo-Nagymaros project. Hungary argued that the treaty was concluded between two communist governments during the Cold War, and that the treaty obligations had since been radically transformed by the following situations:

■ the collapse of communism in Eastern Europe;

■ the rise of concerns for protection of the environment; and

■ the diminishing economic viability of the project.

The ICJ recognised the fundamental changes but was not prepared to accept that the continuant existence of those situations had affected the consent of the parties. The Court held that:

> The treaty provided for a joint investment programme for the production of energy, the control of floods and the improvement of navigation on the Danube. In the Court's view, the prevalent political conditions were thus not so closely linked to the object and purpose of the Treaty that they constituted an essential basis of the consent of the parties . . .[82]

Accordingly, the claim made by Hungary was rejected.

In order to avoid threats to the peace Article 62(2)(a) VCLT excludes the application of the *rebus sic stantibus* to treaties fixing boundaries.

3.13.2.3 Effects of armed conflicts on the termination of a treaty

Historically, war was regarded as ending all treaties between belligerent States. International law has been unclear on whether this view is still acceptable today. For that reason the ILC decided that some clarification on this topic will be useful. Its work culminated in the adoption of Draft Articles on the Effects of Armed Conflicts on Treaties with Commentaries.

DA 3 of the ILC Draft Articles on the Effect of Armed Conflict on Treaties provides that the existence of an armed conflict does not *ipso facto* terminate or suspend a treaty between the States party to the conflict and between a State party to the conflict and a State which is not.[83] Its commentary explains that this is not a presumption. The purpose of DA 3 is to 'dispel any assumption of discontinuity'. However, whether a treaty, or some of its provisions, if severable, will continue to apply depends on the express provisions of the relevant treaty, its subject matter, object and purpose, the number of parties to that treaty and the characteristics of the armed conflict, e.g. its intensity, duration, and in the case of an internal conflict, outside involvement in the conflict.

Notwithstanding the above, DA 7 provides that certain treaties, because of their subject matter are presumed to remain in force. These include treaties declaring, creating or regulating a permanent regime or status or related permanent rights, including treaties establishing or modifying land and maritime boundaries, as well as treaties dealing with the following subjects:

■ IHL (see Chapter 17);

■ HRS treaties (e.g. ICCPR);

■ international criminal law;

■ international environmental law;

---

82   Ibid, para 104.
83   A/RES/66/99.

■ constituent instruments of international organisations (e.g. the UN Charter); and

■ multilateral law-making treaties.

The Draft Articles consider a special situation of an aggressor State and a State which exercises its right to self-defence in conformity with Article 51 of the UN Charter. While an aggressor State is prohibited from terminating, suspending or withdrawing from a treaty if the effect of such a termination, suspension or withdrawal would be to benefit the aggressor State, a State which acts in self-defence is entitled to suspend the operation of a treaty, or some of its provisions, insofar as that operation is incompatible with the exercise of the right to self-defence.

3.14 Settlement of disputes

Articles 65–68 VCLT provide for the situation where a State invokes either a defect in its consent to be bound by a treaty or a ground for impeaching the validity of a treaty, as the reason for terminating it, withdrawing from it or suspending its operation.

Article 65(1) provides that the State must notify the other parties of the 'measure proposed to be taken with respect to the treaty and the reasons therefor'.

Article 65(2) provides that the notification should specify a period within which the other parties may raise objections and this period 'except in cases of special urgency, shall not be less than three months after the receipt of the notification'.

Article 65(3) provides that if an objection is raised the State making the notification and the party or parties 'shall seek a solution' in accordance with Article 33 of the UN Charter *via* 'negotiation, equity, mediation, conciliation, arbitration, judicial settlement, resort to regional agencies or arrangements, or other peaceful means of their own choice'. In circumstances where no solution has been reached by the means specified in Article 65(3) 'within a period of 12 months following the date on which the objection was raised' Article 66 confers jurisdiction on the ICJ over disputes arising from Article 53 (i.e. those concerning the *jus cogens* rules) (see Chapter 2.5) and confers jurisdiction over other disputes on a special conciliation commission set up under an annex to the VCLT.

The above rules represent a significant innovation as compared to the settlement of disputes under customary international law. Under customary international law, international courts and commissions do not have jurisdiction over all cases concerning claims that a treaty is invalid, but only over those cases where the parties to the dispute agree to submit the matter to such a court or commission.

RECOMMENDED READING

Books

Aust, A., *Modern Treaty Law and Practice*, 3rd edn, Cambridge: Cambridge University Press, 2013.

Dörr, O. and Schmalenbach, K. (eds), *Vienna Convention on the Law of Treaties, A Commentary*, Heidelberg/Dordrecht/London/New York: Springer, 2012.

Gardiner, R., *Treaty Interpretation*, Oxford: Oxford University Press, 2010.

Gomaa, M.M., *Suspension or Termination of Treaties on Grounds of Breach*, The Hague: Nijhoff, 1996.

Redgwell, C., 'US Reservations to Human Rights Treaties: All for One and None for All?' in M. Byers and G. Nolte (eds), *United States Hegemony and the Foundations of International Law*, Cambridge: Cambridge University Press, 2003, 363.

Sadat-Akhavi, A., *Methods of Resolving Conflicts between Treaties*, Leiden: Nijhoff 2003.

Articles

Bowman, M., *The Multilateral Treaty Amendment Process – A Case Study* (1995) 44 ICLQ, 540.

Fitzmaurice, M., *Third Parties and the Law of Treaties* (2002) 6 Max Planck Yrbk UNL, 37.

Helfer, L.R., *Not Fully Committed? Reservations, Risk, and Treaty Design* (2006) 31 Yale J Intl L, 367.

Jonas, D.S. and Saunders, T.N., *The Object and Purpose of a Treaty: Three Interpretive Methods* (2010) 43 Vand J Transnatl L, 565.

de Jonge, A., *From Unequal Treaties to Differential Treatment: Is There a Role for Equality in Treaty Relations* (2014) 4 Asian Journal of International Law, 125.

Klabbers, J., How to Defeat a Treaty's Object and Purpose Pending Entry into Force: Toward Manifest Intent (2001) 34 Vand J Transnat L, 283.

Kearney, R.D. and Dalton, R.E., *The Treaty on Treaties* (1970) 64 AJIL, 495.

McCall-Smith, K.I., *Severing Reservations* (2014) 63 ICLQ, 599.

Nahlik, S.E., *The Grounds of Invalidity and Termination of Treaties* (1971) 65 AJIL, 736.

Pellet, A., *The ILC Guide to Practice on Reservations to Treaties: A General Presentation by the Special Rapporteur* (2013) 24/4 EJIL, 1061.

Raustiala, K., *Form and Substance in International Agreements* (2005) 99 AJIL, 581.

Redgwell, C., 'US Reservations to Human Rights Treaties: All for One and None for All?' in M. Byers and G. Nolte (eds), *United States Hegemony and the Foundations of International Law*, Cambridge: Cambridge University Press, 2003, 363.

Tan, Z.P.B., *The International Law Commission's Draft Articles on the Effects of Armed Conflicts on Treaties: Evaluating the Applicability of Impossibility of Performance and Fundamental Change* (2013) 3/1 Asian Journal of International Law, 51

Vagts, D.F., *Rebus Revisited: Changed Circumstances in Treaty Law* (2005) 43 Colum J Transnatl L, 459.

Virally, M., *Review Essay: Good Faith in Public International Law* (1983) 77 AJIL, 130.

Ziemele, I., *Reservations to Human Rights Treaties: From Draft Guideline 3.1.1.2 to Guideline 3.1.5.6* (2013) 24/4 EJIL, 1135.

AIDE-MÉMOIRE

The definition of a treaty under the VCLT

The expression 'treaty' is used as a generic term to cover a multitude of international agreements and contractual engagements concluded between States. These international agreements are called by various names including treaties, conventions, pacts, declarations, charters, concordats, protocols, covenants, or by even less formal names such as 'exchange of notes' and 'memorandum of agreement'. The confusing nomenclature notwithstanding what counts is whether the instrument in question satisfies the following conditions:

It must be concluded between two or more States

Parties to it must have intended to create legal obligations

It must be in writing

It must be governed by international law

The fundamental principles of the law of treaties

The fundamental principles of the law of treaties are:

The principle of free consent. It means that a State cannot be bound by a treaty to which it has not consented although this does not apply:

The principle of good faith. It applies throughout the life of a treaty, from its negotiation, through to its performance and up to its termination.

The principle of *Pacta sunt servanda*. *Pacta sunt servanda* is a latin maxim which literally means that agreements must be kept. It is embodied in Article 26 VCLT which states that: 'Every treaty in force is binding upon the parties to it and must be performed by them in good faith'.

If a treaty provision imposes an obligation on a third party, that treaty provision will become binding on a third party only if that provison contains a rule of customary law (Article 35 VCLT).

If a treaty provision confers a right on a third party, that third party must, in order to take benefit of the right, consent to it (but this is presumed so long as the contrary is not indicated) and the contracting parties must have expressly or by implication, intended to create the right for the third party (Article 36 VCLT).

Stages in the process of concluding a treaty

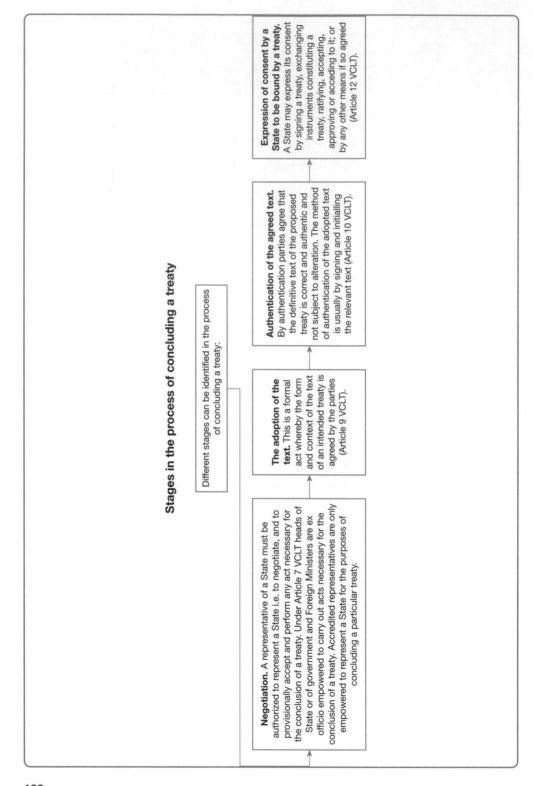

Different stages can be identified in the process of concluding a treaty:

Negotiation. A representative of a State must be authorized to represent a State i.e. to negotiate, and to provisionally accept and perform any act necessary for the conclusion of a treaty. Under Article 7 VCLT heads of State or of government and Foreign Ministers are ex officio empowered to carry out acts necessary for the conclusion of a treaty. Accredited representatives are only empowered to represent a State for the purposes of concluding a particular treaty.

The adoption of the text. This is a formal act whereby the form and context of the text of an intended treaty is agreed by the parties (Article 9 VCLT).

Authentication of the agreed text. By authentication parties agree that the definitive text of the proposed treaty is correct and authentic and not subject to alteration. The method of authentication of the adopted text is usually by signing and initialling the relevant text (Article 10 VCLT).

Expression of consent by a State to be bound by a treaty. A State may express its consent by signing a treaty, exchanging instruments constituting a treaty, ratifying, accepting, approving or acceding to it; or by any other means if so agreed (Article 12 VCLT).

Reservations to treaties and objections to reservations

A reservation is a unilateral statement, however phrased or named made by a State, when signing, ratifying, accepting, approving or acceding to a treaty, or subsequently to entry into force of the treaty, whereby it purports to exclude or to modify the legal effect of certain provisions of the treaty in their application to that State. A reservation to a multilateral treaty must:

- be in writing;
- contain, to the extent possible, the reason why it is being made. This is required under the ILC Guide; and
- be communicated to the other contracting parties and entities who are entitled to become a party to the treaty so they can, within 12 months, accept or reject the reservation by formulating an objection.

Permissible reservations are those which are expressly permitted by the relevant treaty and those which are compatible with the object and purpose of that treaty.

Objections to reservations. The ILC Guide defines an objection as a unilateral statement, however phrased or named, made by a State or international organisation in response to a reservation formulated by another State or international organisation, whereby the former State or international organization purports to preclude the reservation from having its intended effect or otherwise opposed the reservation. It must be in writing and communicated to all contracting States or States entitled to become party to the treaty while the Guide requires that the objection should indicate, to the extent possible, the reasons why it is being formulated.

Non-permissible reservations are:

- Reservations prohibited by the relevant treaty;
- Reservations which are not included in the list of reservations expressly allowed under the relevant treaty (so applying the latin maxim *expressio unius est exclusio alterius*);
- Reservations which are incompatible with the object and purpose of the relevant treaty.

Effects of non-permissible reservations.

There is a controversy on whether non-permissible reservations are 'totally invalid', which means that the reserving State's ratification is ineffective or whether they are 'partially invalid', which means that they are severed from the reserving State's declaration of consent to be bound by the treaty with the consequence that the treaty applies to the reserving State, and the reservation is disregarded. The ILC Guide states that a reserving State which has made an invalid reservation will be a contracting party to a treaty, unless it expresses its intention, at any time, not to be bound by the treaty. If a body monitoring implementation of a particular treaty decides that a reservation is invalid, the reserving State has 12 months from the date at which the treaty body had made such a decision to express its intention not to be bound by the treaty. If it fails then it will be bound by the treaty without the benefit of the reservation.

Ordinary Objections. These concern a situation when a contracting party has objected to the reservation but did not oppose the entry into force of the treaty between itself and the reserving State, the treaty will apply between both parties except for the provisions to which the reservation relates.

Effects of an objection:

Where a contracting State made an objection to a reservation. Its effect depends on whether the objection is simple or qualified.

Qualified Objections. These concern a situation where a contracting party has objected to the reservation and opposed the entry into force of the treaty; the treaty will not enter into force for reserving State.

Where a contracting State has made no objection to a reservation. The treaty will be modified in that the provision to which the reservation relates will not apply between the contracting State and the reserving State, e.g. if State X made a reservation to provison A and State Y accepted the reservation, the treaty will apply to States X and Y with the exception of provision A.

Grounds for nullity of a treaty

Grounds for nullity

Grounds nullifying a treaty for a party to it.

Manifest violation of its internal law (Article 46 VCLT). In order to succeed the alleged violation of domestic law must concern fundamental provisions which relate to the State's treaty-making power and must be evident to any State acting in accordance with normal practice and in good faith.

Violations of specific restrictions on the competence of the representative of a State (Article 47 VCLT). In order to succeed the restrictions on the competence must have been notified to the other parties.

Essential error (Article 48 VCLT). In order to succeed an error, whether unilateral or mutual, must neither concern a question of law nor the wording of text of a treaty agreed by the parties. It must relate to a fact or a situation which was assumed at the time when a treaty was concluded and formed an essential basis of its consent. Further, a State will not be able to claim error if by its own conduct it contributed to it.

Fraud (Article 49 VCLT). This is rarely invoked.

Corruption of a representative (Article 50 VCLT). In order to succeed the 'corruption' must be a 'substantial influence'. A small courtesy or favour shown to a representative will be insufficient.

Coercion of a representative (Article 51 VCLT). In order to succeed coercion must be directed at the representative personally (e.g. blackmailing threats or threats against the representative's family) and not through a threat of action against his State.

Coercion of a State (Article 51 VCLT). In order to succeed, it must be shown that the conclusion of a treaty has been procured by the threat or use of force in violation of the principles of international law embodied in the UN Charter.

Grounds for nullify of a treaty as a whole (i.e. for all contracting parties). This may occur:

If, at the time of the conclusion of the treaty, it conflicts with a rule of *jus cogens* (Article 53 VCLT)

If a new *jus cogens* rule emerges, then any existing treaty which is in conflict with that rule becomes void and terminates (under Article 64 VCLT).

4

INTERNATIONAL LAW AND MUNICIPAL LAW

CHAPTER OUTLINE

1 Introduction

The relationship between international law and municipal law poses two problems:

- theorctical, i.e. whether they form part of one universal legal order or are two distinct systems of law; and

- practical, i.e. how to resolve a conflict between international law and municipal law.

2 The relationship between international law and municipal law

Public international law leaves each country to decide on the relationship between international law and its municipal law. In this respect, there are two main theories, dualist and monist, that have influenced the constitutional law of each country as to the application of international law by municipal courts and other domestic bodies.

- Dualism: according to dualism, international law and municipal law are two independent and separate systems. Neither legal system has the power to create or alter the rules of the other. However, as they may regulate the same subject matter a conflict may arise in which case a municipal court will apply municipal law. Should this cause a breach of international law then this would be a matter to be settled by means of diplomatic protest or of a judgment of an international court.

- Monism. There are many varieties of monism but its main premise is that international law and municipal law are part of the same legal order. As they may regulate the same subject matter any conflict between the two would be solved in favour of international law.

3 Municipal law before international courts and tribunals

The rule is that in the event of a conflict between international law and national law, international law prevails.

4 International law before UK courts

Two doctrines are of relevance to the status and treatment of customary international law and treaties before UK courts: the doctrine of transformation and the doctrine of incorporation. The doctrine of transformation reflects the dualist position according to which international law has no binding effect in municipal law unless it is expressly and specifically transformed into municipal law by the use of the appropriate constitutional machinery such as an Act of Parliament. Under the doctrine of incorporation rules of international law form part of municipal law without the need for further legislative action at the municipal level.

A. Customary international law

Since the judgment in *Trendtex Case* it has been generally accepted that the doctrine of incorporation applies, i.e. customary international law is automatically part of UK law unless it is inconsistent with an Act of Parliament, authoritative judicial decision or established usage. However, following the judgment of the House of Lords in *R v Jones (Margaret)* there is no automatic incorporation of customary international law. This will, in addition to usual restrictions, depend on whether such incorporation is compatible with the UK constitution.

B. International treaties

With regard to international treaties (as well as United Nations Security Council (UNSC) resolutions adopted under Chapter VII of the UN Charter which impose sanctions), the dualist approach has been adopted in the UK (but see the exception relating to EU law). When a change in domestic law is necessary in order to give effect to treaties, they become part of English law only if enabling legislation, primary or secondary, has been passed. In most cases, this is done by Act of Parliament. The justification for the requirement that a treaty which alters UK domestic law must be given effect by enabling legislation is based on the constitutional principle of separation of powers. The conclusion and ratification of treaties is within the prerogative of the Crown. Parliament has no part in this process, but is the ultimate source of law (the doctrine of parliamentary sovereignty). If the courts could apply unimplemented treaties which require a change in domestic law the Crown would be in a position of being able to alter English law without parliamentary consent.

No change in law is necessary:

- with regard to treaties, which wholly or in the major part, regulate international relations between States, e.g. the Vienna Convention on the Law of Treaties (VCLT);

- where implementation of a treaty is a matter of foreign or defence policy and thus within the prerogative of the Crown, e.g. the North Atlantic Treaty Organisation (NATO) requires no implementing measures;

- where implementing a treaty is a matter of domestic policy and no individual rights are affected by it.

It is to be noted that in some dualist common law countries (but not in the UK) municipal courts have given mandatory domestic effect to unimplemented treaties which would normally require enabling legislation. The case law suggests that attentiveness and sensitivity to fundamental human rights values embodied in relevant ratified, but not yet incorporated, treaties provides the main justification for giving them binding domestic effect. As to the legal basis on which these treaties may produce mandatory effect in domestic law, this is highly debated.

C. Treaties and the interpretation of statutes in the UK

So far as rules on interpretation of treaties are concerned, three situations can be distinguished:

- where a treaty that has been transformed into UK domestic law by enabling legislation;

- where there is a statute that is intended to give effect to all or some provisions of a ratified but unenacted treaty;

- where there is a statute that concerns subject matters dealt with by a ratified, but unenacted treaty, and that statute was not intended to give effect to that treaty.

In all the above a general principle of UK constitutional law applies according to which when a provision of a statute is clear and unambiguous a treaty cannot be used to override the plain words of a statute, even if those plain words are inconsistent with the treaty. The UK may, on the international scene, incur liability for a failure to comply with its international obligations in respect of the circumstances covered by bullet points 1 and 2 but, nevertheless, the municipal courts must uphold the statute passed by Parliament.

When a provision of a statute enacting a treaty is obscure or ambiguous, a UK court is allowed to interpret it in the light of the principles set out in *Fothergill v Monarch Airlines*, i.e. to refer to the purpose of the treaty and, if required, take account of *travaux preparatoires*.

When a provision of a statute, which is intended to give effect to an unenacted treaty or some of its provisions, is unclear but is reasonably capable of more than one meaning, a court may have recourse to the treaty as an aid to interpretation in order to select the meaning which conforms with the treaty. This is based on the presumption that Parliament cannot have intended to legislate contrary to international law.

When a provision of a statute, which concerns subject matters dealt with by an unenacted treaty, without having any intention to give effect to that treaty, is obscure or ambiguous, a UK court will attempt to interpret it in the light of the treaty, in accordance with the presumption that Parliament intends to fulfil the UK's international obligations.

It is to be noted that the traditional rules on statutory interpretation have been dramatically altered by s 3(1) of the 1999 Human Rights Act (HRA) which imposes on UK courts a duty to read and give effect to all UK legislation (including international treaties which are part of UK law) 'in so far as it is possible' as being compatible with rights protected by the European Convention on Human Rights (ECHR).

D. European Union (EU) law in UK courts

EU law has a special status in the UK. It forms part of UK law but it applies as EU law not as municipal law. The above rules of interpretation do not apply to EU law. UK courts have a duty to interpret national law in conformity with EU law. The European Court of Justice (ECJ) ensures that the application and interpretation of EU law is uniform in all member States. The EU follows the monist approach. EU law is supreme and thus prevails in the case of a conflict. Further, EU secondary legislation is directly applicable (although there is a debate whether EU directives are directly applicable), and apart from EU directives no implementing measures are necessary for EU law to become part of UK law. Further, provisions of EU law, if they meet some criteria, are directly effective in that they are directly enforceable by individuals before UK courts

5 International law before US courts

The relationship between treaties and US domestic law reflects elements of monism and dualism, with the latter being predominant. Under the Supremacy clause treaties have the same standing as federal statutes. However, the distinction between self-executing and non-self-executing treaties makes domestic law the primary determinant of the domestic legal effects of treaties and constitutes an obvious example of dualism.

The position of customary international law is subject to many controversies but it is clear that only rules of customary international law which are universal, binding and specific, will serve as a basis for successful law suits in US courts.

4.1 Introduction

The relationship between international law and municipal law gives rise to two main problems:

- the theoretical problem as to whether international law and municipal law are part of a universal legal order (the monist doctrine) or whether they form two distinct systems of law (the dualist doctrine);

- the practical problem as to how to solve, before an international tribunal, or before a municipal court, a conflict between the rules of international law and the rules of municipal law.

4.2 The relationship between international law and municipal law

The relationship between international law and municipal law is of more than just academic interest. As well as considering the jurisprudential issues concerning the relationship between the two systems of law (i.e. whether they form part of one all-embracing legal system, but with different spheres of operation, or whether they form two distinct systems) it will often be important to determine the scope of application of rules of international law before domestic tribunals and *vice versa*.

At the jurisprudential level, the relationship between international law and municipal law has been cast in terms of the monist/dualist debate. At the level of the practical application of international law before UK courts, this debate is cast in terms of the incorporation/transformation debate. While these debates are important, it is in the nature of things that they focus on general issues. The actual relationship between international law and UK law can only be properly understood by examining the manner in which UK courts apply treaties, custom and other sources of international law when adjudicating cases.

Public international law leaves each country to decide on the relationship between international law and its municipal law. In this respect, there are two theories: dualist and monist. There are many variations of dualism and monism,[1] but the basic theoretical postulations of each theory can be summarised as follows:

4.2.1 Dualism

Dualism's essential feature is that international law and municipal law are independent systems, separate from each other, and having differing spheres of application. Dualism is based on the view that international law is the law applicable between sovereign States, and that municipal law applies within a State to regulate the activities of its citizens. On this basis, neither legal system has the power to create or alter rules of the other.

The doctrine of transformation reflects the dualist position according to which international law has no binding effect in municipal law unless it is expressly and specifically transformed into municipal law by the use of the appropriate constitutional machinery such as an Act of Parliament. Nevertheless, some dualist States, which are mainly common law States, accept the doctrine of incorporation with regard to customary international law (see Chapter 4.4.1).

With regard to an international treaty entered into by a contracting State the doctrine of transformation applies. Under this doctrine, a treaty, when ratified, creates obligations addressed to the contracting State, but not to individuals. The implications of this are two-fold:

- First, when international law and domestic law regulate the same subject matter a conflict may arise in which case a municipal court would apply municipal law. As a result a State may be in breach of international law, but this will be a matter to be settled by means of diplomatic protest, or by a judgment of an international court.

- Second, an international treaty requires statutory incorporation into municipal law in order to be part of municipal law and thus to be enforceable by individuals albeit only within the extent of the incorporation. However, once a provision of a treaty is implemented into national law, it is applied by national courts as any other municipal provision and not as an international one.

4.2.2 Monism

Monism considers both international law and municipal law to be part of the same legal order, and emphasises the supremacy of international law within the municipal sphere. The doctrine of incorporation is associated with monism. According to that doctrine rules of international law form part of municipal law without the need for further legislative action at the municipal level. Any change in the rules of

---

1   On this topic see P-M. Dupuy, *International Law and Domestic (Municipal) Law, The Max Planck Encyclopedia of Public International Law*, 2011; online edition [www.mpepil.com] (accessed 3 September 2014).

international law brings automatically changes in municipal law. When there is a conflict between international law and municipal law, international law prevails.

The justification for the supremacy of international law is, according to Lauterpacht, that international law is a more trustworthy repository of civilised values than the municipal law of a nation State, and thus better equipped to protect international human rights.[2]

According to Kelsen international law is supreme because it is a higher law than municipal law. This is based on the idea of a basic hypothetical norm (which he calls in the German language 'Grundnorm'), on which all subsequent levels of a legal system are based, i.e. every law can be traced back to another law that validates it as a law until the final source can be found in a 'basic norm'. This basic norm in international law is that 'States should behave as they customarily have behaved.' This norm, because it is derived from the practice of States, is superior to municipal law which derived from law promulgated by States. Because municipal law is derived from international law, all norms of international law are superior to municipal law, with the consequence that when there is a conflict between international law and municipal law, municipal law is automatically null and void.[3]

Under the monist doctrine the unity between international law and municipal law means that international treaties automatically become law within a contracting State. They are directly applicable. There is no need for incorporation of an international treaty as it becomes an integral part of the national law of a contracting State once the procedure for its ratification is completed. An international provision is applied by municipal courts as such and not as a provision of domestic law. Monism is mainly embraced by civil law countries.

4.2.3 Practical relevance of the doctrines

Some commentators claim that the traditional doctrines of monism and dualism have lost their significance. Bogdandy's statement that dualism and monism 'are intellectual zombies of another time and should be laid to rest, or "deconstructed"'[4] is perhaps the most radical.

New approaches have been proposed by commentators. Two of them, legal pluralism and constitutionalisation, are mentioned below.

Legal pluralism claims that the loss of relevance of monism and dualism is shown first, by the changing legal reality in international law in that international law is now fragmented (see Chapter 2.4.2.1.A) and second, by State practice. The main features of legal pluralism are that it recognises the existence of plurality of legal orders, rather than duality of legal orders, and posits that there should be heterarchy of legal orders, i.e. it assumes frequent interaction between overlapping legal orders rather than the separateness of legal orders and refuses to give superiority *per se* to any of them.[5] The main criticism of this theory is that it does not provide for a coherent system of solving conflicts among and between legal orders.

---

2   See *International Law: Collected Papers*, Cambridge: Cambridge University Press, 1957, 151–177 and *International Law* and *Human Rights*, Hamden, CT: Archen, 1968.

3   H. Kelsen, *General Theory of Law and the State*, Cambridge, MA: Harvard University Press, 1945.

4   A. v Bogdandy, *Plurarism, Direct Effect and the Ultimate Say* (2008) 6 International Journal of Constitutional Law, 400.

5   See D. Preshova, 'Legal Pluralism: New Paradigm in the Relationship between Legal Orders, in M. Novaković (ed.), *Basic Concepts of Public International Law: Monism and Dualism*, Belgrade: Faculty of Law University of Belgrad, Institute of Comparative Law and Institute of International Politics and Economics, 2013, 288.

According to the constitutionalisation theory international law is in the process of being (or should be) 'constitutionalised'. There is little agreement on the content of this theory but it can be said that it proposes the transfer of the function of domestic constitutions of liberal democracies to international law in order to improve the effectiveness and fairness of the international legal order.[6] It establishes the presumption that the ultimate beneficiary of the international legal system is humanity as a whole. The main criticism of this theory is that it does not reflect the reality of the international legal order.

It can be said that new theories, whatever their merits or demerits, emphasise the effect of globalisation, the establishment of *jus cogens*, the proliferation of multilateral organisations and the importance of the emergence of non-State actors on changes in the structure and sources of international law. However, as none of the new theories are convincing, the old theories of monism and dualism are still relevant and provide useful tools in examining the relationship between international and national law.

4.3 Municipal law before international courts and tribunals

The general rule is that in the event of conflict between international law and national law, international law prevails. The Draft Declaration on Rights and Duties of States submitted by the International Law Commission (ILC) to the General Assembly of the United Nations (UNGA) in 1949 in its Article 13 states that:

> Every State has the duty to carry out in good faith its obligations arising from treaties and other sources of international law, and it may not invoke provisions in its constitutions or its laws as an excuse not to perform this duty.[7]

In respect of international treaties, Article 27 VCLT states:

> A party may not invoke the provision of its internal law as justification for its failure to perform a treaty. This rule is without prejudice to art 46.

The exception embodied in Article 46 applies only in exceptional circumstances, that is, when a State's consent to a treaty is invalidated by a 'manifest' violation of its internal law and concerns 'a rule of its internal law of fundamental importance'.

There is ample judicial and arbitral authority for the rule that a State cannot rely upon the provisions or deficiencies of its municipal law to avoid its obligations under international law. Some examples are listed below.

---

6   M. Kumm, *The Legitimacy of International Law: A Constitutionalist Framework of Analysis* (2004) 15 Eur J Int'l L, 907; and, 'The Cosmopolitan Turn in Constitutionalism: On the Relationship Between Constitutionalism in and Beyond the State' in J.L. Dunoff and J.P. Trachtman (eds), *Ruling the World? International Law, Global Governance, Constitutionalism*, Cambridge: Cambridge University Press, 2009, 258.

7   The Draft declaration was annexed to UNGA Resolution 375 (IV) of 6 December 1949. It is to be noted that although the UNGA commended the Draft Declaration as a significant contribution to the progressive development and the codification of international law, it has never formally adopted it, mainly because of the lack of interest on the part of States. They provided very little feedback on the ILC Draft, and, since 1949, have never requested the UN to carry out studies concerning rights and duties of States. See H. Kelsen, *The Draft Declaration on Rights and Duties of States* (1950) 44 AJIL, 259–276.

4.3.1 The *Alabama Claims Arbitration*[8]

THE ALABAMA CLAIMS ARBITRATION (1872)

Facts:

Shortly after the beginning of the American Civil War, the UK government made a declaration recognising the Confederates as belligerents and declaring British neutrality. Despite this, during the Civil War, a number of ships were built in England for private buyers.

The vessels were unarmed when they left England but it was generally known that they were to be fitted out as warships by the Confederates in order to attack Union shipping. For example, the Enrica, built in Birkenhead, was designed as a warship. Once she left the UK she sailed to the Azores, where she was fitted with guns, and loaded with ammunition. Her name was changed to Alabama. *During the Civil War,* Alabama *destroyed 64 US vessels before she was herself sunk off Cherbourg in June 1864. The US sought to make the UK liable for these losses on the basis that the UK had breached her obligations as a neutral country during the war, in contravention of Article VI of the Treaty of Washington which laid down the rules of international law on neutrality.*

The UK argued, inter alia, *that under English law as it then stood, it had not been possible to prevent the sailing of vessels constructed under private contracts.*

Held:

The arbitrators rejected the British argument and had no hesitation in upholding the supremacy of international law:

> *the government of Her Britannic Majesty cannot justify itself for a failure in due diligence on the plea of insufficiency of the legal means of action which it possessed . . . . It is plain that to satisfy the exigency of due diligence, and to escape liability, a neutral government must take care . . . that its municipal law shall prohibit acts contravening neutrality.*

4.3.2 The *Polish Nationals in Danzig Case*[9]

In this case the Permanent Court of International Justice (PCIJ) stated that:

> It should . . . be observed that . . . a state cannot adduce as against another state its own constitution with a view to evading obligations incumbent upon it under international law or treaties in force. Applying these principles to the present case, it results that the question of the treatment of Polish nationals or other Persons of Polish origin or speech must be settled exclusively on the basis of the rules of international law and the treaty provisions in force between Poland and Danzig.

---

8   (1872) Moore, 1 Int Arb, 495, 653.

9   *Treatment of Polish Nationals and Other Persons of Polish Origin or Speech in the Danzig Territory (Advisory Opinion)* (1932) PCIJ Ser A/B No 44, 21.

4.3.3   The *UN Headquarters Agreement Case*[10]

The principle of international law that international law prevails over municipal law was affirmed by the International Court of Justice (ICJ) in its Advisory Opinion in the *UN Headquarters Agreement Case*. The principle of primacy of international law over municipal law in proceedings before international tribunals applies to all aspects of a State's municipal law, to its constitutional provisions, its ordinary legislation and to the decisions of its courts.

4.3.4   The *LaGrand Case (Germany v United States of America)*[11] and the *Case Concerning Avena and Other Mexican Nationals (Mexico v United States of America)*[12]

In these cases the ICJ examined the US constitutional rule of 'procedural default' under which a procedural failing which has not been argued at State level cannot be argued at federal level. In *LaGrand* the ICJ stated that although the rule itself did not violate Article 36 of the 1963 Vienna Convention on Consular Relations (VCCR), its application to the *LaGrand* case was in breach of that provision. The procedural default rule prevented a German national from raising a claim on appeal (which had not been raised in earlier proceedings) based on failure of the competent US authorities to comply with their obligations to provide the requisite consular information 'without delay' as set out in Article 36(1) VCCR, thus preventing the German national from seeking and obtaining consular protection from the relevant German authorities. Subsequent to the judgment in *LaGrand* the US did not revise the above rule. In *Avena* the ICJ agreed with the submission of Mexico that the US, by failing to revise the procedural default rule in the light of its implications for defendants seeking to rely on the VCCR in appeal proceedings, had failed to provide 'meaningful and effective review and reconsideration of convictions and sentences impaired by a violation of Article 36(1)' of the Convention (see Chapter 14.7.5.3).

Conflict between a State's municipal law and its international obligations does not necessarily affect the validity of that law on the municipal plane. Thus, a municipal act contrary to international law may be internally recognised as valid but other States will be under no duty to recognise its external effects.

4.4   International law before UK courts

Two doctrines are of relevance to the status and treatment of international law before UK courts: the doctrine of incorporation, and the doctrine of transformation.

Under the doctrine of incorporation international law becomes automatically part of municipal law without any express act of adoption, i.e. any positive act on the part of the State. This entails that a signed and ratified treaty becomes part of municipal law without any need for legislation being passed to give that treaty a binding legal effect in municipal law. Similarly, rules of customary international law will not require any implementing legislation in order to become part of municipal law of the State concerned.

---

10   The Applicability of the Obligation to Arbitrate under Section 21 of the United Nations Headquarters Agreement of 26 June 1947 (1988) ICJ Rep 12, 34.

11   The *LaGrand Case (Germany v United States of America) (Merits)* [2001] ICJ Rep 466, paras 19–21.

12   The *Case Concerning Avena and Other Mexican Nationals (Mexico v United States of America) (Merits)* [2004] ICJ Rep 12.

Under the doctrine of transformation, international law, in order to become part of municipal law, must be 'transformed' into municipal law. This requires a positive act on the part of the State consisting of enacting domestic legislation which will give effect, in municipal law, to international law.

The doctrine of incorporation is a logical consequence of monism in that the automatic incorporation of international law into municipal law is justified on the ground that international law and municipal law form part of the same legal system. So far as the doctrine of transformation is concerned, it constitutes a logical consequence of dualism in that international law and municipal law, being two distinct legal systems, retain the sovereign power to integrate or ignore each other and therefore, international law must be integrated into municipal law by being 'transformed' into municipal law in order to have legal effect in municipal law.

The doctrines of incorporation and transformation are relevant to both customary law and international treaties.

4.4.1 Customary international law

Can English law have regard to rules of customary international law? In the event of a conflict, which rule prevails? In the long debate as to whether the doctrine of transformation or incorporation applies three stages can be distinguished.

4.4.1.1 The preference given to the doctrine of incorporation in cases decided in the eighteenth century

In *Buvot v Barbuit*[13] Lord Chancellor Talbot declared: 'That the law of nations, in its full extent is part of the law of England.'

Holdsworth described the approach of the English courts as follows:

> It would, I think, have been admitted that, if a Statute or a rule of the common law conflicted with a rule of international law, an English judge must decide in accordance with the statute or the rule of common law. But, if English law was silent, it was the opinion of both Lord Mansfield and Blackstone that a settled rule of international law must be considered to be part of English law, and enforced as such.[14]

4.4.1.2 The late nineteenth century and the early twentieth-century cases seemed to favour the doctrine of transformation or, at least, cast ambiguity on the application of the doctrine of incorporation

It has been argued by some writers that in some cases decided since 1876, the doctrine of incorporation has been displaced by that of transformation, i.e. customary international law forms a part of the law of England only in so far as it has been accepted and made part of the law of England by Act of Parliament, judicial decision or established usage. The case of *R v Keyn* [15] is often cited as one which supports the doctrine of transformation.

---

13   (1737) Cases Talbot 281.
14   W. Holdsworth, *Laws of England*, 3rd edn, London, 1968, vol VIII, 264.
15   (1876) 2 Ex D 63.

R V KEYN

Facts:

The Franconia, a German ship, collided with the Strathclyde, a British ship, in British territorial waters. The defendant, the German captain of the Franconia, was prosecuted for the manslaughter of a passenger on board the Strathclyde who was drowned as a result of the collision.

Held:

The defendant was found guilty. However, the question whether an English court had jurisdiction to try the case was reserved for the Court of Crown Cases Reserved which decided by seven votes to six that it did not.

The majority was of the opinion that the English court did not have jurisdiction in the absence of an Act of Parliament granting such jurisdiction. This decision has been interpreted as supporting the 'transformation' approach and as displacing the doctrine of incorporation.

Comment:

Keyn *remains an ambiguous precedent, the true* ratio decidendi *being difficult to establish from among the 11 different judgments delivered. Lauterpacht, commenting on the case, observed:*

[I]t cannot be said that this judgment amounts to a rejection of the rule that international law is a part of the law of England. Writers seem to forget that the main issue of the controversy in the case was not the question whether a rule of international law can be enforced without an Act of Parliament; what was in dispute was the existence and the extent of a rule of international law relating to jurisdiction in territorial waters.[16]

In *West Rand Central Gold Mining Co v R* [17] Lord Alverstone CJ, in an *obiter* statement while appearing to support the principle of transformation, noted that:

It is quite true that whatever has received the common consent of civilised nations must have received the assent of our country, and that to which we have assented along with other nations in general may properly be called international law, and as such will be acknowledged and applied by our municipal tribunals.

However, he softened the above statement by saying that the existence of any rule of customary international law sought to be applied must be proved by satisfactory evidence. These words would seem to rest on an assumption that the doctrine of incorporation holds good, although the requirement of 'assent' suggests his support for the doctrine of transformation. Oppenheim regards the case as 'a reaffirmation of the classical doctrine', i.e. of incorporation, while many scholars emphasised this

---

16   H. Lauterpacht, *International Law: Collected Papers*, Cambridge: Cambridge University Press, 1970, 60.

17   [1905] 2 KB 391, 406–407.

case established that a rule of customary law would be applied if supported by conclusive evidence and not mere opinion of textbook writers.[18]

A remark made by Lord Justice Atkin in *Commercial and Estates Company of Egypt v Board of Trade*[19] is also regarded as supporting the doctrine of transformation. He said:

> International law as such can confer no rights cognisable in the municipal courts. It is only insofar as the rules of international law are recognised as included in the rules of municipal law that they are allowed in municipal courts to give rise to rights and obligations.

In *Chung Chi Cheung v The King*[20] Lord Justice Atkin, delivering the opinion of the Privy Council, adopted a middle of the road approach. He stated:

> It must always be remembered that, so far, at any rate, as the courts of this country are concerned, international law has no validity, save insofar as its principles are accepted and adopted by our own domestic law. There is no external power that imposes its rule upon our own code of substantive law or procedure.
>
> The courts acknowledge the existence of a body of rules which nations accept amongst themselves. On any judicial issue they seek to ascertain what the relevant rule is, and having found it, they will treat it as incorporated into the domestic law, so far as it is not inconsistent with rules enacted by statutes or finally declared by their tribunals.

Accordingly, it is clear that Lord Atkin accepted that when there is evidence of customary international law, the court will apply it; however, when evidence is inconclusive, enabling legislation would be necessary. The above view is not hostile to the doctrine of incorporation but focuses on the difficulty of proving the existence and content of a rule of customary international law.[21]

4.4.1.3 The current approach

Lord Denning in *Trendtex Trading Corporation v Central Bank of Nigeria*[22] confirmed the application of the doctrine of incorporation. He commented on the relationship between customary international law and English law in the following terms:

> A fundamental question arises for decision: what is the place of international law in our English law? One school of thought holds to the doctrine of incorporation. It says that the rules of international law are incorporated into English law automatically and considered to be part of English law unless they are in conflict with an Act of Parliament. The other school of thought holds to the doctrine of transformation. It says that the rules of international law are not to be considered as part of English law except in so far as they have been already adopted and made part of our law by the decisions of the judges, or by Act of Parliament, or long established custom. The difference is vital when you are faced with a change in the rules of international law. Under the doctrine of incorporation, when the rules of international law change, our English law changes with them. But, under the doctrine of transformation, the English law does not change. It is bound by precedent.

---

18   J. O'Brien, *International Law*, London: Cavendish, 2001, 117.

19   [1925] 1 KB 271, 295.

20   [1939] AC 160, 167–168.

21   See I. Brownlie, *Principles of Public International Law*, 7th edn, Oxford: Oxford University Press, 2008 , 41–44.

22   [1977] 2 WLR 356, 365.

As between these two schools of thought, I now believe that the doctrine of incorporation is correct. Otherwise I do not see that our courts could ever recognise or change the rules of international law.

Additionally, in *Trendtex*, Lords Denning and Shaw rejected the doctrine of *stare decisis* on the grounds that international law does not know such a doctrine, and that its application would prevent English law from following changes in international law.[23]

Since *Trendtex* it has been generally accepted that, in so far as customary international law is concerned, the doctrine of incorporation applies, but the doctrine of *stare decisis* does not.[24] The *dictum* of Lord Denning in *Trendtex* has been followed in a number of more recent cases, so supporting the proposition that the doctrine of incorporation has been adopted in English law. Certainly, the courts have been reluctant to apply principles of the common law which conflict with customary international law. For example, in *Westland Helicopters Ltd v Arab Organisation for Industrialisati*[25] Colman J confirmed the doctrine of incorporation and stated:

> Inasmuch as the common law rule is at large before this court, there is, in my judgment, every reason in principle why the approach of the common law should be consistent with that of public international law unless there is some controlling common law principle to the contrary; for it is part of English public policy that our courts should give effect to clearly established rules of international law.

Various judgments in the *Pinochet* case (see Chapter 10.3.3.1.C) provide support for the doctrine of incorporation, for example Lord Lloyd stated that the principles of customary international law 'form part of the common law of England',[26] while Lord Millet emphasised that 'customary international law is part of the common law'.[27] Further, in *John Donnelly* and *Lord Advocate's Reference No 1 of 2000*, the High Court of Justiciary in Scotland held that Scottish law recognises that customary international law forms an integral part of Scottish law.[28]

In *R v Jones (Margaret)*,[29] the House of Lords confirmed that customary international law forms part of the law of England and Wales, or as Lord Bingham stated is 'a source' of the law rather than part of it,[30] but rejected the idea of its automatic incorporation into English law.

R V JONES (MARGARET)

Facts:

Shortly before the UK military intervention in Iraq in 2003, the appellants committed what clearly appeared to be criminal offences consisting of aggravated trespass and criminal

---

23 Ibid, 366.

24 *Thai-Europe Tapioca Service Ltd v Government of Pakistan* [1975] 3 All ER 961.

25 [1995] 2 All ER 387.

26 *R v Bow Street Metropolitan Stipendiary Magistrate, ex p Pinochet Ugarte (No 1)* [2000] 1 AC 61, 98.

27 *R v Bow Street Metropolitan Stipendiary Magistrate, ex p Pinochet Ugarte (No 3)* [2000] 1 AC 147, 276.

28 (2001) SLT 507, 512; see S. Nett, *International Law and Nuclear Weapons in Scottish Courts* (2002) 51 ICLQ, 171.

29 [2006] UKHL 16.

30 On the matter of whether this distinction is of any importance see J.R. Crawford, *International Law in the House of Lords and in the High Court of Australia, 1996–2008: A Comparison* (2009) Australian Yearbook of International Law, 6–7.

damage to various installations and equipment at UK military bases. They argued that they were not committing any crime because they were, in fact, resisting acts by the UK which amounted to crimes of aggression under international law. They submitted that the crime of aggression, although not established and penalised under English law, was well established in customary international law, and thus part of English law. Accordingly, they could rely on s 3 of the UK Criminal Law Act which allows use of reasonable force to prevent the commission of a crime. Indeed, their conduct involved no violence to persons, only damage to property. They argued that while 'the exercise of the prerogatives in respect of foreign policy and deployment of the armed forces cannot be challenged in Courts' i.e. the matter was non-justiciable, they should be allowed to rely on the illegality of the exercise of the Crown's prerogative as a defence to the criminal charges.

The House of Lords had to consider, first whether the prohibition of waging an aggressive war was a rule of customary international law, second, whether it was a crime under English law to wage an aggressive war, and third, whether the appellants could rely on customary international law to justify their prima facie criminal acts.

Held:

The House of Lords held that:

1   the crime of aggression was recognised by customary international law;
2   although a crime recognised in customary international law may be assimilated into domestic law this is not automatic. In this respect Lord Bingham said that 'I think this is true that customary international law is applicable in English courts only where the constitution permits.'[31] Under the UK Constitution only the Parliament can pass legislation creating new triable crimes, as following the unanimous judgment of the House of Lords in Knuller (Publishing, Printing and Promotions) Ltd v Director of Public Prosecutions[32] courts no longer possess any residual power to create new criminal offences. Further, Lord Bingham emphasised, that it is a well established practice in England that crimes recognised by international customary law are given effect in English domestic law by means of a statute.
3   Following from point 2 above, the appellants were not allowed to rely on s 3 of the Criminal Law Act. Lord Bingham stated that there were no compelling reasons to depart from the principle that statutory law is the only source of new criminal offences or to ignore the English practice consisting of passing legislation in order to give domestic effect to crimes established in international law, i.e. there were no compelling reasons to depart from the doctrine of non-justiciability (see Chapter 9.2).

Comment:

The following points should be noted:

1   The sweeping and bold statement that international customary law is automatically part of English law has never been true. Incorporation has never been automatic. It is subject

---

31   Lord Bingham quoted O'Keefe, *Customary International Crime in English Courts* (2001) BYIL, 335.
32   [1973] AC 435.

to many exceptions which are explained in Chapter 4.4.1.4. The commented judgment added a new limitation: i.e. constitutional bars to incorporation of customary international law. However, the new requirement imposed on English courts following the commented judgment, i.e. that courts, after establishing that a particular provision constitutes a rule of customary international law, must consider whether there are any restrictions imposed by the UK constitution on its incorporation into domestic law, entails that the word 'automatic' is not appropriate to describe the operation of the doctrine of incorporation with regard to customary international law.

2   The judgment clearly emphasises the importance of the rule that only the legislature can create new criminal offences. In this respect, Lord Hoffman stated that apart from old offences in customary international law relating to safe conduct, ambassadors and piracy, customary international law should not be used to create new criminal offences in English law. This should be the domain of the Parliament. He said:

> They [i.e. new criminal offences] should not creep into existence as a result of an international consensus to which only the executive of this country is a party. In Sosa v Alvarez-Machain (2004) 159 L Ed 2d 718, 765, Scalia J recently said: 'American law – the law made by the people's democratically elected representatives – does not recognize a category of activity that is so universally disapproved by other nations that it is automatically unlawful here.' At least so far as the criminal law is concerned, I think that the same is true of English law.[33]

4.4.1.4   Situations in which English courts cannot apply customary international law

In the following situations English courts cannot apply customary international law.

A.   If there is a conflict between customary international law and an Act of Parliament, the Act of Parliament prevails.

This was established in *Mortensen v Peters*.[34]

MORTENSEN *V* PETERS

Facts:

The appellant was a Dane and the master of a Norwegian ship. He was convicted by a Scottish court of otter trawling contrary to a bye-law issued by The Fishery Board for Scotland. He argued that the bye-law was in contravention of a rule of international law limiting territorial waters to bays and estuaries of no greater breadth than 10 miles.

---

33   [2006] UKHL 16, para 62.
34   1906 8 F (JC) 93.

Held:

His appeal against conviction was dismissed unanimously by a full bench of 12 judges. The Lord Justice-General, Lord Dunedin said:

In this Court we have nothing to do with the question of whether the Legislature has or has not done what foreign powers may consider a usurpation in a question with them. Neither are we a tribunal sitting to decide whether an Act of the Legislature is ultra vires as in contravention of generally acknowledged principles of international law. For us an Act of Parliament duly passed by Lords and Commons and assented to by the King is supreme, and we are bound to give effect to its terms.

B. Where the UK constitution does not allow it.

The case of *R v Jones* (see Chapter 4.4.1.3) exemplifies this exclusion.

C. Where such matters as the status of a foreign State or the identity of a Head of State, the extent of territorial jurisdiction, or the existence of a state of war, are in issue.

With regard to the above issues, English courts accept a certificate signed by the UK Foreign Secretary as being conclusive. The determination set out in the Foreign Secretary's Certificate is treated by the courts as conclusive and therefore no independent judicial determination will be made by the courts.[35]

It is to be noted, however, that the UK government is no longer issuing certificates regarding the formal recognition of foreign governments (see Chapter 6.4.2).

D. Non-justiciability, State immunity and act of State doctrine
(see Chapter 9.2).

In some circumstances, on the grounds of the doctrine of non-justiciability, or of State immunity or of act of State, an English court will be prevented from exercising its jurisdiction and an individual will, as a result, have no remedy in English law.

4.4.2 International treaties and their relationship with English law

The dualist approach has been adopted in the UK with regard to international treaties and UNSC resolutions imposing sanctions under Chapter VII of the UN Charter. When a change in domestic law is required to give effect to treaties, they become part of English law only if enabling legislation, primary or secondary, has been passed. In most cases, this is done by Act of Parliament.

No change in UK law is necessary:

- with regard to treaties, which wholly or in the major part, regulate international relations between States, e.g. the VCLT;

- where implementation of a treaty is a matter of foreign or defence policy and thus within the prerogative of the Crown, e.g. the North Atlantic Treaty Organisation required no implementing measures;

- where implementing a treaty is a matter of domestic policy and no individual rights are affected by it.

---

35   *The Zamora* [1916] 2 AC 77.

However, the vast majority of treaties require a change in domestic law. Such treaties are not part of UK law and therefore cannot be given effect by domestic courts until enabling legislation is passed. The justification for this is based on the constitutional principle of separation of powers.

In the UK, the conclusion and ratification of treaties is within the prerogative of the Crown. Parliament has no part in this process although under the Ponsonby convention,[36] named after Arthur Ponsonby, the Parliamentary Under-Secretary of State for Foreign Affairs in Ramsay MacDonald's first Labour Government in 1924, every treaty signed by the executive or intended to be acceded to, must be laid before both Houses of Parliament, at least 21 sitting days before ratification. Since 1 January 1997 treaties must be accompanied by an Explanatory Memorandum.[37] The Ponsonby convention ensures democratic scrutiny of treaties, and if a treaty is opposed by Parliament there is a chance that it will not become part of UK law. However, bearing in mind that the UK government normally has a decisive majority in Parliament, there is a high likelihood that it will become part of UK law.

Following from the fact that Parliament is not involved in the negotiation and ratification of a treaty, if the UK courts could apply unincorporated treaties in municipal law, the Crown would be in a position to alter English law without parliamentary consent. To forestall this, treaties are only part of English law if an enabling Act of Parliament has been passed.

In *The Parlement Belge*[38] Sir Robert Phillimore reaffirmed, in that part of the first instance decision which still stands, that the Crown cannot, by entering into a treaty, alter the law of England.

If an Act is not passed by Parliament, the treaty is nevertheless still binding on the UK from the international point of view. There is a distinction, therefore, between the effect of a treaty in international law and the effect of a treaty in municipal law. The treaty is effective in international law when ratified by the Crown. But if the treaty alters the law of England it has no effect in municipal law until an Act of Parliament is passed.

4.4.2.1 Ratified but unenacted treaties which alter the law of England

The general rule that an English court may not take account of an unenacted treaty has been confirmed by a number of decisions. In the *International Tin Council Case*[39] the House of Lords confirmed this rule when it stated that an English court could not examine the International Tin Agreements to establish the liability or otherwise of member States of the International Tin Council. The rule has since been strictly interpreted by the Court of Appeal in *Arab Monetary Fund v Hashim (No 3)*[40] where it held that the decision by the House of Lords in the *International Tin Council Case* precluded the court from having reference to and applying the provisions of a treaty establishing the Arab Monetary Fund. In this case, the Arab Monetary Fund had legal personality, owned assets and conducted business in the UK. The UK was not a party to the treaty of establishment. However, owing to the English constitutional rule requiring transformation in respect of treaties, the Court held that it could not have regard to the treaty. Each of the three Lord Justices of Appeal, however, remarked on the obvious injustice of the result, indicating that it was up to Parliament to legislate to change the matter.

---

36 Constitutional conventions are agreements of political parties on procedural matters. They are unwritten and non-binding. Normally they are observed unless there are good reasons to depart from them.
37 UKMIL (1999) 70 BYIL, 406.
38 (1878–1879) 4 PD 129.
39 [1990] 2 AC 418.
40 [1990] 2 All ER 769.

In *Laker Airways v Department of Trade* [41] Roskill LJ stated:

[W]hen the Crown in the exercise of its prerogative powers concludes a treaty, the subject gains no personal rights under that treaty enforceable in our courts unless the treaty becomes part of the municipal law of this country and provides for the subject to acquire certain specific rights thereunder.

This approach was confirmed by the House of Lords in *R v Bow Street Metropolitan Stipendiary Magistrate, ex p Pinochet Ugarte (No 3)*[42] (see Chapter 10.3.3.1 C).

4.4.2.2 Ratified but unenacted treaties which alter domestic law – a new approach in some dualist common law countries

In respect of ratified but unenacted treaties there is an ongoing debate as to whether mandatory domestic effect can be given to such treaties in commonwealth dualist countries. The case law (see below) shows that municipal and international courts' attentiveness to, and sensitivity to, fundamental human rights values embodied in ratified but unenacted treaties resulted in giving them such mandatory effect in domestic law although all relevant courts had affirmed their adherence to the orthodox view that unenacted treaties are not enforceable in domestic law.

The groundbreaking judgment of the Australian High Court in *Minister of State for Immigration and Ethnic Affairs v Teoh*,[43] initiated the debate. In this case the Court held that an unenacted treaty may give rise to legitimate expectations that federal administrative decision-makers in the performance of their duty, and in the absence of any express law to the contrary, must comply with. In this case the applicant, a Malaysian national who lived in Australia under a temporary permit, was convicted of drug offences and sentenced to 6 years of imprisonment. On the ground that he was a father of children born in Australia he challenged both refusal of his application for resident status in Australia and a deportation order issued at the end of his sentence. Australia had ratified the UN Convention on the Rights of the Child but had not incorporated it into domestic law. The Court, (McHugh dissenting) held that a legitimate expectation raised by the ratification of the UN Convention required that administrative decision-makers act in conformity with the UN Convention, i.e. they would consider as the primary consideration the best interest of the children in making the proposed deportation order. The Court further stated that when a decision is inconsistent with that legitimate expectation, procedural fairness required that the person affected would be given notice and an opportunity to respond. It was held that there was a want of procedural fairness with regard to the proposed decisions and therefore the refusal to grant resident status should be set aside, and the deportation order should be stayed until the Minister had reconsidered the application.

Although in Australia, the importance of the judgment in *Teoh* has waned because of the adoption by the High Court of an expansive principle that rules of natural justice apply to the exercise of any public power that might 'destroy, defeat or prejudice a person's rights, interests or legitimate expectations',[44] it attracted a lot of attention in other common law jurisdictions. In this respect it is interesting to examine three cases, two of them decided by supreme courts and one by an international court.

---

41   [1977] 1 QB 643, 717–718; see also *Rayner (Mincing Lane) Limited v Department of Trade and Industry* [1990] 2 AC 18, at 500.

42   *R v Bow Street Metropolitan Stipendiary Magistrate, ex p Pinochet Ugarte (No 3)* [2000] 1 AC 147. See also *R v Director of Public Prosecution ex p Kebilene and Others* [2000] 2 AC 326.

43   (1995) 183 CLR, 273.

44   See M. Groves, *Treaties and Legitimate Expectations-The Rise and Fall of Teoh in Australia* [2010] 15/4 JR, 323.

BAKER *V* CANADA (MINISTRY OF CITIZENSHIP AND IMMIGRATION)[45]

Facts:

Ms Baker was a Jamaican national who had resided illegally in Canada for 11 years. She was a single mother of four children born in Canada during her illegal stay. She was a paranoid schizophrenic being supported by welfare payments. When the Canadian immigration authorities discovered that she was in Canada illegally, a deportation order was issued against her. She asked for the deportation order to be reconsidered on 'humanitarian and compassionate grounds' given the possible effect of deportation on her children. When the immigration officer refused the requested reconsideration, Ms Baker sought a judicial review of the deportation decision.

Held:

Ms Baker's application was rejected by two lower courts but the Supreme Court of Canada decided that the immigration officer was biased and failed to reasonably exercise his discretionary power. This was because the decision was made without taking into account the interests of Ms Baker's children as required under the UN Convention on the Rights of the Child, which had been ratified by Canada but had not been incorporated into domestic law. The majority of the judges held that although the Convention was not incorporated at the relevant time and thus could not be directly applied by Canadian courts, nevertheless the values it reflected were central in determining whether the decision was reasonable. In conclusion the decision was unreasonable because it did not take account of the rights, interests and needs of children as required by the Convention and other sources.

Comment:

It seems that the ratification of the Convention by Canada gave it, in the view of the Court, a special status which was not equal to incorporation, but which, nevertheless, produced mandatory domestic effect. This effect is however, restricted only to administrative law which allows administrative decisions to be reviewed by the courts for reasonableness.[46] In the commented case the Court held that treaties can 'help show values that are central in determining whether [a particular] decision was a reasonable exercise [of an enabling power]'.[47] The Baker Case, therefore, requires the court to consider the values enshrined in a provision of an unenacted treaty in deciding whether an administrative decision is reasonable. This means that an administrative decision which conflicts with the values enshrined in a provision of a treaty is not automatically invalid. The court may uphold such a decision in so far as it has given careful consideration to the values enshrined in the relevant treaty.[48]

---

45   [1999] 2 SCR 817.

46   *New Brunswick (Board of Management) v Dunsmuir*, 2008 SCC 9, [2008] 1 SCR 190.

47   Supra note 45, at 861–862.

48   Ibid, 863–864.

THE ATTORNEY GENERAL OF BARBADOS *V* JOSEPH AND BOYCE[49] (2006) BEFORE THE CARIBBEAN COURT OF JUSTICE (CCJ) IN ITS APPELLATE JURISDICTION

Facts:

The respondents were found guilty of murder and a mandatory sentence of death by hanging was imposed upon each of them. Their appeal was rejected and the Barbados Privy Council (BPC) refused to commute the death sentences. Death warrants were issued and read to the respondents but the execution was stayed pending the decision of the Judicial Committee of the Privy Council, to which a further appeal had been made. The appeal was dismissed on 7 July 2004. The respondents then filed an application to the Inter-American Commission on Human Rights (the IACommHR) seeking declarations that their rights under the American Convention on Human Rights (ACHR) were breached. Before the IACommHR issued its report the BPC advised the Governor-General of Barbados that the death sentences should be carried out. On 15 September 2004, death warrants were again read to the respondents, who the next day filed a motion before the Barbados High Court seeking commutation of the death sentences. Meanwhile, the IACommHR issued provisional measures requiring Barbados not to execute the respondents until the outcome of the petitions before the Inter-American human rights bodies. The Barbados High Court dismissed the respondents' motion but the respondents were successful before the Barbados Court of Appeal (BCA), which commuted their death sentences to life imprisonment. The BCA had to follow the decisions of the Privy Council in Thomas v Baptiste[50] *and in* Lewis v Attorney General of Jamaica[51] *which required a State to await the outcome of procedures before human rights bodies before issuing death warrants. It also had to follow the Privy Council's judgment in* Pratt v The Attorney General of Jamaica,[52] *according to which if execution is delayed for more than 5 years after sentencing, then normally a death sentence has to be commuted to life imprisonment as such delay will amount to inhuman treatment. By the time the case reached the BCA, 5 years had elapsed since the respondents' conviction. The Barbados Attorney-General appealed the Barbados Court of Appeal's decision to the Caribbean Court of Justice (the CCJ)[53] which, as the highest appellate court for Barbados, is not bound by judgments of any other court including the Privy Council. The issue before the CCJ was whether the decision of the BPC to proceed with execution without awaiting the completion of procedures before the Inter-American Human Rights bodies and without taking into consideration any decision of such bodies when making a recommendation of clemency or otherwise violated*

---

49   [2006] CCJ 3 (AJ).

50   [2002] 2 AC 1.

51   [1999] 3 WLR 249.

52   [1994] AC1; (1993) 43 WIR 340.

53   The CCJ, which has been in operation since 2005, has two-fold jurisdiction: first, under its original jurisdiction it interprets and applies the Revised Treaty of Chaguaramas Establishing the Caribbean Community Including the CARICOM single Market and Economy, i.e. it performs the same function as does the ECJ in respect of EU law, and second, under appellate jurisdiction it is the final appellate court in respect of civil and criminal matters for those Caribbean States which have ceased using the Judicial Committee of the Privy Council as their final court of appeal.

the respondents' right to protection of the law. During the proceedings before the CCJ the IACommHR forwarded the case to the IACtHR for adjudication.

It is important to note that Barbados, a dualist country, had ratified the ACHR, but had not transformed it into domestic law. Barbados also accepted the compulsory jurisdiction of the IACtHR.

Held:

The CCJ dismissed the appeal. It held that with regard to the effect of unincorporated but ratified treaties, a new rule has emerged that, unless municipal law states otherwise, such treaties can give rise to a legitimate expectation. This conclusion was reached by the CCJ after careful and thorough review of cases decided by courts from dualist common law countries. The Court made a distinction between procedural legitimate expectation, and substantive legitimate expectation. In the former the expectation is that an authority will afford certain procedural rights in the course of making a decision, and in the latter, the expectation is of some substantive outcome or benefit. However, in both cases overriding interests of public policy may frustrate legitimate expectations. The CCJ decided that the respondents had not only procedural, but also, substantive legitimate expectations, i.e. a legitimate expectation of a substantive benefit because Barbados had ratified the ACHR; and statements had been made by the government of Barbados expressing an intention or desire to abide by the ACHR. It was, indeed, the practice of the government of Barbados to give an opportunity to condemned persons to have their petitions processed before proceeding to execution.

The CCJ found that there were no overriding interests of public policy to displace the legitimate expectations of the condemned.

Comment:

It is to be noted that the CCJ stated that it did not intend to change the existing rule that unincorporated treaties are not enforceable before domestic courts. Its intention was to restrict the application of the judgment to the specific and special situation of persons condemned to death in order to give them every opportunity to secure the commutation of their sentence.

THOMAS *V* BAPTISTE[54] BEFORE THE JUDICIAL COMMITTEE OF THE PRIVY COUNCIL

Facts:

The facts were similar to those in Joseph and Boyce in that the appellants were convicted of murder and sentenced to death. After exhausting all domestic remedies they lodged a petition with the IACommHR which issued provisional measures which were then ignored

---

54   [1999] 3 WLR 249.

by the government of Trinidad and Tobago. The government of Trinidad and Tobago in an attempt to circumvent the judgment of the Privy Council in Pratt and Morgan *issued instructions establishing time limits within which the petitions of condemned persons were required to be processed before the IACommHR (see Chapter 12.5.2). When the time limit set out in the instructions elapsed, but before a decision of the IACommHR was adopted, death warrants were read to the appellants. Subsequently, they appealed to the Privy Council arguing that it was unlawful to execute them before the relevant body, which could recommend the commutation of their death sentences to life imprisonment, had received and considered the decision of the IACommHR. It is to be noted that Trinidad and Tobago had ratified the ACHR but had failed to implement it into domestic law.*

Held:

The Privy Council held that the instructions of the government of Trinidad and Tobago were unlawful because they were disproportionate and contrary to the due process clause in that country's constitution.

The Privy Council also decided that the ratification of the ACHR extended the meaning of the due process clause in the Constitution of Trinidad and Tobago, even if temporarily. Consequently, a stay of execution was granted pending the decision of the IACommHR. The majority of the Privy Council rejected the doctrine of legitimate expectations.

It transpires from the above cases that the courts have recognised that mandatory effect should be given to unenacted treaties in order to give effect to fundamental values embodied in them. Further, it seems that the courts dissociated the mandatory effect of such treaties from their binding force in domestic law (one is left to wonder how this is possible).

It is submitted that, as the CCJ stated in *Joseph and Boyce*, a new development has taken place with regard to the effect of unenacted treaties, which, under the dualist doctrine, are not part of domestic law. Whether the new development is the commencement of a slow movement of some dualist common law countries towards monism[55] remains to be seen. If this is the case, then the very foundations of dualism are being eroded. Each of the above judgments is based on different legal reasoning. Judge Pollard of the CCJ argued that the doctrine of legitimate expectations does not challenge the traditional approach because '. . . a legitimate expectation is not a principle of law possessing the faculty to amend an ordinary legislative enactment, much less the supreme law of the State'.[56] He then argued that the judgments of the Privy Council in *Thomas v Baptiste* as confirmed in *Neville Lewis v Attorney-General of Jamaica* [57] were wrong as they encroached on the sacrosanct principle of the separation of powers in that the executive became competent to determine unilaterally the administration of criminal justice in a State. It is outside the scope of this book to enter into an in-depth debate on this topic. However, what is clear is that in some common law countries municipal courts and indeed international courts have given mandatory effect to unenacted treaties.

---

55   M. Waters, *Creeping Monism: the Judicial Trend towards Interpretive Incorporation of Human Rights Treaties* (2007) Columbia Law Review, 107.

56   *Unincorporated Treaties and Small States* (2007) 33/3 Commonwealth Law Bulletin, 389, at 403.

57   (2000) 57 WIR 275.

There are powerful arguments supporting the new development:

■ The ratification of international treaties, in particular those aimed at protecting fundamental human rights, by the executive creates legitimate expectations and, therefore, a State should not be allowed to use the excuse that a treaty has not been enacted into domestic law to deny a solemn promise or undertaking made at the international level.[58]

■ The principle of *pacta sunt servanda* imposes upon the contracting parties to a treaty an obligation to execute a treaty in good faith (Article 26 VCLT). This, it is submitted, should logically include an obligation to implement the relevant treaty into domestic law. In the twenty-first century, in particular with regard to human rights treaties, it is unacceptable that a State should complete all the ratification procedures for a treaty and then fail to enact it. This submission is supported by the Advisory Opinion of the PCIJ in *The Exchange of Greek and Turkish Populations*[59] in which the Court held that a State is obliged to bring its municipal law into conformity with its obligations under international law.

■ If the *raison d'etre* of the dualist approach is to protect citizens then, as Justices de la Bastide and Saunders of the CCJ stated in *Joseph and Boyce*:

> The fulfilment of the legitimate expectation of the condemned men here results in the enhancement of the protection afforded those rights and minimises the risk that the Executive may have cause to regret the carrying out of a death sentence.[60]

Although this statement was made in the context of death sentence cases it may be of relevance to all cases where fundamental human rights of alleged victims have been violated.

4.4.3 Treaties and the interpretation of statutes in the UK

A State has exclusive competence to decide how it intends to give effect to a treaty in its domestic law. In the UK, a treaty may be transformed into municipal law either by direct or indirect enactment.

■ In direct enactment a treaty is normally set out as a schedule to a short enacting act and therefore the text of the treaty is not altered. The Act itself only provides that the treaty shall have the force of law.

■ Indirect enactment entails that a draftsman uses his own words to create an Act which in effect (but not in the exact words of the treaty) sets out the provisions and requirements of the treaty. As a result, the relevant provisions of the treaty are translated into the legislative language of domestic law. In so doing a statute may refer to particular terms in a treaty.

When an issue of interpretation of statutes in the light of treaties arises an English court will pay attention to the following:

■ a general principle of British constitutional law that in the case of a conflict, statute prevails over treaty;

■ a rule of construction that where domestic legislation is passed to give effect to a treaty there is a presumption that Parliament intended to fulfil its international obligations.

58　See S. Patel, *Founding Legitimate Expectations on Unincorporated Treaties* [2010] 15/1 JR, 74. He submits interesting arguments in favour of the application of the doctrine of legitimate expectation. Arguments against are examined by S. Vasciannie, *The Relationship between International Law and Caribbean Domestic Law*, (2007) 32/1 West Indian Law Journal , 51.

59　(1925) PCIJ Rec Ser B, 10.

60　Supra note 49, para 127.

4.4.3.1 Interpretation of enacted treaties

Treaties which are directly enacted form an integral part of the enacting Act, being attached to it as a Schedule. Accordingly, there can be no difference between the interpretation of the Act and of the Treaty.

With regard to indirectly enacted treaties, if a provision of a statute enacting the relevant treaty is clear and unambiguous and requires no interpretation, the court must follow the statute[61] even if the words of the statute are inconsistent with those of the treaty. The rationale of this rule is that the sovereign power of Parliament covers both the making and breaking of treaties. Obviously, however, the UK might incur liability at the international level.

In the interpretation of obscure or ambiguous provisions of a statute enacting a treaty a more expansive approach than that accepted under English law in respect of purely domestic statutes is allowed. In *James Buchanan & Co v Babco Forwarding and Shipping (UK)*[62] the House of Lords held that a provision enacting a treaty should be interpreted in a manner unconstrained by technical rules of English law, or by English legal precedent. The House of Lords further explained this approach in *Fothergill v Monarch Airlines Ltd*,[63] in which it stated that in the interpretation of treaties the court will be guided by the following principles:

- The court will give a purposive construction to the treaty taken as a whole.

- Cautious use will be made of *travaux preparatoires*.

- The court will take into consideration the interpretation of the relevant treaty by courts in other contracting States.

- The court will be most anxious to ensure that decisions in different contracting States are, as far as possible, kept in line with each other.

- The court will not give a judgment which would create domestic remedies that would undermine the working of the treaty.

This broad approach was applied in *Sidhu v British Airways plc*[64] in which Lord Hope stated that it was 'well-established that a purposive approach should be taken to the interpretation of an international convention which has the force of law in this country'.

4.4.3.2 Statutes which are intended to give effect to ratified but unenacted treaties

Some statutes are intended to give effect to treaties without making any express reference to the relevant treaty which has been ratified by the UK, e.g. the 1999 Immigration and Asylum Act which partially intends to give effect to the 1951 Geneva Convention on the Status of Refugees. In this respect English courts have developed the following rules.

---

61   *The Ellerman Lines v Murray* [1931] AC 126.
62   [1977] 3 All ER 1048.
63   [1981] AC 251.
64   [1997] 1 All ER 193, 202.

When a provision of an Act is clear and unambiguous, the court will apply that provision even if it is contrary to the treaty.[65] If the relevant provision of an Act is narrower in scope than the relevant provision of the treaty to which it intends to give effect, the narrower provision will prevail.[66]

If a provision of a statute is unclear or ambiguous the approach taken by Lord Diplock in *Salomon v Commissioners of Customs and Excise*[67] will apply. In this case Diplock LJ stated:

> if the terms of the legislation are not clear but are reasonably capable of more than one meaning, the treaty itself becomes relevant, for there is a *prima facie* presumption that Parliament does not intend to act in breach of international law, including therein specific treaty obligations; and if one of the meanings which can reasonably be ascribed to the legislation is consonant with the treaty obligations and another or others are not, the meaning which is consonant is to be preferred.

Lord Diplock went on to hold that provided there is cogent extrinsic evidence that a statute was intended to give effect to a particular international convention, then that convention may be consulted as an aid to interpretation of the statute.

In *R v Chief Immigration Officer, ex p Salamat Bibi*[68] the point at issue was whether immigration rules made under the Immigration Act 1971 should be interpreted and applied by immigration officers in accordance with the right to family life set out in Article 8 of the ECHR, which had been ratified by the UK government but not implemented into UK law. Lord Denning MR stated:

> The position as I understand it is that if there is any ambiguity in our statutes, or uncertainty in our law, then these courts can look to the Convention as an aid to clear up the ambiguity and uncertainty, seeking always to bring them into harmony with it. Furthermore, when Parliament is enacting a statute, or the Secretary of State is framing rules, the courts will assume that they had regard to the provisions of the Convention, and intended to make the enactment accord with the Convention: and will interpret them accordingly. But I would dispute altogether that the Convention is part of our law. Treaties and declarations do not become part of our law until they are made law by Parliament.

4.4.3.3 Statutes which concern subject matters dealt with by a treaty without having any intention to give effect to that treaty

In a situation where an Act of Parliament, without there being any intention that it should give effect to a specific treaty, concerns subject matter dealt with by a treaty to which the UK is a contracting party (but which has not been transformed into domestic law) a court will give effect to clear and unambiguous provisions of the Act of Parliament, even if they conflict with the unenacted treaty. This was examined in *R v Secretary of State for the Home Department, ex p Brind*.[69]

---

65   *Ellerman Lines v Murray* [1931] AC 126.
66   *R (on the application of Pepushi) v Crown Prosecution Service* [2004] EWHC 798 (Admin).
67   [1967] 2 QB 116, 143.
68   [1976] 1 WLR 979, 985.
69   [1991] 1 AC 696.

R V SECRETARY OF STATE FOR THE HOME DEPARTMENT, EX P BRIND

Facts:

Under the 1981 Broadcasting Act, the Home Secretary issued directives to broadcasting authorities prohibiting the broadcast of statements by proscribed terrorist organisations in Northern Ireland. A number of journalists applied for judicial review of the right of the Home Secretary to issue those directives. The applicants contended that the directives were unlawful because they violated Article 10 of the ECHR, which provides that the right to freedom of expression includes the freedom 'to receive and impart information and ideas without interference by public authorities'. According to the applicants, the Home Secretary was obliged to exercise his powers in a manner consistent with the ECHR. The UK was a contracting party to the ECHR but had not incorporated it into domestic law.

Held:

The House of Lords upheld the ban.

Comment:

The Court acknowledged the well established rule that when a provision of a statute is obscure and ambiguous English courts will attempt to construe it in a manner ensuring that the statute conforms to the UK's obligations arising from an unenacted treaty but stated that 'where Parliament has conferred on the executive an administrative decision, without indicating the precise limits within which it must be exercised, to presume that it must be exercised with Convention limits would go far beyond the resolution of an ambiguity.'[70] To have decided otherwise would, in the words of the House of Lords, be equivalent to 'imputing to Parliament an intention to import international conventions into domestic law by the back door, when it has quite clearly refrained from doing so by the front door'. As a result, the House of Lords clearly rejected any form of judicial incorporation of the Convention.

It is to be noted that although in *R v Secretary of State for the Home Department: ex parte Ahmed*,[71] the Court of Appeal stated that the judgment in *Brind* did not prevent the application of the doctrine of legitimate expectations similar in content to that developed by the Australian High Court in *Minister of State for Immigration and Ethnic Affairs v Teoh*[72] (see Chapter 4.4.2.2) the Court of Appeal in *R (European Roma Rights Centre) v Immigration Officer at Prague Airport*[73] clearly rejected the possibility of applying the doctrine based solely on treaty ratification by the government.[74] However, on appeal, the House of Lords did not consider this matter.

---

70   Ibid, 748.
71   1998] INLR 570.
72   (1995) 183 CLR 273.
73   [2004]QB 211(CA).
74   Ibid, per Laws LJ at paras 99 and 101, and per Brown LJ at para 51.

4.4.3.4 The impact of the 1998 Human Rights Act (HRA) on the interpretation of treaties

The UK ratified the ECHR in 1951 but has never incorporated it into UK law. However, in 1998 it enacted the HRA which brought the rights and freedoms contained in the ECHR and in some of its protocols into UK law but not the ECHR itself, which is still neither directly enforceable in the UK nor part of UK law.

Section 3 of the 1998 HRA has dramatically changed the interpretation of all UK legislation including interpretation of international treaties which have been given effect in domestic law. Section 3(1) HRA provides:

> So far as it is possible to do so, primary legislation and subordinate legislation must be read and given effect in a way which is compatible with the Convention rights.

Section 3(2) states that when it is impossible to read and give effect to legislation in a way compatible with Convention rights, that legislation remains valid and courts are required to enforce it. However, s 4 HRA provides that if senior UK courts (i.e. the High Court, Court of Appeal and the Supreme Court of the United Kingdom which latter on 1 October 2009 assumed the judicial functions previously carried out by the House of Lords) are not able to make the legislation fit the Convention, they may, at their discretion, make a 'declaration of incompatibility'. The House of Lords held in *R v A*[75] that a declaration of incompatibility, which may result in incompatible legislation being repealed or amended, should be a last resort.[76] Therefore, s 3(1) HRA imposes a duty on courts to do all they can to read the legislation as being compatible with Convention rights.[77]

How far UK courts are allowed to go to achieve compatibility is debatable. Although they are not allowed to cross the line from interpreting to legislating, the case law shows that they can go quite far as exemplified in *Ghaidan v Godin-Mendoza*.[78]

GHAIDAN *V* GODIN-MENDOZA

Facts:

In this case the interpretation of Schedule 1 of the 1977 Rent Act was at issue. The Schedule stated that 'a person who was living with the original tenant as his or her wife or husband shall be treated as the spouse of the original tenant' for the purposes of succeeding to a protected Rent Act tenancy on the tenant's death. The claimant, a man living with the tenant in a monogamous same-sex relationship, argued that he was entitled to succeed to the tenancy of the deceased male tenant.

Held:

The House of Lords decided that it was 'possible' to read the schedule in a way that included same-sex relationships. Consequently, a declaration of incompatibility was not necessary.

---

75   [2001] UKHL 25, para 44. See also, *R (L) v Commissioner of Police for the Metropolis* [2009] UKSC 3, para 7, per Lord Neuberger.

76   It is to be noted that UK courts have no power to invalidate incompatible law following a declaration of incompatibility. On consequences of incompatibility see H. Davis, *Human Rights Law, Directions,* 3rd edn, Oxford: Oxford University Press, 2013, 75–76.

77   See *R(G) v Metropolitan Police Commissioner* [2011] UKSC 21.

78   [2004] UKHL 30.

However, *Bellinger v Bellinger*[79] shows that a reading of a legislative provision in conformity with Convention rights would not be possible when major changes in law are involved.

BELLINGER *V* BELLINGER

Facts:

This case concerned the interpretation of s 11(c) of the 1973 Matrimonial Causes Act, which makes a marriage void if the parties are not respectively male and female. The claimant was born a man and after undergoing a gender reassignment operation, had gone through a ceremony of marriage with a man. The claimant then sought a declaration that the marriage was valid. It is important to add that the claimant's birth certificate could not be changed under the then existing law and therefore the claimant was legally a man.

Held:

The House of Lords held that it was not 'possible' to read s 11 in a compatible manner with Convention rights. As a result, the marriage was invalid on the ground that English law does not recognise any change of gender. However, the House of Lords issued a declaration of incompatibility of s 11(c) with Article 8 ECHR (which protects the right to private life) and Article 12 ECHR (which protects the right to marry).

Comment:

In this case in order to include transsexual persons within the definition provided in s 11(c) of the 1973 Matrimonial Causes Act it would have been necessary for the House of Lords to create a new definition of those who are 'male and female'. It is for Parliament, not for the courts, to deal with the matter of the right of persons to marry in a new gender after an apparent change of gender.

It can be said that the traditional approach of UK courts to statutory interpretation has profoundly changed. Under s 3(1) HRA, UK courts have a duty to seek for a meaning that would prevent them from making a declaration of incompatibility. To achieve compatibility of an Act of Parliament with Convention rights, UK courts are allowed to:

- 'read in' an Act of Parliament, i.e. to introduce words or meanings into that legislation;

- 'read down' an Act of Parliament, i.e. to give a narrower construction to words of the Act than their ordinary meaning;

- 'read out' an Act, i.e. leave out or not enforce provisions of the Act.[80]

The above techniques, which are used in a situation where it is not possible for a court to read legislation as being compatible with the Convention rights, override the ordinary rules of interpretation. In this respect the House of Lords stated in *Ghaidan v Godin-Mendoza* that:

---

79   [2003] UKHL 21.
80   H. Davis, *Human Rights Law, Directions*, Oxford: Oxford University Press, 2007, 64.

It is now generally accepted that the application of s 3 does not depend upon the presence of ambiguity in the legislation being interpreted. Even if construed according to the ordinary principles of interpretation, the meaning of the legislation admits of no doubt, s 3 may none the less require the legislation to be given a different meaning.[81]

However, UK courts in discharging their duty under s 3(1) are not allowed to adopt a meaning inconsistent with a fundamental feature of legislation under consideration.

Section 3 applies to UK legislation enacted both prior to and after the entry into force of the 1998 HRA (the HRA came into force on 2 October 2000), including that which enacts international treaties, to ensure 'so far as it is possible' that an Act of Parliament under consideration is compatible with Convention rights regardless of the literal meaning of that Act, and of precedents to the contrary. Thus, the implications of s 3 on the interpretation of international treaties in force in the UK are huge, and further emphasised by the fact that human rights are ever pervasive and evolving.

4.4.3.5 European Union (EU) Law in UK Courts

EU law is neither foreign nor external to the legal systems of the member States. To the contrary, it forms an integral part of their national laws. Its peculiar position is due to the manner in which it penetrates into the national legal order of the member States. Three fundamental principles developed by the ECJ – that is, direct applicability, direct effect and supremacy of EU law[82] – strengthen the autonomy of EU law and determine the degree of its integration into the national laws of the member States, as does the fourth which goes side by side with those three. That is the principle that establishes a member State's liability for damage to individuals caused by a breach of EU law for which that member State is responsible. Further, EU law has imposed the duty on national courts to interpret national law in conformity with EU law. This is referred to as indirect effect. However, national courts have neither the duty to interpret national law *contra legem* nor to interpret it in such a way as to ignore the general principles of EU law, in particular the principles of legal certainty and non-retroactivity in criminal matters

EU law endorses the monist theory.[83] This approach derives from the nature of the EU. Only a monist system is compatible with the idea of European integration. In Case 6/64 *Costa v ENEL*[84] the ECJ emphasised the peculiar nature of European Community law (now EU law) by stating that the member States have created:

> a Community of unlimited duration, having its own institutions, its own personality, its own legal capacity and capacity of representation on the international plane and, more particularly, real powers stemming from a limitation of sovereignty or a transfer of powers from the states to the Community, the member states have limited their sovereign rights, albeit within limited fields, and have thus created a body of law which binds their nationals and themselves.

The special nature of EU law is further emphasised in the following passage extracted from the same decision in which the ECJ stated that:

---

81   Supra note 78, para 29.

82   It is to be noted that some supreme national constitutional courts are reluctant to accept the ECJ's unqualified claim that EU law is supreme (e.g. the German Federal Constitutional Court in *Brunner v European Treaty* [1994] 1 CMLR 57).

83   Case 104/81 *Hauptzollamt Mainz v CA Kupferberg & Cie KG* [1982] ECR I-3641.

84   [1964] ECR 585.

By contrast with ordinary international treaties, the Treaty has created its own legal system which, on the entry into force of the Treaty, became an integral part of the legal systems of the member states and which their courts are bound to apply.

As a result, EU law cannot tolerate national divergences as to relations *vis-à-vis* international law since a dualist system would jeopardise the attainment of the objectives of the EU and be contrary to the spirit and objectives of EU law.

Member States may preserve a dualist system in relation to international law, but such a system is excluded in relations between EU law and national law. As a result, EU law is superior to national law and becomes an integral part of that law without any need for its formal enactment (apart from directives which often require further implementing measures on the part of a member State), and national judges are bound to apply it. Furthermore, EU law occupies a special place in the domestic legal systems of the member States as it is applied as EU law and not as municipal law.

4.5 International law before US courts

The relationship between international law and US law is complex.

With regard to treaties it is important to examine their reception in US domestic law in the light of two principles:

- the principle of separation of powers, which is enshrined in the US constitution and which defines powers that each branch of the federal government, i.e. the Congress, the US President and the US courts, is entitled to exercise with regard to matters relating to foreign affairs; and

- the principle of federalism under which all important foreign affairs powers belong to the federal government, not the governments of the states of the federation or sub-states entities. It ensures that when there is a conflict between state law and federal law, which is passed pursuant to these federal constitutional powers in foreign affairs, federal law prevails.

With regard to customary international law, it is part of US law and considered by the US Supreme Court as federal common law (see Chapter 4.5.2).

4.5.1 Treaties

The Supremacy clause enshrined in the US Constitution provides:

> This Constitution, and the Laws of the United States which shall be made in Pursuance thereof, and all Treaties made, or which shall be made under the Authority of the United States, shall be supreme Law of the Land; and the Judges in every State shall be bound thereby, any Thing in the Constitution or Laws of any State to the Contrary notwithstanding.[85]

The Supremacy clause indicates that treaties have the same authority as statutes passed by Congress and signed by the President. They are a source of law and prevail over state law. The Supremacy clause needs to be examined in the light of the following considerations:

---

85   US Constitution, art VI, cl.

1 Under US law international treaties within the meaning of the VCLT, may take the form of treaties or executive agreements. For the purposes of this section treaties refer to both unless otherwise indicated.

2 Under US law there is a distinction between self-executing and non-self executing treaties.

3 The Supremacy clause does not provide for resolution of conflicts between US domestic law, i.e. US Constitution and federal statutes, and treaties.

The above considerations are examined below.

4.5.1.1 Distinction between treaties and executive agreements

Under US law a treaty is an agreement negotiated and signed by the executive (i.e a representative of the US government) that enters into force if it is approved by a two-thirds majority of the Senate and subsequently ratified by the President. The Senate may, when considering whether to give its consent, make reservations, amendments declarations, understandings, and provisos concerning its application. Any changes made by the Senate must be accepted by the other party to the treaty before it takes effect.

Executive agreements are entered into by the executive branch of the government. The majority of international agreements are concluded in this form.[86] There are three types of executive agreement:

■ Congressional-executive agreements. These are executive agreements previously or retroactively authorised by Congress. Such authorisation takes the form of a statute which must be passed by both houses of Congress.

■ Executive agreements made pursuant to an earlier treaty, in which the agreement is authorised by that treaty.

■ Sole executive agreements made on the basis of the President's constitutional authority. They do not require further authorisation by Congress.

4.5.1.2 Distinction between self-executing and non-self executing treaties

US law makes a distinction between 'self-executing' and 'non-self-executing' treaties.[87] Self-executing treaties, will become part of US domestic law immediately upon entry into force of the relevant treaty, and will be applied by US courts in the same way as federal laws. This is not the case with non-self-executing treaties. They require legislation to implement them into US domestic law. Prior to implementation they have no binding effect in domestic law.[88] Whether or not a treaty should be regarded as self-executing is highly debatable following the judgment of the US Supreme Court in the Case of *Medellin v Texas*.[89]

---

86 From 1939 to 2013 the US concluded approx. 17,300 published executive agreements and approx. 1,100 treaties. See M.J. Garcia, *International Law and Agreements: Their Effect upon US Law, Congressional Research Service*, 2014, available at http://fas.org/sgp/crs/misc/RL32528.pdf (accessed 7 August 14).

87 *Foster v Neilson* 27 US (2Pet) 253,314 (1829) and *Whitney v Robertson* 124 US 190, 194 (1888); *Medellin v Texas* 552 US at 502. See: T. Buergenthal, *Self-Executing and Non Self-Executing Treaties in National and International Law* (1992) 235 RCADI, 303, at 370.

88 See R. Crootof, *Judicious Influence: Non-Self-Executing Treaties and the Charming Betsy Canon* (2011) 120 Yale LJ, 1786.

89 552 US 491(2008).

MEDELLIN *V* TEXAS

Facts:

Medellin, a Mexican national on death row in Texas for gang rape and murder of two teenage girls in Houston (Texas), filed a number of habeas corpus *petitions before Texas courts and the US Supreme Court, challenging his conviction and sentence on the ground that he was denied the right to consular protection in breach of Article 36 VCCR. Medellin was one of 51 Mexican nationals, all convicted murderers on death row throughout the US, mentioned in the* Case Concerning Avena and Other Mexican Nationals (Mexico v US)[90] *brought by Mexico against the US before the ICJ. Mexico argued that the right of those nationals under the VCCR to contact their local Mexican consulates for assistance had been violated. Mexico asked,* inter alia, *for the annulment of the convictions. The ICJ ruled that the US had violated its international obligations under the VCCR with regard to certain Mexican nationals in criminal custody of the US. It ordered the US to review and reconsider their sentences to determine whether they had been prejudiced by the violation of their right of consular consultation (for details see Chapter 14.7.5.3). Following the ICJ's judgment President Bush issued a memorandum to the US Attorney General stating that the US would comply with the judgment of the ICJ, and ordered states to review the convictions and sentences of foreign nationals who had not been advised of their VCCR rights. In the Medellin case the Texas courts refused to do so. Medellin appealed to the US Supreme Court.*

Held:

The US Supreme Court held that neither the judgment of the ICJ in Avena nor the President's Memorandum nor the VCCR were directly enforceable federal law. As a result Medellin's petition was dismissed. He was executed on 5 August 2008.

Comment:

Before examining the US Supreme Court's approach to the determination of whether a particular treaty is self-executing, it is to be noted that prior to the judgment in the commented case, US courts had used a multifactor balancing test[91] to determine whether a treaty was self-executing and relied on a number of presumptions, including one in favour of treating treaties as self-executing.[92] This presumption is laid down in the Restatement (Third) of Foreign Relations Law.[93]

---

90   2004 ICJ 12.

91   Under this test the following factors were considered: 'the purposes of the treaty and the objectives of its creators, the existence of domestic procedures and institutions appropriate for direct implementation, the availability and feasibility of alternative enforcement methods, and the immediate and long-range consequences of self or non-self-execution.' See *Postal* 589 F.2d at 877 (quoting *Saipan* 502 F.2d at 97*).

92   See C. Bradley, *Intent, Presumptions, and non-Self-Executing Treaties* (2008) AJIL, 540.

93   The Restatements seek to 'restate' the legal rules that constitute the common law in the particular area. They are prepared under the auspices of the prestigious American Law Institute by eminent professors, judges and lawyers. Their purpose is to distill the 'black letter law' from cases, to determine a trend in common law, and also make recommendation as to what a rule of law should be. They are non-binding, but highly persuasive authority often used by US courts and scholars.

The US Supreme Court carefully examined whether the judgment of the ICJ was a self-executing treaty, i.e. whether it was directly enforceable in state and federal courts. It analysed the four treaties: the Optional Protocol to the VCCR under which the ICJ had jurisdiction to adjudicate the dispute between Mexico and the US arising from the VCCR, the VCCR, the UN Charter and the Statute of the ICJ. There was no implementing legislation for either of them.

In the commented case the US Supreme Court used the textual approach to the determination of whether a particular treaty was self-executing, i.e. it focused on finding indications in the treaty itself, or provided by the President, or the Senate as to whether it should be regarded as self-executing. A treaty is self-executing if it 'contains stipulations which are self-executing, that is, that require no legislation to make them operative'.[94] The textual approach focuses on the intent of the US treaty-makers, rather than on the intent of contracting parties to the treaty.

In applying the textual approach the US Supreme Court departed from the presumption that treaties are self-executing. It also modified the rule set in the case of the US v Percheman under which treaties would be regarded as self-executing unless the treaty itself 'stipulate[es] for some future legislative act'.[95] Finally, in footnote 3 of the judgment[96] the Court seemed to reject the well established presumption in favour of finding that treaties confer a private right of action, whenever they confer a private right, i.e. the possibility for a private party to seek enforcement of a private right, provided by a treaty, in federal courts.

The Court concluded that 'neither Avena nor the President's Memorandum constitutes directly enforceable federal law that pre-empts state limitations on the filing of successive habeas petitions'.[97] The only treaty which could have been potentially self-executing was the UN Charter. Applying the textual approach, the Court found that Article 94(1) of the UN Charter which provides that member States would 'undertake to comply' with ICJ judgments 'does not provide that the United States "shall" or "must" comply with an ICJ decision, nor indicate that the Senate that ratified the UN Charter intended to vest ICJ decisions with immediate legal effect in domestic court. Instead, [t]he words of Article 94 . . . call upon governments to take certain action'.[98] The Court then examined the remaining part of Article 94(1) of the UN Charter which concerns the potential enforcement of ICJ decisions through the Security Council, i.e. a political remedy, and stated that this part did not contemplate the automatic enforcement of ICJ decisions is domestic courts.

The textual approach has been criticised by many, including the dissenting judge of the US Supreme Court who stated that the majority judgment was looking for 'the wrong thing

---

94   552 US 491(2008), at 505–506.

95   *US v Percheman* 32 US (7 Pet.) 51, 89 (1833).

96   The FN reads: 'Even when treaties are self-executing in the sense that they create federal law, the background presumption is that international agreements, even those directly benefiting private persons, generally do not create private rights or provide for a private cause of action in domestic courts.' 552 US 491(2008) at 506, n 3. On this topic see: O.A. Hathway, S. McElroy and S. Aronchick Solow, *International Law at Home: Enforcing Treaties in US Courts* (2012) 37 YJ of Int L, 52.

97   552 US 491(2008), at 498–499.

98   Ibid, at 501.

(explicit textual expression about self-execution) using the wrong standard (clarity) in the wrong place (the treaty language).[99] Teleman criticised the judgment as incompatible with the US Constitution.[100]

The most important aspect of the judgment is that it has had a great impact on the interpretation of treaties by US courts. It has been submitted that research indicates that US courts understand the judgment as establishing strong presumptions that first, treaties are not self-executing, and second, they are not protective of private rights.[101] As a result, the US textual approach to determination as to whether a treaty is self-executing means that the US is in the process of adopting the dualist doctrine with regard to the relationship between treaties in US domestic law.

4.5.1.3 Solving conflicts between treaties and US domestic law

The Supremacy clause does not indicate how to solve conflicts between self-executing treaties including executive agreements and US domestic law, i.e. US Constitution and federal law. Under US law these conflicts are solved as follows:

1 When there is a clash between the US Constitution and a treaty or statute, the Constitution prevails. This was established by the US Supreme Court in the Case of *Reid v Covert*[102] in which both a federal statute and treaties (they were in the form of executive agreements) were in conflict with the US Constitution. In this case the issue was whether civilian wives who killed their military husbands, on whom they were dependent, on US bases in England and Japan were entitled to a jury trial and to have their indictment presented to a grand jury pursuant to the US Constitution. Under the provisions of the federal statute, the Uniform Code of Military Justice (UCMJ), civilian dependent wives were to be tried by court-martial i.e. without a grand jury or a jury trial. These provisions were incorporated into Presidential executive agreements concluded with the UK and Japan, and provided that the US military courts had exclusive jurisdiction over offences committed by US servicemen and their dependents in the military bases situated abroad, i.e. in the UK and Japan. The US Supreme Court held that the rights enshrined in the US Constitution could not be vacated by either the federal statute or by executive agreements.

2 Where there is a conflict between a federal statute and a treaty, the last in time prevails. This was stated in the case of *Reid v Covert*, in which the US Supreme Court said that it 'has . . . repeatedly taken the position that an Act of Congress which must comply with the Constitution, is on full parity with a treaty, and that when a statute which is subsequent in time is inconsistent

---

99   Ibid at 562 (Breyer, J dissenting).
100   J. Teleman, 'A Monist Supremacy Clause and a Dualistic Supreme Court: The Status of Treaty Law as US Law' in M. Novaković (ed.), *Basic Concepts of Public International Law. Monism and Dualism*, Belgrade: Faculty of Law, University of Belgrade, Institute of Comparative Law and Institute of International Politics and Economics, 2013, 585 *et seq.*
101   See O.A. Hathway, S. McElroy and S. Aronchick Solow, *International Law at Home: Enforcing Treaties in US Courts* (2012) 37 YJ of Int L, 52.
102   354 US 1 (1957).

with a treaty, the statute to the extent of conflict renders the treaty null.'[103] Therefore the principle of the *lex posteriori derogat lex prori* (see Chapter 2.4.2.1.C) applies unless Congress evinces a contrary intent. Such intent can be found, for example, in 19 United States Code (USC) para. 3312(a)(1) (2006) which provides that US statutes always prevail over provisions of the North American Free Trade Agreement (NAFTA). Further US courts under the canon of interpretation of treaties known as Charming Betsy,[104] which is enshrined in the Restatement (Third), in order to avoid conflict between a statute which is later in time than a treaty which is prior in time, when there is an ambiguity or the necessity to fill gaps in a treaty, will, if possible, interpret it in such a way as to avoid any conflict with a statute. The Charming Betsy canon applies to both self-executing and non-self-executing treaties. It is to be noted that non-self-executing treaties may nevertheless codify customary international law, and in any event, are part of US international obligations. US courts have used the Charming Betsy canon to ensure that a statute does not violate provisions of a non-self-executing treaty if any other possible interpretation remains.

3 According to the Restatement (Third)[105] sole executive agreements, which are based on the President's constitutional power, may, in some circumstances, not prevail over a conflicting prior federal statute.

4.5.2 Customary international law

The *Paquete Habana* is the most famous case on the relationship between customary international law and US domestic law. In this case the issue was whether international law prohibited the US Navy from capturing as prize of war two small Spanish fishing vessels, the *Paquete Habana* and *Lola*, engaged in catching and bringing in fresh fish off the coast of Cuba, during a naval blockade ordered by the US President in 1898 'in pursuance of the laws of the United States, and the law of nations applicable to such cases'. The original owners of the fishing vessels, which were sold as prize vessels, brought proceedings before US courts trying to recover the proceeds of their sale. The US Supreme Court, sitting as a prize court, found that under international customary law the capture of coast fishing vessels pursuing their vocation of catching and bringing fresh fish during naval blockades was unlawful. It stated:

> International law is part of our law, and must be ascertained and administered by the courts of justice of appropriate jurisdiction, as often as questions of right depending upon it are duly presented for their determination. For this purpose, where there is no treaty and no controlling executive or legislative act or judicial decision, resort must be had to the customs and usages of civilized nations.[106]

The above statement has raised controversy. Some commentators have interpreted it broadly, others have regarded it as a narrow precedent. Under the broad interpretation the above statement means that international customary law is directly and automatically applicable in US courts. It constitutes the 'Laws of the United States' and under the Supremacy clause being the 'supreme Law of the Land' trumps state law and must be faithfully executed by US Presidents under Article II, para. 3 of the US

---

103   354 US 1 (1957) at 18.
104   *Murray v Schooner Charming Betsy* 6 US (2 Cranch) 64, 118 (1804).
105   Restatement (Third) para 115, rptrs.note 5.
106   175 US 677, 700 (1900).

Constitution.[107] In other words, customary international law has the same status as self-executing treaties and federal statutes and when there is a conflict the principle of *lex posteriori derogat lex priori* applies.

Under the narrowed view, the second sentence limits considerably the application of customary international law because it means that customary international law only applies in the absence of a treaty or a 'controlling executive or legislative act' or judicial decision. Accordingly, in the hierarchy of sources of law customary international law yields to the US Constitution, treaties, judicial decisions, statutory federal law and controlling acts of the executive.

The above controversy related to the status of customary international law in US domestic law was reflected in heated debates during the preparation of the Restatement (Third).[108] Its position on this matter is that '[c]ustomary international law is considered to be like common law in the US, but is federal law'. This statement has been subject to heated debates. It raises the issue of whether customary international law is part of federal common law or whether it is an independent source of law which US courts discover through the usual common law method. In the first situation, international customary law could never prevail over an inconsistent legislative enactment. In the second situation, in some circumstances a customary rule may prevail over an inconsistent federal statute.[109] The US Supreme Court treats customary international law as federal common law and not as some other type of law. It noted in *Sosa v Alvarez-Machain* that federal common law exists in various 'havens of specialty' such as international law.[110] This position does not challenge the traditional rule that Congressional legislation may violate international customary law regardless of whether the statute becomes effective before or after custom has emerged[111] and that Congressional legislation on a particular matter prevents federal courts from creating inconsistent common law on the same matter.[112]

The unsettled debate on the place of customary international law in US domestic law should be viewed in the light of the approach of US courts which shows that not only treaties, but also any executive or legislative act, will be superior to customary law and will prevail over any inconsistent rule of customary law, regardless of which is later in time.[113] One possible exception mentioned in Restatement (Third) concerns *jus cogens* rules.[114] US courts, like UK courts, will refuse to apply customary law in cases involving the application of non-justiciability, State immunity and acts of State doctrines and will also defer to executive determination in some circumstances.[115]

Some clarifications relating to the status of customary international law have been provided by US courts, including the US Supreme Court, when applying the Alien Tort Statute, which is the clearest example of US law incorporating customary international law.

---

107   See L. Henkin, *International Law as Law in the United States* (1984) 82 Mich L Rev, 1556.

108   See F.L.Kirgis, *Federal Statutes, Executive Orders and 'Self-Executing Custom'* (1984) 81 AJIL, 371.

109   On this topic see: L. Henkin, *The Constitution and United States Sovereignty: A Century of Chinese Exclusion and its Progeny* (1987) 100 Harv L Rev, 876–877 and A.M. Weisburd, *The Executive Branch and International Law* (1988) 41 Vand L Rev, 1237.

110   542 US 692, 726–730 (2004). See also the case of *Banco National de Cuba v Sabbatino* 376 US 398 (1964) which strongly implies that customary international law is federal common law, see J. Hartman, *'Unusual' Punishment: The Domestic Effects of International Norms Reflecting the Application of the Death Penalty* (1983) 52 UCin LRev, 662. For the opposite view see Weisburd, supra note 109, at 1240–1241.

111   See e.g. *Cunard SS Co v Mellon* 262 US 100, 131 (1923).

112   E.g. *Mobil Oil Corp v Higginbotham* 436 US 618, 625 (1978).

113   See for example, *Tag v Rogers* 267 F2d 664,666 (1959) and *Garcia-Mir v Meese* 788 F.2d 1446, 1453–1455 (11th Cir 1986); *Guzman v Tippy* 130 F.3d 64, 66 (2d Cir 1997); *Gisbert v US Attorney General* 988 F.2d 1437 (5th Cir 1993) and *Committee of United States Citizens Living in Nicaragua v Regan* 859 F.2d 929 (DC Cir 1988).

114   See Restatement (Third), para 102 cmt.k.

115   Ibid, para 112c.

4.5.2.1　The Alien Tort Claims Act (ATCA)

Under the US Alien Tort Claims Act (ATCA), US federal courts have jurisdiction over 'any civil action by an alien for a tort only, committed in violation of the law of nations or a treaty of the United States'.

The statute was enacted in 1789 and left dormant for 200 years (only two cases were decided under ATCA from 1789 to 1980). It was in 1980, in *Filartiga v Pena-Irala*,[116] that a US federal court decided that the claimants, a family from Paraguay who brought an action for damages against a Paraguayan official (a police chief) for torturing and killing a member of their family in Paraguay, could rely on ATCA. The Court found that the act of torture was committed under 'colour of law', that torture constituted a crime under the law of nations and that the fact that it was committed by an official of a foreign government when exercising his official duty was not an excuse. It seems that the position under ATCA is that while foreign officials are immune under the Foreign Sovereign Immunities Act when acting within their lawful duties, they are liable when they commit serious human rights abuses because such acts are considered as illegal or *ultra vires*.

The US Supreme Court in *Sosa v Alvarez-Machain*[117] (for facts see Chapter 9.10) imposed important limitations on the scope of ATCA. It found that ATCA was a jurisdictional statute and thus, in itself, does not provide for a cause of action. However, such a cause of action can be found either in a treaty to which the US is a contracting party or in customary international law. With regard to a rule of customary international law, in order to become a source of actionable tort under ATCA, it must be:

■ universal in acceptance;

■ binding;

■ specific. The US Supreme Court requires specificity comparable to the features of the eighteenth century paradigms contemplated by Congress when it enacted ATCA, e.g. offences against ambassadors, violation of safe conduct and piracy.

In the *Sosa* case, the claimant failed because the Court found that prohibition of arbitrary arrest (as opposed to prolonged arbitrary detention) was neither of the required specificity nor prohibited under any treaty binding on the US. Subsequently, claims based on defamation, environmental tort, fraud, etc were dismissed as they did not pass the test established in *Sosa*.[118] However, claims based on flagrant human rights violations including genocide, torture, war crimes, crimes against humanity, summary execution and disappearances passed the *Sosa* test.[119]

Many issues remain unresolved under ATCA, e.g. whether corporations can be sued under ATCA, the availability of aiding and abetting claims, the scope of the principle of exhaustion of domestic remedies.

One fundamental question was answered by the US Supreme Court in *Kiobel v Royal Dutch Petroleum*.[120] The US Supreme Court unanimously ruled (although judges were divided on the rationale five to four), against extraterritorial application of ATCA, i.e. ATCA does not apply to acts committed on the territory of a foreign State. In this case, a lawsuit was brought by Nigerian plaintiffs against

---

116　630 F 2d 876 (2d Cir 1980).

117　542 US 692, 729 (2004).

118　See e.g. *Hamid v Price Waterhouse* 51 F.3d 1411, 1418 (9th Cir 1995).

119　See B. Stephens, J. Chomsky, J. Green, P. Hoffman and M. Ratner, *International Human Rights Litigation in US Courts*, 2nd edn, The Hague: Martinus Nijhoff Publishers, 2008.

120　133 SCt 1659 (2013).

foreign corporations, *inter alia*, the Royal Dutch Petroleum, for allegedly aiding and abetting human rights violations in Nigeria. The more liberal judges were of opinion that the law suit was not sufficiently related to the US to warrant jurisdiction of a US court. The conservative majority of judges were more radical. They stated that ATCA does not apply to conduct occurring within the territory of a foreign sovereign. This judgment, to a great extent, ends the extraterritorial application of ATCA, i.e. the kind of 'universal jurisdiction in tort' which US courts previously exercised under ATCA. The full implications of *Kiobel* are to be seen,[121] but it remains that the presumption against the extraterritorial application of ATCA is strong. In this respect the Chief Justice stated that when the relevant conduct takes place abroad it must 'touch and concern the territory of the United States . . . with sufficient force to displace the presumption against extraterritorial application [of ATCA]'.[122]

It is submitted that the judgment in *Kiobel* addresses the criticism addressed by many countries against ATCA. For example, Canada submitted an *amicus curiae* in *Presbyterian Church of Sudan v Talisman Energy Inc*[123] challenging the application of ATCA on two grounds. They were, first, that ATCA was contrary to customary international law, which requires a genuine link between the forum State and a person or events it seeks to regulate and, second, that its application to the case at issue would have a negative impact on Canada's foreign policy in Sudan. The three judges Higgins, Koijmans and Buergenthal, in their Joint Separate Opinion in the *Arrest Warrant Case* assessed ATCA as follows:

> While the unilateral exercise of the function of guardian of international value has been much commented on, it has not attracted the approbation of States generally.[124]

Obviously, for victims of serious violations of human rights the judgment in *Kiobel* is a serious setback in obtaining judicial remedies in US courts.

RECOMMENDED READING

Books

Fatima, S., *Using International Law in Domestic Courts*, Oxford: Oxford University Press, 2005.
Novaković, M. (ed.), *Monism and Dualism*, Belgrade: Faculty of Law University of Belgrade, Institute of Comparative Law and Institute of International Politics and Economics, 2013.

Articles

Buergenthal, T., *Self-Executing and Non Self-Executing Treaties in National and International Law* (1992) 235 RCADI, 303.
Crootof, R., *Judicious Influence: Non-Self-Executing Treaties and the Charming Betsy Canon* (2011) 120 Yale LJ, 1786.
Feldman, D., *Monism, Dualism and Constitutional Legitimacy* (1999) 20 Australian YIL, 105.
Groves, M., *Treaties and Legitimate Expectations-The Rise and Fall of Teoh in Australia* [2010] 15(4) JR, 323.

---

121   For example, it is uncertain whether ATCA will apply to conduct of US nationals abroad, whether it will apply to tort committed in a failed State, etc. On this topic see: P.D. Mora, *The Alien Tort Statute After Kiobel: The Possibility for Unlawful Assertions of Universal Civil Jurisdiction Still Remains* (2014) 63 ICLQ, 699.
122   At 1669.
123   582 F.3d 244 (2nd Cir 2009) The US Supreme Court refused to grant a writ of certiorari seeking to review the Second Circuit's decision dismissing the case.
124   The *Case Concerning the Arrest Warrant of 11 April 2000 (Democratic Republic of the Congo v Belgium)* (2002) ICJ Rep 3, para 48.

Hathway, O.A., McElroy, S. and Aronchick Solow, S., *International Law at Home: Enforcing Treaties in US Courts* (2012) 37 YJ Int L., 52.

Keith, K., *International Law Part of the Law of the Land: True or False* (2013) 26 LJIL, 351.

Mendis, D.L., *The Legislative Transformation of Treaties* (1992) 13 Statute Law Review, 216.

Mora, P.D., *The Alien Tort Statute After Kiobel: The Possibility for Unlawful Assertions of Universal Civil Jurisdiction Still Remains* (2014) 63 ICLQ, 699.

Patel, S., *Founding Legitimate Expectations on Unincorporated Treaties* [2010] 15/1 JR, 74.

Pollard, D., *Unincorporated Treaties and Small States* (2007) 33/3 Commonwealth Law Bulletin, 389.

Singh, R., *Interpreting Bill of Rights* (2008) 29 Statute Law Review, 82.

Waters, M., *Creeping Monism: the Judicial Trend towards Interpretive Incorporation of Human Rights Treaties* (2007) Columbia Law Review, 107.

AIDE-MÉMOIRE

Relationship between international and municipal law

Public international law leaves each country to decide on the relationship between international and municipal law. Historically there have been two schools of thought as to the relationship between international law and municipal law:

Dualism. According to dualists international law and municipal law are two independent and separate systems. Neither legal system has the power to create or alter the rules of the other. However, as they may regulate the same subject matter a conflict may arise in which case a municipal court will apply municipal law.

Monism. There are many varieties of monism but its main premise is that international law and municipal law are part of the same legal order. As they may regulate the same subject matter any conflict between international law and municipal law should be solved in favour of international law.

The doctrine of transformation. It requires rules of international law to be transformed into municipal law by the use of the appropriate constitutional machinery such as an act of parliament.

The doctrine of incorporation. Under this doctrine rules of international law form part of municipal law without the need for further legislative action at the municipal level.

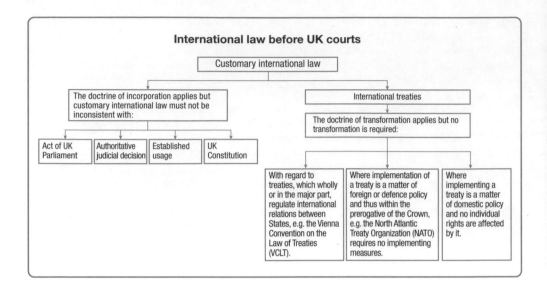

5

INTERNATIONAL PERSONALITY

CHAPTER OUTLINE

1 Introduction

A subject of international law can be defined as an entity capable of possessing international rights and duties and having capacity to protect its rights by bringing international claims. Under the traditional view the only subjects of international law were sovereign States. With the development of international law entities other than States have been granted recognition as subjects of international law. These are:

- entities which can potentially become States (e.g. *de facto* regimes, insurgents and belligerents, and national liberation movements which represent peoples entitled to exercise their right to self-determination);

- entities with State-like qualities such as the Holy See and the Order of Malta;

- IGOs, within which States are co-operating at an international level; and

- individuals.

However, only States and State-like entities have full legal personality, i.e. they have all legal rights, are subject to all international legal obligations, and have unlimited capacity to bring claims against other subjects of international law. Subjects of international law, other than States and State-like entities, have been accorded partial personality i.e. the extent of their rights and obligations as well as their capacity to bring claims against a State are ultimately controlled by States. The distinction between full and partial legal personality has been confirmed by the ICJ in the *Reparation for Injuries Suffered in the Service of the United Nations (Advisory Opinion)*, in which the ICJ stated that 'subjects of law in any legal system are not necessarily identical in their nature or in the extent of their rights'.

Controversial candidates for the status of subjects of international law are non-governmental organisations (NGOs), multinational corporations (MNCs) and indigenous peoples (see Chapter 2.12). Other non-State actors e.g. private armies, international criminal gangs, and terrorist organisations with global reach have tremendous impact on international law, but are unlikely to become subjects of international law bearing in mind the political connotation of recognising an entity as a subject of international law.

2 States and the criteria for statehood

The four traditional criteria for statehood are set out in Article 1(1) of the 1933 Montevideo Convention. Under the traditional view if an entity satisfies all four criteria it is a State. The four criteria are:

A. Permanent population. International law neither prescribes a minimum number of people making up a population nor requires that the population is made up of nationals.

B. Defined territory. International law neither prescribes a minimum surface nor requires that the international boundaries of an entity must be precisely delimited.

C. Government. A government, or at least some governmental control, is required for qualification as a State. The government must maintain some degree of order and stability. However, once a government has been established, the subsequent absence of governmental authority does not affect the existing State's right to be considered as a State.

D.   Capacity to enter into relations with other States/Independence. The capacity of an entity to enter into relations with other States derives from the control the government exercises over a given territory, which in turn is based on the fact that the State is independent. Independence can be described as the right of a State to exercise, to the exclusion of any other State, the functions of a State.

More recently, the following criteria, additional to those set out in the 1933 Montevideo Convention, have assumed prominence:

■ the legality of origin of a State;

■ the willingness and ability of the entity concerned to observe international law including human rights law (HRL). However, State practice shows that this criterion has not become a formative element of statehood.

3   Independent States

Independent States possess full international personality. However, they may enter into various agreements with other States which may affect their international personality such as:

A.   Federation. This occurs when two or more States unite to such an extent that they abandon their separate statehood. Governmental responsibilities are divided between the federal authority and the constituent members of the federation. Usually, the federal government is entrusted with exclusive competence in foreign affairs while the member States have competences in respect of internal domestic matters. Consequently, only the federal State is regarded as a State under international law and possesses international personality. In some federations, however, a component State is allowed to enter into relations with foreign States, e.g. the US, Switzerland, Austria and Germany.

B.   Confederation. This occurs when two or more independent States decide to unite for their mutual welfare and the furtherance of their common aims, but do not abandon their separate statehood. A central government is created that has certain powers, mostly in external affairs, and component States retain their powers for domestic purposes. Each State in a confederation retains its sovereign status.

C.   Personal union. This occurs when two or more States decide to have the same head of State while remaining separate States with distinct international personalities. Great Britain and Hanover formed a personal union from 1714 to 1837. However, in some personal unions a State may cease to be a subject of international law. This occurred in the case of the Channel Islands – Jersey, Guernsey, Alderney and Sark, each of which is united in a personal union with the British monarch.

D.   Real union. This occurs when two or more States share one State organ or more. Whether or not members of a real union enjoy international personality depends upon internal arrangements between them, and the attitude of third States towards them.

E.   The Commonwealth of Nations, formerly known as the British Commonwealth of Nations (the term 'British' was dropped in 1946), is a free association of sovereign States who have decided to maintain ties of friendship and co-operation with each other and recognise the British monarch as a symbolic head of their association. The Commonwealth has no international personality. Its members, sovereign States, are subjects of international law.

4 Dependent States

These are States subject to the authority of one or more other States. There are different forms of dependency and therefore in some situations a dependent State will retain its international personality, in others it will lose it.

A. Colonies. Under the traditional rules colonies did not have international personality but with the emergence of the principle of self-determination they were granted various measures of international personality.

B. Protectorates. Protectorates refer to territories or states that are placed under the diplomatic or military protection of a third State. They are of historical interest only.

C. Satellite States. These are States which are under heavy influence of, or control by, another State but retain their international personality e.g. Central and Eastern European States under the control of the USSR.

D. Condominium. In condominium two or more States exercise joint sovereignty over the same territory and its inhabitants. The territory under condominium has no international personality.

E. Co-imperium. This is similar to condominium but differs from it in that two or more States temporarily exercise joint sovereignty over the territory and inhabitants of a third State, For instance, Germany after WWII was administered by four allied powers but the State of Germany was never dismantled and the situation during co-imperium was described as 'akin to legal representation or agency of necessity'.

F. Diminutive States. These are very small States in terms of the size of their population and territory. Despite this, they have been recognised as possessing full international personality.

5 *Sui generis* entities

These entities do not satisfy the criteria for statehood but are, nevertheless, recognised as States by the majority of States, e.g. the Holy See and the Sovereign Military Hospitaller Order of Malta.

6 Internationalised territories

These are created by international agreements, normally peace treaties, and endowed with a limited international personality, e.g. the Free City of Danzig (now Gdansk) which was created by the 1919 Treaty of Versailles and the 1920 Agreement between the Free City of Danzig and Poland. The Free City of Danzig was neither an independent State nor subordinate to any sovereign State. It was legally dependent on the League of Nations and Poland and as such possessed a limited international personality.

7 *De facto* regimes

De facto regimes can be described as those which have had control of a defined territory for a long period of time, and usually claim to be a State or a government but have failed to achieve recognition by a significant number of States. If an entity controls the whole of a territory of a recognised State the matter is that of recognition or otherwise of a government (see Chapter 6.4). Examples of *de facto* regimes are Taiwan, the Turkish Republic of Northern Cyprus (TRNC), and the Republic of Somaliland. Their status depends on the circumstances of each case.

8 Mandates and trusteeship territories

Colonial territories were placed under the mandate of the League of Nations or the UN trusteeship system to prepare them for the exercise self-determination. Mandates and trusteeship territories had limited international personality. Currently, there are no trusteeship territories. The last one, Palau, became associated with the US in 1994.

9 Insurgents, belligerents and national liberation movements

In the context of armed conflicts some organised groups may become subjects of international law.

A. Limited international personality may be granted to some insurgent groups and belligerents during armed conflicts when they exercise *de facto* control over a part of a national territory provided that the requirements contained in the 1977 Additional Protocol II to the 1949 Geneva Conventions are met (see Chapter 17.5.7).

B. Following the adoption by the UNGA of the 1960 Declaration on the Granting of Independence to Colonial Countries and Peoples, which declared that all colonial people have a right to self-determination, and that colonialism should be brought to a speedy and unconditional end international law has recognised that some 'pre-independent States' and national liberation movements have international personality in various gradations. For example Guinea-Bissau was recognised as a State although only two-thirds of its territory was under the control of the African Party for the Independence of Guinea and Cape Verde (PAIGC) (the liberation movement of that territory), and the Palestine Liberation Organisation (PLO) was recognised as a national liberation movement representing the people of Palestine although, at the time of recognition, it had no control over any territory.

10 Territories under UN administration

On the basis of UNSC resolutions the UN, through its missions, administered the territories of East Timor and Kosovo. In each territory, the UN exercised all functions of a State and thus enjoyed full international personality. Each mission was designed as a mechanism for transition of these territories to self-governance.

11 International governmental organisations (IGOs)

The ICJ in the *Reparation for Injuries Suffered in the Service of the United Nations (Advisory Opinion)* held that the UN was a subject of international law capable of possessing international rights and duties, and the necessary capacity to maintain those rights by bringing international claims. However, the international legal personality of the UN (but see Chapter.5.11.2) and other IGOs is functional in that it depends on powers, express and implied, that member States have conferred on the relevant IGO.

The ICJ, in the above mentioned advisory opinion, held that the UN had objective international personality due to its almost universal membership and its universal mission. The distinction between objective and specific (or relative) personality is that objective international legal personality operates *erga omnes*, i.e. against all subjects of international law while specific (or relative) international personality is bestowed by subjects of international law on an entity, and thus it is relative in the sense that it has to be recognised by other subjects in order to exist.

12 Individuals

International law creates rights and duties for individuals which are capable of being enforced on an international level. Individuals are subjects of international law. However, as their rights and duties including procedural rights allowing them to bring claims against a State are ultimately controlled by States, they are only partial subjects of international law.

13 Non-governmental organisations (NGOs)

NGOs are not subjects of international law. There is, however, one exception, i.e. the ICRC which has international personality similar to that of the UN.

An NGO of interest to international law can be defined as an association, a foundation or other private institution, which has a non-profit making aim of international utility, has been established by an instrument governed by internal law, and operates in at least two States (this is the essence of the definition contained in the 1986 European Convention on the Recognition of the Legal Personality of International Non-Governmental Organisations). The increasing participation of NGOs in international affairs, which has been recognised by the granting of the status of consultants within the United Nations Economic and Social Council (under Article 71 of the UN Charter) to some of them, has bolstered their claim to international personality.

14 Multinational corporations (MNCs)

MNCs can be defined as corporations with wholly or partially controlled subsidiaries in more than one country. MNCs are not subjects of international law although they have rights directly conferred on them by international law and can enforce their claims against a State before international tribunals and bodies such as the International Centre for Settlement of Investment Disputes (ICSID). Although many attempts at imposing obligations on MNCs have failed, the UNHRC has not given up initiatives aimed at holding them accountable for violations of HRs at international level (see Chapter 2.12.3).

5.1 Introduction

A subject of international law is defined as an entity capable of possessing international rights and duties and having capacity to protect its rights by bringing international claims. Professor Brownlie rightly pointed out that this definition is circular because international law recognises the capacity to act at an international level of an entity which is already capable of acting at that level, i.e. it is already a subject of international law.[1] This definition, therefore, leaves unexplained that which the concept of personality ought to explain.

The importance of an entity being recognised as a subject of international law is that without international legal personality it does not exist in international law, i.e. its acts will not be recognised in international law, it will be prevented from starting proceedings against a State and will not be held responsible under international law. Apart from the legal considerations, when an entity is regarded as a subject of international law, it is granted political recognition from other subjects of international law.

The traditional view was that the only subjects of international law were sovereign States. They alone had capacity to make claims on the international plane in respect of breaches of international law, capacity to make treaties and other binding international agreements, and the ability to enjoy privileges and immunities from national jurisdiction. An exception was made for the Holy See (see Chapter 5.5.1).

However, in the eighteenth and nineteenth centuries States accepted that some atypical entities could be recognised as subjects of international law, e.g. the free cities created by the Congress of Vienna in 1815 (such as the city of Cracow) and the component States of federations (such as the cantons of the Swiss Federation). In parallel, under the rules of *jus in bello*, entities which exercised *de facto* control over certain territories were given recognition as insurgents or belligerents.

For the first time, in the nineteenth century, States decided that establishment of inter-governmental organisations (IGOs) would ensure efficient co-operation in areas of common interest. The European Commission for the Danube, created by the 1856 General Treaty for the Re-establishment of Peace,[2] was such an organisation. Its objective was to ensure free navigation on the river Danube. Its legislative and enforcement powers were so extensive that from today's perspective it can be said that it was endowed with international personality and supranational powers comparable to those of the EU. However, the recognition of a sort of international personality to the European Commission for the Danube was, *inter alia*, based on the fact that it had exercised powers over a territory, i.e. the river Danube.

After WWI, with the creation of the League of Nations and the International Labour Organisation (ILO) it became obvious that entities other than States, which had no physical control over any territory, were important players in the international arena. However, during the period between WWI and WWII, the matter of whether the League of Nations had international personality was never conclusively decided.[3]

After WWII with the creation of the UN and the proliferation of international organisations the traditional views on subjects of international law changed. The ICJ in *Reparation for Injuries Suffered in the Service of the United Nations (Advisory Opinion)* [1949][4] had to decide whether the UN had legal capacity to bring a claim for reparations concerning injuries which one of its employees had suffered while in active service of the organisation. The ICJ attributed to the UN legal personality, with the consequence that it was 'a subject of international law, and capable of possessing international rights and duties and that it has the capacity to maintain its rights by bringing international claims'.[5] The ICJ also recognised that 'subjects of law in any legal system are not necessarily identical in their

1   I. Browlie, *Principles of International Law*, 7th edn, 2008, Oxford: Oxford University Press, 57.
2   114 CTS 409.
3   J. Crawford, *The Creation of States in International Law*, 2nd edn, Oxford: Oxford University Press, 2006, 29.
4   [1949] ICJ Rep 173.
5   Ibid, 179.

nature or in the extent of their rights',[6] and made a distinction between partial and full legal personality. Under this distinction only States enjoy full legal personality which implies that, in principle, States possess all international legal rights, and are subject to all international legal duties. Other subjects of international law are regarded as partial subjects in that their rights and duties are limited, in the case of IGOs, by their constitutional treaties or, in the case of individuals, by the relevant treaties and customary international law. The first half of the twentieth century thus ended with the acceptance of IGOs as new subjects of international law.

Since the middle of the twentieth century the perception of who is a subject of international law has been under challenge once again. The growing body of HRL has led to the creation of international rights and duties for individuals, and other non-State actors. Further, globalisation, privatisation, feminism, and the fragmentation of international law have emphasised the impact of the increasingly important role of non-State actors in the making and working of international law. This, in turn, has invigorated the debate on who is to be regarded as a subject of international law. Some scholars have rejected the doctrine of 'subjects' of international law. For example, Higgins considers that 'we have been held captive by a doctrine that stipulates that all international law is to be divided into "subjects" – that is, those elements bearing, without the need for municipal intervention, rights and responsibilities; and "objects" – that is, the rest'.[7] She concludes that the doctrine has no relevance to reality and serves no functional purpose, and proposes replacement of the term 'subjects of international law' with the term 'participants' in international law.[8] Other scholars have been less radical, and tried to reconcile the doctrine of subjects of international law with the appearance of new entities, including individuals.[9]

It is submitted that attacks on the doctrine of 'subjects' of international law are fully justified in that the circularity of the definition of international personality entails that an entity needs to be a subject of international law to have the capacity to act at the international level, yet the fact of having such capacity implies that one is such a subject.

Irrespective of the confusion and controversies surrounding the doctrine, the fact is that the categories of international legal persons recognised under international law have been broadened. Nowadays, not only States are considered as subjects of international law but also:

- entities which can potentially become States;

- some *de facto* regimes;

- insurgents and belligerents;

- national liberation movements which represent peoples who are entitled to exercise their right to self-determination;

- entities with State-like qualities such as the Holy See, and the Order of Malta;

- IGOs, through which States co-operate at an international level;

- individuals, on whom international law confers rights and imposes obligations enforceable before international courts and bodies;

---

6   Ibid,178.
7   R. Higgins, *Problems and Process: International Law and How We Use It*, Oxford: Clarendon Press, Oxford University Press, 1994, 49.
8   Ibid, 48.
9   D.P. O'Connell, *International Law*, Vol 1, 2nd edn, London: Stevens and Sons, 1970, 82.

■ UN missions created by UNSC resolutions to administer certain territories during the transition period leading to self-governance of those territories. Such missions enjoy full legal personality during the transition period.

Non-State actors, who can be described as 'candidates for the status of subjects of international law' are NGOs, MNCs, and indigenous peoples. However, there are other non-State actors, e.g. private armies, international criminal gangs, and terrorist organisations with global reach which have tremendous impact on international law. The 9/11 terrorist attacks on the US demonstrated that activities of terrorist organisations can pose a 'threat to international peace and security'.[10] This is even more evident with the emergence of the Islamic State of Iraq and Syria (ISIS), a criminal terrorist group which, by combining unimaginable cruelty with military expertise has, at the time of writing, achieved control of large swathes of Syria and Iraq. ISIS is so powerful that its defeat and destruction has necessitated an international action. In this respect a US–led coalition conducts airstrikes against ISIS and provide supports for military partners of the coalition on the ground. Bearing in mind the political connotation of the recognition of an entity as a subject of international law, it is unlikely that international criminal organisations will ever be granted international personality.

In conclusion it can be said that the ICJ in its judgment in *LaGrand (Germany v United States of America)(Judgment)*[11] (see Chapter 5.12.1), opened the door for non-State actors such as NGOs and MNCs to be recognised as subjects of international law. In this respect the Special Rapporteur, Giorgio Gaja, in his first report on responsibility of international organisations presented to the ILC stated that the ICJ's recognition of individuals as subjects of international law:

> may lead the Court to assert the legal personality even to non-governmental organisations. It would be difficult to understand why individuals may acquire rights and obligations under international law while the same could not occur with any international organisation, provided that it is an entity which is distinct from its members.[12]

5.2 States and the criteria for statehood

Independent States remain the primary subjects of international law as they occupy the central position in the international community. In order to be regarded as an independent State an entity must satisfy certain criteria. The accepted definition of what constitutes the criteria for statehood is laid down in Article 1(1) of the 1933 Montevideo Convention on Rights and Duties of States[13] which provides:

> The state as a person of International Law should possess the following qualifications:
> (a)   a permanent population;
> (b)   a defined territory;
> (c)   government; and
> (d)   capacity to enter into relations with other states.

The simultaneous existence of these qualifications creates a sovereign entity possessing international personality. However, the absence of some of them over a period of time does not necessarily deprive a State of its international personality.

---

10   S/Res/1373(2001).
11   [2001] ICJ Rep 466.
12   First Report on Responsibility of International Organisations, UN Doc A/CN.4/532, 26 March 2003, para 17.
13   165 LNTS, 19.

The principle of effectiveness is at the root of the criteria set out in the Montevideo Convention. This principle plays a vital role in international law because it recognises that in the absence of any central authority which can decide whether an entity has met the criteria for statehood, any legal fictions should be discouraged. International law in order to be efficient, not a mere speculation, has to take a realistic approach to international matters. With regard to the creation of States, the principle of effectiveness requires that no entity should be regarded as a State within the meaning of international law unless that entity has a government which controls both a defined territory, and its inhabitants, effectively and independently from any other State. Without this the entity in question will neither be able to fulfil obligations deriving from international law, nor benefit from international rights.

Under the traditional view once an entity satisfies the criteria set out in the Montevideo Convention that entity is a State, irrespective of its recognition or non-recognition by other States, and irrespective of any other factors such as its legality or otherwise, or origin, or its compliance with HRL and other rules of international law.[14]

There is a debate on whether the traditional view on the creation of a State based on the principle of effectiveness has been challenged by the development of international law, in particular whether additional criteria to those set out in the Montevideo Convention have become relevant to the establishment of a State. In this respect it can be said that, ignoring the issue of the legal effects of recognition of States, State practice shows that statehood need not necessarily be equated with effectiveness, and thus that conditions unrelated to effectiveness are relevant to the determination of whether an entity should be regarded as a State under international law. In particular, the development of *jus cogens* entails that peremptory rules apply to all aspects of international law including the creation of States. Indeed, if an entity is created in breach of one of those rules it should be denied international legal personality. It is therefore justified to add a new criterion to those set out in the Montevideo Convention, i.e. the legality of origin of the entity in question. However, this criterion is closely linked with the principle of self-determination. If peoples are entitled to exercise their right to self-determination they can use force to break away from their existing State and create a new State. Everything therefore depends on who is entitled to exercise the right, and under what circumstances. The uneasy relationship between statehood and the principle of self-determination is examined in Chapter 12.7.

The debate on the criteria for statehood was revived by the the Badinter Arbitration Commission which was established by the European Community (EC) to respond to the break-up of the former Socialist Federal Republic of Yugoslavia (SFRY), and the subsequent unilateral declarations of independence by its former republics. The EC decided that if the former republics wished to be recognised by the EC as independent States they had to apply to the EC which would then refer their applications to an Arbitration Commission chaired by Robert Badinter (as a result the Commission has become known as the Badinter Commission). The Badinter Commission prepared guidelines for possible recognition of the republics of Yugoslavia which were officially adopted by the EC.[15] Although the Commission's main concern was the recognition of States, its Decisions 1 and 8–11 dealt with issues relating to statehood.[16]

---

14   See J. Crawford, *The Criteria for Statehood in International Law* (1976–77) 48 BYIL, 93.

15   The EC Guidelines on Recognition adopted on 17 December 1991, H. Hannum (ed.), *Documents on Autonomy and Minority Rights*, Dordrecht/Boston/London: Martinus Nijhoff Publisher, 1993, 85.

16   Opinions 10–10 in Opinions 1–10 of *Badinter Commission* (1993) 92 ILR 162; and Opinions 11–15 in International Conference on the Former Yugoslavia Documentation on the Arbitration Commission under the UN/EC (Geneva) Conference: Advisory Opinions Nos 11–15 of the Arbitration *Commission*, July 16, 1993 (1993) 32 ILM, 1587.

5.2.1   The traditional criteria for statehood

5.2.1.1   A permanent population

A State cannot exist without population. The requirement of 'a permanent population' refers to a stable community.

There is no prescribed minimum number of people making up a population. When Nauru became independent its estimated population was 6,500 people. The matter whether a very limited population will preclude the creation of a State was examined by the UN 'Special Committee of Twenty-Four' which was asked to interpret the right to self-determination of colonial peoples in the context of extremely small colonial populations. The smallest entity which was examined by the Committee was Pitcairn Island with a population of 90 inhabitants occupying an area of 5 square kilometres. The Committee affirmed the right of the people of Pitcairn Island to self-determination, but warned them that in deciding their political future they should take into consideration 'the Territory's tiny size, its small and decreasing population, mineral resources and dependence on postage stamps for the bulk of its revenue.'[17]

The criterion of population is not affected if the population of a State is nomadic, that is, it constantly changes its place of residence because of its nomadic mode of life. The nomadic tribes on the Kenya–Ethiopia borders have been a changing element of each nation's population for centuries. The transient nature of some parts of their population has never affected their qualification as independent States.

International law does not require the population of a State to be homogeneous. The notion of a nation State, as opposed to a State, is of historic interest only. It is not necessary that the population is made up of nationals. The determination of nationality is one of the attributes of a State, but not an element of its definition. Therefore, nationality is dependent upon statehood and not the reverse. The criterion of a 'stable population' refers to a group of individuals living within a certain geographical area.

5.2.1.2   A defined territory

A fixed territory constitutes a basic requirement for statehood. Jessup, in his arguments submitted in favour of the admission of Israel to the UN, stated that:

> The reason for the rule that one of the necessary attributes of a state is that it shall possess territory is that one cannot contemplate a state as a kind of disembodied spirit.[18]

However, there is no requirement that the frontiers of a State be fully defined and undisputed, either at the time it comes into being or subsequently. The State of Israel was admitted to the UN in 1949, despite the final delimitation of its boundaries not having been settled. Many of the States created after WWII were recognised by the Allied powers, although their boundaries were only drawn up in the subsequent peace treaties.

What is important is the effective establishment of a political community. In the case of *Deutsche Continental Gas-Gesselschaft v Polish State*[19] the German–Polish Mixed Arbitral Tribunal held that:

---

17   UN Doc A/9623/Add 5 (Part III) (1974), 6–7.
18   3 UN SCOR (383 mtg, 41) (1948).
19   (1928) 2 RIAA 829, 838.

In order to say that a state exists and can be recognised as such . . . it is enough that . . . [its] territory has a sufficient consistency, even though its boundaries have not yet been accurately delimited.

Therefore, there is no State without an area of land being generally defined. For that reason a 'nomad State' cannot exist. However, international law does not require any maximum or minimum size for a territory. For example, Monaco occupies only 1.5 square kilometres. Russia, on the other hand, occupies around 17 million square kilometres.

5.2.1.3 Government

A government, or at least some governmental control, is required for qualification as a State. The government must maintain some degree of order and stability. According to Shaw this criterion:

should be regarded more as an indication of some sort of coherent political structure and society, than the necessity for a sophisticated apparatus of executive and legal organs. The requirement relates to the nineteenth century concern with 'civilisation' as an essential of independent statehood and ignores the modern tendency to regard sovereignty for non-independent peoples as the paramount consideration, irrespective of administrative conditions.[20]

The structure or form of government need not follow any particular pattern.[21] Moreover, once a government has been established, the absence of any effective governmental authority does not affect the existing State's right to be considered as a State. States have often survived periods of anarchy, civil war and hostile occupation. For example, although civil war in Somalia led to the virtual disappearance of all State structures and the current Somali transitional government controls only a fraction of the territory of Somalia, Somalia has never lost its statehood.

5.2.1.4 Capacity to enter into relations with other States/independence

The criterion set out in the Montevideo Convention with regard to the capacity of an entity in question to enter into relations with States has been challenged by many authors as being a consequence of statehood, not a prerequisite. Indeed, such capacity derives from the control a government exercises over a given territory, which in turn is based on the actual independence of that State. It is the case, therefore that the essence of the capacity to enter into relations with other States is independence. As Lauterpacht said:

. . . the first condition of statehood is that there must exist a government actually independent of that of any other state . . . If a community, after having detached itself from the parent state, were to become, legally or actually, a satellite of another state, it would not be fulfilling the primary conditions of independence and would not accordingly be entitled to recognition as a state.[22]

In the *Island of Palmas Arbitration (The Netherlands v US)* (1928)[23] the Permanent Court of Arbitration clearly stated that 'Sovereignty . . . signifies independence. Independence . . . is the right to exercise . . . to the exclusion of any other state, the functions of a state.'

---

20   *International Law*, 2nd edn, Cambridge: Cambridge University Press, 1986, 128.
21   *Western Sahara (Advisory Opinion)* [1975] ICJ Rep 12, para 94.
22   *International Law: Collected Papers*, Cambridge: Cambridge University Press, 1975, 487.
23   2 RIAA 829.

Sovereignty is described as the supreme power of the State over its territory and inhabitants, independent of any external authority. That supreme power exists only inside the independent State not outside.

In respect of independence it is necessary to distinguish between independence as a criterion for the coming into being of a State and as a qualification for the continued existence of a State. Indeed, once a State is established it can reduce its independence through agreements and treaties with other States or IGOs. Judge Anzilotti in *Customs Regime between Germany and Austria*[24] explained that:

> the restrictions upon a State's liberty, whether arising out of ordinary international law or contractual arrangements do not in the least affect its independence. As long as those restrictions do not place the State under the legal authority of another State, the former remains an independent State however extensive and burdensome those obligations may be.

For example, member States of the EU have attributed to the EU exclusive competences in some areas, e.g. the Common Commercial Policy, the Common Agricultural Policy, and monetary policy (in so far as the member States that have adopted the euro are concerned), with the consequence that they are prevented from acting unilaterally or collectively in these areas, irrespective of whether the EU has already acted. Notwithstanding this, member States of the EU are independent and sovereign States enjoying full international personality. Consequently, a State remains independent as long as it has not given up its independence to any other State, since only an entity 'which is subjected to international law through the intermediary of a foreign State is not a sovereign State under international law'.[25] Therefore, if a State has neither abandoned its independence to another State, nor is subject to the intermediary of any other State, such a State is a direct subject of international law.

International law identifies two elements evidencing the existence of independence:

■ The entity exists separately within established boundaries. This emphasises the link between territory, population, government and independence. All four criteria must be present for the purposes of statehood.

■ The entity is not subject to any authority except international law.

Independence as a criterion for statehood can be formal or actual. Formal independence refers to a situation where a State has control over all its functions or competences (the so-called *kompetenz kompetenz*), while actual independence is described as 'the minimum degree of real government power at the disposal of the authorities of the putative state, necessary for it to qualify as independent'.[26]

The relationship between formal and actual independence of an entity will indicate to what extent such entity satisfies the criteria for statehood. A number of possibilities may arise:

■ formal independence is combined with the actual ability to exercise independence. The entity will satisfy the fourth criterion and its recognition should pose no problem;

■ formal independence exists but actual independence is missing. The entity will not meet the fourth criterion and should not be recognised as a State;

■ formal independence is missing but the entity exercises some degree of actual independence. In such a case the fourth criterion is not satisfied. It will be difficult to recognise such an entity, although the circumstances of each case may provide justification for its recognition, e.g. colonial people exercising the right to self-determination.

---

24   [1931] PCIJ Ser A/B no 41, 57–58.,

25   M.S. Korowicz, *Some Present Aspects of Sovereignty in International Law*, Leyden: A. W. Sijthoft, 1961, 108

26   J. Crawford, *The Creation of States in International Law*, Oxford: Clarendon Press, 1979, 56–57.

5.2.2 The legality of origin of a State as a criterion for statehood

In most cases where the issue of statehood is debated in relation to an entity, that entity has likely been created in breach of any of the following three norms of international law:

- the prohibition against aggression and against the acquisition of territory by force;

- the right to self-determination;

- the prohibition against racial discrimination and apartheid.

Normally, an entity created in breach of the above rules will not be regarded as a State because of the lack of actual independence, i.e. because it does not satisfy one of the criteria set out in the Montevideo Convention.

This is illustrated by the case of Manchukuo, a puppet State created by Japan subsequent to its 1931 invasion of Manchuria. The League of Nations sent the Lytton Commission to Manchukuo to observe the situation. It reported:

> In the Government of Manchukuo Japanese officials are prominent and Japanese advisers are attached to all important Departments. Although the premier and his ministers are all Chinese, the heads of the various Boards of General Affairs, which, in the organisation of the new state, exercise the greatest measure of actual power, are Japanese. At first they were designated as advisers, but recently those holding the most important posts have been made full government officials on the same basis as the Chinese.[27]

The League of Nations adopted the recommendations of the Commission and decided not to recognise Manchukuo. Although this issue was not debated it was obvious that the State of Manchukuo could not be recognised as a State because it was not independent.

Similarly, in more recent cases entities which were created with the assistance of foreign military intervention and whose continuous existence depends on foreign support, will not satisfy the criterion of independence. For example, the Republic of Abkhazia, the Republic of South Ossetia, and the TRNC are not independent States, because without foreign support they will not survive (see Chapter 5.7).

The ECtHR decided in *Cyprus v Turkey*[28] that the decisive factor for non-recognition of the TRNC as a State was its dependence on Turkish administration, not the fact that it was an illegal entity from the standpoint of international law. In this respect the ECtHR held that Turkey's responsibility under the ECHR could not be confined to the acts of its own soldiers and officials operating in Northern Cyprus but was also engaged by virtue of the acts of the local administration, whose survival was due to the Turkish military and other support.[29]

When South Africa created the homeland States of Transkei, Ciskei, Bophutatswana and Venda, those entities were not only created in breach of the principle of self-determination, and the prohibition of racial discrimination, but also lacked independence.

If an entity created in violation of one of the three principles of international law set out above becomes genuinely independent, e.g. the case of Bangladesh in 1971, then the issue of illegality of origin arises. In the case of Bangladesh it was generally accepted that Bangladesh, although created in breach of the prohibition of the use of force, was entitled to exercise the right to self-determination.[30]

---

27   League of Nations Publication, 1932, VIIA, 12.
28   (2002) 35 EHRR 30.
29   Ibid, para77.
30   J. Crawford, *The Creation of States in International Law*, Oxford: Oxford University Press, 2006, 140–143 and 393.

It can be said that the weight to be attached to the different criteria of statehood reflects political reality as much as normative concerns. This probably results from the fact that there was circularity in the traditional criteria for statehood in so far as they included relations with other States as a supposed criterion of statehood instead of its consequence. However, self-determination as a peremptory norm is now a factor that strongly reflects what is politically acceptable, but is not absolute, as for example, the realisation of self-determination is subject to the principle of *uti possiditis*, which requires that borders between former colonies, or administrative units in the case of non-self-governing territories, drawn during colonisation or borders between republics as was the case of the SFRY and the Soviet Union, are to be respected (see Chapter 13.7.2).

In conclusion it can be said that the criterion of legality of origin of a State is only of relevance when an entity created in breach of international law achieves, at some stage of its existence, independence from any other State. In such a situation its illegality of origin will be examined, in particular in the light of the principle of self-determination. The criterion of legality of origin of a State as an element of statehood refers back to the debate on the recognition of a State at the international level, i.e. whether the declarative or constitutive theory applies (see Chapter 6.2.1).

5.2.3 Additional criteria for statehood based on HRL and other considerations

The criteria for statehood were not frozen by the 1933 Montevideo Convention. Possible future additions to the Montevideo criteria may be taken from the EC Declaration on the Recognition of New States.[31] Although the Declaration was applied in respect of recognition of new States, some of its principles may be relevant to the criteria for statehood. It is submitted that the following criteria should be included for statehood to exist:

- respect for the provisions of the UN Charter, for the rule of law, democracy and human rights. This would ensure that a State is 'adult' enough to be a member of the international community;

- guarantees for the rights of ethnic and national groups and minorities. This would ensure that such groups are incorporated into the structure of a State from its inception.

State practice, however, does not support the idea that these additional criteria have become formative elements of statehood.

5.3 Independent States

Independent States possess unlimited international personality. However, they may enter into various agreements with other States which may affect their international personality.

5.3.1 Composite States

The following types of composite State can be identified.

5.3.1.1 Federation

In a federation two or more States unite to such an extent that they abandon their separate statehood. Governmental responsibilities are divided between the federal authority and the constituent members

---

31   EC 'Declaration on the "Guidelines on the Recognition of New States in Eastern Europe and in the Soviet Union"' (1992) 31 ILM 1486.

of the federation. Usually, the federal government is entrusted with exclusive competence in foreign affairs while the member States have competences in respect of internal domestic matters. Consequently, only the federal State is regarded as a State under international law and only it will possess international personality.

There is a general principle that member States of a federation cannot enter into separate relations with foreign States. However, there are some federal constitutions which give member States of the federation a limited capacity to enter into international relations with foreign States or IGOs (e.g. the constitutions of the US; Germany; Switzerland; and Austria). In such circumstances, the member State is simply acting as a delegate of the federal State. Such a situation may create separate personality in international law. For example, in 1944 the constitution of the USSR was amended to allow the Ukrainian SSR and Byelorussian SSR, both of which were member States of the USSR, to conclude treaties on their own behalf and become members of the UN alongside the USSR.

5.3.1.2 Confederation

In a confederation two or more independent States decide to unite for their mutual welfare and the furtherance of their common aims but do not abandon their separate legal personality. A central government is created that has certain powers, mostly in external affairs, and component States retain their powers for domestic purposes. The central government acts upon the member States, not upon the individuals. Each member State is fully sovereign and independent and thus possesses international legal personality. Examples of confederations are: Switzerland between 1291 and 1848; the Netherlands between 1581 and 1795; the US between 1776 and 1788 and Germany between 1815 and 1866.

An example of a thriving confederation is the Benelux Union comprising Belgium, the Netherlands and Luxembourg. It started as a customs union after WWII and under a 1958 treaty became an economic union whereby the three countries became one economy where goods, labour, capital and services were in free circulation and where welfare and other policies were co-ordinated. The 1958 Treaty creating the Benelux Economic Union was concluded for 50 years and entered into force in 1960. At its expiry, it was replaced by a new treaty creating the Benelux Union under enlarged co-operation between the three States in the context of greater European integration. The change of name reflects the evolving objectives of the Benelux Union which are no longer of a purely economic nature.

A confederation, because of its loose structure, normally, with time, transforms itself into a unitary State or a federation or disintegrates.

5.3.1.3 Personal union

This occurs when two or more States decide to have the same head of State while remaining separate States with distinct international personalities. Great Britain and Hanover formed a personal union from 1714 to 1837. However, in some personal unions a State may cease to be a subject of international law. This occurred in the case of the Channel Islands – Jersey, Guernsey, Alderney and Sark, each of which is united in a personal union with the British monarch. Each island has sovereignty over its territory, population, administration and judiciary entirely free of the control of the British Parliament, but their external affairs are conducted by the UK. They have no international personality.

5.3.1.4 Real union

In a real union two or more States share one or more State organ. Whether members of a real union enjoy international personality depends upon the internal arrangements between them and upon the attitude of third States towards them. An example of a real union was provided by the Austro-Hungarian dual monarchy from 1723 to 1849 and 1867 to 1918.

5.3.1.5 Commonwealth of Nations

The Commonwealth of Nations, formerly known as the British Commonwealth of Nations (the term 'British' was dropped in 1946), merits special attention. The Commonwealth is a free association of 53 sovereign States, most of them were formerly part of the British Empire.

The Commonwealth has no international personality: its members, each of which is a sovereign State, are subjects of international law. The Commonwealth was established by the 1931 Statute of Westminster which recognised that some British colonies and dependencies, i.e. dominions (e.g. Canada, Australia, New Zealand, South Africa and the Irish Free State), which enjoyed a large degree of self-government granted to them, had a special status within the British Empire. They were autonomous communities, independent from each other but unified through common allegiance to the British Crown.

With decolonisation the Commonwealth redefined its objectives. It allowed its members to resign from membership (which was done by the Irish Republic in 1948, South Africa in 1961 and Pakistan in 1972), but the majority of the former British colonies chose to remain within the Commonwealth. Instead of pledging allegiance to the British Crown, they recognise the British monarch as a symbolic head of their association. The members of the Commonwealth of Nations support each other and work together toward the achievement of common goals consisting of promoting democracy, peace, human rights and development. The activities of the Commonwealth relating to the implementation of the common goals are co-ordinated through the Commonwealth Secretariat located in London. The Commonwealth provides a forum for discussion among its members, including meetings of the heads of governments which take place every 2 years.

5.4 Dependent States

In the *Customs Regime between Germany and Austria* Case,[32] in a separate opinion, Anzilotti J provided some clarifications as to the meaning of 'dependent State' in the context of international law. He stated that:

> These are states subject to the authority of one or more other states. The idea of dependence therefore necessarily implies a relation between a superior state (suzerain, protector, etc.) and inferior or subject state (vassal, protégé, etc.); the relation between the state which can legally impose its will and the state which is legally compelled to submit to that will.

There are different forms of dependency and therefore in some situations a dependent State will retain its international personality, while in others it will lose it.

5.4.1 Colonies

Under the traditional rules of international law colonies were not regarded as possessing international personality. The exercise of their international relations was under the effective control of the colonial power. However, some colonial powers granted limited capacity to their colonies which were in the process of becoming independent. For instance, before its independence the British colony of Singapore

---

32   (1931) PCIJ Rep Ser A/B No 41, 57.

was authorised to enter into commercial treaties and join international organisations subject to the veto of the UK. Another example is provided by India when it became an original member of the League of Nations.

Following the adoption by the UNGA of the 1960 Declaration on the Granting of Independence to Colonial Countries and Peoples[33] which declared that all colonial people have a right to self-determination and that colonialism should be brought to a speedy and unconditional end international law has recognised that some 'pre-independent States' and national liberation movements have a limited international personality (see Chapter 5.9.2).

5.4.2 Protectorates

Protectorates are of historical interest only as they no longer exist on the international scene. Protectorates refer to States or territories which have been placed under the protection of a powerful State. A distinction must be made between protected territories and protected States.

5.4.2.1 Protected territories

In the nineteenth century it was the practice of certain European States to create 'protectorates' over certain 'primitive areas' of Africa and Asia by entering into treaties of protection with the local ruler. The effect of such agreements was that, while the local ruler retained control of his territory's internal affairs, foreign affairs were placed exclusively in the hands of the protecting power. Examples in Africa included Northern Rhodesia (now Zambia) and Nyasaland (now Malawi).

Protectorates did not have international personality before the protectorate was created. They acquired limited personality when they began to operate at the international level. Once the protecting power was removed and the protectorate started to act independently of the protecting power it became an independent State, and, as such, possessed international personality. This is illustrated by the case of Kuwait which became a British protectorate in 1899. It was gradually given responsibility for its own international relations, and this position was formally recognised by the UK in 1961 although, at that time, Kuwait had already achieved *de facto* statehood independently of formal recognition by the UK.

5.4.2.2 Protected States

Protected States are those States which have enjoyed international personality but subsequently surrendered their international competence to one or more protecting States. Protected States retain their original personalities as States in international law notwithstanding any treaty of protection.

Morocco was a protectorate of France and Spain from the beginning of the twentieth century. The General Act of the International Conference of Algeciras of 7 April 1906 governing relations between France and Morocco guaranteed 'the Sovereignty and the Independence of His Majesty the Sultan, the integrity of his Domains, and economic liberty without inequality'. Under the Act, Morocco surrendered to France the right to institute administrative, judicial, educational, financial and military reforms. Additionally, France could maintain its military presence without the permission of the Sultan. The treaty was concluded for an unlimited period and the Sultan had no right to terminate it. In 1912, by the Treaty of Fez, Morocco made another arrangement with France whereby France undertook to exercise certain sovereign powers in the name of and on behalf of Morocco, and all of the international relations

---

33   UNGA Res 1514 (XV) (14 December 1960) GAOR 15th Session Supp 16, 66.

of Morocco. Notwithstanding this, the ICJ in the *Case Concerning Rights of Nationals of the United States of America in Morocco (France v United States of America)*[34] held that the 1912 Treaty of Fez was an international treaty and that Morocco, even under the protectorate, had retained its international personality despite the fact that France exercised certain sovereign powers in the name of, and on behalf of, the Sultan in both internal and external affairs.

5.4.2.3 Satellite States

After WWII the 'liberation' of the Central and Eastern European States by the Soviet army from German occupation gave the Soviet Union military and political control of these States to the point that, in effect, they became satellite States. However, the political and economic power exercised by the Soviet Union and the military presence of its army within the territory of the satellite States did not affect their international personality. Furthermore, the Soviet Union was always very careful to eliminate any semblance of *de jure* dependency on it by the satellite States. Nevertheless, in reality there were no doubts that the satellite States were not fully sovereign, particularly after the Soviet invasion of Hungary in 1956 and Czechoslovakia in 1968.

5.4.2.4 Condominium and co-imperium

In condominium two or more States exercise joint sovereignty over the same territory and its inhabitants. The territory under condominium has no international personality. The best example of condominium was the Anglo-French condominium of the New Hebrides constituted in 1906.[35] This arrangement was said to create 'a region of joint influence . . . each of the two Powers retaining sovereignty over its nationals . . . and neither exercising a separate authority over the group'. The territory achieved its independence in 1980 as the State of Vanuatu.

Co-imperium is different from condominium. The best example is provided by Germany after 1945. After the defeat of Germany in WWII the victors decided neither to annex the enemy territory nor to establish an international territory but to govern it jointly as a distinct international entity. The Allied powers decided to divide Germany into four occupation zones: Berlin was jointly controlled by the four powers and the Control Council, an inter-Allies government which acted on behalf of Germany and was empowered to enter into international agreements. The State of Germany was never dismantled and the situation during co-imperium was described as 'akin to legal representation or agency of necessity'.

5.4.2.5 Diminutive States

Extremely small European States such as Monaco, Andorra, San Marino and Liechtenstein exist as something between being independent and dependent States. Each is regulated under different arrangements. For example, Andorra is governed by two co-princes, the President of the French Republic and the Spanish Bishop of Urgel. And Monaco has various arrangements with France and may *de facto* be considered as her satellite. Nevertheless, these States are recognised by other States as sovereign States and are members of many international organisations, including the UN.

---

34   [1952] ICJ Rep 1/6.

35   Convention between the United Kingdom and France concerning the New Hebrides (adopted 20 October 1906, entered into force 9 January 1907) (1907) 1 AJIL Supp 179–200.

Diminutive States which emerged as a result of decolonisation e.g. Tuvalu, Nauru, Palau, Saint Kitts and Nevis, the Marshall Islands and Dominica are fully independent and their international personality is not in doubt.

5.5 *Sui generis* entities

There are a number of entities that enjoy a special status under international law. They do not satisfy the criteria for statehood but are, nevertheless, recognised as States by the majority of States. Examples are the Holy See, the Vatican City State and the Sovereign Military Hospitaller Order of Malta.

5.5.1 The Holy See and the Vatican City

The Holy See enjoys a special status in international law. The term 'Holy See' is a translation of the Latin expression *'sancta sedes'* which refers to the chair of St Peter. Under canon law, the term 'Holy See' is used to refer to both the Pope and the Roman Curia through which the Pope exercises his powers over the Catholic Church including spiritual power over 1 billion people who profess the Catholic faith. The Holy See has always been recognised as possessing international personality. Even during the period when the Holy See lacked any sovereign territory (from 1870 to 1929) it entered into international agreements (concordats) with many independent States. The Holy See is a member of international organisations (e.g. the OSCE, the UNCTAD, the WIPO, the IAEA); enjoys observer status in many IGOs (the UN, the WHO, UNESCO, FAO); is a contracting party to international treaties (the 1961 Vienna Convention on Diplomatic Relations, the 1963 Vienna Convention on Consular Relations, the 1949 Geneva Conventions and the core human rights treaties (see Chapter 12.2. and 12.3)) and has been granted immunities and privileges in most States in the world. The Holy See is, under international law, a distinct entity from the Vatican City State.

The Vatican City State was created in 1929 when the Holy See signed the Lateran Treaty with Italy under which diplomatic relations were established between them. Under the treaty the 'City of Vatican' was granted to the Holy See as its sovereign territory. Prior to 1929 the Holy See had no territory but occupied *de facto* the Vatican palaces which were regarded as a part of Italy. The Lateran Treaty expressly stated that all customary inhabitants of the Vatican, irrespective of their citizenship, were subject to the sovereign authority of the Holy See while on the territory of the Vatican City. The Vatican City does not have a fixed population within the meaning of the criterion for statehood. In 2014, the Vatican City State had a population of over 800 citizens, of whom over 450 had Vatican citizenship.[36] Vatican citizenship is based on service to the Holy See[37] and is normally revoked upon the termination of such service. Any inhabitant of the Vatican City, irrespective of whether or not he is a citizen of the Vatican, can be expelled at any time from its territory.

Although the Holy See and the Vatican City State have separate international personality so that each has capacity on its own to enter into international relations (e.g. the Vatican City State, not the Holy See, is a member of the Universal Postal Union) and each issues its own passports (the Holy See only issues diplomatic and service passports; the state of Vatican City issues normal passports) both are ruled by the bishop of Rome, i.e. the Pope, who is the head of the Holy See, the head of the Vatican

---

36   See the official website of the Vatican City State www.vaticanstate.va/content/vaticanstate/en/stato-e-governo/ note-generali/popolazione.html (accessed 6 May 2014).

37   E.g., all cardinals have Vatican City citizenship *ex officio*.

City State and the head of government of the Vatican City. It is unclear why the Pope chooses, on some occasions, to act through the Vatican City, and on others through the Holy See, but as God is said to act in mysterious ways perhaps the Pope's choices on these matters are not to be questioned.

5.5.2   The Sovereign Military Hospitaller Order of Malta

The Sovereign Military Hospitaller Order of Malta was founded as a religious military order of the Roman Catholic Church during the Crusades. Initially it had a territory but lost it in 1798. In 1834 the Order established itself in Rome as a humanitarian organisation.

In 1446 Pope Nicholas V acknowledged the Grand Master of the Order as a 'sovereign prince'. From the time of its establishment the Order has always maintained diplomatic relations with States and has been consistently treated as a sovereign State despite its lack of territory or population. Its Knights are citizens of other States.

Italy, being the State where the Order is located, has recognised it as a sovereign State in a number of legislative and administrative acts as well as in decisions of its judiciary.[38]

The Order has established diplomatic relations with more than 100 States; has its own postal service; issues passports which are internationally recognised; is a member of numerous international organisations; has the status of a permanent observer to the UN; enters into treaties and international agreements with many independent States; possesses its own fleet of hospital aircraft carrying its flag, and is independent from other States and jurisdictions except in religious matters in which the Order is subordinated to the Holy See. Its awards (a Bailiff Grand Cross of Honour and Devotion, and the Collar Pro Merito Melitense) have been accepted by heads of State or government.

5.6   Internationalised territories

By virtue of an agreement, normally a peace treaty, some territories may be endowed with limited international personality. The best example is the Free City of Danzig (now Gdansk) which was created by the 1919 Treaty of Versailles and the 1920 agreement between the Free City of Danzig and Poland.[39]

The free city of Danzig occupied 1,890 square kilometres and had 356,000 inhabitants. In Article 100 of the Treaty of Versailles Germany renounced all its rights and title to Danzig in favour of the Allied powers. Article 102 provided for the establishment of the Free City of Danzig under the protection of the League of Nations. The relationship between Poland and the Free City of Danzig was regulated by Article 104 of the Treaty of Versailles. This stated that an agreement between Poland and the Free City of Danzig which would come into force at the time of the establishment of the Free City would ensure:

- the inclusion of the Free City within the Polish Customs frontier and the establishment of a free area in the port;

- free use and service of all waterways, docks, basins etc for Polish imports and exports;

---

38   See G.I. Draper, *Functional Sovereignty and the Sovereign Military Hospitaller Order of Saint John of Jerusalem, of Malta* 1974, Annales de L'Ordre Souverain Militaire de Malte, 78–86.

39   Convention between Poland and the Free City of Danzig (signed 9 November 1920, entered into force 12 December 1921) 6 LNTS 189.

- the control of Poland over the administration of the Vistula and of the whole railway system within the Free City, except streets and railways which served the primary needs for the Free City, and of postal, telegraphic and telephonic communication between Poland and the port of Danzig;

- that Polish citizens and other persons of Polish origin and speech would not be discriminated against within the Free City; and

- that the Polish government would conduct the foreign relations of the Free City and be in charge of the diplomatic protection of all citizens of the city when abroad.

The agreement between Poland and the Free City of Danzig was signed on 9 November 1920 and entered into force on 15 November 1920. The legal status of the Free City was described in its constitution, which provided for a Parliament exercising legislative, executive and administrative powers, as well as a Senate representing the Free City within the limits set out by the treaties. Although Poland was entrusted with the foreign affairs of the Free City, she had no right to initiate or to impose international agreements contrary to the interests of the Free City. The High Commissioner appointed by the League of Nations, who had his headquarters in Danzig, had a general power of supervision in respect of implementation of the League's decisions and resolutions concerning the Free City, and was entitled, in the first instance, to settle disputes between the Free City and Poland. He also had the right of veto in respect of international agreements which, according to the League of Nations, were in breach of the status of the Free City.

From the point of view of international law the Free City of Danzig was neither an independent State nor subordinate to any sovereign State. It was legally dependent on the League of Nations and Poland and as such possessed limited international personality.

The Free City was, however, organised as a State. It had its own constitution, flag and currency, and was entitled to grant citizenship to inhabitants of Danzig. The PCIJ recognised that the Free City had international personality, except in so far as the treaty obligations arising from its special relationship with Poland, and the League of Nations.[40] The Free city of Danzig ceased its *de facto* existence in 1939 upon being annexed to Germany. Under customary international law the annexation to Germany was unlawful and thus *de jure* it was still in existence in 1945 when it was incorporated into the territory of Poland.

In the 1947 Peace Treaty between the Allied and Associated Powers and Italy[41] which was designated to find a solution to a dispute between Italy and Yugoslavia regarding Trieste, envisaged the establishment of the Free Territory of Trieste but this never came into being.

5.7   *De facto* regimes

De facto regimes can be described as those which have had control of a defined territory for a lot of time, and usually claim to be a State or a government but have failed to achieve recognition by a significant number of States. If an entity controls the whole of a territory of a recognised State the matter is that of recognition, or otherwise, of a government (see Chapter 6.3).[42]

---

40   *Free City of Danzig and International Labour Organization (Advisory Opinion)* PCIJ Ser B No 18 and *the Treatment of Polish Nationals and Other Persons of Polish Origin or Speech in the Danzig Territory (Advisory Opinion)* PCIJ Ser A/B No 44.

41   49 UNTS 3.

42   *Arbitration between Great Britain and Costa Rica* (1924) 18 AJIL, 147.

The issue of whether *de facto* regimes are subjects of international law is complex. Nevertheless it is clear that if *de facto* regimes are not independent from other States, they do not qualify for statehood. This is the case of the Turkish Republic of Northern Cyprus (Cyprus), the Republic of Abkhazia and the Republic of South Ossetia (Georgia), Nagorno-Karabakh (Azerbaijan), and Transdniestria (Moldova). However, the existence of Taiwan and the Republic of Somaliland[43] is not dependent on any other State.

Examples of *de facto* regimes are as follows.

5.7.1 The Turkish Republic of Northern Cyprus (TRNC)

The TRNC was created after the Turkish invasion of Cyprus in 1974 which divided the Republic of Cyprus into two sectors: Greek and Turkish. The TRNC unilaterally declared its independence in 1983 but has been recognised as a State only by its creator, Turkey. Indeed the UN Security Council, by Resolutions 541 of 1983 and 550 of 1984, called upon all States not to recognise the TRNC.

5.7.2 The Republic of Abkhazia and the Republic of South Ossetia

The Republic of Abkhazia and the Republic of South Ossetia both lie within the former Soviet republic of Georgia. After 5 days of fighting between, on the one side, the separatist movements in both regions supported militarily by Russia and, on the other, Georgia, in August 2008, Georgia lost *de facto* control over both regions. On 28 August 2008, Russia recognised the Republic of Abkhazia and the Republic of Ossetia as independent States. Apart from Russia, only Nicaragua, Nauru and Venezuela have recognised them as States. Tuvalu and Vanuatu had also previously recognised Abkhazia and South Ossetia but subsequently retracted that recognition.

5.7.3 The national government of Spain during the Spanish civil war (1936–1939)

See Chapter 6.4.2.1.

5.7.4 Taiwan

Taiwan, which fulfils all the criteria for statehood, has not been recognised as a State by the international community.

Taiwan (previously known as Formosa) was ceded by China to Japan in 1895. In 1945, upon the surrender of Japan, all Japanese forces were withdrawn from Taiwan and Japan officially relinquished all claims to Taiwan. At that time, the civil war in China was at its end. The People's Republic forces led by Mao Tse Tung were in control of the Chinese mainland while the Republic of China's forces led by Chiang Kai-Shek had retreated to Taiwan. Each party to the conflict created a State, the People's Republic of China on the mainland (PRC) and the Republic of China (ROC) in Taiwan. Both claimed to be the sole representative of China and of all its territory. During the 1950s and 1960s the UN and most States recognised the ROC as the legitimate government of China. However, as a result of UNGA Resolution 2758 (XXVI) of 25 October 1971[44] the PRC was recognised as the sole *de jure* government of China including Taiwan. Despite this, the ROC did not amend its claim to be the only legitimate

---

43   On this topic see: R., Richards, 'The Road Less Travelled: Self-Led Statebuilding and International "Non-intervention" in the Creation of Somaliland' in B. Bliesemann de Guevara (ed.), *Statebuilding and State- Formation: The Political Sociology of Intervention* (2012), 149–164.

44   GAOR 26th Session Supp 29, 2.

representative of all Chinese people. With regard to the PRC, it declared that Taiwan was a province of the PRC and that any State wishing to maintain relations with the PRC must deny recognition to the ROC. From that time onwards, the ROC's status in international law has been debated.

The ROC satisfies all criteria for statehood. It has capacity to sue and to be sued in national courts of foreign States. It conducts international relations with many countries which have used various means to maintain their relations with Taiwan.[45] For example, when the US recognised the PRC, it passed the 1979 Taiwan Relations Act under which it made a commitment to provide Taiwan with arms of defensive character and to ensure the security of the people of Taiwan. The ROC enjoys sovereign immunity. However, States which have not recognised Taiwan keep a low profile when entering into dealings with it, e.g. they do this through commercial missions and cultural associations.

The ROC is a contracting party to international treaties. On some occasions, clever devices have been employed by the international community to allow Taiwan's participation in multilateral treaties. For example, the 1963 Treaty Banning Nuclear Weapon Tests in the Atmosphere, in Outer Space and under Water[46] designated three States as its depositories: the US, the UK and the USSR. This allowed the German Democratic Republic (unrecognised at that time by the UK and the US) to deposit its instrument of ratification in Moscow, and the Nationalist Chinese Government of Taiwan to deposit its instruments of ratification in Washington. Taiwan is also a member of a number of IGOs, e.g. it was admitted to the WTO as the 'Separate Customs Territory of Taiwan, Penghu, Kinmen and Matsu' with the short name of 'Chinese Taipei',[47] after the PRC agreed to its admission subject to the condition that the ROC would not become a member of the WTO until the PRC had been admitted to the WTO. Additionally, the ROC is a member of the Asian Development Bank under the name of 'Taiwan, China'.

Under international law Taiwan is not a State and is not recognised as being an entity which is separate and distinct from the PRC. However, it enjoys partial international personality which allows it to participate in international relations.

5.8 Mandates and trusteeship territories

Mandates and trusteeship territories are dealt with in Chapter 13.2.1.and 13.2.2.1. Currently, there are no trusteeship territories. Under a Compact of Free Association, which entered into force on 1 October 1994, the last trusteeship territory, Palau, became associated with the US.

The status of the people inhabiting trusteeship territories was defined by Judge Ammoun in the *Namibia* Case,[48] in the following terms:

Namibia, even at the periods when it had been reduced to the status of a German Colony or was subject to the South African Mandate, possessed a legal personality which was denied it only by the law, now obsolete . . . It nevertheless constituted a subject of law . . . possessing national sovereignty but lacking the exercise thereof . . . sovereignty . . . did not cease to belong to the people subject to mandate. It had simply, for a time, been rendered inarticulate and deprived of freedom of expression.

Consequently, such territories could not be regarded as attaining full legal personality until independence was achieved.

---

45   E. Freund Larus, *Taiwan's Quest for International Recognition* (2006) 42 Issues & Studies, 23.
46   480 UNTS 43.
47   WT/ACC/TPKM/18, 5 October 2001.
48   *Separate Opinion of Vice-President Ammoun* (1971) ICJ Rep 16, 68.

5.9   Insurgents, belligerents and national liberation movements

During armed conflicts some organised groups may become subjects of international law.

5.9.1   Insurgents and belligerents

During armed conflicts limited international personality may be granted to some insurgent groups and belligerents when they exercise *de facto* control over a part of a national territory, provided the requirements contained in the 1977 Additional Protocol I to the four 1949 Geneva Conventions are satisfied. The main objective of such recognition is to ensure the compliance of the parties involved in an armed conflict with IHL and HRL.

5.9.2   National liberation movements.

Following the adoption by the UNGA of the 1960 Declaration on the Granting of Independence to Colonial Countries and Peoples,[49] and the subsequent recognition that all colonial people have a right to self-determination, international law recognised that some 'pre-independent States' and national liberation movements have international personality in various gradations. For example, in the case of Guinea-Bissau, the international community decided to recognise it as a State when the African Party for the Independence of Guinea and Cape Verde (PAIGC), the national liberation movement of that territory, exercised *de facto* control over two-thirds of the territory of Portuguese Guinea. The Front for the Liberation of Mozambique (FRELIMO) in Mozambique was recognised as a national liberation movement when, by the late 1960s, it established 'liberated zones' in Northern Mozambique. With regard to Namibia, the South West Africa People's Organisation (SWAPO)[50] was recognised as the liberation movement of Namibia while the UN Council for Namibia, created by the UNGA in 1967[51] was, theoretically, in charge of administering the territory with a view to preparing it for self-governance, and accordingly had full legal personality.

On the basis of the Declaration of Principles of International Law concerning Friendly Relations and Co-operation among States in Accordance with the Charter of the United Nations,[52] the UNGA, granted observer status, which is normally reserved for sovereign States which are non-members of the UN, to many liberation movements in Africa and Asia in the 1970s and 1980s. Among them were: SWAPO in Namibia; the Frente POLISARIO in Western Sahara; FRELIMO in Mozambique and FRETILIN in East Timor.[53] National liberation movements, when recognised at the international level, are considered as representing their peoples. They have the necessary capacity to enter into international agreements with States and IGOs, are required to respect IHL and HRL, and their representatives enjoy the immunities necessary for the performance of their functions in States which have recognised them and in IGOs.

At the time of writing, the number of national liberation movements entitled to represent colonial people in their struggle for freedom is very limited. One of the remaining few is the Palestine Liberation Organisation (PLO). In 1974, the PLO was granted observer mission status at the UN. The head of

---

49   UNGA Res 1514 (XV) (14 December 1960) GAOR 15th Session Supp 16, 66.

50   UNGA Res 3111 (XXVIII) 'Question of Namibia' (12 December 1973) GAOR 28th Session Supp 30 vol 1, 93.

51   UNGA Res 2248 (S-V) 'Question of South West Africa' (19 May 1967) 5th Session Supp 1, 1.

52   UNGA Res 2625 (XXV) [24 October 1970] GAOR 25th Session Supp 28, 121.

53   H.A. Wilson, *International Law and the Use of Force by National Liberation Movements*, Oxford: Clarendon, 1988, 119–125.

the PLO was invited to address the UNGA, and representatives of the PLO have attended conferences and meetings organised under the auspices of the UN. Since 1988, the PLO has been participating in UNSC debates of interest to Palestine and has represented the Palestinian people at the UN under the name 'Palestine'. In September 2011, Mahmoud Abbas as President of Palestine and Chairman of the Executive Committee of the PLO, applied on behalf of Palestine for full admission to the UN.[54] The President of the UNSC referred the application to the Committee on the Admission of New Members which was unable to make a unanimous recommendation to the UNSC.[55] Its members could not agree on whether Palestine satisfied all the requirements of statehood. In particular, questions were raised as to whether Palestine had effective control over its territory in light of the Israeli occupation of the Palestinian territories and the fact that Hamas, not the PLO, controlled the Gaza Strip.[56] The Report did note that Palestine had obtained membership of the Non-Aligned Movement, the Organisation of Islamic Cooperation, the Economic and Social Commission of West Asia, the Group of 77, and the United Nations Education, Scientific and Cultural Organization (UNESCO) and had been recognised as an independent and sovereign State by over 130 States. The UNSC has not yet voted on the application for membership but it is unlikely that such a vote will be successful. In November 2012, however, the UNGA voted to grant Palestine the status of a non-member observer State[57] (see also Chapter 13.5.2). Subsequently, the 'State of Palestine' has become a contracting party to many HRs treaties, the Geneva Conventions and the Statute of the ICC. Nevertheless its statehood is highly debated (see Chapter.13.5.2).

5.10 Territories under UN administration

The UN administered the territories of East Timor and Kosovo on the basis of the following resolutions:

- Resolution 1244 (1999) of 10 June 1999, which established a United Nations Mission in Kosovo (UNMIK);

- Resolution 1272 (1999) of 25 October 1999 which created a United Nations Transitional Administration in East Timor (UNTAET).

During the UN administration, the UN performed all functions of a State i.e. it exercised legislative, executive and judicial functions and was in charge of conducting the external relations of both territories, e.g. the UNTAET, replaced Indonesia as the contracting party, and signed an agreement with Australia concerning the continuation of the operation of a treaty signed between Australia and Indonesia in 1989.

Each mission was headed by a UNS-G's Special Representative whose authority derived directly from the above UNSC resolutions. Each mission was designed as a mechanism for transition of these territories to self-governance. In the case of East Timor, it became an independent State in May 2002

---

54   See Application of Palestine for admission to membership of the UN, A/66/371-S/2011/592. On this topic: J. Vidmar, *Palestine and the Conceptual Problem of Implicit Statehood* (2013) 12/1 Chinese Journal of International Law, 19.

55   See Report of the Committee on the Admission of New Members concerning the application of Palestine for admission to membership of the United Nations, S/2011/705, 11 November 2011.

56   Ibid, paras 11–12.

57   See United Nations, 'General Assembly Votes Overwhelmingly to Accord Palestine 'Non-Member Observer State' Status in United Nations' 29 November 2012 available at www.un.org/press/en/2012/ga11317.doc.htm (accessed 10 September 2014).

and was admitted to the UN as the Democratic Republic of Timor-Leste in 2002.[58] Kosovo declared its independence on 17 February 2008 but is unlikely to become a member of the UN in the light of the strong opposition from Russia although President Putin relied on the case of Kososvo to justify the annexation of Crimea. However, Kosovo has become a member of the World Bank, the IMF and other IGOs and is recognised by many States (see Chapter.13.7.3.1.B).

Neither East Timor, nor Kosovo when they were under the transitional administration of the UN, had international personality because they did not then satisfy the criteria for statehood. The authority exercised by the UN in respect of both territories was *sui generis*. It shows some similarities with the traditional condominium, or the system of protectorate but also displays important differences in that the UN had no claim to permanent sovereignty over those territories. It is to be noted that the UNGA resolutions establishing the missions were not based on the trusteeship provisions of the UN Charter (see Chapter 13.2.2.1).

The above UN missions satisfied all the requirements for international personality and were therefore subjects of international law.

5.11 International governmental organisations (IGOs)

An IGO must satisfy the following conditions to have legal personality under international law:

- it must be a permanent association of States;

- it must be created to attain certain objectives,

- it must have administrative organs;

- it must exercise some power that is distinct from the sovereign power of its member States; and

- its competences must be exercisable on an international level and not confined exclusively to the national systems of its member States.

5.11.1 Legal personality of IGOs

The leading judicial authority on the personality of IGOs is contained in the *Reparation for Injuries Suffered in the Service of the United Nations (Advisory Opinion)* [59]

REPARATION FOR INJURIES SUFFERED IN THE SERVICE OF THE UNITED NATIONS (ADVISORY OPINION)

Facts:

On 17 September 1948, the UN's chief truce negotiator, a Swedish national, Count Folke Bernardotte, and an UN observer, a Frenchman, Colonel André Sérot, were assassinated by Jewish terrorist organisations, while on an official mission for the UN. They were murdered in the eastern part of Jerusalem, which was under Israeli control, at the time when Israel had proclaimed its independence, but had not yet been admitted to the UN. The UN alleged

---

58   S/Res 1414 (2002) of 23 May 202; UNGA Res 57/3 of 27 September 2002.
59   ICJ Rep 174.

that Israel had neglected to prevent or punish the murderers, and wished to make a claim against Israel for compensation under international law. The UNGA sought the advice of the ICJ as to the legal capacity of the UN to make such a claim.

Held:

The Court held that the UN possessed an international judicial personality and was therefore capable of presenting such a claim with a view to obtaining reparation in respect of the damage caused to both its assets and its agents (the so-called functional protection). The ICJ stated that:

> *In the opinion of the Court, the organisation was intended to exercise and enjoy, and is in fact exercising and enjoying, functions and rights which can be explained on the basis of the possession of a large measure of international personality and the capacity to operate upon an international plane. It is at present the supreme type of international organisation, and it could not carry out the intentions of its founders if it was devoid of international personality . . . Accordingly, the Court has come to the conclusion that the organisation is an international person. That is not the same thing as saying that it is a State, which it certainly is not, or that its legal personality and rights and duties are the same as those of a State. Still less is it the same thing as saying that it is a 'super-state', whatever that expression may mean. It does not even imply that all its rights and duties must be upon that plane. What it does mean is that it is a subject of international law and capable of possessing international rights and duties, and that it has capacity to maintain its rights by bringing international claims.[60]*

It must be remembered, however, that when States create an international organisation they set it up for specific purposes and in this respect legal personality must be treated as being relative to those purposes. Therefore, in order to determine whether an organisation has legal competence to perform a particular act both its express and implied purposes and functions must be taken into consideration. As the ICJ emphasised:

> *Under international law, the organisation must be deemed to have those powers which, though not expressly provided in the Charter, are conferred upon it by necessary implication as being essential to the performance of its duties.[61]*

Consequently, the question whether an international organisation possesses international personality can only be answered by examining its functions and powers expressly conferred by, or to be implied from, its constitution and developed in practice.

With regard to the issue of whether the UN had capacity to bring a claim for reparation against a non-State member the ICJ decided that:

> *[F]ifty States, representing the vast majority of the members of the international community, had the power, in conformity with international law, to bring into being an entity possessing objective international personality, and not merely personality recognized by them alone, together with capacity to bring international claims.[62]*

---

60   Ibid, 179.
61   Ibid, 182.
62   Ibid, 185.

Comment:

As can be seen from the above, the ICJ found that the UN had objective international personality. The distinction between objective and specific (or relative) personality is that objective international personality operates erga omnes, i.e against all subjects of international law, while a specific (or relative) international personality is bestowed by subjects of international law on an entity in question, and thus it is relative in the sense that it has to be recognised by other subjects in order to exist. The justification for specific international personality is that the principle of the pacta tertiis nec nocent nec prosunt *requires that a third party to an agreement cannot be bound by it. Only States and the UN possess objective international personality.*

The ICJ explained that the UN possesses an objective international personality because of its almost universal membership. This reasoning is, however, difficult to accept in that it is contrary to the principle that a third State cannot be bound by agreements entered into by other States and therefore as long as there are States which are non-members of the UN, they should not be required to recognise an organisation to which they are not contracting parties. This is despite the fact that, at the time of writing, 193 States are members of the UN. Further, it can be said that nowadays IGOs other than the UN also enjoy quasi-universal membership, and thus should accordingly possess objective international personality. The fact remains that the ICJ decided that the UN was a special case due to its quasi-universal membership and its universal mission.

Follow up:

The UN proceeded with a claim against Israel. In June 1950, Israel paid the sum claimed by the UN and apologised for the assassination and for its failure to find and prosecute the culprits.[63]

5.11.2 Factors relevant to the establishment of legal personality of an IGO.

The following factors are of relevance.

5.11.2.1 Status under municipal law

Most treaties setting up IGOs contain a clause providing for those IGOs to enjoy legal personality under the municipal laws of their contracting States. Usually the clause is similar to Article 104 of the UN Charter which states that:

the organisation shall enjoy in the territory of each of its members such legal capacity as may be necessary for the exercise of its functions and the fulfilment of its purposes.

---

63   'Letter Dated 14 June 1950 from the Minister for Foreign Affairs of the Government of Israel to the Secretary-General concerning a Claim for Damage Caused to the United Nations by the Assassination of Count Folke Bernadotte and a Reply Thereto from the Secretary-General' [14 June 1950] UN Doc S/1506.

It is doubtful that international personality can be deduced from such a grant of municipal personality, although some writers have argued that the granting of this personality may be recognition of that status.

5.11.2.2 Treaty-making power

The most important attribute of an IGO in respect of international personality is the right to enter into international agreements with States who are not members of it on matters within the organisation's competence. Such treaty-making power is strong evidence of international personality.

5.11.2.3 International claims

If the constitution of an IGO provides for the settlement of disputes by arbitration or other international adjudication this may be of relevance in deciding its status, the power to present claims on the international plane being one of the basic rights of international personality.

5.11.2.4 General powers

It is apparent from the Advisory Opinion in the *Reparations for Injuries Suffered in the Service of the United Nations* case (above) that the whole powers of an IGO must be considered. These will include the implied powers conferred on it by its member States in order for it to perform the duties required under its constitution.

One example of an IGO is the EU. Member States conferred distinct legal personality on both the European Community (EC) and the European Atomic Energy Community (Euratom) but for many years the EU itself had no legal personality. This has changed with the entry into force of the Treaty of Lisbon, which in Article 47 TEU recognises the legal personality of the EU. The Treaty of Lisbon merged the EC and the EU with the consequence that the EU replaced and succeeded to the legal personality of the EC.

The EU has the capacity to enter into relations and to conclude treaties with third States and other organisations (*jus tractatus*), to engage in diplomacy (*jus missionis*) and to sue an individual State for injuries to it, and to be sued. Further, the EU is the only international organisation that possesses and exercises the independent power to make decisions binding on its member States, their nationals and corporate bodies and, in some circumstances, foreign corporations. The EU, to a certain extent, exercises powers similar to those of sovereign States.

5.12 Individuals

International law creates rights and duties for individuals capable of being enforced before international courts, tribunals and other bodies. Individuals are subjects of international law. However, as their rights and duties, including procedural rights allowing them to bring claims against a State, are ultimately controlled by States they are only partial subjects of international law.

5.12.1 The acquisition of rights by individuals

The possibility that individuals may have rights and duties deriving directly from international law was recognised for the first time by the PCIJ in the *Case Concerning Competences of the Courts of*

Danzig (Advisory Opinion),[64] in which it was held that an exception to the principle that individuals are not subjects of international law arises if the intention of the contracting parties was to adopt a treaty which creates rights and obligations for individuals capable of being enforced by municipal courts. The PCIJ emphasised that this intention must be express and not inferred from the treaty since this kind of international treaty constitutes an exception to a general principle. Such treaties are defined under international law as 'self-executing'. They become automatically part of the national law of the contracting parties and are directly applicable by the national courts.

Many international human rights treaties entered into after WWII have conferred rights on individuals which can be enforced directly before international courts, tribunals and other bodies (see Chapter 12). In some cases, individuals have acquired those rights without the intervention of municipal legislation.

A new step in the recognition of international personality of individuals was taken by the ICJ in the *Case of LaGrand (Germany v United States of America)*[65] (for facts see Chapter 14.7.5.3). In this case the Court found that Article 36 (1) of the Vienna Convention on Consular Relations (VCCR)[66] created rights for individuals and thus confirmed the fact that individual's rights do not have to derive only from classical human rights treaties or from 'self-executing' treaties but may also flow from any treaty concluded between States, e.g. a treaty concluded between States regulating consular relations between them.

The ICJ held that Article 36(1) VCCR contains rights of individuals which they themselves can invoke, and rights of a State, which a State may invoke on behalf of its nationals. The judgment not only confirms that HRs are a pervasive phenomenon affecting nearly all areas of international law but also challenges the principle set out in the *Case Concerning Competences of the Courts of Danzig (Advisory Opinion)* that the express consent of the parties to a treaty is necessary for a provision to have direct effect, i.e. to be enforceable by an individual before a national court. In this case, the ICJ implicitly agreed that the Article 36 VCCR due process rights of detained foreign nationals have the legal character of HRs. However, the ICJ was unwilling to explore the relationship between an individual's right to receive consular assistance, and procedural human rights, such as the right to a fair trial. This issue was, nevertheless, fully examined by the Inter-American Court of Human Rights (IACHR) in its *Advisory Opinion on the Right to Information on Consular Assistance*.[67] In it the IACHR unanimously stated that Article 36 VCCR confers on all foreign nationals specific legal and human rights including the right to consular notification 'without delay' and the right to consular assistance to ensure due process. The Court emphasised that failure of a contracting State to inform a foreign national of his consular rights followed by execution of that person is in breach of the right to life of the individual concerned, and constitutes an 'arbitrary deprivation of life'. Further, the Court found that the right granted under Article 36 VCCR entails a procedural remedy in international law. The Court linked the right under Article 36 VCCR with the right to due process of law prescribed in Article 14 ICCPR. It concluded that in the light of Article 36 VCCR and Article 14 ICCPR when a contracting State to the VCCR fails to honour rights prescribed in Article 36 VCCR, it violates the foreign national's human right to due process of law and therefore that national can sue directly, or immediately, without having to rely on his or her State to sue on his or her behalf.

---

64   (1928) PCIJ Rep Ser B No 15.
65   [2001] ICJ Rep 466.
66   596 UNTS 261.
67   Advisory Opinion OC-16/99, October 1, 1999, (1999) Inter-Am Ct HR (Ser A) No 16.

5.12.2 The imposition of direct obligations and responsibilities on individuals

The 1946 Judgment[68] of the International Military Tribunal (IMT) at Nuremberg established, for the first time, that individuals have obligations arising under international law. The impact of the judgment on the recognition of individuals as subjects of international law was essential in that it confirmed a direct relationship between individuals and international law. However, the 1946 Judgment, because of defects which are examined below, was challenged as representing 'victor' justice. International criminal courts subsequently created by the international community, i.e. the International Criminal Tribunal for the Former Yugoslavia (ICTY), the International Criminal Tribunal for Rwanda (ICTR) and the International Criminal Court (ICC) are based on different premises. Their creation has not been motivated by the desire for revenge of a winning party in an armed conflict, but constitutes a genuine response of the international community to the worst abuses of HRL and IHL.

5.12.2.1 The International Military Tribunal (IMT) at Nuremberg

At the end of WWII the allied nations had to decide how to deal with high-ranking Nazis. Some proposed that they should be shot without trial; others that they should be prosecuted and brought to justice before an international court. The latter solution was approved by the US, the UK, France and the Soviet Union (and subsequently by another 19 States) whose representatives signed on 8 August 1945 the London Agreement for the Prosecution and Punishment of the Major War Criminals.

On the basis of the London Agreement the International Military Tribunal (IMT)[69] at Nuremberg was established to bring to justice the major Nazi war criminals. It provided for new and original solutions since there was no legal basis under positive international law for prosecuting alleged war criminals (although it was submitted that some of the Geneva Conventions, the Hague Conventions and the 1928 Kellogg-Briand Pact provided a legal basis for such proceedings and, additionally, an argument can be made that the crimes of the Nazis and their collaborators violated natural law).[70]

The Charter of the International Military Tribunal[71] was annexed to the London Agreement. Under the Charter the charges against the accused were to be brought on any of four counts:

- conspiracy to wage wars of aggression;

- crimes against peace;

- war crimes;

- crimes against humanity.

The Tribunal consisted of eight judges, two each from: the US, the UK, the Soviet Union and France. The proceedings were commenced on 20 November 1945 and ended on 1 October 1946.

Charges were brought against 22 defendants, of whom only 21 were present. Bormann, who was never found, was tried *in absentia*.

There were a number of important matters which challenged the neutrality and the legitimacy of the Nuremberg trial.

---

68   *Judgment of the Nuremberg International Military Tribunal* 1946 (1947) 41 AJIL, 172.
69   UN Doc A/CN.
70   T. Mertens, *Radbruch and Hart on the Grudge Informer: A Reconsideration* (2002)15/2 Ratio Juris 186–205.
71   82 UNTS 251.

1   International law did not provide solid grounds for prosecuting alleged war criminals. In this respect, the most relevant were Articles 226–228 of the Treaty of Versailles 1919[72] establishing the right of allied nations to prosecute and punish individuals responsible for 'violation of the laws and customs of war'. Article 228 stated that 'the German Government recognises the right of the Allied and Associated Powers to bring before military tribunals persons accused of having committed acts in violation of the laws and customs of war'. Of relevant interest is the fact that under Article 227 of the Treaty of Versailles German Kaiser Wilhelm II of Hohenzollern was stated to be guilty of 'supreme offence against international morality and the sanctity of the treaties'. The Allied powers agreed to set up a special international tribunal made up of judges from the US, the UK, Italy and France to try him. However, the Allied powers had never submitted a formal request for the surrender of the Kaiser and the idea of an international trial of the German Kaiser Wilhelm II was abandoned.

Furthermore, the 1928 Kellogg-Briand Pact which was ratified by both Germany and Japan outlawed war but did not provide for any enforcement mechanism. Thus, the Pact did not provide for criminal sanctions if its provisions were breached. The IMT Charter, based on the idealistic objective of outlawing war in accordance with Article 2(4) of the UN Charter, created brand new laws and applied them retrospectively to the accused contrary to the fundamental principles of any criminal law, that is *nulla poena sine lege*, *nulla crima sine lege*. As a result, the accused might reasonably have been able to argue that their trial was in breach of those fundamental principles.

2   The defence could neither challenge the legitimacy of the tribunal nor raise some defences. For example, the accused were barred from submitting the argument that the Allied forces themselves committed similar offences (the '*tu quoque*' argument – 'you did it too') such as indiscriminate bombing of civilians in the raids on Hamburg, Berlin and Dresden or waging aggressive war.

3   The defence was seriously handicapped by lack of adequate lawyers, lack of adequate back-up staff, lack of resources, etc. It was paradoxical that the accused, Hermann Goering, submitted personally, and without the aid of the lawyer, the most effective arguments in his defence.

4   The jurisdiction of the IMT was based on the conquest of Germany, and the co-imperium exercised by the occupying powers over Germany.

It is interesting to note that the most important Nazi criminals were already dead. Hitler committed suicide on 30 April 1945 and Goebbels, his minister of propaganda, killed himself and his family on 1 May 1945. Himmler and Heydrich, the principal organisers of the 'final solution' in the course of which six million Jews were killed, were both dead, Himmler by suicide after capture, and Heydrich through assassination earlier in the war. One of the most important Nazi officials captured by the allied forces Reichmarshall Hermann Goering was put on trial despite the fact that there was no documentary evidence linking him conclusively with the 'final solution'. The IMT acquitted only three defendants (Papen, Schacht and Fritzsche), 11 were found guilty on all four counts and condemned to death, the remainder were found guilty and were sentenced to lengthy terms of imprisonment. Reichmarshall Goering was condemned to death but died a few hours before the intended execution by swallowing a concealed cyanide capsule.

The main contributions of the IMT at Nuremberg to the development of international criminal law were as follows.

---

72   225 CTS 189.

1   The Tribunal established the principle that individuals could be liable under international law. In this respect the judgment of the IMT stated that:

> Crimes against international law are committed by men, not by abstract entities, and only by punishing individuals who commit such crimes can the provisions of international law be enforced.[73]

All the accused argued that States were subjects of international law, not individuals, and therefore individuals neither had obligations under international law nor could they be punished under international law. The accused emphasised that their only obligations were to the Nazi state which was liable under international law. Furthermore, they submitted that their acts were acts of State and consequently those who carried them out were not liable because of the doctrine of the sovereignty of the State. Both arguments were rejected by the IMT which stated that:

> individuals have international duties which transcend the national obligations of obedience imposed by the individual state [to which they owe allegiance]. He who violates the laws of war cannot obtain immunity while acting in pursuance of the authority of the state if that state in authorising action moves outside its competence under international law.[74]

2   The Tribunal dealt with the matters of both the official position held by the defendants in the Nazi government and of 'superior orders'. Article 7 of the IMT Charter provided that the official position of the defendant, whether as Head of State or an official in the government would neither exonerate him from responsibility nor mitigate the punishment, while Article 8 rejected any defence based on the following of orders of the government or of a superior, but accepted that this may be considered in mitigation of punishment. The Nuremberg Tribunal stated in this respect that: 'The true test, which is found in varying degrees in the criminal law of most nations, is not the existence of the order, but whether moral choice was in fact possible.'

3   Article 6 of the Charter of the IMT stated that individuals could be liable for crimes against peace, war crimes and crimes against humanity. It defined these crimes as follows:
   (a) Crimes against peace: namely planning, preparing, initiating or waging of a war of aggression, or a war in violation of international treaties, agreements or assurances, or participation in a common plan or conspiracy for the accomplishment of any of the foregoing.
   (b) War crimes: namely, violations of the laws or customs of war. Such violations shall include, but not be limited to, murder, ill-treatment or deportation to slave labour or any other purpose of civilian population of or in occupied territory, murder or ill-treatment of prisoners of war or persons on the seas, killing of hostages, plunder of public or private property, wanton destruction of cities, towns or villages, or devastation not justified by military necessity.
   (c) Crimes against humanity: namely, murder, extermination, enslavement, deportation, and other inhumane acts committed against any civilian population, before or during the war; or persecution on political, racial or religious grounds in execution of or in connection with any crime within the jurisdiction of the Tribunal, whether or not in violation of the domestic law of the country where perpetrated.

The definition of the war crimes given above was in conformity with customary and treaty law in this area. War crimes constitute violations of the rules applicable to the conduct of armed conflict, and

---

73   *Judgment of the Nuremberg International Military Tribunal* 1946 (1947) 41 AJIL, 221.
74   Ibid.

were recognised as crimes under international law by Articles 45, 50, 52 and 56 of the Hague Convention IV 1907, and Articles 2, 3, 4, 46 and 51 of the Geneva Convention Relating to the Amelioration of the Condition of the Wounded and Sick in Armies in the Field 1929.

However, crimes against peace and crimes against humanity were introduced by the IMT Charter into international law. In particular, the recognition that crimes against humanity are so hideous that the international community as a whole is empowered to prosecute and try offenders constitutes one of the most important legacies of the IMT. Under the IMT Charter the Tribunal had jurisdiction over crimes against humanity where such crimes were related to war crimes and over crimes against peace. As a result, crimes committed by the Nazi regime before WWII were left unpunished.

Both, the 'crimes against peace' and the 'crimes against humanity' raised many controversies, especially in respect of the defendants before the IMT as they were charged with these offences which did not exist at the relevant time. These controversies were resolved shortly after the Nuremberg judgment when the UNGA unanimously adopted Resolution 95 (I) on the Affirmation of the Principles of International Law Recognised by the Charter of the Nuremberg Tribunal 1946.[75] The word 'affirmation' is very important. It suggests that the IMT applied principles which already existed under customary law, and thus the IMT had only to 'recognise' them. Consequently the UNGA confirmed them. Further, the UNGA asked the ILC to codify them.[76] On the basis of the UNGA Resolution many countries enacted national legislation in order to prosecute lower level Nazi criminals before national courts.

As a result of the fact that the IMT's Charter definition of crimes against humanity mentioned genocide an autonomous concept of the crime of genocide has evolved. In Resolution 260 of 9 December 1948 the UNGA adopted the Convention on the Prevention and Punishment of the Crime of Genocide,[77] in which genocide is recognised as a crime under international law, which the contracting parties undertake to prevent and punish (Article I of the Genocide Convention).[78]

5.12.2.2   The International Criminal Tribunal for the Former Yugoslavia (ICTY) and the International Criminal Tribunal for Rwanda (ICTR)

Both the above tribunals were created in response to the atrocities committed in the territory of the former Yugoslavia and in Rwanda. Both were set up by UNSC resolutions adopted under Chapter VII.[79]

The ICTY is located at The Hague in the Netherlands while the ICTR is located in Arusha, in the United Republic of Tanzania.

The jurisdiction of the tribunals is as follows:

■ *Ratione materiae*: the ICTY has jurisdiction over grave breaches of the 1949 Geneva Conventions (Article 2 of the Statute of the ICTY), violations of the laws or customs of war (Article 3), genocide (Article 4) and crimes against humanity (Article 5). The ICTR jurisdiction includes: genocide, crimes against humanity, violations of Article 3 common to the 1949 Geneva Conventions and of the 1977 Additional Protocol II to the Geneva Conventions. Its main focus is the crime of genocide.

---

75   UNGA Res 95 (I) (11 December 1946) GAOR 1st Session Resolutions 188.
76   The ILC codified the Nuremberg Principles in 1950, [1950] UNYB 852.
77   78 UNTS 277.
78   On this topic see: W. Schabas, *Genocide in International Law*, 2nd edn, Cambridge: Cambridge University Press, 2009.
79   UNSC Resolution 827 (1993) [25 May 1993] set up the ICTY and UNSC Resolution 955 (1994) [8 November 1994] set up the ICTR.

- *Ratione tempore*: the ICTY has jurisdiction in respect of crimes committed since 1991; that of the ICTR is limited to crimes committed between 1 January and 31 December 1994.

- *Ratione personae* and *ratione loci*: the ICTY has jurisdiction over crimes committed in the territory of the former Yugoslavia; the nationality of the victims and the offenders is irrelevant. The ICTR has jurisdiction over crimes committed by Rwandans in the territory of Rwanda and in the territory of neighbouring States, and crimes committed by non-Rwandans in Rwanda.

Both the ICTY and the ICTR are truly international criminal tribunals in terms of their composition, the condition of their establishment and the principles of international law they apply under their respective statutes. The argument of 'victor' justice (see Chapter 5.12.2.1) cannot apply to them.

5.12.2.3 The International Criminal Court (ICC)

The ICC is the first permanent, independent, international criminal court. It was established on the basis of the provisions of the Rome Statute[80] of the ICC which entered into force on 1 July 2002. As at 9 November 2014, 122 States were contracting parties to it. The ICC is not an organ of the UN but the UNSC has power to intervene in the initiation or deferment of the investigation of some cases (Articles 16 and 13(b) of the Statute) (see Chapter 17.6.2).

The main task of the ICC is to try persons accused of the most serious crimes, namely genocide, crimes against humanity, and war crimes.[81]

The Rome Statute reiterates the general principles of criminal law: *nullum crimen sine lege, nulla poena sine lege*, and the principle of non-retroactivity meaning that no person can be brought before the Court for crimes committed before the entry into force of the Statute. Article 25 confirms individual criminal responsibility. Article 27 states that the official capacity of the accused will have no relevance to his guilt and shall not, in itself, constitute a ground for reduction of sentence. Article 28 deals with the responsibility of commanders and other superiors. Article 33 of the Statute sets out grounds which exempt from criminal responsibility a person who, pursuant to an order of a superior or of his government, committed what would otherwise have been a crime within the Court's jurisdiction. These are where:

- the person was under a legal obligation to obey such an order;

- the person did not know that the order was unlawful;

- the order was not manifestly unlawful. However, Article 33(2) specifies that orders to commit genocide or crimes against humanity are manifestly unlawful.

5.12.3 Access to international bodies and tribunals by individuals

Access to international bodies and tribunals by individuals, who allege that their HRs have been violated, is discussed in Chapter 12.

---

80   2187 UNTS 90.

81   On the future jurisdiction of the ICC over the crime of aggression see Chapter 16.2.2.1.B.

5.13 Non-governmental organisations (NGOs)

In the modern sense NGOs appeared in the nineteenth century, e.g. the ICRC (see Chapter 17.7) and the British and Foreign Anti-Slavery Society. Nowadays, there is a myriad of NGOs with a variety of aims. They are active in all possible areas, *inter alia*, science, culture, health, education, economic matters, the protection of human rights and the protection of the environment. They carry out valuable charitable and philanthropic work in the areas of their competence. Probably the most prominent NGOs are those which are active in the humanitarian and human rights fields, e.g. the ICRC, *Médécins Sans Frontières*, Amnesty International, Human Rights Watch, and in the protection of the environment, e.g. Greenpeace.

It is submitted that, perhaps, the best definition of an NGO of interest to international law is contained in the 1986 European Convention on the Recognition of the Legal Personality of International Non-Governmental Organisations[82] which sets out the following criteria for recognition of an NGO under the Convention:

- it must be an association, a foundation or other private institution;

- it must have a non-profit-making aim of international utility. This means that an NGO may make profit, e.g. selling a publication, but any profit must be used for a non-profit-making aim. Further, the aim must be of international utility and not simply of national or local utility, i.e. the benefit must be to the international community;

- it must be established by an instrument governed by municipal law;

- its activities must be carried on in at least two States;

- it must have its statutory office in a contracting State and its central management and control in that State or another contracting State.

The last two criteria are relevant to NGOs which wish 'as of right' to have the legal personality and capacity which they have acquired in a contracting State where they have their statutory offices recognised by any other contracting party. It is to be noted that the 1986 Convention has not been successful. It is in force but, as at 9 November 2014, it had been ratified by only 11 States of the 47 member States of the Council of Europe.

At the universal level, the UN Economic and Social Council (ECOSOC), acting under Article 71 of the UN Charter confers consultative status on NGOs, the mandates of which accord with 'the spirit, purpose and principles of the Charter'.[83] When a NGO is granted consultative status it may attend the relevant international conferences convened by the UN and participates in preparatory work of the said conferences.

The ECOSOC Committee on Non-Governmental Organisations is in charge of recommending to the ECOSOC whether an applicant NGO should be granted consultative status.[84] The Committee's decision is based on the 1996 criteria which provide that a NGO, whether international, regional, sub-regional or national non-governmental, non-profit public or voluntary organisation, must, *inter alia*, be registered under national law, have an established headquarters, a democratically adopted constitution, authority to speak for its members, a representative structure, appropriate mechanisms of accountability

---

82   ETS 124.
83   ECOSOC Res 1296 (XLIV), 23 May 1968.
84   The list of NGOs which have been granted consultative status is available at: http://esango.un.org/civilsociety/documents/E_2013_INF_6.pdf (accessed 9 November 2014).

and democratic and transparent decision-making processes. Any financial support which a NGO receives from a government must be declared to the Committee. As at 1 September 2013, a total of 3,999 NGOs had been granted consultative status.

Among NGOs one, the ICRC (see Chapter 17.7), a private association established under Swiss law, has been recognised as enjoying partial international personality similar to that of the UN. This was acknowledged by the ICTY in a decision concerning the testimony of an ICRC witness[85] where the ICRC presented evidence based on the recognition of its work by international treaties, its treaty-making capacity which allows it to enter into agreements with States, its immunities which are comparable to those of the UN including inviolability of premises and documents, its immunity from judicial process as well as its testimonial privilege (i.e. the right not to be called as a witness) and its status of observer granted by the UNGA. The prosecutor did not challenge the evidence.

No NGO, other than the ICRC, is recognised as a subject of international law. This is despite the fact that NGOs:

■ participate in the institutional process of international law-making, particularly, in their consultative capacity (see Chapter 2.12);

■ initiate and are often the driving force behind the conclusion of international treaties (e.g. the creation of the ICC; the Ottawa Convention on the Prohibition of the Use, Stockpiling, Production and Transfer of Anti-Personnel Mines and on Their Destruction; the 1984 Torture Convention and the 2002 Optional Protocol to it; and the UNIDROIT Convention on Mobile Equipment;

■ participate in monitoring compliance of States with treaties, and continuously encourage States to ratify treaties (e.g. to accede to the Rome Statute of the ICC);

■ encourage and assist victims of violations of international law to seek judicial remedy;

■ have *locus standi* before some international courts and bodies: e.g. the African Court of Human Rights; the Inter-American Human Rights Commission (IACommHR), and (with the consent of the victim) before the Inter-American Court of Human Rights (IACHR). Further, they can bring proceedings before national courts, even against a State;[86] and

■ submit *amicus curiae* before some international courts (the ECtHR and the IACtHR).

NGOs sometimes prove themselves to be more powerful and efficient than the UN. Their impact on public opinion is tremendous. For example, when the Royal Dutch Shell company, after obtaining approval from the relevant national and international authorities, decided to sink its Brent Spar rig to the ocean floor, Greenpeace launched a campaign to boycott Shell gasoline. Within weeks, Shell's sales in Germany were down by 30 per cent at which point Shell chose a course which avoided the sinking of the rig. Since this incident, Shell consults Greenpeace regarding the decommissioning of its rigs.[87]

The main criticism of NGOs is their lack of transparency and accountability.

---

85   *Prosecutor v Simic*, Decision of 27 July 1999, para 35.

86   *Greenpeace, Inc (USA) v The State of France* 946 F Supp 773 (1996).

87   This example is given by P.J. Spiro, *New Players on the International Stage*, (1997) 2 Hofstra L & Pol'y Sump19, 21.

5.14 Multinational corporations (MNCs)

MNCs, also often referred to as transnational corporations or enterprises, are corporations with wholly or partially controlled subsidiaries in more than one country. Historic examples of powerful MNCs are:

■ The Hanseatic League[88] formed in the 1280s when Northern German towns and merchants which dominated trade in the Baltic Sea region joined in association with merchants operating in Flanders and England. All trade in the region around the Baltic and North Seas was monopolised by the League. Although the League's objectives were mainly commercial, when its interests were threatened in 1368 it raised an army and crushed the Danes who subsequently signed the 1370 Treaty of Stralsund acknowledging free trade in the entire Baltic Sea region and recognising the League's monopoly on the Baltic fish trade. At its zenith, the League had a membership of about 160 towns and its assembly enacted legislation binding on all Hanseatic towns.

■ The British East India Company[89] and the Hudson Bay Company.[90] These two companies were founded in the seventeenth century. Their powers were huge. For example, the British East India Company was allowed to acquire territory, to make war and peace and to exercise civil and criminal jurisdiction over the Indian subcontinent.

MNCs may have a beneficial effect on a country where they operate by creating wealth, employment and introducing new technology, but they may also have disastrous effects. The latter may occur particularly in developing countries where MNCs' dominance may disrupt the traditional economy, distort competition, and allow MNCs to assert their own political and economic agenda on a State. Further, from the perspective of the protection of HRs and the environment, MNCs, not being subjects of international law, can only be held accountable under domestic law. Obviously any claim against them at a national level in a country which they, in effect, run is impractical, and in the country of the parent company is likely not to be successful.[91] Any attempts at imposing binding obligations on MNCs at the international level have so far failed. However, in June 2014 the UN Human Rights Council (UNHRC), adopted a resolution entitled 'Elaboration of an International Legally Binding Instrument on Transnational Corporations and other Business Enterprises with Respect to Human Rights', which provides for the establishment of an open-ended inter-governmental working group with a view to drafting such an instrument[92] (see Chapter 2.12.3). If the initiative of the UNHRC obtains support from States, which seems unlikely, and legally binding rules are imposed on MNCs to respect HRs then it would be difficult to argue that they do not have international personality.[93] In the meantime the main arguments for MNCs' candidacy to international legal personality are that:

---

88   P. Dollinger, *The German Hansa*, London and Basignstoke: Macmillan, 1970.
89   P. Lawson, *The East India Company: A History*, London: Longman, 1993.
90   P.C. Newman, *Empire of the Bay. The Company of Adventurers that Seized a Continent*, New York: Penguin Group, 1998.
91   See e.g. L.J. Connell, Establishing Liability for Multinational Oil Companies in Parent/Subsidiary Relationships, Case Note: *A.Г. Akpan & Anor v Royal Dutch Shell plc & Anor* District Court of The Hague, 30 January 2013, LJN BY9854/HA ZA 09–1580,(2014) 16/1 Environmental Law Review, 50.
92   A/HRC/26/L.22.
93   On the topic of legal personality of MNCs see: K. Nowrot, 'Reconceptualising International Legal Personality of Influential Non-State Actors: towards a Rebuttable Presumption of Normative Responsibilities' in J. Fleurs (ed), *International Legal Personality*, Farnham: Ashgate, 2010, 369 *et seq.*

■ They can bring proceedings against a State before the International Centre for Settlement of Investment Disputes (ICSID) during which they are treated on an equal footing with the respondent State. Further, MNCs have capacity to bring claims against a State before, *inter alia*, the Iran-United States Claims Tribunal, the United Nations Compensation Commission (UNCC); the World Bank Inspection Panels; the ECtHR and the IACHR and to institute process following the complaints procedure under Article 14 of the 1993 North American Agreement on Environmental Co-operation. Therefore, the argument is that as they have international capacity to complain to international bodies, under the relevant treaties, they ought to be regarded as subjects of international law.

■ They participate in treaty-making in the areas of their activities (see Chapter 2.12.3).

RECOMMENDED READING

Books

Clapham, A., *Human Rights Obligations of Non-State Actors*, Oxford: Oxford University Press, 2006.
Crawford, J., *The Creation of States in International Law*, 2nd edn, Oxford: Oxford University Press, 2006
Fleurs, J. (ed.), *International Legal Personality*, Farnham: Ashgate, 2010.
Higgins, R., *Problems and Process: International Law and How we Use it*, Oxford: Clarendon Press, 1994.
Nijman, J.E.,*The Concept of International Legal Personality: An Inquiry into the History and Theory of International Law*, The Hague: Asser, 2004.
Portman, R., *Legal Personality in International Law*, Cambridge; Cambridge University Press, 2010.
Schabas, W.A., *An Introduction to the International Criminal Court*, 2nd edn, Cambridge: Cambridge University Press, 2004.
Wilson, H.A., *International Law and the Use of Force by National Liberation Movements*, Oxford: Clarendon Press, 1988.

Articles

Acquaviva, G., *Subjects of International Law: A Power-Based Analysis* (2005) 38 Vand J Transnatl L, 345.
Alvarez, E., *International Organizations: Then and Now* (2006) 100 AJIL, 324.
Charnovitz, S., *Non-governmental Organizations and International Law* (2006) 100 AJIL, 348.
Crawford, J., *The Criteria for Statehood in International Law* (1976–7) 48 BYIL, 93.
Huang, E.T-L., *Taiwan's Status in a Changing World: United Nations Representation and Membership for Taiwan* (2003) 9 Annual Survey of International and Comparative Law, 55.
Militello, V., *The Personal Nature of Individual Criminal Responsibility and the ICC Statute* (2007) 5 J Int Criminal Justice, 941.
O'Connell, M.E.,*Enhancing the Status of Non-State Actors through a Global War on Terror?* (2005) 43 Colum J Transnatl L, 435.
Vidmar, J., *Palestine and the Conceptual Problem of Implicit Statehood* (2013) 12/1 Chinese Journal of International Law, 19.

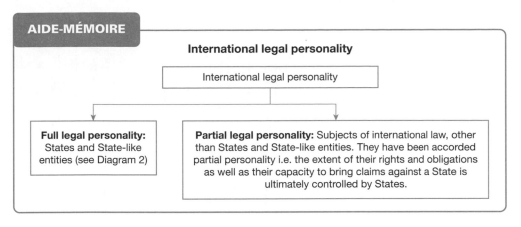

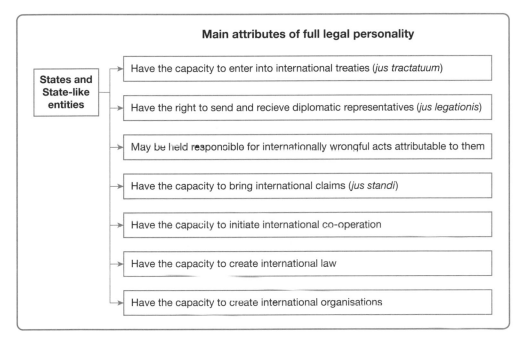

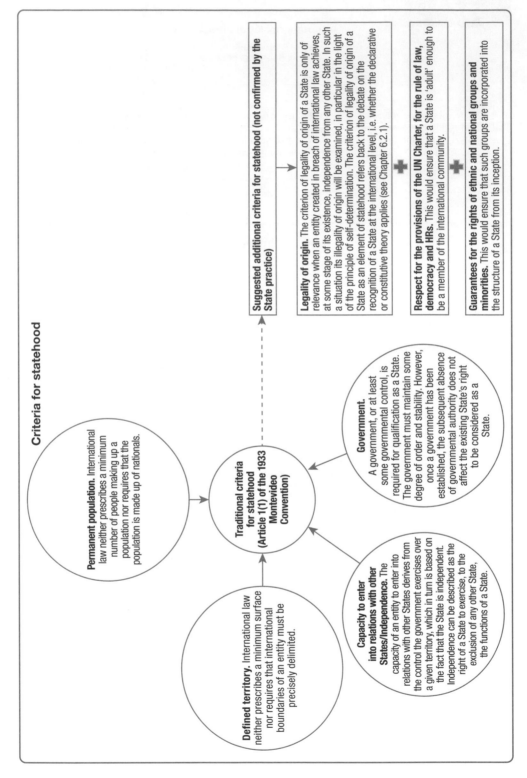

Criteria for statehood

Permanent population. International law neither prescribes a minimum number of people making up a population nor requires that the population is made up of nationals.

Defined territory. International law neither prescribes a minimum surface nor requires that international boundaries of an entity must be precisely delimited.

Traditional criteria for statehood (Article 1(1) of the 1933 Montevideo Convention)

Government. A government, or at least some governmental control, is required for qualification as a State. The government must maintain some degree of order and stability. However, once a government has been established, the subsequent absence of governmental authority does not affect the existing State's right to be considered as a State.

Capacity to enter into relations with other States/Independence. The capacity of an entity to enter into relations with other States derives from the control the government exercises over a given territory, which in turn is based on the fact that the State is independent. Independence can be described as the right of a State to exercise, to the exclusion of any other State, the functions of a State.

Suggested additional criteria for statehood (not confirmed by the State practice)

Legality of origin. The criterion of legality of origin of a State is only of relevance when an entity created in breach of international law achieves, at some stage of its existence, independence from any other State. In such a situation its illegality of origin will be examined, in particular in the light of the principle of self-determination. The criterion of legality of origin of a State as an element of statehood refers back to the debate on the recognition of a State at the international level, i.e. whether the declarative or constitutive theory applies (see Chapter 6.2.1).

Respect for the provisions of the UN Charter, for the rule of law, democracy and HRs. This would ensure that a State is 'adult' enough to be a member of the international community.

Guarantees for the rights of ethnic and national groups and minorities. This would ensure that such groups are incorporated into the structure of a State from its inception.

Subjects of international law

Subjects of international law	**Independent States.** They possess full international personality. However, they may enter into various agreements with other States which may affect their international personality.
	***Sui generis* entities.** They do not satisfy the criteria for statehood but are recognised as States by the majority of States. They are: the Holy See and the Sovereign Military Hospitaller Order of Malta.
	Internationalised territories. These are created by international agreements, normally peace treaties, and endowed with a limited international personality, e.g. the Free City of Danzig (now Gdansk) (1919–1939).
	UN missions established under UNSC resolutions to administer territories of East Timor and Kosovo. In each territory, the UN mission exercised all functions of a State and thus enjoyed full international personality. Each mission was designed as a mechanism for transition of these territories to self-governance.
	IGOs. In *the Reparation for Injuries Suffered in the Service of the United Nations (Advisory Opinion)* the ICJ confirmed that IGOs are subjects of international law and decided that the UN possessed objective international personality. Whether a particular IGO has international personality depends on whether it needs it in order to carry out the tasks entrusted to it by its member States (this is referred to as the functional approach to international personality).
	***De facto* regimes.** They can be described as those which have had control of a defined territory for a long period of time, and usually claim to be a State or a government but have failed to achieve recognition by a significant number of States.
	Insurgents, belligerents and national liberation movements. In the context of armed conflicts they may become subjects of international law if they satisfy certain conditions.
	Individuals. International law creates rights and duties for individuals which are capable of being enforced on an international level. However, as their rights and duties, including procedural rights, allowing them to bring claims against a State are ultimately controlled by States they are only partial subjects of international law.

6

RECOGNITION OF STATES, GOVERNMENTS AND INTER-GOVERNMENTAL ORGANISATIONS IN INTERNATIONAL LAW

CONTENTS

CHAPTER OUTLINE

1 Introduction

Recognition may be defined as a discretionary act exercised unilaterally by the government of a State acknowledging the existence of another State or government.

2 Recognition of a State in international law

The topic of recognition of a new State is one of the most controversial in international law, in theory and in practice. At the theoretical level, there are two competing theories, the constitutive theory and the declaratory theory, both of which try to explain whether recognition is a necessary requirement for the establishment of *de jure* international personality of a new State or, merely, a consequence of international personality.

Under the constitutive theory a State may possess all the formal attributes and qualifications of statehood, but unless recognition is accorded by other States it will not acquire international personality. Therefore, it is the recognition by other States that creates a new State.

According to the declarative theory, recognition is a mere formality. States exist as a matter of fact and the granting of recognition is merely an acknowledgment of that fact. The practical difficulties result from the fact that first, there is no legal duty imposed on States to recognise a new State and second, recognition of a State is not a matter governed by law but a political issue to be decided by the recognising State.

(a)   Recognition may be explicit or implied, but the latter will only be effective if a recognising State unequivocally and clearly indicates that it has a clear and inescapable intention to recognise the entity in question as a State.

(b)   Collective recognition may arise in two contexts:

■ when recognition is accorded collectively by a group of States; or

■ when an entity is admitted as a new member of the UN.

3   Recognition of governments

Under traditional international law, when there is a doubt about whether an authority should be recognised as a government of a State (e.g. when the authority came to power by unconstitutional means including violence or with foreign help), it is sufficient for the authority seeking recognition to show that it has effective control over the relevant territory shown by consent of or tolerance by the population inhabiting that territory. In the European context more is required in that the authority in question must also be democratically elected and respect the rule of law.

(a)   Three approaches to recognition of governments can be identified:

■ The objective approach, under which a State recognises a new government on a factual basis, namely that the new government is independent and has effective control over that State's territory and that this control seems likely to continue, without giving any judgment on the legality of that government or any approval. This approach had, until 1980, been applied by the UK government.

■ The subjective approach, under which a State by recognising a new government expresses its approval and endorses the policy of that new government. The US has always used the recognition of a new government as a powerful political tool.

■ The approach contained in the Estrada doctrine. According to this doctrine no express recognition is necessary. All that is required is to establish that the authority in question exercises effective control over the relevant territory.

(b)   A distinction between *de facto* and *de jure* recognition of governments is no longer of relevance in the UK bearing in mind the announcement made by the UK government in 1980 that from that date it would cease to accord formal recognition to governments.

4 Recognition of States and governments in national law: the UK

(a)   Recognition of States. An executive certificate from the UK Foreign Office will be conclusive for UK courts as to whether the UK recognises the entity in question as a State.

There is not a lot of merit in making a distinction between the legal effects in UK law of non-recognition of States and of non-recognition of governments. They are the same in that non-recognised States and non-recognised governments:

- cannot claim immunity from jurisdiction of UK courts;

- cannot have their laws and acts applied by English courts for the purposes of private international law;

- have no *locus standi* before UK courts and thus cannot sue and be sued.

Nevertheless, in some circumstances the distinction may be relevant, in particular in situations where a State is recognised but not its government; where two or more entities claim to be the government of the same State; and (in the past) where one entity was recognised by the UK government as *de facto* and another as *de jure* government of the same State.

(b)   UK courts, since the announcement made by the UK government in 1980 that it would no longer accord formal recognition to governments (as opposed to States), have the difficult task of determining the status of an entity in question. The test set out by Hobhouse J in *Republic of Somalia v Woodhouse Drake and Carey (Suisse) SA*, is helpful as it sets out four criteria in the light of which a court will decide whether an entity exists as a government of a State. These criteria are:

- whether the entity is the constitutional government of the State;

- the degree, nature and stability of administrative control, if any, that the entity maintains over the territory of the State;

- whether Her Majesty's government has any dealings with the entity and, if so, the nature and extent of those dealings;

- the extent of international recognition afforded by the world community to the entity as the government of the State concerned.

However, the above test is far from solving the difficulties in that, for example, the second criterion refers to a factual situation which may be very difficult to establish. It is to be noted that despite the 1980 announcement, the UK government may choose to issue a certificate recognising or not recognising the relevant government. In such a case a certificate will be conclusive for UK courts and the criteria set out in the *Republic of Somalia* are disregarded.

5 Recognition of IGOs in national law: the UK

An intergovernmental organisation (IGO) of which the UK is a member can acquire legal personality in the UK either:

- through the adoption of an Order in Council which confers upon such an organisation the 'legal capacities of a body corporate'; or

■ through the enactment of specific legislation by the UK Parliament in respect of a given organisation.

An IGO of which the UK is not a member will have legal personality if it satisfies the criteria set out in the 1991 Foreign Corporations Act.

6.1 Introduction

The international community is continuously subject to a process of change. The collapse of the Soviet Union and subsequent emergence of 15 new States, the break-up of the Socialist Federal Republic of Yugoslavia (SFRY) from which seven States have emerged, including the controversial State of Kosovo (see Chapter 13.7.3.1.B), the division of Czechoslovakia into two new States (the Czech Republic and Slovakia), the creation of South Sudan, the disintegration of Iraq, all go to show that few things on the world's political stage are ever static. New States may be created, existing States may disappear, territorial changes may take place. Moreover, revolutions, uprisings and 'coups d'état' may sweep aside existing governments and replace them with new regimes.

To fully operate on the international plane a new State or government must be recognised by other States. Recognition may be defined as a discretionary function exercised, usually unilaterally, by the government of a State acknowledging the existence of another State or government.

State practice shows that the birth of a new State, the establishment of a new government and territorial changes are in general recognised by other States. Recognition practice in respect of the new States established as a result of the collapse of the Soviet Union and the break-up of the SFRY demonstrates that recognition of a State is not a matter governed by law, but depends upon the decisions of individual States based on political expediency.

Usually, once a new State has been recognised, a recognising State will not retract its recognition so long as the requirements of statehood continue to be fulfilled. However, if a recognising State refuses to recognise a new government this refusal will not challenge the existence of a State. The matter of recognition of a new government arises normally when a new government comes to power by unconstitutional means. However, it may also occur, as was the case of Libya in July 2011, that recognition will be withdrawn from the existing government, (i.e. the government of Colonel Qaddafi, which was still in power in parts of the national territory), and a rebel group (i.e. the Libyan National Transitional Council (NTC)), will be recognised as the legitimate government of a State (see Chapter 5.7.1).

Recognition of a State or government is important for two reasons:

■ At the level of international law it shows that the recognised State possesses the attributes of statehood and that the recognising State is willing to engage in foreign relations with the recognised State. The recognition of a new government signifies that it is an effective government and that the recognising State expresses its willingness to initiate, or to continue, relations with that new government.

■ At the level of municipal law, usually only recognised entities will be accorded rights and have obligations under the law concerned.

211

6.2 Recognition of a State in international law

This topic is, at both the theoretical and practical level, one of the most controversial in international law. This is because, so far as the theoretical debate is concerned, two competing theories, the 'constitutive' and the 'declaratory', attempt to explain whether recognition is a necessary requirement for the establishment of *de jure* international personality of a new State or, merely, a consequence of international personality. On the practical level, difficulties arise from the fact that recognition, being a matter of discretion for the recognising State, is based on political rather than legal considerations.

Recognition may be express or implied. It may be effected by one State alone by means of its unilateral act or by a group of States granting collective recognition to a new entity. Further, the UN has acquired an important role in recognition or non-recognition of new States. Member States of the UN by voting in favour of admission to membership of the UN may recognise a new entity as a State. State practice shows that admission to membership of the UN is *prima facie* evidence of statehood.

The above topics are further examined below.

6.2.1 Recognition of States: the declaratory and the constitutive theory of recognition

There are two competing theories as to the recognition of a State, the declaratory and the constitutive theory. They are examined below.

6.2.1.1 The declaratory theory

The declaratory theory states that recognition is a mere formality. States exist as a matter of fact, and the granting of recognition is merely an acknowledgment of that fact. Thus the status of an entity under international law stems from the fact that it does or does not possess the necessary attributes of Statehood, and not from its recognition or non-recognition by the members of the international community. An early example of the endorsement of the declaratory theory is provided by Articles 3 and 6 of the Montevideo Convention.[1] Article 3 states:

> The political existence of the State is independent of recognition by other States. Even before recognition the State has the right to defend its integrity and independence . . . and organise itself as it sees fit.

Article 6 adds that a recognised State by an act of recognition merely accepts the legal personality of a new State. This view was accepted by the mixed arbitration tribunal in *Deutsche Continental Gas-Gesellschaft v Polish State*.[2] It stated that:

> according to the opinion rightly admitted by the great majority of writers on international law, the recognition of a state is not constitutive but merely declaratory. The state exists by itself (par lui-même) and the recognition is nothing else than a declaration of this existence, recognised by the state from which it emanates.

The main advantage of the declaratory theory is that it allows an objective determination of whether an entity is a State in that once an entity satisfies the criteria for statehood, it becomes a State not

---

1   165 LNTS 19.
2   (1929) 5 AD, 11.

merely for States which have recognised it, but for all States. The declaratory theory is favoured by most academics, has been endorsed by international treaties[3] and by both municipal and international courts

The objections to the declaratory theory are:

■ It reduces recognition to an empty formality, ignoring the fact that an act of recognition produces important legal effects.

■ It is workable only if international law and State practice agree as to the criteria for statehood. As Crawford stated: 'If there are no such criteria, or if they are so imprecise as to be practically useless, then the constitutive position will have returned, as it were, by the back door.'[4] As there is no such general agreement, and even if one argues that some generally accepted criteria are in place, State practice has shown that recognition is part of the foreign policy of a State, an instrument by which a State expresses either approval or disapproval of the new situation. For that reason, the constitutive theory regains its importance and cannot be easily dismissed.

■ It does not work in a situation where States are required under international law to withhold recognition. This obligation is well rooted in customary international law,[5] UN practices and reflected in Article 41(2) of the ILS Articles on State Responsibility. This article states that 'no State shall recognize as lawful a situation created by a serious breach [of *jus cogens*] nor render aid and assistance in maintaining that situation'. It further emphasises that States owe an obligation *erga omnes* to withhold formal or implied recognition of an effective territorial situation, created in breach of *jus cogens*. This obligation implies that recognition can have constitutive effect.

■ In a situation where a new entity emerges as a result of unilateral succession to which the parent State, which is still in existence, does not consent the only way for the new entity to become a State is through universal recognition. This was noted by the Supreme Court of Canada in the *Québec Case* when it stated: 'The ultimate success of . . . a [unilateral] succession would be dependent on recognition by the international community, which is likely to consider the legality and legitimacy of succession having regard to, amongst other facts, the conduct of Québec and Canada, in determining whether to grant or withhold recognition.'[6] However, in such a situation, recognition must be universal rather than merely widespread.

The supporters of the declaratory theory have not provided convincing responses to the above arguments.[7]

6.2.1.2   The constitutive theory

The constitutive theory originated in the nineteenth century and is based on the positivist view of international law. According to the constitutive theory a State may possess all the formal attributes

---

3   E.g. Article 12 of the OAS Charter (119 UNTS 3) states: 'The political existence of the State is independent of recognition by other States. Even before being recognized, the State has the right to defend its integrity and independence'.

4   C.J. Crawford, *The Creation of States in International Law*, Oxford: Oxford University Press, 2006, 28.

5   See the ICJ's *Advisory Opinion in Kosovo* in which the ICJ held that a creation of a new State will be illegal where it results from 'unlawful use of force or other egregious violations of norms of general international law, in particular those of a peremptory character (*jus cogens*)' [2010] ICJ Rep, para 81

6   *Reference re Secession of Québec* [1998] 2 SCR 217, para 155.

7   On this topic see: J. Vidmar, *Explaining the Legal Effects of Recognition* (2012) 61 ICLQ, 361.

and qualifications of statehood, but unless recognition is accorded by other States it will not acquire international personality. Therefore, it is the recognition by other States that creates a new State. This is because, international law having no organ or body empowered to determine whether an entity qualifies as a State, it can only be the existing States, acting unilaterally or collectively, which decide the matter.

There are several defects inherent in the constitutive theory:

■ New States are without rights and obligations under international law until recognised.

■ State practice shows that recognition is primarily a political act on the part of the States. Why should the legal status of an entity be dependent upon the performance of such a political act?

■ State practice shows that it may not be possible to ignore completely an unrecognised entity. For instance, while the US did not recognise Communist China, it has nevertheless had to enter into negotiations with it on several occasions, and thereby acknowledge its existence.

■ How many members of the international community must recognise a new entity?

■ Is existence relative only to those States which do extend recognition?

Under the constitutive theory recognition is of a purely political nature. The decision of a recognising State is therefore based on political expediency. Inevitably, therefore, there will be situations in which an entity is recognised as a State by some members of the international community, but denied recognition by others. This was exemplified by the case of Manchukuo and that of the German Democratic Republic (GDR). Manchukuo was recognised by El Salvador, Germany, Hungary, Italy and Japan. Other States, including the US and those of the League of Nations, denied recognition on the ground that Manchukuo was a puppet State of Japan seized from China by illegal force. The GDR was denied recognition by the Western powers for many years on the ground that it was a mere dependent territory of the Soviet Union and not a sovereign and independent State. The UK did not recognise the GDR until February 1973.

In order to overcome the above shortcomings in the constitutive theory, Professor Lauterpacht suggested that once the criteria for statehood are met by an entity aspiring to be recognised as a State, existing States were under a duty to grant recognition.[8] However, actual State practice has clearly challenged his opinion and demonstrated that there is no legal obligation imposed upon States to recognise an entity only because it satisfies the requirements of statehood.

It is submitted that in State practice neither the declarative nor the constitutive theory prevails. A mixture of both is present in that, on the one hand, under the declaratory theory the new entity cannot achieve its objective of participating in the global conduct of international relations, and achieve some equality of status with other members of the community of nations, if the vast majority of States have refused to recognise it, and, on the other, it is difficult to argue that a State, only because it has not been recognised by other States, does not exist.

It is interesting to note that the Badinter Commission (see below) which, while endorsing the declaratory theory in its Opinion 1 by stating that: 'The existence or disappearance of the State is a question of fact', in its Opinion 8 stated that 'while recognition of a State by other States has only declaratory value, such recognition, along with membership of international organisations, bears witness to those States' conviction that the political entity so recognised is a reality and confers on it certain rights and obligations under international law.'[9]

---

8   H. Lauterpacht, *Recognition in International Law*, New York: AMS Press, 1978, 6.
9   92 ILR, 199, 120.

6.2.2 Explicit and implied recognition

The act of recognition may be effected expressly, by a formal announcement or by a bilateral treaty of recognition, or, in some circumstances, impliedly through any act indicating an intention to effect recognition.

6.2.2.1 Explicit recognition

A formal announcement may take the form of a public statement, a congratulatory message on attainment of independence or a simple diplomatic note delivered to the entity which is to be recognised.

Express recognition may be granted by a bilateral treaty formally regulating the relations between the two States. This has been the method usually employed by the UK when establishing the independence of its colonial or other dependent territories. This is exemplified by the treaty the UK government and the provisional government of Burma signed on 17 October 1947 which expressly recognised the Republic of Burma as a fully independent sovereign State.

6.2.2.2 Implied recognition

It is possible under certain circumstances for recognition to be implied from the conduct of one State towards another. It has been stated, however, that recognition, by implication, must be unequivocal and clearly indicate that a recognising State has a clear and inescapable intention to recognise. Lauterpacht was of the opinion that, in the case of recognition of States, only the 'conclusion of a bilateral treaty regulating comprehensively the relation between the two States, the formal initiation of diplomatic relations and, probably, the issue of consular exequaturs' would justify recognition by implication.[10]

State practice shows that recognition is not implied by:

- the fact that a State has become party to a multilateral treaty to which an unrecognised State was already a party;

- the fact that a State remains a party to a multilateral treaty after an unrecognised State becomes a party;

- the establishment of unofficial representatives;

- exchange of trade missions with an unrecognised State;

- the presentation of an international claim against, or by payment of compensation to, an unrecognised State;

- entering into negotiations with an unrecognised State. In practice many States are, for various reasons, forced to negotiate with unrecognised regimes. To avoid embarrassment such negotiations normally take place in secret (see Chapter 5.7);

- the admission of an unrecognised State to an international organisation, in so far as those States opposing the admission are concerned;

- the presence of a State at an international conference in which an unrecognised State participates.

---

10   H. Lauterpacht, *Recognition in International Law*, Cambridge: Cambridge University Press, 1947, 406.

6.2.3 Collective recognition

Collective recognition may arise in two contexts:

■ In a situation where recognition is accorded collectively by a group of States. Traditionally, States have granted recognition to new States by a peace treaty, as illustrated by the 1919 Treaty of Versailles which recognised new States emerging after the end of World War I (WWI). The modern example of collective recognition is that provided by the European Community (now EU), which established a common policy on recognition of new States after the disintegration of the USSR and the SFRY. Member States of the EU did their best to act jointly in conformity with the adopted EC policy (now EU).

■ In a situation where a new State becomes a member of the UN. In respect of this second manner of collective recognition it can be said that the UN has not only acquired an essential role with regard to recognition of new States, but also plays a crucial role in respect of non-recognition of certain entities which have been created in breach of international law. It is important to note that although the admission of a new State to membership of the UN cannot produce the same legal effects as that of recognition, because the UN Charter does not encompass all duties and rights of a State existing under international law, from a practical point of view, membership of the UN constitutes definitive acknowledgment of the existence of a new State.

6.2.3.1 EC policy concerning the recognition of new States in Europe

The EC's policy concerning the recognition of new States was established in order to deal with the emergence of new States in Europe resulting from the break-up of the SFRY and the collapse of the Soviet Union. The policy was carried out in the framework of the European Political Co-operation (EPC) which was initiated by heads of State and government of the EEC (now the EU) following their meeting in The Hague in 1969. EPC consisted of informal consultations between member States, carried out outside the structures of the EEC, with a view, when possible, to achieving a common position. Under the 1986 Single European Act (SEA), which amended the EEC Treaty, EPC was formalised in Title III of the Act, but its inter-governmental nature was retained. The weakness of EPC, in particular in so far as the handling of the Yugoslav wars[11] was concerned, led to the establishment of a Common Foreign and Security Policy (CFSP) under Pillar II of the Treaty of Maastricht, which amended the EEC Treaty and created the EU (it came into force in 1993).

In August 1991, when the Yugoslav armed conflict started, member States of the EEC, under EPC, adopted a Declaration on Yugoslavia under which they established the Peace Conference on Yugoslavia and created the Badinter Commission, an organ of the Conference.[12] The historical context of the disintegration of the SFRY and the EC policy towards the crisis in Yugoslavia are examined below.

The SFRY comprised six republics: Slovenia, Croatia, Serbia, Bosnia-Herzegovina, Montenegro and Macedonia, plus two autonomous regions – Kosovo and Vojvodina. All attempts to impose a national identity upon the people living within the SFRY failed; the only thing that had kept the various ethnic groups together was the 'towering political dominance' of President Tito. His death in 1980

---

11   See D. Dinan, *Ever Closer Union?* London: Anne Rienner, 489 *et seq.*

12   On this topic see S. Terrett, *The Dissolution of Yugoslavia and the Badinter Arbitration Commission*, Aldershot: Ashgate, 2000.

resulted in a lack of political leadership and control, and over the next decade the SFRY slowly began the process of dissolution.[12A]

On 25 June 1991 both Croatia and Slovenia declared their independence. Their attempts to oust the Yugoslav National Army from their territories were met by armed resistance. Violence followed. The EC, as a principal mediator in the conflict, requested both Republics to agree to a three-month moratorium on the implementation of their declarations of independence. In August, after widespread violence in Croatia, the EC decided to establish both a Peace Conference on Yugoslavia and an Arbitration Commission (named the Badinter Commission after its chairman) made up of five presidents of various constitutional courts of the EC countries. After the expiry of the three-month moratorium Slovenia and Croatia formally seceded from Yugoslavia. This, and the unilateral declarations of independence of Ukraine and Byelorussia from the USSR in July 1991, prompted the EC to establish a coherent policy regarding recognition of new States. On 16 December 1991 the EC foreign ministers meeting in Brussels issued two declarations – a 'Declaration on the Guidelines on the Recognition of the New States in Eastern Europe and in the Soviet Union'[13] and a 'Declaration on Yugoslavia'. The Guidelines adopted in the former set out the following requirements for recognition:

- Respect for the:
  - provisions of the UN Charter;[14]
  - final Act of Helsinki;[15]
  - Charter of Paris,[16] especially with respect to the rule of law, democracy and human rights.

- Guarantees for the rights of ethnic and national groups and minorities in accordance with the commitments subscribed to in the context of the Conference on Security and Co-operation in Europe (CSCE).

- Respect for the inviolability of all frontiers, which may only be changed by peaceful means and by common agreements.

- Commitment to settle by agreement or arbitration all issues concerning State secession and regional disputes.

- Acceptance of all relevant commitments with regard to disarmament and nuclear non-proliferation, as well as to security and regional stability.

The Guidelines also contained a clause stating that the EC countries 'will not recognise entities which are the result of aggression'.

Further requirements were laid down in the Declaration on Yugoslavia with regard to the Yugoslav republics wishing to be recognised by the EC, that is, they were required to apply to the EC for recognition by 23 December 1991. Their applications would then be submitted to the Arbitration Commission. Upon its recommendation a decision would be taken by the EC on 15 January 1992. Moreover, the applicants would have to declare that they:

- wished to be recognised as independent States;

- accepted the commitments contained in the 1991 EC Guidelines as mentioned above;

12A   See P. Radan, *The Break-up of Yugoslavia and International Law*, New York: Routledge, 2002.
13   UN Doc S/23293.
14   1 UNTS XVI.
15   (1975) 14 ILM 1292.
16   (1991) 30 ILM 190.

- agreed to accept obligations respecting human rights and the rights of national and ethnic groups;

- supported the continued effort of the UN and EC to resolve the Yugoslav crisis;

- had no territorial claim towards any neighbouring EC Member State.

The Republics of Slovenia, Croatia, Bosnia-Herzegovina and Macedonia applied for recognition through the Badinter Commission.

A. *Slovenia and Croatia*
In mid-January 1992 the EC granted recognition to the States of Slovenia and Croatia despite the fact that the Badinter Commission had found that Croatia did not satisfy the requirements laid down in the EC Guidelines, namely the Croatian constitution did not contain sufficient guarantees in respect of the protection of human rights, especially relating to the status of minorities. Subsequently, the President of Croatia wrote a letter to the Badinter Commission confirming Croatia's acceptance of these obligations, thus satisfying the requirements of the Guidelines. Within a few days of the recognition of Slovenia and Croatia by the members of the EC, others such as Australia, Argentina, Canada and a number of European countries followed suit. Within a few months both countries were recognised by Japan, the US, China, India, and many others. On 22 May 1992 they were admitted to the UN.

B. *Bosnia-Herzegovina*
The recognition of Bosnia-Herzegovina by the EC was subject to the same conditions as Slovenia and Croatia plus one more, that condition being that the Badinter Commission recommended a referendum which would demonstrate whether the people of Bosnia-Herzegovina wished to constitute a sovereign and independent State. In March 1992, the referendum was duly held and of a turnout of 63.4 per cent (the referendum was boycotted by Serbs living in Bosnia-Herzegovina), 92.7 per cent were in favour. At that time the tension in Bosnia-Herzegovina was growing as the Yugoslav National Army was there ready to defend the Serbian minority. On 7 April 1992 the US and the EC recognised Bosnia-Herzegovina. Other countries followed. In response, the Serbian minority in Bosnia-Herzegovina established, in what was the Serb Autonomous Region there, the Republic Srpska.[17] Fighting then broke out between the Yugoslav Army (which had officially withdrawn after the recognition of Bosnia-Herzegovina by the US and the EU but, in fact, its soldiers had changed their insignia and became the Army of Republika Srpska), and Bosnian Muslims loyal to the Bosnian government. The Serbs living in Bosnia-Herzegovina were supported by volunteers and various paramilitary forces from Serbia, and received extensive humanitarian, logistical and financial support from the Federal Republic of Yugoslavia. Bosnia-Herzegovina at the time of recognition was torn by violence and its government had little control over its territory.

In the case of Bosnia-Herzegovina its recognition as a State was prompted by the fact that the principles of non-intervention and the prohibition of the use of force were not applicable to Bosnia-Herzegovina before its recognition as a State. This was because, like other former republics, it was regarded as a constituent part of the SFYR, and the conflict between the Yugoslav National Army and the Bosnian Muslims was seen as an internal conflict to which only the provisions of humanitarian law relating to civil wars and the general rules on the protection of human rights were applicable. By recognising Bosnia-Herzegovina, notwithstanding the fact that the criterion of effective government

---

17   The Republic Srpska continues to exist as a constituent part of Bosnia-Herzegovina which is officially made up of the Federation of Bosnia and Herzegovina and the Republika Srpska.

was not satisfied (as the government of Bosnia-Herzegovina had control only over a small part of the national territory), the EC and the US, by way of a legal fiction, conferred on Bosnia-Herzegovina international legal personality and the status of a State with all ensuing benefits of international law. These were the protection of its territorial integrity and political independence, the prohibition of the use of force, the application of the full Geneva regime to the armed conflict taking place on Bosnia-Herzegovina territory, and the obligation of peaceful settlement of international disputes, etc.

The case of Bosnia-Herzegovina illustrates the importance of recognition, and at the same time, demonstrates the political nature of the act of recognition.

C. *Macedonia*

The recognition, or rather non-recognition by the EC, of Macedonia in January 1992 was also based on political considerations. Macedonia satisfied all the criteria for statehood. The Badinter Commission recommended its recognition, but the EC declined on account of Greek opposition regarding the name and the flag of Macedonia. Neither Macedonia nor Greece was willing to change their position. Only Bulgaria and Turkey recognised Macedonia. A breakthrough came, however, in August 1992 with recognition by Russia dictated by its concern about the security and stability of the Balkan region. For Macedonia, recognition had interesting implications as mentioned next.

On 27 April 1992 the Assembly of the SFRY had enacted the constitution of the Federal Republic of Yugoslavia (FRY) proclaiming that the SFRY was transformed into the FRY, a State comprising two republics – Serbia and Montenegro. On the one hand, the FRY had no claims in respect of Macedonia; on the other, Macedonia was not recognised as a State. Under international law Macedonia became *terra derelicta*, i.e. an abandoned land as the FRY did not wish to maintain sovereignty over Macedonia and Macedonia was not recognised as a State and was therefore, in theory, open to (military) intervention by a third State.[18]

The EC countries, not surprisingly, decided that this situation could not be allowed to continue, especially taking into account the general situation in the Balkan region, and consequently recognised Macedonia as a State in 1993.

When Macedonia had the status of *terra derelicta* the only protection that could be given to it by international law was under Chapter VII of the UN Charter, which empowers the United Nations Security Council (UNSC), in the event of a military conflict occurring between an unrecognised entity and a member of the UN, to use its powers to force a member State to respect the prohibition of the use of force. This is in conformity with the definition of aggression contained in the General Assembly of the United Nations (UNGA) Resolution 3314 (XXIX) which states that every State enjoys protection 'without prejudice to questions of recognition or to whether a state is a member of the United Nations'. As can be seen, therefore, the rules of Chapter VII of the UN Charter are the only protection for new States not universally recognised.

D. *Conclusion*

The EC set an interesting precedent by inviting entities wishing to be recognised as States to apply for recognition. The requirements for recognition went beyond the traditional criteria for statehood, but conformed with existing State practice, and the requirements for admission to the UN. The EC was seeking a commitment from entities waiting to be admitted to the international community in respect of the protection of human rights, especially concerning the protection of minorities, the rule of law and democracy. Consequently, what in respect of existing States, would amount to a violation

---

18   See C. Hillgruber, *The Admission of New States to the International Community* (1998) 9/3 EJIL, 491.

of the prohibition of intervention in internal affairs was made a precondition for recognition in respect of new States. Moreover, the States of the EC, including the UK, altered their national policies on recognition of States in order to be able to act in unison.

It is also interesting to note that

■ most of the world's States were, in the context of the Yugoslav conflict, waiting for formal recognition to be accorded by the EC before themselves recognising the new European States;

■ the application of the criteria set out by the Badinter Commission was disregarded by the EC States when the necessity arose to cope with situations endangering the peace and stability of the Balkan region.

The member States of the EC were able to agree on a collective mechanism for the recognition of the new States emerging immediately after the disintegration of the USSR and Yugoslavia, and subsequently acted jointly in conformity with the adopted EC policy. However, they could not establish a common position so far as Kosovo (which broke away from Serbia later) was concerned with the consequence that each member State was free to proceed according to its national interests (see Chapter 13.7.3.1.B).

6.2.3.2   The role of the UN in the recognition of new States

A.   Admission to the UN

Admission to the UN, has, to a great extent, diminished the importance of recognition or non-recognition of an entity by States.

Article 4 of the UN Charter sets out the conditions and the procedure for admission. Article 4(1) requires that a new member must love peace, must accept the obligations deriving from the Charter, and must be able and willing to carry out those obligations. Under Article 4(2) the absolute masters of the admission procedure are the UNSC and UNGA. The UNSC will verify whether the conditions laid down in Article 4(1) are fulfilled by the applying entity, and, on its recommendation, the UNGA will adopt a final decision.

The interpretation of Article 4 has been the subject of two Advisory Opinions delivered by the International Court of Justice (ICJ). Both were deemed necessary by the UNGA to resolve a deadlock so far as admission of new members was concerned. Between 1951 and 1954 because of the attitude of the USSR no States were admitted to the UN despite the fact that some 25 had applied for membership. Any pro-Western applicant was vetoed by the USSR in the UNSC and any Communist applicant was vetoed by the Western countries. In the first request for an Advisory Opinion[19] the UNGA asked whether the requirements of Article 4(2) were exhaustive in the sense that no requirements could be imposed other than those set out in Article 4(1) of the UN Charter. The ICJ answered that the conditions set forth in Article 4 were exhaustive and should be regarded 'not merely as the necessary conditions but also as the conditions that suffice'.[20] In the second request,[21] the UNGA asked whether a recommendation by the UNSC was necessary for admission. The ICJ's Opinion was in the affirmative.

---

19   *The Conditions of Admission of a State to Membership in the United Nations [Advisory Opinion]* [1948] ICJ Rep 57.

20   Ibid, para 62.

21   *The Competence of the General Assembly for the Admission of a State to the United Nations [Advisory Opinion]* [1950] ICJ Rep 4.

Article 4 was invoked by Greece when the Republic of Macedonia applied for admission. The Greek government argued before the UNSC that the former Yugoslav Republic of Macedonia was not 'peace loving' because by adopting the name 'Republic of Macedonia' 'it has explicitly adopted the name of a wider geographical region extending over four neighbouring countries' and therefore showed its imperialistic attitude. The UNSC recommended admission of Macedonia but only as 'the former Yugoslav Republic of Macedonia'[22] pending settlement of the dispute between Greece and Macedonia. At the time of writing, the dispute has not been settled. Relations between Greece and Macedonia deteriorated to a point where Macedonia has brought proceedings against Greece before the ICJ for blocking its admission to the North Atlantic Treaty Organisation (NATO) in violation of Article 11 of the Interim Accord signed between the two States in September 1995. Under this provision, on the one hand, Greece promised not to object to applications made by Macedonia to any international organisation but, on the other, reserved the right to object if Macedonia were to use in such organisations any name other than 'the Former Yugoslav Republic of Macedonia'. The ICJ in the *Case Concerning the Application of the Interim Accord of 13 September 1995 (The Former Yugoslav Republic of Macedonia v Greece)*[23] did not rule on the difference over the name of the Republic of Macedonia as this matter was excluded from its jurisdiction. However, it found that Greece was in breach of the 1995 Agreement by objecting to Macedonia's application to NATO.

It can be said that while it is clear that non-admission to the UN does not act as an effective denial of the statehood of the entity concerned, and that admission to membership does not establish that the entity concerned has been recognised in so far as the bilateral relationship between the entity and each existing member is concerned, it is clear from State practice that admission to membership will be *prima facie* evidence of statehood.

B. The UN as the forum to co-ordinate both recognition and non-recognition
It is important to note that the UN has acquired a function which was not envisaged in the Charter. That is the legitimation or, in its absence, illegitimation of new States as exemplified in the cases of Rhodesia and Palestine.

With regard to Rhodesia, in response to the Unilateral Declaration of Independence of the Colony of Southern Rhodesia in 1965, under which it declared itself a State of Rhodesia, the UN called upon its members not to recognise the new State, even though the purported State of Rhodesia fulfilled the traditional criteria for statehood. The non-recognition was justified on the ground that Rhodesia was created in violation of the fundamental principles of the UN: the prohibition of racial discrimination and apartheid, and the right of people to self-determination. Under UNSC Resolution 221 (1966) adopted under Chapter VII, and thus binding on all members of the UN, Rhodesia was not recognised as a State.

The situation with Palestine is more complex. On 15 November 1988 the Palestinian National Council at its extraordinary session in Algiers adopted a Declaration Creating the State of Palestine in the Land of Palestine with a Capital at Jerusalem. The State of Palestine did not satisfy the criteria for statehood as it had no defined territory and consequently no government exercising effective control over it. Despite that, the UNGA in Resolution 43/177 officially acknowledged the proclamation of independence of Palestine in December 1988 and 132 States have recognised a new State of Palestine. The justification for the recognition of the State of Palestine was based on the right of the people of Palestine to self-determination.

---

22   UNSC Res 817 [1993] [7 April 1993] UN Doc S/RES 817 [1993].
23   [2011] ICJ Rep 644.

On 31 October 2011, UNESCO admitted Palestine as a full member. On 29 November 2012, the UNGA with 138 votes in favour, nine against and 41 abstentions adopted Resolution 67/19 which accorded Palestine non-member observer State status in the United Nations. Further, the UNS-G, who is a depository of most international treaties, has allowed Palestine to become a contracting party to 13 human rights treaties, while the Swiss government, the depository of the Geneva Conventions and Protocols Additional to them, accepted Palestine as a contracting party to these instruments. The issue which arises here is whether all the above facts entail that Palestine has been recognised as a State by the UN system although its formal admission to the UN as a member State, for which a formal application was submitted by Palestine on 23 September 2011, is unlikely to occur, given that the US clearly opposes it and intends to use its veto at the UNSC to block the admission.

The most significant fact is that the UNGA clearly granted Palestine the status of 'an observer State'. The word 'State' is of importance here. Has Resolution 67/19 created the State of Palestine, and confimed its existence or has it had no impact on the status of Palestine? Commentators express differing views.[24] However, for supporters of the constitutive theory Resolution 67/19 entails that UNGA has implicitly recognised Palestine as a State, although the recognition, being far from universal, may not be sufficient to create the State of Palestine. It is also important to note that for the purposes of the ICC it seems that the statehood of Palestine started with Resolution 67/19. The ICC Office of Prosecutor on 14 August 2014 stated that following Resolution 67/19 Palestine could join the Rome Statute[25] but so far, has not made such request. A previous request made by the Palestinian authorities in May 2009 to join the Rome Statute was rejected by the ICC in April 2012 on the ground that Palestine was 'an observer entity' and, thus could not become a party to the Rome Statute.

It is submitted that the UN has become a forum for recognition, or non-recognition, of new States. The attitude of the UNSC as well as the UNGA toward new entities has produced important legal consequences for entities seeking recognition. In practice, Rhodesia was denied international personality and rejected by the international community, while Palestine continues on its way to becoming a State. Further, UN's decisions, in particular those calling for non-recognition, whether binding or not, have been followed by members of the UN.

6.2.4 The effects of recognition of a State in international law

Recognition confers the legal status of 'State' under international law upon the entity seeking recognition. Such an entity becomes a subject of international law, initially *vis-à-vis* States recognising it, and subsequently upon its admission to the UN as a member of the international community. Upon recognition, all rules of international law apply *ipso facto* to relations between a new State and the recognising States.

---

24 See J. Vidmar, *Palestine and the Conceptual Problem of Implicit Statehood* (2013) Chinese Journal of International Law, 19, who argues that the UNGA resolution has had no impact on the status of Palestine, and that State creation cannot be an implicit side-effect of international treaties or voting procedures in international organisations. See also J. Cerone, *Legal Implications of the UN General Assembly Vote to Accord Palestine the Status of Observer State* (2012) 16/37 Insights, 1.

25 See the Statement of the Prosecutor of the International Criminal Court, Fatou Bensouda: 'The Public Deserves to Know the Truth about the ICC's Jurisdiction over Palestine' available at: www.icc-cpi.int/en_menus/icc/press%20and%20media/press%20releases/pages/otp-st-14-09-02.aspx (accessed 10 September 2014).

6.3 Recognition of governments

The recognition of new States necessarily involves the recognition of new governments. When in a State previously recognised by other States, a government changes through normal constitutional proceedings, its recognition only becomes an issue in exceptional circumstances. This is because a change of government in accordance with national rules is a matter within the domestic competence of a State and does not concern international law. The situation differs when, in a recognised State, a government changes through unconstitutional means, e.g. by violence, by a *coup d'état* or with foreign help. The case of Libya shows that recognition of a government may be withdrawn in a situation where a recognised government violates fundamental human rights and the international community recognises a rebel group, in this case the National Transitional Council (NTC), as the legitimate government of a country. The Libyan Contact Group, established on 29 March 2011 at the London conference with a view to co-ordinating international efforts in support of the struggle of the Libyan people for democratic and free Libya comprising representatives of many States, including the UK, the US, and international organisations, at its fourth meeting issued the following statement:

> The Contact Group reaffirmed that the Qaddafi regime no longer has any legitimate authority in Libya and that Qaddafi and certain members of his family must go. Henceforth and until an interim authority is in place, participants agreed to deal with the National Transitional Council (NTC) as the legitimate governing authority in Libya.[26]

This statement recognised the NTC as the *de jure* government of Libya. Following this, the UNGA passed a resolution recognising the NTC as Libya's representative for its sixty-sixth session.[27] Recognition of the NTC was a political act bearing in mind that legal factors such as effective control over the territory of Libya, (in fact, NTC did not establish effective control over the myriad of armed revolutionary 'brigades' operating in the territory of Libya) and its constitutionality were not considered.[28]

With regard to legal considerations, under traditional international law States normally recognise an authority as a government of a State if that authority is independent, i.e. it is not under foreign control, and is therefore subordinate only to international law, and has effective control over its territory, shown by consent or tolerance of the population inhabiting that territory. However, in the European context, it seems that a new criterion has been added. The authority in question must also be democratically elected and respect the rule of law. This new criterion can be inferred from, *inter alia*:

- the 1990 Charter of Paris for New Europe[29] adopted by the Member States of the Conference on Security and Co-operation in Europe;

- the 1991 EC Guidelines on the Recognition of New States in Eastern Europe and the Soviet Union.[30]

---

26 Chair's Statement at the Fourth Meeting of the Libya Contact Group (Istanbul, 15 July 2011) www.nato.int/nato_static/assets/pdf/pdf_2011_07/20110926_110715-Libya-Contact-GroupIstanbul.pdf (accessed 10 September 2014).

27 UNGA press release stated: 'After much wrangling, General Assembly seats National Transitional Council of Libya as country's representative for sixty-sixth session' (GA/11137, 16 September 2011) available at: www.un.org/News/Press/docs/2011/ga11137.doc.htm (accessed 10 September 2014).

28 See S.Talmon, *Recognition of the Libyan National Transitional Council* (2011) 15/16 Insights, 4. The author argued that recognition of a rebel group which had no broad-based support of the Libyan people constituted an illegal interference in internal affairs of Libya and could give rise to State responsibility.

29 (1991) 30 ILM 190.

30 Supra note 13.

In municipal law there is no difference between the effects of non-recognition of a State, and the effects of non-recognition of a government, save in the case where there is more than one authority requesting recognition as the government of the State concerned.

No legal duty is imposed on States to recognise new governments.[31] Examples include the non-recognition by the US and the Allied powers of the Tinoco regime that ruled Costa Rica between 1917 and 1919; the general non-recognition of the Taliban which was recognised only by three States: Pakistan, Saudi Arabia and the United Arab Emirates; and the non-recognition by the UK until 1921 (and by the US until 1933) of the Soviet government which came into power in 1919.

6.3.1 Approaches to the recognition of governments

Three approaches can be identified in respect of recognition of governments:

■ The objective approach, under which a State recognises a new government on a factual basis, namely that the new government has effective control over that State's territory and that this control seems likely to continue, without giving any judgment on the legality of that government or any approval. This approach had, until 1980, been applied by the UK government.

■ The subjective approach, under which a State by recognising a new government expresses its approval and endorses the policy of that new government. The US has always used the recognition of a new government as a powerful political tool. For example, with regard to Iraq, after the ousting of Saddam Hussein, the US and the UK governed Iraq through the Coalition Provisional Authority which was to be replaced by a permanent government. When in June 2004 an interim Iraqi government was established the US government made the following statement: 'On June 28, 2004, full sovereignty was transferred to a new Iraqi interim government. The Coalition Provisional Authority, led by Ambassador Paul Bremer, ceased to exist. The Iraqi government is now running the day-to-day operations of its country.'[32] By this statement the US recognised the Iraqi government, and subsequently opened an embassy in Baghdad.

■ The approach endorsed by the Estrada doctrine. As a response to the use of recognition by powerful nations as a means of extracting some concessions from new governments of small nations the 'Estrada doctrine' was put forward by the Mexican foreign minister, Genaro Estrada, in 1930.[33] He rejected the doctrine of recognition of new governments because:

> . . . it allows foreign governments to pass [judgment] upon the legitimacy or illegitimacy of the regime existing in another country, with the result that situations arise in which the legal qualifications or national status of governments or authorities are apparently made subject to the opinion of foreigners.

This approach is based on the assumption that a change of government is an internal matter of the State concerned in which other States have no right to intervene. It avoids the disadvantages of the subjective and, the objective, approach. Indeed, if non-recognition can be an expression of disapproval of a new government then it can be argued that recognition may be interpreted as implying approval of a new government even in cases where no such approval was intended. The Estrada doctrine rejects the need for express and formal declarations granting recognition of governments. What is required

---

31   *R (on the application of North Cyprus Tourism Centre Ltd) v Transport for London* (2005) UKHRR 1231.

32   US Dep't of State Fact Sheet on Iraq's Transition to Self-Government (June 28, 2004).

33   Genaro Estrada's statement of this doctrine is reprinted in (1931) 25 AJIL, Supp, 203.

for a new government is to show that it exercises effective control over the relevant territory. The doctrine has gained increasing support.

Under the objective and subjective approaches a recognising State may recognise a foreign entity as either *de jure* or *de facto* government. The terms *de jure* or *de facto* reflect the quality of the government. *De facto* recognition of a new government is an interim step taken where there are doubts as to its legitimacy and stability. The distinction between *de facto* and *de jure* recognition was explained by Bankes J in *Luther v Sagor* [34] as follows:

> A *de jure* government is one which in the opinion of the person using the phrase ought to possess the powers of sovereignty, though at the time it may be deprived of them. A *de facto* government is one which is really in possession of them, although the possession may be wrongful or precarious.

In April 1980 the UK government made an announcement that it would no longer accord formal recognition to foreign governments, i.e. it endorsed the Estrada doctrine. The announcement explains that the practice of making a formal announcement, which was a simply neutral formality, recognising a new government had been sometimes misunderstood, despite explanations to the contrary, and was interpreted as implying approval.[35]

Following from the announcement the distinction between *de facto* and *de jure* recognition became irrelevant.

6.4 Recognition of States and governments in national law: the UK

International lawyers frequently draw a distinction between the effects in municipal law of recognition of States, and of governments. However, for two reasons, the making of this distinction is not always worthwhile:

- ■ It will often be difficult in practice to distinguish, at the international level, between the non-recognition of States, and the non-recognition of governments. For example, was the non-recognition by the UK of the Soviet Union prior to 1924 a choice not to recognise the existence of the Soviet State or to not recognise the legitimacy of the Soviet government? Similarly, was the non-recognition of the Smith regime in Rhodesia post-UDI in 1965 a refusal to recognise an illegal government, or a withholding of recognition from the Rhodesian State? At first sight these questions may appear straightforward. In truth they are more complex.

- ■ The distinction between non-recognition of States and of governments for the purposes of municipal law is seldom significant because the effect of either will invariably be the same. Thus, it will make little difference whether entity 'X', or its government, is not recognised. In either case, 'X' will not be entitled to claim sovereign immunity before English courts or to issue process in England. The reason why non-recognition will have the same effect in the case of a State, and in the case of its government, is that a State is invariably represented on the international plane by its government.

However, in some circumstances, for the purposes of municipal law, it will be important to distinguish between non-recognition of a State, and of its government, that is, when the State in question remains recognised, while the authority in control of the State is an illegal authority. Such a situation arose

---

34   [1921] 3 KB 532.
35   Written answer by the Secretary of State, H.of.Lds, 28 April 1980, reprinted in (1980) 51 BYIL, 367–368.

following the Iraqi invasion of Kuwait in 1990. While it was clear that the State of Kuwait remained a recognised entity, it was equally apparent that the Iraqi-imposed administration was not recognised. At one level, therefore, the non-recognition of the illegal administration was fatal to the international standing of the State. However, the attempts which were made by the deposed, but still recognised and legitimate government of Kuwait, to retain a measure of international personality to act on behalf of the State on the international level were successful. In these circumstances (i.e. where there are competing authorities in respect of the same State) it will be important to distinguish between the non-recognition of a State and the non-recognition of its government. Additionally, the distinction will be useful in a situation where two or more entities claim to be the government of a State, and where one entity is recognised as the *de facto*, and another as the *de jure*, government of the same State.

6.4.1 Recognition of a State in UK law

Generally, UK courts will not recognise a foreign State unless the UK Foreign Office certifies that it has been recognised by the British government. UK courts cannot challenge the determination made by the executive.[36]

The effects of recognition of a State in UK law are examined below.

6.4.1.1 A recognised State has sovereign immunity and cannot be sued in the UK courts without its consent

The issue of sovereign immunity was examined in *Duff Development Company v Government of Kelantan*.[37]

DUFF DEVELOPMENT COMPANY *V* GOVERNMENT OF KELANTAN

Facts:

In this case the House of Lords had to decide whether Kelantan, a State in the Malay Peninsula then under the protection of Great Britain, was an independent State so that it could claim State immunity in the English courts. The Under Secretary of State for the British Colonies submitted a letter stating: 'Kelantan is an independent state in the Malay Peninsula . . . His Majesty the King does not exercise or claim any rights of sovereignty or jurisdiction over Kelantan.'

Held:

The above Colonial Office statement was accepted as binding by the Court. Lord Cave said that 'it is the duty of the Court to accept the statement of the Secretary of State thus clearly and positively made as conclusive upon the point'.

---

36   *Caglar and Others v Billingham (Inspector of Taxes)* 108 ILR 510, 519. In this case the Foreign Office certificate stated that the Turkish Republic of Northern Cyprus (TRNC) was to be regarded as a 'foreign State' despite the fact that 'it is not recognised as such by her Majesty's government'.

37   [1924] AC 797.

6.4.1.2 An unrecognised State cannot sue in UK courts and is not recognised for the purposes of conflict of laws rules

This principle was examined in *Carl-Zeiss-Stiftung v Rayner and Keeler Ltd.*[38]

CARL-ZEISS-STIFTUNG *V* RAYNER AND KEELER LTD.

Facts:

The dispute concerned the use of the trademarks 'Carl-Zeiss-Stiftung', 'Carl Zeiss' and 'Zeiss' for optical and glass instruments which, before WWII, belonged to Carl-Zeiss-Stiftung, a charitable foundation located in Thuringia and controlled by the authorities of Thuringia. After WWII, when Thuringia became part of the German Democratic Republic (GDR), the foundation was nationalised. Meanwhile, the management and many Carl-Zeiss workers had left Thuringia and 're-established' the foundation in the Federal Republic of Germany (FRG). In 1955, the GDR Carl-Zeiss-Stiftung started proceedings in the UK against the FRG Carl-Zeiss-Stiftung, and against two retailers selling FRG Carl-Zeiss-Stiftung glass instruments under the trademark Zeiss in the UK.

It is a rule of English conflict of laws that in cases of dispute over title to property, English courts will apply the lex situs, *i.e. the laws of the State where the property is situated. Accordingly, the Court had to consider the validity of title to intellectual property based upon legislative and administrative acts of the GDR. However, at the time of the court proceedings, the GDR was not recognised by the British government.*

Held:

The Court of Appeal refused to apply East German law. Diplock LJ said that where English rules of private international law made reference to a foreign system of law, that law would only be regarded as effective in so far as it was:

> made by or under the authority of those persons who are recognised by the Government of the United Kingdom as being the sovereign Government of the place where the thing happens.

Notwithstanding the correctness of this decision, the consequences of the application of the relevant rule of law could potentially be very harsh. This approach could lead to hardship in the day-to-day transactions of ordinary people.

With this in mind the House of Lords reversed the decision of the Court of Appeal.[39] Two approaches to the problem of the non-recognition of East Germany were in evidence in their Lordships' decision. First, Lord Wilberforce indicated that English courts should in some circumstances recognise the administrative acts of a non-recognised State (see below). Second, the approach preferred by the majority of the Lords was for the Court to rely on a legal fiction. Thus, the Law Lords accepted that the East German government was an administration or subordinate authority controlled by the Soviet Union. As the Soviet Union

---

38   *Carl-Zeiss-Stiftung v Rayner and Keeler Ltd* (1965) 1 All ER 300.
39   *Carl-Zeiss-Stiftung v Rayner and Keeler Ltd (No 2)* [1967] 1 AC 853.

> was recognised by the UK government, the English courts could grant recognition to the acts of its local authority, namely the East German government.
>
> It was therefore possible for the House of Lords to accept the acts of the unrecognised GDR as being those of a subordinate authority of the USSR.

It is important to note that in 1980 the UK government expressed its position only in respect of formal recognition of governments (as opposed to States) in that it provides certificates when a court has doubts as to whether an entity is a State recognised by the UK government.[40] However, it is submitted that the approach in the *Carl-Zeiss Case* remains, in that an unrecognised State cannot sue or be sued in UK courts, and its acts are not recognised for the purposes of private international law. However, the harshness of the rule in *Zeiss* has been mitigated by the adoption of the subordinated authority theory, by subsequent case law which built upon Lord Wiberforce's approach and by the enactment of the 1991 Foreign Corporations Act.

A. Perfunctonary acts of administration

Lord Wilberforce in the *Carl-Zeiss Case* stated that:

> where private rights, or acts of everyday occurrence, or perfunctory acts of administration are concerned . . . the courts may, in the interests of justice and common sense, where no consideration of public policy to the contrary has to prevail, give recognition to the actual facts or realities found to exist in the territory in question.[41]

This idea was further developed by Lord Denning in *Hesperides Hotels Ltd v Aegean Turkish Holidays Ltd,*[42] in the context of a case concerning the expropriation of property in the TRNC in which he said that he would, give recognition of laws, or act, of an unrecognised government which is in effective control of the relevant territory 'at any rate, in regard to the laws which regulate the day to day affairs of the people, such as their marriages, their divorces, their leases, their occupations, and so forth'.[43] This approach is in line with the so called Namibia exception formulated by the ICJ in its Advisory Opinion on the *Legal Consequences for States of the Continued Presence of South Africa in Namibia (South West Africa) notwithstanding Security Council Resolution 276 (1970).*[44] In its Opinion the ICJ emphasised that the restrictions deriving from the obligation of non-recognition of the unlawful presence of South Africa in Namibia imposed on States were aimed at ensuring that South Africa might not entrench its authority over Namibia. They, however, should not result:

> in depriving the people of Namibia of any advantages derived from international co-operation. In particular, while official acts performed by the Government of South Africa on behalf of or concerning Namibia after the termination of the Mandate are illegal and invalid, this invalidity cannot be extended

---

40 E.g. with regard to Kuwait see: *Kuwait Airways Corporation v Iraqi Airways Company and the Republic of Iraq* ILR 116, 535, 580–581, and in respect of the TRNC see: *Ceglar v Bellingham*, ILR 108, 510, 519.

41 *Carl Zeiss Stiftung v Rayner & Keeler Ltd (No 2)* [1967] 1 AC 853, 954.

42 [1978] 1 QB 205, at 218 G. see also *Caglar v Billingham (Inspector of Taxes)* [1996] STC (SDC) 150, para 121.

43 See Lord Denning's *obiter* statement in *Hesperides Hotels Ltd v Aegean Turkish Holidays Ltd* [1978] QB 205, 218.

44 [1971] ICJ Rep 16.

to those acts, such as, for instance, the registration of births, deaths and marriages, the effects of which can be ignored only to the detriment of the inhabitants of the Territory.[45]

In subsequent cases before UK courts the Namibia exception was applied, but subject to further qualifications. In *Emin v Yeldag*,[46] the Court held that private acts performed in an unrecognised State could be recognised in the UK under two conditions:

■ that such recognition was not prohibited by statute; and

■ that it did not compromise the conduct of UK foreign relations.

In applying this approach, in *Emin v Yeldag* a divorce decree obtained in the TRNC, which was not recognised by the UK (see Chapter 5.7), was given recognition in the UK. However, in *Adams v Adams (Attorney-General Intervening)*[47] the UK courts refused to recognise a divorce granted by the Rhodesian courts, because its recognition would have been contrary to the UK Southern Rhodesia Act 1965, which declared that Southern Rhodesia continued to be part of Her Majesty's dominions and that 'the Government and Parliament of the United Kingdom have responsibility and jurisdiction as heretofore for and in respect of it.' In *R v Kibris Türk Hava Yollari and CTA Holidays* Limited[48] Lord Justice Richards examined *obiter*, the application of the Namibia exception. In this case the Cyprus Turkish Airline, a Turkish registered airline, and its wholly owned subsidiary CTA Holdays, a travel agent registered in England and specialising in providing holidays in the TRNC, applied to the UK Secretary of State for Transport for the grant of an operation permit to conduct direct flights from the UK to the TRNC and *vice versa*. The permit was refused. The Court of Appeal upheld the refusal on the ground that its granting would be in breach of the rights of the Republic of Cyprus (RoC) (the RoC was recognised by the UK but the TRNC was not), under the 1944 Chicago Convention on International Civil Aviation to which both the RoC and the UK were contracting parties. The Court rejected the application of the Namibia exception on the ground that the granting of the permit involved a public law decision which was different from decisions affecting everyday affairs of citizens of an unrecognised State.

B. The 1991 Foreign Corporations Act

The 1991 Foreign Corporations Act provides that if a question of legal personality or any other material question (i.e. concerning the capacity, constitution or otherwise) relating to a foreign corporation which has been incorporated under the laws of a territory which is not recognised as a State by the UK arises, that question should be resolved in accordance with the laws of that territory if it appears that the laws of that territory are applied by a settled court system in that territory. Section 1 of the Act equates the unrecognised territory with a recognised State if that unrecognised territory has a settled court system. This means that UK courts will apply, in the situation described above, the laws of an unrecognised State as if it were a recognised State. The Act was applied in *R v Ministry of Agriculture, Fisheries and Food, ex p S.P. Anastasiou (Pissouri) and Others*.

---

45   Ibid, para 125.
46   [2002] 1 FLR 956.
47   [1971] P 188.
48   (2010) EWCA Civ 1093.

R V MINISTRY OF AGRICULTURE, FISHERIES AND FOOD, EX P S.P. ANASTASIOU (PISSOURI) AND OTHERS

Facts:

Under the 1972 Association Agreement and its Protocol concluded between the Republic of Cyprus and the EEC, citrus fruits and potatoes originating from Cyprus benefited from preferential treatment in terms of customs duties in EEC countries (now the EU) if accompanied by a certificate confirming the originating status of the products, and by other phytosanitary certificates issued by the exporting State. The 1972 Agreement and its Protocol established a system of co-operation between the authorities of the exporting and the importing States, in that the relevant authority in the importing State, if in doubt as to the validity or veracity of the relevant certificates, could consult the relevant authority in the exporting State, and settle any dispute in accordance with the Agreement. Some member States, including the UK, depending upon the circumstances, accepted the certificates issued by the competent authority of the TRNC. The claimants, supported by the Greek government, argued that the acceptance by the UK customs and excise authorities of certificates issued by the TRNC was unlawful. In proceedings before an English court, a company incorporated in the TRNC, Cypfruvex, sought to intervene. Popplewell J applied the 1991 Foreign Corporations Act to Cypfruvex and held that Cypfruvex had locus standi *because it satisfied the conditions of the Act in that there was a territory (the TRNC) unrecognised by the UK, that territory had a settled legal system, and that Cypfruvex was incorporated by the laws of that territory. However, Popplewell J decided to refer the matter of interpretation of EC law to the ECJ within the preliminary ruling procedure.*

Before the ECJ, the UK government and the European Commission submitted that the principle of non-discrimination enshrined in Article 8 EC Treaty required that the whole population of Cyprus (including that of the TRNC) should benefit from any advantage conferred by the EC Treaty, in particular in a situation where it was impossible for exporters from the TRNC to obtain the relevant certificates from the Republic of Cyprus.

Held:

The ECJ:

The ECJ held that the system established under the 1972 Agreement and its Protocol could work properly only if there was total confidence and co-operation between exporting and importing States. The special situation of Cyprus precluded such co-operation between EC member States and the TRNC. Accordingly, the ECJ stated that certificates issued by the authorities in the TRNC could not be accepted by importing States as their acceptance would undermine the object and purpose of the system established by the 1972 Agreement and its Protocol.[49]

The High Court of England and Wales:

In the light of the preliminary ruling delivered by the ECJ, Popplewell J decided that certificates issued by the TRNC could not be accepted in the UK as they were in breach of EC law.

---

49   Case C-432/92 *R v Minister of Agriculture, Fisheries and Food, ex p Anastasiou (Pissouri) Ltd (Anastasiou I)* (1994) ECR I-3087.

It is important to note that EC law, being supreme, prevails over any conflicting national law and therefore in a situation where EC law is relevant it prevails over the 1991 Foreign Corporations Act. However, the reasoning of Popplewell is applicable to any situation which has no connection with EC law.

Comment:

It is submitted that the judgment of the ECJ in the Anastasiou I Case *does not undermine the 1991 Foreign Corporations Act and its objectives, i.e. the settlement of issues relating to 'private international law'. It separates matters of UK foreign policy from matters relating to the legal personality of corporations whatever the status of the territory of their incorporation so far as UK law is concerned. It is submitted that the ECJ's judgment was based on practical rather than political considerations, i.e. the fact that the TRNC was unrecognised. This submission is supported by the fact that the ECJ in* R v Minister of Agriculture, Fisheries and Food, ex p Anastasiou (Pissouri) Ltd (Anastasiou II)[50] *decided that the relevant certificates issued by Turkey in respect of products covered by the 1972 Agreement and its Protocol were not in breach of EC law, i.e. the ECJ accepted indirect imports – via Turkey – of the mentioned produce on the ground that Turkey was a State recognised by the EU and its member States.*

In some situations the interpretation of domestic statutes will reveal that the issue at hand has no connection with the status of an unrecognised State. In *R (on the application of North Cyprus Tourism Centre Ltd) v Transport for London*[51] the claimant sought judicial review of a decision of Transport for London to remove adverts for holidays in the TRNC from buses, on the ground that the TRNC was not recognised in the UK, and therefore tourism in the TRNC should not be promoted. The Court held that the contracts for promotion were with UK companies and therefore no acts of authorities of the TRNC were at issue.

6.4.2 Recognition of governments in UK law

Up to 1980, UK Foreign Office certificates were conclusive evidence for UK courts so far as the recognition or otherwise of a foreign government was concerned. It is to be noted that nothing prevents the UK Foreign Office from issuing such certificates post-1980 if it so wishes. However, this will be a rare occurrence (see below).

In April 1980 the Foreign Office adopted the Estrada doctrine and thus abandoned its practice of expressly recognising foreign governments when they come to power unconstitutionally. As a result, UK courts, instead of relying on a Foreign Office certificate, have to determine whether an entity in question is a government for the purposes of UK internal law. This section examines, first, the effects in UK law of non-recognition of a foreign government, and, second, the case law since the 1980 change in UK practice.

---

50   (2000) ECR I-5241.
51   (2005) UKHRR 1231.

6.4.2.1 The effects of non-recognition of a government in UK law

Non-recognition of a government has the following effects in UK law:

A. If a government is not recognised, it is not entitled to sovereign immunity
The principle that if a government is not recognised by the UK, it is not entitled to sovereign immunity was explained in *Arantzazu Mendi*[52] in which it was established that a plea of immunity can be raised by an authority recognised as being in *de facto* control of territory, even if the proceedings are brought by the *de jure* sovereign.

ARANTZAZU MENDI

Facts:

This case arose out of the Spanish Civil War between, on the one side, Nationalist rebels led by Generals José Sanjurjo, Emilio Mola and Francisco Franco, and, on the other side, the legitimately elected government known as the Popular Front, Republicans or Loyalists.

In June 1937, shortly before the Basque region of Spain fell to the Nationalist rebels, the Spanish Republican government issued a decree requisitioning all ships registered in the Spanish port of Bilbao, including the Arantzazu Mendi *owned by the respondent Spanish company, and which was at sea when the decree was issued. In March 1938 the Nationalist government issued a decree requisitioning ships registered in Bilbao, a city situated in the Basque region. The respondent company did not oppose this second requisition and agreed to hold the ship, then in the Port of London, for the Nationalists. The Republican government then issued an English writ for possession of the* Arantzazu Mendi *on the basis of its 1937 decree. The Nationalist government sought to have the writ set aside on the ground that it impleaded a sovereign State.*

Held:

On the question of whether the Nationalist government of Spain was a sovereign State the judge at first instance directed a letter to be written to the UK Secretary of State for Foreign Affairs as to the status of the Nationalist authorities. In reply it was stated that His Majesty's government recognised Spain as a sovereign State, and recognised the government of the Spanish Republic as the only de jure *government of Spain or any part of it. The reply also stated that:*

1 *His Majesty's government recognises the Nationalist government as a government which at present exercises* de facto *administrative control over the larger portion of Spain.*
2 *His Majesty's government recognises that the Nationalist government now exercises effective administrative control over all the Basque Provinces of Spain.*
3 *His Majesty's government have not accorded any other recognition to the Nationalist government.*
4 *The Nationalist government is not a government subordinated to any other government in Spain.*

---

52   [1939] AC 256.

5 The question whether the Nationalist government is to be regarded as that of a foreign Sovereign state appears to be a question of law to be answered in the light of the preceding statements and having regard to the particular issue with respect to which the question is raised.

Held:

The House of Lords held that the Foreign Office letter established that the Nationalist government of Spain at the date of the writ was a foreign sovereign State and could not be impleaded. Lord Atkin stated:

> this letter appears to me to dispose of the controversy. By 'exercising de facto administrative control' or 'exercising effective administrative control', I understand exercising all functions of a Sovereign Government, i.e. maintaining law and order, instituting and maintaining acts of justice, adopting or imposing laws regulating the relations of the inhabitants of the territory to one another and to the Government ... That the decree, therefore, emanated from the Sovereign in that territory there can be no doubt. There is ample authority for the proposition that there is no difference for the present purposes between a recognition of a state de facto as opposed to de jure. All the reasons for immunity which are the basis of the doctrine in international law as incorporated into our law exist.[53]

B. If a government is not recognised it cannot sue or be sued in UK courts

In *City of Berne v Bank of England* [54] it was held that an unrecognised government has no *locus standi* in English courts.

C. If a government is not recognised its laws are not to be applied in UK courts

The leading case on this topic is *Luther v Sagor.*[55]

LUTHER *V* SAGOR

Facts:

In 1920 the defendant company purchased a quantity of timber from the then recently constituted Soviet government of Russia. The plaintiff Russian company claimed title to the timber on the ground that it had come from a factory in Russia that had been owned by it before being nationalised by the Soviet government in 1919. The plaintiff argued, inter alia, that the nationalising decree should not be recognised by the English court because the Soviet government had not been recognised by Great Britain.

---

53   Ibid, 264–265.
54   (1804) 9 Ves 347.
55   [1921] 1 KB 456.

Held:

Roche J held:

> *If a foreign Government, or its sovereignty, is not recognised by the Government of this country the Courts of this country either cannot, or at least need not, or ought not, to take notice of, or recognise such foreign Government or its sovereignty . . . I am not satisfied that His Majesty's Government has recognised the Soviet Government as the Government of a Russian Federative Republic or of any Sovereign state or power. I therefore am unable to recognise it, or to hold it has sovereignty, or is able by decree to deprive the plaintiff company of its property.*

On appeal this decision in favour of the plaintiff was reversed in the light of the intervening recognition of the Soviet government by the British government.

> *This recognition was held to be retroactive and to be dated back to the date of the actual coming into being of the recognised entity, which in this particular case was when the Soviets seized power in 1917. The nationalising decree confiscating the timber could therefore be recognised.*

> *In the Court of Appeal, Bankes LJ stated that so far as the first instance decision was concerned: 'Upon the evidence which was before the learned judge I think that his decision was quite right.'*[56]

D. If a government is not recognised it is not entitled to the property of the State which it claims to govern

The leading case on this is *Haile Selassie v Cable and Wireless Limited (No 2).*[57]

HAILE SELASSIE *V* CABLE AND WIRELESS LIMITED *(NO 2)*

Facts:

In 1935 Italy invaded Abyssinia (the Empire of Ethiopia was before WWII referred to as Abyssinia) and formally annexed that territory on 9 May 1936. Prior to the invasion the plaintiff had made a contract with the defendants for the transmission of wireless messages between Abyssinia and Great Britain. In 1937 the plaintiff commenced proceedings to recover money due under the contract. At this time the plaintiff was still recognised by Great Britain as the de jure *sovereign of Abyssinia, although Italy was recognised as the* de facto *government. The question before the court was whether the Italian government, which was recognised by the UK as the* de facto *government of Ethiopia, had the right to sue for a debt due and recoverable by the plaintiff before an English court despite the fact that the plaintiff as Emperor of Ethiopia was recognised as the* de jure *sovereign of Ethiopia.*

---

56   [1921] 3 KB 532, 544.
57   [1939] 1 Ch 182.

Held:

At first instance Bennett J held that the plaintiff had not been divested of the right to sue for the debt in spite of the fact that the British government recognised the Italian government as the de facto *government of virtually the whole of Abyssinia.*

The defendants had relied, inter alia, *on the decision in* Luther v Sagor *to establish the exclusive power of the* de facto *government. The learned judge distinguished the current case, saying:*

> *I think the only point established by [Luther v Sagor] is that where the Government of this country has recognised that some foreign Government is* de facto *governing some foreign territory, the law of England will regard the acts of* de facto *Government in that territory as valid and treat them with all the respect due to the acts of a duly recognised foreign Sovereign state. It is clear I think that the acts so treated are acts in relation to persons or property in the territory which the authority is recognised as governing in fact.*

> *It was not suggested in that case nor was anything said in it which supports the view that on or in consequence of such recognition a title to property in this country vests in the* de facto *Government and that a title vested in a displaced Government is divested . . . The present case is not concerned with the validity of acts in relation to persons or property in Ethiopia. It is concerned with the title to a chose in action – a debt, recoverable in England.*[58]

While an appeal by the defendants was pending the British government recognised the King of Italy as the de jure *Emperor of Ethiopia. Sir Wilfrid Greene MR stated:*

> *It is not disputed that in the Courts of this country, His Majesty the King of Italy as Emperor of Abyssinia is entitled by succession to the public property of the state of Abyssinia and the late Emperor of Abyssinia's title thereto is no longer recognised as existent . . . that right of succession is to be dated back at any rate to the date when the* de facto *recognition of the King of Italy as the* de facto *Sovereign of Abyssinia took place . . . in December 1936 . . . Now that being so the title of the plaintiff to sue is necessarily displaced.*

6.4.2.2 The change of the UK policy on recognition of governments

It is important to note that the decision of the UK government in April 1980 to abandon the practice of expressly recognising foreign governments has introduced an element of uncertainty into this particular area of the law.

In the House of Lords in May 1980, the Foreign Secretary, Lord Carrington, was asked:

> How in future, for the purposes of legal proceedings, it may be ascertained whether, on a particular date, Her Majesty's Government regarded a new regime as the government of the State concerned?

---

58   [1939] Ch 182, 190.

The Foreign Secretary replied:

> In future cases where a new regime comes to power unconstitutionally our attitude to the question whether it qualifies to be treated as a government will be left to be inferred from the nature of the dealings, if any, which we may have with it, and in particular on whether we are dealing with it on a normal government-to-government basis.[59]

A.   Possible problems in the implementation of the post-1980 policy of the UK government

The abandonment of express recognition of foreign governments may give rise to several problems for the judges when deciding whether an entity qualifies to be treated as a government. Those problems are:

- the Foreign Office may not make available to the judges details of its dealings with the foreign government;

- even if such details are made available it may be difficult for judges, in the absence of diplomatic experience, to infer from the nature of those dealings whether or not the foreign government qualifies to be treated as a government;

- if a government is in firm control of a State, it may be unjust to refuse to apply its laws in an English court solely because the British government refuses to have dealings with it;

- the extent of a government's control over its territory, and not the extent of its dealings with the British government, remains the best test of its international status;

- if the courts were to adopt the control test and the Foreign Office were to refuse to provide the judges with details of a particular government's control over its territory, the judges might have difficulty in deciding whether such control does in fact exist.

B.   Post-1980 case law

In *Republic of Somalia v Woodhouse Drake and Carey (Suisse) SA*[60] Hobhouse J set out four criteria for the determination of whether an entity should be recognised as a government.

REPUBLIC OF SOMALIA *V* WOODHOUSE DRAKE AND CAREY (SUISSE) SA

Facts:

The incumbent government of Somalia purchased and paid for a cargo of rice for delivery at the port of Mogadishu. However, prior to delivery, the government was overthrown and a provisional government established. In the meantime, the cargo was not delivered to its port of destination due to fighting.

The provisional government of Somalia, which succeeded the above mentioned incumbent government, raised an action for recovery of the price of the undelivered goods and the court had to consider whether the provisional government had standing to bring the action.

---

59   (1980) 51 BYIL, 367–368. See also C. Warbrick, *Recognition of Governments* (1993) 56 MLR, 92.
60   [1992] 3 WLR 744.

Held:

Hobhouse J examined what have become referred to as four criteria in order to decide whether the plaintiff existed as the government of the State of Somalia. They were:

- *whether the plaintiff was the constitutional government of the State;*
- *the degree, nature and stability of administrative control, if any, that the plaintiff maintained over the territory of the State;*
- *whether Her Majesty's government had any dealings with the provisional government and, if so, what were the nature and extent of those dealings; and*
- *the extent of the international recognition afforded by the world community to the provisional government as the government of the State.*

The evidence submitted by the provisional government of Somalia failed to satisfy these criteria and the claim to the price of the consignment was rejected.

The criteria set out in the *Republic of Somalia* case have been applied in subsequent cases. One of those is *Sierra Leone Telecommunications Co Ltd v Barclays Bank plc.*[61]

SIERRA LEONE TELECOMMUNICATIONS CO LTD *V* BARCLAYS BANK PLC

Facts:

Sierra Leone Telecommunications Co Ltd (Sierratel), incorporated in Sierra Leone, wholly owned by the government of Sierra Leone and controlled by it, held a US dollar account at Barclays Bank in London. The relevant bank mandate had been drawn up in July 1996 and provided for four signatories. In May 1997 Sierra Leone's democratically elected government of President Kabbah had been ousted in a military coup and replaced by a military junta. The ministers in the government of President Kabbah had fled to the Republic of Guinea. The UK government had continued to deal with President Kabbah and had been active in demanding the restoration of the democratic government. The military junta's regime was condemned by the UN, the Commonwealth, the AU and the EU.

In December 1997 Barclays Bank in London received a letter purportedly from Sierratel in Freetown which stated that a board meeting had resolved that the original bank mandate be suspended. The London bank was faced with a dilemma as to whether to continue to respect instructions of the original signatories to the mandate or whether to accept new instructions emanating from the head office of Sierratel.

The Sierra Leone High Commissioner in London, who remained loyal to President Kabbah, began proceedings seeking a declaration that the London bank account remained subject to the original mandate of July 1996.

---

61   [1998] 2 All ER 821.

Held:

The Court held that the claimant was entitled to the declaration. The Court stated that the question whether the military junta in Sierra Leone was to be regarded as the recognised government was to be tested by applying the criteria set out by Hobhouse J in Republic of Somalia v Woodhouse Drake and Carey (Suisse) SA *(above). The Court took into consideration the facts:*

- *that the British government was continuing to deal with President Kabbah and had been active in seeking the restoration of his constitutional and democratic regime;*
- *that the military junta did not have effective control beyond Freetown and could not be said to be in control of the entire country;*
- *that the military regime had been condemned by the Commonwealth and the OAU;*
- *that UN sanctions against the regime had been given the force of law by delegated legislation in the UK.*

The application of the criteria established in the Republic of Somalia *case to the above facts convinced the Court that the military junta was not the government of Sierra Leone and thus lacked the legal capacity under the Sierra Leone constitution to alter the board of directors of Sierratel or to suspend the bank mandate.*

Comment:

This case indicates that, whatever the difficulties of English courts in deciding whether or not to accord recognition to governments, the criteria set out by Hobhouse J in the Republic of Somalia *case continue to represent sensible and workable guidelines. They have become the governing orthodoxy on the matter.*

It is to be noted that despite the 1980 statement, in *British Arab Commercial Bank plc v The National Transitional Council of the State of Libya*[62] the UK Foreign Secretary provided the Court with a certificate. He made the following statement:

[T]he United Kingdom recognises and will deal with the National Transitional Council as the sole governmental authority in Libya. This decision reflects the NTC's increasing legitimacy, competence and success in reaching out to Libyans across the country.[63]

In this case the issue was whether the British Commercial Bank was entitled to act on the instruction of the NTC in releasing money from the Libyan government embassy's fund in London to Libyan students in the UK. The Court was satisfied with the statement made by the Foreign Secretary recognising the NTC as the government of Libya. It emphasized that the judiciary and the executive must speak with one voice and therefore there was no need for any factual investigation into the status of the NTC, i.e. there was no need to apply the criteria set out in the *Republic of Somalia*, which the NTC may have failed to satisfy, in particular regarding the effective control over Libya.

---

62   [2011] EWHC 2274.

63   Foreign and Commonwealth Office, 'Libyan Charge d'Affaires to be expelled from UK' (27 July 2011) available at www.fco.gov.uk/en/news/latest-news/?id=635937682&view=News (accessed 10 September 2014).

6.5 Recognition of IGOs in national law: the UK

The most important aspect of conducting international relations for IGOs is their recognition by third States and other IGOs.

If international personality is conferred on an IGO, either expressly or impliedly, its members, by signing the constitutional instrument, *ipso facto* recognise it in their domestic legal order.

A distinction, however, must be made between monist and dualist States (see Chapter 4.2). In monist States international law forms part of the municipal law and as such can be relied upon before national courts. In dualist States an international agreement must be incorporated into the municipal law in order to produce legal effects at national level. The House of Lords in the *International Tin Council*[64] stated that '[the] ITC as a matter of English law owes its existence to the Order in Council. That is what created the ITC in domestic law'. This means that an IGO of which the UK is a member can acquire its personality in the UK either:

- through the adoption of an Order in Council which confers upon such an organisation 'legal capacities of a body corporate'; or

- through the enactment of specific legislation by the UK Parliament in respect of a given organisation.

The situation is more complicated in respect of States which are not members of an IGO. States are entitled to use their discretion. In the absence of recognition, acts of a new entity in international law would not be opposable by those who refuse to recognise it.

6.5.1 The status of an IGO in the municipal law of a State which is not a member of the IGO concerned

The status of IGOs in national law has become a matter of increasing importance. The extent of the rights and duties of IGOs in the UK of which the UK is not a member was clarified by the House of Lords in *Arab Monetary Fund v Hashim (No 3)*.[65]

ARAB MONETARY FUND *V* HASHIM (NO 3)

Facts:

The Arab Monetary Fund (AMF) was established by an international agreement among 20 Arab States and the Palestine Liberation Organisation (PLO). Under Article 2 of the treaty creating the AMF it was granted 'independent judicial personality' which included the rights to own, contract and litigate. The headquarters of the AMF was in Abu Dhabi, and in 1977 the United Arab Emirates (UAE) passed legislation incorporating the treaty which created the AMF into its national law, thereby conferring legal personality within the UAE on the AMF.

Hashim, a former director-general of the AMF, was alleged to have absconded with approximately US$50 million in assets belonging to the AMF. In 1988 Hashim was found

---

64   [1990] 2 AC 418.
65   [1991] 1 All ER 871.

residing in the UK and the AMF raised an action against Hashim, and a number of banks which had allegedly assisted in laundering a substantial part of the embezzled proceeds, for recovery of the stolen money. The defendants argued that the claimant possessed no legal personality, being an international organisation established under a treaty to which the UK was not a party, and therefore had no standing to bring the action.

Held:

The House of Lords made a number of interesting statements concerning the legal personality of IGOs in English law. Most importantly, it held that the UK was not obliged to recognise an entity created by a treaty to which it was not a party. Ultimately, the House of Lords held that the AMF could not have legal personality in English law unless the treaty creating it had been incorporated into English law. The AMF, therefore, had no legal existence in English law.

The commencement and continuation of the action was allowed, not on the ground that the AMF possessed legal personality, but by virtue of the conflict of laws principle that entities which possess legal personality in municipal law of a foreign State are entitled to raise actions by virtue of their status as foreign legal entities.

Comment:

It is to be noted that under the 1991 Foreign Corporations Act the AMF would have had legal personality in the UK as it met the three criteria set out in that Act (see Chapter 6.4.1.2.B). Indeed, the Act was the response of the UK legislature to the case.

RECOMMENDED READING

Books

Crawford, C.J., *The Creation of States in International Law*, Oxford: Oxford University Press, 2006.
Caplan, R., *Europe and the Recognition of New States in Yugoslavia*, Cambridge: Cambridge University Press, 2005.
Radan, P., *The Break-up of Yugoslavia and International Law*, New York: Routledge, 2002.
Talmon, S., *Recognition of Governments in International Law*, Oxford: Oxford University Press, 1998.
White, N.D., *The Law of International Organizations*, 2nd edn, Manchester: Manchester University Press, 2005.

Articles

Hillgruber, C., *The Admission of New States to the International Community* (1998) 9 EJIL, 491.
Mann, F.A., *The Judicial Recognition of an Unrecognised State* (1987) 36 ICLQ, 349.
Murphy, S.D., *Democratic Legitimacy and the Recognition of States and Governments* (1999) 48 ICLQ, 545.
Shaw, M.N., *Legal Acts of an Unrecognised Entity* (1978) 94 LQR, 500.
Warbrick, C., *Recognition of Governments* (1993) 56 MLR, 92.
Vidmar, J., *Explaining the Legal Effects of Recognition* (2012) 61 ICLQ, 361.
Vidmar, J., *Palestine and the Conceptual Problem of Implicit Statehood* (2013) Chinese Journal of International Law, 19.

AIDE-MÉMOIRE

Recognition of States

Recognition may be defined as a discretionary act exercised unilaterally by the government of a State ackowledging the existence of another State: there are two theories on recognition:

According to the declaratory theory recognition is a mere formality. States exist as a matter of fact and the granting of recognition is merely an acknowledgment of that fact. Thus the position of an entity under international law stems from the fact that it possesses the necessary attributes of statehood and not from its recognition or non-recognition by the members of the international community.

According to the constitutive theory a State may possess all the formal attributes and qualifications of statehood but unless recognition is accorded by other States it will not acquire international personality. Therefore, it is the recognition by other States that creates a new State. This is because as international law has no organ or body empowered to determine whether an entity qualifies as a State, the only possible organ to do this is the existing States, acting unilaterally or collectively.

Recognition of governments

Recognition of governments is based on political considerations. There are three approaches to recognition of governments:

An objective approach. Under this approach a State recognises a new government on a factual basis, namely that the new government is independent and has effective control over that State's territory and that this control seems likely to continue, without giving any judgement on the legality of that government or any approval. This approach had, until 1980, been applied by the UK government. It made official announcements according recognition to governments.

A subjective approach. Under this approach a State by recognising a new government expresses its approval and endorses the policy of that new government. The US has always used the recognition of a new government as a powerful political tool.

The Estrada doctrine. Under this doctrine no express recognition is necessary. All that is required is to establish that the authority in question exercises effective control over the relevant territory. Since 1980 this approach has been adopted by the UK.

UK courts have to decide, without any firm guidance from the UK government, whether an entity can be recognised as a government of a State. The test established by Hobhouse J in *Republic of Somalia v Woodhouse Drake and Carey (Suisse) SA*, seems to be generally accepted. The test sets out four criteria in the light of which a court will decide whether an entity exists as a government of a State. These criteria are:

Whether the entity is the constitutional government of the State.

The degree, nature and stability of administrative control, if any, that the entity maintains over the territory of the State.

Whether Her Majesty's government has any dealings with the entity and, if so, the nature and extent of those dealings.

The extent of international recognition afforded by the world community to the entity as the government of the State concerned.

7

TERRITORIAL SOVEREIGNTY

CHAPTER OUTLINE

1 Introduction

Territorial sovereignty was described in the *Island of Palmas Arbitration* as being 'the right to exercise therein [i.e. on the territory], to the exclusion of any other State, the functions of a sovereign'. Territorial sovereignty has two aspects:

- internal, which concerns the authority exercised by a State within its borders over persons and situations/events that occur there. It also encompasses the right to dispose of the territory; and

- external, which entails that a State must respect the territorial integrity of other States, i.e. must not interfere in other States' internal and external affairs and must ensure the safety of foreign nationals present within its territory. This obligation is embodied in the principle of non-intervention.

In addition to territorial sovereignty, there are three other territorial regimes recognised by international law:

- territory not subject to the sovereignty of any State or States and which possesses a status of its own (e.g. mandate and trust territories – See Chapter 13.2.1 and 13.2.2.1);

- *terra nullius*, being land legally susceptible to acquisition by States, but not as yet placed under any territorial sovereignty;

- *res communis*, consisting of the high seas, and also outer space, which is not capable of being placed under the sovereignty of any State as it belongs to the Community of States.

2 Different types of territorial sovereignty

There are different types of territorial sovereignty resulting from the divisibility of territorial sovereignty, and distribution of the components of sovereignty:

A. Titular (or residual sovereignty) and effective sovereignty:

- Titular (or residual sovereignty) is possessed by an entity which has the ultimate capacity to dispose of the territory.

- Effective sovereignty is attributed to an entity which exercises plenary actual power over the territory, but lacks the capacity of ultimate disposal.

Titular and effective sovereignty together make up the totality of sovereignty.

B. Condominium – this occurs when two or more States jointly exercise sovereignty over a piece of territory and its inhabitants.

C. Terminable and reversionary sovereignty. This refers to a situation where sovereignty of a territory changes by operation of law as a result of fulfilment of a condition or a failure to meet an express or implied condition.

D. Indeterminate sovereignty – this may occur when a territory which is not *terra nullius* nevertheless has no determinate sovereign.

3 Principles and rules applicable to the acquisition of title to territory

The following principles and rules can be identified.

A. The rules of *jus cogens* such as: the prohibition (other than in self-defence or as mandated by the UNSC) of the threat or the use of force against the territorial integrity or the political independence of a State, the principle of settlement of disputes in a peaceful manner and the principle of self-determination. However, the content of *jus cogens* is much disputed and even the principles just mentioned, probably, apart from the prohibition of the use of force, may not qualify as being of a *jus cogens* nature (see Chapter 2.5.1). The *jus cogens* rules apply to all modes of acquisition/loss of territory by a State. Thus the validity of and/or effect of any mode of acquiring territorial title or losing it by a State will be tested by reference to these fundamental rules. However, their application is subject to the limitations imposed by the intertemporal law.

B. Specific principles applicable to the acquisition of title to territory. These are:

- The principle of effectiveness. This has many meanings, but in the context of acquisition of title to territory it refers to how a factual situation affects the creation of a right, i.e. the acquisition of legal title to territory. That situation being the exercise of effective authority over the relevant territory. The principle of effectiveness is of relevance to the following modes of acquisition of territory: occupation, acquisitive prescription and (prior to the prohibition of the use of force) the acquisition of territory by conquest. Further, it plays an important role in the settlement of disputes concerning conflicting claims to territory.

- The principle of *uti possidetis*. This was first developed among the Spanish colonies of Latin America in the nineteenth century and later accepted by the Organisation of African Unity in its 1964 Cairo Declaration. The principle provides that the old colonial boundaries will be recognised as the borders of the newly independent ex-colonial States. The principle ensures territorial integrity for newly independent States thus allowing them to survive, consolidate and develop. The Badinter Commission in its Opinions 2 and 3 applied the principle of *uti possidetis* in the European context, that is in dealing with the issues of self-determination and the determination of frontiers of new States which have emerged as a result of the disintegration of the former Socialist Federal Republic of Yugoslavia (SFRY) and of the Soviet Union.

- Intertemporal law concerns the temporal application of legal rules, that is whether a judical fact should be appreciated in the light of the law contemporary with it or in the light of the law in existence when a matter or dispute arose or failed to be settled. The famous Swiss arbitrator M. Hubert in the *Island of Palmas Arbitration* in 1928 acknowledged that while a judical fact should be appraised in the light of the rules of international law contemporaneous with that judicial fact he added that a distinction must be made between the creation of rights and their continued existence. The creation of rights should be assessed in accordance with rules contemporaneous with the time of their creation, while the continued existence of rights is to be determined in accordance with the rules of international law as they exist at the time of dispute. This distinction was criticised as undermining the stability of international relations as it implies that States would constantly have to re-establish title to territory due to the evolving nature of international law. One view is that the two elements in Hubert's definition are complementary and that they ensure stability as to the creation of rights, and flexibility as to the evolutions of rights.

C. The critical date rule. This is a procedural rule which refers to the date on which a territorial dispute crystallised. After that date subsequent events will not be taken into account in the determination of the rights of the parties.

D. Evidentiary rules. These are:

- Recognition. In respect of land claims recognition refers mainly to the attitude of third States, i.e. States not involved in a dispute. By a unilateral declaration or by an international treaty they may show that they have accepted a particular situation. However, recognition will also be of relevance in a situation where a State by positive conduct, even if contrary to an existing treaty, acknowledges that its opponent has a valid title to a disputed territory.

■ Acquiescence. This refers to the attitude of a dispossessed State and is inferred from its failure to protest in circumstances where protest might reasonably have been expected against the exercise of control by its opponent over disputed territory.

■ Estoppel. The situation of estoppel arises when a State's conduct is clear, sustained and consistent and the other party relying on such conduct has changed its position to its own detriment or has suffered some prejudice.

4 Modes of acquisition of title to territory

The traditional five modes are:

A. Occupation. Only *terra nullius* can be acquired by occupation. The condition for the acquisition of title to any territory by occupation is effective possession. Such possession combines the intention of a State to act as sovereign and some actual exercise or display of State activity consistent with sovereignty. Nowadays the acquisition of territory by occupation is of little relevance as there is practically no *terra nullius*.

B. Acquisitive prescription. This concerns the acquisition of territory by a State through continuous and undisturbed exercise of sovereignty for a long period over a territory belonging to another State during which period the latter does not protest the occupation, i.e. the occupying State may claim title on the basis of the implied acquiescence of the alleged dispossessed State and sufficient passage of time.

C. Accretion. This refers to slow, gradual increase of land due to accumulation of soil material such as sand, silt, clay, gravel resulting from natural causes. The opposite of accretion is erosion which occurs when land is gradually washed away by water or in natural course. Sudden or violent changes due to storms, floods, eruptions of a volcano, or sudden changes in course of a body of water are known as avulsion. Accretion entails gradualness while avulsion entails suddenness. With regard to boundary rivers, a State may gain title to land formed by accretion in or near its border river but not as a result of avulsion.

D. Cession. This consists of the peaceful transfer of territory from the grantor State to the grantee State usually by a treaty, although the form in which the States concerned express their understanding is not important. Both States must consent and a consent obtained by the use of or a threat of force is invalid by virtue of Article 52 VCLT. Cession is an example of a derivative title and thus the grantee State cannot possess more rights than the grantor State. The grantee, upon the passing of the title, is responsible under international law for any wrongful acts committed in the territory concerned.

E. Conquest. This was a historical method of establishing sovereignty over a territory. The prohibition of the use of force outlawed this basis for claiming title to territory.

Three additional modes can be added: historical consolidation, novation (replacement of sovereignty rather than succession) and the acquisition of a title to territory resulting from a joint decision of victors of wars in the twentieth century.

5 Other circumstances relevant to the acquisition of territory

These are:

A. Contiguity. This was rejected as a mode of acquisition of title to territory. Nowadays contiguity is regarded as a fact which may influence the decision of an international tribunal.

B. Discovery. In the Middle Ages, mere discovery without actual possession was sufficient to establish a valid title to territory. The modern view is that discovery merely gives an option to the discovering State to consolidate its claim by proceeding to effective occupation within a reasonable time.

C. Symbolic annexation. This will be accepted as establishing a valid title only in special circumstances, such as those described in the *Clipperton Island Arbitration.*

D. Adjudication/arbitration only confirms the existence of a title to territory as courts and arbitral bodies have no power to grant title.

6 Acquisition of territory in polar regions

In the Arctic the race continues between the five coastal States to claim the extension of their continental shelf beyond the 200 nautical miles mark from baselines but all are willing to co-operate in respect of environmental matters. The 1959 Antarctic Treaty, on the one hand, has imposed a moratorium on territorial claims to Antarctica and, on the other, ensures that this region is used for peaceful purposes only.

7 Restrictions on the transfer of territory

It is doubtful whether restrictions normally imposed by treaties on the transfer of territory by a State will affect the title of a grantee State.

8 Loss of territory

This mainly results from cession, acquisitive prescription, emergence of a new State which entails that another State loses territory and, by abandonment. Abandonment requires both physical abandonment of territory and an intention to abandon it. For reasons of stability there is a rebuttable presumption against abandonment of title to territory.

9 Rights over parts of territory of a foreign State: international leases and servitudes

With regard to leases each agreement is *sui generis*, but the general principle is that a leased territory remains under the residual sovereignty of the lessor State, while the lessee State has exclusive jurisdiction over it for the period of the lease. Servitudes occur when territory of one State is made to serve the interests of another State. By treaty or otherwise a State may be entitled to do something on the territory concerned (e.g. to exercise a right of way) or to compel the other State to refrain from doing something, (e.g. fortifying its towns). Servitudes may benefit the international community or a particular State.

7.1 Introduction

The territory of a State is the foundation of its factual existence and the basis for the exercise of its legal powers. Territory has both a physical[1] and a legal dimension.

■ As to the physical element, the territory of a State comprises all land areas (including subterranean areas), waters (including national rivers and lakes), the territorial sea appurtenant to the land, and the sea-bed and subsoil of the territorial sea, and the airspace over the land and the territorial sea[2] (see Chapter 8). Territorial sovereignty may be exercised over various geographical features analogous to land including islands, islets, rocks and reefs.

■ So far as the legal element is concerned, the possession of territory and the exclusive exercise of (territorial) jurisdiction therein is one of the essential elements of State sovereignty.

Territorial sovereignty was described in the *Island of Palmas Arbitration (the Netherlands v US)*[3] as being 'the right to exercise therein [i.e. on the territory], to the exclusion of any other state, the functions of a sovereign'.

Sovereignty understood as *summa potestas*, i.e. supreme power of command within a territory, has both internal and external aspects which coexist, and are omnipresent:

■ The internal aspect concerns the authority exercised by a State within its borders over persons and situations/events that occur there. It encompasses the right to dispose of the territory.

■ The external aspect entails that a State must respect the territorial integrity of other States, must not interfere in the internal affairs of other States and must ensure the safety of foreign nationals present within its territory. Hubert, in the *Island of Palmas Arbitration*, emphasised that a State has a duty to 'protect within the territory the rights of other States, in particular their right to integrity and inviolability in peace and in war, together with the rights which each State may claim for its nationals in foreign territory'.[4] Further, in *the Corfu Channel Case (Merits) (UK v Albania)* the ICJ held that each State has a duty 'not to allow knowingly its territory to be used for acts contrary to the rights of other States'.[5]

In addition to territorial sovereignty three other territorial regimes are recognised by international law:

■ Territory not subject to the sovereignty of any State or States, and which possesses a status of its own (e.g. mandate and trust territories – see Chapter.13.2.1 and 13.2.2.1).

■ *Terra nullius*, being land legally susceptible to acquisition by States but not as yet placed under territorial sovereignty.

■ *Res communis*, consisting of the high seas and outer space, which are not capable of being placed under the sovereignty of any State.

---

1   Article 1 of the 1933 Montevideo Convention which sets out the basic requirements for statehood (see Chapter 5.2).
2   I. Brownlie, *Principles of Public International Law*, 7th edn, Oxford: Oxford University Press, 2008, 115–117.
3   (1928) 2 RIAA 829.
4   Ibid, 839.
5   [1949] ICJ Rep 4, 22.

7.2 Different types of territorial sovereignty

It is sometimes said that territorial sovereignty is indivisible, but there have been numerous instances in international practice, both of division of sovereignty and of distribution of the components of sovereignty. These are examined below.

7.2.1 Titular or residual sovereignty and effective sovereignty

An entity which has the ultimate capacity of disposing of a territory may be said to possess 'titular' or 'residual' sovereignty. The entity which exercises plenary power over a territory but lacks the capacity of ultimate disposal may be said to possess 'effective' sovereignty. For example, with regard to a lease, a lessor State retains residual sovereignty over the leased territory while the lessee State exercises effective control over it. The titular/residual and effective sovereignty make up the totality of sovereignty.

7.2.2 Condominium

Condominium occurs when two or more States jointly exercise sovereignty over a piece of territory and its inhabitants.

The best example was the Anglo-French condominium of the New Hebrides Islands (now Vanuatu) constituted in 1906. Under this arrangement each State was to retain its authority over its nationals and both of them were to exercise joint control over the indigenous inhabitants (see Chapter 5.4.2.4).

7.2.3 Terminable and reversionary sovereignty

Terminable and reversionary sovereignty refers to a situation where sovereignty of a territory may, or will, change by operation of law, for example, when a condition is met, or where a failure to meet an express or implied condition will result in the title to a territory reverting to the grantor.

The fulfilment of a condition under which sovereignty was to revert was envisaged under Article 3 of the 1918 Treaty Establishing the Relations of France with the Principality of Monaco[6] which specified that in the event of vacancy in the Crown of Monaco a new State called 'the State of Monaco' would be established as an autonomous State acting as a protectorate of France. This clause meant that Monaco would revert to France in the case of the absence of a legitimate heir to the Monaco Crown. However, this is of historical interest only, as neither the 2002 Treaty of Friendship between France and Monaco,[7] nor the 2002 Constitution of Monaco make any reference to Article 3 of the 1918 Treaty. Consequently, should there be no heir to carry on the Grimaldi dynasty which has governed Monaco since the thirteenth century, the principality would remain an independent nation State rather than revert to France.

With regard to a failure to satisfy a condition which failure would result in a title reverting to the grantor, in the *South West Africa Cases (Ethiopia v South Africa; Liberia v South Africa) (Preliminary Objections)* Judges Spencer and Fitzmaurice in their joint dissenting opinion stated that the Allied and Associated Powers (Great Britain, France, Italy, Japan and the US) retained a dormant reversionary interest in the territory under mandate until it fulfilled the condition of attaining self-governance or

---

6   981 UNTS 364.

7   Traité destiné à adapter et à confirmer les rapports D'amitié et de coopération entre la République française et la Principauté de Monaco (signed 24 October 2002, entered into force 1 December 2005) (6 January 2006) Journal Officiel de la République Française, 309.

independence.[8] The reference to a 'dormitory reversionary interest' of the principal Allied and Associated Powers by the dissenting judges has proved to be very controversial in that until the termination of the mandate system in 1946 it was unclear as to who had sovereignty in respect of mandated territories. There were three views:

- First, that the Allied and Associated Powers were vested with sovereignity over mandated territories. This was based on the fact that the defeated nations Germany and Turkey had renounced all their rights and titles to their colonial territories (under the 1919 Treaty of Versailles in the case of Germany and under the 1923 Treaty of Lausanne in the case of Turkey) in favour of the Principal Allied and Associated Powers who then conferred mandates directly upon the mandatories. Indeed, the Supreme War Council consisting of the UK, France, Italy, Japan and initially the US, drafted the terms of each mandate and conferred mandates on the selected State. However, with the development of the mandate system, and the growing involvement of the League of Nations it had become clear that the temporary nature of the mandate, the shared responsibility in the administering of mandated territories between mandatories and the League of Nations, and the fact that mandatories had no right to dispose of the territory to a third State undermined the idea that sovereignty was vested in the Principal Allied and Associated Powers.

- Second that sovereignty over mandated territories was attributed to the League of Nations by virtue of Article 22 of the Covenant of the League which stated that mandatories exercised tutelage on behalf of the League of Nations. The counter-arguments were first, that it was doubtful whether the League of Nations had international legal personality, and second, that the League of Nations did not confer mandates on the selected mandatories but merely confirmed the decisions of the Supreme War Council of the Principal Allied and Associated Powers.

- Third that sovereignty was vested in peoples living in the mandated territories. This view was confirmed after WWII. The ICJ in *Legal Consequences for States of the Continued Presence of South Africa in Namibia (South West Africa) Notwithstanding Security Council Resolution 276 (Advisory Opinion)*[9] held that peoples living in the mandated territories had virtual sovereignty over those territories but were temporarily deprived of it by domination or tutelage. From today's perspective, therefore it is clear that sovereignty over mandated territories was vested in people living in those territories and therefore could not revert to the Principal Allied and Associated Powers.

7.2.4 Indeterminate sovereignty

It may be that a piece of territory which is not *terra nullius* nevertheless has no determinate sovereign. This would apply for instance in a situation where a sovereign has renounced his sovereignty and the coming into being of a new sovereign is postponed (i.e. there is an *interregnum*) until a certain condition is fulfilled, or there is a dispute as to who the new sovereign should be. An example is that of Japan's renunciation of any right to Formosa (now Taiwan) and the subsequent claims of both the Communist regime which controls mainland China, and the Nationalist government which controls Taiwan, to represent the whole of China, including Taiwan. Neither government has ever submitted that Taiwan is a separate State. As a result Taiwan is a *de facto* regime (see Chapter 5.7.4) which is *de jure* part of China but under separate administration.

---

8   [1962] ICJ Rep 319, 482.
9   [1970] ICJ Rep 16.

7.3 Principles and rules applicable to the acquisition of title to territory

The title to a territory was described by the ICJ in the *Case Concerning the Frontier Dispute (Burkina Faso/Republic of Mali)*[10] as encompassing both any evidence which may establish the existence of a right, and the actual source of that right. Therefore, the title concerns both the foundation and the cause of the right of a State to a territory. This raises the question of how to distinguish between the title and the modes of acquisition of the title. In this respect, Torres Bernardez contends that if,

> one adopts a conceptual approach which differentiates between the actual process whereby territorial sovereignty is attained and the legal status thereby acquired, the distinction between 'mode' and 'title' is seen as logical, even if over-elliptical terminology and the manner in which territorial claims are normally advanced have tended to mask it.[11]

Accordingly, the mode of acquisition of title to territorial sovereignty refers to material and judicial facts which will be examined by reference to the requirements of international law to decide whether they are sufficient to create a 'title' to territorial sovereignty. This will occur, in particular, in a situation where States make competing claims, and the subsequent exercise of territorial sovereignty is considered as a separate matter.

The principles and rules relating to the acquisition of title to territorial sovereignty can be divided into three categories:

■ *jus cogens* rules of international law;

■ specific principles applicable to the acquisition of title to territory;

■ procedural/evidentiary rules relating to the ascertaining of title to territory.

7.3.1 *Jus cogens* rules of international law

Jus cogens rules such as the prohibition of the use of force (see Chapter 15.3), the principle of peaceful settlements of international disputes (see Chapter 14) and the principle of self-determination of peoples (see Chapter13) apply to all modes of acquisition/loss of territory by a State. Thus the validity of and or/effect of any mode of acquiring territorial title (or losing it) by a State will be tested by reference to these rules. However, their application is subject to the limitations imposed by intertemporal law (see below). Additionally, there is no agreement on what rules have the status of *jus cogens* (see Chapter 2.5.1).

7.3.2 Specific principles applicable to the acquisition of title to territory

These principles are:

7.3.2.1 The principle of effectiveness (or effectivité)

This has many meanings but in the context of acquisition of title to territory it refers to how a factual situation affects the creation of a right i.e. the acquisition of legal title to territory. It can be said that under the principle of effectiveness decisive importance is given to a factual situation in the evaluation

---

10   [1992] ICJ Rep 564, para 18.
11   *Encyclopaedia of Public International Law*, vol 10, Amsterdam: North-Holland, 1987, 496.

of a legal situation i.e. the factual effective situation constitutes a pre-requisite of the existence of the right of a State to claim sovereignty over a territory. The application of the principle of effectiveness is justified on the ground that, because there is no single coercive international authority which decides on States' titles to particular territories, effective control exercised by a State over a territory may create, in some circumstances, a legal title to it. However, the principle of effectiveness does not apply in all circumstances as its main purpose is not to recognise a right based on strength, but to ensure the stability of the international legal order and to guarantee legal security.

The principle of effectiveness is relevant to the following modes of acquisition of territory:

■ Occupation: a State which can show effective control over no man's territory (*terra nullius*) together with the intention to establish sovereign title to it can claim sovereignty over that territory.

■ Acquisitive prescription: continuous, uninterrupted and peaceful control over territory for a long period of time under the implicit or explicit consent of a prior sovereign will be sufficient to prove the title.

■ Conquest: prior to the prohibition of the use of force by Article 2(4) of the UN Charter, save in the exercise of self-defence, it was possible for a State to acquire territory by force if that State proved that it had effective control over the conquered territory accompanied by an intention of annexing that territory.

The principle of effectiveness applies to settlement of disputes between States in the following way: first, if a State cannot show that title was acquired from a prior sovereign through a treaty of cession or through State succession including decolonisation and, second, if the principle of *uti possidetis* (see below) is not applicable, the determination of whether a State can claim sovereignty over a disputed territory or whether a prior sovereign had in fact held title, will be made on the basis of the actual exercise of State power over the disputed territory. This principle was formulated in the *Island of Palmas Arbitration* in the following words: 'continuous and peaceful display of the functions of State within a given region is a constituent element of territorial sovereignty'.

7.3.2.2 The principle of uti possidetis

Uti possidetis, or the principle of territorial integrity, was first developed among the Spanish colonies of Latin America in the nineteenth century. It provides that the old colonial boundaries will be recognised as the borders of newly independent ex-colonial States. This principle was adopted by the Organisation of African Unity (OAU) in the 1964 Cairo Declaration[12] which provides that all States should respect colonial boundaries as they existed at the time of establishment of new independent States in Africa. The successor to the OAU, the African Union (AU), confirmed its adherence to the principle of *uti possidetis* in Article 4(b) of its 2000 Constitutive Act[13] which states that members of the AU should respect borders existing on achievement of independence.

The function of this principle is to ensure stability and certainty in the process of decolonisation and thus avoid continuous territorial disputes among newly independent States. More recently, the Badinter Commission, which was established by the EU in order to deal with problems arising from the disintegration of the former Socialist Federal Republic of Yugoslavia (see Chapters 6.2.3.1 and 13.7.2) in its Opinions 2 and 3 Relating to Self-Determination and the Frontiers of New States, extended

---

12 OAU Res 16(1) (17–21 July 1964) Resolutions Adopted by the First Ordinary Session of the Assembly of Heads of State and Government Held in Cairo, UAR, from 17 to 21 July 1964, 16.

13 Constitutive Act of the African Union (done 11 July 2000, entered into force 26 May 2001) 2158 UNTS 3.

the application of the principle of *uti possidetis* beyond the colonial context. The Commission stated that the internal boundaries of the former Yugoslav republics should become international frontiers protected by international law.[14]

The principle of *uti possidetis* has been rigidly applied by the ICJ in the context of post-colonial border disputes.[15] In the *Frontier Dispute Case (Burkina Faso/The Republic of Mali)*,[16] the ICJ based its judgment on the principal of *uti possidetis*, to which both parties referred. The Court held that the principle of *uti possidetis* was of general application with regard to the determination of borders for all newly established States in Africa, not only those located in South America. Further it held that the recognition of the principle of *uti possidetis* by the new African States, as evidenced, *inter alia*, by the Cairo Declaration, showed that it had become a principle of customary international law.

The application of the principle of *uti possidetis* to the determination of post-colonial boundaries has been criticised on the ground that it confirms the artificial division of Africa by colonial powers which determined the borders of their colonies without any consideration for ethnicity, geography, economy and other local factors. Although the principle of *uti possidetis* has prevented many territorial disputes it has also been a source of many major armed conflicts between African States, e.g. Somalia and Kenya, Ethiopia and Somalia, Togo and Ghana and between tribes living in the same State, e.g. Rwanda and Somalia (see Chapter 13.7.2). Many authors submit that instead of the principle of *uti possidetis*, which is a Eurocentric principle, some genuine African solutions would be more appropriate to solve territorial disputes in Africa.[17]

It is to be noted as follows:

First, that States can always adjust their frontiers by an agreement.

Second, that in some circumstances the principle of effectiveness may prevail over the principle of *uti possidetis*, e.g. a State by carrying out some activities or by being inactive, may acquiesce in the acquisition of title to territory by another State.[18]

Third, that the ICJ is not insensitive to the criticism raised by the application of the principle of *uti possedetis*. In the *Case Concerning Frontier Dispute (Burkina Faso/Niger)*,[19] the Court showed concerns about the impact of the delimitations of the frontier between the parties to the dispute on the local population. The ICJ applied the principle of *uti possedetis*, as directed by the parties to the dispute, but stated that having determined the course of the frontier on the basis of this principle it:

> expresses its wish that each Party, in exercising its authority over the portion of the territory under its sovereignty, should have due regard to the needs of the populations concerned, in particular those of the nomadic or semi-nomadic populations, and to the necessity to overcome difficulties that may arise for them because of the frontier.[20]

Burkina Faso and Niger assured the ICJ that the freedom of movement of these populations across their borders and their access to natural resources would not be affected by the delimitation of the

---

14   [1993] 92 ILR 170, 171.
15   *The Case Concerning the Territorial Dipsute (Libyan Arab Jamahiriya/Chad)* (1994) ICJ Rep 6; *Case Concerning Land, Island and Maritime Frontier Disputes (El Salvador/Honduras: Nicaragua Intervening)* (1992) ICJ Rep 92 and *Case Concerning the Frontier Dispute (Benin/Niger)* (2005) ICJ Rep 90.
16   [1986] ICJ Rep 554.
17   G. Oduntan, *The Demarcation of Straddling Villages in Accordance with the International Court of Justice Jurisprudence: The Cameroon-Nigeria Experience* (2006) 5 Chinese Journal of International Law, 79.
18   *The Case Concerning Land, Island and Maritime Frontier Disputes (El Salvador v Honduras: Nicaragua Intervening)* [1992] ICJ Rep 92.
19   (2013) ICJ Rep 44.
20   Ibid, para 112.

frontier between them because they had already entered into bilateral and multilateral agreements ensuring that the affected populations could keep their *modus vivendi*.

7.3.2.3 Intertemporal law

As a result of changes in the law relating to the acquisition of territory, problems have arisen as to which legal regime should be applied when determining title. For example, should title to territory acquired by conquest in the nineteenth century be assessed according to the rules relating to conquest at the time (in which case title would be lawful) or according to the law on conquest today (so that title would be unlawful)?

The general rule – known as the principle of intertemporal law – is that title should be assessed according to the rules of law that prevailed at the time of the acquisition of territory. In the *Island of Palmas Arbitration*, however, Arbitrator Huber based his decision on the proposition that title to territory needed to be confirmed against the changing standards of international law. He stated:

> As regards the question which of different legal systems prevailing at successive periods is to be applied in a particular case (the so-called inter-temporal law), a distinction must be made between the creation of rights and the existence of rights. The same principle which subjects the acts creative of a right to the law in force at the time the right arises, demands that the existence of the right, in other words its continued manifestation, shall follow the conditions required by the evolution of law.

Accordingly, Arbitrator Huber made a distinction between the creation of rights, which ought to be assessed in the light of the legal system contemporaneous with their creation and the existence of rights, which ought to be assessed in the light of evolving rules of international law. The first mentioned ensures stability in international relations, the second mentioned introduces the necessary flexibility in the assessment of the existence of rights.

A number of writers argued that the modified rule developed by Hubert would be highly disruptive, as every State would constantly have to review and confirm its title.[21]

In practice, the concept of intertemporal law, as Judge Al-Khasawneh in his Separate Opinion in the *Case concerning the Land and Maritime Boundary between Cameroon and Nigeria (Cameroon v Nigeria: Equatorial Guinea Intervening)*[22] stated, is confusing, controversial to the point that the ICL dropped it from the 1969 VCLT, ill-defined and not supported by judicial decisions of international courts including the ICJ. Judge Al-Khasawneh provided, *inter alia*, the following examples of cases in which the ICJ either avoided or rejected the application of intertemporal law:

■ The *Aegean Sea Continental Shelf Case (Greece v Turkey)*.[23] This case concerned a dispute relating to the delimitation of the continental shelf of a Greek island located close to the Turkish coast of Anatolia. In this case, the ICJ interpreted the phrase 'disputes relating to the territorial status of Greece' contained in a Greek reservation to the 1928 Kellogg-Briand Pact in accordance with the law as it was at the time the case was examined by the ICJ and not in accordance with rules in force when the reservation was made, i.e. in 1931. As Judge Al-Khasawneh emphasised 'with the aid of a belated discovery of the intention of the parties',[24] the ICJ avoided the application of intertemporal law.

---

21   R.Y. Jennings, *The Acquisition of Territory in International Law*, Manchester: Manchester University Press, 1963, 28–31.
22   [2002] ICJ Rep 492, para 15 *et seq*.
23   [1978] ICJ Rep 3.
24   Supra note 22, para 15.

■ In the *Namibia Case*,[25] the ICJ held that 'an international instrument must be interpreted and applied within the overall framework of the judicial system in force at the time of interpretation'.

It can be said that intertemporal law has as many critics as supporters.[26] For example the Institute of International Law in its 1975 Resolution on 'The Intertemporal Problems in Public International Law' stated that 'the temporal application of any norm of public international law shall be determined in accordance with the general principles of law by which any fact, action or situation must be assessed in the light of the rules contemporaneous with it'.[27] Further, in many cases the ICJ has relied on intertemporal law.[28]

In conclusion it can be said that Judge Al-Khasawneh's assessment of intertemporal law as a confusing and ill-defined concept is correct. It is submitted that the requirement of stability which intertemporal law, in fact, embodies is vital for harmonious relations between States. In particular in respect of territorial claims which are often based on treaties entered into by States many centuries ago. However, the evolutionary nature of international law is also an important factor to be taken into consideration when title to a territory is disputed. In this respect, the main problem with intertemporal law is when it is at odds with *jus cogens* rules. Judges Shi and Koroma in a Joint Declaration in the *Case Concerning the Application of the Convention on the Prevention and Punishment of the Crime of Genocide (Bosnia and Herzegovina v Serbia and Montenegro)*[29] stated that 'in some respects the interpretation of a treaty's provision cannot be divorced from developments in the law subsequent to its adoption' and that 'even though a treaty when concluded did not conflict with any rule of ius cogens, it will become void if there subsequently emerges a new rule of ius cogens with which it is in conflict' Certainly, the rejection of intertemporal law when its application clashes with *jus cogens* or the requirements of HRL, is justified, but its application to a legal title to territories which were validly acquired before the relevant rule of *jus cogens* has come into existence undermines the requirement of stability

The conflict between the stability guaranteed by intertemporal law and the evolutionary nature of international law is not easy to resolve. The applicability of intertemporal law or otherwise will depend on the facts of each case.

7.3.2.4 *Procedural/evidentiary rules relating to the ascertaining of title to territory*

These are examined below.

A. The critical date
The 'critical date' is the date on which a dispute over territory crystallised. Conduct of the parties or any events that occurred after the critical date will not be taken into account in the determination of title.

---

25 *The Legal Consequences for States of the Continued Presence of South Africa in Namibia (South West Africa) Notwithstanding Security Council Resolution 276 (1970) (Advisory Opinion)* [1971] ICJ Rep 16, 31.

26 See J.D. Fry, *The Roots of Historic Title. Non-Western Pre-Colonial Normative Systems and Legal Resolution of Territorial Disputes* (2014) 27 LJIL, 727.

27 Article 1 of the 1975 Resolution (1975) 56 ANNIDI, 536.

28 E.g. the *Minquiers and Ecrehos Case (France v United Kingdom)* [1953] ICJ Rep 47 and the *Case concerning the Gabčíkovo-Nagymaros Project (Hungary/Slovakia) (Order)* [1997] ICJ Rep 3.

29 (2007) ICJ Rep 43, para 1.

While the critical date will often be apparent from the facts of the case, its determination by the court or tribunal, particularly in the face of conflicting evidence from the parties, may be of great significance to the merits of the dispute. The choice of one or other date may, for example, preclude a party from adducing particular evidence or may alter the case from one of occupation to one of prescription. The choice of the critical date is thus a useful practical tool available to the court to restrict or broaden the scope of the argument.

B. Evidentiary rules: recognition, acquiescence and estoppel

Three evidentiary rules play an important role in the acquisition of title to territory when competing claims are made by States.

(a) Recognition

Recognition in respect of land claims mainly refers to the attitude of third States, i.e. States not involved in the dispute. This may take the form of a unilateral express declaration or may occur in treaty provisions with third States. In the *Legal Status of Eastern Greenland Case*[30] concerning a dispute between Denmark and Norway, the PCIJ referred to treaties between Denmark and States other than Norway, as constituting evidence of recognition of Danish sovereignty over Greenland in general. However, recognition is also relevant in respect of competing claims of two States in a situation where a State by positive conduct, even if contrary to an existing treaty,[31] acknowledges that its opponent has a valid title to a disputed territory.

(b) Acquiescence

This applies to the attitude of a dispossessed State and is inferred from its failure to protest in circumstances where protest might reasonably have been expected against the exercise of control by its opponent. Therefore, as the ICJ held in *the Sovereignty over Pedra Branca/Palau Batu Puteh, Middle Rock and South Ledge (Malaysia/Singapore)*,[32] silence may also speak but only if the conduct of the other State calls for a response. Acquiescence by a State has little or no effect unless it is accompanied by some measure of control over the territory by the other State. So, for instance, failure to protest against a purely verbal assertion of title unsupported by any degree of control does not constitute acquiescence.

(c) Estoppel

Judge Spender in the *Temple of Preah Vihear Case* provided the following definition of estoppel:

> the principle operates to prevent a State contesting before the Court a situation contrary to a clear and unequivocal representation previously made by it to another State, either expressly or impliedly, on which representation the other State was, in the circumstances, entitled to rely and in fact did rely, and as a result that other State has been prejudiced or the State making it has secured some benefit or advantage for itself.[33]

In the above case, the ICJ regarded acquiescence over a long period of time as amounting to estoppel. In subsequent cases the Court upheld this approach. In the *North Sea Continental Shelf Cases*[34] the

---

30   The *Legal Status of Eastern Greenland (Denmark v Norway)* PCIJ Ser A/B No 53.

31   *The Taba Case*, 80 ILR 224.

32   [2008] ICJ 12 at 37, para 121.

33   The *Case Concerning the Temple of Preah Vihear (Cambodia v Thailand) (Merits)*, Dissenting Opinion of Sir Percy Spender [1962] ICJ Rep 6, at 101, paras 143–144.

34   *The North Sea Continental Shelf Cases (Federal Republic of Germany/Denmark; Federal Republic of Germany/The Netherlands) [Judgment]* [1969] ICJ Rep 3.

Court held that only 'a very definite, very consistent course of conduct' on the part of Germany could have been relied upon by States parties to the Geneva Convention on the Continental Shelf to claim that the Convention was binding upon Germany in a situation where Germany was not a contracting party to it (see Chapter 2.3.1.2). Additionally, such consistent, unequivocal conduct of Germany would have had to be detrimental to the position of Denmark or the Netherlands. As this was not the case, the situation of estoppel did not arise. Accordingly, the requirement of detriment or prejudice distinguishes estoppel from acquiescence.

In the *Gulf of Maine Case*[35] the Chamber of the ICJ explained that both acquiescence and estoppel have their origin in the same principles, i.e. the principle of good faith and the principle of equity. However, they are based on different legal reasoning; while acquiescence is equivalent to tacit recognition manifested by unilateral conduct which the other party may interpret as consent, estoppel is linked to the idea of preclusion, and requires the existence of detriment to the States relying on it. In this case the Chamber decided that both acquiescence and estoppel were relevant to the facts of the case and, after reviewing the facts of the dispute, rejected the argument of Canada that the US had by its conduct acquiesced in the idea of the median line applying in particular to the delimitation of the Georges Bank. The Chamber concluded that the conduct of the US was not 'sufficiently clear, sustained and consistent to constitute acquiescence'.[36] Further, it held that estoppel did not arise because in the light of the circumstances of the case a letter written by the competent US administrative authorities (i.e. the Hoffman letter), which contained an implicit acknowledgement that the delimitation should be made on the basis of the median line, was not sufficient to amount to estoppel.[37]

It can be said that a situation of estoppel arises only when a State's conduct is clear, sustained and consistent, and the other party, relying on such conduct, has changed its position to its own detriment, or has suffered some prejudice.[38]

7.4 Modes of acquisition of title to territory

Traditional international law distinguishes several modes by which sovereignty can be acquired over territory. They were based on Roman law rules regarding acquisition of property. The analogy with Roman law was well suited to the system of absolute monarchy prevalent in Europe during the formative years of European expansion in the sixteenth and seventeenth centuries when the monarch was regarded as 'owner' of his State's territory. However, with the decline of private law notions in the eighteenth and nineteenth centuries the analogy with Roman law rules became less distinct, and today, under current international law, it can be argued that such an analogy serves no useful purpose, and indeed gives a distorted view of current practice.

The five modes by which territory has traditionally been said to have been acquired are: occupation; prescription; accretion; cession; and conquest. These modes are not, however, exclusive or exhaustive. In practice it is unlikely that any single mode would be evident in isolation. The modes are interrelated, and in complex cases may be used in conjunction with each other to the extent that no one mode appears dominant. In addition, these modes do not adequately describe the acquisition of territory by

---

35 *Case Concerning Delimitation of the Maritime Boundary in the Gulf of Maine Area (Canada/US) Judgment* [1984] ICJ Rep 246.
36 Ibid, para 146.
37 Ibid, paras 142–145.
38 See also, *the Legality of the Use of Force (Serbia and Montenegro v Canada) Preliminary Objections* [2004] ICJ Rep, 429, para 42.

newly independent States exercising the right to self-determination. It must also be borne in mind that the traditional modes of acquisition of territory found a place in legal reasoning during the formative stages of international law. In a number of cases it will, therefore, be evident that these modes are based on a Western perception of the status of the territory in question prior to acquisition. As is illustrated in more detail below, acquisition of territory by occupation, for example, is based on the fundamental perception that the territory was previously *terra nullius*, i.e. not under the sovereignty of any State. By *terra nullius* it was, however, implied that the territory was not under the sovereignty of any other recognised State, i.e. a State which was one of the small club of States to which international law was deemed to have application.

7.4.1 Occupation

This is the original mode of acquisition whereby a State acquires sovereignty over *terra nullius* (i.e. territory capable of being owned by a State but not under the sovereignty of any State). The territory may be land which has never previously belonged to any State. It may have been abandoned by the former sovereign or it may have been occupied by a people lacking the social and political organisation necessary to constitute a sovereign state under international law.

In the *Advisory Opinion on the Western Sahara*, the ICJ held that areas inhabited by groups which have 'social and political order' were, in the light of the law in force at that time, not to be regarded as *terra nullius*.[39] Accordingly, the colonial powers were not able to establish that they had acquired original titles, i.e. they could not, in respect of the territory inhabited by such groups, successfully claim territorial sovereignty on the basis that the relevant territory had not been claimed by any other State. The colonial powers were, nevertheless, able on the basis of a derivative title, i.e. a title acquired by a cession treaty concluded between the relevant colonial power and local rulers, or by conquest or both, to establish their sovereign power over the territory.

7.4.1.1 What constitutes occupation?

Territory is occupied when it is placed under effective control. This is a relative concept varying according to the nature of the territory concerned. For instance, it will be much easier to establish effective control over territory which is uninhabited than over territory which is inhabited, albeit by a people lacking social and political organisation.

In the *Legal Status of Eastern Greenland Case (Denmark v Norway)*[40] the PCIJ stated:

> a claim to sovereignty based not upon some particular act or title such as a treaty of cession but merely upon a continued display of authority, involves two elements each of which must be shown to exist: the intention and will to act as Sovereign; and some actual exercise or display of such authority.[41]

The two elements are examined below.

A. The intention and will to act as sovereign (*animus possidendi*)
Brownlie argues that intention and will to act as sovereign, being a subjective criterion, involves the imputation of a state of mind involving a legal assessment and 'judgment' to those ordering various

---

39   *Western Sahara (Advisory Opinion)* [1975] ICJ Rep 12, para 80.
40   (1933) PCIJ Rep Ser A/B No 53.
41   PCIJ Ser A/B No 53, 42–43.

State activities. He concludes that this approach expects too much, and is unrealistic in seeking a particular and coherent intention in a mass of activity by numerous individuals.[42]

This requirement of *animus possidendi* also leads to problems where there are competing acts of sovereignty. Today almost all habitable areas of the earth fall under the dominion of some State and, therefore, the importance of acquisition by occupation lies not in the acquisition of new territory but in the solving of competing claims based on past occupation. For that reason, in cases where there are competing acts of sovereignty the subjective requirement of the *animus possidendi* of the competing States may be inconclusive. In such cases the determination of the matter relies on objective elements of State activity, i.e. the actual manifestations of sovereignty.

The intention to act as sovereign as one of the requirements of effective occupation is important in three respects:

■ the activity must be that of the State or its authorised agent and not that of a mere individual;

■ the activity must not be exercised by or subject to consent of another State;

■ the activity, when looked at as a whole, must have no other explanation but the assumption that there was the pre-existing sovereignty.

B. Effective exercise or continued authority

Possession must give the occupying State control over the territory concerned and there must be some display of State activity consistent with sovereignty. The traditional view is one of occupation in terms of settlement and close physical possession. However, what constitutes the necessary degree of control will vary with the circumstances of the case. This is exemplified by the cases below.

THE ISLAND OF PALMAS ARBITRATION (THE NETHERLANDS *V* US)[43]

Facts:

The US claimed the Island of Palmas which lies half-way between the Philippines and what was then the Dutch East Indies. The US founded its title upon the 1898 Treaty of Paris by which Spain ceded the Philippine Islands to the US. In this Treaty the Island of Palmas was described as forming part of the Philippines. However, the island was actually under Dutch control. The issue was therefore whether sovereignty over the island belonged to Spain at the time she purported to cede the island to the US.

Held:

The arbitrator held that even if Spain did originally have sovereignty over the island the Dutch had administered it since the early eighteenth century, thereby supplanting Spain as the sovereign. He stated that:

> *the continuous and peaceful display of territorial sovereignty (peaceful in relation to other states) is as good as a title ... Manifestations of territorial sovereignty assume, it is true, different*

---

42   I. Brownlie, *Principles of Public International Law*, 7th edn, Oxford: Oxford University Press, 2008, 137.

43   (1928) 2 RIAA 829.

forms, according to conditions of time and place. Although continuous in principle, sovereignty cannot be exercised in fact at every moment on every point of a territory. The intermittence and discontinuity compatible with the maintenance of the right necessarily differ according as inhabited or uninhabited regions are involved, or regions enclosed within territories in which sovereignty is incontestably displayed or again regions accessible from, for instance, the high seas.

The learned arbitrator found ample support for the Dutch arguments based upon its peaceful and continuous exercise of State authority over the island. These included the close link existing since 1677 between the people of the island and the Netherlands via the Dutch East India Company and the unchallenged peaceful display of Dutch sovereignty from at least 1700 to the outbreak of the dispute in 1906.

THE LEGAL STATUS OF EASTERN GREENLAND CASE[44]

Facts:

A dispute arose out of the action of Norway in proclaiming its occupation of parts of East Greenland in 1931. Denmark argued that Danish sovereignty extended to the whole of Greenland. On the evidence submitted the Court was satisfied that Denmark's intention to claim title to the whole of Greenland was established, from at the latest 1721. For the Danish claim to succeed it was next therefore, necessary to discover some actual exercise or display of authority by Denmark over the disputed territory. The following factors were submitted by Denmark in evidence:

- *the absence, until 1931, of any competing claim;*
- *the character of the country – the arctic and inaccessible nature of the uncolonised parts of the territory where it would be unreasonable to demand a continuous exercise of authority;*
- *the numerous Danish legislative and administrative acts purporting to apply to the whole of Greenland;*
- *treaties with other States in which those other States recognised the Danish claim to the territory;*
- *the granting of a trade monopoly and the granting of trading, mining and other concessions by Denmark.*

Held:

The Court held that this pattern of activity between 1721 and 1931 was sufficient to establish Danish title to the whole of the territory.

---

44   *The Legal Status of Eastern Greenland (Denmark v Norway)* 1933 PCIJ Ser A/B No 53.

Another example of the practical approach to occupation was provided by the Anglo-French dispute involving the *Minquiers and Ecrehos Islands (France v UK).*[45] In appraising the relative strength of the opposing claims to sovereignty over the Ecrehos Islands the Court stated that it 'attaches, in particular, probative value to the acts which relate to the exercise of jurisdiction and local administration and to legislation'. The Court referred to the exercise of criminal jurisdiction, the holding of inquests, the collection of taxes and to a British Treasury Warrant of 1875 including the 'Ecrehos Rocks' within the Port of Jersey.

A further example of the development of this approach is provided by the *Rann of Kutch Arbitration (India v Pakistan).*[46] In this case the tribunal stated that grazing and other economic activities by private landholders may provide acceptable evidence of title.

7.4.2 Acquisitive prescription

Like occupation, acquisitive prescription is based on effective control over territory, but whereas occupation is acquisition of *terra nullius*, prescription is the acquisition of territory which belongs to another State. Oppenheim describes prescription as:

> The acquisition of territorial sovereignty through continuous and undisturbed exercise of sovereignty over it during such a period as is necessary to create, under the influence of historical development, the general conviction that the present condition of things is in conformity with international order.[47]

According to Brownlie:

> The essence of prescription is the removal of defects in a putative title arising from usurpation of another's sovereignty by the consent and acquiescence of the former sovereign.[48]

Acquisitive prescription should be distinguished from:

■ Immemorial possession. The main difference between acquisitive prescription and immemorial possession is that in the case of immemorial possession the origin of the possession is unknown and therefore it is presumed that the possession combined with the effective exercise of sovereignty is legal while in respect of acquisitive prescription the title is initially illegal.

■ Occupation. Although in situations of both acquisitive prescription and occupation a State exercises, with the intention to act as sovereign, effective control over a territory, in the case of occupation the claim to sovereignty is over *terra nullius* while in the case of acquisitive prescription the claim concerns a territory which belongs to another State. Notwithstanding this, in practice the difference between occupation and acquisitive prescription in claims based upon the nominal exercise of sovereignty may be impossible to ascertain. The very point at issue may be whether the territory was *terra nullius* or whether it was subject to previous sovereignty. In the *Island of Palmas Arbitration* (above), for example, the arbitrator did not make clear whether the island was under Spanish sovereignty before the Dutch began to exercise control.

45   (1953) ICJ Rep 47.
46   (1968) 7 ILM 633.
47   R. Jennings and A. Watts (eds), *Oppenheim's International Law*, 9th edn, vol I, Harlow: Longman, 1992, 706.
48   *Principles of Public International Law*, Oxford: Oxford University Press, 7th edn, 2008, 146.

Accepted criteria for acquisitive prescription are:

1   Possession must be exercised '*à titre de soverain*'. There must be a display of State authority and absence of any recognition of sovereignty of another State. This first condition rules out the possibility of acquisition of territory by means of acquisitive prescription when a State administers a territory, e.g. as its protectorate or as a trustee (see Chapter 5.4.2 and 5.8). It also prevents acquisition of title by a State in circumstances where individuals, not by virtue of authority from any State, but in their private capacity take and retain possession and control of a territory. In *Kasikili/Sedudu Island (Botswana/Namibia) (Judgment)*[49] Namibia argued that it had acquired a disputed island by virtue of the fact that members of the Masubia tribe (who were Namibian nationals) had for a long time occupied and used the island. The ICJ held that members of the tribe did not occupy the island '*à titre de souverain*' since they were not exercising functions of State authority.

2   Possession must be peaceful and uninterrupted. What conduct is sufficient to prevent possession from being peaceful and uninterrupted? Any conduct indicating a lack of acquiescence, e.g. protest. Effective protests prevent acquisition of title by prescription. This is illustrated by the *Chamizal Arbitration (US v Mexico)*.[50]

CHAMIZAL ARBITRATION (US *V* MEXICO)

Facts:

(for detailed facts see Chapter 7.4.3)

The US laid claim to an area of Mexican territory which had become joined to US territory by the movement of the Rio Grande southwards, inter alia, *on the ground of uninterrupted possession.*

Held:

The claim failed because Mexico had made a number of protests to the US, and indeed as a result of the protests a convention had been signed in an attempt to settle 'the rights of the two nations with regard to the changes brought about by the action of the waters of the Rio Grande'. Therefore in the opinion of the commissioners, diplomatic protests by Mexico prevented title arising by acquisitive prescription.

However, it is doubtful whether diplomatic protests alone are sufficient to preserve the rights of a dispossessed sovereign. There must be some serious expression of protest, e.g. the severing of diplomatic relations or the imposition of sanctions as retaliation. The matter should be raised before the UN and reinforced by a *bona fide* suggestion that the dispute be submitted to arbitration or judicial settlement.

In the *Minquiers and Ecrehos Islands Case* (above) the UK argued that French protests against British legislation applying to the disputed islands were ineffective, *inter alia*, on the ground that they should have been reinforced by pressure to have the matter submitted for determination by an international tribunal. The Court did not comment on this issue.

---

49   [1999] ICJ Rep 1045, para 99.
50   (1911) 5 AJIL 782.

While some jurists do regard protest as merely effecting a postponement for a reasonable period of the process of prescription while advantage is taken of the available machinery for the settlement of international disputes, this approach can be criticised. Should failure to resort to certain bodies be penalised by loss of territorial rights? Is it proper to demand that all territorial disputes be referred to international arbitration? Should procedural requirements be introduced into the concept of acquiescence?

3   The possession must be public. If there is to be acquiescence then there must be publicity.

4   The possession must persist. The effective control necessary to establish title by prescription must last for a long period of time. However, the length of time required is not fixed by international law with the consequence that whether the effective control exercised over a territory was of sufficient duration will be a matter of fact depending on the particular case.

The concept of acquisitive prescription in international law is very controversial, mainly because international law does not fix any specific period of time that must elapse before a State can claim that its possession of territory '*à titre de sovereign*' amounts to a good title. The ICJ has avoided making any pronouncement on whether the concept of acquisitive prescription is part of international law. This has been possible as a result of the fact that claims based on acquisitive prescription alone are rare, because by relying on acquisitive prescription the State concerned admits that it has no valid title. Additionally, the application of the principle of *uti possidetis* to territorial claims in the colonial context has further undermined the relevance of the doctrine of acquisitive prescription. However, in many cases before the ICJ parties have relied on acquisitive prescription as an alternative claim. For example, in the *Kasikili/Sedudu Island Case*, Namibia argued that its title to the disputed territory was based on the 1890 Anglo-German Treaty, and in the alternative on acquisitive prescription. Both parties to the dispute, Botswana and Namibia, agreed on the criteria necessary to justify acquisitive prescription as stated above, but the ICJ based its judgment on the first claim and therefore did not examine the alternative claim. As noted by J. Wouters and S. Verhoeven[51] the ICJ has never recognised the existence of a title to territory based on the sole ground of acquisitive prescription. The Court prefers to base its judgments, when acquisitive prescription is invoked, on a tacit agreement or acquiescence. The attitude of the ICJ was explained by Wouters and Verhoeven as follows: 'It is difficult not to regard acquisitive prescription as a form of acquiescence or tacit agreement inferred from the inactivity of a State whose territory is partially occupied by another State'. This is exemplified by the ICJ's judgment in the *Sovereignty over Pedra Branca/Pulau Batu Puteh Case, Middle Rocks and South Ledge (Malaysia/Singapore) (Judgment)*,[52] in which the Court decided that Singapore had acquired title to the disputed islands on the ground of a tacit agreement or acquiescence, 'although the facts of the case warranted the application of acquisitive prescription'.[53]

State practice shows that States recognise acquisitive prescription as a distinct ground of transferring title. Further, there is some support in the opinions of judges of the ICJ, and of other international courts and tribunals, as well as of academics, for the view that acquisitive prescription, although not a rule of customary international law, can be regarded as a general principle of international law.[54]

---

51   *Prescription*, Max Planck Encycopedia of Public International Law available at http://mpepil.com, para 9 (accessed 12 October 2013).
52   (2008) ICJ Rep 12.
53   Ibid.
54   Supra note 51, para 9.

7.4.3 Accretion

A State has the exclusive right of sovereignty over any additions made to its territory as a result of accretion or resulting from the formation of islands within its territorial waters. The slow, gradual increase of land due to accumulation of soil material such as sand, silt, clay, gravel resulting from natural causes is called accretion. The opposite of accretion is erosion which occurs when land is gradually washed away by water or in the natural course of events. Both erosion and accretion must occur naturally i.e. slowly, gradually and imperceptibly in order to affect the title to territory.[55] Sudden or violent change, due to natural forces or disaster, such as storms, floods and hurricanes, in the course of a body of water are known as avulsion.

International law is of relevance with regard to alterations in rivers which form States' boundaries.[56] Normally, the boundary line is the median line in non-navigable rivers, and in navigable rivers, it is the '*thalweg*' – the deepest channel continuously used for navigation. It is to be noted that the *thalweg* is not a boundary line but a boundary area because the channel of a river is never a precise line. Further, there may be more than one navigable channel. If a boundary river changes its course as a result of accretion on one bank and erosion on the other the boundary line will, in the case of a navigable river, continue to be the middle of the *thalweg*, and in the case of a non-navigable river, its middle line. However, if a boundary river changes its course as a result of avulsion the boundary will remain where it was.

The *Chamizal Arbitration*[57] dealt with both accretion and avulsion.

THE CHAMIZAL ARBITRATION

Facts:

The 1848 and 1852 Treaties between the US and Mexico established the Rio Grande as a boundary river between the two countries. However, as the Rio Grande often changed its course a dispute arose. Before 1864, the Rio Grande was gradually changing its course which resulted in the gradual exposure of a tract of land (by way of accretion). In 1864 there was suddenly a very big flood of the river. This flood dramatically altered the course of the river resulting in a tract of some 600 acres, called the Chamizal Tract, which had been on the south bank of the river near the Mexican shore finding itself adjacent to the north bank near the US town of El Paso. The gradual accretion and the sudden flood both altered the course of the Rio Grande.

The US claimed that the Chamizal Tract was formed by slow and gradual erosion while Mexico argued that it was formed by avulsion.

Held:

The Arbitral Tribunal made a distinction between the relevant two periods of alteration in the Rio Grande: prior to 1864, the alteration was due to gradual erosion and accretion and

---

55   *County of St Clair v Lovingston* 90 US 46 [1874], 68.
56   A State's continental shelf may also be extended by accretion. Further, if an island emerges through natural process in the EEZ of a State it will normally belong to that State.
57   (1911) 5AJIL 785.

consequently, the US was entitled to the part of the Chamizal Tract resulting from the gradual southward accretion of land. In 1864 there was a sudden alteration and thus Mexico was entitled to the acres exposed by the flood. Because of different causes of alterations in the two periods, the majority of the arbitration commission awarded 437 acres of the Chamizal Tract to Mexico (i.e. this was an area of the land that was on the Mexico side of the river before the 1864 flood). The US refused to accept the award for more than 50 years. After the intervention of US President J.F. Kennedy, a Treaty was signed between US and Mexico in 1963 under which the 437 acres of Chamizal Tract were transferred to Mexico.

In *Louisiana v Mississippi*[58] the US Supreme Court applied the principles of international law to a boundary dispute between these two federal States whose boundary was formed by the Mississippi River. The Court held that the gradual erosion of soil from the Mississippi bank and its deposit on the Louisiana bank between 1823 and 1912 passed title to the accretion to Louisiana. But when the river suddenly changed course in 1913 across the accretion of the previous 90 years this did not divest Louisiana of the territory already acquired. This change was an avulsion and therefore the pre-1913 boundary remained. The US courts have applied these principles to many cases concerning disputes between states of the federation.[59]

7.4.4 Cession

This is the transfer of territory, usually by treaty, from one State to another. The form is not important, any form of understanding will be sufficient provided that both the grantor State and the grantee State have given their consent. A unilateral declaration of the grantor State will suffice if accepted by the grantee State. However, so called 'consent' obtained by the use of force will be invalid by virtue of Article 52 VCLT.

Cession may be either gratuitous or for some consideration (e.g. the sale to the US by Denmark of the Danish West Indies in 1916, the sale of Louisiana by France to the US in 1803, the sale of Alaska by Russia to the US in 1867) or in exchange for another territory, e.g. the UK ceded Heligoland to Germany in exchange for Zanzibar in 1890. Many cessions were based on peace treaties, e.g. the 1919 Versailles Peace Treaty. Nowadays, cession is usually effected in respect of small pieces of territory along State borders with a view to abolishing complications resulting from historical irrationalities and peculiarities in the border line, e.g. Switzerland and France in 1953.

Cession is an example of a derivative title. If there are defects in the ceding State's title, the purported cession cannot cure them.

In the *Island of Palmas* Arbitration,[60] the US claimed that by the 1898 Treaty of Paris it acquired title to the island of Palmas from Spain. However, the Arbitrator found that at the time of the purported transfer of the island in 1898 sovereignty over the island lay not with Spain but with the Netherlands. Spain could not transfer more rights than she herself possessed. Therefore since Spain had no title to the island in 1898, the US could not have acquired title from Spain.

---

58   (1940) 282 US 458.

59   E.g. *Kansas v Missouri* 322 US 213 (1944); *Arkansas v Tennessee* 246 US 158 (1918); *Georgia v South Carolina* [1990] 91 ILR, 439.

60   Supra note 3.

When title to territory is passed to a grantee State, that State becomes responsible for any act occurring on the territory. This is exemplified by the *Iloilo Case*.[61]

ILOILO CASE

Facts:

The Treaty of Paris, signed on 10 December 1898, provided that on exchange of ratifications, Spain should evacuate the Philippines in favour of the US. However, on 24 December local insurgents forced the Spanish to withdraw and it was not until 10 February that American troops captured Iloilo from the insurgents. On the following day the insurgents set fire to the town damaging property of British subjects.

Held:

The British-American tribunal hearing claims for damaged property held that as the treaty did not take effect until ratification on 11 April, the transfer of de jure *sovereignty to the US, and its resulting obligations, did not commence until that date.*

The issue of nationality of individuals residing in a territory which has been ceded is normally settled between the two States concerned. However, in the absence of any agreement, the successor State will normally grant its nationality to the newly acquired population. This is supported by Article 5 of 1999 Draft Articles on Nationality of Natural Persons in Relation to the Succession of States[62] prepared by the ILC which set a rebuttable presumption that persons habitually resident within the territory concerned should acquire the nationality of the successor State. In order to avoid statelessness, the Council of Europe 2006 Convention on the Avoidance of Statelessness in Relation to State Succession[63] provides that a successor State is obliged to grant its nationality to nationals of the predecessor State who are habitually resident in the relevant territory and who would otherwise became stateless persons (Article 5).

Under international law a State has no obligation to grant to the population concerned an option to choose nationality, although Article 20 of the 1999 Draft Articles provides that such an option should be available. Further, a grantor State has no obligation to consult the affected population as its consent is not required in order to make the cession valid. This is exemplified by the constant practice of States which, before and after WWII, and following the disintegration of the Soviet Union and the Former Yugoslavia, did not consult the affected population when territorial changes were made.

7.4.5 Conquest

Under traditional international law conquest was recognised as a means of acquiring territory even in the absence of a treaty of cession, but the acquisition of territory by conquest was not lawful until hostilities had come to an end. Therefore, in the absence of a peace treaty evidence was necessary that

---

61   (1925) 4 RIAA 158.
62   (1999) *Yearbook of the International Law Commission*, vol II, Part Two, para 48.
63   CETS 200.

all resistance by the enemy State and by its allies had ceased so that there were no longer forces in the field which might free the occupied territory from the control of the conquering power. Thus, the German annexation of Poland during WWII was invalid, because Poland's allies continued to struggle against Germany.

Even when a State has been completely subjugated there will be no transfer of sovereignty in the absence of an intention to annex it. Thus, in 1945 the victorious Allies expressly disclaimed any intention of annexing Germany, although they had occupied all German territory and defeated Germany's allies.

While acquisition of territory by conquest may have been acceptable during the period when there was no legal restriction upon the right of a State to wage war, it is now accepted that the Covenant of the League of Nations, the Pact of Paris, and, more importantly, Article 2(4) of the UN Charter did away with the ability of a State to acquire territory by conquest (see Chapter 15.3).

7.4.5.1 The effect of the prohibition of the use of force on the acquisition of territory

Once the proposition is accepted that an aggressor State cannot acquire territory by conquering another State through the use of force, it follows that an aggressor cannot now acquire territory by conquest and that any treaty of cession imposed by an aggressor will be invalid.

7.4.5.2 Can an 'innocent party' to a war still acquire territory by conquest?

Can a State acting in self-defence acquire territory by conquest? The Soviet Union view was that States acting in self-defence may impose sanctions on a defeated aggressor: in particular, they are empowered to take away part of the territory of the aggressor in order to prevent a recurrence of the aggression. However, the Declaration on Principles of International Law concerning Friendly Relations and Co-operation among States in Accordance with the Charter of the United Nations, (UNGA (Res 2625 (XXV))[64] suggests otherwise. It states that:

> The territory of a state shall not be the object of military occupation resulting from the use of force in contravention of the provisions of the Charter. The territory of a state shall not be the object of acquisition by another state resulting from the threat or use of force.

So any threat of or use of force, whether in contravention of the UN Charter or not, invalidates the acquisition of territory. For example, both the UNGA and the UNSC have repeatedly declared that Israel is not entitled to annex any of the territory it captured following the war of June 1967. The UNSC affirmed in 1967 that the 'acquisition of territory by military conquest is inadmissible' and that all measures taken by Israel in the occupied territories were invalid and ineffective to change the status of that territory.[65] More recently, in the Preamble to Resolution 1472 dealing with the situation in Iraq the UNSC reaffirmed 'the commitment of all Member States to the sovereignty and territorial integrity of Iraq'."[66]

However, it must be remembered that as long as the international community of States is not determined to prevent aggressors from enjoying their spoils the principle that an aggressor cannot acquire a good title to territory is liable to produce serious discrepancies between the law and the facts. It will depend upon political rather than legal circumstances.

---

64   (24 October 1970) GAOR 25th Session Supp 28, 121.

65   UNSC Res 242 [22 November 1967] UN Doc S/RES/242[1967].

66   UNSC Res 1472 [28 March 2003] UN Doc S/RES/1472 [2003].

7.4.5.3 The 1961 invasion of Goa

Portugal retained this colony on the Indian subcontinent until it was invaded by India and incorporated into India's territory. This illegal use of force by India and the subsequent annexation of Goa received the approval of many members of the UN and there was no condemnation of the act by either the UNSC or the UNGA.

Can one argue that India has obtained a basis of title which, even if there is no express recognition of the fact, will become consolidated over a relatively short period of time, by the acquiescence of the international community, into a fully valid title?

It is submitted that in the light of the *jus cogens* rule prohibiting the threat or use of force any annexation which has taken place after the entry into force of the UN Charter e.g. the annexation of Tibet by China in 1951, the annexation of Hyderabad by India in 1948, the annexation of Goa (despite the fact that Portugal relinquished its claim and recognised the sovereignty of India over Goa by a treaty[67]) should be regarded as illegal and thus without any effect under international law. Such fundamental illegality can neither be justified by the subsequent conclusion of a peace treaty nor by the application of the doctrine of historic consolidation (see Chapter 7.4.6). However, in respect of annexations which occurred during the period between the two world wars, and provided that there was acquiescence on the part of the State concerned, it may be that application of the doctrine of historic consolidation can be accepted. This results from the fact that at that time the prohibition of the use of force was not generally accepted. This view was expressed by Judge Fortier in his Separate Opinion in the Case *Concerning the Maritime Delimitatation and Territorial Questions between Qatar and Bahrain (Qatar v Bahrein) (Merit).*[68] He agreed with the majority of the judges that Qatar was the sovereign of the disputed area of Zubarah but, unlike all the other judges, who decided that in 1937 the disputed area belonged to the Skeikh of Qatar, he characterised the events that occurred in 1937 as conquest by Qatar of a territory which belonged to Bahrain. He concluded that Zubarah should be part of Qatar on the ground that the forcible taking of territories in pre-UN Charter days could not be protested today. This was first because of the uncertain position of international law in 1937 on illegality of annexation of a territory by an aggressor State, and second because of the requirements of the principle of stability of international relations.[69]

7.4.5.4 The 1990 invasion of Kuwait

On 2 August 1990 Iraqi armed forces invaded Kuwait and subsequently the Iraqi government announced its intention to establish a 'comprehensive and eternal merger' between Iraq and Kuwait. On 8 August, Iraq declared its intention to annex Kuwait and that it would become the nineteenth province of Iraq and instructed all foreign diplomats to leave Kuwait. Foreign embassies and consulates in Kuwait were closed by the Iraqi authorities.

In response, the UNSC adopted Resolution 662 (1990) of 9 August 1990, which declared that the 'annexation of Kuwait by Iraq under any form and whatever pretext has no legal validity and is considered null and void'.[70] The Resolution also called upon all States to refrain from extending

---

67   Portugal recognised the sovereignty of India over Goa by the 1974 Treaty signed between both States. In this treaty, which came into force in 1975, Portugal accepted that Goa became part of the Indian Union from 1962, the date on which the Indian Parliament passed an amendment to the Indian Constitution to this effect.

68   [2001] ICJ Rep 40.

69   Ibid, 458, paras 96–97.

70   UNSC Res 662 [9 August 1990] UN Doc S/RES/662 [1990].

recognition to the purported annexation and to abstain from any actions that could be construed as indirect recognition of the annexation.

Resolution 662 was ignored by Iraq and preparations were made by the Iraqi government to declare Kuwait as Iraq's nineteenth province. The UNSC therefore adopted a second Resolution relating to the Iraqi claim to have acquired the territory of Kuwait by means of conquest and annexation. Specifically referring to the obligations of Iraq under international law, UNSC Resolution 664 (1990)[71] reaffirmed that the annexation of Kuwait by Iraq was null and void and demanded that the government of Iraq rescind its orders for the closure of the diplomatic and consular missions in Kuwait and the withdrawal of immunity of their personnel (see Chapter 16.2.4.2).

Both the above UN Resolutions are evidence that the acquisition of territory by means of annexation and conquest is no longer a valid method of obtaining title under international law.

7.4.6   Historical consolidation

The doctrine of historical consolidation says that there will come a time when there will be created the belief that however wrongful the original taking of a territory, and despite protests that have been made regarding this, the present condition of things should not be disturbed.

The doctrine was first expressed in the *Anglo-Norwegian Fisheries Case (UK v Norway)*[72] with reference to the Norwegian decrees of 1935 which had the effect of extending the area of Norway's internal waters through the use of straight baselines as the means of delimitation of its territorial sea. This exercise of sovereignty claimed by Norway was over *res communis* and, therefore, the general acquiescence of all foreign States would have been necessary for the Norwegian decrees to be effective.

The Court stated:

> it is indeed this system [of straight baselines] itself which would reap the benefit of general toleration, the basis of an historic consolidation which would make it enforceable as against all states.

De Visscher cites the Court's decision as an example of the 'fundamental interest of the stability of territorial situations from the point of view of order and peace'. According to De Visscher's doctrine, consolidation differs from acquisitive prescription, occupation and recognition:

> consolidation differs from acquisitive prescription . . . in the fact that it can apply to territories that could not be proved to have belonged to another state. It differs from occupation in that it can be admitted in relation to certain parts of the sea as well as of land. Finally, it is distinguished from international recognition . . . by the fact that it can be held to be accomplished . . . by a sufficiently prolonged absence of opposition either, in the case of land, on the part of states interested in disputing possession or, in maritime waters, on the part of the generality of states.[73]

In addition, historic consolidation also takes cognisance of other special factors including economic interests and economic resources.

In the *Case Concerning the Land and Maritime Boundary between Cameroon and Nigeria (Cameroon v Nigeria: Equatorial Guinea Intervening)(Merits)*[74] Nigeria based its claim to the lake Chad area and to the Bakassi Peninsula on the ground of historical consolidation. Cameroon responded that as it held

---

71   UNSC Res 664 [1990] [18 August 1990] UN Doc S/RES/[1990].

72   (1951) ICJ Rep 116.

73   Cited by Johnson, *Consolidation as a Root of Title in International Law* [1955] 12 Cambridge Law Review, 215, 220.

74   [2002] ICJ Rep 303.

a title to these territories it was under no obligation to prove the effective exercise of sovereignty and unless Nigeria could prove that Cameroon had validly acquiesced in the relinquishing of its territory (which was not the case), Nigeria was exercising its authority *contra legem* and thus could not rely on the principle of effectiveness for the assignment of the title. The ICJ agreed with Cameroon. It stated that when a State possesses a legal title to a territory which is effectively administered by another State, the preference should be given to the holder of the title, i.e. Cameroon. The ICJ emphasised that the historic consolidation doctrine was highly controversial and that it could not replace the established modes of acquisition of title.[75] It can be said that in this case the ICJ suggested that a State has no duty under international law to exercise constant and thorough control over remote and inaccessible areas in order to maintain its title and that a claim based on the doctrine of historic consolidation with regard to the acquisition of title to land will perhaps never be successful in depriving the holder of a valid territorial title to the land at issue.

7.4.7 Novation

This is a distinct mode of acquisition defined by Verzijl as follows:

> It consists in the gradual transformation of a right in territorio alieno, for example a lease, or a pledge, or certain concessions of a territorial nature, into full sovereignty without any formal and unequivocal instrument to that effect intervening.[76]

The most famous example is that of British claims to British Honduras (Belize) resulting from the Treaty of Paris 1763 allowing British nationals to cut compeachy wood in the Spanish territories bordering the Bay of Honduras. A dispute between Guatemala, which considered itself as heir to the Spanish territories, and the UK which on the basis of novation claimed sovereignty over Belize, was settled by a treaty signed between Guatemala and Britain in 1859, under which Belize was officially declared a British colony with the name of British Honduras in 1862.

Nowadays, the fundamental principles of international law, i.e. the right of people to self-determination and the prohibition of intervention in a State's affairs will make the acquisition of a title to territory by means of novation highly unlikely. For example, territorial pledges, i.e. arrangements made by one State (the pledgor State) to transfer some of its territory to another State (the pledgee State) as a security for debts or performance of an obligation no longer occur mainly because the territory of a State is no longer considered as personal property of the ruler. A historical example of a pledge that resulted in territorial changes is that of the Shetland and Orkney Islands which were pledged to Scotland by King Christian I of Denmark, Norway and Sweden in 1468–69 *in lieu* of a dowry for his daughter Margaret of Denmark. When King Christian I failed to pay the dowry, James III of Scotland, the husband of Margaret, in 1472 annexed the islands to the Scottish Crown. It is interesting to note that as late as 1967 Norway asked the UK to discontinue the pledge in exchange for repayment of the debt.[77] The request was refused. With regard to leases and servitudes see Chapter 7.9.

---

75   Ibid, para 65.
76   *International Law in Historical Perspective*, vol 3, Leyden: Sijthoff, 1970, 384.
77   T.H. Irmscher, *Pledge of State Territory and Property*, Max Planck Encyclopedia of Public International Law, available at http:www.mpepil.com, para 9.

7.4.8 Acqusition of a title to territory resulting from a joint decision of victors of wars in the twentieth century

Victors of WWI and WWII disposed of certain territories of the defeated States in the following ways:

1 After WWI the mandate system was created under which the defeated States – Germany and the Ottoman Empire (Turkey) – were dispossessed of their colonial territories. Those territories were placed under the protection of the League of Nations and governed on its behalf by the selected States (see Chapter 13.2.1). Further, under peace treaties concluded between the victors and the defeated States, the map of Europe and the world was redrawn. Many new States were created on the territories of defeated nations. The PCIJ recognised this type of transfer of territorial sovereignty in the *Jaworzina Boundary Advisory Opinion.*[78]

2 During and after WWII, the principal Allied Powers (the US, UK and Russia) agreed on major territorial changes to be effected in Europe at the expense of Germany. In the Declaration Regarding the Defeat of Germany and the Assumption of Supreme Authority by Allied Powers of 5 June 1945 ('the Berlin Declaration') the three Powers and France, which had joined them, declared that they had power to 'determine the boundaries of Germany or any part thereof and the status of Germany or of any area at present being part of Germany'.[79] Indeed, the Three Allied Powers decided at the Potsdam Conference in 1945 to place 'under the administration of the Polish State'[80] the former German territories situated east of the Oder-Neisse line pending the determination of the final western border of Poland. Subsequently, the German population living on that territory was transferred to Germany. As to Soviet Russia, the so-called liberated territories were either annexed to Russia (*inter alia*, Estonia, Latvia, and the Eastern part of Poland) or became Soviet satellites.

The territorial changes made by the victors were subsequently formalised by the relevant treaties, e.g. between Poland and the Soviet Union concerning the frontiers between them by a treaty signed on 16 August 1945,[81] by Poland and the German Democratic Republic (GDR) by an agreement of 6 July 1950,[82] between the Soviet Union and the Federal Republic of Germany (FRG) by a treaty signed on 12 August 1970 under which the FRG renounced all territorial claims against anybody and affirmed the inviolability of all existing borders in Europe.[83] It is to be noted that subsequent to the treaty the FRG exchanged notes with the three Allied Powers and informed them that the rights of the former occupying powers were not affected by the agreement and that the FRG acted in the name of the FRG only.[84] Accordingly, this note did not bar the GDR from making territorial claims in the future. After the reunification of Germany, the Treaty on the Final Settlement with Respect to Germany of 12 September 1990,[85] between the two German States and the Four Powers settled the matter of German borders in that it confirmed the existing outer border of unified Germany as that country's final border, and stated that a new treaty with Poland was to be concluded reconfirming the existing border between

---

78   (1923) PCIJ, Ser B, No 8.
79   68 UNTS 190.
80   Report on the Tripartite (Soviet Union, UK and USA) Conference of Berlin or Potsdam (from 17 July to 2 August 1945) XIII (1945) DeptStBull 153.
81   10 UNTS 200.
82   319 UNTS 106.
83   (1970) 9 ILM 1027.
84   (1970) 9 ILM 1027.
85   (1990) 29 ILM 1187.

Germany and Poland. On 14 November 1990 a Treaty on the Confirmation of the Frontier between Germany and Poland[86] was signed in Warsaw which ensures the inviolability of the existing borders and renunciation of all territorial claims between the contracting parties.

The issue of the legal basis on which the victors were entitled to dispose of the defeated States' territories is still controversial[87] but not the existence of the power of disposition of these territories. In any event, the territorial changes were confirmed by the subsequent treaties signed by the FDR and the GDR and confirmed by both after the reunification.

7.4.9 Assessment of traditional modes of acquisition of territory.

It is to be noted that the traditional modes of acquisition of territory are unhelpful in explaining two matters.

The first is that of acquisition of territory during the post-WWII period by newly independent States. Although this can be explained in terms of cession or acquisitive prescription, such analysis fails to take into account the developments in international law since the late 1950s which have underpinned the independence movement. Most significant among these developments has been the recognition of a right to self-determination which has a specific content going beyond the broad principles outlined in, *inter alia*, Article 1(2) of the UN Charter and common Article 1 of the 1966 International Covenant on Civil and Political Rights and the International Covenant on Economic, Social and Cultural Rights 1966 (see Chapter 12.2.2).

The second matter is that the traditional modes of acquisition of territories give little acknowledgment to the fact that title in international law is a *relative* rather than absolute concept. In the *Legal Status of Eastern Greenland Case*, for example, the PCIJ was concerned to assess the strength of the Danish claim relative to that of Norway. This is not to say that a State's control over its own territory will always be open to challenge. Rather, it is recognition of the fact that disputes over territory arise in the context of competing claims. In these circumstances, the function of the Court is to determine which of the competing claims has the greater merit, not which of the claims is good against the world at large.

Given the above outlined two substantive limitations regarding the traditional modes of acquisition of territory, any assessment of current entitlement can only take place on the basis of all relevant facts and circumstances.

7.5 Other circumstances relevant to the acquisition of territory

Other circumstances relevant to the acquisition of territory are examined below.

7.5.1 Contiguity

Under the doctrine of contiguity a State may base a claim to an area of land on the ground that it forms geographical continuation of its territory. Contiguity alone is not a basis of title. However, it is a fact which may influence the decision of an international tribunal in cases, for instance, where sovereignty has not been exercised uniformly in every part of the territory or where only the coast of a barren territory has been occupied, or in cases where it is desired to give effect to principles of

---

86   830 UNTS 332.
87   See I. Brownlie, *Principles of Public International Law*, 7th edn, Oxford: Oxford University Press, 2008, 131.

geographic unity. For example, in the *Legal Status of Eastern Greenland Case*[88] where Danish sovereignty over the whole of Greenland was confirmed, the areas of the disputed territory actually settled by Denmark were few.

Contiguity is also the basis of the law concerning territorial waters, the contiguous zone and the continental shelf (see Chapter 8).

7.5.2 Discovery

It was believed in the sixteenth century that discovery alone conferred a complete title to territory and such discovery was usually accompanied by symbolic acts such as the planting of a flag. The modern view, however, is that discovery merely gives an option to the discovering State to consolidate its claim by proceeding to effective occupation within a reasonable time. This was the view stated by the arbitrator in *the Island of Palmas Arbitration.*[89]

7.5.3 Symbolic annexation

Symbolic annexation has been defined by Brownlie as:

A declaration or other act of sovereignty or an act of private persons duly authorised or subsequently ratified by a state, intended to provide unequivocal evidence of the acquisition of sovereignty over a parcel of territory or an island.[90]

Only in special circumstances, such as those described below in the *Clipperton Island Arbitration,*[91] may a State rely on symbolic annexation to prove its title to territory. Otherwise, symbolic annexation will be regarded as a factor to be taken into consideration in establishing that a State has exercised effective control over *terra nullius*.

CLIPPERTON ISLAND ARBITRATION

Facts:

The island was first discovered by the Englishman Clipperton in 1705 and later rediscovered by French navigators. It is a small uninhabited island located in the Pacific Ocean, some 1,000 kilometres southwest of Mexico, now part of French Polynesia. Neither the UK nor France made any claims to the island prior to 1858. In that year, the French government granted a concession to exploit guano resources on the island and on 17 November 1858, a French navy officer, duly authorised by the French government, proclaimed French sovereignty over the island from the deck of a French merchant ship cruising near the island. Although, at that time, the French landed on the island, no visible marks of the French presence were left on the island. The proclamation was reported to the French consulate in Honolulu and subsequently notified to the government of Hawaii and published in the

---

88   Supra note 44.
89   Supra note 3.
90   Supra note 2, 141.
91   (1933) 27 AJIL, 130.

local Hawaiian newspaper. When in 1897 a French navy vessel found that guano was being collected on the island on behalf of a US company, the French government requested that the US declare that it had no claim to the island. The US confirmed this but Mexico decided to claim sovereignty over the island on the ground that the island was discovered by Spain and that Mexico, as the legal successor to Spain, could claim title to the island. Mexico despatched a warship whose crew landed there and planted the Mexican flag. France and Mexico agreed to refer the dispute to the arbitration of King Victor Emanuel III of Italy.

Held:

The arbitral award stated that Mexico had not acquired sovereignty over the island as it could neither prove that the island was discovered by Spain nor that it had occupied the island prior to 1858. Accordingly, prior to 1858 the island was terra nullius *and could be occupied by France. In the absence of any effective rival claim and taking into account the inaccessible and uninhabited nature of the island, France acquired the island when sovereignty was proclaimed on 17 November 1858. Accordingly, the purported annexation, though symbolic in form, was sufficient to confer on France the legal title to Clipperton Island.*

7.5.4 Boundary treaties

The vast majority of States have agreed their borders with neighbouring States by means of bilateral treaties which determine the respective territories. Periodically, disputes arise between States over the precise delimitations set down in such treaties. In these circumstances, the treaties establishing the borders must be interpreted and applied by an impartial international body such as the ICJ. For example, in *Case Concerning Land, Island and Maritime Frontier Disputes (El Salvador/Honduras, Nicaragua Intervening)*,[92] El Salvador and Honduras submitted a long-standing dispute over an area of territory on the border between them to the ICJ for resolution.

Treaties defining borders have a special status in international law. Borders established by such treaties have a permanence that exists independently from the fate of the treaties which sets them out. This principle has been affirmed by the International Court in the *Case Concerning the Territorial Dispute (Libyan Arab Jamahiriya/Chad)*.[93]

CASE CONCERNING THE TERRITORIAL DISPUTE (LIBYAN ARAB JAMAHIRIYA *V* CHAD)

Facts:

After an armed conflict caused by competing claims to an area of border territory, Libya and Chad agreed to refer the dispute regarding the location of their mutual border to the Court. A Treaty of Friendship and Good Neighbourliness in 1955 had been negotiated between the

---

92   [1992] ICJ Rep 92.
93   [1994] ICJ Rep 6, para 72.

newly independent State of Libya and France as the colonial administrator of the territory which subsequently became Chad. In the treaty, a border had been set down between the two countries but the treaty was expressed to be of limited duration.

Held:

The Court considered the matter and concluded that the border was definitively agreed in the 1955 Treaty to which Chad was a party as the successor State to the French administered territory. The subsequent actions of the parties supported this determination. The fact that the treaty was only concluded for a limited period – 20 years – was not relevant because treaties setting down borders create demarcations which endure independently of the agreement establishing them. In the words of the Court:

> *The establishment of this boundary is a fact which, from the outset, has had a legal life of its own, independently of the fate of the 1955 Treaty. Once agreed, the boundary stands, for any other approach would vitiate the fundamental principle of the stability of boundaries, the importance of which has been repeatedly emphasised by the Court.*

Comment:

The Court's position accords with Article 62(2)(a) VCLT which precludes the application of rebus sic stantibus *to treaties settling international borders.*[94]

In the absence of relevant treaties, an adjudicating body normally applies the principle of *uti possidetis* (which has acquired the status of a norm of customary international law – see Chapter 7.3.2.2) that is, takes into consideration, if relevant, the existing official maps, administrative acts, legislation and unilateral declarations of the relevant colonial power and its conduct to delimit borders at the time of attainment of independence by the States concerned (the critical date). If the principle of *uti possidetis* is not applicable, then the adjudicating body will look at the conduct of the parties to a dispute in terms of which of them has exercised effective control over the disputed area.[95] For example in the boundary dispute between Cameroon and Nigeria,[96] the ICJ held that Cameroon had established a valid title to the disputed area and thus the administrative control exercised by Nigeria was not only ignored but regarded as unlawful. The amount of display of the actual exercise of a State's sovereignty depends upon the specific circumstances of each case, i.e. depends on the territory's accessibility and habitability.[97]

Any adjudication/arbitration only confirms the existence of title to territory, as courts and arbitral bodies have no power to grant title to a party to a dispute. The decisions of such bodies have declaratory rather then constitutive effect. It is on the basis of an international agreement concluded by the parties to the dispute that those bodies are empowered to settle a particular dispute. The implementation of a decision of the adjudicating body is left to the parties, which will normally conclude an international

---

94   Also Article 11 of the Vienna Convention on the Succession of States in Respect of Treaties (17 ILM 1488) provides that succession has no effect on border treaties.
95   See the *Case Concerning the Frontier Dispute (Burkina Faso/Republic of Mali)* [1986] ICJ Rep 554, para 63.
96   *The Case Concerning Land and Maritime Boundary between Cameroon and Nigeria (Cameroon v Nigeria) (Preliminary Objections)* [1998] ICJ Rep 275.
97   *The Island of Palmas Arbitration*, supra note 3, 849, p 24 para 67.

agreement. Further, the parties to a dispute are free to agree on rules and principles applicable to the dispute and the manner of its attempted settlement in order to arrive at a settlement. Consequently, even existing treaties may be ignored and the relevant body may be required to decide the case on the principle of *ex aequo et bono*, i.e. to disregard legal principles and base its decision on what is equitable in the circumstances of the case, although so far, the principle of *ex aequo at bono* has never been applied by the ICJ, and rarely by other international tribunals.[98]

7.6 Acquisition of territory in polar regions

The polar regions create unique problems in the context of acquisition of territory. A distinction must be made between the Arctic and Antarctica.

7.6.1 The Arctic

The Arctic comprises the northern polar region encompassing approximately 20 million square kilometres, half of which consists of ocean almost entirely covered by ice. The remainder is made up of territories and islands belonging to Canada, the US (Alaska), Russia, Norway, Finland, Sweden, Denmark (Greenland) and Iceland. Approximately 4 million people including over 30 different indigenous peoples inhabit the Arctic.[99] Initially, these 'Arctic Eight' States claimed sovereignty over regions beyond their land territories, *inter alia*, on the basis of a sector theory. According to this theory all land lying within the triangle between the east-west extremities of a State contiguous to the Pole and the Pole itself should be subject to that State's dominion, unless the territory already belongs to another State. The sector theory was examined by the PCIJ in *Legal Status of Eastern Greenland (Denmark v Norway).*[100] The PCIJ stated that while the sector theory does not give title which would not otherwise arise, if necessary State activity occurs in the claimed territory such activity represents a reasonable application of the principle of effective occupation. The international community has never accepted the sector theory, which was finally dismissed by the 1982 UN Convention on the Law of the Sea (LOSC).[101]

The Arctic has great military importance for the US and Russia. The economic potential of the Arctic shelf areas, which are rich in oil, gas and other natural resources, has prompted territorial claims to the Arctic. Canada alone is facing a number of actual or potential disputes relating to its control of the Arctic region, for example: as regards the status of the Northwest Passage which Canada claims constitutes part of its internal waters but the US, the EU and possibly Japan regard as being an international strait; relating to the delimitation of a maritime boundary between Alaska and Yukon; concerning the delimitation of the Northern continental shelf to which Russia and the US may submit claims; relating to an existing dispute over Hans Island, a small island between Northern Greenland and Ellesmere Island, to which Denmark asserts claims, etc.

Under the terms of the LOSC, a contracting State may claim an extended continental shelf beyond the normal 200 nautical miles (nm) from its baselines where the outer edge of the continental margin (which includes the shelf, the slope and rise) extends beyond 200 nm, but in no event must the outer

---

98 A.M. McHugh, *Resolving International Boundary Disputes in Africa: A Case for the International Court of Justice* (2005) 49 How LJ 209, at 222.
99 On the Arctic see: M. Byers, *International Law and the Arctic*, Cambridge: Cambridge University Press, 2013.
100 (1933) PCIJ Rep Ser A/B No 53.
101 1836 UNTS 3.

limits of the continental shelf exceed 350 nm from the baselines or 100 nm from the 2,500-metre isobath. Such claims must be submitted to the Commission on the Limits of the Continental Shelf (the CLCS) which gives binding and final recommendation on a State's submissions (see Chapter 8.7.5). Up to the time of writing, no nation has secured territorial rights to the Arctic in this manner, but all coastal States, apart from the US, have ratified the LOSC. Global warming has added to the importance of securing rights to the Arctic because a successful claim to the extended continental shelf may bring the coastal States enormous benefits. This region is warming twice as fast as the rest of the planet. It is likely that the North Pole could be ice-free in summertime by the end of the century. Apart from the treasure of natural resources, which the thaw may make accessible, a Northwest shipping passage may be created, reducing by thousands of miles the length of shipping journeys between the Atlantic and Pacific Oceans, and providing new fishing grounds for claimant States.

Despite the existing legal controversies the Arctic Eight have been willing to co-operate in respect of environmental matters. The first major development was the conclusion of the 1973 Agreement on the Conservation of Polar Bears, followed in 1991 by the creation of the Arctic Environmental Protection Strategy (AEPS) and the establishment of the Arctic Council in 1996.[102]

7.6.2   Antarctica

Antarctica has a surface area of more than 14 million square kilometres. The UK, Russia and the US all claim to have discovered Antarctica. Explorers reached the continent in the late eighteenth century. The whaling and sealing industry was developed in the nineteenth century. This last uncharted and unclaimed land on earth became a target of scientific explorations around the turn of the twentieth century. The first territorial claim was made by the UK. In Letters Patent of 21 July 1908 the UK claimed a large portion of Antarctica with a view to controlling the whaling industry.

In total six nations made territorial claims to Antarctica. They were: Australia, Chile, France, New Zealand, Norway and the UK. They are referred to as claimant States. Their claims were based on various grounds: occupation, contiguity, the sector theory, discovery, exploitation and historic rights. The claimant States, except when claims overlapped, recognised each other's claims, whatever the legal basis.

After WWII five countries: Belgium, Japan, South Africa, the US and the USSR stated that they would neither assert nor recognise any territorial claims to Antarctica. Those States are referred to as non-claimant States.

The above events combined with a claim by the USSR of a right to maintain its bases in Antarctica, and numerous territorial disputes between South American countries and the UK, emphasised the need for a more permanent solution at an international level. The Antarctic Treaty of 1959,[103] which entered into force on 23 June 1961, provided such a solution. This Treaty 'freezes!' all claims to territorial sovereignty in Antarctica. Art IV of the 1959 Treaty states:

> No acts or activities taking place while the present Treaty is in force shall constitute a basis for asserting, supporting or denying a claim to territorial sovereignty in Antarctica or create any rights of sovereignty in Antarctica. No new claim, or enlargement of an existing claim to territorial sovereignty in Antarctica shall be asserted while the present Treaty is in force.

---

102   See the official website of the Arctic Council available at www.arctic-council.org.
103   402 UNTS 71.

The treaty is of unlimited duration. To ensure compliance with the treaty, the contracting parties provided for inspections of 'all areas of Antarctica, including all stations, installations and equipment within those areas'.

Apart from imposing a moratorium on territorial claims, the treaty ensures that Antarctica is used for peaceful purposes only, and that freedom of scientific investigation and co-operation is preserved.

On the basis of the 1959 treaty a system of management of the continent was set up, often referred to as the Antarctic Treaty System (ATS),[104] which over the years has developed new policies to respond to changing circumstances, in particular, to ensure the protection of the environment in Antarctica. Additional components of the ATS include: the 1972 Convention for the Conservation of Antarctic Seals, the 1980 Convention on the Conservation of Antarctic Marine Living Resources, the 1988 Convention on the Regulation of Antarctic Mineral Resource Activities and the 1991 Protocol to the Antarctic Treaty on Environmental Protection.

7.7 Restrictions on the transfer of territory

States may enter into agreements not to alienate certain areas of territory under any circumstances or they may contract not to transfer territory to a particular State or States. An obligation not to acquire territory may also be undertaken. By the State Treaty of 1955 Austria agreed not to enter into political or economic union with Germany. By the Treaty of Utrecht 1713, Great Britain agreed to offer Gibraltar to Spain before attempting to transfer sovereignty over Gibraltar to any other State.

It is doubtful whether a breach of a treaty not to alienate or acquire particular territory will affect the title of a country which is a grantee of that territory.

7.8 Loss of territory

Loss of territory may occur in the following circumstances.

- by treaty of cession – a transfer of rights by one State to another;

- by acquisitive prescription;

- by the creation of a new State which will obviously cause at least one State to lose territory.

- by abandonment otherwise known as *derelicto* – a State may give up part of its territory by:

  - conduct (see below the abandonment of Pedra Branca/Palau Batu Puteh);

  - express admission, e.g. the statement of the Under-Secretary of the UK Foreign Office made before the House of Commons in 1928 declaring the abandonment by the UK of a claim over Bouvet island;

  - treaty e.g. a treaty between the US and Kiribati[105] in which the US abandoned its claims to some islands;

  - acquiescence of another State's claim to its territory e.g. the abandonment of the area of Tepangüisir by Honduras.[106]

---

104   See the official website of the ATS available at www.ats.aq/e/ats.htm (accessed 8 October 2014).

105   Treaty of Friendship between the US and the Republic of Kiribati signed on 20 September 1643 UNTS 239.

106   *The Case Concerning Land, Island and Maritime Frontier Dispute (El Salvador/Honduras: Nicaragua Intervening) (Judgment)* [1992] ICJ Rep 351.

When a State abandons a territory, that territory becomes either *terra nullius* or part of another State's territory.

Abandonment requires both physical abandonment and an intention to abandon dominion. The intention must be clear and proven. In the *Sovereignty over Pedra Branca/Palau Batu Puteh, Middle Rock and South Ledge (Malaysia/Singapore)*[Merits][107] the ICJ, on the basis of the following facts, decided that Malaysia, which held the original title to Pedra Branca/Palau Batu Puteh island – a tiny, uninhabited granite island – had abandoned it:

- that the Johor authorities and their successor (Malaysia) had not taken any action in connection with the island for more than one century from June 1850;

- that the official visits of the Malaysian authorities in the twentieth century were subject to express permission given by Singapore;

- that official maps of Malaysia of the 1960s and the 1970s indicated that Singapore had sovereignty over the island;

- that Singapore conducted itself on many occasions as acting '*à titre de souverain*' e.g. operated the Horsburgh lighthouse, investigated shipwrecks in the waters around the island, installed military equipment in the lighthouse in 1977, and exercised exclusive control over visits to the island and the use of land, in particular after 1953, without any protest from Malaysia although most of the activities carried out by Singapore were notified to Malaysia (apart from the installation of naval communication equipment).

For reasons of stability, abandonment is not to be presumed and certainly in the case of remote, inhospitable and uninhabited areas it would seem that international tribunals require little evidence of maintenance of sovereignty. This was confirmed in the *Clipperton Island Arbitration* and was referred to in the *Legal Status of Eastern Greenland Case*. In territories which are inhospitable it may well be that dominion will remain if a physical manifestation of sovereignty subsists.

7.9   Rights over parts of territory of a foreign State: international leases and servitudes

7.9.1   Leases

One State may lease parts of its territory to another State, usually for an annual fee or other consideration, e.g. in exchange for a debt write-off, or for provision of military, or financial aid. As there is no general international law specifically regulating leaseholds, it is for the lessor State and the lessee State to agree the terms of each lease. Such leases being international agreements are governed by the law of treaties. Examples of leases include those made by China in favour of France, Russia, Germany and Great Britain in 1898, when the European powers entered into leases of areas of Chinese territory in order to gain access to ports and thus increase their influence in the region. More recent examples are leases entered into by Russia as lessee and some of the former republics of the Soviet Union as lessor, which allow Russia to have access to and control of strategic facilities owned by Russia but located on the territories of new independent States. For example, the Baikonur cosmodrome in Kazakhstan is being leased to Russia for a period of 50 years.

---

107   [2008]. ICJ Rep 12.

The leased territory remains under the residual sovereignty of the lessor State, but the lessee State has jurisdiction over it for the period of the lease. Such a lease is a right *in rem*. It attaches to the territory and remains enforceable against the territory even if the territory subsequently finds itself under the dominion of another State.

A lease may be granted for a specific period of time or for perpetuity. For example, Hong Kong, with adjacent areas, was leased by China to the UK for 99 years. When the lease expired in 1997, Hong Kong was handed back to China.

In 1903 Panama granted to the US 'in perpetuity the use, occupation and control' of the Panama Canal Zone. However, following an agreement between the US and Panama in 1977, the lease was terminated in 1999 and Panama restored its full sovereignty over the Panama Canal Zone.

With regard to Guantánamo Bay in Cuba, under the terms of a lease of land there signed between Cuba and the US in 1903[108] as supplemented by a 1934 treaty, the US in effect decides whether it wishes to continue the lease. When Fidel Castro came to power in Cuba, he declared the lease to be void or voidable on the grounds of the doctrine of unequal treaties, coercion during the negotiations and changing circumstances, i.e. the establishment in Cuba of a communist regime. The communist government of Cuba has refused to collect the annual rental (apart from once), but has also constantly declared that Cuba would not have recourse to force to recover Guantánamo Bay. Further, the Cuban government considers that the US was in breach of the lease, in the mid-1990s when Guantánamo Bay was used to process asylum seekers from Haiti and has also been in breach since 2001 at which time it became an interrogation centre for persons taken into custody of the US as terrorist suspects (see Chapter 17.5.4.1). The lease states that Guantánamo Bay is to be used for coaling and naval stations.

7.9.2 Servitudes

Servitudes occur when a territory of one State is made to serve the interests of another State. By treaty or otherwise a State may acquire rights over the territory of another State, i.e. it may be entitled to do something on the territory of another State (e.g. exercise a right of way, use ports or watercourses) or to compel the other State to refrain from doing something (e.g. fortifying its towns). Such rights may be divided into two categories.

1 Rights benefiting the international community: international servitudes may exist, not for the benefit of a single State but for the benefit of the international community. This is exemplified by the *Aaland Islands Case*.[109]

AALAND ISLANDS CASE

Facts:

Russia had entered into a treaty obligation in 1856 not to fortify the Aaland Islands. Although the islands lay near Stockholm, Sweden was not a party to the treaty. In 1918 the islands became part of Finland which started fortifying them. Sweden complained to the League of Nations.

---

108 Agreement between the United States and Cuba for the Lease of Lands for Coaling and Naval Stations (signed 16 February 1903, entered into force 23 February 1903) 192 CTS 429.
109 (1920) LNOJ Spec Supp No 3, 3.

Held:

The Commission of Jurists decided that Finland had succeeded to Russia's obligations and that Sweden could claim the benefit of the 1856 Treaty, although she was not a party to it. The treaty was designed to preserve the balance of power in Europe and could, therefore, be invoked by all the States which were 'directly interested', including Sweden.

2 Rights benefiting only a single State: these include mining rights, rights to run an oil or gas pipeline across a neighbouring state, rights to take water for irrigation, rights of way, etc.

CASE CONCERNING RIGHT OF PASSAGE OVER INDIAN TERRITORY CASE (PORTUGAL *V* INDIA) (MERITS)[110]

Held:

Portugal had a right of passage over Indian territory between the coastal district of Daman and the 'enclaves' in respect of private persons, civil officials and goods in general, and this right was binding on India.

International tribunals seem reluctant to find servitudes in favour of a single State where those servitudes are of an economic nature. For example, in the *North Atlantic Fisheries Arbitration (US v Great Britain)*,[111] it was held that a treaty between the US and Great Britain (the Newfoundland Coast Fishing Treaty 1818), granting the inhabitants of the US the liberty to take fish from the sea off Newfoundland, did not create a servitude preventing Great Britain from limiting the fishing rights of all persons, including US nationals, in the area concerned. However, if clear evidence of the intention to create such servitude is found to exist, on the part of the State granting it, then it will be upheld.

---

110   [1960] ICJ Rep 6.
111   (1910) 11 RIAA 167.

RECOMMENDED READING

Books

Byers, M., *International Law and the Arctic*, Cambridge: Cambridge University Press, 2013.

Higgins, R., 'Some Observations on the Inter-temporal Rule in International Law' in J. Makarczyk (ed.), *Theory of International Law at the Threshold of the 21st Century: Essays in Honour of Krzystof Skubiszewski*, The Hague: Kluwer Law International, 1996, 173.

Jennings, R.Y., *The Acquisition of Territory in International Law*, Manchester: Manchester University Press, 1963.

Korman, S., *The Right of Conquest: The Acquisition of Territory by Force in International Law and Practice*, Oxford: Clarendon, 1996.

Mälksoo, L., *Illegal Annexation and State Continuity*, Leiden: Nijhoff, 2003.

Milano, E., *Unlawful Territorial Situations in International Law: Reconciling Effectiveness, Legality and Legitimacy*, Leiden: Nijhoff, 2006.

Articles

Bouchez, J.L., *The Fixing of Boundaries in International Boundary Rivers* (1963) 12 ICLQ, 789.

Dickinson, E.D., *The Clipperton Island Case* (1933) 27 AJIL, 130.

Elias, T.O., *The Doctrine of Intertemporal Law* (1980) 74 AJIL, 285.

Fry, J.D., *The Roots of Historic Title: Non-Western Pre-Colonial Normative Systems and Legal Resolution of Territorial Disputes* (2014) 27 LJIL, 727.

Lesaffer, R., *Arguments from Roman Law in Current International Law: Occupation and Acquisitive Prescription* (2005) 16 EJIL, 16.

McHugh, M., *Resolving International Boundary Disputes in Africa: A Case for the International Court of Justice* (2005) 49 How LJ, 209.

Marston, G., *Abandonment of Territorial Claims: The Cases of Bouvet and Spratly Islands* (1986) BYIL, 337.

Menon, P.K., *Title to Territory* (1994) 72 RDI, 1.

AIDE-MÉMOIRE

Modes of acquiring title to territory

The traditional five modes of acquisition of a title to territory are:

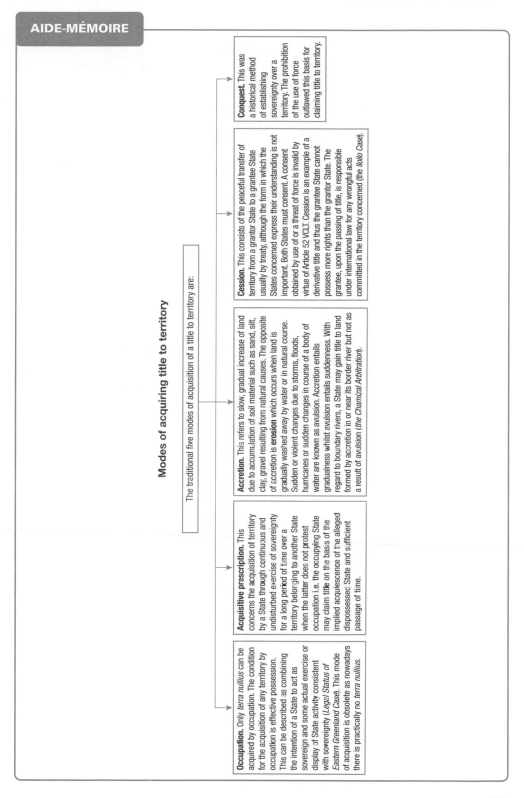

Occupation. Only *terra nullius* can be acquired by occupation. The condition for the acquisition of any territory by occupation is effective possession. This can be described as combining the intention of a State to act as sovereign and some actual exercise or display of State activity consistent with sovereignty (*Legal Status of Eastern Greenland Case*). This mode of acquisition is obsolete as nowadays there is practically no *terra nullius*.

Acquisitive prescription. This concerns the acquisition of territory by a State through continuous and undisturbed exercise of sovereignty for a long period of time over a territory belonging to another State when the latter does not protest occupation i.e. the occupying State may claim title on the basis of the implied acquiescence of the alleged dispossessed State and sufficient passage of time.

Accretion. This refers to slow, gradual increase of land due to accumulation of soil material such as sand, silt, clay, gravel resulting from natural causes. The opposite of accretion is *erosion* which occurs when land is gradually washed away by water or in natural course. Sudden or violent changes due to storms, floods, hurricanes or sudden changes in course of a body of water are known as avulsion. Accretion entails gradualness whilst avulsion entails suddenness. With regard to boundary rivers, a State may gain title to land formed by accretion in or near its border river but not as a result of avulsion (*the Chamizal Arbitration*).

Cession. This consists of the peaceful transfer of territory from a grantor State to a grantee State usually by treaty, although the form in which the States concerned express their understanding is not important. Both States must consent. A consent obtained by use of or a threat of force is invalid by virtue of Article 52 VCLT. Cession is an example of a derivative title and thus the grantee State cannot possess more rights than the grantor State. The grantee, upon the passing of title, is responsible under international law for any wrongful acts committed in the territory concerned (the *Iloilo Case*).

Conquest. This was a historical method of establishing sovereignty over a territory. The prohibition of the use of force outlawed this basis for claiming title to territory.

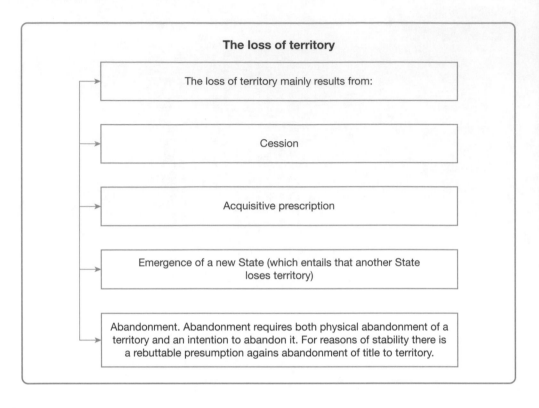

The loss of territory

The loss of territory mainly results from:

Cession

Acquisitive prescription

Emergence of a new State (which entails that another State loses territory)

Abandonment. Abandonment requires both physical abandonment of a territory and an intention to abandon it. For reasons of stability there is a rebuttable presumption agains abandonment of title to territory.

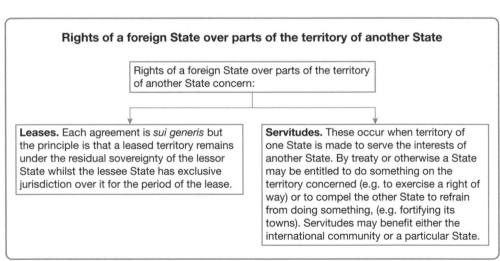

Rights of a foreign State over parts of the territory of another State

Rights of a foreign State over parts of the territory of another State concern:

Leases. Each agreement is *sui generis* but the principle is that a leased territory remains under the residual sovereignty of the lessor State whilst the lessee State has exclusive jurisdiction over it for the period of the lease.

Servitudes. These occur when territory of one State is made to serve the interests of another State. By treaty or otherwise a State may be entitled to do something on the territory concerned (e.g. to exercise a right of way) or to compel the other State to refrain from doing something, (e.g. fortifying its towns). Servitudes may benefit either the international community or a particular State.

8

THE LAW OF THE SEA

CONTENTS

CHAPTER OUTLINE

1 Introduction

As early as AD 533, legal scholars of the Roman Empire declared 'the sea by its nature [to be] open to everyone' and 'for the common use of all men'. This principle, although contested through the centuries, was universally accepted by the end of the first quarter of the nineteenth century. However, rules relating to the law of the sea were based mainly on customary international law and thus their codification and development became the priority of the League of Nations and the UN. The first successful codification was carried out by the First United Nations Conference on the Law of the Sea (UNCLOS I) which in 1958 produced four Geneva conventions, on various aspects of the law of the sea, but failed to resolve the issue of the breadth of the territorial sea. However, UNCLOS III was successful in that it adopted the United Nations Convention on the Law of the Sea (LOSC), which entered into force on 16 November 1994. The LOSC has been ratified by 166 States and is considered as a constitution for the oceans. It is comprehensive in content and scope. Its main provisions are examined in this chapter.

2 Baselines

A baseline is a line which serves as a base or a point of reference for measuring the breadth of the territorial sea. It marks the limit of a State's internal waters with the result that all waters which are landward of the baseline are internal waters, and therefore part of a State's land territory. Every maritime zone extending from a coast is measured from the baseline. Finally, it is used to construe lines of equidistance in disputes concerning the delimitation of territorial sea between opposite or adjacent States. Three types of baselines are used in the law of the sea: normal, straight and straight archipelagic.

3 Internal waters

Internal or national waters are defined by the LOSC as all water landward from the baseline. They include rivers, lakes, canals, bays or other internal waters that come from the sea as well as the water landward from fringing islands off the coast of a State. These waters may be considered as 'legally equivalent to the state's land'. As a result, a coastal State may exercise full jurisdiction over its internal waters, subject only to the limitations imposed by international law, e.g. with regard to foreign warships and ships operated by a foreign State for non-commercial purposes. However, in respect of jurisdiction of a coastal State over commercial ships State practice shows that, based on comity, a port State will not exercise jurisdiction over the internal affairs of the foreign vessel, but it will exercise jurisdiction over any act that may interfere with the peace and tranquility of the port.

It is uncertain whether freedom of access to ports and harbours of a coastal State is a rule of customary international law.

There is no right of innocent passage in internal waters except where the use of the straight baseline method has the effect of enclosing as internal waters what had previously been classified as part of the territorial sea. Under customary international law, States are also obliged to permit entry into internal waters and ports to ships in distress.

4 Territorial sea, international straits and archipelagic waters

Territorial sea. The territorial sea refers to a band or belt of water immediately adjacent to the internal waters, archipelagic waters or coast of a State. The LOCS permits a State to claim a territorial sea up to 12 nautical miles (nm) in length from the baseline. Under customary international law the territorial sea forms part of the State's territory and is subject to its sovereignty but there are some limitations. Customary international law confers upon the foreign vessel of every State the right to innocent passage through the territorial sea of other States. Passage is innocent if it is not prejudicial to the peace, good order or security of the coastal State. There is some disagreement as to whether warships enjoy the right of innocent passage.

A coastal State may exercise criminal jurisdiction in its territorial sea over foreign ships and their crew, but the LOSC specifically provides this should only be exercised where (i) the consequences of the crime extend to the coastal State; (ii) the crime disturbs the peace of the country or the order of the territorial sea; (iii) assistance has been requested either by the captain of the ship or the flag country; and (iv) it is necessary for the suppression of illicit traffic in narcotic drugs.

International straits: Part III of the LOSC divides international straights into two categories: those to which it applies and those to which it does not apply. Part III LOSC applies to straits used for international navigation between one part of the high seas or an Exclusive Economic Zone (EEZ), and another part of the high seas or an EEZ, which are entirely within the territorial waters of States bordering them. It applies not only to ships but also to aircraft. Under Article 44 LOSC bordering States have a duty not to hamper transit passage and not to suspend transit passage, regardless of all circumstances. All ships and aircraft are entitled to transit passage through, or over, as appropriate, international straits. Such passage must be exercised in a continuous and expeditious manner. For international straits outside the scope of Part III, the LOSC establishes special rules.

Archipelagic waters. The LOSC provides a definition of an archipelagic State and of archipelagic waters. Only a State which satisfies the definition of archipelagic State may claim the right to archipelagic waters. Archipelagic States can draw 'archipelagic baselines', i.e. allowing enclosure of their outmost islands and reefs with baselines (see Chapter 8.2.3), from which they delimit their maritime zones, i.e. territorial waters, contiguous zone, and EEZ. Waters landwards of these baselines are 'archipelagic waters', they are neither internal waters nor territorial waters unless they fall landwards of closing lines across river mouths, bays, or harbours of individual islands drawn in accordance with LOSC rules on normal baselines. Like the territorial sea, these waters, the subsoil below and the air column above form part of the territory of the archipelagic State and are subject to its sovereignty. One of the main restrictions imposed on archipelagic States is that they must ensure that ships of all States enjoy the right of innocent passage through archipelagic waters much as they do through the territorial sea.

5 Contiguous zone

This is a zone adjacent to the territorial sea over which a coastal State may exercise limited jurisdiction. However, its importance has diminished as a result of the establishment of the EEZ by the LOSC.

6 The Exclusive Economic Zone (EEZ)

The EEZ is an area beyond and adjacent to the territorial sea in which a coastal State enjoys certain sovereign rights subject to the rights and freedoms accorded to all other States. The EEZ stretches up to 200 nm from the baseline. A coastal State may exercise sovereign rights over the resources contained there including those of the seabed and subsoil and the airspace above for the purpose of exploration, exploitation, conservation and management. A coastal State may exercise legislative and enforcement jurisdiction over foreign ships relating to conservation, pollution and the exploitation and use of EEZ resources. In the EEZ of a coastal State, all other States enjoy the freedom of navigation and overflight, the laying of submarine cables and pipelines and other internationally lawful uses of the seas related to these freedoms.

7 Continental shelf

The continental shelf refers to the seabed and subsoil of the submarine areas adjacent to but outside the territorial sea of a coastal State. The coastal States have the exclusive right to explore and exploit the natural resources of the continental shelf including both mineral and other non-living resources, and no other State may do so without express consent. Every costal State is entitled to claim the continental shelf up to 200nm of the baselines from which the breadth of the territorial sea is measured, regardless of the configuration of the seabed. However, where the outer edge of the continental margin (which includes the shelf, the slope and the rise) extends beyond 200 nm, the coastal State may claim the legal title to a natural prolongation of its continental shelf but in no event can the outer limits of the continental shelf exceed 350 nm from the baselines or 100 nm from the 2,500-metre isobath. If a State wishes to make such a claim it must make a submission to the Commission on the Limits of the Continental Shelf (CLCS) which will then make a final and binding recommendation on the claim.

8 Delimitation of maritime boundaries

Maritime delimitation refers to the process of determining the sovereignty or jurisdiction of a coastal State over its adjacent seas, where its claims overlap with that of one or more States. The corrective equity approach is generally applied to delimitation of maritime boundaries. It involves a three steps procedure:

First, an international court or tribunal draws a provisional equidistance line in the area to be delimited; next, it examines whether that line needs to be adjusted or shifted in the light of the relevant circumstances; finally, it applies the principle of proportionality to ascertain whether the maritime areas attributed to each party in the relevant zone are marked disproportionally to the length of their respective coasts. Under the corrective equity approach the application of the equidistance method is mandatory so this ensures predictability of results, while equity intervenes as a corrective element.

9 The high seas

All parts of the sea not included in the EEZ, the territorial sea or in the internal waters of a State or the archipelagic waters of an archipelagic State form part of the high seas. The high seas are open to all States, and no State may validly purport to subject any part of the high seas to its sovereignty. All States are entitled to make various uses of the high seas including navigation, overflight, laying submarine cables and pipelines, construction of artificial islands, fishing and maritime research. The general rule is that vessels on the high seas are subject to the authority of the State whose flag they fly. However, to maintain peace and order on the high seas, a number of exceptions to the jurisdiction of a flagship State have been developed, most of them under customary international law. These include (i) the hot pursuit of a foreign vessel; (ii) the right to approach and visit; (iii) exceptions under treaties and (iv) UNSC authorisation. As to the right to visit, warships or other duly authorised ships in government service including aircraft may approach a foreign ship that does not enjoy State immunity (see Chapter 10.3.2) where there is reasonable ground for suspecting that the ship is engaged in piracy, slave trade, unauthorised broadcasting, is without nationality, i.e. stateless, or its nationality is uncertain but it can reasonably be assumed that it is of the same nationality as the visiting craft.

10 The Area

The Area is defined as the seabed and ocean floor and subsoil thereof, beyond the limits of natural jurisdiction. It constitutes the 'common heritage of mankind'. The LOSC creates a legal framework for exploring and exploiting resources of the Area. It provides that any activities in the Area are to be organised, carried out and controlled by the International Seabed Authority (ISA). The LOSC provisions relating to the Area were considerably modified by the 1994 Implementation Agreement, first to ensure ratification of the LOSC by developed States and second, to incorporate a market oriented approach to exploitation of the Area. However, exploitation of resources on the seabed has not actually yet taken place and is not likely to commence in the immediate future.

11 Settlement of disputes under the 1982 UN Convention on the Law of the Sea (LOSC)

The LOSC establishes an original two-tier system for settlement of disputes concerning the application and interpretation of its provisions which combines voluntary procedures with compulsory procedures. Under this system, in the first place, parties to a dispute may choose any procedure they wish. In the second place, if they fail to settle a dispute by means of their own choice, they must settle it in accordance with the compulsory procedures set out in section 2 of Part XV. The procedures are:

- the International Tribunal for the Law of the Sea (ITLOS);

- the ICJ (see Chapter 14.6.–14.9);

- an arbitral tribunal under Annex VII of LOSC; and

- a special arbitral tribunal under Annex VII of LOSC which has jurisdiction in respect of disputes relating to fisheries, the marine environment, scientific research and navigation.

However, the compulsory procedures are subject to limitations.

8.1 Introduction

The sea, or the large and connected body of salt water covering approximately 71 per cent of the earth's surface, holds significant economic, social and cultural value. Historically the primary medium of global transport, its importance has constantly increased. It remains the most cost-effective method of transporting cargo and freight, with an estimated 90 per cent of global trade occurring by sea.[1] The sea also produces half of the world's oxygen supply and is home to a variety of marine species. Marine fisheries, in particular, provide a vital food source and also form a significant part of the global economy.[2] Equally important are non-biological resources in the form of mineral deposits (such as gold, tin, titanium and manganese) and oil and gas located on or below the surface of the sea.

---

1   International Maritime Organization (IMO), International Shipping: Facts and Figures –Information Resources on Trade, Safety, Security and Environment (March 2012) available at www.imo.org/KnowledgeCentre/ShipsAnd ShippingFactsAndFigures/TheRoleandImportanceofInternationalShipping/Documents/International%20Shipping %20-%20Facts%20and%20Figures.pdf (accessed 7 July 2014).

2   See A.J. Dyck and U.R. Sumaila, Economic Impact of Ocean Fish Populations in the Global Fishery (2010)12 J Bioecon, 227.

Because of its significance to exploration, trade, transport, defence and warfare, the law of the sea is one of the oldest specialised areas of public international law. Initially consisting almost entirely of customary rules and norms, it was the focus of considerable but gradual codification throughout the course of the twentieth century and now consists of a framework of multilateral and other treaties, together with rules of customary international law.

8.1.1 Historical development

As early as AD 533, legal scholars of the Roman Empire declared 'the sea by its nature [to be] open to everyone' and 'for the common use of all men'.[3]

Such sentiments underlie what has long been a fundamental principle of the law of the sea, the freedom of the seas, under which no State can exercise sovereignty and the seas (at least the high seas) are instead open to navigation and use by all. This principle, as expressed in Roman jurisprudence, may have been adapted from earlier maritime codes such as that developed in the Aegean island of Rhodes.[4]

The principle that the seas are open to all is not a principle that has gone unchallenged. The law of the sea has been marked by tension between this principle and that of State sovereignty. The collapse of the Roman Empire saw the emergence in the Middle Ages of maritime city-States and principalities, such as Venice and Genoa, which began to make claims to large portions of the sea, appropriating, sometimes by force, the waters in which they were interested.[5] The Republic of Venice, for example, claimed sovereignty over the entire Adriatic Sea, while Genoa claimed dominion over the Ligurian Sea. Both asserted exclusive fishing rights and demanded tributes from any foreign ships sailing these waters.[6]

Under King James I, Britain laid claims to the 'Coasts and Seas of Great Britain, Ireland and the rest of the Isles adjacent' and required foreign vessels to recognise British sovereignty in the North Sea, the English Channel and the Irish Sea.[7] The most audacious claim was that of Spain and Portugal, made after Portuguese maritime voyages to Africa, and the Spanish 'discovery' of the Americas by Christopher Columbus. On 7 June 1494 they signed the Treaty of Tordesillas which divided the Atlantic Ocean by means of a 'line' drawn from the North to the South poles, 370 leagues (1,185 miles) to the West of the Cape Verde Islands. Under the Treaty, all land, not in the possession of Christian rulers, discovered or to be discovered West of the line was given to Spain and that to the East to Portugal. The Treaty reaffirmed bulls of Spanish born Pope Alexander VI but the line itself had been moved several hundred miles to the West. The punishment for violating the papal bulls was excommunication. The consequence of the Treaty was that by the mid-sixteenth century, Spain and Portugal became superpowers as prior to the reformation, few rulers dared to blatantly challenge the authority of the Pope.

---

3   G.J. Mangone, *Law for the World Ocean (Tagore Law Lectures)*, Calcutta: University of Calcutta, 1981, 7–8.

4   Ibid, 6; R.P. Anand, *Origin and Development of the Law of the Sea*, The Hague: Martinus Nijhoff Publishers, 1982, 10–12.

5   G.P. Smith II, *The Concept of Free Seas: Shaping Modern Maritime Policy within a Vector of Historical Influence* (1997) 11/2 International Lawyer, 263, 265. See also D. Anderson, 'The Development of the Modern Law of the Sea' in D. Anderson, *Modern Law of the Sea: Selected Essays*, Leiden: Martinus Nijhoff Publishers, 2008, 4–5.

6   H.B. Robertson Jnr, 'The "New" Law of the Sea and the Law of Armed Conflict at Sea' in J.N. Moore and R.F. Turner (eds), *Readings on International Law from the Naval Law College Review: 1978–1994*, Naval War College, 1995.

7   D. Anderson, 'The Development of the Modern Law of the Sea' in D. Anderson, *Modern Law of the Sea: Selected Essays*, Leiden: Martinus Nijhoff Publishers, 2008, 4–5.

Objections to the authority of the Pope to divide the non-Christian world between Spain and Portugal were raised by Hugo Grotius, the author of the first systematic treatise on international law. He was in 1604 hired to represent the Dutch East India Company, which had, despite Portugal's claim to the entire Far East, engaged in trade with India and, in that capacity, he published anonymously in 1609 a treatise entitled *Mare Librum*, i.e. 'in order to defend the interests of the Company'.[8]

Grotius, in addition to arguing that the papal bulls lacked any authority to confer sovereignty on Portugal, relied on Roman law and history to assert that the sea should be open and free to all. He argued that unlike land, the oceans could not be occupied, and could not therefore be claimed as property. Despite the initial criticism from almost all European States, as well as fellow publicists his ideas ultimately prevailed. The principle of the freedom of the seas was universally accepted by the end of the first quarter of the nineteenth century.

Despite the acceptance of the principle of the freedom of the seas, its tension with State sovereignty continued, not by broad claims to swathes of the ocean but by attempts by States to exercise sovereignty over the maritime belt adjacent to their coasts. It was this issue that was the subject of the first attempt at codification of the law of the sea made under the auspices of the League of Nations.[9] However, this attempt failed. It was within the framework of the UN that codification took place.

8.1.2 Codification of the law of the sea under the auspices of the UN

In 1949, the ILC was requested by the UNGA to commence work on the codification of the law of the sea. In 1956 the ILC produced the Draft Articles Concerning the Law of the Sea. They formed the basis of the First United Nations Law of the Sea Conference (UNCLOS I) held in Geneva from February to April 1958.

8.1.2.1 UNCLOS I

UNCLOS I produced the following four conventions:

1 the Geneva Convention on the Territorial Sea and Contiguous Zone (GCTS);[10]

2 the Geneva Convention on the High Seas (GCHS);[11]

3 the Geneva Convention on the Continental Shelf (GCCS);[12] and

4 the Geneva Convention on Fisheries and Conservation of the Living Resources of the High Seas.[13]

The adoption of four separate conventions on specific topics meant that States selected the convention to which they wished to be bound instead of ratifying all, as had been intended. As at July 2014, the conventions had been ratified by 52, 63, 58 and 39 states respectively. UNCLOS I also produced an Optional Protocol for Compulsory Dispute Settlement ratified by 38 States.[14] Although all the conventions

---

8   R.P. Anand, *Origin and Development of the Law of the Sea*, The Hague: Martinus Nijhoff Publishers, 1982, 79.
9   'United Nations Documents on the Development and Codification of International Law' Supplement to American Journal of International Law, vol 41, no 4, October, 1947.
10   516 UNTS 205. Entered into force 10 September 1964.
11   450 UNTS 11. Entered into force 30 September 1962.
12   559 UNTS 285. Entered into force 10 June 1964.
13   499 UNTS 311. Entered into force 30 September 1962.
14   450 UNTS 169. Entered into force 30 September 1962.

entered into force, it is clear that they never gained widespread acceptance. Newly independent States were particularly critical of them.[15]

The issues left outstanding by UNCLOS I, namely 'the breadth of the territorial sea and fishery limits',[16] were referred to the Second United Nations Conference on the Law of the Sea (UNCLOS II) held in 1960. UNCLOS II failed to resolve them.

8.1.2.2 UNCLOS III and the United Nations Law of the Sea Convention 1982 (LOSC)

A number of important developments after UNCLOS II paved the way for UNCLOS III:

1 The number of participating State had increased as a result of decolonisation.

2 Many States began to claim new maritime zones, mainly fishery zones or 'exclusive fishing zones', both unilaterally and through bilateral and regional treaties.

3 Metalliferous nodules (called manganese nodules), predicted to be valuable and capable of exploitation, were discovered on the deep seabed. The Ambassador of Malta persuasively argued before the UN that the seabed and ocean floor were part of the common heritage of mankind and that deep seabed mining should be regulated by the UN. His comments led to the creation of a Seabed Committee which acted as a preparatory committee for UNCLOS III.

4 States were increasingly concerned about the need for protection of the marine environment after a number of high profile environmental disasters such as the shipwreck of the SS Torrey Canyon operated by British Petroleum.[17]

It is against this background that UNCLOS III was convened in 1973 with a broad agenda that encompassed all aspects of the law of the sea from the lingering question of the breadth of the territorial sea to the issues pertaining to the regulation of the deep seabed and the protection of the marine environment. UNCLOS III was by far the most representative conference, attracting delegations from more than 150 countries, both coastal and land-locked.

After 9 years of intermittent negotiations, UNCLOS III concluded with the adoption of the United Nations Convention on the Law of the Sea (LOSC),[18] which opened for signature at Montego Bay, Jamaica on 10 December 1982 and, in accordance with Article 304(1), entered into force on 16 November 1994 upon deposition of the 60th instrument of ratification by Guyana. However, of these 60 ratifications to the LOSC, almost all were from the developing world. Industrial States such as the US, Great Britain and most of Europe, were initially quite reluctant to ratify the LOSC because of its provisions on deep seabed mining (Part XI), only doing so after the Agreement Relating to the Implementation of Part XI of the Convention, which was adopted by a resolution of the UNGA, entered into force[19] (see Chapter 8.10.1). Not all parties to the LOSC have, however, ratified the Implementation Agreement or the subsequent Implementation Agreement pertaining to Straddling Fish Stocks.[20] Further,

---

15 Anand, supra note 8, 194.

16 See Res VIII, adopted on 27 April, 1958, Doc A/CONF. 13/L.56.

17 See R.M. M'Gonigle and M.W. Zacher, *Pollution, Politics and International Law*, Berkeley, CA: California University Press, 1979, 157 *et seq.*

18 1833 UNTS 396; (1982) 21 ILM 1261.

19 GA Res 48/263 (July 28, 1994).

20 The United Nations Agreement for the Implementation of the Provision of the United Nations Convention on the Law of the Sea 10 December 1982 relating to the Conservation and Management of Straddling Fish Stocks and Highly Migratory Fish Stocks, 8 September 1995, Reproduced in (1995) 34 ILM 1542.

a number of States including Afghanistan, Ethiopia, Rwanda, Liechtenstein, Libya and Iran have signed but not ratified the LOSC while others, most notably the US, Israel, Syria, Turkey, Peru, Venezuela and Eritrea have neither signed nor ratified

8.1.3 Scope and status of the LOSC

As at the 4 August 2014, there were 166 parties to the LOSC including the EU and two associated States, the Cook Islands and Niue. Many parties have made declarations on signature or ratification of the LOSC pursuant to Article 310, but these declarations, despite their content, do not modify or exclude the legal effect of any of the treaty's provisions.[21]

The LOSC, lauded as a constitution for the Oceans,[22] is comprehensive in content and scope, containing some 320 articles, set out in 17 parts and 9 annexes dealing with a wide range of maritime issues. It establishes

a legal order for the seas and oceans . . .[to] facilitate international communication, and . . . promote the peaceful uses of the seas and oceans, the equitable and efficient utilization of their resources, the conservation of their living resources, and the study, protection and preservation of the marine environment.[23]

As to its achievements, the LOSC finally settled the breadth of the territorial sea, setting its limit to 12 nm. In order to achieve consensus on the territorial sea, the LOSC had to divide the sea into additional maritime zones, namely the EEZ and 'The Area' and create legal regimes for each.[24] It not only confirmed the continental shelf regime established by the GCCS, but expanded its limit to 200 nm independent of any geomorphologic factors, and further, if certain geomorphologic, depth and distance criteria were satisfied. It also codified the coastal States rights to a contiguous zone, and significantly expanded the rights of coastal States. At the same time, it guaranteed the right of navigation through all maritime zones including the territorial sea, archipelagic waters and international straits, striking a balance between coastal States and maritime powers.

Other innovations of the LOSC include provisions articulating the right of access for landlocked States, detailed provisions concerning marine scientific research, the creation of a framework for the protection of the marine environment, a detailed and comprehensive regime for the peaceful settlement of disputes and the formulation of a legal regime to govern deep seabed mining.

The LOSC began to influence State practice before it entered into force[25] and even before it had been adopted.[26] Many provisions now reflect customary international law and are therefore enforceable by and against the non-parties. However, it cannot be said that all LOSC rules have achieved the status of custom, and even those that have may lose that status as State practice evolves.

---

21   See *Maritime Delimitation in the Black Sea (Romania v Ukraine)* Judgment, [2009] ICJ Rep 61, 78 at para 42.

22   T T.B. Koh, President of the Third United Nations Conference on the Law of the Sea, Remarks at the Final Session of the Conference at Montego Bay 1 (6–11 December 1982), www.un.org/Depts/los/convention_agreements/texts/koh_english.pdf (accessed 5 June 2014).

23   See Preamble to the LOSC.

24   Y. Tanaka, *The International Law of the Sea*, 2012, Cambridge: Cambridge University Press, 31.

25   See, for example, UN Division of Ocean Affairs and Office of Legal Affairs, Current Developments in State Practice No III, New York: United Nations, 1992. Available at www.un.org/Depts/los/LEGISLATIONANDTREATIES/PDFFILES/publications/E.92.V.13%20(Eng.)%20Curr%20Dev.1992.pdf (accessed 5 June 2014).

26   See: D. Anderson, 'The Development of the Modern Law of the Sea' in D. Anderson, *Modern Law of the Sea: Selected Essays*, Leiden: Martinus Nijhoff Publishers, 2008, 14–15.

8.1.4 Maritime zones

The figure below shows the different zones recognised by the LOSC.

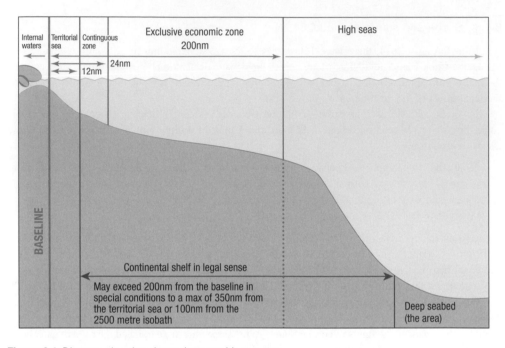

Figure 8.1 Diagram showing the various maritime zones

8.2 Baselines

A baseline is a line which serves as a base or a point of reference for measuring the breadth of the territorial sea. It marks the limit of a State's internal waters with the result that all waters which are landward of the baseline are internal waters, and therefore part of a State's land territory. Also, every maritime zone extending from a coast is measured from the baseline. Finally, it is used to construe lines of equidistance in disputes concerning the delimitation of the territorial sea between opposite or adjacent States.

Three types of baselines are used in the law of the sea: normal, straight and straight archipelagic. They are used either alone or in combination with one another, depending on the geographical features of a coast.

8.2.1 The normal baseline

Article 5 LOSC states that 'the normal baseline for measuring the breadth of the territorial sea is the low water line along the coast as marked on large-scale charts officially recognized by the coastal State'.[27] Accordingly, it is determined using appropriate points along the low water line of the coast.

---

27   Article 3 GCTS and Article 5 LOSC.

In the *Anglo-Norwegian Fisheries Case*, the ICJ held that:

it is the low-water mark as opposed to the high-water mark, or the mean between the two tides, which has generally been adopted in the practice of the States. This criterion is the most favourable to the coastal State and clearly shows the character of territorial waters as appurtenant to the land territory.[28]

8.2.2 The straight baselines

The normal baseline is not suitable for all coasts. Its application can be very difficult where a coast is deeply indented, or fringed with islands. In such a case, it may be more appropriate to use a straight baseline, which 'consists of selecting appropriate points on the low-water mark and drawing straight lines between them'.[29]

Straight baselines are also used: across the mouth of a river; the natural entrance of a juridical bay when it is situated within a single State, but not if it is a historical bay or a bay shared between two or more States; and in respect of low-tide elevations with lighthouses or similar installations built upon them, and when such elevations have received international recognition. Additionally, they are used in circumstances where natural conditions make the coastline highly unstable.

The conditions in which a State is allowed to draw straight baselines were examined by the ICJ in the *Anglo-Norwegian Fisheries Case*.

FISHERIES CASE (NORWAY *V* UK) [1951] ICJ REP 116

Facts:

British fisherman fishing off the coast of Norway had been warned, or arrested, for fishing in Norwegian territorial waters. Norway claimed a territorial sea of 4 miles. The Norwegian Royal Decree of 12 July 1935 provided that the delimitation of its territorial waters would 'run parallel with straight base-lines drawn between fixed points on the mainland, on islands or rocks'. The UK objected to the validity of this method of delimitation, the application of which had led to an increase in the number of British vessels arrested.

Although it was accepted by both parties that the low water mark was to be used as the baseline, the UK argued that it should be drawn from the Norwegian mainland while Norway contended that it should be drawn from the skjaergaard or fringe of islands and rocks fronting the mainland.

Held

Tthe Court recognised that Norway was entitled to use the straight baselines.

Comment:

The Court considered the geographical realities of the Norwegian coast with its many indentations and large and small islands, islets, rocks and reefs (i.e the skjaergaard). It held

---

28   *(Norway v UK)* [1951] ICJ Rep 116, 128.
29   *Anglo-Norwegian Fisheries Case (Norway v UK)* [1951] ICJ Rep 116, 130.

that the skjaergaard formed part of the coast. The mainland did not provide 'a clear dividing line between land and sea' and the baseline therefore had to be drawn from the skjaergaard.

It held that where a coast was deeply indented or fringed by islands the straight baselines were appropriate. This method had been consistently applied by Norway without any objection from other States and was therefore justified.

In giving its decision, Court enunciated the following general principles for drawing baselines:

1. *Baselines must "not depart to any appreciable extent from the general direction of the coast".*
2. *Any areas of the sea falling within the lines must be sufficiently connected to the land.*
3. *In drawing baselines, it may be appropriate to take into account 'economic interests peculiar to the region, the reality and importance of which are clearly evidenced by a long usage'.*
4. *The straight baseline must not cut off from EEZ or high sea the territorial sea of another State.*

The decision in the *Anglo-Norwegian Fisheries Case* was codified in Article 7(1) LOSC and Article 4(1) of the GCTS both of which provide that a system of straight baselines may be used where a coastline is deeply indented or 'if there is a fringe of islands along the coast in its immediate vicinity'. These provisions also reproduce the general principles set out by the ICJ.[30]

8.2.2.1 Bays

The line of closure of bays, i.e. the line which connects two points of the coast which terminate two sides of an indentation in the coast, is of great importance to any coastal State as it separates its internal waters from its territorial sea. It constitutes the baseline from which the breadth of a costal State's territorial sea is measured.

A. Juridical bays

Article 10 LOSC applies only to bays 'the coasts of which belong to a single State'. Under this article a bay is a bay in the juridical sense if it meets the geographic and objective criteria. With regard to geographic criteria it must be a well-marked indentation, as opposed to a mere curvature of the coast, which is in such proportion to the width of its mouth that it contains landlocked waters. Objective criteria are met when the area of a bay is as large, or larger, than a semi-circle whose diameter is a line drawn across its mouth.

Article 10 (4 and 5) LOSC provides that 'if the distance between the low-water marks of the natural entrance points of a bay does not exceed 24 nautical miles, a closing line may be drawn between these two low-water marks'. This line will be the baseline from which the breadth of the territorial sea will be measured. Where an island lies at the mouth of a bay so that the indentation appears to have more than one mouth, the diameter of the semi-circle is a line as long as the sum total of the lengths of the

---

30   Article 4(2) and (4) GCTS) and Article 7(3) and (5) LOSC.

lines across the different mouths.[31] Islands within the bay form part of internal waters.[32] If the length of the line between the natural entrance points of the bay exceeds 24 nm, a straight baseline of 24 nm must be drawn within the bay 'in such a manner as to enclose the maximum area of water that is possible with a line of that length'.[33]

The ICJ has held that the articles in the LOSC regulating the drawing of straight baselines over bays form part of customary international law.[34]

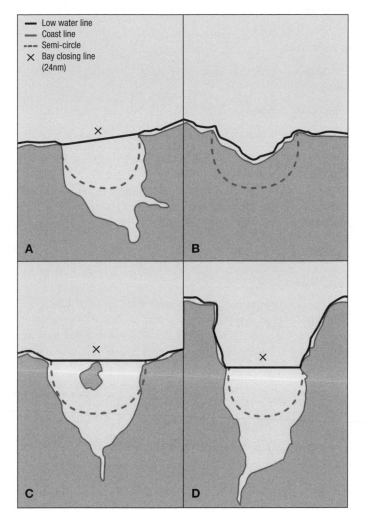

Figure 8.2 A diagram showing indentations on a coast

A, C and D are juridical bays under Article 10

---

31   Article 10(3) LOSC.
32   Ibid.
33   Article 10(5) LOSC.
34   *Land, Island and Maritime Frontier Dispute (El Salvador/Honduras; Nicaragua Intervening)* [1992] ICJ Rep 351, para 383.

B. Historic bays

Neither the LOSC nor the GCTS applies to historic bays. Historic waters (including a historic bay) are waters over which the State exercises territorial sovereignty based on historic title acquired and preserved by long and respected usage.[35]

In the *Fisheries Case*, the ICJ explained that:

> By 'historic waters' are usually meant waters which are treated as internal waters but which would not have that character were it not for the existence of an historic title.[36]

It is generally accepted that in order for a claim to historical waters to succeed, the following three conditions have to be satisfied:

(i) the State making the claim must exercise effective sovereignty over the waters claimed as historic waters;

(ii) the State must have exercised sovereignty for a considerable period of time; and

(iii) other States must have acquiesced to its exercise of sovereignty.[37]

There is no single regime governing historic waters and bays. Each recognised case of historic waters or bays is regulated by its own rules.[38] Most claims to historic bays have received objections from other States. One example is that of Libya's1974 claim made in respect of the Gulf of Sidra. The Gulf was defined by a closing line approximately 300 miles long. In 1974 the US, and many other States, protested the claim that the Gulf of Sidra constituted internal waters of Libya.[39]

8.2.2.2 Rivers

Under Article 9 LOSC, if a river flows directly into the sea, a baseline shall be a straight line drawn across the mouth of the river between points on the low water line of its banks.[40]

A number of observations may be made about this article. First it imposes no limit on the length of the closing line. Second, it is uncertain whether it applies to rivers which form an estuary. The ILC proposed that rules relevant to bays should apply in such a case.[41] Finally, the article provides no guidance as to the selection of appropriate points from which to draw the closing line with regard to a coast with an extensive tidal range.

8.2.3 Straight archipelagic baselines

Archipelagic baselines can only be drawn by States that have declared themselves to be archipelagic States.[42] (see Chapter 8.4.3). Article 47(1) LOCS defines archipelagic baselines as straight baselines

---

35   Ibid. See also UN Secretariat, Juridical Regime of Historic Waters including Historic Bays, UN Doc A/CN.4/143 (1962).

36   *Fisheries Case (United Kingdom v Norway)* [1951] ICJ Rep 116, 130.

37   UN Secretariat, *Juridical Regime of Historic Waters including Historic Bays*, UN Doc A/CN.4/143 (1962) para 80.

38   *Case Concerning the Continental Shelf (Tunisia/Libyan Arab Jamahiriya)* [1982] ICJ Rep 74.

39   See: Y.Z. Blum, *The Gulf of Sidra Incident* (1986) 80 AJIL, 668–677.

40   See also Article 13 GCTS.

41   (1956–2) ILC Yearbook, 253, 271–272.

42   *Maritime Delimitation and Territorial Questions between Qatar and Bahrain (Qatar v Bahrain)* [2001] ICJ Rep 40, para 214.

that join 'the outermost points of the outermost islands and drying reefs of the archipelago'. Archipelagic baselines enclose the archipelagic waters of an archipelagic State. From them an archipelagic State measures the breadth of its territorial sea, contiguous zone, the EEZ and the continental shelf.[43]

In drawing archipelagic baselines, an archipelagic State must satisfy the following conditions:

1   the baselines must include the main islands of the archipelagic State;[44]

2   the ratio of water to land (including atolls) must be between 1 to 1, and 9 to 1;[45]

3   the length of the archipelagic baselines must not exceed 100 nm, except that up to 3 per cent of the total number of baselines enclosing any archipelago may exceed the length of 100 nm, up to a maximum length of 125 nm;[46] and

4   the drawing of the baselines must not depart to any appreciable extent from the general configuration of the archipelago.[47]

The main islands of an archipelagic State may be its largest island, its most populous island or its most economically productive ones.[48] As to the ratio of water to land, the lower ratio excludes archipelagos constituted of one or two large islands with relatively small areas of sea, such as the UK and Australia, while the larger ratio excludes those archipelagoes whose islands are widely dispersed, such as Tuvalu and Kiribati.

Although archipelagic baselines under the LOSC may only be drawn by States that fall within the Article 46 definition of archipelagoes, several States that do not satisfy that definition have attempted to claim archipelagic baselines, much to the objection of other States.[49]

8.2.4   Islands

An island is defined as a naturally-formed area of land that is surrounded by water and stands above water at high tide.[50] This definition distinguishes islands from low tide elevations (which are submerged at high tide – see below) and artificial islands which have been created by human intervention. In their dissenting opinion in *Qatar/Bahrain*, Judges Bedjaoui, Ranjeva and Koroma suggested that geomorphological considerations of the land above high tide must also be taken into account:

> The fact that the land lies above the high-water line is not enough in itself for a feature to be characterized as an island; only areas of terra firma can be accorded the status of island under Article 121.[51]

Islands receive special attention in both the LOSC and the GCTS. However, while the latter only refers to the territorial sea of an island,[52] Article 121(2) of the LOSC explicitly states that every island,

---

43   Article 48 LOSC.

44   Article 47(1) LOSC.

45   Ibid.

46   Article 47(2) LOSC.

47   Article 47(3) LOSC.

48   Office for Ocean Affairs and Law of the Sea, Baselines: An Examination of the Relevant Provisions of the United Nations Convention on the Law of the Sea, New York: United Nations, 1989, 36–37.

49   D.R. Rothwell and T. Stephens, *The International Law of the Sea*, Oxford: Hart Publishing, 2010, 188.

50   Article 10 GCTS and Article 121(1) LOSC.

51   *Case Concerning Maritime Delimitation and Territorial Questions between Qatar and Bahrain (Qatar v Bahrain)* (Joint Dissenting Opinion of Judges Bedjaoui, Ranjeva and Koroma) [2001] ICJ Rep 145, para 198.

52   Article 24(2) GCTS.

regardless of size, can claim a territorial sea, contiguous zone, EEZ and continental shelf. Article 121(3) LOSC then proceeds to exclude rocks incapable of sustaining 'human habitation or economic life' from claiming an EEZ or continental shelf.

Because of Article 121(3), the UK, on ratification of the LOSC, dropped all claims to the EEZ and continental shelf of Rockall although it continued to claim a territorial sea. Rockall is an unoccupied granite islet in the North Atlantic Ocean which is visible at high tide. It had been annexed by the Royal Navy in 1955 and formally incorporated into the UK by the Island of Rockall Act 1972. It cannot sustain human habitation or economic life.

8.2.5 Harbour works

The LOSC provides that permanent harbour works may be considered as part of the coast and the outer limits of these features may therefore be used for drawing baselines.[53] Permanent harbour works do not, however, include offshore installations and offshore islands. It has been held that they also exclude a 7.5 km dyke, because although this structure was permanent in nature, its function was quite distinct from that of a harbour or port.[54]

8.2.6 Low-tide elevations

A low-tide elevation is defined as 'a naturally formed area of land which is surrounded by and above water at low tide but submerged at high tide'.[55] The low-water line of such elevation may be used as the baseline for measuring the breadth of the territorial sea if the elevation is situated wholly or partially at a distance not exceeding the breadth of the territorial sea (i.e up to 12 nm) from the mainland or an island. However, low-tide elevations situated wholly beyond that distance have no territorial sea of their own.[56] This means that a low-tide elevation, which is situated less than the breadth of the territorial sea, say 6 nm from the coast from which normally baselines are drawn, may be used by a costal State to extend its territorial sea up to 18 nm. However, if within the extended territorial sea, there is another low-tide elevation, say 15 nm from the coast a coastal State is not allowed to use that elevation to extend its territorial sea up to 27 nm. Thus the LOSC prevents a coastal State from 'leap frogging' from one low-tide elevation to another in order to extend the outer limit of the territorial sea seawards. The maximum extent of the territorial sea using low-tide elevations as baselines is up to 24 nm.

8.2.7 Conclusion

State practice shows that coastal States have considerable discretion in determining the appropriate method for drawing their baselines; they are entitled to use any combination of methods suited to their specific conditions.[57]

Even where the coast of a State is deeply indented or fringed with islands, there is no obligation imposed on a State to use straight baselines. There is also no objective test for determining when the use of straight baselines is appropriate. States are given considerable latitude in their use. However,

---

53   Article 8 Geneva Convention on the Territorial Sea and Article 11 LOSC.
54   *Maritime Delimitation in the Black Sea (Romania v Ukraine) Judgment [2009]* ICJ Rep. 61, paras 133–138.
55   Ibid.
56   Article 13 LOSC.
57   Article 14 LOSC.

the ICJ has emphasised that straight baselines are an exception to the general rule and 'must [therefore] be applied restrictively'.[58]

Climate change has considerable impact on baselines, in that even a small rise in ocean levels will result in a regression of the normal baseline. For that reason many commentators proposed that baselines should be fixed in their current position, i.e. before any substantial change has occurred.[59]

8.3 Internal waters

Internal waters are defined by the LOSC as all water landward from the baseline.[60] They include rivers, lakes, canals, bays or other internal waters that come from the sea as well as the water landward from fringing islands off the coast of a State.

The internal waters of a coastal State fall squarely within its sovereign territory.[61] These waters may be considered as 'legally equivalent to the state's land'.[62] A coastal State may therefore exercise full jurisdiction over its internal waters, subject only to the limitations imposed by international law, for example in relation to foreign immunity.

As a consequence of a State's sovereignty over its internal waters, there is no general right of innocent passage through those waters, except first, where what is now enclosed as internal waters through the use of straight baselines was previously part of the territorial sea[63] and second, where a foreign ship is in distress (see Chapter 8.3.2).

8.3.1 Access to ports and harbours of a coastal State

The LOSC is silent on whether a coastal State has the right to restrict access to its ports and harbours. The arbitrator in *Saudi Arabia v Arabian American Oil Company (ARAMCO)*[64] stated that:

> According to a great principle of public international law, the ports of every State must be open to foreign merchant vessels and can only be closed when the vital interests of the State so require.[65]

The ICJ in *Military and Paramilitary Activities in and against Nicaragua (Nicaragua v United States) (Merits)*[66] did not address the matter of whether the freedom of access to ports is a rule of customary international law. It however stated that a State by virtue of its sovereignty is entitled to 'regulate access to its ports'[67] and concluded that hindering access of one State to the ports of another

---

58   *Case Concerning Maritime Delimitation and Territorial Questions (Qatar v Bahrain)* [2001] ICJ Rep 40, para 211.

59   See R. Rayfuse, 'Sea Level Rise and Maritime Zones' in M.B. Gerrard and G.E. Wannier (eds), *Threatened Island Nations. Preserving the Maritime Entitlements of 'Disappearing' States*, Cambridge: Cambridge University Press, 2013, 167–197.

60   See Article 8(1) LOSC.

61   *Military and Paramilitary Activities in and against Nicaragua (Nicaragua v United States) (Merits)* [1986] ICJ Rep 144.

62   R. Jennings and A. Watts, *Oppenheim's International Law: Volume 1*, Parts 2 to 4, 9th edn, Oxford: Oxford University Press, 2008, p 572 §171.

63   Article 8(2) LOSC.

64   (1963) 27 ILR 117.

65   Ibid, 212.

66   *Military and Paramilitary Activities in and against Nicaragua (Nicaragua v United States) (Merits)* [1986] ICJ Rep. 144.

67   Ibid, para 213.

State 'prejudices both the sovereignty of the coastal State over its internal waters, and the right of free access enjoyed by foreign ships'.[68]

The US Restatement (Third) of Foreign Relations Law endorses the view that access to ports in peacetime constitutes a rule of international customary law.[69]

Because of the uncertainty as to whether the right to access to ports exists in customary international law States have often entered into multilateral and bilateral treaties to ensure that their ships will have unrestricted access to ports of the other party. With regard to multilateral treaties Article 2 of the Statute on the International Regime of Maritime Ports confers the right to access ports of contracting parties on the basis of reciprocity.[70] However, it ensures that land-locked States may not be denied freedom of access to ports only because they cannot satisfy the requirement of reciprocity. This treaty has not been widely ratified. With regard to bilateral treaties, often States conclude 'Friendship, Commerce and Navigation' treaties under which each contracting party guarantees access to its ports and harbours to the other.[71]

It can be said that traditionally a coastal State may restrict access to its ports and harbours:

1   for national security reasons, e.g. in time of an armed conflict, or to combat maritime terrorism;

2   for other important reasons such as prevention of pollution, e.g. on the basis of Article 211(3) LOSC;

3   with regard to nuclear–powered ships which are nowadays primarily warships (see below);

4   with regard to warships. This is based on customary international law. The PCIJ in *Advisory Opinion in Access to, or Anchorage in, the Port of Danzig, of Polish War Vessels*[72] held that under customary international law a foreign warship, before entering the port of a coastal State, must seek consent of that State, and while in that State's port must refrain from certain activities, e.g. deployment of helicopters from the warship.

8.3.2   Ships in distress

Under customary international law, a ship in distress, i.e. a vessel which it can be said with reasonable certainty is threatened by grave and imminent danger and requires immediate assistance,[73] has the right to enter internal waters of a coastal State and have access to ports and harbours of that State.[74]

However, this rule has become problematic in two situations.

First, where a foreign ship represents a considerable environmental hazard to a coastal State. In such a situation, the coastal State is faced with a dilemma. On the one hand, to refuse access to its ports is well justified by interests of that State, on the other, if a ship in distress is sent back to the sea, the probability of environmental disaster may increase, and thus the ship may anyway cause environmental damage. Additionally, the refusal may endanger the lives of the persons on of ship.

---

68   Ibid, para 214.

69   Para 513, n 3. (1987).

70   9 December 1923, 25 LNTS 202.

71   See, e.g. Article XIX of the Treaty of Friendship, Commerce and Navigation between the Netherlands and Americas signed 27 March 1956 and Article 2 of the Agreement between the Government of the United States of America and the People's Republic of Bulgaria on Maritime Transport signed 19 February 1981.

72   (1931) PCIJ Ser A/B No 43, 128–129.

73   Article 1 of the Convention for Maritime Search and Rescue, 1405 UNTS 97.

74   See *The Eleanor* (1809) Edw 135.

Second, when a ship that carries asylum seekers, who were rescued at sea by it, wishes to disembark them in the nearest available port.[75] For example, in 2001, Australia refused access to its port on Christmas Island to the Norwegian flagged ship *Tampa* which had rescued 433 asylum seekers in the North-Eastern Indian Ocean, and wanted to disembark them at that port. Following this incident, Norway was successful in achieving an amendment to the 1944 International Convention for the Safety of Life at Sea permitting vessels that have carried out search and rescue operations at sea to disembark rescued persons at the nearest available port.

8.3.3 Jurisdiction over foreign vessels

As internal waters form part of State territory, a foreign vessel entering them is normally subject to the full force of that State's laws. The extent of this jurisdiction is examined below.

8.3.3.1 Jurisdiction over foreign warships or ships operated by a State for non-commercial purposes.

Foreign warships or ships operated by a State solely for non-commercial purposes enjoy immunity from the jurisdiction of a costal State.[76] This principle was firmly established by the US Supreme Court in *The Schooner Exchange v* McFaddon,[77] in which plaintiffs sought to obtain possession of a ship, which they previously owned, but which was subsequently seized by the French government and converted into a French warship. At the time of the proceedings the ship was in a US port. The Court held that under international law:

> national ships of war, entering the port of a friendly power open for their reception, are to be considered as exempted by the consent of that power from its jurisdiction.[78]

More recently, when a Ghanaian Court, in an attempt to enforce a debt against Argentina, granted an injunction that had the effect of preventing an Argentinean frigate warship in its port from leaving, the International Tribunal for the Law of the Sea (ITLOS) (see Chapter 8.11.1), noting that the ship was a warship and enjoyed immunity in internal waters, ordered its immediate release. [79]

The immunity of a warship may, however, be waived on the consent of the flag State.[80]

8.3.3.2 Jurisdiction over commercial ships

A foreign ship, while in internal waters of a coastal State, is subject not only to the jurisdiction of that State, but also to that of the State whose flag it flies. State practice shows that, based on comity, the port State will not exercise jurisdiction over the internal affairs of the foreign vessel but it will exercise jurisdiction over any actions that may interfere with the peace and tranquility of the port.

---

75   On this topic see: A Klug, *Strengthening the Protection of Migrants and Refugees in Distress at Sea Through International Co-operation and Burden Sharing* (2014) 26/1 International Journal of Refugee Law, 48.
76   Article 32 LOSC.
77   11 US 116 (1812).
78   Ibid, 145–146.
79   *The 'Ara Libertad' Case (Argentina v Ghana), Request for Provisional Measures*, ITLOS, Case No 20, Order of 15 December 2012.
80   *Cheung (Chung Chi) v R* [1939] AC 160.

R V ANDERSON[81]

Facts:

An American national committed manslaughter aboard a British vessel while it was in French internal waters. He was convicted in Britain of manslaughter, and argued, on appeal, that the British Court had no jurisdiction over the offence.

Held:

There was no doubt that the offence occurred in French internal waters on a ship flying a British flag. Accordingly, both Britain and France had jurisdiction over the offence. The appeal therefore failed.

WILDENHUS' CASE

Facts:

While a Belgian vessel was docked in an American port, a Belgian crew member murdered another Belgian crew member. The incident occurred aboard the ship. He was arrested by American police and charged with murder. The Belgian Counsel sought his release, contending that the Court lacked jurisdiction.

Held:

The Court stated:

> *by comity it came to be generously understood among civilized nations that all matters of discipline and all things done on board which affected only the vessel or those belonging to her, and did not involve the peace or dignity of the country or the tranquility of the port should be dealt with by the flag state . . . but if crimes committed on board of a character to disturb the peace and tranquility of the country to which the offenders have been brought, the offenders have never, by comity or usage, been entitled to any exemption from the operation of the local laws for their punishment if the local tribunals see fit to assert their authority.[82]*

8.3.3.3 Ships in distress.

A port state cannot seek to enforce its laws against a foreign ship that does not voluntarily enter its internal waters but does so as a result of distress. Such ships enjoy some immunity from local laws and under the LOSC are specifically exempted from certain rules regulating pollution.[83] The immunity

---

81   1 Cox's Criminal Cases 198.
82   *Wildenhus' Case* [1887] 120 US 1, 12.
83   Articles 218(1)(3) and 220(1) LOSC.

enjoyed by a ship entering under distress is, however, restricted to laws breached because of *force majeure*.[84]

8.4 Territorial sea, international straits and archipelagic waters

This section examines rules of international law, in particular the LOSC, relating to the territorial sea, international straits and archipelagic waters.

8.4.1 Territorial sea

The territorial sea refers to a band or belt of water immediately adjacent to the internal waters, the archipelagic waters or the coast of a State.

Under customary international law the territorial sea forms part of the State's territory and is subject to the sovereignty of that State.[85] The Permanent Court of Arbitration (PCA) described it as 'maritime territory [that] is an essential appurtenance of land territory'.[86] This rule can be considered one of the original customary international rules relating to the law of the sea and has been codified in Article 1 GCTS and Article 2 LOSC.

The possession of territorial sea has been described as 'compulsory' and 'not dependent upon the will of the [coastal] State'.[87] This is implicit in both the LOSC and the GCTS as neither leaves it to States to claim a territorial sea, but both prescribe the extension of State sovereignty to the sea adjacent to the coastal State's terrestrial territory.[88] While this may be so, the extent of that sovereignty is, in a sense, inchoate until the territorial sea is actually claimed, particularly as international law stipulates no minimal length for the territorial sea.

The State's sovereignty over the territorial sea covers not only the water column but extends to the seabed, the subsoil below, and the airspace above.[89] As a consequence of its sovereignty, only the coastal State has the right to appropriate or exploit any of the natural resources of the territorial sea and its seabed and subsoil, and no foreign vessel or State may do so without its consent.

With regard to the breadth of territorial sea, although there was initially much dispute surrounding its maximum permitted breadth, this issue was resolved during UNCLOS III. Article 4 LOSC, which is generally agreed to be a rule of customary international law, permits a State to acquire a territorial sea that is up to 12 nm in length. For a coastal State, that length is generally measured from its baseline, but where the State is an archipelagic State, as defined by the LOSC (see Chapter 8.4.3), its territorial sea is measured from its archipelagic baselines (see Chapter 8.2.3).

The exercise by a coastal State of its sovereign right over territorial sea is not unlimited, but subject to the rules of international law. This is examined below.

8.4.1.1 The right of innocent passage

The sovereignty of a coastal State over its territorial sea is subject to one very significant limitation. As a corollary to the freedom of navigation, customary international law confers upon the foreign

---

84   See D.P. O'Connell, *The International Law of the Sea*, vol 2, Oxford: Clarendon Press, 1984, 857.

85   *Military and Paramilitary Activities Case (Nicaragua v USA) (Merits)*, [1986] ICJ Rep 14, para 212. See also Articles 1 and 2 GCTS and Article 2 LOSC.

86   *The Grisbadarna Case (Norway v Sweden)* (1910) 4 AJIL 231.

87   *Anglo-Norwegian Fisheries Case (UK v Norway)* [1951] ICJ Rep 116, 160, per McNair J.

88   R.A. Churchill and A.V. Lowe, *The Law of the Sea*, 3rd edn, Manchester: Juris Publishing, 1999, 81.

89   Article 2(1) LOSC and Article 2 GCTS. See also *Military and Paramilitary Activities Case (Nicaragua v USA) (Merits)* [1986] ICJ Rep 14, para 212.

vessel of every State the right to innocent passage through the territorial sea of other States. Neither permission nor consent is required to exercise this right, and no State can impose any charges as a prerequisite of its exercise nor can any State impose any requirement that would have the practical effect of impairing or denying it.[90]

The right of a foreign vessel to innocent passage was not simply codified in Article 14 GCTS and Article 19 LOSC, but, to a large extent, clarified.[91] The guaranteeing in the LOSC of innocent passage through the territorial sea was fundamental to securing the consensus of many developed States to an extension of the maximum length of the territorial sea.[92]

The right of innocent passage applies to the navigation of a foreign vessel through the territorial sea without entering internal waters or without calling at a roadstead or port facility and to the vessel's passage to and from a State's internal waters, port facility or roadstead facility.[93] The exercise of the right of innocent passage would not normally include drifting or hovering in the territorial sea. In this respect the LOSC provides that the passage must not only be continuous and expeditious, but also that stopping and anchoring is only included where incidental to ordinary navigation, or made necessary by *force majeure* or distress, or for the purpose of rendering humanitarian assistance to third parties in danger or distress.[94]

Although the territorial sea includes airspace above, the right of innocent passage does not extend to flight. However, it does apply to underwater vessels such as submarines, when they are navigating on the surface of the territorial sea and show their flag.[95] Failure to abide by these requirements may lead to a request to depart territorial waters, as happened with a Chinese atomic-powered submarine travelling in Japanese waters.[96]

A. When is passage not innocent?

In the *Corfu Channel Case*, the ICJ considered what was meant by 'innocent passage' in relation to the passage of British warships through the Corfu Channel, an international strait.[97]

CORFU CHANEL CASE (UNITED KINGDOM *V* ALBANIA) (FOR FULL FACTS SEE CHAPTER 15.3.2)

Facts:

Albania submitted that the passage of British warships through the Corfu Chanel violated its sovereignty, as it was not innocent. It argued that the warships were manoeuvring in combat formation, and their journey was politically motivated, and not part of the ordinary course of navigation. Their presence was aimed at intimidating Albania and observing and reporting on its coastal defences.

---

90   Article 26 LOSC and Article 18 GCTS.

91   R.A. Churchill and A.V. Lowe, supra note 88, 81.

92   D.R. Rothwell and T. Stephens, *The International Law of the Sea*, Oxford: Hart Publishing, 2014, 76–77.

93   Article 18(1) LOSC and Article 14(4) GCTS.

94   Article 18(2) LOSC.

95   Article 20 LOSC.

96   M. Mashiro, *The Submerged Passage of a Submarine through the Territorial Sea – the Incident of a Chinese Atomic-powered Submarine* (2006) 10 SYBIL, 243–250.

97   *Corfu Channel Case (United Kingdom v Albania) (Merits)* [1949] ICJ Rep 4.

Held:

The ICJ held that ordinary navigation was not the true purpose of the warships' passage. The UK was using the warships to test Albania's attitude to navigation through the Corfu Channel, and to affirm the right of navigation that Albania had previously sought to deny them. Their passage was nonetheless legal but to determine whether it was innocent it was necessary to consider whether it was carried out in a manner *consistent with innocent passage. Thus their passage, as they had travelled in line and had not engaged in combat manoeuvres was innocent.*

Innocent passage refers to passage that 'is not prejudicial to the peace, good order or security of the coastal state'.[98] Article 19(2) LOSC provides an extensive list of activities that will render passage prejudicial to peace, good order or security. These activities include not only such actions as threatening or using force against the sovereignty, territorial integrity or political independence of a State, but extend to engaging in fishing activities or carrying out research and survey activities. The last item listed is 'any other activity not having a direct bearing on passage' which implies that the list is not intended to be exhaustive.

By providing a list of activities the performance of which makes passage cease to be innocent, the LOSC appears to follow the approach of the ICJ in the *Corfu Channel Case* and determines the innocence, or otherwise, of a passage on the manner in which it occurs rather than reasons or the motives for its occurrence which, in any event, might be impossible to prove.

B. Innocent passage and warships

A warship may be defined as a vessel belonging to the armed forces of a State that bears external marks distinguishing its nationality and being under the command of an officer duly commissioned by the government of the State and manned by a crew under regular armed forces discipline.[99]

It has been contended by a number of States including the US and Russia, that the right of a foreign vessel to innocent passage extends to warships of a foreign State. Whether it does so as a matter of customary international law or pursuant to the provisions of the LOSC is open to debate.

There is some disagreement as to whether warships enjoy the right of innocent passage under the LOSC. The right of a warship to innocent passage through territorial sea is neither specifically provided nor negated. A number of comentatotors have argued that the right of passage was intended to apply to warships and may be implied from the treaty's provisions.[100] They correctly point first to the fact that Section 3 of Part II of the LOSC, which applies to innocent passage in the territorial sea, is subtitled 'Rules applicable to all ships' and that in the absence of any evidence to the contrary 'all ships' includes warships. Second, many of the situations listed in Article 19(2) as activities considered prejudicial to the peace, good order and security of a coastal State are activities that are normally only performed by a warship. Third, and perhaps most convincingly, Article 30 provides that if any warship fails to comply with the laws and regulations of a coastal State concerning passage through the territorial sea

---

98   Article 19(1) LOSC.
99   Article 29 LOSC and Article 14.2 GCTS.
100   Y. Tanaka, *The International Law of the Sea*, 2012, Cambridge: Cambridge University Press, 90.

and disregards any request for compliance, the coastal State may require it to leave its territorial sea immediately.

The LOSC's failure to explicitly deal with the right of innocent passage of warships is most puzzling. One suggestion is that perhaps it was deliberately left open because of the absence of any such customary international law right and of the disagreement of States on this matter.[101]

The *Corfu Channel Case* is, at times, cited as authority in support of the right of a warship to innocent passage. However, in its judgment in the *Corfu Channel* Case, the ICJ was careful to avoid expressing any opinion on whether warships had a right of passage through territorial sea, limiting its decision to the case of straits. It stated:

> In these circumstances, it is unnecessary to consider whether the more general question, much debated by the authorities, whether States under international law have a right to send warships through territorial waters not included in a strait.[102]

This judgment cannot therefore stand as any authority for the existence of any such right. State practice does not persuasively demonstrate its existence. Many States require prior authorisation before warships are permitted entry to their territorial sea and have made declarations to that effect.[103] Other States have made declarations that requiring prior permission for the passage of warships is not only unnecessary, but contrary to international law. [104]

8.4.1.2 *Rights and responsibilities of coastal States*

Vessels exercising the right of innocent passage are subject to the laws and regulations of each particular coastal State provided that those laws conform to the LOSC and other rules of international law and are duly publicised.[105] The laws must, however, be in relation to such topics as the safety of navigation and the regulation of maritime traffic, the protection of navigational aids and facilities and other facilities at sea, the protection of cables and pipelines, the conservation of living resources, the preservation of the environment, marine scientific research and hydrographic surveys and the prevention of infringement of customs, fiscal, immigration or sanitary laws and regulations.[106]

A coastal State may take steps to prevent non-innocent passage.[107] It may also temporarily suspend innocent passage in specified portions of its territorial sea, but may only do so where such suspension is 'essential for the protection of its security' and provided that it has duly publicised its intention to do so. Suspension of innocent passage is not, however, permitted over any portion of the territorial sea that constitutes a strait used for international navigation (see Chapter 8.4.2).

---

101   R.A. Churchill and A.V. Lowe, supra note 88, 90.

102   (1949) ICJ Rep 4, 32.

103   See, for example, Declaration of Algeria made upon signature of the LOSC (10 December 1982), Declaration of Cabo Verde made upon signature (10 December 1982) and confirmed upon ratification (19 August 1987) and Declaration made by the People's Republic of China upon ratification (7 June 1996), available at: www.un.org/depts/los/convention_agreements/convention_declarations.htm (accessed 12 July 2014).

104   See, for example, Declaration of Federal Republic of Germany upon accession to the LOSC (14 October 1994), Declaration of the Netherlands upon ratification to the LOSC (28 June 1996), available at www.un.org/depts/los/convention_agreements/convention_declarations.htm (accessed 12 July 2014).

105   Article 21 LOSC.

106   Ibid.

107   Article 25(1) LOSC.

The sovereignty of coastal States brings with it certain responsibilities. In his separate opinion in the *Fisheries Jurisdiction Case*[108] Judge Fitzmaurice explained:

The territorial sea involves responsibilities as well as rights, which many countries were unable to discharge satisfactorily outside a relatively narrow belt, such as for example policing and maintaining order; buoying and marking channels and reefs, sandbanks and other obstacles; keeping navigable channels clear, and giving notice of danger.

Thus, the coastal State is required, both by the LOSC and customary international law, to provide warnings of any dangers to navigation of which it has knowledge, or ought to have knowledge.[109] Failure to do so may make the State liable in international law for any damage caused as a result.[110]

8.4.1.3 Exercise of jurisdiction

A coastal State has exclusive criminal jurisdiction over its territorial sea, but the exercise of its jurisdiction has to be balanced with the right to navigation and the right of foreign vessels to exercise innocent passage.

It is for the above reason that the LOSC specifically provides that the criminal jurisdiction of a coastal State should not be exercised on board a foreign ship passing through the territorial sea except where (i) the consequences of the crime extend to the coastal State; (ii) the crime disturbs the peace of the country or the order of the territorial sea; (iii) assistance has been requested either by the captain of the ship or the flag country; and (iv) it is necessary for the suppression of illicit traffic in narcotic drugs.[111]

The right to exercise civil jurisdiction over a foreign ship in innocent passage or on any person on board that ship is generally only available in relation to obligations or liabilities assumed or incurred by the ship itself in the course of its voyage through the coastal State's territorial waters.[112]

8.4.2 International straits

One of the key issues at the UNCLOS III negotiations concerned the legal regime of international straits. In particular, the possibility of coastal States to claim their territorial waters up to 12 nm from the baseline meant that more than 200 international straits with a width of less than 24 miles would become part of the territorial waters of coastal States.[113] This would considerably restrict freedom of passage of ships and submarines in those straits and of aircraft to overfly them. Accordingly, for most States the extension of their territorial seas was subject to the establishment of a special regime for passage through international straits, different from that regulating the innocent passage through territorial seas. The compromise achieved by UNCLOS III is reflected in its Part III which divides international straits into two categories, i.e. those to which Part III applies and those to which it does not.[114]

---

108 Fisheries Jurisdiction (UK v Iceland) (Jurisdiction) 1973 ICJ Rep 3, 27n8.
109 Article 24(2) LOSC.
110 *Corfu Channel Case (United Kingdom v Albania) (Merits)* [1949] ICJ Rep 4.
111 Article 27 LOSC.
112 Article 28 LOSC.
113 Y. Tanaka, supra note 100, 97.
114 A.G. López Martin, *International Straits: Concept, Classification and Rules of Passage*, Dordrecht/London/New York: Springer, 2010.

8.4.2.1 Straits to which Part III applies

Part III LOSC applies to straits used for international navigation between one part of the high seas or an EEZ, and another part of the high seas or an EEZ, which are entirely within the territorial waters of States bordering them. It applies not only to ships but also to aircraft. It establishes the following regime for transit passage through/over these straits.

With regard to bordering States, Article 44 LOSC imposes on them a duty not to hamper transit passage, and to give appropriate notification of any danger to navigation or overflight of which they are aware. This includes warnings about shipwrecks blocking part of the passage, or severe weather conditions.

Bordering States are prohibited from suspending transit passage in any circumstances. The implications of closing or suspending transit passage are tremendous. For example, the threat by Iran in 2012 to block passage of oil tankers through the Strait of Hormuz could have resulted in serious economic difficulties in Europe, and in the US, given that one-fifth of the world's oil, and 90 per cent of Persian Gulf oil is transported through it. The threat was a response to sanctions imposed on Iran by the UNSC for unlawful development of Iran's nuclear programme[115] (see Chapter 8.9.3.4).

The matter of whether a bordering State is permitted to impose fees for the passage or for pilotage through a strait is highly debated. On the one hand, such payments would alleviate the financial burden imposed on bordering States resulting from their obligation to ensure safe navigation and environmental protection, on the other, they would certainly 'hamper' transit passage.[116]

Under Article 42(1) LOSC a bordering State may enact legislation and regulations ensuring safety of navigation and controlling, *inter alia*, pollution, loading and unloading of any commodity, currency or persons. Bordering States may also designate sea lanes for passage through the strait, and other schemes aimed at regulating traffic in the strait with a view to ensuring safe passage of ships. All national regulations must apply without discrimination to all foreign ships and must not in practice result in hampering or impairing the right of transit passage. The right to transit passage entails that even if a ship violates national regulations its right to transit passage cannot be suspended but a bordering State may take measures to enforce its regulations.[117]

With regard to ships and aircraft, Article 38(2) LOSC states that all ships and aircraft are entitled to transit passage through international straits. Such passage must be exercised in a continuous and expeditious manner. The reference in Article 38(2) LOSC to 'all' ships and aircraft entails that the right to transit passage is enjoyed by warships as well as by military aircraft. With regard to submarines and other underwater vehicles it seems that they are neither required to navigate on the surface nor to show their flag.[118]

Obligations imposed on ships and aircraft are listed in Article 39(1) LOSC. They are required:

1   to proceed without delay through or over the strait, i.e. their passage must be continuous and expeditious;

2   comply with Article 2(4) of the UN Charter, i.e. refrain from any threat or use of force against States bordering the strait, and any violations of principles embodied in the UN Charter;

---

115   M. Wählish, *The Iran-US Dispute, the Strait of Hormuz and International Law* (2012) 37 Yale Journal of International Law Online, 21.

116   Y. Tanaka, supra note 100, 241.

117   Article 233 LOSC.

118   Y. Tanaka, supra note 100, 103.

3　refrain from any activities other than those incidental to their normal modes of continuous and expeditious transit unless rendered necessary by *force majeure* or by distress; and

4　comply with other relevant provisions of LOSC.

Additionally, ships must comply with national regulations of bordering States, and international standards concerning, *inter alia*, safety at sea, and prevention of pollution, while aircraft must comply with the Rules of the Air established by the International Civil Aviation Organisation.

8.4.2.2　International straits outside the scope of Part III

Part III does not apply to the following:

1　International straits which are regulated in whole or in part by long-standing international conventions.[119] Examples of such straits are the Turkish straits that include the Dardanelles, the Sea of Marmara, and the Bosporus. They are governed by the 1936 Montreaux Convention Regarding the Régime of the Straits.[120] The LOSC does not supersede the relevant conventions.

2　Straits through which there is a high seas route, or a route through an exclusive zone, of similar convenience with respect to its navigational and hydrographic characteristics. With regard to such a strait, which must be of more than 24 nm wide, the right of innocent passage is ensured through the bands of territorial seas which lie on either side of it. An example of this kind of a strait is the so called Florida Strait between the US and Cuba.[121]

3　Straits which are located between an island of a bordering State and its mainland in a situation where there exists an equally convenient route through the high seas or through an EEZ seaward of the island.[122] The Strait of Messina located between Italy and Sicily is an example of such a strait.

4　International straits within archipelagic waters. These are governed by archipelagic sea lanes passage (see below).

5　International straits connecting an area of the high seas or an EEZ with the territorial sea of a third State, e.g. the Straits of Tiran. In such straits ships have the right to non-suspendable innocent passage, but aircraft have no freedom to overfly them. Submarines and other underwater vehicles are required to navigate on the surface and show their flags.[123]

8.4.3　Archipelagic waters

The LOSC represents a victory for archipelagic States which had long fought for the recognition of their special status. The two most prominent mid-ocean archipelagic States, the Philippines and Indonesia, have long recognised that the waters between and connecting their islands or parts thereof form part of their territory and are subject to their sovereignty.[124] Until UNCLOS III, however, the special status

---

119　Article 35(c) LOSC.
120　[1937] 31 AJIL Supplement 1–17.
121　Article 36 LOSC.
122　Article 38 LOSC.
123　Article 45(2) LOSC.
124　See Act No 4 Concerning Indonesian Waters, 18 February 1960, and Philippines Republic Act No 3046 of 17 June 1961 cited in *The Law of the Sea: Practice of Archipelagic States*, New York: UN Office of Ocean Affairs and Law of the Sea, 1992, 45–53 and 75–85.

of these waters was not recognised by international law.[125] Recognition of their status under the LOSC was conditional on compliance with the rules of LOSC relating to archipelagic waters.

An archipelagic State is defined in Article 46(a) LOSC as a State 'constituted wholly or by one or more archipelagos and may include other islands'.

Article 46(b) LOSC defines an archipelago as 'a group of islands, including parts of islands, interconnecting waters and other natural features which are so closely related that such islands, waters and other natural features form an extrinsic, geographical, economic and political entity or which has been historically regarded as such'. When a State satisfies this definition it may claim the status of being an archipelagic State.

At the time of writing, 22 States have made formal declarations to the effect that they are archipelagic States. Many Caribbean islands have made such declarations. They include: Barbados, Trinidad and Tobago, Antigua and Barbuda, St Vincent and Grenadines and Grenada. The definition of an archipelago set out in Article 46(b) LOSC entails that mainland States as well as archipelagos that are colonies or dependents of another State, for example the Cook Islands and the Faroe Islands,[126] cannot claim the status of being archipelagic States.

Archipelagic States can draw 'archipelagic baselines', i.e. allowing the enclosure of their outmost islands or reefs within baselines (see Chapter 8.2.3). Waters landwards of these baselines are 'archipelagic waters', they are neither internal waters nor territorial waters unless they fall landwards of closing lines across river mouths, bays, or harbours of individual islands drawn in accordance with LOSC rules on normal baselines.[127]

Archipelagic waters enjoy a unique status. Like the territorial sea, these waters, the subsoil below and the air column above form part of the territory of the archipelagic State and are subject to its sovereignty.[128] The sovereignty of an archipelagic State is, however, restricted in three ways:

1   The existing rights of other States in archipelagic waters are protected. Article 48 LOSC requires recognition of and respect for existing agreements, traditional fishing rights and other legitimate activities of immediately adjacent neighbouring States and the submarine cables of any State. Special protection is accorded to the existing rights and all other legitimate interests exercised by an immediately adjacent neighbouring State where part of the archipelagic waters fall between two parts of that State.[129]

2   Ships of all States enjoy the right of innocent passage much as they do through the territorial sea, although this may be suspended temporarily in the interests of an archipelagic State's security.[130]

3   All ships and aircraft have the right to archipelagic sea lanes passage, i.e. the right of navigation and overflight solely for the purpose of continuous, expeditious and unobstructed transit between one part of the high sea or an EEZ to another part of the high sea or an EEZ.[131]

---

125   See D.R. Rothwell and T Stephens, supra note 92, 172–174.

126   Article 46(a) LOSC.

127   Article 50 LOSC.

128   Article 49 LOSC.

129   Article 47(6) LOSC.

130   Article 52 LOSC.

131   Article 53 LOSC.

An archipelagic State may designate sea lanes suitable for the continuous and expeditious passage of foreign ships through or over its archipelagic waters and adjacent territorial sea.[132] These sea lanes must conform to generally accepted regulations and be adopted by the IMO. Where an archipelagic State does not designate a sea lane, the right of archipelagic sea lane passage may be exercised through the routes normally used for international navigation.[133]

Acceptance of the regime established by the LOSC relating to archipelagic waters is generally accepted by States. This suggests that it forms part of customary international law.[134]

8.5 Contiguous zone

The contiguous zone refers to the zone adjacent to the territorial sea over which a coastal State may exercise limited jurisdiction.

The zone emerged from State practice throughout the nineteenth, and particularly the early twentieth century. Coastal States recognised and exercised jurisdiction in areas of the high seas immediately outside their territorial sea in an attempt to enforce certain laws and regulations, primarily those related to customs. For example, by its 'hovering laws' enacted in the eighteenth century, Britain attempted to prevent ships from anchoring outside its territorial sea in order to act as a base for smuggling. Likewise, the 1930 American Tariff Act, which is still in force, authorised customs officers to enforce US customs laws in waters extending for four leagues (approximately 12 nm) from the US coast. This jurisdiction was considered necessary for 'self-protection in time of war or for the prevention of frauds on [the US] revenue'.[135]

The GCTS provides for the establishment of a contiguous zone.[136] It defines the contiguous zone as a zone of the high seas contiguous to the territorial sea where the coastal State may exercise the control necessary to prevent and punish infringement of its customs, fiscal, immigration or sanitary regulations within its territory.[137] This definition is echoed in the LOSC.[138] However, as the LOSC permits a territorial sea of up to 12 nm, the breadth of the contiguous zone was extended up to 24 nm from the baseline of the coastal State.[139] Further, the establishment of an EEZ by the LOSC has reduced the importance of a contiguous zone in that it now forms part of an EEZ. Even though a coast State has a right to the contiguous zone, that right must be claimed. It can be said that the contiguous is the least popular of the maritime zones asserted by coastal States, although claims to the contiguous zone have reportedly increased as a consequence of the increase in acts of terrorism and ensuing concerns for safety and security.[140]

---

132   Article 53(1) LOSC.
133   Article 53(12) LOSC.
134   D.R. Rothwell and T. Stephens, supra note 92, 189.
135   *Manchester v Massachusetts* (1891) 139 US 240, 258.
136   Article 24 GCTS.
137   Ibid.
138   Article 33 LOSC.
139   Article 33(2) LOSC.
140   D.R. Rothwell and T. Stephens, supra note 92, 79–80. See also S. Kaye, 'Freedom of Navigation in a Post 9/11 World: Security and Creeping Jurisdiction' in D. Freestone, R. Barnes and D.M. Ong (eds), *The Law of the Sea: Progress and Prospects*, Oxford: Oxford University Press, 2006, 347–364.

8.5.1 Jurisdiction of the State

In its contiguous zone, a coastal State is only entitled to punish and prevent infringement of its customs, fiscal, immigration and sanitary laws and regulations. Its jurisdiction does not extend to crimes other than these that may have occurred therein.

In *Sorensen v Jensen*,[141] the Supreme Court of Chile observed that as the Chilean Civil Code provided for a 12 mile 'maritime area contiguous to the territorial sea', Chile could exercise jurisdiction over an area extending to 24 miles, but only in relation to customs, fiscal, immigration and sanitary matters. In stark contrast to the observations of the Supreme Court of Chile stands the decision of the Supreme Court of India in the *Republic of Italy v Union of India*.[142]

In the case just mentioned, two Italian marines aboard the *MV Enrica Lexie*, an Italian merchant vessel in the contiguous zone of India, shot and killed two Indian fishermen whom they had mistaken for pirates. The two marines were arrested and charged with murder under Indian penal law. Objections were raised to India's exercise of criminal jurisdiction. While the Indian Supreme Court concluded that India could not exercise criminal jurisdiction over the EEZ, it held out that India was entitled to exercise 'rights of sovereignty' in its contiguous zone which rights, in its opinion, included the exercise of its criminal jurisdiction:

> India is entitled both under its domestic law and the public international law to exercise rights of sovereignty up to 24 nautical miles from the baseline on the basis of which the width of the territorial waters is measured [. . .]. The incident of firing from the Italian vessel on the Indian shipping vessel having occurred within the contiguous zone, the Union of India is entitled to prosecute the two Italian marines under the criminal justice system prevalent in the country.[143]

The decision appears to have ignored the fact that under Article 33 LOSC the 'sovereign rights' exerciseable in the contiguous zone are limited to very specific circumstances. None of these circumstances appear to have existed. Accordingly, to hold that India was entitled to exercise criminal jurisdiction under international law, because the incident occurred in its contiguous zone, is misconceived.

8.6 The Exclusive Economic Zone (EEZ)

The EEZ is an area beyond and adjacent to the territorial sea. In this area, the coastal State enjoys certain sovereign rights subject to the rights and freedoms accorded to all other States.[144]

The EEZ has been called 'a revolutionary development' of the law of the sea brought about by the LOSC.[145] It emerged primarily through the efforts of developing States seeking to exercise greater control over the exploitation of economic resources offshore. Although the EEZ was created by the LOSC, the concept of it and underlying principles relating to its creation were grounded in emerging State practice prior to UNCLOS III, specifically claims of the US and many Latin American States to fisheries zones.[146] Despite State practice preceding UNCLOS III, it was the incorporation of the concept

---

141   Case No 3134 89 ILR 78.

142   (2013) 4 SCC 721.

143   *Republic of Italy v Union of India* (2013) 4 SCC 721, 110, cited in Y.J. Wu, 'The Enrica Lexie Incident – Jurisdiction in the Contiguous Zone?' *Cambridge Journal of International and Comparative Law*, 19 April 2014 available at http://cjicl.org.uk (accessed 10 July 2014).

144   Article 55 LOSC.

145   D.R. Rothwell and T. Stephens, supra note 92, 82.

146   See R. Jennings and A. Watts, *Oppenheim's International Law, Volume I: Peace, Parts 2 to 4*, 9th edn, Oxford: Oxford University Press, 2008, 784, §327 and D.P. O'Connell, *The International Law of the Sea, Volume I*, Oxford: Clarendon Press, 1984, 553–558.

into the draft Convention during the course of negotiations that directly led to its development as a customary norm. Thus, in the *La Bretagne* Arbitration, the majority judgment stated:

> The Third United Nations Conference on the Law of the Sea and the practice followed by States on the subject of sea fishing even while the Conference was in progress have crystallized and sanctioned a new international rule to the effect that in its exclusive economic zone a coastal state has sovereign rights in order to explore and exploit, preserve and manage natural resources.[147]

Similarly, the ICJ had little difficulty in regarding the EEZ 'as part of modern international law', even before the LOSC entered into force.[148]

A coastal State does not automatically acquire sovereign rights over the EEZ. The EEZ must be claimed. While jurisdiction over the continental shelf arises from 'the innateness of local authority over submarine terrain', there is no inherent quality attached to the EEZ that permits a coastal State to exercise rights over it without first making a claim.[149] In this respect, the EEZ is quite different from the continental shelf, for which no claim needs to be asserted prior to the coastal State's exercise of jurisdiction.[150] The ICJ pointed out that although there can be a continental shelf without an EEZ there cannot be an EEZ without a corresponding continental shelf.[151]

8.6.1 Rights and duties of a coastal State

A coastal State does not exercise sovereignty over the EEZ but may instead acquire, on the basis of the LOSC (and customary international law), certain sovereign rights over the resources contained therein.[152] These rights extend not only to the living resources in the oceans, but also to the resources of the seabed and its subsoil, and also to the airspace above, and are to be exercised for the purpose of exploration, exploitation, conservation and management.[153] A coastal State also has the right to engage in other 'activities for the economic exploitation and exploration of the zone, such as the production of energy from water currents, and winds'.[154]

The EEZ is a slightly deceptive term in that a coastal State is not permitted to claim exclusive rights over the living resources therein, but has preferential fishing rights. This means that a coastal State cannot wholly exclude other States from fishing in its EEZ. A coastal State is required to determine the allowable catch or the extent of fishing which will permit maintenance or, if appropriate, restoration of its fisheries populations.[155] It is also required to determine its capacity to harvest living resources and, if its capacity is insufficient for it to harvest the entirety of its allowable catch, to grant other States access to the surplus.[156] However, a coastal State is granted exclusive rights to non-living resources.

---

147   *Dispute Concerning Filleting within the Gulf of St. Lawrence (France v Canada) ('La Bretagne')* (1986) 19 UN Rep of Intl Arbitral Awards 225, para 49.

148   *The Case Concerning the Continental Shelf (Tunisia/Libyan Arab Jamahiriya) (Merits)* [1982] ICJ Rep 18, 74 at para 100. See also *the Case Concerning the Continental Shelf (Libyan Arab Jamahiriya/Malta) (Merits)* [1985] ICJ Rep 13, 33 at para 34 and *Gulf of Maine Case (Canada/United States) (Merits)* [1984] ICJ 246, para 94.

149   D.P. O'Connell, *The International Law of the Sea, Volume I*, Oxford: Clarendon Press, 570–571.

150   Article 77(3) LOSC.

151   *The Case Concerning the Continental Shelf (Libyan Arab Jamahiriya/Malta) (Merits)* [1985] ICJ Rep. 13, para 34.

152   Article 56(1) LOSC.

153   Article 56(1)(a) LOSC.

154   Ibid.

155   Article 61 LOSC.

156   Article 62 LOSC.

Along with the rights set out above, certain duties are imposed upon a coastal State, for example, in relation to artificial islands, installations and structures. These must be constructed, operated and dismantled in a manner that safeguards navigation.[157] A coastal State is required to give due notice of their construction, and to provide a permanent means of warning of their presence, and also, where necessary, to establish reasonable security zones around them. It is also obliged to remove any abandoned or disused structures and give appropriate publicity to the depth, position and dimensions of any remnants thereof.

8.6.2 Jurisdiction over the EEZ

The LOSC confers jurisdiction on a coastal State in relation to:

- the establishment and use of artificial islands, installations and structures;

- marine scientific research; and

- the protection and preservation of the environment.[158]

A coastal State, enforcing compliance with its laws, and regulations in the EEZ, has some broad powers. It may inspect, arrest and institute legal proceedings, as necessary, over foreign ships in the EEZ.[159] It is not required to have reasonable suspicion before exercising this right, once it considers it necessary.

In order to safeguard the rights of a foreign State the LOSC provides that (i) any vessels or crew arrested, pursuant to the power conferred on a coastal State, be 'promptly released' after a reasonable bond, or other security, has been provided; (ii) imprisonment cannot be imposed as a penalty for any contravention except with the agreement of the flag State; and (iii) the flag State be promptly notified when its vessel has been arrested or detained.[160]

A coastal State is only entitled to enforce laws and regulations relating to matters such as conservation, pollution, and exploitation of and use of the EEZ. Customs laws can only be enforced in the contiguous zone or in relation to any artificial islands and installations that a coastal State may have constructed. This was confirmed by the ITLOS in *M/V Saiga (No 2)*.

M/V SAIGA (NO 2) (ST VINCENT AND THE GRENADINES *V* GUINEA) (1998) 117 ILR 111

Facts:

M/V Saiga, an oil tanker registered in St Vincent and the Grenadines and flying its flag, was engaged in the act of bunkering or selling gas oil to fishing vessels operating in the EEZ of Guinea. In the course of doing so, it was arrested and boarded by Guinean authorities. The master of the vessel was charged with, and found guilty of contraband and fraud offences plus tax evasion for importing into Guinean territory merchandise taxable under Guinean law without declaring it.

---

157   Article 60 LOSC.
158   Article 56(1)(b) LOSC.
159   Article 73(1) LOSC.
160   Article 73(2), (3) and (4) LOSC.

One of the issues before the ITLOS was whether Guinea was justified in applying its customs laws in the EEZ.

Held:

Pursuant to Article 60(2) LOSC, a State was entitled to apply its customs laws and regulations in the EEZ only in relation to artificial islands and structures. The Convention did not empower it to apply its customs laws in respect of any other parts of the EEZ. Accordingly, by applying its customs laws and regulations to parts of the EEZ, Guinea contravened the LOSC.

Similarly, the rights conferred by the EEZ do not entitle a coastal State to exercise criminal jurisdiction, as was decided by the Supreme Court of Chile in *Sorensen v Jensen.*[161]

SORENSEN *V* JENSEN

Facts:

A collision occurred approximately 41 nm off the Chilean coast as a result of which the defendants were charged with certain criminal offences. The question before the Court was whether it could exercise jurisdiction over those offences.

Held

The collision occurred in the EEZ of Chile in which Chile enjoyed exclusive sovereignty solely in relation to economic matters. Chilean criminal jurisdiction, however, could only be exercised over offences that occurred in Chilean national territory. Accordingly, the Court had no jurisdiction.

8.6.3 Rights and freedoms of other States

The LOSC sought to strike a balance between the rights of coastal States and those of others States. It secured for all States, whether coastal or landlocked, the freedom of navigation and overflight, the laying of submarine cables and pipelines and other 'internationally lawful uses of the seas related to these freedoms'.[162] A foreign State does not have the right to carry out marine scientific research in the EEZ of a coastal State, except with that State's consent.[163] However, a coastal State should normally grant such consent once it established that the research is to be conducted for peaceful purposes and to increase scientific knowledge.[164]

---

161   Case No 3134 (1991) 89 ILR 78.
162   Article 58(1) LOSC.
163   Article 246(1) and (2) LOSC.
164   Article 246 (3) and (5) LOSC.

The right to navigation is of particular import as all major shipping routes pass through the EEZ of one State or another.[165] Navigation of foreign vessels through an EEZ is subject to any laws that the coastal State may have enacted to prevent marine pollution. The freedoms enjoyed by a third State over the EEZ are therefore clearly not as extensive as those enjoyed on the high seas.

Article 56(1) LOSC has not set out every activity that may be permissible to a foreign State in an EEZ and there has been some debate as to whether or not certain endeavours should be permitted.

For example, in the *M/V Saiga*, both parties urged the ITLOS to make declarations as to whether offshore bunkering, i.e. the sale of gas oil to vessels at sea, was permitted by a foreign State in the EEZ of another. St Vincent and the Grenadines argued that bunkering was part of the freedom of navigation and therefore an internationally lawful use of an EEZ by a foreign State, while Guinea contended that it was not part of the exercise of the freedom of navigation or any of the internationally lawful uses of the sea related to freedom of navigation, but a commercial activity proscribed in an EEZ except with the consent of the relevant coastal State.[166] Although the ITLOS noted that the LOSC contained no specific provision on this subject, it declined to make any finding on this question, holding that such a finding was unnecessary to resolve the dispute before it.[167]

The conduct of military activities in an EEZ, specifically naval surveillance and the performance of peaceful naval exercises, has been a source of contention, particularly between China and the US.[168] For example, in 2009, China interrupted the USNS Impeccable, an unarmed American navy vessel, from conducting surveillance in the South China Sea, causing a formal protest from the US which believed it was entitled to conduct such exercises in the EEZ without prior notification or consent, while China argued that such activities were not permitted. While the US, France and Italy made declarations to the effect that ordinary naval procedures were lawful in the EEZ of other States, other States such as Pakistan, Uruguay and Cape Verde made declarations alleging otherwise.

8.7 Continental shelf

There are two definitions of 'continental shelf', one scientific and one legal.

8.7.1 Scientific definition

The surface of the earth may be divided not only into continents and oceans, but also, on the basis of its lithosphere (or crust and uppermost mantle), into the continental lithosphere and the oceanic lithosphere.[169] Reference to the continental margin is to that portion of the continental crust that lies beneath the ocean and is recognised as the physical extension of the continental land mass. Although there is considerable diversity in the formation and features of continental margins,[170] they are recognised as having certain common configurations. The continental margin generally consists of a continental shelf, continental slope and continental rise (see Figure 8.3 below).

---

165   R.A. Churchill and A.V. Lowe, *The Law of the Sea*, 3rd edn, Juris Publishing, 1999, 162.

166   *M/V 'SAIGA' (No. 2) Case (St. Vincent and the Grenadines v Guinea)* (1998) 117 ILR 111, para 137.

167   Ibid, paras 137–138.

168   See E. Franckx, *American and Chinese Views on Navigational Rights of Warships* (2011) 10/1 Chinese Journal of International Law, 187.

169   See, P.A. Symonds, O. Eldholm, J. Mascle and G.F. Moore, 'Characteristics of Continental Margins' in P.J. Cook and C.M. Carleton (eds), *Continental Shelf Limits: The Scientific and Legal Interface*, Oxford: Oxford University Press, 2000, 25.

170   Ibid.

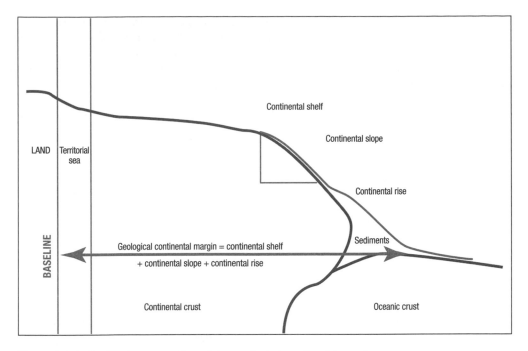

Figure 8.3 A simplified cross-section of the geological continental margin

The continental shelf is a gently sloping platform submerged in relatively shallow water and lies immediately adjacent to the coast. The continental shelf ends in a relatively steep slope known as the continental slope. Sediment accumulates at the base of this slope and forms what is known as the continental rise.

8.7.2 Legal definition of the continental shelf and the development of that definition

The seabed and subsoil of the continental margin is rich in oil and gas deposits. These deposits began to attract the attention of States after WWII. On 28 September 1945, US President Truman issued a Continental Shelf Proclamation stating that 'the government of the United States regards the natural resources of the subsoil and sea bed of the continental shelf beneath the high sea but contiguous to the coast of the United States as appertaining to the United States, subject to its jurisdiction and control . . .'. The Proclamation, however, recognised, that the waters above the continental shelf remained part of the high seas.[171]

The Proclamation thus claimed 'an intrinsic right [to the adjacent continental shelf] independently of the procedures of occupation'.[172] This claim corresponded to the geological understanding of the continental shelf as an extension of the continental mass and was considered by the ICJ to be 'the starting point of the positive law on the subject'.[173]

---

171   Exec Procl 2667, 10 Fed Reg 12, 303 (1945).
172   D.P. O'Connell, *The International Law of the Sea, Volume 1*, Oxford: Clarendon Press, 1984, 470.
173   *The North Sea Continental Shelf Cases (Federal Republic of Germany/Denmark; Federal Republic of Germany/Netherlands)* [1969] ICJ 3, para 47.

319

There were few objections to the US claim. Certain eminent jurists contended that the claim was grounded in already established principles of international law.[174] More importantly, the Truman Proclamation was followed by similar claims by a number of other States although the content of their claims was far from uniform.[175] This emerging State practice was codified by the GCCS. The first three articles of the GCCS (e.g Article 1 defined the term 'continental shelf') were recognised by the ICJ as reflecting 'received, or at least emergent rules of customary international law'.[176]

In the *North Sea Continental Shelf Cases*, the ICJ explained the basis of the entitlement of a coastal State to its continental shelf. It stated:

> What confers the *ipso jure* title which international law attributes to the coastal State in respect of its continental shelf is the fact that the submarine areas concerned may be deemed to be actually part of the territory over which the coastal State already has dominion, – in the sense that, although covered with water, they are a prolongation or continuation of that territory, an extension of it under the sea.[177]

In contrast to the scientific definition of the continental shelf, the legal definition excludes that portion of the continental margin that falls within the territorial sea. The inner limit of the continental shelf begins where the territorial sea ends. This is because the subsoil and seabed of the territorial sea already form part of State territory.

Article 1 GCCS defined the continental shelf as:

> the seabed and subsoil of the submarine areas adjacent to the coast but outside the area of the territorial sea, to a depth of 200 metres or, beyond that limit, to where the depth of the superjacent waters admits of the exploitation of the natural resources of the said areas.

The 200 metre depth limit of the continental shelf was based on the recommendation that the continental margin was normally located at the 200 metre isobath. This restrictive view was not acceptable to coastal States as they had no desire to confine their rights to that limit of the continental shelf.[178] The criterion of exploitability was therefore added, but this displaced the legal definition from its scientific basis. It also made the definition imprecise and uncertain. It was rejected at UNCLOS III which sets out its definition of continental shelf in Article 76(1). This article states:

> The continental shelf of a costal State comprises the seabed and subsoil of the submarine areas extending beyond its territorial sea throughout the natural prolongation of its land territory to the outer edge of the continental margin, or to a distance of 200 nautical miles from the baselines from which the breadth of the territorial sea is measured where the outer edge of the continental shelf does not extend up to that distance.

The above definition shows that the term 'continental shelf' is intended not only to encompass the entire continental margin, but to go further. The continental shelf extends up to a distance of 200 nm from the territorial sea regardless of the configuration of the underlying seafloor i.e. whether or not it contains a continental margin. It is only where the continental margin actually goes beyond the 200 nm limit that the scientific definition of the continental shelf and the concept of natural prolongation come into play. The continental shelf is therefore defined not only by the principle of natural prolongation but by a specified distance from the baselines. These two elements are complementary.[179]

---

174   D.P. O'Connell, supra note 172, 471–472.
175   D.R. Rothwell and T.M. Stephens, supra note 92, 101.
176   *The North Sea Continental Shelf Cases (Federal Republic of Germany/Denmark; Federal Republic of Germany/Netherlands)* [1969] ICJ 3, para 63.
177   Ibid, para 43. See also *Aegean Continental Shelf Case (Greece v Turkey)* [1978] ICJ Rep 1 at para 86.
178   D.R. Rothwell and T.M. Stephens, *The International Law of the Sea*, Oxford: Hart Publishing, 2010, 103.
179   *The Case Concerning the Continental Shelf (Libyan Arab Jamahiriya/Malta)* (1985) ICJ Rep 13, para 34.

8.7.3 Outer limits of the continental shelf when the outer edge of the continental margin extends beyond 200 nm

In a situation where the outer edge of the continental margin (which includes the shelf, the slope and the rise) extends beyond 200 nm from the baseline, the coastal State may claim the legal title to the natural prolongation of its continental shelf, but in no event must the outer limits of the continental shelf exceed 350 nm from the baselines or 100 nm from the 2,500 metre isobath.[180] The 2,500 metre iso-bath is a line every point of which is on the seabed at a depth of 2,500 metres below the sea water's surface.

In order to make a claim to a prolonged continental shelf a coastal State must determine the outer limits of the claimed continental shelf by using methods described in the LOSC, the first, known as the Irish formula, is described in Article 76(4)(a)(i) and the second, known as the Hedberg formula, in Article 76(4)(a)(ii). Each formula is very complex, and the coastal State may request advice from the Commission on the Limits of the Continental Shelf (CLCS) to assist it in the determination of the outer limits of its continental shelf (see Chapter 8.7.5)

It is interesting to note that in 2012 the ITLO in the *Bangladesh/Myanmar Case* rendered its first judgment concerning delimitation of the continental shelf beyond 200 nm.[181]

8.7.4 Rights and duties of coastal States

Coastal States have sovereign rights over the continental shelf for the purpose of exploring and exploiting their natural resources. The rights conferred upon coastal States do not depend upon 'occupation, effective or notional, or on any express proclamation'.[182] These rights are inherent; they arise from the territorial sovereignty of the State. Their exercise requires 'no special legal process . . . nor . . . special acts'.[183]

The rights of a coastal State are exclusive in that no other State may explore or exploit the natural resources of the continental shelf without its express consent.[184] As an extension of this exclusivity, only a coastal State can (i) regulate or authorise any drilling for any purpose on the continental shelf[185] or (ii) construct and authorise and regulate the construction of any artificial islands, installations and structures.[186] Marine research on the continental shelf also requires the consent of the coastal State.[187]

The rights of a coastal State to exploitation and exploration apply only to natural resources of the seabed and subsoil. Such rights do not, for example, confer upon a coastal State any right to wrecked ships or their cargo.[188] The natural resources to which the continental shelf regime apply are (i) mineral and other non-living resources and (ii) sedentary species.[189]

---

180   Article 76(5) LOSC.
181   On this topic see: H. Yao, *Natural Prolongation and Delimitation of the Continental Shelf Beyond 200 nm: Implications of the Bangladesh/Myanmar Case* (2014) 4 Asian Journal of International Law, 281.
182   Article 2(3) GCCS and Article 77(3) LOSC. See also the *North Sea Continental Shelf Cases (Federal Republic of Germany/Denmark; Federal Republic of Germany/Netherlands)* [1969] ICJ Rep 1 at paras 19, 39 and 43.
183   *The North Sea Continental Shelf Cases (Federal Republic of Germany/Denmark; Federal Republic of Germany/Netherlands)* [1969] ICJ Rep 1 at para 29.
184   Article 2(2) GCCS and Article 77(2) LOSC.
185   Article 81 LOSC.
186   Articles 60 and 80 LOSC. See also Article 5 GCCS.
187   Article 246, LOSC.
188   See *Treasure Salvors, Inc. et al. v Unidentified Wrecked and Abandoned Sailing Vessel, etc.* 529 F. 2d 330 (5th Cir 1978).
189   Article 77(4) LOSC.

Sedentary species are defined as 'organisms, which at harvestable stage, either are immobile on or under the seabed or are unable to move except in constant physical contact with the seabed or subsoil'.[190] This definition is imprecise and has been subject to some controversy. Brazil and France, for example, have disagreed as to whether it encompasses lobsters while Japan and the US have disputed the status of crabs.[191]

A State which rightfully claims an extended continental shelf has the right to explore and exploit the natural resources of that extended continental shelf. Where it does so, however, it is required by the LOSC to make payments or contributions in kind to the International Seabed Authority (ISA).[192]

The LOSC emphasises that the rights of a coastal State to the continental shelf must be exercised in a manner that does 'not infringe or result in any unjustifiable interference with navigation and other rights and freedoms of other states'.[193]

8.7.5 The Commission on the Limits of the Continental Shelf (CLCS)

The CLCS was established on the basis of Article 76(8) LOSC. It is made up of 21 experts in the field of geology, geophysics or hydrography elected by contracting States from among their nationals, for a period of 5 years. The members of the CLCS serve in their personal capacities. The CLCS meets twice a year at the UN headquarters in New York. Its meetings are *in camera*.

The main purpose of the CLCS is to implement the provisions of LOSC relating to the establishment by coastal States of the outer limits of the continental shelf beyond 200 nm. Its two functions are:

■ to consider the data and other relevant information submitted by a coastal State wishing to establish the outer limits of its continental shelf beyond 200 nm. This consideration will result in the adoption of recommendations which are final and binding.[194] Under Article 4 of Annex II to the LOSC, a coastal State has 10 years from the entry into force of the LOSC for that State to make a submission. However, this period has been extended for many reasons, one of them is to accommodate developing countries that lack technical capacity to provide the information necessary to make a submission. If a coastal State disagrees with the CLCS' recommendations it may make, within a reasonable time, a revised or a new submission. However, the CLCS will not consider submissions which involve land or maritime disputes unless the parties concerned decide otherwise. So far the CLCS has not adopted any recommendations, but progress of its work and the status of submission of coastal States can be found at the CLCS official website;[195] and

■ at the request of a coastal State, to provide advice concerning the preparation of a submission by that State.

---

190   Ibid.
191   See D.P. O'Connell, supra note 172, 498–503.
192   Article 82 LOSC.
193   Article 78(2) LOSC.
194   On this topic see: B. Kwiatkowska, *Submissions to the UN Commission on the Limits of the Continental Shelf: The Practice of Developing States in Cases of Disputed and Unresolved Maritime Boundary Delimitations or Other Land or Maritime Disputes: Part Two* (2013) 28 International Journal of Marine and Coastal Law, 563.
195   Availavle at www.un.org/depts/los/clcs_new/commission_submissions.htm (accessed 10 November 2014. See also: H. Llewellyn, *The Commission on the Limits of the Continental Shelf: Joint Submission by France, Ireland, Spain, and the United Kingdom* (2007) 56 ICLQ, 677 at 687.

8.8 Delimitation of maritime boundaries

Maritime delimitation refers to the process of determining the sovereignty or jurisdiction of a coastal State over its adjacent seas in circumstances where its claims thereto overlap with those of one or more States. Where the dispute over maritime space arises because of a dispute over land, the territorial dispute must be determined by the rules relating to the acquisition of territorial sovereignty before maritime boundaries can be delimited.[196]

The delimitation of boundaries, including maritime boundaries, is an aspect of State sovereignty. It is both a political and a legal act. A State may unilaterally determine and declare its maritime boundaries and some States do, in fact, do this. While such declarations may be considered valid under national law, without recognition from other States, that delimitation will not be valid under international law nor will it be binding on any other State. Maritime delimitation between States with adjacent or opposite coasts 'must be sought and effected by means of an agreement, following negotiations conducted in good faith and with the genuine intention of achieving a positive result.'[197] In the absence of agreement, the issue of maritime delimitation may be referred to a competent third party for mediation, conciliation, arbitration or adjudication.

Maritime delimitation is fundamental to international peace and security. Uncertainty as to maritime boundaries can create or exacerbate regional tension. Nowhere is this more evident currently than in the disagreement relating to the South China Sea where six countries – China, Brunei, Taiwan, Malaysia, the Philippines and Vietnam – have made competing claims to an area which is believed to be rich in hydrocarbon resources. China, in particular, has forcefully asserted its claims, leading to tensions not only with its neighbours but also with the US.[198]

Delimitation of maritime boundaries may be necessary in two situations. First, where adjacent States have a land boundary and wish to extend that into the sea through the different maritime zones, and second where States have opposite coasts and would have overlapping maritime zones, if both States aimed at the maximum allowable extension.

One of the methods used for delimitation of maritime boundaries is the equidistance method (or principle). This method determines the boundaries in such a way that every point in the boundary is equidistant from the nearest point of the baselines from which the breadth of the territorial sea of each State is measured. When using this method an equidistance line is drawn, i.e. 'a line every point of which is equidistant from the nearest point of two States'. Article 15 LOSC provides that when two States' coasts are opposite or adjacent to each other, unless there is an agreement between the parties, neither State may extend its territorial sea beyond the median line every point of which is equidistant from the nearest points on the baseline from which the territorial sea's breadth is measured. The same formula is used in Article 12(1) GCTS but this provision does not mention the possibility of an

---

196 See: the *Case Concerning the Land and Maritime Boundary between Cameroon and Nigeria (Cameroon v Nigeria; Equatorial Guinea intervening)* [2002] ICJ Rep 303 and *Arbitration between Eritrea and Yemen, Award of the Tribunal in the First Stage of the Proceedings (Territorial Sovereignty and the Scope of the Dispute)* 9 October 1998. Available at www.pca-cpa.org (accessed 9 June 2014).

197 The *Case Concerning the Delimitation of the Maritime Boundary in the Gulf of Maine Area (Canada/United States)* [1984] ICJ Rep 246, para 112.

198 See: e.g. K Hodal 'Despite Oil Rig Removal, China and Vietnam Row Still Simmers' *The Guardian*, 17 July 2014, available at www.theguardian.com/world/2014/jul/17/oil-rig-china-vietnam-row-south-china-sea (accessed 22 July 2014), and B. Xi, 'South China Sea Tensions' *Council on Foreign Relations*, 14 May 2014, available at www.cfr.org/china/south-china-sea-tensions/p29790 (accessed 22 July 2014).

agreement. Article 6(1) GCTS uses the same formula as Article 15 LOSC, but the LOSC's provisions on the continental shelf and the EEC provisions do not (see below).[199]

The case law on the delimitation of maritime boundaries shows that two approaches have developed: the result-oriented approach and the corrective-equity approach. While both were applied by international tribunals and courts between 1969 and 1992, from 1992 onwards, the corrective-equity approach has gained general recognition.[200]

8.8.1 The result-oriented and the corrective-equity approaches (1969–1992)

In 1969 the ICJ in *North Sea Continental Shelf Cases (Federal Republic of Germany/Denmark; Federal Republic of Germany/Netherlands)* established the result-oriented approach.

NORTH SEA CONTINENTAL SHELF CASES (FEDERAL REPUBLIC OF GERMANY/DENMARK; FEDERAL REPUBLIC OF GERMANY/ NETHERLANDS) [1969] ICJ REP 3

Facts:

The case concerned the delimitation of the continental shelf between Germany and the Netherlands and Germany and Denmark beyond the partial boundaries previously agreed upon by these States. The Netherlands and Denmark argued that the equidistance method previously applied should continue applying but Germany objected. Its coastline curved inwards and it believed that the equidistance method would unduly curtail its fair share of the continental shelf.

Denmark and the Netherlands submitted that the use of the equidistance method was mandatory under Article 6 GCCS, and, although Germany had not ratified the GCCS it had indicated that it was bound by Article 6 and that Germany was now estopped from alleging otherwise. Alternatively, the use of the equidistance method was required by customary international law.

Germany contended that the equidistance rule did not form customary international law, and, that even if it did, the configuration of the German coast constituted a special circumstance that justified a departure from its use. According to Germany, each State should obtain a just and equitable share of the continental shelf with their share determined in proportion to the length of their coastal front or facade.

The ICJ was requested to determine the applicable rules and principles.

Held:

The ICJ held that Germany was not bound by Article 6 GCCS. Germany had neither ratified it nor by its conduct indicated that it did accept Article 6 GCCS. Moreover, Article 6 did not codify existing or emerging customary international law.

---

199   Articles 74, 83 and 134(4) LOSC.
200   Y. Tanaka, *The International Law of the Sea*, Cambridge: Cambridge University Press, 2012, 192–197.

Comment:

The equidistance method

The ICJ accepted that the use of the equidistance method was very convenient for the purposes of delimitation of maritime boundaries, noting that no other method possessed the same combination of 'practical convenience and certainty of application'. The ICJ further noted that the use of the equidistance method was justified by cartography, and practical convenience, but not by legal theory as the equidistance method could cause areas that are the natural prolongation of one State's territory to be attributed to another State.

The Court held that the use of the equidistance method was not mandatory and that 'there [is] no other single method of delimitation the use of which is in all circumstance obligatory'.[201] It held that 'It is not necessary to seek one method of delimitation but one goal'. This goal was to achieve equitable results.

The role of equity

The ICJ noted that the equidistance method could in certain geographical circumstances produce results that were unreasonable and inequitable. It magnified the slightest irregularity in the coastline and in the delimitation of concave and convex coastlines, the unreasonable results were more pronounced the greater the irregularity and the further from the coastline the area to be delimited. The Court held that if the equidistance method was to be used Germany would not be treated equally because of the configuration of its coastline which was roughly convex while that of the others was markedly concave.

Equitable principles permit consideration of the relevant facts of each particular situation and allow the Court to arrive at a solution that is crafted to suit the circumstances of a given case. The ICJ explained that:

> It is clear that what is reasonable and equitable must depend on its particular circumstances. There can be no doubt that it is virtually impossible to achieve an equitable result in any delimitation without taking into account the particular relevant circumstances which characterize the area.[202]

The result-oriented approach

The result-oriented approach entails that international courts and tribunals decide each case with a view to achieving equitable results and are not bound by any method of maritime delimitation. This approach confers on them a significant degree of discretion which, however, comes at the cost of consistency and predictability.

The Court of Arbitration in the *Anglo-French Continental Shelf*, which was decided just a few years after the *North Sea Continental Shelf Cases*, criticised the ICJ for failing to provide practical guidance on delimitation of maritime boundaries. It ultimately took a different approach from that of the ICJ to Article 6 GCCS. This new approach can be described as the corrective-equity approach. The Court

---

201   Para 90.
202   The *Case Concerning the Delimitation of Continental Shelf (Tunisia/Libyan Arab Jamahiriya)* [1982] ICJ Rep 18, para 72.

held that the equidistance method, being recognised by customary international law, must be applied in the first stage of delimitation.[203] When justified by geographic and other circumstances the equidistance method should not apply but instead equitable principles should be followed.[204] The Court concluded that in the delimitation of the continental shelf between opposite coasts, the equidistance method, the only predictable method ensuring certainty of results given that once the base points are fixed the delimitation line is mathematically determined, was an appropriate starting point. However, a shift from the equidistance method may be envisaged, if justified by geographic and other circumstances, to achieve equitable results. Accordingly equity intervenes as a corrective element. The advantage of this approach is that it ensures predictability in the delimitation of maritime disputes.

Until 1993, the ICJ maintained the view that the equidistance method was not 'a mandatory legal principle or a method having some privileged status in relation to other methods'[205] and that:

> The result of the application of equitable principles must be equitable. . . . It is . . . the result which is predominant; the principles are subordinate to the goal. The equitableness of a principle must be assessed in the light of its usefulness for the purpose of arriving at an equitable result.[206]

8.8.2 The acceptance of the corrective-equity approach by the ICJ

In 1993, the ICJ in its *Greenland/Jan Mayen*[207] judgment, endorsed the corrective-equity approach and has applied it since that judgment. This case concerned a dispute between Denmark and Norway, both States being contracting parties to the GCCS, relating to maritime delimitation of their continental shelf and the EEZ/fishery zone (FZ). The ICJ accepted that the equidistance method was part of customary law and therefore:

> [I]n respect of the continental shelf boundary in the present case, even if it were appropriate to apply, not Article 6 of the 1958 Convention, but customary law concerning the continental shelf as developed in the decided cases, it is in accord with precedents to begin with the median line as a provisional line and then to ask whether 'special circumstances' require any adjustment or shifting of that line.[208]

In the *Cameroon v Nigeria Case*,[209] the ICJ went further in that it applied the corrective-equity approach to the delimitation of the continental shelf and the EEZ under the LOSC. Article 74(1) LOSC deals with delimitation of the EEZ while Article 83(1) LOSC deals with delimitation of the continental shelf. Both articles are rather vague in terms of the approach which should be applied to delimitation. Article 74(1) LOSC states:

---

203 Ibid, paras 245–249.

204 Ibid, para 70.

205 The *Case Concerning the Delimitation of Continental Shelf Case (Tunisia/Libyan Arab Jamahiriya)* [1982] ICJ Rep 18, paras 109–110.

206 Ibid, para 70, See also: the *Case Concerning the Delimitation of Continental Shelf (Libyan Arab Jamahiriya/Malta)* [1985] ICJ Rep 13, para 45; The *St Pierre and Miquelon Arbitration*, 31 ILM 1145 (1992), para 38. The *Guinea/Guinea-Bissau Arbitration*, (1985) 89 RGDIP 483, 521, para 89 and para 102; and the *Case Concerning the Delimitation of the Maritime Boundary in the Gulf of Maine Area (Canada/US)*, [1984] ICJ Rep 246, at 300, para 112.

207 The *Case Concerning the Delimitation in the Area between Greenland and Jan Mayen (Denmark v Norway)* [1993] ICJ Rep 38, para 58.

208 Para 51.

209 The *Case Concerning the Delimitation of the Land and Maritime Boundary between Cameroon and Nigeria (Cameroon v Nigeria: Equatorial Guinea intervening)* [2002] ICJ Rep 303, at 441–442, paras 288–290.

The delimitation of the exclusive economic zone between States with opposite or adjacent coasts shall be effected by agreement on the basis of international law, as referred to in Article 38 of the Statute of the International Court of Justice, in order to achieve an equitable solution.

Article 83(1) is identical to Article 74(1), save that it refers not to the EEZ but to the continental shelf. In accordance with the ICJ's judgment in the *Cameroon v Nigeria Case* delimitation under both Articles should be made in accordance with the corrective-equity approach.

The ICJ's delimitation methodology was explained in *Maritime Delimitation in the Black Sea (Romania v Ukraine).*[210] It consists of three steps:

First, the ICJ will establish a provisional delimitation line based upon equidistance from adjacent coasts and the median line for opposite coasts. The Court stated that 'No legal consequences flow from the use of the terms "median line" and "equidistance line "since the method of delimitation is the same for both'.[211]

Second, the ICJ will consider whether there are any factors that justify an adjustment of the provisional equidistance line in order to achieve an equitable solution.[212] If the ICJ decides that such circumstances are present, it establishes a different boundary which usually entails such adjustment or shifting of the equidistance/median line as is necessary to take account of those circumstances.

Third, the ICJ will:

verify that the line (a provisional equidistance line which may or may not have been adjusted by taking into account the relevant circumstances) does not, as it stands, lead to an inequitable result by reason of any marked disproportion between the ratio of the respective coastal lengths and the ratio between the relevant maritime area of each State by reference to the delimitation line.[213]

Accordingly in the final stage the ICJ will apply the proportionality test (see Chapter 8.8.3).

The ICJ has applied its delimitation method as a standard method.[214] Other international tribunals and courts have, in general, followed the ICJ, e.g. the Arbitral Tribunal in the 2007 *Guyana v Suriname Arbitration,*[215] the ITLOS in the 2012 *Bangladesh v Myanmar,*[216] the Arbitral Tribunal in 1999 in the *Eritrea v Yemen Arbitration (the Second Phase).*[217] However, in the *Barbados/Trinidad Arbitration,* the Arbitration Tribunal did not accept the existence of any mandatory method of delimitation but, nevertheless, applied the corrective-equity approach.[218]

---

210   (2009) ICJ Rep 61, paras-116–122.
211   Ibid, para 116.
212   Ibid, para 120.
213   Ibid, para 122.
214   See *The Case Concerning the Maritime Dispute between Peru and Chile*, judgment of 27 January 2014, available at the official website of the ICJ
215   The *Guyana/Suriname Arbitration*, paras 335 and 342. The text of the award is available at the official website of the PCA: www/pca-cpa.org (accessed 25 July14).
216   *Dispute Concerning Delimitation of the Maritime Boundary between Bangladesh and Myanmar in the Bay of Bengal (Bangladesh/Myanmar)* [2012] ITLOS Case no 16, para 240.
217   The *Eritrea/Yemen Arbitration (the Second Phase)* 40 ILM 983 (2001), at 1005, paras 131–132.
218   *In the Matter of an Arbitration between Barbados and Republic of Trinidad and Tobago*, Award of Arbitral Tribunal dated 11 April 2006, para 242, available at the official website of the PCA.

8.8.3 Relevant/special circumstances

The term 'special circumstances' was used in the GCCS. Courts and tribunals have used the term 'relevant circumstances' in their interpretation of Articles 74 and 83 LOSC. There is little difference in the meaning of the terms.

Special or relevant circumstances refer to every factor of a case that justifies an adjustment or shifting of an equidistant line. These circumstances are taken into account in the process of delimitation in order to avoid inequitable results arising from a mechanical or unqualified application of the equidistance rule.[219]

The courts and tribunals have emphasised that they are 'not constrained by a finite list of special circumstances' but that relevant factors must be decided on a case-by-case basis.[220] The weight to be accorded to a given factor will also vary depending on the circumstances of the case.[221] In the interests of maintaining consistency and predictability, courts will, however, also have regard to decided cases and state practice.[222] The factors to which the court or tribunal may have regard may be categorised into geographical factors and non-geographical factors.

8.8.3.1 Geographical factors

Geographical factors include the configuration of the coast, the direction of the coastline, the lengths of the parties' respective coasts and the presence of geographical structures such as islands. All geographic peculiarities existing on a particular coast need not be considered in a given case.[223]

As a coastal State's entitlement to its maritime zones is based on sovereignty over its land territory, the configuration of the coastlines of each State is a very important factor. The configuration of the coast was considered crucial in the *North Sea Continental Shelf Case* (above) due to the Court's reliance on the concept of natural prolongation. While the natural prolongation of the continental shelf is no longer as significant, coastal configuration remains important. For example, the ITLOS held that the concavity of a coast was a relevant circumstance where it had the effect of cutting off part of the maritime entitlement of one of the States.[224] The equidistance line was adjusted to abate the cut-off.[225]

The length of the parties' coastlines was regarded as a relevant factor in the *North Sea Continental Shelf case*. This factor is subsumed under the principle of proportionality and therefore considered separately in Chapter 8.8.4.

---

219 *Delimitation in the Area between Greenland and Jan Mayen (Denmark v Norway)* [1993] ICJ Rep 38, para 55.

220 *In the Matter of an Arbitration between Guyana and Suriname*, Award of 17 September 2007 paras 302–303, available at www.pca-cpa.org. See also *Delimitation in the Area between Greenland and Jan Mayen (Denmark v Norway)* [1993] ICJ Rep 38, paras 61–64.

221 *North Sea Continental Shelf Cases (Federal Republic of Germany/Netherlands; Federal Republic of Germany/Denmark)* [1969] ICJ Rep 3, para 93.

222 See *Delimitation in the Area between Greenland and Jan Mayen (Denmark v Norway)* [1993] ICJ Rep 38, para 58.

223 The *Case Concerning the Delimitation of the Land and Maritime Boundary between Cameroon v Nigeria (Cameroon v Nigeria; Equatorial Guinea intervening)* [2002] ICJ Rep 303, para 295.

224 The *Dispute Concerning Delimitation of the Maritime Boundary between Bangladesh and Myanmar in the Bay of Bengal (Bangladesh/Myanmar)* [2012] ITLOS Case no 16, para 292

225 Ibid, para 325.

Although geological structure had initially been considered a relevant factor in the delimitation of the continental shelf,[226] the geology and geomorphology of the seabed and subsoil are no longer considered as relevant since the continental shelf is now generally measured by distance from the coastline.[227]

The presence of an island or islands in waters claimed by more than one State has long been regarded as relevant to the delimitation of maritime boundaries. This is because islands give rise to their own maritime zones under Article 121 LOSC.

Islands vary significantly in their size, importance and location from the coast and have had varied treatment in the delimitation process. They may be given full effect, no effect, partial effect or placed in an enclave.[228]

8.8.3.2 Non-geographic factors

Non-geographic factors are normally subordinate to geographic factors. They include the following:

1 *Navigational interests:* in the *Eritrea/Yemen Arbitration*, the tribunal appeared to take into account the location of a major international shipping route.[229] Navigational interests were found to constitute special circumstances justifying deviation from the median line in the *Guyana/Suriname Arbitration*.[230]

2 *Economic factors:* as the continental shelf and EEZ were both established to facilitate the exploitation of marine resources, States have sought to argue that economic factors including fishery zones and hydrocarbon resources are relevant. The ICJ has made it clear that the economic position of one State relative to that of another is not, however, of any relevance as the objective of the delimitation is not the redistribution of wealth or resources between the parties.[231]

3 *Oil and gas resources:* the unity of mineral deposits straddling the continental shelf of States was considered relevant in the *North Sea Continental Shelf Cases*. However, there has been a clear reluctance to regard any licences for petroleum exploration that may have been granted by a State while the delimitation was in progress as a relevant factor. These are only relevant where they are used as evidence of express or tacit agreement between the parties as to the areas to which they are entitled.[232]

4 *Historic rights:* historic rights are expressly incorporated into articles dealing with delimitation of the territorial sea. They are also mentioned in Article 6 GCCS, but excluded from Articles 74 and 83 LOSC. However, the ICJ has indicated that historic rights, which have been preserved

---

226 *North Sea Continental Shelf Cases (Federal Republic of Germany/Netherlands; Federal Republic of Germany/Denmark)* [1969] ICJ Rep 3 para 101.

227 *Dispute Concerning Delimitation of the Maritime Boundary between Bangladesh and Myanmar in the Bay of Bengal (Bangladesh/Myanmar)* [2012] ITLOS Case no 16, para 322.

228 See Y. Tanaka, *The International Law of the Sea*, Cambridge: Cambridge University Press, 2012, 204–206.

229 *Arbitration between Eritrea and Yemen, Award of the Arbitral Tribunal in the Second Stage of the Proceedings (Maritime Delimitation)*, supra note 217.

230 *In the Matter of an Arbitration between Guyana and Suriname*, Award of 17 September 2007 paras 304–306, supra note 220.

231 The *Case Concerning the Delimitation of Continental Shelf (Libyan Arab Jamahiriya/Malta)* [1985] ICJ Rep 13.

232 The *Case Concerning the Delimitation of the Land and Maritime Boundary between Cameroon and Nigeria (Cameroon v Nigeria; Equatorial Guinea intervening)* [2002] ICJ Rep 303, para 304.

by long usage, should be respected even in the delimitation of the EEZ and continental shelf. Even where such rights have been recognised, as in the *Eritrea/Yemen Arbitration*, they did not affect the drawing of the delimitation line.[233] They will influence the drawing of maritime boundaries only in the most exceptional cases.[234]

5 *Fisheries:* States have attempted to argue that access to fish stocks and fishing ground is a relevant factor. The ICJ in the *Jan Mayen Case* did take into account impact of a median line on access to a migrating fish stock. However, it later held that this resource-related criteria will only influence the delimitation process where the party relying on it can show that failure to take it into account 'will be radically inequitable, that is to say, as likely to entail catastrophic repercussions for the livelihood and economic well-being of the population of the countries concerned'.[235]

6 *Conduct of the parties:* the courts and tribunals have sometimes considered the conduct of the parties to see whether they have, between themselves, established a *de facto* maritime line, or accepted a particular line of delimitation. Such conduct has been said to 'constitute a circumstance of great relevance'.[236] The courts have also had regard to the conduct of colonial powers who had control of a territory before independence, but this conduct is only relevant where the parties had not departed from it after becoming independent.[237]

7 *Security considerations:* in the *Anglo-French Continental Shelf Case*, France argued that a relevant factor was 'the security and defence of its territory' should the Hurd Deep Fault be attributed to Great Britain.[238] The Court of Arbitration accepted that security and defence considerations may be a relevant factor but concluded that in the circumstances of the case it was not decisive.[239] The ICJ has confirmed that security considerations may be a relevant factor, although it has never considered it necessary to consider this factor on the facts before it.[240]

8 *Maritime boundaries of third States:* an equitable delimitation cannot ignore pre-existing boundaries or maritime delimitations that remain to be completed.[241] In the *Barbados-Trinidad Arbitration*, the tribunal considered the boundary agreements made between each party and third States to be relevant, not because they were binding on non-parties but because they determined the limit of each party's zones.

---

233 *Arbitration between Eritrea and Yemen, Award of the Arbitral Tribunal in the Second Stage of the Proceedings (Maritime Delimitation)*, supra note 217.

234 *In the Matter of an Arbitration between Barbados and Republic of Trinidad and Tobago*, Award of Arbitral Tribunal dated 11 April 2006, para 269, supra note 218.

235 The *Case Concerning the Delimitation of the Maritime Boundary in the Gulf of Maine Area (Canada/United States)* [1984] ICJ Rep, para 237.

236 The *Continental Shelf Case (Tunisia/Libyan Arab Jamahiriya)* [1982] ICJ Rep 3, para 97. See also the *Dispute Concerning the Drawing of a Maritime Boundary between Bangladesh and Myanmar in the Bay of Bengal*, para 2.56.supra note 227.

237 *In the Matter of an Arbitration between Guyana and Suriname*, Award of 17 September 2007, para

238 The *Case Concerning the Delimitation of the Continental Shelf between the United Kingdom of Great Britain and Northern Ireland and France (Great Britain v France)* 18 RIAA 3, para 161.

239 Ibid, para 188.

240 The *Case Concerning the Delimitation of the Continental Shelf (Libyan Arab Jamahiriya/Malta)* [1985] ICJ Rep 13 para 51 and *The Delimitation in the Area between Greenland and Jan Mayen (Denmark v Norway)* [1993] ICJ Rep 38, para 81.

241 *Guinea/Guinea-Bissau Arbitration* at para 104; and *Maritime Delimitation in the Black Sea (Romania v Ukraine)* (2009), ICJ Rep 61, paras 43–76.

8.8.4 Proportionality

The principle of proportionality used in maritime delimitation originated in the *North Sea Continental Shelf Cases*. In discussing the factors to be taken into account during negotiations between the parties, the ICJ described the final factor as being 'proportionality ... between the extent of the continental shelf areas appertaining to the coastal State and the length of its coast measured in the general direction of the coastline'.[242] It asserted that 'a reasonable degree of proportionality' was the intended result of any delimitation conducted according to equitable principles.[243]

Proportionality is considered inherent to an equitable maritime delimitation.[244] The concept does not, however, provide any independent source of rights to the maritime space being delimited.[245] Maritime delimitation is not effected by apportioning a disputed area between the States concerned in a manner that is proportional to the respective lengths of their coastlines.[246] It is instead simply a factor by which a court or tribunal determines whether the coastal configuration of the States or some other geographic factor has distorted the course of a boundary and rendered the delimitation inequitable.[247]

Although proportionality was described by the ICJ in the *North Sea Continental Shelf Cases* as one factor to be considered, its role has evolved. In *Tunisia v Libya*, the ICJ held that proportionality formed a third and final step to check the equity of a delimitation.[248] Accordingly the boundary resulting from a provisional delimitation is scrutinised for perceptible disproportionality resulting from geographical configuration or features.[249] A substantial disproportion in the relative lengths of the parties' coasts is regarded as a circumstance that justifies an adjustment of the maritime boundaries.[250]

The application of the principle does not require any mathematical formula. The cases have kept well away from 'a purely mathematical application of the relationship between coastal lengths'.[251] Indeed, the ICJ noted in the *Black Sea Case* that there were no clear requirements under international law as to how this final step was carried out.[252]

8.9 The high seas

Much of the initial development of the law of the sea occurred around the freedom of the high seas. That principle remains essential, but its content has evolved to accommodate the changing needs of the international community. The high seas and the activities engaged upon them are now regulated

---

242 *North Sea Continental Shelf Cases (Federal Republic of Germany/Netherlands; Federal Republic of Germany/Denmark)* [1969] ICJ Rep 3, para 98.

243 Ibid.

244 The *Case Concerning the Delimitation of the Continental Shelf between the United Kingdom of Great Britain and Northern Ireland and France (Great Britain v France)* 18 RIAA 3, para 98.

245 Ibid, para 101.

246 Ibid. See also *The Maritime Delimitation in the Black Sea (Romania v Ukraine)* [2009] ICJ Rep 61, para 167.

247 Ibid.

248 Ibid, paras 122, 210–216.

249 The *Case Concerning Delimitation of the Maritime Boundary in the Gulf of Maine Area (Canada/United States)* [1984] ICJ Rep 246, para 185; and the *Case Concerning Delimitation of the Continental Shelf (Libyan Arab Jamahiriya/Malta)* [1985] ICJ Rep 13, paras 74–75.

250 *Maritime Delimitation in the Black Sea (Romania v Ukraine)* [2009] ICJ Rep 61, para 167.

251 *In the Matter of an Arbitration between Barbados and Republic of Trinidad and Tobago*, para 238, available at www.pca-cpa.org (accessed 7 July 2014).

252 *The Maritime Delimitation in the Black Sea (Romania v Ukraine)* [2009] ICJ Rep 61, paras 212–213.

by a complex network of treaties pertaining to navigational and maritime safety, and the conservation and protection of the marine environment and its resources.[253]

The high seas is a zone of exclusion; it is defined by what it does not include. The GCHS, which codified customary international law, defined the high seas as all parts of the sea not included in the territorial sea or internal waters of a State.[254]

The LOSC deliberately omits any express definition. However, Article 86, the opening provision of Part VII (entitled 'High Seas'), declares that Part VII applies to all parts of the sea except for the EEZ, territorial sea and internal waters of a coastal state and the archipelagic waters of an archipelagic State. Thus, the high seas may be considered all parts of the oceans that do not fall within the internal waters, archipelagic waters, territorial sea, contiguous zone and EEZ of any State.

The legal concept of the high seas is not limited to the water column but extends to the superjacent air space and also to the seabed and subsoil, but only where the seabed and subsoil is not included in the continental shelf or extended continental shelf regime of a coastal State.

8.9.1 The freedom of the high seas

The freedom of the high seas means that no State can subject any part of the high seas to its sovereignty or prevent its access, use or exploitation by any other State. The Court in the *Mariana Flora*[255] stated:

> Upon the ocean, then in time of peace, all possess an entire equality. It is the common highway of all, appropriated to the use of all, and no one can vindicate himself a superior or exclusive prerogative there.

The high seas have thus been recognised as *res communis*, common to all mankind, and *res nullis*, incapable of ownership and, more recently, as the common heritage of mankind.

The principle of the freedom of the high seas is codified in both the GCHS and the LOSC. Freedom of the high seas means that not only can no State subject any part of the high seas to its sovereignty, but that all States, whether coastal or landlocked, have a right to sail their ships there.[256] Part X LOSC specifically provides landlocked States with a right of access to and from the sea. It specifies that they shall enjoy freedom of transit through transit States, although the terms and mode of the transit have to be agreed by bilateral, sub-regional or regional agreements.[257] It also guarantees equal treatment in maritime ports to these States.[258]

Article 87 LOSC lists some of the activities that may be enjoyed by all States on the high seas:

1 freedom of navigation;

2 freedom of fishing;

3 freedom to lay submarine cables and pipelines;

4 freedom of flight;

---

253 See, e.g. the 2005 Convention for the Suppression of Unlawful Acts against the Safety of Maritime Navigation and the 1992 Convention on Biological Diversity; the 1992 Convention on Biological Diversity and the 1974 International Convention for the Safety of Life at Sea.

254 Article 1 GCHS.

255 (1826) 24 US 1, 42.

256 Article 90 LOSC.

257 Article 125 LOSC.

258 Article 131 LOSC.

5 freedom to construct artificial islands and installations permitted under international law;

6 freedom of scientific research.

The list is not exhaustive. Notably absent is the freedom to conduct military activities. The LOSC provides that the high sea is reserved for 'peaceful purposes'.[259] It is generally agreed, however, that military exercises such as naval manoeuvres and conventional weapons testing are permitted.[260] Military activities that are contrary to the UN Charter are implicitly excluded by the LOSC.[261] It remains unclear whether the testing of nuclear weapons on the high seas is permitted (see Chapter 17.3.1.3).

All freedoms of the high seas must be exercised in accordance with the provisions of the LOSC and other rules of international law. In enjoying these freedoms, a State must act in good faith with 'due regard for the interests of other states in their exercise of the freedom of the high seas, and also with due regard for the rights under this Convention with respect to the activities in the Area'.[262]

8.9.2 Jurisdiction of the flag ship

The general rule is that vessels on the high seas are subject to the authority of the State whose flag they fly, but this is subject to exceptions (see Chapter 8.9.3). As with nationality of individuals, it is for the flag State to determine the criteria and procedure for granting and withdrawing nationality.[263] The flag State must issue to a ship flying its flag documents showing that it has been granted the right to do so.[264]

The flag State exercises legislative and enforcement jurisdiction over the internal affairs of the vessel. By permitting a vessel to fly its flag, it also undertakes certain responsibilities, which are set out in the LOSC. It must 'effectively exercise its jurisdiction and control in administrative, technical and social matters' by, *inter alia*, maintaining a register of ships containing the names and particulars of all ships flying its flag. The flag State also has an obligation to take measures to facilitate safety at sea. This requires it to take measures to ensure the seaworthiness of its ships.

8.9.2.1 *The requirement of a genuine link*

LOSC requires that there be a 'genuine link' between the ship and the State whose flag it flies.[265] The term 'genuine link' is borrowed from the *Nottebohm* case[266] (see Chapter 11.11.2.2). The requirement is not always observed. Many ships fly what are known as 'flags of convenience'. They are registered in States with which they have little to no material connection. This is because those States generally impose lower taxes and less stringent regulations.

The absence of a genuine link does not render a ship stateless nor does it entitle a State to refuse to recognise the nationality of a foreign ship. The reason for the requirement and the effect of its absence was explained in the *M/V Saiga (No 2) Case.*

---

259 Article 88 LOSC.

260 See: S.C. Truver, *The Law of the Sea and the Military Use of the Oceans in 2010* (1985) 45 Louisiana Law Review, 1221.

261 Article 301 LOSC.

262 Article 87(2) LOSC.

263 *M/V Saiga (No 2) (St Vincent and the Grenadines v Guinea)* (1998) 117 ILR 111, para 65; *Commission v Ireland* Case C-280/89 1992 ECR I-6185, para 24.

264 Article 91(2) LOSC.

265 Article 91(1) LOSC. See also Article 5(1) GCHS.

266 *(Liechtenstein v Guatemala)* (Second Phase) [1955] ICJ Rep 4.

M/V SAIGA (NO.2) (ST VINCENT AND THE GRENADINES *V* GUINEA)

Facts:

M/V Saiga was an oil tanker registered in St Vincent and the Grenadines. It was owned by a company registered in Cyprus, managed by a Scottish company and chartered to a company in Switzerland. Its master and crew were all Ukrainian other than three Senegalese employed as painters. The vessel was arrested and detained by Guinean authorities. St Vincent and the Grenadines instituted an action seeking, inter alia, *its release. Guinea challenged the jurisdiction of the ITLOS to hear the matter, arguing,* inter alia, *that no genuine link existed between the Saiga and St Vincent and the Grenadines and that St Vincent could not therefore bring the claim on the Saiga's behalf.*

Held:

The ITLOS asked itself whether (i) the absence of a genuine link entitled foreign vessels not to recognise the flag of another; (ii) there was a genuine link between St Vincent and the Grenadines and the Saiga.

Observing that the LOSC did require a flagship to have a genuine link to the State whose flag it flew, the ITLOS held, however, that the purpose of requiring a genuine link was 'to secure more effective implementation of the duties of the flag State, and not to establish criteria by reference to which the validity of the registration of ships in a flag State may be challenged'.[267] *It also found that Guinea had provided no evidence that a genuine link between the flagship and the flag State did not exist.*

8.9.2.2 Statelessness

A vessel that does not fly the flag of any State is stateless. A vessel must fly the flag of one State only and if it flies the flag of more than one State, it is treated as if it is a stateless vessel.[268] Any State may legally exercise jurisdiction over a stateless vessel or one treated as such.

MOLVAN *V* ATTORNEY GENERAL FOR PALESTINE (*THE ASYA*) (1948) 81 LLOYD'S LIST LR 277

Facts:

The Asya was sighted by a British warship. At that time she was flying no flag, but later hoisted the Turkish flag. The British ship asked her destination by signal but received no reply. A party was then sent to board the ship. On its arrival, the Turkish flag was replaced with a Zionist one. The boarding party brought the ship to Haifa where it was discovered

---

267 (1998) 117 ILR 111, para 83.
268 Article 92(2) LOSC.

that the ship had no papers or passenger list and its passengers had no passport or travel documents. Forfeiture of the vessel was ordered and the appellant, its owner, appealed against that order.

One of the arguments made by the appellant was that the seizure of the vessel breached international law.

Held:

The appeal was dismissed. Lord Simmonds stated at 369–370:

> For the freedom of the open sea, whatever those words may connote, is a freedom of ships which fly, and are entitled to fly, the flag of a State which is within the comity of nations. The Asya did not satisfy these elementary conditions. No question of comity nor of any breach of international law can arise if there is no State under whose flag the vessel sails. Their Lordships would accept as a valid statement of the law the following passage from Oppenheim's International Law (6th edn), vol. I., p. 546: 'In the interest of order on the open sea, a vessel not sailing under the maritime flag of a State enjoys no protection whatever, for the freedom of navigation on the open sea is freedom for such vessels only as sail under the flag of a State.' Having no usual ship's papers which would serve to identify her, flying the Turkish flag, to which there was no evidence she had a right, hauling it down on the arrival of a boarding party and later hoisting a flag which was not the flag of any State in being, the Asya could not claim the protection of any State nor could any State claim that any principle of international law was broken by her seizure.

8.9.2.3 Collisions and other incidents of navigation

Where a collision or incident of navigation occurs on the high seas, and involves the penal or disciplinary responsibility of a master or crew member, Article 97(1) LOSC provides that jurisdiction over the incident can only be exercised by the flag State, or the State of which the master or any other person in the service of the ship is a national.[269] Article 97(3) LOSC provides that no arrest or detention of the ship, even as a measure of investigation, shall be ordered by any authorities other than those of the flag State. (The PCIJ in the *SS Lotus Case* took the view that the State of the victim had the right to exercise criminal jurisdiction over the crew member although that crew member was a foreign national, see Chapter 9.2.)

8.9.3 Exceptions to flagship jurisdiction

In order to maintain peace and order on the high seas, a number of exceptions to the flagship jurisdiction were developed, most of them under customary international law. These include (i) the hot pursuit of a foreign vessel; (ii) the right to approach and visit; (iii) exceptions under treaties; and (iv) UNSC authorisation.

---

269   See also Article 11 GCHS.

8.9.3.1 Hot pursuit

Customary international law recognises the right of a coastal State to pursue onto the high seas a foreign vessel that has violated its laws while in one of its maritime zones. This right is known as the right of hot pursuit and was developed to facilitate the effective enforcement of a coastal State's laws and to prevent an offending vessel evading enforcement by hiding behind the freedoms enjoyed on the high seas.

The right has been set out in some detail in Article 23 GCHS and is repeated in Article 111 LOSC, both of which set out certain conditions that must be satisfied before a State can engage in hot pursuit. These are referred to and commented on below:

1 The term 'hot pursuit' suggests that the pursuit must begin immediately and might suggest that once commenced there must be no interruptions. However, the requirement of immediacy is not inflexible.

2 The right may only be exercised by warships or authorised government vessels or aircraft, which are clearly marked and visible.

3 The authorities of the coastal state must have good reason to believe that the foreign vessel is or has engaged in activity which is contrary to the laws and regulations properly enforced in those zones. Mere suspicion is not sufficient.[270]

4 The pursuit is only deemed to begin when the pursuing ship is satisfied that (i) the ship being pursued, or one of its boats; or (ii) other craft working as a team and using the ship pursued as a mother ship, is in the coastal State's territorial sea or one of its maritime zones.

5 Pursuit must begin in one of the maritime zones of the coastal State and may only continue on to the high seas when it has been uninterrupted. Under the LOSC, pursuit is not regarded as interrupted where it is continued by a vessel which replaces the vessel that initiated the pursuit.

6 Pursuit can only be commenced after a visual or auditory signal to stop has been given at a distance which enables it to be seen or heard by the foreign ship.

7 The right of hot pursuit ceases as soon as the vessel pursued enters the territorial waters of another State.

8 Following hot pursuit, the arrested vessel may be escorted across the high seas or an EEZ and back to the port of the coastal State.

In *M/V Saiga (No 2)*, the ITLOS concluded that the conditions set out in Article 111 LOSC are 'cumulative': each had to be satisfied.[271] The right to hot pursuit was considered by the English Court in *R v Mills and Others*.[272]

---

270   See: *M/V Saiga* (1999) 120 ILR 143, para 147.
271   Ibid, para 146.
272   See W.C. Gilmore, *Hot Pursuit: the Case of R v Mills and Others* (1995) 44/4 ICLQ, 954.

R *V* MILLS AND OTHERS (1995) (UNREPORTED)

Facts:

The MV Poseidon *was a vessel registered in St Vincent and the Grenadines. It was involved in an operation to smuggle cannabis to the UK. Under the surveillance of British authorities, the* Poseidon *transported cannabis from Morocco and transferred it to the* Delvan, *a British registered trawler, outside British territorial waters. The* Delvan *continued into British waters and was seized after landing in England.*

The Poseidon *continued on the high seas, shadowed by British vessels. Three days later, it was circled by helicopters that attempted to contact it by radio. The command to stop was also sent by radio. The* Poseidon *did not respond. It was boarded, the vessel was arrested and the crew charged with conspiracy to import cannabis.*

At their trial, the crew applied for a stay of prosecution on the ground that they had been arrested on the high seas contrary to international law. They argued, inter alia, *that no right to hot pursuit arose and that, even if it had, it had not been validly exercised as pursuit had not been commenced immediately, and no auditory or visual signal had been given before boarding.*

Held:

The application for a stay was dismissed.

The Court held that the right of hot pursuit was a rule of customary international law and that the British authorities had validly exercised this right, finding, in particular, that:

1 *The* Poseidon *had a constructive presence inside British waters because it had (i) worked as a team with the* Delvan *in carrying out the offence; and (ii) it had been the* Delvan's *'mother ship'. It was irrelevant that the operation between the ships may have been a one-off or that the daughter ship had not departed from the shore of the pursuing State, but from a third State.*

2 *The requirement for immediacy did not require pursuit to commence immediately. In this case, because of the need to ensure that an offence and 'the ambient conditions, sea state and light' the delay in commencing hot pursuit was justified and was not fatal to the exercise of the right.*

3 *Finally, as to the requirement of giving a valid visual or auditory signal before commencing pursuit, the Court found that radio communication was the standard method of communication and that a valid signal could therefore be transmitted over this medium.*

Comment:

Although the use of radio communication to give the required audio-visual signal to stop had not been originally contemplated, it is clear that it is now permitted in customary international law

During the pursuit of a vessel that has failed to stop despite being requested to do so, the use of force is permitted but only where it is necessary and proportionate.[273] It is only appropriate as a last resort.[274] Finally, a ship that has been stopped or arrested as a result of the unlawful exercise of the right of hot pursuit is entitled to compensation for any loss or damage sustained as a result.[275]

8.9.3.2 Right to approach and visit

Under international law, a warship, military aircraft, or other duly authorised government ship or aircraft (clearly marked and identifiable as being on government service) may approach a foreign ship that does not enjoy State immunity (see Chapter 10.3.2) in order to verify that ship's nationality. The right of approach and visit has been codified in Article 110 LOSC. Article 110(2) provides that where suspicion remains after checking the ship's documents, a further examination on board the ship may be carried out and if this occurs it must be done with all possible consideration.

The right to visit includes boarding and searching the vessel and taking appropriate measures such as seizure of the foreign vessel and punishment of persons on board. It was exercised in *Molvan v AG of Palestine* (above). It may only be carried out in very limited circumstances. According to Article 110 LOSC boarding a foreign ship is justified where there is reasonable ground for suspecting that:

(a) the ship is engaged in piracy, the slave trade or unauthorised broadcasting;

(b) the ship is either without nationality; or

(c) although flying the flag of a foreign ship or refusing to show its flag, the foreign ship has the same nationality as the visiting craft.

Aside from unauthorised broadcasting, which is not included in the GCHS, the circumstances listed above are reflective of customary international law.

A. Piracy

Acts of piracy have long been viewed as crimes over which any State may exercise universal jurisdiction (see Chapter 9.6.2.3). In his dissenting opinion in the *Lotus Case*, Judge Moore explained that on the high seas the pirate 'is denied the protection of the flag which he may carry, and is treated as an outlaw, as the enemy of all mankind – *hostis humani generis* – whom any nation may in the interest of all capture and punish'.[276]

Piracy refers to any illegal acts of violence or detention, or an act of depredation, committed for private ends by the crew and passengers of a private ship or aircraft against another ship or aircraft or against persons or property on board such ship or aircraft.[277] Acts of piracy also refer to the voluntary operation of a pirate ship or aircraft and extend to the incitement or intentional facilitation of acts of piracy. Additionally, the LOSC provides that when acts of piracy are committed by a warship, government ship or government aircraft such craft is to be treated in the same way as a private craft.[278]

---

273   See: *The Investigations of Certain Incidents Involving the British Trawler, Red Crusader Case*, (1962) 35 ILR 485, and *SS I'm Alone Case* (Canada, US) (1935) 3 RIAA 1609.

274   The *M/V Saiga Case (St Vincent and the Grenadines v Guinea)* (1998) 117 ILR 111, para 156.

275   Ibid. See also Article 111(8) LOSC.

276   The *Case of the SS Lotus (France v Turkey)* (1927) PCIJ Ser A/10 70 at para 249; See also *In re Piracy Jure Gentium* [1934] AC 586.

277   Article 15 GCHS and Article 101 LOSC.

278   Article 16 GCHS and Article 102 LOSC.

States are mandated to co-operate in the repression of piracy.[279] A warship may board a foreign ship where it has reasonable grounds for suspecting that the ship is involved in piracy.[280] Any State is entitled to seize pirate ships or aircraft, arrest persons on board and seize any assets.[281] Pirates may be tried by any State before whose courts they are brought, and the courts of that State may determine the appropriate penalties.[282]

Piracy was once considered obsolete. However, it has reemerged as a serious threat to vital shipping routes in the locality of the Horn of Africa, the Indian Ocean and elsewhere. Concerted global efforts have been made to resolve the problem. In particular, since the Somalian civil war in the 1990s, piracy off the Somali coast has become a threat to international peace and security. To tackle the problem, on 2 June 2008, the UNSC in Resolution 1816 (2008), noted the lack of capacity of the government of Somalia to fight the piracy and recommended that other States co-operate with the government of Somalia in the fight against piracy and robbery off the coast of Somalia. For that purpose other States are authorised to enter the territorial sea of Somalia. In August 2009, the 'Combined Task Force 151'established under UNSC Resolution 1816, a multinational coalition task force, took on the role of fighting Somali piracy by establishing a Maritime Security Patrol Area (MSPA) within the Gulf of Aden. It co-operates with NATO's anti-terrorism 'Operation Ocean Shield' and the EU's 'Atalanta Operation' carried out in the MSPA. In 2012 the EU decided to expand its Atalanta Operation to Somalia's beaches with a view to destroying pirates' facilities. This extension has raised some HRs and IHL concerns.[283]

According to the EU, in November 2014, no vessels were held by Somalia's pirates. However, 30 hostages were still in their hands. Since 2009, at least 154 pirates have been transferred to the competent authorities for prosecution. 128 of them were convicted.[284] Apprehended pirates are prosecuted in Kenya following an agreement between the UK, US and other States with the Kenyan government. The EU is not only combating piracy off the coast of Somalia, but is also dealing with its root causes. In this respect the EU has provided all sorts of development aid and humanitarian assistance to ensure that Somalia creates an environment for sustainable and equitable economic growth, while respecting HRs and the principle of democracy. This EU Atalanta Operation is expected to continue until the end of 2016.

B. Slavery

The first attempt at international level to protect human rights concerned the abolition of slavery which, at the end of the eighteenth century, was legal under national laws. England outlawed slavery in England in the *Somersett Case* in 1772,[285] prohibited the slave trade in the British Empire in 1807, and abolished slavery throughout the British Empire in 1833 when the Slavery Abolition Act came into force. In the nineteenth century, the UK established herself as a leading international advocate of the abolition of slavery and of slave trade. In the 1814 Treaty of Paris, France and the UK agreed to co-operate in the

---

279   Article 100 LOSC.
280   Article 22(1) GCHS and Article 110(1) LOSC.
281   Article 19 GCHS and Article 105 LOSC.
282   Ibid.
283   On this topic see: F. Wiesenbach, *Uncertainty on Somalia's Beaches — The Legal Regime of Onshore Anti-Piracy Operations* (2014) 19/1 Journal of Conflict and Security, 85.
284   See http://eunavfor.eu/key-facts-and-figures (accessed 15 November 2014).
285   M. Meltzer, *Slavery: A World History* New York: Da Capo, 1993 and J. Allain, *The Slavery Conventions: The Travaux Préparatoires of the 1926 League of Nations Convention and the 1956 United Nations Convention*, Amsterdam BV: Brill, 2008.

suppression of the traffic in slaves. In 1815 the major European States endorsed the prohibition of the slave trade at the Congress of Vienna.[286] The first multinational treaty prohibiting the slave trade and introducing measures for its suppression, both in Africa and on the high seas, was the Anti-Slavery Act adopted by the Brussels Conference of 1890 and ratified by 18 States, including the US, Turkey and Zanzibar. Under this treaty contracting States had the right to visit and search ships suspected of being involved in the slave trade, confiscate them and punish their master and crew. This right is reflected in the LOSC which requires every State to take 'effective measures to prevent and punish the transport of slaves in ships authorized to fly its flag, and to prevent the unlawful use of its flag for that purpose'.[287] A warship that reasonably suspects a foreign ship of engaging in the slave trade may visit that ship.[288] No further action, however, may be taken. Enforcement remains within the jurisdiction of the flag State.

C.   Unauthorised broadcasting

The LOSC requires States to cooperate in suppressing unauthorised broadcasting on the high seas.[289] A warship may visit a foreign ship reasonably suspected of doing so.[290] However, not all States have jurisdiction to intervene. Such jurisdiction is limited to the flag State of the ship, the State of registry of an installation if broadcasting activity is carried out from that installation, the State of which a person engaged in unauthorised broadcasting is a national, the State receiving the transmissions and any State whose radio communications may suffer interference.[291] In the context of Internet communications, this provision now has little practical relevance.

8.9.3.3   Treaties

The LOSC acknowledges that the exercise of jurisdiction over foreign ships may be expanded by treaty. Many bilateral and multilateral treaties have been concluded in recent years usually in order to suppress certain transnational crimes and to facilitate or ensure maritime security.[292]

The 1988 UN Convention Against Illicit Traffic in Narcotic Drugs and Psychotropic Substances[293] is aimed at facilitating co-operation between parties in an attempt to effectively respond to the illicit traffic in drugs. Article 17 provides that in order to repress illicit traffic by sea, a party which has reasonable grounds to suspect that a flagship of another party is engaged in illicit traffic may request authorisation to take 'appropriate measures' including boarding and searching the vessel, seizing the vessel and its cargo and arresting and charging persons on board. Such measures may also be taken 'in accordance with treaties in force between them or in accordance with any agreement or arrangement otherwise reached'.

---

286   H. Kern, *Strategies of Legal Change: Great Britain, International Law, and the Abolition of the Transatlantic Slave Trade* (2004) 6 Journal of History of International Law 233. See also Chapter 9.6.2.3).

287   Article 99, LOSC. See also Article 13 of the 1958 Geneva Convention on the High Seas.

288   Article 110(1) LOSC. See also Article 22(b) of the 1958 Geneva Convention on the High Seas.

289   Article 109 LOSC.

290   Article 110(1) LOSC.

291   Article 109(3) LOSC.

292   On this topic see: E. Papastavridis, *The Right of Visit on the High Seas in a Theoretical Perspective: Mare Liberum versus Mare Clausum Revisited* (2011) 24 LJIL, 45.

293   1582 UNTS 29. Entered into force 11 November 1990.

The 2000 Protocol Against the Smuggling of Migrants by Land, Sea and Air Supplementing the UN Convention Against Transnational Organized Crime[294] seeks, *inter alia*, to suppress the smuggling of migrants by sea. In this regard, Article 8 provides that, on the authorisation of the flagship, State parties may board and inspect ships on the high seas that are suspected of engaging in the smuggling of migrants.

As to maritime security, the Proliferation Security Initiative (PSI) is intended to provide a 'coordinated and effective basis through which to impede and stop shipments of [weapons of mass destruction], delivery systems, and related materials flowing to and from states and non-state actors of proliferation concern'.[295] The PSI calls upon participating States to take measures to prevent the shipment of WMD including 'under appropriate circumstances the boarding and searching of [their] own flag vessels by other states'.[296]

The interception of ships on the high seas under the PSI is carried out on the authority of bilateral agreements. To this end, the US has entered into agreements with Cyprus, Liberia, Panama, the Marshall Islands, the Bahamas and Antigua and Barbuda, being States that have some of the largest open ships registries and between them attract the registration of a substantial percentage of the ships sailing the seas.[297]

With regard to international terrorism the Rome Convention on the Suppression of Unlawful Acts against the Safety of Maritime Navigation 1988, covers all imaginable acts of maritime violence that could occur and seeks to protect not only individuals but also navigation.

8.9.3.4 UNSC authorisation

The authority to interfere with vessels on the high seas may be found in UNSC Resolutions which impose blockades or embargos on States. For example, by Resolution 1718 (2006) the UNSC imposed an embargo on the Democratic People's Republic of Korea (DPRK) under which all member States of the UN were allowed (i.e. no obligation was imposed on States) to stop and inspect any ship suspected of carrying any materials that could be used in the construction of WMD. In Resolution 1874 (2009) the UNSC sharpened its sanction in response to nuclear tests conducted by the DPRK. The UNSC authorised member States to inspect and destroy all banned cargo (including not only materials relating to the construction of WMDs but also armoured combat vehicles, large calibre artillery systems, attack helicopters, warships and missiles and spare parts). Member States were required to inspect, seize and dispose of the banned items and deny fuel or supply services for the vessels carrying them. Inspections were to be carried out on the high seas, at seaports and airports in a situation where a State had reasonable grounds to suspect a violation of the UN embargo. With regard to inspections of suspected vessels on the high seas the consent of the flag State was required. However, if the flag State did not consent to inspection on the high seas, that State was required to direct the suspected vessel to proceed to an appropriate and convenient port for the required inspection by the local authorities. A similar embargo and thus similar resolutions existed in relation to Iran[298] (see Chapter 17.3.1.3 A).

---

294   Doc A/55/383, 2241 UNTS 501. Entered into force 28 January 2004.
295   The White House, Office of the Press Secretary, Proliferation Security Initiative: Statement of Interdiction Principles, Fact Sheet (Sept 4 2003) available at www.state.gov/t/isn/c27726.htm (accessed 23 July 2014).
296   Ibid.
297   A. Syrigos 'Interdiction of Vessels on the High Seas' in A. Strati, M. Gavouneli and N. Skourtos (eds), *Unresolved Issues and New Challenges to the Law of the Sea, Time Before and Time After* Leiden: Martinus Nijhoff Publishers, 2006, 149–201.
298   See UN Security Council Resolutions 1747, 1803 (2007–8) and 1929 (2010).

8.9.4 Immunity

Under customary international law and the LOSC, (i) warships; and (ii) ships owned and operated by a State and used only for non-commercial government service enjoy immunity from jurisdiction of foreign States.[299] However, under Article 102(1) LOSC the immunity of warships, and non-commercial government vessels, is lost if those vessels engage in piracy or slavery.

8.10 The Area

The need to regulate mining on the deep seabed was one of the factors driving UNCLOS III. That regulation is provided through Part XI LOSC, entitled 'The Area'.

'The Area' is defined as 'the seabed and ocean floor and subsoil thereof, beyond the limits of natural jurisdiction'.[300] Part XI of the LOSC is concerned solely with the regulation of the Area and does not have any legal effect on the waters or the airspace above.[301] The legal regime of the high seas remains applicable and co-exists with that established in Part XI for the deep seabed.

Consistent with UNGA Resolutions adopted prior to UNCLOS III,[302] Part XI provides that the deep seabed and subsoil of the Area are part of the 'common heritage of mankind'.[303] This status has the following consequences:

1   The Area is to be used exclusively for peaceful purposes and in accordance with the principles embodied in the UN Charter and other rules of international law.[304]

2   No State can claim or exercise sovereignty or sovereign rights over it and no such claim shall be recognised.[305]

3   Rights to the Area are vested in mankind as a whole and it is on its behalf that the International Seabed Authority (ISA), established to regulate the exploitation of resources on the seabed, is to act.[306]

4   No State or any other person, whether physical or juridical, can appropriate or exploit the resources of the Area except in accordance with the regime established by Part XI.[307] Resources on the seabed are subject to alienation only in accordance with this regime.[308]

5   Activities in the area are to be carried out for the benefit of mankind and any financial or other economic benefit is to be equitably shared on a non-discriminatory basis.[309]

---

299   Articles 8 and 9 GCHS and Articles 95 and 96 LOSC.
300   Article 1 1 LOSC.
301   Article 135 LOSC.
302   See the Declaration of Principles Governing the Sea-Bed and the Ocean Floor, and the Subsoil Thereof, Beyond the Limits of National Jurisdiction, UNGA Resolution 2749 (XXV), UN Doc A/8028, 24 (1970) and Charter on the Economic Rights and Duties of States, UNGA Resolution 3281 (XXIX), UN Doc N 9631 (1974): Article 29.
303   Article136 LOSC.
304   Articles 138 and 141 LOSC.
305   Article 137 (1) LOSC.
306   Article 137(2) LOSC.
307   Article 137(3) LOSC.
308   Article 137(2) LOSC.
309   Article 140 LOSC.

6 In an effort to ensure equity, the ISA may show special consideration for the interests and needs of developing States by, *inter alia*, promoting the effective participation of developing States including those that are landlocked and geographically disadvantaged.[310]

Additionally, Part XI seeks to ensure that any activities in the Area are conducted in a manner that guarantees the 'effective protection' of the marine environment and human life and with due regard to the rights and legitimate interests of coastal States.[311]

Article 153 creates a legal framework for exploring and exploiting resources. It provides that any activities in the Area are to be organised, carried out and controlled by the ISA. An organ of the ISA, The Enterprise, is permitted to exploit and explore resources.[312] State parties, and State enterprises or natural or juridical persons which possess the nationality of State parties, or are effectively controlled by them or their nationals, when sponsored by such States, may also exploit the Area, but only in association with the ISA.

Part XI proved to be controversial, not in the declaration of the Area as the common heritage of mankind, but in the legal regime set out for its exploration and exploitation. Negotiations of its provisions at UNCOS III were described as 'tortuous', with the developing world advocating for a strong regulatory regime while the developed world urged flexibility.[313] It is probable that industrialised countries only agreed to the inclusion of Part XI after receiving concessions on other issues such as navigation and coastal rights.[314] As a result of the provisions of Part XI, a number of States refused to adopt the LOSC and most industrialised nations took no steps to ratify it. In an effort to facilitate universal participation, informal consultations were held 'on outstanding issues relating to Part XI and related provisions of the Convention'.[315] The consultations culminated in the adoption by the UNGA, on 28 July 1994, of the Agreement relating to the implementation of Part XI of the United Nations Convention on the Law of the Sea ('The Implementation Agreement').[316]

There is some dispute as to the extent to which Part XI is binding on non-parties. Certain developed States led by the US have argued that the freedom of the seas remains applicable to such States.[317] It is possible that the status of the Area as part of the common heritage of mankind has developed into a rule of customary international law precluding unilateral exploration and exploitation of Area resources, but whether it has done so appears uncertain. Should it have crystallised into custom, the US, which would have dissented during the formation of this rule, would have the status of a persistent objector.[318]

---

310   Articles 140 and 148 LOSC

311   See Article 142 and Articles. 145–146 LOSC.

312   Article 158(2) LOSC.

313   See: S. Nandan, 'Administering the Mineral Resources of the Deep Seabed' in D. Freestone, R. Barnes and D.M. Ong, *The Law of the Sea: Progress and Prospects*, Oxford: Oxford University Press, 2006, 75–93.

314   L. Sohn, M. Juras, J. Noyes and E. Franckx, *Law of the Sea in a Nutshell*, Eagan, MN: West Publishing, 1984, 339–340.

315   Preamble of the Agreement relating to the Implementation of Part XI of the United Nations Convention on the Law of the Sea of 10 December 1982.

316   UNGA Resolution on the Agreement Relating to the Implementation of Part XI of the United Nations Convention of the Law of the Sea of 10 December 1982, Resolution 48/263, UN Doc A/RES/48/263 (1994).

317   I. Brownlie, *Principles of International Law*, 7th edn, Oxford: Oxford University Press, 2008, 245–246.

318   Ibid.

8.10.1   The Implementation Agreement

The Implementation Agreement is to be interpreted and applied with the LOSC as if the two are a single instrument,[319] but in the event of any inconsistency between them, the Implementation Agreement prevails.[320] To achieve consistency with the LOSC, the Implementation Agreement provided for its provisional application from the entry into force of the LOSC until the Agreement itself entered into force.[321] The Agreement is not, however, binding on any State until that state accepts it in accordance with Article 4.

The Implementation Agreement consists of 10 articles and an Annex. It is clear from its articles (and Preamble) that the Agreement did not seek to alter the status of the Area as part of the common heritage of mankind or the legal consequences flowing from this designation, but it did seek to incorporate a market oriented approach into Part XI. It did so in a number of ways. These include:

- removing the competitive advantage of the Enterprise and requiring all its organs and subsidiary bodies to be cost-effective and commercially oriented;

- mandating that development of the Area's resources occur in a manner that conforms to sound commercial principles and GATT.[322]

- removing the limitation imposed by Article 151 LOSC on the production and export of minerals from the Area in order to protect developing economies.[323]

- removing the obligation imposed on contractors and their sponsoring States to transfer technology to the Enterprise or developing States although they are to facilitate the acquisition of the technology in a manner consistent with the IPRs.[324]

There is no doubt that without the Implementation Agreement the LOSC would not have obtained universal participation. Its adoption was possible with the changing dynamics facilitated by the end of the Cold War and the realisation that the feasibility of and expected profits from, deep sea mining proved to have been exaggerated. The effect of the Agreement, however, was to amend the LOSC, outside of the amendment procedures provided therein.

8.10.2   The achievements of the Authority

The Authority was established in 1994, although it took some further years for its principal organs to be set up.[325]

Since its establishment, the Authority has convened a number of scientific workshops and meetings of experts to enhance knowledge of the Area. It has also drafted exploration codes for the three primary minerals of interest: polymetallic nodules, polymetallic sulphides and cobalt-rich ferromanganese crusts and, as of 2013, began preparing mining codes for exploration. It has entered into exploration contracts with seven pioneer investors. Pioneer investors are States and national undertakings that expended over $30 million on seabed activities prior to the LOSC, and they are granted priority over other entities in

---

319   Article 2.
320   Ibid.
321   Article 7.
322   See Annex, section 6, 1.
323   See Annex, section 7.
324   See Annex, section 5.
325   See Jean-Pierre Levy, *International Seabed Authority: 20 Years*, Kingston: International Seabed Authority, 2014.

the allocation of contracts for exploitation of the Area.[326] However, exploitation of the resources on the seabed has not yet taken place and is not likely to commence in the immediate future.

8.11 Settlement of disputes under the 1982 UN Convention on the Law of the Sea (LOSC)

Part XV of the LOSC contains provisions relating to settlement of disputes.[327] The conflict between the wish of contracting parties to freely choose means of dispute resolution, and the need to impose on them some compulsory procedures to ensure the proper enforcement of the LOSC led to the establishment of a two-tier system by the LOSC. This system is described in Sections 1, 2 and 3 of Part XV. In accordance with Section 1, parties are required to settle disputes arising out of the interpretation or application of the LOSC by peaceful means of their own choice. If they fail, they must settle such disputes in accordance with compulsory procedures set out in Section 2 of Part XV. The procedures are *via*:

- the International Tribunal for the Law of the Sea (ITLOS);

- the ICJ (see Chapter 14.7);

- an arbitral tribunal under Annex VII of the LOSC; and

- a special arbitral tribunal under Annex VIII of the LOSC which has jurisdiction in respect of disputes relating to fisheries, the marine environment, scientific research and navigation.

Parties to the LOSC may choose in advance one or more of the above by making a written declaration to this effect and depositing it with the UNS-G. If a party has not made a declaration it is deemed to submit to arbitration in accordance with Annex VII. If the parties to a dispute do not accept the same procedures as each other the dispute must be submitted to arbitration in accordance with Annex VII, unless the parties otherwise agree. Irrespective of the procedures selected or imposed on the parties, the ITLOS has compulsory jurisdiction in respect of requests for the prompt release of vessels, and of crews, and requests for provisional measures unless the parties decide otherwise.

Compulsory procedures are subject to limitations imposed by Article 297(1) and 297(3)(a) LOSC. The limitations concern settlement of disputes relating to the exercise of discretionary powers by the coastal State over fishing and marine scientific research in its EEZ.

8.11.1 The ITLOS

The ITLOS was established on 18 October 1996 in Hamburg, Germany. It is an independent tribunal, not an organ of the UN although it closely co-operates with the UN. It is made up of 21 experts in the law of the sea elected by the contracting parties. Access to the ITLOS is not limited to contracting parties to the LOSC. Non-contracting parties, namely, States, international organisations, State enterprises and private entities may also seize the ITLOS. The last two mentioned have access to the ITLOS

---

326 Final Act of UNCLOS III, Annex I: Resolution II governing preparatory investment in pioneer activities relating to polymetallic nodules.

327 On this topic see: S. Yee, *En Route to the Final Shape of the UNCLOS Dispute Settlement System: Some Pivotal Negotiating Procedural Steps Worthy of Considering by Future Treaty-makers and Leaders in Treaty-making* (2014) 13/1 Chinese Journal of International Law, 185.

'in any case expressly provided for in Part XI or in any case submitted pursuant to any other agreement conferring jurisdiction on the Tribunal which is accepted by all the parties to that case'.[328] The ITLOS has jurisdiction in respect of all disputes under the LOSC and also in respect of cases arising out of other agreements that confer jurisdiction on the Tribunal. Disputes relating to activities in the International Seabed Area are submitted to the Seabed Disputes Chamber of the ITLOS, consisting of 11 judges.

To date 22 cases have been submitted to ITLOS and two requests have been made for advisory opinions.[329] Its judgments are final and binding on the parties to a dispute but the ITLOS has no means of enforcing them. Despite this, so far its decisions have been complied with.

8.11.2 The ICJ

See Chapter 14.7.

8.11.3 An arbitral tribunal constituted in accordance with Annex VII

This is a traditional arbitration tribunal made up of five members (see Chapter 14.5).

8.11.4 A special arbitral tribunal constituted in accordance with Annex VIII

An arbitral tribunal constituted in accordance with Annex VIII consists of five experts in the areas of: fisheries; protection and preservation of the maritime environment; marine scientific research and navigation, including pollution from vessels and by dumping. The jurisdiction of the arbitral tribunal is confined to the areas of expertise of its members. A special arbitral tribunal has competence to carry out an inquiry in accordance with the agreement by the parties to the dispute. Its findings are binding on the parties to a dispute. However, the parties may request a special arbitral tribunal to adopt non-binding recommendation for review by them.

RECOMMENDED READING

Books

Anand, R.P., *Origin and Development of the Law of the Sea*, The Hague: Martinus Nijhoff Publishers, 1983.

Churchill, R.R. and Lowe, A.V., *The Law of the Sea*, 3rd edn, Manchester: Manchester University Press, 1999.

Gerrard, M.B. and Wannier G.E. (eds), *Threatened Island Nations. Preserving the Maritime Entitlements of 'Disappearing' States*, Cambridge: Cambridge University Press, 2013.

Karim, M.S. 'Litigating Law of the Sea Disputes Using the UNCLOS Dispute Settlement System' in N. Klein (ed.), *Litigating International Law Disputes: Weighing the Balance*, Cambridge: Cambridge University Press, 2014, 260–83.

López Martin, A.G., *International Straits: Concept, Classification and Rules of Passage*, Dordrecht/London/New York: Springer, 2010.

Rothwell, D.R. and Stephens T.M., *The International Law of the Sea*, Oxford: Hart Publishing, 2010.

---

328   Article 20 of the Statute of the ITLOS.
329   For a review of cases decided by the ITLOS see: P. Gautier, *The International Tribunal for the Law of the Sea: Activities in 2012* (2013) 12/3 Chinese Journal of International Law, 613. See also the official website of the ITLOS at www.itlos.org

Sohn, L., Juras, K.G., Noyes, J. and Franckx, E., *Law of the Sea in a Nutshell*, 2nd edn, Eagan, MN: West Publishing, 1984.

Tanaka, Y., *Predictability and Flexibility in the Law of Maritime Delimitation*, Oregon: Hart Publishing, 2006.

Tanaka, Y., *The International Law of the Sea*, Cambridge: Cambridge University Press, 2012.

United Nations Division for Ocean Affairs and the Law of the Sea, *Definition of the Continental Shelf: An Examination of the Relevant Provisions of the United Nations Convention on the Law of the Sea*, New York: United Nations, 1993.

Articles

Dyck, A.J. and Sumaila, U.R. *Economic Impact of Ocean Fish Populations in the Global Fishery* (2010)12 J. Bioecon, 227.

Franckx, E., *American and Chinese Views on Navigational Rights of Warships* (2011) 10/1 Chinese Journal of International Law, 187.

Klug, A., *Strengthening the Protection of Migrants and Refugees in Distress at Sea through International Co-operation and Burden Sharing* (2014) 26/1 International Journal of Refugee Law, 48.

Kwiatkowska, B., *Submissions to the UN Commission on the Limits of the Continental Shelf: The Practice of Developing States in Cases of Disputed and Unresolved Maritime Boundary Delimitations or Other Land or Maritime Disputes: Part Two* (2013) 28 International Journal of Marine and Coastal Law, 563–614.

Molenarr, E.J., *Multilateral Hot Pursuit and Illegal Fishing in the Southern Ocean: The Pursuits of Viarsa I and South Tomi* (2004) 19 International Journal of Maritime and Coastal Law, 19.

Papastavridis, E., *The Right of Visit on the High Seas in a Theoretical Perspective: Mare Liberum versus Mare Clausum Revisited* (2011) 24 LJIL, 45.

Wiesenbach, F., *Uncertainty on Somalia's Beaches – The Legal Regime of Onshore Anti-Piracy Operations* (2014) 19/1 Journal of Conflict and Security, 85.

Yao, H., *Natural Prolongation and Delimitation of the Continental Shelf Beyond 200 nm: Implications of the Bangladesh/Myanmar Case* (2014) 4 Asian Journal of International Law, 281.

Zekos, G.I., *Constitutionality of Commercial/Maritime Arbitration* (2014) 45 Journal of Maritime Law and Commerce, 35.

Table 8.1 The different maritime zones recognised by the LOSC

Zone and definition	Sovereignty and jurisdiction of coastal State	Rights of other states in respect of zone
Internal waters All waters (ports, rivers, lakes, canals and sometimes also small bays) on the landward side of the baseline of a State's territorial waters other than archipelagic waters. In order to be considered the internal waters of a State, the waters must be closely linked to its land.	Constitutes part of the territory of the State over which it exercises full sovereignty. Foreign warships and ships operated by a State for non-commercial purposes are immune from jurisdiction of a coastal State. With regard to jurisdiction over commercial ships, State practice shows that, based on comity, a port State will not exercise jurisdiction over the internal affairs of a foreign vessel but it will exercise jurisdiction over any actions that may interfere with the peace and tranquility of its port.	There is no right of innocent passage in internal waters except where the use of the straight baseline method has the effect of enclosing as internal waters what had previously been classified as part of the territorial sea. However, under customary international law, States are obliged to permit entry (including to their ports) to ships in distress.
Territorial sea/waters A belt of sea adjacent to the land of a State the breadth of which must not extend beyond 12 nm from the baseline.	A coastal State has sovereignty over its territorial sea and the airspace, seabed and subsoil above and below it. A coastal State may exercise criminal jurisdiction in its territorial sea over foreign ships and its crew but the LOSC specifically provides this should only be exercised where (i) the consequences of the crime extend to the coastal State; (ii) the crime disturbs the peace of the country or the order of the territorial sea; (iii) assistance has been requested either by the captain of the ship or the flag country; and (iv) it is necessary for the suppression of illicit traffic in narcotic	All ships (but there is a disagreement whether warships, foreign nuclear powered ships and ships carrying inherently noxious substances) have the right of innocent passage. Submarines and other underwater vehicles are required to navigate on the surface and to show their flag. However, the right of innocent passage is subject to any laws and regulations adopted by the coastal State relating to, *inter alia*, the safety of navigation and regulation of maritime traffic, the conservation of maritime resources, and the preservation of the environment.

drugs in relation to criminal offences and breaches of the peace. However, it has no jurisdiction over foreign warships and ships operated by a foreign State for non-commercial purposes.

Archipelagic waters

An archipelago is defined as referring to a group of islands, interconnecting waters and other natural features which are so closely interrelated that such islands, waters and other natural features form an intrinsic geographical, economic and political entity or has been historically regarded as such.

The LOSC defines an archipelagic State as a State constituted of one or more archipelagos and may include other islands.

Archipelagic waters are waters enclosed by the baselines drawn between the outermost points of the outermost islands of the archipelagic State, subject to these points being sufficiently close to one another and the ratio between the enclosed water surface area and the land area being between 1 to 1, and 9 to 1.

Archipelagic waters, the airspace above and the seabed and subsoil and the resources contained therein form part of the territory of the archipelagic State and are subject to its territorial sovereignty.

All States enjoy the right of innocent passage through archipelagic waters although the archipelagic State may designate sea lanes for such passage. It may also designate air routes for aircraft.

The archipelagic State is required to respect the traditional fishing rights of third States and existing submarine cables.

Where the archipelagic waters lay between two parts of an immediately adjacent neighbouring State, the archipelagic State must also recognise rights and interests traditionally exercised in its waters by those States.

Zone and definition	Sovereignty and jurisdiction of coastal State	Rights of other States in respect of zone
Contiguous zone A zone contiguous to the territorial sea that extends up to 24 nm from the baseline of a coastal State.	In its contiguous zone, the coastal State has the power to prevent and punish any infringement of its customs, fiscal, immigration or sanitary laws and regulations occurring within its territory or territorial sea.	The contiguous zone forms part of the EEZ (where claimed) and therefore the rights that may be exercised by States in that zone, such as the freedom of navigation and overflight and freedom to lay submarine cables apply.
Exclusive Economic Zone (EEZ) The EEZ is an area beyond and adjacent to the territorial sea subject to the specific legal regime established in Part V of LOSC. It extends up to 200 nm from the baselines from which the territorial sea is measured.	Coastal States exercise sovereign rights over the exploration, exploitation, conservation and management of living and non-living resources. Only the coastal State may construct and operate artificial islands and installations in that area and conduct marine scientific research.	Subject to the rights of coastal States to explore, exploit, conserve and manage maritime resources, the freedom of the high seas may be enjoyed by all other States in the waters of the EEZ, most importantly the freedom of navigation and overflight and the freedom to lay submarine cables.
Continental shelf The continental shelf refers to the seabed and subsoil of the submarine areas adjacent to, but outside, the territorial sea of a coastal State. Every coastal State is entitled to claim the continental shelf within 200 nm from the baseline. In a situation where the outer edge of the continental margin (which includes the shelf, the slope and rise) extends beyond 200 nm, the coastal State may claim the legal title to the natural prolongation of its continental	The coastal States have the exclusive right to explore and exploit the natural resources of the continental shelf including both mineral and other non-living resources, and no other State may do so without its express consent. The coastal State's rights over the continental shelf do not alter the legal status of the waters or airspace above its continental shelf.	All States are entitled to lay submarine cables and pipelines on the shelf although the coastal State may delineate the course of such cables (Art. 79) All States are entitled to exercise the freedom of navigation and overflight in the waters and airspace above the continental shelf.

		All States enjoy the freedom of the high seas which includes the freedom of navigation, the freedom of overflight, the freedom to lay submarine cables and pipelines, the freedom to construct artificial islands and installations, the freedom to conduct scientific research and the freedom to fish.
shelf but in no event must the outer limits of the continental shelf exceed 350 nm from the baselines or 100 nm from the 2,500 metre isobath. If a State wishes to make such a claim it must make a submission to the Commission on the Limits of the Continental Shelf (CLCS) which gives final and binding recommendations on such claims.		
High seas All parts of the sea not included in the EEZ, the territorial sea or in the internal waters of a State or the archipelagic waters of an archipelagic State.	The high seas are open to all States and no State may validly purport to subject any part of the high seas to its sovereignty. Jurisdiction over vessels on the high seas is exercised by the flag State. However, to maintain peace and order on the high seas, a number of exceptions to the flagship jurisdiction have been developed, most of them under customary international law. These include (i) the hot pursuit of a foreign vessel; (ii) the right to approach and visit; (iii) exceptions under treaties; and (iv) UNSC authorisation. With regard to the right to visit, a warship, a military aircraft, or other duly authorised government ship or aircraft may approach a foreign ship that does not enjoy State immunity where there is reasonable ground for suspecting that the ship is engaged in piracy, slave trade, unauthorised broadcasting, is without nationality, i.e. stateless, or although it flies the flag of a foreign ship or refuses to show its flag, has the same nationality as the warship.	

9

JURISDICTION

CHAPTER OUTLINE

1 Introduction

The term jurisdiction has many meanings but in the present context it refers to the legal competence of a State to make, apply, and enforce rules with regard to persons, property and situations/events outside its territory, and to the limits of that competence. Three types of jurisdiction can be distinguished. The best description of each is contained in Restatement (Third) of the Foreign Relations Law of the United States of which the major aspects are set out in the following three points:

■ Jurisdiction to prescribe, 'i.e. to make its [a State's] law applicable to the activities, relations, or status of persons, or the interests of persons in things, whether by legislation, by executive act or order, by administrative rule or regulation, or by determination of a court' (s 401(a)).

■ Jurisdiction to adjudicate, under which a State has the authority 'to subject persons or things to the process of its courts or administrative tribunals, whether in civil or criminal proceedings, whether or not the state is a party to the proceedings' (s 401(b)).

■ Jurisdiction to enforce, under which a State is empowered to 'induce or compel compliance or to punish non compliance with its laws or regulations, whether through courts or by use of executive, administrative, police or other non- judicial action' (s 401(c)).

This chapter deals mainly with jurisdiction to prescribe. However, it is to be noted that jurisdiction to prescribed is closely connected with jurisdiction to adjudicate given that jurisdiction to adjudicate follows jurisdiction to prescribe.

It is open to debate whether international law allows a State to exercise extraterritorial jurisdiction in civil matters. With regard to criminal matters, the exercise of extraterritorial jurisdiction by States is uncontroversial, but it must fit within one of the five principles of jurisdiction set out in the 1935 Harvard Research Draft Convention on Jurisdiction with Respect to Crime. These five principles are: the territoriality principle; the nationality principle; the protective principle; the passive personality principle; and the universality principle.

2 The territoriality principle

Territorial jurisdiction is most commonly relied upon by States. It means that every State has jurisdiction over persons and events within its territory. In addition, a State is allowed to exercise subjective and objective territorial jurisdiction over acts that occur partly outside its territory. Under subjective territorial jurisdiction a State will have jurisdiction over conduct that commences within the State but is completed abroad. Objective territorial jurisdiction concerns conduct that commences outside the State and is completed within it.

3 The nationality principle

A State may exercise jurisdiction over:

■ its nationals when they commit offences abroad. It is universally accepted that nationals are required to comply with the domestic law of their State even when they are outside the territory of that State;

■ corporations when they are incorporated in that State (the common law countries approach) or have their seat there (the civil law countries approach), but based on the judgments of the ICJ in *Barcelona Traction*, not on the ground that the majority of shareholders are nationals of that State;

■ ships registered in accordance with that State's domestic law and sailing under its flag (ships sailing on the high seas under more than one flag are regarded as being without nationality);

■ aircraft registered with that State.

4 The protective principle

Under this principle a State may exercise jurisdiction over foreigners for acts committed outside its territory if such acts are directed against the security of the State or threaten its overriding interests or the integrity of its governmental functions.

5 The passive personality principle

Under this controversial principle a State may exercise jurisdiction over foreigners for acts committed outside its territory if a victim of the act is a national. In the US, the passive personality principle is not recognised for 'ordinary torts or crimes' but has been applied to crimes against diplomats (assassination and kidnapping), and has been accepted in respect of terrorist acts directed against a State's nationals by reason of their nationality, and in respect of international crimes such as torture and extrajudicial killings. In civil law countries, the principle of passive personality is applied not only in respect of international crimes but also in respect of serious common crimes (e.g. Article 113–7 of the French Civil Code). However, in some civil law countries, the principle *ne bis in idem*, known in common law as the principle of double jeopardy, i.e. no legal action can be instituted twice for the same cause of action, limits the application of this principle (e.g. s 7(1) of the German Penal Code).

6 The universality principle

This is based on the nature of the crime, not on any nexus between the forum State and the matter under consideration. Although the existence of the universality principle is well established in customary international law, the modality of its exercise is highly disputed.

The contentious issues are:

1 Must the accused be present within the *forum* State, at least at the beginning of a trial, or in other words, can the prosecuting State exercise jurisdiction *in absentia*?

2 Whether universal jurisdiction is a default jurisdiction in that it should only be exercised if the State on whose territory the crime has occurred and the State of the nationality of either the alleged perpetrator or the victims are unable or unwilling to exercise their jurisdiction?

3 What international crimes should be within the *ratione materiae* of universal jurisdiction?

No clear answer to any of the above is provided by international customary law.

7 Jurisdiction based on a treaty dealing with international crimes

This concerns a situation where a State, on the basis of a binding international treaty, exercises jurisdiction over international crimes. Treaties do not allow the exercise of jurisdiction *in absentia*, but contain an obligation to either prosecute, or extradite an alleged offender when he is found on the territory of a contracting State. This obligation is often referred to as the *aut dedare aut judicare*. Its meaning was elucidated by the ICJ in *Case Concerning Questions Relating to the Obligation to Extradite or Prosecute (Belgium v Senegal)* in respect of the 1984 UN Convention against Torture and Other Cruel, Inhuman and Degrading Treatment or Punishment (The CAT). It held that:

■ The CAT creates an obligation *erga omnes* which entails that all contracting parties to the CAT have a 'common interest' in ensuring compliance with its provisions. On this basis Belgium's claim was admissible.

■ Extradition and prosecution are not, to be given the same weight. Extradition is an option while prosecution is an international obligation. Accordingly, a State must prosecute; if it does not it can relieve itself from the obligation to prosecute by extraditing the person concerned. If it neither prosecutes nor extradites it commits a wrongful act for which it may incur international responsibility. However, this does not mean that a State has an obligation to extradite. Accordingly, in the absence of prosecution a State on whose territory a suspect is found is not required, and the State which seeks extradition is not entitled, to have the person concerned extradited.

It is to be noted that the judgment of the ICJ concerns only the CAT and, therefore in respect of other international treaties which require a contracting party to prosecute or extradite, whether there is a duty to extradite will depend on the wording of the relevant treaty.

8 Jurisdiction in competition matters: the US 'effects doctrine' and the EU 'implementation doctrine'

The 'effects doctrine', which derives from the principle of objective territoriality, was first developed in the US to deal with jurisdictional problems in competition law. Under the doctrine US courts have jurisdiction to apply US anti-trust law to conduct which:

■ occurred outside the US territory;

■ was intended to, and did in fact, harm competition in the US; and

■ had a direct, substantial and reasonably foreseeable adverse effect on US commerce or US export.

The EU endorsed the 'implementaiton doctrine' in the *Wood Pulp Cases*. This doctrine is similar, but not identical to the 'effects doctrine'.

9 Concurrent jurisdiction

Under international law more than one State may have jurisdiction over a person or event as well as a legitimate interest in dealing with that same person or event. In the absence of a centralised enforcer of international law, it is for each State to decide whether to exercise its jurisdiction as well as to assess the impact of any such exercise on international relations. The concepts of reasonableness and comity are often relied upon by the US courts in such circumstances. It is a matter of controversy whether the standard of reasonableness is recognised under international law, but principles such as the principle of non-intervention, the requirement of a genuine connection between the case and the forum State and the principles of equity and proportionality will impose limitations/restraints on the exercise of jurisdiction by a State. Further, the principle of *ne bis in idem* may help to resolve concurring jurisdiction claims.

10 Jurisdiction to enforce

International law prohibits a State from exercising sovereign functions in the territory of another State without that State's consent. The illegal seizure of foreign offenders in the territory of another State, although it violates international law, in some States, such as the US and Israel, does not prevent municipal courts from exercising criminal jurisdiction.

9.1 Introduction

The term jurisdiction has many meanings but in the context of public international law it refers to the legal competence of a State to make, apply, and enforce rules with regard to persons, property and situations/events outside its territory, and to the limits of that competence. Professor Mann described the term 'jurisdiction' as 'a State's right under international law to regulate conduct in matters not exclusively of domestic concern'.[1]

Described in the above terms, jurisdiction is fundamental to the concept of sovereignty. It concerns both the extent of sovereign powers and the scope or limitation of those powers at the international level. It is an aspect of State sovereignty which relates to the legislative, executive and judicial competence of a State.

Three types of jurisdiction can be distinguished. The best description of each is contained in the Restatement (Third) of the Foreign Relations Law of the United States of which the major aspects are set out in the following three points:

- Jurisdiction to prescribe, 'i.e. to make its [a State's] law applicable to the activities, relations, or status of persons, or the interests of persons in things, whether by legislation, by executive act or order, by administrative rule or regulation, or by determination of a court' (s 401(a)).

- Jurisdiction to adjudicate under which a State has authority 'to subject persons or things to the process of its courts or administrative tribunals, whether in civil or criminal proceedings, whether or not the State is a party to the proceedings' (s 401(b)).

- Jurisdiction to enforce under which a State is empowered to 'induce or compel compliance or to punish noncompliance with its laws or regulations, whether through courts or by use of executive, administrative, police or other non-judicial action' (s 401(c)).

The distinction between these three types of competence is of importance when determining the limit of a State's jurisdiction.

In international law the matter of whether a State is allowed to exercise its jurisdiction to prescribe, adjudicate and enforce outside its territory involves a fundamental dilemma. On the one hand, State sovereignty entails that a State cannot legislate, enforce and punish breaches of its law outside its territory. On the other, individuals and businesses in the age of globalisation are increasingly engaged in conduct which produces effects across State borders. The answer to this dilemma is that international law allows a State to exercise extraterritorial jurisdiction under well established rules.

With regard to criminal jurisdiction in 1935 the Harvard Law School conducted an extensive study on jurisdiction to prescribe in the light of, on the one hand, the increasing need for co-operation between States and, on the other hand, problems arising from conflicts between different States which wanted to exercise their jurisdiction to prosecute the same criminals as each other.[2] The Study resulted in the Draft Convention on Jurisdiction with Respect to Crime which has been accorded high standing in doctrine.[3] It identified five traditional bases upon which a State is allowed to regulate an individual's conduct occurring wholly or partially beyond its borders. They are:

- the territoriality principle;

- the nationality principle;

---

1   F.A. Mann, *The Doctrine of Jurisdiction in International Law* (1964-I) 111 RCADI, 9.
2   *The Research in International Law of the Harvard Law School, Jurisdiction with Respect to Crime* (1935) 29 AJIL (Special Supplement).
3   D. Harris, *Cases & Materials on International Law*, 6th edn, London: Sweet & Maxwell, 2004, 266.

■ the protective principle;

■ the passive personality principle;

■ the universality principle.

Of these, according to the Harvard Draft Convention, the principles most widely accepted were territoriality and nationality. The Harvard researchers also found evidence in State practice for the protective and universality principles. Although some evidence of passive personality was apparent, the researchers were of the opinion that this was insufficient to bring it within the ambit of customary law.

This chapter deals mainly with jurisdiction to prescribe, i.e. concerning the geographical reach of national laws. Jurisdiction to prescribe must fit within one of the five principles of jurisdiction set out in the 1935 Harvard Draft Convention. Obviously, a State may rely on more than one of these principles and usually does this when asserting jurisdiction in any particular case.

The governing principle with regard to jurisdiction to enforce is that one State cannot take measures on the territory of another State by way of enforcement of its national laws without the consent of that other State. For example, a person may commit an offence in England and then escape to Brazil. The English courts have jurisdiction to try him, but the English police cannot enter Brazilian territory and arrest him. If they did, this would be contrary to the well established rule of international law that one State may not commit acts of sovereignty on the territory of another State. So persons may not be arrested, police investigations may not be mounted and summonses may not be served on the territory of another State except with consent of that other State, or under the terms of a treaty. However, under customary law of the sea a State has the right of hot pursuit (see Chapter 8.9.3.1).

The existence of extraterritorial jurisdiction in civil matters is highly disputed although some commentators argue that similar jurisdiction to that in criminal matters exists in particular when enforcement of civil jurisdiction involves criminal sanctions.[4] Some States, in particular the US, using globalisation as a pretext, have extended the right to exercise jurisdiction outside the national territory to defend its economic interests and national security. With regard to economic matters the US now exercises jurisdiction over anti-trust cases under the 'effects doctrine' (see Chapter 9.8). Further, in respect of obtaining documents or evidence which is located abroad, but relevant to proceedings taking place in the US, the US courts (instead of relying on international co-operation based on the Hague Convention on Taking of Evidence Abroad in Civil and Commercial Matters), believing that international co-operation based on international treaties is insufficient to protect the rights of the plaintiff, order the defendant to produce evidence under threat of *subpoena*. Aggressive assertion of jurisdiction by the US to defend its national security is exemplified by its so-called secondary boycotts. These are effected by US legislation prohibiting foreign companies which operate outside the US, from doing business dealings with a State (or that State's companies or nationals) on which sanctions/embargos have been imposed to achieve the US' foreign policy objectives. In response the affected countries often enact so-called blocking legislation, e.g. the 1980 UK Protection of Trading Interests Act blocking any enforcement of US anti-trust law including discovery orders. Another example is that of the EU, which in Regulation 2271/96 Protecting against the Effects of the Extraterritorial Application of Legislation Adopted by a Third Country,[5] responded to the enactment by the US of the 1996 Helms-

---

4   Supra note 1, see also, the same author, *The Doctrine of Jurisdiction Revisited after Twenty Years* (1984-III) RCADI, 20–33 and 67–77.

5   (1997) 36 ILM 125.

Burton Act[6] imposing trade sanctions against Cuba. Under that Act any person, whatever his nationality, is prohibited from allegedly 'trafficking' in property expropriated by Cuba after the Cuban revolution previously belonging to Americans or Cubans who subsequently acquired US citizenship. It is outside the scope of this book to deal with the US's aggressive use of jurisdiction to achieve foreign policy objectives. However, bearing in mind that the EU, as well as the US, has been applying competition law to companies established outside their territorial jurisdiction, Chapter 9.8 deals with jurisdiction in anti-trust cases. As Professor Brownlie rightly noted, 'anti-trust legislation often involves a process which, though formally "civil", is in substance coercive and penal'.[7]

9.2 The territoriality principle

Each State enjoys full sovereign powers within its territory. In *The Christina Case* Lord Macmillan stated:

> It is an essential attribute of the sovereignty of this realm, as of all sovereign independent States, that it should possess jurisdiction over all persons and things within its territorial limits and in all cases, civil and criminal, arising within these limits.[8]

The principle of territoriality is universally recognised and raises no controversy. It is a manifestation of State sovereignty, and the most common basis of jurisdiction.

Under US law there is a presumption that US statutes only apply to acts performed within US territory unless the statute was expressly enacted to apply outside US territory[9] or Congress manifested a clear intent to the contrary.[10] For example, in *US v Bin Laden* [11] the defendants, who allegedly conspired in the bombing of two US embassies in East Africa in 1998, and were brought to stand trial in the US, argued that the US statute under which they were charged did not apply outside US territory. The statute prohibited the malicious destruction of property owned or possessed by the US but was silent on whether the property had to be situated in the US. The Court, on the authority of *US v Bowman*,[12] held that the intention of Congress was to apply the statute to property located abroad as well as in the US.

The essence of the territoriality principle is that every State has jurisdiction over crimes committed in its own territory. Normally, the application of the principle will be straightforward. An individual, present within a State, committing a crime in that State, will be subject to the enforcement jurisdiction of that State. In two circumstances, however, the application of the territorial principle will be more complicated – where an offence commenced within the territory of another State and is completed in the territory of the State concerned, and where the offence was commenced within the territory of the State concerned but only completed in the territory of another State.

---

6   See K.J. Kuilwijk, *Castro's Cuba and the US Helms-Burton Act. An Interpretation of the GATT Security Exception* (1997) 31 JWT, 49.

7   I. Brownlie, *Principles of International Law*, 7th edn, Oxford; Oxford University Press, 2008, 302.

8   (1938) AC 485, 496–497.

9   E.g. murder of US nationals in a foreign country (18 USC § 1119(2006)); foreign terrorist activities (18 USC § 2332b(e) (2006)). See also *EEOC v Arabian Am. Oil Co.*, 499 US 244, 248, 113 L Ed 2d 274, 111 S Ct 1227 (1991).

10   *Foley Bros. v Filardo*, 336 US 281, 285 (1949).

11   92 F Supp 2nd 189 (SDNY 2000).

12   260 US 94, 98 (1922).

The 1935 Harvard Draft Convention approached the above problem by providing that a State would have territorial jurisdiction in respect of acts which occur in whole or in part within the territory of that State. 'In part' was defined as an essential constituent element of the act in question. Thus, whether the act commenced in the territory (subjective jurisdiction) or was completed in the territory (objective jurisdiction) the State concerned would be able to exercise its authority.

The leading case on the territoriality principle is the *SS Lotus Case (France v Turkey)*.[13]

SS LOTUS CASE (FRANCE *V* TURKEY)

Facts:

The SS Lotus *was a French ship that collided on the high seas with a Turkish collier, the* Boz-Kourt, *which sank with loss of life. When the* SS Lotus *reached Constantinople (now Istanbul), the French officer of the watch at the time of the collision was arrested, tried before a Turkish court and convicted of involuntary manslaughter. France protested about the legality of the Turkish action, and the Permanent Court of International Justice (PCIJ) was asked to decide whether Turkey had acted in conflict with international law by instituting proceedings and thereby exercising criminal jurisdiction.*

Held:

The following three aspects of the PCIJ's judgment are of importance:

- *The Court distinguished between jurisdiction to prescribe and jurisdiction to enforce. While in the absence of a permissive rule of international law States are precluded from enforcing their law outside the national territory (jurisdiction to enforce), they are free to make rules in respect of persons, property and situations outside their territory in the absence of a prohibitive rule (jurisdiction to prescribe).*

- *With regard to jurisdiction to prescribe the Court adopted the approach under which any assertion of jurisdiction is lawful unless there is a specific prohibitive rule. This approach is contrary to that of customary law under which jurisdiction to prescribe is prohibited unless there is a permissive rule, e.g. the principle of territoriality, nationality, etc. This aspect of the judgment has been and is, by some, considered as obsolete.[14] Notwithstanding this, States still rely upon it.[15] Although the application of either approach may lead to the same result, the burden of proof under* Lotus *is on a State which asserts jurisdiction, and under customary law on the State which opposes another State's jurisdiction.[16]*

- *By the casting vote of the President, the Court decided that Turkey had not acted in conflict with the principles of international law. The Court rejected the contention made by the French government that international law recognised the exclusive jurisdiction of the flag State over events occurring on board a ship on the high seas. In this respect*

---

13   (1927) PCIJ Rep Ser A No 10.

14   C.A. Bradley, *Universal Jurisdiction and US Law* (2001) University of Chicago Legal Forum, 323.

15   E.g. the Belgian government in the *Case Concerning Arrest Warrant of 11 April 2000 (Democratic Republic of Congo v Belgium)* (hereafter referred to as the *Arrest Warrant Case*) [2002] ICJ Rep 3, paras 48–51.

16   See C. Ryngaert, *Jurisdiction in International Law*, Oxford: Oxford University Press, 2008, 21–31.

the PCIJ held that '. . . the offence produced its effects on the Turkish vessel and consequently in a place assimilated to Turkish territory in which the application of Turkish criminal law cannot be challenged, even in regard to offences committed there by foreigners'. The majority of the Court, therefore, by assimilating the Turkish vessel to Turkish territory, brought the case under the principle of objective territorial jurisdiction.[17]

9.3 The nationality principle

The competence of a State to prosecute and punish its nationals on the sole basis of their nationality is based upon the allegiance which the person charged with a crime owes to the State of which that person is a national. It is now universally accepted that a State may prosecute its nationals for crimes committed anywhere in the world. In *Joyce v Director of Public Prosecutions*[18] the House of Lords considerably extended the application of this principle.

JOYCE *V* DIRECTOR OF PUBLIC PROSECUTIONS

Facts:

The accused, William Joyce, was charged with treason under the Treason Act 1951 for having made propaganda broadcasts to the UK from Germany during WWII. Joyce was a US citizen born in the US of Irish parents but he had spent most of his adult life in England. It was contended that because the accused was a US citizen he did not owe allegiance to the Crown and could not, therefore, be guilty of treason.

Held:

The House of Lords accepted that allegiance was necessary and found that the accused, who also held a British passport, still in force at the time of his broadcasts, was entitled to protection by the Crown and, therefore, owed the Crown allegiance. The fact that the passport had been obtained by fraud was immaterial. Additionally, the House of Lords relied on the protective principle and found that a proper regard for the security of the UK required that an alien who committed treason whether abroad or within the realm should be amenable to British laws.

---

17   This part of the PCIJ's judgment has not been confirmed by practice. International Conventions such as the 1952 Brussels Convention for the Unification of Certain Rules Relating to Penal Jurisdiction in Matters of Collision or Other Incidents of Navigation (439 UNTS 233, Articles 1 and 3) and the 1958 Geneva Convention on the High Seas (450 UNTS 82, Article 11), provide for the exclusive jurisdiction of the flag State or of the State of nationality of the offender. That approach is also followed by the 1982 United Nations Convention on the Law of the Sea (see Chapter 8.9.2) UNTS 3, Article 97).

18   [1946] AC 347.

In the UK, Parliament enacted legislation under which UK citizens and habitual residents may, in respect of certain acts, be criminally liable regardless of where the relevant conduct occurred. Examples are terrorism, murder, bigamy, offences against children, bribery, money laundering, fraud, soccer hooliganism and breaches of the Official Secrets Acts.

It is, however, recognised that the application of the nationality principle may create parallel jurisdiction, i.e. jurisdiction by more than one State, and possible double jeopardy in cases of dual nationality, and where territorial and national jurisdictions overlap. Many States, therefore, place limitations on the nationality principle. For instance, UK courts may only claim jurisdiction in the case of serious offences as mentioned above. The UK does not, however, challenge the application of the principle by other States in less serious criminal cases.

The issue of nationality of corporations is dealt with in Chapter 11.11.3 while that of ships and aircraft in Chapter 8.9.2.1.

9.4. The protective principle

Almost all States assume jurisdiction to punish acts prejudicial to national security or other vital interests of a State, even when they are committed by aliens abroad. Such acts, not necessarily confined to political matters, include spying, plots to overthrow the government, forging currency, immigration and economic offences.

The protective principle was accepted by the courts as providing alternative bases for jurisdiction in both the *Joyce* case and the *Eichmann* case[19] (for facts see Chapter 9.6.1.1). In the latter case, the Court assimilated the State of Israel – which did not exist at the time of the offences – to the Jewish people, holding that the protective principle permitted the Israeli Court to exercise jurisdiction in respect of crimes against the Jewish people.

Although most States use the protective principle to some extent, thereby confirming its legitimacy, there is nevertheless always the danger that some States may abuse the principle by giving a very broad interpretation to the concept of protection.

The growth in international terrorism and drug smuggling has made the courts of Western democratic countries less hostile to the reception of the protective principle of jurisdiction. Even the courts of the common law countries, which traditionally rejected the protective principle, have been compelled to have a change of heart.

The above change of policy was most evident in the Judicial Committee of the Privy Council's decision in *Liangsiriprasert (Somchai) v United States Government*.[20]

LIANGSIRIPRASERT (SOMCHAI) *V* UNITED STATES GOVERNMENT

Facts:

This case involved the extradition of a Thai national from Hong Kong to the US on charges of drug smuggling. However, the defendant had been lured into Hong Kong territory by an American agent posing as a fellow smuggler, and the defendant had committed no offence

---

19   *Attorney-General of the Government of Israel v Eichmann* (1961) 36 ILR 5.
20   [1991] 1 AC 225, 251.

under Hong Kong law. The charges used as grounds for extradition related to offences outside Hong Kong's territory and in fact the only connection of the defendant with the territory was his physical presence.

Held:

The Privy Council rejected the contention that the courts could not exercise jurisdiction to extradite the defendant to the US. The Court continued to reject the notion that the protective principle could not be relied upon by pointing out that:

> *Unfortunately in this century crime has ceased to be largely local in origin and effect. Crime is now established on an international scale and the common law must face this new reality. Their Lordships can find nothing in precedent, comity or good sense that should inhibit the common law from regarding as justiciable in England inchoate crimes committed abroad which are intended to result in the commission of criminal offences in England . . .*

Comment:

The Court, however, qualified its decision by deciding that the charge in question could be construed as involving illicit trade in drugs which could be considered to amount to a potential conspiracy to traffic drugs in Hong Kong. Despite this qualification, the decision signalled a definite change of policy on the part of the British courts towards the acceptance of the protective principle.

The US courts have relied on the protective principle in immigration cases,[21] in espionage cases,[22] in cases concerning illegal drug smuggling and with the rise of terrorism, have used it to justify the application of US criminal law to terrorist offences.[23] The protective principle has also been relied upon by the US in the situation of the so-called secondary boycotts, i.e. US legislation prohibiting foreign companies operating outside the US from any business dealings with a State (or that State's companies or nationals) on which sanctions/embargos have been imposed with a view to achieving US foreign policy objectives (see Chapter 9.1).

Cameron identifies two main problems relating to the application of the protective principle. First, it may be easily abused by States in that, for example, political offences such as 'speech crime' and other vague offences against economic interests may justify imposition of criminal/administrative penalties on individuals or companies, and second, it may be 'hard' on individuals in that an individual may be convicted for acts which had not been regarded as criminal offences in a State where they were committed and, additionally, that individual may be convicted twice for the same offence because 'the application of the principle of *ne bis in idem* is often excluded by States as far as offences covered by the protective principle are concerned'.[24]

---

21 *Rocha v US* (288 F 2d 545 9th Cir 1961) and *US v Pizzarusso* (388 F 2d 8 2nd Cir 1968).

22 *US v Zehe* (601 F Supp 196 D Mass 1985).

23 *US v Yousef* (327 F 3d 56 2nd Cir 2003); *US v Yunis* (924 F 2d 1086 DC Cir 1991) and *US v Bin Laden*, supra note 12.

24 I. Cameron, 'International Criminal Jurisdiction, Protective Principle' *Max Planck Encyclopedia of Public International Law*, available at www.mpepil.com>, para 21 (accessed 10 August 2012).

The fact that a person has been tried or punished by a foreign court cannot impair a sovereign State's right to punish that person. It is for a State to determine which offences it wants to punish, but normally it would exercise its right to punish in respect of offences which affect the very fabric of society of that State. Nevertheless, many States have endorsed the principle of *ne bis in idem* (i.e. 'not twice for the same', meaning that no legal action can be instituted twice for the same cause of action) and *ne bis poena in idem* ('not double punishment for the same', meaning that an offender should not be punished twice for the same offence) by becoming parties to international treaties and other international instruments incorporating these principles.

The principle of *ne bis in idem* constitutes an important safeguard for an individual as it protects him from unacceptable repetition of the exercise of the right of a State to punish. The principle *ne bis in idem* is enshrined in Article 19 of the Arab Charter on Human Rights,[25] which entered into force in 2008 and, at the time of writing, is in force in 13 Arab States. It constitutes an accepted ground for refusal to surrender a person in many extradition treaties. In particular, in the European context, the principle is contained in Article 9 of the European Convention on Extradition,[26] which is in force in all 47 member States of the Council of Europe (see Chapter 12.7.1) and in its First Additional Protocol[27] which bars extradition in respect of political offences.

So far as the EU is concerned, Article 5 of the Charter of Fundamental Rights of the European Union[28] embraces the principle *ne bis in idem*. EU conventions and secondary legislation further implement the principle, e.g. Articles 3 and 4 of the Framework Decision on the European Arrest Warrant.[29] In Joined Cases C-187/01 and C-385/01 *Hüseyin Gözütok and Klaus Brügge*[30] the ECJ interpreted the scope of application of the principle *ne bis in idem* generously. It held that under the 1990 Convention implementing the Schengen Agreement of 14 June 1985 on the Gradual Abolition of Checks at Common Borders, the principle applies to a situation where criminal proceedings have been discontinued in a member State as a result of a settlement of the case between the accused and the relevant public prosecutor's office.

It is important to note that international treaties contain exceptions to the principle *ne bis in idem* to ensure that a contracting State retains its right to punish if either a foreign trial turns out to have been a sham, or any penalty, if a person has been convicted, is not enforced or will not be enforced. For example, Article 10 of the Statute of the International Criminal Tribunal for the Former Yugoslavia (ICTY) prohibits national courts from trying a person already tried by the ICTY but not *vice versa*. The ICTY is competent to try a person, despite the fact that the person has already been tried by a national court, in the following circumstances:

- if the act for which the offender was tried was characterised as an ordinary crime under national law;

- if national proceedings were not impartial or independent;

- if national proceedings were designed to shield the accused from international criminal responsibility;

- if the case was not diligently prosecuted.

---

25   12 IHRR 893.
26   CETS No 24.
27   30 CETS No.
28   [2000] OJ C 364/1.
29   [2002] OJ L 190/1.
30   [2003] ECR I-1345.

It can be said that the principle *ne bis in idem* only works when there is mutual trust between States in their criminal justice systems, and that in Europe in general, and within the EU in particular, the principle is respected and ensures that, on the one hand, the human rights of persons concerned are adequately protected and, on the other, the problem of competing jurisdiction is reduced.[31]

9.5 The passive personality principle

According to the passive personality principle a State has jurisdiction to punish aliens for harmful acts committed abroad against its nationals. This has been described as the most difficult principle to justify in theory and, while many civil law countries claim jurisdiction on this ground, others, such as the UK and the US, tend to regard it as contrary to international law so far as ordinary torts and crimes are concerned, but not in respect of terrorist killings and the taking of hostages, etc. (see below).

Although the passive personality principle was in evidence in State practice at the time, it was not indicated as one of the accepted bases of jurisdiction in the 1935 Draft Harvard Convention because of opposition from the common law countries. In the *SS Lotus Case*, for example, although the PCIJ ultimately did not have to decide on jurisdiction under the passive personality principle because they had already accepted the principle of territoriality, all of the dissenting judges expressly rejected the application of the passive personality principle.

Reliance on the passive personality principle has been firmly accepted in the US in the context of combating international terrorism. The US Congress has enacted statutes making it a criminal offence, *inter alia*, to attack US diplomats abroad,[32] to kidnap a protected US government employee abroad,[33] to take a US national hostage abroad,[34] and to kill a US national abroad by a terrorist act.[35] The US Congress also created a civil cause of action for US nationals, as well as foreigners, who are victims of torture and/or extrajudicial killings allowing them to recover 'treble damages' under the Torture Victim Protection Act of 1991 (TVPA). Under TVPA[36] a victim or his legal representatives, or his beneficiaries in the case of extrajudicial killing, can bring a civil action in US courts for recovery of damages from a natural person (but not a corporation or a political group[37]) who, acting in an official capacity for any foreign government, has committed an act of torture and/or extrajudicial killing. The defendant must have acted 'under actual or apparent authority, or colour of law'. The claimant must first exhaust adequate and available domestic remedies in the place where the conduct giving rise to the claim occurred. The TVPA was enacted to give US nationals the same remedy as that enjoyed by foreign nationals under the Alien Tort Claims Act (ATCA) (see Chapter 4.5.2.1). It is important to note that under the TVPA only individuals who reside or are temporarily on the territory of the US can be sued and that the TVPA does not override the US Foreign Sovereign Immunity Act and thus foreign heads of State or other persons enjoying diplomatic or consular immunity cannot be sued under its provisions.

---

31   See G. Conway, *Ne Bis in Idem in International Law* (2003) 3/3 International criminal Law Review, 217.
32   18 USC § 1116 (c) (2006).
33   18 USC § §1201(a) (4), 1201(e) (2006).
34   18 USC § 1203 (2006).
35   18 USC § 2332 (2006).
36   18 USC §2333 (2006).
37   *Mohamad v Palestinian Authority* 566 US, 132 S Ct 1702 (2012).

US courts have, however, refused to apply the passive personality principle to ordinary crimes and torts which take place abroad. This was confirmed in *US v Columba-Colella*[38] in which the Fifth Circuit Court of Appeal dismissed charges against the defendant, who allegedly 'fenced' a car stolen in the US and then taken to Mexico. The defendant was arrested in Mexico and brought to stand trial in the US. The case was dismissed on the ground that the US courts had no jurisdiction over such acts.

9.6 The universality principle

Under this principle a State may exercise jurisdiction in respect of persons accused of international crimes committed anywhere in the world and irrespective of the nationality of the accused and of the victim. A 2005 Resolution of the Institut de Droit International (the Institute of International Law (IDI)) states in point 1 that universal jurisdiction in criminal matters means 'the competence of a State to prosecute alleged offenders and to punish them if convicted, irrespective of the place of commission of the crime and regardless of any link of active or passive nationality, or other grounds of jurisdiction recognised by international law'.[39] A very similar definition was set out in the AU-EU Expert Report on the Principle of Universal Jurisdiction.[40] It states that 'Universal criminal jurisdiction is the assertion by one State of its jurisdiction over crimes allegedly committed in the territory of another state by nationals of another state against nationals of another state where the crime alleged poses no direct threat to the vital interest of the state asserting jurisdiction.'[41]

The legal justification for the existence of the principle of universal jurisdiction is that some crimes are so universally repugnant that their perpetrators are considered as *hostis humani generis*, i.e. enemies of all mankind. The prosecuting State acts, therefore, on behalf of all States. The practical justifications are that first, international crimes are normally committed by a State and their perpetrators are therefore unlikely to be prosecuted by that State, and second, that some States are unable to prosecute for lack of institutional, financial and human resources.

This section, examines first, the most controversial cases of the application of the principle of universality by national courts, and second, controversies surrounding modality of the exercise of universal jurisdiction by national courts.

9.6.1 The audacious application of the principle of universality by national courts

The most famous and probably the first case of the application of the principle of universality by a national court is the case of *Eichmann*.[42]

---

38   604 F 2d 356 (5th Cir 1979).

39   Available at www.idi-iil.org/idiF/navig_res_them.html (accessed 22 April 2014).

40   The AU EU Expert Report on the Principle of Universal Jurisdiction, 8772/1/09 Rev. 1.

41   Ibid, para 8.

42   For in-depth examination of the *Eichmann Case* see: G.J. Bass, 'The Adolf Eichmann Case: Universal and National Jurisdiction' in S Macedo (ed.), *Universal Jurisdiction: National Courts and the Prosecution of Serious Crimes Under International Law*, Philadelphia, PA: University of Pennsylvania Press, 2004, 77 and L. Bilsky, 'The Eichmann Trial and the Legacy of Jurisdiction' in S. Benhabib, R.T. Tsao and P. Verovšek (eds), *Politics in Dark Times: Encounters with Hannah Arendt*, Cambridge: Cambridge University Press, 2010, 198.

9.6.1.1 The Eichmann Case

ATTORNEY-GENERAL OF THE GOVERNMENT OF ISRAEL *V* EICHMANN

Facts:

In 1960, Adolf Eichmann was illegally abducted from Argentina by members of the Israeli secret service, by order of the then Prime Minister of Israel, David Ben-Gurion, to stand trial in Israel. He was charged under Israel's Nazi and Nazi Collaborators (Punishment) Law 1950 with 15 counts of war crimes and crimes against humanity. Under the Nazi regime Eichmann, by his own admission, was in charge of 'cleansing' or forcing the emigration of 150,000 Jews from Austria. From 1942 he was one of the main persons responsible for Hitler's 'final solution', i.e. the systematic execution of some 6 million Jews. After the war he escaped to Argentina and lived there with his family for 10 years before being abducted.

Eichmann challenged the jurisdiction of the Israeli Court on the grounds that: first, he was illegally abducted and thus Israel had no right to hold him; second, he was charged with crimes that did not exist at the time when he was alleged to have committed them, i.e. crimes against humanity; and third, he stood trial in a country that did not exist at the time of the commission of the alleged crimes.

Held:

All arguments submitted by Eichmann were rejected. The Israeli District Court stated that the crimes committed by Eichmann were international crimes in nature and therefore it applied the universality principle of jurisdiction.

The Court stated that:

> *The crimes defined in this [Israeli] law must be deemed to have always been international crimes, entailing individual criminal responsibility: customary international law is analogous to the common law and develops by analogy and by reference to general principles of law recognised by civilised nations, these crimes share the characteristics of crimes . . . which damage vital international interests, impair the foundations and security of the international community, violate universal moral values and humanitarian principles . . . and the principle of universal jurisdiction over 'crimes against humanity' . . . similarly derives from a common vital interest in their suppression. The state prosecuting them acts as agent of the international community, administering international law.[43]*

Eichmann was found guilty by the Israeli courts and was executed on 31 May 1962.

Comment:

In the Eichmann Case, *the District Court relied mainly on the principle of universality. This was explained by the Israeli Supreme Court on appeal, as follows:*

> if in our judgment we have concentrated on the international and universal character of the crimes . . . one of the reason for so doing is that some of them were directed against non-Jewish groups.[44]

Israel also relied on the protective and passive personality principles.

---

43 *Attorney-General of the Government of Israel v Eichmann* (1961) 36 ILR 5, 15 (District Court of Jerusalem).
44 (1968) 36 ILR 277, para 12 (SC).

The principle of universality was not subject to any special controversy until Belgium and Spain enacted far reaching legislation based on the principle of universality, vigorously applied by their judiciary.

9.6.1.2   Belgian Law of 1993 and of 1999 amended in 2003

The Belgian law of 1993 and of 1999 (now amended) gave Belgian courts jurisdiction over war crimes, genocide and crimes against humanity. The '*Butare Four*' *Case*, was the first one concluded under that Belgian law.[45]

THE 'BUTARE FOUR' CASE

Facts:

Four accused, two Rwandan nuns, i.e. Sister Gertrude and Sister Maria Kisito, and two ethnic Hutu militants, Alphonse Higaniroa, a businessman and former Rwandan transport minister, and Vincent Ntezimana, a university professor at Butare, were brought before the Belgian Court. The Catholic nuns were accused of aiding the massacre of 6,000 Tutsis in April and May 1994 in Butare. Sister Gertrude was a mother superior at a convent in the town of Sovu. She collaborated with a local militia leader to kill Tutsis who sought sanctuary in the convent. Both nuns were accused of forcing Tutsis to leave the convent when armed Hutu militia were gathering outside the convent waiting to massacre them. Sister Maria Kisito was accused of providing jerry cans filled with petrol to local Hutu militias to help them to set fire to up to 700 people who refused to leave the convent and were locked in a garage at the convent's health clinic. The two Hutu militants were accused of helping to plan massacres and of spreading ethnic hatred. All four pleaded not guilty.

Held:

On 8 June 2001 the four accused were found guilty of international crimes arising from the Rwandan genocide. All were sentenced to at least 12 years' imprisonment.

Comment:

Between 500,000 and 800,000 ethnic Tutsis and Hutus were killed in Rwanda in 1994. The Belgian trial was a triumph for justice and a step towards the ending of the impunity of human rights abusers. They were found guilty by a civil jury made up of 12 ordinary people, which included a hairdresser, a lorry driver and a university professor.

---

45   L. Reydams, *Belgium's First Application of Universal Jurisdiction in the "Butare Four" Case* (2003)1 J Int'l Criminal Justice, 428.

The application of the Belgian Law became highly contested when, under the above mentioned 1999 law, immunity with regard to heads of State and high-ranking State officials was removed. This resulted in many claims being made in respect of such persons for committing core crimes outside the territory of Belgium.[46] Additionally, the Belgian Supreme Court allowed Belgian judges to issue international arrest warrants against accused persons located outside Belgium.[47] Such a warrant was issued on 11 April 2000 against Abdulaye Yerodia Ndombasi, the then Minister for Foreign Affairs of the Democratic Republic of Congo (DRC), for serious violations of international humanitarian law. On 17 October 2000 the DRC filed an application before the ICJ against Belgium challenging the arrest warrant. On 14 February 2002 the ICJ delivered its judgment in *Case Concerning the Arrest Warrant of 11 April 2000 (Democratic Republic of the Congo v Belgium)*, in which it found Belgium in breach of international law (see Chapter 10.3.3.1).

Belgium, following the judgment in the *Arrest Warrant Case*, revised its 1993 and 1999 legislation,[48] first in order to comply with that judgment and second, to avoid a conflict with the US. Indeed, the US had threatened to take measures against Belgium, such as removing the headquarters of NATO from Brussels,when criminal proceedings were brought there against, *inter alia*, US General, Tommy Franks, for alleged war crimes committed when he was commanding US forces during the invasion of Iraq in March 2003; high-ranking officials of NATO; and US President George W. Bush and UK Prime Minister Tony Blair for unlawful use of force against Iraq and Afghanistan. As a result of the revision, Belgian courts are now allowed to assert jurisdiction in situations where the victim is a national of Belgium, or has resided in Belgium for at least 3 years. Prosecution is excluded in respect of persons enjoying immunity under international law, such as incumbent heads of State, heads of government and ministers of foreign affairs, and other persons enjoying immunity from civil and criminal proceedings as recognised under international law or granted on the basis of international treaties to which Belgium is a contracting party. Under the amendments no act in furtherance of commencing criminal proceedings will be allowed against any person who has been officially invited to Belgium by the Belgian authorities, or by an international organisation located in Belgium, during the period of stay of such a person in Belgium.

9.6.1.3 Spanish law of 1985 amended in 2009 and 2014

Article 23.4 of the Spanish Judicial Power Organisation Act (LOPJ), enacted on 1 July 1985, empowered Spanish courts to exercise universal jurisdiction. This was tested in decisions of the Spanish Supreme Court in the *Guatemala Genocide Case*[49] and in the *Peruvian Genocide Case.*[50] The Spanish Supreme Court decided, by a majority of eight to seven, not to apply the principle of universal jurisdiction as a basis for the prosecution in Spain of former Guatemalan officials and former Peruvian officials for acts of torture committed respectively in Guatemala and in Peru, and decided instead to apply the passive personality principle. The Supreme Court limited the jurisdiction of Spanish courts over the

---

46   Claims were brought against then incumbent heads of State, i.e. Cuban President Fidel Castro, Iraqi President Saddam Hussein, Palestinian leader Yasser Arafat, Israeli Prime Minister Ariel Sharon, US President George W. Bush and UK Prime Minister Tony Blair.

47   (2003) 42 ILM 596.

48   Moniteur Belge 40506 (7 August 2003). Amendment on 7 August 2003 to Law of 15 June 1993 (English Translation) (2003) 42 ILM 1258.

49   (2003) 42 ILM 686.

50   (2003) 42 ILM 1200.

most serious international crimes, such as genocide and torture, to cases where there were close connections between the victim of the crime and Spanish nationality. These connections included: that victims were of Spanish nationality or citizenship; that victims or their survivors had dual nationality (the country where the alleged crime was committed and Spanish nationality); and that victims or their survivors had some close familial lineage of Spanish origin. Further, it introduced the principle of subsidiarity according to which the State where the alleged crime had been committed had priority over Spanish jurisdiction. The judgment meant that cases concerning torture and killing of Spanish citizens in Guatemala, and in Peru, could continue while claims of non-Spanish nationals were dismissed. The decision of the Spanish Supreme Court in the *Guatemalan Genocide Case* was appealed to the Spanish Constitutional Court. In October 2005, it ruled that 'the concept of universal jurisdiction in contemporary international law is not predicated on links to the individual interests of states'[51] or on the suspect's presence in the territory of the forum state'.[52]

Following the ruling of the Spanish Constitutional Court, numerous investigations were commenced, *inter alia*, in respect of a targeted killing attack in Gaza in 2002 against the former Israeli Defence Minister, Binyamin Ben-Eliezer; the former defence chief-of-staff Moshe Ya'alon and four others, for crimes against humanity; against seven former Chinese officials, including the former President of China Jiang Zemin and former Prime Minister Li Peng, for their alleged participation in genocide in Tibet; and against six former Bush administration officials for allegedly giving legal cover to torture committed at the US detention centre in Guantánamo Bay, Cuba. Those investigations created diplomatic friction, in particular when arrest warrants were issued in November 2013 against former high ranking Chinese officials including the former President of China. Many considerations, including the fear that China would use economic sanctions to punish Spain, led to amendments of the 1985 law. Indeed, the fear was well justified in the light of the fact that China imposed economic sanctions on Norway in response to the award, by the Norwegian Nobel Committee, of the Nobel Peace Prize to Liu Xiaobo, a dissident serving an 11-year prison term in China, which sanctions are still in place. Further, China is the biggest trading partner of Spain outside the EU and the second largest foreign holder of Spanish debt.[53]

The first amendment of the 1985 law took place in 2009. The amended legislation provides that Spanish courts may exercise jurisdiction over international crimes if the suspect resides in Spain, or the victims are Spanish nationals or there is a link of relevant connection with Spain. It also requires Spanish authorities to verify whether there are 'effective' proceedings outside Spain concerning the same allegations. If, so the Spanish proceedings must be suspended.[54]

The second amendment occurred in 2014. Under amended legislation, apart from piracy, universal jurisdiction exists for crimes of genocide, crimes against humanity and war crimes only when the accused is a Spanish national, or a foreigner habitually resident in Spain, or a foreigner present in Spain whose extradition has been denied by Spanish authorities. With regard to acts of torture and forced disappearance, universal jurisdiction exists if the accused is a Spanish citizen, or the victims were (at the time of the events in question) Spanish citizens and the person accused of the crime is in Spanish territory. Only public prosecutors and victims may initiate criminal proceedings under universal

---

51   *Menchú v. Two Guatemalan Government Officials* ILDC 137 (ES 2005), para 9, author's translation.
52   Ibid, para 7.
53   S. Kern, Spain Rethinks Universal Jurisdiction available at www.gatestoneinstitute.org/4149/spain-universal-jurisdiction (accessed 15 September 2014).
54   See E.C. Rojo, *National Legislation Providing for the Prosecution and Punishment of International Crimes in Spain* (2011) 9/3 J Int Criminal Justice, 699.

jurisdiction. Cases which, before the amendment, were pending trial are required to be stayed and thereafter dismissed if they cannot satisfy the new conditions.[55]

9.6.2 Controversies surrounding the exercise of universal jurisdiction by national courts

As can been seen from the experience of Spanish and Belgian courts, the principle of universality has come under attack.[56] Although some scholars have denied the existence of universal jurisdiction,[57] customary international law shows otherwise. It also shows that what is contested is the modality of the exercise of universal jurisdiction.

State practice supports the existence of universal jurisdiction. According to an Amnesty International survey a total of 163 States can exercise universal jurisdiction over one or more of the following four crimes: war crimes, crimes against humanity, genocide and torture, either as international crimes or as ordinary crimes.[58] The African Union (AU), which comprises 54 African States, while initiating debate at the UNGA concerning alleging abuses of the exercise of universal jurisdiction by some States, made a declaration in which it 'recognize[d] that universal jurisdiction is a principle of international law whose purpose is to ensure that individuals who commit grave offences such as war crimes and crimes against humanity do not do so with impunity and are brought to justice in line with ... the Constitutive Act of the African Union'.[59] This Declaration shows that the AU does not challenge the existence of universal jurisdiction, but its abuse. The Declaration should be assessed in the light of the fact that the conduct of many officials of the member States of the AU was or is being investigated on the basis of universal jurisdiction by some European States. Further, in 2011, the AU prepared a Draft (Model) Law on Universal Jurisdiction over International Crimes.[60] Its Article 1 states that the purpose of the Draft, which the AU hopes will be adopted by its member States, is to provide for the exercise by them of universal jurisdiction over international crimes. It is also important to note that the US has enacted legislation allowing its courts to exercise universal jurisdiction over some crimes, including the use of child soldiers, based on customary international law,[61] and China accepts the principle of universal jurisdiction.[62]

International criminal tribunals such as the ICTY and ICTR, as well the Special Court for Sierra Leone recognise that States may assert universal jurisdiction over international crimes. So do the ECtHR, and the IACtHR.[63]

---

55   See New, *Spain Eases Law After China Pressure* (2014) 6/2 LSGAz.

56   According to Professor H. van der Wilt, this attack is unjustified. The review of cases and legal trends shows that Western courts have made prudent use of universal jurisdiction, See *Universal Jurisdiction under Attack* (2011) 9/5 I Int Criminal Justice, 1043.

57   See, e.g. A. Rubin, *Action Popularis, Jus Cogens and Offences Erga Omnes* (2001) 35 New England Law Review, 265.

58   See 'Universal Jurisdiction. A Preliminary Survey of Legislation around the World'available at www.amnesty. org/ar/library/asset/IOR53/004/2011/en/d997366e-65bf-4d80–9022-fcb8fe284c9d/ior530042011en.pdf (accessed 19 June 2014).

59   Decision on the Report of the Commission on the Abuse of Universal Jurisciction (Assembly/AU/14/XI) annexed to Letter from the AU Permanent Observer to the President of the Security Council (UN Doc S/2008/465).

60   Hereafter Model Law, its text is available at www.ejiltalk.org/wp-content/uploads/2012/08/AU-draft-model-law-UJ-May-2012.pdf (accessed 2 March 2014).

61   Child Soldier Accountability Act 2007, S 2135.

62   Z. Lijiang, *Chinese Practice in Public International Law* (2014) 13/2 Chinese Journal of International Law, 405.

63   See R. Cryer, H. Friman, D. Robinson and E. Wilmshurst, An Introdcution to International Criminal Law and Procedure, 2nd edn, Cambridge: Cambridge University Press, 2010, 59.

With regard to the ICJ, the Court in the *Arrest Warrant Case*[64] declined to examine the matter of whether or not Belgium was entitled to enact national legislation under which its municipal courts had broad universal jurisdiction in respect of international crimes. Even though the DRC decided to withdraw its original argument which challenged the legality of the Belgian law under international law, the ICJ could have taken the opportunity to clarify the issue of universal jurisdiction. However, the majority of the ICJ ruled that under the *non ultra petita* rule the Court was bound to abstain from deciding issues not included in the submissions of the parties. This was challenged by dissenting judges who considered that the Court was not prevented from examining issues relevant to the case, even if they were not raised by the parties. The dissenting judges considered that the principle of *jura novit curia* could supersede the *non ultra petita* rule and thereby the ICJ could have inherent competence to decide on the relevant issues of international law, irrespective of the absences from the submissions of the parties to the proceedings. Notwithstanding this, many judges, either in dissenting or separate opinions, expressed their views on the legality or otherwise of the exercise of universal jurisdiction in international law. However, their views concerned the modality of the exercise of universal jurisdiction rather than its existence.

The modality of exercise of universal jurisdiction is unclear as evidenced by the fact that the topic of universal jurisdiction is in its fifth year of discussion at the UNGA, in particular before its Sixth Committee. The discussion at the UNGA was initiated by the AU which considered that African States have been singled out in terms of the indictment and arrest of their officials and that the exercise of universal jurisdiction by some European States has been politically motivated. The AU requested the inclusion on the UNGA agenda for its 63rd session of the topic of 'abuse of the principle of universal jurisdiction'. The request was accepted and the heated debate has initiated a series of measures taken by the UNGA with a view to clarifying the scope and application of universal jurisdiction. This includes reports presented by the UNS-G based on observations and information provided by the member States and by international organisations such as the ICRC,[65] and the establishment of a working group on this topic by the UNGA Sixth Committee.[66] So far the UNGA has acknowledged the existence of a diversity of views presented by the member States on the principle of universal jurisdiction and the need for further work in this area.

The three most controversial matters concerning the modality of exercise of universal jurisdiction are examined below.

9.6.2.1 Must the accused be present within the prosecuting State, at least at the beginning of a trial?

Two approaches have been adopted. The first requires the presence of the accused within the *forum* State. The second considers that a State may exercise jurisdiction regardless of whether or not the alleged offender is in its custody.

The first approach is that of the majority of common law countries which consider that 'due process' guarantees require that the accused must be present within the *forum* State. Thus, criminal trials *in absentia* are normally not authorised. Under US law the defendant must be before the court at the time the trial begins.[67] The second approach is embraced by many civil law countries which allow a

---

64   [2002] ICJ Rep 3.
65   A/65/181 and A/67/116.
66   A/RES/66/103.
67   §§ 422 and 423 of the US Restatement (Third) and *Crosby v United States* 506 US 255. However, if the accused
      is disruptive or absconds, as long as he was present at the initiation of proceedings, the trial will continue in

trial to take place in the absence of the accused. The main justification is that justice should not be frustrated by delays. Accordingly trials *in absentia* will either force the accused to submit to the court or allow the court to proceed.

The first approach is not without controversy in that it is unclear whether the prosecuting State is entitled under international law to issue an arrest warrant, or an extradition request, when the suspect is not present within the jurisdiction. Famous examples where arrest warrants were issued by the prosecuting States are: first the case of Pinochet and second, the case of Cavallo.

- In the *Pinochet Case* (for facts see Chapter 10.3.3.1 C) Spain requested extradition of the former dictator and President of Chile, Augusto Pinochet, from the UK pursuant to the 1972 European Convention on Extradition to which Spain and the UK are contracting parties. The Law Lords in the UK ruled that he was not immune, as a former Head of State, from charges of systematic torture in Chile and therefore his extradition to Spain for a trial could proceed.

- In the *Cavallo Case*, Spain requested that an Argentinean national on a visit to Mexico be extradited to Spain to stand trial there for genocide and terrorism. The Supreme Court of Mexico allowed the extradition. The *Cavallo Case* is important because, for the first time, a State requested an extradition solely on the basis of the universal jurisdiction principle (based on the nature of the crime, not on a connection between the *forum* and either the victims, or the perpetrator, or the territory, where the crime occurred). The Supreme Court of Mexico honoured the extradition treaty between Mexico and Spain and did not contest the jurisdictional legitimacy of the requesting State.[68]

It is submitted that international law allows the prosecuting State to take initial procedural steps *in absentia*. This is confirmed by the 2005 Resolution of the IDI[69] and the 2009 resolution of the International Association of Penal Law (IAPL). [70] However both resolutions, which require the presence of the suspect in the *forum* State, include in the initial procedural steps the issuance of an arrest warrant or a request for extradition. In this respect Section II(2) of the 2009 Resolution of the IAPL states: 'Investigation is admissible *in absentia*; States can initiate criminal proceedings, conduct an investigation, preserve evidence, issue an indictment, or request extradition.'[71] This is to be contrasted with the position of the AU which complained to the EU and the UNGA that public issuance of indictment and arrest warrants by some European States against sitting African officials constitutes a new form of colonialism, i.e. legal colonialism, undermines the dignity of the State officials against whom such measures are

---

his absence. Rule 43(b) of the Federal Rules of Criminal Procedure allows a trial to take place 'and the defendant shall be considered to have waived the right to be present whenever a defendant, initially present, (1) is voluntarily absent after the trial has commenced'. The purpose of the 'initial presence' requirement is to ensure that the accused has notice of the charges and proceedings. The position of the UK is similar to that of the US. If the accused absents himself or herself from a trial for a non-capital offence, after the start of the trial, the trial may nonetheless proceed. See *R v Ellis* (1973) 57 Cr App R 571 and *R v Jones (REW) (No 2)* [1972] 2 All ER 731, cited in R. Pattenden, *Judicial Discretion and Criminal Litigation*, Oxford: Oxford University Press, 1990, 59 *et seq*.

68 See Extradición del oficial de contrainteligencia de la Armada Argentina, Ricardo Miguel Cavallo, Suprema Corte de Justicia de la Nación [Mexican Supreme Court] (10 June 2003) available at www.derechos.org/nizkor/arg/espana/cortemex.html> (accessed 18 July 2010).

69 See Article 3(b) of the Resolution available at www.idi-iil.org/idiE/resolutionsE/2005_kra_03_en.pdf (accessed 10 July 2014).

70 The Resolution can be found at www.cairn.info/revue-internationale-de-droit-penal-2008–1-page-151.htm (accessed 10 July 2014).

71 Ibid.

taken and creates an international stigma against them.[72] Not surprisingly, Article 4 of the AU Model National Law on Universal Jurisdiction over International Law, which requires, for the exercise of universal jurisdiction, the presence of the suspect within the jurisdiction of the prosecuting State is silent on whether the issuance of an indictment and arrest warrants is allowed.[73]

The position of international law on trials *in absentia* is unclear. It seems that international law neither prohibits nor allows them and that State practice is too scarce and inconsistent to decide either way. This is exemplified by divergent opinions expressed by judges in the *Arrest Warrant Case*.[74] President Guillaume, Judge Ranjeva, and Judge *ad hoc* Bula-Bula considered the exercise of universal jurisdiction as violating international law. President Guillaume, in particular, in his Separate Opinion submitted that neither international customary law nor international conventions, which oblige contracting States either to try, or to extradite, the alleged offender, permit a State to assert jurisdiction for crimes against international law *in absentia*.[75] He emphasised that the exercise of universal jurisdiction would encourage powerful States to act as agents of an 'ill-defined inter- national community', and therefore had no place in international law.[76] Judge Rezek accepted universal jurisdiction as a subsidiary basis of jurisdiction if the suspect is present on the territory of the prosecuting State.[77] The opposite position was taken by the three judges Higgins, Kooijmans and Buergenthal in their Joint Separate Opinion. They submitted that a State may choose to exercise universal criminal jurisdiction *in absentia* subject to certain safeguards.[78] Similarly, Judge *ad hoc* Van den Wyngaert in her dissenting opinion endorsed the exercise of universal jurisdiction *in absentia*.[79]

Both, the statutes and the practice of international criminal tribunals on trials *in absentia* are inconclusive.[80] With regard to the Statute of the ICC, after many years of heated debates at the UNGA and at the 1998 Rome Conference which finalised the Statute, it was agreed that the presence of the accused during the trial is required unless the accused continues to disrupt the trial in which case he may be removed from the proceedings.[81] This clearly rules out trials *in absentia*. The Statutes of the ICTY and the ICTR mirror Article 14 ICCPR, which provides for the right to a fair trial. This provision says nothing about the prohibition or otherwise of trials *in absentia*. Both the ICTY and the ICTR, as well as the Human Rights Committee, which interprets and applies the ICCPR (see Chapter 12.2.2.2), have construed Article 14 ICCPR as meaning that trials *in absentia* are allowed. Specialised courts such as the Special Court for Sierra Leone, the Extraordinary Chambers of the Court of Cambodia and the Special Tribunal for Lebanon conduct trials *in absentia*.[82]

With regard to the ECtHR, its position on trials *in absentia* was stated in *Sejdovic v. Italy*.[83] The Court held that a person charged with criminal offences is entitled to take part in the hearing. However, Article 6 ECHR, which ensures the right to a fair trial, will not be breached if an accused who is

---

72   See The Report at http://ec.europa.eu/development/icenter/repository/troika_ua_ue_rapport_competence_universelle_EN.pdf (accessed 25 July 2014).

73   Supra note 60.

74   (2002) ICJ Rep 3.

75   Ibid, paras 34–45.

76   Supra note 74, Separate Opinion, para 43.

77   Supra note 74, Separate Opinion, paras 91–92.

78   Supra note 74, Joint Separate Opinion, para 59.

79   Supra note 74, Dissenting Opinion, para 67.

80   On this topic see: G.J. Shaw, *Note. Convicting Inhumanity in Absentia: Holding Trials in Absentia at the International Criminal Court* (2012) 44 Geo Wash Int'l L Rev, 107.

81   Article 63 of the Rome Statute.

82   Supra note 80,118 *et seq*.

83   *Sejdovic v Italy* (2006) 42 EHRR 17.

sentenced in his absence is entitled to 'to obtain from a court which has heard him a fresh determination of the merits of the charge, in respect of both law and fact'.[84] However, there is no need to secure the possibility of a retrial if the person 'has waived his right to appear and to defend himself or intended to escape trial'.[85] The ECtHR added that, in order to be effective, 'a waiver of the right to take part in the trial must be established in an unequivocal manner and be attended by minimum safeguards commensurate to its importance'.[86]

9.6.2.2 Whether universal jurisdiction is a default jurisdiction in that it should only be exercised if the State on whose territory the crime has occurred or the State of the nationality either of the alleged perpetrator or the victims are unable or unwilling to exercise jurisdiction?

The idea that there is a hierarchy among the various bases of jurisdiction in criminal matters entails that universal jurisdiction is subsidiary or complementary to jurisdiction which States may claim on the basis of territoriality, nationality or the passive personality principles. It is important to note that subsidiarity arises when a State has a real choice either to prosecute on the basis of the principle of universality, or to extradite to a State which can assert jurisdiction on the principles of territoriality, nationality, or passive personality. Accordingly subsidiarity should not be relied upon to justify inaction based on unclear intentions of the territorial State or its vague investigations with regard to general situations rather than specific individual cases.[87]

Views differ as to whether subsidiarity is a rule of customary international law. Many commentators including A. Cassese submit that subsidiarity is established in customary law. Cassese explained that subsidiarity as a rule of customary international law is partly based on treaty law.[88] However, the ICJ in *Case Concerning Questions Relating to the Obligation to Extradite or Prosecute (Belgium v Senegal)*,[89] at least with regard to the 1984 Convention against Torture (CAT), clearly stated that the obligation to prosecute exists independently of any request for extradition, and that extradition is only an option, not a duty under the CAT (see Chapter 9.7).

It is submitted that the AU-EU Report on the Principle of Universal Jurisdiction is probably the best summary of the current position of customary international law on subsidiarity. It states that: 'Positive international law recognises no hierarchy among the various bases of jurisdiction that it permits'[90] (i.e. a State is not obliged to give priority to another State to prosecute a suspect, only because that State can assert jurisdiction based on territoriality or the nationality of victims). However, Recommendation 9 of the Report provides that 'states should, as a matter of policy, accord priority to territoriality as a basis of jurisdiction'. Recommendation 9 justifies this on two very convincing arguments, first, that although international crimes are offences against the international community as a whole they primarily injure the community where they are committed and violate not only the rights of the victims but also of that community. The second reason is practical. It concerns procedural economy. The State on whose territory the relevant crime was committed is the best place to gather

---

84   Ibid, para 82.
85   Ibid, para 82.
86   Ibid, para 86.
87   F. Lafontaine, *Universal Jurisdiction – the Realistic Utopia* (2012) 10/5/ J Int Criminal Justice, 1287.
88   A. Cassese, *Is the Bell Tolling for Universality?' A Plea for a Sensitive Notion of Universal Jurisdiction* (2003) 1 JICJ, 593–594.
89   (2012) ICJ Rep 422.
90   Supra note 74, para 14.

and process evidence. Indeed, it would be very difficult for a State exercising universal jurisdiction to conduct a trial without the co-opertation of the State where the relevant crime took place. Such co-operation between the State on whose territory the crime took place and the prosecuting State resulted in successful prosecutions in such cases as the '*Butare Four*' (see Chapter 9.6.1.2) in Belgium, Afghan warlord Faryadi Zardad, convicted in the UK for conspiracy to take hostages and conspiracy to torture during the 1990s in Afghanistan, and the *Case of Niyontenze*, convicted in Switzerland for war crimes committed during the conflict in Rwanda.[91]

9.6.2.3   Which international crimes should be within the ratione materiae of universal jurisdiction?

The right of States to exercise universal jurisdiction over piracy is universally recognised and rooted in international customary law. President Guillaume of the ICJ in his Separate Opinion in the *Arrest Warrant Case* stated that customary international law knows of only one true case of universal jurisdiction – piracy.[92] Piracy is not the most heinous crime but customary international law allows any State to try pirates. This offence is usually committed on the high seas rather than within the territorial waters of any nation. The nationality and passive personality principles are not practical alternatives because it is difficult to establish the nationality of pirates, and the State apprehending them will not necessarily be the State of the victims. Therefore pragmatic reasons rather than the nature of the crime justify the existence of universal jurisdiction over piracy (see Chapter 8.9.3.2A).

It seems that the universality principle is recognised with regard to traditional chattel slavery and the Atlantic slave trade, but not in respect of new forms of slavery such as debt bondage, serfdom, forced labour, and trafficking and exploitation of women and children, mainly for sexual purposes.[93]

With regard to other international crimes, controversy persists.

Various lists of international crimes have been suggested.

Article 404 of the US Restatement (Third) provides a list identifying international crimes. It states that:

A State has jurisdiction to define and prescribe punishment for certain offences recognised by the community of nations as of universal concern, such as piracy, slave trade, attacks on or hijacking of aircraft, genocide, war crimes, and perhaps certain acts of terrorism.

According to the Restatement the above list is based on customary law. Universal jurisdiction for additional offences is provided by international treaties. The above list is very controversial. It is, at the same time, too broad and too restrictive. It is too restrictive because some crimes not mentioned in Article 404 of the Restatement (Third) are seen as violating the rules of *jus cogens* and therefore should be included in the list – for example, torture and the crime of aggression. It is too broad because there is no sufficient evidence based on State practice to classify some crimes, such as attacks on, or hijacking of, aircraft, as crimes in international customary law. Further, the US Restatement (Third)

---

91   See R. Cryer, H. Friman, D. Robinson and E. Wilmshurst, *An Introduction to International Criminal Law and Procedure*, 2nd edn, Cambridge: Cambridge University Press, 2010, 60.

92   The *Arrest Warrant of 11 April 2000 (Democratic Republic of the Congo v Belgium) (Judgment)* [2002] ICJ Rep 3. Separate Opinion, para 12.See also: E. Kontorovich, *The Piracy Analogy: Modern Universal Jurisdiction's Hollow Foundation* 45 Harvard International Law Journal (2004) 183, at 186; and Goldwin, *Universal Jurisdiction and the Pirate: Time for an Old Couple to Part* (2003) 19 Vanderbilt Journal of Transnational Law, 995.

93   On this topic see S. Scarpa, *Trafficking in Human Beings: Modern Slavery*. Oxford: Oxford University Press, 2008.

makes no distinction between international crimes which violate *jus cogens* and international crimes which breach other norms of international customary law.

In 2001 a group of international experts participating in the Princeton Project on Universal Jurisdiction published a set of guidelines known as the 'Princeton Principles on Universal Jurisdiction', which according to the participants constitutes a progressive restatement of the international law in this area (*de lega lata*) and 'encourages its further development' (*de lege feranda*).[94] The Princeton Principles on Universal Jurisdiction propose the following as serious crimes under international law: piracy; slavery; war crimes; crimes against peace; crimes against humanity; genocide; and torture. One may argue that other crimes such as apartheid, terrorism, and drug-related crimes should be included and that the above list is still very controversial, i.e. what exactly do 'crimes against peace' encompass? Should 'war crimes' be understood as 'grave' breaches of the 1949 Geneva Convention and its Protocol I?

Important clarifications in determining crimes which should be considered as international crimes are provided by the Statutes of both the International Criminal Tribunal for the Former Yugoslavia (ICTY) and the International Criminal Tribunal for Rwanda (ICTR). It may be implied that since both Tribunals were established on the basis of UNSC resolutions the international community considers crimes falling within the jurisdiction of both courts as international crimes. The ICTY can adjudicate cases involving grave breaches of the 1949 Geneva Conventions, violations of the laws or customs of war, genocide and crimes against humanity. The ICTR jurisdiction covers genocide, crimes against humanity, violations of Article 3 common to the 1949 Geneva Conventions and the 1977 Additional Protocol II to the 1949 Geneva Conventions.

The Statute of the International Criminal Court (ICC), which sets out only the most serious violations of international law, provides that the ICC has jurisdiction *rationae materiae* in respect of genocide, war crimes, crimes against humanity and the crime of aggression.

9.7 Jurisdiction based on a treaty dealing with international crimes

A State may assert jurisdiction on the basis of a treaty dealing with international crimes to which it is a contracting party. Crawford called it 'treaty based quasi-universal jurisdiction'.[95] This is because 'it arises from *sui generis* treaty regime incorporating penal characteristics'.[96] Indeed, a contracting State exercises its jurisdiction on the basis of the terms of the treaty rather than on any generally accepted principle of customary international law. Examples of such international treaties are: the 1970 Hague Convention for the Suppression of Unlawful Seizure of Aircraft,[97] the 1984 UN Convention against Torture and other Cruel, Inhuman or Degrading Treatment or Punishment,[98] the 1948 UN Convention on the Prevention and Punishment of the Crime of Genocide,[99] the 1948 Geneva Conventions,[100] the 1988 Rome Convention for the Suppression of Unlawful Acts against the Safety of Maritime Navigation[101] and the 1999 UN Convention for the Suppression of the Financing of Terrorism.[102]

---

94 The Princeton Principles can be found at www1.umn.edu/humanrts/instree/princeton.html (accessed 27 July 2014).

95 J. Crawford, *Brownlie's Principles of Public International Law*, 8th edn, Oxford: Oxford University Press,2012, 469.

96 Ibid.

97 860 UNTS 105.

98 1465 UNTS 85.

99 78 UNTS 277.

100 GC-I (75 UNTS 31); GC-II (75 UNTS 85); GC-III (75 UNTS 135); GC-IV (75 UNTS 287).

101 1678 UNTS 221.

102 2178 UNTS 197.

The key elements of most treaties dealing specifically with crimes of an international nature are as follows:

- the provision of definitions of the international crimes dealt with by the particular treaty;

- the establishment of an obligation on a contracting State to make acts considered as international crimes offences under their municipal legal systems;

- the requirement that a contracting State must be in a position to establish jurisdiction over international crimes. Invariably, territoriality and nationality are indicated as mandatory bases of jurisdiction. Other principles are permitted as optional grounds of jurisdiction;[103]

- the offences created are deemed to be extraditable offences;

- the imposition of a duty on a contracting State to either extradite or prosecute the offender. This is often referred to as the *aut dedare aut judicare* obligation. The ICJ in *Case Concerning Questions Relating to the Obligation to Extradite or Prosecute (Belgium v Senegal)*[104] elucidated the meaning of this obligation.

CASE CONCERNING QUESTIONS RELATING TO THE OBLIGATION TO EXTRADITE OR PROSECUTE (BELGIUM *V* SENEGAL)

Facts:

On 19 February 2009, Belgium brought proceedings against Senegal for failure to either extradite Mr Habré, the former Chadian President, to Belgium (despite repeated requests submitted by Belgium), or to prosecute him under the 1984 UN Convention against Torture and Other Cruel, Inhuman and Degrading Treatment or Punishment (CAT), to which both States were contracting parties. Belgium alleged that during the 8-year presidency in Chad, Mr Habré committed crimes against humanity, acts of torture and acts of barbarity. Mr Habré, after the overthrow of his regime in 1990, fled to Senegal where he was granted political asylum and where he has subsequently resided. When Belgium first issued a request for extradition to Senegal in 2005, the Chambre d'accusation of the Dakar Court of Appeal rejected Belgium's request on the ground that Mr Habré was immune, as a former Head of State, from the jurisdiction of Belgian courts for acts 'allegedly committed in the exercise of his functions'.[105] Senegal referred the matter to the AU. Before the AU rendered its decision, Belgium submitted to Senegal a series of Notes Verbales stating that Senegal had not complied with its obligation to extradite or prosecute Mr Habré by referring to the AU. In July 2006, the AU requested Senegal to prosecute Mr Habré 'on behalf of Africa'.[106] In response Senegal amended its Penal Code to comply with Article 5(2) CAT, placed Mr Habré under house arrest, but claimed that financial difficulties prevented the bringing of the accused to trial. Belgium requested the dispute between Belgium and Senegal to be

---

103   See S. Yee, *Universal Jurisdiction: Concept, Logic, and Reality* (2011) 10/3 Chinese Journal of International Law, 518.

104   (2012) ICJ Rep 422.

105   Ibid, para 22.

106   Decision 137(VII) of the African Assembly of Heads of State and Government.

submitted to arbitration in conformity with Article 30 CAT as it had not been settled by negotiation, and offered its judicial co-operation. Although Senegal indicated that it would accept Belgium's assistance, matters did not progress. In those circumstances Belgium brought proceedings before the ICJ alleging that Senegal was in breach of:

- *Article 5(2) CAT which requires a contracting party to take measures to establish jurisdiction over acts of torture;*
- *Article 6(2) CAT which requires a contracting party to immediately initiate a preliminary inquiry into allegations of acts of tortures when the person accused is found within that State territory; and*
- *Article 7(1) CAT which requires a contracting party, in the territory of which a person alleged to have committed acts of torture is found, 'if it does not extradite him, submit the case to its competent authorities for the purpose of prosecution'.*

Held:

The ICJ held that Senegal was in breach of Articles 6(2) CAT and 7(1) CAT, but not of Article 5(2) as it had implemented the CAT in 2007/2008, i.e. before Belgium filed its application to the ICJ.

Comments:

The ICJ made a number of important statements in the commented case.

1   With regard to the admissibility of the Belgian claim, Belgium first relied on the principle of passive personality, i.e. the prosecution commenced on the basis of a complaint filed by a Belgian of Chadian origin. Senegal disputed this by pointing out that at the time the acts occurred the alleged victims were not Belgian nationals. Second, Belgium argued that it was entitled to rely on the CAT to invoke the responsibility of the party which had failed to comply with obligations arising out of the CAT.

The ICJ held that the second basis was sufficient to establish the admissibility of Belgium's claim because the CAT creates an obligation erga omnes which entails that all contracting parties to the CAT have the 'common interest' in ensuring compliance with its provisions. The Court held:

The obligations of a State party to conduct a preliminary inquiry into the facts and to submit the case to its competent authorities for prosecution are triggered by the presence of the alleged offender in its territory, regardless of the nationality of the offender or the victims, or of the place where the alleged offences occurred. All the other States parties have a common interest in compliance with these obligations by the State in whose territory the alleged offender is present. That common interest implies that the obligations in question are owed by any State party to all the other States parties to the Convention. All the States parties 'have a legal interest' in the protection of the rights involved.[107]

---

107   Ibid, para 68, The ICJ made reference to *Barcelona Traction, Light and Power Limited* [1970] ICJ Rep 32, para 33.

2   In respect of the obligation to extradite or prosecute the ICJ held that this obligation is part of 'a single conventional mechanism aimed at preventing suspects from escaping the consequences of their criminal responsibility'.[108] The judgment stated:

> *The Court considers that Article 7, paragraph 1, requires the State concerned to submit the case to its competent authorities for the purpose of prosecution, irrespective of the existence of a prior request for the extradition of the suspect. . . . However, if the State in whose territory the suspect is present has received a request for extradition in any of the cases envisaged in the provisions of the Convention, it can relieve itself of its obligation to prosecute by acceding to that request. It follows that the choice between extradition or submission for prosecution, pursuant to the Convention, does not mean that the two alternatives are to be given the same weight. Extradition is an option offered to the State by the Convention, whereas prosecution is an international obligation under the Convention, the violation of which is a wrongful act engaging the responsibility of the State.[109]*

The above citation clearly states that extradition and prosecution are not, as Judge Donoghue stated 'of equal footing'.[110] Extradition is an option, while prosecution is an international obligation.[111] Accordingly, a State must prosecute, if it does not it can relieve itself from the obligation to prosecute by extraditing the person concerned. If it neither prosecutes nor extradites it commits a wrongful act for which it may incur international responsibility. However, this does not mean that Senegal had an obligation to extradite. Judge Donoghue explained the position of the ICJ on this point by stating that: ' . . . extradition is not required by this provision [Article 7(1) CAT] or by any other provision of the Convention [the CAT]'.[112] Accordingly, in the absence of prosecution Senegal is not required and Belgium is not entitled to have the person concerned extradited.

It is to be noted:

- *First, that the interpretation by the ICJ of Article 7(1) CAT differs from that of the Committee against Torture[113] which considered that Senegal was under an obligation to extradite if it failed in its obligation to prosecute.[114]*
- *Second, the judgment of the ICJ concerns only Article 7(1) CAT and therefore in respect of other international conventions which require a contracting party to prosecute or extradite, whether there is a duty to extradite will depend on the wording of the convention.[115]*

---

108   Ibid, para 91.

109   Ibid, paras 94 and 95.

110   See Declaration of Judge Donoghue, para 3.

111   Ibid.

112   Ibid, para 3.

113   See Chapter 12.3.4.3.

114   Communication No 181/2001 *Guengueng et al v Senegal*, Date of adoption of Views by the Committee of Torture: 17 May 2006. The text of the decision is reproduced in Selected Decisions of the Committee against Torture, UN Office of High Commissioner for Human Rights, 2013, 97.

115   On the relationship between prosecution and extradition enshrined in international treaties see: A. Nollkaemper, *Wither Aut Dedere? The Obligation to Extradite or Prosecute after the ICJ's Judgment in Belgium v Senegal* (2013) 4/3 J Int Disp Settlement, 501.

3   The ICJ made important statements regarding the jus cogens and erga omnes obligations which are examined in Chapter 2.5. Although the ICJ found that the prohibition of torture was a rule of jus cogens and thus existed prior to the entry into force of the CAT for Senegal, the obligation to extradite, or prosecute, arose only after the CAT entered into force for Senegal.

Follow up of the judgment:

In February 2013, Senegal inaugurated the Extraordinary African Chambers in the Court of Senegal to deal with international crimes committed in Chad between 1982 and 1990. In July 2013 Mr Habré was charged, by the Chambers, with crimes against humanity, torture and war crimes.[116]

Problems in establishing jurisdiction over persons accused of crimes specified in multi- lateral treaties were highlighted in the following case.

CASE CONCERNING QUESTIONS OF INTERPRETATION AND APPLICATION OF THE 1971 MONTREAL CONVENTION ARISING FROM THE AERIAL INCIDENT AT LOCKERBIE (LIBYA V UK) (PROVISIONAL MEASURES)[117]

Facts:

Libya sought from the ICJ an order for provisional measures to protect its rights under the Montreal Convention for the Suppression of Unlawful Acts against the Safety of Civil Aircraft 1971 and thus to prevent the United Nations Security Council (UNSC) from imposing sanctions in response to the refusal of the Libyan authorities to extradite two of its nationals suspected of carrying out the destruction of Pan Am Flight 103 which exploded when flying over the Scottish town of Lockerbie. All 234 passengers were killed, as well as 16 crew members and 11 residents of Lockerbie.

The application was based on the contention made by Libya that the matter was governed by the 1971 Montreal Convention and not an issue that constituted a threat to international peace and security justifying the UNSC's decision to adopt sanctions.

The Montreal Convention specifies that if a person suspected of a terrorist act is arrested in the territory of a contracting party, that State is required to prosecute the accused for the offences or, alternatively, it must extradite the accused to any contracting State that is seeking to exercise jurisdiction over the accused. Thus, the State in which an accused person is found has the option of prosecuting or extraditing to a requesting State.

---

116   See Chronology of Habré Case, available at www.hrw.org/news/2012/03/09/chronology-habr-case (accessed 3 August 2014).

117   (1992) ICJ Rep 3.

Since the accused were Libyan nationals, Libya opted to conduct the prosecution itself and refused to extradite the suspects to either the UK or the US. Both the UK and the US feared that the trial of the accused in Libya would be a sham, and the accused would escape proper trial. Hence, both States sponsored UNSC Resolution 748 (1992)[118] imposing sanctions against Libya, involving the severance of all economic, commercial and diplomatic links by all member States of the UN. The UK and the US wanted to compel Libya to extradite the suspects as opposed to conducting the trial itself. Resolution 748 (1992) was adopted three days after the closing of oral hearings by the ICJ.

Held:

The ICJ refused the application on the ground, inter alia, *that Libya was required to carry out the decisions of the UNSC in accordance with Article 25 of the UN Charter. To permit Libya to rely on the 1971 Montreal Convention would have been inconsistent with the principle that the UN Charter prevails over the inconsistent terms of any international agreements. In the end the Court could not protect the rights conferred upon Libya by the Convention because there were no longer any rights to protect in the light of the UNSC Resolution 748. The ICJ held that:*

> *Whatever the situation previous to the adoption of that resolution, the rights claimed by Libya under the Montreal Convention cannot now be regarded as appropriate for protection.[119]*

Comment:

It should be noted that:

- *The ICJ did not make any definitive ruling on whether it had jurisdiction to review UNSC resolutions made under Chapter VII. This was because the case had been discontinued following an agreement between Libya, the US and the UK in 2003, under which the two suspects Megrahi and Fhimah were surrendered by Libya to the UK and the US to stand trial in the Netherlands before a Scottish court made up of three Scottish judges. The outcome of the trial was that charges against Fhimah were dismissed while Megrahi was sentenced to a mandatory term of life imprisonment.[120] However, on 20 August 2009, on compassionate grounds, he was released from the Scottish prison and returned to Libya.*
- *The taking into account of Resolution 748 (1992) by the ICJ when it was examining the issuing of provisional measures of protection was criticised by Judge Bedjaoui who questioned how the Court could 'take into account a resolution passed after the closure of the proceedings and apply it, retroactively, as it were, to the case which had been submitted to it'.[121] However, it is difficult not to agree with the majority of the ICJ. To do otherwise would result in ignoring a binding resolution of the UNSC.*

---

118   UN Doc S/RES/748.
119   (1992) ICJ Rep 3, 15.
120   The trial and subsequent appeals of Megrahi are analysed in depth in R. Black and J.P. Grant, *The Lockerbie Trial and Its Implications*, Edinburgh: Dunedin Academic Press, 2006.
121   Supra note 117, Dissenting Opinion, para 17.

> • *The ICJ did not proceed to the judgment. Consequently, it did not give any definite ruling on whether UNSC resolutions can override international treaties, in this case the 1970 Montreal Convention.*
>
> *While in this particular case Libya was not allowed to avoid its UN Charter obligations, the existence of alternative grounds for exercising jurisdiction will clearly cause problems when one of two or more States are permitted to exercise jurisdiction over the same person.*

9.8 Jurisdiction in competition matters: the US 'effects doctrine' and the EU 'implementation doctrine'

If two companies enter into an agreement in State Y to co-ordinate their pricing policy for goods marketed in the territory of State X, the question arises as to whether the agreement infringes the municipal law of State X and, if so, whether State X is in a position to do anything about it. These questions concern the extraterritorial application of competition law and are examined below.

The traditional principles establishing prescriptive jurisdiction apply to criminal matters. Competition law is not within the scope of criminal matters although some commentators argue that jurisdiction similar to that in criminal matters exists, in particular when enforcement of civil jurisdiction involves criminal sanctions (see Chapter 9.1). Further, competition law is acquiring an increasingly international dimension. Trade and investment on a global scale have mushroomed, and the geographic reach of the effects of cartels, mergers and abuses by dominant firms is ever expanding.

The extraterritorial application of competition law creates many problems:

- it is contrary to international comity and fairness;

- it encourages confrontation between States rather than co-operation;

- investigation, outside the territory of a State or regional organisation such as the EU or CARICOM, of alleged breaches of competition law often necessitates the co-operation of competent authorities of a third State;

- enforcement of decisions of competition authorities outside their jurisdiction is difficult because a third State, where the offending undertaking is located, has no obligation, unless there is some arrangement to this effect, to co-operate, to assist foreign authorities or to recognise and enforce their decisions;

The best way forward would be to establish multilateral universal rules under the auspices of the WTO, however, all attemps in this direction have so far failed.[122] However, many States and international organisations such as the EU, exercise extraterritorial jurisdiction in competition law.

The application of competition law to foreign firms was initially developed in the US under the 'effects doctrine', which was first applied in *Aluminium Co of America*.[123] The question there was whether a Canadian company could be liable under US anti-trust legislation. The US Court held that

---

122   On this topic see: D.J. Gerber, *Competition Law and the WTO: Rethinking the Relationship* (2007) 10/3 Journal of International Economic Law, 707.

123   (1945) 148 F 2d 416.

it had jurisdiction as the acts of the Canadian company were intended to, and did indeed, have effects within the US.

This doctrine has since undergone a measure of refinement. In *Timberlane Lumber Co v Bank of America* [124] the issue was whether foreign companies, acting outside the US, could be subject to US anti-trust jurisdiction. The Court of Appeals held that it was too simplistic to look only at the effect that the agreement in question would have on trade within the US. This approach failed to take into account the interests of other States. The Court indicated, therefore, that a balancing of interests approach should be applied to determine whether the US courts should assume jurisdiction. This balancing of interests approach was further developed in the *Mannington Mills v Congoleum Corporation* [125] where the Court indicated a number of factors that should be taken into account before jurisdiction could be assumed. This weighing of competing interests required the US court before which the case was heard to consider such matters as the nature of the alleged violation, the nationality of the parties, the interests of other States and the effect of an assumption of jurisdiction. However, in 1982 the Foreign Trade Anti-Trust Improvement Act (FTAIA) amended the Sherman Act [126] and provided for application of US anti-trust law in a situation where the conduct of a foreign company has direct, substantial and reasonably foreseeable effect on US commerce or US export. Further, the 'competing interests' or 'reasonableness' approach was rejected in *Hartford Fire Insurance Co v California* [127] in which the US Supreme Court held that conduct by foreign parties violates the Sherman Act if it satisfies both the 'intent' and the 'effects' tests. As to the intent, the party must have intended to hurt, and in fact have hurt, competition in the US market. With regard to the effect, its conduct must have had a direct, substantial and reasonably foreseeable effect on US commerce or US exports. The only defence available to the defendant is based on foreign legal compulsion. This means that comity will limit the assertion of jurisdiction of US courts only when a foreign State compels particular conduct that US anti-trust law prohibits. The intent and effect tests have also been applied in criminal proceedings against foreign companies and their officials. [128] However, following from the *Empagran Case*, [129] the Sherman Act does not apply in a situation in which foreign claimants seek damages in respect of conduct prohibited under the Act, which conduct has produced harmful effects only outside the United States.

EU competition law has established its own basis for the extraterritorial application of EU law. It is based,

- ■ first, on the 'single economic unit' doctrine. Under EU law, a number of entities, although legally distinct, may nevertheless, for competition purposes, form one legal entity when they are controlled by a common mind and in a cohesive manner. The implication of this doctrine is that a controlling entity can be liable for the conduct of a subordinate entity. [130]

---

124   (1976) 549 F 2d 597.

125   (1979) 595 F 2d 1287.

126   The Sherman Act is the main anti-trust legislation of the US.

127   *Hartford Fire Insurance Co. v California* 509 US 764,113 SCt 2891, 125 L.Ed.2d 612 (1993).

128   *United States v Nippon Paper Indus. Co.* 109 F3d 1 (1st Cir 1997).

129   *Hoffmann-La Roche Ltd v Empagran SA* 124 SCt 2359 (2004).

130   Case 15/74 *Centrafarm v Sterling Drug Inc.* [1974] ECR 1147. The matter of the attribution of responsibility for an infringement of EU competition law by a subsidiary to its parent company is highly debated: see M. Bronckers and A. Vallery, *No Longer Presumed Guilty? The Impact of Fundamental Rights on Certain Dogmas of EU Competition Law* (2011) 34 World Competition, 535; S. Thomas, *Guilty of a Fault that One Has not Committed: The Limits of the Group-Based Sanction Policy Carried out by the Commission and the European Courts in EU-Antitrust Law* (2012) 3(1) JECLAP, 11; L. La Rocca, *The Controversial Issue of the Parent-Company Liability for the Violation of EC Competition Rules by the Subsidiary* (2011) 32(2) ECLR, 68.

- second, on the 'implementation doctrine' established by the ECJ in the *Wood Pulp Cartel* cases[131] (see below); and

- third, on the EU Merger Regulation,[132] which applies to undertakings satisfying the turnover threshold in the European Union.

The implementation doctrine was formulated by the ECJ in *Wood Pulp Cartel*,[133] in which the European Commission found 40 undertakings supplying wood pulp to be in violation of EU competition law, despite the fact that they were not resident within the European Union. The ECJ held that:

> It should be observed that an infringement of [Article 101 TFEU], such as the conclusion of an agreement which has had the effect of restricting competition within the Common Market, consists of conduct made up of two elements: the formation of the agreement, decision or concerted practice and the implementation thereof. If the applicability of prohibitions laid down under competition law were made to depend on the place where the agreement, decision or concerted practice was formed, the result would obviously be to give undertakings an easy means of evading these prohibitions. The decisive factor is therefore the place where it is implemented.[134]

This statement established the doctrine of 'implementation'. The doctrine is particularly relevant where a foreign undertaking has no subsidiaries, no agents and no branches in the EU, and thus the Union has no jurisdiction under the doctrine of the single economic unit. In *Wood Pulp Cartel*, the ECJ held that it had jurisdiction in a situation in which a foreign undertaking sells directly to EU purchasers.

Under the implementation doctrine, it is irrelevant for the application of EU law where an agreement, decision or a concerted practice was formed; what counts is where it was implemented. Implementation in the EU is the first condition for the application of the doctrine. The second is that the agreement, decision or concerted practice in question must have appreciable effect on intra-Union trade.[135]

The implementation doctrine developed by the ECJ does not exactly match the US effects doctrine: intent to harm intra-Union trade is irrelevant; what counts is the place of implementation of the relevant agreement, decision, concerted practice or abusive practice, and its appreciable impact on intra-Union trade. Further, in the EU, the implementation doctrine will not apply to a situation in which undertakings conclude an agreement outside the Union under which they agree not to sell within the Union, or not to purchase from EU producers, while the US effects doctrine will apply if such an agreement is directed at the US market.[136]

The ECJ has never formally recognised the US effects doctrine as part of EU competition law.[137] This is for many reasons, the most important being that the US effects doctrine ignores the role of comity in dealing with issues of extraterritorial jurisdiction. This is well illustrated in the *Hartford*

---

131   Joined Cases 89, 104, 114, 116, 117 and 125–129/85 *A. Ahlström Osakeyhtiö and ors v Commission (Re Wood Pulp Cartel)* [1988] ECR 5193.

132   Council Regulation (EC) 139/2004 on the control of concentrations between undertakings [2004] OJ L 24/1.

133   Joined Cases 89, 104, 114, 116, 117 and 125–129/85 *A. Ahlström Osakeyhtiö and {?}ors v Commission (Re Wood Pulp Cartel)* [1988] ECR 5193.

134   Ibid.

135   Case T-329/01 *Archer Daniels Midland Co. v Commission (Re: Sodium Gluconate Cartel)* [2006] ECR II-3255.

136   J. Griffin, *Reactions to US Assertions of Extraterritorial Jurisdiction* [1998] ECLR 64.

137   It is to be noted that the General Court in Case T-102/96 *Gencor Ltd v Commission* [1999] ECR II-753, [87], seemed to recognise the effects doctrine. Some AGs and the European Commission endorse it. See: D. Geradin, M. Reysen and D. Henry, 'Extraterritoriality, Comity, and Cooperation in EU Competition Law' in A.T. Guzman (ed.), *Cooperation, Comity, and Competition Policy*, New York: Oxford University Press, 2011, 27–28.

Case,[138] in which the UK government's *amicus* to the US Supreme Court submitted that US courts had no jurisdiction over conduct occurring in London, because the UK had a regulatory scheme in place for the reinsurance industry and the challenged reinsurance agreements were exempt, under that scheme, from UK competition law. Nevertheless, UK law, although it permitted the agreements, did not compel them. Accordingly, under UK law, a defendant was not required to act in the impugned manner, and thus a defence based on foreign legal compulsion was not available to it. Bearing in mind that most competition laws are normally prescriptive in nature and thus do not require undertakings to act in any particular manner, under the effects doctrine, US courts have no discretion to take account of foreign interests, because the only instance in which a defence pursuant to comity is accepted is when a foreign sovereign compels a foreign firm to act in a manner prohibited by US anti-trust law.[139] The wide extraterritorial scope of the US effects doctrine, combined with the manner in which US anti-trust law is enforced (for example the possibility of imposition of treble damages, the possibility of foreign individuals being sentenced to imprisonment (anti-trust violations are criminal offences), and the possibility of class action), has led to the enactment of blocking legislation in many States,[140] such as the UK, and to accusations that US anti-trust law is 'imperialistic' in nature.

9.9 Concurrent jurisdiction

The existence of different grounds of jurisdiction inevitably means that several States may have concurrent jurisdiction over a particular person or event.

The matter of concurrent jurisdiction is illustrated by the disagreement between Saudi Arabia and the US in respect of the indictment on 21 June 2001 by a US federal grand jury of 13 Saudi Arabian nationals and one Lebanese national in connection with the bombing in 1996 of a building in Saudi Arabia which was used as a barracks for US military service personnel.[141] A bomb left in a truck near the building exploded, killing 19 members of the American military services and wounding nearly 400 others in an apartment building. The bombing was allegedly committed by a terrorist organisation and was intended to drive the US out of the Persian Gulf.

Saudi Arabia claimed that it had exclusive jurisdiction in the matter. Indeed, it could claim that it had jurisdiction under either the territorial or the nationality principle since the bombing took place on its territory and the accused were its nationals. However, the US also had strong arguments as to its right to assert jurisdiction because the victims were nationals of the US and thus it could invoke the passive personality principle, and additionally justify the exercise of universal jurisdiction on the ground that the offenders committed terrorist offences and were in the custody of the US.

At the time of the disagreement, neither the US nor Saudi Arabia were contracting parties to the 1997 Convention for the Suppression of Terrorist Bombings which entered into force in May 2001. The Convention has, however, some significance for non-contracting parties because it expresses the need to suppress acts of terrorism and codifies general principles in this area, including the issue of jurisdiction. The Convention recognises that the State of nationality of victims is entitled to prosecute

---

138   *Hartford Fire Insurance Co. v California*, 509 US 764,113 SCt 2891, 125 L.Ed.2d 612 (1993).

139   C. Ryngaert, *Jurisdiction in International Law*, 2008, Oxford: Oxford University Press, 134ff.

140   Under blocking statutes, States prohibit national firms from providing documents to foreign competition authorities or courts. See D.A. Sabalot, *Shortening the Long Arm of American Antitrust Jurisdiction: Extraterritoriality and the Foreign Blocking Statutes* (1982) 28 Loyola L Rev, 213. An example of a blocking statute is the UK Protection of Trade Interest Act 1980.

141   New York Times, 23 June 2001, A6.

the offenders. It also sets out grounds for universal jurisdiction in that a contracting State must prosecute the offenders if it decides not to extradite them to a State with a more direct interest. Further, the Convention states that it does not exclude the exercise of any criminal jurisdiction established by a contracting State in accordance with its domestic law.

In the US, the issue of concurrent jurisdiction is solved by reference to the reasonableness standard, i.e. the forum should take account of the different factors set out in the US Restatement (Third) to decide whether it is reasonable for US courts to assert jurisdiction in a particular case. Even if the reasonableness test is passed, US courts may decline jurisdiction on the ground of comity. Therefore the standard of reasonableness refers to the power of a State to exercise its jurisdiction over a person or event while the duty of comity concerns the wisdom of its exercise.[142]

It is a matter of controversy as to whether international law endorses the reasonableness standard. The only authority to support the existence of this standard in international law is the following statement made by Judge Fitzmaurice in his separate opinion in the *Barcelona Traction Case*:

> under present conditions, international law does not impose hard and fast rules on States delimiting spheres of national jurisdiction . . . It does however . . . involve for every State an obligation to exercise moderation and restraint as to the extent of the jurisdiction assumed by its courts in cases having a foreign element, and to avoid undue encroachment on a jurisdiction more properly appertaining to, or more appropriately exercisable by another State.[143]

It is submitted that principles of international law such as the principle of non-intervention, proportionality, equity, good faith and the requirement of a genuine link between the matter at hand and the *forum* State certainly play a role in restraining jurisdictional assertions of States.

Ryngaert, in his book on jurisdiction in international law,[144] proposes that the conundrum of jurisdiction should be solved in the following ways: instead of relying on the strongest nexus between the case and the forum, States should be entitled to exercise subsidiary jurisdiction over persons and events in a situation where a State with the strongest nexus fails to adequately deal with the case. Accordingly, States should 'exercise their jurisdiction with a view to furthering the interests of the international community rather to [*sic*] advancing their own interests'. He, however, admits that this solution may not be workable in the field of economic law, where the effect of violation may affect all States.[145]

9.10 Jurisdiction to enforce

Under customary international law, as confirmed by the PCIJ in the *SS Lotus Case*, extraterritorial enforcement of municipal law on the territory of another State is prohibited unless the other State consents. This is because any measure of enforcement violates the other State's sovereignty and its right to territorial integrity. Accordingly, the offended State is entitled to protest and, in some circumstances, has the right to receive reparation from the offending State. However, this is subject to the exception that, under the law of the sea, States have the right to hot pursuit (see Chapter 8.9.3.1).

---

142   *Lauritzen v Larsen* 345 US 571, 582 (1953).
143   *Barcelona Traction, Light and Power Company Ltd (Belgium v Spain)* (1970) ICJ Rep 3, 105.
144   C. Ryngaert, *Jurisdiction in International Law*, Oxford: Oxford University Press, 2008.
145   Ibid, 227.

If a State seeks custody of an individual who is in the territory of another State it must proceed through diplomatic channels, or according to the procedures specified in any relevant extradition treaty. However, despite the rule on extraterritorial enforcement being absolute and straightforward, some States have brought foreign nationals suspected of committing criminal offences before municipal courts through irregular means. Examples are: the abduction of Adolf Eichmann by the Israeli secret services from Argentina; the abduction of General Manuel Noriega by the US army from Panama; the abduction of Mordechai Vanunu by Israeli secret services from Italy; the abduction of Dr Alvarez-Machain sponsored by the US Drug Enforcement Administration from Mexico; the abduction of Abu Khattalah, the suspected leader of the 2012 attack on the US Consulate in Benghazi resulting in death of four US diplomats, including US Ambassador Stevens, from Libya by the US special forces in June 2014; and finally, the attempted abduction of Osama Bin Laden in May 2011 by US special forces, which resulted in the death of Osama Bin Laden. He was killed in the firefight and subsequently buried at sea. The last two situations are more complex given that the governments of the relevant States were either 'unwilling or unable' to co-operate with the US and that the US justified its actions on Article 51 of the UN Charter, i.e. the right to self-defence (see Chapter 15.4.5.3).

In respect of the abduction of Eichmann, following a protest from Argentina, it was subject to a debate at the UNSC resulting in the adoption of Resolution 138 (1960) declaring that repetition of such acts: 'would involve a breach of the principles upon which international order is founded, creating an atmosphere of insecurity and distrust incompatible with the preservation of peace'.[146] Under the resolution Israel was required to make appropriate reparation. Subsequently, it settled the matter with Argentina.

Bearing in mind the illegality of international abduction, in that it violates sovereignty and the territorial integrity of a State, the issue arises whether abductions will prevent municipal courts in offending States from trying foreign nationals abducted abroad, and brought to stand trial in the offending States. In this respect, most States agree that their courts will lack jurisdiction in a situation where a person is brought to trial by illegal means.[147] However, in each of the above examples municipal courts decided otherwise. The position of the US is that in conformity with the doctrine of *male captus bene detentus*, the US will have jurisdiction irrespective of whether a person is abducted by a private individual, i.e. normally a bounty hunter, or a State agent, and irrespective of whether there is an extradition treaty between the US and the relevant State. [148]

In *US v Alvarez-Machain* [149] the US Supreme Court confirmed the above position despite the protest of Mexico, the State of nationality of the abducted person, and despite the existence of an extradition treaty between the US and Mexico, under which the US authorities did not make any formal request for extradition of the accused.

---

146   Para 4 of the Preamble to UNSC Res 138 (1960).

147   In the UK this approach was confirmed by the House of Lords in *R v Horseferry Road Magistrates' Court ex p Bennett* [1994] 1 AC 42.

148   In *Ker v Illinois* (119 US 436,444 (1886)) the defendant, despite there being an extradition treaty between the two countries, was abducted by a private individual from Peru and brought to the US where he was tried and convicted for larceny. The US Supreme Court held that because there was no governmental involvement, and Peru did not object to the abduction, the US court had jurisdiction to try him.

149   *The SS 'I'm Alone' Case* (1949) 3 RIAA 1609.

US *V* ALVAREZ-MACHAIN

Facts:

The abduction of Dr Alvarez-Machain, a medical doctor, was sponsored by the US Drug Enforcement Administration (DEA) which believed that the doctor had taken part in the murder and torture of one of its agents in Mexico by prolonging the agent's life so that others could torture and interrogate him. DEA agents, after making some attempts to persuade the Mexican authorities to deliver the suspect, offered a reward for his delivery to them. Subsequently, Alvarez-Machain was abducted from his office in Mexico by bounty hunters and delivered to the DEA officials in Texas who arrested him. He argued that his unlawful abduction prevented US courts from trying him.

Held:

The US Supreme Court held that the extradition treaty between the US and Mexico did not expressly prohibit such abduction and that 'General principles of international law provide no basis for interpreting the Treaty [Extradition Treaty] to include an implied term prohibiting international abductions.' The Supreme Court ignored the argument of the defendant that abductions are so clearly prohibited in international law that there was no reason to include the prohibition in the Treaty itself. Further, the Court did not rule on the issue whether the abduction constituted a violation of the general principles of international law and if so, whether the defendant should be returned to Mexico.

Comment:

The case against Dr Alvarez-Machain was remanded to the District Court of Texas which dismissed all charges against him on the ground of lack of evidence. Subsequently, he sued one of his kidnappers under ATCA but the Supreme Court found that arbitrary arrest was not actionable under that Act (see Chapter 4.5.2.1).

RECOMMENDED READING

Books

Reydams, L., *Universal Jurisdiction: International and Municipal Legal Perspectives*, Oxford: Oxford University Press, 2003.

Ryngaert, C., *Jurisdiction in International Law*, Oxford: Oxford University Press, 2008.

Articles

Cassese, A.,*When May Senior State Officials be Tried for International Crimes? Some Comments on the Congo v Belgium Case* (2002) 13 EJIL, 853.

Conway, G., *Ne Bis in Idem in International Law* (2003) 3/3 International Criminal Law Review, 217.

Dinstein, Y.,*The Extra-Territorial Jurisdiction of States: The Protective Principle* (1994) 65 ANNIDI, 305.

Fachiri, A.P., *The Case of the SS Lotus* [1928] 9 BYIL, 131.

Gerber, D.J., *Competition Law and the WTO: Rethinking the Relationship* (2007) 10/3 Journal of International Economic Law, 707.

Lafontaine, F., *Universal Jurisdiction – the Realistic Utopia* (2012) 10/5/ J Int Criminal Justice, 1287.

Lowe, A.V., *US Extraterritorial Jurisdiction: The Helms-Burton and D'Amato Acts* (1997), 46 S.

McNeal, G.S. and Field, B.J., *Snatch-and-Grab Ops: Justifying Extraterritorial Abduction* (2007) 16 Transnatl L&Contemp Probs, 491.

Nollkaemper, A., *Wither Aut Dedere? The Obligation to Extradite or Prosecute after the ICJ's Judgment in Belgium v Senegal* (2013) 4/3 J Int Disp Settlement, 501.

Rojo, E.C., *National Legislation Providing for the Prosecution and Punishment of International Crimes in Spain* (2011) 9/3 J Int Criminal Justice, 699.

Shaw, G.J., *Note. Convicting Inhumanity in Absentia: Holding Trials in Absentia at the International Criminal Court* (2012) 44 The Geo Wash Int'l L Rev, 107.

Yee, S., *Universal Jurisdiction: Concept, Logic, and Reality* (2011) 10/3 Chinese Journal of International Law, 518.

AIDE-MÉMOIRE

The permissible bases for exercising criminal jurisdiction	Conduct for which State A may prosecute individual Z
The principle of territoriality. It constitutes the most used basis of jurisdiction. Every state has jurisdiction over property and persons within its territory, and over events occurring there.	When Z, a national of State B, is on the territory of State A and his conduct violates the law of State A.
The subjective territorial principle	Z breaches the law of State A. His conduct had commences in State A but was completed in State C.
The objective territorial principle	Z breaches the law of State A. His conduct had commenced in State C but was completed in State A.
The principle of nationality. Under this principle a State may exercise its jurisdiction over natural and juridicial persons (companies, ships, etc) that have its nationality in respect of offences committed by them abroad	Z, a national of State A, breaches the law of State A. His conduct may commence or end anywhere in the world.
The protective principle. This allows a State to exercise jurisdiction over foreigners for acts committed outside its territory if such acts are directed against the security of the State or threaten the integrity of governmental functions	Z, a national of State B, commits acts directed against the security of State A or threaten the integrity of governmental functions of State A. His conduct may commence and end anywhere in the world.
The passive personality principle. Under this principle a State may exercise jurisdiction over foreigners for acts committed outside its territory if the victim of the act is a national of that State	Z, a national of State B, commits acts against nationals of State A in State C. Conduct may start and end anywhere in the world.

The permissible bases for exercising criminal jurisdiction	Conduct for which State A may prosecute individual Z
The universality principle This is based on the nature of the crime, not on any nexus between the forum State and the matter under consideration. The reasoning behind this principle is that some crimes are so universally repugnant that their perpetrators are considered as *hostis humani generis*, i.e. enemies of all mankind. The prosecuting State acts, therefore, on behalf of all States. Although the existence of the universality principle is well established in customary international law, the modality of its exercise is highly disputed.	Z, a national of State B commits heinous crimes in State C. Z's conduct may start and end anywhere in the world. All States may prosecute Z, including State A.
Please note: Universal jurisdiction when exercised on the basis of a treaty dealing with international crimes is often referred to as **quasi universal jurisdiction.** Treaties do not allow to exercise jurisdiction *in absentia* but contain an obligation to either prosecute or extradite an alleged offender when he is found on the territory of a contracting State. This obligation is often referred to as the *aut dedare aut judicare*.	Z, a national of State B, commits an international crime, e.g. acts of torture in State C. State A is a contracting party to the CAT. If Z happens to be on the territory of State A, State A is required under the CAT either to prosecute Z or extradite him.

10

IMMUNITY FROM NATIONAL JURISDICTION

CONTENTS

CHAPTER OUTLINE

1 Introduction

Under international law some persons enjoy varying degrees of immunity from the jurisdiction of the municipal courts in a foreign country. These are: sovereigns and sovereign States, ambassadors and other diplomatic officers, consular officers, and members of foreign armed forces. With regard to international governmental organisations (IGOs) and their representatives, immunity normally derives from the constituent treaties creating the relevant organisation. In the UK, Orders in Council will determine first whether an IGO is eligible for any immunity and, second, the extent of immunity it is to enjoy in the UK.

2 State immunity, non-justiciability and the act of State doctrine

A distinction must be made between State immunity, and the doctrines of non-justiciability, and act of State. While a successful plea of State immunity, non-justiciability or act of State, prevents a municipal court from adjudicating a dispute, the ground on which a municipal court declines its jurisdiction will differ in respect of each plea. Under the plea of State immunity, a national court is barred from exercising its adjudicative and enforcement jurisdiction on the ground of the quality of the defendant, i.e. because the defendant is a foreign State or its agent. Under the plea of non-justiciability a municipal court has no jurisdiction because of the subject matter of the proceedings. The act of State doctrine was described by Lord Hope in *Kuwait Airways v Iraqi Airways* as applicable

> to the legislative or other governmental acts of a recognised foreign state or government within the limits of its own territory. The English court will not adjudicate upon, or call into question, any such acts.

However, there are limits to the doctrine. The Court of Appeal in *Yukos Capital* noted that the doctrine of act of State is a subset of the doctrine, or of the principle of non-justiciability. State immunity may be waived by a foreign State, resulting in proceedings being continued, but successful pleas of non-justiciability and of act of State always terminate proceedings before a municipal court.

3 State immunity and its evolution

State immunity is a rule of customary international law under which municipal courts of one State (the *forum* State) are prevented from exercising their adjudicative and enforcement jurisdiction in disputes where a foreign State is named as defendant (direct impleading) or where a foreign State intervenes by means of interpleader proceedings (indirect impleading), e.g. proceedings are commenced against individual State officials for alleged official torture abroad but the foreign State is indirectly impleaded because acts of its officials are attributable to it, or the disputed property is in possession or under control of a foreign State.

The doctrine of State immunity has evolved over the centuries:

- Initially, a State enjoyed absolute immunity from proceedings in municipal courts.

- Subsequently, State immunity was recognised with regard to sovereign or public acts (*jure imperii*) of a State but not with regard to private acts (*jure gestionis*).

- Currently, with regard to acts *jure imperii* an exception to immunity from foreign criminal proceedings exists in a situation where a former head of State or other high ranking official is accused of committing international crimes. However, no exception exists in respect of immunity from foreign civil proceedings, even if they involve the commission of international crimes, with respect to a State, or a head of State and other officials, irrespective of whether they are in office or have vacated it.

4 The terrorism exception to State immunity under the 1976 US Foreign Sovereign Immunities Act (FSIA) and its amendments

The US Foreign Sovereign Immunities Act (FSIA) and its amendments provides for the terrorism exception to State immunity. The exception permits civil suits for monetary damages, including punitive damages, against foreign States (and their officials), designated by the US Secretary of State as States sponsoring terrorism (a Designated State Sponsoring Terrorism (DSST)), in a situation where 'by an act of torture, extrajudicial killing, aircraft sabotage, hostage taking, or the provision of material support or resources for such an act' a DSST has caused personal injury or death. However, in practice, this remedy has not been of great importance because the enforcement of judgments poses many problems. Either victims are not compensated or are compensated through the US Treasury which seems counterintuitive to deterring State-sponsored terrorism.

5 UK law on State immunity: the 1978 State Immunity Act (SIA) and the common law

The 1978 UK State Immunity Act (SIA), which broadly implements the provisions of the 1972 European Convention on State Immunity, embodies the restrictive theory of State immunity, i.e. States can claim immunity only in respect of *acta jure imperii*. The SIA applies worldwide, i.e. not only to contracting parties to the 1972 European Convention, and governs foreign States' immunity from civil proceedings in UK courts. All civil matters falling outside the scope of the SIA and all cases involving criminal proceedings are decided under the relevant common law.

6 The 2004 UN Convention on Jurisdictional Immunities of States and Their Property (the UN Immunity Convention)

The first global codification of rules on State immunity was successfully achieved by the Convention on Jurisdictional Immunities of States and Their Property (the UN Immunity Convention) adopted by the UNGA in December 2004. The UN Immunity Convention has not yet entered into force. It has been signed by the UK, but it is still uncertain whether the UK will decide to become a contracting party to it. The UN Immunity Convention embraces the restrictive theory on State immunity, and thus removes immunity in respect of *acta jure gestionis*. It applies only to civil proceedings.

7 Diplomatic immunity

The Vienna Convention on Diplomatic Relations 1961, which was implemented in the UK through the Diplomatic Privileges Act 1964, regulates the extent of immunity granted to diplomats and the staff of a diplomatic mission.

8 Quasi-diplomatic privileges and immunities

Consular officers are not diplomatic representatives. Under the provisions of the 1968 Consular Relations Act, which gives effect to the 1963 Vienna Convention on Consular Relations, consular officers enjoy a limited degree of immunity in respect of their official functions.

9 Immunities of international governmental organisations (IGOs)

The immunity of international governmental organisations (IGOs) is not based on international customary law, but derives from the terms of the particular treaty creating the IGO. These treaties, almost without exception, specify the privileges and immunities accorded to the IGO by the contracting parties to the relevant treaty. An IGO, in States which are members of that organisation, is generally granted immunity from all types of legal process in respect of all acts carried out with a view to achieving the purposes set out in the constituent treaty. Thus, immunities are based on the principle of functionality, i.e. an IGO is immune in respect of all activities related to the exercise of its functions necessary to fulfil its international mandate. Immunity enjoyed by IGOs has been challenged because, in practice, it frees IGOs from the obligation to settle disputes with third parties such as contractors, persons tortiously injured, employees, etc. Such persons, if an IGO decides not to waive its immunity, have no forum in which to bring their claims and therefore are denied access to justice. With regard to employment contracts, the European Court of Human Rights (ECtHR) in *Waite and Kennedy v Germany* held that Article 6(1) of the European Convention on Human Rights (ECHR) (which ensures the right of access to a court) requires that when a claimant has no reasonable alternative means to protect effectively his rights under the Convention, i.e. no alternative forum is available to the claimant, a contracting party is obliged to remove immunity of the relevant IGO and to allow its national courts to entertain the claim. However, the UN is in a special position in that it enjoys absolute immunity from all proceedings in its member States.

10 Immunities of visiting armed forces

Members of the armed forces, who are in the territory of a host State with its consent, enjoy limited immunity from jurisdiction of that State. This is necessary in order to ensure that the integrity and the efficiency of a visiting army are not jeopardised. Normally, specific arrangements are made between a host State and a sending State.

10.1 Introduction

Under international law the following categories of persons and bodies enjoy varying degrees of immunity from the jurisdiction of the municipal courts in a foreign State:

- Foreign sovereigns, heads of State and other high ranking officials and a foreign State itself (i.e. State immunity). From the European perspective the extent of State immunity in respect of foreign civil proceedings for acts *jure imperii* was set out in the 1972 European Convention on State Immunity[1] (which was given effect in the UK by the 1978 State Immunity Act) and from the universal perspective it was set out in the 2004 UN Convention on Jurisdictional Immunities of States and their Property.[2] which to a great extent, codifies customary international law. Neither the UK nor the US are contracting parties to the last mentioned. In respect of acts *jure imperii* the above persons enjoy absolute immunity from foreign criminal proceedings subject to one

---

1   CETS 74.
2   UN doc A/RES/59/38, Annex.

exception. Immunity may be removed when a former head of State and, or, any other high ranking official is accused of the commission of international crimes.

■ Diplomatic agents of a foreign State. The scope of diplomatic immunity was the subject of the 1961 Vienna Convention on Diplomatic Relations[3] adopted on 16 April 1961 by the UN Conference on Diplomatic Intercourse and Immunities. It entered into force on 24 April 1964. The 1964 Diplomatic Privileges Act implements the Convention in the UK.

■ International organisations and their representatives. This immunity is based on the constituent treaties creating international organisations, not on customary international law. In the UK, the 1968 International Organisations Act as amended[4] regulates the extent of exemptions from jurisdiction of UK courts of an international organisation and of representatives of an international organisation.

■ Consular officers. Although consular officers of a foreign State are not diplomatic representatives, they enjoy some measure of immunity. This matter is governed by the 1963 Vienna Convention on Consular Relations[5] which was implemented in the UK in the 1968 Consular Relations Act.

■ Armed forces in the territory of a foreign State when they are present with the consent of that State. They enjoy limited immunity necessary to ensure that the integrity and the efficiency of a visiting army are not jeopardised. Normally, specific arrangements are made between a host State and a sending State.

10.2   State immunity, non-justiciability and the act of State doctrine

It is important to make a distinction between three doctrines which often apply in cases involving foreign governments: State immunity, non-justiciability (sometimes this is referred to as the principle of non-justiciability), and act of State. While under each of them a national court is prevented from determining a dispute, the bar to adjudication is based on differing grounds.

10.2.1   A plea of State immunity

Under the plea of State immunity, a national court is barred from exercising its adjudicative and enforcement jurisdiction because of the status of the defendant, i.e. because the defendant is a foreign State or the agent of such.

10.2.2   A plea of non-justiciability

Under the plea of non-justiciability a municipal court has no jurisdiction because the subject matter of the proceedings is not suitable for judicial determination. In *Kuwait Airways v Iraqi Airways*[6] the Court of Appeal summarised the doctrine as follows:

> In essence, the principle of non-justiciability seeks to distinguish disputes involving sovereign authority which can only be resolved on a state to state level from disputes which can be resolved by judicial means.

---

3   500 UNTS 95.
4   The Act is available at: www.legislation.gov.uk/ukpga/1968/48 (accessed 10 August 2014).
5   596 UNTS 261.
6   [2000] EWCA Civ 284 at [319].

10.2.3   The act of State doctrine

The Court of Appeal in *Yukos Capital SARL v OJSC Rosneft Oil Company*[7] provided much needed clarifications of the doctrines of act of State and of non-justiciability. It stated that the act of State doctrine is a subset of a wider doctrine of non-justiciability, both closely connected to the doctrine of State immunity, all three being based on international law, public and private, and the concept of comity.[8] The Court of Appeal considered that the 'clearest modern formulation of the doctrine [of act of State] at the highest level' is that provided by Lord Hope in *Kuwait Airways v Iraqi Airways* when he said:

> [the doctrine] applies to the legislative or other governmental acts of a recognised foreign state or government within the limits of its own territory. The English court will not adjudicate upon, or call into question, any such acts.[9]

The Court of Appeal considered that the above definition needs to be understood as qualified by Lord Wilberforce's two insights[10] provided in *Buttes Gas v Hammer*.[11] The first 'insight' is that the doctrine may apply to acts of more than one State. In *Buttes Gas v Hammer*, in the context of an action for defamation brought by one company against another, the House of Lords was required to consider the executive and diplomatic acts of more than one foreign State for which there were 'no judicial or manageable standards by which to judge those issues'.[12] Accordingly, the House of Lords declined to adjudicate the dispute on the ground of the principle of non-justiciability. The second 'insight' requires that in applying the principle of non-justiciability judicial restraint must be exercised but not judicial abstention.

The Court of Appeal reviewed the development and content of the act of State doctrine in the UK and in the US. It stated that 'the act of state doctrine cannot be reduced to a single formula' and observed that 'increasingly in the modern world the doctrine is being defined, like a silhouette, by its limitations'.[13] The Court found that its application is subject to the following limitations:

1   The acts of a State must generally take place within the territory of the foreign State itself although in some exceptional circumstances, such as in *Buttes*, acts may take place beyond the territory of one State.

2   The doctrine will not apply to foreign acts of a State which are in breach of international law, English principles of public policy and grave violations of HRs. For example in *Kuwait Airways Corp v Iraqi Airways Co* (Nos 4 and 5)[14] the House of Lords refused the enforcement and recognition of Resolution 369 enacted by the government of Iraq in the following circumstances. After the invasion of Kuwait by Iraq on 2 August 1990, 10 commercial aircraft belonging to Kuwait Airways Corporation (KAC), were forcibly confiscated by Iraqi Airways Company (IAC), a State-owned corporation. The confiscation of the aircraft was ordered by the Iraqi Minister of Transport and the aircraft were seized from Kuwait territory and removed to Iraq where they were indefinitely retained. On 9 September 1990, Iraq enacted legislation Resolution 369 granting

---

7   [2012] EWCA Civ 855.
8   Para 66.
9   Para 115.
10   Ibid.
11   [1982] AC 888.
12   Ibid, para 938.
13   Para 115.
14   [2002] UKHL 19.

IAC ownership of the confiscated aircraft. In proceedings brought in England IAC argued that Resolution 369, although a confiscatory decree which provided for no compensation, was enacted by the recognised government of Iraq and thus on the authority of *Luther v Sagor* [15] should be recognised as valid in England. Consequently, IAC's title to the aircraft, valid according to the law of the *situs* at the time of acquisition, should be recognised in England, and the claim of KAC should be dismissed on the ground of the doctrine of act of State and the principle of non-justiciability. The House of Lords held that Resolution 369 was not simply a confiscatory decree, but was part of an attempt by Iraq to extinguish every vestige of Kuwait as an independent State and as such constituted 'a gross violation of established rules of international law of fundamental importance',[16] one of them being the principle of *jus cogens* which prohibits the use of force against the territorial integrity of any State. Further, the House of Lords held that there was universal consensus that Iraq's aggression was illegal. Accordingly, the recognition of Resolution 369 would be contrary to the public policy of English law.

3   A judicial act will not be regarded as an act of State. This was one of the main issues in *Yukos Capital SARL v OJSC Rosneft Oil Company in* which the appellant Yukos Capital, alleged that judicial proceedings of Russian courts which set aside four arbitral awards totaling US \$425 million in favour of Yukos Capital, were a travesty of justice and part of the policy of the Russian State to bankrupt Yukos Capital. The awards were issued against OJSC Yuganskneftegaz (YNG), a private company which was subsequently taken over by State-owned Rosneft while Yukos Capital had survived in private hands. Rosneft, after the takeover of YNG, applied to Russian courts for annulment of the awards. The Russian courts ruled that the contracts between Yukos Capital and YNG under which the awards had been made were part of an unlawful tax scheme. Yukos Capital successfully enforced the awards before the Court of Appeal of Amsterdam which had found that the decision of the Russian courts setting aside the awards was 'partial and dependent', in other words was dictated by bias or intimidation. In proceedings in England Yukos Capital sought to enforce the awards and obtain post-award interest totalling US \$160 million. The awards were enforceable in the Netherlands as a result of a failed appeal of Rosneft, but the claim concerning post-award interest remained. Rosneft in its defence relied on the doctrine of act of State, and the plea of non-justiciability, on the ground that it is not appropriate for an English court to deal with allegations of governmental interference in judicial proceedings of Russian courts. The Court of Appeal rejected the application of both doctrines and stated that judicial acts are not acts of State and that there is no rule in English law against passing judgment on judiciary of a foreign State.[17]

4   The act of State doctrine does not apply to *acte jure gestions*, i.e. to commercial activities of a State (see Chapter 10.3.2).

5   The act of State doctrine does not apply when acts of a foreign State are only considered as a question of fact, i.e. from the perspective of whether an act had occurred without its validity or effectiveness being called into question. This is known as the *Kirkpatrick exception.*[18]

---

15   [1921] 3 KB 532.

16   [2002] UKHL 19, per Lord Nicholls, para 29.

17   For comments on this case see: A. Mills, *From Russia with Prejudice? The Act of State Doctrine and the Effect of Foreign Proceedings Setting Aside an Arbitral Award* [2012] 71 The Cambridge Law Journal, 465. See also: *Yukos Capital SARL v OJSC Rosneft* [2014] EWHC 2188.

18   *Kirkpatrick v Environmental Tectonics Corporation International* 493 US 400 (1990).

10.3 State immunity and its evolution

The main legal and political justifications for the existence of State immunity are as follows:

1 The principle of sovereign equality and independence. Since States are independent and equal, no State should be subjected to the jurisdiction of another State without its consent. This is encompassed in the maxim *par in parem non habet imperium* – legal persons of equal standing cannot have their disputes settled in the courts of one of them. Otherwise there would be an attack on the dignity of a foreign State. This is exemplified in *De Haber v Queen of Portugal*,[19] in which the claimant issued writs in the UK against the defendant and a number of agents of the Portuguese government, claiming that the Portuguese government had wrongfully received money which was in fact due to him. The defendant succeeded in having all proceedings stayed. Lord Campbell CJ stated that: 'to cite a foreign potentate in a municipal court . . . is contrary to the law of nations and an insult which he is entitled to resent'. Domestically in the UK, the monarch personally is immune from suit, and although in *M v Home Office*[20] it was held that a minister could be held in contempt of court, it was also held that an enforcement order could not be directed against a minister by a court.

2 The inability to enforce judgments of a forum State against a foreign State. Immunity remains absolute in respect of *acta de jure imperii*, i.e. acts of a public and governmental nature, as opposed to *acta jure gestionis*, i.e. private acts of State such as commercial transactions. Any attempt to enforce a judgment rendered against a foreign State, even if some assets of that State are within the forum, would not only create tension between the two States and upset friendly relations but also be contrary to the principle of non-intervention.[21] Further, in a situation where assets of a foreign State are outside the jurisdiction of the forum State, enforcement measures would simply be ineffective.

3 Entitlement of foreign sovereigns to immunity similar to that enjoyed by them in the municipal law of their home State. This entitlement rests upon the historical proposition that a sovereign could not himself be sued before his own municipal courts, so the sovereign of another State was similarly exempt from jurisdiction of the local law. Obviously, this argument is largely of historical value bearing in mind that in a democratic State the principles of transparency and accountability require that only in exceptional cases can a sovereign not be sued in his own courts.

The ICJ in the *Arrest Warrant Case*[22] recognised State immunity as a rule of international customary law and in the *Case Concerning Jurisdictional Immunities of the State (Germany v Italy: Greece intervening)*[23] confirmed that State immunity is not based on comity, but on customary international law.[24] Similar recognition was given in *Holland v Lampen-Wolfe*,[25] where Lord Millet said that:

---

19   (1851) 17 QB 171, 196.

20   [1993] 3 WLR 433.

21   See the ICJ's definition of the principle of non-intervention in the *Case Concerning Military and Paramilitary Activities in and against Nicaragua (Nicaragua v United States of America) (Merits)* [1986] ICJ Rep 14, para 205, which reflects current international customary law. On the prohibition of intervention see Chapter 15.3.

22   *The Arrest Warrant of 11 April 2000 (Democratic Republic of the Congo v Belgium) (Judgment)* [2002] ICJ Rep 3. Hereafter referred to as the *Arrest Warrant Case*.

23   Hereafter referred to as the *Jurisdictional Immunities* Case, (2012) ICJ Rep 99.

24   Ibid, para 53.

25   [2000] 1 WLR 1573, 1588, para 101 (for facts see Chapter 10.5.2).

State immunity is not a self-imposed restriction on the jurisdiction of the courts which the United Kingdom has chosen to adopt and which it can, as a matter of discretion, relax or abandon. It is imposed by international law without any discrimination between one State and another.

The doctrine of State immunity has evolved over the centuries. Initially, a State enjoyed absolute immunity from proceedings in municipal courts; subsequently, the immunity came to be recognised with regard to sovereign or public acts (*jure imperii*) of a State but not with respect to private acts (*jure gestionis*). As from the last years of the twentieth century, State immunity is being challenged on three grounds:

- First, because it is incompatible with the development of international criminal law as it shields heads of State and other high-ranking officials from being accountable for grave human rights abuses before otherwise competent courts.

- Second, the recognition by the international community that some rules of inter-national law are of *jus cogens* character (i.e they are superior to any other rules, including the rules on State immunity) entails that the prohibition of crimes having the character of *jus cogens*, such as genocide, crimes against humanity, war crimes, torture, should prevail over the rules on State immunity which do not enjoy the status of *jus cogens*.

- Third, that it clashes with basic human rights such as the right of access to a court, the right to a remedy and/or the right to effective protection.

The plea of immunity can be raised before any court, tribunal or quasi-judicial body of the forum State in respect of civil, criminal, administrative or any other proceedings. If a State raises the plea of immunity in respect of *acte jure imperii* in criminal proceedings the immunity is absolute. This is justified on the ground that criminal proceedings, if successful, result in the imposition of a penalty on, or imprisonment of, the accused. This is an unacceptable result in terms of its impact on international relations between the *forum* State and the defendant State. However, as a State can only act through its officials, acts of State officials are actually acts of the State itself and are attributable to that State.[26] In this context it is important to make a distinction between immunity *ratione personae* and *ratione materiae*.

- Immunity *ratione personae* is enjoyed by heads of State and some other high-ranking officials while in office and covers all acts, official and private. It ends when the head of State or the official vacates the post.

- Immunity *ratione materiae* or subject matter or functional immunity protects all State officials from jurisdiction of municipal courts of the forum State in respect of acts committed in their official capacities irrespective of whether they are still occupying the post or have vacated it. Accordingly, the scope of *ratione materiae* immunity is much broader than that of immunity *ratione personae* in that it applies to all State officials including ex-heads of State and high-ranking officials who have been involved in performing the functions of State.

---

26   See *Prosecutor v Tihomir Blaškić*, ICTY Appeal Chamber Judgment on the request of the Republic of Croatia for review of the Decision of Trial Chamber II of 18 July 1997, 29 October 1997, Blaškić, IT-95–14-AR108bis, para 38.

The distinction was well explained in the *Pinochet Case*,[27] in which Augusto Pinochet, as a former head of State, was denied immunity *ratione personae* because he was no longer a head of State (see Chapter 10.3.3.1. C). As to immunity *ratione materiae* in relation to acts done in his official function while in office, this was denied on the ground that the 1984 Torture Convention implemented in the UK through the Criminal Justice Act 1988 could not confer jurisdiction on a contracting party over acts of torture performed in an official capacity and, at the same time, maintain immunity from extradition or prosecution on the ground that they were of an official nature. As Lord Millet stated 'no rational system of criminal justice can allow an immunity which is coextensive with the offence',[28] i.e. immunity can only rationally exist in relation to acts that are an offence, otherwise there is nothing from which to be immune. However, the above judgment was made in the context of criminal proceedings.

A distinction must be made between State immunity for *acte jure imperii* in criminal and in civil foreign proceedings. On the authority of the ICJ judgment in the *Jurisdictional Immunities Case*[29] there is no exception to State immunity, including the commission of international crimes, from foreign civil proceedings, with regard to a State itself and its officials, irrespective of whether they are in office or have vacated it. However, such an exception applies to foreign criminal proceedings with regard to a head of State and other high-ranking officials accused of international crimes when they have left office. This, as Judge Kalaydjieva stated in *Jones v United* Kingdom,[30] means that parallel systems of State immunity apply to State officials: no immunity in relation to criminal proceedings for international crimes (which are analysed as personal acts of the perpetrator), but immunity in relation to civil proceedings against them for the same acts (which are analysed as acts of the State).

The evolution of the doctrine of State immunity is examined below.

10.3.1 Absolute immunity

The concept of absolute immunity was endorsed and explained by Chief Justice Marshall of the United States Supreme Court in *Exchange v McFaddon*[31] in the context of a dispute involving the ship, the *Exchange*, whose ownership was claimed by both the government of France, and a number of US nationals. In this case it was held that:

> The full and absolute territorial jurisdiction being alike the attribute of every sovereign, and being incapable of conferring extraterritorial power, would not seem to contemplate foreign sovereigns nor their sovereign rights as its objects. One sovereign being in no respect amenable to another; and being bound by obligations of the highest character not to degrade the dignity of his nation, by placing himself or its sovereign rights within the jurisdiction of another.

In England, the issue of whether a foreign sovereign enjoyed absolute immunity was first answered in the negative in *The Charkich*[32] but this case's approach to that issue, founded on a division between acts *jure imperii* and *jure gestionis*, did not survive the century. In *The Charkich*, Sir Robert Philimore

---

27   *R v Bow Street Metropolitan Stipendary Magistrate ex p Pinochet Ugarte (No 3)* [1999] 2 All ER 97, 113 and
      119.
28   Ibid, para 277.
29   (2012) ICJ Rep 99.
30   [2014] ECHR 32. See The Dissenting Opinion of Judge Kalaydjieva.
31   (1812) 7 Cranch 116, 138.
32   (1873) LR 4 A & E 59.

held that a vessel owned by the Khedive of Egypt forfeited its immunity because it was chartered to a private individual, but engaged in commercial activity.

In *The Parlement Belge*[33] the principle of absolute immunity was firmly established.

THE PARLEMENT BELGE

Facts:

The defendant ship was owned by the King of Belgium. It was a mail boat engaged in channel crossings.

Held:

Sir Robert Philimore remained faithful to his reasoning in The Charkich *in deciding that because the mail ship was involved in a commercial enterprise it was not to be accorded immunity.*

His decision was reversed by the Court of Appeal, which had the option of deciding that the vessel was primarily operating for the public benefit, the carrying of cargo and passengers being secondary to the carrying of mail. However, the principle applied by the Court of Appeal was that of absolute immunity resting on the theory of the independence of States.

The principle was confirmed in *The Porto Alexandre*.[34]

THE PORTO ALEXANDRE

Facts:

The Porto Alexandre, *a Portuguese ship, had gone aground in the River Mersey in the UK and had been refloated with the assistance of three tugs. The tug owners could not obtain payment and so issued a writ* in rem *against the ship itself. The facts were that the ship had been requisitioned by the Portuguese government, but was being employed entirely for carrying cargoes for private individuals.*

Held:

A claim of immunity was upheld. The judges in the Court of Appeal were aware of the blatant injustice of the decision, but demurred that they had no alternative in the light of the strong dicta in The Parlement Belge.

---

33   (1878–79) 4 PD 129.
34   [1920] P 30.

Foreign governmental agencies like the US Shipping Board and the TASS News Agency were accorded immunity by the English courts, but in 1957 in *Baccus SRL v Servicio Nacional del Trigo*[35] the Court of Appeal went further.

BACCUS SRL *V* SERVICIO NACIONAL DEL TRIGO

Facts:

The defendant was a department of the Spanish Ministry of Agriculture but, according to expert advice, was an independent legal personality.

Held:

The majority of the Court of Appeal upheld the plea of immunity, even though the defendant was in Spanish law a separate company, and the subject matter of the dispute was a commercial transaction.

The above cases are largely of historical interest only. The doctrine of absolute immunity was justifiable when it applied to a sovereign in person, but was called into question with the increased participation of States in commercial activities.

10.3.2 The restrictive approach – the removal of immunity in respect of *acte jure gestionis*

The need to impose restrictions on State immunity became apparent with the development of international trade at the end of the nineteenth century when States were becoming increasingly involved in commercial activities. The emergence of Communist States in the twentieth century further accentuated this tendency as Communist States, and their trading organisations, entered into commercial dealings with foreign individuals and companies. The latter had no remedy under their national laws, if a dispute arose because a foreign State or its trading organisation could rely on the concept of sovereign immunity and claim immunity from the judicial process of the courts of that State. Growing pressure toward establishing a more realistic and pragmatic approach gradually led municipal courts to a distinction between public acts of a State (acts *jure imperii*) and private acts such as trading and commercial activities (acts *jure gestionis*). As a result of this, a State could claim immunity only in relation to acts *jure imperii*. The Supreme Court of Austria in *Dralle v Republic of Czechoslovakia*[36] endorsed this distinction. Other States have followed.

In the UK, the stranglehold of precedent regarding absolute immunity was broken in 1975 in the case of *The Philippine Admiral*.[37] A writ *in rem* was issued by two Hong Kong shipping corporations against the owner of the ship, *The Philippine Admiral*. She was owned by the Philippine Reparation Commission, an agency of the Philippines government, but was being operated at the relevant time by the Liberation Steamship Company under a conditional sale agreement with the Commission.

---

35   [1957] 1 QB 438.
36   (1950) 17 ILR 165.
37   [1977] AC 373.

The company had employed the ship for normal commercial purposes. The Privy Council refused to uphold the plea of immunity.

This was followed in *Trendtex Trading Corp v Central Bank of Nigeria Co.*[38]

TRENDTEX TRADING CORP *V* CENTRAL BANK OF NIGERIA

Facts:

The plaintiffs sued the Central Bank of Nigeria for refusing to honour a letter of credit in respect of a contract for the supply of cement. The defendant claimed sovereign immunity.

Held:

Lord Denning MR stated that international law recognised the doctrine of restrictive immunity and that a distinction must be drawn between acts jure imperii *and acts* jure gestionis. *He quoted what Galileo said of the earth, and said that like the earth, international law also 'does move'. Accordingly, courts can take cognisance of changes in international law without any act of transformation by previous decisions of the English courts or an Act of Parliament. It is important to note that in this case Lord Denning stated that the doctrine of* stare decisis *does not apply to international law. Further, he said that the only satisfactory test to distinguish between* acte jure imperii *and* acte jure gestionis *was to look to the functions and control of the organisation, i.e. the Central Bank of Nigeria, not the purpose of a contract. Thus, it was necessary to examine all the evidence to see whether the organisation was under governmental control, and exercising governmental functions.*

At common law, therefore, the UK courts abandoned the doctrine of absolute immunity in respect of both actions *in rem* and actions *in personam*, thereby anticipating the enactment of the 1978 State Immunity Act which implemented in the UK the 1972 European Convention on State Immunity. That Convention, which was prepared under the auspices of the Council of Europe, confirms the restrictive approach to the concept of State immunity. However, the UK State Immunity Act 1978 does not address the issue of how to identify *acte jure gestionis*. In this respect Lord Wilberforce, elaborating on the position of Lord Denning taken in *Trendtex* stated in *I Congreso del Partido:*[39]

in considering, under the 'restrictive' theory whether state immunity should be granted or not, the court must consider the whole context in which the claim against the state is made, with a view to deciding whether the relevant act(s) upon which the claim is based, should, in that context, be considered as fairly within an area of activity, trading or commercial, or otherwise of a private law character, in which the state has chosen to engage, or whether the relevant act(s) should be considered as having been done outside that area, and within the sphere of governmental or sovereign activity.[40]

It flows from the above quotation that Lord Wilberfoce endorsed the 'overall context' approach which looks at all circumstances of the act including not only its nature but also its purpose. This approach has been applied by courts to cases decided under the UK Sovereign Immunity Act (SIA)

---

38   [1977] 1 QB 529.
39   *I Congreso del Partido* [1981] 2 All ER 1064.
40   [1983] I AC 244, 267.

and under the common law (see Chapter 10.5.2).[41] Other States which have adopted the 'overall context' approach are Australia, Ireland, Israel, Malaysia, New Zealand and Sweden. However, most States have endorsed the 'nature' approach.[42] Under this approach the nature of the transaction alone is considered in that if an act or transaction can be performed by a private individual it is of a commercial nature. Some States, such as Italy, prefer the 'purpose' approach under which it is not relevant whether an individual can be engaged in the relevant transaction, what counts is that it serves a sovereign or public purpose. The lack of an agreement as to whether the nature or the purpose of a transaction should be the determinative factor is reflected in Article 2(2) of the 2004 United Nations Convention on Jurisdictional Immunities of States and their Property, which states:

> In determining whether a contract or transactions is a commercial transaction under paragraph 1(c), reference should be made primarily to the nature of the contract or transaction, but its purpose should also be taken into account if the parties to the contract or transaction have so agreed, or if, in the practice of the State of the Forum, that purpose is relevant to determining the non-commercial character of the contract or transaction.

10.3.3 Challenges to the doctrine of State immunity based on the development of international human rights law, international criminal law and the existence of peremptory rules of international law – *jus cogens*

The doctrine of State immunity has been challenged on the following bases:

1 The development of international criminal law which has firmly established that an individual can be held responsible for grave human rights and humanitarian law abuses. The removal of immunity with regard to those accused of international crimes culminated with the establishment of the International Criminal Court (ICC). Article 27(2) of the Statute of the International Criminal Court states:

> Immunities or special procedural rules which may attach to the official capacity of a person, whether under national or international law, shall not bar the court from exercising its jurisdiction over such a person.

2 The recognition by the international community that some rules of international law are of *jus cogens* character. That is, that they are superior to any other rules. Consequently, the rules of international law prohibiting crimes, such as genocide, crimes against humanity, war crimes and torture, having the character of *jus cogens* should prevail over the rule on State immunity which does not enjoy the status of *jus cogens*. This entails that a State and its representatives should be denied immunity for acts performed in the course of official duties if such acts have violated a *jus cogens* rule.

3 The development of human rights law (HRL) which makes individuals subject to international law, and which confers important rights upon them which rights should be protected at both national and international level. Indeed, HRs are no longer an internal matter within the jurisdiction

---

41   See: X. Yang, *State Immunity in International Law*, Cambridge: Cambridge University Press, 2012, 103 *et seq.*
42   See M. Sornarajah, *Problems in Applying the Restrictive Theory of Sovereign Immunity* (1982) 31/4 ICLQ, 668– 671.

of a State but are of concern to the international community as a whole. In this context, the submission is that immunity should not be available when it clashes with the basic requirements of HRL, in particular if it results in denial of justice.

The manner in which international law has dealt with the above challenges is examined in the light of the distinction between immunity, which a State and its agents enjoy, in respect of foreign criminal and civil proceedings.

10.3.3.1 Immunity from foreign criminal proceedings

It is necessary to distinguish between the scope of immunity from criminal proceedings enjoyed by incumbent heads of State and other incumbent high ranking officials, from that enjoyed by them when they are no longer in office.

A. *Ratione Personae* immunity enjoyed by incumbent heads of State and other incumbent high ranking State officials

The ICJ in the *Arrest Warrant Case and in the Dijbouti v France Case* clearly stated that high ranking State officials, when in office, enjoy *ratione personae* immunity from foreign criminal jurisdiction. The ICJ held that under customary international law, incumbent foreign ministers, when abroad, enjoy full immunity from criminal jurisdiction as well as inviolability protecting them from 'any act of authority' by another State which would hinder them in the performance of their duties. The majority of the ICJ rejected any distinction between acts performed in an official capacity and those performed in a private capacity, or acts performed before or during the holding of the office of foreign minister. Accordingly, immunity is absolute in nature and suffers no exception.[43]

When a head of State acts in his/her official capacity as an organ of State his/her acts or omissions are attributable to the State itself and therefore any breach of international law committed by a head of State is considered as a breach of the international obligations of that State for which the State may be held accountable (see Chapter 11). The special position of a head of State in international law is recognised by the SIA and the FSIA (see Chapters 10.4 and 10.5.1.2). Under both Acts, a head of State enjoys the same immunity as the State itself. The UN Immunity Convention (see Chapter 10.6) does not directly regulate this issue but its Article 3(2) provides that its provisions are without prejudice to privileges and immunities accorded under international law to heads of State *ratione personae*.

A disputed matter is whether only heads of State, heads of government and foreign ministers, namely the troika (a group of three highest governmental officials), enjoy immunity, or whether it extends to other State officials when performing official functions. The language employed by the ICJ in the *Arrest Warrant Case*[44] and in the *Dijbouti v France Case*[45] indicates that the Court used the example of the troika rather than limiting immunity *ratione personae* only to these three highest ranking officials of a State. Discussions on this within the ILC and the Sixth Committee of the UNGA are inconclusive.[46]

In the light of the absolute nature of *ratione personae* immunity of high ranking State officials the question arises whether, when such persons are accused of commission of international crimes immunity

---

43   See *The Arrest Warrant Case* [2002] ICJ Rep 3, paras 51, 54, 56 and 58. See also Case *Concerning Certain Questions of Mutual Assistance (Djibouti v France)*, (2008) ICJ Rep 177, paras 170, 174.

44   *The Arrest Warrant Case*, supra note 43, para 51.

45   *Djibouti v France* Judgment, supra note 43, para 170.

46   See H. Huikang, *On Immunity of State Officials from Foreign Jurisdiction* (2014) 13/1Chinese Journal of International Law, 8.

means impunity. In the *Arrest Warrant Case* the majority of the judges noted that immunity does not mean impunity in that immunity from jurisdiction does not affect individual criminal responsibility. Accordingly, an individual can be held liable:

- before the courts of his own country; or

- when his State waives his immunity and allows another State to bring him to justice; or

- after he ceases to hold public office which means he may then be tried by any State which has jurisdiction under international law to do so; or

- before the ICC.

The dissenting judges in the *Arrest Warrant Case*, Higgins, Kooijmans and Buergenthal[47] were sceptical as to the likelihood of an individual being held liable for international crimes in the above circumstances.

The issue of whether and to what extent the ICC and other international criminal tribunals contribute to the fight against immunity is examined below.

B. Immunity of incumbent heads of State and other high ranking State officials before international criminal tribunals

Any attempt by heads of State, either incumbent or former, to rely on immunity once they have been indicted, or an arrest warrant has been issued against them by an international criminal court, or they have been brought before such a court, has, so far, failed.

With regard to the Nuremberg International Tribunal, the defendants, the most important leaders of Nazi Germany, were already in the custody of the Court and in accordance with Article 7 of the Charter of the Nuremberg Tribunal their official position neither freed them from responsibility nor mitigated punishment. Article 7 of the Nuremberg Charter was adopted in 1950 by the UNGA as Principle III of the International Law Recognized in the Charter of the Nuremberg Tribunal and in the Judgment of the Tribunal. These principles were formulated by the ILC at the request of the UNGA (Resolution 1777(II)), and have since been widely recognised by all States.[48]

Provisions similar to Article 7 of the Nuremberg Charter are embodied in the statutes of special criminal courts (e.g. Article 7(2) of the Statute of the International Criminal Tribunal for the Former Yugoslavia (ICTY), Article 6(2) of the Statute of the International Criminal Tribunal for Rwanda (ICTR), Article 6(2) of the Statute of the Special Court for Sierra Leone (SCSL)). Principal III refers to substantive immunity and as such is applied by both international and national courts, i.e. immunity which concerns the claimant's substantive rights or the defendant's responsibility.

Article 27(2) of the Statute of the International Criminal Court is unique in that, unlike statutes of other international criminal courts, it deals with procedural jurisdictional immunity. It states:

Immunities or special procedural rules which may attach to the official capacity of a person, whether under national or international law, shall not bar the court from exercising its jurisdiction over such a person.

The lack of any provision similar to that stated in Article 27(2) of the Statute of the ICC in statutes of other international criminal courts resulted in a debate as to whether special international criminal

---

47   Supra note 43., Joint Separate Opinion of Judges Higgins, Kooijmans and Buergenthal, para 78.

48   UNGA Resolution 95(1), 11 December 1946, UN Doc A/64/Add 1 (1947). The Principles were confirmed in the 1996 ILC's Draft Code of Offences Against the Peace and Security of Mankind.

courts are empowered to indict incumbent heads of State and to issue arrest warrants against them. A judgment on this issue was given by the Appeals Chamber of the SCSL in *Prosecutor v Charles Ghankay Taylor*.[49]

PROSECUTOR *V* CHARLES GHANKAY TAYLOR

Facts:

The accused, Charles Ghankay Taylor, the former President of Liberia, challenged his indictment on 17 counts. These included the commission of crimes against humanity, and grave breaches of the Geneva Conventions. He also challenged the warrant for his arrest. These challenges were on the ground that at the time the warrant was issued he was the President of Liberia and, in addition, on an official visit to Ghana. He argued that, on the authority of the Arrest Warrant Case, *he was not only entitled to immunity* ratione personae *for conduct performed when in office but also the indictment and the arrest warrant were invalid because they were issued when he was in Ghana, and so violated the principle of sovereign equality of States.*

Held:

The Appeals Chamber of the SCSL dismissed Taylor's challenges on the following grounds:

1 *Under the rules of procedure of the SCSL an accused is required to submit himself to the Court before he can raise the issue of his immunity. As Taylor made no appearance before the SCSL he could not bring a preliminary motion.*
2 *The SCSL had jurisdiction because it was an international court. Despite the fact that it was not established by resolutions of the UNSC, as was the case of the ICTY and the ICTR, the UN's involvement in the creation of the SCSL was essential bearing in mind that it was established on the basis of an agreement between the UNSC and Sierra Leone in pursuance of UNSC Resolution 1315 (2000). This Resolution, while reaffirming that the situation in Sierra Leone continued to constitute a threat to international peace and security, authorised the Secretary General of the United Nations (UNS-G) to negotiate the creation of the Court. The power of the UNSC to enter into the agreement with Sierra Leone derived, first, from the general purposes of the UN as expressed in Article 1 of the Charter and, second, from the specific powers under Articles 39 and 41 of the UN Charter to undertake appropriate measures to maintain or restore international peace and security. Therefore, the Chamber stated that whether or not the SCSL was established under Chapter VII of the UN Charter was irrelevant for the determination of its legal status. What was essential was that the agreement establishing the SCSL was an agreement between the UN and Sierra Leone expressing the will of the international community to punish those responsible for serious violations of international humanitarian law (IHL) in Sierra Leone. Accordingly, the circumstances of the establishment of the SCSL showed that it was a truly international court and as such its competence and jurisdiction* ratione materiae *and* ratione personae *were broadly similar to that of the ICTY, the ICTR and the ICC.*

---

49   SCSL-2003–01-I (3014–3039) of 31 May 2004.

Comment:

The above reasoning of the SCSL can be challenged. Indeed, it is questionable whether Resolution 1315 which determined the situation in Sierra Leone as constituting a threat to international peace and security should be given the same weight as UNSC resolutions establishing the ICTY and ICTR under which both courts are regarded as subsidiary organs of the UN. Further, the Appeals Court did not refer to the fact that the SCSL was actually a 'mixed tribunal' (see Chapter 17.6.2).

3 *The accused, as the head of a State, could not rely on jurisdictional immunity. Jurisdictional immunity of the accused was removed because the SCSL, as an international court, could rely on the authority of the following passage of the* Arrest Warrant Case: *'an incumbent or former Minister for Foreign Affairs may be subject to criminal proceedings before certain criminal courts, where they have jurisdiction. Examples include the International Criminal Tribunal for the former Yugoslavia, and the International Tribunal for Rwanda, established pursuant to Security Council resolutions under Chapter VII of the United Nations Charter, and the future International Criminal Court created by the 1988 Rome Convention.'[50]*

Comment:

In this respect it can be said that the above statement clearly indicates that not all international criminal courts have jurisdiction over persons clothed with personal immunity. Whether the SCSL belongs to the club of 'certain criminal courts' or not can be argued bearing in mind the SCSL's nature as a 'mixed tribunal' and the manner in which it was constituted as compared to both the ICTY and ICTR.

4 *The issue of the arrest warrant and its transmission to Ghana did not violate the sovereignty of Ghana. This was because, first, it was for Ghana to raise the issue, not for Taylor, and, second, an arrest warrant is not a self- executing instrument as it requires the co-operation and authority of the receiving State to achieve its execution. A receiving State has no obligation to assist the issuing authority in the execution of an arrest warrant unless such an obligation is imposed on it by the UN Charter or by an international treaty. When Ghana refused to enforce the arrest warrant it merely refused to assist the SCSL. Thus a request by the SCSL for assistance was in fact a recognition of the sovereignty of the receiving State, not its infringement.*

Follow up:

Charles Ghankay Taylor ceased to be the President of Liberia in 2003. He accepted exile in Nigeria where he was arrested and then taken before the SCSL. In 2013 he was sentenced by the SCSL to 50 years of imprisonment.[51]

---

50   *The Arrest Warrant Case* [2002] ICJ Rep 3, para 16.
51   *Prosecutor v Charles Ghankay Taylor*, Judgment of the Appeals Chamber, SCSL-03–01-A (10766–11114), A Ch, 26 September 2013.

Has establishment of the ICC ended impunity?

The answer to this question involves the examination of jurisdictional restrictions imposed on the ICC (see Chapter 17.6.2). One of them is that a State must be a contracting party to the Rome Statute. Accordingly, President Mugabe of Zimbabwe is unlikely to stand trial under the Statute of the ICC as Zimbabwe has not ratified that Statute, and a referral to the ICC by the UNSC is not to be expected. Further, even if he travels abroad, under Article 98 of the Statute:

> The Court may not proceed with a request for surrender or assistance which would require the requested State to act inconsistently with its obligations under international law with respect to the State or diplomatic immunity of a person or property of a third State, unless the Court can first obtain the cooperation of that third State for the waiver of the immunity.

Similarly, although Sudanese President Omar al-Bashir is, at the time of writing, indicted by the ICC on charges of genocide, crimes against humanity and war crimes in connection with the slaughter in Darfur, he will probably remain comfortably in his seat. Additional, political considerations play a significant role in ensuring impunity. In this respect the AU in 2010 called upon its member States not to co-operate in the arrest of al-Bashir on the ground of the destabilising impact of the al-Bashir arrest warrant.[52] Similar circumstances may be in existence with regard to the proposed arrest warrant for Syrian President Bashar al-Assad. In conclusion it can be said that as international law stands now, immunity means impunity and a State can, indeed, 'get away with murder'.

C. *Ratione materiae* immunity of former heads of State and other high ranking official from foreign criminal jurisdiction

In the *Arrest Warrant Case*, the ICJ made an unclear statement on whether former heads of State and other high ranking officials are entitled to immunity from foreign criminal jurisdiction. It stated that:

> *after a person ceases to hold the office* of Minister for Foreign Affairs, he or she will no longer enjoy all of the immunities accorded by international law in other States. Provided that it has jurisdiction under international law, a court of one State may try a *former* Minister for Foreign Affairs of another State in respect of acts committed *prior* or *subsequent* to his or her *period of office*, as well as in respect of acts committed *during* that period of office *in a private capacity*.[53]

The Court was criticised for not making a distinction between immunity *ratione personae* and *ratione materiae*.[54] In this respect the 2009 Resolution[55] of the IDI on Immunity and International Crime, in its Article 3, provides that persons who act on behalf of a State enjoy only immunity *ratione personae*. When it ceases such persons cannot claim immunity from foreign criminal jurisdiction with regard to international crimes committed when in office. The position of the IDI is well reflected in the famous *Pinochet Case* adjudicated by English courts. As judgment in *Pinochet I*[56] was set aside in the judgment of *Pinochet II*,[57] only the judgment in *Pinochet III*[58] is examined below.

---

52   See J. Flint and A. de Waal, *To Put Justice Before Peace Spells Disaster for Sudan*, The Guardian, 5 March 2009.

53   The *Arrest Warrant* Case, supra note 50, para 61.

54   See A. Watts, *The Legal Position of Heads of States, Heads of Governments and Foreign Ministers* 247 Recueil des Cours de l'Académie de droit international de la Haye (1994-III) 35–81.

55   The Resolution can be found at www.idi-iil.org/idiE/resolutionsE/2009_naples_01_en.pdf (accessed 25 August 2014).

56   *R v Bow Street Stipendiary Magistrate, ex parte Pinochet Ugarte (No 1)* [2000] 1 AC 61.

57   *R v Bow Street Metropolitan Stipendiary Magistrate, ex p Pinochet Ugarte (No 2)* [1999] 2 WLR 272.

58   *R v Bow Street Metropolitan Stipendiary Magistrate, ex p Pinochet Ugarte (No 3)* [1999] 2 WLR 827.

R V BOW STREET METROPOLITAN STIPENDIARY MAGISTRATE, EX P PINOCHET UGARTE (NO 3)

Facts:

Augusto Pinochet was President of the Chilean military junta which overthrew the government of President Allende and then ruled Chile from 11 September 1973 until June 1974. From 1974 until March 1990 Pinochet, although unelected, held office as President of Chile. He was at all material times a Chilean national and had never held Spanish citizenship. Throughout this period Chilean nationals and citizens of Spain, Switzerland, France and other countries were arbitrarily imprisoned and tortured and up to 4,000 persons disappeared or were killed as part of a government policy to eliminate political opposition.

In 1998 Pinochet travelled to the UK to receive medical treatment. During his stay in the UK, Spain applied for a warrant to extradite him to face charges of genocide, attempted murder, torture, hostage-taking and conspiracy. Two provisional warrants were issued in October 1998 for his arrest in London pursuant to s 8(1) of the UK Extradition Act 1989. The first, for the murder of Spanish citizens in Chile, and second concerned allegations of torture, the taking of hostages and conspiracy to murder.

The Divisional Court quashed both warrants on the ground, inter alia, *that Pinochet, as a former head of State, was entitled to absolute immunity from the jurisdiction of UK courts. The matter then went to the House of Lords,*

Held:

The House of Lords by a majority of six to one (Lord Goff dissenting) held the following:

1 *Section 2 of the UK Extradition Act 1989 required that the alleged conduct that was the subject of the extradition request was a crime in the UK at the time the alleged offences were committed. Extraterritorial torture did not become a criminal offence in the UK until s 134 of the Criminal Justice Act 1988, which had implemented the 1984 Convention against Torture and other Cruel, Inhuman or Degrading Treatment or Punishment (CAT), came into effect on 8 December 1988. It therefore followed that all allegations of torture prior to that date were not extraditable offences.*

2 *In principle a head of State had immunity from the criminal jurisdiction of the UK for acts done in his official capacity as head of State by virtue of s 20 of the State Immunity Act 1978 when read with Article 39(2) of Sch 1 to the 1964 Diplomatic Privileges Act. However, torture was an international crime and after the coming into effect of the CAT it was a crime of universal jurisdiction.*

3 *Since the CAT had been ratified by Spain, Chile and the UK by 8 December 1988, there could be no immunity for offences of torture or conspiracy to torture from 8 December 1988 at the latest.*

4 *Extradition proceedings on the charges of torture and conspiracy to torture could therefore proceed.*

Comment:

The above judgment can be summarised as follows:

1 *The issue of universal jurisdiction: The House of Lords based its judgment on the CAT which was implemented in the UK by the Criminal Justice Act 1988. Six out of seven*

Law Lords decided that universal jurisdiction could only be assumed on the basis of an international treaty (see Chapter 9.7), and not on customary international law, including the rules of jus cogens.

2 *The issue of double criminality: The double criminality rule in extradition proceedings requires that the conduct be an offence in both the requesting State and the requested State. The issue before the House of Lords was to decide on the critical date for the application of the principle of double criminality, i.e. whether the critical date was the date of the extradition request, or whether it was the date at which the actual conduct constituted an offence in both the requesting State and the requested State. The large majority of the Law Lords agreed that the critical date was the date of actual conduct. As a result, only acts of torture committed after the entry into force of s 134 of the Criminal Justice Act 1988, i.e. 8 December 1988, were extraditable offences. This interpretation of the UK Extradition Act was contrary to the wording of the Act and to settled practice.*[59]

3 *The issue of immunity of a former head of State: In this respect there were four possible approaches:*

- *to examine whether any rule of customary international law provided for immunity;*
- *to examine the statutory provisions;*
- *to consider whether the immunity was ratione materiae or ratione personae;*
- *to consider the effect of the CAT.*

In respect of the first two approaches the majority of Law Lords felt that immunity arose either by virtue of the rules of customary international law or under the terms of s 20 of the State Immunity Act 1978 as read with s 2 and Articles 29, 31, and 39 of Schedule 1 of the Diplomatic Privileges Act 1964. In respect of such immunity the question arose as to whether it was ratione personae or ratione materiae. In the circumstances of the case the majority categorised it as ratione materiae. This meant that the alleged acts of torture were carried out by Pinochet in his official capacity. Lord Millet was of the opinion that: 'These were not private acts. They were official and governmental or sovereign acts by any standard.'[60] This opinion was shared by the majority of the Law Lords. Consequently, Pinochet was prima facie entitled to immunity ratione materiae in respect of them.

Under s 134 of the Criminal Justice Act 1988 it was possible to remove the sovereign immunity in respect of the former head of State. That section provides a specific exception to the immunity ratione materiae of a former head of State in the case of acts of torture as defined therein. Thus, it is the nature of the offence that permits removal of the immunity. In this respect Lord Browne-Wilkinson stated:

Finally, and to my mind decisively, if the implementation of a torture regime is a public function giving rise to immunity ratione materiae, this produces bizarre results . . . If immunity ratione materiae applied to the present case, and if the implementation of the torture regime is to be treated as official business sufficient to found an immunity for the former Head of State, it

59   See A. Bianchi, *Immunity v Human Rights: The Pinochet Case* (1999) 10/2 EJIL, 237.
60   *R v Bow Street Metropolitan Stipendiary Magistrate, ex p Pinochet Ugarte (No 3)*[1999] 2 WLR 827, per Lord Millet, para 277.

must also be official business sufficient to justify immunity for his inferiors who actually did the torturing. Under the Convention the international crime of torture can only be committed by an official or someone in an official capacity. They would all be entitled to immunity. It would follow that there can be no case outside Chile in which successful prosecution for torture can be brought unless the state of Chile is prepared to waive its right to officials' immunity . . . In my judgment all these factors together demonstrate that the notion of continued immunity for ex-Heads of State is inconsistent with the provisions of the Torture Convention.[61]

The majority of their Lordships held that any immunity ratione materiae *was displaced at the latest at the time when the CAT had come into effect in all of Spain, Chile and the UK. Accordingly, they decided that after 8 December 1988 no immunity arose in international law in respect of any torture charge and thus extradition could proceed. In other words, the CAT had the effect of displacing any existing immunity after 8 December 1988.*

Follow up:

Pinochet was not extradited to Spain because the UK Home Secretary refused his extradition on medical grounds. He returned to Chile. In August 2000 the Chilean Supreme Court removed immunity from prosecution under Chilean law in respect of Pinochet. He was indicted on charges of kidnapping arising out of the disappearance of 19 political opponents in the first months of his leadership in 1973. On 9 July 2001 the panel of three judges of the Santiago Appeals Court found him, on the basis of dementia, unfit to face any trial. On appeal on 26 August 2004, the Supreme Court of Chile held that Pinochet was fit to face trial. It is highly likely that the Court's decision was influenced by the release of a report by the US Senate's Permanent Subcommittee on Investigations providing details concerning Pinochet's personal involvement in financial operations with Riggs National Bank from 1996 to 2002. The report showed that although Pinochet had, in 2001, been declared to be suffering from dementia he carried out several financial transactions through offshore corporations in the Bahamas relating to his assets at the Riggs National Bank. In Chile there were more than 230 lawsuits outstanding against him, filed by families of more than 3,000 people who disappeared or were tortured. Pinochet died of a heart attack on 10 December 2006 while under house arrest for tax evasion and for the kidnapping and murder in 1973 of two body guards of former Chilean President Allende. In the end, Pinochet was neither held accountable for crimes nor faced trial for the crimes alleged against him.

10.3.3.2   *Immunity from foreign civil proceedings*

The matter of whether a State and its officials are entitled to immunity from foreign civil proceedings involving allegations of the commission of international crimes has been very controversial. The ICJ, in the *Jurisdictional Immunities Case*,[62] gave a clear and unequivocal answer. Under customary international law both a State and its officials enjoy immunity from foreign jurisdiction in civil proceedings relating to the alleged commission of an international crime, irrespective of whether State

---

61   Ibid, per Lord Brown-Wilkinson, para 205.
62   (2012) ICJ Rep 99.

officials are in office or have left the office. In order to understand the judgment of the ICJ it seem necessary to examine judgments given by Greek and Italian courts which were challenged by Germany before the ICJ in the above mentioned case.

The ICJ is not alone in upholding absolute State immunity in foreign civil proceedings. The same position has been taken by the ECtHR and the House of Lords. This position is to be contrasted with the judgment of the US Supreme Court in *Samantar v Yousuf*.[63]

The above topics are examined below as well as the implications of the judgment of the ICJ in *Jurisdictional Immunities Case*.

A. The background to the dispute adjudicated by the ICJ in the *Jurisdictional Immunities Case*[64]

The Greek case

In *Prefecture of Voiotia v Federal Republic of Germany*,[65] for the first time, a Supreme Court of a State, in the context of civil proceedings, removed immunity in respect of *acta jure imperii* which were in breach of *jus cogens*. In this case the Greek Supreme Court gave a judgment in which it decided that Germany could not rely on State immunity in respect of acts *jure imperii* which were in breach of *jus cogens*. In so doing it upheld the Greek district court's award of damages of nearly 9.5 billion drachmas as indemnity for atrocities, including murder and destruction of private property, committed by the Nazi Germany occupation forces in the Greek village of Dimosio on 10 June 1944.

However, the Greek Minister of Justice refused to enforce the judgment, which refusal was confirmed by the Greek Supreme Court as being in conformity with Greek law. This refusal was challenged before the ECJ on the basis of its incompatibility with the 1968 Convention on Jurisdiction and the Enforcement of Judgments in Civil and Commercial Matters. The ECJ held that the matter was outside the material scope of the Convention as military operations of armed forces during WWII as a matter of law were performed by public authorities in the exercise of public powers and thus were not within the meaning of 'civil matters'.[66] The reaction of the Greek judiciary to the ECJ's judgment was to establish an *ad hoc* Special Supreme Court charged with the task of deciding the relevant issues of international law. The *ad hoc* Court, made up of judges and academics, decided, by six votes to five, that Germany was entitled to enjoy immunity without any restriction or exception and therefore could not be sued before any Greek civil court for torts committed.[67] The decision of the Special Supreme Court in fact nullified the prior judgment of the Greek Supreme Court, and thus it was not surprising that when the claimants sought to enforce the judgment of the Greek Supreme Court in Germany, this was refused by the German Federal Supreme Court on the ground that the conduct of German military troops, even if in violation of the laws of war, was of an *acta jure imperii* nature.[68] Next, the claimants brought proceedings against Greece and Germany before the ECtHR[69] which refused to remove the cloak of immunity from Germany. The ECtHR rejected the submission of the applicants that the

---

63   560 US (2010).

64   (2012) ICJ Rep 99.

65   Case No 11/2000 (2001) 95 AJIL 95.

66   Case C-292/05 *Irini Lechouritou and Others v Dimosio tis Omospondiakis Dimokratias tis Germanias* [2007] ECR I-1519.

67   M. Panezi, *Sovereign Immunity and Violation of Jus Cogens Norms* (2003) 56 RHDI, 199.

68   *Greek Citizens v Federal Republic of Germany*, BGH-III ZR 245/98, German Supreme Ct, 26 June 2003, BGH-1112R 248/98; (2003) 42 ILM, 1030.

69   *Kalogeropoulou v Greece and Germany*, ECtHR Reports 2002-X 389. On this topic see K. Bartsch and B. Elberling, *Jus Cogens vs. State Immunity, Round Two: The Decision of the European Court of Human Rights in the Kalogeropoulou et al. v Greece and Germany Decision* (2003) 4(5) German Law Journal, 477–491.

prohibition of crimes against humanity, being a rule of *jus cogens*, prevails over the principle of sovereign immunity.

Notwithstanding this, the Court of Appeal of Florence decided to enforce the Greek judgment in Italy and this decision was later confirmed by the Italian Corti di Cassazione (the highest Italian court in all matters except regarding the constitutionality of Italian laws).[70] Measures of enforcement were authorised against Villa Vigori, a German property located in Italy and used for cultural purposes.

The Italian cases

The Italian Corti di Cassazione in *Ferrini v Federal Republic of Germany*[71] refused to follow the ECtHR's judgments and based its decision on the superiority of *jus cogens* rules in the hierarchy of international rules and on the consequences attached to their breaches. This resulted in the Court's refusal to grant immunity to acts *jure imperii* which violated *jus cogens* rules.

FERRINI *V* FEDERAL REPUBLIC OF GERMANY

Facts:

M. Ferrini, who was forcibly deported from Italy to Germany for the purpose of forced labour in Germany, by the German military forces during WWII, brought civil proceedings against Germany for compensation before the Italian courts. Previous proceedings by him before the German courts had failed on the ground that his claim was outside the scope of the German law relating to reparation claims arising out of WWII.

Held:

The Italian Corte di Cassazione held that although Germany's military actions were acta jure imperii and thus Germany would normally have been entitled to immunity from proceedings in the Italian courts, the pleas of State immunity had to be rejected in this particular case because of the jus cogens *exception to State immunity. The Court found that the prohibition of forced labour being a peremptory norm under international law 'trumps' the plea of State immunity which is just 'an ordinary customary international law'. The absolute nature of a* jus cogens *rule entails that its violation: 'offend[s] universal values which transcend the interest of individual national communities'.*[72]

The Court further held that a State has an obligation not to recognise and lend its support to acts contrary to jus cogens *which are repugnant to the international community.*

Comment:

The judgment in Ferrini *stands alone as the one and only judgment where a supreme court of a State fully acknowledged the consequences deriving from the recognition of* jus cogens *rules as superior, peremptory norms of international law. It was applied to subsequent cases and even expanded in the case of Max Joseph Milde*[73] *(see below).*

---

70   See C. Espósito, *Of Plumbers and Social Architects: Elements and Problems of the Judgment of the International Court of Justice in Jurisdictional Immunities of States* (2013) 4/3 J Int Dis Settlement, 444.

71   (Cass Sez Un 5044/04) reproduced in the original Italian text in (2004) 87 Rivista di Diritto Internazionale, 539;128 ILR 659.

72   Ibid, paras 7 and 7.1.

73   (2009) 92 Riv Dir Int, 618.

B. The judgment of the ICJ in the *Jurisdictional Immunities Case*[74]

JURISDICTIONAL IMMUNITIES CASE

Facts:

As can be seen from the above cases, claims by Italian and Greek nationals arose from their exclusion from the conventional and unilateral schemes of reparation for victims, and their successors in respect of crimes committed by the German Third Reich during WWII in Greece and Italy.

Germany brought three types of claims against Italy:

- *First, challenging judgments of the Italian courts refusing Germany, and in the case of Max Josef Milde (a German official condemned in absentia by Italian courts for his participation in the massacres of civilians in Italy in 1944), immunity from civil jurisdiction on the ground that such immunity does not apply when a State, and/or its officials, commit grave international crimes.*
- *Second, alleging that the Italian judges in the above cases violated Germany's immunity by allowing the enforceability of Greek judgments in Italy.*
- *Third, alleging that Germany's immunity was violated by allowing measures of constraint against Germany's property in Italy, i.e. against Villa Vigoni.*

The first argument of Italy was based on the development of international law in that it no longer upholds State immunity in respect of acts jure imperii *when such acts constitute international crimes of* jus cogens *nature. Accordingly,* jus cogens *rules when in conflict with any other rules, including those on State immunity, should prevail. The second argument was that the victims would have been left without any kind of redress as a consequence of the application of the doctrine of State immunity. Therefore, the exercise of jurisdiction by Italian courts was a measure of last resort to avoid injustice.*

Held:

The ICJ rejected all arguments of Italy. It held that customary international law allows no exception to immunity for acte jure imperii of a State, or its officials, with regard to foreign civil proceedings and foreign enforcement measures. Accordingly, Italy was found in breach of international law.

Comment:

The ICJ established, by examining the law and practice of States, that customary international law allows no exception to State immunity from foreign civil proceedings with regard to acte jure imperii. It held a State's immunity for acte jure imperii encompasses acts committed by its armed forces during the conduct of armed conflict. This leads to the astonishing conclusion that the commission of international crimes by a State, and by its agents, can be considered as a legitimate exercise of sovereign power of a State. This conclusion, as pointed out by Espósito, requires a more sophisticated approach to the distinction between

---

74   (2012) ICJ Rep 99.

acte juris imperii and acte juris gestionis *so that it reflects the importance of developments of human rights, and its fight against impunity.*[75]

The most interesting part of the commented judgment concerns the relationship between the rules of jus cogens *and the rules on State immunity. The Court made a distinction between substantive and procedural rules, i.e. the Court held that rules of* jus cogens *are substantive while rules relating to State immunity from jurisdiction of another State are procedural, and consequently, a conflict between them is conceptually impossible. This means that procedural rules will never cross paths with rules of* jus cogens *(see Chapter 2.5 and 2.5.1.1). This approach to the relationship between the rules of* jus cogens *and the rules on State immunity mirrors the approach taken by the House of Lords in* Jones v Minister of Interior of Kingdom of Saudi Arabia[76] *and was accepted by the Fourth Chamber of the ECtHR when dealing with the same case (see below). Its main merit lies in its simplicity, but, as noted by Judge Bennouna in his Separate Opinion, this approach 'raises fundamental ethical and legal problems for the international community as a whole, which cannot be evaded simply by characterizing immunity as a simple matter of procedure'.[77] Indeed, one of the consequences of the commented judgment is that victims of international crimes are left without judicial redress. In this respect the ICJ expressed its regret for the victims, and suggested that their claims 'should be the subject of further negotiations involving the two States concerned'.[78]*

C. Implications of the judgment of the ICJ in the *Jurisdictional Immunities Case*[79]

There are many implications of the above judgment. However, the main is that the judgment does not solve in a satisfactory manner the conflict between State immunity and human rights law in terms of the right of victims of international crimes to adequate judicial remedy.

The right to a remedy has been recognised as a fundamental human right in customary international law and has been enshrined in global and regional human rights instruments.

The UN Basic Principles and Guidelines on the Right to Remedy and Reparations for Victims of Gross Violations of International Human Rights and Serious Violations of International Humanitarian Law adopted by the UNGA in Resolution 60/147 of 16 December 2005 states in Principle VIII that victims should have equal and effective access to justice and adequate, effective and prompt reparation for harm suffered.

The concept of remedies, according to D. Shelton, refers 'to the range of measures that may be taken in response to an actual or threatened violation of HRs. They embrace the substance of relief as well as the procedures through which relief may be obtained'.[80]

It flows from the judgment in the *Jurisdictional Immunities Case* that State immunity, as a procedural rule of municipal law will determine whether or not a municipal court has jurisdiction to adjudicate a

---

75   See C. Espósito, *Of Plumbers and Social Architects: Elements and Problems of the Judgment of the International Court of Justice in Jurisdictional Immunities of States* (2013) 4/3 J Int Dis Settlement, 455.

76   [2006] UKHL 26.

77   Supra note 74, para 9.

78   Ibid, paras 195–198.

79   (2012) ICJ Rep 99.

80   D. Shelton, *Remedies in International Human Rights Law*, Oxford: Oxford University Press, 2006, 8.

dispute involving a foreign State, or the officials of a foreign State. Although procedural immunity is, theoretically, a separate matter from that of substantial immunity, as procedural immunity merely indicates that once immunity is granted, the claimant must submit his claim to an alternative forum, in practice, in most cases of serious violations of HRs, there is no alternative forum. This results, on the one hand, in a victim being denied any reparation, and on the other, in impunity for the perpetrator. The case of Mr Al-Adsani provides an example. For Mr Al-Adsani, who was allegedly tortured in prison in Kuwait, no judicial remedy was available in Kuwait. Further, although he was a holder of dual citizenship, UK and Kuwait, the UK authorities refused to espouse his case. The Court of Appeal of England and Wales acknowledged that Mr Al-Adsani had made attempts to use diplomatic channels, but the UK was unwilling to assist him.[81] Indeed, diplomatic protection is of a discretionary nature and therefore it is exercised subject to political considerations. Accordingly, often the rights of victims are sacrificed by a State because of the importance to a State of maintaining friendly relations with the offending State. The judicial battle of Mr Al-Adsani ended before the Grand Chamber of the ECtHR, which held that there was no violation of the ECHR by the UK. The most controversial issue was whether there was a breach of Article 6 which guarantees the right to a fair trial. The judges of the ECtHR decided by nine votes to eight that there had been no violation of Article 6(1) of the Convention.[82] The Court noted that the right protected by Article 6(1) ECHR is not absolute. Limitations are allowed provided that they do not restrict or reduce access to a national court in such a manner, or to such an extent, as to impair the very essence of the right. Those limitations must pursue a legitimate aim, and must be proportionate to the objective sought to be attained by a contracting State. The Court accepted that the application of the doctrine of sovereign immunity, under which a State grants sovereign immunity to another State in respect of civil proceedings, had pursued the legitimate aim of complying with international law to promote comity and good relations between States.

The issue of proportionality was, however, more controversial. The ECtHR took account of the relevant rules of international law. While it acknowledged that those rules could not, in principle, be considered as imposing a disproportionate restriction on the right of access to a court it found that:

the Court, while noting the growing recognition of the overriding importance of the prohibition of torture, does not accordingly find it established that there is yet acceptance in international law of the proposition that States are not entitled to immunity in respect of civil claims for damages for alleged torture committed outside the forum State.[83]

However, in *Jones v Minister of Interior of Saudi* Arabia,[84] a case previously decided by the House of Lords,[85] the Fourth Chamber of the ECtHR had to deal not only with a civil claim against a foreign State, but also against its officials who allegedly tortured four British expatriates and detained them for up to 3 years in Saudi Arabia. The Court upheld immunity of Saudi Arabia as well as its officials from civil proceedings and thus confirmed the judgment of the House of Lords. However, the matter is not closed because the claimants asked for their case to be reconsidered by the Grand Chamber of the ECtHR. In this context the matter arises as to whether the claimants have a realistic chance to obtain a judgment in their favour. In this respect it is to be noted that the Fourth Chamber of the ECtHR was fully aware of the injustice the judgment causes to the claimants. It stated that: 'In the

---

81   107 ILR 536.
82   *Al-Adsani v UK* (2002) 34 EHRR 11.
83   Ibid, para 66.
84   [2014] ECHR 32.
85   (2006) UKHL 26.

light of the developments currently underway in this area of public international law, this is a matter to be kept under review by contracting parties.'[86] Therefore it remains to be seen whether the Grand Chamber will go against the traditional view on State immunity favoured by the ICJ or whether it will recognise that time for a change has come.

It is to be noted that not all national courts share the view of the ICJ. Apart from Italian Corte di Cassatione, the US Supreme Court in *Samantar v Yousuf*,[87] a case concerning a civil lawsuit against a former Somali prime minister accused of serious human rights violations, decided unanimously that the US Foreign Sovereign Immunities Act (FSIA) which governs the immunity of foreign States in US courts does not apply to suits against foreign officials, irrespective of whether they are in office or have left office. Accordingly, the FSIA, which applies to suits against a foreign State, will not apply to suits against officials of a foreign State. Although in *Samantar v Yousuf* statutory provisions were involved, i.e. the Alien Tort Claim Act (see Chapter 4.5.2.1) and the Torture Victims Protection Act the judgment applies to all suits against foreign officials, including those brought on the basis of common law. The defendant is entitled to rely on common law immunity, and other defences to jurisdiction, *inter alia*, statements of interest (SOI) filed by the US State Department.[88] Although on remand to the district court, the matter of immunity was settled in accordance with the SOI filed by the US State Department, which had refused immunity on the basis of its impact on the foreign relations interests of the US.[89] The main reason, not mentioned in the SOI, was, as the District Court stated, that 'under international and domestic law, officials from other countries are not entitled to foreign official immunity for *jus cogens* violations, even if the acts were performed in the defendant's official capacity'.[90]

It is important to mention that under the terrorist exception (see below), States which are considered by the US government as sponsoring terrorism cannot rely on immunity in tort suits brought against them.

10.4 The terrorism exception to State immunity under the 1976 US Foreign Sovereign Immunities Act (FSIA) and its amendments

The US seems to be the only country which has enacted legislation expressly providing for an exception to State immunity in a situation where a foreign State has committed terrorist acts.

The FSIA was amended in 1996 through the Antiterrorism and Effective Death Penalty Act (AEDPA) to include the terrorist State exception to State immunity.

Under the terrorist exception, US federal courts have jurisdiction over claims for monetary damages filed by a clamant or victim, as defined in the exception, against an agent of a foreign State who acts under the conditions specified in the exception, and since 2008 also against a foreign State itself, for injury or death caused 'by an act of torture, extrajudicial killing, aircraft sabotage, hostage taking, or the provision of material support or resources'.[91]

---

86   [2014] ECHR 32, para 215.

87   *Samantar v Yousuf* 130 S Ct 2278 (2010). On this topic see H.H. Koh, *Foreign Official Immunity After Samantar: A United States Government Perspective* (2011) 44 Vanderbilt Journal of Transnational Law, 1141.

88   It is unclear whether SOI are binding on US courts, see I. Wuerth, *Foreign Official Immunity Determinations in U.S. Courts: The Case Against the State Department* (2011) 51 Va J Int'l L, 915.

89   *Yousuf v Samantar* No 1:04cv1360 (ED Va Feb 11, 2012), aff'd, 699 F.3d 763 (4thCir 2012).

90   *Yousuf v Samantar* (4th Cir 2012) No. 11–1479, Slip Op Nov 2, 2012, at 21–22.

91   28 USC § 1605(a)(7) (2000).

Five months after establishing this exception, Congress passed a civil liability statute – the Civil Liability for Acts of State Sponsored Terrorism Act (known as the Flatow Amendment).[92] This amendment allows US courts to award punitive damages for claimants.[93]

Initially, claimants brought many successful claims under the above legislation, including Mr Flatow. However, after the judgment of the DC Circuit Court of Appeals in *Cicippio-Puleo v Iran*,[94] claimants under the FSIA and the Flatow Amendment found it almost impossible to succeed. In this case, the Court found that neither the terrorist exception to the FSIA nor the Flatow Amendment creates a private right of action against the foreign government itself, including its agencies and instrumentalists. Accordingly, a suit could only succeed against officials, employees, or agents of a foreign State for conduct performed in their private capacity (i.e. only to the extent that US officers and employees are amenable to lawsuits for similar conduct) as they retain immunity for conduct performed in their official capacity. To remedy this, in 2008 Congress amended the FSIA by creating a private right of action against the State itself.[95] However, the terrorist exception has the following limitations:

- the claimant or victim must have been a US national at the time the terrorist attack occurred; or be a member of the armed forces, or employee of the government; or an individual performing a contract awarded by the US government acting within the scope of the employee's employment;

- the foreign State must have been designated, by the US Secretary of State, as a State sponsoring terrorism (DSST), i.e. a rogue State. At the time of writing, four States are on the list: Cuba, Iran, Sudan, and Syria;[96]

- if the act occurs within the territory of a terrorism sponsoring State the claimant must give the State responsible a reasonable opportunity to arbitrate the claim;[97]

- if a foreign State fails to appear, the plaintiff must establish to the requisite standard of proof that the foreign State was liable for the conduct in question.

In assessing the terrorist exception to the FSIA it is submitted that in practice it has not provided the expected results. It has failed to achieve the two objectives for which it has been created:

- first, it has failed to deter State sponsors of terrorism. This is mainly because victims have been unsuccessful in enforcing their judgments, but and also because the list of DSST is based on the policy of the US government, and some States, like Cuba, can hardly be regarded as DSST; and

- second it has failed to compensate victims.[98] Most victims remain uncompensated as a result of factors such as scarcity of assets of DSST on the US territory, and unwillingness of the US government to allow payments being made from the defendant State's blocked assets, i.e. assets

---

92   28 USCS § 1605 note (2000). Flatow was a successful claimant in a suit against the Shagagi faction of Palestine Islamic Jihad, sponsored by Iran, responsible for death of his daughter, 22-year-old Alisa Michelle Flatow, who was killed when a suicide bomber drove a van loaded with explosives into a bus passing through the Gaza Strip, killing her, a US national and seven Israeli soldiers. In March 1998, he was awarded US$ 247 million in compensatory and punitive damages, *Flatow v Iran* 999F Supp 1 (DDC 1998).

93   28 USC § 1605 note (2000).

94   353 F 3d 1024, 1033–36 (DC Cir 2004).

95   28 USCA §1605A (2008).

96   The list is available at www.state.gov/j/ct/rls/crt/2013/224826.htm (accessed 10 August 2014).

97   *Simpson v Libya* 326 F 3d 230, 233–234 (DC Cir 2003).

98   For the in depth examination of failures of the terrorist exception see I. Arnowitz Drescher, *Seeking Justice for America's Forgotten Victims: Reforming the Foreign Sovereignty Immunities Act Terrorist Exception* (2012) 15 Legislation and Public Law, 806.

frozen by the US government as part of economic sanctions against the relevant State. An attempt to resolve the enforcement problem took place in 2000 when Congress passed legislation to pay to successful plaintiffs portions of 11 selected judgments, 10 against Iran and one against Cuba. Only the Cuban judgment was paid from Cuban assets in the US blocked in 1962. The Iranian judgments were to be paid from the US Treasury with the idea that later the US government would be able to seek reimbursement from Iran. This attempt was criticised for its selectiveness, and for the fact that compensation *via* the US Treasury is contrary to the aims of deterring State-sponsored terrorism. The same can be said about the 9/11 Victim Compensation Fund established by Congress in 2001 to compensate relatives of those who died in the World Trade Center.[99]

Notwithstanding the above, it can be said that the existence of the terrorist exception and the possibility, even remote, for victims to be compensated is certainly a move in the right direction.

10.5   UK law on State immunity: the 1978 State Immunity Act (SIA) and the common law

This section examines the main provisions of the UK State Immunity Act 1978 and the relationship between the SIA and the common law.

10.5.1   The 1978 UK State Immunity Act (SIA)

The position of UK law on State immunity is regulated by the State Immunity Act 1978, which entered into force on 22 November 1978.[100]

This SIA, which broadly implements the provisions of the 1972 European Convention on State Immunity, embodies the restrictive theory of immunity. It sets out in s 1(1) the general principle of absolute immunity and then goes on to indicate a number of exceptions to this principle. It applies only to civil proceedings, but on the authority of the judgment of the House of Lords in *Jones v Ministry of the Interior of the Kingdom of Saudi Arabia*[101] not to civil claims for alleged torture against a foreign State or its officials. Criminal proceedings are governed by the rules of common law. Because of this, in the *Pinochet Case* the House of Lords could not apply s 14(1)(a) which grants immunity to a head of State acting in his public capacity. The SIA applies *erga omnes*, i.e it is not confined to the States which are contracting parties to the 1972 Convention.[102]

The most important exceptions to the basic rule of absolute immunity, i.e concerning the *acte jure gestionis* exception, are set out in s 3, which provides that a State will not be immune in respect of proceedings relating to commercial transactions or obligations which under contract stand to be performed in whole or in part in the UK. Section 3(3) defines commercial transactions as:

(a)   any contract for the supply of goods or services;

(b)   any loan or other transaction for the provision of finance and any guarantee or indemnity in respect of any such transaction or of any other financial obligation; and

(c)   any other transaction or activity . . . into which a state enters or in which it engages otherwise than in the exercise of sovereign authority.

---

99   Air Transportation Safety and System Stabilization Act of 2001, Pub L No 107–42, §§ 401–409, 115 Stat 230, 237–241 (2001).

100   SI 1978 No 1572.

101   [2006] UKHL 26.

102   H. Fox, *The Law of State Immunity*, Oxford: Oxford University Press, 2008, 239.

A transaction that falls within any one of (a), (b), and (c) above will be a commercial transaction for the purpose of the Act with the exception that a contract of employment is not to be regarded as a commercial transaction within the meaning of the section (see below).

With regard to the determination of whether an act or transaction is within the scope of s 3 (a)–(c) UK courts will apply the 'overall context' approach, explained in Chapter 10.3.2.

Contracts of employment are specifically covered by s 4 which provides, *inter alia*, that a State will not be able to claim immunity in respect of such a contract made in the UK, or in respect of work to be performed in whole or in part in the UK. However, some exceptions are provided in s 4(2), one of them is set out in s 4(2)(b) which states that immunity will apply in respect of employment contracts if:

> at the time when the contract was made the individual was neither a national of the United Kingdom nor habitually resident there.

The above provision together with s16 SIA, which confirms this exception, and the UK Diplomatic Privileges Act were at issue in two cases: *Benkharbouche v Embassy of the Republic of Sudan* and *Janah v Libya*[103] which were heard together before the UK Employment Appeal Tribunal.

BENKHARBOUCHE *V* EMBASSY OF THE REPUBLIC OF SUDAN AND JANAH *V* LIBYA

Facts:

A cook of Moroccan nationality working at the Sudanese embassy in London, and a member of the domestic staff of the Libyan embassy in London who was also a national of Morocco, made claims arising out of their employment contracts. They alleged, inter alia, harassment, racial discrimination and a breach of EU Working Time Regulations. In proceedings before the UK Employment Tribunal their claims were rejected twice on the basis of their employers' pleas of State immunity based on ss 4(1)(b), 16 SIA, and the Diplomatic Privileges Act of 1964. On appeal to the Employment Appeal Tribunal, the appellants argued that the pleas of immunity first, denied them access to a court in breach of Article 6 ECHR as confirmed by the ECtHR in Cudak v Lithuania[104] *and* Sabeh el Leil v France[105] *and, second, were in breach of EU law, in particular Article 47 of the Charter of Fundamental Rights of the European Union[106] which recognises the same principle as that contained in Article 6 ECHR, and in breach of the EU Working Time Regulations 1998. With regard to the breach of EU law, the appellants claimed that the Tribunal was bound to disapply the relevant provisions of the SIA in accordance with the principle of supremacy of EU law.*

Held:

Langsaff P held that on the basis of EU law it was the duty of the tribunal to disapply the relevant sections of the SIA, i.e. the EU Working Time Regulations 1998 and Article 47 of

---

103   *Benkharbouche v Embassy of the Republic of Sudan and Janah v Libya* [2013] UKEAT/0401/12/GE; 0020/13/GE.
104   (2010) 51 EHRR 15.
105   (2012) 54 EHRR 14.
106   [2010] C83/389.

the Charter as they were in conflict with EU law. Article 47 of the Charter was breached because to deny the claimants access to court would constitute disproportional restrictions on the exercise of the rights conferred on claimants by EU law. The appeal was allowed.

Comment:

With regard to the ECHR, the appellants argued that to deny them access to court constituted unlawful discrimination based on their national origin in breach of the principle of proportionality as applied by the ECtHR in Cudak v Lithuania *and* Sabeh el Leil v France. *The Tribunal accepted that there had been a breach of Article 6 ECHR as far as the SIA was concerned. However, as the UK Human Rights Act of 1998, which incorporated the ECHR into domestic law of the UK, did not allow courts to disapply it, the claimants' remedy was to appeal to the Court of Appeal to seek a declaration of incompatibility under s 4 of the Human Rights Act 1998 (see Chapter 4.4.3.4.).*

It is important to note that Langsaff P accepted the interpretation of Article 6 ECHR by the ECtHR in which the ECtHR found that in the light of new developments in international and comparative law toward limiting State immunity in respect of employment related disputes, with the exception related to the recruitment of staff in embassies, the denial to access to court constituted disproportionate restriction on the right protected by Article 6 ECHR. This new development was based on Article 11 of the 2004 UN Convention on Jurisdictional Immunities of States and Their Property[107] (see Chapter 10.6) which according to the ECtHR reflected customary international law and therefore was binding on all States irrespective of whether a State has ratified the Convention. However, in Jarallah al-Malki v Reyes and Suryadi[108] *Langsaff P stated that a plea of diplomatic immunity must be treated differently (see Chapter 10.7.2) from that of sovereign immunity, the first mentioned being wider in scope, and thus respondents who were domestic workers employed by the appellant, a diplomat, were barred from pursuing their claims because of the purpose of the pleas of diplomatic immunity and lack of new developments similar to those regarding State immunity so far as the scope of diplomatic immunity was concerned. Langsaff P emphasised that the seriousness of claims made by respondents, i.e. that they had been trafficked, denied contractual wages or minimum agreed wages and discriminated against because of their race, had no bearing on the scope of the exception. Although the respondents did not rely on EU law, if the reasoning of Langsaff P is correct, the outcome would not have been different had they done so. The appeal was allowed.*

The SIA establishes substantive exceptions (additional to those examined above) to absolute immunity in the case of:

■ proceedings for personal injury, death or loss or damage to tangible property in the UK (s 5);[109]

■ proceedings relating to any interest in or possession or use of immovable property in the UK (s 6);

---

107   (2005) 44 ILM 801.

108   (2013) UKEAT/0403/12/GE.

109   On the authority of *Jones v The Kingdom of Saudi Arabia* [2006] UKHL 26, this exception does not apply to

- proceedings relating to patents or trademarks registered or protected in the UK (s 7);

- proceedings relating to a State's membership of a body corporate and unincorporated association or partnership which has members other than States and one which is incorporated or constituted under UK law or controlled from or has its principal place of business in the UK (s 8);

- proceedings in the UK courts with respect to arbitration to which the State has agreed to submit (s 9);

- actions *in rem* against a ship belonging to a State or actions *in personam* for enforcing a claim in connection with such a ship (s 10);

- proceedings in respect of liability for VAT, customs and excise duties, agricultural levies or rates in respect of premises occupied for commercial purposes (s 11).

Immunity from indirect taxes does not, however, extend to liability for income tax payable by foreign governments on earnings from investments in the UK.[110]

10.5.1.1 Remedies

Section 13 of the SIA establishes the general rule that relief may not be given against a State by way of injunction, specific performance or order for the recovery of land or other property, and that the property of a State shall not be subject to enforcement save where the State concerned has consented to such measures being taken. The principle of absolute immunity in respect of enforcement is, however, subject to an important limitation in the case of 'property which is for the time being in use or intended for use for commercial purposes' (s 13(4)). Section 13(5) provides that the head of a State's diplomatic mission shall be deemed to have authority to certify whether or not the property in question is in use or intended for use for commercial purposes. Such a certificate shall constitute sufficient evidence unless the contrary is proved.

The effect of a s 13(5) certificate was considered in *Alcom v Republic of Colombia*.[111]

ALCOM *V* REPUBLIC OF COLOMBIA

Facts:

The question arose as to whether the claimants could enforce an order for execution against monies in a bank account in the UK in the name of the Colombian mission.

Held:

The House of Lords, refusing enforcement, accepted a certificate from the head of the mission under s 13(5) that the funds were not used for the day-to-day running of the mission and were thus not property used for commercial purposes within the meaning of the section.

---

tort resulting from torture or other similar international crimes committed by a State or its official when acting in their official capacity (see Chapter 4.4.1.3).
110   *R v IRC, ex p Camacq Corp* [1990] 1 All ER 173.
111   [1984] 2 WLR 750.

10.5.1.2 Entities entitled to claim immunity

The immunities and privileges conferred by the SIA apply to any foreign State. Within the term of State the following bodies are eligible for immunity:

■ the sovereign or other head of State when acting in a public capacity (s 14(1)) and members of his family forming part of his household (s 20(1)(b));

■ the government of a State (s 20(1));

■ any department of the government of a State (s 20(1)) 'but not any entity (thereafter referred to as "separate entity") which is distinct from the executive organs of the government of the State and capable of suing or being sued' (s 14(2)).

A. Head of State and 'members of his family forming part of his household'
By s 21 of the SIA, the question whether an entity is a State is conclusively determined by a certificate of the UK Secretary of State for Foreign and Commonwealth Affairs, and may not be questioned in the courts (see Chapter 6.4.1).

Similarly, the question of whether a person is a head of State for the purposes of immunity is conclusively determined by a certificate of the Secretary of State for Foreign and Commonwealth Affairs and may not be questioned in the courts.[112] The matter of whether a person is a member of a family of a head of State forming part of his household was elucidated by the Court of Appeal in *Apex Global Management Ltd v Fi Call Ltd.*[113]

APEX GLOBAL MANAGEMENT LTD *V* FI CALL LTD

Facts:

Section 20(1)(b) SIA states that the Diplomatic Privileges Act 1964 (see Chapter 10.7.2) applies not only to a sovereign or other head of State, but also to 'members of his family forming part of his household'. In the context of a dispute concerning a commercial contract, each of two Saudi Arabia princes, a brother of the king of Saudi Arabia, and the son of the brother, argued that they were entitled to immunity from civil proceedings because they were within the scope of s 20(1)(b) SIA. The brother of the king had for many years performed significant royal and constitutional duties on behalf of the king. However, he had his own household and lived separately from the king. The same applied to his son.

Held:

The Court of Appeal held that there was no interpretational basis for giving the phrase 'members of his family forming part of his household', as contained in s 20(1)(b) of the 1978 Act, a wider meaning in relation to heads of State than in relation to diplomats. Under s 20(1)(b) SIA members of the family forming part of the household of a diplomat included

---

the spouse, or a civil partner, minor children of a diplomat and in exceptional circumstances older children dependent on a diplomat while in education and a dependent parent of a diplomat normally residing with him. Accordingly, the princes were not within the categories of persons covered by s 20(1)(b) SIA and therefore could not rely on State immunity for the purpose of setting aside the proceedings instituted against them. The Court emphasised that the granting of immunity to family members forming part of a sovereign's or a head of State's household was conferred solely for the protection of the dignity and independence of the head of State himself in the performance of his functions, and was not intended to apply to those assisting him or members of his family for the better performance of their own royal, governmental or constitutional duties.

B. The government of a State

Section 20(1) SIA does not expressly refer to State officials or representatives. Lord Hoffman in *Jones v Minister of Interior of Saudi Arabia*[114] stated that the words 'State' and 'government' have to be given a wide meaning, and be interpreted by reference to the UN Convention of Jurisdictional Immunities of States and Their Property (see Chapter 4.4.1.3). Wide interpretation means that a representative of a State acting in a public capacity is entitled to the same immunities as the State itself.

C. State entity

Under s 14(2) SIA a 'separate entity' is defined as 'any entity . . . distinct from the executive organs of the government of the state and capable of suing or being sued'. It benefits from immunity if:

■ the proceedings relate to anything done by the entity in the exercise of sovereign authority; and

■ the circumstances are such that a State would have been so immune.

In modern international life, there are many entities which are related to States or conduct quasi-State activities. The issue of whether or not an entity is a 'separate entity' or a department of a State or the *alter ego* of a State was discussed in *Trendtex Trading Corp v Central Bank of Nigeria.*[115] The Court of Appeal held that in order to decide whether an entity was an organ of a State UK courts should examine the functions, control, powers, duties and activities of the entity in question. This test has been applied by UK courts.[116]

However, the Privy Council in *La Générale des Carrières et des Mines (Gecamines) v FG Hemisphere Associates LLC*[117] departed from the Trendtex test.

---

114 Supra note 109, para 69.
115 [1977] 1 QB 529.
116 For example in *Kensington International Ltd v Republic of the Congo* [2005] EWCH 2684 (Comm) the Court of Appeal.
117 [2012] UKPC 27, FG.

LA GÉNÉRALE DES CARRIÈRES ET DES MINES (GECAMINES) V FG HEMISPHERE ASSOCIATES LLC

Facts:

FG Hemisphere Associates LLC (FGH), an investor in distressed assets, purchased the assignment of two ICC arbitral awards against the Democratic Republic of Congo (DRC). FGH sought to enforce those awards against the assets of Gecamines, a mining company wholly owned by the DRC, but possessing a distinct legal personality under the law of DRC. Gecamines owned shares in a Jersey joint venture group, Groupement du Terril de Lumbashi (GTL). FGH started proceedings against the DRC and Gecamines in Jersey. The SIA 1976 was incorporated into Jersey law by the State Immunity (Jersey) Order 1985.

The Jersey Court of Appeal held that Gecamines was an organ of the DRC and thereby the assets in Jersey could be used to pay the sums due under the arbitral awards. The matter went before the Privy Council.

Held:

The Privy Council allowed the appeal. It held that Gecamines was a separate entity and therefore its assets were not answerable for the DRC's debt.

Comment:

The Privy Council stated that even if the test established in Trendtex is satisfied, i.e. it is established that a State has constitutional and factual control over the entity and that the entity exercises some sovereign authority, this is not sufficient to convert a separate judicial entity into an organ of the State. Lord Mance explained that:

> *where a separate juridical entity is formed by the State for what are on the face of it commercial or industrial purposes, with its own management and budget, the strong presumption is that its separate corporate status should be respected, and that it and the State forming it should not have to bear each other's liabilities. The presumption will be displaced if in fact the entity has, despite its juridical personality, no effective separate existence.[118]*

This is indeed a very strong presumption and will only be displaced where the affairs of the State-owned entity, and the State, would have to be 'so closely intertwined and confused that the entity could not properly be regarded for any significant purpose as distinct from the State and vice versa'.

It results from the above judgment that a State-owned entity which has a separate juridical personality will be entitled to immunity under the SIA only when it can be shown that the State has constitutional and factual control of the entity, and that the entity has no separate existence from the State. Obviously, companies which trade in distressed sovereign debts will not like the outcome of the commented judgment, but those that carry out commercial transactions with sovereign States, often via wholly owned State companies, will welcome it.

---

118   Ibid, para 29.

10.5.1.3 Waiver of immunity

Waiver of immunity is covered by ss 2 and 13 of the SIA. The position regarding this waiver may be summarised as follows:

- A State may waive its immunity from jurisdiction either expressly or by conduct.

- This may occur by treaty, diplomatic communication or by actual submission to the jurisdiction in respect of the proceedings in question and all matters incidental to them.

- If a foreign sovereign comes to the court as claimant, or appears without protest as defendant in an action, he has submitted to the jurisdiction in respect of those proceedings, and all matters incidental to them.

- Even if a sovereign waives his immunity and a decision is given against him, it is not immediately possible for the successful claimant to execute a judgment against the sovereign. A separate act by the sovereign of waiver of immunity from execution will be necessary before execution can be levied.

- Whether a foreign sovereign appears as claimant or defendant, he submits not only to the jurisdiction of the court of first instance, but also to all stages of appeal.

- The submission must be a genuine act of submission in the face of the court.

10.5.2 State immunity under common law

The entry into force of the SIA did not abolish the common law rules on State immunity. These rules remain relevant to all cases falling outside the scope of the SIA in respect of civil proceedings, and to all cases involving criminal proceedings. The best example of the application of common law rules on State immunity in civil proceedings is provided by *Holland v Lampen-Wolfe*[119] in which the House of Lords considered that the SIA did not apply to the circumstances and based its judgment on State immunity at common law.

HOLLAND *V* LAMPEN-WOLFE

Facts:

The claimant was a US citizen and a professor at a US university that provided courses at a number of US military bases in Europe. From 1991 the claimant taught courses on international relations at a military base in England which was operated by the US under the terms of the NATO alliance. The defendant was a US citizen who was responsible for educational programmes at a military base in Yorkshire and was employed by the US Department of Defence. In March 1997 pursuant to his duties the defendant wrote a letter to the US University's European programme director in Germany stating that the claimant had been subject to criticism by students and that the writer questioned her professional competence. The letter concluded with a request that an alternative tutor be appointed to

---

119   [2000] 1 WLR 1573.

replace the claimant. Following the letter the claimant issued a writ for defamation. The defendant applied to a High Court Master for the setting aside of the writ on the ground that as an employee of the US Department of Defence he was immune from the jurisdiction of the court.

Held:

The Master set aside the writ. The claimant appealed. The appeal was subsequently rejected by the High Court, the Court of Appeal and the House of Lords. The House of Lords reached the same conclusions as the Court of Appeal in Littrell v United States of America (No 2).[120] *The appeal was unanimously rejected by the House of Lords on the grounds that, although the 1978 State Immunity Act did not apply, the defendant was entitled to immunity at common law.*

Comment:

This case raised a number of interesting issues.

- *By virtue of s 16(2) SIA, which provides that the Act 'does not apply to proceedings relating to anything done by or in relation to the armed forces of a State while present in the United Kingdom and, in particular, has effect subject to the Visiting Forces Act 1952', the House of Lords decided that the SIA could not apply to the circumstances.*
- *The Law Lords found that the applicable law was the common law on State immunity as stated in the case of* I Congreso del Partido[121] *which was decided before the entry into force of the SIA. The* I Congreso Case *endorsed the restrictive doctrine of State immunity based on the distinction between acts* jure imperii *and* jure gestionis. *Therefore, the question to be decided by the House of Lords was whether the tort of defamation was covered by the* I Congreso Case *and, if so, to determine the nature of the acts. The House of Lords ruled that the* I Congreso Case *applied not only to contract but also to tort.*
- *The crucial matter was to classify whether tort claims were attached to acts* jure imperii *or* jure gestionis. *The House of Lords, in determining the issue, decided to take into consideration the whole context of the claim, including the place where the educational programme was being provided and the persons to whom it was provided as well as its beneficiaries. The unanimous conclusion reached by the House of Lords was that the letter in question was classified as an act* jure imperii *and therefore covered by State immunity at common law.*
- *The House of Lords stated that its decision was in line with Article 6(1) ECHR. In this respect Lord Millet stated:*

    At first sight [the right to a fair trial] may appear to be inconsistent with the doctrine of comprehensive and unqualified state immunity in those cases where it is applicable. But in fact there is no inconsistency. This is not because the right guaranteed by article 6 is

---

120   [1995] 1 WLR 82.
121   [1981] 2 All ER 1064.

not absolute but subject to limitations, nor is it because the doctrine of state immunity serves a legitimate aim. It is because article 6 forbids a contracting State from denying individuals the benefit of its powers of adjudication; it does not extend the scope of those powers.[122]

His lordship therefore, dismissed the claim on the ground that a State has no power to adjudicate a dispute when a respondent State has not waived its immunity from legal proceedings, that is, on the ground that a court cannot exercise powers which it does not possess. The doctrine of State immunity constitutes an absolute bar on the exercise, by a forum State, of jurisdiction to adjudicate. In these circumstances, State immunity prevails over the Convention right contained in Article 6 ECHR.

10.6 The 2004 UN Convention on Jurisdictional Immunities of States and Their Property (The UN Immunity Convention)[123]

The UN Immunity Convention is the first global treaty codifying customary international law on State immunity. For the first time the ILC was, in 1977, asked by the UNGA to examine the topic of State immunity. This resulted in the ILC submitting a final set of Draft Articles in 1991. However, the Draft Articles did not meet with universal approval. Nevertheless, the work on the ILC Draft continued within the ILC, and among States' representatives in the UN Six (Legal) Committee. In 2000, the UNGA decided to establish an Ad Hoc Committee on Jurisdictional Immunities of States and Their Property with a view to furthering the work already done, to resolving the most contentious issues, and to preparing a generally acceptable convention in this area. The Committee succeeded and, after 27 years of work, the final text of the UN Immunity Convention was adopted by the UNGA on 2 December 2004. As at 27 September 2014, the Convention had not come into force; it had, however, attracted the signatures of 28 States and had been ratified by 16 States but not by the US or the UK. It requires 30 ratifications in order to enter into force. An Annex of Understandings is attached to the Convention and forms an integral part of it. The main role of the Annex is to clarify the meaning of certain terms used in Articles 10, 11, 13, 14, 17 and 19 of the Convention.

For interpretative purposes, the following are useful:

■ UNGA Resolution 59/39 of 16 December 2004 on Jurisdictional Immunities of States and Their Property.[124]

■ The Statement of the Chairman of the Ad Hoc Committee on Jurisdictional Immunities of States and Their Property (this committee was established by the UNGA under Resolution 55/150 to continue the earlier work done by the ILC in this area and to prepare generally acceptable rules on State immunities).

■ The Commentary prepared by the ILC on its 1991 Draft Articles on State Immunity.

---

122   [2000] 1 WLR 1573, para 52.
123   (2005) 44 ILM 801.
124   A/59/508.

The most important features of the UN Immunity Convention are:[125]

1 It establishes a general rule that States and their property enjoy immunity from the adjudicating jurisdiction of courts of other States (Article 5) and then sets out the following exceptions to that general rule:

■ Commercial transactions (Article 10). The Convention embraces the restrictive theory on State immunity and thus removes immunity in respect of *acta jure gestionis*. The term 'commercial transaction' means any commercial contract or transaction for the sale of goods or supply of services, any contract for a loan or other transaction of a financial nature and 'any other contract or transaction of a commercial, industrial, trading, or professional nature, but not including a contract of employment' (Article 2(1)(c)). On the controversial issue of what criterion should be used to determine whether a contract or transaction is commercial, the Convention achieved a compromise between States favouring reference to the nature of the act/transaction and those preferring its purpose as the defining criterion. Article 2(2) provides that reference should be made primarily to the nature of the act/transaction although its purpose can also be used 'if the contract or transaction so agreed, or if, in the practice of the State of the forum, that purpose is relevant to determining the non-commercial character of the contract or transaction' (Article 2 (2)).

■ Contracts of employment (Article 11). A State is not entitled to immunity with regard to employment contracts between that State and an individual for work performed or to be performed in the State where proceedings are commenced. This exception is, however, itself subject to numerous exceptions *ratione personae* and *ratione materiae*. With regards to persons, it excludes employees who are nationals of the employing State unless they are permanent residents in the *forum* State; those who were recruited to perform particular functions in the exercise of governmental authority; those who are diplomatic agents, consular officers or other persons enjoying diplomatic immunity. *Ratione materiae* exclusions concern: proceedings relating to recruitment, renewal of employment or reinstatement; proceedings relating to dismissal or termination of employment; proceedings which would interfere with the security interest of the employer State.

■ Personal injuries and damage to property (Article 12). There is no immunity in respect of proceedings for death or personal injury, or damage to, or loss of tangible property caused by an act or omission which occurred in whole or in part in the *forum* State if the author of the act or omission was present in the forum State at the time of the act or omission. This means that, on the one hand, a foreign State will be entitled to plead immunity in respect of acts or omissions committed outside the territory of the *forum* State, but in a situation where acts or omissions occurred wholly or partially within the forum State only if the wrongdoer was present in the forum State at the time of the act or omission. On the other hand, a foreign State will not be entitled to immunity on the ground that acts were performed in its official capacity. Both private and official activities are within the scope of the exception. The personal injuries and damage to property exception applies solely to proceedings concerning financial compensation. Consequently, a foreign State will be immune, for example, from proceedings aimed at obtaining an injunction.

---

125   For in depth examination of the UN Immunity Convention see R. O'Keefe and C. Tams (eds), *The United Nations Convention on Jurisdictional Immunities of States and Their Property. A Commentary*, Oxford: Oxford University Press, 2013.

It is unclear whether Article 12 applies to the activities of troops of a foreign State in armed conflict in the territory of the forum State. The Chairman of the *ad hoc* Committee stated that when this issue was debated an agreement was reached amongst the Committee members that military activities were outside the scope of the Convention. He also stated that the ICL's Commentary on Article 12 confirmed the view that Article 12 should not apply to situations involving an armed conflict.[126] As there is nothing in the Convention to support the Chairman's statement it is debatable whether military activities will be regarded as being outside the scope of the Convention.

In respect of victims of international crimes, for example, torture, they will be able to commence proceedings only if the act/omission complained of occurred in the territory of the *forum* State. Consequently, a foreign State will enjoy immunity from civil proceedings in the municipal courts of the *forum* State if the relevant act/omission occurred outside the territory of the forum State. The absence from the Convention of any human rights exception to State immunity was explained by the UNGA's Sixth Committee Working Group on two grounds: first that it 'did not fit into the present draft' and, second, that the matter was not 'ripe enough . . . to engage in a codification exercise'.[127] The real reason, however, is more practical. It is that many States, in particular those with a bad human rights record, will not agree on the imposition of an exception which even the ICJ in the *Arrest Warrant* Case rejected.

■ Arbitration agreements (Article 17). No immunity is provided for a foreign State in respect of court proceedings which relate to an arbitration concerning a commercial transaction unless the arbitration agreement provides otherwise. The relevant proceedings must be before a court which would otherwise have jurisdiction and relate to the validity, interpretation or application of the arbitration agreement, the arbitration procedure, or a confirmation of the setting aside of the award.

■ Other exceptions to immunity from adjudication of a forum State concern: legal proceedings relating to immovable property located in the territory of the forum State, succession and administration of estates (i.e. inheritance rights) (Article 13); infringement of industrial or intellectual property rights (Article 14); participation in a company or other collective body (Article 15); and operation of commercial ships (Article 16).

2   The Convention provides a broad definition of a State. Apart from the State and its various organs, Article 2(1)(b) includes units and subdivisions, agencies and other entities which are entitled to perform and indeed do perform acts in the exercise of sovereign authority, and representatives of the State acting in that capacity.

3   The Convention contains a provision relating to State enterprises, that is enterprises and entities set up by a State but which have an independent legal personality from that State, and are capable of suing and being sued. When State enterprises are involved in proceedings relating to a commercial transaction, the immunity from jurisdiction enjoyed by that State will not be affected.

---

126   A. Dickinson, *Status of Forces under the UN Convention on State Immunity* (2006) 55 ILLQ, 427.

127   UNGA Sixth Committee Convention on Jurisdictional Immunities, Report of the Chairman of the Working Group, 12 November 199, AC 6/54/L 12 para 46–08.

4   The Convention does not apply to criminal proceedings against a foreign State in a *forum* State. There is no provision in the Convention itself to this effect, but UNGA Resolution 59/39 expressly states in point 2 that the UNGA agrees with the general understanding reached by the *Ad Hoc* Committee that the Convention does not cover criminal proceedings.

5   The Convention maintains almost absolute immunity of a State from any measures of enforcement. Prior to a judgment, without the express consent of a State, no constraint measures, such as attachment or arrest, can be taken against its property. However, no such consent is required in circumstances where a State has, in advance of any claim being made, allocated or earmarked property as being available to satisfy such a claim as that actually being made (Article 19(b)). This is because it is assumed that by acting in a very specific manner the State has sufficiently demonstrated its consent. Subsequent to a judgment, a State is, subject to what is said below, entitled to immunity from enforcement of that judgment unless it has expressly consented, or by earmarking available property, implicitly demonstrated its consent. However, enforcement measures may be taken, without a State's consent, if it has been established that the State property against which the enforcement action is being taken:

■ is specifically in use or intended for use for commercial purposes; and

■ is located in the territory of the *forum* State; and

■ has a connection with the entity against which the proceedings were directed.

An Understanding attached to the Immunity Convention specifies that the term 'connection' is to be understood as broader than ownership or possession. Article 21 of the Convention lists the categories of property which should not be considered as property specifically in use or intended for use for commercial purposes by a State.

10.7   Diplomatic immunity

Diplomatic immunity has evolved from State immunity. For centuries kings and other heads of State appointed agents to represent their interests in other States. Ancient Greece first established the inviolability of the persons of heralds who were intermediaries bringing messages between warring States. In the Middle Ages papal diplomacy, conducted through papal legates and *nuncii*, contributed to the development of diplomacy as secular rulers started to follow the example of the Holy See in their modelling of the conduct of international relations. From the twelfth century, agents representing foreign rulers were called ambassadors. Italian city States, in particular Venice, conducted the most extensive diplomatic relations. During the period of the crusades, Venice entered into commercial relations with Byzantium and endorsed some of its practices. For example, Venice started to give its agents written instructions and established an archive containing a registry of all diplomatic documents. Its agents also reported on the conditions in host countries. Venice's practice was followed by other Italian city States, and later by France and Spain. Diplomatic rules, procedures and protocols were established in the sixteenth century when foreign ambassadors began to reside permanently in the capitals of host States. In 1626, Cardinal Richelieu established the first Ministry of External Affairs in France. He regarded diplomacy as a continuous process of negotiations which should ensure that national interests, not rulers' wishes or dynastic considerations, were pursued by diplomats. He believed that the '*raison d'état*' should be recognised and acted upon by those in charge of international relations. The Peace Treaty of Westphalia 1648 terminating the Thirty Years War was the first major meeting of heads of State in Europe, but diplomats were in charge of its preparations. Four years before the Treaty's signature they were working together and became well acquainted with each other. Experience gained by representatives of European rulers during negotiation of the Peace Treaty of Westphalia served as a base for the establishment of networks of embassies and legations throughout Europe. By the seventeenth century, diplomacy had become a profession for the aristocracy. For three centuries following the Peace Treaty of Westphalia, diplomats played the principal role in conducting international relations, and enjoyed a large measure of autonomy in a host State. However, the coming of a technological age, speedy transport, instant communications, plus a growing and evolving global agenda of States, and the emergence of new international non-State actors, has changed the way in which inter-State relations are conducted. This has resulted in 'diplomacy at a distance', and indeed diplomats themselves are losing importance.

In *US Diplomatic and Consular Staff in Iran (US v Iran)*,[128] the ICJ stated that diplomatic immunity is 'essential for the maintenance of relations between states and [is] accepted throughout the world by nations of all creeds, cultures and political complexions'. Diplomatic relations are based on mutual consent between the sending State and the receiving State. Since almost every State is both a receiving and a sending State the rules on diplomatic immunity are universally respected and rarely breached (for example, during the Iran–US crisis, when US diplomats were held hostage from 1979 to 1981, no country supported Iran's actions). The protection of the representatives of another State is necessary to ensure that they can perform their international political functions without fear of prosecution. In England the first statute in this area, the Diplomatic Privileges Act 1708, was passed as a result of the arrest and detention of the Russian Ambassador and his coach by the English authorities in order 'to prevent like insolence for the future'.[129]

In the UK, the rules in force on diplomatic immunity are embodied in the 1964 Diplomatic Privileges Act, which is based on the 1961 Vienna Convention on Diplomatic Relations which was approved by the UN Conference on Diplomatic Intercourse and Immunities held in 1961. The Vienna Convention on Diplomatic Relations came into force on 24 April 1964 and, as at 2 October 2014, had been ratified by 190 States.

10.7.1 Functions of missions

The functions of diplomatic missions are specified in Article 3 of the Vienna Convention. They consist, *inter alia*, of representing the sending State in the receiving State, protecting the interests of the sending State and its nationals, gathering, by lawful means, information about conditions and developments in the receiving State, and reporting them to the government of the sending State, negotiating with the government of the receiving State, and promoting friendly relations in all areas between both States.

10.7.2 Staff of the mission

Under the 1964 UK Diplomatic Privileges Act the UK's common law rule of absolute immunity was abolished and a qualified immunity now applies even to the head of a diplomatic mission. The 1964 Act divides the staff of a diplomatic mission into three categories as to the extent of immunity they enjoy.

1 The first category comprises 'diplomatic agents', such as the head of the mission or chargé d'affaires, and members of his diplomatic staff – counsellors, attachés, secretaries. Provided they are

---

128   (1980) ICJ Rep 3, para 24.

129   See *Empson v Smith* [1965] 2 All ER 881 at 883 discussing the case law on this subject.

not nationals or permanent residents of a receiving State they are entitled to complete immunity (in both official and private acts) from criminal, civil (including divorce petitions[130]) and administrative jurisdiction, and from measures of execution except in three cases. These are:

- in actions relating to private immovable property located in the UK, provided it is not held on behalf of the sending State for the purposes of the mission;[131]

- in actions relating to succession in which the diplomatic representative is an executor, administrator, heir or legatee as a private person;

- in actions relating to any professional or commercial activity exercised by the diplomatic representative in the UK outside his official functions.[132]

This immunity is also granted to the family of a diplomatic agent which forms part of his household, unless they are nationals of a receiving State.[133]

2   The second category encompasses the members of the administrative and technical staff of the mission, which includes clerks, typists, translators, radio and telephone operators etc. and their families which form part of their household provided they are neither nationals nor permanent residents of the receiving State. The second category does not enjoy immunity from civil and administrative jurisdiction in relation to acts performed outside the course of their duties.

3   The third category comprises members of the service staff such as butlers, maids, cooks, chauffeurs, porters, cleaners. Provided they are not nationals or permanent residents of a receiving State, they enjoy immunity only from the civil jurisdiction in respect of acts performed in the course of their duties.[134]

10.7.3   Expulsion of individual diplomats

A receiving State is entitled at any time and without any explanation to declare a head of a mission or members of its diplomatic staff or a consular agent as unacceptable, i.e. *persona non grata*. This long accepted rule of customary law has been enshrined in both the 1961 Vienna Convention on Diplomatic Relations (Article 9) and the 1963 Vienna Convention on Consular Relations (Article 23).

In this event the sending State normally recalls the diplomat concerned. However, if no such step is taken the receiving State may refuse to consider him as being a member of the mission. The declaration of *persona non grata* may be made either before or after the diplomat's arrival in the territory of the receiving State. There are three main reasons for which a diplomat may be declared *persona non grata*:

- the diplomat's personal behaviour, such as the commission of a criminal act or anti-social conduct, or an abuse of his diplomatic status such as when he acts as a spy or in any other manner endangers the security and other interests of the receiving State;

---

130   *Shaw v Shaw* [1979] Fam 62.
131   State Immunity Act 1978, s 16(1)(b).
132   Diplomatic Privileges Act 1964, Sched 1, Art 31.
133   Diplomatic Privileges Act 1964, Sched 1, Art 37(1); *Re C* [1959] Ch 363; and *R v Guildhall Magistrates' Court, ex parte Jarren-Thorpe* (1977) *The Times*, 6 October 1977.
134   Diplomatic Privileges Act 1964, s 2(4); Sched 1, Arts 33, 37.

- a receiving State may declare a diplomat *persona non grata* as a retaliation against a sending State which has so declared one of its own diplomats. This practice is quite common;

- a receiving State is required to make a *persona non grata* declaration with regard to diplomats of a sending State to comply with a binding resolution of the UNSC. Often UNSC resolutions, as part of sanctions imposed on a sending State, require the severance, or substantial reduction of diplomatic relations with a State under sanctions, e.g. UNSC Res 748 (1992) (31 March 1992) or UNSC Res 1353 (2001) (13 June 2001).

10.7.4 Inviolability of diplomatic agents

All diplomats, as well as members of their families forming part of their households, provided they are not nationals or permanent residents of a receiving State, enjoy personal inviolability. A receiving State must treat them with due respect and is also bound to ensure complete protection of all members of a foreign mission and their families against physical violence, and attacks on their dignity and freedom. Inviolability is extended to the private residence of a diplomat, his papers, correspondence and his other property.

10.7.5 Inviolability of the mission, its records and communications

Article 1(1) of the Vienna Convention defines 'premises of the mission' as:

> the buildings or parts of buildings and the land ancillary thereto, irrespective of ownership, used for the purposes of the mission including the residence of the head of the mission.

By Article 22 of the Vienna Convention the premises of the mission are inviolable. They may not be entered by agents of the receiving State without the permission of the head of mission. This rule is universally accepted and was applied by the High Court of England and Wales when it refused to issue a writ of *habeas corpus* in respect of the incident in 1896 concerning a Chinese refugee Sun Yat Sen who was held against his will in the Chinese mission in London.

The receiving State is bound to take all appropriate measures to protect such premises against intrusion and damage and to prevent any disturbance of the peace of the mission or impairment of its dignity. This obligation is embodied in Article 22 of the Vienna Convention. In the *Case of US Diplomatic and Consular Staff in Iran (US v Iran)*[135] the ICJ emphasised the imperative nature of the rules of diplomatic inviolability and in the *Case Concerning Armed Activities on the Territory of the Congo (Democratic Republic of Congo v Uganda)*[136] in the context of an armed conflict, again stressed their fundamental character.

---

135   [1980] ICJ Rep 3 at 24.
136   [2005] ICJ Rep 168, para 20.

CASE OF US DIPLOMATIC AND CONSULAR STAFF IN IRAN (US *V* IRAN)

Facts:

On 4 November 1979, after the overthrow of the Shah of Iran in that year, the US embassy in Teheran was overrun by hundreds of Iranians who had been demonstrating at the embassy gate. They seized diplomats, consuls and marine personnel there, and occupied the premises of the embassy. The embassy personnel were physically threatened and refused all communication with either US officials or relatives. The US consulates in other Iranian cities were also subjected to similar attacks. Subsequently, US personnel and one private citizen were apprehended and taken to the US embassy in Teheran where they were kept hostage.

The US government instituted proceedings against Iran before the ICJ alleging violations by Iran of the 1961 Vienna Convention on Diplomatic Relations, the 1973 Vienna Convention on the Prevention and Punishment of Crimes against Internationally Protected Persons[137] and the 1955 US-Iran Treaty of Amity 1955.

Iran refused to participate in the proceedings before the ICJ but presented its official position in correspondence sent to the Court, in which it stated that the matter of the hostages at the US embassy in Teheran was secondary or marginal in the light of 25 years of interference by the US in the internal affairs of Iran, namely that crimes were committed by the US – such as the preparation by the CIA of the coup d'état *in 1953 which overthrew the lawful government of Dr Mossadegh and resulted in the restoration of the Shah and his regime, and the subsequent subjugation of Iran's interest in all matters to the interests of the US – which led to a shameless exploitation of Iran contrary to international law and to humanitarian norms. Iran asked the ICJ not to take cognisance of the case.*

Held:

Provisional Measures of Protection
On 15 December 1979 the ICJ issued an order indicating provisional measures to be taken by Iran, that is, the immediate release of all hostages.[138]

In its judgment the ICJ disagreed that the detention of US diplomats was a secondary matter and emphasised the importance of the legal principle involved in the dispute. The Court confirmed that it had compulsory jurisdiction under the protocols to the two Vienna Conventions to which both States were contracting parties as well as under the US-Iran Treaty of Amity 1955. Moreover, the ICJ stated that under the ICJ Statute and its Rules of Procedure, there was no provision contemplating that the Court should decline jurisdiction merely because a dispute had other aspects, however important.

Judgment:

As to the merits, the ICJ distinguished two sets of circumstances.[139]

---

137   1035 UNTS 167.

138   *The Case Concerning United States Diplomatic and Consular Staff in Teheran (US v Iran) (Order)* [Removal from the List] [1981] ICJ Rep 45.

139   [1980] ICJ Rep 3

First, it dealt with the armed attack on the US embassy and consulates and the taking of their staff hostage by the Iranian militants. The ICJ held that the attacks on the US embassy in Teheran and consulates in other Iranian cities could not be imputable to the Iranian State. However, Iran's inaction after the attack and the taking of hostages was in breach of Articles 22(2) and 29 of the Vienna Convention as Iran failed to take appropriate measures to ensure the protection of the US embassy and consulates, their staff, their archives, their means of communications and the freedom of movement of the members of staff. The Court emphasised that this failure was due to 'more than negligence or lack of appropriate means'.

Second, with regard to events occurring after the occupation of the embassy by the militants and the detention of hostages, Iran's official position was that of approval of acts committed by the militants. As the ICJ stressed, the approval and the decision taken by Iran to perpetuate the situation translated continuing occupation of the Embassy and the detention of the hostages into acts of that State. The militants, authors of the invasion and jailers of the hostages, had now become agents of the Iranian State for whose acts the State itself was internationally responsible.[140]

The Court ordered Iran to immediately release all hostages and make reparations to the US.

Iran did not comply with the judgment, but the dispute was subsequently settled through negotiations. Under the 1979 International Convention against the Taking of Hostages all hostages were released after 15 months of captivity and the Iranian-United States Claims Tribunal was established to deal with claims of US nationals against Iran. A special fund created from a portion of Iranian government assets in the US frozen by President Carter at the beginning of the hostage crisis was set aside to satisfy the claims.

Comment:

In this case the ICJ stated that diplomatic law constituted a self-contained regime. However, this statement has been challenged in that the special counter-measures provided for under diplomatic law are neither exhaustive nor comprehensive, with the consequence that, on occasions, the law of State responsibility can take effect when diplomatic law runs out (see Chapter 2.4.2.1 A).

10.7.6 Cessation of immunities and privileges

Under Article 39(2) of the Vienna Convention immunities and privileges normally cease at the moment when a diplomat leaves the receiving country, or upon the expiry of reasonable time for that diplomat to do so, even during an armed conflict. Therefore, the termination of his functions in a receiving State does not coincide with the cessation of immunity. It extends for a reasonable time to allow a diplomat to complete his arrangements and leave the receiving State.

In respect of the cessation of immunities it is important to make a distinction between functional and personal immunity. Functional immunity covers acts and transactions performed by a diplomat in his official capacity and is everlasting (Article 39 of the Vienna Convention). Personal immunity covers

---

140   Ibid, para 74.

all private activities of a diplomat performed during the period of his mission in a receiving State, but expires at the end of that period. Therefore, if after the termination of his diplomatic functions and his subsequent return to his country he goes back to a receiving State as a private individual he may be accountable for his personal activities carried out during his mission and may be arrested and brought to trial there.

The matter of functional immunity as well as the relationship between diplomatic and State immunity was examined in *P v P (No 2)*.[141]

P V P (NO 2)

Facts:

A US diplomat who worked as a cultural attaché at the US Embassy in London was ordered by the US government to return to the US with his family. Shortly after the termination of his diplomatic functions, his wife commenced divorce proceedings in London. During child custody proceedings, the entire family returned to the US, but the wife went under protest having beforehand issued an originating summons in the English court seeking a declaration under s 8 of the 1985 Child Abduction and Custody Act that the removal of the children from the UK by her husband was a wrongful removal within the meaning and terms of Article 3 of the 1980 Hague Convention on the Civil Aspects of International Child Abduction.

The US government was given leave to intervene and sought dismissal of the proceedings on the grounds of diplomatic immunity and sovereign immunity.

The divorce proceedings were set aside on the basis of diplomatic immunity enjoyed by the husband. Under the Diplomatic Privileges Act 1964, a cultural attaché is regarded as a diplomatic agent and thus is exempt from the civil and criminal jurisdiction of the English courts in respect of both official and private acts. It should be noted that in Shaw v Shaw[142] *it had been held that civil proceedings include a divorce petition.*

The matter whether the husband could rely on his status of a diplomatic agent when, against his wife's wishes, he removed their children at the end of the diplomatic posting was assessed in the light of Article 39(2) of the 1961 Vienna Convention on Diplomatic Relations which provides that:

> *When the functions of a person enjoying privileges and immunities have come to an end, such privileges and immunities shall normally cease at the moment when he leaves the country, or on expiry of a reasonable period in which to do so, but shall subsist until that time, even in case of armed conflict. However, with respect to acts performed by such a person in exercise of his function as a member of the mission, immunity shall continue to subsist.*

Held:

His Lordship, Sir Stephen Brown, President of the Family Division, emphasised that diplomatic privileges and immunities were functional in character, aimed at ensuring the efficient performance of the functions of diplomatic missions representing States, and not to benefit

---

141   (1998) 114 ILR 485.
142   [1979] Fam 62.

> individual diplomats. His Lordship held that the removal of children from the UK by a father at the end of his diplomatic posting could not be construed as an act performed in the exercise of a diplomat's functions within the scope of Article 39(2) of the 1961 Vienna Convention on Diplomatic Relations.
>
> However, the jurisdiction of the English court was also challenged on the ground of State immunity. The husband had been ordered by the government of the US to leave the UK with his family. The Court found that his action in removing the children was of a governmental nature and therefore subject to State immunity from legal proceedings in the UK.

Foreign diplomats and their families are not entitled to the right of residence or to expedited immigration procedure after the expiry of the secondment to their mission. If they remain in the UK it is without the leave of the immigration authorities.[143]

10.7.7 Waiver of immunity

Article 32(1) of the Vienna Convention provides that it is for the sending State to waive immunity at its discretion and under Article 32(1) 'Waiver must always be express.' Section 2(3) of the 1964 UK Diplomatic Privileges Act provides that the waiver by the head of a mission shall be deemed to be a waiver by the State he represents. Such a waiver of the immunity is that of the State and not of the diplomatic representatives themselves.[144]

Article 32(4) provides that if a diplomatic agent commences proceedings, he/she is precluded from invoking immunity from jurisdiction in respect of any counterclaim directly connected with the principal claim. Article 32(4) provides that waiver of immunity from civil or administrative jurisdiction shall not be held to imply waiver in respect of the execution of a judgment, for which a separate waiver shall be necessary.

10.8. Quasi-diplomatic privileges and immunities

Consuls, although representatives of their States in another State, are not accorded the same degree of immunity within the receiving State as that enjoyed by diplomatic agents. Their functions are varied and include the protection of the interests of the sending State and its nationals, the development of economic and cultural relations, the issuing of passports and visas, the registration of births, marriages and deaths, and the supervision of vessels and aircraft attributed to the sending State.

However, while as a general rule a consul is not immune from local jurisdiction, under the provisions of the 1968 Consular Relations Act, which gives effect to the 1963 Vienna Convention on Consular Relations, a consul does enjoy a limited degree of immunity in respect of his official functions. Article 41 of the Convention provides that:

---

143   *R v Secretary of State for the Home Deparment, ex p Bagga* [1990] 3 WLR 1013.
144   See *Fayed v Al-Tajir* [1987] 2 All ER 396.

1   Consular officers shall not be liable to arrest or detention pending trial, except in the case of grave crime and pursuant to a decision by the competent judicial authority.

2   Except in the case specified in paragraph 1 of this article, consular officers shall not be committed to prison or liable to any other form of restriction on their personal freedom save in execution of a judicial decision of final effect.

3   If criminal proceedings are instituted against a consular officer, he must appear before the competent authorities. Nevertheless, the proceedings shall be conducted with the respect due to him by reason of his official position and, except in the case specified in paragraph 1 of this article, in a manner which will hamper the exercise of consular functions as little as possible. When, in the circumstances mentioned in paragraph 1 of this article, it has become necessary to detain a consular officer, the proceedings against him shall be instituted with the minimum delay.

The Convention provides that career consuls (as opposed to honorary consuls) are exempt from taxation and customs duties in the same way as diplomats, and that consular premises, archives and documents are inviolable and given exemption from taxation. It also states that immunity and protection afforded by customary law is maintained.

10.9   Immunities of international governmental organisations (IGOs)

The immunity of IGOs is not based on international customary law but derives from the terms of the particular treaty creating the particular IGO. Such treaties, almost without exception, specify privileges and immunities accorded to the IGO which are shaped by the functions that the relevant IGO is intended to fulfil.[145] The founding treaties usually impose an obligation on the contracting parties to enact national legislation granting the relevant international governmental organisation and its representatives specific immunities and privileges.

Normally, a headquarters agreement is concluded between the relevant IGO and its host member State which regulates the extent of immunities and privileges granted to the organisation in the national territory.

The reason behind granting immunities and privileges to an IGO and its representatives is that in order to fulfil particular tasks assigned to it by its members an organisation must be independent from any member State. Accordingly, if a State is not a member of a particular IGO it is not obliged under international law to grant immunity to that IGO. In the UK, Article 4A of the 1981 International Organisations Act specifies that international governmental organisations of which the UK is not a contracting party (apart from international commodity organisations and such organisations which by special Act have immunities conferred upon them) are not immune from the jurisdiction of UK courts. However, it is widely accepted that an IGO in a non-member/host State will have legal capacity on the assumption that an IGO, as a subject of international law, has a separate legal personality from that of its members.[146] In the UK, under the 1991 Foreign Corporations Act, English courts will recognise the legal capacity of IGOs incorporated in countries whose governments are not recognised in the UK, if those countries have a stable regime with settled law (see Chapter 6.4.1.2.B).

Although the scope of immunities and privileges that IGOs enjoy, either under bilateral or multilateral treaties and national legislation, differs from one IGO to another, it is, nevertheless, submitted that there are substantial similarities as to their international immunities. IGOs are generally granted absolute

---

145   On this topic see K. Wellens, *Remedies against International Organizations, 21 Cambridge Studies in International and Comparative Law*, Cambridge: Cambridge University Press (2002), 114–135.

146   *International Tin Council v Amalgamet Inc* 524 NYS 2d 971 (1988) and *Branno v Ministry of War* 22 ILR, 756.

immunity from all types of legal process in respect of all acts carried out with a view to achieving the purposes set out in the constitutional treaty in a host member State and in States which are members of the organisation. Thus, immunities are based on the principle of functionality, i.e. an IGO is immune in respect of all activities related to the exercise of its functions necessary to fulfil its international mandate. The immunity covers not only immunity from the adjudicative and enforcement jurisdiction of municipal courts, but also inviolability of an IGO's property, immunity from direct taxes and customs duties on transactions and on property, and often from indirect taxes, except public utility fees (VAT and local taxes on sales are normally reimbursed by the host State); and immunity from censorship of official correspondence and communications. However, IGOs do not enjoy immunity for *ultra vires* acts (but see Chapter 10.9.2).

10.9.1   Immunity of IGOs and the right of access to a court

Jurisdictional immunity enjoyed by IGOs (bearing in mind that it covers all acts carried out within the scope of their functions, i.e. involving internal constitutional and administrative acts, including employment conditions) has been under attack because, in practice, it frees IGOs from the obligation to settle disputes with third parties such as contractors, persons tortiously injured, employees, etc. Such persons are, indeed, in a worse legal position than those who have a claim against a foreign State. While the rejection of claims against a foreign State by municipal courts of the *forum* State is based on the assumption that there is an available *forum* abroad: with regard to IGOs, there is no other *forum* and therefore the claimant is denied access to justice. For that reason constitutional treaties of many IGOs contain provisions for resolving private law disputes to which the organisation is a party and those concerning its officials whose immunity the organisation declines to waive.[147] In many cases, however, IGOs have no arrangements for resolving private law disputes and even if there are some specific methods of settlement of disputes otherwise covered by immunities, those methods may not be adequate. In particular with regard to employment disputes between an employee and an IGO an important principle was set out by the ECtHR in *Beer and Regan v Germany* and *Waite and Kennedy v Germany*.[148]

BEER AND REGAN *V* GERMANY AND WAITE AND KENNEDY *V* GERMANY

Facts:

The applicants, who were employed in Germany by private companies, were placed at the disposal of the European Space Agency (ESA) to perform services at the European Space Operations Centre in Darmstadt. When their contracts were not renewed they brought proceedings before the German Labour Court against the ESA, arguing that, on the basis

---

147   With regard to the EU, Article 340 TFEU deals with liability of the EU. Article 340(1) TFEU governs contractual liability of the EU and provides that such liability shall be governed by the law applicable to the contract. The EU's contracts normally contain a choice of law clause. Article 340(2) TFEU deals with non-contractual liability of the EU by providing that the EU must make good any damage caused by its institutions and by its servants in the performance of their duties. Further, a Special Tribunal was created to deal with employment disputes.

148   (1999) 118 ILR 121.

of German legislation (German Provision of Labour (Temporary Staff) Act (Arbeitnehmer-überlassungsgesetz), they had acquired the status of employees of the ESA. Their claims were dismissed by the German Labour Court and their appeal rejected by the German Federal Constitutional Court (Bundesverfassungsgericht) on the ground that the ESA was entitled to immunity from the jurisdiction of the German courts. The applicants brought proceedings before the ECtHR on the ground that their right of access to a court under Article 6(1) of the ECHR was breached by the refusal of the German courts to adjudicate their claims.

Held:

The ECtHR held that the right protected by Article 6(1) was not absolute but subject to limitations. Accordingly, contracting parties when exercising their discretion under Article 6(1) should take into account three criteria:

- *whether the limitations imposed restricted the access to court in such a way or to such an extent that the very essence of the right was impaired;*
- *whether the limitations pursued a legitimate aim;*
- *whether there was a reasonable relationship of proportionality between the means employed and the aim sought to be achieved.*

The ECtHR found that the limitations had pursued a legitimate objective, i.e. ensuring the proper functioning of an international organisation and thus protecting it from unilateral interference by individual governments. As to the proportionality of the limitations the Court held that: 'a material factor in determining whether granting ESA immunity from German jurisdiction is permissible under the Convention is whether the applicants had available to them reasonable alternative means to protect effectively their rights under the Convention'. The limitations were proportional because the applicants had alternative means to protect their rights. In particular they could have had recourse to the ESA Appeals Board competent to hear disputes relating to decisions taken by ESA and arising between it and a staff member.

Comment:

Although the applicants failed, an important principle was established by the ECtHR to be followed in Europe. An IGO will not be entitled to immunity in a situation where no alternative forum is available to a claimant and thus that claimant would be deprived of his right of access to a court. The disappointing aspect of the judgment is that the ECtHR did not examine whether the arrangements for settlement of disputes within the ESA met the standard set out in Article 6(1) of the ECHR.

Cases decided by municipal courts in Europe, subsequent to the above judgment, show that it has, indeed, been followed.[149] However, it is submitted that even if a national court decides to remove immunity, which is very unlikely, it may employ the so called 'avoidance techniques' in order to

---

149   See e.g. *Lutchmaya v ACP*, JTDE (2003) 684, Note David, Gaz Pal 16017, 24 April 2004; *Banque Africaine de Developpement (BAD) v Degboe, decided by the French Court de Cassation,* (2004) 93 Revue Generale de Droit International Public, 409, and *S v Western European Union (WEU)* (2004) Journal du Tribunal, 617. See also

dismiss cases on grounds other than that of immunity.[150] The reluctance of national courts to adjudicate private law claims against IGOs is understandable. They are not appropriate *fora* because whatever they do will be inappropriate. If they maintain immunity this will constitute a denial of justice which, as the French Court de Cassation held in the *Degboe* Case,[151] would violate the international public order. If they decide to follow the judgment of the ECtHR in *Waite and Kennedy*, there would be a great risk that the independence of an IGO and its proper functioning will be jeopardised.

10.9.2   Special status of the UN and its implications

Article 105(1) and (2) of the UN Charter states that the UN and its officials shall enjoy, in the territory of each of its members, functional immunity. Article 105(3) gives the UNGA powers to further determine the immunity of the UN and its officials. It did this by adopting the 1946 Convention on Privileges and Immunities of the United Nations (CPIUN).[152] This Convention is special in that the UN is not a contracting party to it. The ICJ in its Advisory Opinion on *the Reparation for Injuries Suffered in the Service of the United Nations* stated that CPIUN has created rights and obligations between each member State and the UN.[153]

Although under Article 105(1) of the UN Charter the UN enjoys only functional immunity, s 2 CPIUN grants it absolute immunity.[154] National courts have always respected UN immunity, even though this means denial of access to a court and the right to an effective remedy.[155] The most spectacular case in that of *Mothers of Srebrenica v The State of the Netherlands and the UN* in which the association 'Mothers of Srebrenica' on behalf of its 6,000 members (Bosnian women who lost members of their family in genocide which took place in Srebrenica in 1995) and ten individuals brought civil proceedings against the government of the Netherlands and the UN for failure to prevent the 1995 Srebrenica genocide. The background of this case was that in 1993 the UN declared the besieged enclave of Srebrenica in the Drina Valley of North Eastern Bosnia a 'safe area' under UN protection. This area was protected by 600 lightly armed Dutch infantry forces, who were peacekeepers there. When in 1995 Srebrenica was attacked by Serbian forces, despite its UN status, the Dutch peacekeepers were completely overrun. As a result Srebrenica was captured. Subsequently, the Serbian forces under the command of General Ratko Mladić separated Bosnian Muslim men and boys from women, and executed around 8,000 Bosnian Muslim males in and around Srebrenica. In 2004, the Appeals Chamber of the ICTY in *Prosecutor v Krstić*[156] ruled that the massacre of the Bosnian Muslim males constituted genocide. In the proceedings against the government of the Netherlands and the UN the claimants alleged that these respondents were jointly and severally responsible for genocide in

A. Reinisch, *The Immunity of International Organizations and the Jurisdiction of their Administrative Tribunals*, (2008) 7 Chinese Journal of International Law, 285–306, at 294–303.

150   A. Reinich in *International Organisations before National Courts*, Cambridge: Cambridge University Press, 2000, 99–127 provides the following examples of 'avoidance techniques': non-recognition of an IGO as a legal person under domestic law; non-recognition of a particular act as being *ultra vires*; the reliance on the doctrine of act of State, political questions and non-justiciability; absence of subject matter jurisdiction; lack of controversy; the exercise by a court of its discretion to avoid harassing lawsuits and mock trials as abuse of process.

151   Supra note 149.

152   1 UNTS 15.

153   (1949) ICJ Rep 174, 179.

154   This was confimed by the ICJ in its Advisory Opinion in *Differences relating to Immunity from Legal Process of a Special Rapporteur of the Commission on Human Rights*, (1999) ICJ Rep 66, para 66.

155   See R. Freedman, *UN Immunity or Impunity? A Human Rights Based Challenge* (2014) 25/1 Eur J Int L, 252.

156   Case No IT-98-33-A, 19 April 2004.

Srebrenica and accordingly sought compensation. Initially, leave to proceed against the UN had been allowed on the ground that the UN failed to appear. However, all Dutch courts involved in the proceedings, including the Supreme Court,[157] and subsequently the ECtHR decided that the UN enjoys absolute immunity from national proceedings.

Although there are mechanisms introduced by the UN to ensure that an injured party's right to access to a court and the right to remedy are protected through alternative means,[158] the fact remains that the use of those means is entirely at the discretion of the UN. If the UN decides not to use that discretion its immunity is not affected.[159] For example, the UN has consistently refused to compensate victims of the outbreak of cholera in 2010 in Haiti attributable to the negligence of the UN peacekeeping forces.[160]

10.9.3 Immunities of IGOs in the UK

In the UK immunities and privileges of IGOs and their representatives are governed by the 1968 International Organisations Act as amended.[161] Under the 1968 Act the Crown is empowered by an Order in Council to confer immunity on any organisation in which the UK is a member, and to specify what immunities are to be granted to a particular IGO and its representatives. The UK applies functional immunity, i.e. immunity is granted in respect of all official acts carried out in the performance of official functions and activities of the organisation. As to IGOs' officials, high-ranking officials normally enjoy immunities and privileges similar to those granted to heads of diplomatic missions, while other officials are entitled to immunity in respect of acts done in the course of their employment. There is no limitation on jurisdiction in actions brought by an IGO against its employees.[162]

10.10 Immunities of visiting armed forces

Members of the armed forces, who are in the territory of a host State with its consent, enjoy limited immunity from the jurisdiction of that State. This is necessary in order to ensure that the integrity and the efficiency of a visiting army are not jeopardised. Normally, specific arrangements are made between a host State and a sending State. In the UK special arrangements were made for visiting forces of the North Atlantic Treaty Organisation (NATO) of which the UK is a member. The 1951 NATO Status of Forces Agreement (SOFA)[163] which was implemented in the UK by the 1952 Visiting Forces Act, and amended by the 1995 Partnership for Peace Agreement (which extends the 1951 SOFA to visiting armed forces which had joined NATO after the fall of the Soviet Union) governs the issue of immunities and the jurisdiction of UK courts in respect of armed forces from other NATO countries visiting or

---

157 *LJN: BW1999, Hoge Raad [Supreme Court]*, 10/04437 (Apr 13, 2012).
158 S 29 CPIUN imposes an obligation on the UN to make arrangements for settlement of private disputes arising out of contracts or other disputes of private law character to which the UN is a party and disputes involving any official of the UN who by reason of his official position enjoys immunity, if this has not been waived by the UNS-G. Further in respect of peacekeeping operations alternative modes of dispute resolution include establishment of claims commissions, administrative tribunals and *ad hoc* negotiations, mediation and arbitration. See supra note 150 p. 247–250.
159 A. Miller, *The Privileges and Immunities of the United Nations* (2009) 6 Int'l Orgs L Rev, 7.
160 Supra note 155.
161 Amended by the Diplomatic and other Privileges Act 1971, the European Communities Act 1972, s 4(1), Sched 3, Pt IV, the International Organisations Act 1981 and the International Organisations Act 2005.
162 *Arab Monetary Fund v Hashim* [1996] 1 Lloyd's Rep 589, CA.
163 199 UNTS 67.

stationed on the national territory. The SOFA is based on two principles: first, reciprocity, in that UK armed forces enjoy the same benefits when in the territory of a sending State as foreign armed forces when in the UK and, second, equivalence, in that visiting armed forces enjoy only the benefits and privileges which are granted to the UK armed forces at home.

RECOMMENDED READING

Books

van Alebeek, R., *The Immunities of States and Their Officials in International Criminal Law*, Oxford: Oxford University Press, 2008.

Denza, E., *Diplomatic Law: A Commentary on the Vienna Convention on Diplomatic Relations*, 3rd edn, Oxford: Clarendon Press, 2008.

Fox, H., *The Law of State Immunity*, 2nd edn, Oxford: Oxford University Press, 2008

O'Keefe, R. and Tams, C. (eds), *The United Nations Convention on Jurisdictional Immunities of States and Their Property. A Commentary*, Oxford: Oxford University Press, 2013.

Yang, X., *State Immunity in International Law*, Cambridge: Cambridge University Press, 2012.

Articles

Arnowitz Drescher, I., *Seeking Justice for America's Forgotten Victims: Reforming the Foreign Sovereignty Immunities Act Terrorist Exception* (2012) 15 Legislation and Public Law, 806.

Cassese, A., *When May Senior State Officials be Tried for International Crimes? Some Comments on the Congo v. Belgium Case* (2002) 13 EJIL, 853.

Espósito, C., *Of Plumbers and Social Architects: Elements and Problems of the Judgment of the International Court of Justice in Jurisdictional Immunities of States* (2013) 4/3 J Int Dis Settlement, 439.

Evans, R., *Pinochet in London-Pinochet in Chile: International and Domestic Politics in Human Rights Policy* (2006) 28 Hum Rts Q, 207.

Fox, H., *The Resolution of the Institute of International Law on the Immunities of Heads of State and Government* (2002) 51 ICLQ, 119.

Freedman, R., *UN Immunity or Impunity? A Human Rights Based Challenge* (2014) 25/1 Eur J Int L, 252.

Huikang, H., *On Immunity of State Officials from Foreign Jurisdiction* (2014) 13/1 Chinese Journal of International Law, 8.

Koh, H.H., *Foreign Official Immunity After Samantar: A United States Government Perspective* (2011) 44 Vanderbilt Journal of Transnational Law, 1141.

McGregor, L., *Torture and State Immunity: Deflecting Impunity, Distorting Sovereignty* (2008) 18/5 EJIL, 903.

Mills, A., *From Russia with Prejudice? The Act of State Doctrine and the Effect of Foreign Proceedings Setting Aside an Arbitral Award* [2012] 71 The Cambridge Law Journal, 465.

Witiw, E.P., *Persona non Grata: Expelling Diplomats Who Abuse Their Privileges* (1988) 9 New York Law School Journal of International and Comparative Law, 345.

AIDE-MÉMOIRE

Important points on immunity from foreign jurisdiction

1   The ICJ in the *Arrest Warrant* Case recognised State immunity as a rule of international customary law, and in the *Case Concerning Jurisdictional Immunities of the State (Germany v Italy: Greece intervening)* confirmed that State immunity is not based on comity, but on customary international law. Under this rule municipal courts of one State (the *forum* State) are prevented from exercising their adjudicative and enforcement jurisdiction in disputes where a foreign State is named as defendant (direct impleading), and where a foreign State intervenes by means of interpleader proceedings (indirect impleading) e.g. proceedings are commenced against individual State officials for alleged official torture abroad, but the State is indirectly impleaded because acts of its officials are attributable to the State, or the disputed property is in possession or under control of a foreign State.

2   It is important to distinguish between:

Acta jure imperii ('Acts by right of dominion')
They concern activities of a governmental or public nature carried out by a foreign State or one of its subdivisions, which qualify for State immunity under the doctrine of restrictive foreign sovereign immunity.

AND

Acta jure gestionis ('Acts by right of management')
They concern activities of a commercial nature carried out by a foreign State or one of its subdivisions or agencies, which are **not** immune from the jurisdiction and process of local courts under the doctrine of restrictive foreign sovereign immunity.

3   It is important to distinguish between:

Immunity ratione personae
This is enjoyed by heads of State and other high-ranking officials while in office and covers all acts official and private, but ends when the officials vacate the post or, earlier, if their State waives it. Such immunity derived from the office that the individual concerned holds.

AND

Immunity ratione materiae
All representatives of a State who are acting in that capacity enjoy immunity *ratione materiae* (also called 'official acts immunity') for the acts so performed, even if they have acted *ultra vires*. Such immunity attaches to the official act, not to the office of the individual concerned, and can therefore be relied upon by former officials as well as incumbent officials (but see point 5). It may also be relied upon by non-State actors who have acted on behalf of a State.

4   It is important to distinguish between

Procedural (or jurisdictional) immunity
This is a procedural rule under which a municipal court is barred from adjudicating a case to which a foreign State, or its officials, is a party.

AND

Substantive immunity
This concerns the substance of the immunity in that it concerns the claimant's substantive rights or the defendant's responsibility.

In the *Arrest Warrant* case, the ICJ held that while 'jurisdictional immunity is procedural in nature, criminal responsibility is a question of substantive law'.

---

5   It is important to distinguish between:

Immunity from foreign civil proceedings (not involving acte jure gestionis)
On the authority of the ICJ judgment in the *Jurisdictional Immunities* Case, there is **no** exception to State immunity. Accordingly, civil actions are barred before courts of third States even if they concerned commission of international crimes by a State itself and by its officials, irrespective of whether those officials are in office or have vacated it (but see the position of the US Supreme Court in *Samantar v Yousuf*).

AND

Immunity from foreign criminal proceedings
States are always immune from foreign criminal proceedings.

Heads of State and other high ranking officials when in office
The ICJ in the *Arrest Warrant* Case and in *Dijbouti v France* stated that heads of State and other high ranking officials, when in office, enjoy *ratione personae* immunity from foreign criminal jurisdiction. The ICJ held that
under customary international law, incumbent foreign ministers, when abroad, enjoy full immunity from criminal jurisdiction as well as inviolability protecting them from 'any act of authority' by another State which would hinder them in the performance of their duties. The majority of the ICJ rejected any distinction between acts performed in an official capacity and those performed in a private capacity, or acts performed before or during the holding of the office of foreign minister. However, this immunity suffers two exceptions. First, heads of State and other high ranking official cannot rely on immunity in a situation where they have been indicted, or an arrest warrant has been issued against them by an international criminal court, or they have been brought before such a court and second, when their home State has removed immunity (unlikely to occur!).

Heads of State and other high ranking officials when they are no longer in office
They cannot rely on immunity *ratione personae* but immunity *ratione materiae* may be removed in respect of international crimes allegedly committed by them while in office. In *Pinochet III* the House of Lord held that acts of torture are within the scope of immunity *ratione materiae*. Also, Judges Higgins, Kooijmans and Buergenthal in the *Arrest Warrant* Case in their joint separate opinion indicated that the current trend of State practice is that for international crimes immunity *ratione materiae* may be removed with regard to former State officials.

11

STATE RESPONSIBILITY FOR WRONGFUL ACTS

CONTENTS

CHAPTER OUTLINE

1 Introduction

Every State which is in breach of an obligation imposed upon it by international law must bear responsibility for that breach. It is important to note that traditional rules on State responsibility have evolved. In particular:

■ The development of human rights resulted in the establishment of a common international standard of treatment of aliens, thus resolving the disagreement between supporters and opponents of the 'national treatment', and the 'minimum international treatment', standards.

■ The importance of the exercise of diplomatic protection by a State, on behalf of its nationals injured by a wrongful act of another State, has greatly diminished because individuals, as subjects of international law, have access to international courts and tribunals and thus able to make claims independently of any espousal by the State of their nationality.

■ As to corporations, two factors, first the settlement of disputes between States and foreign private persons through arbitration, and second, the proliferation of Bilateral Investment Treaties (BITs), result in diplomatic protection being less relevant than hitherto. This applies not only to cases of expropriation, but also to those cases where a State violates the international minimum standard of treatment of aliens by its conduct in connection with investment contracts, commercial contracts and loan contracts.

■ The use of force in international relations has been banned and the principle of peaceful settlement of international disputes has modified the manner in which an injured State is allowed to exercise its right to reparation.

■ The concept of aggravated responsibility has been introduced to deal with gross and systematic violations of *jus cogens* rules.

The International Law Commission (ILC) has clarified and developed the rules: on State responsibility in its 2001 Draft Articles on Responsibility of States for Internationally Wrongful Acts (hereafter the 2001 DARSIWA); on diplomatic protection in its 2006 Draft Articles on Diplomatic Protection (hereafter the 2006 DADP); and on the expulsion of aliens in its 2014 Draft Articles on the Expulsion of Aliens (hereafter DAEA).

2 Theories on State responsibility

There are two theories on State responsibility:

■ the objective theory, which relies on the premise that a State is liable once an unlawful act which violates an international obligation has been done by that State, regardless of any fault or intention on the part of that State;

■ the subjective theory, which states that *culpa* (the term *culpa* is used to describe blameworthiness based upon fault arising from any sort of conduct from negligence to recklessness) or fault is a necessary basis for State responsibility.

The 2001 DARSIWA gives preference to the objective theory while not completely rejecting the subjective theory.

3 Imputability

A State is only responsible for acts that are attributable to it. The matter of attribution may arise with regard to:

- acts of State officials;
- acts of private persons;
- acts of insurrectionaries.

4 Direct and indirect international wrongs

A direct wrong arises when one State is in direct breach of an obligation owed to another State, e.g. a breach of a treaty to which both a delinquent State and a claimant State are contracting parties. An indirect wrong arises when a State is in breach of an obligation owed to a national of another State, irrespective of whether that national is a natural or juristic person.

5 Direct international wrongs: aggrieved responsibility

The 2001 DARSIWA introduces a new category of direct international wrong which arises when a State is in direct, gross and systematic breach of a rule of *jus cogens* and thus in breach of an obligation owed to the international community as a whole. This is known as the case of aggrieved responsibility in that any State, whether injured or not, may invoke and enforce the responsibility of the delinquent State (i.e. the breach is of an *erga omnes* nature), in particular it may:

- demand the cessation of the internationally wrongful act, plus assurances and guarantees of non-repetition;
- claim reparation in the interest of the injured State or of the beneficiaries of the obligation breached, for example in respect of victims of gross violations of human rights;
- take countermeasures, either on behalf of an injured State with its consent, or, when no State is 'injured', on behalf of the beneficiaries of the obligation breached.

6 Direct international wrongs: ordinary responsibility

For a direct international wrong the State may incur ordinary responsibility.

7 Indirect international wrongs: the treatment of aliens

There are two views regarding the matter. The first favours the standard of national treatment under which aliens are to be treated in the same way as nationals. The second considers that an 'international minimum standard' of treatment must be accorded to aliens by all States irrespective of how they treat their nationals. The international minimum standard as established by human rights law (HRL) is generally accepted.

8 The treatment of aliens: admission and expulsion

While HRL, whether customary or based on treaties, guarantees that fundamental HRs such as the right to life, the right to be free from torture, the right not to be discriminated against on the ground of race, must be observed by all States in respect of all persons, whether nationals or foreigners, under the jurisdiction of a State, the matter of admission and expulsion of aliens is more controversial. With regard to admission of aliens this area still remains, to a great extent, within the exclusive domain of each State although under HRs treaties a State may have a duty to accept an alien, e.g. in order to give effect to the right to family life or in light of the refugee law principle of non-refoulement. Whether the expulsion of aliens is subject to customary international law is debatable. The ILC in 2014 adopted Draft Articles on the Expulsion of Aliens (DAEA) which both reflect customary international law and propose development of that law.

9 The treatment of aliens: denial of justice

A State will be held responsible in international law if a denial of justice occurs in the treatment of an alien. Denial of justice can be defined as any gross miscarriage of justice by domestic courts resulting from wrongful administration of justice to aliens. The wrongful administration of justice may arise from acts of the executive, the legislature or the judiciary.

10 The treatment of aliens: expropriation of foreign property

In the nineteenth and twentieth centuries the main problem which existed in connection with expropriation was one of the destruction or direct expropriation of the property of one individual; in the twenty-first century it is likely to be one concerning indirect expropriation and the exercise by a State of powers in the public interest which may affect property rights of foreign persons. Accordingly, most disputes focus on the violations by a foreign State of the fair and equitable standard of treatment of foreign natural and legal persons rather than claims based on alleged expropriation.

11 Admissibility of State claims: diplomatic protection

Espousal by a State of a claim by its nationals, whether natural or juristic persons, against another State is known as the exercise of diplomatic protection. Such a claim may be defeated by the respondent State on the following grounds:

- non-compliance with the rules regarding nationality of a claim;

- failure, by the national concerned, to exhaust local remedies;

- unreasonable delay by the claimant State in bringing the claim;

- waiver by the claimant State of the claim;

- improper behaviour by the injured national.

(a)   Nationality of the claim. Under the continuity rule, a claimant must be a national of the claimant State at both the date of injury (known as the *dies a quo*) and the date of presentation of the claim (known as the *dies ad quem*). The 2006 DADP introduced some flexibility to the rules (Articles 5(2) and 10(3)). The rules on the nationality of individuals differ from those on nationality of corporations and their shareholders:

Individuals:

- Where an injured person has nationality of both the claimant State and the respondent State, the claimant State may exercise diplomatic protection if its nationality is predominant (i.e. under the principle of effective nationality) both at the *dies a quo* (the date of injury) and the *dies ad quem* (the date of the presentation of the claim).

- Where an injured person has a dual or multiple nationality, any State of nationality may exercise diplomatic protection, separately or jointly against a State of which that person is not a national. It is to be noted that the principle established by the International Court of Justice (ICJ) in the *Nottebohm Case* which requires a claimant State to have a 'genuine connection' with an injured person in a situation where that person has acquired nationality of the claimant State by naturalisation should be confined to that case.

Corporations and their shareholders:

- Corporations: the State of incorporation and registered office of a corporation is entitled to exercise diplomatic protection. Although in the *Barcelona Traction Case* the ICJ rejected the principle of a 'genuine link', it nevertheless stated that in addition to incorporation and a registered office, 'a close and permanent connection' is required between a corporation and a State espousing its claim.

- Shareholders: only in any of the following exceptional circumstances will the national State of the shareholders be entitled to assert a claim for diplomatic protection:

  - the wrong alleged was directed against the shareholders by reason of their nationality;

  - the corporation has ceased to exist as a result of a wrongful act;

  - the national State of the corporation lacks the capacity to bring an international claim;

  - the corporation had, at the time of injury, the nationality of the respondent State but its incorporation in that State was required as a precondition of doing business there.

(b)   Exhaustion of domestic remedies. The injured person must exhaust domestic remedies before a claim can be espoused by his national State. However, exceptions to this requirement are set out in Article 15 of the 2006 DADP.

(c)   Unreasonable delay by the claimant State in bringing the claim. There is no time limit within which claims must be presented. Nevertheless, a claim will fail if it is presented after unreasonable delay by the claimant State. What is reasonable is a question for the tribunal to decide at its discretion.

(d)   Waiver by the claimant State of the claim. A claim, once waived by the claimant State, cannot be resurrected. But as the claim belongs to the State and not the injured national, any waiver of the claim by the national in his private capacity does not bind his government.

(e)   Improper behaviour by the injured alien. Under the doctrine of 'clean hands' if an alien is involved in activities which are illegal, either under municipal or international law, this may bar the claim. However, the claim will not be barred if the injury caused to him is unreasonable and disproportionate to the illegality committed by him.

12 Circumstances precluding wrongfulness

These are:

■ Consent. Under the principle *volenti non fit injuria*, when an injured State consents to an act or conduct, which without that consent will be considered as a wrongful act, the delinquent State cannot be held responsible in international law.

■ Countermeasures. As countermeasures constitute a response to an unlawful act they are allowed provided they are not forcible and are exercised in accordance with international law.

■ Self-defence (see Chapter 15.4).

■ *Force majeure*. Article 23 of the 2001 DARSIWA defines *force majeure* as 'the occurrence of an irresistible force or of an unforeseen event, beyond the control of the State, making it materially impossible in the circumstances to perform the obligation'. However, para 2 of Article 23 excludes a defence based on *force majeure*:

■ when the situation of *force majeure* is due, either alone or in combination with other factors, to the conduct of the State invoking it; or

■ the State has assumed the risk of that situation occurring.

■ Necessity. A State is entitled to rely on necessity, only if the act in question constitutes the only way for it to safeguard an essential interest against a grave and imminent peril, provided that the act does not seriously impair an essential interest of a State or States towards which the obligation exists, or of the international community as a whole.

■ Distress. This occurs when the author of the act in question, in a situation of distress, has no other reasonable way of saving the author's life or the lives of other persons entrusted to the author's care. However, distress cannot be invoked if:

■ the situation of distress is due, either alone or in combination with other factors, to the conduct of the State invoking it; or

■ the act in question is likely to create a comparable or greater peril.

■ Compliance with peremptory rules. Wrongfulness is excluded if an act of a State is required by a peremptory rule.

13 Consequences of invoking a circumstance precluding wrongfulness

The fact that an act of State is lawful will not necessarily mean that the respondent State will have no duty to pay compensation. In particular, in a situation of distress or necessity there is no reason why a State, which acts for its own benefit, should not pay compensation for any material harm or loss caused by its act. The circumstance where liability arises in the absence of an international wrong is sometimes referred to as 'international liability' rather than 'international responsibility'.

14 Reparation for injury

A delinquent State must make full reparation for the injury caused by the commission of the internationally wrongful act. Reparation may take the form of restitution, compensation or satisfaction, either separately or in combination.

11.1   Introduction

All legal systems provide for consequences arising from failure to observe obligations imposed by their rules. International law is no different in that every State which is in breach of the obligations imposed upon it by international law must bear responsibility for that breach. In the *Spanish Zones of Morocco Claims (Great Britain v Spain)*[1] Judge Hubert said that:

> Responsibility is the necessary corollary of a right. All rights of an international character involve international responsibility. If the obligation in question is not met, responsibility entails the duty to make reparations.

Traditionally, responsibility of States for internationally wrongful acts was based on customary rules originating from the practice of States as applied by the Permanent Court of International Justice (PCIJ) and the International Court of Justice (ICJ) and by international arbitral tribunals.

Only a very limited number of international treaties contain provisions providing for liability of a contracting State for violations of their provisions. An example of such a provision is Article 3 of the 1907 Hague Convention IV Respecting the Laws and Customs of War on Land which states that the violation of the Regulations annexed to that Convention by a contracting State gives rise to liability. By virtue of this provision, a contracting State is required to pay compensation in respect of all wrongful acts committed by its armed forces.

The matter of State liability was on the agenda of the League of Nations. A Codification Conference convened under the auspices of the League of Nations in 1930 at The Hague to codify rules in a number of areas, including rules on State responsibility, failed to produce any internationally binding instruments with regard to State responsibility. The Hague Conference showed deep disagreement between participating States in respect of State responsibility for the treatment of aliens. Some States wanted to apply 'national' treatment; others were in favour of the application of the 'minimum international treatment standard'.

In an assessment of the early twentieth century customary law on State responsibility it can be said that:

- it focused on the treatment of aliens;

- there were gaps in it;

- it was unclear on a number of important issues, such as whether a State could be liable irrespective of any fault or intention on the part of an agent of that State whose conduct caused injury (the subjective theory) or whether its liability arose when an unlawful act attributable to a State constituted a breach of international law, without any necessity to show some fault or intention on the part of the official concerned (the objective theory);

- an injured State was allowed to resort to armed force without first requesting reparation. Further, if an offending State failed to make reparation the injured State was free to decide whether to use peaceful means to resolve the matter or whether to enforce its right to reparation by using military or economic force.

---

1   (1925) 2 RIAA 615, 641.

The following are relevant to the evolution of the rules on State responsibility:

- The development of HRL resulted in the establishment of a common international standard of treatment of aliens thus resolving the disagreement between supporters and opponents of the 'national treatment' and the 'minimum international treatment standards'.

- The use of force in international relations has been banned and the principle of peaceful settlement of international disputes has modified the manner in which an injured State is allowed to exercise its right to reparation.

- In respect of certain activities – such as the use of, and experiments with, nuclear technology, the exploration of space, etc. – only the principle of strict or absolute liability (see this Chapter later) of a State is appropriate because, on the one hand, it is impossible to prove the commission of a wrongful act taking into account the precautions which are normally taken and, on the other hand, it is unrealistic to prohibit such activities altogether. International co-operation in the prevention of disasters arising from such activities is paramount.

- The importance of a State exercising diplomatic protection on behalf of its nationals, whether individuals or corporations, has greatly diminished. This is because individuals, being subjects of international law, have direct access to international courts and tribunals to enforce their rights (see Chapter 5.12). In the past individuals were not considered subjects of international law and thus generally had no standing before international courts and tribunals. Further, disputes concerning expropriation and nationalisation are now largely settled under bilateral and multilateral trade and investment treaties. Those treaties often either establish a body competent to deal with disputes or confer jurisdiction over disputes on the International Centre for Settlement of Investment Disputes (ICSID).

The topic of State responsibility has been greatly clarified and developed by the ILC. At its first session in 1949 the ILC selected this topic for future codification. The ILC adopted the final text of the DARSIWA at its 53rd session held in August 2001.[2] In December 2001 the UNGA recommended the 2001 DARSIWA to the attention of governments and attached it to its Resolution 56/83.

The 2001 DARSIWA was prepared under the leadership of special rapporteurs – Alberto Ago (1962–1979), Willem Riphagen (1979–1986), Gaetano Arangio-Ruiz (1987–1996) and James Crawford (1997–2001). The basic concepts, structure and content of the 2001 DARSIWA were prepared by Alberto Ago. His successors improved and substantially revised the initial Draft. Its final version deals comprehensively with the most important aspects of State responsibility for wrongful acts, including the definition of such acts, the consequences of an internationally wrongful act, the circumstances precluding wrongfulness, the rights of an injured State, the means of reparation at its disposal, and the circumstances in which it is allowed to resort to countermeasures. Moreover, the ILC has made three essential contributions to the development of the rules on State responsibility:

- Alberto Ago introduced a distinction between 'primary rules', which impose certain rules of conduct (obligations to do or not to do something), and 'second level rules' (secondary rules) which define the consequences of internationally wrongful acts attributable to a State. Primary rules are of a substantial nature as they define international obligations of a State in each particular context. Secondary rules contain principles which govern State responsibility. The 2001 DARSIWA is solely concerned with 'second level rules'.

---

2   A/CN4/L602/Rev.

■ The ILC promotes two regimes of State responsibility – 'ordinary responsibility' and 'aggrieved responsibility' – while maintaining the unitary nature of a wrongful act. The emphasis is on the character of the obligation breached. Aggrieved responsibility occurs when a State breaches peremptory norms of international law.

■ Damage has been dissociated from a wrongful act and is no longer considered as a constituent element. The Special Rapporteur explained this solution as follows:

> It will be a matter for the primary rules in question to determine what is the threshold for a violation: in some cases this may be the occurrence of actual harm, in others a threat of such harm, in others again, the mere failure to fulfil a promise, irrespective of the consequences of the failure at the time. Similarly, it will be a matter for the primary rules and their interpretation to specify what are the range of interests protected by an international obligation, the breach of which will give rise to a corresponding secondary obligation of reparation.[3]

The dissociation of damage from a wrongful act will allow the secondary rules to cover all possible breaches of primary rules without excluding responsibility of the delinquent State in cases where there is no damage or the damage is not compensable.

In is important to note that the ILC, as part of its work on State responsibility, examined the topic of diplomatic protection but subsequently decided to deal with diplomatic protection separately. This resulted in the adoption by the ILC of the 2006 DADP at its 58th Session. The Draft was submitted to the UNGA in 2006.[4] It defined diplomatic protection in its Article 1 as consisting of:

> the invocation by a State, through diplomatic action or other means of peaceful settlement, of the responsibility of another State for an injury caused by an internationally wrongful act of that State to a natural or legal person that is a national of the former State with a view to the implementation of such responsibility.

In 2014 the ILC completed its work on the Draft Articles on the Expulsion of Aliens (DAEA),[5] a topic which is very relevant to the exercise of diplomatic protection by States (see Chapter.11.8.2.2).

11.2 Theories on State responsibility

International law makes no distinction between tortious (delictual) and contractual liability. The breach of a treaty or of a customary obligation will give rise to the same remedy, usually an award of damages or a declaration.

The matter of whether States may be criminally liable is very controversial. The ILC adopted, at the first reading of the Draft text of the Articles on Responsibility of States for Internationally Wrongful Acts, Article 19 which referred to international crimes and thus made a distinction between 'international delicts' and 'international crimes'. At the second reading of the Draft, which began in 1998, the ILC, in the light of comments from governments, deleted Article 19, and the term 'crime' disappeared from the Draft. The ILC decided that internationally wrongful acts should form a single category. The idea embodied in Article 19 was dealt with in a different way so that Chapter III of Part II of the final version refers to serious breaches of obligations under peremptory norms of general international law,

---

3   *Fourth Report on State Responsibility*, Mr James Crawford, Special Rapporteur, A/CN4/517, para 28.
4   [2006] GAOR 61st Session Supp 10, 16.
5   A/69/10.

and Article 41 of the 2001 DARSIWA deals with some particular consequences of such breaches which are added to the general consequences attached to 'ordinary' breaches of international law.

11.2.1   The basis of responsibility

There are two theories as to the basis of State responsibility: the 'risk' or 'objective theory' of responsibility and the 'fault' or 'subjective theory' of responsibility.

11.2.1.1   Objective responsibility

The principle of strict liability on the part of States has been followed both in State practice and in the jurisprudence of the PCIJ and ICJ and that of arbitral tribunals.

Objective responsibility relies on the premise that a State is liable once an unlawful act which violates an international obligation has taken place, regardless of any fault or intention on the part of the State concerned.

This is exemplified in the *Caire Claim (France v Mexico)*.[6]

CAIRE CLAIM (FRANCE *V* MEXICO)

Facts:

Caire, a French national, was tortured and killed in Mexico by Mexican soldiers after they had demanded money from him which he was unable to obtain. France, on his behalf, presented a claim against the Mexican government before the Franco-Mexican Claims Commission.

Held:

The Commission found the Mexican government liable for the actions of its military personnel regardless of the fact that they were acting without orders and against the wishes of the commanding officer. The President of the Franco-Mexican Claims Commission applied the doctrine of objective responsibility and explained its meaning in the following terms:

> *the doctrine of the 'objective responsibility' of the state, that is the responsibility for the acts of the officials or organs of a state . . . may devolve upon it even in the absence of any 'fault' of its own . . . The state also bears an international responsibility for all acts committed by its officials or its organs which are delictual according to international law, regardless of whether the official organ has acted within the limits of its competence or has exceeded those limits . . . However, in order to justify the admission of this objective responsibility of the state for acts committed by its officials or organs outside their competence, it is necessary that they should have acted, at least apparently, as authorised officials or organs, or that, in acting, they should have used powers or measures appropriate to their official character.*

---

6   (1929) 5 RIAA 516, 529–531.

11.2.1.2 Subjective responsibility

Subjective responsibility originates from the Grotian view that *culpa* or *dolus malus* provides the proper basis of State responsibility in all cases.

The term *culpa* is used to describe types of blameworthiness based upon fault arising from any sort of conduct from negligence to recklessness. The view that *culpa* or fault is a necessary basis for State responsibility has been supported in some arbitral awards, e.g. in *Home Missionary Society Claim (United States of America v Great Britain).*[7]

HOME MISSIONARY SOCIETY CLAIM (UNITED STATES OF AMERICA V GREAT BRITAIN)

Facts:

The collection of a new tax imposed by Britain in 1898 on the natives of the Protectorate of Sierra Leone led to serious and widespread revolt during which missions were attacked and either destroyed or damaged, and some missionaries were murdered. On behalf of its nationals the US brought a claim against the UK.

Held:

The arbitral tribunal dismissed the claim. It stated that:

> It is a well established principle of international law that no government can be held responsible for the act of rebellious bodies of men committed in violation of its authority, where it is itself guilty of no breach of good faith, or of no negligence in suppressing insurrection.

Comment:

This statement has often been invoked by the supporters of the subjective doctrine as justifying its existence, while its opponents argue that the case involved the specific topic of a State's responsibility for the acts of rebels rather than establishing a general rule on a State's responsibility based on culpa.

In addition to the above, the supporters of the doctrine of subjective responsibility rely on the judgment of the ICJ in the *Corfu Channel Case (Merits)*[8] in which the fault was assessed in the form of knowledge.

The UK argued that Albania had laid the mines which caused the sinking of a British warship in Albanian territorial waters. However, the lack of evidence in this respect forced the UK to reformulate its argument whereupon the UK government submitted that the mines could not have been laid without the knowledge or connivance of the Albanian authorities.

The ICJ found that the laying of mines 'could not have been accomplished without the knowledge of the Albanian Government' and further stated that every State has a duty 'not to allow knowingly its territory to be used for acts contrary to the rights of other States'.

---

7   (1920) 6 RIAA 42, 44.
8   (1949) ICJ Rep 4, 22.

11.2.1.3 Assessment of the objective and subjective approaches

Of these two approaches, the objective school appears to have wider support. However, a number of writers have argued that to see State responsibility exclusively in the light of either approach is misleading. The better view, according to Brownlie, is that:

> the content of a particular duty . . . will not depend upon a general principle but upon the precise formulation of each obligation of international law. The relevance of fault, the relative 'strictness' of the obligation, will be determined by the content of each rule.[9]

The above statement also emphasises the necessity of examining 'the secondary level rules' in the context of primary rules.

The ILC gives preference to the objective theory in its Articles 1 and 2 of the 2001 DARSIWA. Article 1 provides that 'every internationally wrongful act of a state entails international responsibility', while Article 2 specifies an internationally wrongful act as being an action or omission on the part of a State which:

- is attributable to a State under international law; and

- constitutes a breach of an international obligation.

Articles 1 and 2 do not mention any fault on the part of a State. The notion of fault or *culpa* is particularly inappropriate in respect of State responsibility for wrongful acts because:

- it requires the discovery of the intentions or motives of a wrongful act; and

- it misunderstands the main purpose of imposing responsibility on a State which is to restore the equality of States *vis-à-vis* their international obligations which has been disturbed by the commission of a wrongful act.

However, the 2001 DARSIWA has not completely abandoned subjective responsibility in that:

- lack of fault may still be invoked as an excuse and thus preclude State responsibility in certain circumstances. A State may rely on the defence of necessity to preclude the wrongfulness of its act provided that the relevant act did not contribute to the situation of necessity. The definition of necessity is very strict and presupposes an absolute impossibility of taking any other course of action than that which led to the violation of an international obligation. Necessity may excuse the wrongful act but a State may still be obliged to make compensation (see Chapter. 11.12.5);

- fault is taken into account in the determination of the amount of compensation. Article 39 of the 2001 DARSIWA specifies that if the injured State has contributed to the injury by willful or negligent action or omission the amount of reparation should be reduced accordingly;

- fault in the form of knowledge, and not as wrongful intent or negligence, is referred to in Chapter IV of the 2001 DARSIWA dealing with responsibility of a State in connection with the commission of a wrongful act by another State. Under this Chapter a State is internationally responsible if it has knowledge of the circumstances of a wrongful act of another State and notwithstanding this provides aid and assistance to that State (Article 16), or directs and controls another State in the commission of a wrongful act (Article 17) or coerces another State to commit such an act (Article 18).

---

9   I. Brownlie, *The System of the Law of Nations: State Responsibility*, Part 1, Oxford: Clarendon Press, 1983, 40.

11.3 Imputability

State responsibility is engaged by the acts or omissions of individuals. It is a fundamental matter of responsibility, therefore, to distinguish those acts that are attributable to a State from those which are not. Attribution has the effect of indicating that the act in question is an act of the State concerned.

The matter of attribution may arise in any of the following:

■ acts of State officials;

■ acts of private persons;

■ acts of insurrectionaries.

11.3.1 Acts of State officials

A State can only act through its organs and representatives. The organs and representatives of a State include the following: the executive and administration; the judiciary; the legislature; the armed forces; and federal States and their component States.

The general rule regarding State organs and officials is found in Article 4 of the 2001 DARSIWA which provides that:

1 The conduct of any state organ shall be considered an act of that state under international law, whether the organ exercises legislative, executive, judicial or any other functions, whatever position it holds in the organisation of the state, and whatever its character as an organ of the central government or of a territorial unit of the state.

2 An organ includes any person or entity which has that status in accordance with the internal law of the state.

A State will incur responsibility for a wrongful act of an official, irrespective of the position of that official, e.g. whether superior or subordinate. This situation was examined in the *Massey Case (United States of America v Mexico).*[10]

MASSEY CASE (UNITED STATES OF AMERICA *V* MEXICO)

Facts:

A US national was murdered in Mexico by a Mexican named Saenz. Saenz was later arrested, but escaped from prison when the assistant warder allowed him to leave. The Mexican government argued that it was not liable for this denial of justice because it stemmed from the misconduct of a minor official who was acting in violation of Mexican law and of his duty.

Held:

Commissioner Nielson stated that:

To attempt by some broad classification to make a distinction between some 'minor' or 'petty' officials and other kinds of officials must obviously at times involve practical difficulties.

---

10   (1927) 4 RIAA 155, 159.

> *Irrespective of the propriety of attempting to make any such distinction at all, it would seem that in reaching conclusions in any given case with respect to responsibility for acts of public servants, the most important considerations of which account must be taken are the character of the acts alleged to have resulted in injury to persons or to property, or the nature of functions performed whenever a question is raised as to their proper discharge.*

Article 4(2) by using the word 'includes' entails that individuals who have no official status, but *de facto* exercise State functions, are within the scope of this provision. The ICJ endorsed this interpretation in the *Case Concerning the Application of the Convention on the Prevention and Punishment of the Crime of Genocide Case (Bosnia and Herzegovina v Serbia and Montenegro)*.[11] The Court stated that in a situation where individuals or entities act, in fact, in 'complete dependence' on the State they can be equated with an organ of a State.

Article 6 of the 2001 DARSIWA provides that the conduct of an organ placed at the disposal of one State by another State shall be considered as an act of the former State if that organ was acting in the exercise of elements of governmental authority of the providing State at whose disposal it acts. Under this provision, for example, the conduct of the Judicial Committee of the Privy Council, which acts as the highest appeal body for some Commonwealth countries, will not be attributable to the UK but to the country at the disposal of which it has been placed.

11.3.2 Liability of the State for *ultra vires* acts of its organs or officials

A State is responsible for *ultra vires* acts of its organs or officials if committed within the scope of their apparent authority. Article 7 of the 2001 DARSIWA provides that:

> The conduct of an organ of a state or of a person or entity empowered to exercise elements of the governmental authority shall be considered an act of the state under international law if the organ, person or entity acts in that capacity, even if it exceeds its authority or contravenes instructions.

Article 7 embodies a well established customary rule that wrongful acts may be imputed to the State when its organs or its officials act beyond their legal capacity but act to all appearances as competent officials or organs. This is exemplified in two cases, *The Jessie*[12] and *The Wonderer*.[13]

THE JESSIE AND THE WONDERER

Facts:

US revenue officers exercised their right of visit and search over British ships on the high seas. The officers had acted in good faith, but had exceeded their powers under the relevant Anglo-American agreement.

---

11 Hereafter referred to as the *Genocide* Case (2007) ICJ Rep 43, paras 393–395.
12 (1921) RIAA 57.
13 (1921) RIAA 68.

Held:

The Tribunal held that the US was responsible for the acts of its revenue officers although they acted outside their actual authority. The Tribunal confirmed that so long as the officers were acting within the scope of their duties the State would be responsible.

Other examples are provided below.

In the *Union Bridge Company Claim (United States of America v Great Britain)* [14] in 1899, shortly after the outbreak of war between Great Britain and the Orange Free State, a British official of the Cape Government Railway appropriated neutral property under the mistaken belief that it was not neutral. The Arbitration Tribunal held that:

> liability is not affected either by the fact that [the official appropriated the property] under a mistake as to the character and ownership of the material or that it was a time of pressure and confusion caused by war, or the fact, which, on the evidence, must be admitted, that there was no intention on the part of the British authorities to appropriate the material in question.

The official acted within the scope of his general duty, and liability was, therefore, attributed to the British government.

In the *Youmans Case (United States of America v Mexico)* [15] a group of three US nationals was being attacked by a Mexican mob. Troops sent to protect them joined in the attack, which resulted in the death of the Americans. The Mexican government argued that as the soldiers had acted in complete disregard of the government's instructions, Mexico could not be responsible for the deaths.

The Commission rejected the Mexican argument that the soldiers having disregarded their orders were acting in a private capacity. The Commission stated:

> We do not consider that the participation of the soldiers in the murder . . . can be regarded as acts of soldiers committed in their private capacity when it is clear that at the time of the commission of these acts the men were on duty under the immediate supervision and in the presence of a commanding officer. Soldiers inflicting personal injuries or committing wanton destruction or looting always act in disobedience of some rules laid down by superior authority. There could be no liability whatever for such misdeeds if the view were taken that any acts committed by soldiers in contravention of instructions must be considered as personal acts.

A distinction exists between the case law and Article 7 of the 2001 DARSIWA in that the cases stress the requirement of apparent authority, while Article 7 is silent on this matter. This notwithstanding, it is probably the case that some notion of apparent authority or use of official powers will be necessary for a claim to succeed. Further, Article 9 of the 2001 DARSIWA may be of assistance as it states that responsibility will be attributed to a State if a person or a group of persons was in fact exercising elements of governmental authority in the absence or default of the official authorities and in circumstances such as to call for the exercise of those elements of authority. [16] However, Article 9 mainly deals with so-called failed States. [17]

---

14   (1924) 6 RIAA 138.
15   (1926) 4 RIAA 110, 116.
16   *Yeager v Iran* (1987) 17 Iran-USCTR 92.
17   D. Thürer, *The 'Failing State' and International Law* (1999) 81 IRRC, 731.

11.3.3 Acts of private persons

The DARSIWA provides for two situations in which a State may be responsible for unlawful acts committed by private persons:

- when their conduct is directed or controlled by a State (Article 8); and

- when their conduct is acknowledged and adopted by a State as its own (Article 11).

11.3.3.1 The situation of control

Two tests have been applied to determine whether conduct of private individuals/entities can be attributed to the State:

- The 'effective control test'. Under this test, in order to hold a State responsible for conduct of private individuals/entities it is necessary to show that it had effective control over each act carried out by such persons/entities.

- The 'overall control' test. Under this test, in order to hold a State responsible for conduct of private individuals/entities it suffices to show that it has overall control over acts carried out by such persons/entities. If so, each act of a relevant private individual/entity will be attributable to the State irrespective of whether any particular act had been specifically subjected to the control of the State.

The effective control test was applied by the ICJ in the *Nicaragua Case (Nicaragua v US) (Merits)*.[18] In this case the question arose as to whether the acts of the Contras could be attributed to the US. In considering the matter the ICJ had to determine the relationship between the Contras[19] and the US government. The Court stated that it was not sufficient to establish that the US government financed, organised, trained, supplied and equipped the Contras as well as providing logistical assistance in terms of planning their operations. The Court stated that:

> despite the heavy subsidies and other support provided to them by the United States, there is no clear evidence of the United States having actually exercised such a degree of control in all fields so as to justify treating the *contras* as acting on its behalf ... For this conduct to give rise to legal responsibility of the United States, it would in principle have to be proved that the State had effective control of the military or paramilitary operations in the course of which the alleged violations were committed.[20]

The Court found that acts of the Contras were not generally attributable to the US, but on occasions where the US was directly involved, e.g. mine-laying, acts of the Contras were imputable to the US.

The 'overall test' was applied by the Appeals Chamber of the International Criminal Tribunal for the Former Yugoslavia (ICTY) in the *Tadic Case*[21] in which the Chamber criticised the ICJ, and held

---

18   [1986] ICJ Rep 14.

19   'Contras' was a name given to various rebel groups in Nicaragua opposing the Sandinista Junta of National Reconstruction Government that came to power in 1979 after a successful *coup d'état* that overthrew the dictatorship of Anastasio Somoza. The US government assisted the Contras in various ways with a view to removing the Sandinistas from power.

20   Supra note 18, paras 109, 115.

21   Case No IT-94-1-A, Judgment, ICTY AC, 15 July 1999, at para 145. The Chamber supported the 'overall test' by citing the case law from national courts and from the ECtHR in the Case of *Loizidou v Turkey* (1997) 23

that with regard to the Bosnian Serb armed forces, the control of the Federal Republic of Yugoslavia (FRY) was overall control 'going beyond the mere financing and equipping of such forces and involving also participation in the planning and supervision of military operations'. The Chamber stated that international law does not require that such control should extend to the issuance of specific orders or instructions relating to single military actions. However, it is to be noted that the issue dealt with by the Appeals Chamber was not the attribution of responsibility for acts of the Bosnian Serb forces to the FRY, but the determination of whether the conflict was internal or international. The Chamber decided that as the Serbian forces were under the control of the FRY the conflict was international and therefore the relevant applicable rules were rules of humanitarian law applicable in international armed conflicts.

In the *Genocide Case*[22] the ICJ restated its position and said that 'effective control' is required in respect of 'each operation in which the alleged violations occurred, not generally in respect of the overall actions taken by the persons or groups of persons having committed the violations'. Accordingly, under the effective control test the threshold of attribution is very high, but as the ICJ stated the test of 'overall control' 'has the major drawback of broadening the scope of State responsibility well beyond the fundamental principle governing the law of international responsibility'.[23]

The ILC's position is stated in Article 8 of the 2001 DARSIWA which provides that the conduct of a person or group of persons is attributable to the State 'if the person or group of persons is in fact acting on the instructions of, or under the direction or control of, that State in carrying out the conduct'. As can been seen, Article 8 supports the view of the ICJ.

The choice between the two tests is very important. For example, with regard to the conflict in 2006 between Israel and Hezbollah, i.e. between a State and a non-State actor, the question whether the acts of Hezbollah can be attributed to Lebanon, Syria or Iran would be answered differently depending upon the test to be applied (see Chapter 15.4.5.2).

11.3.3.2   The situation where a State acknowledges the conduct of a private individual or entity

This situation is illustrated by the *Case Concerning United States Diplomatic and Consular Staff in Tehran (United States of America v Iran)*[24] (for detailed facts see Chapter 10.7.5) in which the ICJ held that Iran, by adopting the acts of the revolutionary guards, became responsible for them. However, in respect of the first phase of the taking of the US embassy and of the US hostages, which acts had been carried out by the revolutionary guards, the Court was quite clear that even congratulatory and approving statements made by the Iranian leadership did not have the effect of attributing the acts to the State. It was only when, on 17 November 1979, Ayatollah Khomeini, the then spiritual and *de facto* leader of Iran, issued a decree which maintained the occupation of the US embassy and the detention of hostages until the US handed over the Shah for trial in Iran that the acts were adopted by the State and therefore responsibility arose.

EHRR 513. See also J. De Hoogh, *Articles 4 and 8 of the 2001 ILC Articles on State Responsibility, the Tadic Case and Attribution of Facts of Bosnian Serb Authorities to the Federal Republic of Yugoslavia* (2001) 72 BYIL, 255.

22   Supra note 11, para 400. See also *Armed Activities on the Territory of the Congo (Democratic Republic of the Congo v Uganda)* (Judgment) [2005] ICJ Rep 168, para 160.

23   Ibid, para 406.

24   (1980) ICJ Rep 3.

11.3.4 Liability for acts of insurrectionaries

The development of the law in this area has been complicated by the existence of a very fine line between insurrection and mob violence. In the case of mob violence, the contention has long been that a State would be liable for failure to take the necessary measures. In the case of insurrections such a view was less certain as a number of writers argued that a State engaged in repressing insurgents was not responsible for harm caused to foreigners.

Article 10 of the 2001 DARSIWA encompasses the general proposition that a State will not be responsible for acts of any insurrectionary movement. The position changes if the movement subsequently becomes the government of the State or establishes a new State in part of the territory of a pre-existing State. In such cases the new government formed by the insurgents will be responsible for the acts of the movement during the insurgency. It will also bear responsibility for any acts committed by the previous government.

A number of cases on the responsibility of the State in respect of insurrection were submitted to the Iran-US Claims Tribunal. One of them in *Short v Iran*.[25]

SHORT *V* IRAN

Facts:

A US national was forced to leave Iran after threats from private persons during the Iranian revolution. He claimed against Iran for wrongful expulsion.

Held:

The Tribunal, while accepting that the revolutionary government was liable for acts committed during the revolution, held that Iran was not responsible for acts of private persons who had no status within the revolutionary movement. The claimant would have been able to recover had he been compelled to leave by revolutionary officials. In a dissenting opinion, the US member of the Tribunal queried how to distinguish between mere enthusiastic supporters and members of the revolutionary movement.

In *Yeager v Iran*[26] the applicant was expelled by revolutionary guards. The Tribunal decided in his favour since these acts were clearly attributable to the new government.

11.4 Direct and indirect international wrongs

An indirect wrong arises when a State is in breach of an obligation owed to a national of another State, e.g. an unlawful expropriation of private property. In contrast, a direct wrong occurs when one State is in direct breach of an obligation owed to another State. This gives rise to 'ordinary responsibility'. The 2001 DARSIWA introduces a new category of direct international wrong which arises when a State is in direct breach of *jus cogens*, and thus in breach of an obligation owed to the international community as a whole. This gives rise to 'aggrieved responsibility'. These two categories of direct international wrongs are examined below.

---

25   (1987) 16 Iran-USCTR 76.
26   (1987) 17 Iran-USCTR 92.

11.5   Direct international wrongs: aggrieved responsibility

Article 19 of the ILC Draft Articles adopted at the first reading in 1996 dealt with international crimes. The Draft defined an international crime as:

> an internationally wrongful act which results from the breach by a state of an international obligation so essential for the protection of fundamental interests of the international community that its breach is recognised as a crime by that community as a whole.

Article 19 identified some of these crimes as being:

- serious breaches of the law on peace and security, such as aggression;

- serious breaches of the right to self-determination, such as the establishment or maintenance by force of colonial domination;

- serious breaches of international duties on safeguarding human rights, such as slavery, genocide and apartheid;

- serious breaches of an obligation to protect the environment, such as massive pollution of the atmosphere or the seas.

Article 19 was strongly criticised. Many States felt that the seriousness of the breach of an obligation was not a matter of kind but of degree. On the one hand, breaches other than those set out in Article 19 may also be very serious in terms of their consequences and, on the other hand, there are ways of imposing a stricter form of responsibility for serious breaches of international law without introducing a distinction between international crimes and international delicts. Moreover, in the context of other articles of the Draft, Article 19 gave rise to many problems, especially in respect of the consequences attached to international crimes and the definition of an injured State. For the above-mentioned reasons the ILC, at its session in 1998, decided to put aside Article 19 and to consider 'whether the systematic development in the draft articles of key notions such as obligations (*erga omnes*), peremptory norms (*jus cogens*) and a possible category of the most serious breaches of international obligation could be sufficient to resolve the issues raised by Article 19'.[27] As a result, Article 19 was deleted, the term 'international crime' was abandoned and the distinction between criminal and delictual responsibility was abolished.

The problems raised in connection with Article 19 have been solved as follows: the notion of international crimes is envisaged through the concept of peremptory rules and obligations to the international community as a whole. Peremptory rules are expressly or implicitly invoked in the context of non-derogability, while international obligations to the international community as a whole are expressed through the wide determination of the legal interests of injured States. Chapter III of the 2001 DARSIWA deals with serious breaches of obligations under peremptory rules of international law. Article 40(2) states:

> A breach of such obligation is serious if it involves a gross or systematic failure by the responsible state to fulfil the obligation.

---

27   *First and Second Reports on State Responsibility*, James Crawford, UN Doc A/CN 4/490 & Adds 1–7 (1998), para 331.

The 2001 DARSIWA's definition of a wrongful act remains the same with regard to 'ordinary' and 'aggrieved responsibility' of a State. However, for aggrieved responsibility requirements additional to those for ordinary responsibility are set out in Article 40(2). These are:

■ the obligation which has been breached by a State must be of *jus cogens* character (see Chapter 2.5); and

■ it must be serious, that is it must involve a gross or systematic breach of that obligation. Therefore, sporadic, or minor breaches, are not covered by Article 40(2).

The requirement that the obligation breached must be owed to the international community as a whole, that must be of *erga omnes* character, is present in a number of articles contained in Chapter III of the 2001 DARSIWA relating to the implementation of the international responsibility of a State. This is further emphasised by the right given to any State, whether injured or not, to enforce an *erga omnes* obligation. Moreover, some obligations are imposed on all States other than a delinquent State. In this respect Article 41 of the ILC Articles requires:

■ all States to co-operate to bring the breach to an end through lawful means;

■ all States not to recognise the situation created by such a breach;

■ all States not to provide any aid or assistance to the delinquent State in maintaining the situation so created.

The possibility for States, other than the injured State, to invoke and enforce the responsibility of a delinquent State constitutes the main legal consequence of the commission of a wrongful act in cases of aggrieved responsibility. In this respect the distinction between an injured State and other States is vital. Article 42 defines an injured State in the following terms:

A state is entitled as an injured state to invoke the responsibility of another state if the obligation breached is owed to:
(a)   that state individually; or
(b)   a group of states including that state, or the international community as a whole, and the breach of the obligation:
   (i)   specifically affects that state; or
   (ii) is of such a character as radically to change the position of all the other states to which the obligation is owed with respect to the further performance of the obligation.

Article 42(b)(ii) refers to the so-called 'integral obligations' which, the Special Rapporteur noted, 'operate in an all-or-nothing fashion'.[28] The consequences of the breach of an 'integral obligation' are envisaged in Article 60(2)(c) VCLT. In the event of such a breach any party, other than the defaulting party, is entitled to suspend the operation of the whole treaty or part of it in respect of all other parties to the treaty because its breach by a defaulting party radically changes the position of every other party. In other words, the treaty is devoid of its substance, and its further performance is purposeless. Examples of integral treaties are the Treaty on the Non-Proliferation of Nuclear Weapons (see Chapter 17.3.1.3A), the Antarctic Treaty (see Chapter 7.6.2), and the disarmament treaties. The compliance of all contracting parties with integrated obligations ensures their effectiveness. There are a very limited number of such treaties but, according to the Special Rapporteur, their importance justifies the granting

---

28   A/CN4/517 § 38.

of the status of an injured State to a contracting party when another contracting party is breaching an integral obligation. Human rights treaties can never be considered as integrated treaties taking into account that a breach of their provisions by one contracting party has no effect on the performance of obligations by all other parties. To the contrary, a contracting State cannot justify the suspension of, for example, the European Convention for the Protection of Human Rights (ECHR) on account of the fact that another contracting party has violated fundamental rights and freedoms guaranteed under the ECHR (see Chapter 12.7.2).

The rights given to any State to invoke the responsibility of a delinquent State entitle an invoking State to:

- demand the cessation of the international wrongful act and assurances and guarantees of non-repetition; and

- claim reparation in the interest of the injured State or of the beneficiaries of the obligation breached, e.g. in respect of victims of gross violations of HRs.

The 2001 DARSIWA also allows any State to take countermeasures. This may occur in two situations:

- when a State acts on behalf of an injured State. However, the injured State must give its consent and any actions of the State acting on its behalf must be confined to the scope of the consent; and

- when no State is 'injured'. This situation concerns, in particular, violations of human rights obligations, owed to the international community as a whole, which are committed against nationals of the delinquent State. Any State may take lawful countermeasures acting in the interests of the beneficiaries of the obligation breached (Article 54 of the 2001 DARSIWA). All the limitations on the taking of countermeasures by an injured State set out in the 2001 DARSIWA apply in this event.

11.6   Direct international wrongs: ordinary responsibility

The following are examples of direct wrongful acts by one State against another.

11.6.1   Breach of a treaty

A breach of a treaty by a State is a breach of an obligation owed by that State to the other party or parties to the treaty whereby it, or they, suffers a direct wrong.

In the *Chorzów Factory Case (Indemnity) (Germany v Poland)*[29] the PCIJ stated that it was 'a principle of international law that the breach of an engagement involves an obligation to make reparation' and that reparation was therefore 'the indispensable complement of a failure to apply a convention'.

11.6.2   Damage to State property

If a State, through its acts or omissions, is the direct cause of damage to the property of another State, then it is liable to make reparation for the damage caused.

---

29   [1928] PCIJ Rep Ser A No 17, 29.

For example, in December 1999 the US and China agreed on US$28 million in damages payable to China for the mistaken bombing of the Chinese embassy in Belgrade by NATO forces led by the US. At the same time, China agreed to pay US$2.87 million in damages to the US for mob damage of the US diplomatic mission in China during demonstrations subsequent to the above-mentioned bombing.

In the *Corfu Channel Case (United Kingdom v Albania) (Merits)*[30] the ICJ held Albania responsible for the loss of life and the damage sustained by UK warships which were struck by mines laid in Albanian territorial waters.

11.6.3   Failure to respect the territorial rights of other States

A failure to respect the territorial rights of another State may consist of a straightforward breach of the prohibition of the use of force contained in Article 2(4) of the UN Charter which will give rise to 'aggrieved responsibility' of the offending State.

11.6.4   The unlawful arrest of a wanted criminal on the territory of another State

Eichmann, who played a key role in planning and carrying through the Nazi 'final solution' consisting of the extermination of some six million Jews, was found in Argentina in 1960 by the Israeli Secret Service, and abducted without the knowledge of the Argentinean government. Argentina complained to the United Nations Security Council (UNSC) which adopted a resolution stating that 'acts such as that under consideration, which affect the sovereignty of a member state ... endanger international peace and security' and requested the government of Israel to make appropriate reparations to the government of Argentina (see Chapter 9.6.1.1).

11.6.5   Illegal flights in the airspace of another State

In the U-2 incident of May 1960 (*Lissitzyn*[31] and *Wright*[32]) a US aircraft engaged in espionage activities over the Soviet Union was forced to land on Russian soil. The US did not protest at the shooting down of the aircraft and the subsequent trial of the pilot.

11.6.6   The carrying out of activities in the territorial waters of a State

In the *Corfu Channel Case (United Kingdom v Albania) (Merits)*[33] the ICJ held that the Royal Navy, in carrying out minesweeping operations in Albanian territorial waters, violated the sovereignty of the Albanian Peoples Republic.

11.6.7   By allowing toxic fumes to escape into the territory of another State

This is illustrated by the *Trail Smelter Arbitration (United States of America v Canada)*.[34]

---

30   [1949] ICJ Rep 4.
31   (1962) 56 AJIL 135.
32   (1960) 54 AJIL 836.
33   [1949] ICJ Rep 4.
34   (1938 and 1941) 3 RIAA 1905; 1965.

TRAIL SMELTER ARBITRATION (UNITED STATES OF AMERICA V CANADA)

Facts:

A Canadian company began smelting lead and zinc at Trail, on the Columbia River about 10 miles from the US-Canadian border, on the Canadian side. By 1930 over 300 tons of sulphur, containing considerable quantities of sulphur dioxide, were being emitted daily. Some of the fumes were being carried down the Columbia River valley and across into the US where they were allegedly causing considerable damage to land and other interests in the state of Washington. The US claimed compensation, and the matter was referred to the International Joint Commission.

Held:

The Commission found that 'under the principles of international law . . . no state has the right to use or permit the use of its territory in such manner as to cause injury by fumes in or to the territory of another or the properties of persons therein'.

11.6.8 Insult to the State

Such acts are generally termed 'insults to the flag' and constitute international wrongs for which the State responsible should make suitable reparations. An example is provided by the *I'm Alone Case (Canada v United States of America).*[35]

I'M ALONE CASE (CANADA V UNITED STATES OF AMERICA)

Facts:

The I'm Alone, a British schooner, registered in Canada, was ordered to heave to by a US coastguard vessel, on suspicion of smuggling liquor at the time of prohibition in the US. She fled, and when more than 200 miles from the US coast (on the high seas) was fired upon and sunk, with the loss of the boatswain and the cargo.

Held:

The Arbitration Commission, to which the case was referred, found that the sinking of the vessel was unlawful. It accepted that the US had the right to hot pursuit but that its exercise was unlawful in that the US by intentionally sinking the ship used force which went beyond what was reasonable and necessary in the circumstances. It was also established that the vessel was de facto owned by citizens of the US and therefore no compensation ought to be paid in respect of the ship or cargo. However, the Commission considered that the US ought to formally acknowledge the illegality of its act, apologise to His Majesty's Canadian government, and further, pay the sum of US$25,000 to that government as material compensation.

---

35   (1933–1935) 3 RIAA 1609.

In the majority of flag insult cases a public apology and an undertaking to punish those responsible for the act will constitute adequate amends.

11.7 Indirect international wrongs: the treatment of aliens

Vattel stated that an injury to a citizen is an injury to the State.[36] The relationship between the individual and his State gives rise to two principles:

■ the State is responsible for the acts of its citizens of which its agents know or ought to know and which cause harm to the legal interests of another State; and

■ the State has a legal interest in its citizens, and in protecting this interest, the State may call to account those harming its citizens.

In the *Mavrommattis Palestine Concessions Case (Jurisdiction) (Greece v United Kingdom)*[37] the Court said:

it is an elementary principle of international law that a state is entitled to protect its subjects, when injured by acts contrary to international law committed by another state, from whom they have been unable to obtain satisfaction through the ordinary channels. By taking up the case of one of its subjects and by resorting to diplomatic action or international judicial proceedings on his behalf, a state is in reality asserting its own right – its right to ensure, in the person of its subjects, respect for the rules of international law.

The respondant State's duties are owed not to the injured alien, but to the alien's national State. Thus:

■ The claimant State may refrain from making a claim as there is no obligation to espouse a claim. Each State exercises its discretion in this respect. In deciding whether to espouse a claim, irrespective of the merits of the claim, many factors will be taken into account, in particular the consequences of the espousal for relations between the injured State and the foreign State against which a person has a claim.

■ The claimant State may abandon its claim.

■ The claimant State is under no obligation to pay any compensation obtained to its injured national. In *Rustomjee v The Queen*[38] money had been paid to Great Britain by China as compensation for damage suffered by British nationals in China. Lush J stated:

No doubt a duty arose as soon as the money was received to distribute that money amongst the persons towards whose losses it was paid by the Emperor of China; but then the distribution when made would be, not the act of an agent accounting to a principal, but the act of the Sovereign in dispensing justice to her subjects. For any omission of that duty the Sovereign cannot be held responsible.

---

36 E. de Vattel *Le Droit des Gens ou Principes de la Loi Naturelle* (trans. C. Fenwick) The Law of Nations or the Principles of Natural Law (1758), Washington, DC: Carnegie Institution of Washington, 1916, vol 1, 309, para 71.

37 [1924] PCIJ Rep Ser A No 2, 12.

38 (1876) 1 QBD 487.

However, the ILC 2006 DADP recommend that a State transfers to the injured persons any compensation obtained from the responsible State subject to any reasonable deductions (Article 19(c)).

■ A private claim becomes an international claim over which the State enjoys exclusive control. As a result a claimant is barred from pursuing or disposing of the claim on his own. The advantage to the claimant is, however, that his State is supporting the claim and thus the chances of him being compensated are greatly improved (see Chapter.11.11).

11.7.1 The treatment of aliens

The importance of espousal of claims by a State has been reduced due to the development of HRL (see Chapter 12). This is because:

■ individuals, as subjects of international law, have access to international courts and tribunals and thus will be able to make claims independently of any espousal by the State;

■ corporations, on the basis of BITs, will be able to settle disputes through arbitration;

■ the minimum standard of treatment of aliens has been defined by reference to IHL. Accordingly, every State is required to respect fundamental human rights, in particular those which are of a *jus cogens* nature.

Much of the controversy regarding the treatment of aliens stems from the difference in approach between those States that consider that there is an 'international minimum standard' of treatment which must be accorded to aliens by all States irrespective of how they treat their own nationals, and those that argue that aliens may only insist upon 'national treatment', i.e. treatment equal to that given by the State concerned to its own nationals.

11.7.1.1 The standard of national treatment

The principle of national treatment has been favoured by the newer and developing States. It has received support in Latin American countries which have developed the Calvo doctrine, or clause, on the basis of which an alien is not entitled to seek the diplomatic protection of his national State and instead, in accord with the standard of national treatment, seeks redress before local courts in the same way as nationals of the relevant State. The commentary of the ILC on Article 14 of the DADP states that the Calvo clause:

> is difficult to reconcile with international law if it is to be interpreted as a complete waiver of recourse to international protection in respect of an action by the host State constituting an internationally wrongful act (such as a denial of justice), or where the injury to the alien was of direct concern to the State of nationality of the alien.[39]

Nevertheless, the use of the Calvo clause, mainly inserted in contracts between a State and a natural/legal person, is not dead, although the development of settlement of disputes procedures in respect of commercial activities and investment has, to a great extent, made the clause irrelevant (see Chapter 11.10.3).

---

39   The Report of the International Law Commission, 58th Session (1 May–9 June and 3 July–11 August 2006) GAOR, 61st Session Supp 10, 73.

The main justifications for granting aliens equality of treatment under the local law have been stated as follows:

■ to give an alien a special status would be contrary to the principles of territorial jurisdiction and equality of States; and

■ by residing in the particular State the alien is deemed to have submitted to both the benefits and the burdens incidental to residence in that State, i.e. he takes conditions as he finds them. This means, for example, that if a national of a State does not receive compensation for expropriation, an alien will similarly have no right to such compensation.

The national standard does not apply to every area of activity. Customary international law recognises that in certain areas of activity States may treat aliens less favourably than their own nationals. For example, aliens may be restricted in: the ownership of property; participation in public life and politics; the taking of employment; and receiving legal aid and welfare benefits. In the UK, for instance, an alien may not own a British ship (but this does not apply to citizens of the EU), may not vote in parliamentary elections, and may face restrictions in joining the civil service.

11.7.1.2 The international minimum standard

The older and more economically developed States of Western Europe and North America have generally supported the international minimum standard of treatment of aliens, which unlike the national standard, is based solely on international law. The international minimum standard does not require that nationals and aliens are treated equally, but ensures that there is a common international standard of treatment of aliens. The international minimum standard, as defined by HRL, is supported by the great majority of international tribunals.

11.7.1.3 The treatment of aliens: fundamental human rights

It is generally accepted that, the standard of treatment to be accorded to non-nationals should be the standard established by HRL. This is further supported by the fact that all HRs treaties contain a clause ensuring that their provisions will apply to any person within the jurisdiction of a contracting State, irrespective of whether the person is a national or an alien.

Traditionally, the minimum standard was very relevant in ensuring that aliens were not killed, tortured and otherwise physically mistreated in another State, and that, if they suffered harm, they had access to justice in a foreign State. However, with the development of HRL, the traditional areas relevant to the exercise of diplomatic protection by a State have lost their importance. Nevertheless, new areas have emerged, namely those concerning the protection of property of aliens, including their investments in a foreign State, which pose challenges to international law. The above topics are examined below.

11.8 The treatment of aliens: admission and expulsion

HRL *via* the rules of *jus cogens*, customary international law and international treaties requires that fundamental human rights must be observed by all States. Thus, for example, the right to life, the right to be free from torture and the right not to be discriminated against on the ground of race, are universally accepted. The UNGA Declaration on the Human Rights of Individuals Who are Not Nationals of the Country in which They Live emphasises the importance of respect for human rights of aliens.[40] However, the issue of admission and expulsion of aliens is somewhat controversial.

---

40   Resolution 40/144 of 13 December 1985.

11.8.1 Admission

The admission of aliens remains essentially within the domestic jurisdiction of States. A State may refuse to admit aliens or may impose conditions or restrictions upon their admission.

In *Attorney-General for Canada v Cain*[41] the Privy Council stated:

> One of the rights possessed by the supreme power in every state is the right to refuse to permit an alien to enter that state, to annex what conditions it pleases to the permission to enter it, and to expel or deport from the State, at pleasure, even a friendly alien, especially if it considers his presence in the state opposed to its peace, order and good Government, or to its social or material interests.

The only restrictions imposed by international law on a State with regard to the admission of aliens are those provided for in international treaties. For example, the European Court of Human Rights (ECtHR) in *Mubilanzila Mayeka and Kaniki Mitunga v Belgium*[42] emphasised that when a State is exercising its sovereign right to control its border, and the entry and stay of aliens, it must comply with its obligations deriving from the ECHR, in particular Article 3 (Prohibition of torture), Article 5 (Right to liberty and security), and Article 8 (Right to respect for private and family life), and from the Convention on the Rights of the Child.

11.8.2 Expulsion

With regard to expulsion, treaties (e.g. the International Covenant on Civil and Political Rights (ICCPR), the CAT, the 1951 Convention of the Status of Refugees, and regional conventions protecting HRs such as the ECHR) guarantee, in certain circumstances, not only a substantive right against expulsion, but also provide for procedural rights to ensure that expulsion is not administered in an arbitrary manner. It is important to emphasise that under HRs treaties there is an absolute prohibition from extradition, or expulsion in a situation where there are substantial grounds to believe that the person in question will be in danger of being subjected to torture, even if the person is a terrorist,[43] or a murderer,[44] or his presence is considered as being against the public interest of a contracting party, e.g. the person poses a threat to national security.

11.8.2.1 *The position of the ECtHR.*

According to the case law of the ECtHR, prohibition of expulsion/extradition/deportation/removal of a person to a country in which there is a 'real risk' that he/she might be killed, tortured or suffer other ill treatment in breach of Articles 2 (the right to life) or 3 ECHR (the right not to be tortured or subjected to inhuman, degrading treatment or punishment) is well established.[45] Further, the ECtHR has ruled that expulsion/deportation may engage rights protected under Article 5 (the right to liberty and security)[46] and Article 6 (the right to a fair trial – see below the *Case of Abu Qatada*), although

---

41   [1906] AC 542, 546.
42   (2008) 46 EHRR 23.
43   The Decision of the Committee against Torture in *Paez v Sweden* (CAT 39/96), the judgment of the ECtHR in *Chahal v UK* (1997) 23 EHRR 413.
44   The decision of the UN Human Rights Committee in *NG v Canada* (469/91); the judgment of the ECtHR in *Soering v UK* (1989) 11 EHRR 439.
45   *Soering v UK* (1989) 11 EHRR 439; *Chahal v UK* (1997) 23 EHRR 413; and *Saadi v Italy* [2009] 49 EHRR 30.
46   *Tomic v UK*, Application 17837/03, Judgment of 14 October 2003 (unreported), and *Othman (Abu Qatada) v UK*, ((2012) 55 EHRR 1, para 233) in which the ECtHR gave examples of flagrant breaches of Article 5 ECHR.

it has refused to accept that the violation of the right of freedom of religion (protected under Article 9 ECHR) may bar deportation.[47] Examples of the broad interpretation of the ECHR are provided in the judgments of the ECtHR in *D v UK*[48] in which it held that in exceptional circumstances a State is prohibited from deporting an alien on the ground that he would not be able to obtain necessary medical treatment in another State, and in *Othman (Abu Qatada) v UK*[49] in which it ruled that deportation is prohibited in a situation where it would give rise to a flagrant denial of justice in violation of Article 6 ECHR, which ensures the right to a fair trial. Both judgments are examined below.

D *V* UK

Facts:

D, a national of St Kitts and Nevis, was convicted of serious drug offences in the UK and was to be deported to St Kitts at the end of his sentence. He challenged the deportation order on the ground that it would violate Article 3 ECHR (prohibition of torture and other similar treatment) because he was in advanced stages of AIDS and his deportation to St Kitts, where he would not receive the treatment for AIDS he was receiving in the UK, would expose him to risk of dying in distressing circumstances. Further, in St Kitts he would be alone as he had no friends or family there.

Held:

The ECtHR held that D's deportation, because of exceptional humanitarian reasons, should not proceed, i.e. D was in the critical stage of his illness and his removal would expose him to a real risk of dying under the most distressing circumstances. This would amount to inhuman treatment. No such circumstances were present in Bensaid v UK,[50] *where deportation of a schizophrenic to Algeria, where medical treatment was not as good as in the UK, was allowed.[51] However, so far, the threat that removal would expose the person concerned to harsh social and economic circumstances has not been sufficient to constitute a violation of Article 3 ECHR.*

OTHMAN (ABU QATADA) *V* UK[52]

Facts:

Othman, known under the name of Abu Qatada, a Jordanian national who was granted political asylum in the UK in 1994, and lived there until his voluntary departure in 2013, was

---

47   *Z and T v UK*, Application 27034/05, Judgment of 28 February 2006.
48   (1997) 24 EHRR.
49   (2012) 55 EHRR 1.
50   (2001) 33 EHRR.
51   See also *R (N) v Secretary of State for the Home Department* [2005] UKHL 31, in which, in circumstances similar to those of D, the House of Lords held that there was no violation of Article 3 of the ECHR.
52   (2012) 55 EHRR 1.

a radical cleric and a mentor to jihadists, who in 2001 issued some sort of so called ruling justifying suicide attacks. According to the UK government he not only publicly supported terrorist groups, but also raised funds for them, including for groups linked to al Qaeda. From 2002 to 2005 he was detained in the UK under the Anti-terrorism, Crime and Security Act 2001, but never charged with any criminal offence. When the Act was repealed in 2005 he was released on bail, and served by the UK Secretary of State with notice of intention to deport him to Jordan. In 1999, in Jordan he had been convicted in absentia on two charges of conspiracy to cause explosions, i.e. concerning the successful bombing of the American School and the Jerusalem Hotel in the capital of Jordan, Amman. Abu Qatada argued, inter alia, that his deportation from the UK would be in breach of Article 3 ECHR, just because on return to Jordan he would be tortured and second, in breach of Article 6 ECHR because in his retrial in Jordan for offences he had been convicted in absentia in 1999 on evidence obtained by torture of co-defendants in that trial that evidence will be used against him.

Held:

The ECtHR held that there was no breach of Article 3 ECHR because the UK government obtained sufficient assurances from the Jordanian government that there would be no risk of ill-treatment of Abu Qutada. However, the ECtHR held that his deportation would breach Article 6 ECHR because there was a 'real risk' that, in the retrial, incriminating evidence obtained by torture would be admitted against him. The Court held that the use of any evidence obtained by torture during a criminal trial would amount to a flagrant denial of justice.

Comment:

Evidence of the involvement of Abu Qatada in terrorism had been provided by two co-defendants in the 1999 trial in Jordan who claimed that their statements were obtained by torture. The Jordanian Court had not taken any action in relation to their complaints. Further, the ECtHR found that evidence obtained by torture was used by Jordanian courts. In these circumstances the ECtHR ruled that there was a 'real risk' that incriminating evidence would be admitted to any retrial of Abu Qatada and that such evidence would be of considerable importance. The Court emphasised that there would be a flagrant denial of justice if evidence obtained by torture were admitted in a criminal trial, and that allowing a criminal court to rely on torture evidence would legitimise the torture of witnesses and suspects pre-trial. It also stated that in the absence of any assurances obtained by the UK from Jordan that evidence obtained by torture would not be used against Abu Qatada his deportation to Jordan to be retried would give rise to a flagrant denial of justice in violation of Article 6 ECHR.

Follow up:

The UK government reached an agreement with the Jordanian government that no evidence against Abu Qatada obtained by torture of his co-defendants in an earlier trial would be used against him at his retrial. Following this Abu Qatada voluntarily departed to Jordan. In September 2014 he was acquitted of all charges by the Jordanian court and released from prison.

11.8.2.2 The position of the ILC – The Draft Articles on the Expulsion of Aliens (DAEA)

The topic of expulsion of aliens was of interest to the ILC for more than 60 years. However, it was in 2004 that the ILC started preparing draft articles. They were adopted at the ILC's 66th session in 2014 together with a commentary, and submitted to the UNGA with recommendations that the UNGA first takes notice of the DAEA by adopting a resolution to which the DAEA would be annexed, so ensuring the widest possible dissemination of the DAEA and, second, at some future date, prepare a convention based on the DAEA.[53]

The DAEA are divided into five parts. Each is briefly examined here:

1   Part One, sets out 'General provisions', defines the key words: 'expulsion' and 'alien', and establishes a few general rules relating to expulsion of aliens.

The most controversial is the definition of 'alien' in that the DAEA recognises that aliens, who are lawfully in the State territory, and aliens who are not, should enjoy almost[54] similar rights. In this respect, HRs treaties make a distinction between lawful and unlawful presence in terms of the scope of international protection accorded to aliens.

Draft article (DA) 2 defines 'expulsion' as:

> a formal act or conduct attributable to a State by which an alien is compelled to leave the territory of that State; it does not include extradition to another State, surrender to an international criminal court or tribunal, or the non-admission of an alien to a State.

The commentary explains that the term 'non-admission' refers to a situation where an alien is refused entry, but special rules relating to asylum seekers are fully recognised by the DAEA. Accordingly, a person stopped at the border, apart from an asylum seeker, is not within the scope of the DAEA.

DA 3 confirms the right of a State to expel an alien from its territory but this is subject to the requirements set out in the DAEA, those of international law, and in particular those of HRL.

2   Part Two of the DAEA deals with cases of prohibited expulsion. These cases concern:

- refugees, who apply for refugee status, and stateless persons. They cannot be expelled save on grounds of national security or public order;

- nationals, in the State of intended expulsion, who have been stripped of their nationality for the sole purpose of expulsion;

- aliens who are subjected to expulsion for the specific purpose of confiscation of their assets;

- collective expulsions, save when permitted by the *jus in bello* in time of armed conflicts; and

- disguised expulsions.

3   Part III deals with the protection of the rights of aliens subjected to expulsion.

First, Chapter I deals with general rights granted to aliens subjected to expulsion. At all times, they should be treated with humanity, respect to their human dignity, and protected from discrimination on

---

53   A/69/10.

54   Only Draft Articles 6–7, 26–27 and 29 differentiate between aliens who are lawfully in a State's territory and those who are not.

grounds of race, colour, sex, language, religion, political or other opinion, national or social origin, property, birth or other grounds impermissible under international law.

Second, Chapter II defines the extent of protection of aliens in the expelling State. Various HRs apply to them, including the right to life, the right to be free from torture and cruel, inhuman or degrading treatment, the right to private and family life, the right to property, and the right to non-discrimination. The matter of detention of aliens for the purpose of expulsion is dealt with in DA 19. Such detention should not be arbitrary or punitive in nature, as short as reasonably possible, and based on a judicial decision, which must be subject to review by another competent authority. If expulsion cannot proceed, detention must end except where reasons attributable to the alien concerned justify it.

Third, Chapter III deals with the protection of aliens due to be expelled in relation to the State of destination. Ideally, an alien who is required to leave a State will depart therefrom voluntarily. However, when a forcible expulsion is necessary that expulsion is subject to the 'core' requirements of HRL. Accordingly it is prohibited to expel an alien to a State where he/she has a justified fear of being killed. Indeed, a State which has abolished the death sentence is prohibited from expelling an alien already sentenced to death, or being at real risk of the imposition of the death sentence, unless it has obtained adequate assurances from the State of destination. Further an intended expulsion is prohibited to a State where an alien may be subjected to torture or cruel, inhuman or degrading treatment or punishment. This goes beyond the requirements of the CAT which prohibits expulsion/extradition, etc., when there is a risk of the person being tortured (see Chapter 12.3.4).

Fourth, Chapter IV deals with the protection of the expelled person in a transit State. DA 25 requires the State of transit to protect the rights of an expelled person in conformity with its obligations under international law.

4   Part IV sets out specific requirements concerning the procedural rights of persons subjected to expulsion. Those are the rights normally guaranteed under international law, including the right to consular assistance.

5   Part Five sets out the legal consequences of an unlawful expulsion for the expelling State, and the State of nationality of the expelled alien. The State of nationality is entitled to exercise diplomatic protection while the alien has the right to readmission save when she/he constitutes a threat to national security or no longer satisfies the condition for admission to the territory of the expelling State.

It is submitted that DAEA reflects the law on this topic *de lega lata* i.e. customary international law, and *de lege feranda*, i.e. its proposed development. Whether customary international law imposes any restrictions on the expulsion of aliens is a matter of controversy. State practice suggests that only if an obligation is imposed by HRs treaties will States refrain from expelling persons whose presence within their territory is regarded as unwelcome and undesirable. It should perhaps be said that the DAEA are more *de lege feranda* than *de lege lata* and consequently many of its provisions will not be accepted by the majority of States.

11.9   The treatment of aliens: denial of justice

The term 'denial of justice' has been given widely differing interpretations by international tribunals and its precise meaning is, therefore, uncertain and controversial. In its widest sense it has been equated with any wrongful treatment of aliens for which a respondent State would be accountable. In its narrowest sense it has been used to cover only those situations in which foreigners have either been refused access to local courts, or where such access has been hindered.

A definition somewhere between the above interpretations is contained in the 1929 Harvard Draft Convention on the Responsibility of States for Damage Done in Their Territory to the Person or Property of Foreigners,[55] Article 9 of which states:

> Denial of justice exists when there is a denial, unwarranted delay or obstruction of access to courts, gross deficiency in the administration of judicial or remedial process, failure to provide those guarantees which are generally considered indispensable to the proper administration of justice, or a manifestly unjust judgment. An error of a national court which does not produce manifest injustice is not a denial of justice.

This draft article has been criticised as being too general. It is such generality which has resulted in the wide interpretation given to the term 'denial of justice' and has led to its erratic application and uncertainty of meaning.

Although no universally accepted definition of denial of justice to aliens has been agreed, it is submitted that denial of justice can be defined as any gross miscarriage of justice by domestic courts resulting from wrongful administration of justice to aliens. The wrongful administration of justice may arise from acts of the executive, the legislature or the judiciary.

The material content of the concept of denial of justice has, to a great extent, been defined by international courts and bodies dealing with human rights treaties, e.g. the UN Human Rights Committee while interpreting Article 14 of the International Covenant on Civil and Political Rights (ICCPR) which guarantees the right to fair trial and equality before the courts, and sets out a number of rights to be respected in both criminal and civil proceedings; the ECtHR when interpreting Article 6 of the ECHR; and the Inter-American bodies in charge of the interpretation and application of Article 8 of the American Convention on Human Rights (ACHR).

It is submitted that denial of justice will occur, *inter alia*, in the following situations:

- Where a claimant has no access to a court. Cases decided by human rights bodies, however, emphasise that the right to access to a court is not absolute and that in some circumstances a refusal may be justified, e.g. where national and international courts on the ground of State immunity have refused to adjudicate cases, even where a *jus cogens* rule was violated[56] (see Chapter 10.3.3.2.C).

- Where a trial does not proceed within a reasonable time. The determination of a reasonable time depends upon the circumstances of the case: i.e. the complexity of the case, whether the proceedings concern civil or criminal matters, the conduct of the claimant, the conduct of the authority concerned and the importance of the case to the claimant.[57]

- Where the court dealing with a claim is not independent and impartial. This embodies the principle of separation of powers which is normally enshrined in the constitution of any democratic State. In the *Petrobart v Kyrgis Republic Arbitration* the Stockholm Chamber of Commerce held that collusion between the Government of the Kyrgis Republic and the court amounted to 'a clear breach of the prohibition of denial of justice under international law'.[58] Partiality includes bias by an adjudicating body, e.g. when the judge has a personal (including moral) interest in the outcome of the trial.[59]

---

55   (1929) 23 AJIL Spec Supp 131–239.
56   *Al-Adsani v UK* (2002) 34 EHRR 11.
57   See e.g. *Philis v Greece (No 2)* (1998) 25 EHRR 417.
58   Award of 29 March 2005, SCC Case No 126/2003.
59   R v Bow Street Magistrates ex p Pinochet (No 2) [2000] AC 119.

■ Where due process guarantees are not respected, e.g. in respect of criminal proceedings this refers to the right to be presumed innocent, the right to be informed of charges, the right to counsel of one's own choice, or as in the case of Abu Quatada, non-admission of evidence obtained by torture.

■ Where the relevant authority of a foreign State refuses to enforce an arbitral award or a foreign judgment in breach of an international treaty, or just refuses to enforce a judgment rendered by a local court.[60]

11.10   The treatment of aliens: expropriation of foreign property

A State may restrict or place conditions upon the acquisition of certain kinds of property by aliens. In the absence of such restrictions an alien is free to acquire and enjoy property in accordance with the provisions of the local law.

Expropriation, or the compulsory taking of private property by the State, has always been considered as a ground for diplomatic intervention based on a breach of international law. Whereas in the nineteenth and twentieth centuries the problem was usually one related to the destruction or direct expropriation of the property of an individual, in the twenty-first century, it is likely to be one concerning indirect expropriation and the exercise by a State of powers in the public interest which may affect the property rights of foreign persons. Accordingly, most disputes focus on violations by a State of the fair and equitable standard of treatment of foreign natural and legal persons rather than claims based on alleged expropriation.[61]

The acquisition and control of property by aliens is of considerable political importance to States. The economies of many States, both underdeveloped and developed, are dominated by foreign companies and foreign investors. Many States resent this foreign dominance and see it as a threat to their independence, and as inhibiting their freedom to implement their chosen economic and social policies. However, the same States are usually seeking to attract foreign investors. Consequently, direct expropriations are rare.

11.10.1   The rules on expropriation

Although it is generally agreed that expropriation may occur, the wide divergence of political and economic beliefs among States has resulted in little agreement as to the rules to be applied in cases of expropriation.

Communist States believe that States may expropriate, i.e. confiscate the means of production, distribution and exchange without paying any compensation.

Developing States believe the matter of expropriation of property should be left to the expropriating State to regulate at its discretion and in accordance with its national law.

Western capital-exporting States have, however, advocated an international minimum standard based on four requirements:

■ the requirement of non-discrimination;

■ the requirement that the expropriation must be for a public purpose;

---

60   *Timofeyev v Russia* (2004) ILM 768.

61   In 2011, the ILC recognised the importance of clarifying the meaning and scope of the 'fair and equitable treatment' by including it onto its long-term work plan. Report of the ILC, 63rd Session, April 26–June 3, July 4–August 12, 2011,para 365.

■ the requirement that expropriation must be adequately compensated;

■ the requirement that expropriation must be carried out in accordance with due process of law.

11.10.1.1   The requirement of non-discrimination based on nationality

While the requirement of non-discrimination is not expressly stated in either of the principal international instruments dealing with this matter (see below UN General Assembly resolution (UNGAR) 1803 and UNGAR 3281), it is based on a general principle of good faith, and has been widely upheld in arbitral awards such as *LIAMCO v Libya*[62] or in *Aminoil v Kuwait*.[63] The last mentioned is examined below.

AMINOIL *V* KUWAIT

Facts:

Kuwait was pursuing a general policy of nationalisation, but was doing so in stages. At the time of the nationalisation of Aminoil, a Japanese company also operating in the same region was left unnationalised. Aminoil alleged discrimination.

Held:

The Tribunal rejected the claim on the grounds that there were legitimate reasons for the nationalisation not having included the Japanese company. To establish an unlawful discrimination a company would, therefore, have to show that it had been singled out on the basis of its nationality.

The case of *BP v Libya*[64] provides the most striking example of a company being singled out. In this case Libya expressly stated that it was expropriating BP's assets in response to what was regarded as improper action by the British government in the Persian Gulf. The expropriation thus arose directly as a result of the British nationality of BP.

11.10.1.2   The public purpose requirement

In *Certain German Interests in Polish Upper Silesia*[65] the PCIJ acknowledged that 'expropriation for reasons of public utility, judicial liquidation and similar measures' was permissible in international law.

The public purpose requirement is stated in UNGAR 1803 (XVII) but not in UNGAR 3281 (XXIX) (see Chapter 11.10.1.4).

According to the United Nations Conference on Trade and Development (UNCTAD) document entitled 'Expropriation', the requirement of public purpose is recognised by most legal systems and constitutes a rule of customary international law.[66] For the expropriatory measure to be lawful it is

---

62   (1981) 20 ILM 1.

63   (1982) 21 ILM 976.

64   (1974) 53 ILR 297.

65   [1925] PCIJ Rep Ser A No 6, 22.

66   Hereafter referred to as 'UNCTAD expropriation document', UNCTAD/DIAE/IA/2011/7, 28. The UNCTAD expropriation document forms part of a series on Issues in International Investment Agreements (IIAs) which is considered as a standard reference tool for the preparation and interpretation of IIAs.

necessary that it seeks to achieve some legitimate welfare purpose which is of genuine interest to the public. The existence of 'public interest' is assessed by reference to the time when the expropriatory measure was effected and therefore the matter of whether the original purpose has been achieved is irrelevant.[67] This entails that if initially an expropriatory measure did not pursue a public purpose, but subsequently started to serve such purpose, the measure will be unlawful.

11.10.1.3 The requirement of compensation

While there is general acceptance that there is a requirement to compensate in the case of expropriation, the standard of the compensation required has been much in issue. The debate has focused on the divide between those seeking an international standard of compensation and those in favour of a standard of compensation determined in accordance with the municipal law of the State concerned, i.e. under this standard the exact market value of the expropriated property should not necessarily be paid as factors such as history, wealth, etc. should be taken into account.

Those in favour of an international standard of compensation have pointed to numerous examples of State practice in support of the proposition. US Secretary of State Hull, in 1940, argued that the right to expropriate was 'coupled with and conditioned on the obligation to make adequate, effective and prompt compensation'.[68]

In the *Anglo-Iranian Oil Co Case (United Kingdom/Iran) (Request for the Indication of Interim Measures of Protection)*[69] the UK pleaded the following before the ICJ:

> it is clear that the nationalisation of the property of foreigners, even if not unlawful on any other ground, becomes an unlawful confiscation unless provision is made for compensation which is adequate, prompt and effective . . . By 'adequate' compensation is meant 'the value of the undertaking at the moment of dispossession, plus interest to the day of judgment' . . . There have, in fact, been pronouncements that prompt compensation means immediate payment in cash. Thus in the arbitration between the United States and Norway relating to the requisitioning of contracts for the building of ships in the United States, it was held: the Tribunal is of opinion that full compensation should have been paid . . . at the latest on the day of the effective taking . . . The Government of the United Kingdom is, however, prepared to admit that deferred payments may be interpreted as satisfying the requirement of payment in accordance with the rules of international law if: (a) the total amount to be paid is fixed promptly; (b) allowance for interest for late payment is made; (c) the guarantees that the future payments will in fact be made are satisfactory, so that the person to be compensated may, if he so desires, raise the full sum at once on the security of the future payments . . . The third requirement is summed up in the word 'effective' and means that the recipient of the compensation must be able to make use of it. He must, for instance, be able, if he wishes, to use it to set up a new enterprise to replace the one that has been expropriated or to use it for such other purposes as he wishes . . . The compensation . . . must be freely transferrable from the country paying it and, so far as that country's restrictions are concerned, convertible into other currencies.

---

67   See *Siag and Vecchi v Egypt*, Award, 1 June 2009, cited in the UNCTAD expropriation document.
68   R.A. Brand, *Fundamentals of International Business Transactions*, The Hague: Kluwer Law International, 2000, 981–982.
69   [1951] ICJ Rep 81, 83.

The ICJ ordered interim measures but later found that it had no jurisdiction to adjudicate the dispute.[70]

Not unlike the thrust of the UK pleading quoted above, UNGA Resolution 1803 (XVII) on Permanent Sovereignty over Natural Resources[71] requires payment of 'appropriate compensation . . . in accordance with international law'. While the resolution left what was meant by 'appropriate' unstated, it was generally accepted that the resolution firmly established an international standard of compensation. The international standard has been applied in numerous cases since that resolution (e.g. *Texaco, BP, Aminoil*).

There are nevertheless exceptions to the requirement of compensation:

■ if a treaty so provides;

■ in the case of confiscation as a penalty for crimes;

■ if confiscation occurs in the course of legitimate exercise of police power;

■ if confiscation is a measure of defence;

■ if the property is seized by way of taxation;

■ if the destruction of property of neutrals results from military operations;

■ if the enemy takes property as reparation.

Developing States have argued in favour of a standard of compensation set by the municipal law of the State concerned. They point in particular to UNGAR 3281 (XXIX) – the Charter of Economic Rights and Duties of States[72] – which provides, in para 2(c), that 'where the question of compensation gives rise to a controversy, it shall be settled under the domestic law of the nationalising state'.

In terms of this debate, the weight of opinion would appear to rest with an international standard of compensation. The arbitrator in *Texaco v Libya*,[73] following an assessment of the two UNGA resolutions, came to the conclusion that UNGAR 1803 reflected customary law while UNGAR 3281 did not. This conclusion notwithstanding, the debate on the international versus domestic standard of compensation, has lost much of its vigour for two main reasons:

■ In an attempt to encourage foreign investment in order to stimulate economic growth, a large number of developing States have been willing to conclude bilateral investment treaties (BITs) containing clauses that subject the investment agreement to international law, and that provide for the submission of any dispute to international settlement. Further, the vast majority of BITs include the Hull formula requiring prompt, adequate and effective compensation.

■ BITs as well as multilateral trade and investment treaties require fair and equitable treatment and full protection and security with regard to direct foreign investment, e.g. Article 1105 of the 1992 North American Free Trade Agreement (NAFTA).

---

70   *The Anglo-Iranian Oil Co Case (United Kingdom v Iran) (Request for the Indication of Interim Measures of Protection)* [1951] ICJ Rep 89, Memorial submitted by the government of the UK, para 30.
71   UN Doc A/RES/1803 (XVII) GAOR 17th Session Supp 17, 15.
72   UN Doc A/RES/29/3281, GAOR 29th Session Supp 31 Vol 1, 50, (1975) 69 AJIL 484.
73   (1977) 53 ILR 389.

11.10.1.4 Requirement that expropriation must be carried out in accordance with due process law

According to UNCTRAL's Expropriation document the review of IIAs shows that the requirement that expropriation must be carried out in accordance with due process of law entails that, first, any measure of expropriation must be taken in accordance with domestic legislation and the relevant rules of international law, second, the affected person must be given an opportunity to challenge the measure before an independent and impartial body, and third that the expropriation procedure is free from arbitrariness.[74] The ICJ in *Elettronica Sicila S.p.A. (ELSI) v United States of America*[75] defined arbitrariness as: 'A wilful disregard of due process of law, an act which shocks, or at least surprises, a sense of juridical propriety.'

11.10.1.5 UNGA resolutions relevant to the topic of expropriation

It is important to examine the two most significant UNGA resolutions relevant to the topic of expropriation.

A. The 1962 UNGA Resolution on Permanent Sovereignty over Natural Resources
(UNGA 1803 (XVII))

Widespread nationalisation following WWII and the emergence of the new post-colonial States in Africa and Asia led to a dramatic shift in international opinion regarding the expropriation of foreign property. This resolution of the UNGA illustrates the emerging attitudes of the developing States by emphasising that foreign ownership of the means of production should not deprive a State of its sovereignty or its ability to control and plan its economy.

The UNGA in the above resolution declares that:

1 The right of peoples and nations to permanent sovereignty over their natural wealth and resources must be exercised in the interest of their national development and of the well-being of the people of the state concerned;

2 The exploration, development and disposition of such resources, as well as the import of the foreign capital required for these purposes, should be in conformity with the rules and conditions which the peoples and nations freely consider to be necessary or desirable with regard to the authorisation, restriction or prohibition of such activities;

3 In cases where authorisation is granted, the capital imported and the earnings on that capital shall be governed by the terms thereof, by the national legislation in force, and by international law. The profits derived must be shared in the proportions freely agreed upon, in each case, between the investors and the recipient state, due care being taken to ensure that there is no impairment, for any reason, of that state's sovereignty over its natural wealth and resources;

4 Nationalisation, expropriation or requisitioning shall be based on grounds or reasons of public utility, security or the national interest which are recognised as overriding purely individual or private interests, both domestic and foreign. In such cases the owner shall be paid appropriate compensation in accordance with the rules in force in the state taking such measures in the

---

74   The UNCTAD expropriation document, supra note 66, 36–40.
75   (1989) ICJ Rep 15 para 128.

exercise of its sovereignty and in accordance with international law. In any case where the question of compensation gives rise to a controversy, the national jurisdiction of the state taking such measures shall be exhausted. However, upon agreement by Sovereign states and other parties concerned, settlement of the dispute should be made through arbitration or international adjudication;

5 The free and beneficial exercise of the sovereignty of peoples and nations over their natural resources must be furthered by the mutual respect of states based on their Sovereign equality;

6 International co-operation for the economic development of developing countries, whether in the form of public or private capital investments, exchange of goods and services, technical assistance, or exchange of scientific information shall be such as to further their independent national development and shall be based upon respect for their sovereignty over their natural wealth and resources;

7 Violation of the rights of peoples and nations to sovereignty over their natural wealth and resources is contrary to the spirit and principles of the Charter of the United Nations and hinders the development of international co-operation and the maintenance of peace;

8 Foreign investment agreements freely entered into by, or between sovereign states shall be observed in good faith; states and international organisations shall strictly and conscientiously respect the sovereignty of peoples and nations over their natural wealth and resources in accordance with the Charter and the principles set forth in the present resolution.

As suggested above, para 4 of the Resolution would seem to reflect the Western States' position regarding expropriation.

B. The 1974 Charter of Economic Rights and Duties of States (UNGA Resolution 3281 (XXIX))
The Charter, adopted by a resolution of the UNGA, reflects the viewpoint of the developing States on the matter of expropriation of foreign property. The Charter illustrates the great strength of support within the UN for the developing States' viewpoint.

Article 2 of the Charter provides:

1 Every state has and shall freely exercise full permanent sovereignty, including possession, use and disposal, over all its wealth, natural resources and economic activities.

2 Each state has the right:

(a) To regulate and exercise authority over foreign investment within its national jurisdiction in accordance with its laws and regulations and in conformity with its national objectives and priorities. No state shall be compelled to grant preferential treatment to foreign investment;

(b) To regulate and supervise the activities of transnational corporations within its national jurisdiction and take measures to ensure that such activities comply with its laws, rules and regulations and conform with its economic and social policies. Transnational corporations shall not intervene in the internal affairs of a host state. Every state should, with full regard for its sovereign rights, co-operate with other states in the exercise of the right set forth in this sub-paragraph;

(c) To nationalise, expropriate or transfer ownership of foreign property in which case appropriate compensation should be paid by the state adopting such measures, taking into account its relevant laws and regulations and all circumstances that the state considers pertinent. In any case where the question of compensation gives rise to a controversy, it shall be settled under the domestic law of the nationalising state and by its tribunals, unless it is freely and mutually agreed by all states concerned that other peaceful means be sought on the basis of the Sovereign equality of states and in accordance with the principle of free choice of means.

C. Assessment of the above UNGA resolutions

The two resolutions differ in a number of important aspects. While both accept that there is a right to nationalise, UNGAR 1803 specifies the requirement of public purpose, whereas UNGAR 3281 does not.

Both acknowledge the requirement for compensation to be paid. UNGAR 1803, however, specifies that this should accord with international law, while UNGAR 3281 establishes a domestic standard of compensation.

The status of these resolutions was reviewed by arbitrator Dupuy in *Texaco* (above). He stated that:

- in contrast to UNGAR 1803, which had the support of both developed and developing States, UNGAR 3281 had little or no support from industrialised nations (i.e. the investors);

- the nature of the opposition to the Charter was of sufficient size and significance to deny it the status of customary international law. The Charter was adopted by 120 votes to six, with ten abstentions. The States voting against were Belgium, Denmark, the Federal Republic of Germany, Luxembourg, the UK and the US. The abstaining States were Austria, Canada, France, Ireland, Israel, Italy, Japan, the Netherlands, Norway and Spain.

11.10.2 Disguised expropriation

This may occur by the placing of a company under 'temporary' government control which is then maintained indefinitely, or by more subtle processes of discrimination against foreign companies. These may take the form of controls on prices or profits, promoting nationally owned companies or creating delays in the granting of licences, supplying equipment, manpower etc. This matter was considered by the Iran-US Claims Tribunal in *Starrett Housing Corporation v The Government of the Islamic Republic of Iran*.[76] The Tribunal concluded that any significant interference with property rights, such that these rights were rendered useless, would amount to an expropriation even though there was no actual change in ownership or legal title. Thus, the appointment by Iran of a temporary manager, with a right to control and use the assets of a housing project, amounted to a taking.

The matter was raised again in *Elettronica Sicula SpA (ELSI) (US v Italy)*.[77] The US argued that the taking of property would include not only an outright expropriation but also any unreasonable interference with the use, enjoyment or disposal of that property. While the Court did not rule directly on this point, it implied that any act that amounted to a significant deprivation of interest would satisfy the requirement of a taking.

11.10.3 Investment protection

Many different methods have been used to protect foreign investments. For example:

- Many developing countries in order to attract new investment have passed laws, or in some cases inserted provisions into their constitutions, guaranteeing foreign investments against expropriation or providing for payment of compensation in the event of expropriation.

---

76   (1984) 23 ILM 1090.
77   [1989] ICJ Rep 15.

- Some Western States, including the US and the UK, have encouraged their nationals to invest in developing countries by insuring their nationals against the risk involved in such investment, in return for a small premium.

However, the most popular and effective way of protecting foreign investments is through BITs. Their popularity is reflected in their proliferation. At the time of writing, there are more than 2,500 BITs in existence.[78] The purpose of a BIT is to encourage, promote and protect investors of one party in the territory of another party. A typical BIT ensures:

- that a foreign investor receives national treatment or at least the most favoured nation treatment in the territory of the other party;

- that an investor is entitled to compensation in the event of expropriation or damage to the investment. Almost all BITs clearly define the limits of expropriation and provide, in accordance with the Hull formula, that in cases of expropriation an investor should receive adequate, prompt and effective compensation;

- transferability of investment related funds to and from a host country without delays and at the market rate of exchange;

- settlement of disputes between investors and the government of the other party outside national courts, usually by arbitration.

With regard to the last above point, the majority of BITs specify the World Bank's International Centre for the Settlement of Investment Disputes (ICSID) as the arbitral body. The ICSID was established under the 1965 Convention on the Settlement of Investment Disputes Between States and Nationals of Other States. The ICSID settles investment disputes by conciliation and arbitration and has jurisdiction over:

> any legal dispute arising directly out of an investment, between a contracting state . . . and a national of another Contracting state, which the parties to the dispute consent in writing to submit to the Centre.

The ICSID is competent to settle disputes only if both the home State and the host State of an investor are contracting parties to the Convention. ICSID awards are final and binding on all contracting parties.

As at 1 August 2014, 150 States had ratified the Convention, including the US, the UK, Canada, the majority of Western States and most Afro-Asian States.

The settlement of disputes between States and foreign private persons through arbitration combined with the proliferation of BITs results in diplomatic protection being less relevant not only to cases of expropriation but also to those where a State violates the international minimum standard of treatment of aliens by its conduct in connection with investment contracts, commercial contracts and loan contracts.

11.11 Admissibility of State claims: diplomatic protection

When a national of a State, whether a natural or a juristic person, is harmed by a wrongful act of another State, the State of nationality may espouse the claim of its national by exercising diplomatic protection. If it does this, a claim may be found inadmissible as a result of a preliminary objection raised by the respondent State.

---

78   R. Dolzer and C. Schreuer, *Principles of International Investment Law*, Oxford: Oxford University Press, 2008, 2.

The principal grounds giving rise to a preliminary objection are:

- non-compliance with the rules regarding the nationality of claims;

- failure to exhaust local remedies;

- unreasonable delay in bringing the claim;

- waiver of the claim;

- improper behaviour by the injured alien.

11.11.1 Nationality of claims – continuous nationality

The general rule on the nationality of claims is that only a State may assert a claim on behalf of its nationals. Article 44 of the DARSIWAprovides that the responsibility of a State may not be invoked if the claim is not brought in accordance with any applicable rule relating to nationality of claims.

Article 3 of the 2006 DADP sets a general rule that only a State of nationality is entitled to exercise diplomatic protection, but provides for an exception to the rule with regard to refugees and stateless persons.

Rule I of the UK Rules Applying to International Claims provides that 'Her Majesty's Government will not take up a claim unless the claimant is a UK national and was so at the date of the injury'.[79]

This rule on continuous nationality was stated by Oppenheim as follows:

> from the time of the occurrence of the injury until the making of the award the claim must continuously and without interruption have belonged to a person or to a series of persons: (a) having the nationality of the state by whom it is put forward, and (b) not having the nationality of the state against whom it is put forward.[80]

The requirement of continuity, evident in the rule, has been criticised on two main grounds:

- it allows incidental matters, e.g. a change of nationality by operation of law, to defeat a valid claim; and

- if an injury to an individual is an injury to the State of origin, then the wrong matures at the time of the injury, and should not be affected by any subsequent change in the status of the individual.

The continuity requirement has, however, been justified on the ground that it prevents the claimant from changing nationality in order to find what is, for the claimant, the most advantageous State to pursue the claim on his behalf.

The position of customary international law is uncertain but the 2006 DADP supports the view that a claimant should be a national of the claimant State at both the date of injury (known as the *dies a quo*) and the date of presentation of the claim (known as the *dies ad quem*).

The 2006 DADP, however, introduces some flexibility in order to avoid injustice:

- With respect to natural persons where a change of nationality is compulsory (e.g. upon a cession of territory, or succession of States or in the case of adoption, divorce or marriage) Article 5(2)

---

79 UKMIL (1983) 54 BYIL 520.

80 R. Jennings and A. Watts (eds), *Oppenheim's International Law*, 9th edn, Harlow: Longman, 1992, 512–513.

of the 2006 DADP provides that a State is allowed to exercise diplomatic protection in respect of a person who is its national at the date of presentation of a claim but not at the date of injury provided 'that the person had the nationality of a predecessor State or lost his or her previous nationality and acquired, for a reason unrelated to the bringing of the claim, the nationality of the former State in a manner not inconsistent with international law'.

■ With regard to corporations, in particular when a corporation, as a result of a wrongful act of a foreign State, ceases to exist in the State of its nationality, the continuous nationality rule will make it impossible for its State of nationality, or the State of nationality of the shareholders, to bring a claim.[81] Article 10(3) deals with this situation and provides that a State is entitled to exercise diplomatic protection in respect of a corporation which was its national at the time of injury, but has, as a result of the injury, ceased to exist according to the law of the State of incorporation.

It is to be noted that when a natural/legal person changes its nationality between the *dies a quo* and the *dies ad quem* from that of a claimant State to that of a respondent State, the claimant State loses its right to proceed with the claim.[82]

11.11.2 State protection over its nationals as individuals

The judgment of the ICJ in the *Case Concerning Ahmadou Sadio Diallo (Preliminary Objections) (Republic of Guinea v Democratic Republic of the Congo*[83]*)* and the *Case Concerning Ahmadou Sadio Diallo (Merits) (Republic of Guinea v Democratic Republic of the Congo)*[84] provides an example of how a State of nationality exercises its diplomatic protection over an injured national (see Chapter 11.11.3). However, the *Diallo Case* was straightforward in that Mr Diallo was a national of one State only – Guinea. In some cases, the matter of determination of the nationality of the injured individual for the purposes of admissibility of State claims may be complex, in particular:

■ where the injured person is a national of more than one State;

■ where the injured person has a stronger link with the respondent State than with the national State seeking to exercise diplomatic protection.

11.11.2.1 Protection in cases of dual or multiple nationality

Two situations can be distinguished:

■ where the individual is both a national of the claimant State and the respondent State;

■ where the individual is a national of the claimant State and a third State not involved in the dispute.

---

81 Article 5(4) of the 2006 DADP; see also the *Barcelona Traction Case* [1970] ICJ Rep 3, Separate Opinion of Judge Jessup, 193.
82 See *Loewen Group Inc v US* (Award) (2005) 7 ICSID Rep 442.
83 Hereafter both cases will be referred to as the *Diallo* Case (2007) ICJ Rep 582.
84 (2010) ICJ Rep 639.

A. The situation where the individual is a national of the claimant State and of the respondent State

The test for deciding whether a claimant State can exercise diplomatic protection against a respondent State is that of 'dominant nationality' (also referred to as 'effective nationality') of an injured person.

The traditional rule was that one State of nationality was barred from exercising diplomatic protection against another State of nationality. This position was expressed in Article 4 of the 1930 Hague Convention on Certain Questions Relating to the Conflict of Nationality Laws.

A number of cases have sought to modify the rule against dual nationality. One of them was the *Mergé Claim*.[85]

MERGÉ CLAIM

Facts:

The US brought a claim against Italy under the Italian Peace Treaty 1947. The claimant was, however, of both US and Italian nationality and the Treaty, which permitted claims on behalf of 'United States nationals', contained no provisions governing the case of dual nationality.

Held:

The Commission decided that the question whether the US could bring the claim against Italy must be answered according to 'the general principles of international law' and agreed that these included the principle of the dominant and effective nationality. The Commission gave the following examples of persons having dominant US nationality:

(i)   children born in the United States of an Italian father when the children have habitually lived there;

(ii) Italians who, having acquired United States nationality by naturalisation and having thus lost their Italian nationality, later re-acquire it by Italian law by staying in Italy for more than 2 years though without the intention of residing there permanently;

(iii) American women married to Italian nationals where the family has had habitual residence in the United States and the interests and the permanent professional life of the head of the family were established in the United States;

(iv) a widow who at the termination of her marriage transfers her residence from Italy to the United States when her conduct, especially with regard to the raising of her children, shows her new residence to be of a habitual nature.

The principle of dominant and effective nationality has since been upheld in two cases before the Iran-US Claims Tribunal, namely, *Esphahanian v Bank Tejarat*[86] and *Case A/18*.[87]

Despite these decisions, however, it is by no means clear that the principle of dominant and effective nationality has become part of customary international law, although its endorsement by the ILC in Article 7 of the 2006 DADP suggests that it may have attained the status of a customary rule. It is to be noted, however, that Article 7 requires that the person concerned has a predominant nationality of the claimant State, both at the date of injury, and at the date of the official presentation of the claim.

---

85   *The Mergé Claim (United States v Italy)* (1955) 22 ILR 443.

86   (1983) 2 Iran-USCTR 157.

87   (1984) ILR.

B. The position where an individual is a national of a third State as well as of the claimant
State or States

The practice of international tribunals seems to indicate that an individual's connection with a third
State is immaterial.

In the *Mergé Claim* (above) the Italian-US Conciliation Commission accepted the principle that the
respondent State could not raise the second dominant nationality of a third State. It said:

> United States nationals who do not possess Italian nationality, but the nationality of a third state can
> be considered 'United States nationals' under the Treaty, even if their prevalent nationality was the
> nationality of the third state.

Article 6 of the 2006 DADP endorses the above statement and adds that in the case of dual or
multiple nationality any State of nationality may, separately or jointly, exercise diplomatic protection
against any State of which the injured person is not a national.

11.11.2.2 The situation where an individual has close ties with, but not the nationality of, the respondent State and has acquired nationality of the claimant State by naturalisation

The above situation was examined in the *Nottebohm Case (Liechtenstein v Guatemala) (Second Phase).*[88]

NOTTEBOHM CASE (LIECHTENSTEIN *V* GUATEMALA) (SECOND PHASE)

Facts:

*Nottebohm was born in Hamburg and held German nationality by birth. In 1905, he went
to Guatemala, took up residence there and made that country the headquarters of his
business activities. He had business connections in Germany and sometimes went there
on business. He also paid a few visits to a brother who had lived in Liechtenstein since
1931. In 1939 Nottebohm applied for citizenship of Liechtenstein. His request was granted,
the 3 years' waiting period for citizenship was waived and his passport was issued. By
operation of German law, when Nottebohm acquired the citizenship of Liechtenstein, he
simultaneously lost his German citizenship. Subsequent to naturalisation Nottebohm travelled
to Guatemala on a visa (duly obtained from the consulate of Guatemala in Zurich) stamped
in his Liechtenstein passport. At the time of naturalisation no state of war existed between
Guatemala and Liechtenstein. However, in 1940, when Guatemala entered WWII on the
Allied side, Nottebohm was arrested, deported to the US, where he was interned, and his
property in Guatemala was confiscated. He was released in 1946 and went to live in
Liechtenstein. Guatemala refused Nottebohm entry to its territory.*

*In 1951 the government of Liechtenstein instituted proceedings before the ICJ in which
it claimed restitution and compensation on the ground that the government of Guatemala
had 'acted towards the person and property of Mr Friedrich Nottebohm, a citizen of
Liechtenstein, in a manner contrary to international law'.*

---

88   [1955] ICJ Rep 4.

Held:

The Court held that Liechtenstein was not entitled to exercise diplomatic protection and present a claim to the Court on behalf of Nottebohm against Guatemala because there was no genuine link between Nottebohm and Liechtenstein. The ICJ asked a question and then answered it:

> *At the time of his naturalisation does Nottebohm appear to have been more closely attached by his tradition, his establishment, his interests, his activities, his family ties, his intentions for the near future to Liechtenstein than to any other state?. . .*
>
> *He had been settled in Guatemala for 34 years. He had carried on his activities there. It was the main seat of his interests. He returned there shortly after his naturalisation, and it remained the centre of his interests and of his business activities. He stayed there until his removal as a result of war measures in 1943. He subsequently attempted to return there, and he now complains of Guatemala's refusal to admit him. There, too, were several members of his family who sought to safeguard his interests.*
>
> *In contrast, his actual connections with Liechtenstein were extremely tenuous. No settled abode, no prolonged residence in that country at the time of his application for naturalisation: the application indicates that he was paying a visit there and confirms the transient character of this visit by its request that the naturalisation proceedings should be initiated and concluded without delay. No intention of settling there was shown at that time or realised in the ensuing weeks, months or years – on the contrary, he returned to Guatemala very shortly after his naturalisation and showed every intention of remaining there . . . There is no allegation of any economic interests or of any activities exercised or to be exercised in Liechtenstein and no manifestation of any intention whatsoever to transfer all or some of his interests and business activities to Liechtenstein. . .*
>
> *These facts clearly establish, on the one hand, the absence of any bond of attachment between Nottebohm and Liechtenstein and, on the other hand, the existence of a long-standing and close connection between him and Guatemala, a link which his naturalisation in no way weakened.*[89]

The judgment of the ICJ is very controversial in that it establishes a new principle according to which a State is only entitled to exercise diplomatic protection in respect of its national who has acquired nationality by naturalisation if there exists 'a genuine connection' between the State and the individual concerned. The main criticism of this principle is that:

- *the ICJ, in fact, applied to Nottebohm the principle of effective nationality which is appropriate in respect of multiple nationalities but so far as a case of one nationality is concerned, results in excluding any State from exercising diplomatic protection on behalf of persons in the same situation as Nottebohm; and*
- *the principle entails that in each State there are different classes of nationals, i.e. persons in a situation similar to Nottebohm who have acquired nationality by naturalisation and*

---

89   Ibid, 24 and 25.

> *those who have acquired it by birth. This is, obviously, in breach of the prohibition of non-discrimination and suggests that once the genuine link is lost by a naturalised person, and such a person has not acquired the nationality of another State, that person's State of nationality will no longer be allowed to espouse his claim.*

The above judgment remains controversial. Indeed, the ILC in its 2006 DADP explained that it did not endorse the principle established in the *Nottebohm Case* because it regarded it as confined to the facts of that case and did not think that the ICJ intended to establish a general rule. Article 4 of the 2006 DADP does not make the exercise of diplomatic protection dependent upon any kind of link.[90]

11.11.2.3   The position where a person is a refugee or a stateless person

Before the establishment of international protection for stateless persons their situation was precarious. In the *Dickson Car Wheel Company Case (United States of America v Mexico)*[91] it was held:

> A state . . . does not commit an international delinquency in inflicting an injury upon an individual lacking nationality and consequently, no state is empowered to intervene or complain on his behalf either before or after the injury.

The modern view is embodied in Article 8(1) of the 2006 DADP. It states that a State may espouse a claim of a stateless person or a refugee officially recognised as such if that person was, at the date of injury and is, at the date of the official presentation of the claim, a habitual resident of that State. However, in the case of a refugee, if a claim is against the State of nationality of the refugee, the State of habitual residence is barred from exercising diplomatic protection.

11.11.3   State protection over its corporations and shareholders.

Under customary international law a State of nationality of a corporation, i.e. a State under whose law the corporation has been incorporated, may espouse its cause. However, the matter of whether and under what circumstances a State may exercise its diplomatic protection on behalf of nationals who are shareholders in a foreign corporation whenever the corporation has been a victim of a wrongful act committed by the State under whose law it has been incorporated is very controversial. This type of exercise of diplomatic protection is known as the exercise of diplomatic protection 'by substitution' and was examined by the ICJ in two cases: in *Barcelona Traction, Light and Power Co Ltd Case (Belgium v Spain)*[92] and in the *Diallo Case*. Further in the *Diallo Case* the ICJ dealt with claims brought by a State of nationality of an individual who was not only a shareholder in a foreign company, but also its manager and principal investor. Both cases are examined below.

---

90   A view similar to that expressed by the ILC, i.e. that the judgment in the *Nottebohm Case* is of limited application, was stated by the Italian US Conciliation Commission in the *Flegenheimer Claim* (1958) 25 ILR 91.
91   (1931) 4 RIAA 669, 678.
92   [1970] ICJ Rep 4.

BARCELONA TRACTION, LIGHT AND POWER CO LTD CASE (BELGIUM *V* SPAIN)

Facts:

The Barcelona Traction, Light and Power Company, Limited (Barcelona Traction) was established under Canadian law in 1911. As its purpose was to develop electricity supplies in Spain, it formed a number of subsidiaries, some of them incorporated and having their registered office in Canada, some in Spain. In 1948 the company was declared bankrupt by a Spanish Court. Canada intervened on behalf of the company but later withdrew. At the time 88 per cent of the shares in the company were allegedly owned by Belgian nationals. When they were unsuccessful in challenging the bankruptcy judgment, and subsequent decisions of the appointed trustees in bankruptcy, before Spanish courts, Belgium espoused the cause of the Belgian shareholders. It brought a claim in the ICJ against Spain in respect of the injury to its nationals who were shareholders, resulting from the injury to the company, i.e. it exercised diplomatic protection by 'substitution'

Spain objected that since the injury was to the company, not the shareholders, Belgium lacked locus standi *to bring the claim.*

Held:

The ICJ made the following important findings:

With regard to the exercise of diplomatic protection by 'substitution'
The Court ruled in favour of the respondent State, Spain, upon the ground that Belgium had no locus standi. *Belgium was not entitled to espouse before the Court claims of Belgian nationals who were shareholders in the company, inasmuch as the company was incorporated in Canada and was, in an international legal sense, of Canadian nationality. The reasoning relied upon by the Court may be expressed as follows:*

- *International law must recognise the general principle of municipal legal systems which provides that an infringement of the rights of a company by outsiders does not involve liability towards the shareholders, even if their interests are detrimentally affected by the infringement. The Court will not look behind the corporate veil.*
- *It is a general rule of international law that it is the national State of the company concerned which is entitled to exercise diplomatic protection, and seek redress for an international wrong done to a company.*
- *A different principle might apply if the wrong were aimed at the direct rights of the shareholders, e.g. their right to attend and vote at general meetings. However, the present case was not concerned with the infringement of the shareholders' direct rights but with the alleged illegal measures taken by Spain against the company.*
- *The exclusive entitlement of the national State of the company to exercise diplomatic protection might conceivably, in certain cases, give way to right of the national State of the shareholders, e.g. where the company itself had ceased to exist, or the protecting national State of the company lacked capacity to exercise diplomatic protection.*

However, in the present case, the company had not ceased to exist as a corporate entity in Canada, nor was the Canadian government incapable of exercising diplomatic protection – it merely chose not to do so.

Comment:

The Court rejected the argument that for reasons of equity a State should be entitled in certain cases to take up the protection of its nationals who were shareholders in a company, which was the victim of a breach of international law. The Court was afraid that any such alleged equitable justification would open the door to competing claims on the part of different States thereby creating an atmosphere of confusion and insecurity in international economic relations.

The ICJ was reluctant to 'pierce the corporate veil' in order to allow a State other than the national State of the company concerned to seek redress for an international wrong done to that company.

Further, the Court stated that, as a general rule, the genuine link principle does not apply to companies. However, in three cases the national State of the shareholders will be entitled to assert a claim for diplomatic protection. These three exceptions have been incorporated into the UK Rules Applying to International Claims and are as follows:

- *the wrong alleged was directed against the shareholders by reason of their nationality (Rule III, UK Rules);*
- *the company has ceased to exist as a result of a wrongful act (Rule V, UK Rules);*
- *the national State of the company lacks the capacity to bring an international claim (Rule VI, UK Rules).*

Articles 11 and 12 of the 2006 DADP endorse the above principles and add, in Article 11(b), that a State of nationality of shareholders will be entitled to exercise diplomatic protection in a situation where a corporation had, at the time of injury, the nationality of the respondent State, but its incorporation in that State had been required as a precondition of doing business there (on this point see the Diallo Case *below).*

With regard to the determination of nationality of a corporation in international law

The ICJ held that:

- *it was the State of incorporation and registered office that was entitled to exercise diplomatic protection. This was in accordance with customary international law;*
- *the principle of a 'genuine link' established in the Nottebohm Case was not applicable. However, the ICJ stated that, in addition to incorporation and a registered office, 'a close and permanent connection' is required between a corporation and a State espousing its claim. In this case the additional factors allowing establishment of a connection between Canada and Barcelona Traction were:*
  - *Barcelona Traction maintained its registered office, its accounts and its share registers in Canada;*
  - *its board meetings were held there; and*
  - *the company was listed in the records of the Canadian tax authorities.*

Comment:

It is submitted that although the Court rejected the analogy to the Nottebohm Case *its conclusion on the 'genuine connection' may not be regarded as authoritative because:*

- *neither Belgium nor Spain contested the Canadian character of the Barcelona Traction Company so the reference to 'genuine connection' was not at issue;*
- *the Court did in fact set out the 'manifold' links of the company with Canada;*
- *many jurists are in favour of the application of the* Nottebohm *principle to the diplomatic protection of limited companies.*

It is interesting to note that Article 9 of the 2006 DADP provides that a State may espouse a claim on behalf of a corporation incorporated in that State. However, that article also endorses the close and permanent connection test by stating that:

> *. . . when the corporation is controlled by nationals of another State and has no substantial activities in the State of incorporation, and the seat of management and the financial control of the corporation are both located in another State, that State shall be regarded as the State of nationality.*

THE DIALLO CASE

Facts:

Guinea started proceedings against the Democratic Republic of Congo (DRC) alleging that the rights of its national, Mr Diallo, had been violated by the DRC. Mr Diallo, until his expulsion from the DRC lived there and conducted business via two corporations Africom-Zaire and Africontainers-Zaire, set up by him and of which he was a major shareholder and manager. The corporations were incorporated in the DRC and thus had Congolese nationality. Their primary business was conducted within the DRC. They were involved in numerous legal disputes with several other corporations in the DRC regarding the payment of various debts owed to Africom-Zaire and Africontainers-Zaire. Guinea claimed that the purpose of Mr Diallo's expulsion was to prevent him from recovering the debts owed to his corporations, inter alia, *by the DRC and companies in which the DRC had substantial interest. In any event, it was established that a judgment in favour of Mr Diallo's corporations had been stayed. In the course of these disputes, Mr Diallo was detained first on suspicion of fraud, and later pending an expulsion order, which was finally executed in January 1996. Guinea alleged that:*

1 *Mr Diallo, as an individual, was unlawfully detained, mistreated while in detention, illegally expelled from the DRC, deprived of his property (movable and immovable), and suffered a denial of justice;*
2 *Mr Diallo's rights as a shareholder and manager of his two corporations were violated,* inter alia, *his right to attend general meetings and to appoint, or be appointed as a manager. Accordingly this claim concerned the direct rights of Mr Diallo as a shareholder.*

3 The rights of both corporations were violated and thus Guinea wished to exercise diplomatic protection by 'substitution' i.e. in respect of the corporations of which Mr Diallo was a shareholder and manager. Guinea had argued that the corporations were not able to protect themselves anymore and that, for this reason, Mr Diallo as a major shareholder and manager who, for all intents and purposes, practically incorporated the businesses, could pursue the claim, and by 'substitution' Guinea could exercise diplomatic protection being the State of nationality of Mr Diallo.

Held:

The ICJ found that Mr Diallo's human rights had been violated by the DRC. However, his rights as a shareholder, manager of, and investor in his two corporations had not been violated. Further, the Court rejected Guinea's right to exercise diplomatic protection by 'substitution', thus confirming its judgment in the Barcelona Traction Case.[93]

Comment:

1 Mr Diallo's human rights as an individual

The ICJ examined whether the human rights of Mr Diallo, as an individual, had been breached in the light of HRs treaties to which Guinea and the DRC were contracting parties, i.e. the ICCPR and the African Charter on Human and Peoples' Rights (see Chapter 12.6.1), rather than on the basis of customary international law to which Guinea had referred in respect of the prohibition of arbitrary expulsion, denial of justice and deprivation of property. The ICJ focused on the lawfulness, or otherwise, of the expulsion and detention. It found that Mr Diallo's expulsion and detention were in breach of the law of the DRC, which in itself must be compatible with HRL, and were also arbitrary in nature.[94]

With regard to deprivation of property the ICJ dealt with it in the context of expulsion rather than as a separate item. As Vermeer-Künzli noted: 'Does this lead to the conclusion that there is no independent right to property? It is a rather dangerous precedent to discuss only the primary or underlying violation and not the others that this violation caused. Expulsion, particularly when arbitrary, will often lead to deprivation of property, but the connection between the two is not inevitable. It would have clarified matters for both parties with respect to reparation and compensation had the Court explicitly discussed the extent of expropriation.'[95]

2 Mr Diallo's rights as a shareholder, manager and investor

The ICJ held that the DRC had not violated any of his rights.

Mr Diallo's rights as a shareholder. The ICJ based its finding on the factual situation, e.g. the fact that no shareholders meetings had been convened after his expulsion, rather than

---

93   (1970) ICJ Rep 4

94   For in depth examination of the judgment see S. Ghandhi, *Human Rights and the International Court of Justice, The Ahmadou Sadio Diallo Case* (2011) 11/3 Human Rights Law Review, 527 and A.M.H. Vermeer-Künzli, *Diallo and the Draft Articles: The Application of the Draft Articles on Diplomatic Protection in the Ahmadou Sadio Diallo Case* (2007) 20 LJIL, 941.

95   A.M.H. Vermeer-Künzli, *The Subject Matters: The ICJ and Human Rights, Rights of Shareholders and the Diallo Case* (2011) 24 LJIL, 610.

on the fact that MR Diallo had a right to participate in such meetings, notwithstanding whether or not he had exercised it. This position was criticised by Judges Al-Khasawneh and Yusuf in their Joint Dissenting Opinion. They wondered how the Court envisaged such general meetings: 'an exiled destitute associé/gérant (French words which can be translated as "shareholder/manager") participating in a general meeting with himself?'[96] They considered that to require a shareholder to actually organise a general meeting in order to demonstrate his inability to do so due to expulsion was 'quite surrealistic'.[97]

Mr Diallo's rights as a manager and supervisor of the two corporations. With regard to Mr. Diallo's right to manage and supervise commercial activities of his corporations, the ICJ held that Guinea did not show that it was impossible for Mr Diallo to carry out those tasks. Accordingly there was no breach of Mr Diallo's rights. The position of the ICJ suggests that there would have been a breach if it had been impossible for Mr Diallo to exercise managerial and supervisory tasks, but not when such exercise was more difficult as a result of unlawful acts of a State, i.e. detention of the manager and his subsequent expulsion.

Mr Diallo's rights as an investor. Notwithstanding the unclear and complex factual context of the case regarding the actual financial situation of Africom-Zaire and Africontainers-Zaire, it is clear that Mr Diallo had lost his investment, i.e. his shares in the corporations. The ICJ ruled that a distinction must be made between the corporation and its shareholders. It reiterated its position in the Barcelona Traction Case and stated that 'when corporations suffer losses, this will be reflected in losses by shareholders without, however, giving them any right to claim'.[98] This means that Mr Diallo's only rights as an investor were in the right to dividends and to share in the money in case of liquidation. His loss of investment was not compensated. The message of the ICJ to foreign investors is clear: their investment is not protected under customary international law. This emphasises the importance of BITs and also entails that without BITs, or other forms of State protection for investors (see Chapter 11.10.3), a State where an investment has been made may arbitrarily expel a foreign investor who may be compensated but will not be able to recover his investment.

3 Guinea's rights to exercise diplomatic protection by 'substitution'

Article 11(b) of the DADP, based on the judgment of the ICJ in the Barcelona Traction Case,[99] states that there are two exceptions to the principle that only a State of nationality of shareholders in a corporation is entitled to exercise diplomatic protection in respect of the shareholders in the case of an injury to the corporation. These are:

* when the corporation has ceased to exist under the law of the State of incorporation for reasons unconnected with the injury;
* the corporation at the time of injury has the nationality of the State of incorporation which is responsible for the injury and incorporation was required by that State as a precondition of doing business there. It is clear from the Commentary of the ILC that both de facto and de jure forced incorporation are contemplated.[100]

---

96   Diallo (Merits), supra note 84, Joint Dissenting Opinion of Judges Al-Khasawneh and Yusuf, at 6.
97   Ibid.
98   Diallo (Merits), supra note 84, para 156.
99   (2006) ILC Report, at 58–59 and 65.
100   A/61/10, 65.

The question before the ICJ was whether Guinea could rely on the latter exception bearing in mind that Africom-Zaire and Africontainers-Zaire were incorporated in the DRC and thus were of Congolese nationality. Further, both carried on business mainly in the territory of the DRC. A negative answer was given by the ICJ. It is to be noted that Judge ad hoc Mahiou in his Declaration[101] stated that the Court took a very narrow interpretation of the facts of the case and of Article 11(b) of the DADP because it had disregarded the fact that under the DRC law unless a corporation has its registered office and the seat of administration in the DRC it will be unable to conduct business there. Accordingly Mr Diallo had, in fact, no choice but to incorporate his corporations in the DRC.

11.11.4 Exhaustion of local remedies

It is a well established rule of international law that a claim brought by a State on behalf of its national, whether a natural or a juristic person, will not be admissible before an international tribunal unless the national has exhausted all the legal remedies available under national law of the respondent State.

Justifications for the above rule are as follows:

- The foreign State should be given the opportunity of doing justice in its own way and of having an investigation and adjudication of the issues of law and fact and thus righting any wrong it has committed. Accordingly, to force a State to immediate submission to international adjudication would be an interference with its sovereignty.

- National courts, and other appropriate bodies, of the respondent State are the most suitable and convenient forum for hearing the claims of individuals and corporations. In particular, they are in the best position to establish the facts of the case, and assess the damage caused.

- By residing and operating within a foreign State the individual or corporation has associated himself/itself with the local jurisdiction.

- The principle of exhaustion avoids the multiplication of small claims based on diplomatic protection.

It is for the protecting State to show that local remedies were exhausted or to establish that exceptional circumstances justify their non-exhaustion. Then it is for the respondent State to establish that there were effective remedies in its domestic law which were not exhausted by the person concerned.

11.11.4.1 The scope of 'local remedies'

Article 14(2) of the 2006 DADP defines local remedies as being 'legal remedies which are open to an injured person before the judicial or administrative courts or bodies'. They do not include extra-legal remedies or remedies as of grace. For example, the right to petition the Queen under the Royal Prerogative is an act of grace, and not a local remedy which must be exhausted under the principle. In the *Diallo Case*, the ICJ stated that:

---

101   Supra note 83, Declaration of *Ad Hoc* Judge Mahiou, para 10.

while the local remedies that must be exhausted include all remedies of a legal nature, judicial redress as well as redress before administrative bodies, administrative remedies can only be taken into consideration for purposes of the local remedies rule if they are aimed at vindicating a right and not at obtaining a favour, unless they constitute an essential prerequisite for the admissibility of subsequent contentious proceedings.[102]

In the *Diallo Case*, the ICJ held that to require Mr Diallo to make an appeal from the expulsion decision to the Minister of Interior of the DRC, who was the person who took that decision, could not be deemed as a local remedy to be exhausted because the reconsideration of the decision by the Minster was a matter of grace.[103]

11.11.4.2 Exceptions to the rule of exhaustion of local remedies

Article 15 of the 2006 DADP sets out exceptions to the rule of exhaustion of domestic remedies. These are where:

(a) there are no reasonably available local remedies to provide effective redress, or the local remedies provide no reasonable possibility of such redress;

(b) there is undue delay in the remedial process which is attributable to the State alleged to be responsible;

(c) there was no relevant connection between the injured person and the State alleged to be responsible at the date of injury;

(d) the injured person is manifestly precluded from pursuing local remedies; or

(e) the State alleged to be responsible has waived the requirement that local remedies be exhausted.

A. When remedies are futile

It is not necessary for the individual to exhaust remedies which, though available in theory, would nevertheless be ineffective or insufficient to redress the injury of which he complains.

For example, there are no effective remedies to exhaust where:

■ the local courts are bound by statute or precedent which compels them to reject the claim;[104]

■ the local courts are notoriously corrupt or known to discriminate against foreigners;[105]

■ the wrong has been committed by the legislature itself or by some high official and the local courts refuse to challenge that authority;

■ the claim having been unsuccessful in the lower court, appeal would be futile because the point at issue is one of fact, and the court of appeal only has power to deal only with points of law.[106]

---

102   (2007) ICJ Rep 582, para 48.

103   Ibid, para 47.

104   *Norwegian Loans Case (France v Norway)* [1957] ICJ Rep 9.

105   *Robert E Brown Case (United States of America v Great Britain)* (1923) 6 RIAA 120.

106   *The Finnish Ships Arbitration (Finland v Great Britain)* (1934) 3 RIAA 1479.

B. Unreasonable delay: extinctive prescription

There is no rule of international law which lays down a time limit within which claims must be presented. Nevertheless, a claim will fail if it is presented after an unreasonable delay by the claimant State. What is reasonable is a question for the tribunal to decide at its discretion.

A claim which is delayed may be denied:

- where the delay creates difficulty for the defendant State in establishing the facts alleged by the claimant State;

- where the delay is evidence of acquiescence or waiver on the part of the claimant State.

C. Waiver of the claim

A claim, once waived by the claimant State, cannot be resurrected. But as the claim belongs to the State and not the injured national, any waiver of the claim by the national in his private capacity does not bind his government.

D. Improper behaviour by an injured alien

The doctrine of 'clean hands' means that where the alien was at the relevant time involved in activities which are illegal, either under municipal or international law, this may bar the claim. However, the claim will not be barred if the injury caused to him is unreasonable and disproportionate to the illegality committed by him.

E. Where a claim is brought preponderantly on the basis of an injury to a State itself rather than to its national

The principle of exhaustion of domestic remedies applies with regard to claims by a State on behalf of its national. It does not apply to claims by a State in respect of direct injuries to itself. For example, if a State's embassy is damaged there is no obligation upon that State to seek redress in the municipal courts of the foreign State concerned.

In the *Aerial Incident of 27 July 1955 Case* [107] an Israeli airliner which had strayed into Bulgarian airspace was shot down by Bulgarian fighter aircraft. Bulgaria argued, *inter alia*, that the ICJ had no jurisdiction over the Israeli claim concerning this because Israel had failed to exhaust local remedies. Israel contended that as the incident had been a direct interstate wrong, the local remedies principle was inapplicable. The ICJ agreed with Israel.

However, in some situations a claim by a State and a claim by its national are closely connected. For example, in the *Case concerning Avena and Other Mexican Nationals (Mexico v United States of America) (Merits)*,[108] Mexico submitted that the US was in breach of Article 36(1) of the Vienna Convention on Consular Relations, because it had 'violated its international legal obligations to Mexico, in its own right and in the exercise of its right of diplomatic protection of its nationals'. The ICJ held that:

> [V]iolations of the rights of the individual under [the Convention] may entail a violation of the rights of the sending State, and . . . violations of the rights of the latter may entail a violation of the rights of the individual. In these special circumstances of interdependence of the rights of the State and of individual rights, Mexico may, in submitting a claim in its own name, request the Court to rule on

---

107   [1959] ICJ 127.
108   [2004] ICJ Rep 12.

the violation of rights which it claims to have suffered both directly and through the violation of individual rights conferred on Mexican nationals under [the Convention]. . . . The duty to exhaust local remedies does not apply to such a request.[109]

In order to decide whether the rule of exhaustion applies in any particular case, the test of preponderance set out in Article 14(3) of the 2006 DADP is used. This article states that:

Local remedies shall be exhausted where an international claim, or request for a declaratory judgment related to the claim, is brought preponderantly on the basis of an injury to a national or other persons referred to in draft article 8.

It can be said, therefore, that in the case of direct injury to a State, the rule of exhaustion of domestic remedies does not apply but it is relevant when a State has suffered indirect injury, i.e. through its nationals.

F. Where there is no relevant connection between the injured alien and the respondent State
The general principle is that by entering the territory of a foreign State, an individual is presumed to subject himself to the jurisdiction of the local courts. However, it can be argued that where the connection between the injured national and the respondent State is involuntary or purely fortuitous then the local remedies principle should not be applied.

In the *Aerial Incident of 27 July 1955 Case (Israel v Bulgaria) (Preliminary Objections)*,[110] for example, Israel argued, *inter alia*, that there was no link between the victims and the Bulgarian State. Therefore, even assuming the claim could be regarded as being made on behalf of Israeli nationals, there was no need to exhaust local remedies because the connection with Bulgaria was only caused by the illegal act of the Bulgarian authorities in bringing down the plane. The ICJ agreed with the Israeli argument.

Article 15(c) of the 2006 DADP endorses the judgment in the above case. The article provides that the rule of exhaustion of domestic remedies does not apply when there is a lack of relevant connection between the injured party and the respondent State.

The relevant connection might be the residence of a victim on the territory of the respondent State, his presence within that territory[111] or the fact that the injured party entered into a contractual relationship with the respondent State.[112]

G. Where the State concerned has not committed a breach of international law
If there has been no breach of international law, but only a breach of local law, then no responsibility arises on the international plane in respect of the breach, unless the individual concerned is denied justice in the local courts. If this occurs it would seem absurd to require the individual to seek redress in those same courts. In such a case there may be no justice to exhaust and therefore it would be inappropriate for the principle to be applied.

H. Where the State concerned has not committed a breach of local law
Where there is a breach of international law which does not involve any breach of local law then the principle is inapplicable.

---

109   Ibid, para 40.
110   [1959] ICJ Rep 127.
111   *The Finnish Ships Arbitration (Finland v Great Britain)* (1934) 3 RIAA 1479.
112   *The Ambatielos Case (Greece v United Kingdom) (Merits: Obligation to Arbitrate)* (1953) ICJ Rep 10.

11.12 Circumstances precluding wrongfulness

The 2001 DARSIWA identifies circumstances under which a wrongful act will not give rise to international responsibility. Under the ILC Articles these circumstances preclude wrongfulness and thus provide defences to international claims. Chapter V entitled 'Circumstances Precluding Wrongfulness' specifies the following as defences: consent of an injured State; self-defence; compliance with peremptory norms; countermeasures in respect of an internationally wrongful act; *force majeure*; distress; and necessity. The circumstances precluding wrongfulness do not authorise or excuse any derogation from a peremptory norm of international law. This means that genocide cannot justify counter-genocide and a defence based on necessity cannot excuse the breach of a peremptory norm.

In addition, under Article 18 of the 2001 DARSIWA a State may avoid international responsibility by pleading coercion to commit a wrongful act, but such an act will nevertheless be a wrongful act for which the coercing State will be held internationally responsible.

11.12.1 Consent

Under the principle of *volenti non fit injuria*, when an injured State consents to an act or conduct, which without that consent would be considered as a wrongful act, the delinquent State cannot be held responsible in international law. For this defence to succeed, it is necessary that a valid consent exists and that the delinquent State acts within the scope of the consent. However, a consent given to another State to act in violation of *jus cogens*, for example to enter its territory and massacre civilians, does not amount to a valid consent.

11.12.2 Countermeasures

The ILC Draft Articles on State Responsibility recognise that States are entitled to resort to countermeasures. Countermeasures must not be forcible. Further, non-forcible anticipatory countermeasures are unlawful given that countermeasures constitute a response to an unlawful act. Countermeasures are temporary, reversible steps aimed at inducing the wrongdoing State to comply with its obligations under international law. In the *Case Concerning the Gabčíkovo-Nagymaros Project (Hungary/Slovakia) (Judgment)*[113] the ICJ, relying on the 2001 DARSIWA, defined the conditions under which a State may resort to countermeasures. The ICJ stated that:

> In order to be justifiable, a countermeasure must meet certain conditions . . . In the first place it must be taken in response to a previous international wrongful act of another state and must be directed against that state . . . Secondly, the injured state must have called upon the state committing the wrongful act to discontinue its wrongful conduct or to make reparation for it . . . In the view of the Court, an important consideration is that the effect of a countermeasure must be commensurate with the injury suffered, taking account of the rights in question . . . [and] its purpose must be to induce the wrongdoing state to comply with its obligations under international law, and . . . the measure must therefore be reversible.

11.12.3 Self-defence

Self-defence as defined in international law, especially under Article 51 of the UN Charter and in customary law, will preclude the wrongfulness of the conduct concerned (see Chapter 15.4).

---

113   [1997] ICJ Rep 7, para 83.

11.12.4   *Force majeure*

Article 23 of the 2001 DARSIWA defines *force majeure* as 'the occurrence of an irresistible force or of an unforeseen event, beyond the control of the State, making it materially impossible in the circumstances to perform the obligation'. However, para 2 of Article 23 excludes a defence based on *force majeure*:

(a)   when the situation of *force majeure* is due, either alone or in combination with other factors, to the conduct of the State invoking it; or

(b)   the State has assumed the risk of that situation occurring.

Force majeure was pleaded by Albania in the *Corfu Channel Case*.[114] The ICJ rejected the defence on the ground that Albania did not show that it was an absolute impossibility to notify to the UK warships the existence of a minefield in its territorial waters.

Force majeure was also at issue in the *Rainbow Warrior Arbitration (New Zealand v France)*.[115]

RAINBOW WARRIOR ARBITRATION (NEW ZEALAND *V* FRANCE)

Facts:

Two French members of the French Secret Service, who were apprehended by New Zealand after boarding the Rainbow Warrior *and placing explosive devices which, when they were detonated, caused extensive damage to the vessel and also the death of one crew member, were tried under the law of New Zealand and sentenced to 10 years' imprisonment. The French government and the government of New Zealand accepted the proposal of the Secretary General of the United Nations (UNS-G) which consisted of handing over the two agents to the French authorities on the basis that they would be transferred immediately to the French military base on the Island of Hao in French Polynesia and detained there for 3 years. France, once they were handed over, without the consent of New Zealand and in breach of the above agreement, immediately returned one of them, Major Mafart, to France. The French government justified its decision to repatriate him on urgent medical reasons which, according to France, amounted to* force majeure.

Held:

The French defence was rejected by the Arbitral Tribunal on the ground that the medical emergency did not amount to 'absolute and material impossibility' which is a necessary requirement for a successful defence based on force majeure.

11.12.5   Necessity

The criteria for the defence of necessity are very stringent under international customary law. They are:

---

114   [1949] ICJ Rep 4.
115   (1987) 26 ILM 1346.

■ there must be exceptional circumstances of extreme urgency;

■ as soon as possible the *status quo ante* must be re-established;

■ the State concerned must act in good faith.

Article 25 of the 2001 DARSIWA defines the conditions for invoking a defence based on necessity. A State is entitled to rely on necessity only if the act in question constitutes the only way for it to safeguard an essential interest against a grave and imminent peril, and provided that the act does not seriously impair an essential interest of a State or States towards which the obligation exists, or of the international community as a whole. In its commentary the ILC defined a state of necessity as being:

> The situation of a state whose sole means of safeguarding an essential interest threatened by a grave and imminent peril is to adopt conduct not in conformity with what is required of it by an international obligation to another state.[116]

In the *Case Concerning the Gabčíkovo-Nagymaros Project (Hungary/Slovakia) (Judgment)*[117] Hungary pleaded necessity when it suspended and abandoned works on a project for a hydro-electric dam which was intended to be built to harness the waters of the River Danube. Hungary alleged that the exploitation of the dam would have grave consequences for the environment. The ICJ relied heavily on the 2001 DARSIWA article on necessity. The Court rejected the defence. It stated that Hungary had neither proved the existence of the perils nor that they were imminent. Moreover, at the time of suspension Hungary had available to it other means of responding to these perceived perils.

The defence of necessity was successfully invoked by the United Kingdom when it bombed the crewless *Torrey Canyon*,[118] a ship flying the Liberian flag which was grounded outside British territorial waters and the oil it had carried constituted a potential ecological disaster which it was believed would or might be avoided as a result of the bombing (see Chapter 8.1.2.2).

11.12.6 Distress

Article 24 of the 2001 DARSIWA provides that a situation of distress occurs when 'the author of the act in question has no other reasonable way, in a situation of distress, of saving the author's life or the lives of other persons entrusted to the author's care'. Paragraph 2 of Article 24 states that distress cannot be invoked if:

■ the situation of distress is due, either alone or in combination with other factors, to the conduct of the State invoking it; or

■ the act in question is likely to create a comparable or greater peril.

In a situation of distress there is always a choice: to respect an international obligation, or to sacrifice one's life or the lives of others who are in one's care. It is generally accepted that an international obligation cannot be observed at the price of human life. Thus, there is no serious alternative for the author. The ILC in its commentary, to illustrate the situation of distress, gave an example of the unauthorised entry of an aircraft into foreign territory to save the life of passengers.

---

116   (1989) Yearbook of the ILC, Vol II, Part 2, 34, para 1.

117   [1997] ICJ Rep 7.

118   E. Brown, *The Lessons of the Torrey Canyon: International Law Aspects* (1968) 21 CLP 113–136.

11.12.7 Compliance with peremptory rules

Article 21 of the 2001 DARSIWA provides that: 'The wrongfulness of an act of a state is precluded if the act is required, in the circumstances, by a peremptory norm of general international law.'

11.13 Consequences of invoking a circumstance precluding wrongfulness

The exculpatory defences preclude the wrongfulness of an act, but not necessarily the responsibility of the perpetrating State. The matter of whether, in a situation where a State takes action which causes loss to another State or its nationals, but the action is not unlawful, that State will be under an obligation to pay compensation is addressed in Article 27 of the 2001 DARSIWA. This provision states that 'the invocation of a circumstance precluding wrongfulness . . . is without prejudice to . . . the question of compensation for any material harm or loss caused by the act in question'.

The exclusion of any right to compensation is certainly justified in circumstances where a State is acting with the consent of the injured State, where it acts in self-defence, and where it takes countermeasures. If an injured State gives its consent and the other State acts within the scope of that consent there is no breach of international law. Consequently, there should be no duty to pay compensation. Also in a situation where a State takes countermeasures to respond to prior violation of its rights, or where a State exercises its right to self-defence in conformity with international law, no claim to compensation by an injured State can arise.

However, in a situation of distress or necessity a State has, at least theoretically, a choice between taking no action or breaching an international obligation. There is no reason why in such circumstances a State, which acts for its own benefit, should not bear the cost of its action. Therefore, both distress and necessity may involve a duty to make compensation for the breach of the right of another State.

11.14 Reparation for injury

Article 34 of the 2001 DARSIWA sets out the principle that a delinquent State must make full reparation for injury caused by its commission of an internationally wrongful act. In this respect it is interesting to note that in the *Case Concerning Oil Platforms (Islamic Republic of Iran v United States of America)*[119] the ICJ found that the respondent acted unlawfully but it did not order any reparation, however symbolic, in favour of the claimant. Judge Kooijmans in his dissenting opinion was especially critical about this aspect of the Court's judgment. He stated:

> It is, however, unprecedented in the history of both Courts for a claim against a respondent to be rejected while earlier in the same paragraph the respondent is found to have acted unlawfully even though that finding is not – and is not said to be – determinative or even relevant for the dismissal of the claim. This novum can be seen as setting a precedent which in my view is a highly hazardous one since it raises questions about the scope of a judgment of the Court, e.g. with regard to its *res judicata* character.[120]

---

119   [2003] ICJ Rep 161.
120   Ibid, Separate Opinion, para 3.

Reparation may take the form of restitution, compensation or satisfaction, either separately or in combination. Indeed, international law recognises various forms of reparation. The choice of a particular form of reparation varies depending upon the content of the obligation that has been breached and the nature of the injury sustained. In the *Chorzów Factory Case*,[121] involving a claim by Germany against Poland arising out of the expropriation of a factory, the PCIJ established the essential principle in this area. The Court held that:

> The essential principle contained in the actual notion of an illegal act – a principle which seems to be established by international practice and in particular by the decisions of arbitral tribunals – is that reparation must, as far as possible, wipe out all the consequences of the illegal act and re-establish the situation which would, in all probability, have existed if that act had not been committed. Restitution in kind, or, if this is not possible, payment of a sum corresponding to the value which a restitution in kind would bear; the award, if need be, of damages for loss sustained which would not be covered by restitution in kind or payment in place of it – such are the principles which should serve to determine the amount of compensation due for an act contrary to international law.

The above principle was endorsed by the 2001 DARSIWA. Reparation may take the following forms:

- Restitution. This is the restoration of the *status quo ante*.

- Compensation. This refers to monetary payments.

- Satisfaction. This concerns reparation not involving material consideration.

Article 39 of the 2001 DARSIWA provides that in determining reparation, the contribution to the injury of the State claiming reparation should be taken into account, in particular any wilful or negligent act or omission by the injured State or by any person or entity in relation to whom the injured State seeks reparation. Article 39 has been criticised by the UK government. It felt that there was no reason why the 2001 DARSIWA should emphasise negligence and wilful wrongdoing, taking into account that, on the one hand, there might be other factors that might be equally worth express mention, given that the provision relates to reparation as a whole and not merely to compensation and, on the other hand, the introduction of a doctrine of contributory tort, or negligence, as a general principle of State responsibility is inappropriate since the primary rule that has been violated will deal with all these aspects itself.

11.14.1 Restitution

Restitution may take the form of 'legal restitution' or restitution in kind or *in integrum*. Legal restitution consists of a declaration that an offending treaty, or act of the executive, judiciary or legislature is invalid. Legal restitution is rare. One such example is provided by the *Martini Case*.[122] Legal restitution can be considered as restitution *in integrum* or as a kind of satisfaction.

Restitution in kind is the primary remedy at international law. The re-establishment of the *status quo ante* is, however, in most cases impossible. There have, nevertheless, been circumstances in which courts and tribunals have awarded restitution in kind. In the *Free Zones of Upper Savoy and the District*

---

121   [1928] PCIJ Rep Ser A No 17, 47.
122   (1930) 2 RIAA 975.

of Gex Case (France v Switzerland)[123] the PCIJ ordered France to withdraw her customs line in the district of Gex from the political frontier with Switzerland and to return to the *status quo ante* regarding the border and customs arrangements between France and Switzerland. Similarly, in the *Temple of Preah Vihear Case (Cambodia v Thailand)*[124] the ICJ ordered Thailand to return to Cambodia religious objects removed unlawfully from the Temple of Preah Vihear.

More controversial has been the question of the power of the court or tribunal to award restitution or specific performance in expropriation cases. The matter was discussed in the Libyan oil nationalisation cases. In one of these, i.e. in *Texaco v Libya*,[125] Arbitrator Dupuy, relying on the judgment of the ICJ in the *Chorzów Factory Case*, accepted that restitution was the primary remedy under international law. This aspect of his judgment has, however, come in for severe criticism on the grounds that an order requiring a State to perform its obligations under a concession agreement does not sit easily with the principle of permanent sovereignty over natural resources. It is also unrealistic to assume that an order for restitution will be effective in the circumstances of expropriation. Certainly, in the *BP v Libya Case*[126] Arbitrator Lagergren accepted that restitution would not be an appropriate remedy.

The criticisms levelled at the Dupuy approach were taken into account in the drafting of Article 35 of the 2001 DARSIWA. It provides that restitution will not be available if it is not materially possible or if it would involve 'a burden out of all proportion to the benefit deriving from restitution instead of compensation'.

This provision clearly rejects the Dupuy approach in the *Texaco* case.

11.14.2 Compensation

The most frequent form of reparation is compensation. Article 36 of the ILC Draft Articles on State Responsibility provides that compensation should cover any financially assessable damage (*damnum emergens*) and, if applicable, any loss of profits (*lucrum cessans*).

Article 38 of the 2001 DARSIWA provides important clarifications in respect of interest:

■ It states that interest on any principal sum 'shall be payable when necessary in order to ensure full reparation. The interest rate and mode of calculation shall be set so as to achieve that result'. This provision has been criticised by the UK government, which feels that the payment of interest should not be an optional matter but an obligation imposed on a delinquent State taking into account that it represents the actual loss suffered by the claimant; Article 38(2) specifies that, if payable: 'Interest runs from the date when the principal sum should have been paid until the date the obligation to pay is fulfilled.'

■ The 2001 DARSIWA, in conformity with the actual state of international law, rejects the concept of punitive, vindictive or exemplary damages.

---

123   [1932] PCIJ Rep Ser A/B No 46.
124   [1962] ICJ Rep 6.
125   (1977) 53 ILR 389.
126   (1974) 53 ILR 297.

11.14.3 Satisfaction

Article 37 of the 2001 DARSIWA defines satisfaction as a remedy for the injury caused by a wrongful act which cannot be made good by restitution or compensation. Paragraph 2 of Article 37 states that satisfaction may consist of an acknowledgment of the breach, an expression of regret, a formal apology or another appropriate modality. Indeed, satisfaction usually involves three facets:

- apology or other acknowledgment of wrongdoing by means of a salute to the flag or payment of indemnity;

- the punishment of the individual concerned;

- the taking of measures to prevent recurrence of the harm.

The forms that satisfaction may take are illustrated by the *Borchgrave Case (Belgium v Spain)*.[127] In that case a Belgian national working at the Belgian embassy in Madrid was found dead on the roadside in Spain in 1936. Belgium sought the following reparation in diplomatic proceedings with Spain:

- an expression of excuses and regrets by the Spanish government;

- the transfer of the corpse to the port of embarkation with military honours;

- the payment of an indemnity of one million Belgian francs;

- the punishment of the guilty.

A declaration by a court or tribunal that a State has acted illegally may itself be sufficient satisfaction in some cases. For example, in the *Corfu Channel Case (UK v Albania) (Merits)*[128] the ICJ declared that the mine-sweeping operation by the British Royal Navy in Albanian territorial waters was a violation of Albanian sovereignty. Albania did not seek damages and the Court held that 'This declaration is in accordance with the request made by Albania through her counsel, and is in itself appropriate satisfaction'.

Article 37(3) of the 2001 DARSIWA clearly establishes that satisfaction should not be out of proportion to the injury and should not take a form which humiliates the delinquent State.

---

127   [1937] PCIJ Rep Ser A/B No 72.
128   [1949] ICJ Rep 4, 35.

RECOMMENDED READING

Books

Amerasinghe, C.F., *Local Remedies in International Law*, 2nd edn, Cambridge: Cambridge University Press, 2004.

Crawford, J., *The ILC's Articles on State Responsibility: Introduction, Text and Commentaries*, Cambridge: Cambridge University Press, 2002.

Crawford, J., *State Responsibility. The General Part*, Cambridge:Cambridge University Press, 2014.

Dolzer, R. and Schreuer, C., *Principles of International Investment Law*, Oxford: Oxford University Press, 2008.

Paulsson, J., *Denial of Justice in International Law*, Cambridge: Cambridge University Press, 2005.

Ragazzi (ed.), M., *International Responsibility Today: Essays in Memory of Oscar Schachter*, Leiden: Nijhoff, 2005.

Tams, C.J., *Enforcing Obligations Erga Omnes in International Law*, Cambridge: Cambridge University Press, 2005.

Articles

Alland, D., *Countermeasures of General Interest* (2002) 13 EJIL, 1221.

Gattini, A., *Smoking/No Smoking: Some Remarks on the Current Place of Fault in the ILC Draft Articles on State Responsibility* (1999) 10 EJIL, 397.

Ghandhi, S., *Human Rights and the International Court of Justice, The Ahmadou Sadio Diallo Case* (2011) 11/3 Human Rights Law Review, 527.

Koskenniemi, M., *Solidarity Measures: State Responsibility as a New International Order?* (2001) BYIL, 337.

Porterfield, M.C., *An International Common Law of Investor Rights?* (2006) 27 University of Pennsylvania Journal of International Economic Law, 79.

Vermeer-Künzli, A. *A Matter of Interest: Diplomatic Protection and State Responsibility Erga Omnes* (2007) 56 ICLQ, 553.

Vermeer-Künzli, A., *As if: The Legal Fiction in Diplomatic Protection* (2007) 18 EJIL, 37.

Vandevelde, K.J., *A Brief History of International Investment Agreements* (2005) 12 UC Davis Journal of International Law and Policy, 157.

Vermeer-Künzli, M.H., *The Subject Matters: The ICJ and Human Rights, Rights of Shareholders and the Diallo Case* (2011) 24 LJIL, 610.

Imputability of a wrongful act

A customary rule of international law requires that every State which is in breach of an obligation imposed on it by international law must bear responsibility for that breach (*Spanish Zones of Morocco Claims (Great Britain v Spain)*). However, a State is responsible only if an act is **attributable** to it. The following conduct can be attributed to a State:

Conduct by the organs of a State. The organs and representatives of a State are the executive and administration; the judiciary; the legislature; the armed forces; and in the case of a federal State, the State itself and its component States. A State will also be responsible for conduct of its officials who act beyond their legal capacity but act to all appearances as competent officials, but, de facto, exercise State functions.

Conduct directed or controlled by a State. There are two competing tests to determine whether conduct of private individuals/entities can be attributed to the State:

Conduct acknowledged and adopted by a State as its own.

Conduct by an organ of a State placed at the disposal of another State (e.g. an army, or the Judicial Committee of the Privy Council acting for some countries in its appellate capacity).

Conduct of insurrectionaries that become the new government of a State.

The '**effective control**' test. Under this test, in order to hold a State responsible for conduct of private individuals/entities it is necessary to show that the State concerned has effective control over each act carried out by such persons/entities.

The '**overall control**' test. Under this test, in order to hold a State responsible for conduct of private individuals/entities it suffices to show that the State concerned has overall control over acts carried out by such persons/entities. If so, each act of private individuals/entities will be attributable to a State irrespective of whether any particular act has specifically been subjected to the control of the State.

Wrongful acts

A breach of an obligation may give rise to:

A direct wrong. This arises:

When one State is in direct breach of an obligation owed to another State. In such a case the State which is in breach may incur **ordinary responsibility** (*the Chorzow Factory Case (Indemnity) (Germany v Poland)*) or,

When a State is in gross and systematic breach of *jus cogens* and thus in breach of an obligation owed to the international community as a whole. Such a breach entails **aggrieved responsibility** under which any State, whether injured or not, may invoke and enforce the responsibility of the delinquent State.

An indirect wrong. This arises when a State is in breach of an obligation owed to a national of another State. In such a case the State of nationality of the injured person is entitled to exercise **diplomatic protection** by espousing the person's claim. The espousal is discretionary and its consequence is that the private claim becomes an international claim over which the State enjoys exclusive control.

Diplomatic protection

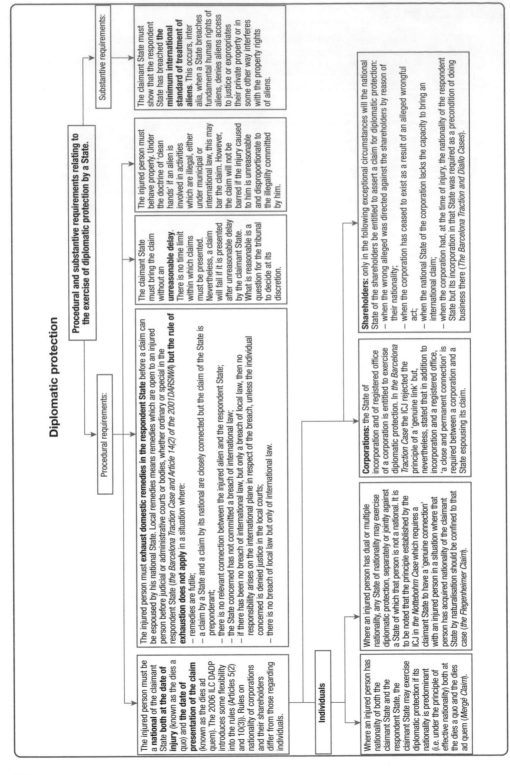

Procedural and substantive requirements relating to the exercise of diplomatic protection by a State.

Substantive requirements:

The claimant State must show that the respondent State has breached **the minimum international standard of treatment of aliens.** This occurs, inter alia, when a State breaches fundamental human rights of aliens, denies aliens access to justice or expropriates their private property or in some other way interferes with the property rights of aliens.

Procedural requirements:

The injured person must **exhaust domestic remedies in the respondent State** before a claim can be espoused by his national State. Local remedies means remedies which are open to an injured person before judicial or administrative courts or bodies, whether ordinary or special in the respondent State (*the Barcelona Traction Case and Article 14(2) of the 2001DARSIWA*) **but the rule of exhaustion does not apply** in a situation where:
– remedies are futile;
– a claim by a State and a claim by its national are closely connected but the claim of the State is preponderant;
– there is no relevant connection between the injured alien and the respondent State;
– the State concerned has not committed a breach of international law;
– if there has been no breach of international law, but only a breach of local law, then no responsibility arises on the international plane in respect of the breach, unless the individual concerned is denied justice in the local courts;
– there is no breach of local law but only of international law.

The claimant State must bring the claim without an **unreasonable delay.** There is no time limit within which claims must be presented. Nevertheless, a claim will fail if it is presented after unreasonable delay by the claimant State. What is reasonable is a question for the tribunal to decide at its discretion.

The injured person must behave properly. Under the doctrine of 'clean hands' if an alien is involved in activities which are illegal, either under municipal or international law, this may bar the claim. However, the claim will not be barred if the injury caused to him is unreasonable and disproportionate to the illegality committed by him.

The injured person must be a **national** of the claimant State **both at the date of injury** (known as the dies a quo) and **the date of presentation of the claim** (known as the dies ad quem). The 2006 ILC DADP introduces some flexibility into the rules (Articles 5(2) and 10(3)). Rules on nationality of corporations and their shareholders differ from those regarding individuals.

Individuals

Where an injured person has nationality of both the claimant State and the respondent State, the claimant State may exercise diplomatic protection if its nationality is predominant (i.e. under the principle of effective nationality both at the dies a quo and the dies ad quem (*Mergé Claim*).

Where an injured person has dual or multiple nationality, any State of nationality may exercise diplomatic protection, separately or jointly against a State of which that person is not a national. It is to be noted that the principle established by the ICJ in *the Nottebohm Case* which requires a claimant State to have a 'genuine connection' with an injured person in a situation where that person has acquired nationality of the claimant State by naturalisation should be confined to that case (*the Flegenheimer Claim*).

Corporations: the State of incorporation and of registered office of a corporation is entitled to exercise diplomatic protection. In *the Barcelona Traction Case* the ICJ rejected the principle of a 'genuine link' but, nevertheless, stated that in addition to incorporation and a registered office, 'a close and permanent connection' is required between a corporation and a State espousing its claim.

Shareholders: only in the following exceptional circumstances will the national State of the shareholders be entitled to assert a claim for diplomatic protection:
– when the wrong alleged was directed against the shareholders by reason of their nationality;
– when the corporation has ceased to exist as a result of an alleged wrongful act;
– when the national State of the corporation lacks the capacity to bring an international claim;
– when the corporation had, at the time of injury, the nationality of the respondent State but its incorporation in that State was required as a precondition of doing business there (*The Barcelona Traction and Diallo Cases*).

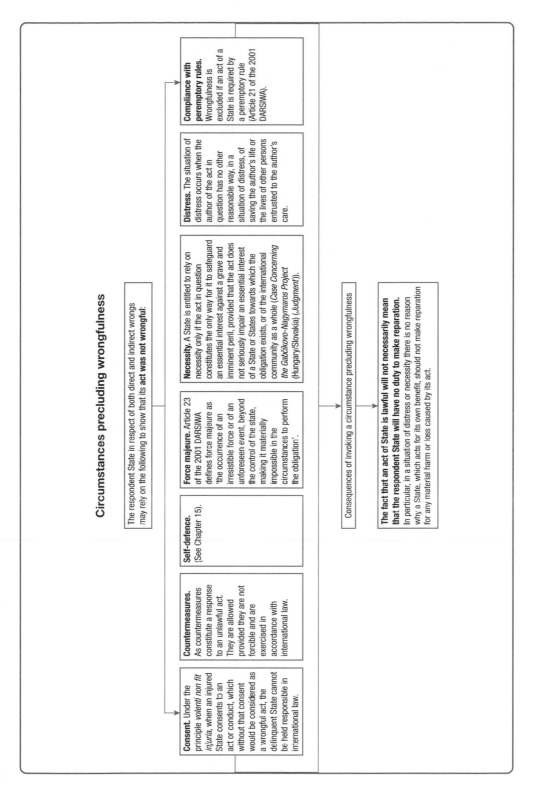

Circumstances precluding wrongfulness

The respondent State in respect of both direct and indirect wrongs may rely on the following to show that its **act was not wrongful:**

| Consent. Under the principle *volenti non fit injuria*, when an injured State consents to an act or conduct, which without that consent would be considered as a wrongful act, the delinquent State cannot be held responsible in international law. | Countermeasures. As countermeasures constitute a response to an unlawful act. They are allowed provided they are not forcible and are exercised in accordance with international law. | Self-defence. (See Chapter 15). | Force majeure. Article 23 of the 2001 DARSIWA defines force majeure as 'the occurrence of an irresistible force or of an unforeseen event, beyond the control of the state, making it materially impossible in the circumstances to perform the obligation'. | Necessity. A State is entitled to rely on necessity only if the act in question constitutes the only way for it to safeguard an essential interest against a grave and imminent peril, provided that the act does not seriously impair an essential interest of a State or States towards which the obligation exists, or of the international community as a whole (*Case Concerning the Gabčíkovo-Nagymaros Project* (Hungary/Slovakia) (*Judgment*)). | Distress. The situation of distress occurs when the author of the act in question has no other reasonable way, in a situation of distress, of saving the author's life or the lives of other persons entrusted to the author's care. | Compliance with peremptory rules. Wrongfulness is excluded if an act of a State is required by a peremptory rule (Article 21 of the 2001 DARSIWA). |

Consequences of invoking a circumstance precluding wrongfulness

The fact that an act of State is lawful will not necessarily mean that the respondent State will have no duty to make reparation. In particular, in a situation of distress or necessity there is no reason why a State, which acts for its own benefit, should not make reparation for any material harm or loss caused by its act.

12

AN OVERVIEW OF THE INTERNATIONAL PROTECTION OF HUMAN RIGHTS

CONTENTS

CHAPTER OUTLINE

1 Introduction

Human rights (HRs) are those rights which are inherent in all human beings by virtue of their humanity alone. They are not only inherent but also inalienable, universal, indivisible, interrelated, and apply equally to all human beings.

The first national instruments guaranteeing some rights to individuals, for example, the 1215 English Magna Carta, granted certain rights and freedoms to some individuals or groups of individuals by virtue of their rank or status. The idea of HRs as natural rights inherent to all human beings, although implicit in the classical natural law tradition associated with Cicero, Aristotle, and Saint Thomas Aquinas, was first advocated in the writings of Francisco de Vittoria and Bartholomy de Las Casas and further developed by Grotius and philosophers of the period of the Enlightenment. At the end of the eighteenth century, the idea of natural rights served as a justification for both the American Declaration of Independence (1776) and the French Declaration des Droits de l'Homme et du Citoyen (1789). In the nineteenth century, slavery, and slave trading, became the first HRs matters of concern to international law. In the twentieth century, with the establishment of the League of Nations, international protection was granted to some specific groups of people, e.g. European minorities, refugees, and populations living in mandate territories. During the period between WWI and WWII, the International Labour Organisation (ILO) established the first universal standards for labour and social welfare. However, until the end of WWII a State's treatment of individuals was considered as a domestic matter of the State and thus of no interest to international law. This changed after WWII with the creation of the UN.

2 The International Bill of Human Rights: The Universal Declaration of Human Rights and its implementation through the 1966 Covenants

Article 1(3) of the UN Charter states that one of the purposes of the UN is to provide comprehensive HRs protection to all individuals. The UN Charter contains many references to HRs, in particular, its Articles 55 and 56 impose obligations on the UN and its member States to achieve the purpose set out in Article 1(3). These provisions constitute the foundation of modern human rights law (HRL) as they 'internationalise' HRs (i.e. HRs are no longer considered to be within the exclusive jurisdiction of a State), and impose obligations on member States to promote HRs and to co-operate with the UN, *inter alia*, with a view to defining and codifying those rights. As the language of the UN Charter with regard to HRs is vague and general it was the task of the UN Commission on Human Rights to define the fundamental HRs, and to provide specific standards for the guidance of the international community. The UN Human Rights Commission successfully achieved this task by preparing the International Bill of Human Rights consisting of:

- ■ The Universal Declaration of Human Rights (UDHR), which was adopted by the General Assembly of the United Nations (UNGA) on 10 December 1948. The UDHR sets out a wide range of human rights and freedoms to be protected, ranging from traditional civil and political rights to economic, social and cultural rights. Formally, the UDHR has no binding legal force, but with the passage of time, many provisions of the UDHR have acquired the status of customary rules, some of them even of a *jus cogens* nature. Further, the UDHR constitutes an authoritative interpretation of the UN Charter so far as HRs are concerned. The rights set out in the UDHR were translated into binding obligations in two Covenants.

- ■ The 1966 International Covenant on Civil and Political Rights (ICCPR). It deals with civil and political rights. Under its First Optional Protocol (OPT-I) the Human Rights Committee (HRC) was established with a view to monitoring compliance of contracting parties with the ICCPR. The HRC oversees compliance in the following ways:
    - – it examines periodic reports submitted by contracting parties;
    - – it adopts General Comments which state the HRC's views on how the provisions of the ICCPR should be interpreted;

- it examines inter-State complaints (if authorised by a contracting party);
- it examines individual complaints under the OPT-I (if authorised by a contracting party).

However, the HRC is not a judicial body and its decisions, although of high moral authority, are not binding. If a contracting party refuses to comply with its decisions the only sanction is bad publicity as the HRC will note a State's refusal in its annual report.

■ The 1966 International Covenant on Economic, Social and Cultural Rights (ICESCR). The ICESCR, unlike the ICCPR, does not require immediate implementation, but allows progressive realisation of its obligations by a contracting party, apart from rights that can be implemented without any burden being imposed on a State, e.g. the right of non-discrimination. The Committee on Economic, Social and Cultural Rights is in charge of monitoring compliance with the ICESCR in ways similar to the monitoring of the ICCPR by the HRC.

3 Other 'core' UN human rights treaties

In addition to the International Bill of Human Rights (consisting of the UDHR, the ICCPR and the ICESCR) an impressive number of HRs treaties have been adopted under the auspices of the UN. Some of the so-called 'core' human rights treaties, i.e. the most important in terms of their subject matter and widespread acceptance, are examined in this chapter. These are:

■ The 1966 Convention on the Elimination of All Forms of Racial Discrimination (CERD). It contains a definition of 'racial discrimination' and imposes a duty on contracting parties to eliminate any racial discrimination direct or indirect and to prevent, prohibit and eradicate the practice of apartheid. Under CERD, the Committee on the Elimination of Racial Discrimination (the CERD Committee) was set up with the task of monitoring the CERD's implementation. Its monitoring functions are similar to those exercised by the HRC.

■ The International Bill of Rights for Women which comprises the 1979 Convention on the Elimination of All Forms of Discrimination against Women (CEDAW) and the 1999 New York Optional Protocol to the CEDAW. Under the CEDAW the Committee on the Elimination of Discrimination against Women was set up to supervise the CEDAW's implementation with similar functions to those of the HRC.

■ The International Bill of Rights of the Child. This consists of the 1989 New York Convention on the Rights of the Child and its two optional protocols:
- the 2000 New York Optional Protocol on the Involvement of Children in Armed Conflicts; and
- the 2000 New York Optional Protocol on the Sale of Children, Child Prostitution and Child Pornography.

The Convention sets out a minimum standard of treatment of children in contracting States and leaves a contracting State the discretion as to the manner in which its provisions are to be implemented. Under the Convention the Committee on the Rights of the Child was set up in 1991. It, *inter alia*, receives, and deals with, reports from contracting States on the implementation of the Convention. However there is no procedure for individual petitions.

■ The 1984 Convention against Torture and other Cruel, Inhuman or Degrading Treatment or Punishment (CAT). The CAT prohibits both torture and cruel, inhuman or degrading treatment or punishment and confirms that freedom from torture is an absolute right from which no derogation is permissible whatever the circumstances including a state of war or other public emergency (Article 2(2) CAT). Under Article 17 of CAT the Committee against Torture was established which supervises the implementation of the Convention in contracting States. Its tasks are similar to those exercised by the HRC. Additionally, the Committee is empowered to conduct investigations if it has evidence that torture is being practised in the territory of a contracting State.

4 The UN human rights enforcement machinery

The UN Charter authorises various bodies to monitor compliance of UN member States with HRL. These include:

■ The UN Human Rights Council (UNHRC), which in 2006, replaced the UN Commission on Human Rights. It is made up of 46 members (elected for 3-year terms by the UNGA) who represent their governments. The UNCHR monitors compliance with HRL through:

■ a Universal Periodic Review (UPR) of the HRs record of each UN member once every 4 years;

■ special procedures consisting of establishing 'Special Rapporteurs', 'Special Representatives' or 'Independent Experts' to examine HRs violations in a specific State or to examine a specific HRs problem in a global context;

■ a complaints procedure, which deals with individual communications concerning 'a consistent pattern of gross and reliably attested violations of human rights and fundamental freedoms'. This procedure applies to large-scale violations of HRs, and thus is not appropriate to deal with violations of the rights of one individual only, unless a complaint lodged by an alleged victim, backed up by credible evidence, reveals a consistent pattern of gross HRs violations.

■ The Office of High Commissioner for Human Rights. This was created in 1993 by the UNGA. The Commissioner, together with the Secretary General of the United Nations (UNS-G), oversees all UN HRs activities.

■ The treaty bodies. These have been established on the basis of 'core' HRs treaties (see above). The 2014 UNGA Resolution on 'Strengthening and Enhancing the Effective Functioning of the Human Rights Treaty Body System' brought significant improvements to this system.

5 Regional arrangements for the promotion and protection of human rights – the inter-American system

This is based on the 1948 Charter of the Organisation of American States (OAS), the 1948 American Declaration of the Rights and Duties of Man, and the 1969 American Convention on Human Rights (ACHR) and its two additional Protocols. There are two bodies in charge of the enforcement of HRs in the Americas: the Inter-American Commission on Human Rights (IACommHR) and the Inter-American Court of Human Rights (IACtHR).

6 Regional arrangements for the promotion and protection of human rights – the African system

This is based on the African Charter on Human and Peoples' Rights (the African Charter) together with its Protocols, i.e.:

- the 1998 Protocol Establishing the African Court of Human and Peoples Rights (ACtHPR Protocol);

- the 1990 African Charter on the Rights and Welfare of the Child;

- the 2003 Protocol on the Rights of Women in Africa.

Two bodies have been created in Africa to ensure the promotion and protection of human and peoples' rights: the African Commission on Human and Peoples' Rights (ACommHPR) and the African Court of Human Rights (ACtHPR).

7 Regional arrangements for the promotion and protection of human rights – the European system

The main element of the European system is the 1950 European Convention for the Protection of Human Rights and Fundamental Freedoms (ECHR), together with its enforcement mechanisms. The ECHR was prepared under the auspices of the Council of Europe (COE). In addition, the European Union (EU) is a stout defender and promoter of HRs and greatly contributes to respect for HRs in the EU and worldwide. The ECHR protects civil and political rights. The European Court of Human Rights (ECtHR) is in charge of applying and interpreting the ECHR.

The European Union (EU):

- protects and promotes HRs as it recognises that HRs are general principles of EU law (Article 6(3) TEU);

- the Treaty of Lisbon, which entered into force on 1 December 2009, reinforces the EU's commitment to the protection of HRs. It required that the EU accede to the ECHR and made the Charter of Fundamental Rights in the European Union a binding instrument.

8 General conclusions

The UN system for the enforcement of HRs is weak for the following reasons:

- It is not mandatory, apart from the UPR, and as a result many States choose not to submit themselves to any external scrutiny.

- There is no judicial mechanism within the UN to deal with individual complaints.

- The reporting and monitoring system is, in many cases, based on confidentiality.

- In most cases the main sanction for non-compliance is merely bad publicity.

- The UNSC has not taken any consistent and firm stand in respect of States violating basic HRs. Regrettably, the principle of non-interference in domestic matters, and the political assessment of human rights situations, often prevails.

The European system is the most efficient, sophisticated and mature of the regional arrangements. The Inter-American system is gaining recognition among the peoples of the Americas but needs major reform to overcome its deficiencies and become effective; *inter alia*, in order for it to be efficient individuals must be granted the right to seize the ACtHR directly, and thus be placed on an equal footing with the State concerned. The African system is less developed, and needs international and regional support in order to make any worthwhile difference to the lives of ordinary people living in Africa.

12.1 Introduction

Human rights (HRs) are those rights which are inherent in all human beings by virtue of their humanity alone. They are inherent in that the mere fact of being human entails enjoyment of human rights, i.e. they do not have to be purchased or granted; they are inalienable so are not able to be transferred or taken away; and they are applicable to all human beings equally. HRs are universal, i.e. the same rights are enjoyed by every human being irrespective of cultural, economic, social or other factors; indivisible, which means that no right is more important than any other right; and interrelated which means that, for example, political and civil rights cannot be dissociated from social, economic or cultural rights, as the satisfaction of the first mentioned guarantees the enjoyment of the second mentioned and *vice versa*. It needs to be mentioned that there is tension between this view of HRs, and that advocated by some non-Western States which is based on cultural relativism, and which asserts that human values, far from being universal, vary a great deal according to different cultural perspectives (see below).

The leading tenet of human rights law (HRL) is that individuals should be protected against arbitrary interference by a State. In this connection, the primary responsibility for the protection of HRs is imposed on a State. A State has a duty to ensure that all persons within its jurisdiction are protected against any violations of HRL, and that when an individual alleges violation of his rights a competent, impartial and independent court, which must apply procedures ensuring equality and fairness, will decide, on the basis of clear, specific and pre-existing laws, whether any breach has occurred. A State has not only a negative duty to refrain from violating HRs, but also a positive duty to protect an individual from infringement of his rights by others. However, with the development of international law, many scholars argue that HRL should not be solely State-focused, but should also encompass non-State actors.[1] Indeed, in June 2014 the United Nations Human Rights Council (UNHRC) adopted its resolution entitled 'Elaboration of an International Legally Binding Instrument on Transnational Corporations and other Business Enterprises with Respect to Human Rights' which provides for the establishment of an open-ended inter-governmental working group (IWG) with a view to drafting such an instrument[2] (see Chapter 5.14).

The first national instruments guaranteeing some rights to individuals were the 1215 English Magna Charta Libertatum (Magna Carta); the 1222 Hungarian Golden Bull; the 1282 Danish Erik Klippings Håndfaestning; and the 1356 Brabant Joyeuse Entrée. All recognised that some individuals or groups of individuals by virtue of their rank or status should enjoy certain freedoms. For example, the Magna Carta was, in fact, a contract between the King and the barons, who, dissatisfied with the unfair and erratic manner in which the King administered justice, and the way taxes were levied on them, forced

---

1   A. Clapham, *Obligations of Non-State Actors*, Oxford: Oxford University Press, 2006.
2   A/HRC/26/L.22.

the King to confer on them certain liberties and legal procedures, e.g. due process guarantees, the *habeas corpus* writ, equality under the law, trial by a jury of one's peers, freedom from excessive bail and fines and cruel and unusual punishment. However, almost from its inception the Magna Carta was interpreted as meaning much more than the mere entitlement of barons to enjoyment of certain rights. Indeed, it was interpreted as expressing the idea of freedom of man under the rule of law.

The idea of HRs as natural rights inherent to all human beings, although implicit in the classical natural law tradition associated with Cicero, Aristotle and Saint Thomas Aquinas, was first explicitly advocated in the writings of Francisco de Vittoria (1486–1546) and Bartholomy de Las Casas (1474–1566) who defended the rights of indigenous peoples living in the Spanish colonies. In the seventeenth and eighteenth centuries Hugo Grotius (1583–1645), Samuel von Pufendorf (1632–1694) and Jean Jacques Rousseau (1712–1778) contributed to the development of the concept of HRs considering them as natural rights.

The idea of natural rights served as a justification for both the American Declaration of Independence (1776) and the French Declaration des Droits de l'Homme et du Citoyen (1789) (the French Declaration of the Rights of Man and Citizen). In North America the settlers living in British colonies argued that they 'were free people claiming their rights as derived from the laws of nature and not as the gift of their Chief Magistrate'. The Declaration of Independence 1776 drafted by Jefferson emphasised that human beings have natural rights, in particular:

> We hold these truths to be self-evident, that all men are created equal, that they are endowed by their Creator with certain unalienable rights, that among these are life, liberty and the pursuit of happiness.

This philosophy was reflected in the French Declaration of the Rights of Man and the Citizen 1789, in particular its Article 2 which states that:

> The aim of all political association is the conservation of the natural and inalienable rights of man. These rights are: liberty, property, security and resistance to oppression.

The basic principle of the French Declaration was that all men are born and remain free and equal in their rights. In particular the Declaration referred to civil and political rights such as equality before the law, freedom from arrest except in conformity with the law, the presumption of innocence, protection against retroactivity of the law, freedom of expression, and the freedom to do anything which is not harmful to others.

The first attempt at the international level to protect HRs concerned the abolition of slave trading and slavery which were legal under national laws at the end of the eighteenth century. In the nineteenth century, the 1815 Vienna Congress[3] (see Chapter 1.2.4) declared the slave trade as repugnant to morality and humanity, and the 1841 Treaty for the Suppression of the African Slave Trade concluded between Austria, Great Britain, Prussia and Russia[4] outlawed it. However, the first truly international treaty which prohibited slavery was the 1926 Convention on the Abolition of Slavery and the Slave Trade[5] adopted under the auspices of the League of Nations. This was complemented by the UN 1956 Supplementary Convention on the Abolition of Slavery, the Slave Trade, and Institutions and Practices Similar to Slavery.[6]

---

3   Act of the Congress of Vienna (signed 9 June 1815) (1815) 64 CTS 454.
4   (1841) 92 CTS 438.
5   60 LNTS 253.
6   266 UNTS 3.

Another important development which took place in the nineteenth century was the gradual protection of human beings involved in armed conflicts through the advancement of international humanitarian law (IHL) (see Chapter 17).

During the nineteenth century some HRs were enshrined in national constitutions, but the number of democratic countries was so limited, even in Europe, that the idea of international protection of HRs did not have any place in international law. At that time, international law recognised that the treatment of nationals was a matter within the exclusive domestic jurisdiction of a State. Aliens were treated according to a certain minimum standard. This standard was respected on the basis of reciprocity rather than any obligation to aliens themselves. In parallel, international law made no provision for refugees and stateless, or displaced, persons. Only States were subjects of international law. Individuals had no enforceable rights in international law.

Following WWI some progress was made towards the establishment of international protection of HRs in the sense that certain rights and certain categories of persons were recognised as being of concern to the international community. However, in the years between WWI and WWII no attempt was made to protect HRs generally. The 1919 Peace Treaties created new States after the dissolution of the Austrio-Hungarian Empire, the collapse of the Ottoman Empire, and the defeat of Germany, and redrew the frontiers in Europe. It was not always possible to respect the principle of nationality while creating new States, and changing the frontiers of others. As a result, it was necessary to introduce mechanisms protecting minorities. These took three forms:

- Special treaties on minorities were signed between the Allied powers and the newly created States, i.e. Poland (the 1919 Treaty of Versailles), Czechoslovakia and Yugoslavia (the 1919 Treaty of St Germaine-en-Laye), Romania (the 1920 Treaty of Trianon) and Greece (the 1920 Treaty of Sevres).

- Chapters on the protection of minorities were included in the peace treaties between the Allied powers and ex-enemy States, i.e. Austria (the 1919 Treaty of St Germaine-en-Laye); Bulgaria (the 1919 Treaty of Neuilly); Hungary (the 1920 Treaty of Trianon); and Turkey (the 1923 Treaty of Lausanne).

- Admission to the newly created League of Nations was made conditional upon a declaration before the Council of the League ensuring the protection of rights of minorities living within the territory of the candidate States, i.e. Finland in 1921, Albania in 1921, Lithuania in 1922, Latvia in 1923, Estonia in 1923 and Iraq in 1932.

The above arrangements were intended to ensure that minorities were not discriminated against and that they were entitled to freedom of religion, and freedom to use their own language, together with the right to protect their cultural identity including the right to maintain educational establishments. The League of Nations was to supervise the system of protection of minorities.

Other initiatives towards the international protection of HRs under the auspices of the League of Nations included: the creation of the mandate system in respect of colonies belonging to the ex-enemy States (see Chapter 13.2.1); the supervision of the prohibition of trafficking of women and children; the supervision of the prohibition of traffic in dangerous drugs; and the establishment of the first arrangements for the international protection of refugees.

The International Labour Organisation (ILO), which was established as a part of the 1919 Treaty of Versailles, initiated the protection of workers through international conventions.

Genocide, atrocities and suffering inflicted upon millions of human beings by the Nazi and totalitarian regimes in the 1930s and 1940s gave a new impetus to those demanding international recognition and enforcement of fundamental human rights and freedoms. As a result, the concept of the protection of

HRs has been internationalised and universalised since WWII. According to Henkin 'universalisation' means general acceptance of HRs by national governments, while 'internationalisation' refers to the recognition that the 'treatment of citizens in one country has become the business of other countries'.[7]

Since the end of WWII an impressive number of legal rules – conventional and customary, universal and regional – have been created to ensure the protection of HRs. The most important HRs treaties in terms of their content and the high number of contracting States are examined in this chapter.

The demise of the Soviet Union has had an important impact, not only on the structure of the international community and the functioning of IGOs, but also on the development of HRs. The international community becomes now directly involved when situations of grave violations of HRs develop. As the Secretary General of the United Nations (UNS-G) emphasised at the opening of the World Conference on Human Rights held in Vienna in June 1993 the language of human rights has become universal in the twentieth century.[8] HRs have the same meaning for all the world's people.

It is to be noted that some States have been challenging the universality of HRs on the basis of cultural relativism, i.e. on the ground that HRs are based on Western morality and disregard cultural values and traditions of non-Western States and thus the imposition of HRs on non-Western States constitutes a form of cultural imperialism.[9] Without entering into a lengthy debate, it can be said, and should perhaps be noted, that:

■ The ratification of the UN Charter by 193 States and the ratification of the core HRs treaties by the vast majority of non-Western States (as well as Western States) shows that HRs are in fact universally recognised by States belonging to various cultures and being at various stages of economic and social development.

■ Culture is not static but evolves to reflect the changing values in a society. Values and traditions which were acceptable 100 years ago in Western societies, e.g. discrimination and violence against women, child labour, corporal punishment of children and social stigma of people with disabilities, are now condemned and considered unacceptable. Perpetuation of traditional structures of power, e.g. male domination and the absence of democracy, has nothing to do with culture but everything to do with discrimination and maintenance of the *status quo* by repressive regimes.

■ HRs represent the minimum protection necessary to ensure dignity to every human being. HRs do not impose any cultural standard. They require that a State ensures that its nationals enjoy the right to freedom, equality and adequate conditions of life.

■ HRs are flexible enough to accommodate cultural diversity and to reinforce real cultural values.

■ Cultural diversity is precious and should be protected. The UNGA recognised in its Resolution 62/155[10] the necessity to prevent and mitigate cultural homogenisation 'through increased intercultural exchange guided by the promotion and protection of cultural diversity'. Further, the 2005 World Summit, which was attended by 167 heads of State and government, acknowledged the 'importance of respect and understanding for religious and cultural diversity'.[11]

---

7   Internationalisation of Human Rights, Human Rights: A Symposium, Columbia University, *Proceedings of the General Education Seminar*, 6, No 1 (1977), 5.

8   *Vienna Declaration and Programme of Action*, UN World Conference on Human Rights (25 June 1993) UN Doc A/CONF.157/23.

9   J. Waldron, *Law and Disagreement*, Oxford: Oxford University Press, 1999.

10   (18 December 2007) GAOR 62nd Session Supp 49 vol 1, 384 para 5.

11   UNGA Res 60/1 (12 September 2005) GAOR 60th Session Supp 49 vol 1, 3 para 14. See also the UNESCO Convention on the Protection and Promotion of the Diversity in Cultural Expressions (adopted 20 October 2005,

Thus cultural diversity should enhance tolerance and non discrimination, and should not be used as a justification for violations and restrictions of HRs.

■ challenges to the universality of HRs are made by governments, never by victims of violations of HRs.

The 1993 World Conference on Human Rights held in Vienna,[12] witnessed a confrontation between universalism and cultural relativism. In particular, Asian States in the Final Declaration of the Regional Meeting for Asia of the World Conference on Human Rights (the 'Bangkok Declaration')[13] notwithstanding their confirmation of belief in the universality of HRs stated that HRs 'must be considered in the context of a dynamic and evolving process of international norm-setting, bearing in mind the significance of national and regional particularities and various historical, cultural and religious backgrounds' (Para 8 of the Declaration).

Notwithstanding the differences a compromise was achieved. The 'Vienna Declaration and Programme of Action' (VDPA)[14] in para 5 confirms that HRs are universal, indivisible, interdependent and interrelated. However, VDPA, being a compromise, also states in para 5 that:

> While the significance of national and regional particularities and various historical, cultural and religious backgrounds must be borne in mind, it is the duty of States, regardless of their political, economic and cultural systems, to promote and protect all human rights and fundamental freedoms.

It is submitted that while cultural diversity is to be taken into account and accommodated within the system of HRL, cultural relativism, in its extreme form, would jeopardise the achievement of HRL bearing in mind that it would serve as a legitimate justification for States to apply local laws and traditions contrary to HRL.

The international community has reaffirmed many times the universality, indivisibility, interdependence and interrelatedness of all HRs, whether civil, political, economic, social or cultural. Every person is entitled to them by virtue of being a human being. Humans have inalienable rights, irrespective of whether they exercise them individually or collectively. They live in both material and spiritual worlds. That is why economic, social, cultural, and the so-called 'solidarity rights' (i.e. collective rights granted to groups of individuals, e.g. the right to development, the right to peace, the right to protection, the right to self-determination) are as fundamental to their welfare as civil and political rights. The fact that violations of human rights continue to take place demonstrates that the attempts to provide international protection are not as effective as they ought to be, and that much remains to be done to improve existing international procedures.

---

entered into force 18 March 2007) http://unesdoc.unesco.org/images/0014/001429/142919e.pdf (accessed 10 July 2014) and the UNESCO Action Plan adopted at the Intergovernmental Conference on Cultural Policies for Development (adopted 2 April 1998).

12 The main objectives of the Conference were to assess progress made in the implementation of HRs since the adoption of the UDHR, to identify the main obstacles to their development and to find the best ways to further develop HRs.

13 UN Doc A/CONF.157/ASRM/8–A/CONF.157/PC/59. It is interesting to note that the 'Final Declaration of the Regional Meeting for Africa of the World Conference on Human Rights' (the 'Tunis Declaration') reaffirmed that 'the universal nature of human rights is beyond question; their protection and promotion are the duty of all States, regardless of their political, economic or cultural systems' (Para 2 Tunis Declaration) UN Doc A/CONF. 157/AFRM/ 14–A/CONF.157/PC/57.

14 UN World Conference on Human Rights (25 June 1993) UN Doc A/CONF.157/23.

12.2 The International Bill of Human Rights: The Universal Declaration of Human Rights and its implementation through the 1966 Covenants

The draftsmen of the UN Charter included among its provisions the foundations for the international protection of HRs. At the 1945 San Francisco Conference a proposal was submitted to insert a 'Declaration on the Essential Rights of Man' into the Charter. It was rejected on the ground that more time was required in order to elaborate that idea. Nevertheless, the Charter contains many provisions on HRs. In the preamble, the Peoples of the United Nations reaffirm their:

> faith in fundamental human rights, in the dignity and worth of the human person, in the equal rights of men and women . . .

Article 1(3) of the Charter enumerates among the purposes and principles of the UN the promotion of, and respect for, human rights and for fundamental freedoms for all 'without distinction as to race, sex, language and religion'.

The most important provisions are contained in Articles 55 and 56 of the Charter. Article 55 states that:

> With a view to the creation of conditions of stability and well-being which are necessary for peaceful and friendly relations among nations based on respect for the principle of equal rights and self-determination of peoples, the United Nations shall promote . . .
>
> (c) universal respect for, and observance of, human rights and fundamental freedoms for all without distinction as to race, sex and language or religion.

Under Article 56 of the Charter:

> All members pledge themselves to take joint and separate action in co-operation with the Organisation for the achievement of the purposes set forth in art 55.

Articles 55 and 56 constitute the foundation of modern HRL as they 'internationalise' HRs (i.e. HRs are no longer considered to be within the exclusive jurisdiction of a State) and impose obligations on member States to promote HRs and to co-operate with the UN, *inter alia*, with a view to defining and codifying those rights.

The Charter assigns important responsibility for discharging the functions contained in Articles 55 and 56 to various organs of the UN. The UNGA (Article 60) and the Trusteeship Council (Article 76) are charged with the promotion of human rights within the general framework of their obligations, and the Economic and Social Council (ECOSOC), under Article 68, 'shall set up commissions in economic and social fields and for the promotion of human rights'.

At the recommendation of the Preparatory Commission of the United Nations the ECOSOC established, in 1946, the Commission on Human Rights for the promotion of HRs as provided for in Article 68.

However, the fundamental HRs which the members of the UN have to respect are not defined by the Charter, apart from the right to non-discrimination ('without distinction as to race, sex, language or religion'). This is the only human right which explicitly derives from the Charter. In the *Advisory Opinion on the Legal Consequences for States of the Continued Presence of South Africa in Namibia (South West Africa) Notwithstanding Security Council Resolution 276 (1970)*[15] the ICJ confirmed that:

---

15   [1971] ICJ Rep 16, para 57.

to establish . . . and to enforce distinction, exclusion, restrictions and limitations exclusively based on grounds of race, colour, descent or national or ethnic origin which constitute a denial of fundamental human rights is a flagrant violation of the purposes and principles of the Charter.

12.2.1   The Universal Declaration of Human Rights (UDHR)[16]

The language of the UN Charter with regard to HRs is vague and general. In order to define the fundamental HRs and to provide specific standards for the guidance of the international community the UNGA, at its first session in 1946, decided to charge the Commission on Human Rights established by the ECOSOC with the task of preparing a Draft Declaration of Fundamental Human Rights and Freedoms.[17]

The Commission, at its first session held in 1947, decided to prepare a preliminary draft of an International Bill of Human Rights, and set up a Drafting Committee. During its second session held in December 1947 the Commission, after examining a proposal from the Drafting Committee, decided that the term 'International Bill of Human Rights' would be applied to the series of documents under preparation by three working groups, one on the declaration, one on the convention (which was later called 'covenant') and one on implementation.

The draft declaration was submitted to the UNGA meeting in Paris. On 10 December 1948 the UNGA adopted the UDHR. Forty-eight States voted in favour, none against, and eight abstained. Among the abstaining States were: the Soviet Union and its allies on the basis that the UDHR undermined States' sovereignty, lacked implementing mechanisms and was not appropriate to apply to a communist society; South Africa, which, in particular in the light of its policy of apartheid, did not like the non-discrimination provisions; and Saudi Arabia, which objected to the equal rights of men and women to marry and the right to change one's religion.

The UDHR consists of a preamble and 30 articles. Articles 1 and 2 state that all human beings 'are born equal in dignity and rights' and are 'entitled to enjoy all the rights and freedoms set forth in the Declaration, without distinction of any kind, such as race, sex, language, religion, political or other opinion, national or social origin, property, birth or other status'.

The UDHR sets out a wide range of human rights and freedoms to be protected, ranging from traditional civil and political rights to economic, social and cultural rights. Articles 3–21 refer to civil and political rights and freedoms being:

- The right to life, liberty and security (Article 3).

- Freedom from slavery and servitude (Article 4).

- Freedom from torture or cruel, inhuman or degrading treatment or punishment (Article 5).

- The right to recognition as a person before the law (Article 6).

- The right to equal protection of the law (Article 7).

- Rights to due process in civil and criminal matters (Articles 8–11).

- Freedom from arbitrary interference with privacy and family (Article 12).

- Freedom of movement (Article 13).

---

16   UNGA Res 217 A (III) (10 December 1948) GAOR 3rd Session Part I 71.
17   Resolution 43 (I) [11 December 1946] A/234.

- The right to seek and enjoy asylum (Article 14).

- The right to a nationality (Article 15).

- The right to marry and to found a family (Article 16).

- The right to own property (Article 17).

- Freedom of thought, conscience and religion (Article 18).

- Freedom of opinion and expression (Article 19).

- The right to peaceful assembly and association (Article 20).

- The right to take part in government (Article 21).

Articles 22 to 27 define the economic, social and cultural rights, including the rights to work, social security, equal pay, join trade unions, rest and leisure, an adequate standard of living, education, and the right to participate in the cultural life of the community.

Article 28 states that everyone is entitled to a social and international order in which the HRs set forth in the UDHR may be fully realised, and emphasises that each person has duties to the community in which he lives. Articles 29 and 30 impose limitations on rights. Article 29(1) refers to duties of an individual towards the community while Article 29(2) states that:

> In the exercise of his rights and freedoms, everyone shall be subject only to such limitations as are determined by law solely for the purpose of securing due recognition and respect for the rights and freedoms of others and of meeting the just requirements of morality, public order and the general welfare in a democratic society.

In its Preamble, the UDHR sets out:

> a common standard of achievement for all peoples and nations, to the end that every individual and every organ of society, keeping this Declaration constantly in mind, shall strive by teaching and education to promote respect for these rights and freedoms and by progressive measures, national and international, to secure their universal and effective recognition and observance, both among the peoples of Member States themselves and among the peoples of territories under their jurisdiction.

Formally, the Declaration has no binding legal force and therefore does not impose any immediate duty upon member States to implement its provisions. However, more than 60 years after the adoption of the UDHR the question arises whether its provisions have achieved the status of customary law? In other words, has the UDHR, independently of specific treaties, imposed a wide range of obligations in the field of HRs?

It is uncontested that the UDHR has been used on numerous occasions to interpret human rights obligations arising out of the UN Charter. Furthermore, the UNGA has always emphasised in its declarations and resolutions the binding nature of the UDHR. For example, the UNGA's 1960 Declaration on the Granting of Independence to Colonial Countries and Peoples states that: 'All states shall observe faithfully and strictly the provisions of . . . the Declaration of Human Rights'. A very similar statement can be found in the 1963 UNGA Declaration on Elimination of All Forms of Racial Discrimination. Also, in its resolutions the UNSC has referred to the binding nature of the UDHR, e.g. its resolutions condemning apartheid. The Commission on Human Rights' Special Rapporteur on the situation in Iran, Mr Galindo Pohl, had no hesitations in affirming that: 'The rights and freedoms set out in the Universal Declaration have become international customary law through state practice and *opinio juris*'.

The Commission accepted his report without any debate on the matter of the binding force of the UDHR.[18] As can be seen from the above, for the organs of the UN, the binding nature of the UDHR is evident.

There is no doubt that the UDHR has had considerable impact on the development of HRs: it has been partially incorporated into many national constitutions (including those of the Soviet Union and China), has served as a basis for national legislation, has been referred to in court opinions and has constituted a source of inspiration for many internationally binding treaties.

With regard to member States, they have made statements expressly acknowledging the binding force of the UDHR. The UDHR was unanimously proclaimed by the International Conference on Human Rights held in Teheran in 1968 as representing 'a common understanding of the peoples of the world concerning the inalienable and inviolable rights of all members of the human family and constitutes an obligation for the members of the international community'.[19] Its binding force was further confirmed, *inter alia*, in the 1975 Final Act of the Helsinki Conference on Security and Co-operation in Europe and, in the 1993 Vienna Declaration. The argument that States cannot, on some occasions, accept the binding force of the UDHR, and, on others occasions reject it, is very convincing.

It emerges from State practice that the UDHR, despite being recognised as a binding instrument on some occasions, is not binding in its entirety. Some rights set out in the UDHR are widely recognised by States and their violation by a State is strongly condemned by the international community (e.g. genocide and torture), while violations of other rights do not provoke such a reaction (e.g. violations of equality between men and women and of the right to nationality). Accordingly, it can be said that with the passing of time many provisions of the UDHR have acquired the status of customary rules, but not all of them. It is submitted that the UDHR:

- provides the first comprehensive universal catalogue of fundamental human rights and that many of its rights have acquired the status of customary rules or even achieved the status of *jus cogens*;

- constitutes an authoritative interpretation of the UN Charter's HRs obligations;

- serves as a basis for HRs treaties, both at the universal and regional levels;

- represents a consensus of the international community regarding HRs, which each of its members must respect, promote and observe.

12.2.2 The 1966 international covenants on human rights

In order to translate the UDHR into binding instruments the UNGA requested the Commission on Human Rights, on the same day it adopted the UDHR, to prepare, as a matter of priority, a draft covenant on HRs, together with draft measures for its implementation. During the preparatory work the UNGA decided that the covenant should also include economic, social and cultural rights, considering them interconnected with, and interdependent on, civil and political rights. Practical reasons led the UNGA in 1951/1952 to request the Commission on Human Rights to prepare two covenants, rather than one, with as many similar provisions as possible, one on civil and political rights and the other on economic, social and cultural rights.[20]

---

18   UN Doc E/CN4/1987/SR56/Add 1 paras 10–37.
19   H. Hannum, *The Status of the Universal Declaration in National and International Law* (1995) 25 Ga J Intl &Comp L, 287.
20   Resolution 543 (VI).

On 16 December 1966 the UNGA adopted the International Covenant on Civil and Political Rights (ICCPR),[21] together with an Optional Protocol to the ICCPR[22] (which provides a mechanism for dealing with communications from individuals claiming to be victims of violations of the rights set out in the Covenant), and the International Covenant on Economic, Social and Cultural Rights (ICESCR).[23]

The preambles and Articles 1, 3 and 5 of the two Covenants are almost identical. The preambles refer to the obligation of States under the UN Charter to promote HRs and they confirm the connection between, on the one hand, civil and political rights and, on the other hand, economic, social and cultural rights, in the achievement of the ideals set out in the UDHR.

The substantial provisions common to both Covenants are:

■ Article 1 which states that all people have the right to self-determination (see Chapter 13.6);

■ Article 3 which refers to equality between men and women in the enjoyment of human rights and enjoins States to take steps to implement that equality.

The differences between the Covenants is that the ICCPR is immediately applicable upon ratification, while contracting States to the ICESCR are obliged to ensure 'progressively' the full enjoyment of the rights recognised under it. The justification for the differentiation is that the implementation of civil and political rights requires minimum economic input from a contracting party, while the implementation of economic, social and cultural rights may impose a considerable burden on a contracting party in terms of changing its social, economic and cultural conditions to make necessary adjustments with a view to ensuring the full enjoyment of the rights set out in the ICESCR. Accordingly, a contracting party to the ICESCR may need time and considerable financial resources before adopting the necessary measures.

12.2.2.1 The ICCPR and its implementation

The ICCPR and its First Optional Protocol entered into force on 23 March 1976. As at 9 October 2014 the ICCPR had been ratified by 168 States, its First Optional Protocol, which provides for a mechanism for the Human Rights Committee (HRC), a body created under Article 28 ICCPR, to monitor compliance with the ICCPR and to receive individual complaints alleging violations of the Covenant by a State party, by 115 States and its Second Optional Protocol,[24] which deals with the abolition of the death penalty, by 81 States.

The ICCPR generally reflects the civil and political rights contained in the UDHR, although some rights listed in the UDHR do not appear in the ICCPR (e.g. the right to property, the right to seek and enjoy asylum, and the right to nationality) and *vice versa*, i.e. the ICCPR contains rights which are not mentioned in the UDHR. These are: the right of a person in detention to be treated with humanity and dignity (Article 10(1)), the right of a person not to be imprisoned and punished for inability to fulfil a contractual obligation (Article 11); and the right of every child to nationality and to be accorded special protection by virtue of his/her status as a minor (Article 24).

---

21   Resolution 2200A (XXI); 999 UNTS 171. On the ICCPR and its implementation see S. Joseph and M. Castan, *The International Covenant on Civil and Political Rights, Cases, Materials and Commentary*, 3rd edn, Oxford: Oxford University Press, 2013.

22   999 UNTS 302.

23   993 UNTS 3.

24   Second Optional Protocol to the International Covenant on Civil and Political Rights, aiming at the Abolition of the Death Penalty (adopted 15 December 1989, entered into force 11 July 1991) GAOR 44th Session Supp 49 vol 1, 207.

The ICCPR is divided into six parts. Parts I and II contain general provisions applicable to all rights protected under the ICCPR. Part III lists the substantive individual rights. The remaining parts concern the establishment of the Human Rights Committee (HRC), and its functions and some technical matters.

Parts I and II (Articles 2–5) of the ICCPR contain so-called supporting guarantees, i.e. overreaching provisions or provisions of a structural nature.

Article 2 imposes on a contracting State an obligation immediately, upon ratification, to implement the substantive rights contained in the ICCPR and to 'respect and ensure enjoyment by all individuals within its territory and subject to its jurisdiction' of the substantive rights contained in the ICCPR 'without distinction of any kind' (Article 2(1)). This provision therefore imposes on a contracting party a positive duty consisting of taking the necessary measures to ensure the enjoyment by individuals of the rights guaranteed in the Covenant (i.e. to ensure that the rights are enforceable, and that remedies are available to victims of infringements of those rights; to investigate alleged violations; to remove all obstacles which impede effective realisation of the Covenant rights; to train the relevant personnel) and a negative duty consisting of refraining from violating the rights granted to individuals under the ICCPR.

Article 3 imposes an obligation on a contracting party to ensure the equal right of men and women to the enjoyment of all civil and political rights set out in the ICCPR.

Article 4 allows a contracting party to derogate from the ICCPR 'in times of public emergency'. However, the right to derogate is strictly limited and important safeguards are provided in Article 4 to ensure that a contracting party will not abuse this right.

Article 5 provides that rights guaranteed under the ICCPR must not be abused by States, groups or individuals so as to undermine the enjoyment of ICCPR rights by others (e.g. by promoting fascist or racist ideas which call for destruction of the rights of others). Article 5(2) contains a 'saving provision' in that the ICCPR cannot be used as a pretext to lower the standard of protection which individuals enjoy under national law, specific HRs treaties or customary law.

An individual cannot successfully complain to the HRC that a contracting party has violated Articles 2 to 5 ICCPR unless a simultaneous violation of a substantive right has occurred, i.e. an individual cannot complain that his right to a remedy under Article 2(3) has been violated unless he shows that a substantive right, let's say, his right to privacy, has been infringed by a contracting party.

Part III of the ICCPR lists the following substantive rights and fundamental freedoms:

- Articles 6 to 11 are the core provisions as they seek to ensure the protection of life, liberty and the physical security of the individual. The imposition of the death penalty is allowed in States which have not abolished it but its use is strictly limited (Article 6). The following are prohibited: torture, cruel, inhuman or degrading treatment or punishment (Article 7); slavery, servitude and forced or compulsory labour (Article 8); and arbitrary arrest or detention (Article 9). Article 10 enshrines the right to human treatment for all persons deprived of their liberty while Article 11 ensures freedom from imprisonment for inability to fulfil contractual obligations.

- Articles 12 and 13 concern free movement into, out of, and within a contracting State. In particular, Article 12 imposes limitations on expulsion of aliens lawfully admitted to the territory of a contracting State.

- Articles 14 to 16 concern guarantees relating to judicial process: the right to fair trial (Article 14); freedom from the retroactive application of criminal law (Article 15); and the right to recognition as a person before the law (Article 16).

- Articles 17 to 22 ensure that an individual is protected from arbitrary or unlawful interference with his privacy (Article 17) as well as from interference with enjoyment of his freedoms: of thought, conscience and religion (Article 18); of opinion and expression (Article 19); from war propaganda, and the advocating of racial or religious hatred (Article 20); and of assembly and association (Articles 21 and 22).

■ Articles 23 to 24 emphasise the role of the family in society and protect right to family life, the right to equality between spouses in respect of their rights and responsibilities as to marriage, during marriage and at its dissolution (Article 23), and the rights of children (Article 24).

■ Article 25 ensures the right to participate in public affairs and elections.

■ Articles 26 and 2(1) contain a general prohibition on discrimination which is reinforced by Article 3 which prohibits discrimination based on sex. Additionally, the ICCPR makes reference to the prohibition of discrimination in Article 4(1) with regard to the application of derogations. Further, Articles 23, 24 and 25 state that the rights protected under those articles shall be enjoyed without any discrimination.

■ Article 27 ensures protection of the rights of minorities.

Contracting parties are not allowed to impose any restrictions or limitations on absolute rights, either in times of peace or in times of national emergency. Absolute rights are embodied in particular in Article 6, which protects the right to life; Article 7, which prohibits torture, cruel, inhuman and degrading treatment and punishment; and Article 8(1), which prohibits slavery. Other rights may be limited as follows:

■ Some limitations are expressly allowed by the ICCPR. These are contained in Articles 12(1); 13, part of Article 14(1), 18(1); 19(2); 21 and 22. The limitations must be prescribed by law and be necessary in a democratic society.

■ By Articles 25 and 26 which explicitly state that reasonable action of a contracting party is permissible.

■ Some limitations are implicitly allowed in respect of rights protecting against 'arbitrary' action on the part of the contracting State (Articles 6(1); 9(1); 12(4); and 17). In respect of these rights reasonable measures are permissible.

Draft General Comment 31 of the HRC provides the following guidance on the assessment of legitimacy of limitations:

> Where such limitations are permitted, States must in any case demonstrate their necessity and only take measures which are proportionate to the pursuance of legitimate aims in order to ensure continuous and effective protection of Covenant rights. In no case may the limitations be applied or invoked in a manner that would impair the essence of a Covenant right.[25]

12.2.2.2 Enforcement of the ICCPR

Article 28 of the ICCPR provides for the establishment of the HRC which is responsible for the supervision and monitoring of the implementation of the ICCPR. The HRC is made up of 18 members elected by the contracting parties for terms of 4 years on the basis of equitable geographical representation

---

25   S. Joseph, J. Schultz and M. Castan, *The International Covenant on Civil and Political Rights*, 2nd edn, Oxford: Oxford University Press, 2005, 33.

and with due consideration to an adequate representation of the different forms of civilization, and of the principal legal systems. Members of the HRC must be persons of high moral character who are experts in the field of human rights. They serve in their personal capacity, not as representatives of their government. The HRC oversees compliance with the ICCPR in the following ways:

■ It examines periodic reports submitted by the contracting parties. Contracting States are required to submit reports on measures taken to implement the ICCPR. A contracting party has to provide a report within a year of its ratification of the ICCPR, and subsequent reports are required at a time individually specified by the HRC for each contracting party, normally every 5 years.[26] For each contracting party's report a country task force (CRTF) is established, which is in charge of preparing a list of issues to be addressed to the particular contracting party and of leading the dialogue with that party when a report is under consideration. The HRC discusses reports with the State concerned in a constructive way. At the conclusion of the examination of a report, the HRC adopts, by consensus, its Concluding Observations which normally indicate measures which a contracting party is required to take to comply with the ICCPR. If the HRC decides that it requires information on a specific topic it will appoint a Special Rapporteur to follow up on the report's concluding observations. Normally within a year, the Special Rapporteur examines the information and prepares a report on the basis of which the HRC decides whether the date for the next periodic report of a contracting party should be adjusted. If a contracting party fails to submit the required information the HRC will note this in its annual report. If a contracting party does not submit a periodic report to the HRC, or if it submits a report but sends no delegation to defend it, the HRC will proceed with the examination. When a contracting party fails to submit a report, the HRC after notifying the relevant State of the date of examination, will deliberate (in the absence of the report) in private, and will not make public its Concluding Observations although they will be sent to the contracting State. In situations where a contracting party is not co-operating with the HRC, a Special Rapporteur will be appointed to restore dialogue between the relevant party and the HRC.

■ It adopts General Comments. By virtue of Article 40 ICCPR the HRC is empowered to make 'general comments as it may deem appropriate'. Since 1980 such comments are permitted provided that they:

■ promote co-operation between States in the implementation of the Covenant;

■ summarise the experience of the Committee in examining the States' reports;

■ draw the attention of the contracting States to matters relating to the improvement of the reporting procedures and the implementation of the Covenant.

The HRC has adopted numerous 'General Comments' which clarify the meaning of the provisions of the ICCPR. Comments are adopted by consensus and are of a general character. Therefore, they are not controversial. They can be found at the official website of the HRC.[27]

■ It examines inter-State complaints. Under Article 41 of the ICCPR the HRC is entitled to hear inter-State complaints providing that both States are contracting parties to the Covenant and have made a declaration recognising its competence. At the time of writing, the inter-State complaints procedure has never been used.

---

26 The Rules of Procedure of the HRC: Rule 66(2).
27 See the official website of the HRC at www.ohchr.org/en/hrbodies/ccpr/pages/ccprindex.aspx (accessed 5 May 2014).

■ It examines individual complaints under the First Optional Protocol (OPT-I) to the ICCPR. Under OPT-I a contracting party to both OPT-I and the ICCPR must recognise the competence of the HRC to receive and consider individual communications (this is the name given to a complaint lodged by an individual under the ICCPR) alleging violations of the ICCPR by that party. In order to establish *locus standi* under OPT-I, an applicant:

■ must be an individual, i.e. a natural person;

■ must be an alleged victim of violation of his rights guaranteed by the ICCPR, i.e. must be personally affected by a violation.[28] However, in two situations a third party may submit a complaint:

   ■ when the victim appoints a person to act on his behalf;

   ■ when the alleged victim is not able to submit the communication; i.e. he has been killed, is kept incommunicado, or as a result of mistreatment, is physically or mentally unable to authorise the submission of a communication. In these cases, the applicant must show that there is a sufficient connection between him and the alleged victim (e.g. normally a member of a family) to justify the presumption that the alleged victim would consent to submission of a complaint on his behalf by the person concerned;

■ must show that the event generating the complaint had occurred after the entry into force of OPT-I for the relevant party. However, OPT-I applies if a violation which had begun before the date of entry into force continues after that date;[29]

■ must show that the event generating the complaint took place within the jurisdiction of a contracting State. However, the alleged victim does not have to be a national of a contracting party as the ICCPR applies to all individuals, regardless of their nationality, who are in the territory of a contracting party or subject to its jurisdiction;

■ must show that the subject matter of the complaint is not being concurrently considered by an international body similar to the HRC;

■ must exhaust all available domestic remedies. However, the applicant is not required to exhaust remedies which are objectively futile,[30] unreasonably prolonged[31] and in some circumstances too costly;[32]

■ must present a *prima facie* case, i.e. substantiate the complaint by submitting sufficient evidence that there is a case to answer.

An application must be submitted in writing. If a communication is considered by the HRC as admissible it is forwarded to the State concerned which must within six months submit written explanations or statements relating to the alleged violation of the ICCPR and, if appropriate, indicate the measures it intends to apply to remedy the violation.

On the basis of information submitted by the individual and the State in question the HRC, at a closed meeting, considers the matter and then issues its 'views' on the merits under Article 5(4) of the

---

28   *Morrison v Jamaica* (663/95).
29   *Könye and Könye v Hungary* (520/92).
30   *Pratt and Morgan v Jamaica* (210/86; 225/87).
31   *Fillastre and Bizoarn v Bolivia* (336/88).
32   *Henry v Jamaica* (230/87).

OPT-I. The views of the HRC are not legally binding although they are issued 'in a judicial spirit'.[33] In this respect it must be remembered that the HRC is not a judicial body but its high moral authority is often sufficient to ensure compliance. However, if a contracting party refuses to comply the only sanction is bad publicity as the HRC notes a State's refusal to comply in its annual report.

12.2.2.3 The Second Optional Protocol (OPT-II) to the ICCPR

Although Article 1 of OP-II abolishes the death penalty, Article 2(1) allows its imposition in time of war pursuant to a conviction for a most serious crime of a military nature committed during wartime. Article 3 requires that a contracting party submits reports to the HRC on measures taken to implement the Protocol. Under Article 5 OPT-II the HRC is entitled to receive and consider an individual communication so long as a contracting party to OPT-I had not, at the moment of ratification or accession, stated to the contrary.

12.2.3 The ICESCR and its implementation

The ICESCR entered into force on 3 January 1976. As at 9 October 2014 it had been ratified by 162 States. The Covenant covers three categories of rights:

- rights to work and to the enjoyment of just and favourable conditions of work, including the right to form and join trade unions;

- rights to social protection, to an adequate standard of living, and to the enjoyment of the highest attainable standard of physical and mental health;

- rights to education and to participation in cultural life.

The main feature of the ICESCR is that it does not require immediate implementation, but allows progressive realisation of its obligations by a contracting party. However, there are some exceptions to this rule. The first is in respect of rights which can be implemented without any burden being imposed on a State, e.g. the right of non-discrimination. Second, under Article 2(1) a contracting party has a duty, regardless of the level of economic development, to ensure that persons under its jurisdiction are provided with a 'bare' minimum in terms of food, housing and access to health services and education. In this respect Article 2(1) states:

> Each State Party to the present Covenant undertakes to take steps, individually and through international assistance and co-operation, especially economic and technical, to the maximum of its available resources, with a view to achieving progressively the full realization of the rights recognized in the present Covenant by all appropriate means, including particularly the adoption of legislative measures.

The reference to 'the maximum of its available resources' emphasises that when a party is not able to ensure the 'bare minimum', it has an obligation to seek international assistance and co-operation with a view to fulfilling its obligations under the ICESCR.[34]

---

33   S. Joseph and M. Castan, *The International Covenant on Civil and Political Rights*, 3rd edn, Oxford: Oxford University Press, 2013, 22.

34   The Limburg Principles on the Implementation of the International Covenant on Economic, Social and Cultural Rights (8 January 1987) UN Doc E/CN.4/1987/17 Annex.

Once progress has been achieved in the realisation of ICESCR rights a State is prohibited from taking any deliberate step backward that cannot be justified on the grounds of severe economic difficulties, *force majeure* or similar circumstances.

Some limitations are permitted under Article 4 ICESCR which provides that:

> The States Parties to the present Covenant recognize that, in the enjoyment of those rights provided by the State in conformity with the present Covenant, the State may subject such rights only to such limitations as are determined by law only in so far as this may be compatible with the nature of these rights and solely for the purpose of promoting the general welfare in a democratic society.

However, the essence of the Covenant's rights must at all times be guaranteed by national law.

Under the ICESCR the contracting parties are obliged to send periodic reports to the ECOSOC on progress in implementation of its provisions. In order to ensure that this task was fulfilled ECOSOC, in 1978, set up a sessional working group of 15 members to meet annually and to report to it. The group was not successful and in 1985 ECOSOC decided to establish a new Committee on Economic, Social and Cultural Rights made up of 18 independent experts to study reports from contracting States and discuss them with the governments concerned. The Committee is not autonomous and is accountable to ECOSOC. The Committee may make recommendations to ECOSOC based on annual reports.

On 10 December 2008, the UNGA unanimously adopted an Optional Protocol[35] to the ICESCR under which the Committee has jurisdiction to receive and consider individual petitions. Further it has competence to deal with inter-State complaints and conduct an inquiry into serious, grave or systematic violations by a contracting party of the ICESCR, but only if a State party accepts this. The Protocol entered into force on 5 May 2013 and as at 9 October 2014 had been ratified by 16 States, four of which accepted the competence of the Commission to conduct inquiries.

12.3 Other 'core' UN human rights treaties

In addition to the International Bill of Human Rights, an impressive number of human rights treaties have been adopted under the auspices of the UN. This section examines some so-called 'core' HRs treaties, i.e. the most important in terms of their subject matter, the widespread acceptance they have achieved and the manner in which their implementation is monitored by the treaty bodies. The author's choice of the treaties examined may be challenged, but it is outside the scope of this book to examine all 'core' HRs treaties.

12.3.1 The 1966 Convention on the Elimination of All Forms of Racial Discrimination (CERD)[36]

In 1966, the UNGA adopted the Convention on the Elimination of Racial Discrimination (CERD) which entered into force in 1969. As at 9 October 2014, it had been ratified by 177 States.

The CERD defines 'racial discrimination' as:

> any discrimination, exclusion, restriction or preference based on race, colour, descent or national or ethnic origin which has the purpose or effect of nullifying or impairing the recognition, enjoyment or exercise, on an equal footing, of human rights and fundamental freedoms in the political, social, cultural or any other field of public life (Article 1).

---

35   UNGA Resolution A/RES/63/117.
36   660 UNTS 195.

A contracting party is required to eliminate any racial discrimination direct or indirect and to prevent, prohibit and eradicate the practice of apartheid. Article 1(4) CERD permits, in some circumstances, the taking of special measures to secure advancement of racial or ethnic groups, provided that those measures do not result in the maintenance of separate rights for different racial groups and that they are terminated after the objective for which they were taken have been achieved. The meaning of 'special measures' has been clarified by the CERD Committee in its General Recommendation No 32 on the Meaning and Scope of Special Measures issued in August 2009.[37] The Recommendation emphasises that such measures are temporary and should be taken with a view to securing enjoyment of fundamental rights by disadvantaged groups and individuals. According to the CERD Committee such measures include legislative, executive, administrative, budgetary, and other measures taken at any level in the State's apparatus as well as 'plans, policies, programmes and preferential regimes in areas such as employment, housing, education, culture, and participation in public life for disfavoured groups, devised and implemented on the basis of such instruments'. Therefore a State's policy consisting of giving persons belonging to an underrepresented minority group preference over a person with similar qualifications/credentials/needs who does not belong to such a group, may be justified under Article 1(4) CERD.[38]

The Committee on the Elimination of Racial Discrimination (the CERD Committee) was set up under the Convention with the task of monitoring its implementation. Its functions are similar to those exercised by the HRC in that the CERD Committee examines periodic reports submitted by contracting States, issues General Comments, processes inter-State complaints (at the time of writing no such complaints have been received by the CERD Committee) and, if authorised by a contracting party, petitions from individuals or groups of persons who claim to be victims of violations of the Convention by a contracting State. As at 9 October 2014, 55 contracting States had made a declaration recognising the competence of the CERD Committee to receive individual complaints. Since 1994 the Committee may use early warning measures and urgent procedures to try to prevent serious violations of the CERD.

12.3.2 The International Bill of Rights for Women

The International Bill of Rights for Women comprises the 1979 Convention on the Elimination of All Forms of Discrimination against Women (CEDAW),[39] which, as at 9 October 2014 had been ratified by 188 States, and the 1999 New York Optional Protocol to the Convention[40] which, as at 9 October 2014, was in force in 105 States.

The International Bill of Rights for Women was prepared by the Commission on the Status of Women created in 1946 by ECOSOC. The Commission is responsible for advancing the status of women around the world. It is made up of representatives of 45 member States representing the world's major legal systems and reflecting the geographical distribution of UN membership. The Commission, in addition to initiating and drafting the above Bill of Rights for Women, and other instruments intended to improve the status of women, is empowered to make recommendations and reports to ECOSOC on

---

37 See the official website of the CERD Committee at www.ohchr.org/EN/HRBodies/CERD/Pages/CERDIntro.aspx (accessed 10 May 2014).

38 See e.g. the US Supreme Court in *Grutter v Bollinger* (539 US 306 (2003)) in which the Court found that a University of Michigan law school admission policy consisting of giving applicants belonging to underrepresented minority groups (e.g. African Americans, Hispanics, and Native Americans) a significantly greater chance of admission than White and Asian American applicants with similar qualifications was not in breach of the Equal Protection Clause of the Fourteenth Amendment (the US ratified the CERD in 1994).

39 1249 UNTS 13.

40 2131 UNTS 83.

the promotion of the rights of women in political, economic, social and educational fields and in respect of urgent problems requiring immediate attention in the field of women's rights, with a view to implementing the principle of equality between men and women. The Commission drafts proposals for the implementation of its recommendations.

It was the Commission on the Status of Women that initiated the work on the Optional Protocol. The Commission did this because it was dissatisfied with the pace of implementation of the Nairobi Forward-looking Strategies for the Advancement of Women to the Year 2000 produced by the Third World Conference on Women. In 1995, at the Fourth World Conference on Women held in Beijing, the Commission decided to press for the establishment of an individual complaints procedure to the Committee on the Elimination of Discrimination against Women in respect of violations of the Convention by a contracting State.

The CEDAW describes discrimination against women as:

Any distinction, exclusion or restriction made on the basis of sex which has the effect or purpose of impairing or nullifying the recognition, enjoyment or exercise by women, irrespective of their marital status, on a basis of equality of men and women, of human rights and fundamental freedoms in the political, economic, social, cultural, civil or any other field.

The CEDAW sets out comprehensive global standards for women's HRs. It seeks to eliminate discrimination against women in all areas. A contracting State is required to take all necessary measures to ensure equality between men and women and to eliminate existing stereotyped perceptions of women due to socio-cultural factors. A contracting State has also an obligation to prevent and punish private discrimination, e.g. sexual harassment at a work place and domestic violence.[41]

The Committee on the Elimination of Discrimination against Women was set up to supervise implementation of the CEDAW and receive reports from contracting States.

Under the Optional Protocol individuals and groups of persons who claim to be victims of violations of their rights under the CEDAW can complain against the State concerned to the Committee, provided that the State concerned is a contracting party to both the CEDAW and its Optional Protocol. Under the Protocol the Committee on the Elimination of Discrimination against Women is entitled to make inquiries into serious or systematic violations of the Convention in a State which has ratified both instruments, provided that such State did not opt out of the inquiry procedure by making a declaration to this effect. Further, the Committee issues General Recommendations.

The effectiveness of the CEDAW has been undermined by many reservations made by contracting States, in particular almost all Islamic countries have made reservations to Article 2 (which requires a contracting party to take the necessary measures to ensure equality between men and women); Article 15(4) (which prohibits any discrimination against women in terms of the right to free movement and the freedom to choose residence and domicile); and Article 16 (which requires elimination of discrimination in matters relating to marriage and family relations, including the right to freely choose a spouse). Usually, a reserving State declares itself not bound by the relevant provisions if they are in conflict with national law, Islamic tradition or Islamic Sharia. These reservations are contrary to the fundamental rights protected by the CEDAW and obviously incompatible with the object and purpose of the Convention. The CEDAW Committee has on many occasions expressed its frustration with incompatible reservations. However, Islamic countries are not keen on removing them.[42]

---

41   Committee on the Elimination of Discrimination against Women, 'General Recommendation No 19: Violence against women' (1992) GAOR 47th Session Supp 38, 1.

42   Committee on the Elimination of Discrimination against Women 'General Recommendation No 20: Reservations to the Convention (1992) GAOR 47th Session Supp 38, 7.

12.3.3   The International Bill of Rights of the Child

The International Bill of Rights of the Child consists of the 1989 New York Convention on the Rights of the Child[43] which had, as at 9 October 2014, been ratified by 194 States, and its two optional protocols: the 2000 New York Optional Protocol on the Involvement of Children in Armed Conflicts[44] and the 2000 New York Optional Protocol on the Sale of Children, Child Prostitution and Child Pornography.[45] Both Protocols are in force: the first had been ratified by 157 States and the second by 168 as at 9 October 2014.

The 1989 Convention is not very ambitious. While it sets out a minimum standard of treatment of children in contracting States it leaves those States discretion as to the manner in which its provisions are to be implemented.

The Convention is based on four principles:

- the principle of non-discrimination, including equality of opportunity between boys and girls;

- the principle that a contracting State must, when taking any measures affecting children, act in their best interests;

- the principle that children's opinions should, with due regard to their age and maturity, be taken into consideration in all matters affecting them; and

- the principle that children have the right to life, survival and development which a contracting State must ensure 'to the maximum extent possible'.

Under the Convention the Committee on the Rights of the Child was set up in 1991 with the task of receiving reports from contracting States on the implementation of the Convention. However, there is no procedure for individual petitions under the Convention, although the Committee may request a contracting State to forward additional information relevant to the implementation of the Convention if it is seriously concerned about the situation of children in that State. In 1992 the Committee initiated a study leading to the adoption of two Optional Protocols to the Convention.

Under the First Optional Protocol on the Involvement of Children in Armed Conflicts, contracting States are required to take all necessary measures to ensure that children under the age of 18 are not directly participating in hostilities, that any compulsory recruitment is fixed above the age of 18, and that the minimum age for voluntary recruitment is above the current international standard of 15. Contracting States are also required to take all measures to prevent non-governmental groups from using and recruiting children under the age of 18.

Under the Second Optional Protocol contracting States are required to criminalise the sale of children, child prostitution and child pornography.

The Chairman of the UN Commission on Human Rights stated that the effective implementation of these Protocols 'should greatly contribute to seeing children take up books not arms, seeing them in school not in brothels'.[46]

---

43   1577 UNTS 3.

44   UNGA Res 54/263 (25 May 2000) UN Doc A/RES/54/263 Annex I.

45   2171 UNTS 247.

46   At the closing of the 56th session of the Commission on 28 April 2000.

12.3.4 The 1984 Convention against Torture and Other Cruel, Inhuman or Degrading Treatment or Punishment (CAT)[47]

The CAT entered into force on 26 June 1987 and, as at 9 October 2014, had been ratified by 156 States. It prohibits torture and other cruel, inhuman or degrading treatment or punishment. Torture, like slavery, is one of the very worst assaults on human physical and mental integrity and dignity. However, unlike slavery, torture is still widespread and after the 9/11 attacks on the US the Bush administration claimed that in some circumstances the prohibition may be overridden on the ground that by torturing one person one can save the lives of hundreds of innocent people.[48] This argument is morally wrong and legally unacceptable. Torture, like slavery, is universally condemned and any attempt to justify it has been firmly rejected by international[49] and national courts[50] and bodies monitoring the implementation of the core human rights treaties.[51]

The CAT and the Committee against Torture, a body created to monitor the implementation of CAT, condemn in absolute and unequivocal terms any act of torture. Freedom from torture is a non-derogable and absolute right which allows no exceptions or qualifications. It is also a rule of *jus cogens*[52] and thus binding on all States whether or not they are a contracting party to CAT or other regional conventions prohibiting torture.

12.3.4.1 The definition of torture

Article 1(1) CAT provides the following definition of torture:

> For the purposes of this Convention, the term 'torture' means any act by which severe pain or suffering, whether physical or mental, is intentionally inflicted on a person for such purposes as obtaining from him or a third person information or a confession, punishing him for an act he or a third person has committed or is suspected of having committed, or intimidating or coercing him or a third person, or for any reason based on discrimination of any kind, when such pain or suffering is inflicted by or at the instigation of or with the consent or acquiescence of a public official or other person acting in an official capacity. It does not include pain or suffering arising only from, inherent in or incidental to lawful sanctions.

---

47   1465 UNTS 85.

48   US Department of Justice, Office of Legal Counsel 'Legal Standards Applicable under 18 USC §§ 2340–2340A' (Memorandum, 30 December 2004) available at www.usdoj.gov/olc/18usc23402340a2.htm (accessed 12 October 2013).

49   E.g. the IACtHR in *Velásquez Rodríguez v Honduras (Judgment)* IACtHR Series C No 4 (29 July 1988); the ICJ in the *Case Concerning Questions Relating to the Obligation to Extradite or Prosecute (Belgium v Senegal)* (2012) ICJ Rep 422; and the ECtHR *in Saadi v Italy* (2009) 49 EHRR 30.

50   E.g. *Filártiga v Peña-Irala* (30 June 1980) 630 F 2d 876 (2nd Cir 1980); *Public Committee Against Torture v Prime Minister* HCJ 5100/94 [Supreme Court of Israel sitting as the High Court of Justice] (6 September 1999) (1998–99) Israel Law Reports 567–610; *Regina v Bow Street Metropolitan Stipendiary Magistrate and Others, ex p Pinochet Ugarte (No 3)* UK House of Lords [2000] 1 AC 147; *AS &DD v Secretary of State for the Home Department* [2008] EWCA Civ 289 (Ct App).

51   UN Committee against Torture, 'Conclusions and Recommendations concerning the Third Periodic Report of Israel' (23 November 2001) UN Doc CAT/C/XXVII/Concl.5; UN Committee against Torture, 'Consideration of Reports Submitted by States Parties under Article 19 of the Convention: Conclusions and Recommendations of the Committee against Torture: United States of America' (18 May 2006) UN Doc CAT/C/USA/CO/2.

52   The ICTY in *Prosecutor v Furundžija* (Judgment) ICTY-95–17/1 (10 December 1998) and the ICJ in the *Case Concerning Questions Relating to the Obligation to Extradite or Prosecute (Belgium v Senegal)* (2012) ICJ Rep 422, para 99.

The following elements of the definition can be identified:

■ There must be conduct on the part of national authorities. This includes not only affirmative conduct but also encompasses deliberate omission, e.g. the denial of food or medical care to a detained person.[53]

■ There must be infliction of severe mental or physical pain or suffering. The interpretation of this element by the Committee against Torture is that the severity of pain or suffering, a constitutive element of the definition of torture, is not crucial in terms of distinguishing torture from cruel and inhuman treatment. Unlike the ECtHR which uses a 'threshold of severity', i.e. the force of the violence and the degree of the physical/moral suffering[54] to distinguish the two, the Committee considers that every form of cruel and inhuman treatment (including torture) entails the infliction of severe pain or suffering. Consequently, what distinguishes torture from other forms of ill treatment is whether elements other than severe pain and suffering as referred to in the definition contained in Article 1(1) have been in existence.

■ There must be intention to inflict severe pain or suffering. That intention must be directed at the conduct of inflicting severe pain or suffering as well as at the purpose to be achieved by such conduct.

■ The infliction of severe pain or suffering must be done for a purpose. Article 1(1) provides a non-exhaustive list of such purposes being:
  - extracting a confession;
  - obtaining from the victim, or a third person, information;
  - punishment;
  - intimidation and coercion;
  - discrimination.

The existence of the purpose emphasises that a victim is 'at least under the factual power or control of the person inflicting the pain and suffering'. It follows that torture, as the most serious violation of the human right to personal integrity, presupposes a situation of powerlessness of the victim which usually means deprivation of personal liberty.[55]

■ Public officials must be involved. Under the CAT severe pain or suffering amounts to torture if it is 'inflicted by or at the instigation of or with the consent or acquiescence of a public official or other person acting in an official capacity'. Instigation means incitement, inducement or solicitation and thus requires the direct or indirect involvement and participation of a public official. The concept of acquiescence was explained by the Committee in *Dzemajl et al v Yugoslavia*[56] in which the police present at the Roma settlement in Galvica failed to act in accordance with their duties and instead of stopping an attack by non-Roma residents of Danilovograd, who were destroying the settlement, stood and watched the violence. Therefore, acquiescence means that a contracting party will be held responsible for acts of private torturers when it does not respond adequately to them or fails to take preventive measures.

---

53   *The Greek Case* (1969) YB XII.
54   *Ireland v UK* (1978) 2 EHRR 25; *Tyrer v UK* (1979–80) 2 EHRR 1; and *Selmouni v France* (2002) 29 EHRR 403.
55   M. Nowak and E. McArthur, *The United Nations Convention against Torture, A Commentary*, Oxford: Oxford University Press, 2008, 75.
56   CAT 161/2000.

Although both torture and cruel, inhuman or degrading treatment or punishment are prohibited the distinction is important, not only because the freedom from torture is an absolute right from which no derogation is permissible whatever the circumstances including a state of war or other public emergency (Article 2(2) CAT), but also because Article 3 CAT prohibits a contracting party from expelling, returning or extraditing a person to another State where there is a real risk that the person will be tortured. It is to be noted that Article 3 CAT is often relied on by two categories of persons.

First, persons who do not qualify as refugees under Article 1F of the 1951 Convention relating to the Status of Refugees (i.e. they are war criminals, or they have committed serious non-political crimes prior to their admission to the country of refuge or they have committed acts contrary to the purposes and principles of the UN).

Second, refugees lawfully admitted to a territory of a State. Although Article 33 of the 1951 Convention protects a person who has been granted the status of a refugee from being sent to a country 'where his life or freedom would be threatened on account of his race, religion, nationality, membership of a particular social group or political opinion', the protection is not absolute. Under Article 33(2) refoulement[57] is permitted in a situation where a State in which the refugee is, has reasonable grounds to believe that his presence poses a danger to national security or, if a refugee has been convicted of a particularly serious crime by a final judgment, or his presence constitutes a danger to the community of that State. For an asylum seeker who has failed to obtain refugee status or a refugee who is in the situation described by Article 33(2) of the 1951 Convention the only hope to avoid being returned to a home State where there is a real risk of him being tortured is the protection embodied in Article 3, i.e. the absolute prohibition of expulsion.[58]

In practice, more than 80 per cent of individual complaints submitted to the Committee against Torture allege a breach of Article 3 CAT by a contracting party.[59] The Committee interprets Article 3 as meaning that it applies only where there is a real risk of torture and does not cover situations of ill-treatment described in Article 16.[60] As a result, a person will not be deported if there is a risk of him being tortured in a receiving State, but deportation will be allowed if he faces 'mere' ill treatment in a receiving State. It is important to note that the prohibition in Article 3 is absolute, whereas the prohibition contained in Article 33 of the 1951 UN Convention Relating to the Status of Refugees[61] is not so, in that it allows expulsion of a refugee whose presence on the national territory is considered to be against the public interest, i.e. constitutes a danger to the security of that State or to the community of that State.[62] Under Article 3 CAT a State is prohibited from expelling a person even if that person is a terrorist[63] or a murderer.[64]

---

57   The French word 'refoulement' has been used in the English text of the 1951 Convention. In French it means 'turn back' an immigrant. In refugee law it is used to refer to all measures of expulsion taken by a State against an asylum seeker or a refugee. Article 33(2) enshrines the principle of non-refoulement which by many is considered as being of a *jus cogens* nature.

58   *Paez v Sweden* (CAT 39/1996).

59   See the official website of the Committee against Torture atwwww2.ohchr.org/english/bodies/cat (accessed 8 October 2014).

60   *TM v Sweden* (CAT 226/2003).

61   189 UNTS 150.

62   *Mutombo v Switzerland* (CAT 13/1993).

63   *Paez v Sweden* (CAT 39/1996).

64   *Soering v UK* (1989) 11 EHRR 439.

12.3.4.2 The obligations imposed on a contracting party under the CAT

Under the CAT a contracting State is obliged to:

■ take all necessary measures to prevent, investigate and punish acts of torture, cruel, inhuman or degrading treatment;

■ make torture a criminal offence;

■ compensate victims of torture and of other ill treatment defined in Article 16 even in the absence of a criminal conviction of the alleged offenders;

■ ensure that any evidence obtained by torture should never be taken into account by a judicial body in any legal proceedings, except against a person accused of torture, as evidence against that person;

■ either punish or extradite an alleged torturer when he is within the territory of a contracting State (see Chapter 9.7);

■ not expel a person to a State where he may be subjected to torture.

12.3.4.3 The implementation of the CAT

The Committee against Torture was established under Article 17 CAT. It started work in 1987. Its main task is to supervise the implementation of the Convention in contracting States. It is charged with examining periodic reports submitted by each of the contracting States and on the basis of such examination to adopt recommendations in respect of the State concerned. It has, under Article 21 CAT, competence to deal with inter-State complaints. As at 9 October 2014, this competence had been accepted by 70 States. The Committee may hear individual petitions under Article 22 provided that the State concerned has recognised the Committee's competence in respect of such petitions. As at 13 October 2009, 64 States had recognised the Committee's competence. The Committee is also empowered to conduct inquiry (unless a contracting State to the CAT declared at the time of its ratification that it did not recognise this competence of the Committee – so far 12 contracting States have made such a declaration) if it has evidence that torture is being practised in the territory of a contracting State (Article 20 CAT). The inquiry, including site visits, is confidential and carried out in co-operation with the State concerned. The Committee discusses its findings with the State concerned. However, the Committee, after consultation with that State, may decide to publicise the result of its investigation in its annual report.

12.3.4.4 The Optional Protocol to the CAT

On 18 December 2002 the UNGA approved an Optional Protocol to the CAT.[65] It entered into force on 22 June 2006. As of 9 October 2014, the Protocol had obtained 74 ratifications.

The Optional Protocol establishes procedures for systematic visits by independent international and national bodies to 'places where people are deprived of their liberty' to ensure that these people are not tortured or submitted to cruel, inhuman and degrading treatment or punishment. Within the Committee against Torture a new body was established, i.e. the Sub-committee on Prevention of Torture

---

65   (2003) 42 ILM 26.

and Other Cruel, Inhuman and Degrading Treatment or Punishment, to supervise practical arrangements regarding the visits. Under the Protocol, at national level, a contracting party is required to set up one, or several, domestic 'visiting bodies' to detention places.

The Protocol provides an exception to such visits based on 'urgent and compelling grounds of national defence, public safety, natural disasters or serious disorder in the place to be visited which temporarily prevent the carrying out of such visits'. However, the existence of a State of emergency cannot be relied upon by a contracting party to object to a visit.

12.4   The UN human rights enforcement machinery

The UN HRs enforcement machinery consists of three categories of bodies:

- bodies which have been established directly on the basis of the UN Charter, such as the UNGA, the UNSC, and the ECOSOC;

- bodies which have been established indirectly by the UN Charter, that is whose creation was authorised by one of the bodies belonging to the first category, e.g. the UN Human Rights Council (UNHRC), the Office of High Commissioner for Human Rights (OHCHR) or the Commission on the Status of Women;

- bodies which have been established on the basis of HRs treaties, e.g. the HRC under the ICCPR, the Committee against Torture under the CAT or the Committee on the Elimination of All Forms of Racial Discrimination under the CERD.

The following bodies are examined in this section: the UNHRC and the OHCHR because of their universal mission and, the UN treaty bodies system made up of bodies established under the ten UN HRs treaties. These are considered by the High Commissioner for HRs as 'core' treaties,[66] because of their great contribution to the protection of HRs worldwide.

12.4.1   The Commission on Human Rights and its successor the UN Human Rights Council

The Commission on Human Rights was created in 1946 as a subsidiary organ of ECOSOC in order to draft the International Bill on Human Rights and on 27 March 2006 concluded its 62nd and final session. The Commission was made up of 53 representatives of member States of the UN who were selected for a 3-year term by ECOSOC on the basis of equitable geographic distribution. The members of the Commission were not independent as they represented their States.

---

66   Apart from the treaties examined in this chapter, the UN High Commissioner considered the following treaties as being 'core treaties' UN Convention on the Protection of the Rights of All Migrant Workers and Members of Their Families; UN Convention on the Rights of Persons with Disabilities; and the UN Convention for the Protection of All Persons from Enforced Disappearance. See The Report of the UN High Commissioner for Human Rights, 16, available at www2.ohchr.org/english/bodies/HRTD/docs/HCReportTBStrengthening.pdf (accessed 7 May 2014). It is submitted that these treaties may not be the most important, but under their terms contracting parties have agreed to establish a body of independent experts to monitor their implementation. For many treaties no such agreements have ever been reached, e.g. the UN Convention on the Prevention of the Crime of Genocide.

The Commission was abolished as a result of growing dissatisfaction based on the fact that from 2001 States sought to be elected to the Commission in order to shield themselves from international scrutiny. For example, in 2001 the following countries, with a very poor human rights record, were elected: Algeria, the Democratic Republic of Congo, Kenya, Saudi Arabia, Syria and Vietnam; but the US failed to be elected (although it was elected a year later). In 2003 Libya chaired the Commission. Obviously, the choice of members influenced the Commission's agenda, in that States which ought to have been examined were the very States which selected the States to be scrutinised. Further, the Commission failed to act in situations where its action was necessary, e.g. it failed to condemn the atrocities committed in Chechnya, slavery in Sudan or the massive violation of HRs in Zimbabwe, or to properly assess the situation in Iraq after the US invasion, or the alleged HRs abuses in Afghanistan.

As part of the reform of the UN it was decided that the Commission should be abolished and replaced by a new body – the UN Human Rights Council (UNCHR)[67] which was established on 15 March 2006.

12.4.1.2 The UNHRC

The UNCHR, a subsidiary organ of the UNGA, is made up of 47 members elected for 3-year terms by the UNGA. It holds no fewer than three sessions per year for a total duration of no less than 10 weeks.

The members of the UNHRC represent their governments. In order to ensure that the membership reflects the main legal systems and geographical regions, a fixed number of seats has been allocated as follows: 13 for Africa; 13 for Asia; 6 for Eastern Europe; 8 for Latin America and the Caribbean; and 7 for the Western European and Others Group.

The main task of the UNCHR is to strengthen the promotion and protection of HRs worldwide and to address situations of HRs violations and make recommendations on them to the UNGA.

On 18 June 2007, the UNHRC adopted its institution-building package which establishes the procedures, mechanism and structures of its work. These are as follows:

- A Universal Periodic Review (UPR) of the HRs record of all UN members including members of the Council. Each member is reviewed once every 4 years, i.e. 48 States are reviewed each year. The process of review ends with the adoption of recommendations by the UNCHR for implementation by the State under review. The review is based on a report submitted by the State under review, information provided by IGOs and national HRs institutions, plus recommendations from HRs bodies monitoring the implementation of the core human rights treaties.

- Special procedures consisting of establishing 'Special Rapporteurs' 'Special Representatives' or 'Independent Experts' to examine HRs violations in a specific State or to examine a specific human rights problem in the global context.

- The Human Rights Council Advisory Committee. It is described by the UNHRC as its 'think tank', i.e. its main role is to advise the UNHRC on thematic issues at the request of the UNHRC. The Advisory Committee is made up of 18 experts serving in their personal capacity.

- A complaints procedure.[68] Under the complaints procedure the complainant (an individual or groups of individuals, whether alleged victims of violations of HRs or not, or an NGO or other

---

67   UNGA Res 60/251. (A/RES/60/251).
68   A/HRC/3/CRP.3, A/HRC/4/CRP.6 and A/HRC/5/CRP.6.

organisation) must show that there is a consistent pattern of gross and reliably attested violations of HRs. Under this procedure the UNHRC examines a situation in a particular country, not a situation of a particular individual. Therefore it is not appropriate to address a complaint brought by an individual concerning violations of his rights unless that complaint is one of many, i.e. shows that there is a consistent pattern of violations. Further, violations must be very serious, e.g. concerning acts of torture, arbitrary executions and forced disappearances, and backed up by credible evidence. The UNHRC set up two working groups to deal with communications received: the Working Group on Communications (WGC) and the Working Group on Situations (WGS). The main features of the procedure are as follows:

- the Chairperson of the WGC screens communications and forwards those which meet the admissibility criteria to the relevant States for comments;

- the WGC (made up of five independent experts in the field of HRs who meet twice a year for five working days) decides on both the admissibility and the merits of a communication. It also decides whether the communication alone or together with other communications reveals a consistent pattern of gross and reliably attested violations of HRs. The WGC forwards all admissible communications with its recommendations to the WGS;

- the WGS (made up of five independent experts who meet twice a year for 5 working days) deals with communications transmitted by the WGC and with situations of gross violations of HRs already under consideration by the UNHRC. With regard to communications received from the WGC, it decides, on the basis of all available information, whether a communication or a number of communications show that there is a consistent pattern of gross violations of HRs. If so, it prepares a report, with recommendations on how to deal with a new situation. The report is submitted to the UNHRC, which will decide what to do next.

The entire procedure is confidential although the UNHRC may decide, in particular in a situation where the State concerned refuses to co-operate, to discontinue confidentiality.

12.4.1.3 Assessment of the UNHRC

The question of how the UNHRC should be assessed is difficult to answer.[69] Certainly, the UPR procedure is to be welcomed. It ended the political manoeuvring as to the choice of a State to be examined, which had greatly undermined the authority of the Commission on Human Rights. The first cycle of the UPRs (2008–2011) was completed. The HRs situation in all 192 members of the UN was assessed, which in itself is a success, although as Freedman noted some States have used various tactics: 'to deflect attention from sensitive issues or to protect [them] from particular scrutiny'.[70] More than 20,000 recommendations were made to the member States of which two-thirds were accepted. The second cycle of UPRs will be critical as it will show whether, in fact, recommendations have been implemented and thus whether the UPRs work as they should.

The main deficiencies of the UNHRC, as any UN body which is made up of members representing their governments are, first, 'politisation' which was defined by Freedman as 'the introduction of unrelated controversial issues by countries seeking to further their own political objectives', and

---

69   For in depth assessment of the first 5 years of the UNHRC see R. Freedman, *The United Nations Human Rights Council: A Critique and an Early Assessment*, London/New York: Routledge, 2013.
70   Ibid, 278.

'regionalism' which is 'the most important kind of politicisation at the HRC, useful for understanding HRC proceedings in relation to regional group power and influence at that body'.[71] Indeed, the deep political and ideological divide between South (Africa, Latin America and developing Asia and the Middle East) and West (North America, the EU and developed part of East Asia), as to the role of the UNHRC and the nature and scope of responsibility of individual States for the protection of HRs is reflected in the agenda and outcome of UNHRC work.[72] For example, the UNHRC was criticised for the excessive focus on one country, i.e. Israel. Of the 25 resolutions adopted by the UNHRC from its inception until its 12th Session in September 2009, 20 targeted Israel.[73] Many States considered that this excessive focus on Israel showed, once again, bias in its agenda, and that this is detrimental to the prestige of the UNHRC and to its work, in that other urgent human rights situations occurring during that period were not dealt with, e.g. the situations in Darfur, Pakistan, and Myanmar (Burma).

However, with the 'Arab Spring',[74] the divide between South and West has, on some occasions, been overcome. For example, the UNHRC unanimously decided to suspend Libya, then governed by Colonel Quadaffi from membership of the UNHRC for gross and systematic violations of HRs.[75] Another example was the UNHRC's decision to change the confidential complaint mechanism to a public procedure in respect of the government of Eritrea concerning its intimidation practices targeting HRs defenders and journalists. Eritrea denied any wrongdoing, and the need to take such a step. With regard to Eritrea, the UNHRC established the mandate of a Special Rapporteur to follow up complaints.[76] Additionally, there has been an increasing number of cross-regional initiatives both thematic and concerning country situations, one of them is the adoption by the UNHRC of a resolution on the situation of human rights in Iran.[77] Notwithstanding this, it is clear that political reality will affect the agenda and outcome of the UNHRC and thus certain HRs matters are unlikely to be debated and dealt with bearing in mind that the West–South divide makes it unlikely that members of the UNHRC will, in many case, act outside regional and other political block allegiances.

Additionally, the UNHRC has been criticised:

■ by non-governmental organisations (NGOs) for the inappropriate outcome of its election process for membership. For example, currently, Russia, China, Cuba, Vietnam and Saudi Arabia are members of the Council despite the fact that none of them is a champion of HRs;

■ because, under the UN system, there is no individual complaints procedure other than that relating to a consistent pattern of widespread and serious violations of HRs. As a result, individuals who are victims of sporadic HRs violations have no available *forum* in a situation where a State, which is a member of the UN, has not ratified the relevant HRs treaty or, even if it has ratified the relevant treaty, made a declaration excluding the competence of a treaty body to deal with individual petitions.

---

71   Ibid, 11–13 and 122.

72   See Th. Weiss, *What's Wrong with the United Nations and How to Fix It*, 2nd edn, Cambridge: Polity Press, 2012, in particular 50 *et seq.*

73   'A Farcical Attempt to Paint Israel Black' Times Online, 29 September 2009.

74   The name 'Arab Spring' was given to internal conflicts and changes of governments in some Arab countries which started in Spring 2011. On this topic see M.C. Bassiouni, Editorial (2014) 8/3 International Journal of Transitional Justice, 325.

75   A/HRC/RES/S-15/1.

76   A/HRC/RES/20/20.

77   A/HRC/RES/16/9.

12.4.2 The Office of High Commissioner for Human Rights (OHCHR)

The 1993 Vienna Declaration and Programme of Action[78] adopted by 171 States at the World Conference on Human Rights called for the strengthening and harmonising of the monitoring of the implementation of HRs under the UN system. To this effect, among other concrete actions, a proposal for the establishment of the Office of the High Commissioner for Human Rights was put forward. The UNGA created such a post on 20 December 1993[79] and listed the main tasks of the High Commissioner as being:

- to promote and protect the enjoyment of all HRs, including the right to development;

- to provide all forms of assistance (including financial and technical aspects) in the

field of HRs at the request of a State;

- to stimulate and to co-ordinate action on HRs within the UN system and at international level;

- to prevent and to respond to serious violations of HRs throughout the world.

The High Commissioner is appointed by the UNS-G with the approval of the UNGA for a period of 4 years, renewable for a further 4 years. The High Commissioner is in charge of all UN HRs activities. He acts under the direction and authority of the UNS-G, and within the framework of the overall competence, authority and decisions of the UNGA, ECOSOC and the UNCHR.

The mandate of the first High Commissioner commenced on 5 April 1994. Since then the OHCHR has become widely known and respected. It has developed many initiatives to fulfil its task, including the establishment of field offices and operations which provide advice, training and assistance to governments and, if required, supervise the observance of HRs in particularly sensitive places, or work with local NGOs.

12.4.3 Bodies established on the basis of the 'core' HRs treaties

Treaty bodies[80] such as the HRC, the Committee against Torture, the ICESCR Committee, the CEDWE Committee, are made up of members who, unlike the members of the UNHRC, act in their personal capacity. Membership of such bodies must reflect the different forms of civilisation and the principal legal systems. Members, being independent politically and economically from their governments, although obviously a person who fiercely opposes the policy of her/his government is unlikely to be nominated by a State party to a particular treaty to be a candidate for membership, are subject to certain additional safeguards ensuring their impartiality, e.g. members of the HRC do not participate in the examination of cases brought against their home State.

The treaty bodies, within their main task of monitoring the implementation of the relevant treaty, have made tremendous impact on the development of HRs.

First, they ensure that the relevant HRs treaty is correctly implemented by its contracting parties. To this effect they regularly conduct periodic, non-politicised, non-discriminatory reviews of compliance of the contracting parties with their obligations deriving from the particular treaty, and when authorised by a contracting party, deal with complaints from individuals so allowing those individuals to have access to an independent, international forum, in some cases, the only forum.

---

78   'Vienna Declaration and Programme of Action' UN World Conference on Human Rights (25 June 1993) UN Doc
      A/ CONF.157/23.
79   Resolution 48/141.
80   There are 10 treaty bodies within the UN HRs system.

Second, decisions of treaty bodies reflect universal HRs values rather than values of a particular region or State or religion; and

Third, jurisprudence generated by treaty bodies, usually of high quality, provides guidance for the interpretation of the relevant treaty for all contracting parties, and serves as a basis for any desired future reform.

However, there are two main problems with the UN treaty body system. First, while the number of ratifications of the 'core' HRs treaties doubled between 2000 to 2012,[81] this has not been matched by an increase in resources allocated to treaty bodies. They have remained part-time bodies, whose members, being volunteers, have not been paid, although their expenses during meetings are paid. The increased workload has resulted in delays in dealing with individual complaints, the processing of State reports and the carrying out of other mandated tasks. The second problem is the lack of respect on the part of contracting parties for the work of these bodies. There have been numerous instances where contracting parties have refused to provide information, delayed submission of reports, refused to comply with decisions and recommendations made by such bodies and, in brief, generally obstructed, frustrated and undermined their work.[82]

In the light of the above, calls, in particular by the OHCHR, were made for the strengthening of the UN treaty body system.[83] They were, to some extent, answered by the UNGA which in February 2014 adopted a resolution on 'Strengthening and Enhancing the Effective Functioning of the Human Rights Treaty Body System'.[84] This resolution may not solve all the problems, but certainly provides a useful platform for further improvement. It provides for measures to be adopted by the treaty bodies to streamline their efficiency, and enhance their visibility and accessibility to individuals who need it most. It also ensures a better resourcing. Under the resolution supplementary funds will be allocated to treaty bodies so allowing them time for additional meetings with a view to dealing with State reports and clearing backlogs. Further, additional resources will be allocated for capacity building for States so enabling them to comply with their treaty obligations to submit reports. It is, however, disappointing that States could not agree to immediately fund webcasting of the public sessions of treaty bodies thereby increasing the visibility and accountability of the treaty bodies. Also no resources were allocated to support and encourage efforts towards the universal ratification of the 'core' HRs treaties. Further, the UNGA did not deal with the matter of reprisals and intimidation suffered by some members of the treaty bodies and by those who seek to rely on their rights protected by the 'core' HRs treaties.

12.5 Regional arrangements for the promotion and protection of human rights – the Inter-American system

The inter-American HRs system is based on the 1948 Charter of the Organisation of American States (OAS),[85] the American Declaration of the Rights and Duties of Man[86] adopted in Bogota, Colombia in 1948, and the 1969 American Convention on Human Rights (ACHR).[87] Two additional Protocols are attached to the ACHR:

---

81   See The Report of the UN High Commissioner for Human Rights, 17, available at www2.ohchr.org/english/bodies/ HRTD/docs/HCReportTBStrengthening.pdf (accessed 7 May 2014).
82   Ibid, 20–23.
83   Ibid.
84   A/68/L.37.
85   119 UNTS 3.
86   Reprinted in Basic Documents Pertaining to Human Rights in the Inter-American System OEA/Ser L V/II.82 Doc 6 Rev 1 at 17 (1992).
87   1144 UNTS 123.

■ The 1988 Additional Protocol to the American Convention on Human Rights in the Area of Economic, Social and Cultural Rights (known as the San Salvador Protocol).[88] This in terms of the rights protected, is similar to the ICESCR. The obligations imposed on contracting parties are not immediate, but progressive and pragmatic. The Inter-American Commission on Human Rights (IACommHR) monitors the implementation of the Protocol, *via* the periodic reports procedure, and by attending to individual petitions. The Protocol entered into force in 1999 and, as at 10 October 2014, had been ratified by only 16 States. This low number implies that the protection of economic, social and cultural rights is not a high priority for the States of the Americas.

■ The 1990 Additional Protocol Relating to the Abolition of the Death Penalty, which entered into force on 28 August 1991 and, as at 10 October 2014, had achieved 13 ratifications. The Protocol does not totally abolish the death penalty, as the contracting parties may declare, upon signing, their intention to apply the death penalty in times of war for serious military crimes, but this reservation must be in conformity with international law.

There are two bodies in charge of the enforcement of HRs in the Americas: the Inter-American Commission on Human Rights (IACommHR) with its headquarters in Washington, DC, and the Inter-American Court of Human Rights (IACtHR) which is located in San José, Costa Rica.

In May 1948, the ninth Inter-American Conference set up the Organisation of American States (OAS) which, as at 7 October 2014, had membership of 35 States. The OAS Charter contains two provisions relating to HRs:

■ Article 3(l), which provides that 'American states proclaim the fundamental rights of the individual without distinction as to race, nationality, creed and/or sex'; and

■ Article 17, which requires that a Member State respects the rights of the individual and the principle of universal morality.

These provisions were inspired by the UN Charter and constitute statements of moral principles rather than conferring any specific rights on individuals. The same Conference adopted the American Declaration of the Rights and Duties of Man which contains 27 human rights and ten duties. The Declaration sets out civil, political, economic, social and cultural rights and duties. These duties include a general duty contained in Article 29 to conduct oneself in relation to others in such a way that 'each and everyone may fully form and develop his personality', and specific duties such as duties to society, to children and parents, to receive instruction, to vote, to obey the law, to serve the community and the nation, to pay taxes, to work, and to refrain from political activities in a foreign country.

The issue whether the American Declaration, which was adopted as a simple non-binding resolution of the Conference, has any binding force is of importance with regard to member States of the OAS which have not ratified the ACHR. The issue here is whether the IACommHR is empowered to scrutinise a State's compliance with the requirements of HRs, including dealing with individual complaints against a State party to the OAS Charter in the light of the American Declaration.

The Drafters of the American Declaration, that is the inter-American Judicial Committee, regarded the American Declaration as a non-binding document.[89] The issue of whether, with the passage of time, its status has changed has been viewed as follows:

---

88   [1989] 28 ILM 156.

89   Pan American Union, Human Rights in the American States 164–65 [1960].

■ The IACommHR in the *Baby Boy Case*[90] in 1981 found that the Declaration had acquired 'binding force', i.e. enjoys the status of a legally binding treaty by reason of its incorporation into the OAS Charter system. The Statute of the IACommHR confirms this position, e.g. its Article 1(2).

■ The IACtHR's assessment was more confusing as it stated in the Interpretation of the American Declaration of the Rights and Duties of Man within the Framework of Article 64 of the American Convention on Human Rights (Advisory Opinion)[91] that the Declaration was not a treaty but this did not lead to 'the conclusion that it does not have legal effect, nor that the Court lacks power to interpret it'.[92] The reasoning of the IACtHR is not entirely clear as the Court chose not to specify the nature of the legally binding obligation which the Declaration imposes on OAS member States.

■ The ACHR recognises the binding force of the American Declaration in Article 29(d) which states that its provisions shall not be interpreted in such a way as to exclude or limit the effect of the Declarations and other international acts of the same nature.

In conclusion it can be said that the Declaration is not a treaty, but constitutes an authoritative interpretation of Article 3(l) of the OAS Charter, and creates legally binding obligations based on two sources. First, member States of the OAS have interpreted the Declaration as creating legal obligations. This is evidenced by the fact that they granted the IACommHR competence to examine communications from individuals and States and adopt recommendations to States based on the American Declaration (Article 49 of the IACommHR Statute). The ACtHR confirmed this position in the Tenth Advisory Opinion (above) in which it stated that it had jurisdiction to interpret the American Declaration because 'by means of an authoritative interpretation, the Member States of the Organisation have signalled their agreement that the Declaration contains and defines the fundamental human rights referred to in the [OAS] Charter'.[93] Second, many provisions of the American Declaration have, with the passage of time, become rules of customary international law, and some of them have acquired the status of *jus cogens*, e.g. the prohibition of torture and the prohibition of arbitrary deprivation of life.

12.5.1 The ACHR

The ACHR was signed on 22 November 1969 at San José, Costa Rica. It entered into force in 1978 and, as at 10 October 2014 it had been ratified by 25 States of the Americas but two of them subsequently withdrew their ratifications. Trinidad and Tobago (T&T) denounced the ACHR on 26 May 1998, effective on 26 May 1999, and Venezuela on 10 September effective on 10 September 2013.

T&T's denunciation was the response to an order issued by the IACommHR requiring suspension of the execution of prisoners on death row in T&T while their petitions were under review by the IACommHR.[94] The real meaning of the denunciation can only be understood in the light of the judgment

---

90   Case No 2141, Annual Report of the Inter-American Commission on Human Rights (1980–1981) OEA/Ser.L/V/II.54 Doc 9rev 1.

91   IACtHR A No 10 (14 July 1989), para 45.

92   See also the Interpretation of the American Declaration of the Rights and Duties of Man within the Framework of Article 64 of the American Convention on Human Rights (Advisory Opinion) IACtHR A No 10 (14 July 1989), para 45.

93   Supra note 91., para 48.

94   James, *et al.* (Trinidad and Tobago), Provisional Measures, Inter-Am CT HR, Order of 29 August 1998, Se[r]e. On this topic see E.N. Parassram Conceptión, *The Legal Implications of Trinidad and Tobago's Withdrawal from the American Convention on Human Rights* (2001) 16 American University International Law Review, 847.

of the Judicial Committee of the Privy Council in *Pratt and Morgan v Attorney General for Jamaica*[95] which stated that if in any case in which execution was to take place more than 5 years after the sentence of death there would be strong grounds for believing that the delay was such as to amount to inhuman or degrading punishment or other treatment, with the consequence that after the expiry of 5 years no person condemned to death could be executed, and therefore all death sentences had to be commuted to life imprisonment. Obviously condemned persons were making use of all available national and international procedures, which in most cases took more than 5 years to be concluded, to challenge their sentences. The IACommHR was unwilling to give T&T any assurances that its proceedings would be completed within the timeframe sought by T&T. In these circumstances T&T denounced the ACHR so that by depriving persons on death row of the possibility of having their case being reviewed by international treaty bodies, it could execute them within the 5-year period.

Venezuela's denunciation followed a longstanding tension between late President of Venezuela, Hugo Chávez, and the IACommHR and the IACtHR. He accused both bodies of bias against him, interfering in internal affairs of Venezuela, acting at the behest of the US and constantly breaching the IACHR. Chávez was particularly infuriated by the 2009 Report prepared by the IACommHR on 'Democracy and Human Rights in Venezuela' which found Venezuela in persistent breach of many HRs, and by a number of unfavourable judgments of the IACtHR condemning attacks on the independence of judiciary, politically-motivated prosecution of opposition leaders, and in some cases their extrajudicial execution by police, restrictions on freedom of expression, and poor conditions in prison.[96]

The ACHR protects civil and political rights and contains a general provision (Article 26) referring to economic, social and cultural rights. Apart from civil and political rights identical to those contained in the ICCPR, it contains the following additional rights: the right of reply to injurious statements in legally regulated media of communication (Article 14); the right to compensation for a miscarriage of justice (Article 10); the right to a name (Article 18); the rights of the child (Article 19); the right to nationality (Article 20); and the right to property (Article 21). It also contains extended guarantees in respect of the right to a fair trial in that it covers not only criminal proceedings but also 'the determination of rights and obligations of a civil, labour, fiscal, or any other nature' (Article 8(1)). Unlike similar HRs treaties, the ACHR contains anti-abortion provisions in Article 4(1) which states that the right to life should be protected 'by law, in general, from the moment of conception'. This provision, on the one hand, reflects the position of the predominantly Roman Catholic States of Central and Latin America on abortion, and, on the other, is the main reason why Canada has been unwilling to become a contracting party.

A contracting party to ACHR is required to apply it to all persons, including legal persons, within its jurisdiction, without any discrimination based on 'race, colour, sex, language, religion, political or other opinion, national or social origin, economic status, or any other social condition'.

Restrictions and derogations are permitted within strictly defined limits. Article 30 deals with restrictions which a contracting party is permitted to impose on enjoyment or exercise of rights or freedoms recognised under the ACHR. The following principles apply to restrictions:

- A restriction must be provided for by a provision of the ACHR. This means that absolute rights, e.g. the right to life or the right to be free from torture, can never suffer any restrictions.

---

95   [1991] 4 All ER 769.

96   For example see *Case of the Barrios Family v Venezuela*, Merits, reparations and costs. Judgment of November 24, 2011. Series C No 237; *Case of López Mendoza v Venezuela*, Merits, reparations and costs. Judgment of September 1, 2011. Series C No 233; *Case of Apitz Barbera et al. ('First Court of Administrative Disputes') v Venezuela*, Preliminary Objection, merits, reparations and costs. Judgment of August 5, 2008. Series C No. 182.

■ Rights and freedoms, which the ACHR recognises as capable of being restricted, may only be restricted 'in accordance with laws enacted for reasons of general interest and in accordance with the purpose for which such restrictions have been established'. This means that any arbitrary restrictions are prohibited.

■ The grounds upon which a restriction may be imposed are indicated in the relevant provisions, e.g. to protect public order, public health or morals or the rights or freedoms of others.

■ Some provisions require that the enjoyment or exercise of a protected right can only be restricted if a restriction is necessary in a democratic society, e.g. Article 15 which protects the right of assembly.

With regard to derogations, Article 27 provides that only in situations of war, public danger or other emergency threatening the independence or security of a State party may some rights be suspended but only:

■ to the extent and for the period of time strictly required by the exigencies of the situation;

■ if the derogations are consistent with obligations arising under international law for the State concerned;

■ if the derogations do not involve any discrimination on the grounds of race, colour, sex, language, religion or social origin.

Any measures taken under Article 27 must be notified to the other State parties through the Secretary General of the OAS. Article 27(2) lists rights which can never be suspended, i.e. those contained in Articles 3, 4, 5, 6, 9, 12, 17, 18, 19, 20 and 23 ACHR, as well as 'the judicial guarantees essential for the protection of such rights'. The IACommHR and the IACtHR will, at the end of the day, decide whether the requirements of Article 27 are satisfied if a contracting party suspends the operation of certain rights. Further, the IACtHR has confirmed that the remedies of *habeas corpus* and *amparo* [97] are non-derogable in times of emergency.[98]

Article 75 ACHR permits reservations to the ACHR but these must be compatible with the object and purpose of the treaty (see Chapter 3.6.2).

Under the ACHR two bodies are in charge of enforcing its provisions: the pre-existing IACommHR and the new IACtHR.

12.5.2 The IACommHR

The IACommHR is made up of seven members, acting in their personal capacity, elected by the OAS General Assembly in a secret ballot from a list of candidates submitted by members of the OAS, for a 4-year term, which may be renewed. The Commission is a part-time body and meets for no more than a total of eight weeks a year. Its meetings are held *in camera*.

---

97 This is a form of constitutional relief found in the legal systems of various Latin American countries. While *habeas corpus* remedies protect physical liberty the *amparo* seeks to protect all rights other than physical liberty.

98 *Habeas Corpus in Emergency Situations (Arts. 27(2), 25(1) and 7(6) of the American Convention on Human Rights) (Advisory Opinion)* IACtHR Series A No 8 (30 January 1987).

12.5.2.1 The formative years of the IACommHR

In 1959 the OAS established the IACommHR as its autonomous organ. The main task of the Commission is to ensure the respect of HRs and to serve as a consultative body in this area for the OAS.

The IACommHR conducted its first ever investigation into violations of HRs in 1959. This was in relation to Cuba following the overthrow of the Batista government by Fidel Castro. The government of Fidel Castro did not allow the Commission to visit Cuba and therefore the Commission carried out investigations in Florida, where it interviewed Cuban refugees. The result of the Commission's investigation was the expulsion of Cuba from the OAS. Regrettably, during the following two decades when military dictatorships took over democratic governments in most Latin American countries, and subsequently gross and systematic violations of HRs occurred in these countries, the OAS did not impose any sanctions on any of the member States.

From 1961 the IACHR carried out on-site visits to verify the HRs situations in specific countries. In 1965 the IACHR was authorised by the OAS to examine complaints concerning alleged violations of HRs in Member States of the OAS. However, its powers were limited:

- in the light of its limited resources it investigated the general situations of HRs in each member State rather than individual cases; and,

- it had no teeth as it had no power to impose sanctions on a State found to be breaching HRs. The best it could do was to make a declaration that a member State had violated the American Declaration.

Before the entry into force of the ACHR, as Medina said:

the Commission was the sole guarantor of human rights in a continent plagued with gross, systematic violations, and the Commission was part of an international organisation for which human rights were definitely not the first priority, and these facts made an imprint on the way the Commission looked upon its task ... Apparently, the Commission viewed itself more as an international organ with a highly political task to perform than as a technical body whose main task was to participate in the first phase of quasi-judicial supervision of the observance of human rights. The Commission's past made it ill-prepared to efficiently utilise the additional powers the [American] Convention subsequently granted it.[99]

12.5.2.2 The role of the IACommHR under the Charter and under the ACHR

The Commission has retained its status and functions under the OAS Treaty and acquired new functions under the ACHR. Consequently, it derives its powers from two sources, the OAS Charter and the American Declaration being the first source, and the ACHR being the second. This dual character allows the IACommHR, on the one hand, to ensure uniform interpretation and application of both the American Declaration and the ACHR but, on the other, when dealing with individual petitions and inter-State complaints under the OAS Charter, the Commission's effectiveness is impaired in that for inter-State complaints, explicit acceptance of its jurisdiction is required from States, and in respect of individual complaints the Commission has no power to bring them for judicial determination by the IACtHR (see Chapter 12.5.3.1).

Under both the OAS Charter and the ACHR, the IACommHR exercises promotional, protective and consultative functions.

---

99   C. Medina, *The Inter-American Commission on Human Rights and the Inter-American Court of Human Rights: Reflections on a Joint Venture* (1990) 12 Hum Rts Q, 441.

A. Promotional activities of the IACommHR

Within promotional activities, the IACommHR organises seminars and conferences, publishes information on HRs in the Americas; prepares studies and reports; and prepares treaties on HRs, e.g. it drafted the ACHR, the two Additional Protocols to it, the 1985 Inter-American Convention to Prevent and Punish Torture and the 1994 Inter-American Convention on the Forced Disappearances of Persons.

B. The IACommHR as a protector of HRs

Within its role as a protector of HRs, the Commission:

- monitors the general HRs situations in the Member States and publishes special reports when appropriate;

- conducts on-site visits[100] and investigations in respect of specific situations. After examining the situation the Commission will publish a report and send it to the OAS;

- recommends to the member States of the OAS the adoption of measures aimed at improving the protection of HRs in the Americas;

- requests a State to adopt 'precautionary measures'. Since 1980 such requests are binding on all OAS Member States as confirmed in IACommHR Resolution 1/05 of 8 March 2005. If a State refuses, and is a contracting party to the ACHR, the IACommHR may ask the IACtHR to order 'provisional measures';

- requests advisory opinions from the IACtHR on the interpretation of the ACHR;

- submits cases to the IACtHR against States which are contracting parties to the ACHR and which have accepted jurisdiction of the Court;

- receives and examines individual petitions alleging violations of the ACHR.

Under both the OAS Charter and the ACHR the Commission is competent to deal with inter-State complaints if both States have explicitly accepted its competence. With respect to individual petitions, when a State ratifies the OAS Charter or the ACHR, it automatically confers on the IACommHR jurisdiction over individual petitions, i.e. no special declaration is required. However, their treatment differs as explained below.

12.5.2.3 Individual petitions before the IACommHR

The IACommHR has power to deal with individual petitions under both the OAS Charter and the ACHR. The Commission decides on both the admissibility and the merits.

The following persons have *locus standi* before the IACommHR:

- any natural person;

- any group of persons;

- an IGO recognised in one or more member States of the OAS.

---

100   The IACommHR visits are subject to two conditions: first the government concerned must consent to a visit, and second, that government must give assurances to the IACommHR that it will have unrestricted freedom to visit any place of interest and to organise its own schedule of activities.

Under the inter-American system it is not required that, in order to have *locus standi*, a person be an alleged victim of a violation of his HRs or that such a person consents to the lodging of a petition.[101] The granting of *locus standi* to an NGO (which does not need to be recognised by a respondent State as it is sufficient that an NGO is recognised in any member State of the OAS) ensures that those who are too poor or too frightened can effectively defend their rights *via* an NGO. However, a party who is unrelated to an alleged victim needs permission to represent him before the IACtHR. Further the IACtHR in *Cantos v Argentina (Preliminary Objections)*[102] held that companies also have *locus standi*.

Requirements for admissibility of petitions are set out in Article 28 of the Commission's Rules of Procedure. Those relating to the exhaustion of domestic remedies have been broadly interpreted by the IACtHR. In line with decisions of similar HRs treaty bodies, the Court decided that a petitioner is not required to exhaust domestic remedies which are inadequate or were denied, or where there has been undue delay in the rendering of a final domestic judgment. However, it added a new exception to the requirement of exhaustion of domestic remedies. In the *Advisory Opinion OC-11/90*[103] the IACtHR held that the duty of exhaustion does not apply if the victim is indigent or unable to find a lawyer due to fear of governmental reprisals. However, this requirement is not mentioned in Article 28 of the Commission's Rules of Procedure.

If a case is admissible the Commission forwards the relevant part of the petition to the government concerned with a request for relevant information. Each party is asked to comment on the reply of the other. At this stage the Commission may carry out its own investigations including site visits. The Commission may also decide to have a hearing in the presence of both parties and ask them to submit their legal and factual arguments. The Commission will try to reach a friendly settlement. If this is not possible it will prepare a preliminary report on merits with proposals and recommendations. The report is confidential and the Commission will give the State concerned a fixed period of time to resolve the matter and to comply with its recommendations. After the expiry of that time and provided the respondent State refuses to comply with the recommendations, the Commission has different options to deal with the respondent State, depending upon whether a case has been processed under the OAS Charter or under the ACHR and depending on whether the respondent State has accepted jurisdiction of the IACtHR.

- With regard to petitions brought under the OAS Charter, and under the ACHR in respect of States which have ratified the ACHR, but have not recognised the competence of the IACtHR, the IACommHR will adopt a 'final report on merits' in which it sets out its recommendations. If a respondent State fails to comply, the Commission may publish the report and include it in its annual report to the OAS General Assembly, which so far has not been keen on imposing any sanctions on a defaulting State. To deal with this lack of enthusiasm, the IACommHR has instituted a follow-up procedure, which may ultimately conclude with another report on non-compliance.

- with regard to petitions brought under the ACHR in respect of States which have accepted jurisdiction of the IACtHR, the IACommHR will adopt its final report on merits setting out its recommendations and sends it to the respondent State. That State has three months to comply

---

101   *Constitutional Court v Peru* (Competence), Inter-Am Ct HR, 24 September 1999, SerC, No 55.

102   Inter-Am Ct HR, 7 September 2001, Ser C, No 85.

103   *Exceptions to the Exhaustion of Domestic Remedies (Arts 46(1), 46(2)(a) and 46(2)(b)) of the American Convention on Human Rights*, Inter-Am CtHR, Advisory Opinion OC-11/90 of 10 August 1990, Ser A, No11, paras 30 and 35.

or to react to them, for example, it may bring the matter before the IACtHR. If the respondent State refuses to comply with recommendations, in accordance with Article 45 of the IACommHR Rules of Procedure, the Commission 'shall' refer the case to the IACtHR unless there is a reasoned opinion by an absolute majority of its members to the contrary. In reaching the decision the IACommHR will take into account factors specified in Article 45(2) of its Rules of Procedure, *inter alia*, views of the petitioners and nature and seriousness of the violation. In cases in which the IACommHR decides not to refer to the ICtHR and if the respondent State refuses to comply, the IACommHR may decide, by an absolute majority vote, to publish its report, and determines whether to include it in the Annual Report to the OAS General Assembly (see above).

12.5.3 The IACtHR

The IACtHR was inaugurated on 3 September 1979. It is made up of seven judges who must be jurists 'of the highest moral authority' recognised for their expertise in HRL. Judges are elected by the State parties to the ACHR, although they are not required to be nationals of contracting parties. It suffices that they are nationals of Member States of the OAS. The IACtHR is a part-time body which holds regular sessions and may, if needed, convene special sessions. Five judges constitute a *quorum*.

The IACtHR's main task is to apply and to interpret the ACHR. It has contentious and advisory jurisdiction.

12.5.3.1 *Contentious jurisdiction*

In respect of contentious jurisdiction the IACtHR determines cases brought by contracting States to the ACHR, and by the Commission, and may order provisional measures in urgent cases involving danger to persons, even when a case has not yet been submitted to it. However, two-fold restrictions are imposed on the Court's contentious jurisdiction:

- Only contracting States and the IACommHR may commence proceedings. Individuals have no direct access to the Court, even if a contracting State is willing to waive the requirement of exhausting domestic remedies against it in national courts and before the Commission.[104] Individuals must first seize the IACommHR which decides, subject to the respondent State's acceptance of jurisdiction of the ACtHR (see below), whether to bring the case before the Court.

- Both inter-State and individual cases can be determined by the Court but only if a contracting State permits this by making a general declaration to this effect, although a contracting State which has not made such a declaration may authorise the Court to exercise its jurisdiction in a specific case. Out of 23 contracting States to the ACHR, nine have, at the time of writing, accepted the general competence of the Court in inter-State cases, and 20 have done this in respect of cases concerning individual applications. For States which have recognised the Court's jurisdiction the judgments are binding. However, there is no way to force a contracting State to comply with the judgment. The only sanction is bad publicity in that the IACtHR may, in its annual report to the OAS General Assembly, note that a State party refused to comply with its judgment, and, may formulate appropriate recommendations.

---

104   *Re Viviana Gallardo* (1981) 20 ILM 1424.

12.5.4 Advisory jurisdiction

In its advisory capacity the Court is empowered, at the request of member States and organs of the OAS, to give opinions on the interpretation of the ACHR and other treaties relating to the protection of HRs. Also, a Member State may ask the Court to give its opinion on the compatibility of its internal laws with the ACHR and other international instruments in the field of HRs.

12.5.5 Assessment

For many years the IACommHR and the IACtHR dealt with atrocious crimes committed by dictatorships in power in almost all States of South and Central America. Extra-judicial killings, torture and forced disappearances were constant occurrences. This, together with extreme poverty in many member States of the OAS, shaped the approach of the IACommHR and the IACtHR to the interpretation of the ACHR. In particular, both bodies were keen to ensure the broadest possible access to them, and to provide adequate compensation to victims. In this respect, the IACtHR has extended the categories of victims to encompass not only next of kin, but also persons described as 'dependants',[105] i.e. non-successor dependants such as relatives, partners, and other persons who were financially supported by the victim. It has awarded compensation for both material and non-material damage to victims, as well as to persons with close emotional relationships with a victim who have suffered emotional distress.

The IACtHR has been creative in awarding the most appropriate reparation to victims. In the *Loayza Tamayo Case*,[106] the IACtHR introduced a new type of damage, i.e. damage to the victim's life plan (*proyecto de vida*). The Court described the concept of a 'life plan' as 'akin to the concept of personal fulfilment which in turn is based on the options that an individual may have for leading and achieving the goal that he sets for himself'.[107] If those opportunities to attain the realisation of a person's potential are taken away from an individual, he loses a valuable asset and therefore such a loss must be compensated. In many cases the IACtHR has decided that as part of reparation of the consequences of violations of rights and freedoms of the victim, a contracting party was required to investigate, identify, publicise and punish those responsible for the violations. It has also ordered other non-monetary reparation, such as commutation of death sentence, release of prisoners, public acts of apology, erection of memorials to deceased victims, and search for and return of their remains. Unlike other HRs courts, the IACtHR is empowered to order a State party to amend or repeal domestic law which is in breach of the ACHR or to enact legislation to comply with its obligations deriving from the ACHR.

Despite many achievements, the inter-American system has many deficiencies. The task of the IACommHR and the IACtHR is not easy in an environment where, after years of dictatorships and atrocious abuses of HRs, many Member States, now democratic and theoretically committed to the protection of HRs, when charged with HR violations, refuse to acknowledge their responsibility, and instead accuse both bodies of 'politisation' and 'selectivity'. Even though such accusations, in some cases, have been justified, they will persist:

> as long as the States do not take seriously the necessity that members of the Commission and the Court are persons who enjoy absolute independence and they no longer consider these positions as a treasure to be distributed through agreements of reciprocal support and accept that the members

---

105   *Aloeboetoe et al v Suriname (Reparation)*, Inter-Am Ct HR, 10 September 1993, Ser C, No 15, para 71.
106   *Loayza Tamayo v Peru (Reparations)*, Inter-Am Ct HR 27 November 1998, Ser C, No 42.
107   Ibid, para 147.

be elected in the framework of an absolutely transparent process, the system will be defective with little credibility.[108]

In recent years member States' frustration with unfavourable rulings has taken the form first, of calls for reforms aimed at weakening the authority and independence of the Commission (e.g. those concerning the procedure for filing precautionary measures and the work of the Special Rapportuer on Freedom of Expression) and second, threats to withdraw or, as was the case of Venezuela, the actual denunciation of the ACHR, rather than strengthening their committments to the protection of HRs in the Americas by creating an efficient and credible system, and providing it with the measures necessary to achieve its purpose.

It is submitted that the inter-American system is in crisis.

First, the lack of necessary material resources has resulted in unreasonable delays on the part of the IACommHR when dealing with individual petitions.[109]

Second, the process of 'strengthening' the IACommHR initiated in 2009 by the OAS General Assembly, as a result of dissatisfaction by States such as Venezuela, Bolivia, and Brazil, with unfauvorable decisions issued by the IACommHR, has brought relatively minor changes to the rules of procedure of both institutions.[110] These changes, although important will not make a great impact on the overall functioning of the system.

Third, the lack of political will of the member States to create an efficient and credible system is evidenced not only in terms of lack of funding, but also in terms of a lack of enforcement mechanisms relating to decisions of the IACommHR and judgments of the IACTHR. There are no provisions in the OAS Charter which the OAS General Assembly 'could adopt or for the coercive mechanisms that it could use to achieve compliance of the judgment'.[111] The member States are not keen to change this.

Fourth, the Anglo-Latin divide in the OAS is unlikely to disappear. Although the system applies to the Americas, the US has never ratified the ACHR on the ground that it could not determine the extent of its commitment under the 'full and free exercise of human rights' provision of the ACHR. Further, the US, which should have been the leading light in the implementation and the enforcement of the ACHR, has never been interested in ensuring its effectiveness. Apart from Barbados and Grenada no English speaking country in the Americas has ratified the ACHR.

In conclusion it can be said that a profound reform of the system for the protection and promotion of HRs in the Americas is needed. Such system requires, *inter alia*, the establishment of a full time Court and Commission, if the later mentioned is retained, and the allocation by the OAS of necessary

---

108   H.F. Ledesma, *The Inter-American System for the Protection of Human Rights*, 3rd edn, Inter-American Institute of Human Rights: San Jose, 2008, 936.

109   Cases pending decisions on admissibility and merits rose from 976 in 1997 to 1753 in 2013. Annual Report of the IACHR 2013, Ch II. Of the 2061 petitions received in 2013, only about 35 per cent (736) were reviewed, leaving 65 per cent pending. Of those reviewed, 123 were accepted for processing, roughly 17 per cent of the those reviewed (and 6 per cent of the total number filed), and 613 were rejected, i.e. 83 per cent of reviewed petitions. See also A. Dulitzky, *Too Little, Too Late: The Pace of Adjudication of The Inter-American Commission on Human Rights* (2013) 35 Loy L A Int'L and Cimp L Rev, 131,134, 136. His research shows that it takes an average of 4 years for a petition to reach a decision on admissibility and another 2½ years to reach a decision on merits.

110   The Rules of Procedure of the IACtHR were adopted by the Court during its LXXXV Regular Period Session held on 16–28 November 2009. The IACommHR approved its new Rules of Procedure at its 137th regular period of sessions, held from 28 October to 13 November 2009, and modified them on 2 September 2011 and again during its 147th Regular Period of Sessions, held from 8 to 22 March 2013. They entered into force on 1 August 2013.

111   Supra note 108, 856.

funds to ensure independence and efficient functioning of both bodies. In this respect Ledesma stated: 'it is uncomfortable, not to say embarrassing, that the latest judgments and advisory opinions of the Court were published thanks to funds from the European Union'.[112] Further, transparency in the nomination and election process of members of both bodies is needed to ensure that they are impartial and independent from the member States. Finally, the OAS needs to adopt measures ensuring that member States comply with decisions of the IACommHR and judgments of the IACtHR.

12.6 Regional arrangements for the promotion and protection of human rights – the African system

The 1963 Charter of the Organization of African Unity (the OAU Charter)[113] contains some references to the protection of HRs. Like other documents of this type the Charter's provisions were moral rights which awaited implementation. This was done by the African Charter on Human and Peoples' Rights (the African Charter)[114] adopted by the OAU in 1981 in Nairobi which entered into force on 21 October 1986. At the time of writing it is in force in 54 African States. It is to be noted that the 2001 Constitutive Act of the African Union (the AU Act)[115] replaced the Charter of the OAU. The Act makes a much stronger commitment to the protection of HRs than its predecessor. In particular, Article 3 of the Act provides that one of the objectives of the AU is to promote and protect HRs, while Article 4 states that the AU is based on the respect of democratic principles, HRs and the rule of law. Although the AU is an IGO similar to the EU and therefore its main concern is to achieve political and socio-economic integration of the African continent, it is, in fact, the only organisation in Africa which can ensure effective enforcement of HRs (see below), whereas in Europe the primary protector of human rights has been the Council of Europe, rather than the EU.

The African Charter, together with its Protocols: the 1998 Protocol Establishing the African Court of Human and Peoples Rights (APCtHPR)[116] which entered into force on 25 January 2004 and, as at 13 October 2014, had been ratified by 26 States; the 1990 African Charter on the Rights and Welfare of the Child[117] which entered into force on 29 November 1999; and the 2003 Protocol on the Rights of Women in Africa[118] which entered into force on 25 November 2005, constitutes the cornerstone of the protection of HRs in Africa.

The system of protection established under the African Charter is complemented by the 1969 Convention Governing the Specific Aspects of Refugee Problems in Africa[119] which entered into force on 20 June 1974. The Convention extends the definition of a refugee taking account of the peculiarity of the refugee situation in Africa. Its Article 1 states that the term 'refugee' applies not only to a person who has 'well-founded fear of persecution' but also to every person who, 'owing to external aggression, occupation, foreign domination or events seriously disturbing public order in either part or the whole of his country of origin or nationality, is compelled to leave his place of habitual residence in order to seek refuge in another place outside his country of origin or nationality'.

---

112   Ibid, 937.
113   479 UNTS 39.
114   1520 UNTS 217.
115   2158 UNTS 3.
116   (1999) 20 HRLJ 269.
117   OAU Doc CAB/LEG/24.9/49 (1990).
118   OAU Doc CAB/LEG/66.6 reprinted in (2001) 1 Afr Hum Rts LJ 53.
119   1001 UNTS 45.

12.6.1 The 1981 African Charter on Human and Peoples' Rights (the African Charter)

The African Charter is very ambitious in that it is the only international human rights treaty which incorporates three types of HRs:

- Civil and political rights. The Charter lists the most important civil and political rights and freedoms: the right to life, liberty, fair trial, equality before the law, property (although this is limited by 'public need'), to seek asylum, to participate in government, to freedom from torture, cruel, inhuman and degrading treatment, from slavery, freedom of association and assembly, of conscience and religion, of movement and residence, of speech, and the prohibition of mass expulsion of non- nationals. However, some important civil and political rights are not mentioned in the Charter, e.g. the right to privacy, to vote in periodic and genuine elections, to marry with full and free consent of the intended spouses, to change one's religion. Some provisions are drafted in a general and vague manner, e.g. the right to fair trial, which does not specify the usual guarantees contained in other regional human rights treaties or in the ICCPR, such as the right to be informed of the charges brought against the person concerned, the right to speedy trial, the right to a public hearing, the right to appeal. Further, limitations imposed on the exercise of the rights refer to limitations 'within the law' (Article 9(2)), or 'in accordance with the law'(Articles 12(4) and 13(1). In other similar HRs treaties limitations are more precise, i.e. only allowed are those which are necessary in a democratic society to achieve a specific objective (see Chapter 12.7.2.1). Despite this, the African Commission on Human and Peoples' Rights (ACommHPR) has interpreted limitations such as those mentioned above in a manner similar to interpretations adopted by other HRs treaties bodies.[120] Further, this deficiency can be cured by the ACtHPR, which under Article 60 APCtHPR, should, in the interpretation of the Charter, pay due regard to the UDHR and other HRs treaties adopted by the UN and by African countries.

- Economic, cultural and social rights. The African Charter provides for the right to work under equitable and satisfactory conditions, and to receive equal pay for equal work; the right to the best attainable state of physical and mental health; the right to receive medical attention when in poor health; the right to education, and the freedom to take part in the cultural life of the community.

- 'Solidarity' rights. The Charter recognises the right to development, the right of peoples to the equal enjoyment of the common heritage of mankind, the right to peace and security and the right of peoples to a generally satisfactory environment favourable to their development.

The African Charter, by incorporating the above three types of HRs, enshrines the principle of the indivisibility and the interdependence of all HRs. Its preamble states:

> It is henceforth essential to pay particular attention to the right to development and that civil and political rights cannot be dissociated from economic, social and cultural rights in their conception as well as their universality and that the satisfaction of economic, social and cultural rights is a guarantee for the enjoyment of civil and political rights.[121]

---

120 E.g. *Media Rights Agenda v Nigeria*, Comm Nos 105/93, 128/94 and 152/96.
121 Para 8 of the Preamble.

Under Article 2 of the African Charter all rights and freedoms shall be enjoyed by individuals without any discrimination based on race, ethnic group, colour, sex, language, religion, political or any other opinion, national and social origin, birth or other status.

Another feature of the African Charter is that it imposes duties on individuals. Unlike other universal and regional HRs treaties, it puts a strong emphasis on duties of individuals, and this is reflected in the fact that a whole chapter of the Charter is devoted to them. Among the duties are the duty to preserve family, society, the State and the AU; the duty to consider another human being without discrimination; the duty to maintain relations aimed at promoting, safeguarding and reinforcing mutual respect and tolerance; and the duty to contribute, to the best of a person's abilities, at all times and at all levels, to the promotion and achievement of African Unity.

The Charter reflects the specificity of the African continent in terms of its perception of HRs and their enforcement. The importance of a strong feeling of community reflected in the social structures of African societies explains the emphasis on solidarity rights. The economic rights have a special place in the light of the underdevelopment of the continent. The references in the Charter to the 'unity and solidarity' of African people is directly connected to the African experience of colonialism. The initial 'weak' enforcement mechanism through the Commission, not a court, underlines the traditional African way of settlement of disputes through negotiation, conciliation and other non-judicial methods.

12.6.2 The enforcement of HRs in Africa

Two bodies have been created in Africa to ensure the promotion and protection of human and peoples' rights: the African Commission on Human and Peoples' Rights (ACommHPR), which was established in 1987, and the African Court of Human and Peoples' Rights (ACtHPR) which was established in 2004.

12.6.2.1 The ACommHPR

The guardian of the African Charter is the ACommHPR made up of 11 independent members elected by the Assembly of Heads of State and Government of the AU from a list submitted by the contracting parties to the Charter. The ACommHPR meets twice a year, usually for 15 days, in any location of its choice, although it often holds its sessions in Banjul (in The Gambia) where it has its headquarters. The ACommHPR may also, if necessary, convene extraordinary sessions. The ACommHPR may invite States, national liberation movements, specialised institutions, National Human Rights Institutions, NGOs and individuals to take part in its sessions.

The important feature of the ACommHPR is its close working relationship with NGOs which may request and obtain observer status with the Commission, allowing them to participate in Commission sessions, including the making of oral statements on items on the public agenda, to distribute documents during sessions, and to receive official documents of the Commission on a regular basis.[122] Approximately 300 NGOs have acquired observer status with the Commission. Any NGO may make proposals for inclusion of items on the provisional agenda of the Commission, submit information and comments regarding periodic State-reports (see below), request specific time to consult with the Commission and be invited by the Commission to participate in its sessions.

---

122   Resolution on the Cooperation between the African Commission on Human and Peoples' Rights and NGOs having Observer Status with the Commission (1998), ACommHPR Res 30(XXIV) 98.

The main functions of the ACommHPR are: to promote human rights and to assess the situations of violations, including inter-State and individual complaints; to interpret the Charter; and, since the establishment of the ACtHPR, to prepare submissions for the Court.

A. The ACommHPR as a promoter of HRs

The most important part of the promotional activities of the ACommHPR is the examination of periodic reports which contracting parties to the African Charter are required to submit every 2 years on measures taken with a view to implementing the rights and freedoms set out in the African Charter. Almost from its inception the ACommHPR decided that it was the proper body to examine these reports. The reporting system is similar to that established by other bodies monitoring the implementation of HRs treaties. Its main objective is to engage a contracting party in a constructive dialogue with the ACommHPR on how to achieve the full and effective implementation of the African Charter by a contracting party. Compliance of member States with the reporting obligation is weak. For example, the ACommHPR's Activity Report covering the period from April to October 2013 states that 7 out of 53 contracting parties had never submitted any report, while only 13 States have submitted and presented all reports.[123] Apart from lack of commitment on the part of States, there are other difficulties with the reporting system, such as lack of financial resources of a State to send a delegation to a session or to prepare a proper report; and lack of resources on the part of the ACommHPR to translate a report with the consequence that only some commissioners are able to read it.[124]

The ACommHPR, additionally, exercises its promotional functions by:

- appointing special rapporteurs or working groups to deal with a particular general topic, e.g. freedom of expression in Africa, or with a particular country;

- organising seminars, symposia and conferences;

- disseminating information on universal and regional human rights treaties and the mandate of the Commission concerning the implementation of the African Charter;

- co-operating with international, national and local institutions concerned with the promotion and protection of HRL.

B. The ACommHPR as a protector of HRs

As a protector of HRs the ACommHPR carries out its function in the following ways:

- Attending to communications submitted by individuals, groups of individuals, indigenous people, NGOs and State parties to the African Charter alleging violations of human rights by a contracting party. With regard to communications made by complainants other than States, it is very difficult to find information relating to the overall activities of the ACommHPR. However, its 35th Activity Report submitted to the AU Assembly covering the period from April to October 2013 shows that during that period it ACHPR received 11 new communications, adopted 12 decisions on admissibility and six decisions on merits.[125] As can been seen, the ACommHPR has not been

123   35th Activity Report of the African Commission on Human and Peoples' Rights, submitted in Conformity with Article 54 of the African Charter on Human and Peoples' Rights, 3, available at www.achpr.org/files/activity reports/35/achpr54eos14_actrep35_2014_eng.pdf (accessed 10 October 2014).

124   R. Murray, 'African Commission on Human and Peoples' Rights (ACommHPR)' in *Max Planck Encyclopedia of Public International Law*, Oxford University Press, 2008, online edition www.mpepil.com, paras 14 and 15 (accessed 7 October 2009).

125   Supra note 123, 25–26.

overwhelmed with complaints, probably because of a low level of awareness about the individual complaints procedure, its structural deficiencies, and the lack of any effective enforcement of its decisions on communications (see below). Bekker examines in depth failures of the ACommHPR, emphasising that the greatest is the Commission's refusal to provide genuine redress to victims of HRs violations.[126]

■ Writing 'Urgent Appeals' to contracting parties in response to allegations of HRs violations.

■ Setting up fact-finding missions.

■ Adopting resolutions on particular topics, e.g. the 2014 Resolution on Protection against Violence and Other Human Rights Violations against Persons on the Basis of Their Real or Imputed Sexual Orientation or Gender Identity,[127] or condemning a contracting party for violations of HRs, e.g. the 2014 Resolution on the Human Rights Situation in the Democtractic Republic of the Congo (DRC).[128]

The main problem with the ACommHPR is that it has no teeth. It may only examine situations, make reports and make recommendations. It has no enforcement powers. The only sanction against a State in breach of HRs is the publication of a report.

The real enforcement power lies with the Assembly of Heads of State and Government of the AU (AU Assembly) to which the ACommHPR forwards its decisions on the merits of all cases. This body has powers under the AU Act to force a Member State to comply with HRL. In this respect Article 30 of the AU Act states that any governments which 'come to power through unconstitutional means shall not be allowed to participate' in AU activities, and under Article 23(2) the AU may suspend membership and impose sanctions on a Member State which fails to comply with its decisions and policies. However, so far the AU Assembly has not shown any willingness to have recourse to meaningful enforcement measures in a situation where a State has refused to comply with a decision rendered by the ACommHPR.

It is important to note that the AU's membership covers the entire continent, 54 African States are members of the AU.

C.   The ACommHPR as an interpreter of the African Charter

With regard to interpretative function, the ACommHPR has fulfilled this with aplomb. In many instances it has been innovative, e.g. inferred from Article 55(1) of the African Charter that the term 'other communications', that is those which are not submitted by State parties, means communications from individuals and NGOs and as authorising it to deal not only with communications concerning 'flagrant and massive human rights violations' but also particular and sporadic violations of rights of individuals. The ACommHPR has taken the same broad approach to the interpretation of substantive rights.[129]

---

126   G. Bekker, *The African Commission on Human and Peoples' Rights and Remedies for Human Rights Violations* (2013) 13/3 Human Rights Law Review, 499.

127   Available at www.achpr.org/sessions/55th/resolutions/275 (accessed 12 September 2014).

128   Available at www.achpr.org/sessions/44th/resolutions/139 (accessed 12 September 2014).

129   E.g. see *The Social and Economic Action Center for Economic and Social Rights v Nigeria*, Comm No 155/96.

12.6.2.2 The ACtHPR

In 1998 the OAU adopted a Protocol to the African Charter establishing an African court to 'complement and reinforce the functions' of the Commission. The Protocol (hereafter referred to as the Protocol) entered into force on 25 January 2004, after receiving the 15 required ratifications.

The ACtHPR is made up of 11 judges who are elected for renewable 6-year terms. It is a part-time body located in Arusha, Tanzania. It has contentious and advisory jurisdiction.

A. Contentious jurisdiction
This is as follows:

1 *Ratione materiae.* Under Article 3(1) of the Protocol the Court has jurisdiction over all cases and disputes submitted to it concerning the interpretation and application of the Charter, the Protocol 'and any other relevant Human Rights instrument ratified by the states concerned'. This broad jurisdiction is confirmed by Article 7 of the Protocol entitled 'Sources of Law' which provides that the Court 'shall apply the provisions of the Charter and any other relevant human rights instruments ratified by the State concerned'. On the basis of the above provisions when a State party to proceedings has, for example, ratified the ICCPR, the Court is allowed to apply its provisions to a dispute;

2 *Ratione personae.* The ACtHPR has compulsory jurisdiction when the proceedings are brought by:

- the ACommHPR against:
  - (a) a State party against whom a complaint has been lodged before the ACommHPR,
  - (b) a State party, a national of which has allegedly been a victim of violation of his HRs;
  - (c) an African IGO;
- an individual and an NGO who has observer status with the ACommHPR.

However, the ACtHPR will have jurisdiction only if a State party consents, i.e. if a State party has made a declaration recognising the ACtHPR's competence to deal with cases brought by individuals and NGOs.

Under Article 5(3)(e) of the Protocol applicants may bypass proceedings before the ACommHPR and bring a case directly before the Court.

The Court's proceedings are public. The Court has jurisdiction to promote amicable settlement in cases pending before it. If such settlement does not occur, the ACtHPR must render a judgment within 90 days of finishing hearing a case. Judgments are come to by a majority vote, although judges are allowed to deliver a separate or dissenting opinion. If the ACtHPR finds that there has been violation of human or peoples' rights it must provide for remedies, including 'the payment of fair compensation or reparation' (Article 27(1) of the Protocol). The Court may also order provisional measures in cases of extreme gravity and urgency, and when necessary to avoid irreparable harm to persons. Contracting parties are bound to comply with a judgment. The Council of Ministers of the AU is charged with the task of monitoring compliance but it has no enforcement powers. However, the Court can report cases of non-compliance to the AU Assembly, which is the supreme political organ of the AU, and may take the necessary enforcement measures, in particular, under Article 23(2) AU Act.

B. Advisory jurisdiction
Under Article 4 of the Protocol the Court may deliver an advisory opinion on any legal matter relating to the Charter or any relevant human rights instrument at the request of any member State of the AU,

irrespective of whether that State is a party to the Protocol, the AU itself or any of its organs, and any organisation recognised by the AU. The only limitation is that the subject matter of the request must not be related to a communication under examination by the ACommHPR.

12.6.3 Assessment

The African regional arrangements for the promotion and protection of HRs are not very effective. The main problem is that there is no political will on the part of contracting parties to the African Charter to make it work, although the Preamble to the AU Act states that the contracting parties will take 'all necessary measures to strengthen [their] common institutions and provide them with the necessary powers and resources to enable them to discharge their respective mandates effectively'. Further, the ACommHPR lacks human, material, and financial resources. Obviously, some urgent action is needed because, as the ACommHPR stated in its 35th Activity Report, despite some positive developments that have taken place in Africa, the list of areas of concern is long and shows that the most serious abuses of HRs, such as torture, extra-judicial killing, disappearances, FGM, and child labour, are taking place in many contracting States.[130]

With regard to the Court, out of 26 States which have ratified the Protocol establishing the ACtHPR only seven have accepted its jurisdiction to receive cases from individuals and NGO's. From its inception to 1 December 2013, the Court received 29 applications and six requests for advisory opinions.[131] The low number of applications shows that the ACtHR has a long way to go before it is of any relevance to African peoples.

12.7 Regional arrangements for the promotion and protection of human rights – the European system

The main element of the European system for the protection of HRs is the 1950 European Convention for the Protection of Human Rights and Fundamental Freedoms (ECHR),[132] together with its enforcement mechanisms. The ECHR was prepared under the auspices of the Council of Europe (COE). In addition, the European Union (EU) is a stout defender and promoter of HRs and greatly contributes to the respect for HRs in the EU and worldwide.

12.7.1 The Council of Europe (COE)

The COE, which has its headquarters in the Palais de l'Europe, in Strasbourg, is one of the most efficient and competent IGOs in Europe. The Statute of the COE was signed in London on 5 May 1949.[133] At its inception it had only ten members. Now, it encompasses almost the entire European continent (the exception being Belarus) and, as at 10 October 2014, claimed a membership of 47 States. Only democratic States which ensure the protection of HRs may become members of the COE.

The main objectives of the COE are:

■ the promotion of European unity by proposing and encouraging common European action in economic, social, legal and administrative matters;

---

130   Ibid, 10–11.
131   See The Activity Report of the African Court for the Year 2013, EX.CL, 825(XXIV), 4.
132   213 UNTS 221.
133   CETS No 1.

- the protection of HRs, fundamental freedoms and pluralist democracies;

- the development of a European cultural identity.

Under the auspices of the COE, more than 200 conventions, agreements and protocols have been established, the majority of them are in force in member States, and hundreds of recommendations have been adopted in the light of which member States subsequently harmonise and modernise their own legislation.

The greatest achievement of the COE is undoubtedly the adoption of the ECHR based on Article 3 of the Statute of the COE under which a member State 'must accept the principles of the rule of law and of the enjoyment by all persons within its jurisdiction of human rights and fundamental freedoms'.

The ECHR[134] was opened for signature on 4 November 1950 and entered into force in September 1953. Since then additional protocols, which are separate treaties, have been adopted, adding further rights and liberties to those guaranteed by the Convention[135] or modifying the control mechanism established by the ECHR. As at 10 October 2014, 47 European States were contracting parties to the ECHR. The ECHR, together with its Protocols and procedures for enforcement, constitutes the first and the most efficient regional arrangement for the protection of HRs. The ECHR protects civil and political rights.

12.7.2   The ECHR

The ECHR recognises and protects the following rights and freedoms:

- Right to life (Article 2).

- Freedom from torture, cruel and inhuman treatment or punishment (Article 3).

- Freedom from slavery and forced labour (Article 4).

- Right to liberty and security (Article 5).

- Right to a fair trial (Article 6).

- Right to no punishment without law (Article 7).

- Right to respect for private and family life (Article 8).

- Freedom of thought, conscience and religion (Article 9).

- Freedom of expression (Article 10).

- Freedom of assembly and association (Article 11).

- Right to marry (Article 12).

---

134   CETS No 5.

135   Protocol 1 protects the right to property, education and free elections by secret ballots; Protocol 4 prohibits imprisonment for civil debts, provides for the right to free movement within a country, the right to leave any country, prohibits expulsion of nationals, and collective expulsion of foreigners; Protocol 6 abolishes the imposition of the death penalty in times of peace; Protocol 7 provides for additional rights concerning criminal proceedings, e.g. the right to appeal, the right to compensation for victims of miscarriages of justice, and in family matters, i.e. the right to equality between spouses; Protocol 12 prohibits discrimination; and Protocol 13 abolishes the death penalty at all times.

■ Right to an effective remedy (Article 13).

■ Prohibition of discrimination (Article 14).

Under Article 1 contracting States are obliged to secure to everyone within their jurisdiction the rights and freedoms contained in the ECHR.

12.7.2.1 Restrictions on the enjoyment and exercise of rights and freedoms protected under the ECHR

Some rights and freedoms protected under the ECHR, e.g. freedom from torture and from slavery, are absolute. Thus, no restrictions or derogations are permitted. However, most rights are subject to limitations and qualifications as follows:

■ Some restrictions are expressly authorised by the very article which sets out the relevant rights, e.g. Articles 8–11.

■ Some restrictions are contained in the articulation of the article, e.g. under Article 12 the right to marry is to be exercised in accordance with the national laws of a contracting party.

■ Some restrictions are formulated as specific exceptions in the article which sets out the right, e.g. Article 1 contains exceptions to the right to life which allows the use of lethal force in particular circumstances.

■ Some restrictions, which indicate the limits of the right guaranteed, are contained in the definition of the right, e.g. Article 4 ECHR defines the term 'forced or compulsory labour' as not including certain forms of work.

The principles relating to permissible restrictions are as follows:

■ Whatever the way in which restrictions are articulated, only the restrictions expressly authorised by the ECHR are allowed.

■ Under Article 18 restrictions permitted under the ECHR 'shall not be applied for any purpose other than those for which they have been prescribed'.

■ Any restrictions must satisfy the three-part test established by the ECtHR, under which a contracting State must show that:

■ the restriction is 'in accordance with the law' or 'prescribed by law'. This means that any interference with a protected right must be based on national law, statutory or unwritten, which is adequately accessible to citizens and formulated with sufficient precision to enable the citizen to regulate his conduct;[136]

■ the restriction seeks to achieve one of the specific legitimate aims. Those aims are set out in the relevant articles and are exhaustive, e.g. the protection of health or morals;

■ the restriction is necessary in a democratic society. What is necessary in a democratic society is assessed in the light of the principle of proportionality, i.e. whether the interference by public authority with the rights protected is no greater than is necessary to achieve the specific

---

136   *Sunday Times v UK* (1979) 2 EHRR 245, para 49.

legitimate aim. The ECtHR has established the doctrine of the margin of appreciation to decide whether a particular action of a State is necessary in a democratic society. Under this doctrine the Court has recognised that a contracting party enjoys a certain margin of discretion in the matter of the imposition of restrictions because it is in principle in a better position than the ECtHR to evaluate the particular local needs and conditions and to adequately address them. However, the decision of a contracting party is subject to review by the Court. In some instances a contracting party may enjoy a wide margin of appreciation, i.e. adopt measures considerably restricting the enjoyment of the right in question, and in others very little or no margin of appreciation, i.e. in respect of absolute rights or matters on which Europe-wide consensus has been reached, e.g. the abolition of the death penalty. The doctrine of margin of appreciation is very controversial because, on the one hand, it undermines the universality of HRs but, on the other, as Howard Davis states:

> Defenders of the margin of appreciation see it as recognising the reality of existence of different cultural and political standards in different countries which is necessary to ensure the continuing support of the Convention amongst governments and people. It also supports the Convention value of democracy by ensuring that, where appropriate, decisions are taken by elected or accountable bodies rather than handed over to judges.[137]

Article 15 of the ECHR provides that in times of war or other emergencies threatening the life of the nation, a contracting State is allowed to take measures derogating from its obligations to the 'extent strictly required by the exigencies of the situation, provided that such measures are not inconsistent with its other obligations under international law'. Furthermore, no derogations are permitted from Article 2, apart from those concerning deaths resulting from lawful acts of war, or from Articles 3, 4(1) and 7. A contracting State must inform the Secretary of the COE of the emergency measures taken as well as of their termination.

12.7.2.2 Interpretation of the ECHR

The ECtHR has interpreted the ECHR as a 'living instrument which . . . must be interpreted in the light of present-day conditions'[138] with a view to ensuring that rights protected under the ECHR are not theoretical and illusory but practical and effective.[139]

12.7.2.3 The scope of application of the ECHR ratione personae

There are two categories of applicants under the ECHR: contracting States and individuals.

- ■ Contracting States. Any contracting State is entitled to submit an application in respect of any alleged violation of the ECHR by another contracting State. The violation may be against any person, not necessarily a national of the complaining State. Also an application regarding an abstract situation, for example incompatibility of a State's legislation or administrative practices with the ECHR, is admissible. Inter-State applications have not proved to play an important role in the protection of HRs. Contracting States prefer not to get involved in a situation which is

---

137   H. Davis, *Human Rights Law, Directions*, 3rd edn, Oxford: Oxford University Press, 2013, 133.
138   *Tyrer v UK* (1978) 2 EHRR 1, para 31.
139   *Marckx v Belgium* (1989) 2 EHRR 330, para 31.

not of any direct concern to them. However, the ECtHR has dealt with inter-State applications on a number of occasions.[140]

■ Individuals. They have unfettered access to the ECtHR provided they meet the necessary admissibility criteria (see below). Individuals, under the ECHR encompass:

■ natural persons;

■ companies, but not their shareholders;[141]

■ NGOs.

There is no *actio popularis* under the ECHR. Therefore a group of persons or an IGO cannot bring proceedings unless it is a direct or potential victim of a violation of rights protected under the ECHR.

12.7.3 The ECtHR

The ECtHR was established in 1959. Between its inception and the end of 2013 the Court delivered more than 17,000 judgments. It oversees the protection of HRs of 800 million Europeans who live in the 47 States which have ratified the Convention. Its popularity is steadily growing. In 2013, the ECtHR dealt with 93,397 applications, more than half of which were against four member States: Russia, Italy, Ukraine and Serbia. On 1 December 2013, approximately 99,000 applications were pending before it.[142] In order to deal with the excessive caseload a new Protocol 15 has been adopted but, as at the time of writing, has not come into force (see Chapter 12.7.3.2). In 2013 the ECtHR was mainly seized of cases alleging violations of Article 6 ECHR (the right to a fair trial), Article 2 ECHR (the right to life) and 3 ECHR (the prohibition of torture and other similar treatment).[143]

The ECtHR is made up of 47 judges. The number of judges is the same as the number of contracting States. A judge sits in his individual capacity and does not represent any State. He must be of high moral standing, have relevant qualifications in his own country for holding a position of high office, and must act with total impartiality and independence.

Judges are nominated by contracting States and elected for 9 years by the General Assembly of the COE. They are not to be re-elected. A judge can be dismissed if two-thirds of the judges other than the judge in question consider that he has failed to maintain the standards required for being a judge.

The Court may sit in the following formations: as a single judge, but only to decide on admissibility of applications, as a Committee of three judges, as a Chamber of seven judges and as a Grand Chamber of 17 judges.

12.7.3.1 *Jurisdiction of the ECtHR*

The ECtHR exercises both contentious and advisory jurisdiction.

A. Contentious jurisdiction

The ECtHR exercises its contentious jurisdiction over inter-State and individual complaints. Inter-State applications are dealt with directly by a Chamber. All proceedings before the ECtHR are public;

---

140   E.g. *Ireland v UK* (1978) 2 EHRR 25 and *Cyprus v Turkey* (2002) 35 EHRR 30.

141   *Agrotexim v Greece* (1996) 21 EHRR 250.

142   See the official website of the ECtHR at www.echr.coe.int/Documents/Facts_Figures_2013_ENG.pdf (accessed 7 June 2014).

143   Ibid.

however, the judges deliberate in private and their deliberations are secret. The procedure before the ECtHR in respect of individual applications is as follows:

Admissibility procedure. The Court sitting in single judge formation decides on inadmissibility of applications. Most applications are disposed of by a single judge. His decision is final. If the application is not straightforwardly inadmissible it is forwarded to a Committee of three judges or a Chamber of seven judges. If a Committee disagrees on admissibility it forwards the application to a Chamber. There is no appeal when an application is declared inadmissible although the Committee or the Chamber dealing with the application on merits may consider admissibility if related to the merits.[144] The criteria of admissibility are:

- the applicant must be an alleged victim of a violation of his rights by a contracting party, and be either directly or potentially affected[145] by an act or omission on the part of a contracting State;

- there must be a *prima facie* violation of one or more of the provisions of the ECHR;

- the applicant must have exhausted domestic remedies;

- the application must have been lodged within six months of the final decision of the highest domestic court or authority;

- the application must not be anonymous;

- the application must not concern a factual situation the same as a factual situation that has already been examined by the ECtHR in an earlier case;

- if an applicant has not suffered any significant disadvantage as a result of any violation of his rights his application will be inadmissible. This is known as the 'significant disadvantage' criterion. The criterion is subject to the satisfaction of either of two safeguards. The first is that his case does not otherwise require an examination on the merits by the Court. The second is that he, even when his complaint is of a trivial nature, is not left without any judicial remedy. The second safeguard requires that no case may be rejected under this criterion which has not been duly considered by a domestic authority;

- the application must not concern issues which have been submitted to another procedure or international investigation or settlement;

- the application must not abuse the Convention system, e.g. this would be the case if an applicant repetitively submitted ill-founded and querulous complaints.

Procedure on the merits. Committees normally decide on admissibility. However, they may also decide on the merits in respect of cases which do not involve difficult issues of law, and thus well established principles of the ECHR will apply to them. In most cases, Committees deal with repetitive cases, i.e. cases which arise from the same structural defect at national level (a structural defect may relate to the existence of particular legislation or administrative practice capable of generating a significant number of repetitive applications). There is no appeal from decisions taken by Committees. Chambers normally decide cases on merits, although when a Committee disagrees on admissibility, the Chamber will decide on both. Chambers decide cases by majority vote, and judges are allowed to give separate,

---

144   *Yumak and Sadak v Turkey* (2009) 48 EHRR 4, para 72.
145   *Open Door Counselling v Ireland* (1993) 15 EHRR 244.

dissenting or concurrent judgments. There is an appeal procedure. Within three months of the judgment of a Chamber, any party may ask for a referral to a Grand Chamber. When this occurs, a panel of judges decides whether or not to allow an appeal to be made. The panel must be convinced that the 'case raises a serious question affecting the interpretation or application of the Convention or the protocols . . . or a serious issue of general importance'.[146] Therefore, an appeal will only be allowed to occur in exceptional circumstances. If the request to appeal is granted the Grand Chamber will examine the merits of the case and, by majority vote, give a final judgment. A Chamber may decide to relinquish jurisdiction in favour of a Grand Chamber where the case raises serious questions affecting the interpretation of the Convention. Such relinquishment is mandatory if there is a possibility of conflict with a previous judgment, unless one of the parties objects within one month of notification of the intention to relinquish.

B.   Advisory opinions.

The Committee of Ministers of the COE, which is made up of one representative from the government of each member State of the COE, usually the minister for foreign affairs,[147] may request advisory opinions from the ECtHR on the interpretation of the ECHR and its Protocols. An advisory opinion is given by the Grand Chamber by majority vote. Judges are allowed to submit a separate opinion or a simple statement of dissent.

Under Protocol 16 the highest domestic courts and tribunals of the contracting States will be allowed to request the ECtHR for advisory opinions on the interpretation and application of the ECHR and its Protocols. 10 ratifications are required for Protocol 16 to enter into force. It will apply only in respect of those States which have ratified it.

12.7.3.2   Enforcement of ECtHR's judgments

A final judgment is binding on the respondent State, and its execution is supervised by the Committee of Ministers of the COE. A judgment finding a breach of the ECHR is forwarded to the Committee of Ministers which then invites the respondent State to inform it of measures taken to comply with the judgment. This may include the payment of compensation/costs and expenses to the applicant and, if relevant, introducing measures into national law such as repealing, amending, enacting legislation to comply with the law as defined by the judgment. In order to ensure compliance with judgments delivered by the Court, the Committee of Ministers may decide, by a two-thirds majority, to bring proceedings before the Grand Chamber against any contracting party which, after having been given appropriate notice, refuses to comply with a final judgment. The Court will have jurisdiction to declare the failure of such a contracting party to fulfil its obligations under Article 46(1) ECHR. A special Department for the Execution of Judgments of the ECtHR has been established by the COE to assist the Committee of Ministers in the follow-up procedures.

12.7.3.3   Assessment

The ECHR is very popular with Europeans. This is because:

■   individuals have direct and automatic access to the ECtHR in respect of rights protected under the ECHR;

---

146   Article 43(2) ECHR.
147   Its composition and functions are governed by the Statute of the COE (Articles 13–21).

- individuals' applications are dealt with and decided by a judicial process;

- individuals can request an appeal;

- individuals' applications are dealt with speedily and cheaply, and there is even a possibility for an applicant to obtain legal aid from the COE;

- the Court sits on a full time basis; and

- acceptance of the judgment is compulsory for all contracting States and its execution is supervised by the Committee of Ministers of the COE.

However, the ECHR is a victim of its own success. Notwithstanding the entry into force of Protocols 11 and 14, which have greatly enhanced effectiveness of the mechanism for dealing with individual complaints under the ECHR, the ECtHR can hardly cope with the increasing number of applications. For that reason the ECtHR has been engaged in a process of reform which started in 2010 and is expected to end in 2015.[148] So far the outcome of the reform process is the adoption of Protocols 15 and 16 (see Chapter 12.7.3.1.B).

With regard to Protocol 15, its entry into force requires ratification by all 47 contracting States. The main amendments proposed by Protocol 15 are:[149]

- changes to the Preamble of the ECHR. It will make reference to the doctrine of the margin of appreciation (see Chapter 12.7.2.1) and to the principle of subsidiarity. The last mentioned emphasises that the primary responsibility for enforcement of rights protected by the ECHR lies with a contracting State;

- the tightening of the admissibility criteria, first, the time-limit for lodging individual applications will be reduced from six months to four months of final domestic decision, and second with regard to the 'significant disadvantage' criterion (see Chapter 12.7.3.1) the proviso that the case has been duly considered by a domestic tribunal will be removed; and

- the removal of the possibility for one of the parties to object when a Chamber seeks to relinquish jurisdiction to the Grand Chamber.

12.7.4 The European Union (EU) and HRs

In the EU the protection of HRs has acquired two dimensions, internal and external.

So far as the internal dimension is concerned, the EU, when exercising its internal competences, deals with HRs on a daily basis. This is especially the case in the area of gender discrimination and social policy where the protection conferred by EU law upon EU citizens goes far beyond that which the national law of most member States provides. Further, HRs are envisaged in a broad context in respect of all EU policies as being part of the general principles of EU law, which principles have resulted in amendments to the EU Treaties. The most recent, the Treaty of Lisbon, which entered into force on 1 December 2009, requires the EU to accede to the ECHR and makes the Charter of Fundamental Rights of the European Union a binding document.

---

148 For details see the official website of the ECtHR.

149 See the Explanatory Report to Protocol 15 and other relevant documents on the official website of the ECtHR. Views of the leading international human rights NGOs on the proposed amendments can be found at: www.hrw.org/sites/default/files/related_material/2013_Europe_Joint%20NGO%20Statement%20ECHR.pdf (accessed 10 May 2014).

The Charter contains 50 articles. Its main purpose is to make fundamental rights and freedoms more visible, more explicit and more familiar to EU citizens. The Charter expresses the fundamental human values shared by all member States. Unlike the ECHR, it contains not only civil and political but also economic, social and societal rights. The main criticism concerns the scope of application of the Charter. It is addressed to the institutions of the EU and the member States 'only when they are implementing EU law' and Article 6(1) TEU emphasises that the Charter neither extends the scope of application of EU law, nor creates any new competences for the EU, nor any new tasks for the Union.

As to the accession of the EU to the ECHR, the Draft Revised Agreement on the Accession of the European Union to the Convention for the Protection of Human Rights and Fundamental Freedoms,[150] which was a result of the Fifth Negotiation Meeting between the Council of Europe's Human Rights Steering Committee's *ad hoc* Negotiation Group and the European Commission, is being assessed by the European Court of Justice in terms of its compatibility with EU law.[151] If the Court delivers a favourable opinion then only some formal steps will need to be completed before the EU accedes to the ECHR.[152]

With regard to external competences, the grant of development aid and other forms of assistance or co-operation with a third State are subject to observance by that State of HRL. This is in accordance with Article 21 TEU which confirms that in external matters, the EU should seek to advance worldwide indivisibility of HRs, respect for human dignity, the principle of equality, solidarity, and principles on which the UN is based.

12.8 General conclusions

Efforts made by the international community to ensure the protection of HRs are certainly encouraging, but those efforts must be assessed in the light of what many nations are actually doing. The respect for HRs must not and should not be confined to mere declarations. So far as the UN system is concerned, its effectiveness in enforcing HRs is weak for many reasons, the most important being:

- the monitoring system is not mandatory, apart from the URP, and until it is mandatory many States will not submit themselves to any external scrutiny;

- there is no judicial mechanism within the UN to deal with individual complaints regarding violations of HRs;

- the reporting and monitoring system is, in many cases, confidential;

- the UNSC has not taken any consistent and firm stand in respect of States violating basic HRs. Regrettably, the principle of non-interference in domestic matters, and the political assessment of human rights situations, often prevail. The current attempts to formulate and enforce the right to protect (R2P) is selective and based on political interests of permanent members of the UNSC (see Chapter 16.2.7).

---

150   The Draft Revised Agreement is attached in Appendix I to the Final Report to the Council of Europe's Human Rights Steering Committee, 47+1(2013)008rev2, and available at: www.coe.iint/t/dghl/standardsetting/hrpolicy/Accession/Meeting_reports/47_1(2013)008rev2_EN.pdf (accessed 4 March 2014).

151   The European Commission, Request for an Opinion of 4 July 2013, SJ.F (2012) 2701339.

152   On the topic of accession of the EU to the ECHR see T. Schilling, *On Equal Footing: The Participation Rights Envisaged for the European Union After Its Accession to the European Convention on Human Rights* (2014) 14/2 Human Rights Law Review, 197.

At the regional level (apart from Europe where the protection of HRs is well advanced) there is a very large credibility gap between promises, which are easy to make, and performance, which either seems to be very hard to effect or in respect of which there is not the will to carry through.

RECOMMENDED READING

Books

Clapham, A., *Human Rights Obligations of Non-State Actors*, Oxford: Oxford University Press, 2006.

Davis, H., *Human Rights Law, Directions*, 3rd edn, Oxford: Oxford University Press, 2013.

Freedman, R., *The United Nations Human Rights Council: A Critique and an Early Assessment*, London/New York: Routledge, 2013.

Harris, P.J., O'Boyle, M., Warbrick, C., Bates, E. and Buckley, C., *Law of the European Convention on Human Rights*, 2nd edn, Oxford: Oxford University Press, 2009.

Joseph, S., Schultz, J., and Castan, M., *The International Covenant on Civil and Political Rights: Cases, Materials, and Commentary*, 2nd edn, Oxford: Oxford University Press, 2004.

Ledesma, H.F. ,*The Inter-American System for the Protection of Human Rights*, 3rd edn, Inter-American Institute of Human Rights: San Jose, 2008.

Nowak, M. and McArthur, E., *The United Nations Convention against Torture, A Commentary*, Oxford: Oxford University Press, 2008.

Steiner, A.J., Alston, P. and Goodman, R., *International Human Rights in Context, Law, Politics, Morals*, 3rd edn, Oxford: Oxford University Press, 2007.

Senyonjo, M. (ed.), *The African Regional Human Rights System. 30 Years after the African Charter on Human and Peoples' Rights*, Brill/Nijhoff, 2011.

Tomuschat, C., *Human Rights: Between Idealism and Realism*, 2nd edn, Oxford: Oxford University Press, 2008.

Articles

Bekker, G., *The African Commission on Human and Peoples' Rights and Remedies for Human Rights Violations* (2013) 13/3 Human Rights Law Review, 499.

Bianchi, A., *Human Rights and the Magic of Jus Cogens* (2008) 19 EJIL, 491.

Dulitzky, A., *Too Little, Too Late: The Pace of Adjudication of The Inter-American Commission on Human Rights* (2013) 35 Loy L A Int'L and Comp L Rev, 131.

Feria Tinta, M., *Justiciability of Economic, Social, and Cultural Rights in the Inter-American System of Protection of Human Rights: Beyond Traditional Paradigms and Notions*, (2007) 29 Hum Rts Q 431.

Hannum, H., *Human Rights in Conflict Resolution: The Role of the Office of the High Commissioner for Human Rights in United Nations Peacemaking and Peacebuilding*, (2006) 28(1) Hum Rts Q, 1.

Schilling, T., *On Equal Footing: The Participation Rights Envisaged for the European Union after Its Accession to the European Convention on Human Rights* (2014) 14/2 HR L Rev, 197.

Upton, H., *The Human Rights Council: First Impressions and Future Challenges* (2007) 7 HR L Rev, 29.

Waltz, S., *Universalizing Human Rights* (2001) 23 Hum Rts Q, 44.

AIDE-MÉMOIRE

An overview of the international protection of HRs

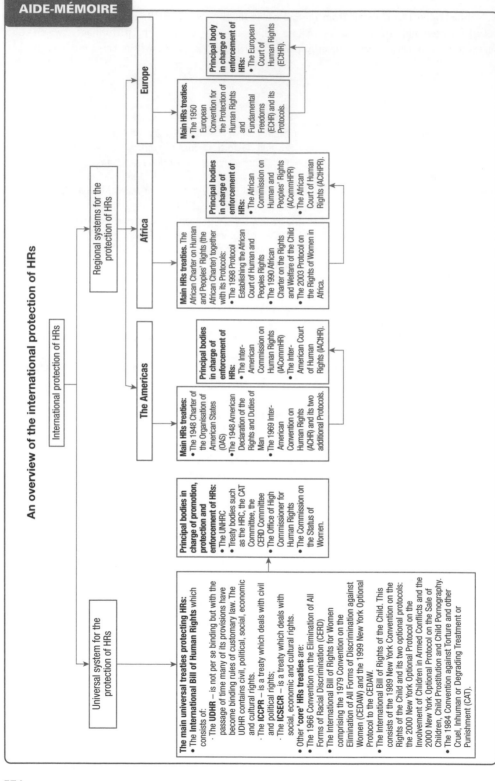

International protection of HRs

Universal system for the protection of HRs

The main universal treaties protecting HRs:
- The **International Bill of Human Rights** which consists of:
  · The **UDHR** – is not per se binding but with the passage of time many of its provisions have become binding rules of customary law. The UDHR contains civil, political, social, economic and cultural rights.
  · The **ICCPR** – is a treaty which deals with civil and political rights;
  · The **ICSECR** – is a treaty which deals with social, economic and cultural rights.
- Other '**core**' **HRs treaties** are:
- The 1966 Convention on the Elimination of All Forms of Racial Discrimination (CERD)
- The International Bill of Rights for Women comprising the 1979 Convention on the Elimination of All Forms of Discrimination against Women (CEDAW) and the 1999 New York Optional Protocol to the CEDAW.
- The International Bill of Rights of the Child. This consists of the 1989 New York Convention on the Rights of the Child and its two optional protocols: the 2000 New York Optional Protocol on the Involvement of Children in Armed Conflicts and the 2000 New York Optional Protocol on the Sale of Children, Child Prostitution and Child Pornography.
- The 1984 Convention against Torture and other Cruel, Inhuman or Degrading Treatment or Punishment (CAT).

Principal bodies in charge of promotion, protection and enforcement of HRs:
- The UNHRC
- Treaty bodies such as the HRC, the CAT Committee, the CERD Committee
- The Office of High Commissioner for Human Rights
- The Commission on the Status of Women.

Regional systems for the protection of HRs

The Americas

Main HRs treaties:
- The 1948 Charter of the Organisation of American States (OAS)
- The 1948 American Declaration of the Rights and Duties of Man
- The 1969 Inter-American Convention on Human Rights (ACHR) and its two additional Protocols.

Principal bodies in charge of enforcement of HRs:
- The Inter-American Commission on Human Rights (IACommHR)
- The Inter-American Court of Human Rights (IACtHR).

Africa

Main HRs treaties. The African Charter on Human and Peoples' Rights (the African Charter) together with its Protocols:
- The 1998 Protocol Establishing the African Court of Human and Peoples Rights
- The 1990 African Charter on the Rights and Welfare of the Child
- The 2003 Protocol on the Rights of Women in Africa.

Principal bodies in charge of enforcement of HRs:
- The African Commission on Human and Peoples' Rights (ACommHPR)
- The African Court of Human Rights (ACtHPR).

Europe

Main HRs treaties.
- The 1950 European Convention for the Protection of Human Rights and Fundamental Freedoms (ECHR) and its Protocols.

Principal body in charge of enforcement of HRs:
- The European Court of Human Rights (ECtHR).

13

SELF-DETERMINATION OF PEOPLES

CONTENTS

CHAPTER OUTLINE

1 Introduction

The concept of self-determination refers to the right of a people to determine its own political destiny. This can be achieved through:

- internal self-determination which gives peoples the right to participate in the conduct of their common affairs within a State and to pursue political, economic, social and cultural development without outside interference. Internal self-determination means that people living within a State have the right to have a government which represents all of them without any discrimination. However, it is uncertain whether the right to democratic governance is part of international law;

■ External self-determination which gives peoples the right to secede from the existing State either to create a new State or to be incorporated into or to associate with another State. As a result, external self-determination challenges the national unity and territorial integrity of a State and, when people are using force to exercise their right, poses a threat to international peace and security. International law has recognised the right of colonial people to external self-determination. However, outside the context of decolonisation, the scope of the principle of external self-determination is uncertain. Notwithstanding this, State practice suggests that it applies:

　　■ in situations where a territorial sovereignty is lacking, either because the State is in the process of formation or because it is undergoing transformation or dissolution;

　　■ when parties agree that the principle of self-determination will apply to settlement of a territorial dispute between them, e.g. the 1919 Treaty of Versailles and the case of East Timor as confirmed by the ICJ in *East Timor (Portugal v Australia)*; and

　　■ in situations where people live under foreign domination, e.g. Palestinians living in the occupied territory.

Peoples who, under international law, have the right to self-determination are entitled to use armed force to achieve external self-determination. The issue of whether, in some circumstances, the right to internal self-determination may transform itself into the right to external self-determination has been highly debated since Kosovo's 2008 unilateral declaration of independence from Serbia.

2　The evolution of the principle of self-determination: from a political concept to a legal concept

In the evolution of the principle of self-determination two periods can be distinguished. The first period is the period up to the end of WWII during which time self-determination was regarded as a political principle, and the second is the period after the end of WWII when the principle of self-determination became a legal principle.

3　Decolonisation

The 1960 Declaration on the Granting of Independence to Colonial Countries and Peoples (UNGA Resolution 1514 (XV)) constitutes the foundation in international law of the right to self-determination. It calls for immediate emancipation of colonial peoples 'without any condition or reservation in order to allow them to enjoy full independence' and irrespective of the stage of their political, economic social or educational development.

Resolution 1514 (XV) has been further developed by numerous UNGA resolutions. In particular, by Resolution 1541 (XV) which provides that the right to self-determination may be exercised by the peoples concerned, through voting in free and fair elections, in three ways:

■ they may decide to constitute themselves as a sovereign independent State;

■ they may decide to associate freely with an independent State;

■ they may integrate with an independent State already in existence.

In order to transform Resolution 1514 into an instrument for action the UNGA set up the Special Committee of Twenty-Four. Its task is to examine the application of the 1960 Declaration and to make recommendations on its implementation.

4   The limit of the right to self-determination in the colonial context

The principle of *uti possidetis* imposes a limitation on the exercise of the right to self-determination by colonial people. Colonial borders are to be maintained even though they were artificially drawn by colonial powers without any consideration of the ethnic or historical tradition of the people or peoples living in that area. This limitation has been confirmed in UNGA Resolution 2625, by African leaders in the 1964 Cairo Declaration and the case law of the ICJ, e.g. in the *Case Concerning the Frontier Dispute (Burkina Faso v Republic of Mali)*.

5   The extension of the right to self-determination to people living under racist regimes and foreign domination

Until the end of the Cold War the international community rarely agreed to recognise the existence of the right to self-determination beyond the context of decolonisation. The rare occasions when this did occur concerned black and coloured people living in South Africa under the system of racial separation called apartheid (apartness) and peoples living in occupied territories such as the Palestinians, or the inhabitants of Afghanistan after the Russian invasion of that country in 1979.

6   The right to self-determination as a human right

International law recognises that the right to self-determination constitutes a fundamental human right, and applies to all people. It is a collective right and under Article 1(3) common to the ICCPR and the ICSECR it is granted to all people, not only to colonial people, people subjected to a racist regime, or foreign or alien domination. Despite the clear recognition of the right to self-determination as a fundamental human right the reality is that in circumstances where a people wishes to secede from a State of which they form part (and this is almost the only circumstance in which the right has any relevance) the international community has been extremely reluctant to recognise or support their right. This being the case even in circumstances where the people concerned were victims of extreme oppression, and thus their physical existence as a 'people' was seriously threatened.

7   Self-determination in the post-Cold War era

With the collapse of communism, old States, e.g. the Soviet Union and the Socialist Federal Republic of Yugoslavia (the SFRY), ceased to exist and were replaced by new States created on the territory of the old States, and minority groups living within those old or newly created States started to demand political rights ranging from internal autonomy to secession. In these circumstances claims of indigenous peoples to self-determination gained a new momentum. The complexity of these issues has emphasised the controversies surrounding the right to self-determination. This right, therefore, must be examined in different contexts:

A.   Dissolution of a State and self-determination. International law recognises the right to dissolve a State in a peaceful way and to create new States on the territory of the former State. The agreement of all parties concerned is at the centre of this principle. The right to self-determination also applies to dissolution of a State by force and the subsequent creation of a new State or States on the territory of the former State. With regard to the dissolution of the SFRY, the international community has always maintained the view that the right to self-determination was granted to the inhabitants of each of its republics as a whole and not to each minority grouping living within a particular republic. However, the case of Kosovo challenges this view.

B. *Uti possidetis* and self-determination. Apart from the case of Kosovo, the principle of *uti possidetis* has always been applied with the consequence that the right to self-determination must not involve changes to existing frontiers (either international or internal e.g. in the case of the SFRY pre-existing frontiers between the republics) at the time of independence except where the States concerned agree otherwise.

C. Peoples and self-determination. Apart from colonial peoples, international law is unclear as to who are 'people' or 'peoples' entitled to exercise the right to external self-determination.

D. Minorities and self-determination. International law refuses to grant minority groups living within a State the right to secession, but ensures that their rights as minorities are respected. The main reason why secession is unlawful is that if the right to secession were to be granted to minorities this would threaten the stability of the State concerned as well as the stability of the international legal order in that one secession would lead to another and could result in the creation of numerous new States. It has been stated that international law should treat oppressed minorities differently from minorities living in a democratic State which respects their right to internal self-determination. So far, State practice has not followed this approach, although the case of Kosovo, if it becomes a precedent, may change the position.

E. Indigenous people and self-determination. Indigenous people are most entitled to be considered as 'people' as they have been the longest victims of colonisation. Despite this, under international law they are not considered as colonial people and have only been granted the right to internal self determination as evidenced by the 2007 Declaration on the Rights of Indigenous Peoples. However, they may become 'people' entitled to external self-determination in cases of extreme oppression if the example of Kosovo becomes a precedent.

8 Conclusion

Self-determination is a complex right which has an internal and external aspect. As a result, it entails different levels of entitlement to political emancipation for 'people' or 'peoples' ranging from the right to exercise meaningful political participation within a State to the right to external self-determination by way of secession. However, international law remains unclear as to the exact meaning and scope of the right to self-determination. Only in the context of decolonisation, provided one is not too precise about the definition of 'decolonisation', is self-determination clearly recognised as a legal right. It is submitted that as claims to self-determination are not abating, it is necessary for the international community to develop a more comprehensive and coherent approach.

13.1 Introduction

There is universal agreement that the concept of self-determination refers to the right of a people to determine its own political destiny. Beyond this vague definition it can be said that in some guises the concept of self-determination exists in a clearly defined form; in others it is ambiguous and uncertain. It has throughout history meant different things to different people and continues to do so today. It was invoked by the founding fathers of the US, the French revolutionaries, Lenin and Wilson during WWI, Gandhi and Nkrumah in the period of decolonisation, and is today relied upon by various groups such as ETA, the Chechens, the Kurds, and the Sri Lankan Tamils, and by many minorities that are seeking to secede from existing States. The right to self-determination has both justified the establishment of new States and, at a later time, justified the disintegration of some of those same States. Because the application of the right undermines the sovereignty and territorial integrity of States it challenges the stability of the international community.

There are two basic theories on self-determination:

■ One links the concept of self-determination with the existence of a State-decision procedure which allows peoples to participate in the conduct of their common affairs within a State. According to this theory a nation, being an artificial community, is composed of individuals linked by the existence of such a State-decision procedure. A nation identifies with a State. The presence and proper functioning of a decision-making procedure constitutes the essence of the right to self-determination.

■ The other theory is more romantic. It emphasises the importance of nationhood as the common identification of a people or a nation and minimises the role of statehood. Nationhood is much more than a decision-making procedure.

There is a conflict between the two theories which international law has, to date, failed to resolve. Koskenniemi has described this conflict as follows:

National self-determination, has an ambiguous relationship with statehood as the basis of the international legal order. On the one hand, it supports statehood by providing an explanation for why we should honour existing *de facto* boundaries and the acts of the state's power-holders as something other than gunman's orders. On the other hand, it explains that statehood *per se*, embodies no particular virtue and that even as it is useful as a presumption about the authority of a particular territorial rule, that presumption may be overruled or its consequences modified in favour of a group or unit finding itself excluded from those positions of authority in which the sustenance of the rule is determined:[1]

In international law these two theories represent the two aspects of self-determination: internal and external.

■ Internal self-determination means that peoples have the right to participate in the conduct of their common affairs within a State in order to pursue their economic, social and cultural development without outside interference. They have the right to have a government which represents all of them without any discrimination 'as to race, creed, or colour'.[2] The Supreme Court of Canada in *Reference re Secession of Quebec* in answering the question of whether Quebec had the right to secede from Canada stated that international law recognises that 'the

---

1   M. Koskenniemi, *National Self-determination Today: Problems of Legal Theory and Practice* (1994) 43 ICLQ, 248.

2   Principal 5 of the Declaration on Principles of International Law concerning Friendly Relations and Co-operation among States in Accordance with the Charter of the United Nations, UNGA Res 2625 (XXV) (24 October 1970) GAOR 25th Session Supp 28, 121.

right to self-determination is normally fulfilled through internal self-determination'.[3] However, it is uncertain whether the right to democratic governance is part of international law.[4] International law has recognised that in situations where people live under racist regimes, e.g. black and coloured people living in South Africa under the regime of racial segregation known as apartheid (which existed from 1948 to1994). They have the right to internal self-determination.[5]

■ External self-determination concerns a situation where people exercise the right to self-determination by seceding from the existing State either to create a new State or to be incorporated into, or to associate with, another State. As a result, external self-determination challenges the national unity and territorial integrity of a State and, other than in situations where all involved parties agree to separation (e.g. the dissolution of Czechoslovakia or the break up of the Soviet Union), entails the use of force by the people concerned, which in turn poses a threat to international peace and security. International law has recognised the right of colonial peoples to external self-determination. They are entitled to use force to achieve self-governance, and any use of force to prevent the realisation of self-determination is unlawful.[6] However, outside the context of decolonisation, the content of the principle of self-determination is uncertain. There is no agreement as to who are to be regarded as a 'people' entitled to exercise the right nor as to how to identify, in any particular set of circumstances, who belongs to a 'people', e.g. for the purpose of participating in a referendum or a plebiscite. Whether or not, and to what extent, the right to self-determination applies in circumstances other than decolonisation is subject to substantial controversy. However, State practice suggests that the right to external self-determination exists in the following situations:

■ where territorial sovereignty is lacking, either because the State is in the process of formation or because it is undergoing transformation or dissolution;

■ where parties agree that the principle of self-determination will apply to settlement of a dispute between them, e.g. the 1919 Treaty of Versailles and in, and, more recently, the Comprehensive Peace Agreement signed between the Government of Sudan and the Sudan People's Liberation Movement/Sudan People's Liberation Army[7] as well as the case of East Timor where the parties concerned agreed that the people of East Timor had the right to self-determination;[8]

■ where people live under foreign domination, e.g. Palestinians living in the occupied territory.

The issue of whether, in some circumstances, the right to internal self-determination may transform itself into the right to external self-determination has been highly debated (see Chapter 13.7.3).

In this chapter the right to self-determination is examined from a historical perspective, its content is analysed in the context of decolonisation and, finally, its relevance and application to the post-Cold War era is explored.

---

3   The Supreme Court of Canada (20 August 1998) (1998) 2 Canada Supreme Court Reports 217, para 126.
4   R. Burchill (ed.), *Democracy and International Law*, Aldershot: Ashgate, 2006.
5   E.g. UNGA Resolution 2775E (XXVI) of 29 November 1971.
6   See J. Crawford, *The Creation of States in International Law*, Oxford: Oxford University Press, 2006, 134–149.
7   The agreement is available at: http://peacemaker.un.org/sites/peacemaker.un.org/files/SD_060000_The%20 Comprehensive%20Peace%20Agreement.pdf (Accessed 7 October 2014).
8   In the *East Timor Case (Portugal v Australia)* [1995] ICJ Rep 90, the ICJ stated that as both parties to the dispute agreed that the people of East Timor were entitled to exercise the right to external self-determination, the population of East Timor was a 'people', paras 31 and 37.

13.2 The evolution of the principle of self-determination: from a political concept to a legal concept

In the evolution of the principle of self-determination two periods can be distinguished. The first is the period up to the end of WWII during which time self-determination was regarded as a political principle and the second is the period after the end of WWII when the principle of self-determination became a legal principle.

13.2.1 Self-determination before 1945

Self-determination as a political concept was for the first time invoked by two revolutionary movements that succeeded in their aspirations. The American War of Independence and the French Revolution both legitimated new governments on the basis of defending the inalienable right of people to organise their own government which, in turn, having been established on the basis of peoples' consent, was accountable to them.

The French National Assembly stated on 17 November 1792 that:

> In the name of the French people, the National Assembly declares that it will give help and support to all peoples wanting to recall their freedom. Therefore, the Assembly considers the French authorities responsible to give orders to grant all means of assistance to those people, to protect and compensate the citizens who might be injured during their fight for the cause of liberty.[9]

The concept of self-determination played an important role in the formation of European nations in the nineteenth century. At that time national liberation movements were relying on it to claim that every nation has the right to become an independent State and that only homogeneous States in terms of their population were legitimate States. This 'national' self-determination led to the unification of Germany in 1870, the establishment of Greece in 1827 and other European States in the nineteenth century and after WWI. However, colonisation was legitimated by international law e.g. by the Treaty of Berlin of 28 February 1885.[10]

Towards the end of WWI US President W. Wilson, in his Fourteen Point Address to the US Congress on 8 January 1918, presented his vision of the post-war world. This was based on idealistic ideas intended to ensure lasting peace. In his speech he embraced the concept of self-determination. He emphasised that the new world order must respect the 'voice of people'. However, the content of his concept of self-determination was vague. It referred to democratic forms of government, defined as government by consent of people, rather than to the right to self-determination.[11] Although his concept applied to all people, in reality it was only relevant to European people living in the territories of defeated nations. He advocated that national aspirations of oppressed minorities and ethnic nationalities living in these territories should be given 'the utmost satisfaction' in terms of becoming independent States. However, he also emphasised that this should be done 'without introducing new or perpetuating old elements of discord and antagonism'.[12]

---

9   J.E.S. Hayward, *After the French Revolution: Six Critics of Democracy and Nationalism*, New York, London: Harvester Wheatsheaf, 1991.

10   Convention Revising the General Act of Berlin, 26 February 1885, and the General Act and Declaration of Brussels, 2 July 1890 (signed 10 September 1919, entered into force 31 July 1920) 8 LNTS 26.

11   N.G. Levin, *Woodrow Wilson and World Politics: America's Response to War and Revolution*, New York: Oxford University Press, 1968, 247–251.

12   A. Whelan, *Wilsonian Self-Determination and the Versailles Settlement* (1994) 43 ICLQ, 102.

The Wilsonian perception of self-determination was reflected in the 1919 Treaty of Versailles which:

■ granted statehood to identifiable peoples;

■ provided that territorial disputes concerning the boundaries of newly created States should be settled on the basis of plebiscites;

■ set up a system of protection for ethnic minorities which were too small to be accorded statehood. The system of protection of minorities was supervised by the Council of the League of Nations (see Chapter 12.1).

The issue of colonialism was directly addressed in the fifth point of Wilson's Address where he advocated impartial adjustment of all colonial claims. According to President Wilson, in settlement of those claims the interests of the populations concerned must have equal weight with the equitable claims of the governments whose title was to be determined. Indirectly, it was understood that the concept of self-determination, which inspired great expectations for colonial people, may apply to colonies, but this would be through a gradual process of tutelage and reform, not by immediately granting to colonial people the right to self-determination. The practical consequence of the application of the concept of self-determination to colonial people was the creation of the mandate system under the League of Nations in relation to colonies of the defeated powers. They became property of the League and were allocated to the Allied powers for tutelage. In respect of such territories the 'advanced nations' were to exercise their tutelage under the principle that 'the well-being and development of such people form a sacred trust of civilisation'.[13] The Council of the League of Nations was responsible for supervising the mandate system. The terms of each mandate were agreed between the Council and each mandatory, but without any consultation with the local population concerned.

The territories under mandate were divided into three categories.

■ Mandate A. These territories were considered nearly ready for self-government. They were the former Turkish territories, Lebanon and Syria which were placed under French mandate, and Iraq, Palestine and Trans-Jordan which were placed under British mandate. All Mandate A territories (other than Palestine) became sovereign States between 1932 and 1947.

■ Mandate B. These constituted territories in Africa that had belonged to Germany before WWI. The Council regarded them as being further away in time from attaining self-government than Mandate A territories. Mandate B territories were as follows: Togoland which was divided into two territories, one governed by France and one by the UK, Cameroons which was also split between France and the UK; and German East Africa, which was split between the UK (Tanganyika) and Belgium (Ruanda-Urundi).

■ Mandate C. The territories which were considered by the Council as being incapable of self-government in the then foreseeable future. Mandatories were allowed to govern Mandate C territories as an integral part of their own territory because of the small population of Mandate C territories or because of their contiguity to the mandatory's territory. Mandate C territories were: the former German colonies of South West Africa which were placed under the tutelage of South Africa; the Marianas, Caroline and Marshall Islands which were mandated to Japan; German Samoa which was allocated to New Zealand, German New Guinea which was mandated to Australia and Nauru which was placed under the mandate of the UK, but was actually administered by Australia and New Zealand.

---

13   Article 22 of the Covenant of the League of Nations.

All Mandate B and C territories except South West Africa became, in due course, trust territories under the UN trusteeship system (see Chapter 13.2.2.1).

The principle of self-determination was examined by the Council of the League of Nations in the *Åland Islands Case.*[14]

ÅLAND ISLANDS CASE

Facts:

The Åland Islands were ceded by Sweden to Russia in 1809. When Finland achieved independence from Russia in 1917, the islands became part of Finland but their inhabitants, 92 per cent of whom were of Swedish origin, requested Sweden to support their claim to return to Swedish jurisdiction. Finland refused to hold a plebiscite and claimed that the matter was within its exclusive domestic jurisdiction. Under Article 15 of the Covenant of the League of Nations disputes between members of the League were to be brought before the Council in certain circumstances and the Council could hear the facts and make recommendations. Disputes within the domestic jurisdiction of a party to the dispute were excluded from the scope of Article 15. In respect of the dispute concerning the Åland Islands the Council set up a Commission of Jurists charged with the preparation of an advisory opinion on whether or not the matter was within the scope of Article 15, Following the Report of the Commission of Jurists the Council established a second body, a Commission of Rapporteurs, to give advice on the same matter.

Held:

The Commission of Jurists
The Commission of Jurists decided that the dispute was outside the exclusive domestic jurisdiction of Finland because, first, the government of Finland was not sufficiently established and, second, the dispute between Sweden and Finland did not concern 'a definitive established political situation depending exclusively upon the territorial sovereignty of a state'. Further, the Commission of Jurists stated that the principle of self-determination was not a rule of law and that in a situation where territorial sovereignty is lacking, either because a State is in the process of formation or because it is undergoing transformation or dissolution 'the principle of self-determination of peoples may be called into play'. However, it did not apply to the dispute at hand because other considerations e.g. economic, geographic and the interests of peace, required a compromise 'based on an extensive grant of liberty to minorities'.[15]

The Commission of Rapporteurs
The Commission of Rapporteurs, as did the Commission of Jurists before it, confirmed that self-determination of people was not a general rule of international law, but concluded that

---

14   (1920) LNOJ Spec Supp No 3, 3.
15   League of Nations 'Report of the International Committee of Jurists Entrusted by the Council of the League of Nations with the Task of Giving an Advisory Opinion upon the Legal Aspects of the Aaland Islands Question' (October 1920) League of Nations Official Journal, vol 1, Special Supplement No 3.

> *although the dispute was, in principle, within the domestic jurisdiction of Finland, it was also within the competence of the Council because 'it had acquired such considerable international importance that it was necessary to submit it to the high authority which the League of Nations represents in the eyes of the world'.*
>
> *The Commission of Rapporteurs stated that in exceptional circumstances and as a remedy of last resort 'when a State lacks either the will or the power to enact and apply just and effective guarantees'[16] a minority living within the territory of a State had the right to separate itself from a State. This was not the case in the Ålands dispute as Finland was indeed willing to grant the Åland islanders satisfactory guarantees to protect their cultural autonomy. Consequently, the Council of the League of Nations granted the inhabitants of the Åland Islands only the right to be protected as a minority rather than the right to external self-determination.*

13.2.2 Self-determination under the UN Charter

The transformation of self-determination from a political concept into a legal rule was envisaged by the 1941 Atlantic Charter[17] signed between Churchill and Roosevelt. They agreed that self-determination would become a basic right upon the termination of WWII. This was achieved under the UN Charter. Its Articles 1(2), 55 and 73 and Chapter XII recognise the right to self-determination. Article 1(2) of the UN Charter states that one of the purposes of the UN is 'to develop friendly relations among nations based on respect for the principle of equal rights and self-determination of peoples'. Similar terms are used in Article 55 of the Charter.

The meaning of self-determination under the UN Charter is unclear: the right to self-determination is mentioned in the context of friendly relations among nations. This gave rise to various interpretations of the principle of self-determination, the most likely being that Articles 1(2) and 55 of the UN Charter refer to the right of the peoples of one State to be protected from interference by other States or governments and thus both provisions emphasise the equal rights of States, rather than the right of dependent peoples to be independent.[18] However, Article 73 and Chapter XII of the UN Charter, which apply to trusteeship and to non self-governing, territories impose specific legal obligations on colonial powers deriving from the principle of self-determination, i.e. under Article 73 they recognise that the interests of inhabitants of these territories are paramount and that the colonial powers have a duty to promote to the utmost the well being of the inhabitants of these territories.

13.2.2.1 The international trusteeship system

Chapter XII of the UN Charter sets up the international trusteeship system under which the Trusteeship Council, one of the main organs of the UN, is charged with the task of supervising and administering trust territories placed under the system.

---

16   League of Nations 'The Aaland Island Question: Report Submitted to the Council of the League of Nations by the Commission of Rapporteurs 16 April 1921' League of Nations Council Doc B.7 21/68/106, 28.
17   204 LNTS 381.
18   R. Higgins, *Problems and Process: International Law and How We Use it*, Oxford: Clarendon Press, 1995, 112.

The Trusteeship Council, which is made up of the five permanent members of the UNSC, is still in existence but suspended its operation on 1 November 1994 when the last trust territory under its supervision, Palau, exercised freely its right to self-determination in a series of plebiscites and decided to become an independent State. The Trusteeship Council by a resolution adopted on 25 May 1994 decided to meet 'only on an extraordinary basis, as the need arose'.

The trusteeship system was intended to promote the welfare of native inhabitants, to advance them toward self-government, to further peace and security and to encourage respect for human rights and for fundamental freedoms.

The trust territories consisted of the following:

■ territories held under mandates established by the League of Nations apart from South West Africa which remained under mandate until it achieved independence as Namibia in 1990;

■ territories taken away from enemy States after WWII. This included Pacific islands over which the US was granted a strategic trusteeship, and Italian Somaliland which was assigned by the UNGA to Italy as trustee for the period of 10 years starting in 1950. In 1960 Italian Somaliland together with former British Somaliland became Somalia;

■ territories voluntarily placed under the system by States responsible for their administration. No colonial power volunteered to place any of its territories under the UN's supervision and administration. Thus, in fact, the trust territories encompassed only the two above-mentioned categories.

The Trusteeship Council was placed under the authority of the UNGA in respect of trust territories, and under the authority of the UNSC in respect of 'strategic trusteeship' territories. Only the Pacific islands, at the request of the US, were designated as a strategic area in the Trusteeship Agreement between the UN and the US. The main advantage of this arrangement was that the US had full control over the Pacific islands.

In order to fulfil its tasks the Trusteeship Council was authorised to examine and discuss annual reports from the administering authorities, in consultation with the administering authorities to examine petitions from individuals and groups, and to conduct visiting missions to verify the manner in which trust territories were administered, in particular to compare the reports from the administering authority with the actual conditions within the territory.

Eleven territories administered by seven member States were placed under the system. They were:

■ Togoland (UK) which united with the Gold Coast to become Ghana in 1957;

■ Togoland (France) which become Togo in 1960;

■ Cameroons (France) which become the Republic of Cameroon in 1960;

■ Cameroons (UK) the northern part of which joined Nigeria in 1961, while the southern part joined the Republic of Cameroon in the same year;

■ Somaliland (Italy) which become Somalia in 1960;

■ Tanganyika (UK) which become independent in 1961 and joined with Zanzibar in 1964 to become the United Republic of Tanzania;

■ Western Samoa (New Zealand) which become Samoa in 1976;

■ Nauru (Australia) which become independent in 1968;

- Ruanda-Urindi (Belgium) which become the States of Rwanda and Burundi in 1962;

- New Guinea (Australia) which become independent as Papua New Guinea in 1975;

- The Pacific Islands Territory (US) which either obtained commonwealth status as the Northern Mariana Islands or became independent under a compact of free associations with the US (the Marshall Islands and the Federation of States of Micronesia in 1986 and Palau in 1994).

13.2.2.2 Non-self governing territories

Chapter XI of the UN Charter entitled 'Declaration Regarding Non-Self-Governing Territories' provides fundamental guarantees for subjected peoples who have not yet attained a full measure of self-government. Non self-governing territories are outside the trusteeship system.

Chapter XI neither imposes any legal obligations on the administering powers nor contains any enforcement mechanism. Under Article 73 administering powers recognise the principle that 'the interest of the inhabitants of these territories are paramount' and accept 'as a sacred trust the obligation to promote to the utmost ... the well-being of the inhabitants of these territories'. In order to fulfil this obligation the administering powers promised:

- to ensure political, economic, social and educational advancement of these people and their just treatment;

- to develop self-government and free political institutions in these territories not necessarily leading to independence;

- to transmit regularly to the UNS-G statistical and technical reports concerning economic, social and educational conditions in these territories.

The reports were intended for information purposes only and no provision was made for their further use. In 1946 the colonial powers submitted a list of 74 territories on which they were willing to transmit reports. However, with time, many colonial powers decided not to submit reports, arguing that changes in the status of some of the non-self-governing territories had extinguished their obligation to do so. The UK decided not to report on any matters on which local autonomy had been granted, France considered that her overseas territories, being a part of the French Union, were outside the scope of Article 73, and Portugal and Spain when they joined the UN in 1955 claimed that their overseas territories formed an integral part of their national territories.

Many colonial powers claimed that they had an exclusive right to determine the status of territories under their jurisdiction. The system set up by Article 73 lacked teeth as the administering powers were entitled to decide unilaterally what territories were non-self-governing. They could also, at any time, cease to perform their obligation of submitting reports to the UNGA. The matter of the international accountability of the administering powers for their administration of dependent territories was of considerable concern to the UNGA which had sought to exercise some measure of control in deciding whether to accept the cessation of information. However, the UNGA had no enforcing powers and could use only persuasion and adverse publicity in respect of the defaulting States. In some cases the termination of reports on non-self-governing territories (i.e. Puerto Rico, Greenland, Alaska, Hawaii) was accepted by the UNGA, but in most cases the matter was decided unilaterally by the administering power.[19]

---

19   R.E. Gordon, *Some Legal Problems with Trusteeship* (1995) 28 Cornell Intl LJ 301.

At the time of writing there are 17 non-self-governing territories recognised by the UN: American Samoa, Anguilla, Bermuda, the British Virgin Islands, the Cayman Islands, the Falkland Islands, Gibraltar, Guam, Montserrat, New Caledonia, Pitcairn, St Helena, the Tokelau, Turks and Caicos Islands, the US Virgin Islands, the Western Sahara and French Polynesia. The current administering powers are France, New Zealand, the UK and the US. In the case of Western Sahara, the original administrating power, Spain, withdrew from the territory in 1976 and the territory was claimed by Mauritania and Morocco, both of which annexed portions of it although the ICJ had found that neither had established any right to territorial sovereignty.[20] Mauritania has since then relinquished all claims and withdrew from the territory it occupied, but Morocco continues to occupy the Western Sahara although its claims to sovereignty are not recognised and it is not regarded as replacing Spain as the administering power.

The case of French Polynesia is interesting. French Polynesia had been on the UN list of non-self-governing territories in 1946, but appears to have been excluded from subsequent lists. Under pro-independence leader, Oscar Temuru, the Assembly of French Polynesia sought to be re-inscribed onto the List, and with the support of the Pacific Island Forum achieved this objective on 17 May 2013 when the UNGA adopted GA Res A/Res/67/265. France described this resolution as a blatant interference in its internal affairs.[21] As a result of its recognition as a non-self-governing territory, French Polynesia hopes to have a referendum on independence from France similar to that planned for New Caledonia, which was itself re-inscribed onto the list in 1986.[22]

The anti-colonial movement invoked the principles contained in Article 73 of the UN Charter to support the immediate granting of self-government and independence to all colonial people. Article 73 continues to be invoked by pro-independence movements in the remaining non-self-governing territories.

13.3 Decolonisation

The list of non-European countries which have never been colonies is very short. It comprises: Thailand, Iran, Turkey, Liberia, Afghanistan and Japan. In the nineteenth century China was a semi-colony in that European empires had 'spheres of influence' set up along its coast. At the beginning of the twenty-first century, however, there were no European colonial powers.

First to declare their independence were the 13 colonies of the UK in North America which in 1776 became the United States of America. In the early nineteenth century Spain and Portugal lost its colonies in South America.

The substantial decolonisation occurred after WWII, although from 1930 onwards nationalist movements in European colonial empires, especially in Asia, were growing in power. However, they were not then strong enough to achieve independence.

WWII was the catalyst for the realisation of the aspirations of colonial peoples for a number of reasons:

- the pattern of control over colonies was interrupted;

- European colonial empires, in order to ensure the support of their colonies, promised them various degrees of autonomy after the end of WWII;

---

20   The *Western Sahara* Advisory Opinion [1975] ICJ Rep12.

21   See. www.diplomatie.gouv.fr/fr/politique-etrangere-de-la-france/onu/evenements-et-actualites-lies-aux/actualites-21429/article/resolution-adoptee-par-l-assemblee (accessed 10 September 2014).

22   A/RES/41/4 and A/RES/66 (I).

- European colonial empires were weakened or destroyed by the war. They no longer had resources to control their colonies;

- many colonies in Asia were occupied by Japan. After Japan's withdrawal in 1945 nationalist movements took advantage of the power vacuum so created. Civil wars erupted in China, Burma, Korea and Indochina. Anti-colonial movements, often inspired by communist ideology, fought hard for independence.

The first wave of decolonisation was confined to Asia. Newly independent Asian States were committed to destroying the colonial system. In 1955 at the Bandung Conference,[23] the first meeting of Asian and African heads of State, they clearly expressed in the final communication that colonialism in all its manifestations was an evil which must be immediately terminated. The fight against colonial domination was supported by both the Soviet Union and the US. After the death of Stalin in 1953, the Soviet Union offered all colonies 'friendship treaties', military advice, trade credits and measures of general support to liberate them from colonial domination.

The US has never forgotten that it was the first colony to achieve independence. Furthermore, the US had a clear conscience as in 1948 the only colony of the US, the Philippines, became independent.

The second wave of decolonisation took place in Africa in the late 1950s and early 1960s. The year 1960 was a turning point in decolonisation. With a growing number of new independent States and their admission to the UN they became the majority in the UNGA. In this context on 14 December 1960 the UNGA adopted Resolution 1514 (XV) on the Declaration on the Granting of Independence to Colonial Countries and Peoples[24] by a vote of 89 for, none against, and nine abstentions (the abstentions being: Portugal, Spain, South Africa, the UK, the US, Australia, Belgium, the Dominican Republic and France). The Declaration constitutes the foundation in international law of the right to self-determination. It calls for immediate emancipation of colonial people 'without any condition or reservation in order to allow them to enjoy full independence' and irrespective of the stage of their political, economic social or educational development. The Declaration calls into question the system set out in the UN Charter in Chapters XI and XII consisting of progressive accession to independence of colonial people under the supervision of administering powers.

The main provisions of the 1960 Declaration state that:

- The subjugation, domination and exploitation of people constitutes a denial of HRs contrary to the principles of the UN Charter.

- All peoples have a right to self-determination.

- The inadequacy of political, economic, social or educational preparedness should not serve as a pretext for delaying independence.

- Any repressive measures or any armed action directed against dependent people should cease.

- Non-self-governing territories should be granted immediately all necessary powers to achieve complete independence and freedom.

- Any attempt to disrupt partially or totally the territorial integrity of a State is incompatible with the principles and purposes of the UN.

---

23 'The Final Communiqué of the Asian-African Conference of the Non-Aligned Countries (24 April 1955)' in G. McTurnan Kahin, The Asian-African Conference, Bandung, Indonesia, 24 April 1955, New York: Cornell University Press, 1956, 76.

24 UNGA Res 1514 (XV) (14 December 1960) GAOR 15th Session Supp 16, 66.

■ All States must observe the Charter, the UDHR, the present Declaration, and the principle of non-intervention in the internal affairs of another State.

Exceptional importance has been conferred to the 1960 Declaration. Its scope of application has been further defined by subsequent resolutions, in particular Resolution 1514 (XV)[25] which defines the concept of 'full measure of self-government'. It provides that self-determination may be exercised by the people concerned, through voting in free and fair elections, in three ways:

■ they may decide to constitute themselves as a sovereign independent State;

■ they may decide to associate freely with an independent State;

■ they may integrate with an independent State already in existence.

In order to transform Resolution 1514 into an instrument for action the UNGA in 1961 set up the Special Committee on the Situation with Regard to the Implementation of the Declaration on the Granting of Independence to Colonial Countries and Peoples which in 1962 became the Special Committee of Twenty-Four. Its task, was and remains, to examine the application of the 1960 Declaration and to make recommendations on its implementation. The Committee meets annually, hears reports from appointed and elected representatives of the territories and petitioners, and decides on visiting missions to the territories. During the First International Decade for the Eradication of Colonialism (1990–2000) the Committee was very active in making proposals and carrying out actions, previously approved by the UNGA, relevant to the objective of the Decade. In 2001, the UN proclaimed the Second, and in 2011 the Third, International Decade for the Eradication of Colonialism.[26] However, the process of decolonisation has not been successfully concluded as 17 non-self–governing-territories remain (see Chapter13.2.2.2).

The right to self-determination in the colonial context has been recognised as one of the fundamental principles of international law equal in importance to the principle of the prohibition of aggression. Resolution 2625 (XXV) entitled 'Declaration on Principles of International Law Concerning Friendly Relations and Co-operation among States in Accordance with the Charter of the UN',[27] which is regarded as interpreting and clarifying the UN Charter taking into account that it was adopted by consensus (i.e. passed by the UNGA without a vote), provides that every State has a duty 'to bring a speedy end to colonialism having regard to the freely expressed will of the peoples concerned'.

The ICJ discussed the right to self-determination in the *Legal Consequences for States of the Continued Presence of South Africa in Namibia (South West Africa) Notwithstanding Security Council Resolution 276 (1970) (Advisory Opinion)*[28] and the *Western Sahara (Advisory Opinion)*.[29] In respect of Namibia the Court held that 'the subsequent development of international law in regard to non self-governing territories as enshrined in the UN Charter made the principle of self-determination applicable to all of them'.[30] In the *Western Sahara* the Court stated that:

In the domain to which the present proceedings relate [the application of the principle of self-determination to non-self-governing territories], the last 50 years ... have brought important developments. These developments leave little doubt that the ultimate objective of the sacred trust

---

25   UNGA Res 1514 (XV) (15 December 1960) GAOR 15th Session Supp 16, 29.
26   A/RES/65/119.
27   UNGA Res 2625 (XXV) (24 October 1970) GAOR 25th Session Supp 28, 121.
28   [1971] ICJ Rep 16.
29   [1975] ICJ Rep 12.
30   [1971] ICJ Rep 16, 52.

was the self-determination and independence of the people concerned. In this domain, as elsewhere, the corpus iuris gentium has been considerably enriched, and this the Court, if it is faithfully to discharge its functions, may not ignore.[31]

In the *East Timor Case (Portugal v Australia)*[32] the ICJ emphasised that the right of peoples to self-determination was 'one of the essential principles of contemporary international law'. In the *Legal Consequences of the Construction of a Wall in the Occupied Palestinian Territories (Advisory Opinion)*[33] the ICJ emphasised that the right of the Palestinian people to self-determination has acquired an *erga omnes* character (see Chapter 13.5.2).

13.4 The limit of the right to self-determination in the colonial context

The right to self-determination of colonial people is limited by the principle of *uti possidetis*, i.e. their claim is limited to territory which is defined by colonial boundaries or in the case of non-self-governing territories, by administrative borders drawn during colonisation. This is expressed in Paragraph 6 of UNGA Resolution 1514 (XV) which seeks to preserve the identity of colonial States when dependent people attempt to attain independence. It provides that:

> Any attempt aimed at partial or total disruption of the national unity and territorial integrity of a country is incompatible with the purposes and principles of the Charter of the United Nations.

As a result, Resolution 1514 does not consider that decolonisation affects the territorial integrity of the colonial power, although it does affect 'the national and territorial integrity of a state'. This clause is very important since self-determination without the counter-balancing force of territorial integrity would, according to many, run the risk of anarchy.[34] Resolution 2625 on Friendly Relations (XXV) emphasises this interpretation in paragraph 7 of its principle 5, by stating that:

> Nothing in the foregoing paragraphs shall be construed as authorising or encouraging any action which would dismember or impair, totally or partially, the territorial integrity or political unity of sovereign and independent states conducting themselves in compliance with the principle of equal rights and self-determination as described above and thus possessed of a government representing the whole people belonging to the territory without distinction as to race, creed or colour.

This entails that colonial frontiers must be respected even though they were drawn by the colonial powers without any consideration as to the ethnic or historical traditions of the peoples living there. The African leaders in the 1964 Cairo Declaration confirmed their adherence to this principle and Judge Djibo in the *Case Concerning the Frontier Dispute (Burkina Faso/Republic of Mali)*[35] explained that the African people consented, through the Cairo Declaration, to the maintenance of colonial boundaries because this was an essential requirement for the stability necessary to develop and consolidate their independence.

There are only two cases in Africa where colonial borders were redrawn. The first concerns the secession of Eritrea from Ethiopia in 1993, and the second the secession of South Sudan from Sudan in 2011.

---

31   [1975] ICJ Rep 12, 31.
32   [1995] ICJ Rep 90.
33   [2004] ICJ Rep 136.
34   L. Brilmeyer, *Secession and Self-Determination: A Territorial Interpretation* (1991) 16 YIL 177–202.
35   (1986) ICJ Rep 554, 567.

It is to be noted that the principle of *uti possidetis* expressed in Principle 5 of Resolution 2625, and confirmed in the 1993 Vienna Declaration adopted by the UN World Conference on Human Rights,[36] applies to all cases of external self-determination, whether realised in colonial or other contexts (see Chapter 7.3.2.2).

13.5 The extension of the right to self-determination to people living under racist regimes and foreign domination

Until the end of the Cold War the international community rarely agreed to recognise the existence of the right to self-determination outside the context of decolonisation. However, in some situations the right of self-determination has been extended to people other than colonial people. This occurred in respect of black and coloured peoples living in South Africa under the system of racial separation called apartheid (apartness) and to peoples living in occupied territories such as the Palestinians and inhabitants of Afghanistan after the Russian invasion of that country in 1979.

13.5.1 South Africa

Between 1948 and 1994 black and coloured people living in South Africa were subjected to apartheid, a policy of racial segregation and political and economic discrimination.

In 1652 the Dutch East India Company set up a 'refreshment station' at the Cape of Good Hope. This was the beginning of South Africa as a Dutch colony. With time, Dutch farmers known as Boers moved inland taking whatever land they wanted and subjugating the native population. During the Napoleonic wars the British took the Cape and the province of Natal. This incited the Boers, who hated the British presence, to establish two small republics, the Transvaal and the Orange Free State. When the British started to fight the Boers in 1899 in order to get hold of their land that was rich in gold and diamonds the Boers fought back with such determination and desperation that the British, in order to win the war, resorted to such extreme measures as putting Boer families into 'concentration camps', where some 26,000 died from typhoid. In 1902 the Boers capitulated, however, their descendants (Afrikaners) won control of the political system in South Africa. Afrikaners consider themselves as having been colonised by the British and not as colonialists.

In 1948 the Afrikaners, who constituted 60 per cent of the white population, won elections to govern South Africa and started to introduce apartheid, a system of strict racial segregation and discrimination reinforced by 'influx control' under which black and coloured people were kept out of cities. These people had no rights whatsoever, any protest was illegal and consequently severely punished. Deprived of any form of democratic participation many turned to violence. The African National Congress (ANC) which was founded in 1912 tried for many years to fight apartheid by peaceful means. After the Sharpeville incident in 1960 when the police panicked and opened fire on peaceful black protesters killing 69 of them, the ANC under the leadership of Nelson Mandela turned to violence. The ANC was banned and many of its leaders including Nelson Mandela were tried and condemned to life imprisonment. The ANC went underground and continued the fight against apartheid.

The international community strongly condemned apartheid. Under Article 1 of the 1973 International Convention on the Suppression and Punishment of the Crime of Apartheid, apartheid is a crime against humanity.[37] Similarly, Article 7 (2) (h) of the Rome Statute of the ICC confirms that apartheid (which

---

36   The United Nations World Conference on Human Rights, Vienna Declaration and Programme of Action, 25 June 1993, (1993) 32 ILM, 1665.

37   (30 November 1973) GAOR 28th Session Supp 30, 75.

is mentioned in Article 7(1)(j)) and similar acts 'committed in the context of an institutionalized regime of systematic oppression and domination by one racial group over any other racial group or groups and committed with the intention of maintaining that regime' are crimes against humanity. The UNGA adopted many resolutions supporting the fight of 'oppressed people of South Africa' by all possible and appropriate measures, including the use of armed force against the racist, minority and illegitimate regime of apartheid. The right to self-determination was conferred on the people of South Africa in its entirety (e.g. Resolution 33/183 of 24 January 1979). Consequently, the right to self-determination entailed the suppression of the racist regime and the establishment of a democratic government, but not the right to secession.

As a result of many factors, but mainly perhaps the political wisdom and vision of South African President F.W. de Klerk who replaced P.W. Botha in 1989, Nelson Mandela and other ANC activists were released from prison in 1990. Subsequently, the South African Parliament repealed the apartheid laws and lifted the ban on the ANC. As a result of negotiations between blacks and whites the first free election, based on the principle of one-person-one vote, took place in 1994. In the new multiracial and multi-party parliament the ANC won a majority. Nelson Mandela was elected President of South Africa.

13.5.2 The Palestinians

The right to self determination of the Palestinian people has been confirmed many times by the UNGA which has passed an impressive number of resolutions on the matter. These started with Resolution 3236 (XXIX) of November 1974 confirming the inalienable right of the Palestinian people to self-determination, the right to national independence, and the right to return to their homes and property. In 1975 the UNGA, frustrated by the lack of progress in the implementation of Resolution 3236, set up the Committee on the Exercise of the Inalienable Rights of the Palestinian People. Its initial task was to prepare a programme of action for the achievement of the Palestinian peoples' rights to self-determination. The programme was endorsed by the UNGA in 1976, but not by the UNSC due to the veto of the US. Despite this, the UNGA extended and expanded the Committee's mandate and established the Division for Palestinian Rights, which provides secretarial and other support for the Committee. The main task of the Committee is now to promote support for the Palestinian cause world-wide, report annually to the UNGA, make suggestions to the UNGA and the UNSC relating to the Palestinian question, and support the Israeli-Palestinian peace process. Also, the UN Commission on Human Rights, and the UN Council on Human Rights, which replaced the Commission, have repetitively condemned Israel for its violations of the HRs of the Palestinian people (see Chapter 12.4.1.3).

The ICJ's position on the right of the Palestinian people to self-determination was stated in the *Legal Consequences of the Construction of a Wall in the Occupied Palestinian Territories (Advisory Opinion)*.[38]

LEGAL CONSEQUENCES OF THE CONSTRUCTION OF A WALL IN THE OCCUPIED PALESTINIAN TERRITORIES (ADVISORY OPINION)

Facts:

Following the beginning of the Second Intifada (i.e. violence that erupted in 2000 between Palestinians and Israelis and resulted in the death of numerous Palestinians and Israelis),

---

38   [2004] ICJ Rep 136.

Israel started to build a 720 kilometres long wall in the region of the boundary between Israel and Palestine. The 'wall', however, does not follow the Green Line which marks the de facto boundary between Israel and Palestine fixed by the general armistice agreement of 3 April 1949 between Israel and Jordan. It deviates in certain places to bring 'within' the wall, i.e. in effect to include into Israel illegal Israeli settlements and Palestinian land. The main justification submitted by Israel for building the wall was based on self-defence. Israel claimed that it had the right and duty to protect its people against terrorist attacks, in particular to prevent suicide bombers penetrating into Israeli territory from the West Bank. According to the Palestinians the construction of the wall constituted an attempt by Israel to fix borders unilaterally ahead of any future settlement between Israel and the Palestine people and to annex territory wrongfully.

Held

On 9 July 2004 the ICJ delivered its Advisory Opinion. The ICJ ruled that:

- *Israel was in breach of international law and requested Israel to dismantle the wall immediately and make reparation for any damage caused;*
- *Israel could not rely on self-defence to justify the building of the wall as a measure taken in order to defend itself from terrorist attacks;*
- *the IV Geneva Convention and international human rights treaties such as the International Covenant on Civil and Political Rights (ICCPR), the International Covenant on Economic, Social and Cultural Rights (ICESCR), and the UN Convention on the Rights of the Child applied to the Occupied Palestinian Territory.*

The Advisory Opinion constitutes confirmation from the Court that Israel has violated a large number of international conventions, and completely ignored a multitude of legally binding UN Resolutions. In the Advisory Opinion the ICJ firmly confirmed the right of the Palestinian people to self-determination.

In the Advisory Opinion the ICJ determined the legal consequences for Israel, for other States, and for the UN following upon violations by Israel of international law, and determined the impact of the construction of the wall on the right of the Palestinian people to self-determination.

In this respect, the ICJ observed that Israel, by constructing the wall had, de facto annexed territories over which the Palestinian people are entitled to exercise their right to self-determination. Israel submitted assurances that the wall constituted a temporary measure and that Israel was ready to adjust and dismantle the wall if so required by a political settlement, and that with the termination of the terrorist attacks launched from the West Bank the wall would no longer be necessary. The Court stated that the construction of the wall amounted to de facto annexation of those territories, and as such was in breach of customary international law prohibiting the acquisition of territory by the use of force. This prohibition is enshrined in the 1928 Kellog-Briand Pact and in art 2(4) of the UN Charter. Further, the Declaration of Principles of International Law Concerning Friendly Relations and Co-operation among States in Accordance with the UN Charter (GA Resolution 2625 (XXV) of 24 October 1970) states that: 'the territory of a state shall not be the object of acquisition by another state resulting from the threat or use of force. No territorial acquisition resulting from the threat or use of force shall be recognised as legal.' Also, the Oslo Accords provide that the status of the West Bank and Gaza shall not be changed pending the outcome of permanent status negotiations and that protected persons under art 47 of the IV Geneva Convention should not be deprived of the benefits of the territory 'by an annexation . . . of the occupied territory'.

The Court noted that the route of the wall includes some 80 per cent of the land occupied by Jewish settlers living in the Occupied Territories (including Jerusalem). The establishment of Jewish settlements, the ICJ emphasised, was in breach of international law, in particular art 49(6) of the IV Geneva Convention, and in breach of binding UN Security Council Resolutions. The Court considered that the construction of the wall and its associated regime created a 'fait accompli' given that this temporary situation could easily become permanent. The ICJ ruled that the construction of the wall in conjunction with the measures taken previously by Israel, namely the establishment of Jewish settlements in the Occupied Territories, severely impeded the exercise by the Palestinian people of their right to self-determination, being a right which had been recognised by the international community and by Israel itself. Consequently, Israel was in breach of the obligation to respect the right of the Palestinian people to self-determination.

The ICJ specified the legal consequences for Israel, for other States and for the United Nations arising from the violation by Israel of international law.

Legal consequences for Israel

With regard to Israel the ICJ noted that any breach of international law triggered the responsibility of the culprit State under international law. The ICJ noted the following points.

- *Israel is obliged to comply with the obligation to respect the right of the Palestinian people to self-determination and its obligations under IHL and HRL;*
- *Israel must ensure freedom of access to the Holy places that came under its control subsequent to the 1967 war;*
- *Israel must put an end to the violations of its international obligations relating to the construction of the wall in the Occupied Territory;*
- *Israel must immediately cease the works of construction of the wall being built in the Occupied Territories, including in and around East Jerusalem, and must dismantle the existing parts of the wall;*
- *Israel must repeal all legislative and regulatory measures adopted with a view to the wall's construction, and to the establishment of the associated regime except insofar as those acts provide for compensation for the Palestinian population;*
- *Israel must make reparation for the damage caused to all natural and legal persons concerned in accordance with the principle of international law as explained in* Chorzów Factory Case (Indemnity) (Merits) (Germany v Poland),[39] *that is, that reparation must, as far as possible, wipe out all the consequences of the illegal act and re-establish the situation which would, in all probability, have existed if that act had not been committed. Consequently, Israel must return the land and other immovable property seized or, if*

---

39   (1928) PCIJ Rep Ser A No 17.

such restitution is materially impossible, compensate the persons concerned for the damage suffered;

- *Israel must compensate any natural or legal person having suffered any form of material damage resulting from the construction of the wall.*

Legal consequences for States other than Israel

The ICJ noted that the obligations violated by Israel included certain erga omnes *obligations such as the right of the Palestinian people to self-determination, and some intransgressible principles of customary humanitarian law. The* erga omnes *character of the above obligations requires that no States must recognise the illegal situation created by the construction of the wall in the Occupied Territory, and that all States must abstain from rendering any aid or assistance in maintaining the situation resulting from such construction and must bring to an end any impediment resulting from the construction of the wall to the exercise by the Palestinian people of their right to self-determination.*

Legal consequences for the UN

The ICJ considered that the UN, in particular the UNSC and the UNGA, should decide what further action is required in order to bring to an end the illegal situation created by the construction of the wall in the light of the present Advisory Opinion. The ICJ urged the UN as a whole to 'redouble its efforts to bring the Israeli-Palestinian conflict, which continues to pose a threat to international peace and security, to a speedy conclusion, thereby establishing a just and lasting peace in the region'.

Follow up:

The UNGA fully endorsed the Advisory Opinion at its Tenth Special Emergency Session held on 20 July 2004 by adopting Resolution 10/18 (150 votes in favour, six votes against and ten abstentions) which demanded that Israel and all States comply with the legal obligations specified in the Opinion, requested the UNS-G to set up a register of all damage caused to all natural and legal persons resulting from the construction of the wall in the Occupied Territory, and reaffirmed the right and duty of all States to take necessary actions in accordance with international law to counter deadly acts of violence against the civilian population. However, the wall through the Palestinian territory remains in place, very much to the annoyance of the Palestinians.

13.6   The right to self-determination as a human right

International law recognises that the right to self-determination constitutes a fundamental human right and applies to all people. It is probably unfortunate that the principle of self-determination was, at its inception, so closely linked with the issue of decolonisation. As a result, it has hardly developed outside the colonial context, even though Resolution 1514 states that any people being subjected to 'subjugation, domination or exploitation' have an inherent right to self-determination. Despite this, the context in which the Resolution was adopted strongly suggests that its addressees were primarily people living under colonial rule.

The right to self-determination as a right granted to all people was clearly set out in the ICCPR and the ICESCR. Both instruments contain an identical Article 1 (3) which provides that 'all people have the right to self-determination. By virtue of that right they are entitled to freely determine their political status and freely pursue their economic, social and cultural development'. Under this provision contracting States 'shall promote the realisation of the right of self-determination and shall respect that right in conformity with the provisions of the Charter of the United Nations'. General Comment 12 on Article 1 of the ICCPR adopted by the Human Rights Committee (HRC)[40] emphasises that the realisation of the right to self-determination is of particular importance because it is an essential condition for the effective guarantee and observance of individual human rights.[41] However, the HRC has not provided any definition of 'peoples' and its case law on Article 1 ICCPR is very limited, mainly because it has decided that Article 1 is non-justiciable under the First Optional Protocol to the ICCPR. In this respect the HRC has stated that under the First Optional Protocol it has competence to deal with individual complaints only (i.e. brought by individuals alleging violations of their individual rights guaranteed under the ICCPR), and not with complaints alleging violation of a collective right. In *Kitok v Sweden*[42] the HRC held that an individual had no *locus standi* under Article 1 because he could not claim to be a victim of a violation of the right to self-determination, i.e. only 'peoples' could claim it. This, however, does not preclude an individual from relying on other rights protected under the ICCPR, e.g. the right to life under Article 6[43] or the right to vote under Article 25 ICCPR[44] to bring a complaint which indirectly concerns violations of Article 1. Nevertheless, the inadmissibility of complaints brought under Article 1 ICCPR is disappointing because it not only precludes alleged victims of violations of Article 1 from bringing their complaints before the HRC, but also precludes the HRC from contributing to the proper construction of the right to self-determination.[45]

The UN Commission on Human Rights has always interpreted Article 1 literally, so confirming the right of all people to self-determination and not merely colonial peoples.[46]

Among other international instruments which confirm that self-determination is not restricted to colonial people, people subjected to a racist regime, or to foreign or alien domination are: the Helsinki Final Act 1975 adopted by the Conference on Security and Co-operation in Europe,[47] and the African Charter on Human and Peoples' Rights 1981 (Article 20).

Despite the right to self-determination being recognised as a fundamental human right the reality is that in circumstances where a people wishes to secede from a State of which they form part (and this is almost the only circumstance in which the right has any relevance) the international community has been extremely reluctant to recognise or support their right, even in circumstances where they were victims of extreme oppression and thus their physical existence as a people was seriously threatened.

The right to self-determination has been marginalised by the principle of territorial integrity. The 1970 Declaration on Principles of International Law[48] clearly subjugates the right of self-determination to the principle of territorial integrity. Furthermore, the main purpose of the UN, which is the maintenance of international peace and stability, has imposed important restrictions on the exercise of the right to

---

40　The HRC is a body created to monitor the implementation of the ICCPR. The HRC is, *inter alia*, entitled to examine individual petitions under the First Optional Protocol to the ICCPR when authorised by a contracting State (see Chapter 12.2.2.2).

41　See the official website of the HRC.

42　197/85.

43　*Bordes and Temeharo v France* (645/95).

44　*Gillot et al. v France* (932/00).

45　On this topic see S. Joseph and M. Castan, *The International Covenant on Civil and Political Rights, Cases, Materials and Commentary*, 3rd edn, Oxford: Oxford University Press, 2013, 153–165.

46　Concluding Comments on Azerbaijan, (1994) UN Doc. CCPR/C/79/Add, para 6.

47　Principle VIII of the Final Act.

48　UNGA Res 2625 (XXV) GAOR 25th Session Supp 28, 121.

external self-determination, taking into account that the result of successful struggle for independence would entail disintegration of an existing State. In this context, neither the UN nor the AU recognised any right to self-determination of the Ibo Community in Biafra which was fighting from 1967–1970 to break away from Nigeria although thousands, if not millions, of Ibos were killed or starved to death. Further, the UN made no statement in respect of the secession of East Pakistan from the State of Pakistan in 1971 although there were serious allegations of genocide by the Pakistani army committed on the Banglas. Additionally, the UN was paralysed when Albanian Kosovars were being exterminated (Chapter 15.6.2.1).

The position of the UN was summarised by U. Thant, the then UNS-G, in 1970 when he said that:

As far as the question of secession of a particular section of a member state is concerned, the United Nations attitude is unequivocal. As an international organisation, the United Nations has never accepted and does not accept and I do not believe it will ever accept, a principle of secession of a part of a member state.[49]

However, the above stated position of the UN is in contrast with the UN position on Kosovo (see Chapter 13.7.3.1 B).

13.7 Self-determination in the post-Cold War era

The collapse of communism resulted in many subjugated nations claiming their right to self-determination through secession.

People of eastern European countries living under the hegemony of the Soviet Union since the end of WWII took advantage of the changing situation and speedily dismantled 'socialism', proving how little legitimacy these regimes enjoyed in their eyes. With the end of the Cold War new problems emerged. Old states ceased to exist and were replaced by new States created on the territory of an old State, and minority groups living within old, or newly created States, started to demand political rights ranging from internal autonomy to a right to secession. In these circumstances claims of indigenous people to self-determination have gained a new momentum. The complexity of these issues has emphasised the controversies surrounding the right to self-determination.

It seems that each situation is different, although some general principles can be applied to all of them. These are examined below.

13.7.1 Dissolution of a State and self-determination

International law recognises the right to dissolve a State in a peaceful way and to create new States on the territory of the former State. The agreement of all concerned parties is at the centre of this principle.

The Final Act of the Helsinki Conference on Security and Co-operation in Europe (CSCE) of 1 August 1975 in its Principle III states that changes of frontiers in Europe are allowed provided they are peaceful and have the consent of the parties involved. This principle was applied when the Soviet Union was replaced by 15 new independent States, 11 of which became loosely associated with Russia within the Commonwealth of Independent States (CIS). It was also respected by Czechoslovakia where a referendum was held which led to the so-called 'Velvet Divorce' between the Czech and the Slovak Republics. The Union between them was dissolved and they became independent States.

---

49   UN Monthly Chronicle, No 2 (1970) 36.

International law does not consider dissolution of a State by force and the creation of new States on the territory of the former State as an internal matter of the State concerned. This is a matter of international law to which the principle of self-determination applies. A good example relates to the dissolution of the former Yugoslavia. The international community has always maintained the view that the right to self-determination was granted to inhabitants of each republic as a whole and not to each minority grouping living within a particular republic. However, the case of Kosovo challenges this view.

13.7.2 *Uti possidetis* and self-determination

The concept of self-determination has been greatly influenced by the doctrine of *uti possidetis* which derives from Roman law and which was applied in the context of the decolonisation of Latin America in the nineteenth century.[50] According to the doctrine, when Spain lost its Latin American territories the boundaries left behind were to be respected and could not be changed under any circumstances. The principle of *uti possidetis* has become recognised in customary law and was applied in the context of later decolonisation (see Chapter 7.3.2.2). In the *Case Concerning the Frontier Dispute (Burkina Faso/Republic of Mali)*[51] the ICJ stated that the doctrine of *uti possidetis*:

> is a general principle, which is logically connected with the phenomenon of the obtaining of independence, whenever it occurs. Its obvious purpose is to prevent the independence and stability of states being endangered by fratricidal struggles provoked by the challenging of frontiers following the withdrawal of the administering power.

In 1991 the Badinter Arbitration Commission which was charged by the then EC (now the EU) with preparing guidelines on the recognition of new States emphasised the importance of *uti possidetis* by stating that:

> it is well established that, whatever the circumstances, the right to self-determination must not involve changes to existing frontiers at the time of independence [*uti possidetis juris*] except where the states concerned agree otherwise.[52]

The Commonwealth of Independent States (CIS), which emerged after the break-up of the Soviet Union, upheld the principle of *uti possidetis*. The Charter of the CIS signed at Minsk on 8 December 1991 provides that 'the High Contracting Parties acknowledge and respect each other's territorial integrity and the inviolability of existing borders within the Commonwealth'. This was further confirmed by the Alma Ata Declaration of 21 December 1991.

The main drawback of the principle of *uti possidetis* is that it freezes the pre-existing borders, whether colonial, or between republics, and thus pays no attention to ethnic, tribal and other considerations which encourages secessionist movements and armed conflicts. At its extreme, it paved the way for the genocide in Darfur, Rwanda and Bosnia-Herzegovina.

The relationship between the principle of *uti possidetis* and the principle of self-determination is not easy. This uneasy relationship was acknowledged by the ICJ in *Burkina Faso v Mali*. In that case, the ICJ held that although it seems, at first glance, that there is an outright conflict between the two principles 'in fact, . . . , the maintenance of the territorial status quo in Africa is often seen as

---

50   The *Case concerning the Land, Island and Maritime Frontier Dispute (El Salvador/Honduras: Nicaragua Intervening)* [1992] ICJ Rep 351.
51   [1986] ICJ Rep 554, 565.
52   (1991) 92 LLR, 168.

the wisest course to preserve what has been achieved by peoples who have struggled for their independence . . .'[53] The ICJ further held that the principle of *uti possidetis* prevailed over the principle of self-determination.

The position of international law on the relationship between the two principles has been stated by the Badinter Commission in its Opinion No 2 when it held that although the Serbian population of Croatia and Bosnia-Herzegovina had the right to self-determination, the exercise of this right must not involve change to the borders existing at the time of achievement of independence by the former republics of Yugoslavia, unless the States concerned agreed otherwise.[54] However, the Kosovo case negates this statement (see Chapter 12.7.3.1.B).

In assessing the principle of *uti possidetis* it can be said that it is not a rule of *jus cogens* taking into account that interested parties, by mutual agreement, are allowed to depart from it. This was confirmed by the ICJ in *Case Concerning Land, Island and Maritime Frontier Dispute (El Salavador/Honduras, Nicaragua Intervening)*[55] in which the ICJ stated that the parties involved were allowed to modify the existing frontiers through an exchange of territory. Following from this, it is clear that existing boundaries are not immutable and may be changed, but the consent of all parties concerned is required. This is exemplified by the secession of Eritrea from Ethiopia in 1993, and the secession of South Sudan from Sudan in 2011, both occurred with the agreement of the Ethiopian and North Sudanese governments respectively.[56]

13.7.3 'People' and the right to self-determination

International law is clear that colonial peoples, i.e. peoples living in mandate, trusteeship, and non-self-governing-territories under a colonial regime are 'people' entitled to exercise the right to external self-determination. Under the principle of *uti possidetis*, former colonial boundaries will become international boundaries, and no regard will be paid to the fact that original colonial boundaries were drawn arbitrarily with the consequences that they in most cases divide ethnic, religious, linguistic groups.

Apart from colonial peoples, international law does not determine who are the 'people' or 'peoples' entitled to exercise their right to self-determination. As Lâm put it 'the meanings of both "self-determination" and "people" remain contentious, and fluctuate with the UN practice'.[57] For that reason often States use the term 'minorities', instead of 'people', when they refer to certain groups, in order to emphasise that such groups have no claims to external self-determination.

It results from the relevant international instruments and from State practice that by 'all people' international law refers to all the people of a given territory and that they are entitled to exercise the right to self-determination in the following circumstances:

■ when they are subjected to alien subjugation, domination or exploitation in violation of international law; and

---

53   Supra note 53, p. 567, para 25.

54   Supra note 52.

55   (1992) ICJ Rep 92, 408.

56   See, for example, P. Malanczuk, *Aekhurst's Modern Introduction to International Law*, London: Routledge, 1997, 163.

57   M.C. Lâm, *Making Room for Peoples at the United Nations: Thoughts Provoked by Indigenous Claims to Self-Determination* (1992) 25 Cornell Int LJ, 615–616. See also the definition of 'people' formulated by the African Commission on Human and Peoples' Rights in *Kevin Mgwange Gunme v Cameroon*, Communication 266/2003, Twenty Sixth Annual Activity Report (2008–2009), online: http://xa.yimg.com/kq/groups/18367317/1483467726/name/Verdict1of1Communication1No1266–2003.pdf (accessed 10 September 2014).

■ when they live in a State guilty of massive, systematic and grave violations of the basic human rights of its citizens.

In both cases they will be entitled to use force. It is clearly stated in the preamble to the UDHR that: 'Whereas it is essential, if a man is not to be compelled to have recourse, as a last resort, to rebellion against tyranny and oppression, that human rights should be protected by the rule of law.'

In the second case, a government may target only part of its population. The Supreme Court of Canada in *Re Secession of Quebec*[58] stated that:

> It is clear that 'a people' may include only a portion of the population of an existing state. The right to self-determination has developed largely as a human right, and is generally used in documents that simultaneously contain reference to 'nation' and 'state'. The juxtaposition of these terms is indicative that the reference to 'people' does not necessarily mean the entirety of a state's population . . .

In such a situation the problem remains: who are the beneficiaries of the right to self-determination?

13.7.3.1 Minorities and self-determination

Probably the best definition of a minority has been formulated by Special Rapporteur Francesco Capotorti. It provides that a minority is:

> [a] group numerically inferior to the rest of the population of a State, in a non-dominant position, whose members – being nationals of the State – possess ethnic, religious or linguistic characteristics differing from those of the rest of the population and show, if only implicitly, a sense of solidarity, directed towards preserving their culture, religion or language.[59]

International law refuses to grant minority groups living within a State the right to secession, but ensures that their rights as minorities are respected. The obvious problem would be that if one group was to be granted a right to break away from an existing State, unless such a group lived within a well defined territory and was almost 100 per cent homogenous other minorities might be forcibly included in the prospective new State's territory unless that intended new State gave the same right to secede to its minorities. A refusal would prove that the new State applied a 'racist double standard', while the granting of such a right would lead to the creation of numerous new States. Max van der Stoel, who advocated internal self determination of minorities, stated that the granting of external self-determination to minority groups would result in the creation of approximately 2000 States.[60] This problem has been illustrated by the Canadian province of Quebec in which the French speaking majority wished to secede from Canada. Aboriginal people living in Quebec challenged the right of Quebec to secede. They argued that in the province of Quebec there are more than one distinct Quebecois 'people' taking into account that there are many distinct aboriginal peoples living there. Their claim to self-determination is much stronger than that of other peoples in Quebec (see below).

As stated above international law does not prohibit secession with the consent of the interested parties. Therefore, it is always possible for a State to allow a minority to determine freely its destiny

---

58   [1998] 2 SCR 217, para 124.

59   Francesco Capotorti, Special Rapporteur, Study on the Rights of Persons Belonging to Ethnic, Religious and Linguistic Minorities, UN Doc E/CN.4/Sub.2/384/Rev.1 (1977).

60   See 'High Commissioner on National Minorities: Speech by Max van der Stoel', 13 May 1994, available at www.osce.org/hcnm/37259 (accessed 10 September 2014).

including choosing to secede. This occurred when the UK of England, Wales, Scotland and Northern Ireland agreed to allow Scotland to hold an independence referendum on 18 September 2014. The result was that the majority voted against Scotland becoming an independent country.[61]

It has been said that international law should treat differently oppressed minorities and minorities living in a democratic State which respect their right to internal self-determination. So far, State practice has not followed this approach, although the case of Kosovo, if it becomes a precedent, may change the current position. In this respect it is interesting to compare the case of Quebec with that of Kosovo.

A. Quebec

Quebec nationalism and its quest for independence has led, so far, to one referendum in 1980 and one in 1995. The final objective of the nationalist movement is to separate Quebec completely from the Canadian Federation and to create an independent State. A majority vote in favour of independence in a referendum would give legitimacy to a claim by Quebec. In both referenda the majority of residents of Quebec said 'No'. However, in the 1995 referendum the nationalist movement was close to victory. It failed by just over 1 per cent of the vote (the 'no' vote was 50.58 per cent, the 'yes' vote 49.42 per cent). The government of Quebec has not given up its objective and one may expect yet another referendum in the future. Meanwhile, the Supreme Court of Canada examined the implication of the possible secession of Quebec in *Re Secession of Quebec*.[62]

RE SECESSION OF QUEBEC

Facts:

The spectre of a unilateral declaration of independence by Quebec and its implications prompted the Canadian Federal government to refer three questions to the Supreme Court of Canada regarding the legality under both the Canadian constitution and international law of such a declaration.

Held:

The Supreme Court reply was that unilateral secession was illegal under both. The second question is of particular interest as it was formulated in the following manner:

Does international law give the National Assembly, legislature or government of Quebec the right to effect the secession of Quebec from Canada unilaterally? In this regard, is there a right to self-determination under international law that would give the National Assembly, legislature or government of Quebec the right to effect the secession of Quebec from Canada unilaterally?

The Supreme Court of Canada answered that international law 'does not specifically grant component parts of sovereign states the legal right to secede unilaterally from their "parent" state'. It emphasised that the protection of territorial integrity prevails over the right to external self-determination since 'A state whose government represents the whole of the people or

---

61   See: S. Tierney, *Legal Issues Surrounding the Referendum on Independence in Scotland* (2013) 9 European Constitutional Law Review, 359.

62   [1998] 2 SCR 217.

> *peoples resident within its territory, on a basis of equality and without discrimination, and respects the principles of self-determination in its own internal arrangements, is entitled to the protection under international law of its territorial integrity'. The Supreme Court of Canada concluded that:*
>
> > *In summary, the international law right to self-determination only generates, at best, a right to external self-determination in situations of former colonies; where a people is oppressed ... or where a definable group is denied meaningful access to government to pursue their political, economic, social and cultural development ... Such exceptional circumstances are manifestly inapplicable to Quebec under existing conditions.*[63]

B. Kosovo

Albanians living in Kosovo (Albanian Kosovars) were victims of massive, systematic and serious human rights violations carried out by the Federal Republic of Yugoslavia (the FRY) under the leadership of Serbian President Slobodan Milošević. When the FRY's atrocities towards Albanian Kosovars intensified in 1999 NATO decided to intervene militarily to prevent a humanitarian disaster, in particular, to prevent the FRY from committing genocide on Albanian Kosovars (for the factual background see Chapter 15.6.2).

The intervention was successful and when FRY forces withdrew from Kosovo, the UNSC adopted Resolution 1244 (1999) authorising an international civil and military presence there, and placing Kosovo under transitional UN administration, i.e. the United Nations Interim Administration Mission in Kosovo (UNMIK), which, at the time of writing, remains in existence but has significantly scaled down its operations (see Chapter 5.10). UNMIK initially performed all the functions of a government, while building national institutions in Kosovo, and ensuring the protection of the rights and interests of all of Kosovo's communities. The Constitutional Framework for Provisional Self-Government in Kosovo was signed by the head of UNMIK on 15 May 2001. On its basis new provisional institutions, including a legislative assembly (Parliament), were established. Since then UNMIK has gradually handed over its responsibility to local institutions.

On 17 February 2008, Kosovo's Parliament unilaterally declared independence from Serbia. Almost immediately the US and major European States, the UK, France, Germany and Italy, recognised Kosovo as an independent and sovereign State. Serbia rejected the declaration. As at August 2014, Kosovo had been recognised by at least 107 States[61] (including 23 out of 28 EU member States) as well as the Republic of Taiwan, and the Sovereign Order of Malta.[65]

States which are uncertain about the implications of recognising Kosovo for their own restless ethnic or political minorities seeking secession are not so keen on recognising Kosovo, e.g. Spain because of its concern about the Basque and Catalan regions; India because of Kashmir; China because of Xinjiang, Tibet and Taiwan. Russia (which has not recognised Kosovo) is in an interesting situation; apart from the fact that it has always supported Serbia it is, on the one hand, uneasy about Chechnya and other regions aspiring for independence, but on the other hand, Kosovo provides a strong argument for the recognition of the Republics of Ossetia and Abhazia (see Chapter 5.7.2). Moreover, the situation in

---

63   Ibid, para 126.
64   Kosovo contends that it has been recognised by Nigeria, Uganda and Sao Tome and Principe, but recognition by these States has been disputed.
65   See www.kosovothanksyou.com/statistics (accessed 7 November 2014).

Kosovo has been used by Russia to justify its 2014 annexation of Crimea.[66] Turkey has recognised Kosovo, although Turkey faces a dilemma in that it seeks the recognition of the Turkish Republic of Northern Cyprus but has to worry about the demands by its own Kurdish separatists.

The pattern of recognition and non-recognition of Kosovo shows that its declaration of independence may have a tremendous impact on international relations. Indeed, if the case of Kosovo establishes a precedent, the Western powers, by recognising Kosovo, may have opened a Pandora's box. Fully aware of the implications of the recognising of Kosovo, the then US Secretary of State, Rice, when making an announcement officially recognising Kosovo, stated:

> The unusual combination of factors found in the Kosovo situation – including the context of Yugoslavia's breakup, the history of ethnic cleansing and crimes against civilians in Kosovo, and the extended period of UN administration – are not found elsewhere and therefore make Kosovo a special case. Kosovo cannot be seen as precedent for any other situation in the world today.[67]

Kosovo's secession from Serbia is, in some respects, exceptional. The following facts emphasise the uniqueness of Kosovo's claim to secession:

■ Kosovo, when it made the declaration of independence, had been under UN administration for more than 9 years.

■ The international civil and military presence in Kosovo was due to gross, systematic and serious violations of HRs of Albanian Kosovars by the parent State-Serbia.

■ UNSC Resolution 1244 (1999) authorised the UN to facilitate a political process to determine Kosovo's future status. A comprehensive proposal for status settlement was developed by the UNS-G's Special Envoy for Kosovo who was appointed by the UNS-G in November 2005. His mission had collapsed after 15 months of negotiation between Kosovo and Serbia. He reported to the UNS-G that in the light of the failure to reach any political settlement he recommended that Kosovo become independent after a period of international supervision. Subsequently, negotiations between Serbia and Kosovo were resumed under the auspices of the 'Troika': the EU, Russia and the US. Once again the negotiations were fruitless. The 'Troika' reported to the UNS-G in December 2007 that the parties were entrenched in their positions and could not reach an agreement as to the final status of Kosovo.

■ UNSC Resolution 1244 was ambiguous as to the final status of Kosovo. Its preamble affirmed 'the commitment of all member states to the sovereignty and territorial integrity of the Federal Republic of Yugoslavia [Serbia]' but its operative part, in particular Para 11(a), stated that the UNMIK was to promote 'the establishment, pending a final settlement, of substantial autonomy and self-government in Kosovo' As can be seen, Resolution 1244 neither prohibits nor promotes Kosovo's secession from Serbia.

A. The Kosovo Advisory Opinion
On 8 October 2008, the UNGA, at Serbia's initiative, adopted resolution 63/3[68] requesting the ICJ to give an advisory opinion on whether Kosovo's declaration of independence from Serbia conforms to international law. The vote in the UNGA on this resolution was 77 in favour, 74 abstentions and

---

66 See Address by President of the Russian Federation, 18 March 2014 http://eng.kremlin.ru/transcripts/6889 (accessed 1 November 2014).
67 See www.state.gov/secretary/rm/2008/02/100973.htm (accessed 17 October 2014).
68 A/RES/63/3.

6 against. It is to be noted that although opinions of the ICJ are non-binding they are highly persuasive among the international community and are generally followed (see Chapter 14.8).

On 22 June 2010, the ICJ delivered its Opinion entitled: 'Accordance with International Law of the Unilateral Declaration of Independence in Respect of Kosovo.'[69]

ACCORDANCE WITH INTERNATIONAL LAW OF THE UNILATERAL DECLARATION OF INDEPENDENCE IN RESPECT OF KOSOVO

Facts:

The UNGA asked the following question: 'Is the unilateral declaration of independence by the Provisional Institutions of Self Government (PISG) of Kosovo in accordance with international law?'

Held:

The ICJ held that the adoption of the unilateral declaration did not violate any applicable rule of international law.

Comment:

The Court pointed out that the question was 'very narrow and specific'.[70] It was very different from the question put before the Supreme Court of Canada in Re Secession of Quebec. The UNGA had requested an opinion on whether the unilateral declaration of independence by the PISG of Kosovo was in accordance with international law. Thus the question neither asked about the legal consequences of that declaration (i.e. whether Kosovo had achieved statehood) or whether international law conferred a positive entitlement on Kosovo unilaterally to declare its independence or, a fortiori, on whether international law generally confers an entitlement on entities situated within a State to unilaterally break away from it. Accordingly, the Court held that it was not necessary for it to address these issues. It was also not necessary for it to answer the specific question of whether a remedial right to secession[71] had arisen in relation to Kosovo.

The Court held that there was no rule of international law prohibiting an entity from making a unilateral declaration of independence.[72] The ICJ referred to the extensive practice of States relating to instances of issuing unilateral declarations of independence. It concluded that declarations of independence were not illegal in international law.[73] However, they were capable of being illegal if they violate general public international law or an applicable lex specialis.

With regard to general international law, in para 81 the ICJ stated that illegality of unilateral declarations result not from the fact that they were unilateral but: 'from the fact that they

---

69   [2010] ICJ Rep 403.

70   Ibid, 51.

71   Remedial secession is a reference to the idea that the oppression of a group within a State can eventually lead to a right of secession from the state for the group: see J. Vidmar, *Remedial Secession in International Law: Theory and (Lack Of) Practice* (2010) 6 St Anthony's International Review, 37.

72   For in depth examination of the Kosovo Opinion see M. Weller, *Modesty Can be a Virtue: Judicial Economy in the ICJ Kosovo Opinion?* (2011) 24 LJIL, 127.

73   Supra note 69, para 79.

were, or would have been, connected with the unlawful use of force or other egregious violations of norms of general international law, in particular those of a peremptory character (jus cogens)'.

In the light of the above, the Kosovo declaration did not violate general public international law but for example similar declarations that had been made by Rhodesia, TRNC and the Republika Srpska were illegal because they were in breach of jus cogens. Further, the ICJ noted that the principle of territorial integrity is neutral with regard to unilateral declarations of independence,[74] i.e. it neither prohibits issuing declarations of independence nor accepting such declarations.

With regard to the lex specialis, i.e. Resolution 1244 and UNMIK regulations, including regulation 2001/9, which promulgated the Constitutional Framework for Kosovo, adopted on the authority of Resolution 1244 (1999), the Court noted that Resolution 1244(1999) had established a temporary, exceptional legal regime that had superseded the Serbian legal order. It was aimed at addressing the crisis existing in the territory in 1999 and designed for humanitarian purposes to provide a means for stabilisation and reconstruction. It was not intended to create a permanent institutional framework. The Court found that Resolution 1244 did not contain specific provisions prohibiting independence or a declaration of independence. Likewise subsidiary documents, i.e. UNMIK regulation the Constitutional Framework, and subsequent practice of UN administration did not preclude the achievement of independence by Kosovo. Accordingly, the Kosovo declaration did not violate the lex specialis.

The next matter considered by the ICJ concerned the author of the Declaration. This was the crucial matter given that the Provisional Institutions of Self Government (PISG) had to act within the restrictive framework of Resolution 1244 and subsidiary instruments. The ICJ held that although the question asked by the UNGA clearly stated that the author of the declaration was the PISG, it was part of the judicial function of the ICJ to determine who, in fact, was the author of the declaration. In this respect the Court found that the members the Kosovo Assembly, an element of the PISG, were not acting as members of the Assembly, but as the democratically elected leaders of the people of Kosovo, i.e. 'as persons who acted together in their capacity as representatives of the people of Kosovo outside the framework of the interim administration.'[75]

Many commentators and judges consider that the question posed by the UNGA was not the question answered by the Court. Judge Simma pointed out in his separate opinion that the Court's interpretation of the question put before it (i.e. whether the declaration was in violation of international law?) goes against the plain and ordinary meaning of that question asked which was whether the declaration of independence was in accordance with international law.[76] In answering that question the Court should have provided a comprehensive analysis of whether the principle of self-determination or some other rule permitted, or even entitled, an entity to declare independence when certain conditions were

---

74 On this point see J. Vidmar, *Conceptualising Declarations of Independence in International Law* (2012) 32/1 Oxford Journal of Legal Studies, 161–167.

75 Supra note 69, para 109.

76 *Declaration of Judge Simma* [2010] ICJ Rep 473, para 1.

> *satisfied.*[77] *He opined that the Court's methodology reflected 'an old, tired view of international law, which takes the adage, famously expressed in the* Lotus *Judgment, according to which restrictions on the independence of States cannot be presumed because of the consensual nature of the international legal order'.*[78] *It did not follow, however, that simply because there were no rules prohibiting a particular course of action that action is ipso facto in accordance with international law.*[79]
>
> *Judge Yusuf agreed that the Court's interpretation of the question was unnecessarily narrow and restrictive. He pointed out that a declaration of independence was 'the expression of a claim to separate statehood and part of a process to create a new State'.*[80] *The Court was not simply being asked about a unilateral declaration of independence as in the mere proclamation or statement made by the seceding entity, but about a unilateral action of independence or secession from an existing State.*

B. The legality of Kosovo's secession from Serbia

The ICJ's opinion leaves open the question of the legality or otherwise of Kosovo's secession from Serbia. It is well recognised that secession of a constituent part of a State territory is allowed with the consent of the parties involved. State practice also supports the possibility of a State giving retrospective consent for a secession to which it had not initially consented. For example, in 1974 Pakistan, by recognising Bangladesh (which was formerly Eastern Pakistan), retrospectively consented to Eastern Pakistan's secession which in reality had occurred in 1971.

On 19 April 2013, Serbia and Kosovo signed a normalisation agreement mediated by the EU.[81] This agreement was a precondition to negotiations on Serbia's accession to the EU. The normalisation agreement deals only with the autonomy of Kosovar Serbs.[82] In light of Serbia's forceful assertions that Kosovo remains part of its territory, this agreement cannot be regarded as Serbia's implicit recognition of Kosovo's existence as a separate State.

The matter of whether international law recognises the right to secession, without the consent of the parent State when that State systematically oppresses a part of its population, is controversial. As previously discussed, the Commission of Rapporteurs in the *Åland Islands Case* [83] and the Canadian Supreme Court in the *Reference re Secession of Quebec* [84] decided that in such a situation the oppressed minority has the right to external self determination. The UN[85] and State practice does not support this view.

---

77   Ibid, para 7.

78   Ibid, para 2.

79   Ibid, para 5.

80   *Separate Opinion of Judge Yusuf* [2010] ICJ Rep 418, para 2.

81   A. Vasovic and J. Kawlak, 'EU Brokers Historic Kosovo Deal, Door Opens to Serbia's Accession', *Reuters*, 19 April 2013, available at www.reuters.com/article/2013/04/19/us-serbia-kosovo-eu-idUSBRE93I0IB20130419 (accessed 8 November 2014).

82   C. Ashton, 'A Different Balkan Story', *NY Times*, 25 April 2013.

83   Supra note 14.

84   Supra note 62.

85   See *An Agenda for Peace, Preventive Diplomacy, Peacemaking and Peace-keeping.* A Report prepared by the UNS-G, 17 June 1991, A/ 47/277 – S/24111, paras 17 *et seq* and General Recommendation 21 adopted by the CERD Committee (see its official website).

Even if external succession is accepted, the following conditions must be met by the seceding entity:

(1) Only 'people' are entitled to secede.

(2) The oppression must be extreme, i.e. 'people' must be victims of widespread, systematic and grave violations of HRs.

(3) External self-determination must be the only available option, i.e. it must be the remedy of last resort.

Kosovo satisfied conditions (2) and (3) in that massive and serious violations of fundamental HRs of Albanian Kosovars occurred and, as indicated above, a political settlement was impossible. However, the issue whether Albanian Kosovars are 'people' is debatable (see Chapter 13.7.3).

The uniqueness of the situation of Kosovo is underlined by all supporters of its independence, but in fact, the only distinction between Albanian Kosovars and other oppressed minorities is the involvement of the international community in managing the humanitarian disaster that took place in Kosovo. In particular, NATO's unlawful intervention was the cause of the UN's subsequent involvement. It seems contrary to the basic tenets of HRL to argue that because NATO intervened in Kosovo (which occurred mainly because Kosovo is located in Europe and therefore of direct concern to the EU and NATO, and thus the decision to intervene was based on political rather than legal considerations) its case is unique. This line of reasoning entails that when minorities are of no great interest to the major powers, or unlucky enough to be part of the population of a major power, international law will deny them the right to external self-determination even when they are being subjected to genocide. Thus, to claim that the Kosovo case does not constitute a precedent is unacceptable. Kosovo should be regarded as a precedent to be followed by all oppressed minorities when the oppression is extreme. This will, on the one hand, force States to treat their minorities in conformity with the requirements of HRL, and, on the other, force the UN to act within its duty resulting from the responsibility to protect (see Chapter 16.2.7), i.e. to intervene in all cases of widespread, serious and systematic violations of HRs orchestrated by a State and not, as is currently the case, only selectively and arbitrarily depending on political factors.

It is to be noted that the right to self-determination and the recognition of a new State which has been established as a result of people exercising that right are two different matters. The recognition of a State involves a political decision of other States which legitimises and validates, *post factum*, the successful exercise of the right to self-determination of a particular group of people. Therefore, recognition, essentially political in content, provides retroactive legitimacy to the act of self-determination. A claim to secession, though not justified on any coherent theory of self-determination, will not preclude or prevent recognition of a new State, although the legality or otherwise of the steps leading to its creation will be assessed by States and will, as a result, either facilitate or hinder its recognition (see Chapter 6.2).

13.7.3.2 Indigenous people and self-determination

There are an estimated 300 million indigenous people living across the world.

Indigenous people are more than any others entitled to be considered as 'people' in the context of self-determination. Their very nomenclature appears to qualify them for such consideration in that they are identified as 'people' and the word 'indigenous' implies that intrinsically they are a special category of colonial people and therefore should benefit from the right to self-determination as envisaged in UNGA Resolution 1514. International law, however, did not include them in the decolonisation movement, although they have been the longest victims of colonisation. Indigenous people have always considered themselves as equals within the international community.

The concept of *terra nullius* was used to justify the claims of the Europeans to the title to land in territories which, at the time of discovery and subsequent colonisation or first settlement, were inhabited by indigenous people. That concept was first contested by Francisco de Vittoria, a Spanish Dominican and a professor of theology at the University of Salamanca in the sixteenth century. He argued that indigenous people enjoyed intrinsic sovereignty and consequently were entitled to negotiate with the European nations on equal terms and to enter into international agreements. De Vittorio's justification for the European conquest of the Americas was based on the inferiority of indigenous civilisations.

Indigenous people were, more often than not, formally recognised by colonial powers which, at first entered into commerce or friendship treaties with local populations, but subsequently denied them any rights. In North America during the time when England, France and Spain were fighting each other in order to conquer the continent these States often entered into international agreements with Indian tribes and treated them as sovereign and independent nations. With the end of the intra-European rivalry and the final withdrawal of European powers from the US (e.g. the cession of Louisiana by France in 1803 and of Florida by Spain in 1819) the US federal government no longer needed Indian tribes. They were dealt with by force of arms.

In the nineteenth century, the colonial powers extended the concept of *terra nullius* to encompass land used and occupied by aboriginal and indigenous peoples in order to justify title to that land. The colonial powers claimed that aboriginal and indigenous peoples, as they did not meet the European standards of civilisation, had no pre-existing interests in and/or rights to land they inhabited. The extended concept of terra nullius, being both inappropriate and unjust, has no place in modern international law. Its rejection has been confirmed by many international instruments, e.g. Articles 13 (1) and 14 (1) of the Convention concerning Indigenous and Tribal Peoples in Independent Countries[86] and Articles 25, 26, 28 and 29(1) of the UN Declaration on the Rights of Indigenous Peoples.[87] It has also been found unacceptable by the ICJ and by national courts.[88] In the *Western Sahara (Advisory Opinion)* the ICJ stated that:

> [A] determination that Western Sahara was a '*terra nullius*' at the time of colonisation by Spain would be possible only if it were established that at that time the territory belonged to no one in the sense that it was open to acquisition through the legal process of 'occupation'.[89]

The ILO was the first to show any interest in indigenous people. This resulted in the adoption of ILO Convention 107 of 1957 on Living and Working Conditions of Indigenous Populations, later replaced by Convention 107.

The issue of whether indigenous people have the right to external self determination was debated on and off for more than 20 years within the UN. The debate ended with the adoption by the UNGA of the Declaration on the Rights of Indigenous Peoples on 13 September 2007 (147 votes in favour, 4 against (Australia, Canada, New Zealand and the US, all of them having a large indigenous population) and 11 abstentions). The Declaration does not recognise the right of indigenous people to external self-determination. In this respect, Article 3 of the Declaration provides that:

---

86   28 ILM 1382.
87   A/Res/61/295.
88   See, e.g. *Mabo* v *Queensland* (1992) 66 ALJR 408 and *Guerin v Her Majesty The Queen* Supreme Court of Canada (1 November 1984) (1984) 2 Canada Supreme Court Reports 376.
89   (1975) ICJ Rep 12, 56.

Indigenous people have the right of self-determination. By virtue of that right they freely determine their political status and freely pursue their economic, social and cultural development.

This article, however, must be read in the light of Article 46(1) of the Declaration which contains the 'safeguard clause' stating that:

Nothing in this Declaration may be interpreted as implying for any State, people, group or person any right to engage in any activity or to perform any act contrary to the Charter of the United Nations or construed as authorising or encouraging any action which would dismember or impair, totally or in part, the territorial integrity or political unity of sovereign and independent States.

Article 46(1) leaves no doubt that when a State where indigenous people live treats them on the basis of equality and without discrimination they can only exercise the right to internal self-determination, i.e. seek various forms of autonomy within that State. As a result, indigenous people are not 'people' within the meaning of international law on self-determination. However, they may become 'people' entitled to external self-determination in cases of extreme oppression, if remedial succession is recognised in international law (see Chapter 13.7.3.1 B).

13.8 Conclusion

The right to self-determination has been declared as a fundamental human right by all important HR instruments, including the UDHR. Self-determination is regarded as the right of all peoples to control their destiny, to choose their political status and to make decisions about their own development. However, international law remains unclear as to the exact meaning and scope of application of the right to self-determination. Only in the context of decolonisation, provided one is not too precise about the definition of 'decolonisation', is self-determination clearly recognised as a legal right. In all other cases political considerations determine which 'oppressed' people gain sufficient acceptance and support to merit their being recognised as having the right to external self-determination. This recognition has most often been expressed by UN resolutions which 'grant' to certain oppressed groups the status of peoples possessing legitimate aspirations to external self-determination. Left unanswered is the question of the legal competence of the UN to grant this recognition in the first place.

It is probably safe to say that the content and the understanding of the right to self-determination has evolved as a result of the end of the Cold War. Some authors have argued that State practice started to recognise a more expansive right to secede in the light of the cases of Bangladesh, the Baltic republics, Slovenia, Croatia, Bosnia-Herzegovina, Eritrea, Kosovo, and by virtue of the velvet divorce, of Slovakia and the Czech Republic. Nevertheless, each case is different, and it is impossible to deduce any clear rules from the above cases. The position expressed by the Supreme Court of Canada in its decision concerning the Secession of Quebec from Canada seems to have been accepted by many States. According to it international law does not recognise any right of a political sub-unit to secede so long as the government of the State 'represents the whole of the people or peoples resident within its territory, on a basis of equality and without discrimination' and the State 'respects the principles of self-determination in its own internal arrangements'.[90] The ICJ has offered no views on this in its Advisory Opinion on the *Accordance with International Law of the Unilateral Declaration of Independence in*

---

90   (1998) 2 SCR 217, para 130.

Respect of Kosovo. This is not surprising given that the Court was not asked to do so. Accordingly, this area of international law remains unclear, but many commentators suggest that:

> Political importance could be a reason for states to prefer that the right remains ill-defined. This is because the international community are more likely to respond to the breach of a norm that is perceived as politically significant, but if the norm is kept ill-defined, states will retain a leeway to resist claims that they are not fulfilling obligations to peoples under their authority.[91]

RECOMMENDED READING

Books

Crawford, J., *The Creation of States in International Law*, 2nd edn, Oxford: Clarendon, 2006.
Sterio, M., *The Right to Self-Determination under International Law. 'selfistans', Secession, and the Rule of the Great Powers*, Abingdon: Routledge, 2013.
Summers, J., *Peoples and International Law: How Nationalism and Self-Determination Shape a Contemporary Law of Nations*, Leiden: Nijhoff, 2007.

Articles

Brilmayer, L., *Secession and Self-Determination: A Territorial Interpretation* (1991) 16 YJIL, 177.
Klabbers, J.,*The Right to be Taken Seriously: Self-Determination in International Law* (2006) 28 Hum Rts Q, 186.
McCorquodale, R., *Self-Determination: A Human Rights Approach* (1994) 43 ICLQ, 857.
Saul, M., *The Normative Status of Self-Determination in International Law: A Formula for Uncertainty in the Scope and Content of the Right?* (2011) 11/4 Human Rights Law Review, 609.
Tierney, S., *Legal Issues Surrounding the Referendum on Independence in Scotland* (2013) 9 European Constitutional Law Review, 359.
Weller, M., *Modesty Can be a Virtue: Judicial Economy in the ICJ Kosovo Opinion?* (2011) 24 LJIL, 127.

---

91   M. Saul, *The Normative Status of Self-Determination in International Law: A Formula for Uncertainty in the Scope and Content of the Right?* (2011) 11/4/ Human Rights Law Review, 612.

Self-determination of peoples

Self-determination refers to the right of a people to determine its own political destiny. It is a collective right. It is enshrined in Articles 1(3), 55, 73 and Chapter XII of the UN Charter and further developed and defined in Article 1(3) common to the ICCPR and ICSECR, in the 1960 Declaration on the Granting of Independence to Colonial Countries and Peoples (UNGA Res 1514 (XV) and in the 1970 Declaration on Principles of International Law concerning Friendly Relations and Co-operation among States (UNGA Res2625 (XXV)).

Internal self-determination. The right to internal self-determination is given to all people living within a State and its exercise does not involve any territorial changes for that State. They have the right to pursue freely their political, economic, social and cultural development without outside interference. In particular, the right is of relevance to:

Minorities.

Indigenous, including tribal, peoples (Article 46(1) of the 2007 Declaration on the Rights of Indigenous Peoples).

People who live under racist regimes, e.g. black and coloured people living in South Africa under the regime of racial segregation known as apartheid (1948–1994).

External self-determination. The right to external self-determination gives peoples the right to secede from an existing State either to create a new State or to be incorporated into or to associate with another State (UNGA Res. 1541). As a result, external self-determination challenges the national unity and territorial integrity of a State and, when people are using force to exercise their right, poses a threat to international peace and security.

The right to external self-determination applies in the following situations:

Where colonial people fight for independence from a colonial power but the principle of *uti possedetis* applies.

Where territorial sovereignty is lacking, either because the State is in the process of formation or because it is undergoing transformation or dissolution.

Where parties agree that the principle of self-determination will apply to settlement of a territorial dispute between them (The Case of *East Timor* (*Portugal v Australia*)).

Where people live under foreign domination, e.g. Palestinians living in the occupied territory.

It is uncertain whether oppressed minorities have the right to external self-determination. So far, State practice has not followed the 'remedial succession' approach, although the case of Kosovo, if it becomes a precedent, may change the current position. They would be entitled to secede if:

They have been subjected to massive, systematic and serious violations of their fundamental HRs, in particular if they have been victims of genocide.

External self-determination is the only available option, i.e. it must be the remedy of last resort.

14

PEACEFUL SETTLEMENT OF DISPUTES BETWEEN STATES

CONTENTS

CHAPTER OUTLINE

1 Introduction

Article 2(3) of the UN Charter imposes an obligation on all its member States to settle their international disputes by peaceful means in such a manner as not to endanger international peace, security and justice. This obligation is also imposed by customary international law.

2 Diplomatic means of dispute settlement between States

Diplomatic means of settlement of international disputes tend to facilitate an agreement between the parties as, in contrast to legal means, such means are not binding on the parties and place less emphasis on their formal position under the law. Such methods include:

A. Negotiation. This concerns discussions between representatives of the parties to a dispute with a view to settling that dispute. No third party is involved.

B. Good offices. This involves the participation of a third party, i.e. a State, an individual or a body, in the settlement of a dispute with a view to bringing the parties together. The main role of a third party is to provide a channel of communication thus facilitating the establishment of dialogue between the parties.

C. Mediation. This occurs when a third party becomes actively involved in the settlement of a dispute and makes proposals for its solution. These proposals can be accepted or refused.

D. Inquiry. Inquiry involves a third party investigation of the facts surrounding the dispute and as such is normally of a technical character.

E. Conciliation. Conciliation is a quasi-judicial procedure. It occurs by agreement between the parties, whereby a third party is appointed to investigate the dispute and to suggest terms for a settlement. The parties, are not, however, bound to accept the terms suggested. A third party entrusted with conciliation examines all aspects of the dispute.

14.3 Arbitration

The ILC defined arbitration as 'a procedure for the settlement of disputes between States by a binding award on the basis of law as a result of an undertaking voluntarily accepted'. Recourse to arbitration is based on the consent of the parties to a dispute and may be based on:

A. Arbitration clauses. They are inserted into a treaty and provide that if a dispute arises between the contracting parties in respect of the interpretation or application of that treaty they will be bound to submit it to arbitration.

B. *Compromis*. This is a formal agreement concluded between States, after the dispute has occurred, to submit the dispute to arbitration. *Compromis* will normally stipulate the terms under which the arbitration tribunal will function, its composition, competences and the law applicable to the dispute.

C. A treaty of arbitration. Arbitration as a method of settlement of international disputes is provided for in numerous treaties the subject of which is arbitration only, *inter alia*, the 1957 European Convention for the Peaceful Settlement of Disputes.

Arbitration has a long history, but in modern times it began with the Jay Treaty of 1774 concluded between Great Britain and the US to settle highly controversial matters after the War of Independence which had not been settled by diplomacy. Its popularity culminated with the establishment of the Permanent Court of Arbitration (PCA), in 1900 on the basis of the 1899 Convention for the Pacific Settlement of International Disputes as amended by the 1907 Convention for the Pacific Settlement of

International Disputes, both adopted by The Hague Peace Conference. The name given to the Permanent Court of Arbitration is highly misleading as it is neither a court nor an arbitration tribunal, nor does it involve any permanency. The PCA can be described as 'a permanent arbitration administration service' as it consists of a list of individuals who declare themselves available, for a renewable term of 6 years, to serve as arbitrators in the case of a dispute.

4 Mixed claims commissions

These are established on an *ad hoc* basis to deal with large numbers of claims arising out of an internal or an international conflict. The claims to be settled may be between nationals of one State and nationals of another State, or between nationals of one State and another State or between two States.

5 From the Permanent Court of International Justice (PCIJ) to the International Court of Justice (ICJ)

There are many international courts, but the International Court of Justice (ICJ) has a special place among them. It is the successor to the Permanent Court of International Justice (PCJ), which was the first permanent world court ever created by the international community open to all States with jurisdiction over all international disputes, and it is thus sometimes informally referred to as the World Court.

A. The PCIJ was established on the basis of Article 14 of the Covenant of the League of Nations. It held its opening ceremony on 15 February 1922 at its seat at the Peace Palace in The Hague and was officially dissolved on 18 April 1946 by a UNGA Resolution. On the same day the ICJ was inaugurated. The PCIJ during its existence rendered 32 judgments and 27 advisory opinions. Despite many criticisms of the PCIJ the fact remains that it was the first permanent court available to all States of the world and that it considerably contributed to the development of international law.

The ICJ is a judicial organ of the UN. Under Article 93(1) of the UN Charter all members of the UN are automatically contracting parties to the Statute of the ICJ. Non-members of the UN may also become parties to the Statute of the ICJ but a special procedure is applied to them. Under Article 94(1) of the Charter each member of the UN is obliged to comply with decisions of the ICJ.

6 The ICJ: functions, composition and organisation

A. Function. The main function of the ICJ is to decide cases on the basis of the law as it stands at the time of the judgment. The ICJ is competent to decide legal disputes only.

B. Judges. The ICJ is made up of 15 judges, who hold office for 9 years, and no two of whom may be nationals of the same State. They may be re-elected.

They are elected by a majority vote taking place simultaneously in the UNGA and the UNSC.

C. Chambers. The ICJ normally decides cases as a full court (a quorum of nine judges, excluding judges *ad hoc*, is required to decide a case). However, under the Statute the ICJ may form permanent or temporary chambers of three kinds. So far only chambers provided for under Article 26(2) of the Statute have been established. Such chambers, made up of three or more judges, deal with a particular case at the request of the parties to that case.

7 The ICJ: contentious jurisdiction

A. Before any State becomes a party to a case before the ICJ it must have access to the Court. There are basically three ways whereby a State may have access to the Court:

■ member States of the UN, being *ipso facto* parties to the Statute, have automatic access to the ICJ;

■ non-member States of the UN:

■ who want to become parties to the Statute have to meet the conditions specified by the UNGA upon the recommendation of the UNSC;

■ who are not parties, and do not wish to become parties, to the Statute have to comply with conditions determined by UNSC Resolution 9(1946).

B. Jurisdiction of the ICJ in contentious proceedings is based on the consent of the parties to a dispute. The consent may be given in the following ways:

■ the parties may conclude a special agreement known as a '*compromis*' under which they agree to submit an already existing dispute to the ICJ;

■ by virtue of a jurisdictional clause. Such a clause has been inserted in numerous international treaties;

■ by express or tacit acceptance by the respondent State of the jurisdiction of the ICJ once the case has already been brought by the claimant State before the Court. This is known as *forum prorogatum*;

■ by virtue of Article 36(2) of the ICJ Statute which confers on the Court the so-called compulsory jurisdiction. Under this article a State may make a declaration recognising the compulsory jurisdiction of the ICJ. A declaration is often subject to reservations. Acceptance of the ICJ's jurisdiction is compulsory but only within the limits of the declaration. However, there is no obligation upon a State to make such a declaration which means that jurisdiction cannot be regarded as compulsory in the true sense. The effect of a declaration is that it creates bilateral relations with other States which have made declarations of acceptance, and as a result, relations between such States are based on reciprocity i.e. a State accepts the Court's jurisdiction with regard to any other State only in so far as that State has also accepted the Court's jurisdiction. In other words, if State A makes a declaration subject to reservation Y and State B makes a declaration subject to reservation Z, the Court has jurisdiction to hear disputes between States A and B only in so far as they are not within reservations Y and Z.

C. Procedure before the ICJ. This consists of written and oral phases. Once the oral phase is concluded, the ICJ deliberates *in camera* and then takes a decision by absolute majority of the judges present. The judgment is delivered in public.

D. Incidental jurisdiction. Independently of the main proceedings the Court may be called upon to exercise incidental jurisdiction: hearing preliminary and admissibility objections, determining applications to intervene and ordering interim measures.

E. Limitation period. There is no limitation period within which a case must be brought before the ICJ, but the Court would be reluctant to adjudicate disputes that have their origin in the distant past. However, all depends on the circumstances of each case.

F. Judgments. They are final, without appeal, and binding on the parties to the case. However, under Article 60 of the Statute, at the request of either party, the Court may interpret its judgment when there is a disagreement between the parties as to its exact meaning. Further, either party may ask the ICJ to revise the judgment, but so far the Court has never revised its judgment. The conditions for revision are specified in Article 60 of the Statute.

8   The ICJ: advisory jurisdiction

This possibility is open exclusively to organs of the UN and international organisations. Under Article 96(1) of the UN Charter the UNGA and the UNSC are entitled to request an advisory opinion and by virtue of Article 96(2) of the UN Charter other organs and specialised agencies, when authorised by the UNGA, may also make such a request. The purpose of the advisory role of the Court is to provide legal advice in respect of the submitted matter and not to settle any particular dispute, even though a request is often related to, or has its origin in, an existing dispute. Article 65(1) of the Statute specifies that:

- an advisory opinion must be confined to a legal question; and

- the Court has discretion to decline its jurisdiction on the ground of judicial propriety.

9   Assessment of the ICJ

The ICJ has greatly contributed to the development and clarification of international law. In its judgments the Court has always paid attention to the evolving nature of international law and has itself contributed to its evolution.

14.1   Introduction

The principle of peaceful settlement of disputes is enshrined in Article 2(3) of the UN Charter[1] which provides that in the pursuit of the fundamental objectives of the UN, namely the maintenance of peace and security, its member States are bound to settle their international disputes by peaceful means in such a manner as not to endanger international peace, security and justice. This obligation is reinforced in Article 33(1) of the UN Charter which provides that:

> The parties to any dispute, the continuance of which is likely to endanger the maintenance of international peace and security, shall, first of all, seek a solution by negotiation, enquiry, mediation, conciliation, arbitration, judicial settlement, resort to regional agencies or arrangements, or other peaceful means of their own choice.

---

1   892 UNTS 119.

Article 33 leaves the parties free to choose the means which they consider as the most appropriate to the circumstances and nature of their dispute. However, if the parties fail to make any meaningful attempt to resolve a dispute which threatens international peace and security then, under Article 33(2), the UNSC may call upon the parties to settle the dispute but without specifying what means to use. However, it may recommend a particular means of settlement, it may recommend the actual terms of settlement, it may investigate the dispute and it may set up machinery for settlement.

The principle of peaceful settlement of international disputes has been reaffirmed by numerous declarations and resolutions of the UNGA, in particular:

■ UNGA Resolution 2625 (XXV) which extends the obligation of peaceful settlement of international disputes to all States and not only to the member States of the UN;[2]

■ the UNGA 1982 Manila Declaration on the Peaceful Settlement of International Disputes[3] which imposes on States the obligation to seek in good faith and a spirit of co-operation an early and equitable settlement of their disputes;

■ the UNGA 1988 Declaration on the Prevention and Removal of Disputes and Situations Which May Threaten International Peace and Security and on the Role of the UN in This Field,[4] which emphasises the need for the ICJ to play a greater role in the settlement of international disputes and recommends the adoption of a universal convention on peaceful settlement of disputes.

The principle of peaceful settlement of international disputes has been recognised by the ICJ in the *Nicaragua Case (Nicaragua v US) (Merits)*[5] as having the status of customary law.

Traditionally, States were free to choose between various peaceful means of settlement of international disputes and thus to select the most appropriate to the circumstances and nature of the dispute. This freedom has been considerably limited in favour of compulsory recourse to specific procedures provided for by an increasing number of multilateral treaties.

In the twenty-first century the principle of peaceful settlement of international disputes is universally accepted. However, the path towards its recognition was long, and bristling with difficulties. Indeed, before the views of humanity on war and peace became more sophisticated the main method of resolving disputes was war. From the historical perspective, two methods have developed in the search for the peaceful settlement of international disputes:

■ The first method consists of settling of such disputes through the channels of diplomacy. Within this, various forms of negotiation, mediation and conciliation have been developed in response to the need to resolve international conflicts in the context of the gradual expansion of an international legal order.

■ The second method consists of settling such disputes through legal processes, in particular by arbitral tribunals and international courts. These being more complex and controversial, took longer to attain recognition.

Alongside State practice efforts were made by pacifists, anti-war movements and idealists, to ban the use of force in international relations. It was towards the end of the nineteenth and the beginning

---

2   UNGA Res 2625 (XXV) 'Declaration on Principles of International Law concerning Friendly Relations and Co-operation among States in Accordance with the Charter of the United Nations' (24 October 1970) GAOR 25th Session Supp 28, 121.

3   A/Res/37/10 (1982).

4   A/Res/43/51 (1988).

5   [1986] ICJ Rep 14.

of the twentieth centuries, at the two Hague Peace Conferences of 1899 and 1907, that restrictions on the use of force and the necessity for the peaceful settlement of international disputes were effectively linked. The Hague Conferences laid down the foundations of the Permanent Court of Arbitration (PCA).

14.2 Diplomatic means of dispute settlement between States

Diplomatic means of settlement of international disputes tend to facilitate an agreement between the parties as, in contrast to legal means, they are not binding on the parties and place less emphasis on their formal position under the law. Such methods include negotiation, good offices, enquiry and conciliation. Diplomatic means are flexible. The parties to a dispute exercise full control over these procedures.

14.2.1 Negotiation

Negotiation is the most frequently and probably the only universally accepted means of dispute settlement. It is also the normal method of diplomatic interchange and as such in certain cases negotiation constitutes a necessary first step before the parties decide to use other procedures to resolve their dispute. Moreover, often, international treaties include clauses providing for negotiation as a prerequisite to other forms of settlement.

Negotiation is more than mere deliberation, and thus may lead to an agreed solution. Negotiation may be bilateral or multilateral. In the latter case it often takes the form of conferences. The value of negotiation as a method of settlement of international disputes has been acknowledged by both the PCIJ[6] and the ICJ.[7]

The main drawback of negotiation is that when a party denies the existence of a dispute or refuses to conduct meaningful negotiations or refuses to follow through on a negotiated agreement other means of dispute settlement must be used.

14.2.2 Good offices and mediation

In most cases, good offices are confused with mediation. For example, when UN Secretary-Generals were asked to render good offices, in fact, they acted as mediators, i.e. beyond what it meant by offering good offices (e.g. Cyprus, East Timor, Iraq, Libya, Nigeria and West Sahara). However, there is an important distinction between good offices and mediation which is explained below.

14.2.2.1 Good offices

Good offices involves the participation of a third party (whether a State, an individual or a body) in bringing the parties together. An offer of good offices is subject to acceptance by the parties to a dispute. The impartiality of a third party is of the essence as confidence in its reliability constitutes a necessary condition of establishing contact between the parties in dispute. The main role of a third party is to provide a channel of communication thus facilitating the establishment of a dialogue between the parties. The third party does not participate in the actual settlement of the dispute.

---

6   *Free Zones of Upper Savoy and the District of Gex Case* [1932] PCIJ Rep Ser A/B No 46.
7   *North Sea Continental Shelf Cases (Federal Republic of Germany v the Netherlands)* [1969] ICJ Rep 3.

Good offices is based on customary international law and has been included in many international agreements, such as the 1907 Hague Convention I for the Pacific Settlement of International Disputes,[8] the UN Charter, the 1948 Bogotá Pact[9] and the 1961 Vienna Convention on Diplomatic Relations.[10]

There is probably only one true example of good offices, i.e. when Norway in 1993 offered its services to facilitate secret talks, which took place in Norway, between the Palestinian Liberation Organisation (PLO) and Israel, which culminated in the signing of the Oslo Agreement.

14.2.2.2 Mediation

This occurs when a third party is actively involved in the solution of a dispute in that the third party makes non-binding proposals to both parties. Often good offices turn into mediation. This is facilitated by the fact that the third party has already been accepted by the parties in dispute. Mediation therefore can be an extension of good offices.

Successful mediation was carried out, *inter alia*, by Germany during the 1878 Berlin Congress, by the Soviet Union during the 1966 Indo-Pakistan conflict, by the US in the 1978 peace talks between Egypt and Israel, by Alexander Haig in the Falklands Islands conflict in 1982, by the UNS-G in 1988 in respect of the termination of war between Iran and Iraq, and by the US in the conflict in the former Yugoslavia which led to the conclusion of the Dayton Peace Agreement in 1995.

Most conflicts in the post-Cold War era have involved attempts to use mediation to achieve peace.

14.2.3 Inquiry

Inquiry involves third-party investigation of the facts surrounding the dispute and as such is normally of a technical character. Many conventions adopted by the 1899 and 1907 Hague Peace Conferences (see Chapter 17.3) expressly refer to the establishment of an international commission of inquiry in order to 'elucidate through an impartial and conscientious examination the question of facts' and thus to facilitate the settlement of disputes.

The Treaties of Bryan (the name of the US Secretary of State who initiated them) concluded between the US and various States in 1913–1914 set up a permanent commission of inquiry under which contracting States were, in the case of a dispute, bound to wait for a report from such a Commission before starting war.[11]

The involvement of a third party, although customary, is not imperative. Many international treaties provide for the establishment of permanent commissions of inquiry, fact-finding or investigation, in particular, conventions relating to the protection of HRs. In the context of HRs, an inquiry is often used as a preventive measure to serve political objectives rather than to actually investigate in a comprehensive manner the facts of a dispute.

Normally, at the conclusion of an inquiry a report containing the factual findings is submitted to the parties. It may also contain non-binding recommendations. Inquiry requires that the parties involved in a dispute provide their assistance and co-operation during the investigation which often involves the examination of witnesses, and on-site visits.

---

8   205 CTS 233.
9   30 UNTS 55.
10   500 UNTS 95.
11   G.A. Finch, *The Bryan Peace Treaties* (1916) 10 AJIL, 882.

14.2.4 Conciliation

Conciliation is a quasi-judicial procedure. It occurs by agreement between the parties, whereby a third party is appointed to investigate the dispute and to recommend terms for a settlement. The parties are not, however, bound to agree to these. A third party entrusted with conciliation examines all aspects of the dispute. In this respect conciliation exceeds the inquiry procedure as not only are the facts of the dispute established, but the dispute is also examined in its entirety.

Pragmatism rather than legal considerations governs conciliation proceedings. Conciliation is a flexible method of settlement of disputes which leaves the parties free to reject the proposed solution, to accept it, or to consider it as a source of inspiration for the future resolution of the dispute. Conciliation has frequently been used in cases of a politically delicate nature, and in non-justiciable disputes.

Numerous conventions concluded under the auspices of the League of Nations provide for the establishment of commissions of conciliation. Modern multilateral treaties often provide for compulsory conciliation which, for two reasons, is a popular alternative to binding procedures:

■ it satisfies States which wish to have some pre-established mechanism relating to the settlement of disputes that may arise under a particular treaty; and

■ it is acceptable to States which do not wish to have imposed upon them any legally binding solution to a future dispute.

Examples of treaties which provide for compulsory conciliation are: the VCLT;[12] the 1978 Vienna Convention on Succession of States in Respect of Treaties;[13] the 1982 UN Convention on the Law of the Sea[14] and the 1986 Vienna Convention on the Law of Treaties between States and International Organisations or between International Organisations.[15]

14.3 Arbitration

Arbitration between States is a different form of arbitration from that used in the settlement of civil disputes between individuals or other non-State actors, and from the concept of mixed arbitral tribunals dealing with claims by natural or legal persons.

The 1899 Convention for the Pacific Settlement of International Disputes[16] states that:

> International arbitration has for its object the settlement of disputes between States by judges of their own choice and on the basis of respect for law. Recourse to arbitration implies an engagement to submit in good faith to the award.

The ILC defined arbitration in its Model Rules on Arbitral Procedure as 'a procedure for the settlement of disputes between states by a binding award on the basis of law as a result of an undertaking voluntarily accepted'.[17]

---

12   1155 UNTS 331.

13   1946 UNTS 3.

14   1833 UNTS 396.

15   (1986) 25 ILM 543.

16   187 CTS 410.

17   UN ILC 'Model Rules of Arbitral Procedure' (28 April–4 July 1958) GAOR 13th Session Supp 9, 5–8.

Recourse to arbitration relies on the consent of the parties to a dispute and may be based on:

- Arbitration clauses. These are inserted into a treaty and provide that if a dispute arises between the contracting parties in respect of the interpretation or application of that treaty they will be bound to submit it to arbitration.

- *Compromis*. This is a formal agreement concluded between States, after the dispute has occurred, to submit the dispute to arbitration. *Compromis* will normally stipulate the terms under which the arbitration tribunal will function, its composition, competences and the law applicable to the dispute. Although the parties are free to organise the procedure as they wish, often they refer to the rules of procedure set out in the 1899 Hague Convention (as revised in 1907) rather than the 1958 Model Rules drafted by the ILC, and recommended for use by member States by UNGA. The reason is that the procedure under the 1899 Hague Convention, unlike the 1958 Model Rules, ensures that the parties enjoy the greatest possible autonomy.

- A treaty of arbitration. Arbitration as a method of settlement of international disputes is provided for in numerous treaties, including the 1928 Geneva General Act for the Settlement of Disputes adopted by the League of Nations and 'reinvigorated' by the UNGA in 1949;[18] the 1929 Washington Treaty of Inter-American Arbitration;[19] the 1948 American Treaty on Pacific Settlement of Disputes[20] (known as the 1948 Bogotá Pact); and the 1957 European Convention for the Peaceful Settlement of Disputes[21] which was prepared under the auspices of the COE. Unfortunately these treaties are for various reasons, e.g. lack of a sufficient number of ratifications and many reservations inserted by contracting parties, of little practical significance.

The importance of arbitration justifies a short summary of its history, followed by the examination of various legal aspects of arbitration including the effect of the arbitral award.

14.3.1 History of arbitration

Arbitration was first used by the ancient Greek city-States to settle their disputes. Although during the Middle Ages arbitration found some favour in respect of disputes between Italian city States, the Swiss Cantons and the Hanseatic League, its use declined with the rise of independent sovereign States.

Modern arbitration dates from the establishment of three mixed claims commissions under the Jay Treaty of 1774 between Great Britain and the US, after the War of Independence, to settle highly controversial matters which had not been settled by diplomacy. Both nations appointed an equal number of British and American nationals to serve on an arbitral commission. The Jay Arbitration was very successful and stimulated international interest in arbitration as a dispute-resolution mechanism. This also encouraged the US to conclude similar arbitration treaties with young South American States which were very interested in introducing arbitration to settle regional disputes, as exemplified by the 1880 General, Permanent and Absolute Arbitration Treaty between Colombia and Chile.

---

18   71 UNTS 101, revised by the UN in 1949, UN GA Res 268A (III) of 28 April 1949.
19   OASTS No 16.
20   30 UNTS 55.
21   CETS No 57.

Further development of arbitration was prompted by the conclusion of the 1871 Treaty of Washington[22] between Great Britain and the US which defined the rights and duties of neutral States. The famous Alabama Claims Arbitration[23] was settled under the Treaty.

ALABAMA CLAIMS ARBITRATION

Facts:

In this case, the US accused Great Britain of infringing customary rules on neutrality by helping the southern States during the US Civil War. In particular, the UK was reproached for its covert conduct while building ships which were intended for the Confederates. The ships while in the UK and its territorial waters did not have the outward appearance of warships but had, in fact, been constructed as warships so that once in the hands of the Confederates they could be fitted with guns and provided with ammunition. Two of these ships, Florida *and* Alabama *inflicted great damage on the Union ships. Alabama destroyed some 64 ships of the Union before, itself, being sunk.*

Held:

The arbitral tribunal found against the UK and ordered Great Britain to pay US $15.5 million in compensation for indirect injury to US commerce. Great Britain complied.

Comment:

The Alabama Case *contributed to the popularity of arbitration and initiated the practice of inserting arbitration clauses into international treaties. It also clarified certain matters relating to neutrality and the composition and competence of arbitral tribunals.*

During the last quarter of the nineteenth century many arbitration tribunals were established on an *ad hoc* basis to settle a particular dispute or to deal with pecuniary claims for compensation for injury to aliens who could not obtain justice in foreign courts.[24]

Arbitration was further developed by The Hague Peace Conferences which adopted two conventions for the pacific settlement of international disputes, one in 1899 and one in 1907. The first provided for the establishment of the Permanent Court of Arbitration (PCA) which materialised in 1900.

14.3.2   The Permanent Court of Arbitration (PCA)

The name given to the Permanent Court of Arbitration is highly misleading as it is neither a court nor an arbitration tribunal nor does it involve much permanency. The PCA can be described as 'a permanent arbitration administration service' as its principal constituent consists of a list of individuals who declare themselves available, for a renewable term of 6 years, to serve as arbitrators in the case of a dispute.

---

22   Treaty between Great Britain and the United States of America for the Amicable Settlement of all Causes of Difference between the Two Countries (signed 8 May 1871, entered into force 17 June 1871) (1870–71) 61 BSP 40.

23   (1872) Moore, 1 Int Arb 495. See also T Bingham, *The Alabama Claims Arbitration* (2005) 54 ICLQ, 1–25.

24   J.H. Ralston, *International Arbitration from Athens to Locarno*, Stanford: Stanford University Press, 1929.

The list is made up of arbitrators whose names have been submitted by the contracting States. Such States may submit up to four names which may be of their nationals or foreigners selected on the basis of their expertise and the highest moral reputation. The PCA, therefore, constitutes an institutional mechanism to facilitate the formation of an arbitration tribunal when contracting States choose arbitration to settle a dispute. At the time of writing there are 116 contracting parties to one or both of the 1899 and 1907 Hague Conventions.

When a dispute is submitted to the PCA an *ad hoc* arbitral tribunal is established comprising arbitrators from the list or in some cases outside the list. Three different systems have been used with regard to the composition of an arbitral tribunal. An arbitration tribunal may consist of a single arbitrator (e.g. arbitrator Asser when he acted in the *Island of Palmas Arbitration (The Netherlands v US))*[25] or a panel of three or five arbitrators. If the parties decide to have a panel of three or five arbitrators but fail to agree on its composition, then in the case of a panel of three each party nominates one arbitrator, and the two who are nominated select the third and in the case of a five member panel each party nominates two and the four who are nominated select the fifth. If they fail to choose a fifth the contracting parties will select a third contracting State which will nominate the fifth. If the parties to a dispute cannot agree on a third State, each will nominate one contracting State, and then the two nominated contracting States will select the fifth member of the panel. If this procedure fails to produce a fifth member within a period of two months, each of these States will nominate two arbitrators from the list, who should neither be a national of the party to the dispute, nor already selected by the parties to the dispute. The selected arbitrators will draw lots to determine which of them will be the fifth member.

The International Bureau and the Administrative Council are the only permanent bodies of the PCA. The International Bureau serves as the registry of the PCA, compiles the list of arbitrators, organises meetings of the PCA and performs all other administrative tasks including acting as a registry for commissions of inquiry. Such Commissions have been established on four occasions (in 1904, 1912, 1921 and 1961). In 1937 the Bureau was authorised by the Administrative Council to set up conciliation commissions. Such commissions have been set up on three occasions, in 1937, 1954 and 1965.

The executive body of the PCA, i.e. its Administrative Council, supervises the work of the International Bureau and is in charge of such administrative tasks as the preparation of a budget and of an annual report on the activities of the PCA for the contracting parties. On some occasions it has taken important decisions, for example concerning the revision of the PCA's rules of procedure. The Council comprises diplomatic representatives of the contracting States and is chaired by the Foreign Minister of The Netherlands, being the person who is the depository of the Hague Conventions. The Administrative Council meets when necessary, but at least once a year.

The importance of the PCA declined with the establishment of the PCIJ and its successor the ICJ, but after falling into relative disuse in the 1950s it successfully reinvented itself, and in the twenty-first century has again become a thriving institution:

■ The PCA from 1902 to 1914 dealt with 17 cases and rendered 16 awards. Its most significant awards were given in the *Muscat* Dhows;[26] the *North Atlantic Fisheries* Arbitration;[27] *Savarkar*,[28] and *the Canevaro Claim*.[29]

---

25   (1928) 2 RIAA 829.
26   (1905) 1 Scott 95.
27   (1910) 11 RIAA 167.
28   (1911) 1 Scott 276.
29   (1912) 11 RIAA 397.

- In the period between the two world wars, the PCA rendered seven awards. The most famous is certainly the *Island of Palmas* Arbitration.[30]

- From 1945 to 1956 it merely dealt with four cases.

As can be seen the PCA was very successful during the period up to the beginning of WWII. However, since 1959 the PCA, in its search for revitalisation, has introduced many initiatives, such as offering its services for arbitrations between States and individuals or between a State and a corporation, or between individuals in commercial matters. Further initiatives,[31] *inter alia*, are:

- Under the UNICITRAL Arbitration Rules,[32] the Secretary-General of the PCA is entrusted with the role of designating an 'appointing authority' if parties to a dispute so agree. Also the PCA provides administrative support in arbitration conducted under the UNCITRAL Arbitration Rules.

- Under the 2002 Optional Rules for Arbitration of Disputes Relating to the Environmental and/or Natural Resources, Specialised Panels have been established who are available for appointment to arbitral tribunals or conciliation commissions.

- Under 'Host Country Agreements' concluded between the PCA and a contracting party, a host country and the PCA may establish a legal framework under which future PCA proceedings in the territory of the host State can, on an *ad hoc* basis, be carried out without permanent physical presence of the PCA.

- Under the 1994 Energy Charter Treaty,[33] the Secretary-General of the PCA acts as an 'appointing authority'.

- Under the PCA's auspices the Eritrea-Ethiopia Claims Commission was established to delimit and demarcate the colonial treaty border between the two States.

- The PCA has acted as a registry in arbitration between contracting States. Some examples are:[34]

  - Arbitration between Barbados and Trinidad and Tobago relating to the Delimitation of the Exclusive Economic Zone and Continental Shelf between them submitted under Part XV of UNCLOS (2006);

  - Arbitration between Guyana and Surinam Concerning the Delimitation of Maritime Boundary between them submitted under Annex VII of the UNCLOS (2007);

  - Arbitration between Ireland and the UK (MOX Plant case) submitted under Annex VII of UNCLOS (2008).

As at 31 December 2013, on the docket of the PCA were eight State-to-State arbitration cases, 62 cases concerning disputes arising under bilateral/multilateral investment treaties and national investment laws, 30 cases concerning disputes between a State and private party, and four other disputes.[35]

---

30   (1928) 2 RIAA 829.
31   See the official website of the PCA at www.pca-cpa.org.
32   UNGA Res 31/98, 9th Session, 99th plen mtg (15 Decemeber 1976).
33   34 ILM 381.
34   All cases can be found at the official website of the PCA.
35   Permanent Court of Arbitration, 113th Annual Report, 2013, 16, available at www.wx4all.net/pca/maintop/PCA-121307-v1-PCA_Annual_Report_2013_FINAL.pdf (accessed 20 October 2014).

The PCA actively co-operates with the UN and in 1993 was granted the status of a Permanent Observer at the UNGA.[36]

14.3.3 The main features of arbitration.

The main features of arbitration are examined below.

14.3.3.1 The selection of the arbitrator is made by the parties themselves or by means of a mechanism agreed between the parties

This distinguishes arbitration from judicial settlement. The freedom that the parties enjoy as to the appointment of the arbitrator may undermine the arbitration agreement itself. Such undermining may occur if one of the parties resiles from its obligation to arbitrate by deliberately failing to appoint its own member or members of the arbitral tribunal. This occurred in respect of the 1947 Allies' peace treaties with the former enemy States of Bulgaria, Hungary and Romania and was the subject of the ICJ's Advisory Opinion on the *Interpretation of Peace Treaties with Bulgaria, Hungary and Romania.*[37]

INTERPRETATION OF PEACE TREATIES WITH BULGARIA, HUNGARY AND ROMANIA

Facts:

The Peace Treaties contained a clause relating to the protection of HRs. In the first years of the Cold War the Allied States accused the former enemy States of the violation of that clause. The treaties required the establishment of an arbitration commission in the event of a dispute. The former enemy States deliberately failed to appoint members of the arbitral commission, thereby rendering the arbitral provision of the treaties inoperative. The UNGA asked the ICJ for an advisory opinion on the matter.

Held:

The ICJ held that although the governments of Bulgaria, Hungary and Romania were obliged to appoint arbitrators, upon their failure to do this the UNS-G was not authorised to appoint arbitrators on their behalf.

To avoid problems similar to those dealt with in the Advisory Opinion on the *Interpretation of Peace Treaties with Bulgaria, Hungary and Romania*, provisions have been adopted in arbitration treaties to provide for the appointment of arbitrators where one of the parties to the dispute fails to co-operate. For example, Article 21 of the 1957 European Convention for the Peaceful Settlement of Disputes provides:

> If the nomination of the members of the Arbitral Tribunal is not made within a period of three months from the date on which one of the parties requested the other party to constitute an Arbitral Tribunal,

---

the task of making the necessary nomination shall be entrusted to the Government of a third state chosen by agreement between the parties, or failing agreement within three months, to the President of the International Court of Justice. Should the latter be a national of one of the parties to the dispute, this task shall be entrusted to the Vice-President of the Court, or to the next senior judge of the Court who is not a national of the parties.

14.3.3.2 The arbitration tribunal may consist of a single arbitrator or be a collegiate body

The arbitration tribunal may consist of a single arbitrator or be a collegiate body, comprising two or more arbitrators appointed in equal numbers by each of the parties separately, plus an umpire appointed jointly by the parties or by the arbitrators appointed by them. Heads of State or judges from neutral countries are the most likely candidates to be a sole arbitrator. In 1931 the King of Italy was appointed as a sole arbitrator in the *Clipperton Island Arbitration*[38] between France and Mexico, and in the *Tinoco Arbitration*[39] between Great Britain and Costa Rica Chief Justice Taft of the US Supreme Court acted as a sole arbitrator.

An arbitral tribunal as a collective body may take two forms: a joint commission, or a mixed commission. A joint commission consists of an equal number of arbitrators nominated by each party. In such a case arbitrators represent the State that has appointed them. The main disadvantage of a joint commission is that often it is not able a reach any kind of agreement. In order to avoid a stalemate the second form of arbitration is the most frequently used, i.e. a mixed commission which is one consisting of an odd number of arbitrators. They do not represent the parties, and being neutral increase the likelihood of successful arbitration. In the *Alabama Claims Arbitration* (above) the UK and the US each appointed an arbitrator. The two arbitrators then asked Brazil, Italy and Switzerland to appoint one arbitrator each, making a total of five.

14.3.3.3 The law applicable to arbitration

The law applicable to arbitration between two States is usually international law, in particular, the general principles of international law. Article 37 of the Hague Convention 1899 provides that the object of arbitration is the settlement of disputes 'on the basis of respect for law'. However, the parties are free to specify in the *compromis* the law applicable to their dispute and may decide to apply the principles of equity or justice or ask the arbitrators to find an equitable solution to their dispute. This is especially appropriate in respect of disputes of a political rather than legal nature.

14.3.3.4 Arbitral tribunals are usually created to deal with a particular dispute or class of disputes

14.3.4 The effect of the arbitral award

Normally arbitration between States is intended to be final so that the award is binding as final settlement of a dispute.[40] The general principle is that the decision of the arbitral tribunal should not be disturbed

---

38   (1932) 26 AJIL 390.
39   (1923) 1 RIAA 369.
40   Article 81 of the 1899 Hague Convention.

except in the event of a manifest error of law or fact, irregularity in the appointment of arbitrators, or an essential procedural error.

Appeal of an arbitral award to the ICJ by a dissatisfied State was permitted in the *Arbitral Awards of 31 July 1989 (Guinea-Bissau v Senegal)*.[41]

The ICJ in its decision clarified a number of points concerning the grounds on which such appeals may be made. There appear to be three separate grounds on which an appeal against an arbitral award will be accepted:

- *Excés de pouvoir* (abuse of authority) – if an arbitral body exceeds its competence, its decision is null and void. Arbitrators have only such powers as the parties have conferred upon them.

- Failure to reach a decision by a true majority – in the above case Guinea-Bissau argued that the award was null and void because President of the Arbitral Tribunal Barberis who voted in favour of the award, had stated in his declaration an opinion contrary to that indicated by his vote.[42] The ICJ found that the view expressed by President Barberis in his declaration 'represented not a position taken by him as to what the Tribunal was required to do, but only an indication of what he considered would have been a better course.'[43] Further, the ICJ stressed that even if there had been any contradiction, the practice of international tribunals showed that the validity of a vote 'remains unaffected by the expression of any such differences in a declaration or separate opinion of the member concerned, which are therefore without consequence for the decision of the tribunal.'[44] As a result, the ICJ rejected the argument of Guinea-Bissau.

- Insufficiency of reasoning – the decision of the arbitral tribunal must be supported by adequate legal arguments. A statement of reasoning, although relatively brief and succinct, if clear and precise, does not amount to an insufficiency of reasoning.

If an arbitral decision is overturned on appeal, the award is null and without binding force. In some cases the issue of nullity will itself be referred to further arbitration. However, there is always a possibility for the parties to ask the arbitral tribunal to interpret the award.

14.4 Mixed claims commissions

Mixed claims commissions are established on an *ad hoc* basis to deal with large numbers of claims arising out of an internal or international conflict. Depending on their mandate, their jurisdiction will be to settle claims between nationals of one State and nationals of another State, or between one State and nationals of another State or between two States or any or all of these.

The first mixed claims commissions were established under the Jay Treaty in 1794 to deal with claims presented by British creditors against US citizens and residents for outstanding pre-peace debts (the British Debts Commission) and by US nationals whose vessels or cargoes were seized or destroyed by Great Britain during the War of Independence (the Maritime Claims Commission).[45] Their success prompted the establishment of numerous mixed claims commissions during the nineteenth century.

---

41   (1991) ICJ Rep 53.

42   *Guinea-Bissau v Senegal* Arbitration Tribunal for the Determination of the Maritime Boundary (Award of 31 July 1989) 83 ILR 1.

43   (1991) ICJ Rep 53, para 32.

44   Ibid, para 33.

45   Treaty of Amity, Commerce and Navigation between Great Britain and the United States (signed 19 November 1794, entered into force 29 February 1796) (1793–95) 52 CTS 243.

After WWII recourse to mixed claims commissions as a method of settlement of disputes lost its importance. However, subsequently there was a revival which started with the Iran-US Claims Tribunal which dealt, and at the time of writing continues to deal, with economic claims which arose from the taking of US hostages in Iran following the 1979 Islamic Revolution in Iran. The Tribunal has jurisdiction over:

- claims made by nationals, including corporations, of Iran against the US government, and claims by nationals of the US (including corporations) against the government of Iran;

- claims by corporations incorporated in third countries, i.e. not in the US or in Iran, if they satisfy the control test of nationality, i.e. a claim by a company with the nationality of a third country having been incorporated there, would nevertheless be admitted if the majority of its shares were owned by nationals of Iran or the US;

- claims made by the US government against the government of Iran and vice-versa.

However, the Tribunal has no jurisdiction over claims by one government against a national of the other, except where made as a counterclaim.

At the time of writing the Tribunal has dealt with more than 3,900 cases.

Other examples of mixed claims Commissions are:

- The Bosnia-Herzegovina Commission for Real Property Claims of Displaced Persons and Refugees which was established under the Dayton Peace Agreement (1995) to deal with claims of persons who lost property during the conflict in Bosnia-Herzegovina (1992–1995). Between 1996–2004, when the Commission was active, it rendered 310,000 decisions concerning the determination, recognition and where possible, restoration of individual property rights to those who were displaced as a result of the conflict.[46]

- The Eritrea-Ethiopia Claims Commission was established under the 2000 peace agreement between Eritrea and Ethiopia to deal with claims resulting from an armed conflict between the two countries (1998–2000) over a boundary dispute. The Commission dealt with claims concerning State responsibility for treatment of prisoners of war, the conduct of hostilities, the treatment of civilian populations and claims of individuals/businesses relating to economic losses they have suffered as a result of the conflict.[47] Its final decision was rendered in 2009.

- Mixed claims commissions were set up by Germany and Austria to provide reparations to victims of slave and forced labour during the Nazi regime.[48]

Mixed claim commissions can also be established by international organisations. For example, the UNSC created the UN Compensation Commission, as its subsidiary organ, to deal with claims made by individuals, corporations and States who had suffered damages as a result of Iraq's 1991 invasion of Kuwait.[49] Using funds from Iraq's oil revenues, the Commission compensated millions of people forced to flee Iraq and Kuwait during the Gulf War.[50] Further, the UN Interim Administration Mission

---

46 H. van Houtte, *Mass Property Claim Resolution in a Post-War Society: The Commission for Real Property Claims in Bosnia and Herzegovina* (1999) 48 ICLQ, 625.

47 See for an example of an award: *Eritrea-Ethiopia Claims Commission, Partial Awards on Prisoners of War* (July 2003)(2003) 42 ILM 1056 and 1083.

48 R. Bank, *The New Programs for Payments to Victims of National Socialist Injustice* (2001) 44 GYIL, 307–352.

49 UNSC Res 687 (1991) (3 April 1991) UN Doc S/RES/687 (1991).

50 D. Caron and B. Morris, *The United Nations Compensation Commission: Practical Justice, not Retribution* (2002) 13/1 EJIL, 183.

in Kosovo set up a Claims Commission in Kosovo to deal with claims for protection and restitution of lost residential property rights in Kosovo.[51]

14.5 From the Permanent Court of International Justice (PCIJ) to the International Court of Justice (ICJ)

There are many international courts, but the International Court of Justice (ICJ) has a special place among them. It is the successor to the Permanent Court of International Justice (PCIJ), which was the first permanent world court ever created by the international community, was accessible to all States and had jurisdiction over all international legal disputes.

14.5.1 The Permanent Court of International Justice (PCIJ)

Article 14 of the Covenant of the League of Nations[52] provided for the establishment of the PCIJ. In 1920 the Council of the League of Nations set up the Commission of Jurists which was entrusted with the preparation of the draft Statute of the Court. The draft, which was unanimously approved by the Council and the Assembly of the League, was contained in the so-called 'Protocol of Signature'[53] which was opened for signature as a separate international convention on 17 December 1920. After obtaining 22 ratifications, it entered into force on 1 September 1921.

The PCIJ held its opening ceremony on 15 February 1922 at its seat at the Peace Palace in The Hague. The PCIJ held its last public sitting on 4 December 1939 when it dealt with the request for interim measures in the *Electricity Company of Sofia* Case.[54] Before the German invasion of the Netherlands, in early May 1940, the PCIJ moved from The Hague to Geneva. All judges of the PCIJ resigned on 30th January 1946 and the PCIJ was dissolved by a Resolution of the UN General Assembly on eighteenth April 1946. On the same day the International Court of Justice (ICJ) was inaugurated.

Between 1922 and 1940 the PCIJ was seized of 66 cases and 28 requests for advisory opinions. Twelve cases were settled out of court. Altogether the PCIJ rendered 32 judgments and 27 advisory opinions. Despite many criticisms of the PCIJ it should be emphasised that it was the first permanent court available to all States of the world. Further, its contribution to the development of international law is significant. As Rosenne said:

> From its experimental beginnings it established the point that a permanent international judicial organ integrated with the political organisation of the international community is both feasible and necessary, even without going so far as to be accompanied by any true compulsory jurisdiction . . . The experience of the Permanent Court, its dispassionate and unhurried consideration of issues brought before it, the high standard of personal integrity and professional competence, and worldly wisdom, of its members, the fact that the judicial pronouncements were endowed with strong moral authority in addition to their formal finality, provided the foundations for the reconstructed system of international adjudication after the dust of the Second World War had started to settle.[55]

---

51   UN Interim Administration Mission in Kosovo Regulation on the Establishment of the Housing and Property Directorate and the Housing and Property Claims Commission (15 November 1999) UN Doc UNMIK/REG/1999/23.

52   225 CTS 195.

53   6 LNTS 379.

54   [1939] PCIJ Rep Ser A/B No 77.

55   S. Rosenne, *Law and Practice of the International Court*, Leyden: Sithoff, 1965, 13–14.

Three factors greatly undermined the work of the PCIJ:

■ The PCIJ was not an organ of the League of Nations.

■ Although its Statute was ratified by 48 States, the leading powers – the US and the Soviet Union – had never become contracting parties. The US signed the 1920 Protocol but the US Senate failed to ratify it on two occasions, first in 1920 and again in January 1935. The Soviet Union became a member of the League of Nations in 1934 but never ratified the Statute of the PCIJ and never participated in any litigation.

■ The outbreak of WWII destroyed the potential effectiveness of the PCIJ.

14.5.2 WWII and the World Court

During WWII the need for an international court of justice was never challenged. However, the idea of reorganisation of the international judicial system was present in many places, including the following:

■ Washington: an announcement concerning the willingness of the US to establish such a court after the war was made by US Secretary of State Hull in July 1942.

■ South America: in January 1942, the foreign ministers of the South American republics requested the Inter-American Judicial Committee to prepare recommendations in this respect.

■ Moscow: a similar approach to that made by the US was developed by Sergei Krylov who later become a judge of the Court.

■ London: the British government addressed an invitation to the government of the US in October 1941 to discuss the future of the PCIJ.[56] This invitation was declined.

In 1943, a new initiative commenced when representatives of ten governments in exile in the UK met in London to discuss the matter and subsequently set up the Informal Inter-Allied Committee of Experts chaired by Sir William Malkin, which in 1944 presented a report on the future of an International Court. The report made three recommendations:

■ The Statute of the PCIJ was considered to be highly appropriate for any future court.

■ Political matters should be excluded from the jurisdiction of a future court.

■ An international court should have both contentious and advisory jurisdiction.

The matter of whether the PCIJ should be reactivated was not examined. The report served as a source of discussion at the Dumbarton Oaks Conference in August-September 1944 where the establishment of the UN was the main topic. The Conference decided to link any new court with the UN and to retain the Statute of the PCIJ. However, the most controversial matters – such as whether or not a new court should be established, its compulsory jurisdiction, and the number of judges – were left to the examination of a newly set up Committee of Jurists.

The Committee of Jurists, which was made up of representatives of 44 nations invited by the US government to meet in April 1945 in Washington, prepared its recommendations relating to the Statute of the Court. In fact these recommendations consisted of making minor technical amendments to the

---

56   See A. Eyffinger, *The International Court of Justice 1946–1996*, The Hague: Kluwer Law International, 1996, 94–99.

Statute of the PCIJ. However, the Committee could not resolve the main issues. Next, the San Francisco Conference which took place from April to June 1945 and was in charge of preparing the UN Charter, decided to establish a new court, the ICJ, as a component part of the UN, i.e. as its judicial body, while maintaining continuity between the ICJ and the PCIJ. The Statute of the ICJ was based on a slightly amended version of the PCIJ Statute. It contains two provisions, Articles 36 (5) and 37, regarding the transfer to the ICJ of jurisdiction vested in the PCIJ as at the date of entry into force of the UN Charter. The Statute of the ICJ is annexed to and forms part of the UN Charter. The UN Charter itself contains provisions referring to the ICJ, in particular, in its Chapter XIV (Articles 92–96).

On 26 June 1945 the Charter of the UN was adopted, together with the Statute of the ICJ, by 51 States and entered into force on 24 October 1945.

14.5.3 The provisions of the UN Charter relating to the ICJ

The UN Charter forged a direct link between the ICJ and the UN. Under the Charter, the Court is one of the six principal organs of the UN.

Under Article 93(1) of the UN Charter, all members of the UN are automatically parties to the Statute of the ICJ. Non-members of the UN may also become parties to the Statute of the ICJ but a special procedure is applied to them.

Under Article 94(1) of the Charter, each member of the UN is obliged to comply with the decisions of the ICJ.

Article 94(2) provides that if a party to a dispute fails to comply with a judgment the other party may have recourse to the UNSC which may make recommendations or take enforcement measures to give effect to the judgment. On a number of occasions States have refused to comply with the judgment of the ICJ. For example, the US refused to recognise the judgment given against it in the *Military and Paramilitary Activities in and against Nicaragua (Merits).*[57]

The UNSC has limited experience in respect of enforcing compliance with ICJ's judgments. In the *Nicaragua Case*, when Nicaragua asked the UNSC to enforce the judgment against the US, the US vetoed the Nicaraguan request.

14.6 The ICJ: functions, composition and organisation

14.6.1 The function of the ICJ

The main function of the ICJ is to decide cases on the basis of the law as it stands at the time of its judgment.

Judge Lachs said in *Case Concerning Questions of Interpretation and Application of the 1971 Montreal Convention Arising from the Aerial Incident at Lockerbie (Libyan Arab Jamahiriya v United Kingdom) (Provisional Measures)*[58] that the Court is the guardian of the legality of the international community as a whole within and without the UN.

The ICJ is competent to decide legal disputes only. The fact that such disputes often involve political issues, and on a number of occasions have been the subject of consideration before political organs of the UN or international organisations, does not deprive the ICJ of its jurisdiction.

There is no definition of a legal dispute but the Court has developed its own approach to what

---

57   [1986] ICJ Rep 14.
58   [1992] ICJ Rep 3.

should be considered as a legal dispute. In the *Mavromattis Palestine Concessions Case*[59] the PCIJ stated that a dispute is a disagreement over a point of law or fact, a conflict of legal views or of interests between two persons. The ICJ, in a number of cases, emphasised that a legal dispute arises when the respondent State before the ICJ denies the allegations of the claimant State. In the *East Timor Case (Portugal v Australia)*[60] the ICJ stated that: 'Portugal has rightly or wrongly formulated complaints of fact and law against Australia, which the latter has denied, by virtue of this denial there is a legal dispute.' Similarly, in the *Case Concerning the Application of the Convention on the Prevention and Punishment of the Crime of Genocide (Bosnia and Herzegovina v Yugoslavia) (Preliminary Objections)*[61] the Court stated that 'by reason of the rejection by Yugoslavia of the complaints formulated against it by Bosnia-Herzegovina there is a legal dispute between them'.

It can be seen that the 'threshold' for a dispute to be a legal dispute is low.

The jurisdiction of the ICJ is twofold:

- The Court decides disputes between States. This is the contentious jurisdiction of the ICJ. Only States can be parties to the proceedings.

- The Court gives advisory opinions at the request of entities which have been given *locus standi* to this effect.

14.6.2 Judges

The ICJ is made up of 15 judges, five of whom are elected at three yearly intervals to hold office for 9 years, and no two of whom may be nationals of the same State. They may be re-elected. A *quorum* of nine judges is required to decide a case. Judges, when engaged on the business of the Court, enjoy diplomatic privileges and immunities. Their salary in fixed by the UNGA and may not be decreased during their term of office.

14.6.2.1 Election of judges

Article 2 of the Statute of the ICJ sets out the eligibility requirements for judges. They must be of high moral character and possess the qualifications necessary for appointment to the highest judicial offices in their respective countries or be jurisconsults of recognised competence in international law.

The judges are elected by the UNGA and by the UNSC from a list of persons nominated by the national groups in the PCA. Members of the UN not represented in the PCA may create national groups for this purpose. In making their nominations each national group may nominate no more than four persons, not more than two of whom shall be of their own nationality. The system of election involves independent, simultaneous voting by the UNSC and the UNGA. Those States which are parties to the Statute of the ICJ but not members of the UN are permitted to participate in the nomination and election procedures.

Article 10 of the Statute provides that to be elected candidates must obtain an absolute majority in each of the UNGA and the UNSC. Article 9 of the Statute of the ICJ requires that in the election procedure both the UNGA and the UNSC must bear in mind that the ICJ as a whole body must represent the main forms of civilisation and the principal legal systems of the world.

---

59   [1924] PCIJ Rep Ser A No 2, 11.
60   [1995] ICJ Rep 90, para 22.
61   [1996] ICJ Rep 595, para 29.

14.6.2.2 Independence and impartiality of judges

Independence of the judges is essential to the proper functioning of the ICJ. Indeed, if the ICJ is to serve any effective purpose it is vital that States have confidence in the integrity of its judges. The Statute of the ICJ reinforces the impartiality and freedom of judges from governmental influence by stating in Article 20 that each judge, before taking up his duties, must make a solemn declaration in open court that 'he/she will exercise his/her powers impartially and conscientiously'. Judges are not allowed to perform any political or administrative function or to engage in any other occupation of a professional nature. Under Article 17 of the Statute:

(1) No member of the Court may act as agent, counsel, or advocate in any case.

(2) No member may participate in the decision of any case in which he has previously taken part as agent, counsel, or advocate for one of the parties, or as a member of a national or international court, or of a commission of enquiry, or in any other capacity.

On the basis of the above provision Judge Zaffrula Khan was excluded from participation in the *South West Africa Cases (Second Phase)(Ethiopia v South Africa; Liberia v South Africa)*[62] because he had played a major role as a member of the delegation of Pakistan to the UN when matters pertaining to South West Africa had been under discussion.

In the *Legal Consequences for States of the Continued Presence of South Africa in Namibia (South West Africa) Notwithstanding Security Council Resolution 276 (1970) (Advisory Opinion)*[63] South Africa opposed the participation of several judges, including Judge Zaffrula Khan of Pakistan, Judge Nervo of Mexico and Judge Morozov of the Soviet Union. These judges, when members of their national delegations to the UN, had participated in activities directed against South Africa's presence in South West Africa. The objections were overruled by the ICJ. The Court noted that the fact that a judge may have participated in his former capacity as a representative of his government while the subject matter of the dispute was under discussion did not bring Article 17(2) of the Statute into application. Being a governmental spokesman in the area of dispute did not necessarily preclude an individual from subsequently exercising judicial impartiality. Judge Zaffrula Khan, excluded from the 1966 case, was no longer prevented from sitting as a judge in the proceedings under consideration as they were entirely separate from the earlier contentious case. However, some members of the ICJ were critical of this decision especially in relation to Judge Morozov, who as a previous UN representative of the Soviet Union had played a leading role in the preparation of UNGA and UNSC resolutions the validity of which were to be assessed in the advisory opinion.

In the *Legal Consequences of the Construction of a Wall in the Occupied Palestinian Territories (Advisory Opinion)* (Order of 30 January 2004),[64] the ICJ referred to the Namibia Advisory Opinion to confirm that there were no grounds to exclude Judge Elaraby from participation in the case. The government of Israel challenged Judge Elaraby's impartiality on the basis that he had played a leading role in the Emergency session of the UNGA which adopted the request for an advisory opinion, and for many years as a diplomat represented Egypt in supporting the Palestinian cause. Further, the judge's personal views confirmed his bias as evidenced by a published report of an interview given to an Egyptian newspaper in 2001. The ICJ held that Judge Elaraby had acted for the Egyptian government many years before the question of the construction of a wall arose, that he had ceased to participate in the UNGA emergency session before the request was made, and that in the interview he expressed

---

62   [1966] ICJ Rep 6.
63   [1971] ICJ Rep 16, para 9.
64   [2004] ICJ Rep, 3, para 8.

'no opinion on the question put in the present case'. As a result, Article 17(2) of the Statute did not apply because Judge Elaraby could not be regarded as having previously taken part in the case in any capacity.

Under Article 18(1) of the Statute of the ICJ a member of the Court can be dismissed if according to the unanimous opinion of other members he has ceased to fulfil the required conditions.

14.6.2.3 Ad hoc *judges*

The Statute of the ICJ provides for *ad hoc* judges. Its Article 31 states that:

(1)   Judges of the nationality of each of the parties shall retain their right to sit in the case before the Court.

(2)   If the Court includes upon the Bench a judge of the nationality of one of the parties, any other party may choose a person to sit as a judge . . .

(3)   If the Court includes upon the Bench no judge of the nationality of the parties, each of these parties may proceed to choose a judge as provided in paragraph 2 of this Article.

Thus, the fact that a judge is a national of one of the parties before the Court does not prevent him from continuing to sit. Also in cases where a party has no national representative in the Court, it may appoint a national judge *ad hoc* for the purpose of the case.

The appointment of *ad hoc* judges has been criticised as being incompatible with the concept of impartiality and independence of the judiciary, in particular Fitzmaurice[65] argued that:

■ those who claim that the presence of such judges increases confidence in the Court argue from an impermissible premise that judges, particularly *ad hoc* judges, will necessarily espouse the view of their government;

■ once a case has been decided, a judge *ad hoc* may feel himself free from any obligation of confidence and reveal to his government what was said in the deliberations of the Court.

Nevertheless, this practice has been justified as being an incentive to States, who may submit more readily to the jurisdiction of the Court and have more confidence in it if there is a judge of their own choice sitting on the bench. It has also been said that such judges are useful as they supply local knowledge and a national point of view.

In practice judges *ad hoc* usually give judgments in favour of the State which appointed them. Thus where two parties appoint judges *ad hoc* their votes will usually cancel each other.

14.6.3 Chambers of the ICJ

Three types of chamber are envisaged by the Statute of the ICJ. These are:

■ The Chamber of Summary Procedure. Article 29 of the Statute provides that the Court is required to establish this type of chamber annually for summary proceedings to deal speedily with court matters. It should be made up of five judges (including the President and Vice-President). As at October 2014 no such chamber has ever been established.

■ Under Article 26(1) of the Statute, a chamber, comprising at least three judges, may be established to deal with certain categories of cases, such as labour or communications. In 1993, the ICJ, for

---

65   *The Law and Procedure of the International Court of Justice*, Cambridge: Cambridge University Press, 1986.

the first time, established a Chamber for Environmental Matters. However, in 2006, its services never having been required, the ICJ decided not to hold elections for a bench for the said chamber.

■ Under Article 26(2) of the Statute a chamber of three or more judges may be established to deal with a particular case. This procedure was used for the first time in the *Delimitation of the Maritime Boundary in the Gulf of Maine Area (Canada/US).*[66] In this case Canada and the US threatened to withdraw from the case if their wishes as to the composition of the chamber were not met. Their request was complied with by the ICJ. Chambers have also been used in subsequent cases: the *Case Concerning the Frontier Dispute (Burkina Faso/Republic of Mali);*[67] the *Elettronica Sicula SpA (ELSI) (US v Italy Case)*[68] and the *Case Concerning Land, Island and Maritime Frontier Dispute (El Salvador/Honduras, Nicaragua Intervening).*[69] Chambers constituted under Article 26(2) offer the parties necessary flexibility in that they are formally consulted as to the number of judges forming a chamber and informally as to the names of the judges they wish to sit in a chamber. Also, their case is decided more speedily as it is decided by three or more judges (usually by five judges) instead of the ICJ sitting in its full composition of 15 judges or in some cases up to 17 judges if the parties appoint *ad hoc* judges.

14.7   The ICJ: contentious jurisdiction

Article 35 of the Statute defines the conditions of access for States to the Court. While paragraph 1 of that Article opens it to the State parties to the Statute, paragraph 2 regulates access to the Court by States which are not parties to the Statute. The conditions of access of such latter States are, subject to the special provisions contained in treaties in force at the date of the entry into force of the Statute, to be determined in accordance with Article 93 (1) and (2) of the UN Charter.

14.7.1   Access to the ICJ in contentious cases

Before a State becomes a party to a case before the ICJ it must have access to the Court. The ICJ is accessible to States only in respect of contentious cases and any State in the world has access to it provides it complies with certain conditions and requirements. There are basically three ways open to a State to have access to the Court. These are set out below.

14.7.1.1   *States which are members of the UN.*

Under Article 93(1) of the UN Charter all members of the UN are *ipso facto* parties to the Statute of the ICJ. By becoming a member of the UN a State is bound by the provisions of the Statute of the Court and therefore has access to it. At the time of writing, 193 States are members of the UN.

14.7.1.2   *Non-members of the UN who wish to become contracting parties to the ICJ Statute*

Non-members of the UN may become parties to the Statute under Article 93(2) of the UN Charter.

---

66   [1984] ICJ Rep 246.
67   [1986] ICJ Rep 554.
68   [1989] ICJ Rep 15.
69   [1992] ICJ Rep 92.

The conditions for their admission are to be determined in each case by the UNGA upon the recommendation of the UNSC. In practice the conditions laid down in the first occurrence, namely the request of Switzerland of December 1946, have always been applied. In respect of Switzerland the UNGA, in its Resolution 91(1) of 11 December 1946, laid down the following conditions:

(a) Acceptance of the provisions of the Statute of the International Court of Justice;

(b) Acceptance of all obligations of a Member of the United Nations under art 94 of the Charter;

(c) An undertaking to contribute to the expenses of the Court such equitable amount as the General Assembly shall assess from time to time after consultation with the Swiss Government.[70]

States becoming parties in this way are entitled to nominate candidates for election to the Court and take part in the election, in the UNGA, of the members of the Court. In the past Liechtenstein, Nauru, Japan, San Marino and Switzerland were in that category before actually becoming members of the UN.

14.7.1.3   States who are not parties to the Statute

The conditions for access to the ICJ for such States were determined by the UNSC in 1946 on the basis of Article 35(2) of the Statute. On 15 October 1946, the UNSC adopted Resolution 9 (1946) which sets out the conditions for access to the ICJ. It states that:

The International Court of Justice shall be open to a state which is not a party to the Statute of the International Court of Justice upon the following conditions, namely, that such state shall previously have deposited with the Registrar of the Court a declaration by which it accepts the jurisdiction of the Court, in accordance with the Charter of the United Nations and with the terms and subject to the conditions of the Statute and Rules of the Court, and undertake to comply in good faith with the decision or decisions of the Court and to accept all the obligations of a Member of the United Nations under art 94 of the Charter.[71]

Mainly in the 1950s, when admission to the UN was blocked by the veto of the USSR with regard to Western States, and by the US with regard to communist States such declarations were made by States which were refused admission to the UN. They are of two kinds: special declarations and general declarations.

Under a special declaration a State accepts the Court's jurisdiction in a particular dispute. Special declarations by non-parties were filed by Albania as respondent in the *Corfu Channel Case*[72] and Italy as a claimant in *Monetary Gold Removal from Rome in 1943(Italy* v *France, United Kingdom and US).*[73]

Under a general declaration a State accepts the Court's jurisdiction over all disputes or a particular class of disputes which have already arisen or which may arise in the future. General declarations were, *inter alia*, filed by Cambodia (1952), Ceylon (1952), the Federal Republic of Germany (1955, 1956, 1961, 1965 and 1971), Finland (1953 and 1954), Italy (1955), Japan (1951), Laos (1952) and the Republic of Viet Nam (1952).

---

70   A/RES/91(1) (1946).
71   S/RES/9(1946) para 1.
72   [1949] ICJ Rep 4.
73   [1954] ICJ Rep 19.

14.7.2   Access to the ICJ of States which have limited recognition by the
             international community

In the *Case Concerning the Application of the Convention on the Prevention and Punishment of the Crime of Genocide (Bosnia and Herzegovina v Yugoslavia)* the Court had to consider, for the first time, the standing of a newly independent State which had only limited recognition from the international community.

BOSNIA AND HERZEGOVINA *V* YUGOSLAVIA

Facts:

The State of Bosnia and Herzegovina brought an action against the State of Yugoslavia (the Federal Yugoslav Republic (FRY)) consisting of Serbia and Montenegro. The applicant alleged that the FRY and its armed forces had been guilty of genocide against the peoples of Bosnia and Herzegovina.

The Socialist Federal Republic of Yugoslavia (SFRY) was a party to the Statute of the ICJ, but, pursuant to a recommendation of the UNSC, the UNGA decided in Resolution 47/1 of 22 September 1992 that the FRY, which declared itself a successor State of the SFRY, 'should apply for membership of the United Nations and that it shall not participate in the work of the General Assembly'.

However, the Legal Council of the UN stated that UNGA Resolution 47/1 did not terminate Yugoslavia's membership.

Held:

The ICJ decided in the Case Concerning the Application of the Convention on the Prevention and Punishment of the Crime of Genocide (Further Request for the Indication of Provisional Measures) (Bosnia and Herzegovina v Yugoslavia)[74] *to grant a request for provisional measures, and in its judgment of 11 July 1996 held that it had jurisdiction to adjudicate the case.*[75]

Comment:

The factual situation was confusing and complex. In particular because of the ambiguous relationship between the FRY and the UN. On the one hand, the FRY, following a Joint Declaration of the National Assembly of Serbia and of Montenegro of 27 April 1992 declared itself a successor State of the SFRY, and stated that it would assume all international obligations of the SFRY. On the other hand, the UNGA resolution, as explained by the Legal Council of the UN neither terminated nor suspended Yugoslavia's membership of the UN, with the consequence that the FRY could participate in the work of organs of the UN other than the UNGA. However, this was not possible as the UNGA blocked any attempt at any participation by adopting a resolution to that effect, e.g. excluding the FRY from work in the ECOSOC. The ICJ, in reaching the decision that it had jurisdiction, took into consideration the facts that the FRY persistently claimed to be a successor of the SFRY and that the position of the UN with regard to the FRY was not entirely clear.

---

74   [1993] ICJ Rep 325.
75   [1996] ICJ Rep 595.

APPLICATION FOR THE REVISION OF THE JUDGMENT OF 11 JULY 1996

After the ousting of Slobodan Milošovič, who had been the President of the FRY for many years, the new democratically elected government of the FRY, on 24 April 2001, filed an application for revision of the judgment of 11 July 1996, claiming that it had become clear that the FRY was not a successor to the SFRY as the FRY had been admitted to the UN on 1 November 2000, and thus was, at the relevant time, not a party to the Statute of the Court and was not a party to the Genocide Convention.

The application of the FRY was rejected by the ICJ on 3 February 2003[76] mainly on the ground that no new facts were presented by the FRY (see Chapter 14.7.7.2). However, the ICJ in its final judgment on merits (see next para) came back to the issue of jurisdiction, in particular because the FRY presented a powerful new argument. This was that in Cases Concerning the Legality of the Use of Force *in which the FRY claimed that NATO States, by bombing its territory in 1999, had been in breach of the prohibition of the use of force,[77] the ICJ declined jurisdiction, inter alia, on the ground that the FRY had not been a member of the UN prior to its admission in 2000, and thus was not then a contracting party to the ICJ's statute, and as such could not appear before the ICJ.*

In the final judgment delivered on 26 February 2007 concerning the Application of the Convention on the Prevention and Punishment of the Crime of Genocide (Bosnia and Herzegovina v Serbia and Montenegro) (Judgment),[78] *the ICJ held that it had jurisdiction on the basis of* res judicata, *i.e. its previous 1996 judgment. In this respect the Court held that the purposive interpretation of Article 60 of its statute, which provides that the ICJ's judgments are final and without appeal, has the following consequences:*

> *First, the stability of legal relations requires that litigation comes to an end. The Court's function, according to Article 38 of its Statute, is to 'decide', that is, to bring to an end, 'such disputes as are submitted to it'. Secondly, it is in the interest of each party that an issue which has already been adjudicated in favour of that party be not argued again. Article 60 of the Statute articulates this finality of judgments.[79]*

Consequently, the Court held that it was not free to reconsider its preliminary judgment finding that it had jurisdiction at the merits stage as to do this would breach the principles governing the legal settlement of disputes.

Many judges dissented, in particular Judge Al-Khasawneh, criticised the ICJ's earlier ruling in the Legality of the Use of Force Case. *He was of the view that the FRY had been the successor of the SFRY from 1992 onward, and thus a party to the ICJ statute.*

---

76   The Application for Revision of the Judgment of 11 July 1996 in the *Case concerning Application of the Convention on the Prevention and Punishment of the Crime of Genocide [Bosnia and Herzegovina v Yugoslavia] (Preliminary Objections)* [2003] ICJ Rep 7.

77   The *Case Concerning the Legality of the Use of Force (Serbia and Montenegro v Belgium et al) (Preliminary Objections)* [2004] ICJ Rep 279.

78   (2007) ICJ Rep 43.

79   Ibid, para 116.

14.7.3   Jurisdiction of the ICJ in contentious cases

The ICJ can only determine cases with the consent of the State parties. In the *Advisory Opinion on Eastern Carelia*[80] the PCIJ stated that:

> it is well established in international law that no state can, without its consent, be compelled to submit its dispute with other states either to mediation or to arbitration, or to any other kind of pacific settlement.

Article 36(1) of the Statute confirms the necessity for a State's consent in the following terms:

> The jurisdiction of the Court comprises all cases which the parties refer to it and all matters specially provided for in the Charter of the United Nations or in treaties and conventions in force.

The importance of consent was emphasised by the ICJ in the *Case concerning Armed Activities on the Territory of the Congo (New Application: 2002) (Democratic Republic of the Congo v Rwanda) (Jurisdiction and Admissibility)*[81] in which the ICJ held that neither the *erga omnes* character nor the *ius cogens* character of the prohibition of genocide could by itself provide a basis for the Court's jurisdiction since the jurisdiction of the ICJ must always be based on the consent of the parties.

The words, 'matters specially provided for in the Charter of the United Nations' were included in the draft Statute in the belief that the UN Charter would provide for compulsory jurisdiction of the Court. A proposal intended to provide for such jurisdiction was rejected at the San Francisco Conference, but the words were not deleted from the Statute. Consequently, as a result of rejection of the proposal, there are no 'matters specially provided for in the Charter of the United Nations'.

The necessary consent may be expressed in a number of ways:

- by a special agreement between the parties to submit the dispute to the ICJ. This is also known as *compromis*;

- by virtue of a jurisdictional clause known as a compromissory clause. Such a clause has been inserted in numerous international treaties. It provides that in the event of a dispute concerning the interpretation or the application of the treaty, one of the parties may refer the dispute to the ICJ and the other party to the treaty is bound to submit to the Court's jurisdiction;

- under the principle of *forum prorogatum*, i.e. by express or tacit acceptance by the respondent State of the jurisdiction of the ICJ at a time when the case has already been brought by the claimant State before the Court;

- by virtue of Article 36(2) of the Statute which confers on the ICJ the so-called compulsory jurisdiction.

14.7.3.1   Jurisdiction by a special agreement

Parties to an already existing dispute may decide by a special agreement to submit it to the ICJ.

In all 11 disputes were submitted to the PCIJ by way of special agreements and subsequently a number of cases have been referred to the ICJ in the same way. The jurisdiction of the Court is defined within the agreement itself and the Court becomes seized of the case by mere notification of the agreement

---

80   [1923] PCIJ Rep Ser B No 5, 27.
81   (2006) ICJ. Rep. 6, para 64.

to its Registrar. A special agreement, being a treaty, entails that all rules of the VCLT apply to it. Normally, by signing a special agreement parties are giving their consent to the Court's jurisdiction. However, in the *Maritime Delimitation and Territorial Questions between Qatar/ Bahrein (Jurisdiction and Admissibility)*,[82] the ICJ had to decide whether a unilateral application by a single State was valid in a situation where there was an incomplete agreement to submit to the jurisdiction of the Court.

MARITIME DELIMITATION AND TERRITORIAL QUESTIONS BETWEEN QATAR AND BAHREIN (JURISDICTION AND ADMISSIBILITY)

Facts:

A tri-party committee was established among Saudi Arabia (who exercised good offices), Qatar and Bahrein to prepare a document to be submitted to the ICJ to settle a number of complex matters on territorial sovereignty and the maritime delimitation between Qatar and Bahrein. A dispute arose as to the drafting of the terms of reference. Bahrein wished to submit all disputed matters to the Court for adjudication, while Qatar wanted to submit only a number of selected issues. Nevertheless, the parties did agree on five areas of territory which were the subject of dispute. Ultimately, however, no completed submission was agreed. At a later meeting of the committee in December 1990, the parties agreed to a further period of good offices of Saudi Arabia and decided that if these discussions did not produce a settlement by the end of May 1991, then the matter could be brought before the ICJ for resolution. Minutes of this meeting were signed by the foreign ministers of both Qatar and Bahrein.

No settlement was reached by the stipulated date and Qatar unilaterally applied to the Court for the settlement of a selected number of issues. Bahrein objected that the Court had no jurisdiction unless there was a mutually agreed bilateral submission from both parties.

Held:

The ICJ found that the minutes of the meeting of December 1990 amounted to an agreement on which the Court could found jurisdiction. The ICJ stated that the minutes 'do not merely give an account of discussions and summarise points of agreement and disagreement. They enumerate the commitments to which the parties have consented. They thus create rights and obligations in international law for the parties'.

In the circumstances the Court held that it had jurisdiction and on 16 March 2001 delivered its judgment on the merits in the Maritime Delimitation and Territorial Questions between Qatar and Bahrein (Qatar/Bahrein).[83]

More recent examples of States bringing proceedings based on a special agreement are: the *Case Concerning Border Dispute between Burkina Faso and Niger* in July 2010, and the *Case Concerning Sovereignty over Pedra Branca/Pulau Batu Puteh, Middle Rocks and South Ledge (Malaysia/Singapore)* in July 2003.[84]

---

82   [1994] ICJ Rep 112, para 25.

83   [2001] ICJ Rep 40.

84   See the official webside of the ICJ at www.icj-cij.org/homepage (accessed 24 September 2014).

14.7.3.2   Jurisdiction based on jurisdictional clauses

Another basis of jurisdiction is envisaged in Article 36(1) of the Statute. It relates to treaties and conventions in force which confer jurisdiction on the Court over disputes arising from them. It has become general practice to insert into an international agreement, whether multilateral or bilateral, the so-called jurisdiction clause also known as a compromissory clause (but do not confuse a compromise with a compromissory clause).

There are hundreds of treaties which confer jurisdiction on the ICJ. For example, in the *Case Concerning the Application of the Convention on the Prevention and Punishment of the Crime of Genocide (Bosnia and Herzegovina v Yugoslavia) (Preliminary Objections)*[85] the ICJ founded jurisdiction on Art IX of the Genocide Convention 1948 and in the *US Diplomatic and Consular Staff in Teheran Case (US v Iran)*[86] it founded its jurisdiction on art 1 of the 1961 Optional Protocol to the Vienna Convention on Diplomatic Relations 1961.

Many treaties and conventions contained clauses conferring jurisdiction on the PCIJ, in effect, the predecessor of the ICJ. When the Statute of the PCIJ was redrafted in 1945 in anticipation of the establishment of the ICJ as the replacement of the PCIJ, in order to save such clauses, Article 37 was added to the Statute of the ICJ. It provides:

> Whenever a treaty or convention in force provides for reference of a matter to a tribunal to have been instituted by the League of Nations, or to the Permanent Court of International Justice, the matter shall, as between the parties to the present Statute, be referred to the International Court of Justice.

Therefore, in order for a treaty which confers jurisdiction on the PCIJ to bestow jurisdiction on the ICJ two conditions must be met:

- The treaty must still be in force. Normally the treaty will have been registered with the Secretariat of the League of Nations or the United Nations and will have been published by them. However, in some cases it is difficult to determine if a treaty is still in force. In the *South West Africa Cases (Preliminary Objections) (Ethiopia v South Africa; Liberia v South Africa)*[87] the Court had to decide whether Article 37 of its Statute could apply in respect of the Mandate between South Africa and the League of Nations. The ICJ decided that Article 7(2) of the Mandate, which provided for compulsory jurisdiction of the PCIJ in the event of disputes arising between the Mandatory and another member of the League relating to the interpretation and application of the provisions of the Mandate, was still in force taking into account that the Mandate had never been terminated.

- The States concerned must not only be the contracting parties to the relevant treaty but also to the Statute of the ICJ. However, the date of accession of the respondent State to the Statute of the ICJ is irrelevant, i.e. it is irrelevant whether that State is or is not the original Member of the UN (see Chapter 14.7.3.4 C). This matter was examined by the ICJ in *Barcelona Traction, Light and Power Company Ltd Case (Belgium v Spain)(Preliminary Objections)*.[88]

---

85   [1996] ICJ Rep 1.
86   [1980] ICJ Rep 3.
87   [1962] ICJ Rep 319.
88   [1964] ICJ Rep 6.

BELGIUM *V* SPAIN (PRELIMINARY OBJECTIONS)

Facts:

Belgium made an application to the ICJ on the basis of Article 17 of the 1927 Spain-Belgian Treaty of Conciliation, Judicial Settlement and Arbitration, which provided that either party had an ultimate right to commence proceedings before the PCIJ in the event of a dispute arising out of its provisions. Spain objected to the ICJ's jurisdiction, inter alia, on the ground that Spain became a party to the Statute when admitted to the UN in 1955, but was not a party to the Statute for the 9 years, between the dissolution of the PCIJ and Spain's admission to the UN and, consequently, Article 17 of the 1927 Treaty ceased to operate.

Held:

The ICJ held that Article 37 of the Statute was not to be interpreted in this way and that the date on which Spain became a party to the Statute was irrelevant. In this respect the ICJ stated that:

> *States joining the United Nations or otherwise becoming parties to the Statute at whatever date, knew in advance (or must be taken to have known) that, by reason of art 37, one of the results of doing so would, as between themselves and other parties to the Statute, be the reactivation in relation to the present Court, of any jurisdictional clauses referring to the Permanent Court, in treaties still in force, by which they were bound.*[89]

Comment:

It is important to distinguish the jurisdiction of the ICJ based on a jurisdictional clause from that based on a declaration made under Article 37(5) of the Statute (see Chapter 14.7.3.4.C). In the commented case the ICJ explained that the main purpose of Article 37, which transferred jurisdiction from the PICJ to the ICJ, was to preserve as many jurisdictional clauses as possible from becoming inoperative because of the dissolution of the PCIJ. The ICJ's jurisdiction based on a declaration made under Article 37(5) of the Statute, if such a declaration had not been renewed at the dissolution of the PICJ, lapsed. For original members of the UN any declaration made under Article 37(5) of the Statute of the PCIJ was automatically renewed when they signed the UN Charter in 1945. For non-original members it lapsed. The situation is different with regard to ICJ's jurisdiction based on a jurisdictional clause. As the ICJ held in the commented cases when a State becomes a member of the UN, irrespective of the date, the ICJ's jurisdiction based on jurisdictional clauses revives.

14.7.3.3 *Jurisdiction of the ICJ based on forum prorogatum*

On the basis of *forum prorogatum* the Court may exercise jurisdiction in those cases where, after the applicant State has instituted proceedings, it is established that the respondent State has consented to submit to the jurisdiction. The consent may be express or may be deduced from conduct of the defendant State in relation to the Court or in relation to the applicant State.

---

89   Ibid, 36.

In the *Rights of Minorities in Polish Upper Silesia Case*[90] the PCIJ stated:

[T]here seems to be no doubt that the consent of a state to the submission of a dispute to the Court may not only result from an express declaration, but may also be inferred from acts conclusively establishing it. It seems hard to deny that the submission of arguments on the merits, without making reservation in regard to the question of jurisdiction, must be regarded as an unequivocal indication of the desire of a state to obtain a decision on the merits of a suit.

Therefore, more is required than the negative fact that the State raises no objection to the Court's jurisdiction. The Court will not accept jurisdiction unless there has been real consent, although this may be explicit or implied from the behaviour of the respondent State.

In the *Corfu Channel Case (Preliminary Objections) (United Kingdom v Albania)*,[91] the UK brought a claim against Albania before the Court by unilateral application. Albania in its reply declared that it:

would be within its rights in holding that the Government of the United Kingdom was not entitled to bring the case before the International Court by unilateral application without first conducting a special agreement with the Albanian Government ... However ... it is prepared notwithstanding this irregularity in the action taken by the Government of the United Kingdom, to appear before the Court.

The ICJ inferred from this reply that Albania voluntarily and indisputably accepted its jurisdiction. Jurisdiction based on *forum prorogatum* is rare. In most cases the Court has exercised it in circumstances where the consent was inferred from conduct of the State concerned: e.g. the *Mavromattis Palestine Concessions Case*,[92] the *Rights of Minorities in Polish Upper Silesia*[93] and the *Corfu Channel Case (Preliminary Objections)*.[94]

On occasions a State has started proceedings before the ICJ knowing that the other party has not accepted the Court's jurisdiction, and inviting it to do so. Many invitations have been made but, few have been accepted.[95]

14.7.3.4 Compulsory jurisdiction of the ICJ based on the optional clause contained in Article 36(2) of the Statute

Article 36(2) and (3) of the Statute describes the compulsory jurisdiction of the ICJ in the following terms:

(2) The states, parties to the present Statute, may at any time declare that they recognise as compulsory ipso facto and without special agreement, in relation to any other state accepting the same obligation, the jurisdiction of the Court in all legal disputes concerning:

---

90   [1925] PCIJ Rep Ser A No 6, 24.

91   [1948] ICJ Rep 15, 27.

92   *The Case of the Readaptation of the Mavrommatis Jerusalem Concessions (Greece v Great Britain) (Jurisdiction)* [1924] PCIJ Rep Series A No 12.

93   Supra note 90.

94   [1948] ICJ Rep 15.

95   E.g. the *Case Concerning Certain Criminal Proceedings in France (Republic of Congo v France)*, removed from the list of cases at the request of the Congo, Ord of 16 November 2010, (2010) ICJ Rep 635; and the *Case Concerning Certain Questions of Mutual Assistance in Criminal Matters (Djibouti v France)* (2008) ICJ Rep. 177.

(a)   the interpretation of a treaty;

(b)   any question of international law;

(c)   the existence of any fact which, if established, would constitute a breach of an international obligation;

(d)   the nature or extent of the reparation to be made for the breach of an international obligation.

(3) The declaration referred to above may be made unconditionally or on condition of reciprocity on the part of several or certain states, or for a certain time.

This so-called 'optional clause' is a compromise between the advocates and the opponents of compulsory jurisdiction. Under this article jurisdiction is only compulsory once the declaration is made, and then, only within the limits of that declaration. However, there is no obligation upon a State to make such a declaration, and therefore jurisdiction cannot, in the true sense, be regarded as compulsory.

Declarations are deposited with the UNS-G and are usually signed by the foreign minister of the State making the declaration, or by its representative at the UN. Despite efforts of the UNS-G,[96] as at 31 December 2014 only 70 States out of 193 member States of the UN have made declarations recognising compulsory jurisdiction of the ICJ.[97] it is very disappointing that out of five permanent members of the UNSC only the UK has accepted the compulsory jurisdiction of the ICJ. As at 31 December 2013, 15 States had withdrawn their acceptance, some of them after unsuccessfully challenging the jurisdiction of the ICJ in cases brought against them. Examples are:

■   Thailand did not renew its declaration upon its expiry on 20 May 1960, after it challenged the jurisdiction of the Court in the *Temple of Preah Vihear Case (Preliminary Objections)(Cambodia v Thailand)*.[98]

■   France withdrew its declaration on 2 January 1974 after the *Nuclear Tests Cases (Interim Protection)*[99] brought against her in May 1973.

■   The US, after unsuccessfully challenging the Court's jurisdiction in the *Case Concerning Military and Paramilitary Activities in and against Nicaragua (Nicaragua v US) (Jurisdiction and Admissibility)*[100] brought by Nicaragua in April 1984, withdrew its declaration on 8 October 1985.[101]

The majority of declarations contain reservations, thus further limiting the ICJ's jurisdiction. As at 31 December 2013, 52 out of the 70 declarations in force contained reservations in respect of various matters[102] (see below).

96   See The 2010 Report of the UNS-G 'Delivering Justice: Programme of Action to Strengthen the Rule of Law at the National and International Levels', A/66/749.

97   See the 2013 Handbook of the International Court of Justice (hereafter referred to as the 2013 ICJ's Handbook), 41. It can be found at www.icj-cij.org/publications/en/manuel_en.pdf (accessed 17 September 2014).

98   [1961] ICJ Rep 17.

99   *Nuclear Tests Case (New Zealand v France) (Judgment)* [1974] ICJ Rep 457 and *Nuclear Tests Case (Australia v France)* [1974] ICJ Rep 253.

100   [1984] ICJ Rep 392.

101   See Department of State letter and Statement of Acceptance of the ICJ Compulsory Jurisdiction (7 October 1985) reprinted in (1985) 24 ILM 1742.

102   The 2013 ICJ's Handbook, supra note 97, 41.

A. The effects of a declaration recognising the compulsory jurisdiction of the ICJ

The effects are as follows:

- An optional clause declaration, although a unilateral act of a State, creates bilateral relations with those other States which have also made declarations of acceptance.[103] As the ICJ stated in the *Case Concerning Land and Maritime Boundary between Cameroon and Nigeria (Cameroon v Nigeria) (Preliminary Objections)*, a declaration constitutes a 'standing offer to the other States party to the Statute which have not yet deposited a declaration of acceptance'."[104]

- Once the Court is seized of a case on the basis of a declaration, the subsequent lapse or withdrawal of the acceptance cannot deprive the Court of jurisdiction. In the *Nottebohm Case (Preliminary Objections) (Liechtenstein v Guatemala)*[105] the declaration of the respondent government, Guatemala, expired a few days after the government of Liechtenstein had seized the Court. It was argued on behalf of Guatemala that upon the expiry of the Guatemalan declaration the Court no longer had jurisdiction to hear the dispute. The Court rejected this argument and stated that its jurisdiction, once established, cannot be challenged by the subsequent lapse of the declaration due to the expiry of the period for which it was valid, or by denunciation, in relation to a case already pending before the Court.

B. The commencement of the obligations under Article 36(2) of the ICJ's Statute

The contractual relations between the States concerned, and the compulsory jurisdiction of the Court resulting therefrom, come into being on the day the new declarant State deposits with the UNS-G its declaration of acceptance and not at the day when parties to the ICJ Statute receive notification from the UNS-G to this effect. The distinction between the two dates is important in that between the date of the deposit of a declaration and the date of receipt of notification from the UNS-G many months may elapse, with the consequence that a prospective respondent State may not be aware that another State has recently accepted the compulsory jurisdiction of the ICJ and thus the latter may start proceedings against the prospective respondent State. This occurred in the *Case Concerning Right of Passage over Indian Territory (Portugal v India)* (Preliminary Objections).[106]

CASE CONCERNING RIGHT OF PASSAGE OVER INDIAN TERRITORY (PORTUGAL *V* INDIA) (PRELIMINARY OBJECTIONS)

Facts:

Portugal deposited its optional clause declaration on 19 December 1955 and brought proceedings against India three days later. India was not aware of the fact that Portugal had accepted the optional jurisdiction of the ICJ and argued that the commencement of proceedings by Portugal before notice of its declaration could be transmitted to other parties to the Statute constituted a violation of equality, mutuality and reciprocity guaranteed under Article 36(2) of the Statute of the ICJ.

---

103   [1984] ICJ Rep 392, para 60.
104   [1998] ICJ Rep 275, para 25.
105   [1953] ICJ Rep 111.
106   [1957] ICJ Rep 125.

Held:

The ICJ held that although during the interval between the deposit of an optional clause declaration with the UNS-G and receipt by the parties to the ICJ Statute of notice of that deposit some element of uncertainty existed, such uncertainty was, nevertheless, inherent in the optional clause system and did not affect the validity of the Portuguese declaration. The ICJ emphasised that:

> *with regard to any degree of uncertainty resulting from the right of Portugal to avail itself at any time of the Conditions in its Acceptance, the position was substantially the same as that created by the right claimed by many Signatories of the Optional Clause, including India, to terminate their Declarations of Acceptance by simple notification without notice.[107]*

The Court added that when a case was brought before it the reciprocal obligations that existed between the parties could be determined with certainty on the basis of their respective declarations.

Many States, in order to avoid being surprised by suits against them brought by States that have, without their knowledge, joined the system created by the existence of the optional clause, have made a reservation excluding the ICJ's jurisdiction over applications filed less than 12 months prior to the other party's acceptance of the optional clause. For example, in the *Case Concerning Legality of Use of Force (Yugoslavia v United Kingdom) (Provisional Measures)*[108] the ICJ, on the basis of such a reservation, dismissed the case against the UK.

C. Special cases of States that had made declarations accepting the jurisdiction of the PCIJ, but remained silent as to their position with regard to the compulsory jurisdiction of the ICJ

Article 36 (5) of the ICJ's Statute deals with a situation where a State has made a declaration of acceptance of the jurisdiction of the PCIJ but has not expressly stated its position as to the acceptance of the jurisdiction of the ICJ. This Article states that declarations made under the PCIJ Statute 'which are still in force shall be deemed, as between the parties to the present Statute, to be acceptances of the compulsory jurisdiction of the International Court of Justice for the period which they still have to run and in accordance with their terms'.

However, in order for a declaration made under the PCIJ Statute to be valid under the ICJ Statute, the PCIJ's jurisdiction had to be in existence when the ICJ Statute came into force. This means that Article 36(5) of the ICJ Statute applies only to the original members of the UN, as specified in Article 3 of the UN Charter. This is exemplified by the *Case Concerning Aerial Incident of 27 July 1955 (Israel v Bulgaria) (Preliminary Objections).*[109]

---

107   Ibid, 143.
108   [2004] ICJ Rep 1307.
109   [1959] ICJ Rep 127.

ISRAEL *V* BULGARIA (PRELIMINARY OBJECTIONS)

Facts:

Israel filed an application against Bulgaria concerning the shooting down of an Israeli passenger aircraft on a regular commercial flight between Austria and Israel by the Bulgarian armed force after it entered, without permission, into Bulgarian airspace.

Held:

The Court found that it had no jurisdiction because, despite the fact that Bulgaria had made a declaration in 1921 accepting for an unlimited period the compulsory jurisdiction of the PCIJ, it was not an original member of the UN as it only became a member of the UN in 1955.

Comment:

As a result of this judgment, it is clear that declarations made by States accepting the compulsory jurisdiction of the PCIJ, which States were not original members of the UN, ceased to be in force on the dissolution of the PCIJ. It is important to note that when the ICJ's jurisdiction is based on a jurisdictional clause, the date at which the respondent State becomes a party to the Statute, i.e. whether it is or is not an original member of the UN, is irrelevant (See Chapter 14.7.3.2).

One of the most interesting cases concerning the application or otherwise of Article 36(5) of the ICJ Statute is the *Case Concerning Military and Paramilitary Activities in and against Nicaragua (Nicaragua v United States) (Jurisdiction and Admissibility).*[110]

In this case one of the preliminary objections raised by the US was that Nicaragua was not a party to the ICJ Statute and as a result the ICJ had no jurisdiction to adjudicate the case.

NICARAGUA *V* UNITED STATES

Facts:

In 1929 Nicaragua signed the Statute of the PCIJ and, at the same time, made a declaration of unconditional and unlimited acceptance of the PCIJ's jurisdiction. Subsequently, Nicaragua completed, under its domestic law, all requirements for ratification. Nicaragua claimed that it had both dispatched the necessary instrument of ratification and had sent a confirmatory telegram to the S-G of the League of Nations to that effect in November 1939. However, no such instrument was on record in the file of the League of Nations and no evidence was provided that Nicaragua had ever sent such an instrument to the S-G of the League of Nations. After WWII, Nicaragua became an original member of the UN and ratified the UN

---

110   [1984] ICJ Rep 392.

Charter on 6 September 1945. The ICJ had to decide whether Article 36(5) of its Statute applied to Nicaragua.

Held:

The ICJ held that the Nicaragua 1929 declaration had a 'potential effect' which Article 36(5) transformed into a binding effect. It is rather unclear how this was supposed to have occurred. Perhaps for that reason the ICJ referred to its practice, of more than 40 years, of listing Nicaragua as a party to the optional clause in its yearbook and in other official documents which showed that the conduct of State parties to the Statute confirmed the Court's interpretation of Article 36(5). Further, the Court accepted the argument of Nicaragua that by its conduct, for more than 38 years, Nicaragua unequivocally showed its consent to be bound by the Statute.

Comment:

It can be said that the above arguments are not very convincing. The fact remains that Nicaragua never specifically ratified the statute of the PCIJ and, as many dissenting judges noted, it is rather difficult to explain how Nicaragua's ratification of the UN Charter, without making any declaration as to the acceptance of compulsory jurisdiction of the ICJ under Article 36(2), could transform a 'potential' acceptance of the PCIJ's Statute into its actual ratification.

D. Reciprocity

An important aspect of the optional clause is that the principle of reciprocity applies to the relations between States that have accepted the compulsory jurisdiction of the ICJ. By virtue of Article 36(2) of the Statute a State accepting the jurisdiction of the Court does so only 'in relation to any other state accepting the same obligation'.

According to this principle, a State accepts the Court's jurisdiction with regard to any other State only in so far as that other State has also accepted the Court's jurisdiction. This means that:

If State A has made a declaration subject to reservation Y and State B has made a declaration subject to reservation Z, the ICJ has jurisdiction to hear disputes between States A and B but only in so far as they are not within reservations Y and Z.

An interesting issue relating to reservations was examined in the *Right of Passage over Indian Territory Case (Preliminary Objections)(Portugal v India).*[111]

PORTUGAL *V* INDIA

Facts:

The Portuguese Declaration accepting the compulsory jurisdiction of the Court contained, inter alia, the following reservation:

---

111   [1957] ICJ Rep 125, 141.

3 *The Portuguese Government reserves the right to exclude from the scope of the present declaration, at any time during its validity, any given category or categories of disputes, by notifying the Secretary-General of the United Nations and with effect from the moment of such notification.*

India argued that this reservation was invalid because it had retrospective effect in that it allowed Portugal to exclude from its declaration at any time, any dispute by mere notification of the category of disputes to be excluded to the UNS-G and thus was incompatible with Article 36(2) of the Statute.

Held:

The ICJ rejected this argument and interpreted the reservation as meaning that the notification applied to disputes brought before the ICJ after the date of notification. The ICJ stated the reservation could not apply to cases already pending before the court and thus have a retrospective effect. Only when Portugal had notified the UNS-G would the reservation become automatically operative against it, in relation to other parties to the optional clause.

Reservations under Article 36(3) of the Statute refer to reciprocity and time. In the early years of the ICJ it was argued that only reservations in accordance with Article 36(3) were admissible. However, it is now accepted that many other reservations may be made, and the validity of such reservations is no longer called into question. In the *Case Concerning the Aerial Incident of 10 August 1999 (Pakistan v India) (Jurisdiction)*,[112] Pakistan argued, *inter alia*, that the permissible conditions to which an optional clause declaration may be subject were enumerated exhaustively in Article 36(3) of the Statute. The ICJ disagreed. It stated that Article 36(3) of the Statute has never been regarded as laying down exhaustively the conditions under which declarations may validly be made, and affirmed its opinion, expressed in previous case law,[113] that States are absolutely free to decide whether or not they wish to make declarations accepting the compulsory jurisdiction of the ICJ either unconditionally and without temporal restrictions, or by qualifying the acceptance through conditions and reservations.

The most frequently made reservations relate to disputes:

- for which other methods of settlement are envisaged. According to the 2013 ICJ'S Handbook, at 31 December 2013, 42 States had made such a reservation;[114]

- which had arisen before a certain date and concerning certain situations or facts that took place before that date. In general the date in question refers to the time when a State first accepted the compulsory jurisdiction of the ICJ. As at 31 December 2013, 33 States had made such a reservation;[115]

- which are considered as falling within the domestic jurisdiction of that state (the so called Connally reservation). As at 31 December 2013, 28 States had made such a reservation;

---

112   [2000] ICJ Rep 12.
113   *The Military and Paramilitary Activities in and against Nicaragua (Nicaragua v US) (Jurisdiction and Admissibility)* [1984] ICJ Rep 392.
114   Supra note 97, 41.
115   Ibid, 41.

■ concerning certain multinational treaties (the so called Vandenberg reservation). As at 31 December 2013, 18 States had made such a reservation;[116]

■ relating to the law of the sea or in respect of certain States or concerning disputes relating to conduct of a State's armed forces.

The most important of the above reservations are examined below.

A. Reservations relating to matters falling within the domestic jurisdiction of a State

These are based on Article 2(7) of the UN Charter which provides that nothing in the Charter 'shall authorise the United Nations to intervene in matters which are essentially within the domestic jurisdiction of any state'.

In 1946 the US made such a reservation which became known as the 'Connally reservation' named after Senator Tom Connally of Texas who wanted to ensure that the ICJ would not interfere in domestic affairs of the US, and thus proposed a clause to be inserted in the US declaration of acceptance to this effect.[117] This provided that the declaration accepting the jurisdiction of the Court would not apply to:

disputes with regard to matters which are essentially within the domestic jurisdiction of the United States of America as determined by the United States of America.

A Connally reservation operates automatically in the sense that, once a State which has made it declares that a matter which is the subject of proceedings initiated before the ICJ falls within its domestic jurisdiction, the ICJ is deprived of jurisdiction over the dispute.

The validity and application of such reservations came up for consideration in the *Norwegian Loans Case (France v Norway)*.[118]

FRANCE *V* NORWAY

Facts:

France brought a claim against Norway under the optional clause on behalf of French holders of Norwegian bonds. The French declaration accepting the compulsory jurisdiction of the Court contained the following reservation:

This Declaration does not apply to differences relating to matters which are essentially within the national jurisdiction as understood by the Government of the French Republic.

Norway which did not make any such reservation in its declaration challenged the Court's jurisdiction by relying on the French declaration. Norway considered that the dispute was within the domestic jurisdiction within the meaning of the French declaration.

Held:

The ICJ agreed with Norway. The Court held that:

---

116   Ibid, 43.
117   J.H.Crabb, *On Judging the Connally Amendment* (1962) 50 Geo LJ, 529.
118   [1957] ICJ Rep 9.

> *France has limited her acceptance of the compulsory jurisdiction of the Court by excluding beforehand disputes 'relating to matters which are essentially within the national jurisdiction as understood by the Government of the French Republic'. In accordance with the condition of reciprocity to which acceptance of the compulsory jurisdiction is made subject in both Declarations and which is provided for in art 36 paragraph 3 of the Statute, Norway equally with France, is entitled to except from the compulsory jurisdiction of the Court disputes understood by Norway to be essentially within its national jurisdiction.[119]*
>
> *The Court considers that the Norwegian Government is entitled, by virtue of the condition of reciprocity to invoke the reservation contained in the French Declaration of 1 March, 1949; that this reservation excludes from the jurisdiction of the Court the dispute which has been referred to it by the Application of the French Government; that consequently the Court is without jurisdiction to entertain the application.[120]*

This successful application of the condition of reciprocity led several States which had previously inserted such reservations in their declarations of acceptance to abandon them.

In the *Norwegian Loans Case*, Judge Lauterpacht in his separate opinion[121] considered that an 'automatic' reservation, i.e. one in which the State itself claims the power to determine what matters are within its domestic jurisdiction, and thus decide on the jurisdiction of the ICJ, were invalid, as contrary to the fundamental principle of national and international jurisprudence according to which it is within the inherent competence of the court to determine its own jurisdiction. Consequently, he argued that an instrument in which a party is allowed to determine the existence of its obligation is not a valid and enforceable legal document of which the Court should take cognisance and that this kind of instrument is a declaration of a political nature, not a legal instrument. Lauterpacht further contended that any declaration under Article 36(2) which included an automatic reservation would itself be void, i.e. it would be insufficient to establish the jurisdiction of the Court. The reasoning behind this conclusion was that the invalid reservation was to be regarded as an essential part of the optional clause declaration. As such, it could not be severable from the declaration as a whole. The only result was, therefore, that the declaration itself was to be regarded as void.

Judge Lauterpacht, together with other members of the Court, returned to consider the matter discussed in the *Norwegian Loans Case* when they dealt with the *Interhandel Case (Switzerland v USA)*.[122] In this case, Lauterpacht in his dissenting opinion,[123] reiterated arguments he advanced in the *Norwegian Loans Case*. However, Judges Kleastad[124] and Armand-Ugon[125] were of the view that in any event reservations were severable from the rest of a declaration of acceptance and therefore a declaration was valid while reservations, being severable, were void.

---

119   Ibid, 24.
120   Ibid, 27.
121   Ibid, Separate Opinion, 44.
122   [1959] ICJ Rep 6.
123   Ibid, 101.
124   Ibid, Dissenting Opinion, 77–78.
125   Ibid, Dissenting Opinion, 93.

The matter of whether or not a reservation should be considered as an integral part of a declaration was examined by the Court in the *Fisheries Jurisdiction Case (Spain v Canada) (Jurisdiction)*.[126] The Court stated that 'declarations and reservations are to be read as a whole'.[127] Thus, depending upon the circumstances of the case a reservation may or may not be severable from a declaration. In the *Anglo-Iranian Oil Co (UK v Iran)(Preliminary Objection)*,[128] the ICJ stated that it could not 'base itself on a purely grammatical interpretation of the text. It must seek the interpretation which is in harmony with a natural and reasonable way of reading the text'. In the *Fisheries Jurisdiction Case* (above) in para 59 the ICJ found that the reservation formed not only 'an integral part of the current declaration but also an essential component of it, and hence of the acceptance by Canada of the Court's compulsory jurisdiction'.

It seems that the ICJ has not clearly stated its position on the effect and validity of the Connally reservation.

Subsequent to the criticism expressed in respect of automatic reservations, the Institute of International Law in 1959 called upon governments which had inserted such reservations in their declarations to withdraw them. Some governments have done this.

B. Multilateral treaty reservations – the Vandenberg reservation

Multilateral treaty reservations provide that a State which is a contracting party to a multilateral treaty, accepts the compulsory jurisdiction of the ICJ in so far as all the parties to the treaty which are involved in the dispute are also parties to the case before the Court. The main reason for making the Vandenberg reservation is to protect the reserving State from the prejudicial effects of partial adjudication of complex multilateral disputes. The Vandenberg reservation was examined by the ICJ in the *Nicaragua Case (Jurisdiction and Admissibility)*.[129]

NICARAGUA CASE (JURISDICTION AND ADMISSIBILITY)

Facts:

The US included in its declaration under Article 36(2) of the ICJ Statute a multilateral treaty reservation, otherwise known as the Vandenberg reservation. The issues before the Court involved, inter alia, the interpretation of the UN Charter, particularly Articles 2(4) and 51. The US argued that as Costa Rica and El Salvador – parties to the UN Charter (and the OAS) and involved in the dispute – were not parties to the proceedings before the Court, the Court lacked jurisdiction to hear the dispute under the terms of the US declaration.

Held:

The ICJ decided that El Salvador was affected by the dispute as it was a party to both the UN Charter and the OAS. The Court stated that the effect of the Vandenberg Reservation was 'confined to barring the applicability of the United Nations Charter and the Organization of American States Charter as multilateral treaty law, and has no further impact on the

---

126   [1998] ICJ Rep 432.
127   Ibid, para 47.
128   [1952] ICJ Rep, 93, 104.
129   [1984] ICJ Rep 392.

source of international law which Article 38 of the Statute requires the Court to apply'. As a result, the Court had jurisdiction on the basis of customary international law, which was the same as the provisions of the relevant treaties.

Comment:

The position of the ICJ was criticised by many. In particular Crawford stated that:

> *the Court found little or no difference between the two [i.e. the UN Charter and the OAS Charter, on one hand and customary international law on the other]. It entirely failed to distinguish the issue of jurisdiction under a treaty from the question of applicable law – an elementary error. Thus, the Vandenberg Amendment had little or no effect, despite the manifest intent of the United States in making the reservation.*[130]

It is also important to note that in the Genocide Case *the ICJ clearly states that it has no jurisdiction based on customary law, even of a jus cogens nature (see Chapter 2.5).*

In the *Case Concerning the Aerial Incident of 10 August 1999 (Pakistan v India) (Jurisdiction)*[131] India relied on the argument that on the basis of its multilateral reservation the ICJ had no jurisdiction. However, the Court decided neither to elaborate on this argument nor to comment on the response of Pakistan invoking the *Nicaragua* precedent.

C. Time – limitations and reservations *ratione temporis*

These reservation clauses are worded in a variety of ways. For example, the 2004 UK declaration, states that it applies to disputes arising after 1 January 1974, with regard to situations or facts subsequent to the same date.[132]

If a declaration contains a time reservation a State may object in appropriate circumstances to the Court's jurisdiction *ratione temporis*, that is it may allege that the dispute or the facts upon which it is based occurred outside the period common to declarations of all parties to the proceedings. In its case law the Court has taken the view that for temporal limitations and reservations to be effective the situations or the facts which are the source of the dispute must not occur outside the period of acceptance. This is exemplified in the *Phosphates in Morocco Case (Preliminary Objections).*[133]

PHOSPHATES IN MOROCCO CASE (PRELIMINARY OBJECTIONS)

Facts:

T, an Italian national, was assigned in 1918–19 various phosphate prospecting licences in French Morocco. In 1920 France, allegedly in contravention of French Treaty obligations,

---

130 J.R. Crawford, *Jurisdiction and Applicable Law, Hague International Tribunals* (2012) 25 LJIL, 477.

131 [2000] ICJ Rep 12.

132 The declaration is available at: www.icj-cij.org/jurisdiction/?p1=5&p2=1&p3=3&code=GB (accessed 17 September 2014).

133 [1938] PCIJ Rep Ser A/B No 74.

established a monopoly over phosphate mining, and T's rights were denied recognition by the French Moroccan Mines Department. In 1931 France made a declaration accepting jurisdiction of the PCIJ over 'any disputes which may arise after the ratification of the present Declaration with regard to situations or facts subsequent to such ratification'.

Held:

The PCIJ found that the facts and situations giving rise to the dispute were earlier than the 1931 exclusion date. Although the alleged illegality continued after the French declaration of 1931 the operative event was the creation of the monopoly in 1920. The dispute, the situation and the facts out of which it had arisen preceded the period covered by the French declaration of acceptance and thus fell outside the Court's jurisdiction.

14.7.4 The procedure before the ICJ

In contentious cases, the procedure consists of written and oral phases. In the written phase the parties file and exchange pleadings. The oral phase comprises public hearings at which agents and counsel of the parties address the Court.

Once the public hearings are over the Court deliberates *in camera* (i.e. in private) The deliberations normally last between three and nine months. Each judgment is decided by an absolute majority of judges present. No abstentions are permitted on any point voted upon. However, if a judge who participated in the proceedings is physically unable to attend the meetings but wishes to vote, he may be allowed to do so, by correspondence, if necessary. Also judges who did not participate in the oral proceedings or the deliberations, but despite this did not miss anything essential may be allowed to vote. In any case a quorum of nine judges is required. If the vote is equally divided, the President of the Court has a casting vote.[134]

The judgment is delivered at a public sitting held in the Great Hall of Justice of the Peace Palace in The Hague in the presence of all judges who participated in voting on the judgments unless for serious reasons they are preventing from attending. The President of the Court reads publicly the judgment in French or English, i.e. one of the official languages of the Court.

14.7.5 Incidental jurisdiction

Independently of the main proceedings the Court may be called upon to exercise incidental jurisdiction: hearing preliminary objections, determining applications to intervene and ordering interim measures.

14.7.5.1 Preliminary objections

In numerous cases, before examining the merits of a particular case, the Court has to consider preliminary objections to its jurisdiction. Such objections are usually dealt with in a separate preliminary judgment, but in some cases the objection is 'joined to the merits' and dealt with together with the merits in a

---

134 E.g. *SS Lotus Case* [1927] PCIJ Rep Ser A No 10 and *South West Africa Cases (Second Phase)* [1966] ICJ Rep 6.

single judgment. By virtue of Article 36(6) of the Statute the Court has jurisdiction to determine its own competence and to decide whether or not it has jurisdiction in a particular case.

In *The Panevezys-Saldutiskis Railway Case (Estonia v Lithuania) (Judgment)*,[135] the PCIJ defined preliminary objections as 'any objection of which the effect will be, if any objection is upheld, to interrupt further proceedings in the case and which it will therefore be appropriate for the Court to deal with before enquiring into the merits'.

The Court may have jurisdiction but an objection may be submitted by a party concerning admissibility of the claim. Preliminary objections to the admissibility of the claim can be based on a number of grounds, such as the failure of the claimant State to exhaust local remedies, failure to comply with the procedures required by the treaty or other instrument which confers jurisdiction upon the Court, failure to comply with the nationality of the claim, etc.

14.7.5.2 Intervention

The Statute of the ICJ provides for two forms of intervention by a third State in cases already before the Court.

A. 'Intervention as of right'

This right is contained in Article 63 of the ICJ Statute. In cases where the main issue in dispute is the construction of a multilateral treaty to which the intervening State is a party, that State has the right to intervene in the proceedings. Article 63 provides that a State that uses this right is bound by the construction given by the judgment.

The registrar of the Court must notify all potentially relevant States of the proceedings.

Notwithstanding the fact that this type of intervention is of right it does not mean that it is sufficient for a State party to a multilateral convention to submit its declaration for intervention to automatically obtain the status of intervener. The right to intervene exists only if the declaration satisfies the condition of Article 63 of the Statute, namely that it is within the scope of the subject matter of the main proceedings. For that reason in some cases it was allowed, e.g. Poland's intervention in the *Wimbledon Case*[136] and Cuba's intervention in the *Haya de la Torre Case (Colombia/Peru) (Judgment)*[137] in other refused, e.g. El Salvador's intervention in the *Case Concerning Military and Paramilitary Activities in and against Nicaragua (Nicaragua v. United States of America)*[138] in which El Salvador stated that its intervention had the 'sole and limited purpose' of claiming that the Court did not have jurisdiction to hear Nicaragua's Application.[139]

In the *Order Concerning Declaration of New Zealand of Intervention*[140] in the *Case Concerning Whaling in the Antarctic (Australia v Japan: New Zealand Intervening)*,[141] New Zealand sought to intervene in order to elucidate the meaning of Article VIII of the Convention for the Regulation of Whaling, to which Japan, Australia and New Zealand were contracting parties. New Zealand's interpretation of this provision was identical to that of Australia. New Zealand's declaration was certainly within the scope of the subject-matter of the main proceedings, but raised an issue of fair

---

135   [1939] PCIJ Rep Series A/B No 76, at 16.
136   [1923] PCIJ Rep Ser A No 1.
137   [1951] ICJ Rep 71.
138   (1986) ECJ Rep, pp1–2.
139   Order of 4 October 1984), pp.1–2.
140   (2013) ICJ Rep, 3.
141   Judgment in this case was delivered on 31 March 2014 and is available at the official website of the ICJ.

administration of justice. Japan, without formally objecting to the intervention of New Zealand argued that the admissibility of New Zealand's intervention would result in 'certain serious anomalies'.[142] In particular, Japan argued that Australia and New Zealand were 'the parties in the same interest' within the meaning of Article 31(5) of the Statute, and therefore, an *ad hoc* judge appointed by Australia should not take part in the proceedings because there had already been a judge from New Zealand on the bench. If New Zealand was allowed to intervene Australia would have two judges on its side and this would undermine the principle of equality of the parties before the ICJ. This argument was examined and rejected by the ICJ. The Court held that the status of an intervener did not confer on New Zealend the status of being a party in the main proceedings, and thus Australia and New Zealand could not be regarded as 'parties in the same interest' and consequently 'the presence on the Bench of a judge of the nationality of the intervening State has no effect on the right of the judge *ad hoc* chosen by the Applicant to sit in the case pursuant to Article 31, paragraph 2, of the Statute.'[143]

B. 'Discretionary intervention'.

This is provided for in Article 62 which says that a State may seek to intervene in a case in which it has an interest of a legal nature which may be affected by the decision. In such cases there is no absolute right to intervene and the Court decides, as a preliminary matter, whether an interest so to do exists. The conditions under which the Court will allow a third State to intervene were elucidated in the *Case Concerning Land, Island and Maritime Frontier Dispute (El Salvador/Honduras, Nicaragua Intervening)*[144] in which Nicaragua was given permission to intervene in a dispute between Honduras and El Salvador. Relevant matters are as follows:

- ■ the intervening State must prove that it has a legal interest which may (rather than will) be affected by the judgment;

- ■ the intervening State does not become a party to the proceedings and consequently the final decision of the Court is not binding on it, i.e. it does not affect its rights.

It is well established that objections of one party or both parties to a dispute to the intervention of a third State will not prevent the ICJ from granting permission to intervene.[145]

Under Article 62 of the Statute a State may intervene not only as an intervener but also as a party. This is subject to two conditions, first, a State must establish the existence of a legal interest in a dispute and second, there must exist a valid basis of jurisdiction between all the States concerned.[146] So far no such a situation has occurred. If it does then the intervening State will be bound by the judgment with respect to all aspects of the case, on which it was allowed to intervene.

14.7.5.3 Provisional measures

Under Article 41 of the Statute the ICJ is empowered, if it considers it appropriate, to indicate any provisional measures 'which ought to be taken to preserve the respective rights of each party'. Either party to the proceedings may make a request for provisional measures.

---

142   (2013) ICJ Rep, 3, para 7.

143   Ibid, para 21.

144   [1992] ICJ Rep 92; see also the *Case Concerning Land and Maritime Boundary between Cameroon and Nigeria Case (Cameroon v Nigeria, Equatorial Guinea Intervening) (Merits)* [2002] ICJ Rep 303.

145   See the *Case Concerning the Territorial and Maritime Dispute (Nicaragua v Colombia), Application by Honduras for Permission to Intervene* (2011) ICJ Rep 420.

146   Ibid.

The difficulty facing the Court when deciding whether or not to indicate provisional measures is that of reconciling the fact that ultimately the Court may decide it lacks jurisdiction to decide the case, with the fact that meanwhile a party's rights may be irreparably damaged pending the making of a decision as to jurisdiction. To avoid this situation the ICJ will indicate provisional measures only if it finds that it has *prima facie* jurisdiction, that the rights claimed by the applicant State appear to be at least plausible, that there exists a link between the rights whose protection is being sought and the measures requested, and that there is a risk of imminent and irreparable damage to the rights of the party seeking protection.

The above conditions were applied in the *Case Concerning Questions of Interpretation and Application of the 1971 Montreal Convention Arising from the Aerial Incident at Lockerbie (Libyan Arab Jamahiriya v US) (Provisional Measures)*.[147]

LIBYAN ARAB JAMAHIRIYA *V* US

Facts:

Libya alleged that the interpretation of UNSC Resolution 748 (1992) imposing certain sanctions in response to Libya's refusal to hand over two Libyan nationals suspected of destroying Pan Am Flight 103 over Lockerbie amounted to a prima facie *case over which the Court should exercise its jurisdiction. Further, Libya argued that the use of sanctions, and possible use of force, put Libya's interests at risk of suffering irreparable and imminent damage.*

Held:

The ICJ declined to find, at the early stage of the proceedings where the Court was dealing with provisional measures, that the UNSC's Resolution was ultra vires. *Neither did the Court find the existence of a risk of imminent and irreparable damage to Libya's rights. In fact, the Court found quite the reverse. The refusal of Libya to comply with the terms of the UNSC Resolution was more likely to impair the rights enjoyed by the UK and the US than the rights of Libya.*

In the circumstances the application for provisional measures was rejected and the grant was therefore refused. The decision of the Court was, however, by a majority with five votes against and strong dissenting opinions were submitted by the minority. The issue of judicial review of UNSC resolutions[148] which arose in this case is dealt with in Chapter 2.10.1

Compliance with interim measures ordered by the Court has always been poor. If a State fails to implement an order of the Court for interim measures of protection, no sanction can be imposed by the Court. The Court merely has power to reiterate the terms of its earlier order in a subsequent order. In the *Case Concerning the Application of the Convention on the Prevention and Punishment of the Crime of Genocide (Further Request for the Indication of Provisional Measures)(Bosnia and*

---

147   [1992] ICJ Rep 114.

148   See also B. Martenczuk, *The Security Council, the International Court and Judicial Review: What Lessons from Lockerbie?* (1999) 10(3) EJIL, 517 and I. Petculescu, *The Review of the United Nations Security Council Decisions* (2005) 52/2 NILR, 167.

Herzegonina v Yugoslavia),[149] where the FRY had effectively ignored the Court's first order, the Court could only order the FRY to give immediate and effective implementation to the earlier order.

In numerous cases the ICJ has issued interim measures without ever determining their binding force with regard to the parties to the proceedings. This matter was, for the first time, comprehensively examined by the Court in the *Case Concerning the Vienna Convention on Consular Relations (Germany v United States of America) (Provisional Measures)*[150] and in the judgment of the ICJ on the merits.[151]

LAGRAND CASE (GERMANY *V* UNITED STATES OF AMERICA)

Facts:

Walter LaGrand and his brother, both German nationals, while living in the US, were arrested in Arizona in 1982 on a charge of armed robbery and murder and later convicted and sentenced to death. During the proceedings before the court in Arizona they were never informed of their rights under the 1963 Vienna Convention on Consular Relations (VCCR) to which both Germany and the US are contracting parties. Under Article 36(1)(b) VCCR a contracting State has a duty to inform a national of another contracting State who is arrested or committed to prison or to custody pending trial or detained in any other manner on its territory that he is entitled to consular assistance of his country. The non-compliance of the US with the VCCR was neither raised during the proceedings against the LaGrand brothers, nor on appeal nor in the post-conviction proceedings in the Arizona courts. It was eventually raised in a federal habeas corpus petition but the petition was rejected on the ground that the matter was not properly raised in the state court. The German government learnt about the matter in February 1999, practically on the eve of the scheduled execution of the brothers. By the time the German government filed the proceedings against the US before the ICJ, Walter LaGrand's brother had already been executed and Walter LaGrand himself was scheduled to be executed the next day. The German government sought a judgment on the merits against the US and requested the Court to issue provisional measures.

LaGrand (Provisional measures)

The ICJ issued provisional measures calling upon the United States to take all necessary measures to ensure that a German national, Walter LaGrand who was sentenced to death in Arizona, not be executed pending the final decision of the ICJ in the proceedings brought by Germany against the US.

The ICJ considered the purpose and the nature of Article 41 of the Statute. It found that the purpose of provisional measures is to enable the Court to settle interim disputes by binding decisions, in particular to preserve the respective rights of the parties pending the final decision in the proceedings. Consequently, the ICJ stated that it has the power to indicate provisional measures which are binding and create legal obligations.[152]

---

149   [1993] ICJ Rep 325.

150   [1999] ICJ Rep 9.

151   *LaGrand Case (Germany v United States of America) (Merits)* [2001] ICJ Rep 466.

152   *The Case Concerning the Vienna Convention on Consular Relations (Germany v United States of America) (Provisional Measures)* [1999] ICJ Rep 9, para 109.

LaGrand (Merits)

Walter LaGrand was executed a few hours after the ICJ issued provisional measures. The position of the US government was that the provisional measures order was not binding. Although the US government transmitted the order to the governor of Arizona, the US Supreme Court decided not to intervene and the governor proceeded with the execution.

In its judgment of 27 June 2001 the ICJ held that it had jurisdiction to adjudicate the matter on the ground of Article 1 of the Optional Protocol attached to the VCCR which provides for the Court's jurisdiction over disputes arising out of the interpretation and application of the VCCR. The ICJ found the US in breach of the VCCR, and in breach of its obligation to comply with the order of provisional measures that the Court had issued.

The Court stated that the measure of a fax transmission by the US authorities to notify the order of the ICJ to the Governor of Arizona was not sufficient to ensure the compliance with the order. The requirement for the US to take all necessary measures goes further. The ICJ stated that it would, for example, have been satisfied by the US Supreme Court granting a preliminary stay of the execution order.

The treatment of aliens on death row by the US, in breach of the VCCR, was the subject of two more cases, one brought by Mexico and one brought by Paraguay. In both the issue of interim measures was relevant.

THE MEXICAN CASE: THE CASE CONCERNING AVENA AND OTHER MEXICAN NATIONALS (MEXICO V UNITED STATES OF AMERICA) (PROVISIONAL *MEASURES*)[153]

Facts:

Subsequent to the judgment in LaGrand the US instituted measures aimed at ensuring the effective review of every case within the scope of the VCCR. These measures, however, were judged as being insufficient by the government of Mexico, which on 9 January 2003 instituted proceedings against the US before the ICJ alleging the violation of Article 36 VCCR in respect of 51 of its nationals who were arrested, detained, tried, convicted and sentenced to death by the US courts without being informed of their right to consular assistance. The government of Mexico requested the ICJ to indicate provisional measures consisting of suspending execution of all Mexican nationals scheduled for execution, or to be executed in the US pending final judgment in this case. The US replied that the request submitted by Mexico would be tantamount to a 'sweeping prohibition on capital punishment for Mexican nationals in the USA' and thereby would transform the ICJ into a 'general criminal court of appeal'.

---

153   [2003] ICJ Rep 2.

Held:

On 5 February 2003 the ICJ granted the request.[154] *The Court rejected the argument put forward by the US. However, the ICJ limited the order requesting the suspension of the execution of Mexican nationals to those who had already been identified in the request as being victims of the violation of the VCCR, and not to all nationals of Mexico in the US currently on death row. However, the US did not comply with the interim order.*

In the case of Paraguay,[155] *the situation was similar to that in Avena. The ICJ issued a provisional measures order which was not complied with by the US. Mr Breard, a national of Paraguay, was executed despite the provisional measures order issued by the ICJ. After the order from the ICJ was received but before the execution, the US government sent a letter to the governor of Virginia, where Breard was awaiting execution, asking the governor to comply with the ICJ's order. In the meantime, the US Supreme Court refused to intervene and stated in* Breard v Greene[156] *that:*

> *While we should give respectful consideration to the interpretation of an international treaty rendered by an international court with jurisdiction to interpret such, it has been recognized in international law that, absent a clear and express statement to the contrary, the procedural rules of the forum State govern the implementation of the treaty in that State.*

On the basis of the above the governor of Virginia allowed the execution of Breard.

The ICJ in judgments on merits in both *LaGrand*[157] and Avena,[158] found that the US was in breach of the VCCR by failing to inform the aliens of their rights of consular notification, by not notifying their consulate of their detention and by depriving the consular representatives of access to the persons in detention. The US was also found in breach of the interim measures order. In *Avena*, the Court held that the failure of the US to provide judicial review of the convictions in the light of the lack of notification constituted a further violation of the VCCR. Additionally, in *Avena*, the ICJ found that Article 36 VCCR created individual rights, which are arguably enforceable in US courts (see Chapter 5.12.1). Finally, the ICJ stated that the US clemency processes through governors and parole boards were not appropriate procedures to guarantee that 'full weight is given to the violations of the rights set forth in the Vienna Convention'.[159]

On 25 February 2005, President Bush issued a memorandum to the Attorney General stating that the US will discharge its obligations under the judgment of *Avena* in accordance with the principle of comity with regard to 51 Mexican national concerned by that decision.[160] However, on 25 March 2008,

---

154   Ibid.

155   *The Application of the Government of Paraguay (Apr. 3, 1998), Vienna Convention on Consular Relations (Paraguay v U.S.), (Request for the Indication of Provisional Measures)* [1988] ICJ Rep 248.

156   523 US 371, 375 (1998).

157   *The LaGrand Case (Germany v United States of America) (Merits)* [2001] ICJ Rep 466.

158   *The Case Concerning Avena and Other Mexican Nationals (Mexico v United States of America) (Merits)* [2004] ICJ Rep 12.

159   Ibid, paras 139–140.

160   Memorandum of the President, 28 February 2005, available at www.whitehouse.gov/news/releases/2005/02/20050228–18.html (accessed 20 June 2009).

in *Medellin v Texas*,[161] the US Supreme Court held that neither the judgment of the ICJ in *Avena* nor the 2005 memorandum issued by President Bush were binding in federal law and therefore not enforceable against Texas (see Chapter 4.5.1.2). The execution of Medellin (who had been expressly mentioned in the *Avena Case*) on 5 August 2008 prompted Mexico to ask the ICJ for interpretation of its judgment of 31 March 2005 in *Case concerning Avena and Other Mexican Nationals (Mexico v United States of America) (Merits)*[162] (see Chapter 14.7.7.1).

It is to be noted that on 7 March 2005, the US government informed the UNS-G of its intention to withdraw from the Optional Protocol to the VCCR.[163] Consequently, no more cases will be able to be brought against the US before the ICJ once the notification takes effect.

It is clear from the case law of the ICJ that an order indicating provisional measures is binding, and that a failure of a State to comply with such an order constitutes an international wrong for which that State may be required to compensate the injured State.

14.7.6 Limitation periods for international actions

The Statute of the ICJ contains no express provision relating to a period within which a case must be brought to its attention. However, this is not to say that such a period of limitation does not exist, for clearly the Court would be reluctant to adjudicate disputes that have their origins other than in the recent past.

The issue of a limitation period arose in the *Certain Phosphate Lands in Nauru Case (Preliminary Objections) (Nauru v Australia)*.[164]

NAURU *V* AUSTRALIA

Facts:

In a dispute between Australia and Nauru concerning compensation for the rehabilitation of certain mines, the matter arose of whether the action was time-barred. Australia challenged the admissibility of the application on the ground, inter alia, that Nauru had achieved independence in 1968 and had ample opportunity to initiate proceedings in this matter but had chosen not to do so until 1988.

Held:

The Court acknowledged that a delay in initiating proceedings might have rendered an application inadmissible if the delay had prejudiced the rights of the other party. The overriding principle was that it was for the Court to decide 'in the light of the circumstances of each case whether the passage of time renders an application inadmissible'. A number of factors have to be taken into consideration in assessing whether the circumstances of the case

---

161 See M. McGuinness, *Medellin v Texas: Supreme Court Holds ICJ Decision not Binding Federal Law, Rejects Presidential Enforcement of ICJ Judgments over State Proceedings* (2008) 12/6 ASIL Insights, available at www.asil.org/insights080418.cfm (accessed 12 April 2014).

162 [2004] ICJ Rep 12.

163 It is to be noted that under the Optional Protocol the ICJ has compulsory jurisdiction over any disputes arising out of the interpretation of the VCCR.

164 [1992] ICJ Rep 240.

render the application inadmissible, including the relationship between the parties and the steps that had been taken prior to litigation to resolve the matter. Further, the Court has a responsibility to ensure that any future delay in proceedings does not prejudice the rights of the defending State with regard to both the establishment of the facts and the determination of the content of the applicable law.

Comment:

It should be noted that, if an action is time-barred, the underlying rights of the parties do not cease to exist. It is only the right of the party raising the action to bring proceedings that is affected. In other words, the rights of the parties under international law do not expire, only their right to vindicate those rights before the Court.

14.7.7   Judgments of the ICJ

The judgment of the ICJ is binding on the parties to any case in respect of that case only. For that reason the principle of *stare decisis*, that is the binding nature of precedents as known at common law, is foreign to the Court. However, in practice the Court often follows its previous decisions and tries to ensure consistency in its decisions.

A judgment is divided into three parts:

- the introduction, which contains a summary of the proceedings, the submissions of the parties, the names of the participating judges and the representatives of the parties;

- the grounds on which the judgment is based;

- the operative part, which contains the actual decision of the Court in respect of the disputed matters submitted by the parties.

Since 1978 each judgment must indicate the number and the names of judges constituting the majority. Judges are allowed to express their opinion on disputed matters in writing and these are attached to the judgment. They may take three forms:

- A judge may write a dissenting opinion in which he submits his reasons for disagreeing with the operative provisions of the judgment as a whole or some aspects of it.

- A judge who voted in favour of the judgment may write a separate opinion in which he may express his disagreement in respect of some or all of the reasoning of the Court or approve the operative provisions of the judgment on the basis of a different method of reasoning or submit additional reasons for approving the judgment.

- A judge may write a declaration which contains a brief indication of his approval or dissent of the judgment.

A judgment of the Court may affect the interests and rights of a third State. This occurs especially in respect of disputes involving the interpretation and application of multilateral treaties since other contracting parties will, to some extent, be affected by such a judgment. The Court has developed the so-called 'necessary third party rule' to deal with cases involving the determination of the rights and obligations of an absent third party which has not consented to the proceedings. In such cases the Court will decline its jurisdiction. Based on the 'necessary third party' rule the Court refused to deliver a decision on merits in the *Monetary Gold Removal from Rome in 1943 (Italy v France, United Kingdom and US)*[165] and in the *East Timor Case (Portugal v Australia)* (1995).[166]

When a case involves the interpretation of a multilateral treaty, the Registrar of the Court is required to notify all contracting parties to the treaty of the proceedings brought before the Court. Whether contracting States have been notified or not by the Registrar they may always submit a declaration of intervention and thus ensure that the Court takes their legal interests into consideration when deciding the case (see Chapter 14.7.5.2).

14.7.7.1 Interpretation

Under Article 60 of the ICJ Statute judgments of the Court are final and without appeal. However, at the request of either party the Court may interpret its judgment when there is a disagreement between the parties as to its exact meaning and scope. This occurred in the *Case Concerning the Request for Interpretation of the Judgment of 15 June1962 in the Case Concerning the Temple of Preah Vihear (Cambodia v Thailand)*.[167]

CASE CONCERNING THE REQUEST FOR INTERPRETATION OF THE JUDGMENT OF 15 JUNE1962 IN THE CASE CONCERNING THE TEMPLE OF PREAH VIHEAR (CAMBODIA *V* THAILAND)

Facts:

The background of this case was that in 1952 Thailand occupied the Temple of Preah Vihear situated on a promontory of the same name in the eastern part of the Dangrek range of mountains, which in a general way constituted a boundary between Cambodia and Thailand. Cambodia claimed that the occupation of the Temple by Cambodia was unlawful relying on the map entitled 'Dengrek – Commission of Delimitation between Indio-China and Siam' (thereafter referred to as 'the Map'), which Thailand had accepted (see Chapter 3.9.1.3).

In its 1962 judgment the ICJ ruled in favour of Cambodia. It held 'that Thailand is under an obligation to withdraw any military or police forces, or other guards or keepers, stationed by her at the Temple, or in its vicinity on Cambodian territory' and return any artefacts removed from the Temple by the Thai authorities to Cambodia. Subsequent to the judgment Thailand withdrew from the Temple but erected a barbed wire fence, which separated the Temple from the rest of the promontory of Preah Vihear on which the Temple sits. This fence followed the course of a line depicted on the map attached to a resolution adopted by the Council of Ministers of Thailand on 10 July1962 but not made public until the proceedings on the interpretation of the 1962 judgment. By that resolution, the Thai Council of Ministers had fixed what it considered to be the limits of the area from which Thailand was required to withdraw. Cambodia argued that the 'vicinity of the Temple' extended to territory far beyond the promontory of Preah Vihear.

---

165   [1954] ICJ Rep 19.
166   [1995] ICJ Rep 90.
167   [2013] ICJ Rep 281.

Held:

The ICJ held that it had jurisdiction to interpret the 1962 judgment as there was a dispute relating to its meaning and scope. It defined the meaning of the 'vicinity of the Temple'.

Comment:

The only precondition of the ICJ's jurisdiction to interpret a previous judgment is that the ICJ must establish that there is a dispute as to the meaning or scope of that judgment. The ICJ found that there was a dispute with regard to three matters:

1. Whether its 1962 judgment decided with binding force that the border between Cambodia and Thailand as drawn in the Map constituted the border between the parties;
2. The meaning and scope of the phase 'vicinity of the Temple' used in its 1962 judgment.
3. The nature of Thailand's obligation to withdraw imposed by the 1962 judgment.

The ICJ, upon finding that it had jurisdiction to interpret the 1962 judgment, stated that its interpretation is strictly confined to the 1962 judgment and thus conduct of the parties subsequent to that judgment could not be taken into account. It also found that the Map, being accepted by both parties in the 1962 proceedings was a basic tool for the determination of the dispute.

With regard to the first matter, the ICJ held that although the Map used by the Court to define the border between Cambodia and Thailand in the region of the Temple also traced the border between the parties throughout the Dengrek region, it was not necessary for the Court to address the question whether the 1962 Judgment determined with binding force the boundary line between the two States as traced by the Map. This was because the Court was not asked to delimit a boundary in the original case, and therefore could not do so in its interpretation, except to the extent that it had to clarify the limits of Cambodian sovereignty in the small area around the Temple of Preah Vihear that was the subject of the original case.

With regard to the second and third matter, the term 'vicinity of the Temple' in the 1962 judgment was unclear. The ICJ, based on evidence presented by the parties, decided that the term 'vicinity' had to be construed as meaning 'the whole territory of the promontory of Preah Vihear' and defined the area of the promontory with reference to natural features and the Map. Consequently, the line identified by the Thai Council of Ministers and physically represented by the fence, could not be regarded as the correct interpretation of the territorial scope of Thailand's obligation imposed by the 1962 judgment. Accordingly, Cambodia was required to withdraw from the entire promontary on which the Temple sits. However, as the ICJ was confined to defining the boundary only in the small region in the vicinity of the Temple in its 1962 judgment it could not rule on whether Cambodia's sovereignty extended beyond the promontory of the Temple.

Follow up:

Cambodia and Thailand welcomed the judgment of the ICJ. They still need to define their boundary throughout the Dengrek region over which they have long disagreed. However, they acknowledge the need for co-operation and negotiations in good faith, so hopefully will be able to at last end a long standing conflict over the Temple, which in 2008 was declared a World Heritage Site by UNESCO, and the territory extending beyond the promontory of Preah Vihear.

In some cases the Court has refused to interpret its judgment.[168] This occurred in the *Request for Interpretation of the Judgment of 31 March 2004 in the Case Concerning Avena and Other Mexican Nationals (Mexico v US)*.[169]

MEXICO *V* US

Facts:

Mexico asked the ICJ to interpret, inter alia, *para153(9) of its judgment in the* Avena Case *which stated that the appropriate reparation to be provided by the US consisted of reviewing and reconsidering, by means chosen by the US, 'the conviction and sentences of the Mexican nationals . . ., by taking account both of the violation of the rights set forth in Article 36 of the [Vienna] Convention [on Consular Relations] and of paragraphs 139 to 141 of the present judgment.'*

Held:

The Court decided that there was no dispute between the parties since both agreed that para 153(9) of the judgment created an obligation of result. The question which was of a real concern to Mexico was the effect of the ICJ's judgment in US domestic law. In this respect the ICJ held that this matter was outside the scope of its judgment in Avena *and therefore outside the jurisdiction of the Court. Although the ICJ did not interpret its previous judgment, as there was no dispute between the parties concerning its meaning, it strongly condemned the US for breaching its obligation by ignoring the ICJ's order issuing provisional measures concerning Medellin, who was subsequently executed. Further, the Court reaffirmed the continuing binding character of the US obligations under para 153(9) of the* Avena *judgment.*

14.7.7.2 Revision of judgments

The Court has jurisdiction to revise its judgment. Article 61 of the Statute sets out the conditions for revision in the following terms:

(1) An application for revision of a judgment may be made only when it is based upon the discovery of some fact of such a nature as to be a decisive factor, which fact was, when the judgment was given, unknown to the Court and also to the party claiming revision, always provided that such ignorance was not due to negligence . . .

(4) The application for revision must be made at least within six months of the discovery of the new fact.

(5) No application for revision may be made after the lapse of 10 years from the date of the judgment.

---

168   E.g. *the Request for Interpretation of the Judgment of 20 November 1950 in the Asylum Case (Columbia v Peru)* [1950] ICJ Rep 395.

169   (2009) ICJ Rep 3.

So far, the Court has never revised any of its judgments. The Application for Revision and Interpretation of the Judgment of 24 February 1982 in the *Case Concerning the Continental Shelf (Tunisia/Libyan Arab Jamahiryya (Judgment))*[170] was rejected by the Court. The same treatment was applied to the Application filed by Yugoslavia on 24 April 2001 requesting the revision of the Judgment of 11 July 1996[171] in which the ICJ declared that it had jurisdiction in the *Case Concerning the Application of the Convention for the Prevention and Punishment of the Crime of Genocide (Bosnia and Herzegovina v Yugoslavia) (Preliminary Objections).*

APPLICATION FOR REVISION OF THE JUDGMENT OF 11 JULY 1996 IN THE CASE CONCERNING THE APPLICATION OF THE CONVENTION FOR THE PREVENTION AND PUNISHMENT OF THE CRIME OF GENOCIDE (BOSNIA AND HERZEGOVINA *V* YUGOSLAVIA (PRELIMINARY OBJECTIONS) (YUGOSLAVIA *V* BOSNIA AND HERZEGOVINA) (JUDGMENT)

Facts:

The Federal Republic of Yugoslavia (the FRY) argued that a new fact which justified the revision of the relevant judgment was the admission of the FRY to the UN on 1 November 2000. This fact showed that the FRY did not continue the international legal and political personality of the Socialist Federal Republic of Yugoslavia (the SFRY), was not a member of the UN, and therefore was not a party to the Court's Statute and was not a party to the Genocide Convention. The FRY asserted that since the Court based its jurisdiction on the above-mentioned instruments, in particular Article IX of the Genocide Convention, no further basis for the Court's jurisdiction existed or could have existed in the case. The FRY further argued that in its notification to the UNS-G submitted on 8 March 2001, relating to accession to the Genocide Convention, the FRY had made a reservation to Article IX. According to the FRY, its accession could not have retroactive effect, and even if it did, this could not possibly encompass the compromissory clause in Article IX taking into account the fact that the FRY never accepted Article IX and as stated in its notification seeking accession to the Genocide Convention did not intend to accept it.

Held:

The ICJ held that the admission of the FRY to the UN in 2000, 4 years after the ICJ delivered its judgment, 'cannot have changed retroactively the sui generis position in which the FRY found itself vis-à-vis the United Nations over the period 1992 to 2000'. The ICJ noted that when, on 27 April 1992, the FRY informed the UN that Serbia and Montenegro 'decided to live together in Yugoslavia' the SFRY was transformed into the FRY, and thereafter had continued the legal personality of the SFRY. The FRY was never formally expelled from the United Nations: it was only barred from participating in the work of the UN bodies. This 'practical consequence' of the situation of the FRY from 1992 to 2000 could not be regarded as a fact within the meaning of Article 61 of the Statute of the ICJ.

---

170   [1985] ICJ Rep 192.

171   *The Application for Revision of the Judgment of 11 July 1996 in the Case Concerning the Application of the Convention for the Prevention and Punishment of the Crime of Genocide (Bosnia and Herzegovina v Yugoslavia (Preliminary Objections) (Yugoslavia v Bosnia and Herzegovina) (Judgment)* [2003] ICJ Rep 7.

14.8 The ICJ: advisory jurisdiction

The Court has jurisdiction to give advisory opinions but only to organs of the UN and international organisations. Under Article 96(1) of the UN Charter the UNGA and the UNSC are entitled to make a request for an advisory opinion on any legal question and by virtue of Article 96(2) of the UN Charter other organs and specialised agencies, when authorised by the UNGA, may also make such a request, but only relating to legal issues arising within the scope of their activities. Additionally, under the advisory jurisdiction, in some circumstances, the ICJ may be requested to review judgments of administrative courts and tribunals. This is a special case of advisory jurisdiction of the ICJ to which special rules apply (see Chapter 14.8.5).

At 28 October 2014, five organs of the UN and 16 international organisations are entitled to request the ICJ to give an advisory opinion.

On many occasions, States have contested the jurisdiction of the ICJ to give an advisory opinion. This occurred in the *Advisory Opinion on the Legal Consequences of the Construction of a Wall by Israel in the Occupied Palestinian Territory*.[172]

ADVISORY OPINION ON THE LEGAL CONSEQUENCES OF THE CONSTRUCTION OF A WALL BY ISRAEL IN THE OCCUPIED PALESTINIAN TERRITORY

Facts:

The government of Israel argued that the UNGA exceeded its competence when making the request for an advisory opinion, given that the UNSC was actively engaged with the situation in Palestine. According to Israel, in the light of Article 12 of the UN Charter the UNGA acted ultra vires *when making its request. Article 12 provides that:*

> *While the Security Council is exercising in respect of any dispute or situation the function assigned to it in the present Charter, the General Assembly shall not make any recommendation with regard to that dispute or situation unless the Security Council so requests . . .*

Held:

The ICJ answered that a distinction must be made between a 'recommendation' within the meaning of Article 12 of the UN Charter, and a request for an advisory opinion. These two measures are of a different legal nature. A request for an advisory opinion cannot be regarded as a 'recommendation' referred to in Article 12(1) of the UN Charter. Further, the ICJ decided to examine Article 12(1) of the UN Charter in the light of the practice of the UN in matters such as this. In this respect the ICJ stated that the interpretation of Article 12(1) had evolved. Initially both the UNSC and the UNGA interpreted this provision as meaning that the UNGA could not make recommendations on a matter concerning the maintenance of international peace and security while that matter was on the UNSC's agenda, given that by virtue of Article 24 of the Charter, the UNSC is entrusted with the main responsibility for the maintenance of international peace and security. Subsequently, the interpretation of Article 12(1) has changed. The ICJ found evidence of the changing nature of the practice in a note

---

172   [2004] ICJ Rep 136.

of interpretation of Article 12(1) given by the UN Legal Counsel at the Twenty-third Session of the UNGA and in the increasing tendency of both the UNSC and the UNGA to deal in parallel with the same matter. The ICJ stated that the accepted practice of the UNGA, as it had evolved, was consistent with Article 12(1) of the UN Charter. Consequently, the UNGA did not exceed its competence by adopting Resolution ES–10/14 seeking to obtain an advisory opinion from the ICJ.

The conditions necessary for the Court to exercise its advisory jurisdiction in respect of specialised agencies of the UN were confirmed in the *Legality of the Threat or Use of Nuclear Weapons Case*[173] in which the World Health Organisation (WHO) requested an advisory opinion. These conditions are:

■ the UNSC must authorise the relevant specialised agency to submit such a request;

■ the opinion requested must concern a legal question;

■ the question must be one arising within the scope of the activities of the requesting agency.

In the above case the Court rejected the WHO's request on the ground that the third condition was not satisfied. The Court held that although the matters of the effects on health of the use of nuclear weapons and the issue regarding preventive measures to be taken in order to protect the health of populations in the event of such weapons being used were within the scope of the WHO's activities, the requested opinion did not concern these matters, but focused on the legality of the use of nuclear weapons in the context of their health and environmental effects, a matter which was outside the scope of activities of the WHO. For that reason the Court held the WHO's request for an advisory opinion was inadmissible. It is to be noted that the ICJ did deliver an advisory opinion on this issue when asked by the UNGA (see Chapter 17.3.1.3).

The purpose of the advisory role of the Court is to provide legal advice in respect of the submitted matter and not to settle any particular dispute, even though a request is often related to, or has its origin in, an existing dispute. Article 65(1) of the Statute specifies that:

■ an advisory opinion must be confined to a legal question; and

■ the Court has discretion to decline its jurisdiction on the basis of judicial propriety.

14.8.1 Legal question within the meaning of Article 96(1) of the UN Charter and Article 65(1) of the Statute of the ICJ

In *Western Sahara Case (Advisory Opinion)*,[174] the ICJ provided a definition of a legal question. It held that questions 'framed in terms of law and rais[ing] problems of international law . . . are by their very nature susceptible of a reply based on law . . . [and] appear . . . to be questions of a legal character'.

Very often, a request for an advisory opinion involves a political element. In the *Conditions of Admission of a State to Membership of the United Nations Case*[175] the ICJ stated that it examines the question 'only in the abstract form' without taking into consideration the motives which may have

---

173   [1996] ICJ Rep 90.

174   [1975] ICJ Rep 12, para 15.

175   [1948] ICJ Rep 57, 61–62.

inspired the request or the distribution of votes with regard to the relevant resolution. Also, the political implications of the Court's opinion would not deprive it from exercising advisory jurisdiction. The Court has acknowledged many times that questions referred to it often have political significance. This does not, however, deprive them of being, at the same time, legal questions. The Court has emphasised on a number of occasions that it is the nature of things that international law and international politics are inevitably intertwined, but it has always stressed that whatever the political aspects of the question 'the Court cannot refuse to admit the legal character of a question which invites it to discharge an essentially judicial task, namely, an assessment of the legality of the possible conduct of states with regard to the obligations imposed upon them by international law'.[176]

In the *Interpretation of the Agreement of 25 March 1951 between the WHO and Egypt*,[177] the Court stated that in situations where political considerations are prominent a request for an advisory opinion may be especially necessary since the requesting organisation would particularly need the Court's advice as to the legal principles applicable to the matter under debate.

In the *Certain Expenses of the United Nations* Case,[178] the legal issues regarding the interpretation of the Charter were bound up with the differing political views of the members of the UN as to the UN peacekeeping role.

CERTAIN EXPENSES OF THE UNITED NATIONS CASE

Facts:

The Court was asked to advise whether the costs of the UN operations in Congo and in the Middle East constituted expenses of the Organisation that could be apportioned between members of the UN.

It was argued that the matter was of a political nature and therefore incapable of solution by legal means.

Held:

The Court decided that the political factors did not constitute sufficiently compelling reasons to refuse an Opinion. In this respect the Court stated that:

It is true that most interpretations of the Charter of the United Nations will have political significance, great or small. In the nature of things it could not be otherwise. The Court, however, cannot attribute a political character to a request which invites it to undertake an essentially judicial task, namely, the interpretation of a treaty provision.

The fact that the subject matter of a request may also involve the determination of facts by the Court does not affect the advisory jurisdiction of the Court. In the *Namibia Case*[179] the Court rejected South Africa's argument that the Court could only answer the question submitted to it by considering the factual issues relating to South Africa's conduct in the disputed territory, and that the Court had

---

176   *The Legal Consequences of the Construction of a Wall in the Occupied Palestinian Territories (Advisory Opinion)*
      [2004] ICJ Rep 136, para 41.
177   [1980] ICJ Rep 73, para 13.
178   [1962] ICJ Rep 151,155.
179   [1971] ICJ Rep 16, para 46.

no more competence to decide such disputes as to the facts than it had jurisdiction over legal disputes between states. The Court answered that:

In the view of the Court, the contingency that there may be factual issues underlying the question posed does not alter its character as a 'legal question' as envisaged in Article 96 of the Charter.

In the *Legal Consequences of the Construction of a Wall by Israel in the Occupied Palestinian Territory (Advisory Opinion)*,[180] arguments that the ICJ had no jurisdiction to give an advisory opinion because of the lack of clarity of the terms of the request, and because the request did not raise a 'legal question' within the meaning of Article 96(1) of the UN Charter and Article 65(1) of the Statute of the ICJ, were dismissed by the ICJ. The ICJ emphasised that lack of clarity did not deprive the Court of jurisdiction. To the contrary, any uncertainty arising from lack of clarity in the drafting of a question requires clarification, which the Court, by way of interpretation, has frequently provided. The ICJ observed that in the past, both the PCIJ and the ICJ were required to broaden, interpret and reformulate the question submitted.[181]

The ICJ was also satisfied that the UNGA's request related to a 'legal question' given that the question concerned the assessment of the legal consequences arising from a given factual situation in the light of the rules and principles of international law. The answer to the question submitted required a reply based on law.[182] The ICJ stated that the question was not an abstract one but in any event the Court was competent to give an advisory opinion in respect of an abstract question.[183] The ICJ affirmed that the political motives inspiring the request, the political implications of any advisory opinion, and any political aspects of the legal question were irrelevant to the establishment of its jurisdiction.[184]

The argument that the political pressures put on the Court and its members were so great as to make it 'impossible for the Court to exercise its judicial function properly' advanced by South Africa in the *Namibia Case*[185] was rejected by the Court. The Court stated that it acts only on the basis of the law, independently of all outside influence or intervention.

14.8.2 Judicial propriety

By virtue of Article 65(1), on the ground of judicial propriety, the ICJ enjoys a discretionary power to decline to give an advisory opinion even if the requirements for jurisdiction are satisfied. Only 'compelling reasons' would force the Court to use this discretionary power.

In the *Advisory Opinion on the Legal Consequences of the Construction of a Wall by Israel in the Occupied Palestinian Territory (Advisory Opinion)*,[186] the ICJ emphasised that, as a matter of principle, the Court should not decline to give an advisory opinion given its responsibilities as the principal judicial organ of the UN. The ICJ affirmed that there was no 'compelling reason' which would force the Court to use its discretionary power to decline to give an advisory opinion despite having jurisdiction

---

180   [2004] ICJ Rep 136.

181   Ibid, para 38. See also the *Jaworzina (Advisory Opinion) [1923] PCIJ Series B No 8; the Admissibility of Hearings of Petitioners by the Committee on South West Africa (Advisory Opinion)* [1956] ICJ Rep 20, 25; *the Certain Expenses of the United Nations (Advisory Opinion)* [1962] ICJ Rep 151, 157–162.

182   The *Western Sahara (Advisory Opinion)* (1975) ICJ Rep 12, para 15.

183   Supra note 180, para 40 and *the Conditions of Admission of a State to Membership in the United Nations (Advisory Opinion)* [1966] ICJ Rep 57, 61.

184   *The Advisory Opinion on the Legal Consequences of the Construction of a Wall by Israel in the Occupied Palestinian Territory*, supra note 176, para 40.

185   [1971] ICJ Rep 16.

186   [2004] ICJ Rep 136, para 44.

to do so. The ICJ emphasised that so far it has never, in the exercise of this discretionary power, declined to give an advisory opinion.

In the *Legality of the Use by a State of Nuclear Weapons in Armed Conflict (Advisory Opinion)*,[187] the ICJ refused to accept a request from the World Health Organisation for an advisory opinion because it lacked jurisdiction and not because it considered that it would be improper and inconsistent with the Court's judicial function to exercise its jurisdiction

As to the PCIJ, a request for an advisory opinion was refused on the ground of judicial propriety on one occasion only. This was in the *Eastern Carelia Case (Advisory Opinion)*.[188] The refusal was due to the unusual circumstances of the case which were:

■ the question directly concerned an already existing dispute;

■ one of the parties to the dispute refused to participate in the proceedings; and

■ the refusing party was neither a party to the Statute of the PCIJ, nor a member of the League of Nations.

The ICJ decided in the *Legal Consequences of the Construction of a Wall by Israel in the Occupied Palestinian Territory (Advisory Opinion)*[189] to examine the arguments based on the decision of the PCIJ in Eastern Carelia challenging the propriety of the exercise of its judicial function. Israel argued that the request for an advisory opinion concerned a contentious matter between Israel and Palestine, in respect of which Israel did not consent to the ICJ's jurisdiction. The ICJ replied that there is a vital difference between the contentious and the advisory jurisdiction of the ICJ with regard to the consent of a party to a dispute. While in contentious cases consent of all parties to the dispute is necessary in order to establish the Court's jurisdiction, in advisory proceedings the consent of all parties, although desirable, is not necessary taking into account the fact that an advisory opinion has no binding force and is given not to the States but to an international organisation which is entitled to request it. Only when an advisory opinion 'would have the effect of circumventing the principle that a state is not obliged to allow its dispute to be submitted to judicial settlement without its consent' may the issue of lack of consent of an interested state compel the Court to decline its jurisdiction on the basis of judicial propriety.[190]

Further, in the *Legal Consequences of the Construction of a Wall by Israel in the Occupied Palestinian Territory*, the ICJ found that the principle set out in *Eastern Carelia* did not apply because the question on which the UNGA requested an opinion was posed in a much broader frame of reference than that of the bilateral dispute between Israel and Palestine, and was indeed of direct concern to the UN and its responsibility for the maintenance of international peace and security.[191]

14.8.3 The Procedure

The procedure before the Court in respect of advisory opinions is modelled on that for contentious proceedings. The only difference between the two is that when the Court receives a request for an advisory opinion it invites States and international organisations which may provide useful information to present written or oral statements.

---

187   [1996] ICJ Report 226, 235.
188   [1923] PCIJ Rep Ser B No 5.
189   Supra note, para 46.
190   The *Western Sahara (Advisory Opinion)* [1975] ICJ Rep 12, paras 32–33.
191   Supra note 180, para 50.

14.8.4 The nature of advisory opinions

Advisory opinions are of a consultative character and therefore not binding on the requesting entities. It is up to these entities to decide on the usefulness of an advisory opinion and on the appropriate course of action. In most cases advisory opinions have been accepted and acted upon by any State concerned.

Some international instruments can, however, provide in advance that the advisory opinion shall be binding.[192]

14.8.5 The special case of advisory opinions on application for review of judgments of administrative courts and tribunals

Currently, only judgments of the Administrative Tribunal (AT) of the International Labour Organisation (ILO) can be reviewed by the ICJ. The AT of the ILO, has jurisdiction over disputes between 58 international organisations and members of their staff in respect of contracts of employment and the condition of employment of staff of these organisations. Under the Statute of the ILO, in some circumstances either the Governing body of the ILO or its Executive Board may request an advisory opinion on the validity of a judgment given by the AT. In order to ensure that the right to equality before courts of an individual affected by the proceedings before the ICJ is respected such an individual is allowed to prepare written observations and submit them to the ICJ through the chief administrative officer of the organisation concerned. Additionally, bearing in mind that an individual has no access to the ICJ only written proceedings are carried out before the ICJ, i.e. there are no oral proceedings. Some judges of the PCIJ and the ICJ have submitted that the safeguards provided are not sufficient, in particular bearing in mind the development of HRs after WWII, and thus the ICJ should withdraw from the ILO procedure.[193] However, it is submitted that the ICJ has taken account of those developments as exemplified in its *Advisory Opinion Concerning Judgment No 2867 of the Administrative Tribunal of the International Labour Organization upon a Complaint Filed against the International Fund for Agricultural Development*[194] the Court relied on the interpretation of Article 14 ICCPR, which ensures the right to a fair trial, by the Human Rights Committee, a body entrusted with monitoring compliance of contracting parties to the ICCPR, to ensure that the rights of the individual affected by proceedings before it were not prejudiced.

As at 28 October 2014, the ICJ had delivered five advisory opinions under the above procedure. They have binding force.

14.9 Assessment of the ICJ

In assessing the ICJ it is very important to note that States are extremely reluctant to submit disputes with other States to any form of international adjudication. Despite cynical views to the contrary, this reluctance is seldom caused by a desire to breach international law with impunity, although the absence of any compulsory adjudicatory system is a temptation! The distrust of States in respect of international

---

192   For example, the Convention on the Privileges and Immunities of the United Nations; the Convention on the Privileges and Immunities of the Specialized Agencies of the United Nations, and the Headquarters Agreement between the United Nations and the United States of America.

193   On this topic see E. de Brabandere, *Individuals in Advisory Proceedings before the International Court of Justice: Equality of the Parties and the Court's Discretionary Authority* (2012) 11 The Law and Practice of the International Courts and Tribunals, 253.

194   (2012) ICJ Rep 10.

adjudication arises from the fear that judicial decisions can be unpredictable. The reason for this unpredictability is not only that international law is uncertain, but also because of the fact that when a particular dispute is not capable of settlement through diplomatic channels it suggests that the relevant law or facts are uncertain.

States also point to the number of dissenting judgments as evidence of judicial unpredictability. They argue that if different judges come to different conclusions, it is evident that the outcome of litigation is pure chance! They further argue that where the law is uncertain, a judge may be influenced by political considerations. However, the fears expressed about the unpredictable nature of international law are, in reality, mere excuses. The most important reason for States' reluctance is that they do not wish to take the risk of exposing serious political issues to adjudication. In addition to all the above, an important psychological factor is that States do not like taking other States to court as this may be construed as an unfriendly act. Moreover, if a State loses its case, it suffers an inevitable loss of prestige.

The manifestation of States' fears can be found in the Statute of the ICJ:

■ Its contentious jurisdiction is not compulsory as it depends on the acceptance of the optional clause, which in turn is often limited by reservations inserted into a State's declaration of acceptance of the 'compulsory jurisdiction'.

■ Under Article 59 of the Statute the judgments of the Court have binding force only in respect of the parties to the dispute and only in respect of that particular case. Therefore, the Court's decisions are not precedents. Nevertheless, the Court has often used its previous decisions as evidence of the content of international law.

■ Under Article 33 of the UN Charter judicial settlement of disputes is one of many means available to States to solve their disputes.

In assessing the ICJ it is necessary to note that the Court is a part of a collective security system envisaged by the UN Charter which has never materialised as intended (see Chapter 16). Article 36(3) of the UN Charter states that 'legal disputes should as a general rule be referred by the parties to the International Court of Justice in accordance with the provisions of the Statute of the Court'. The *raison d'etre* of the ICJ was to provide judicial means for resolving disputes between States and thus deter them from resorting to force to settle their differences. If a party fails to comply with the Court's judgments or interim measures, the UNSC is empowered to take appropriate measures to ensure compliance. Until the end of the Cold War the UNSC was ineffective and unlikely to take measures to enforce the ICJ's decisions. Indeed, the credibility of the entire UN was at a low ebb. Consequently, the ICJ was not particularly popular as its popularity tends to follow upon the ups and downs of the UN. Having said this it must be acknowledged that the Court faced two crises of its own, one in the 1950s in respect of its controversial handling of the *South West Africa Cases* and the other in 1984 when the USA refused to participate in the case brought by Nicaragua, withdrew its acceptance of the Court's jurisdiction on the eve of the filing of the *Nicaragua Case*, and implemented a policy consisting of refusing to become a contracting party to treaties which provide for jurisdiction of the ICJ or of making reservations to the treaty to that effect, e.g. the Convention against Genocide.

The Court being an institution modelled from, and sustained by, essentially Western ideals of justice, tended to be associated with the colonial powers. It blotted its copybook very badly in the *South West Africa Cases*.[195] Here Ethiopia and Liberia sought a declaration from the Court to the effect that the

---

195   The *South West Africa Cases (Ethiopia v South Africa; Liberia v South Africa) (Preliminary Objections)* [1962] ICJ Rep 319 and *the South West Africa Cases (Ethiopia v South Africa; Liberia v South Africa) (Second Phase)* [1966] ICJ Rep 6.

Mandate for South West Africa was still in effect, and that South Africa remained under obligations placed upon it under the Mandate and was subject to the supervision of the UN. South Africa raised a preliminary objection on the basis of *locus standi* of the applicants, which was rejected by the Court. After 4 years of dispute, the Court then said that the applicants did not have *locus standi*! Between the first and second decision the composition of the Court had changed. In the earlier vote a narrow majority had prevailed; in the subsequent vote the Court was equally divided and the President of the Court decided the matter by a casting vote. The *volte-face* was effected by the Court by recourse to the most specious legal reasoning. This decision of the Court marked the beginning of the disillusionment of developing countries with the Court and its increasing unpopularity with them.

In the *Nicaragua Case* the Court proceeded with the case (despite the US's objections and subsequent withdrawal of its acceptance of the Court's compulsory jurisdiction) and rendered a judgment against the US. The US did not comply with the judgment. Moreover, the US's veto of the Nicaraguan application to the UNSC for the enforcement of the judgment in conformity with Article 94(2) of the UN Charter did not reflect well on the political credibility or status of the Court. After the end of the Sandinista regime in Nicaragua the US and Nicaragua settled the matter. The Court took cogniscence of the settlement in its order of 26 September 1991.[196] It must be noted, however, that the Court showed courage and determination when dealing with the US in the *Nicaragua Case*. The non-appearance of the US did not prevent the Court from giving a judgment against it.

The non-appearance of a State is a problem often faced by the Court. In the *Nuclear Tests Cases (Australia v France) (New Zealand v France)*,[197] France did not appear. In the *Fisheries Jurisdiction Case (United Kingdom v Iceland)*,[198] Iceland did not appear. In the *Aegean Sea Continental Shelf Case (Greece v Turkey)*,[199] Turkey not only failed to appear but also ignored the interlocutory orders. Similarly, in the *Hostages Case*,[200] Iran failed to appear. Notwithstanding the non-appearences, the Court proceeded in the absence of defendants, and established principles of significant importance to the development of international law.

From 1946 to 27 October 2014, the ICJ delivered 117 judgments and 27 advisory opinions on a wide range of issues, the most prominent are examined in this book. The advisory jurisdiction of the Court is a necessary complement to its contentious jurisdiction as it allows international organisations, including the political organs of the UN, to voice their concerns, and to be advised on legal issues relevant to their activities. The advisory jurisdiction of the Court has been very useful in clarifying international law in a non-contentious context.

Since the end of the Cold War, the number of cases submitted to the Court has considerably increased. In the 1970s the Court had only one or two cases pending, whereas on 27 October 2014, 14 cases were pending. This is a visible sign of the Court's revival. In the new post-Cold War climate the Court seems well used, and may be in danger of having insufficient capacity to deal with all of the matters before it.

The Court has greatly contributed to the development and clarification of international law. In its judgments the Court has always paid attention to the evolving nature of international law and has itself contributed to the evolution of that law.

---

196   [1991] ICJ Rep 47.
197   [1974] ICJ Rep 253.
198   [1974] ICJ Rep 3.
199   [1978] ICJ Rep 3.
200   (1980) ICJ Rep 3.

RECOMMENDED READING

Books

Hernández, G., *The International Court of Justice and the Judicial Function*, Oxford: Oxford University Press, 2014.

Indlekofer, M., *International Arbitration and the Permanent Court of Arbitration*, London: Kluwer Law International, 2013.

The International Bureau of the Permanent Court of Arbitration (ed), *Redressing Injustices Through Mass Claims Processes: Innovative Responses to Unique Challenges*, Oxford; Oxford University Press, 2006.

Klein, N. (ed.), *Litigating International Law Disputes: Weighing the Balance*, Cambridge: Cambridge University Press, 2014;

Merrills, J.G., *International Dispute Settlement*, 5th edn, Cambridge: Cambridge University Press, 2011.

Zimmerman, A., Tomuschat, C. and Oellers-Frahm, K (eds), *The Statute of the International Court of Justice*, Oxford: Oxford University Press, 2006.

Handbook, The International Court of Justice, 2013, available at www.icj-cij.org/publications/en/manuel_en.pdf (accessed 25 November 2014).

Articles

Alexandrov, S.A., *Accepting the Compulsory Jurisdiction of the International Court of Justice with Reservations: An Overview of Practice with a Focus on Recent Trends and Cases* (2001) 14 LJIL, 89.

de Brabandere, E., *Individuals in Advisory Proceedings before the International Court of Justice: Equality of the Parties and the Court's Discretionary Authority* (2012) 11 The Law and Practice of the International Courts and Tribunals, 253.

Crabb, J.H., *On Judging the Connally Amendment* (1962) 50 Geo LJ, 529.

Donner, R., *The Procedure of International Conciliation: Some Historical Aspects* (1999) 1 Journal of the History of International Law, 103.

Fitzmaurice, M. and Vogiatzi, M., 'Optional Clause Declarations and the Law of Treaties' in M. Fitzmaurice and O. Elias (eds), *Contemporary Issues in the Law of Treaties*, Utrecht: Eleven International Publishing, 2005, 201–253.

Kleiboer, M., *Understanding Success and Failure of International Mediation* (1996) 40 J Conflict Resol, 360.

Oda, S., *The Compulsory Jurisdiction of the International Court of Justice: A Myth?* (2000) 49 ICLQ, 251.

Rosenne, S., *Controlling Interlocutory Aspects of Proceedings in the International Court of Justice* (2000) 94 AJIL, 307.

Shifman, B., 'The Permanent Court of Arbitration: An Overview' in P.J. van Krieken and D. McKay (eds), *The Hague: Legal Capital of the World*, The Hague: TMC Asser Press, 2005, 127–180.

AIDE-MÉMOIRE

Peaceful Settlement of Disputes between States

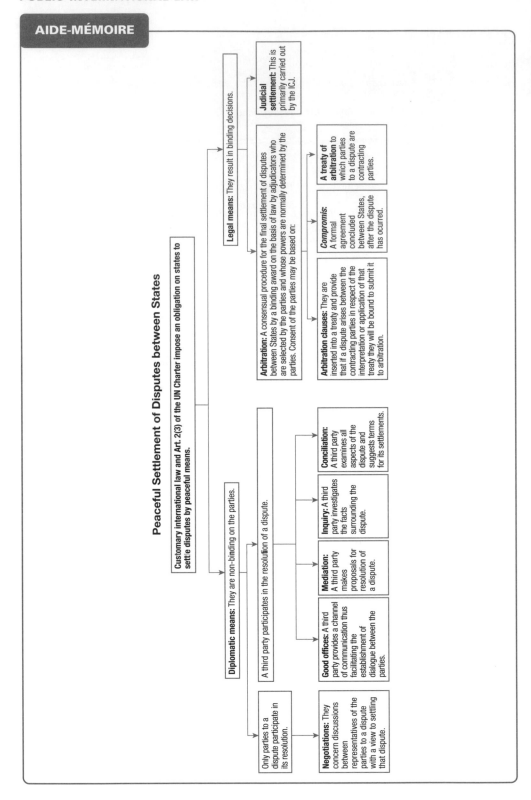

Customary international law and Art. 2(3) of the UN Charter impose an obligation on states to settle disputes by peaceful means.

Diplomatic means: They are non-binding on the parties.

A third party participates in the resolution of a dispute.

Only parties to a dispute participate in its resolution.

Negotiations: They concern discussions between representatives of the parties to a dispute with a view to settling that dispute.

Good offices: A third party provides a channel of communication thus facilitating the establishment of dialogue between the parties.

Mediation: A third party makes proposals for resolution of a dispute.

Inquiry: A third party investigates the facts surrounding the dispute.

Conciliation: A third party examines all aspects of the dispute and suggests terms for its settlements.

Legal means: They result in binding decisions.

Arbitration: A consensual procedure for the final settlement of disputes between States by a binding award on the basis of law by adjudicators who are selected by the parties and whose powers are normally determined by the parties. Consent of the parties may be based on:

Arbitration clauses: They are inserted into a treaty and provide that if a dispute arises between the contracting parties in respect of the interpretation or application of that treaty they will be bound to submit it to arbitration.

Compromis: A formal agreement concluded between States, after the dispute has occurred.

A treaty of arbitration to which parties to a dispute are contracting parties.

Judicial settlement: This is primarily carried out by the ICJ.

Jurisdiction of the International Court of Justice (ICJ)

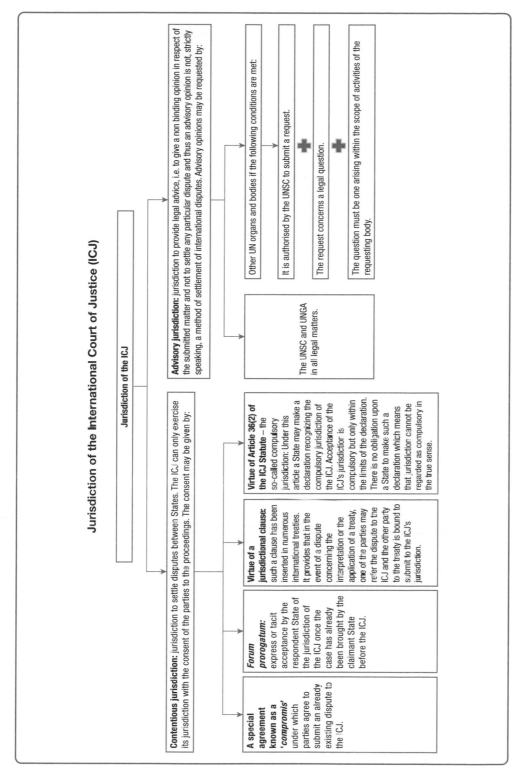

Jurisdiction of the ICJ

Contentious jurisdiction: jurisdiction to settle disputes between States. The ICJ can only exercise its jurisdiction with the consent of the parties to the proceedings. The consent may be given by:

A special agreement known as a '*compromis*' under which parties agree to submit an already existing dispute to the ICJ.

Forum prorogatum: express or tacit acceptance by the respondent State of the jurisdiction of the ICJ once the case has already been brought by the claimant State before the ICJ.

Virtue of a jurisdictional clause: such a clause has been inserted in numerous international treaties. It provides that in the event of a dispute concerning the interpretation or the application of a treaty, one of the parties may refer the dispute to the ICJ and the other party to the treaty is bound to submit to the ICJ's jurisdiction.

Virtue of Article 36(2) of the ICJ Statute – the so-called compulsory jurisdiction: Under this article a State may make a declaration recognizing the compulsory jurisdiction of the ICJ. Acceptance of the ICJ's jurisdiction is compulsory but only within the limits of the declaration. There is no obligation upon a State to make such a declaration which means that jurisdiction cannot be regarded as compulsory in the true sense.

Advisory jurisdiction: jurisdiction to provide legal advice, i.e. to give a non binding opinion in respect of the submitted matter and not to settle any particular dispute and thus an advisory opinion is not, strictly speaking, a method of settlement of international disputes. Advisory opinions may be requested by:

The UNSC and UNGA in all legal matters.

Other UN organs and bodies if the following conditions are met:

It is authorised by the UNSC to submit a request.

➕

The request concerns a legal question.

➕

The question must be one arising within the scope of activities of the requesting body.

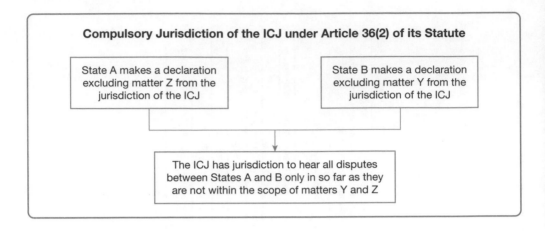

Compulsory Jurisdiction of the ICJ under Article 36(2) of its Statute

State A makes a declaration excluding matter Z from the jurisdiction of the ICJ

State B makes a declaration excluding matter Y from the jurisdiction of the ICJ

The ICJ has jurisdiction to hear all disputes between States A and B only in so far as they are not within the scope of matters Y and Z

15

THE USE OF FORCE

CHAPTER OUTLINE

1 Introduction

The prohibition of the threat of, or the use of force contained in Article 2(4) of the UN Charter constitutes a cornerstone of international law and is also a rule of customary law. However, the prohibition is not absolute as the UN Charter recognises two exceptions: the right to self-defence and the use of force by the UNSC when appropriate. Other exceptions, which are not mentioned in the UN Charter, have been established under international law, some are recognised by the international community, others are of a more doubtful nature.

2 From the right to wage war to a total prohibition of war

From the time of the Roman Republic to the 1648 Peace of Westphalia war was lawful although the doctrine of 'just war' imposed some restrictions on when a State was justified to resort to war.

After the 1648 Peace of Westphalia the doctrine of just war disappeared from international law. States were sovereign and equal and therefore one State had no authority to judge whether or not the cause of another State was just. By the end of the eighteenth century, and throughout the nineteenth century, war was recognised as an instrument of national policy, and customary law placed no limitations on the rights of States to resort to war.

After WWI, the Covenant of the League of Nations:

- outlawed wars of aggression;

- provided that if a dispute arose between members of the League they were obliged to submit the matter either to arbitration or to inquiry by the Council of the League and they agreed 'in no case to resort to war until three months after the award by the arbitrators or the report by the Council'. Any war in breach of this commitment or against a party complying with an award or decision was unlawful. Additionally, the Covenant established the first collective security system and provided for sanctions against a member who violated the specific prohibitions against war.

The 1928 General Treaty for the Renunciation of War, also known as the Kellogg-Briand Pact, was the first universal treaty which outlawed war, but did not provide for sanctions against a State who broke the Pact by resorting to war in violation of its provisions.

3 The prohibition of the threat or use of force under the UN Charter

A. Article 2(4) of the UN Charter states that all members of the UN 'shall refrain in their international relations from the threat or use of force against the territorial integrity or political independence of any State, or in any other manner incompatible with the purposes of the United Nations'. The prohibition, being also a rule of customary international law, applies to all States, irrespective of whether or not they are members of the UN.

B. Article 2(4) prohibits the use or threat of armed force against another State except in self-defence (Article 51) or in execution of collective measures authorised by the UNSC or the UNGA (see Chapter 16).

C. Article 2(4) mentions 'the threat or use of force' and not of 'war'. Thus, all hostilities are covered even where no formal declaration of war has been issued and the parties have denied that a technical state of war exists.

D. The force prohibited is armed force which may be direct e.g. an intentional attack by regular armed forces of one State against another State, or indirect, e.g. sending armed bands or groups from one State into another to carry out acts of armed force of such gravity as to amount to an armed attack. Both such uses of armed force, being acts of aggression, are prohibited under Article 2(4).

E. Article 2(4) does not prohibit the use of economic coercion or resort to other non-violent measures, although those may be unlawful under specific treaty provisions or under customary law.

F. The words 'international relations' mean that States are not prohibited from using force domestically, e.g. to deal with a rebellion or to win a civil war. However, when using force they must observe the relevant rules of IHL and HRL.

G. The phrase 'against the territorial integrity or political independence of any State' was interpreted by the ICJ in the *Corfu Channel Case* as meaning that any use of force contrary to the purposes of the UN, even when not directed against territorial integrity or political independence of any other State, is prohibited. Whether the use of force, not directed against territorial integrity or political independence of any other State, and which is in conformity the with purposes of the UN (e.g. humanitarian intervention) is lawful remains uncertain.

4 Exceptions to the prohibition of the threat or the use of force based on self-defence

A. Article 51 of the UN Charter preserves the inherent right of individual and collective self-defence, if an armed attack occurs, until the UNSC has taken necessary measures to maintain international peace and security.

B. Any action taken in self-defence must be reported to the UNSC as soon as possible. The reporting requirement is of a procedural nature and a failure to report will not make a claim of self defence invalid.

C. Article 51, as the ICJ held in the *Nicaragua Case*, preserves the pre-existing customary law on self-defence by making reference to the 'inherent' right to self-defence.

D. One of many controversial issues under Article 51 is whether this article limits the customary right of self-defence to cases where the attack provoking it has actually been launched. In this respect three approaches are present:

- Some authorities have interpreted 'if an armed attack occurs' to mean 'after an armed attack has occurred'.

- Some authorities argue that a State is allowed to resort to self-defence to respond to an imminent armed attack that has not yet occurred (i.e. anticipatory self-defence).

- Some authorities say that a State is allowed to resort to self-defence to respond to an armed attack which is neither actual nor manifestly imminent but which may take place in the future if no action is taken (i.e. pre-emptive self-defence).

While the third approach was relied upon by former US President G.W. Bush it seems to be rejected by the international community. It is perhaps correct to say that the right to self-defence may be exercised in a case of an actual or manifestly imminent armed attack.

E. A State claiming the right to self-defence must be a victim (or an imminent victim) of an 'armed attack'.

F. Depending on the scale and effect of the force used it may, or may not, amount to an 'armed attack'. Accordingly, less grave forms of the use of force, e.g. mere frontier incidents, will not trigger the right of self-defence.

G. State practice shows that a State can resort to self-defence in the event of an armed attack by non-State actors located on the territory of another State, when the latter is unwilling or unable to take measures to combat non-State actors.

H. Measures of self-defence must be taken as a last resort, i.e. they must be necessary, and must be proportionate to the end of halting or repelling the attack while taking account of side-effects on other interests and values affected by the response.

5 Collective self-defence

Collective exercise of the right of self-defence is expressly incorporated in Article 51. In the *Nicaragua Case*, the ICJ stated the State under attack must:

- have declared itself to be under attack, and

- have requested the assistance of a third State.

in order for a third State to justify the exercise of the right to collective self-defence.

6 Controversial uses of force

These are:

A. Intervention to protect a State's own nationals abroad. It is submitted that the right of a State to use force to protect its nationals abroad will not breach Article 2(4) of the UN Charter in the following circumstances:

- when there is a threat of imminent injury or death to nationals:

- when a State in whose territory they are located is unwilling or unable to protect foreign nationals in danger;

- when the intervention of a State is exclusively confined to the rescuing of its nationals;

- when there is a reasonable chance that the action will save more lives than it will destroy.

B. Humanitarian intervention. Humanitarian intervention can be defined as a unilateral coercive interference by one State or a group of States in the internal affairs of another State, involving the use of armed force, with the purposes of addressing massive human rights violations or preventing widespread human suffering. There is a week support in State practice for the proposition that humanitarian intervention is lawful.

7 Prohibition of reprisals

Reprisals can be defined as coercive measures directed by one government against another government in retaliation for alleged wrongful acts committed by the latter. Reprisals involving the use of force during peace time are unlawful and amount to acts of aggression.

15.1   Introduction

International law prohibits the threat of, and the use of, force in international relations. The prohibition is both embodied in Article 2(4) of the UN Charter and in customary law.[1] However, it is not absolute. The UN Charter itself recognises the right to self-defence and allows the UNSC to use force when appropriate. Other exceptions, outside the UN Charter, have been established under international law – for example, the use of force by people in the exercise of their right to self-determination. Furthermore, States have invoked a number of justifications for the use of force, some of which have gone unchallenged by the international community. This raises a strong presumption in favour of their acceptance.

15.2   From the right to wage war to a total prohibition of war

Humanity needed many centuries before agreeing on the prohibition of the use of force. A short history of the use of force is presented below.

15.2.1   Ancient Rome

The Romans under *jus fetiale* (see Chapter 1.2.1.2), which was a religious law, developed certain procedures that had to be observed in respect of the declaration of war on an enemy State. Only *fetiales* (priests) had the authority to declare war on an offending State and this could only be done after making three trips to that State and reciting Rome's grievances before the relevant authority there. However, *fetiales* had no power to negotiate Rome's demands which were intentionally unacceptable to the offending State which had, in practice, only two options, either surrender or fight. Before the procedure was commenced, a war had already been decided by the Senate, or later by an emperor. The procedure, therefore was a mere formality, but served an important purpose. It made resort to war lawful as its outcome was to demonstrate to the gods and to the people of Rome that the intended war was 'just', i.e. justified on moral and religious grounds.[2]

Marcus Tullius Cicero (106 BC–43 BC), statesman, philosopher and Rome's greatest orator, is considered as the author of the term 'just' war. He argued that no war was lawful unless it was declared openly, had 'just cause' and was conducted justly. However, his understanding of 'just' war was different from that of Christian medieval philosophers. According to Cicero whether or not war was 'just' depended upon the identity of the enemy, e.g. Barbarians were to be fought to death, and the purpose for which a war was fought, i.e. survival or supremacy.

15.2.2   From the first centuries of Christianity to the Middle Ages

The principal theories on war were formed in the first centuries of Christianity. These theories gave rise to the foundations of the law of war in the Middle Ages. The matter of whether the recourse to war was lawful was considered from two perspectives:

- ■ Pacifists condemned any recourse to collective violence irrespective of its objectives and purposes. In the very first centuries of Christianity many pacifists challenged the presence of Christians

---

1   On whether the prohibition of the use of force is a rule of *jus cogens* see U. Linderfalk, *The Effect of Jus Cogens Norms: Whoever Opened Pandora's Box, Did you Ever Think About the Consequences?* (2008) 18 EJIL, 853.

2   W. Murray, M. Knox and A. Bernstein (eds), *The Making of Strategy. Rulers, States, and War*, Cambridge: Cambridge University Press, 1994, 64–65.

in the Roman legions. Tertulien in his work *De Corona (The Crown)*, written in approximately 211 AD, asked the question: 'Can a Christian, in general, be a part of the army?' He answered in the negative. However, pacifism was rejected when the barbarian invasions threatened the Roman civilisation with which, at that time, Christianity had identified itself.

■ The doctrine of 'just' war allowed the use of force provided that the 'cause' was 'just'. This doctrine was formulated by St.Augustine of Hippo (354–430) in the following terms:

> Just wars are usually defined as those which avenge injuries, when the nation or city against which warlike action is to be directed has neglected, either to punish wrongs committed by its own citizens or to restore what has been unjustly taken by it.

Further, that kind of war is undoubtedly just which God Himself ordains.[3] The doctrine of 'just war' accepted war as a necessary instrument to preserve the Christian civilisation. However, St Augustine did not advocate war. To the contrary, he considered war as an evil and specified conditions under which Christians could participate in wars. He also stated that an initially 'just war' may become 'unjust' if pursued to vindictive excess beyond what is necessary to remedy the original wrong. This was the first expression of the idea of proportionality.

With the conversion to Catholicism of Emperor Constantine the interests of the Roman Empire became associated with the interests of Christianity. Consequently, the Catholic Church began distancing itself from its pacifist traditions. By the tenth century Christianity had become the official religion of all European States.

In the Middle Ages the Crusaders' ideal, which emphasised that war was justified by the holy cause (that is rescuing the Holy Land from the Muslims), associated the Church with warring activities. The Church policy was to fight 'infidel Muslims' and stop European States fighting each other. However, as it was not realistic to achieve peace between European States, the Church imposed severe restrictions on the conduct of wars between Europeans. One of these was the institution of the Peace of God, which restricted the times for fighting as it required the observance of a truce during the 'Passion days' of the week, i.e. from Thursday night to Monday morning, subject to ecclesiastical penalties. Further, the Church banned clerical participation in wars and made a distinction between combatants and non-combatants.

The doctrine of 'just war' was further refined by St Thomas Aquinas in the thirteenth century in his *Summa Theologica* (Summary of Theology).[4] He set out three conditions for a just war:

■ Only a sovereign ruler was entitled to resort to force in defence of the interests of the State.

■ The cause must be 'just' in the sense advocated by St Augustine, i.e. the other party must provide a 'just cause' by its culpable conduct.

■ The sovereign ruler must have a just intention, which was to punish the wicked, to help the good and thereby to restore peace as soon as possible. Therefore, just wars were those which were not made by ambition or cruelty but in the spirit of love of peace with a view to helping the righteous by vanquishing the evil ones.

The doctrine imposed some limitations on the authority of sovereign rulers to make war, namely they had to remedy the original wrong without pursuit to excess.

---

3   J. Eppstein, *The Catholic Tradition of the Law of Nations*, London: Burnes, 1935, 65.

4   P. *Schaff, Thomas Aquinas in the New Schaff-Herzog Encyclopedia of Religious Knowledge*, Grand Rapids, MI: Baker Book House, 1953, 422–423.

However, it can be said that the above conditions were sufficiently flexible to justify almost any resort to force.

15.2.3 Renaissance

In the period of the Renaissance the concept of 'just war' continued to be invoked but by then its content had changed. Grotius in *De Jure Belli ac Pacis* (On the Law of War and Peace), the first definitive text on international law, considered that natural law prescribes rules of conduct not only for nations but also for private individuals. He condemned war but agreed that war pursued for a 'just cause', i.e. protecting rights and punishing wrong, was permissible. He identified three causes for the 'just war': self-defence, reparation of injury, and punishment. For him war was a mode of judicial procedure. Further, he defined the state of war, the legal consequences flowing from it, and the rules of conduct of war which should bind all parties, whether their cause was just or not. He advocated that disputes between nations should be settled by independent judges and arbitrators to limit the recourse to war.

Erasmus represented the pacifist approach based on such philosophical and theological principles as the common humanity and brotherhood of all persons as children of God.

15.2.4 From the 1648 Peace of Westphalia to WWI

With the development and consolidation of the modern State system the predominant view was that the right of a State to wage war was inherent in the concept of State sovereignty. After the 1648 Peace of Westphalia the doctrine of just war disappeared from international law.[5] States were sovereign and equal and therefore one State had no authority to judge whether or not the cause of another State was just. By the end of the eighteenth century and throughout the nineteenth century the attitude that it was the right of every State to resort to war prevailed. As a matter of positive law, war was recognised as a legally admissible instrument for attacking and altering existing rights of States. It had become an instrument of national policy, and customary international law placed no limitations on the right of States to resort to war.

The first attempts to limit the right to wage war took place at the end of the nineteenth and the beginning of the twentieth centuries at the Hague Peace Conferences of 1899 and 1907 (see Chapter 17.3).

15.2.5 The period between the two World Wars

A major breakthrough took place after WWI with the creation of the League of Nations and the adoption of the 1928 General Treaty for the Renunciation of War known as the Kellogg-Briand Pact.

15.2.5.1 *The League of Nations*

Towards the end of WWI, US President Woodrow Wilson in his Fourteen Point Plan presented on 8 January 1918 to the US Congress set his vision for the post-war world. He advocated the establishment of a collective security system which would ensure lasting peace and would make WWI the 'war to end all wars', the last war in the history of mankind. According to Wilson, in order to oversee the new system:

---

5   L. Gross, *The Peace of Westphalia* (1948) 42 AJIL, 20.

a general association of nations must be formed under specific covenants for the purpose of affording mutual guarantees of political independence and territorial integrity to great and small states alike.[6]

Under the chairmanship of Wilson, a Drafting Committee was set up to prepare the Covenant of the League of Nations and to establish that League. The Covenant of the League was included in the 1919 Treaty of Versailles which concluded the peace settlement with Germany. The main purpose of the League was to maintain peace and security through international law and the maintenance of justice. The Covenant introduced two major innovations in respect of the right to wage war:

■ It imposed some limitation upon the use of force. Although the preamble to the Covenant refers to a duty on the part of its members not to resort to war, no general duty was contained in the Covenant itself. Under Article 12(1) of the Covenant if a dispute arose between members of the League they were obliged to submit the matter either to arbitration or to inquiry by the Council of the League and they agreed 'in no case to resort to war until three months after the award by the arbitrators or the report by the Council'. The three months' 'cooling off period' was intended to prevent 'accidental' outbreaks of hostilities. The Covenant expressly outlawed wars of aggression (Article 10); wars commenced in breach of Article 12(1), that is when a member State had not submitted a dispute to arbitration or to the Council; wars started in defiance of a judicial or arbitral decision rendered under the auspices of the League of Nations (Article 13(4)), and wars declared despite recommendations adopted unanimously by the Council of the League. The latter possibility was provided for under Articles 15 and 16 of the Covenant. It required that disputes which were not submitted to arbitration or judicial settlement were to be submitted to the Council. If the Council (ignoring any votes of the parties to a dispute) unanimously agreed on a report settling a dispute, the members of the League were bound not to go to war with any party that complied with the recommendations. However, if no such agreement was reached by the Council, the only sanction was the publication of the report, provided its members, unanimously or by a majority vote, agreed to publication. This provision implies that in the situation where the Council could not reach an agreement on a report, members of the League were allowed to take measures which they considered necessary for the maintenance of law and justice (Article 15(7)), including resort to war.

The above provisions are of major importance as they introduced obligations for the members of the League to settle their disputes by peaceful means and not to resort to war without first exhausting those means.

■ Article 16 of the Covenant established the first collective security system and provided for sanctions against a Covenant-breaking member. This article stated that:

> Should any member of the League resort to war in disregard of its Covenants under Article 12, 13, 15, it shall, *ipso facto*, be deemed to have committed an act of war against all other Members of the League, which hereby undertake immediately to subject it to the severance of all trade or financial relations, the prohibition of all intercourse between their nationals and the nationals of the Covenant-breaking state, and the prevention of all financial, commercial or personal intercourse between the nationals of the Covenant-breaking state and the nationals of any other state, whether a Member of the League or not.

---

6   Point XIV in *Selected Literary and Political Papers and Addresses of Woodrow Wilson*, vol 2, New York: Grosset and Dunlop, 1927.

The system developed by the League of Nations did not work in practice for two main reasons:

First, not all States were members of the League of Nations. Initially, 45 States become members by the early 1920s. At its zenith the membership of the League had reached 63 States. Germany was admitted in 1926 and the Soviet Union in 1934. However, the US, the driving force in the creation of the League, did not ratify the Covenant as it did not to obtain the required two-thirds majority before the US Senate.

Second, the major disappointment was the failure of members of the League to impose effective sanctions against a Covenant-breaking State. Under Article 16 economic sanctions were intended to be applied automatically and collectively. Article 16 also provided for military sanctions. In this respect, the Council was empowered to make recommendations to its members asking for contributions to such forces. Under Article 17 collective measures could also be applied against a non-member State.

In practice, military sanctions were never imposed and even economic sanctions were only applied on a selective and optional basis. In 1921 the Assembly of the League adopted a resolution stating that for each member State the imposition of economic sanctions was optional, not mandatory. As a result, the system of sanctions was a failure:

- In 1931 when Japan invaded Manchuria no sanctions were imposed. The League sent a League Commission of Inquiry to the Far East. Apart from a report produced by the Commission, which was adopted by the Assembly and which condemned the act of aggression committed by Japan and refused to recognise the State of Manchukuo created by Japan on the invaded territory, the League did nothing. However, following the condemnation Japan formally withdrew from the League.

- No sanctions were imposed when Germany under Hitler invaded the Rhineland, Austria and Czechoslovakia. Germany, however, withdrew from the League.

- Inefficient sanctions were imposed on Italy after its invasion of Abyssinia (now Ethiopia) in 1935. Although 50 members of the League agreed on an embargo on arms and on financial aid to Italy and on certain Italian exports, the most important product, oil, was not subjected to an embargo. Furthermore, the League neither blockaded the Italian ports nor prevented access of Italy to sea routes, in particular the Suez Canal, through which its forces in Abyssinia were kept supplied. All sanctions were revoked in 1936 when Italy, because of its internal problems, not because of the sanctions, was at the point of economic collapse.

The only occasion of apparently serious action by the League of Nations was in 1939 when it imposed sanctions and ultimately expelled the Soviet Union from the League subsequent to its invasion of Finland. However, at that time the world was at war.

15.2.5.2 The 1928 General Treaty for the Renunciation of War (also known as the Kellogg-Briand Pact)

The comprehensive prohibition of war as an instrument of national policy was achieved under the 1928 General Treaty for the Renunciation of War.[7] On 27 August 1928 at the initiative of the French Minister for Foreign Affairs, Aristide Briand, and the US Secretary of State, Frank Kellogg, representatives of 15 governments signed at Paris the General Treaty for the Renunciation of War and, on the same day, invited other governments to ratify the Treaty. By 1939, 63 States were contracting States to the Treaty. It is very short containing only a preamble and two provisions.

---

7   94 LNTS, 57.

Article I states that:

The High Contracting parties solemnly declare in the names of their respective peoples that they condemn recourse to war for the solution of international controversies, and renounce it as an instrument of national policy in their relations with one another.

Article II provides for the settlement of international disputes or conflicts 'of whatever nature or of whatever origin' exclusively by peaceful means.

The Kellogg-Briand Pact was enthusiastically endorsed by the international community as a breakthrough in the search for peace. However, it had many shortcomings, the most important being that it did not provide for sanctions against a State who broke the Pact by resorting to war in violation of its provisions. The Pact was inefficient in preventing conflicts. It was violated many times during the period preceding the outbreak of WWII by contracting States, namely by Japan, Italy, Germany and the Soviet Union. Consequently, the Pact failed to complement the Covenant of the League of Nations by reinforcing the prohibition of the use of force. Other drawbacks included the following:

■ It emerges from the negotiations leading to the adoption of the Pact that the contracting States considered that the right to self-defence was implicitly incorporated into the Pact. The Pact was silent on this point.

■ Recourse to war remained lawful as between a contracting party and a non-contracting party.

■ The prohibition of merely the recourse to war implied that not all use of force is covered by the Pact.

The Kellogg-Briand Pact has never been terminated. For practical purposes it has, however, been superseded by Article 2(4) of the UN Charter.

15.3   The prohibition of the threat or use of force under the UN Charter

The general prohibition of the threat of, or the use of, force in international relations is contained in Article 2(4) of the UN Charter which states that:

All Members shall refrain in their international relations from the threat or use of force against the territorial integrity or political independence of any state, or in any other manner inconsistent with the purposes of the United Nations.

This provision is complemented by Article 2(3) of the UN Charter which states that:

All members shall settle their international disputes by peaceful means, in such a manner that international peace and security, and justice, are not endangered.

The purposes of the UN set out in Article 1 of the UN Charter are widely drawn so that any use of force by a State outside its own borders is likely to be inconsistent with the maintenance of international peace and security or of promoting friendly relations among nations.

The following points regarding Article 2(4) should be noted:

■ In the *Nicaragua Case (Nicaragua v US) (Merits)*[8] the ICJ accepted that Article 2(4) reflects a rule of customary international law applying to all States whether or not members of the UN.

---

8   [1986] ICJ Rep 14.

■ The article applies only to resort to force in 'international relations' against another State and does not affect a State's legal right to use armed force in the suppression of internal disturbances. In practice, the UN has interpreted a wide range of 'domestic' activities as falling within the ambit of the UN for these purposes. Nevertheless, domestic uses of force (e.g. to quash a rebellion or end a civil war) must conform to the relevant rules of international humanitarian law and of international human rights law.[9]

■ The article entirely prohibits the threat of, and the use of armed force against another State except in self-defence (Article 51) or in execution of collective measures authorised by the UNSC or the UNGA.

■ Article 2(4) talks of the threat or use of force and not of war. Thus, all hostilities are covered even where no formal declaration of war is made, and the parties deny that a state of war exists.

15.3.1 The meaning of 'threat of or use of force'

The force prohibited is armed force. The general view is that the article does not preclude a State from taking unilateral economic or other measures not involving the threat or use of armed force, in retaliation for a breach of international law by another State.[10] However, non-violent actions may be in breach of other provisions of the UN Charter, treaty obligations, or customary international law on State responsibility.

Threats of use of force sometimes materialise in the use of force but sometimes stand alone. The ICJ in its Advisory Opinion on *Legality of the Threat or Use of Nuclear Weapons (Advisory Opinion)*[11] provided important clarifications relating to threats of use of force. It states that:

> The notions of 'threat' and 'use' of force under Article 2, paragraph 4, of the Charter stand together in the sense that if the use of force itself in a given case is illegal – for whatever reason – the threat to use such force will likewise be illegal. In short, if it is to be lawful, the declared readiness of a State to use force must be a use of force that is in conformity with the Charter.

The above statement emphasises that the ICJ gives the same status to threats, and to use, of force in that when the use of force is unlawful, the threat to use force is also unlawful. The ICJ further stated that in order to decide whether a signalled intention to use force constitutes a threat within the meaning of Article 2(4) of the Charter all circumstances of the case must be taken into account. It provided two examples of unlawful threats of use of force, the first concerning a situation where threats of use of force are aimed at forcing a State to yield its territory, and the second, when they aimed at forcing a State to follow a certain political or economic path.

Bearing in mind that under the UN Charter there are only two exceptions to the prohibition of use of force, i.e. first, a State may use force when authorised by the UNSC, and second, in self-defence, in particular when threats of use of force clearly indicate that an armed attack is imminent (see Chapter 15.4.2.2).

---

9   *Prosecutor v Tadić (Judgment)* ICTY-94–1 (15 July 1999).

10 Y. Dinstein, *War, Aggression and Self-defence*, 3rd edn, Cambridge: Cambridge University Press, 2001, 81. See also Report of the Special Working Group on the Crime of Aggression (ICC ASP/6/20/Add.1/Annex II), para 35 which excluded economic aggression from the definition of aggression (see Chapter 16.2.2.1).

11 [1996] ICJ Rep 226, para 47.

15.3.2 The meaning of the phrase 'against the territorial integrity or political independence of any state'

There was a debate on whether the phrase 'against the territorial integrity or political independence of any state':

■ should be interpreted as meaning that the use of force is permissible if the purpose of an armed attack is not to alter the territorial integrity or political independence of a State but, for example, to rescue nationals abroad or to protect human rights;[12] or

■ should be interpreted as meaning that no use of force is permissible irrespective of its purpose.

The second interpretation has been endorsed by the UNGA and the ICJ. The UNGA's position has been stated, *inter alia*, in the Declaration on the Inadmissibility of Intervention in the Domestic Affairs of States and the Protection of Their Independence and Sovereignty,[13] and the Declaration on Principles of International Law concerning Friendly Relations and Co-operation among States in Accordance with the Charter of the United Nations.[14] Both Declarations rule out any kind of military intervention irrespective of its purpose.

The ICJ stated its position on the interpretation of the phrase 'against the territorial integrity or political independence' contained in Article 2(4) of the UN Charter in the *Corfu Channel Case (United Kingdom v Albania) (Merits)*.[15]

UNITED KINGDOM *V* ALBANIA

Facts:

Following an incident when two British warships had been struck by mines while exercising a right of innocent passage in Albanian territorial waters, the UK carried out minesweeping operations (code named Operation Retail) in the Corfu Channel. The UK argued her action was not in breach of Article 2(4) since it 'threatened neither the territorial integrity nor the political independence of Albania. Albania suffered thereby neither territorial loss nor (loss to) any part of its political independence'. Further, the UK argued that its unilateral action was necessary because of the UNSC's inability or unwillingness to act.

Held:

The ICJ rejected the British arguments by stating that:

The Court can only regard the alleged right of intervention as the manifestation of a policy of force, such as has in the past given rise to more serious abuses and such as cannot, whatever be the present defects in international organisation, find a place in international law . . .

. . . The United Kingdom Agent . . . has further classified 'Operation Retail' among methods of self-protection or self-help. The Court cannot accept this defence either. Between independent states respect for territorial sovereignty is an essential foundation of international relations.

---

12   D.W. Bowett, *Self-Defence in International Law*, Manchester: Manchester University Press, 1958, 152.

13   UNGA Res 2131 (XX) (21 December 1965), Supp 14, 11.

14   UNGA Res 2625 (XXV) (24 October 1970), Supp 28, 121.

15   [1949] ICJ Rep 4.

The position of the ICJ in the *Corfu Channel Case* has been accepted by States. This interpretation reinforces the prohibition of the use of force and ensures that States will not have much discretion in deciding whether to use force. The position of most scholars has been expressed by Professor Brownlie as follows:

> The conclusion warranted by the Travaux preparatoires is that the phrase under discussion was not intended to be restrictive but, on the contrary, to give more specific guarantees to small states and that it cannot be interpreted as having a qualifying effect.
>
> . . . The phrase 'political independence and territorial integrity' has been used on many occasions to epitomise the total of legal rights which a state has. Moreover, it is difficult to accept a 'plain meaning' which permits evasion of obligations by means of a verbal profession that there is no intention to infringe territorial integrity and which was not intended by the many delegations which approved the text. Lastly, if there is any ambiguity the principle of effectiveness should be applied.[16]

However, the proponents of humanitarian intervention argue that when the UNSC is unable or unwilling to take any action to respond to the most serious violations of HR by a State the use of force is allowed as it furthers the purposes of the UN. They submit that a State can only rely on Article 2(4) to exclude the use of force against it if it fulfils its duty to protect the rights of persons within its jurisdiction. If it fails, then other States are entitled to intervene (see Chapter 15.6.2). Belgium relied on this interpretation before the ICJ in the *Case Concerning Legality of Use of Force (Serbia and Montenegro v Belgium) (Preliminary Objections).*[17] Unlike other NATO countries against whom Serbia and Montenegro brought proceedings for breach of Article 2(4) of the UN Charter consisting of taking part in bombing of its territory in 1999, Belgium, at the early stage of proceedings where Serbia and Montenegro requested provisional measures,[18] decided to justify its intervention by stating that its action was compatible with Article 2(4) as its purpose was to prevent a humanitarian disaster. Belgium invoked as precedents the intervention of India in Pakistan (1971) which resulted in the creation of Bangladesh, Tanzania in Uganda (1979) which resulted in the overthrow of Idi Amin's regime, Viet Nam in Cambodia (1978) which resulted in the overthrow of the Pol Pot regime, and the actions of the Economic Community of West African States (ECOWAS) in Liberia in 1990/92 and in Sierra Leone in 1998. The ICJ did not consider the merits. It, by order of 2 June 1999, rejected the application for interim measures and then, dismissed the case on the ground of lack of jurisdiction because at the time of the institution of proceedings Serbia and Montenegro was not a member of the UN and consequently, was not, on that basis, a party to the ICJ Statute. The precise scope of Article 2(4) is thus somewhat unsettled.

It is to be noted that, within the meaning of Article 2(4) of the Charter, attacks on the territory of a State include attacks against emanations of the State such as its embassies and its armed forces.[19]

15.4 Exceptions to the prohibition of the threat or the use of force based on self-defence

The UN Charter expressly mentions an exception to the prohibition of the threat of or the use of force based on self-defence.

---

16   *International Law and the Use of Force by States*, Oxford: Clarendon Press, 1963, 268.
17   (2004) ICJ Rep 279.
18   (1999) ICJ Rep 124.
19   The *Case Concerning Armed Activities on the Territory of the Congo (Democratic Republic of the Congo v Uganda) (Judgment)* [2005] ICJ Rep 168, para 333.

In this respect the meaning of self-defence under the UN Charter and under customary law must be examined.

15.4.1 Self defence under customary law

The most important case on the law of self-defence is the *Caroline Case.*[20]

THE *CAROLINE* CASE

Facts:

The case arose out of the Canadian Rebellion of 1837 against the British colonial power. The rebel leaders, despite steps taken by the US authorities to prevent assistance being given to them, managed on 13 December 1837 to enlist at Buffalo in the US the support of a large number of American nationals. The resulting force established itself on Navy Island in Canadian waters from which it raided the Canadian shore and attacked British ships. The force was supplied from the US by an America ship, the Caroline. *On the night of 29–30 December a small Canadian force, loyal to the British, seized the* Caroline, *which was then in the American port of Schlosser, set her on fire and sent her drifting over Niagara Falls. Two US nationals were killed – Amos Durfee, whose body was found on the quay with a bullet through his head, and a cabin boy known as 'little Billy', who was shot while attempting to leave the vessel. The US claimed reparation to which Great Britain replied that the destruction of the* Caroline *had been a necessary act of self-defence.*

Three years later a British subject, McLeod, who unwisely boasted in the US of his participation in the incident on the side of the British was arrested and tried for murder in New York state. Britain demanded his release on the ground that those who participated in the operation against the Caroline *had been engaged in the execution of an act of State for which they were not answerable personally in a municipal court.*

The US government conceded that the public character of McLeod's acts relieved him of personal responsibility and sought to put an end to the proceedings against him in the New York courts. At the same time, it again disputed the British claim that the case was one of legitimate self-defence and the diplomatic correspondence contains the classical statement of the limits of self-defence.

The two governments, although they disagreed about the facts of the particular case, entirely agreed upon the principles applicable to the exercise of the right of self-defence– i.e. there must be a clear and absolute necessity for the intervention, namely:

- *there must, initially, be a necessity of self-defence, instant, overwhelming, leaving no choice of means and no moment for deliberation; and*
- *the acts done in self-defence must be necessary and proportionate (see Chapter 15.4.5).*

---

20   (1837) 29 BFSP 1137–1138.

15.4.2   Self-defence under the UN Charter

Article 51 of the UN Charter provides:

> Nothing in the present Charter shall impair the inherent right of individual or collective self-defence if an armed attack occurs against a member of the United Nations, until the Security Council has taken the measures necessary to maintain international peace and security. Measures taken by members in the exercise of this right of self-defence shall be immediately reported to the Security Council and shall not in any way affect the authority and responsibility of the Security Council under the present Charter to take at any time such action as it deems necessary in order to maintain or restore international peace and security.

Unlike the Covenant of the League of Nations, the right of self-defence under the Charter system is not left outside the collective system for maintaining peace. Self-defence is recognised to be a necessary exception to the fundamental principle in Article 2(4) that resort to force by an individual State is illegal without the prior authority of the UN. However, the exercise of the right of self-defence is made subject to the control of the international community – the individual State decides whether or not to use force in self-defence but the propriety of its decision is a matter for the UN.

Any action taken in self-defence must be reported to the UNSC as soon as possible. The ICJ in the *Case concerning Military and Paramilitary Activities in and against Nicaragua (Nicaragua v United States of America) (Merits)*[21] spelled out the consequences of a failure to report. In this respect the Court held that '. . . the absence of a report may be one of the factors indicating whether the State in question was itself convinced that it was acting in self-defence'.[22] Although the reporting requirement is of a procedural nature and a failure to comply will not make a claim to self-defence invalid, the warning of the ICJ has been taken seriously by the great majority of States.

The fact that resort to force in self-defence is lawful without the prior authority of the UNSC is of vital importance from the point of view of the State which has resorted to force. A State may begin action in self-defence without prior recourse to the UNSC and, therefore, no single permanent member may veto the action being initiated. Moreover, once the action in self-defence is being taken it requires an affirmative decision of the UNSC to order the cessation of that action.

The inherent right of self-defence, as it existed in international law before the Charter, was a general right of protection against a forcible threat to a State's legal rights. Article 51, however, speaks only of an inherent right of self-defence 'if an armed attack occurs'.

15.4.2.1   Does Article 51 cut down the customary right of self-defence?

There is some uncertainty as to the effect of Article 51 upon the customary international law right of self-defence. Kelsen reads Article 51 as meaning that for United Nations members the right of self-defence 'has no other content than the one determined by art 51'.[23] Brownlie also argues that Article 51 says everything and that a State cannot be acting in self-defence unless within Article 51.[24]

Bowett, however, argues that customary international law remains intact unless cut down by the Charter and that if there is any ambiguity it is proper to look at customary international law:

---

21   [1986] ICJ Rep 14.
22   Ibid, para 200.
23   *The Law of Nations, A Critical Analysis of Its Fundamental Problems*, London: Steven & Sons, 1950, 914.
24   Supra note 16, 1123 and 264 *et seq*.

> It is . . . fallacious to assume that members have only those rights which the Charter accords them; on the contrary they have those rights which general international law accords to them except in so far as they have surrendered them under the Charter.[25]

Supporters of Bowett's view argue that the right of individual self-defence was regarded as an automatic exception in both the Covenant of the League of Nations and the Pact of Paris without any mention of it. The same would have been true of the Charter if there had been no Article 51. Indeed, the original Dumbarton Oaks proposals did not contain the Article 51 provisions. Committee 1 at the San Francisco Conference, commenting upon Art 2(4), reported that 'the use of arms in legitimate self-defence remains admitted and unimpaired'.[26]

Article 51 was inserted in the Charter to clarify the position with respect to collective arrangements for mutual self-defence and in particular the Pan-American treaty known as the Act of Chapultepec. The official British government commentary on the Charter reads:

> It was considered at the Dumbarton Oaks Conference that the right of self-defence was inherent in the proposals and did not need explicit mention in the Charter. But self-defence may be undertaken by more than one state at a time, and the existence of regional organisations made this right of special importance to some states, while special treaties of defence made its explicit recognition important to others. Accordingly the right is given to individual states or to combinations of states to act until the Security Council itself has taken the necessary measures.[27]

Therefore, it could be said on the one hand, that Article 51 of the Charter is exhaustive and says all there is to know about self-defence and, on the other hand, that when Article 51 talks about the inherent right of self-defence it refers to customary international law.

The position that Article 51 preserves the pre-existing customary law on self-defence was endorsed by the ICJ in the *Military and Paramilitary Activities in and against Nicaragua (Nicaragua v US) (Merits)*[28] in which the Court stated that:

> As regards the suggestion that the areas covered by the two sources of law [art 51 of the UN Charter and customary international law] are identical, the Court observes that the United Nations Charter, the convention to which most of the United States arguments is directed, by no means covers the whole area of the regulation of the use of force in international relations. On one essential point, this treaty itself refers to pre-existing customary international law: this reference to customary law is contained in the actual text of Article 51, which mentions the 'inherent right' [in the French text the 'droit naturel'] of individual or collective self-defence, which 'nothing in the present Charter shall impair' and which applies in the event of an armed attack. The Court therefore finds that Article 51 of the Charter is only meaningful on the basis that there is a 'natural' or 'inherent' right to self-defence, and it is hard to see how this can be other than of a customary nature, even if its present content has been confirmed and influenced by the Charter.

Customary law does not clearly distinguish between self-defence, self-preservation and self-help. Prior to the Kellogg-Briand Pact there were no restrictions on the right to wage war. As a result, States did not always distinguish between self-defence and their other customary rights to use force. For

---

25   Supra note 12, 185–186.
26   6 UNCIO, Documents.
27   I. Brownlie, *International Law and the Use of Force*, Oxford, Clarendon Press 1963, 265.
28   [1986] ICJ Rep 14, para 176.

example, in the *Caroline Case* it was unclear whether Great Britain was acting in self-defence or in self-preservation when she attacked the *Caroline*. The UN Charter, however, refers to the inherent right of self-defence. Therefore, when referring to customary law does one consider the whole ambit of self-defence, self-preservation and self-help, which mean slightly different things, or is one restricted to clear and unambiguous examples of self-defence?

It must be remembered that customary international law changes with the practice of States. Has the content of self-defence changed with time or was it frozen in 1945? Some argue that the concept of self-defence was fixed once and for all in 1945. Others see it as a dynamic concept which evolves and changes over time.[29] The ICJ in the *Nicaragua Case* viewed the concept as dynamic and evolving over time through State practice. It held that: 'The UN Charter . . . by no means covers the whole area of the regulation of the use of force in international relations' and emphasised that its provisions on self-defence needed to be interpreted in the light of customary law.[30] However, as both parties to the proceedings agreed that Article 2(4) represented customary law there was no need for the Court to elaborate on this matter. Further, the response of the international community to the 9/11 terrorist attacks on the US as evidenced by UNSC Resolutions1368 adopted on 12 September 2001 and 1373 adopted on 28 September 2001 supports the view that the concept of self-defence evolves with time. The preamble to both resolutions states that the UNSC is 'determined to combat by all means threats to international peace and security caused by terrorist acts' and that it recognises 'the inherent right of individual or collective self-defence in accordance with the Charter'.[31]

15.4.2.2 Does Article 51 limit the customary right by restricting forcible self-defence to cases where the attack provoking it has actually been launched?

Article 51 refers solely to situations 'if an armed attack occurs'. The question arises, therefore, as to the legality of anticipatory self-defence. Is an imminent threat sufficient to create a right to resort to force in self-defence or must the victim wait until the aggressor has struck the first blow before it can resort to force in self-defence? Can a State resort to self-defence to pre-empt danger in the future (i.e. in the absence of an imminent threat) in order to stop rogue States and their terrorist organisations before they are able to threaten to use weapons of mass destruction?

In order to answer the above questions it is necessary to note that there are three main approaches as to when a State is allowed to resort to self-defence. They are examined below.

A. Restrictive interpretation under which a State is allowed to rely on self-defence only 'if an armed attack occurs'

Some authorities have interpreted 'if an armed attack occurs' to mean 'after an armed attack has occurred'. In particular Brownlie argues that: 'the view that Article 51 does not permit anticipatory action is correct and . . . arguments to the contrary are either unconvincing or based on inconclusive pieces of evidence'.[32]

---

29 Corten, *The Controversies over the Customary Prohibition on the Use of Force*, (2005) 16 F.JIL, 803.

30 Supra note 28, para 176.

31 For a very interesting debate on this point see Ch. Gray, Chapter 6, 'The Use of Force against Terrorism: A new War for a New Century?' in *International Law and the Use of Force*, 3rd edn, Oxford: Oxford University Press, 2008, 193.

32 I. Brownlie, *Law and the Use of Force by States*, 1963, 278.

Further arguments in support of the restrictive interpretation are:

■ Article 51 is an exception to Article 2(4). The general rule of interpretation is that exceptions to a principle should be interpreted restrictively, so as not to undermine the principle.

■ Some collective defence treaties such as the North Atlantic Treaty, based on Article 51, provide only for defence against armed attacks, and not for defence against imminent danger of armed attacks.

■ The question whether an attack is imminent is subjective and open to abuse. A State can never be absolutely certain about the other side's intentions and may mistakenly launch a pre-emptive strike in a moment of crisis when no real threat exists.

■ Allowing an aggressor State to strike the first blow may not in practice result in military disadvantage to the innocent State as first strikes in inter-state hostilities are seldom conclusive.

However, even the proponents of the strict interpretation of Article 51 admit that anticipatory or pre-emptive resort to self-defence, which is unlawful, in some circumstances 'may be justified on moral and political grounds and the community will eventually condone . . . or mete out lenient condemnation'.[33]

B. Interpretation under which a State is allowed to resort to self-defence to respond to an imminent armed attack that has not yet occurred (anticipatory self-defence).

Many scholars reject the strict interpretation of Article 51 and argue that anticipatory self-defence is allowed. They rely on the following arguments:

1 When Article 51 was drafted it was unlikely that there was any intention to cut down the right of self-defence beyond the already narrow doctrine of the *Caroline Case*. That doctrine allows the exercise of the right of self-defence where there is an imminent threat of attack, and is recognised under Article 51 as being an inherent right which continues to exist. In the *Nicaragua Case* (above) the ICJ accepted that the word 'inherent' in Article 51 was a reference to customary law. The Court declined, however, to rule one way or another on the question of anticipatory self-defence as this was not required by the case.

2 The UN Charter imposes an obligation upon States, before they take any action in anticipatory self-defence, to seek to settle their disputes by peaceful means. In parallel, the UN Charter empowers the UNSC to take the steps necessary to ensure the maintenance of international peace and security (see Chapter 16.2). Members have, therefore, an imperative duty to invoke the jurisdiction of the UN whenever a grave menace to their security develops carrying the probability of armed attack. However, if the action of the UN is delayed, or inadequate, and the armed attack becomes imminent it would be contrary to the purposes of the Charter to compel the defending State to allow the aggressor to deliver the first, and perhaps, fatal blow.

3 To cut down the customary right of self-defence beyond the *Caroline* doctrine does not make sense in times when the speed and power of weapons of attack have greatly increased. For instance, in the case of nuclear missiles, when does an armed attack occur: when the missile lands, when it takes off or on the development of the intention to fire it? It may well be argued that Article 51 is couched in terms appropriate to the middle of the last century and does not properly allow for the nuclear weapons

---

33 A. Cassese, *International Law*, 2nd edn, Oxford: Oxford University Press, 2005, 362.

era. Article 51 is not specific enough for a commander in chief who must determine if an armed attack has occurred despite there being no invading army.

4   The interpretation under which a State can rely on anticipatory self-defence accords with the practice of States and the generally accepted view of international law at the time when Article 51 was drafted. For example, it was argued before the International Military Tribunal at Nuremberg that the German invasion of Norway in 1941 was an act of self-defence in the face of an imminent Allied landing there.[34] The Tribunal held that preventive action in foreign territory is justified only in the circumstances laid down in the *Caroline Case*, and that as there was no imminent threat of an Allied landing in Norway the argument must fail.

However, the International Military Tribunal for the Far East had no hesitation in deciding that the Dutch declaration of war upon Japan in December 1941 was justifiable on the grounds of self-defence. When considering the legality of Japan's invasion of Dutch territory in the Far East the Tribunal stated:

> The fact that the Netherlands, being fully appraised of the imminence of the attack, in self-defence declared war against Japan on 8 December and thus officially recognised the existence of a state of war which had been begun by Japan cannot change that war from a war of aggression on the part of Japan into something other than that.

5   The Institute of International Law in its Resolution on Present Problems of the Use of Armed Force in International Law (Self-defence) adopted at the session in Santiago on 27 October 2007, stated in point 3 that:

> The right to self-defence arises for the target State in case of an actual or manifestly imminent armed attack. It may be exercised only when there is no lawful alternative in practice in order to forestall, stop or repel the armed attack, until the Security Council takes effective measures necessary to restore international peace and security.[35]

6   The UN High Level Panel on Threats, Challenges and Change recognised the lawfulness of anticipatory self-defence.[36]

C.   The interpretation under which a State is allowed to resort to self-defence to respond to an armed attack which is not imminent but may take place at some point in the future if action is not taken (pre-emptive self-defence).

The doctrine of pre-emptive self-defence was rarely relied upon by States prior to the 9/11 terrorist attacks on the US. One example is that of Israel when it attacked an Iraqi nuclear reactor in 1981 claiming that the Iraqi nuclear reactor under construction was designed to produce nuclear weapons which would subsequently have been used against Israel. The attack was condemned by both the UNSC and by the UNGA. In particular, the UNGA classified the attack as a premeditated and unprecedented act of aggression.[37]

---

34   US Department of State, Trial of War Criminals 23, Dep Of State Pub No 2420 (1945).

35   Available at the official website of the Institute of International Law at www.idi-iil.org (accessed 12 August 2014).

36   The UNGA, 'A More Secure World: Our Shared Responsibility', Report of the High-Level Panel on Threats, Challenges and Change in UNGA 'Note by the Secretary-General' (2 December 2004) UN Doc A/59/565, 8, para 188.

37   Resolution 36/27, 109 votes in favour, two against and 34 abstentions.

After the 9/11 terrorist attacks, US President George W. Bush endorsed the doctrine of pre-emptive self-defence.[38] On 17 September 2002 in his speech on the National Security Strategy of the US he stated that 'as a matter of common sense and self-defence, America will act against [. . .] emerging threats before they are fully formed'. The Report of the Bush Administration to the US Congress on The National Security Strategy of the United States of America of September 2002[39] describes how the Bush doctrine intended to deal with the 'war against terrorism' in particular it states that:

> We must be prepared to stop rogue states and their terrorist clients before they are able to threaten or use weapons of mass destruction against the US. The doctrine of self-defence needs to be revised in the light of modern conditions. In particular the requirement that a threat be imminent needs to be revisited.

The possible consequences of the Bush doctrine were summed up by Alan Simpson (a UK MP) in the following terms:

> if the world is being asked to move from a doctrine of containment and deterrence and towards a different doctrine about pre-emptive strikes, regime change, attacks and displacement of potential enemies or unsympathetic regimes, the implications for the planet are enormous.[40]

The doctrine of pre-emptive self-defence was rejected by two reports, first, the Report of the High-Level Panel on Threats, Challenges and Change and, second, the UNS-G's Report entitled 'In Larger Freedom'.[41] When the UNGA discussed the latter report, most States rejected not only pre-emptive but also anticipatory self-defence.[42] Further, the Institute of International Law, in point 6 of its Resolution of 27 October 2007 on Present Problems of the Use of Armed Force in International Law condemned the doctrine of pre-emptive self defence and stated that it has no basis in international law.[43]

The ICJ has consistently refused to make a statement on the issue of pre-emptive or anticipatory self-defence, perhaps because the ICJ has never been directly asked to do so. On the one hand, one understands that the ICJ should limit its judgments to the subject matter of disputes brought before it but, on the other hand, some *obiter dicta* would have been particularly welcome.[44]

The debate on the lawfulness of pre-emptive self-defence was revived by the 2003 US invasion of Iraq. Initially, the US and its allies when launching their invasion relied on anticipatory self defence, but as this failed, the only available justification was based on pre-emptive self defence. They submitted that Iraq had stockpiled chemical weapons, had an advanced nuclear development programme, and a substantial biological weapons programme, which posed clear and immediate threats to the security of the US, its allies and Iraq's neighbours.

The context of the 2003 invasion was as follows:

---

38   Some authors argue that the US adopted this approach much earlier: see Reisman and Armstrong, *The Past and Future of Claims of Pre-emptive Self-defence*, (2005) 100AJIL, 525.

39   Available on the US Department of State website: www. state.gov (accessed 20 July 2004).

40   Alan Simpson, *Hansard*, 24 September 2002, Col 81.

41   A/59/2005.

42   UN Doc GA/10377, 10388, 10399, 6–8 April 2005.

43   Supra note 35.

44   See the criticism expressed by Judge Elaraby in his Dissenting Opinion in the *Case concerning Oil Platforms (Islamic Republic of Iran v United States of America)* [2003] ICJ Rep 161, 295.

Under UNSC Resolution 668, which formalised a ceasefire after the defeat of Iraq in the 1991 Gulf War, Iraq was called upon to destroy, remove and render harmless all chemical and biological weapons and all stocks of agents and components, together with all research, development, support and manufacturing facilities for ballistic missiles with a range greater than 150 kilometres. In order to ensure compliance with the Resolution an international body was set up (UNSCOM) to inspect Iraq's weapons facilities. From October 1997 onwards Iraq had refused to co-operate with UNSCOM, in that Iraq had denied access to the so-called sovereign and presidential sites and had excluded some members of UNSCOM from carrying out inspections. This being on the ground that they worked for intelligence agencies in their respective countries. In 1998 the UNSCOM inspectors left Iraq.

Since the 9/11 terrorist attacks the US administration has taken a very strong stand against terrorism and rogue States. On 29 January 2002 President George W. Bush in his first State of the Union Address said that Iran, Iraq and North Korea 'constitute an axis of evil, aiming to threaten the peace of the world'. After that the US President focused on Iraq, threatening to launch a military campaign to force Iraq to comply with UNSC resolutions. Under growing pressure from the US, Iraq, on 16 September 2002 expressed its willingness to readmit weapons inspectors.

On 8 November 2002 the UNSC, after lengthy negotiations, adopted Resolution 1441 which confirmed that Iraq had been in breach of its obligations under UN resolutions. Resolution 1441 warned Iraq that it would face 'serious consequences' for non-compliance and required Iraq to 'immediately, unconditionally and actively' co-operate with weapons inspectors from the UN Monitoring, Verification and Inspection Commission (UNMOVIC) and the International Atomic Energy Agency (IAEA), and to give immediate, unimpeded, unconditional and unrestricted access to, inter alia, 'any and all, including underground, areas, facilities, buildings, equipment, records and means of transport which they wish to inspect'. Also Resolution 1441 required the Iraqi government to provide, within 30 days, full and complete declaration of all aspects of its programme relating to the development of chemical, biological and nuclear weapons. A 12,000-page declaration on weapons of mass destruction was submitted by Iraq to the UN on 8 December 2002. It was very soon challenged by the US.

At no time did the inspectors from UNMOVIC and the IAEA find any convincing evidence of the existence of weapons of mass destructions (WMD). On 27 January 2003 both Hans Blix (in charge of UNMOVIC) and Mohamed El Baradei (from IAEA) reported to the UNSC that they only found a dozen empty chemical warheads and some documents relating to a past nuclear programme. Two months' inspections had brought no conclusive evidence that Iraq was pursuing its weapons programmes. Hans Blix in his report stated that although there was no overt obstruction of the inspectors there was lack of 'pro-active co-operation' from Iraq. The UN inspectors asked the UNSC for more time to complete their mission. However, the US administration was unwilling to wait much longer and argued that after 12 years of non-compliance with UN resolutions the burden of proof must be on Iraq.

Within the UNSC, the permanent members, other than the US and the UK, voiced their opposition to a quick decision made by the US to take early military action against Iraq. They were unconvinced that Iraq posed an immediate danger and argued that inspections, backed up by the threat of force, were sufficient to ensure that Iraq was kept under control. Furthermore, the lack of evidence of any weapons of mass destruction, and the fact that Saadam Hussein, the then President of Iraq, was co-operating with the UN inspectors, played an important role in the refusal of the majority of the UNSC to adopt a resolution authorising the use of force against Iraq. Even non-permanent members of the UNSC traditionally within the US sphere of influence – such as Mexico, Chile and Pakistan – did not back the idea of a US-led military intervention in Iraq.

The UN inspectors were ordered by the UN to leave Iraq just before a US/UK invasion started. According to Hans Blix, evidence for war was 'very, very shaky'. On 22 April 2003 Hans Blix accused the US and the UK of deliberately undermining his efforts to locate the banned weapons alleged to be in Iraq. He warned the UNSC that only UN inspectors, and not a team being assembled by the US, would be able to provide an objective assessment of any materials that might be found in Iraq.[45]

After the invasion, neither a US team of experts set up to investigate Iraq's programmes on nuclear, chemical, biological and missile weapons[46] nor a UN commission that was in charge of disarming Iraq of weapons of WPD found any credible evidence of their existence. The failure to uncover any evidence of nuclear weapons or of any significant capability to develop other WMD threw extreme doubt on the US's rationale for invading Iraq.

It results from the above that the US administration could not rely on the concept of anticipatory self-defence to justify its intervention. With regard to pre-emptive self-defence, State practice indicates that this concept has no place in international law, and that self-defence can be relied upon only on the clearest evidence of a great emergency, and as a measure of last resort. This was not the case in respect of Iraq as there was no evidence of any imminent armed attack to be launched by Iraq against the US. Further, the use of force by the US was in breach of the principles of proportionality and necessity (see Chapter 15.4.5).

The International Commission of Jurists, a consultative body of the UN, on 18 March 2003, warned the US that any military action without authorisation from the UNSC would constitute an act of aggression. The Commission stated that:

> The [Commission] today expressed its deep dismay that a small number of states are poised to launch an outright illegal invasion of Iraq, which amounts to a war of aggression. The United States, the United Kingdom and Spain have signalled their intent to use force in Iraq in spite of the absence of a Security Council Resolution. There is no other plausible legal basis for this attack. In the absence of such Security Council authorisation, no country may use force against another country, except in self-defence against an armed attack.[47]

Kofi Annan, the UNS-G at the time of the US invasion of Iraq, condemned that invasion as illegal, and in breach of the UN Charter.[48]

Since the establishment of the UN the international community, and the world, until the events just recited, have never been faced with a situation where two founding members of the UN who are permanent members of the UNSC decide to ignore international law, and the fundamental principles of the UN Charter. The US and the UK seriously damaged the UN and NATO. The war of aggression against Iraq constitutes a great threat to the rule of international law and may well be said to have turned the clock back to 1945 when 'might was right'.

No State, even the most powerful in the world, should be careless of, or arrogant towards, the institutions and ideals that have, for very many years underpinned our civilisation.

15.4.3 The requirement of an 'armed attack'

An examination and comparison of Articles 2(4) and 51 of the UN Charter indicates that their provisions are not entirely compatible. Article 2(4) prohibits the threat or use of force. Article 51 provides that there is a right of self-defence if an armed attack occurs. This entails that while every threat or use of

---

45   D. Usborne, *Hans Blix v The US*, The Independent, 23 April 2003, 1.

46   See 'The Report of the Special Advisor to the Director of Central Intelligence on Iraq's Weapons of Mass Destruction' (The Duelfer Report) available at www.cia.gov/cia/reports/iraq_wmd_2004 (accessed 12 November 2004).

47   Available at www.ulb.ac.be/droit/cdi/appel_irak.htlm (accessed 12 November 2004).

48   BBC News, 18 September 2004.

force is prohibited, not every use of force will amount to an 'armed attack' allowing a State to have recourse to the right of self-defence. For that reason it is necessary to determine what constitutes an 'armed attack' under Article 51, or in other words, whether there is a threshold of gravity which will distinguish any use of force from that amounting to an 'armed attack'.

The ICJ in *Case Concerning Military and Paramilitary Activities in and against Nicaragua (Nicaragua v United States of America) (Merits)*[49] stated that it is 'necessary to distinguish the most grave forms of the use of force (those constituting an armed attack) from other less grave forms'.[50] Accordingly the conduct depending on its scale and effect may be classified either as an 'armed attack' or a mere frontier incident. Further it stated that an armed attack may not only be carried out by regular army units across an international border, but also by the sending of armed bands, groups, irregulars, or mercenaries into the territory of a State. In some circumstances, the magnitude of their acts (in scale and effects) may be of such gravity as to amount to an actual attack carried out by regular armed forces.

The position of the ICJ on the threshold of 'scale and effect' has been criticised by some authors. For example, Dinstein accepts that while there is some *de minimus* threshold below which the use of force will not amount to an armed attack, all use of force causing human causalities or serious damage to property, including small scale frontier incidents, triggers the right of self-defence.[51] The leading UK experts in international law, who had participated in the preparation of the *Chatham House Principles of International Law on the Use of Force in Self-Defence*,[52] rejected the threshold of 'scale and effects'. According to the Chatham House Principles:

> an armed attack means any use of armed force and does not need to cross some threshold of intensity. Any requirement that a use of force must attain a certain gravity and that frontier incidents, for example, are excluded is relevant only in so far as the minor nature of an attack is prima facie evidence of absence of intention to attack or honest mistake.

The Chatham Principles state that the position of the ICJ is not generally accepted, but without providing any evidence to this effect. Certainly, neither experts in international law in the UK who participated in the Chatham House project, nor the governments of the US,[53] and Israel accept the ICJ' threshold of 'scale and effect'. There is no sufficient evidence that this position has been rejected by other States and the UN.[54]

In the context of low scale attacks, Israel and other States have relied on the 'accumulation of events theory' or 'needle prick' theory to justify the defensive use of armed force. According to this theory each specific low scale incident, or needle prick, which on its own may not be regarded as an armed attack could, taking into consideration the totality of incidents, amount to an armed attack allowing the victim State to have recourse to the right of self-defence. According to Tams, this theory has been gaining support from States although it was widely rejected in the past. This apparent acceptance can

---

49 [1986] ICJ Rep 14. Confirmed in the *Case Concerning Oil Platforms (Islamic Republic of Iran v United States of America)* [2003] ICJ Rep 161, para 51.

50 Ibid, 191.

51 Y. Dinstein, War, *Aggression and Self-Defence*, 4th edn, Cambridge: Cambridge University Press, 2005, 195.

52 E. Wilmshurst, *The Chatham House Principles of International Law on the Use of Force in Self Defence* [2006] 55 ICLQ, 966.

53 A.D. Sofaer, *Terrorism, the Law, and the National Defense* 126 Military L Rev (1989) 89.

54 See for example the decision of the Eritrea Ethiopia Claims Commission, Partial Award, *Jus ad Bellum*, Ethiopia's Claims 1–8, The Hague, 19 December 2005, at para 11, which endorsed the position of the ICJ. The decision is available at: www.pca-cpa.org/showpage.asp?pag_id=1151 (accessed 8 August 2014).

be explained by the fact that the theory of 'needle prick' may be used to justify the use of force by States against non-State actors[55] (see Chapter 15.4.5).

It is important to note that the term 'armed attack' is understood as the use of armed force. Accordingly an 'economic' attack or a 'cyber' attack will not be sufficient to allow a State to use armed force (Chapter 16.2.2.1.C). Further, 'an armed attack' must be aimed intentionally at the victim State.[56]

15.4.4 The principles of necessity and proportionality

The principles of necessity and proportionality are not mentioned in Article 51. However, customary international law clearly states that force used in self-defence must be no more than is necessary and proportionate. The ICJ in the *Case concerning Military and Paramilitary Activities in and against Nicaragua (Nicaragua v United States of America) (Merits)*[57] stated that the requirements of proportionality and necessity are fundamental to any exercise of the right of self-defence.

Whether the requirements of necessity and proportionality have been satisfied depends on the particular circumstances. Each case must be assessed separately in order to establish whether or not, on a factual basis, the use of force can be considered as necessary and proportionate.

Necessity requires that a State first, has exhausted all non-forceable measures and second, that it would be wholly unreasonable to expect a State to attempt non-forceable response. This was well summarised by Judge Roberto Ago, acting as an ILC Special Rapporteur on State Responsibility, in his Addendum to his Eighth Report on State Responsibility when he said:

> the reason for stressing that action taken in self-defence must be necessary is that the State attacked . . . .must not, in the particular circumstances, have had any means of halting the attack other than recourse to armed force.[58]

Accordingly forceable response must be a measure of last resort in that a State has no alternative but the use of armed force. The principle of necessity has a second dimension in that it is assesses whether the use of force was necessary to achieve the legitimate end of self defence. In this context it is closely related to the principle of proportionality because means can only be proportionate when they are necessary to achieve legitimate ends.

Proportionality means that a State relying on self defence must not use force which exceeds that required to achieve the end of abating or repelling the attack. This is the 'means-ends proportionality' or qualitative proportionality which is generally accepted as appropriate in the context of self defence.[59] It differs from the 'eye for an eye' or 'tit for tat' or quantitative proportionality used in criminal law, (i.e. the punishment must fit the crime), in some aspects of IHL and, in the past, when assessing armed reprisals (see Chapter 15.7).

Qualitative proportionality requires that the means employed are appropriate to the end sought by the response. As such, a proportionate response is one which is necessary and appropriate to halt or

---

55   C.J. Tams, *The Use of Force against Terrorists* (2009) 20 EJIL, 388.

56   The *Case Concerning Oil Platforms (Islamic Republic of Iran v United States of America)* [2003] ICJ Rep 161, para 64.

57   [1986] ICJ Rep 14.

58   (1980) YILC Vol II (Part One)69, para 120 (addendum).

59   C. Greenwood, 'Self-Defence and the Conduct of International Armed Conflict' in Y. Dinstein (ed.), *International Law at a Time of Perplexity: Essays in Honour of Shabtai Rosenne*, Dordrecht: Martinus Nijhoff Publishers, 1989, 273.

repel the attack and which takes account of side-effects on other interests and values affected by the response, e.g. harm to the environment.

In assessing whether a response was proportionate the entire operation relating to the use of force in self-defence must be taken into account.

The issue of proportionality and necessity was examined by the ICJ in the *Case Concerning Oil Platforms (Islamic Republic of Iran v United States of America).*[60]

CASE CONCERNING OIL PLATFORMS (ISLAMIC REPUBLIC OF IRAN *V* UNITED STATES OF AMERICA)

Facts:

The actions giving rise to the dispute occurred in the context of an armed conflict between Iran and Iraq which started on 22 September 1980, when Iran was invaded by Iraqi military forces. The conflict (which lasted 8 years) started as a land armed conflict, but from 1984, when Iraq began attacking oil tankers on their way to and from Iranian ports in order to disrupt Iran's oil exports, also affected the Persian Gulf. This so-called 'Tanker War' lasted till 1988. During that time commercial vessels and warships of various nationalities, including neutral vessels, were attacked by aircraft, missiles or warships, or struck mines in the waters of the Persian Gulf. While Iran denied any responsibility for these attacks, other than incidents involving vessels refusing a proper request for stop and search, the US attributed responsibility for some of these incidents to Iran and saw fit to make attacks against Iran.

The ICJ examined two specific attacks made by US military forces on Iran as a result of US' believe concerning Iranian involvement in incidents above. The first took place on 19 October 1987. On 16 October 1987 the Kuwaiti tanker Sea Isle City, *which had been reflagged to the US, had, according to the US, been struck by an Iranian missile near Kuwait harbour. In response, three days later, the US attacked and destroyed Iranian offshore oil production installations in the Reshadat (Rostam) complex.*

The second attack took place on 18 April 1988. On 14 April 1988 the US warship USS Samuel B Roberts *struck a mine in international waters near Bahrein. Four days later, in retaliation, the US attacked and destroyed Iran's oil production installations in the Nasr (Sirri) and Salman (Sassan) complexes. The alleged justification for the attacks was presented by the US to the UNSC. The US claimed that it acted in self-defence. Unlike the incident of 19 October 1987 the attacks on the Salman and Nasr platforms were not isolated operations as they, in fact, formed part of a much more extensive military operation called 'Praying Mantis', during which the US attacked other Iranian naval vessels and aircraft.*

It is important to note that the Rostam, the Salman and the Nasr complexes were not producing any oil at the time of the US attacks. These installations were under repair as they had been badly damaged by earlier Iraqi attacks.

Held:

The ICJ followed the customary international law on the use of force while defining and applying the concept of 'an armed attack', and the principles of proportionality, and necessity.

---

60   [2003] ICJ Rep 161.

> In respect of the principle of necessity it held that 'the requirement of international law that measures taken avowedly in self-defence must have been necessary for that purpose is strict and objective, leaving no room for any measure of discretion.[61] In respect of the requirement of proportionality, the Court observed that the attack of 19 October 1987 might (had the Court found that it was necessary in response to the Sea Isle City incident as an armed attack committed by Iran) have been considered proportionate.
>
> In the case of the attack of 18 April 1988, however, which was conceived and executed as part of a more extensive operation entitled 'Operation Praying Mantis' (and constituted a response to the mining, by an unidentified agency, of a single US warship, which was severely damaged but not sunk, and without loss of life) the ICJ found that neither 'Operation Praying Mantis' as a whole, nor even that part of it that destroyed the Salman and Nasr platforms, could, in the circumstances of the case, be regarded as a proportionate use of force by the US in self-defence.

It is important to note that in many cases where a State justifies the use of force on the basis of self-defence, proportionality and necessity will be of assistance in rejecting that justification without the need to embark upon a more controversial doctrinal dispute regarding the extent of the right to self-defence under customary international law.

15.4.5 Non-State actors as perpetrators of an armed attack

One of the most controversial issues under Article 51 of the UN Charter is whether a State can rely on self-defence in the event of an armed attack by non-State actors when they are located on the territory of another State. This issue has become of particular relevance in the context of the 'war on terrorism'.

Article 51 does not address this matter. Article 2(4) clearly states that the prohibition of the use of force operates 'against any other State'. It thus seems to rule out the use of force against non-State actors.

There is no doubt that in customary international law the use of force against an attack by a non-State actor is allowed. Indeed, in the *Caroline Case* force was used by the UK against US nationals who went into Canada (then a UK colony) to support a rebellion there. The US did not challenge the UK's right to intervene although it argued that the circumstances of the case did not justify the UK's use of force.

With regard to Article 51, as Judge Higgins emphasised in her Separate Opinion in the *Legal Consequences of the Construction of a Wall in the Occupied Palestinian Territories (Advisory Opinion)* that nothing in Article 51 precludes a State from defending itself from armed attacks launched by non-State actors.[62]

The controversial matter is whether a State can justify the use of force based on its right of self defence in a situation where acts of non-State actors against it are not attributable to a State.

---

61   Ibid, para 73.
62   *The Legal Consequences of the Construction of a Wall in the Occupied Palestinian Territories (Advisory Opinion)* [2004] ICJ Rep 136, Separate Opinion of Judge Higgins, 33.

The position of the ICJ was stated in the *Legal Consequences of the Construction of a Wall in the Occupied Palestinian Territories (Advisory Opinion)*[63] (for facts see Chapter 17.5.5) in which the Court rejected the argument that the construction of a wall was necessary to prevent terrorist attacks on civilian population of Israel and thus consistent with the right to use force in self-defence. The Court stated that: 'Article 51 of the Charter . . . recognizes the existence of an inherent right of self-defence in the case of armed attack by one State against another State' and found that Article 51 had no relevance to the case.[64] The ICJ examined UNSC resolutions 1368(2001) and 1343(2001), in which the UNSC recognised that a State has the right of self-defence in a situation where acts of non-State actors cannot be attributable to a State, and decided that those resolutions did not apply to the occupied territories from where terrorist attacks were launched against Israel because those territories were under Israeli control. The ICJ held that such attacks to be within the scope of Article 51 must be directed from abroad.

The judgment of the ICJ in the *Armed Activities on the Territory of the Congo (Democratic Republic of the Congo v Uganda) (Judgment)*[65] which, *inter alia*, concerned the exercise of the right of a State to use force in self-defence against non-State actors, has been subject to differing interpretations. In this case the DRC argued that Uganda had organised military and paramilitary activities against the DRC in breach of Article 2(4) of the Charter. Uganda, argued that while its presence on the territory of the DRC was initially based on a treaty concluded between the DRC and Uganda, and this was established as a fact by the ICJ, subsequently, it was justified on self-defence. This was because it had to fight rebel groups which were launching attacks against Ugandan forces. Rebel groups were located on the territory of the DRC, and according to Uganda, supported by the DRC, Sudan and Chad. The ICJ held that there was no evidence that attacks by rebel groups were attributable to the DRC within the meaning of Article 3(g) of the definition of aggression set out in Resolution 3314 (see Chapter 16.2.2.1.A). Accordingly, the Court held that: '[t]he attacks did not emanate from armed bands or irregulars sent by the DRC or on behalf of the DRC' and therefore Uganda's actions could not be justified on the ground of self-defence. The Court then stated that with regard to attacks by irregular forces, not attributable to a State, it would not address this matter as this was unnecessary in this case.[66] The majority of commentators interpreted the statements of the ICJ as implying that the ICJ ruled out the possibility for a State to rely on the right of self-defence against non-State actors.[67] This interpretation is supported by views of judges Kooijmans and Simma who considered that the Court did not pay enough attention to the exercise of the right of self-defence by a State against non-State actors, and that self-defence did not require that an armed attack originate from a State.[68] Another interpretation

---

63   [2004] ICJ Rep 136.

64   Ibid, 194.

65   [2005] ICJ Rep 168. It is to be noted that Judge Simma in his Separate Opinion opposed the view of the majority of judges. He stated that: 'Such a restrictive reading of Article 51 might well have reflected the state, or rather the prevailing interpretation, of the international law on self-defence for a long time. However, in the light of more recent developments not only in State practice but also with regard to accompanying *opinio juris*, it ought urgently to be reconsidered', para.11. He was supported by Judge Kooijmans in his Separate Opinion, ibid, para 30. According to Judges Kooijmans and Simma armed action by non-State actors entitles a State to exercise its right of self-defence, if such action, because of its scale and effects, amounts to an armed attack and provided that the requirements of necessity and proportionality are met. Both judges referred in this context to developments triggered by the 9/11 terrorist attacks on the US.

66   Ibid, 147.

67   J. Kammerhofer, *The Armed Activities Case and Non-State Actors in Self-Defence Law* (2007) 20 LJIL, 96.

68   *The Case Concerning Armed Activities on the Territory of the Congo (Democratic Republic of the Congo v Uganda) (Judgment)* [2005] ICJ Rep 168, (Separate Opinion of Judge Kooijmans at para 25 and separate opinion of Judge Simma at para 6–8).

of the judgment is that the ICJ confined its judgment to the dispute between the DRC and Uganda and bearing in mind that Ugandan forces did not attack the bases of the rebel forces, but towns and villages situated far way from those bases, a discussion on the distinct acts of self-defence against the rebel groups was not relevant.[69]

In the light of the above a question arises as to States practice on the right to use force in self defence against non-State actors. In this respect the law on the use of force in self-defence by a State against non-State actors pre- the 9/11 attacks by al-Qaeda on the World Trade Centre was well established. It was generally accepted that this was not allowed. With regard to State practice after the 9/11 attacks it is submitted that three situations should be distinguished.

15.4.5.1 A situation where a State on the territory of which non-State actors are located acquiesces or consents to their presence, but in international law no responsibility can be imputed to that State for acts committed by those non-State actors

The best illustration of this situation is the use of force by the US and its allies against Afghanistan following the 9/11 attacks by al-Qaeda on targets in the US.

On 11 September 2001 four US civilian planes with passengers on board were hijacked from various US airports. They were on internal flights. The hijackers murdered some passengers and crew, took control of the planes and deliberately crashed two of them into the twin towers of the World Trade Centre in New York and one into the Pentagon building in Washington DC. The fourth plane was probably intended to be crashed into Camp David, the summer residence of the US President, but it seems that the passengers and the crew attacked the hijackers and the plane crashed in a wooded area in Pennsylvania. Thousands of people died as a result of the attacks.

US President George W. Bush blamed Islamic fundamentalists, i.e. al-Qaeda, led by Osama bin Laden, for the carnage. He stated that there was compelling evidence pointing to Osama bin Laden and al-Qaeda being involved in the attacks. However, for security reasons, this evidence could not be made public.

Al-Qaeda is a terrorist organisation which was founded in the early 1990s and was led by Osama bin Laden, a national of Saudi Arabia, until his death in 2011. Al-Qaeda's main objective is to destroy the US and its allies. In February 1998 Osama bin Laden issued a 'fatwa', a decree addressed to all Muslims to fight jihad or 'holy war', which calls for the killing of Americans and their civilian and military allies as a religious duty for each and every Muslim to be carried out in whichever country they are. It is alleged that al-Qaeda had been responsible for conducting a number of terrorist attacks against the US, in particular the bombing of US embassies in Kenya and Tanzania on 7 August 1998.

Osama bin Laden established a dozen camps for training militants in Afghanistan. His relationship with the Taliban, the ruling Afghan regime in Afghanistan until the military intervention of the US, started when the Taliban was engaged in a civil war to control the whole of Afghanistan in the 1990s. At that time Osama bin Laden provided the Taliban regime with troops, arms and money to fight its opponents. Once the Taliban won the civil war it provided Osama bin Laden with a safe haven and allowed him to establish training camps.

The Taliban refused many times to extradite Osama bin Laden to the US. It also refused to comply with the UNSC resolutions[70] which requested the Taliban to surrender bin Laden so he could be brought

---

69   M.N. Shaw, *International Law*, 6th edn, Cambridge: Cambridge University Press, 2008, 1136.

70   Resolutions: 1189 (1998); 1193 (1988); 1214 (1998); 12767 (1999), 1277 (1999).

to justice. From 1998, various non-military sanctions have been imposed by the UNSC upon the Taliban for harbouring Osama bin Laden and his organisation. In 1999 the UNSC determined that the Taliban's failure to comply with its resolutions constituted a 'threat to international peace and security'.

In the aftermath of the attacks on the World Trade Centre and Washington the US President requested the Taliban to hand over Osama bin Laden or to face the consequences. The Taliban regime refused.

The UNSC strongly condemned the terrorist attacks on the US in two resolutions: Resolution 1368 (2001) passed on 12 September 2001 and Resolution 1373 (2001) passed on 28 September 2001. Both explicitly recognised the right of self-defence on the part of member States against non-State actors and both determined that the attacks constituted 'a threat to international peace and security'.

On 7 October 2001 the US and the UK, started a military intervention in Afghanistan called Enduring Freedom aimed at hunting down Osama bin Laden, bringing him to justice, and destroying his terrorist organisation, al-Qaeda, and the Taliban regime that had supported them. The US and the UK justified their military action on the ground of the inherent right to self-defence. On the day of commencement of the military intervention in Afghanistan the Chargé d'Affaires of the Permanent Mission of the UK to the UN sent a letter to the President of the UNSC informing him that military forces were employed against targets in Afghanistan 'in exercise of the inherent right of individual and collective self-defence recognised in art 51 [of the UN Charter], following the terrorist outrage of 11 September, to avert the continuing threat of attacks from the same source'.[71] The same justification was provided by the US's representative to the UN.[72]

The first point which needs to be addressed is whether the military intervention of the US and its allies was authorised by the UNSC; if so, the legitimacy of their action would be established under international law. In this respect it is important to examine UNSC Resolutions 1368 (2001) and 1373 (2001). Both Resolutions in their preamble refer to the inherent right of self-defence in the context of terrorist attacks. The matter arises whether or not that reference may be construed as authorisation by the UNSC for the US to use force. It is important to emphasise a number of points:

■ Resolution 1368 was passed the day after the terrorist attacks took place and at that time it was unclear who was behind the terrorist attacks and whether they were directed from abroad or internally. Resolution 1373 was passed on 28 September 2001 and, although the members of the UNSC had by then had time to reflect upon the matter, the Resolution neither mentions the Taliban nor Osama bin Laden as being responsible for the terrorist attacks on the US.

■ The reference to the right of self-defence was part of the preamble of both Resolutions and not of their operative part.

■ No explicit authorisation was granted in the above Resolutions to the US to use armed force. In the past when the UNSC was authorising the use of force the relevant resolutions were very clear and unambiguous given the seriousness of the measures to be taken against a culprit State.

■ Resolution 1368 explicitly expressed the UNSC's readiness to take all necessary steps to respond to the terrorist attacks of 11 September. Resolution 1373, relying on Chapter VII, called on all States to 'prevent and suppress the financing of terrorist acts in general, and international terrorism in particular, by freezing financial assets of persons who commit, or attempt to commit, terrorist

---

71   Available at http://globalresearch.ca.articles/VAR109A.html (accessed 14 April 2004).
72   Ibid, see the US Ambassador to the UN John D. Negroponte's letter of 7 October 2001 informing the President of the Security Council of the commencement of the US military action in Afghanistan.

acts or participate in or facilitate the commission of terrorism acts'. Furthermore, Resolution 1373 called on all States to refrain from providing any support to persons or entities involved in international terrorism.

- Neither Resolution specified any State against which the US is allowed to use armed force. At that time about 60 States supported terrorist organisations. Therefore, it seems preposterous to conclude that the UNSC was authorising the US to use force against all States supporting international terrorism without specifically mentioning any of them, and in circumstances where it was uncertain who was behind the terrorist attacks carried out against the US on 11 September 2001.

- In the letters addressed to the UNSC neither the government of the US nor the government of the UK referred to any existing, actual or implied, authorisation of the UNSC to commence a military intervention in Afghanistan. Certainly, had such an authorisation been in existence both governments would have made an explicit reference to it.

In the light of the above it is submitted that neither Resolution authorised the US and its allies to use force against Afghanistan. The Resolutions linked the terrorist attacks with the right to self-defence and consequently recognised that a State may be entitled to invoke the right to self-defence in the context of terrorist attacks, provided that the requirements of Article 51 of the UN Charter are satisfied.

Once any authorisation by the UN has been ruled out as a possible justification for the military intervention of the US and its allies in Afghanistan the only possible ground for such an intervention in conformity with international law would be the right of self-defence.

The US received extensive support for its Enduring Freedom Operation and offers of assistance.[73] The majority of States seem to accept the declaration of President Bush stating that: 'We will make no distinction between the terrorists who committed these acts and those who harbor them'.[74] It is to be noted that the US seems to rely on pre-emptive self-defence rather than on anticipatory self-defence although this may be disputed.

15.4.5.2 A situation where non-State actors are located on the territory of a State which is unable to take measures to combat them

This situation concerns mainly so called 'failed' States, i.e. States in which all governmental structures have collapsed and as a result, there is no government, there is no order, there is no rule of law. State failure may have various origins, e.g. it may result from ethnic and religious wars (Somalia); illegal military intervention in domestic affairs of a State (Iraq and Libya), and crippling effects of civil war (Uganda and the Central African Republic). US Secretary of Defence Robert Gates stated in 2010 that 'the most lethal threat to the Unites States' safety . . . [would] emanate from states that cannot adequately govern themselves or secure their own territory'.[75] Indeed, failed States represent a serious threat to international security, *inter alia*, their territories often become a safe haven for various terrorist groups, atrocious HRs abuses usually take place there, there is a danger that chemical or biological weapons may fall into the hands of the wrong people, and an influx of refugees may destabilise neighbouring States. A good example is that of Isis, a merciless, barbaric group which was born out of the chaos

---

73   B. Langille, *It's 'Instant Custom': How the Bush Doctrine became Law after the Terrorist Attacks of September 11, 2001* (2003) 26 Boston College International and Comparative Law Review, 155.

74   US President George W. Bush, Statement by the President in His Address to the Nation (11 September 2001).

75   R. Gates, *The Future of US Security Assistance* (2010) 89 Foreign Affairs 2,2.

and sectarian hatred unleashed by the end of the Iraq war. Isis has become so powerful that it has proclaimed itself a State, the caliphate of Iraq and Syria. It has, in fact, all attributes of a State other than international recognition (see Chapter 5.2).

In respect of failed States the Westphalian system of non-intervention (see Chapter 1.2.3) does not make sense. State practice shows that a State may rely on the right of self-defence to fight non-State actors located in a failed State. This is exemplified below.

In 2011, Kenya relied on the right of self-defence when invading Somalia, its neighbour, in order to respond to a series of kidnappings and other terrorist acts committed on its territory by the militant group Al-Shabaab, a non-State actor affiliated with al-Qaeda, which has its base in Somalia. Kenya informed the UNSC of its action emphasising the consequences of the collapse of Somalia on Kenya's national security over the preceding two decades. The Kenyan invasion was supported by the AU, Israel, the US and France.[76] The UNSC did not discuss the Kenyan invasion, probably because the Transnational Federal Government of Somalia (TFGS) (which at the relevant time did not have effective control over the territory of Somalia) approved the Kenyan operation. A joint Communiqué issued by Kenya and TFGS stated that Kenya's intervention in Somalia 'is based on the legitimate right to self-defence under Article 51 of the UN Charter'.[77]

In the 2006 conflict between Israel and Hezbollah in Lebanon, Israel relied on the right of self-defence in the situation where Hezbollah was in effective control of a part of Lebanese territory from which it had launched terrorist attacks. Hezbollah, a radical Shia paramilitary organisation, on 12 July 2006, captured two Israeli soldiers in a surprise attack along the Israeli-Lebanese border. Israel responded by carrying out air strikes against suspected Hezbollah targets in Lebanon, and Hezbollah countered with rocket attacks against cities and towns in northern Israel. In order to push Hezbollah back from its border, Israel launched a full-scale ground operation in Lebanon.

At the first meeting of the UNSC, after the commencement of the conflict, members of the UNSC overwhelmingly supported the argument of Israel that it had acted in self-defence.[78] The then UNS-G Kofi Annan condemned Hezbollah's attacks on Israel and stated that Israel had the right to defend itself under Article 51 of the Charter.[79] However, the disproportionate use of force by Israel (Israeli attacks caused a massive destruction of Lebanon's infrastructure, including thousands of houses, the death of about one thousand civilians, injury to more than 3,500 people and displacement of almost one million) in response to a cross-border attack launched by Hezbollah on 12 July 2006, in which eight Israeli solders were killed and two were abducted, made many States less sympathetic to Israel's claim. Had Israel respected the principle of proportionality, its actions would have been justified by the UNSC as self-defence.

15.4.5.3 A situation where non-State actors are located on the territory of a State which has not been asked for its consent by an alleged victim State to use force against non-State actors

Perhaps the best illustration of the above situation is provided by the 2011 US operation in Pakistan to capture or kill Osama bin Laden. The operation was carried out by US special forces and was successful in that Osama bin Laden was killed and then buried at sea. Although Pakistan generally

---

76   D.J. Birkett, *The Legality of the 2011 Kenyan Invasion of Somalia and its Implications for the Jus ad Bellum* (2013) 18/3 Journal of Conflict and Secuirty Law, 440.

77   Ibid, 449.

78   See e.g. UN Doc S/P. 5489.and UN Doc S/P 5493.

79   UN Doc S/PV.5492.

co-operates with the US in combating terrorists, on this occasion, the US government did not ask Pakistan for any consent. US reasons for this were that asking for consent would almost certainly undermine the operation because, the compound where bin Laden lived was in very close proximity to Pakistani military installations. Some members of the military must have been aware of Osama's whereabouts and might have informed Osma bin Laden about the proposed operation so enabling him to escape. Additionally, Osama's compound was well protected and thus Pakistani's forces would have been unlikely to be able to carry out a successful operation. The then President of Pakistan complained that the US operation violated Pakistani's sovereignty.[80] No further action was taken by the government of Pakistan. Henriksen submits that, in fact, the Pakistani government consented to the operation on the basis of a secret agreement between former President W. Bush and the government of Pakistan under which the US was permitted to conduct unilateral raids in Pakistan in search of Osama bin Laden, and his two closest officials. Under such agreement 'Pakistan would vociferously protest the incursion.'[81]

Whatever the arrangements between the US and Pakistan, customary international law, embodied in Article 2(4) of the UN Charter, is clear that a State may justify the use of force against the territorial integrity of another State only in the legitimate exercise of self-defence, or when authorised by the UNSC. If a State, where non-State actors are operating, is willing and able to fight them, or to co-operate with a victim State, the later will not be entitled to use defensive force against those non-State actors as this will violate the territorial sovereignty of the State where non-State actors are located.

The operation against Osama bin Laden raises another important, and very controversial, issue in international law, i.e. targeted killing of non-State actors located on the territory of a State by special forces or drone aircraft of another State. Targeted killings refer to 'military operations involving the use of lethal force with the aim of killing individually selected persons who are not in the physical custody of those targeting them'.[82] Drone aircraft, or drones, are remotely piloted aircraft, i.e. without a human pilot on board (see Chapter 17.3.2.1).

It is submitted that a victim State may rely on the right of self-defence in situations described in Chapter 15.4.5.1 and 15.4.5.2 but not Chapter 15.4.5.3. It is important to note that in order to assess lawfulness or otherwise of targeted killing areas of international law other than that dealing with the use of force in self-defence are relevant, i.e. IHR and IHL.[83]

15.5 Collective self-defence

Article 51 of the UN Charter was introduced primarily to safeguard the compatibility of the Pan-American regional system of mutual defence with the new regime for maintaining peace established by the Charter. To the South American States the most significant aspect of self-defence was that it could justify collective action.

---

80   See, e.g. John Bacon, *Musharraf: U.S. Violated Pakistani's Sovereignty*, USA Today, 3 May 2011, available at http://content.usatoday.com/communities/ondeadline/post/2011/05/musharraf-us-violated-pakistan-sovereignty/1.(accessed 9 July 2014).

81   A. Henriksen, *Jus as Bellum and American Targeted Use of Force to Fight Terrorism Around the World* (2014) 19/2 Journal of Conflict and Security Law, 235–236.

82   N. Melzer, 'Targeted Killings in Operational Law Perspective' in T.D. Gill and D. Fleck (eds), *Handbook of International Law of Military Operations*, Oxford: Oxford University Press, 2010, 277.

83   On this topic see S. Casey-Maslen, *Pandora's Box? Drone Strikes under Jus ad Bellum, Jus in Bello and International Human Rights Law* (2012) 94 International Review of the Red Cross, 597.

By referring to the 'inherent right of individual or collective self-defence' Article 51 has provided a legal basis upon which a number of regional security systems have been founded. However, Article 51 does not form part of Chapter VIII which regulates regional arrangements. This is important because Chapter VIII subordinates regional arrangements to the UNSC and specifically directs, in Article 53, that enforcement action should not be begun regionally without the UNSC's approval.

At the 1945 San Francisco Conference, Article 51 was deliberately transferred from Chapter VIII to Chapter VII with the result that the right of collective self-defence is entirely independent of the existence of a regional arrangement, and is immune from the paralysing effect of the veto.

15.5.1 Mutual assistance treaties for collective self-defence

The 1949 North Atlantic Treaty[84] provides under Article 5:

> The Parties agree that an armed attack against one or more of them in Europe or North America shall be considered an attack against them all; and consequently they agree that, if such an armed attack occurs, each of them, in exercise of the right of individual or collective self-defence recognised by Article 51 of the Charter of the United Nations, will assist the Party or Parties so attacked by taking forthwith, individually and in concert with the other Parties, such action as it deems necessary, including the use of armed force, to restore and maintain the security of the North Atlantic area.
>
> Any such armed attack and all measures taken as a result thereof shall immediately be reported to the Security Council. Such measures shall be terminated when the Security Council has taken the measures necessary to restore and maintain international peace and security.

The 1947 Inter-American Treaty of Reciprocal Assistance (the Rio Treaty)[85] provides under Article 3:

> (1) The High Contracting Parties agree that an armed attack by any state against an American state shall be considered as an attack against all the American states and, consequently, each one of the said Contracting Parties undertakes to assist in meeting the attack in the exercise of the inherent right of individual or collective self-defence recognised by Article 51 of the Charter of the United Nations . . .
>
> (4) Measures of self-defence provided for under this Article may be taken until the Security Council of the United Nations has taken the measures necessary to maintain international peace and security.

The provisions of these mutual assistance treaties should accord with the UN Charter. If there is any conflict, Article 103 of the Charter applies. It provides that:

> In the event of a conflict between the obligations of the Members of the United Nations under the present Charter and their obligations under any other international agreement, their obligations under the present Charter shall prevail.

15.5.2 The scope of collective self-defence

Article 51 of the UN Charter refers to 'individual or collective self-defence'.

In the *Nicaragua* Case,[86] the ICJ put forward a twofold test regarding the exercise of collective self-defence. According to this test the State under attack must:

---

84   82 UNTS 251.
85   21 UNTS 93.
86   [1986] ICJ Rep 14, paras 103–105.

■ have declared itself to be under attack; and

■ have requested the assistance of a third State.

in order for that third State to justify the exercise of the right to collective self-defence.

Many have criticised the ICJ for requiring a formal declaration and a request by the victim State as being unrealistic and constituting a 'wholly new and unconsidered limitation on the right to collective self defence'.[87] It can be said, however, that these requirements ensure that what might actually be an act of aggression will not be disguised as protection. A further criticism was expressed by Judge Jennings in his dissenting opinion. He argued that the Court missed a vital requirement, i.e. the need for a third State to have its own interest in exercising collective self-defence. The criticism was formulated as follows:

> Whatever collective self-defence means, it does not mean vicarious defence; for that way the notion is indeed open to abuse . . . The assisting state surely must, by going to the victim state's assistance, be also . . . in some measure defending itself.[88]

Kelson in his *Law of the United Nations*[89] has pointed out the dangers to world order which are involved in Article 51. Two groups of States centred on rival Great Powers may each decide that resort to force is justifiable in collective self-defence against the other, and the exercise of the veto may prevent the UNSC from making a determination under Article 39. This may result in a war between the two rival groups, each allegedly acting in self-defence, and the UNSC being unable to make a determination even of a threat to the peace.

The above outlined difficulty has in some respects been overcome by the Uniting for Peace Resolution,[90] which is founded upon the principle that the UNGA and individual members have a secondary responsibility for the maintenance of international peace which comes into play when the UNSC has failed to discharge its primary responsibility. Under the Resolution the UNGA may investigate and pronounce upon any resort to force, including alleged acts of self-defence, provided that a two-thirds majority can be obtained (see Chapter 16.3).

It is important to note that measures adopted by the UNGA under the Uniting for Peace Resolution are non-binding.

15.6 Controversial uses of force

Since the adoption of the UN Charter member States have, in addition to the right of self-defence, relied on a number of controversial grounds to justify their use of military force. Furthermore, international law itself has evolved in that it allows the use of force by people entitled to exercise their right to self-determination (see Chapter 12).

This section examines the possible exceptions, based on customary international law, to the prohibition of the use of force.

---

87   B. Simma (ed.), *The Charter of the United Nations: A Commentary*, Oxford: Oxford University Press, 2nd edn, 2002, 803 at para 38.

88   *The Nicaragua Case* [1986] ICJ Rep 14, Dissenting Opinion of Judge Sir Jennings, 535.

89   H. Kelson, *Law of Nations, The Law of the United Nations. A Critical Analysis of Its Fundamental Problems*, New York: Frederick A. Praeger, 1964.

90   UNGA Res 377 (V) (3 November 1950) UN Doc A/1775, 10.

15.6.1 Intervention to protect a State's own nationals

Nineteenth century jurists considered as lawful the use of force by a State to protect the lives and property of its nationals. The theory behind this is that nationals of a State are an extension of the State itself. In this way intervention to protect the State's nationals is reconcilable with the theory of self-defence – an injury to a national is an injury to the State. This theory has, however, been the subject of much debate and controversy, in particular subsequent to the Anglo-French invasion of the Suez Canal in 1956 and the Israeli raid on Entebbe in 1976.

15.6.1.1 The Anglo-French Invasion of Suez in 1956

In July 1956 Egypt nationalised the Suez Canal Company, a company in which there were considerable British and French interests. On 29 October 1956 Israel invaded Egyptian territory in the area of the Suez Canal zone. Two days later, French and British troops joined the Israeli forces and, within 10 days, completely occupied the Suez region.

Both the UK and France justified their action on the grounds of the protection of their nationals in Egypt, although other justifications were also invoked such as the danger to shipping in the Canal, the danger to the enormously valuable installation of the Canal itself and the effect on many nations of the blocking of the Canal. The international community regarded the Suez invasion by the British and the French as illegal.[91]

15.6.1.2 The 1976 Entebbe raid

On 27 June 1976 an Air France airliner bound for Paris from Tel Aviv was hijacked over Greece. Two of the hijackers were West German nationals and the other two held Arab passports. The airliner was diverted to Entebbe airport in Uganda. The Jewish passengers, some 100 persons, were separated from the other passengers and detained, while the others were released. The hijackers demanded the release of some 50 Palestinian terrorists imprisoned in various countries.

Following reports that Uganda was in fact helping the hijackers, on 2 July 1976 Israel flew soldiers to Entebbe and rescued the hostages by force. The hijackers were killed together with some Ugandan soldiers. Extensive damage was caused to Ugandan aircraft and the airport.

Subsequent to the Israeli intervention in Entebbe, two draft resolutions were submitted to the UNSC: one by Tanzania, Libya and Benin condemning Israel for the violation of the territorial integrity and sovereignty of Uganda; and the other by the UK and the US condemning hijacking but affirming the necessity to respect the territorial integrity and sovereignty of all States. After much debate within the UNSC neither resolution was adopted: the UK/US resolution failed to obtain the required nine votes in favour; the resolution proposed by African States was not submitted to a vote.

The right to intervene to protect nationals abroad has been advanced as an alternative ground for intervention in a number of other cases. In December 1989, for example, following the intervention by 20,000 US troops in Panama, one of the grounds advanced by the US Secretary of State, James Baker, to justify the action was that US nationals in Panama were under threat. The US had advanced similar arguments six years previously in justification of the landing of US troops in Grenada. Both interventions were condemned by the UNGA.

---

91   G. Marston, *Armed Intervention in the 1956 Suez Canal Crisis: the Legal Advice Tendered to the British Government* (1988) 37 ICLQ, 773.

It may well be said that in most cases where a State has relied on the justification that it was protecting its nationals abroad, the main objective of its military action has not been the protection of its nationals but the furthering of its own foreign policy objectives!

15.6.1.3 Conclusion

It is submitted that the use by a State of force to protect its nationals abroad will not breach Article 2(4) of the UN Charter in the following circumstances:

■ when there is a threat of imminent injury or death to nationals:

■ when a State in whose territory they are located is unwilling or unable to protect foreign nationals in danger;

■ when the intervention of a State is exclusively confined to the rescuing of its nationals; and

■ when the action is expected to save more lives than are likely to be lost.

There is sufficient evidence in State practice to suggest that there is a right to use force to protect nationals abroad when all of the above criteria are satisfied. In this respect the main criticism of the US intervention in 1980 intended to rescue the US hostages held in Iran concerned the strategy and tactics used by the US rather than the legality of the mission itself. The rescue mission got stuck in a sandstorm in the Iranian desert during which time much of its equipment was destroyed. Neither Iran nor other countries challenged the legality of the US mission although the ICJ, which at that time was adjudicating the *US Diplomatic and Consular Staff in Teheran Case (US v Iran)*,[92] stated in its judgment that it 'cannot fail to express its concern in regard to the United States' incursion into Iran'. This was not because the US rescue mission was contrary to Article 2(4) of the UN Charter, but because it could 'undermine respect for the judicial process' as it occurred when the Court was deliberating.

Post 9/11 developments on the right of self-defence further support the legality of the use of force by a State to protect its nationals in danger abroad, provided that the requirements specified above are satisfied.

15.6.2 Humanitarian intervention

Humanitarian intervention can be defined as 'coercive interference in the internal affairs of a State, involving the use of armed force, with the purposes of addressing massive human rights violations or preventing widespread human suffering'.[93]

With the development of the concept of Responsibility to Protect (R2P) (see Chapter 16.2.7) the term humanitarian intervention describes a situation where a State or a group of States, without authorisation from the UNSC, intervene militarily in order to protect nationals of a third State. Among academic commentators the majority opinion is that international law does not allow such humanitarian interventions for the following reasons:

■ The strict interpretation of Article 2(4), which prohibits any use of force against another State, and the principle of non-intervention in the internal and external affairs of a State make any intervention, even for humanitarian purposes, unlawful.

---

92   [1980] ICJ Rep 3.

93   J.M. Welsh, *Humanitarian Intervention and International Relations*, Oxford: Oxford University Press, 2006, 3.

■ Article 1 of the Declaration on the Inadmissibility of Intervention in the Domestic Affairs of States and the Protection of Their Independence and Sovereignty adopted in 1965 by the UNGA clearly prohibits any intervention by one State in the internal and external affairs of another State. It provides that:

> No state has the right to intervene, directly or indirectly, for any reason whatever, in the internal or external affairs of any other state. Consequently, armed intervention and all other forms of interference or attempted threats against the personality of the state or against its political, economic and cultural elements, are condemned.[94]

The Declaration makes no provision for humanitarian intervention:

■ UNGA Resolution 3314(XXIX) on the Definition of Aggression reinforces the prohibition of intervention by stating that 'no consideration of whatever nature, whether political, military or otherwise, may serve as a justification for aggression'.[95] This resolution was almost verbatim reproduced in the definition of a crime of aggression agreed in 2010 by contracting States to the Statute of the ICC (see Chapter 16.2.2.1).

■ The 2000 Declaration of the South Summit by the G77 composed of about 130 Member States stated that 'We reject the so-called "right" of humanitarian intervention, which has no legal basis in the United Nations Charter or in the general principles of international law'.[96]

■ If allowed, humanitarian interventions would provide a pretext for powerful States, as only they have the necessary military capacities to carry out large military operations, to intervene in the internal affairs of weaker States. Indeed, it is difficult to find any example, apart from NATO's intervention in Kosovo, where military intervention by a State has not been a cover for pursuing its national interests.

The topic of humanitarian intervention has been the subject of many debates since the intervention of NATO in Kosovo. Despite the creation of R2P, lawfulness or otherwise of humanitarian intervention is still of relevance, in particular, when the UNSC fails to deal with situations where there are massive violations of human rights inside the domestic jurisdiction of a State (e.g. Rwanda, Darfur, Kosovo and Syria), or where a State's structures have collapsed with the consequences that rival bands of criminal, terrorists and bandits are in control of a State (e.g. Somalia).

15.6.2.1   The intervention of NATO in Kosovo.

Before the disintegration of the Socialist Federal Republic of Yugoslavia (SFRY) Kosovo, a province of Yugoslavia, had 2.2 million inhabitants, 90 per cent of whom were ethnic Albanians. These Kosovar Albanians had enjoyed a large measure of autonomy during the many years of the regime of President Tito of the SFRY. However, from 1989, when the Federal Republic of Yugoslavia (FRY)[97] came into existence, that autonomy was taken away and the Kosovar Albanians became targets of the Serbian policy of 'ethnic cleansing'.

---

94   Supra note 13.
95   See 16.2.2.1.A.
96   Para 54.The Declaration is available at www.g77.org/summit/Declaration_G77Summit.htm (accessed 10 April 2014).
97   Serbia and Montenegro, considering themselves to be the successor of the SFRY, formed the FRY.

When Serbian atrocities towards Kosovar Albanian intensified, the situation in Kosovo became of concern to the UNSC. Its Resolution 1160 (1998) adopted on 31 March 1998 imposed a mandatory arms embargo on the Federal Republic of Yugoslavia (FRY). It also called upon the government of the FRY, and the Kosovar Albanians, to work together towards a political solution, and stated that failure to achieve such solution would prompt 'additional measures'. Almost immediately after the adoption of Resolution 1160 violence in Kosovo became even worse and the UNS-G, Kofi Annan, discussed possible military intervention in Kosovo with NATO.

In September 1998 the UNSC adopted Resolution 1199 (1998) which determined the situation in Kosovo as a 'threat to peace and security in the region'. Resolution 1199 requested both parties to the conflict to stop hostilities and to return to negotiations. Within the UNSC it become obvious that Russia would not support any further measures against the FRY, in particular measures involving the use of force. As a result of Russia's attitude, Resolution 1199 (1998) did not authorise NATO intervention. However, the escalation of violence, rape and general 'ethnic cleansing' being perpetrated by Serbian forces against Kosovar Albanians living in Kosovo prompted NATO to announce imminent military action against the FRY for failure to comply with Resolution 1199 (1998). At that point the FRY agreed to a cease-fire and decided to sign two agreements: one with the Organisation for Security and Co-operation in Europe (OSCE), establishing a verification mission in Kosovo and containing an undertaking of the FRY to comply with the UNSC resolutions; and one with NATO establishing an air-verification mission over Kosovo.

On 29 October 1998 the UNSC adopted Resolution 1203 (1998) under Chapter VII endorsing both agreements and urging the FRY to promptly implement them. It also stated that the situation in Kosovo constituted a continuing threat to peace and security in the region. Soon after this Serb forces intensified their policy of 'ethnic cleansing' in Kosovo. In response NATO resumed its threats to intervene. Meanwhile, the situation in Kosovo became alarming, an estimated 1.5 million people had been expelled from their homes, 5,000 Kosovars had been executed and some 225,000 Kosovar men were missing. The FRY did not intend to stop atrocities but under NATO's threats it started peace negotiations with Albanian Kosovars in Rambouillet, France in February 1999. Subsequently, the government of the FRY rejected a peace plan for Kosovo and in the face of inaction of the UNSC, which was paralysed by the threat of Russia's veto, NATO forces began an aerial bombing campaign against FRY military targets on 23 March 1999. The campaign ended on 10 June 1999 with the withdrawal of Serbian forces from Kosovo and the signing of the Military-Technical Agreement on 9 June 1999. The agreement was notified to the UNS-G who urged both sides to comply. The UNSC adopted Resolution 1244 (1999) endorsing the termination of hostilities provided for by the agreement.

15.6.2.2 Assessment

In international law there were, and still are, no convincing legal arguments justifying NATO's intervention in Kosovo. In fact, the Independent International Commission on Kosovo (IICK) concluded that NATOs intervention was illegal.[98] Nevertheless, as many authors emphasise, the real justification lies in the reaction of the international community to NATO's intervention. The legitimacy of the intervention of NATO, despite it illegality, has been widely accepted and appears to be based on the following:

■ The rejection on 26 March 1999 by a majority of 12 votes of a draft resolution submitted by Belarus and Russia to the UNSC with a view to declaring the NATO bombing of Yugoslavia illegal.

---

98   Independent International Commission on Kosovo, *Kosovo Report: Conflict, International* Response, Lessons Learned (2000) 164.

■ On 13 April 1999, at the initiative of the Islamic Conference, the UN Commission on Human Rights adopted a resolution declaring the intervention of NATO lawful by 44 votes in favour, only two against (Russia and Cuba).

■ The UNGA never condemned NATO's intervention, although it did condemn the US intervention in Grenada in 1983 and Panama in 1989.

■ The UNGA in Resolution 1244 (1999) endorsed the 9 June 1999 Military-Technical Agreement between NATO and the FRY.

The IICK emphasised that the intervention of NATO was legitimate and proposed that the doctrine of humanitarian intervention be further developed in order to allow the closing of the gap between legality and legitimacy.[99] Indeed, a new approach is needed bearing in mind that the international community should not stand by and allow atrocities to be committed anywhere when the UNSC is paralysed. This is well exemplified by the failure of the UNSC to intervene in Syria (see Chapter 16.2.7.1).

15.7   Prohibition of reprisals

Reprisals can be defined as coercive measures taken during peacetime, directed by one government against another government in retaliation for alleged wrongful acts committed by the latter, and which would, if taken in any other circumstances, be unlawful.

Prior to the adoption of the UN Charter, reprisals involving armed force were lawful in the circumstances which were defined in the *Naulilaa Case (Portugal v Germany).*[100]

NAULILAA CASE (PORTUGAL *V* GERMANY)

Facts:

In October 1914, when Portugal was a neutral State during WWI, three members of a party of German soldiers lawfully in the Portuguese colony of Angola were killed by Portuguese soldiers. On the evidence it was clearly established that the incident arose out of a misunderstanding.

Germany, however, as a measure of reprisal sent into Angola a military force which attacked several frontier posts and destroyed property including the port at Naulilaa. Portugal claimed reparation for damage attributable to the German action. Germany argued that it was a case of legitimate reprisal.

Held:

The German plea was rejected by the Arbitral Tribunal which held that:

Reprisals are acts of self-help by the injured state, acts in retaliation for acts contrary to international law on the part of the offending state, which have remained unredressed after a demand for amends. In consequence of such measures, the observance of this or that rule of

99   Ibid. On legality and legitimacy of humanitarian interventions see: T. Franck, *Recourse to Force: State Action Against Treats and Armed Attacks*, Cambridge: Cambridge University Press, 2002, 174, and A. Roberts, 'Legality v Legitimacy. Can Use of Force be Illegal but Justified?' in A, Alston and E. Macdonald, *Human Rights, Intervention and the Use of Force*, Oxford: Oxford University Press, 2008, 179.

100   (1928) 2 RIAA 1013.

international law is temporarily suspended in the relations between the two states. They are limited by considerations of humanity and the rules of good faith, applicable in the relations between states. They are illegal unless they are based upon a previous act contrary to international law. They seek to impose on the offending state reparation for the offence, the return to legality and the avoidance of new offences.

The Tribunal laid down three conditions for the legitimacy of reprisals:

- *there must have been an act contrary to international law on the part of the other State.*
- *the reprisal must be preceded by an unsatisfied request for redress of the wrong committed;*
- *the measures adopted as reprisals must not be excessive, in the sense of being out of all proportion to the wrong committed.*

While traditional law recognised that, subject to the above conditions being satisfied, a State could engage in reprisals, the UN Charter, in prohibiting the threat or use of force, negated the position under traditional law by making any use of force by a State, including reprisals, illegal. Article 51 of the UN Charter, however, preserves a State's inherent right of self-defence. It is therefore necessary to distinguish between acts of self-defence, which are permitted, and reprisals, which are not.

The position of the UNSC on reprisals was made clear when it discussed the Harib Fort Incident of 1964. In 1963 and 1964, the British government had complained to the UNSC of a large number of shooting incidents on the Yemeni-South Arabian border and of aerial raids into South Arabian territory from the Yemen. In March 1964, three raids had taken place in which Bedouin and their flocks had been attacked from the air. Thereupon on 28 March 1964 British military aircraft bombed Harib Fort in the Yemen after having first dropped leaflets advising people to leave the area. The Yemen brought the matter before the UNSC.

The British representative denied that the attack had been a reprisal. He argued that:

> there is, in existing law a clear distinction to be drawn between two forms of self-help. One, which is of a retributive or punitive nature – 'retaliation' or 'reprisals'; the other, which is expressly contemplated and authorised by the Charter – self-defence against an armed attack. . . . it is clear that the use of armed force to repel or prevent an attack – that is, legitimate action of a defensive nature – may sometimes have to take the form of a counter attack.[101]

He pointed out that aggressive acts from the Yemen had resulted in loss of life and emphasised that the fort at Harib was not merely a military installation, but was known to be a centre of aggressive action against the Federation of South Arabia (then a British Protectorate).

> To destroy the fort with the minimum use of force was therefore a defensive measure which was proportionate and confined to the necessities of the case.
>
> It has no parallel with acts of retaliation or reprisals, which have as an essential element the purposes of vengeance or retribution. It is this latter use of force which is condemned by the Charter, and not the use of force for defensive purposes such as warding off future attacks.[102]

---

101 Statement of Sir Patrick Dean in UNSC, Official Records, 1109th meeting, 7 April 1964, 5, para 31.
102 Statement of Sir Patrick Dean in UNSC, Official Records, 1111th meeting, 9 April 1964, 6, para 30.

The UNSC did not accept the UK view and adopted Resolution 188 (1964) by nine votes in favour, none against and two abstentions: i.e. the US and the UK. The resolution:

■ condemned reprisals as incompatible with the purposes and principles of the UN;

■ deplored the British military action at Harib on 28 March 1964;

■ deplored all attacks and incidents which occurred in the area.[103]

The position of the ICJ on reprisals was stated in the *Legality of the Threat or Use of Nuclear Weapons (Advisory Opinion)*[104] as follows:

> armed reprisals in time of peace . . . are considered as unlawful . . . any right to [belligerent] reprisals would, like self-defence, be governed inter alia by the principle of proportionality.

It is to be noted that reprisals which do not involve the use of armed force are usually regarded as lawful. They may consist of, e.g. seizure of the offending State's property, refusal to carry out obligations deriving from international treaties *vis-à-vis* the offending State, freezing of financial assets, and refusal to grant visas to nationals of the offending State.

RECOMMENDED READING

Books

Bowett, D.W., *Self-Defence in International Law*, Manchester: Manchester University Press, 1958.

Colin, A.M., *The Inherent Right of Self-Defence in International Law*, Dordrecht: Springer, 2013.

Dinstein, Y., *War, Aggression and Self-Defence*, 4th edn, Cambridge: Cambridge University Press, 2005.

Gray, C., *International Law and the Use of Force*, Oxford: Oxford University Press, 3nd edn, 2008.

Roscini, M., *Cyber Operations and the Use of Force in international Law*, Oxford: Oxford University Press, 2014.

Ruys, T., *'Armed Attack' and Article 51 of the UN Charter: Evolutions in Customary Law and Practice*, Cambridge: Cambridge University Press, 2010.

Shiner, P. (ed.), *The Iraq War and International Law*, Oxford: Hart, 2008.

Welsh, J.M., *Humanitarian Intervention and International Relations*, Oxford: Oxford University Press, 2006.

Articles

Birkett, D.J., *The Legality of the 2011 Kenyan Invasion of Somalia and its Implications for the Jus ad Bellum* (2013) 18/3 Journal of Conflict and Secuirty Law, 440.

Brownlie, I., *The Use of Force in Self-Defence*, (1961) 37 BYIL, 183.

Corten, O. *The Controversies over the Customary Prohibition on the Use of Force* (2005) 16 EJIL, 803.

Czaplinski, W., *Sources of International Law in the Nicaragua Case* (1989) 38 ICLQ, 151.

Henriksen, A., *Jus at Bellum and American Targeted Use of Force to Fight Terrorism Around the World* (2014) 19/2 Journal of Conflict and Security Law.

Jennings, R.Y., The *Caroline and McLeod Cases* (1938) 32 AJIL, 82.

Kammerhofer, J.,*The Armed Activities Case and Non-State Actors in Self-Defence Law* (2007) 20 LJIL, 96.

Murphy, S.D., *Terrorism and the Concept of 'Armed Attack' in Article 51 of the UN Charter* (2002) 43 Harvard ILJ 41.

Tams, C.J., *The Use of Force against Terrorists* (2009) 20 EJIL, 388.

---

103   SCOR, 19th Year,111th meeting, 8 April 1964.
104   [1996] ICJ Rep 226, 246.

The prohibition of the threat or use of force in international law

1907

The Hague Convention II Respecting the Limitation on the Employment of Force for the Recovery of Contract Debt prohibited the use of force in respect of contract debts claimed from the government of one State by the government of another State due to its nationals.

From the time of the Roman Republic to 1648 Peace of Westphalia war was lawful although the doctrine of 'just war' imposed some restrictions on when a State was justified to resort to war. After the 1648 Peace of Westphalia the doctrine of just war disappeared from international law. States were sovereign and equal and therefore one State had no authority to judge whether or not the cause of another State was just. By the end of the eighteenth century and throughout the nineteenth century war was recognised as an instrument of national policy and customary law placed no limitations on the rights of States to resort to war.

1914

The Bryan Treaties prohibited resort to war prior to the report of a conciliation commission.

1919

The Covenant of the League of Nations:
- Outlawed wars of aggression,
- Provided that if a dispute arose between members of the League they were obliged to submit the matter either to arbitration or to inquiry by the Council of the League and they agreed 'in no case to resort to war until three months after the award by the arbitrators or the report by the Council'. Any war in breach of this commitment or against a party complying with an award or decision was unlawful; and
- Established the first collective security system and provided for sanctions against a member who violated the specific prohibitions against war.

1928

The General Treaty for the Renunciation of War also known as the Kellogg-Briand Pact was the first universal treaty which outlawed war but did not provide for sanctions against a State who has broken the Pact by resorting to war in violation of its provisions.

1945

Article 2(4) of the UN Charter states that all members of the UN 'shall refrain in their international relations from threat or use of force against the territorial integrity or political independence of any State, or in any other manner incompatible with the purposes of the United Nations'. The prohibition, being also a rule of customary international law, applies to all States, irrespective of whether or not they are members of the UN.

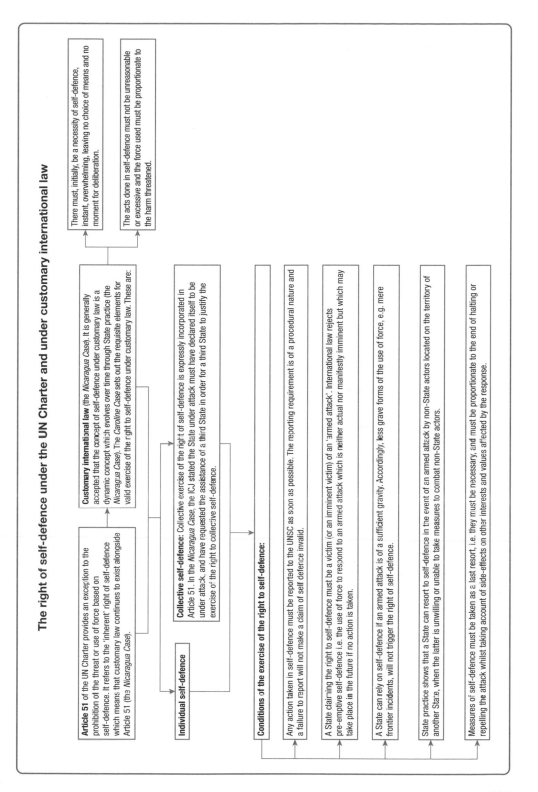

The right of self-defence under the UN Charter and under customary international law

Article 51 of the UN Charter provides an exception to the prohibition of the threat or use of force based on self-defence. It refers to the 'inherent' right of self-defence which means that customary law continues to exist alongside Article 51 (the *Nicaragua Case*).

Customary international law (the *Nicaragua Case*). It is generally accepted that the concept of self-defence under customary law is a dynamic concept which evolves over time through State practice (the *Nicaragua Case*). The *Caroline Case* sets out the requisite elements for valid exercise of the right to self-defence under customary law. These are:

There must, initially, be a necessity of self-defence, instant, overwhelming, leaving no choice of means and no moment for deliberation.

The acts done in self-defence must not be unreasonable or excessive and the force used must be proportionate to the harm threatened.

Individual self-defence

Collective self-defence: Collective exercise of the right of self-defence is expressly incorporated in Article 51. In the *Nicaragua Case*, the ICJ stated the State under attack must have declared itself to be under attack, and have requested the assistance of a third State in order for a third State to justify the exercise of the right to collective self-defence.

Conditions of the exercise of the right to self-defence:

Any action taken in self-defence must be reported to the UNSC as soon as possible. The reporting requirement is of a procedural nature and a failure to report will not make a claim of self defence invalid.

A State claiming the right to self-defence must be a victim (or an imminent victim) of an 'armed attack'. International law rejects pre-emptive self-defence i.e. the use of force to respond to an armed attack which is neither actual nor manifestly imminent but which may take place in the future if no action is taken.

A State can rely on self-defence if an armed attack is of a sufficient gravity. Accordingly, less grave forms of the use of force, e.g. mere frontier incidents, will not trigger the right of self-defence.

State practice shows that a State can resort to self-defence in the event of an armed attack by non-State actors located on the territory of another State, when the latter is unwilling or unable to take measures to combat non-State actors.

Measures of self-defence must be taken as a last resort, i.e. they must be necessary, and must be proportionate to the end of halting or repelling the attack whilst taking account of side-effects on other interests and values affected by the response.

16

COLLECTIVE SECURITY

CONTENTS

CHAPTER OUTLINE

1 Introduction

The UN Charter confers the main responsibility for the maintenance of international peace and security on the UNSC. It has the authority to determine the existence of a threat to the peace, a breach of the peace or act of aggression and to decide what measures, both forcible and non-forcible, are necessary to maintain international peace and security. Member States are bound by such measures.

The failure of the UNSC to fulfil its primary purpose of maintaining international peace and security resulting from the widespread use of a right of veto by one or more of its permanent members has led to three major developments:

■ The assumption by the UNGA of the role of determining a threat to the peace, a breach of the peace, or act of aggression, and of recommending action by members including the use of armed force. During the Korean War in 1950, the UNGA adopted the Uniting for Peace Resolution under which it is empowered to recommend collective measures. However, the UNGA, unlike the UNSC, cannot adopt binding decisions. It may only adopt recommendations on matters of collective security.

■ The development of peacekeeping operations under either Chapter VI or Chapter VII of the Charter.

■ The development of powerful regional military alliances outside the UN, e.g. NATO, the Warsaw Pact, and, the OAS. Since the end of the Cold War, due to a new spirit of co-operation between the UN and its member States, regional arrangements and agencies, not only of a military nature, are often used to enforce measures taken by the UNSC under Article 42 of the UN Charter and to conduct peacekeeping operations, alone or together with the UN.

2 The role of the UNSC in the maintenance of international peace and security

Under Article 24 of the UN Charter, the UNSC is invested with primary responsibility for the maintenance of international peace and security. In order to discharge it, the UNSC enjoys wide powers under Chapter VII in that it may make recommendations or binding decisions when dealing with situations which endanger international peace and security. The Charter contains the following procedure for dealing with such situations:

A. Under Article 40 of the UN Charter the UNSC may order provisional measures to ensure that a conflict does not escalate. Provisional measures do not prejudice the rights of the parties and the UNSC is not required to make any determination under Article 39 of the UN Charter prior to the taking of a decision on the imposition of provisional measures.

B. Under Article 39, the UNSC determines whether the situation under consideration constitutes a threat to the peace, a breach of the peace or act of aggression. None of these is defined by the UN Charter and thus the UNSC enjoys wide discretionary powers in determining what constitutes a 'threat to the peace', 'a breach of the peace' and 'act of aggression'. This is understandable given that such determination involves political assessment of usually very complex and delicate situations. The practice of the UNSC shows that:

■ The UNSC has been very reluctant to find that a situation at issue constitutes an act of aggression and accordingly to name the 'aggressor'. UNGA Resolution 3314 (XXIX) on the Definition of Aggression provides some indication as to what is meant by the term 'aggression'.

■ On the following four occasions the UNSC found that there was a breach of peace: when North Korea invaded South Korea (Resolution 1/1501 (1950)); when Argentina invaded the Falkland Islands (Resolution 502(1982)); when Iraq invaded Iran (Resolution 514 (1982)) and when Iraq invaded Kuwait (Resolution 660(1990)).

■ The concept of 'a threat to the peace' is more flexible than the concepts of 'a breach of the peace' or 'an act of aggression'. As a result of the concept of 'a threat to the peace' being flexible the UNSC has used it as a vehicle to deal with situations such as internal conflicts, widespread violations of fundamental human rights, serious threats to democracy, terrorism and spread of deadly diseases such as Ebola.

C. If the UNSC determines that the situation at issue constitutes a threat or a breach of the peace or act of aggression it then decides what measures should be used to maintain or restore peace. Under Article 41 it may decide to apply diplomatic, economic or other sanctions which do not involve the use of force. Prior to 1990 Article 41 sanctions were used only twice, in 1966 against Rhodesia and in 1977 against South Africa. Since the end of the Cold War in 1990 sanctions have been imposed frequently not only on States, but also on military and paramilitary organisations, and even on individuals.

D. If measures taken under Article 41 fail or would be inadequate, the UNSC may, under Article 42, take measures involving the use of armed force. Military sanctions have never been utilised in the form envisaged under Article 42 bearing in mind that the standing army at the disposal of the UNSC provided for in Article 43 has never materialised. In practice the UNSC has authorised regional arrangements or agencies or members of the UN to use armed force to enforce measures taken under Article 42. Such authorisations, since the 1950 Korean operation, have become the standard procedure.

3 The role of the UNGA in the maintenance of international peace and security: the Uniting for Peace Resolution

Under Article 11(2) of the UN Charter the UNGA may discuss any dispute or a situation relating to the maintenance of international peace and security and may make recommendations relating to them to the State or States concerned or to the UNSC or both. However, under the Uniting for Peace Resolution adopted in 1950 by the UNGA, it exercises a secondary or residual responsibility for the maintenance of international peace and security. This resolution was particularly important during the Cold War as it allowed the UNGA to circumvent any paralysis of the UNSC resulting from a negative vote or a threat of it by one or more of its permanent members. The UNGA is allowed to act if two conditions set out in Resolution 377(V) are met:

- the UNSC has failed to exercise its primary responsibility for the maintenance of international peace and security because of a veto by one its permanent members;

- the situation under consideration falls under Chapter VII in that it constitutes a threat to the peace, a breach of the peace or act of aggression.

However, the UNGA, unlike the UNSC, cannot adopt binding decisions. In practice Resolution 377(V) has never become of great significance although it has been used occasionally.

4 UN peacekeeping and its role in the maintenance of international peace and security

Peacekeeping is not mentioned in the UN Charter. It constitutes a practical answer to the malfunction of collective security as envisaged in the UN Charter. The three fundamental principles of peacekeeping are: the impartiality of peacekeepers, the use of force by them in self-defence or to defend the mandate under which they operate, and the consent of the parties involved to the deployment of peacekeeping forces.

Since the end of the Cold War, peacekeeping has evolved considerably in terms of:

- the nature of missions carried out in that it has been increasingly concerned with intra-State conflicts and civil wars rather than inter-State conflicts;

- complexity as it often involves peacebuilding and even peace enforcing, i.e. it has become multidimensional; and

- composition of multinational forces in that the participation of both civilian police and civilian staff in peacekeeping operations has considerably increased.

UN peacekeeping is under constant review, reform and development.

5 Regional arrangements and agencies and their role in the maintenance of international peace and security

Chapter VIII of the UN Charter brings regional arrangements and agencies into the UN collective security system. However, it does not provide any definition of these terms. The absence of a definition is advantageous as it allows the fitting into the UN collective security system of any arrangements/agencies which contribute to the maintenance of international peace and security. Among organisations which have been recognised as falling within the scope of Article 52 are: the OAS; the Arab League; the AU, the Islamic Conference; the Conference on Security and Co-operation in Europe (CSCE); the Commonwealth of Independent States (CIS); NATO; the Western European Union (WEU); and the EU. All were accorded observer status by the UNGA.

Since 1990 a new era of co-operation between the UN and regional organisations has commenced with the consequence that regional arrangements/agencies are often not only authorised to enforce measures adopted by the UNSC under Article 42 of the UN Charter but also to perform peacekeeping functions, alone or in co-operation with the UN peacekeeping missions.

16.1 Introduction

At the heart of the UN Charter are the provisions relating to the maintenance of international peace and security. They confer on the UNSC the main responsibility for carrying out its tasks. Article 24(1) of the UN Charter states:

> In order to ensure prompt and effective action by the United Nations, its Members confer on the Security Council primary responsibility for the maintenance of international peace and security, and agree that in carrying out its duties under this responsibility the Security Council acts on their behalf:

The UNSC is made up of 15 members, five permanent: the US; the UK; Russia; France; and China, and ten non-permanent who are elected by the UNGA for 2 years. Each member has one vote. However, a distinction is made between voting:

- On substantive matters, also referred to as non-procedural matters. To take a decision on non-procedural matters at least nine affirmative votes are required and these must include a unanimous vote of the five permanent members of the UNSC. Therefore, each permanent member may veto any decision to be taken by the UNSC. However, any abstention among the five permanent members does not prevent the adoption of a non-procedural decision. This has been a long accepted practice of the UNSC, which was confirmed by the ICJ in the *Legal Consequences for States of the Continued Presence of South Africa in Namibia (South West Africa) Notwithstanding Security Council Resolution 276 (1970) (Advisory Opinion).*[1]

- On procedural matters. To take a decision on procedural matters an affirmative vote of nine members is required, but no veto system applies.

If there is a disagreement as to whether a matter concerns substance or procedure, the matter is treated as concerning substance. With regard to disputes either under Chapter VI of the UN Charter or Article 52, a party to the dispute is required to abstain from voting.

---

1   [1971] ICJ Rep 16.

Under Chapters VI and VII of the UN Charter the UNSC decides what type of diplomatic economic or military measures must be taken to prevent or terminate threats to international peace, breaches of the peace and acts of aggression. Chapter VI of UN Charter deals with peaceful settlement of international disputes. Under its provisions the UNSC can make non-binding recommendations (see Chapter 14.1). Under Chapter VII entitled 'Action with Respect to Threats to the Peace, Breaches of the Peace and Acts of Aggression' the UNSC can adopt binding measures.

The competence of the UNSC under Chapter VII is excluded in respect of maters of 'domestic jurisdiction' of a member State. This exclusion is imposed by Article 2 (7) of the UN Charter which defines the relationship between the UN and its members in that it embodies the principle of non-intervention of the UN 'in matters which are essentially within the domestic jurisdiction of any state'. The crucial issue is how to define matters which are within the domestic jurisdiction of a State bearing in mind that such a definition will not only delimit competences between the UN and the member States but also be of assistance to establish whether one State has unlawfully interfered in the domestic affairs of another in breach of customary international law[2] which prohibits any intervention conducted through forcible or dictatorial means. The PCIJ in its *Advisory Opinion of 7 February 1923 concerning Nationality Decrees in Tunis and Morocco* held that:

> The question whether a certain matter is or is not solely within the jurisdiction of a state is an essentially relative question: it depends upon the development of international relations.[3]

This statement holds true today. No satisfactory definition can be provided as there is a constant increase in matters which are within the scope of international law with the consequence that those regarded as being within the exclusive domain of a State are shrinking. Article 2(7) reflects this reality as it states in its final paragraph that the principle of non-intervention 'shall not prejudice the application of enforcement measures under Chapter VII'. This means that when the UNSC decides that a matter is within its competence, i.e. when a situation poses a threat to peace (see Chapter 16.2.2.3), it becomes of concern to the international community. Since the end of the Cold War the UNSC has considerably widened the definition of threat to peace to encompass situations where a State is engaged in serious violations of HRs of its citizens, or where a State's structures collapse with the consequence that anarchy prevails (Somalia and Haiti), or where a State is developing nuclear weapons in breach of international law (North Korea and Iran).

The system of collective security was conceived with the idea that the UNSC would act unanimously as an international gendarme. Regrettably, the Cold War proved the system to be ineffective and even after the end of the Cold War the agreement of all five permanent members of the UNSC to apply measures involving the use of force or other non-violent means is not always guaranteed. This was evident when the UNSC failed to prevent widespread and flagrant breaches of HRs and IHL in Kosovo (see Chapter 15.6.2.1). The need for a substantial reform of the UNSC has been debated for decades. At the time of writing any attempts to reform the UNSC have failed and while attempts continue it is unlikely that any will succeed. This is despite the agreement reached by 170 heads of State and government attending the 2005 World Summit that such a reform was required 'in order to make [UNSC] more broadly representative, efficient and transparent and thus to further enhance its effectiveness and the legitimacy and implementation of its decisions'[4] but not on how and when to achieve it.

---

2   The *Case concerning Military and Paramilitary Activities in and against Nicaragua (Nicaragua v United States of America) (Merits)* [1986] ICJ Rep 14, para 202.

3   (1923) Ser B, No 4, 23.

4   UNGA Res 60/1 (16 September 2005), para 153.

When measures are taken by the UNSC every member of the UN is bound, by virtue of Article 2(5), to provide assistance to the UN and to refrain from giving assistance to a State against whom the measures are directed. This obligation is reinforced by Article 25 of the UN Charter which requires all members to accept and carry out UNSC decisions adopted under any chapter of the Charter. Further, under Article 103 of the UN Charter, when there is a conflict between the obligations of the members of the UN under the UN Charter and their obligations arising from any other international agreements, the obligations under the Charter prevail. However, the question as to whether a UNSC's resolution adopted under Chapter VII prevails over an international agreement has not been definitively settled.[5]

Under Chapter VII the UNSC may take the following measures:

■ under Article 40, before making any recommendation or decisions, order provisional measures to prevent an aggravation of the situation at issue;

■ subsequent to making a determination that a situation at issue constitutes either a threat to the peace, or a breach of the peace, or act of aggression it may:

  ■ under Article 41 of the UN Charter impose measures not involving the use of force;

  ■ under Article 42 of the UN Charter take measures involving the use of force.

With regard to Article 41, measures not-involving the use of force consist mainly of the imposition of economic sanctions. Since the end of the Cold War the UN collective security system has undergone important changes in terms of the use of the UNSC's authority to impose sanctions. Prior to 1990, the UNSC had applied economic sanctions only twice, i.e. in 1966 against Rhodesia and in 1977 against South Africa.

In the decades immediately pre and post 2000 sanctions have been imposed frequently, not only on States but also on military and paramilitary organisations and even on individuals. With regard to sanctions imposed on States, the matter of their effectiveness, their humanitarian impact on the civilian populations and their effect on third States has become an important consideration for the UNSC. In this respect, the UNSC set up on 17 April 2000 the Working Group on General Issues on Sanctions to develop recommendations on how to improve the effectiveness of sanctions. The Group produced a Report in 2006.[6] Many recommendations contained in the Report have been implemented. In particular, the UNSC is putting a special emphasis on the so-called 'smart sanctions', i.e. sanctions which focus on a targeted leadership or group and therefore have little or no effect on civilian populations and third States. As to sanctions imposed on individuals, the main issue is how to make those sanctions conform to international human rights standards.

As to measures involving the use of force under Article 42 of the UN Charter, the standing army at the disposal of the UNSC provided for in Article 43 to give 'teeth' to the collective security system, has never materialised. Consequently, military sanctions have never been utilised in the form envisaged under Article 42. Instead, in practice the UNSC has authorised regional arrangements or agencies or members of the UN to use armed force to enforce measures taken under Article 42. Such authorisations have, since the 1950 Korean operation (see Chapter 16.2.4.1), become the standard procedure.

The UNSC is the main, but not the only, organ of the UN with has the responsibility for the maintenance of international peace and security. Other organs such as the UNGA, the ICJ and the

---

5   The *Case Concerning the Questions of Interpretation and Application of the 1971 Montreal Convention Arising from the Aerial Incident at Lockerbie (Libyan Arab Jamahiriya v United States of America) (Provisional Measures)* [1998] ICJ Rep 115.

6   UN Doc S/2006/997.

UNS-G are vital elements in the collective security system. In particular, as the UNSC has often been deadlocked, the UNGA has filled the gap. During the 1950 Korean war the UNGA adopted Resolution 377(V) entitled 'Uniting for Peace'[7] under which it is empowered to recommend collective measures in a situation where the UNSC is paralysed because of a veto. However, the UNGA, unlike the UNSC, cannot adopt binding decisions. It may only adopt recommendations on matters of collective security.

The deficiencies of the collective security system were the catalyst for the creation of a new technique to deal with the maintenance of peace and security which was not provided for in the UN Charter – UN peacekeeping. As a result, there are two approaches to situations which endanger international peace and security: the collective security approach and the peacekeeping approach.

It is important to note that the UNSC has, since the 9/11 terrorist attacks on the US, gone beyond its function of dealing with specific disputes and situations and adopted two resolutions under Chapter VII which can be qualified as 'legislation': one on terrorism,[8] and one on weapons of mass destructions[9] (see Chapter 2.12.2).

Another consequence of the failure of the UNSC to discharge its primary responsibility for the maintenance of international peace and security has been the development of powerful regional security systems outside the UN, e.g. NATO, the Warsaw Pact, and the OAS. Since the end of the Cold War regional arrangements and agencies of both a military and non-military nature are often used by the UNSC to enforce measures taken under Article 42 and to conduct peacekeeping operations, alone or together with the UN.

The above topics are examined in this chapter.

16.2 The role of the UNSC in the maintenance of international peace and security

Under Article 24 of the UN Charter, the UNSC is invested with primary responsibility for the maintenance of international peace and security. In order to discharge this responsibility it enjoys broad powers under Chapters VI and VII.

Chapter VI is concerned with the pacific settlement of disputes and confers on the UNSC mainly recommendatory, i.e. non-binding powers (see Chapter 14.1). Under Chapter VII, the UNSC may make recommendations or binding decisions when dealing with situations which endanger international peace and security. The Charter contains the following procedure for dealing with such situations:

■ Under Article 40 the UNSC may order provisional measures to ensure that a conflict does not escalate.

■ Under Article 39, the UNSC determines whether the situation under consideration constitutes a threat to the peace, a breach of the peace or act of aggression.

■ If the UNSC determines that the situation at issue constitutes a threat or a breach of the peace or act of aggression it then decides what measures should be used to maintain or restore peace. Under Article 41 it may decide to apply diplomatic, economic or other sanctions which do not involve the use of force and, if measures taken under Article 41 fail or would be inadequate, it may take military sanctions by virtue of Article 42 of the UN Charter.

---

7   UNGA Resolution 377 (V) (3 November 1950) UN Doc A/1775,10.

8   S/Res/1373 (2001).

9   S/Res/1540 (2004). On the topic of the UNSC's exercise of legislative powers see J. Wouters and J.Odermatt, *Quis Custodiet Consilium Securitatis? Reflections on the Law Making Powers of the Security Council*, Working paper No 9, June 2013. Available at https://ghum.kuleuven.be/ggs/publications/working_papers/new_series/wp101–110/wp109-wouters-odermatt.pdf (accessed 2 October 2014).

16.2.1 Provisional measures

Article 40 of the Charter provides:

> In order to prevent an aggravation of the situation, the Security Council may, before making the recommendations or deciding upon the measures provided for in art 39 call upon the parties concerned to comply with such provisional measures as it deems necessary or desirable. Such provisional measures shall be without prejudice to the rights, claims, or position of the parties concerned. The Security Council shall take account of failure to comply with such provisional measures.

Article 40 is mainly used to order a cease-fire and withdrawal. Provisional measures may provide a basis for the settlement of the dispute without the need for further action by the UNSC. These provisional measures do not prejudice the rights of the parties. They are simply a means of preventing aggravation of a situation.

One issue arising under Article 40 is whether the adoption of a resolution providing for provisional measures creates an obligation upon the parties to whom the resolution is directed. In this respect it is generally agreed that the words 'called upon' when used in Article 40 means 'ordered' and should be read in conjunction with Article 25 of the UN Charter.[10] For this reason, to avoid having to take enforcement action against States, the powers under Article 40 are rarely used and most resolutions passed are phrased as recommendations and not orders.

The UNSC may order provisional measures before or after making any determination as to whether the situation at issue constitutes a threat to the peace, a breach of the peace or act of aggression.

When acting under Article 40 of the UN Charter the UNSC will normally call for ceasefires and, depending upon the circumstances, for the withdrawal of military forces of one party from the territory of another. For example, in Resolution 1701(2006) of 11 August 2006, the UNSC, when dealing with the continuing escalation of hostilities between Lebanon and Israel resulting from Hizbollah's[11] attack on Israel on 12 July 2006, called on Hizbollah to cease all attacks on Israel immediately and on Israel to cease all offensive military operations in Lebanon immediately and to withdraw its military forces from Southern Lebanon.

16.2.2 The determination by the UNSC of whether a situation at issue constitutes a threat to the peace, a breach of the peace or of an act of aggression

The meaning of the three above concepts is not defined in the UN Charter. The UNSC exercises its discretion when making Article 39 determinations and proceeds on a case-by-case basis. Further, the determination, or lack of it, depends very much on whether any permanent member of the UNSC has any interest in the situation under consideration. If so, it may, by using its right of veto, prevent the UNSC from making any determination.

The issue of whether a determination made by the UNSC under Article 39 can be challenged before the ICJ has not been decided by the Court. However, Judge Elihu Lauterpacht, an *ad hoc* judge in the *Case Concerning Application of the Convention on the Prevention and Punishment of the Crime of*

---

10   B. Simma, *The Charter of the United Nations: A Commentary*, Oxford: Oxford University Press, 2nd edn, 2002, 729–735, in particular paras 14–17.

11   It seems there are two spellings of the name of this organisation, i.e. Hizbollah and Hezbollah.

Genocide (Bosnia and Herzegovina v Serbia and Montenegro) (Further Request for the Indication of Provisional Mesures)[12] in his Separate Opinion stated:

> that the Court has some power of this kind [judicial review] can hardly be doubted, though there can be no less doubt that it does not embrace any right of the Court to substitute its discretion for that of the Security Council in determining the existence of a threat to the peace, a breach of the peace or an act of aggression, or the political steps to be taken following such a determination.

16.2.2.1 Acts of aggression

Article 1 of the UN Charter lists, as one of the purposes of the UN, 'the suppression of acts of aggression'. Therefore, if a State commits acts of aggression this will be a breach of Article 2(4) of the Charter.

As previously mentioned, the determination by the UNSC of whether an act of aggression has occurred is normally motivated by political interests of each permanent member of the UNSC. For that reason it is very important that a definition of aggression is agreed by the UN Members so to ensure that the determination under Article 39 of the UN Charter is based on objective criteria. Further, such a definition 'supported by the vast majority of Member States, even if it was opposed by the great Powers, would give notice to world public opinion of the restrictions placed on the use of violence in international relations'.[13]

A. Definition of aggression under Resolution 3314(1974)

Prior to the adoption by the UNGA of Resolution 3314 in 1974 all attempts at defining 'aggression' had failed although the crime of aggression, without being defined, was mentioned in the Covenant of the League of Nations and in the Charters of the Military Tribunals at Nuremberg and Tokyo.[14]

It took the UN member States many years to agree on the definition. This was because there was a deep disagreement between Third World States and Western States on this matter and additionally the Soviet Union had its own view as to what a definition should encompass. While the Third World States, as well as the Soviet Union, pushed for a strict definition because they wanted to curtail the possibility that the Western States would rely on anticipatory and pre-emptive self defence or humanitarian considerations to justify military interventions mainly carried out in Third World States, the Western States were not keen on defining aggression arguing that whether an act should be qualified as such depended upon circumstances.[15]

The 1974 UNGA Resolution 3314 (XXIX) on the Definition of Aggression[16] constitutes a compromise between the above mentioned views. It makes war of aggression a crime against international peace giving rise to international responsibility. It excludes the possibility for a State to justify acts of aggression by political, economic, military or other considerations (Article 5). Its Article 1 provides a generic definition of aggression based on Article 2(4) of the UN Charter, but does not mention the 'threat of the use of force'. This means that threats of aggression, whatever their seriousness cannot be regarded as acts of aggression. Article 1 states:

---

12   Order of 13 September [1993] ICJ Rep 325, Separate Opinion of Judge Lauterpacht, para 99.

13   See C. de Bock, *The Crime of Aggression: Prospects and Perils for the Third World* (2014) 13/1 Chinese Journal of International Law, 99.

14   A/CN.4/44, p. 69.

15   On this topic see See C. de Bock, *The Crime of Aggression: Prospects and Perils for the Third World* (2014) 13/1 Chinese Journal of International Law, 91.

16   14 December 1974, GAOR 29th Session Supp 31 vol 1, 142.

Aggression is the use of armed force by a state against the sovereignty, territorial integrity or political independence of another state, or in any other manner inconsistent with the Charter of the United Nations, as set out in this Definition.

Article 2 gives the UNSC flexibility as to whether to make a determination. It establishes a presumption that 'the first use of armed force' by a State in contravention of the UN Charter constitutes an act of aggression, but this is subject to the proviso that the UNSC may decide not to make a determination of aggression in the light of the circumstances, including the fact that the acts or their consequences are not of sufficient gravity.

Article 3 sets out a non-exhaustive list of acts of aggression which encompasses:

(a) The invasion or attack by the armed forces of a State of the territory of another State, or any military occupation, however temporary, resulting from such invasion or attack, or any annexation by the use of force of the territory of another State or part thereof.

(b) Bombardment by the armed forces of a State against the territory of another State or the use of any weapons by a State against the territory of another State.

(c) The blockade of the ports or coasts of a State by the armed forces of another State.

(d) An attack by the armed forces of a State on the land, sea or air forces, or marine and air fleets of another State.

(e) The use of armed forces of one State which are within the territory of another State with the agreement of the receiving State, in contravention of the conditions provided for in the agreement or any extension of their presence in such territory beyond the termination of the agreement.

(f) The action of a State in allowing its territory, which it has placed at the disposal of another State, to be used by that other State for perpetrating an act of aggression against a third State.

(g) The sending by or on behalf of a State of armed bands, groups, irregulars or mercenaries, which carry out acts of armed force against another State of such gravity as to amount to the acts listed above, or its substantial involvement therein.

Article 4 provides that acts other than those listed in Article 3 may constitute acts of aggression.

It can be said that the very existence of the definition was a victory for the Third World States as well as the provisions of Article 3 which set out a list of acts of aggression even though the list is not exhaustive. The Western States, however, were also satisfied with the definition in that it was adopted as a non binding UNGA resolution so could be easily ignored and if applied, was flexible enough either to avoid the making of an Article 39 determination or to expand it, by virtue of Article 4 of the Resolution, to acts not listed in Article 3.

In practice, Resolution 3314 has been rarely, if at all, used by the UNSC when making a determination under Article 39 of the Charter. The UNSC has been very careful in apportioning the blame for an unlawful use of force by pointing out the 'aggressor'. So far it has found that three States have committed acts of aggression: Israel, South Africa and Rhodesia.[17] However, the UNGA on numerous occasions has not hesitated to find that a particular State has committed an act of aggression. Additionally, the ICJ has referred to Resolution 3314 when deciding whether instances of the use of force amounted to acts of aggression. The ICJ in the *Case Concerning Military and Paramilitary Activities in and*

---

17   S/Res/387 (1976); S/Res/455 (1979); S/Res/568(1985); S/Res/567(1985); S/Res/571 (1985); S/Res/573 (1985); S/Res/574 (1985); S/Res/577 (1985); S/Res/611 (1988).

against Nicaragua (Nicaragua v. US), Merits[18] held that the definition set out in Article 3, para(g) reflected customary international law. However, whether Resolution 3314 as a whole is part of customary international law is uncertain.[19]

B. Definition of aggression under Article 8bis(2) of the Statute of the ICC
(also known as the Rome Statute)

Resolution 3314 served a very important purpose. It was used as a basis for negotiations aimed at defining the crime of aggression under the Rome Statute of the ICC, which entered into force in 2002. Its Article 5(2) gives the ICC jurisdiction over the crime of aggression. However, at the time of adoption of the Statute the State parties were unable to reach an agreement on the definition of the crime of aggression.[20] This was achieved by the Review Conference of the Rome Statute held in Kampala, Uganda between 31 May and 11 June 2010 which adopted, by consensus, amendments to the Statute incorporating a definition of the crime of aggression, and establishing conditions relating to the exercise of jurisdiction of the ICC over that crime. The amendment is set out in Article 8bis of the Rome Statute and will enter into force when at least 30 State parties have ratified or accepted the amendment; and following a decision by two-thirds of States parties to activate the jurisdiction of the ICC in respect of the amendment to be taken at any time after 1 January 2017.[21]

The definition of aggression contained in Article 8bis(2) of the Rome Statute, which is necessary to define the crime of aggression, mirrors that contained in Resolution 3314. Further, it reproduces a non-exhaustive list of acts of aggression which constitutes an exact replica of acts listed in Article 3 of Resolution 3314.[22]

C. The meaning of 'use of armed force' under Article 8bis(2) of the Rome Statute

Article 8bis(2) of the Rome Statute, being adopted 37 years after the adoption of Resolution 3314, adds a new gloss to the current understanding by the majority of States of the concept of 'aggression', in particular of the meaning of 'use of armed force'.

At the Kampala Conference States agreed that the words 'use of armed force' should be understood as use of force in the military sense.[23] Accordingly, political or economic aggression, no matter how serious, and cyber warfare[24] are excluded from the definition of aggression. While it has long been accepted that political and economic aggression is outside the scope of the definition of aggression, cyber attacks, which may be as harmful as conventional attacks, are more controversial.

---

18   [1986] ICJ Rep 14, para 3. See also *Armed Activities on the Territory of the Congo (Democratic Republic of the Congo v Uganda)* (2005) ICJ Rep 168, para 146.

19   See the views of Judge Kooijmans in *Armed Activities on the Territory of the Congo (Democratic Republic of the Congo v Uganda)*, Separate Opinion, para 63.

20   P. Kirsch and J.T. Holmes, *The Rome Conference on an International Criminal Court: The Negotiating Process* (1999) 93 AJIL, (1999), 10.

21   Article 15*bis* and *ter* of the Rome Statute.

22   See Report of the Special Working Group on the Crime of Aggression (ICC-ASP/6/20/Add.1/Annex II), para 34. It states that: 'Those delegations that supported the drafting of paragraph 2 [Article 8bis(2)] expressed their understanding that the list of crimes was, at least to a certain extent, open. Acts other than those listed could thus be considered acts of aggression, provided that they were of a similar nature and gravity to those listed and would satisfy the general criteria contained in the chapeau of paragraph 2.'

23   See T. Ruys, *'Armed Attack' and Article 51 of the UN Charter: Evolutions in Customary Law and Practice*, Cambridge: Cambridge University Press, 2010.

24   See Report of the Special Working Group on the Crime of Aggression (ICC-ASP/6/20/Add.1/Annex II), para 35.

In Spring 2007, for example, Estonia suffered major cyber attacks on its public and private institutions. These attacks paralysed the country for three weeks. Estonia believes that this was a response by Russia to its removal of a Soviet era war memorial from the centre of the capital of Estonia to the military cemetery. Russia denied any responsibility. Other cyber attacks, such as those allegedly launched by Russia against Georgia in 2008 during the armed conflict, or more recently during the crisis in Ukraine, and a cyber attack in 2010, widely accepted as being a joint cyber operation of the US and Israel, on nuclear processing centrifuges in Iran, which is thought to have set back the Iranian nuclear programme by many years, show that in the age of increased dependency on technology a State may achieve its objective of destabilising and seriously harming another State without a single shot being fired. This was acknowledged by the Heads of State and Government of the Member States of NATO at a Summit meeting in September 2014 in Wales. They agreed that a large-scale cyber attack on one member State could be considered as an attack on all its members and potentially trigger a military response.[25] The NATO sponsored 'Manual on the International Law Applicable to Cyber Warfare', known as the Tallinn Manual, states that 'whether a cyber operation constitutes an armed attack depends on its scale and effects'.[26] However, in the light of Resolution 3314 and the definition of aggression in the Rome Statute cyber attacks cannot be regarded as acts of aggression, and consequently cannot justify the use of armed force in self-defence, either individual or collective. Even though in some circumstances cyber attacks may be of such a scale and impact, e.g. triggering the detonation of nuclear weapons in a victim State, that it may give rise to the right of self-defence, it is normally very difficult, if not impossible, to establish where a cyber attack came from, and who organised it. However, the Tallinn Manual rightly emphasised that any response to a cyber attack must be in accordance with IHL.

16.2.2.2   A breach of the peace

On the following four occasions the UNSC found that there had been a breach of the peace:

- when North Korea invaded South Korea (Resolution 1/1501 (1950));

- when Iraq invaded Iran (Resolution 514 (1982));

- when Argentina invaded the Falkland Islands (Resolution 502(1982)); and

- when Iraq invaded Kuwait (Resolution 660(1990)).

It is to be noted that when an inter-States armed conflict commences, the first duty of the UNSC is to ensure that the conflict will not escalate and that the parties end immediately their military operations and return to peaceful means of settling their dispute. Therefore, a determination under Article 39 indicating that one party is an 'aggressor' may be counterproductive in terms of achieving peace. Further, at the beginning of the conflict facts may be unclear and therefore any determination of 'an aggressor' may not be possible (e.g. this occurred with regard to the war between Iran and Iraq (1980–88)).

---

25   See the Wales Summit Declaration available at www.nato.int/cps/en/natohq/official_texts_112964.htm (accessed 25 October 2014).

26   On this topic see D. Fleck, *Searching for International Rules Applicable to Cyber Warfare – a Critical Assessment of the New Tallinn Manuel* (2013) 18/2 Journal of Conflict and Security Law, 331.

16.2.2.3   A threat to the peace

Threats to the peace are a broader category than that of breaches of the peace or acts of aggression. While the latter two concepts are more amenable to legal definition, the concept of a breach of the peace offers the UNSC more flexibility in deciding, mainly on political considerations, whether the situation at issue creates a threat to the peace.

The concept of 'a threat to the peace', being more flexible than the concepts of 'a breach of the peace' and 'act of aggression' has indeed expanded over the years. The UNSC has decided that there was a threat to the peace, not only in the context of classical international conflicts (e.g. its first determination of a threat to the peace was made in 1948 when the newly created State of Israel was invaded by armed troops of its neighbouring Arab countries), but also when an internal situation in a State could, if continued, escalate and threaten the peace and stability of a particular region. In this context, the UNSC determined that threats to the peace were created by:

- civil war in Somalia in 1991 (Resolution 733(1992));

- serious threats to democracy in Haiti (Resolution 841 (1993));

- genocide in Rwanda in 1994 (Resolution 912 (1994));

- humanitarian catastrophe in Darfur (Resolution 1556 (2004)); and

- the Ebola outbreak in West Africa (Resolution 2177(2014)).

Further, the UNSC, in many resolutions, has declared that terrorism in all its forms and manifestations constitutes one of the most serious threats to peace and security. A refusal of States to surrender individuals suspected of committing serious terrorist crimes for prosecution by the State concerned has been qualified as a threat to the peace, e.g. the refusal of the Taliban to extradite Osama bin Laden to the US after the 9/11 terrorist attacks (Resolution1277(1999)), the refusal of Sudan to extradite to Ethiopia individuals wanted in 1996 in connection with the attempted assassination of the President of Egypt in 1981 (Resolution 1044 (1996)), and the refusal of Libya to surrender terrorist suspects responsible for the destruction of Pan American Flight 103 over Lockerbie on 21 December 1988 (Resolution 748 (1992)).

Finally, in Resolution 1874 (2009) the UNSC determined that North Korea, by carrying out nuclear tests and missile activities, had generated increased tension in the region and beyond, which activities pose a clear threat to international peace and security.

16.2.3   Enforcement action under Article 41 of the UN Charter not involving the use of armed force

Article 41 provides:

> The Security Council may decide what measures not involving the use of armed force are to be employed to give effect to its decision, and it may call upon the Members of the United Nations to apply such measures. These may include complete or partial interruption of economic relations and of rail, sea, air, postal, telegraphic, radio and other measures of communication, and the severance of diplomatic relations.

Sanctions under Article 41 of the UN Charter play an important role in the maintenance of peace and security, without resorting to force, as they put pressure on States or entities to comply with international law and with the objectives of the UN. They are also widely accepted by public opinion.

Prior to the end of the Cold War the UNSC had taken action under Article 41 only twice, i.e. with regard to Rhodesia in 1965, and South Africa in 1977.

Since 1990 the situation has dramatically changed in terms of the frequency and scope of sanctions. Further, to make sanctions effective, for each country or entity under sanctions the UNSC sets up a Sanctions Committee to supervise their implementation. The Committee relies on co-operation with States, IGOs and NGOs to provide it with information concerning violations of sanctions.

16.2.3.1 Reform of the UN sanctions system

It emerges from the above that sanctions imposed by the UNSC are often in place for a very long time. The positive effect of sanctions has been acknowledged by the international community. However, sanctions may also have negative effects, in particular on civilian population of a country under UN sanctions, and on third States. This matter was considered in the report on *Agenda for Peace*[27] and its Supplement[28] prepared by former UNS-G, Boutros Boutros-Ghali. Following his report there have been ongoing discussions on how to improve the effectiveness of UNSC sanctions and how to alleviate their negative effects. One answer to this problem has been the application of so-called 'smart sanctions' directed against leaders, or target groups, consisting of imposing travel bans, freezing of foreign bank accounts of individuals or groups, imposing arms embargos or, as in the case of Sierra Leone, a diamonds embargo. These smart sanctions have very important psychological effects. It will be impossible for the political elite of a target State to blame UN sanctions for hardship suffered by the civilians.

On 17 April 2000 the UNSC set up the Working Group on General Issues on Sanctions with a view to preparing a document on the use of sanctions by the UNSC as a policy instrument. The Working Group submitted its report in 2006.[29] The report contains many recommendations concerning the administration of sanctions, their design, implementation, duration and termination. A large number of these recommendations have been put into practice.

It is important to note that as sanctions can be imposed on individuals the UNSC must ensure that they are in conformity with international human rights law. Following the judgment of the ECJ in *Kadi and Al Barakaat v Council of the EU and the European* Commission,[30] the UNSC Sanctions Committees have introduced new procedures to conform more fully with human rights standards.[31]

16.2.4 Enforcement action under Article 42 of the UN Charter involving the use of armed force

Article 42 states:

> Should the Security Council consider that measures provided for in Article 41 would be inadequate or have proved to be inadequate, it may take such action by air, sea or land forces as may be necessary to maintain or restore international peace and security. Such action may include demonstrations, blockade and other operations by air, sea or land forces of Members of the United Nations.

---

27   A/47/277-S/24111.
28   A/50/60-S/1995/1.
29   UN Doc S/2006/997.
30   Joined Cases C-402/05P and C-415/05P [2008] ECR I-6351.
31   On this topic see E. de Wet, *From Kadi to Nada: Judicial Techniques Favouring Human Rights over United Nations Security Council Sanctions* (2013) 12/4 Chinese Journal of International Law, 787.

Strictly speaking, action under this provision has never been taken, e.g. the UN forces in Korea were created on the basis of a UNSC recommendation following an Article 39 determination, and in the case of the Gulf War UNSC Resolution 678 (1990), which authorised the use of force, did not refer to Article 42. Nevertheless, the UNSC, has found a different way to enforce Article 42. This being by authorising a State or a group of States or regional organisations such as NATO, the OAS, or the AU to use armed force to restore international peace and order. It is considered that this kind of authorisation is implied in the UNSC's general competence to maintain international peace and security under Chapter VII.

Prior to the end of the Cold War, the UNSC, on a few occasions, authorised the use of force. In 1950, in Resolution 84 (1950) of 7 July 1950, the UNSC recommended that all Members provide military assistance to South Korea under the unified command of the UN (see below). In 1966, the UK was authorised to use force, if necessary, to prevent breach of an oil embargo imposed against Southern Rhodesia.

Since the end of the cold War, the UNSC has authorised the use of force many times, for differing purposes and to varying degree:

1 To repel or reverse aggression by one State against another, e.g. in the Gulf War (1990) when Iraq invaded Kuwait;

2 To enforce sanctions against a member State when it authorised naval blockades, e.g. in Iraq, Haiti, Sierra Leone and the former Yugoslavia;

3 To allow peacekeepers to use force to defend themselves and to protect civil populations: the former Yugoslavia, Somalia, the Democratic Republic of the Congo, Kosovo and East Timor, and by regional arrangements (such as the ECOWAS Mission in Côte d'Ivoire (ECOMICI), the EU force in the Democratic Republic of the Congo (EUFOR R.D. Congo) and the African Union Mission in Somalia (AMISOM).

Additionally the UNSC has authorised the use of 'necessary measures' by multinational forces e.g. in Somalia, Haiti, Rwanda, Eastern Zaire, Albania, Bosnia and Herzegovina, East Timor, Bunia in the DRC, Liberia and Iraq.

Two military interventions authorised by the UNSC are particularly interesting, i.e. that in Korea in 1950 because of its implications for the development of international law on collective security and that in the 1990 Gulf War because it was the most comprehensive. These are discussed next.

16.2.4.1 The 1950 Korean war

Korea became a part of Japan in 1910. In 1943 the Allied powers agreed that it would become an independent State when WWII ended. In 1945 Japanese troops in Korea, North of the 38th Parallel, surrendered to the USSR and those South of the 38th Parallel surrendered to the US. This divided surrender had the long term effect of creating the separate States of North Korea and South Korea. Meanwhile, on 25 June 1950 Korean armed forces from North of the 38th Parallel crossed that Parallel into the Southern part of Korea and fighting broke out. The resulting crisis was immediately debated by the UNSC which (in the absence of the Russian representative adopted the following series of resolutions.

Security Council Resolution 82 (1950) of 25 June 1950:

The Security Council:
. . . noting with grave concern the armed attack upon the Republic of Korea by forces from North Korea. Determines that this action constitutes a breach of the peace.

736

(I) Calls for the immediate cessation of hostilities; and calls upon the authorities of North Korea to withdraw forthwith their armed forces to the 38th Parallel . . .

(III) Calls upon all Members to render every assistance to the United Nations in the execution of this resolution and to refrain from giving assistance to the North Korean authorities.

Security Council Resolution 83 (1950) of 27 June 1950:

The Security Council:

. . . recommends that the Members of the United Nations furnish such assistance to the Republic of Korea as may be necessary to repel the armed attack and to restore international peace and security in the area.

Security Council Resolution 84(1950) of 7 July 1950:

The Security Council:

(3) Recommends that all Members providing military forces and other assistance pursuant to the aforesaid Security Council resolutions make such forces and other assistance available to a unified command under the United States.

(4) Requests the United states to designate the commander of such forces.

(5) Authorises the unified command at its discretion to use the United Nations Flag in the course of operations against North Korea forces concurrently with the flags of the various nations participating.

(6) Requests the United States to provide the Security Council with reports as appropriate on the course of action taken under the unified command.

In response to the UNSC resolutions, 16 member States sent armed forces to Korea.

Some writers are doubtful as to whether the forces in Korea constituted a UN force. Although they were called a UN force, flew the UN flag and were awarded UN medals by the UNGA, nevertheless all operational decisions concerning the force were taken by the US. The Commander took his orders from the US, not from the UN.

However, on the question of whether the forces in Korea were UN forces, Bowett concludes that: 'There can be no doubt that, in practice, the overwhelming majority of states involved in the Korean action were fully prepared to regard it as a United Nations action involving United Nations Forces.'[32]

The UNSC ceased to play an active part in the conduct of the Korean war after the USSR representative resumed his seat on 1 August 1950 and vetoed all possible actions. In October 1950 China entered the war in support of North Korea. After the USSR had, on 30 November 1950, vetoed a draft resolution condemning the Chinese action the UNGA became the organ effectively seized of the Korean war (see Chapter 16.3).

16.2.4.2 The Iraqi invasion of Kuwait

On 2 August 1990, Iraqi armed forces invaded the neighbouring sovereign State of Kuwait and ousted the incumbent Kuwaiti government. The UNSC was immediately called into emergency session and on the same day passed Resolution 660 (1990) which condemned the Iraqi invasion of Kuwait, demanded the immediate and unconditional withdrawal of all Iraqi forces from Kuwait and called upon Iraq and Kuwait to settle their international differences by peaceful means.

---

32   D.W. Bowett, *United Nations Forces: A Legal Study of United Nations Practice,* London: Stevens & Sons, 1964, 47.

After Iraq refused to withdraw its troops from Kuwait, the UNSC passed Resolution 661 (1990) of 6 August 1990. This Resolution imposed mandatory sanctions and an embargo on Iraq. Under the terms of the Resolution, all States (not just members of the UN) were prohibited from permitting:

■ trade in commodities and products originating in either Iraq or Kuwait, other than medicine and humanitarian aid;

■ the transportation or transshipment of any Iraqi and Kuwaiti products, by land, air or sea, and the transfer of funds for payment of related transactions;

■ the supply of weapons or any other military equipment; and

■ the grant of financial assistance, credit, or any other economic resources to either Iraq or Kuwait.

In addition, all States were required to take 'appropriate measures' to protect the assets of the legitimate government of Kuwait and Resolution 661 instructed all States to refrain from recognising any regime set up by the occupying power.

Iraq claimed that the Kuwaiti government had been overthrown by an internal revolution and, on 5 August, a new Kuwaiti government was announced by Iraq. Later, Iraq announced its intention to annex Kuwait, a move which was subsequently renounced by the UNSC in Resolution 662 (1990). Nevertheless, on 28 August, Iraq declared that Kuwait had become its nineteenth province and passed constitutional amendments to that effect.

On 29 November1990, after numerous fruitless attempts to achieve a peaceful settlement, the UNSC passed Resolution 678 (1990) which demanded that Iraq 'comply fully with Resolution 660 (1990) and all subsequent relevant resolutions' and authorised 'Member states co-operating with the Government of Kuwait . . . to use all necessary means to uphold and implement Security Council Resolution 660 (1990) and all subsequent relevant Resolutions and to restore international peace and security in the area'. The deadline of 15 January was set for Iraqi compliance with the Resolutions of the UNSC.

No Iraqi withdrawal was initiated before the deadline specified in Resolution 678 (1990) and on 16 January 1991 coalition forces which were by then stationed in Saudi Arabia commenced an aerial bombardment of military installations and strategic targets inside Iraq and Kuwait. After less than a month, the coalition forces commenced ground operations to liberate Kuwait, and within four days the territory of Kuwait was surrendered to those forces.

Resolution 678 (1990) is of particular significance because, for the first time in the history of the UN, the use of military force was authorised by the UNSC on the basis of a unanimous affirmative vote among the permanent members. However, the multilateral force was not a UN force in the sense of Chapter VII of the Charter, but rather a coalition of military forces organised under the command of the US.

16.2.5 Agreements on the provision of armed forces by UN member States.

The basis of the scheme envisaged in Chapter VII lay in the provision to the UNSC of the armed forces necessary to enforce its decisions against recalcitrant States. This was to be effected by agreements between the UNSC and the member States.

Article 43 of the Charter provides:

(1) All Members of the United Nations, in order to contribute to the maintenance of international peace and security, undertake to make available to the Security Council, on its call and in accordance with a special agreement or agreements, armed forces, assistance, and facilities, including rights of passage, necessary for the purpose of maintaining international peace and security.

(2) Such agreement or agreements shall govern the number and types of forces, their degree of readiness and general location, and the nature of the facilities and assistance to be provided.

(3) The agreement or agreements shall be negotiated as soon as possible on the initiative of the Security Council.

As can be seen, a State is not obliged to take part in military operations under Article 42 unless it has concluded a 'special agreement' under Article 43. This is inferred from Article 43(3) under which member States are not obliged to conclude such agreements, i.e. their consent is required. No such agreements have ever been made. However, the absence of agreements under Article 43 does not prevent States agreeing *ad hoc* to place forces at the disposal of the UNSC in particular cases.

16.2.6   The Military Staff Committee

Article 46 of the Charter provides that:

Plans for the application of armed force shall be made by the Security Council with the assistance of the Military Staff Committee.

Article 47 provides:

(1) There shall be established a Military Staff Committee to advise and assist the Security Council on all questions relating to the Security Council's military requirements . . .

(2) The Military Staff Committee shall consist of the Chiefs of Staff of the permanent members of the Security Council or their representatives . . .

Although established in 1946 the Military Staff Committee has no real function so far as enforcement actions under Article 42 are concerned.[33] In practice the existence of this committee has been disregarded by the UNSC, and responsibility for carrying out the Council's military requirements has been entrusted to the UNS-G.

16.2.7   The exercise by the UNSC of the Responsibility to Protect (R2P).

The concept of the R2P entered the legal vocabulary in 2001 when the International Commission on Intervention and State Sovereignty (ICISS) established by the Canadian Foreign Minister in 2000, and made up of recognised experts in international law, published its report entitled 'The Responsibility to Protect'.

The idea behind the responsibility to protect is that a State has primary responsibility to protect its nationals from avoidable disasters such as mass killing, mass rape, starvation, etc. If a State fails because it is unable or unwilling to protect its nationals, then the international community has collective responsibility to take the necessary action including military intervention.

The Report emphasised that military intervention for humanitarian purposes is a measure of last resort and should be used in accordance with the following principles:

■ The just cause threshold. This ensures that military intervention is only permissible if there is large scale loss of life or large scale 'ethnic cleansing' or a threat of this.

---

33   However, it has carried out many important tasks. For details see its official website at www.usunnewyork.usmission.gov/Issues/msc.html (17 August 2014).

- The precautionary principles. The application of these ensures that there is the right intention on the part of an intervening entity; that military intervention is the remedy of last resort; that it is proportional to what is required to achieve the human protection objective; and that it has a reasonable chance of success.

- Right authority. The most appropriate body to deal with military intervention is the UNSC and therefore any intervention should be subject to authorisation by the UNSC. However, if the UNSC is paralysed because of a veto by one permanent member, then the UNGA should consider the matter under the 'Uniting for Peace' procedure, and if this fails, the relevant sub-regional organisations should be allowed to take action under Chapter VIII of the UN Charter, subject to retrospective authorisation from the UNSC. The Report, however, does not specify what would occur if the UNSC refused to give 'retrospective' authorisation, and how this could be expected to be given bearing in mind the failure of the UNSC to act in the first place.

- Operational Principles. Any military intervention should be carried out in accordance with sound operational principles, e.g. having the protection of a population as its prime objective, having unified command, observing appropriate rules of engagement and having the maximum possible co-ordination with humanitarian organisations.

Even before the publication of the above repost, the then UNS-G Kofi Annan, at the UNGA in 1999, advocated the rethinking of the concept of sovereignty and called on States to 'forge unity behind the principle that massive and systematic violations of human rights should not be allowed to stand.'[34] Again, in 2000, in the Millennium Report he made persuasive pleas to the international community to find the answer to the following question:

> If humanitarian intervention is, indeed, an unacceptable assault on sovereignty, how should we respond to a Rwanda, to a Srebrenica – to gross and systematic violations of human rights that affect every precept of our common humanity.[35]

Subsequently, the High-Level Panel on Threats, Challenges and Change (High-Level Panel) established by Kofi Annan was asked to examine this matter among others. Its conclusions were submitted in the Report entitled 'A More Secure World: Our Shared Responsibility', published in December 2004. The High-level Panel examined and praised the ICISS Report and when commenting on Chapter VII of the UN Charter accepted 'the emerging norm that there is a collective international responsibility to protect, exercisable by the Security Council authorising military intervention as a last resort, in the event of genocide and large-scale killing, ethnic cleansing or serious violations of international humanitarian law which sovereign Governments have proved powerless or unwilling to prevent'.[36] The High-level Panel identified five criteria which should always be used to assess whether military intervention is justified. The criteria are very similar to those proposed by the ICISS and are as follows:

- the seriousness of the threat i.e. only the most serious international crimes will justify the use of military force;

- the proper purpose; i.e. the purpose must be to stop or avert humanitarian disaster or a threat of it;

---

34   UN Doc A/54/PV.4.
35   UN Doc A/54/2000, 48.
36   Para 203.

■ last resort. All non-military options and their potential effectiveness must be considered before resort is made to military intervention;

■ proportional means. The scale, duration and intensity of the proposed military intervention must be proportional to the threat in question;

■ balance of consequences. The proposed intervention must have a reasonable chance of success. In particular, the consequences of action must not be worse than the consequences of inaction.

The next step in the development of the R2P was the Report entitled 'In Larger Freedom' prepared by Kofi Anann. This Report was submitted to and endorsed by 170 heads of State and government attending the 2005 World Summit session of the UNGA.[37] The Report:

■ advocated the establishment of criteria which would guide the UNSC when considering whether to authorise or endorse the use of military force;

■ recommended the adoption of the criteria set out by the High-level Panel;

■ called upon the UNSC to adopt a resolution setting out these criteria and expressing its intention to refer to them when deciding whether to authorise the use of force.

In 2006, the UNSC discussed the UNS-G's Report. It unanimously adopted Resolution 1674 on the Protection of Civilians in Armed Conflict which, for the first time, referred to the R2P.[38] It also passed Resolution 1706 authorising the deployment of UN Peacekeepers in Darfur mentioning the R2P.[39]

The UNGA, in its Resolution 1674 (2006), a thematic resolution on the protection of civilians in armed conflicts, endorsed paras 138 and 139 of the World Summit Outcome Document, i.e. the proposals submitted by UNS-G Kofi Anann on the R2P which were accepted by the 2005 World Summit.

The next step in the development of the R2P was the appointments by the UNS-G Ban ki-Moon of a Special Adviser on the Prevention of Genocide and a Special Adviser to the UNS-G on the R2P.

In January 2009 the UNS-G presented a Report entitled 'Implementing the Responsibility to Protect'[40] which proposes a three pillar strategy for implementing the R2P, as endorsed by the 2005 World Summit. The Report emphasises that the R2P should first and foremost lie with a State and that the best way to discourage a State or a group of States from misusing the R2P is to develop the UN strategy, standards, processes, and practice for the implementation of the R2P.

The three Pillars, which are of equal value, are:

■ The protection responsibility of a State. This responsibility derives from the nature of State responsibility and a State's international obligations. The Report specifies that the R2P applies to four specific crimes: genocide, war crimes, ethnic cleansing and crimes against humanity.

■ International assistance and capacity-building. The Report examines ways in which the UN, States, international organizations and the private sector can assist a State in meeting its obligations deriving from the R2P.

■ Timely and decisive response. The Report emphasises the need for setting up an early warning and assessment system and advocates the use of all available means, coercive, and non-violent by States to respond collectively in a timely and decisive manner to a situation when a State is

---

37   World Summit Outcome Document, in particular paras 138 and 139.
38   S/RES/1674(2006).
39   S/RES/1706 (2006).
40   A/63/677.

failing to protect its nationals. Further, the Report urges the permanent members of the UNSC to refrain from employing or threatening to employ the veto when the intervention of the UNSC is clearly required.

The Report contained a broad-based approach to the implementation of the R2P and invites the UNGA to examine strategies necessary for the R2P to become a reality. In July 2009, the UNGA debated the issues of R2P while taking note of the UNS-G Report. It passed a consensus resolution overwhelmingly reaffirming the 2005 commitment of the member States to the R2P.[41] It has also commenced an informal interactive dialogue between the UNGA and representatives of member States, regional organisations and civil society to be take place each year after the release by the UNS-G of its annual report on various aspects of the R2P. This is to be followed by a debate at the UNGA. So far the UNS-G has released the following reports:

- in July 2010 on the necessity to strengthen the early warning mechanisms;

- in July 2011 on the role of regional and sub-regional arrangements in the implementation of the R2P;

- in July 2012 on the R2P on the necessity of timely and decisive response to violations of HRs covered by the R2P;

- in July 2013 on R2P on State responsibility with regard to the R2P, in particular in the prevention of the occurrences of crimes covered by the R2P;

- in July 2014 on the responsibility of the international community to assist States in implementing the R2P.

The importance of the role of the UNHRC in the implementation of the R2P has been emphasised by the UNHCHR and taken seriously by the UNHRC, in particular in the recognition of early warning signs, and the need for a timely response to HRs crisis.[42]

On the basis of all the above documents the R2P has taken shape. Its main components are:

1 The R2P lies primarily with a State.

2 Crimes which are covered by the R2P are: genocide, war crimes, crimes against humanity and ethnic cleansing.

3 The R2P is based on three Pillars: the first concerns the responsibility to prevent, the second concerns the responsibility to react, and the third concerns the responsibility to rebuild; Obligations deriving from each Pillar for a State, and for the international community have been clarified by the annual reports of the UNS-G and debates at the UNGA.

4 If all non forceable measures fail, military intervention to enforce the R2P may be taken. This is, however a last resort measure and must comply with the principles set out in the 2004 High-Level Panel Report (see above).

The UNSC has referred to the R2P on many occasions when adopting resolutions under Chapter VII: three times in 2006, once in 2009, six times in 2011, twice in 2012, seven times in 2013 and at least four times in 2014.

---

41 A/RES/63/308.
42 A/HC/22.

16.2.7 Assessment of the R2P

The most problematic aspects of the R2P are, first, what occurs when the UNSC fails to take measures, and second the proper supervision by the UNSC of the use of military measures authorised by it. Both aspects are examined below.

The UNSC has consistently failed to authorise measures both non-forceable and forceable to respond to the humanitarian crisis in Syria. This is because China and Russia (as well as some non-permanent members of the UNSC) have vetoed any resolution to this effect.

The attitude of permanent members and non-permanent members of the UNSC must be seen in the light of the developments concerning the 2011crisis in Libya. In February 2011, a political protest had taken place in Tripoli, which spread to other cities, in particular to Bengazi. Protesters demanded the end of the 41-year reign of Qadhafi. Governmental forces brutally attacked the protesters. When they organised themselves and formed the National Transitional Council in Bengazi, Qadhafi publicly expressed his intention to massacre the population of Bengazi. Subsequently his forces began targeting civilians in aerial bombardments. The UNSC, the EU and several States imposed various sanctions on Qadhafi, his family and his regime. None worked. In these circumstances, the UNSC, referring to its obligations deriving from the R2P, adopted on 17 March 2011 Resolution 1973 establishing a no-fly zone to protect civilians in Libya and authorising Member States, in cooperation with the UNSC to take 'all necessary measures (. . .) to protect civilians and civilian populated areas under threat'.[43] The Resolution was adopted with abstention by two permanent members Russia and China, and non-permanent members: India, Brazil and Germany. A Coalition of States, made up of 15 members of NATO led by the US, Sweden, Jordan, Qatar and the United Arab Emirates was formed to enforce Resolution 1973. The enforcement action by the Coalition was successful but criticised on the following grounds.

First, the Coalition overstepped its mandate in that in addition to protecting civilians it substantially helped the rebel forces to overturn the Qadhafi regime. It is well documented that the Coalition continued its mission long after the immediate threat to civilians in Bengazi was averted and Qadhafi's forces were in retreat.[44] Further, the Coalition provided training and supplied rebel forces with weapons, although rebels had been committing war crimes and crimes against humanity.[45]

Second, the Coalition's aerial bombardments were indiscriminate and caused civilian causalities.[46] These allegations were not investigated.

Perhaps, the most disappointing aspect of the intervention in Libya is its outcome. Libya has become a failed State.

It is submitted that no real progress can be achieved in the implementation of the R2P without establishing binding criteria on UNSC with regard to enforcement, or otherwise, of the R2P.

---

43 S/RES/1973.

44 J. Eyal, 'The Responsibility to Protect: A Chance Missed' in A.J. Johnson and S. Mueen (eds), *Short War, Long Shadow – The Political and Military Legacies of the 2011 Libya Campaign*, London: Royal United Services Institute, 2012, 53.

45 See the Report of the International Commission of Inquiry on Libya established by the UNHRC, A/HRC/17/44.

46 For the criticism of Libyan operation of NATO see M.E. O'Connell, 'How to Lose a Revolution', *E-International Relations*, 3 October 2011. Available at: www.e-ir.info/2011/10/03/how-to-lose-a-revolution (accessed 19 July 2014).

16.3 The role of the UNGA in the maintenance of international peace and security: the Uniting for Peace Resolution

The competences of the UNSC and the UNGA concerning the maintenance of international peace and security are set out in Articles 10, 11 14 and 24 of the UN Charter. The main provision concerning the role of the UNGA is contained in Article 11(2) which specifies that it may discuss any dispute or any situation relating to the maintenance of international peace and security and may make recommendations relating to them to the State or States concerned or to the UNSC or both. However, Article 12 imposes a limitation on the UNGA in that it provides that the UNGA is precluded from making any recommendation with regard to a dispute or a situation in respect of which the UNSC is exercising the functions assigned to it by the UN Charter.

The situation in Korea in 1950 (see Chapter 16.2.4.1) was the catalyst for the UNGA to play a new role in the collective security system, and to act independently of the UNSC in a situation where the UNSC was blocked by a veto of one or more of its permanent members and military action was ongoing.

In the Korean conflict, the creation of the unified command in Korea by the UNSC was only possible because of the fortuitous absence of the Soviet representative who boycotted the UNSC in June/July 1950. When he returned, his veto paralysed any further action on Korea. To respond to this, as well as to ensure that the UN would not be powerless in a future case similar to that of Korea, the Western countries, under the leadership of the US, examined methods whereby the UNGA could assume some of the responsibilities of the UNSC at times when use of the veto prevented it from acting. At that time, those countries were in the majority in the UNGA and it was therefore logical to make good use of the UNGA.

On 3 November 1950 the UNGA passed Resolution 377(V) entitled 'Uniting for Peace'[47] Part A of the Resolution states:

> if the Security Council because of lack of unanimity of the Permanent Members, fails to exercise its primary responsibility for the maintenance of international peace and security in any case where there appears to be a threat to the peace, breach of the peace, or act of aggression, the General Assembly shall consider the matter immediately with a view to making appropriate recommendations to members for collective measures, including in the case of a breach of the peace or act of aggression the use of armed force when necessary, to maintain or restore international peace and security. If not in session at the time, the General Assembly may meet in emergency special session ... Such emergency special session shall be called if requested by the Security Council on the vote of any seven Members, or by a majority of the Members of the United Nations.

Following the passing of the Resolution the UNGA established two bodies:

- a Peace Observation Commission which can be despatched to any troublespot and then advise the UNGA of any necessary action;[48]

- a Collective Measures Committee to co-ordinate actions taken on the basis of UNGA's recommendations.[49]

The justification for the UNGA assuming powers under Resolution 377(V) was that although Article 24 of the Charter gives the UNSC primary responsibility for the maintenance of international peace and security, it does not preclude the UNGA from exercising a secondary or residual responsibility.

---

47   UNGA Res 377 (V) (3 November 1950) UN Doc A/1775, 10.
48   On the basis of Part B of Resolution 377(1950).
49   On the basis of Part D of Resolution 377(1950).

The foundation of this justification is the wide scope of Article 10 of the Charter which enables the UNGA to discuss and make recommendations on any matter 'within the scope of the present Charter' in a situation where the UNSC is not exercising the functions assigned to it in accordance with Article 12 of the UN Charter.

Opponents of Resolution 377(V) argue that it is illegal and dangerous in that it amends the UN Charter in breach of its Articles 108 and 109, and that only the UNSC is entitled to take coercive action. Further, they submit that the Resolution is contrary to Article 12(1) of the UN Charter bearing in mind that even when paralysed the UNSC is still exercising its functions in that the relevant matters remain on its agenda and therefore the UNGA should not be allowed to act.

State practice shows that member States have accepted the new competence of the UNGA although there is controversy as to whether the Uniting for Peace Resolution has ever been used as a legal basis to recommend the use of force. In the Korean conflict, the two resolutions recommending such measures did not refer to Resolution 377(V) as such a reference was removed before their adoption. In subsequent resolutions, which are unclear on the issue of their relationship with Resolution 377(V), the UNGA has never recommended the use of force but has recommended other measures such as:

- cessation of all hostilities, in the Suez Canal crisis in 1956;

- imposition of sanctions on South Africa, after its illegal occupation of Namibia in 1981;

- cessation of all dealings with South Africa, in 1982, and with Israel in the same year, in order to isolate them;

- delivery of humanitarian aid by members of the UN, during the Suez Canal crisis in 1956;

- establishment of peacekeeping forces, with regard to the Suez Canal crises in 1956;

- preparation of an advisory opinion by the ICJ, following the construction of a wall by Israel in the occupied Palestinian territory in 2003 (see below).

The powers of the UNGA, as well as procedural matters regarding the use of Resolution 377(V), were clarified in two advisory opinions delivered by the ICJ. These are examined below.

THE CASE CONCERNING CERTAIN EXPENSES OF THE UNITED NATIONS (ARTICLE 17, PARAGRAPH 2, OF THE CHARTER) (ADVISORY OPINION)[50]

Facts:

Some members of the UN fell seriously behind in the payment of the financial contributions assessed to them by the UNGA under Article 17 of the Charter. This was because they refused to accept the assessments in so far as they related to the financing of two peacekeeping operations: the United Nations Emergency Force (UNEF) and the United Nations Operations in Congo (ONUC) on the ground that both of those forces were unconstitutional and had been created illegally.

The UNGA requested the advice of the ICJ as to whether the expenses of the two forces were expenses of the UN within the meaning of Article 17(2) of the Charter.

---

50   [1962] ICJ Rep 151.

The main argument against the legality of the creation of UNEF by the UNGA was that 'action' in the field of international peace and security was the sole prerogative of the UNSC. The UNGA had argued that Article 24 of the Charter only gave the Security Council 'primary' responsibility for the maintenance of international peace and security. This did not therefore preclude the UNGA from exercising a secondary or residual responsibility, in accordance with its wide general powers under Articles 10 and 14 of the Charter. However, it was contended that if the UNGA did exercise such responsibility it would be in breach of that part of Article 11(2) of the Charter which states that any question relating to the maintenance of international peace and security upon which action is necessary must be referred to the UNSC.

Held:

The Court, in a majority opinion (nine votes to five) advised that the UNSC had 'primary' and not exclusive authority, and that while the taking of enforcement action was the exclusive prerogative of the UNSC under Chapter VII this did not prevent the UNGA from making recommendations under Articles 10 and 14. The limitation in Article 11(2) does not apply in such cases, since the 'action' referred to in that paragraph means only 'enforcement action' which is in the nature of coercive action directed against a State. The UNEF action was not, in the Court's view, enforcement action, but rather 'measures' recommended under Article 14.

Under Article 11(2) the UNGA is entitled to organise peacekeeping operations at the request or with the consent of the State concerned. Further, Article 14 can also be relied upon to recommend such an operation.

The ICJ extended the budgetary powers of the UNGA in that it held that all expenses incurred for fulfilling one of the purposes of the UN, even if the measures taken are not coercive, mandatory or binding upon the member States, are within the scope of Article 17(2).

Comment:

It is to be noted that the validity of the Congo operation was not contested because it was the UNSC and not the UNGA that initiated it, therefore the Uniting for Peace Resolution was not in issue. The main argument relating to the Congo was that the UNS-G had exceeded and abused the powers conferred on him. This allegation was rejected by the Court.

THE LEGAL CONSEQUENCES OF THE CONSTRUCTION OF A WALL ON THE OCCUPIED PALESTINIAN TERRITORY (ADVISORY OPINION)[51]

Facts:

(For detailed facts see Chapter 17.5.5.)

Following the beginning of the Second Intifada Israel started to build a 720 kilometres long wall in the region of the boundary between Israel and Palestine, which did not follow

---

51   [2004] ICJ Rep 136.

the de facto *boundary (commonly known as the Green line) fixed by the general armistice agreement of 3 April 1949 between Israel and Jordan. In particular, the wall deviated from the Green line so as, in effect, to include within the territory of Israel illegal Israeli settlements; fertile Palestinian land, and the most important, water wells in the region. Further the Green line often separated Palestinian lands from their owners. Additionally, the wall affected many thousands of Palestinians who, once the wall was completed, would be 'encircled', i.e. be living in enclaves between the wall and the Green Line. The movement of the Palestinian population was thus seriously restricted, or would be so, even though check-points were established through which Palestinians and their goods could pass. The justification of Israel for the construction of the wall was that Israel was acting in self-defence, or in the alternative, out of necessity, to protect its nationals from terrorist attacks originating in the Palestinian territory.*

When the US vetoed a Palestinian drafted resolution condemning the construction of the wall and seeking to ban Israel from extending it deep into the West Bank, the UNGA convened in 1997 its 10th emergency session that passed a resolution demanding that Israel stop and reverse the construction of the wall (Resolution ES-10/2 of 25 April 1997). When Israel refused to comply, the UNGA adopted Resolution ES-10/14 on 8 December 2003 requesting the ICJ to give an advisory opinion on the legal consequences of the construction of the wall.

Israel contested the competence of the UNGA to make the request. It submitted three arguments:

- *that the UNSC was actively engaged with the situation in Palestine and therefore the request by the UNGA for an advisory opinion was ultra vires;*
- *the request did not satisfy the requirements set out in Resolution 377(V)*
- *the emergency session was convened in breach of certain procedural requirements.*

Held:

The ICJ rejected all arguments submitted by Israel:

With regard to the first argument the ICJ held that a distinction must be made between a 'recommendation' within the meaning of Article 12 of the UN Charter and a request for an advisory opinion. These two measures are of a different legal nature and thus a request for an advisory opinion was not a 'recommendation'. The ICJ also noted that the interpretation given to Article 12 UN Charter had evolved, and 'that there has been an increasing tendency over time for the General Assembly and the Security Council to deal in parallel with the same matter concerning the maintenance of international peace and security'[52] The ICJ found this accepted practice to be consistent with Article 12 (1) UN Charter. Consequently, the UNGA had not exceeded its competence by submitting the request for an advisory opinion.

With regard to the second argument the ICJ examined the two conditions set out by Resolution 377(V) under which the UNGA is allowed to act. The first being that the UNSC has failed to exercise its primary responsibility for the maintenance of international peace and security as a result of the veto of one of its permanent members. The second being

---

52   Ibid, 149.

that the situation is one in which there appears to be a threat to the peace, breach of the peace, or act of aggression. The ICJ held that the UNSC was consistently unable to take any decision regarding the situation in the occupied Palestinian territory. Obviously the second condition was also met.

As to the third argument concerning procedural irregularities relating to the 10th Emergency session, namely that it was held at a time when a regular session of the UNGA was in progress, the ICJ held that this issue had no relevance to the validity of the request made by the UNGA. Although the possibility of holding both sessions at the same time was not originally contemplated, the ICJ could not identify any UN rule that would be violated by holding them simultaneously.

16.4 UN peacekeeping and its role in the maintenance of international peace and security

Peacekeeping is not mentioned in the UN Charter. It constitutes a practical answer to the malfunction of collective security as envisaged in the UN Charter.

During the term of office of Dag Hammarskjöld (1953–1961), as the UNS-G, peacekeeping became recognised as a *sui generis* UN contribution to the settlement of international disputes, although *de facto* peacekeeping operations had been carried out on a number of occasions before his entry into office. The UN, retroactively recognised the United Nations Truce Supervision Organisation (UNTSO) created in 1948 to supervise the truce in Palestine as its first peacekeeping operation. Dag Hammarskjöld referred to peacekeeping as belonging to 'Chapter Six and Half' of the Charter. Indeed, peacekeeping represents a middle way between the classical pattern of peaceful settlement of international disputes and collective security measures such as embargos or military actions.

The three fundamental principles of peacekeeping are: the impartiality of peacekeepers, the use of force by them in self-defence and to defend the mandate under which they operate, and the consent of the parties to the conflict to the deployment of peacekeepers.

The following three organs of the UN are involved in peacekeeping operations:

- The political aspects of peacekeeping operations are within the competence of the UNSC. Peacekeeping operations are normally established on the basis of UNSC resolutions which also determine the mandates of the peacekeepers and authorise their deployment.

- The financial aspect is within the domain of the UNGA which is in charge of the budget of individual operations. From 1965 the UNGA has been considering peacekeeping operations under the agenda item 'Comprehensive review of the whole question of peacekeeping operations in all their aspects'. From 1993, this item has been prepared by the Fourth Committee (one of the six main committees of the UNGA) which submits reports, and drafts resolutions/decisions/ recommendations, for adoption by the plenary sessions of the UNGA. As previously mentioned the UNGA may establish a peacekeeping operation under the Uniting for Peace Resolution (see Chapter.16.3).

- The UNS-G directs and manages UN peacekeeping operations and reports on their activities, problems and progress to the UNSC.

16.4.1 Present and past UN peacekeeping operations

Between 1948 and November 2014 the UN set up 69 peacekeeping operations, of which 56 were set up in the years 1990–2014. In November 2014 the UN was maintaining 16 peacekeeping operations.[53]

In respect of the peacekeeping operations current as at the end of August 2014, 122 countries have contributed a total of 118,000 military, police and civilian personnel. The terms and conditions of peacekeepers' service under the UN flag are negotiated between the UN and the governments that volunteer to send their military personnel for a specific mission.

Peacekeeping missions are dangerous – as at the end of September 2014 approximately 3,277 personnel had died while serving on missions. As a result of the increasing number of peacekeeper deaths and injuries the 1994 Convention on the Safety of United Nations and Associated Personnel[54] was adopted requiring contracting States to take all necessary measures to ensure the safety and security of UN personnel and premises.

16.4.2 The evolving nature of UN peacekeeping

Peacekeeping has evolved considerably. From the first peacekeeping operations to the end of the Cold War, the primary task was to prevent further fighting, to act as a buffer between hostile parties, and to help control any armed conflict.

Since the end of the Cold War peacekeeping has changed in terms of the nature of the missions, the composition of multinational forces and the contributions from member States.

The nature of missions has evolved as peacekeeping forces have been increasingly deployed in intra-state conflicts and civil wars. As a result, they have to operate in particularly hostile environments and, on occasions, their missions have exceeded the traditional peacekeeping and become peace-enforcing (see below).

UN peacekeeping operations often involve peacebuilding, in that their mandates include the creation of the foundations for sustainable peace and development in a host country. The multidimensional approach to peacekeeping was endorsed by the UNSC in Resolution 2086 (2013).[55] Its para 8 provides a non-exhaustive list of tasks that a multidimensional peacekeeping should aim to achieve.[56] Peacebuilding measures range from providing electoral support (e.g. Nepal, Afghanistan, Burundi, Haiti, Iraq, Liberia and the DRC) to administering the relevant territory by performing all the function of a State, e.g. UNTAET in East Timor and UNMIK in Kosovo (see Chapter 5.10).

16.4.2.1 Peace-enforcement by UN peacekeepers

UN peacekeeping missions in Somalia in 1992 and 1993 and in Bosnia-Herzegovina in 1994, challenged the traditional principles of peacekeeping, i.e. the impartiality of peacekeeping forces, the use of force only in self-defence, and the consent of parties to deployment of peacekeeping forces. For example in Bosnia-Herzegovina, the UNSC authorised the United Nations Protection Force (UNPROFOR) to use a wide range of coercive measures, including the use of military force not only in self-defence but also for the following purposes:

---

53   See the official website of IUN Peacekeeping at www.un.org/en/peacekeeping/
54   UN Doc A/49/742 (1994).
55   A/RES/2086 (2013).
56   On this topic see V. Bernard, *Multinational Operations and the Law-Great Expectations, Great Responsibilities* (2013) 95 International Review of the Red Cross, 475.

- to respond to attacks on 'safe havens' established by the UNSC in Sarajevo and around five Bosnian towns including Srebrenica;

- to enforce the 'no-fly' zone, banning all military flights over Bosnia and Herzegovina;

- to ensure a stable environment for the delivery of humanitarian assistance; and

- to protect convoys of released civilian detainees as and when requested by the International Committee of the Red Cross.

Some argue that UNPROFOR breached the principle of impartiality because it protected only one ethnic group: i.e. the Bosnian Muslims. Further, as there was neither a ceasefire nor the consent of all parties to the conflict to the deployment of UNPROFOR it has been argued that the deployment of UNPROFOR breached the principle of consent. It should be noted that the commitment of member States was weak. Instead of providing the necessary 30,000 troops States contributed a total of merely 7,000 troops with which UNPROFOR was unable to fully accomplish its mandate. Its biggest failure was that it did not prevent the 1995 massacre in Srebrenica.

The deficiencies of the operations in Bosnia-Herzegovina and in Somalia led to a period of reflection and self-examination regarding UN peacekeeping (see below). One of the outcomes is that the multidimensional nature of UN peacekeeping may require the use of force by UN peacekeepers to protect civilians in a host State. Of major importance is Resolution 2086 (2013) which, while reaffirming that the basic principles of peacekeeping are consent of the parties, impartiality and the use of force in self defence adds that the use of force is also permitted to defend the mandate. Para 8(h) of Resolution 2086 (2013) states that one of the main tasks of UN peacekeeping is to protect civilians, in particular when they are under imminent threat of physical violence. For example, Resolution 1925 (2010)[57] authorises UN peacekeepers in the DRC within the UN Stabilisation Mission in the DRC (MONUSCO) to use all necessary means to protect civilians, humanitarian personnel and human rights defenders, threatened with physical violence, in particular violence emanating from any of the parties engaged in the conflict.

Resolution 2098 (2013)[58] is unique in that it authorises the deployment of an International Brigade acting with the support of and in co-operation with, MONUSCO to use force to protect civilians in the eastern part of the DRC against foreign and domestic armed bands. The International Brigade, made up of 3,069 troops acting alone or in co-operation with the DRC authorities, has as its main task the protection of civilians by preventing the expansion of all armed groups, and neutralising and disarming them. The International Brigade is led by a Tanzanian general, and is made up of three infantry battalions, one artillery unit, one Special Forces unit and a reconnaissance unit. The Resolution also allows the use of drones or unmanned aerial vehicles (UAVs) to provide reconnaissance of militia activity to the International Brigade.

Resolution 2098 (2013) shows, on the one hand, the commitment of the UNSC to attack the roots of the problem, i.e. the existence of armed bands destabilizing the RDC without destruction of which no peace can be established in the DRC, and on the other, the acceptance that UN peacekeepers are sometimes peace enforcers within their multidimensional mandates.[59]

---

57   S/RES/1925(2010).

58   S/RES/2098 (2013).

59   On the protection of civilians by UN peacekeepers see H. Willmot, *The Protection of Civilians Mandate in UN Peacekeeping Operations: Reconciling Protection Concepts and Practices* (2013) 95 International Review of the Red Cross, 517.

16.4.2.2 Ongoing reform of UN peacekeeping

In 2000 the Panel on United Nations Peace Operations produced the so called Brahimi Report[60] that initiated a major and ongoing reform of peacekeeping. One objective of the reform is to ensure that after the withdrawal of peacekeeping forces a host State will not relapse into conflict as occurred in Haiti, Liberia and East Timor. In this respect, the UNSC established a Peacebuilding Commission under Resolution 1645 (2005), which works in co-operation with peacekeeping operations in host countries. While peacekeepers create a stable environment, peace-builders create the conditions for sustainable peace. Further the United Nations Department of Peacekeeping Operations (DPKO) and the Department of Field Support (DFS) initiated a major reform called 'Peace Operations 2010' in order to find the best ways of, on the one hand, strengthening and professionalising the planning, management and conduct of UN peacekeeping operations, and, on the other, responding to an ever-increasing demand for UN peacekeeping and peacebuilding. Building upon past reform the 'new Horizon Initiative' launched in 2009 has two objectives, first to assess the major policy and other dilemmas facing UN peacekeeping and, second, reinvigorate a dialogue with stakeholders on the best ways, by UN peacekeeping, to meet current and future challenges. As can be seen from the above UN peacekeeping is under constant review, reform and development.

It is important to note that the UN has reformed its rules relating to conduct and discipline of UN peacekeepers following allegations of sexual exploitation and abuses by UN peacekeepers in some host countries. The zero tolerance policy formulated by former UNS-G Kofi Annan applies.[61]

16.5 Regional arrangements and agencies and their role in the maintenance of international peace and security

Provisions concerning regional arrangements/agencies are contained in Articles 52 and 53 of the UN Charter.

Article 52 of the UN Charter provides:

(1) Nothing in the present Charter precludes the existence of regional arrangements or agencies for dealing with such matters relating to the maintenance of international peace and security as are appropriate for regional action, provided that such arrangements or agencies and their activities are consistent with the Purposes and Principles of the United Nations.

(2) The Members of the United Nations entering into such arrangements or constituting such agencies shall make every effort to achieve pacific settlement of local disputes through such regional arrangements or by such regional agencies before referring them to the Security Council.

(3) The Security Council shall encourage the development of pacific settlement of local disputes through such regional arrangements or by such regional agencies either on the initiative of the states concerned or by reference from the Security Council.

(4) This Article in no way impairs the application of Articles 34 and 35.

Article 53 provides:

(1) The Security Council shall, where appropriate, utilise such regional arrangements or agencies for enforcement action under its authority. But no enforcement action shall be taken under regional

---

60   Available at www.un.org/peace/reports/peace_operations (accessed 12 July 2014).
61   ST/SGB/2003/13.

arrangements or by regional agencies without the authorisation of the Security Council, with the exception of measures against any enemy state, as defined in paragraph 2 of this Article, provided for pursuant to Article 107 or in regional arrangements directed against renewal of aggressive policy on the part of any such state, until such time as the Organisation may, on request of the Government concerned, be charged with the responsibility for preventing further aggression by such a state.

(2) The term enemy state as used in paragraph 1 of this Article applies to any state which during the Second World War has been an enemy of any signatory of the present Charter.

Article 54 provides:

The Security Council shall at all times be kept fully informed of activities undertaken or in contemplation under regional arrangements or by regional agencies for the maintenance of international peace and security.

A regional arrangement or agency must therefore satisfy three conditions stipulated in Article 52:

- it must be concerned with the maintenance of international peace and security;

- it must be consistent with the Purposes and Principles of the UN:

- it must in some way be regional.

Chapter VIII of the UN Charter brings regional arrangements and agencies into the UN security system. No definition of regional arrangements/agency is given in the UN Charter. The lack of any definition has, however, proved beneficial as it allows any sort of arrangement or agency that contributes to the maintenance of peace and security to be fitted into the UN collective security system.[62]

Among organisations that have been recognised as falling within the scope of Chapter VIII are: the OAS; the Arab League; the AU, CARICOM the Islamic Conference; the Conference on Security and Co-operation in Europe (CSCE); the Commonwealth of Independent States (CIS); NATO; the Western European Union (WEU); and the EU. All have been accorded observer status by the UNGA.

Since the end of the Cold War the relevance of regional arrangements to the maintenance of peace and security has been greatly increased. Not only because of the changed political climate but also because, as examined above, of the changing nature of peacekeeping operations. The consequence of this is that, on the one hand, there is a growing demand for peacekeeping missions with increasingly complex and multidimensional mandates and, on the other, the UN's human and financial resources are diminishing. The need for greater involvement and co-operation of regional organizations with the UN was acknowledged by the 2005 World Summit, endorsed by the UNSC in its Resolution 1631 (2005) and further developed in the 2006 UNS-G's report entitled 'A Regional-Global Partnership: Challenges and Opportunities'.[63]

In practice, on many occasions, regional organisations have been authorised by the UNSC to enforce measures taken under Article 42 of the UN Charter, and to perform peacekeeping functions. Many so called peacekeeping hybrid operations have been established that are carried out by the UN in concert with a regional organisation, e.g. the AU in Darfur (since 2007).

The main drawbacks of allowing regional organisations to intervene, without specific and clearly defined authorisation from the UNSC, is that some operations tend to change their nature from peacekeeping to peace enforcement (e.g. the ECOWAS operation in Sierra Leone (1997–2000)) and

---

62   The 1995 UNS-G's Report to the UNGA, 1995 UNYB 116.
63   UN Doc A/61/204 (2006).

that the fundamental principle of peacekeeping –impartiality, may be undermined by a regional organisation intervening in a regional conflict (e.g. ECOWAS' operation in Liberia (1990–97), and CIS' operation in Georgia in 1994, and in Tajikistan in 1993).

16.5.1 Enforcement actions by regional arrangements/agencies without authorisation from the UNSC

Article 53 of the UN Charter states that 'no enforcement action shall be taken . . . by regional agencies without the authorisation of the Security Council'. On some occasions, this prohibition has not been observed. The most recent example is that of NATO's intervention in Kosovo (see Chapter 15.6.2). In the past, the OAS made attempts to overcome the prohibition in a number of ways. They are examined below.

16.5.1.1 Measures short of the use of force

In 1962 the OAS imposed economic sanctions against the Castro regime in Cuba. The USSR argued in the UNSC that such a measure constituted enforcement action that was illegal without the authorisation of the UNSC. However, the majority of UNSC members considered that economic sanctions did not constitute enforcement action. The OAS was merely doing collectively what any of its members could have done individually – as under customary law, every State is at liberty to sever its economic relations with another State.

16.5.1.2 Measures involving the use of force: the 1962 Cuban Missiles Crisis

The USSR was shipping to Cuba missiles and other weapons and materials that could be seen as a threat to US security. On 22 October 1962 President Kennedy announced America's intention to impose a 'strict quarantine on all offensive military equipment under shipment to Cuba'. (This was essentially a blockade, but a blockade can only exist if there is a state of war and as the term 'war' was not politically acceptable the US called it 'quarantine'.)

There was a great deal of concern on the part of the US to make what they were doing look to be consistent with international law. Two justifications were possible.

■ Self-defence under Article 51 of the UN Charter: the missiles in Cuba would pose a threat to the US. But the action taken by the US would be pre-emptive self-defence. They were not only stopping the missiles being fired but were also stopping them being placed in Cuba.

■ The US also had to consider the American missiles in Turkey aimed at Russia. Could Russia also attempt to remove these in self-defence? Reliance on Article 51 could therefore have created a dangerous precedent which could have been used by many other States. So politically it was felt that claiming self-defence was not the approach to take.

■ Regional action under Chapter VIII of the Charter: the quarantine would have been contrary to Article 2(4) of the Charter unless justified. Self-defence could not seriously be used as a justification. The alternative was to ask the UNSC to act under Chapter VII, but Russia would then use its veto. The UNGA could, of course, then decide to act in accordance with the Uniting for Peace Resolution but it was doubtful that the US would receive the support of the UNGA. The only alternative therefore was action under Chapter VIII of the Charter. This proved to be the best approach and it was followed.

On 23 October, at the suggestion of the US, the UNSC met and discussed the proposed quarantine but took no action. On the same day, the Council of the OAS adopted a resolution recommending that:

> Member states, in accordance with Articles 6 and 8 of the Inter-American Treaty of Reciprocal Assistance, take all measures, individually and collectively, including the use of armed force, which they may deem necessary to ensure that the Government of Cuba cannot continue to receive from the Sino-Soviet powers military material and related supplies which may threaten the peace and security of the Continent and to prevent the missiles in Cuba with offensive capability from ever becoming an active threat to the peace and security of the Continent.[64]

On 23 October the US President issued the following Proclamation:

> Any vessel or craft which may be proceeding towards Cuba may be intercepted and may be directed to identify itself, its cargo, equipment and stores and its ports of call, to stop, to lie to, to submit to visit and search, or to proceed as directed. Any vessel which fails or refuses to respond or to comply with directions shall be subject to being taken into custody.[65]

The US Deputy Legal Adviser, Meeker, justified the US action as follows:

> The quarantine was based on a collective judgment and recommendation of the American Republics made under the Rio Treaty. It was considered not to contravene Article 2, paragraph 4, because it was a measure adopted by a regional organisation in conformity with the provisions of Chapter VIII of the Charter. The purposes of the Organisation and its activities were considered to be consistent with the purposes and principles of the United Nations as provided in Article 52. This being the case, the quarantine would no more violate Article 2, paragraph 4, than measures voted for by the Council under Chapter VII, by the General Assembly under Articles 10 and 11, or taken by United Nations Members in conformity with Article 51.[66]

There was a problem, however, in that enforcement action under Article 53 could not be taken by regional agencies without the authorisation of the UNSC. The Soviet veto in the UNSC would have ensured that this authorisation was not given. The US therefore argued that the concept of 'enforcement action' subject to prior authorisation by the UNSC does not include measures falling short of the use of armed force or taken voluntarily. The US maintained that enforcement action – the term used in the Charter – meant enforcement action that was compulsory upon a State. If enforcement action was not compulsory but merely voluntary it would not be enforcement action within the meaning of the Charter. The action taken by the OAS was not therefore enforcement action within the meaning of the Charter because it was only a recommendation to States that was not binding upon them and thus any action taken by them was purely voluntary.

---

64   47 US Department of State Bulletin, 1962, 722.
65   47 US Department of State Bulletin, 1962, 717.
66   L. Meeker, *Defensive Quarantine and the Law* (1963) 57 AJIL, 515 at 523–524.

RECOMMENDED READING

Books

Bellamy, A.J. and Williams, P., *Understanding Peacekeeping*, Cambridge: Polity Press, 2010.

Bosco, D.L., *Five to Rule Them All: The UN Security Council and the Making of the Modern World*, Oxford: Oxford University Press, 2009.

Luck, E., *UN Security Council: Practice and Promise*, London: Routledge, 2006.

Manusama, K., *The United Nations Security Council in the Post-Cold War Era*, Leiden: Nijhoff, 2006.

Orford, A. *International Authority and the Responsibility to Protect*, Cambridge: Cambridge University Press, 2011.

de Wet, E., *The Chapter VII Powers of the United Nations Security Council*, Oxford: Hart, 2004.

Articles

Bernard, V., *Multinational Operations and the Law: Great Expectations, Great Responsibilities* (2013) 95 International Review of the Red Cross, 475.

de Bock, C., *The Crime of Aggression: Prospects and Perils for the Third World* (2014) 13/1 Chinese Journal of International Law, 99.

Chesterman, S., 'Humanitarian Intervention and R2P' in T.G. Weiss and R. Wilkinson (eds), *International Organization and Global Governance*, London/New York: Routledge, 2013, 488–499.

Fleck, D., *Searching for International Rules Applicable to Cyber Warfare: A Critical Assessment of the New Tallinn Manuel*, (2013) 18/2 Journal of Conflict and Security Law, 331.

Frowein, J.A., and Krisch, N., 'Articles 39–43' in B. Simma (ed.), *The Charter of the United Nations*, 2nd edn, Oxford: Oxford University Press, 717–763.

Hogg, J.F., *Peace-Keeping Costs and Charter Obligations: Implications of the International Court of Justice Decision on Certain Expenses of the United Nations* (1962) 62 Colum L Rev, 1230.

Meeker, L., *Defensive Quarantine and the Law* (1963) 57 AJIL, 515.

Stahn, C., *Between Law-breaking and Law-Making: Syria, Humanitarian Intervention and 'What the Law ought to Be'* (2014) 19/1 Journal of Conflict and Security Law, 25.

de Wet, E., *From Kadi to Nada: Judicial Techniques Favouring Human Rights over United Nations Security Council Sanctions* (2013) 12/4 Chinese Journal of International Law 787.

AIDE-MÉMOIRE

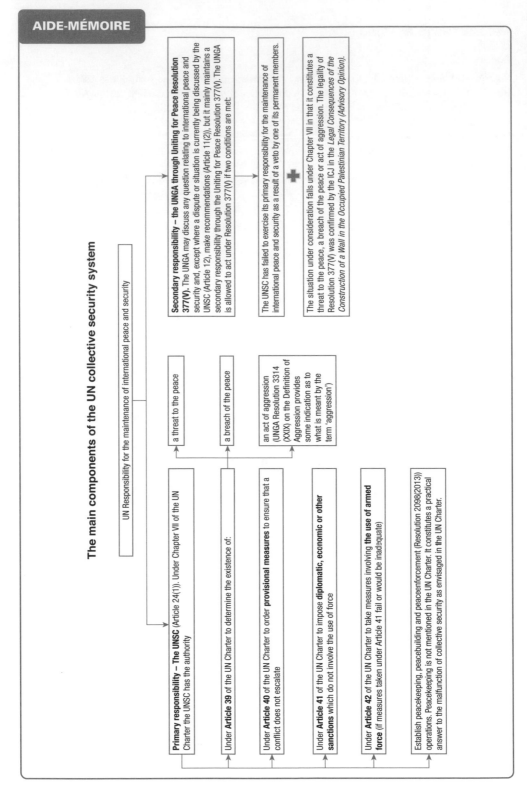

The main components of the UN collective security system

UN Responsibility for the maintenance of international peace and security

Primary responsibility – The UNSC (Article 24(1)). Under Chapter VII of the UN Charter the UNSC has the authority

Under **Article 39** of the UN Charter to determine the existence of:

- a threat to the peace
- a breach of the peace
- an act of aggression (UNGA Resolution 3314 (XXIX) on the Definition of Aggression provides some indication as to what is meant by the term 'aggression')

Under **Article 40** of the UN Charter to order **provisional measures** to ensure that a conflict does not escalate

Under **Article 41** of the UN Charter to impose **diplomatic, economic or other sanctions** which do not involve the use of force

Under **Article 42** of the UN Charter to take measures involving **the use of armed force** (if measures taken under Article 41 fail or would be inadequate)

Establish peacekeeping, peacebuilding and peaceenforcement (Resolution 2098(2013)) operations. Peacekeeping is not mentioned in the UN Charter. It constitutes a practical answer to the malfunction of collective security as envisaged in the UN Charter.

Secondary responsibility – the UNGA through Uniting for Peace Resolution 377(V). The UNGA may discuss any question relating to international peace and security and, except where a dispute or situation is currently being discussed by the UNSC (Article 12), make recommendations (Article 11(2)), but it mainly maintains a secondary responsibility through the Uniting for Peace Resolution 377(V). The UNGA is allowed to act under Resolution 377(V) if two conditions are met:

The UNSC has failed to exercise its primary responsibility for the maintenance of international peace and security as a result of a veto by one of its permanent members.

The situation under consideration falls under Chapter VII in that it constitutes a threat to the peace, a breach of the peace or act of aggression. The legality of Resolution 377(V) was confirmed by the ICJ in the *Legal Consequences of the Construction of a Wall in the Occupied Palestinian Territory (Advisory Opinion)*.

17

INTERNATIONAL HUMANITARIAN LAW (IHL)

CHAPTER OUTLINE

1 Introduction

IHL is a body of rules established by treaty and by custom designed to:

- restrict the methods and means of warfare employed by belligerents against each other. This area of IHL relates to the law of armed conflicts and was mainly developed by The Hague Conventions (The Hague law); and

- protect persons who are not, or are no longer, participating in hostilities, i.e. civilians, prisoners of war, the sick and wounded. This area of IHL concerns the protection of victims of armed conflicts and was primarily regulated by the four 1949 Geneva Conventions (the Geneva law).

The Hague law and the Geneva law were merged with the adoption of Protocols I and II to the Geneva Conventions in 1977.

2 The fundamental principles of IHL

These are of great importance because they fill gaps in IHL and all provisions and rules of IHL are interpreted and applied in their light.

A. The principle of humanity. This is embodied in the famous Martens Clause contained in the Preamble to the Hague Convention IV, which provides that in situations which are not covered by humanitarian law 'civilians and combatants remain under the protection and authority of the principles of international law derived from established custom, from the principles of humanity and from the dictates of public conscience'.

B. The principle of necessity. This provides legal justification for the use of force but outlaws any violence that goes beyond what is strictly necessary to achieve military objectives, i.e. any means or method of warfare that is not justified by military necessity.

C. The principle of proportionality determines whether the nature and degree of the actions taken are proportionate to the military advantage to be gained. Any kind or degree of force that exceeds what is needed to achieve the military objective is unlawful. The main function of the principle of proportionality is to strike a balance between the requirements of military necessity and the requirements of humanity.

D. The principle of the prohibition of use of weapons of a nature to cause superfluous injury or unnecessary suffering (see point 3A).

E. The principle of distinction between civilians and combatants. Under the principle of distinction the parties to a conflict must, at all times, distinguish the civilian population from combatants. The distinction is vital because civilians should be protected when in the hands of the enemy, and against attacks, and the effects of hostilities. However, they lose this protection if they 'directly participate in hostilities'.

F. The principle of independence of *jus in bello* from *jus ad bellum*. Three main arguments support the view that *jus in bello* and *jus ad bellum* should have separate existence. They are:

- Armed conflicts have not been eliminated despite the prohibition of the use of force contained in Article 2(4) of the UN Charter. Further, internal conflicts have become more frequent and more deadly than ever.

- The distinction between *jus ad bellum* and *jus in bello* is vital to ensure that belligerents are treated equally before IHL and that they observe the rules of IHL irrespective of the cause of a conflict.

- victims of armed conflicts are not responsible for violations of the prohibition of the use of force by their governments and need protection irrespective of the merits of their side.

3 The law relating to the conduct of armed conflicts (The Hague law)

The Hague law codifies and crystallises the customary rules of war and also clearly establishes that certain weapons, and certain methods of warfare are prohibited.

A. Prohibited weapons.

- chemical: are prohibited under the 1992 Convention on the Prohibition of the Development, Production, Stockpiling and Use of Chemical Weapons and on Their Destruction (CWC);

- biological: are prohibited under the 1971 Convention on the Prohibition of the Development, Production and Stockpiling of Bacteriological (Biological) and Toxin Weapons and on Their Destruction (BWC);

- nuclear: whether they are prohibited is unclear. The ICJ in the *Legality of the Threat or Use of Nuclear Weapons (Advisory Opinion)* stated that:

  > in view of the current state of international law, and of the elements of fact at its disposal, the Court cannot conclude definitely whether the threat or use of nuclear weapons would be lawful or unlawful in an extreme circumstance of self-defence, in which the very survival of a state would be at stake.

  This uncertainty enhances the importance of the 1968 Non-Proliferation Treaty; the 1996 Comprehensive Nuclear-Test-Ban Treaty (not yet in force) and the creation of nuclear-weapon-free-zones.

- conventional. There is no overall prohibition but many international treaties prohibit some of them. Among the relevant treaties the 1980 Convention on Prohibitions or Restrictions on the Use of Certain Conventional Weapons Which May be Deemed to be Excessively Injurious or to Have Indiscriminate Effects (CCW) has a special place. This Convention does not itself have any directly substantive provisions, but it constitutes an umbrella allowing protocols which ban specific conventional weapons to be annexed to it. So far 5 such protocols have been annexed.

The 1997 Ottawa Convention on the Prohibition of the Use, Stockpiling, Production and Transfer of Anti-personnel Mines and on Their Destruction, and the 2008 Oslo Convention on Cluster Munitions (CCM) complement the CCW.

B. Prohibited conduct. Protocol I expands on the prohibition of specific methods of warfare contained in Article 23 of the Regulations Respecting the Laws and Customs of War on Land, which Regulations are annexed to the Hague Convention IV. The following are, *inter alia*, unlawful: denial of quarter or to threaten an adversary therewith or to conduct hostilities on this basis; perfidy, but not the use of ruse; destruction and seizure of property of an enemy unless required by imperative military necessity (but, this does not apply to war booty); pillage; the use of starvation of civilian population; attacking persons who are *hors de combat*, i.e. persons who by choice, or by circumstances, no longer participate in hostilities; and the improper use of internationally recognised emblems (e.g. the emblem of the UN, and emblems used under the Geneva law: the red cross, the red crescent, and the red crystal). The use of targeted killings is not prohibited if carried out in conformity with the fundamental principles of IHL as stated in point 2 above.

4 The law relating to the protection of victims of armed conflicts (the Geneva law) – its origin and development

The Geneva law originates with two proposals made by Henri Dunant in his booklet *Memory of Solferino* published in 1862.

- the first called for the establishment of a voluntary relief society for the aid of those wounded on battlefields; and

- the second urged for the conclusion of an international agreement on the basis of which such a voluntary society might provide relief for the sick and injured in wartime.

Dunant's proposals led to the creation of the International Committee of the Red Cross (ICRC) and the adoption on 22 August 1864 of the first Geneva Convention for the Amelioration of the Condition of the Wounded in Armies in the Field. Subsequently, under the auspices of the ICRC many conventions aimed at protecting victims of armed conflict were concluded. After WWII the four Geneva Conventions were adopted (G-C I-IV). They have been ratified by 196 States. They are complemented by Additional Protocols I and II adopted in 1977, which merged the Geneva Law with The Hague law, and the 2005 Additional Protocol III.

5   The scope of application and the content of IHL

A.   Distinction between international and non-international conflicts. An international conflict is defined as an armed conflict between States (including a conflict where people are fighting against colonial domination and alien occupation, and against racist regimes in the exercise of their right of self-determination). According to the ICRC non-international conflicts 'are protracted armed confrontations occurring between governmental armed forces and the forces of one or more armed groups, or between such groups arising on the territory of a State [party to the Geneva Conventions]. The armed confrontation must reach a minimum level of intensity and the parties involved in the conflict must show a minimum of organisation'. The definitions of international and non-international conflicts contained in the relevant provisions of G-C I-IV and their Protocols have become subject to debate as to their appropriateness to deal with armed conflicts between a State and non-State actors such as ISIS, or Al-Qaeda and its affiliates. To non-international conflicts Article 3 common to the Geneva Conventions applies, and, in a situation where an armed group controls part of a territory both Article 3 and Protocol II apply if the State concerned has ratified it.

B.   G-C I provides detailed rules concerning the protection of the sick and wounded on land.

C.   G-C II provides detailed rules applicable to the sick, the wounded, and to shipwrecked armed forces at sea.

D.   G-C III concerns the treatment of prisoners of war (POWs). It is complemented by Protocol I that extends the categories of persons entitled to the status of combatant and, if they fall into the hands of the enemy, to the status of prisoners of war and provides some fundamental guarantees in respect of the treatment of persons in the power of a party to a conflict (Article 75). It is to be noted that G-C III does not apply to mercenaries and spies.

E.   G-C IV ensures the protection of civilians in times of war. It contains detailed provisions relating to the treatment of civilians who, at any time and in any manner whatsoever, find themselves (whether in occupied territory or in internment) in the hands of a party to a conflict of which they are not nationals. It also deals with the protection of civilians from the effects of hostilities. G-C IV applies to territories occupied by a party to a conflict. The concept of occupied territory was clarified by the ICJ in the *Case concerning Armed Activities on the Territory of the Congo (Democratic Republic of the Congo v Uganda)*. The obligations of an occupying power towards the civilian population were clarified in *the Legal Consequences of the Construction of a Wall by Israel in the Occupied Palestinian Territory (Advisory Opinion)*.

F. Protocol I seeks to ensure the protection of victims of international armed conflicts. It contains provisions concerning the protection of the wounded and sick, the methods and means of warfare, and the protection of civilian population and civilian objects from the effects of hostilities.

G. Protocol II applies to non-international conflicts. It seeks to ensure application of the basic rules of IHL to non-international conflicts, and to extend the scope of protection that, until its adoption, was insufficient under Article 3 common to G-C I-IV.

6 Breaches of IHL

Grave breaches are defined in Article 50 G-C I, Article 51 G-C II, Article 130 G-C III; Article 147 G-C IV and Articles 11(4), 85 and 86 of Protocol I.

With regard to Protocol II no grave breaches of its provisions are listed. It is assumed that domestic penal law is sufficient to punish the offenders. Article 6 of Protocol II offers an additional guarantee by restating the general rules on the prosecution and punishment of criminal offences related to armed conflicts.

If a State commits a grave breach of IHL it can be held responsible under international law (see Chapter 11). If an individual commits a grave breach of IHL he commits a criminal offence punishable through penal proceedings. Breaches that are not considered as grave are punished through disciplinary procedures

A. The enforcement of IHL at national level. IHL imposes an obligation on each contracting party to implement and enforce its provisions and confers on them quasi universal jurisdiction over a suspected offender. A contracting State must either prosecute or extradite such a person (see Chapter 9.7).

B. The enforcement of IHL at international level. This is through international courts such as the ICC, the ICTY, the ICTR or hybrid or mixed or internationalised criminal tribunals such as those established in Sierra Leone, East Timor, Kosovo and Cambodia, which are seated in the States where the crimes were committed, and have both local and international judges and prosecutors.

7 The role of the International Committee of the Red Cross (ICRC)

The ICRC was established in 1863. Its mission is to bring relief and assistance to the victims of armed conflicts and internal violence. It is detached from all political issues relating to conflicts. The ICRC is independent from any government (including the Swiss government) and from any international organisation. It initiates and develops IHL and disseminates knowledge of IHL. Further, it is the founder of the International Red Cross and Red Crescent Movement, the largest humanitarian network in the world.

17.1 Introduction

International law makes a distinction between rules concerning the resort to war (*jus ad bellum*) (see Chapter 15) and rules governing the conduct of war (*jus in bello*). IHL is concerned with *jus in bello*. IHL is a body of rules established by treaty and by custom designed to:

■ limit the methods and means of warfare. These rules relate to the law of armed conflicts and were mainly developed by the Hague Conventions[1] (The Hague law);

■ protect persons who are not, or no longer, participating in the hostilities. These rules concern the protection of victims of armed conflicts and were primarily regulated by the four Geneva Conventions of 1949 (the Geneva law).

The Hague law and the Geneva law were merged, with the adoption of the 1977 Additional Protocols I and II (thereafter referred to as Protocol I and Protocol II) to the Geneva Conventions, and therefore the distinction is now merely historical but is maintained in this chapter for pedagogical purposes.

There is an ongoing debate as to whether IHL should be updated. Many scholars, NGOs and politician believe that it is ill equipped to deal with twenty-first century challenges. Indeed since 1977 the context in which force is used has changed. In particular:

■ International wars have become less frequent, but local wars and internal conflicts occur more often then ever.

■ Wars have become shorter but more destructive taking into account modern military technology. Some weapons, e.g. nuclear weapons, are so powerful that their use will have a horrendous impact on humans and on the environment.

■ The development of modern weaponry means that wars are no longer confined to members of armed forces but may involve entire populations living in territories where hostilities are taking place.

■ Modern international law requires that the protection of HRs in peace-time is matched by the necessity of ensuring that individuals are treated with humanity in wartime.

■ The fight against terrorism requires the establishment of a new legal framework.

It is unlikely that any major reform of IHL will take place in the near future. However, IHL does not remain static. Since the end of the Cold War the major factors contributing to the development of IHL have been, and remain, as follows.

■ UNSC resolutions stating that large-scale violations of HRs and IHL constitute a threat to international peace, taking into account that local armed conflicts have a tendency to become international conflicts and have serious consequences on the international community as a whole. Examples are: UNSC Resolution 770 (1992) on Bosnia and Herzegovina; UNSC Resolution 794 (1992) on Somalia; UNSC Resolution 929 (1994) on Rwanda; and UNSC Resolution 1244 (1999) on Kosovo. In such circumstances the UNSC is empowered to take all measures at its disposal, in particular measures under Chapter VII of the UN Charter, to bring to an end such violations. The UNSC has authorised the use of force in several humanitarian disasters, and has set up two

---

1   The full text of all treaties mentioned in this chapter can be found at the official website of the International Committee of the Red Cross (ICRC) at www.icrc.org. For that reason no citations are provided in the footnotes of this chapter.

international criminal tribunals to deal with the most serious violations of HRs and IHL that took place in the former Yugoslavia and Rwanda.

■ The growing relationship between HRL and IHL. Internal conflicts in Cambodia, Rwanda and in the former Yugoslavia demonstrated that armed violence used in internal conflicts has no limitations. Atrocities committed in internal conflicts violate both HRL and IHL. HRL fills gaps in IHL, whenever necessary.

■ IHL has been developed not only through decisions of the UN and judgments of the ICJ, but also through international treaties. There is a growing number of States ready to accept important limitations upon their internal affairs. Among the most important treaties are those banning chemical and biological weapons; landmines; limiting proliferation of nuclear weapons; establishing the International Criminal Court (ICC); and protecting cultural property in the event of armed conflicts.

17.2 The Fundamental principles of IHL

The following principles are recognised by IHL as being of a fundamental nature:[2]

■ the principle of humanity;

■ the principle of military necessity;

■ the principle of proportionality;

■ the principle of the distinction between civilians and combatants;

■ the principle of prohibition of use of weapons of a nature to cause superfluous injury or unnecessary suffering;

■ the principle of independence of *jus in bello* from *jus ad bellum*.

The above principles fill gaps in IHL and all provisions and rules of IHL are interpreted and applied in their light. The principle of humanity and the principle of necessity are at the heart of IHL. From them are derived the principles of proportionality, the distinction between civilians and combatants and the prohibition of causing unnecessary suffering.

17.2.1 The principle of humanity

The principle of humanity in wartime finds its expression in the famous Martens clause contained in the Preamble to the Hague Convention IV (see Chapter 17.3), which states:

Until a more complete code of laws of war is issued, the High Contracting Parties think it right to declare that in cases not included in the Regulations adopted by them, populations and belligerents remain under the protection and empire of the principles of international law, as they result from usages established between civilised nations, from the laws of humanity, at the requirements of the public conscience.[3]

---

2   M. Sassòli and A. A. Bouvier, *How Does Law Protect in War?* Volume I, 2nd edn, ICRC: Geneva, 2006, 141–142.
3   Reprinted in D. Schindler and J. Toman, *The Laws of Armed Conflicts*, 3rd edn, Dordrecht/Geneva: Martinus Nijhoff Publisher/Henry Dunant Institute, 1988, 70.

The clause was named after Professor von Martens, a Russian delegate to the 1899 Hague Conference, who, during the Conference, made a declaration, subsequently incorporated into the Preamble, with a view to reaching a compromise between participants who could not agree as to whether civilians who took arms against an occupying force by forming *irregular military* formations (i.e. partisans and franc-tireurs) should be treated as civilians (and consequently when captured executed) or as combatants (and thus released after the termination of hostilities).

The interpretation of the Martens clause is subject to controversy. Under its narrowest interpretation it means that customary law continue to be applicable despite the adoption of a treaty norm. The middle of the road interpretation is that the clause provides that when particular conduct is not expressly prohibited it does not mean that it is permitted. According to the most extensive interpretation the clause means that conduct in armed conflict is not only judged according to treaties and customary law but also according to the principles of international law referred to by the clause.[4]

Professor Cassese, while agreeing that the clause is very confusing stated that the clause could operate on two levels, first as an interpretative device, i.e. in case of doubt IHL should be interpreted in accordance with standards of humanity and the dictates of the public conscience and second:

> the clause, while operating within the existing system of international sources, could serve to loosen – in relation solely to the specific field of humanitarian law – the requirements prescribed for *usus* [practice] while at the same time raising *opinio* [*opinio juris*] to a rank higher than that normally admitted.[5]

It is submitted that Professor Cassese's perception of the principle of humanity as an interpretative device accords with State practice and the practice of the ICRC. With respect to the second legal meaning of the principle of humanity, Professor Cassese argues that his interpretation is justified by the need for humanitarian considerations to prevail over military requirements in some areas of IHL, e.g. the use of nuclear weapons. According to him, in specific areas of IHL to wait for a practice to develop would undermine the very existence of IHL. His view is that when a group of States believe that there is a binding rule in international law or there is a social need for the observance of a rule, this attitude may be conducive to the formation of a customary rule, even when there is no widespread and consistent State practice, or even if there is no practice at all.[6]

The Martens clause was incorporated in treaties similar to the Hague Convention IV and appears in Article 1(2) of Protocol I. The ICJ in the *Legality of the Threat or Use of Nuclear Weapons (Advisory Opinion)*,[7] stated that the clause constitutes a rule of customary law and that 'it has proved to be an effective means of addressing the rapid evolution of military technology'.[8] However, the Court did not elaborate on the meaning of 'the laws of humanity'.

Pictet interpreted the 'laws of humanity' to mean that:

> capture is preferable to wounding an enemy, and wounding him better than killing him; that non-combatants shall be spared as far as possible; that wounds inflicted be as light as possible, so that

---

4   See R. Ticehurst, *The Martens Clause and the Laws of Armed Conflict* (1997) 317 International Review of the Red Cross, 125.

5   A. Cassese, *The Martens Clause: Half a Loaf or Simply Pie in the Sky* (2000) 11EJIL, 187.

6   Ibid, 214.

7   [1996] ICJ Rep 226.

8   Ibid, para 78.

the injured can be treated and cured; that wounds cause the least possible pain; that captivity be made as endurable as possible.[9]

Despite differing views, it can be said that the principle of humanity, as a general principle of IHL, establishes the requirement of minimal conditions of humanity applicable to all acts of warfare, and in particular to situations not covered by treaty provisions or customary law.

17.2.2 The principle of military necessity

The best definition of military necessity was provided by an American Military Tribunal in the 1948 *Hostage Case* in the following terms:

Military necessity permits a belligerent, subject to the laws of war, to apply any amount and kind of force to compel the complete submission of the enemy with the least possible expenditure of time, life, and money.[10]

IHL accepts that winning a war or a battle is a legitimate objective and that to achieve the submission of an enemy as quickly as possible the use of lethal force is necessary. However, under the principle of necessity IHL prohibits any violence that goes beyond what is strictly necessary to achieve legitimate military objectives. This requires that a distinction be made between military objectives and civilian objectives or civilian objects given that IHL permits attack on military objectives but prohibits attack on civilian objectives or civilian object (see below the principle of distinction).

A definition of what constitutes a military objective is provided in Article 52(2) of Protocol I which sets out a two-pronged test which an object must satisfy cumulatively to be a military objective:

- ■ it must by its nature, location, destination or use effectively contribute to the military might of one party; and

- ■ its total or partial destruction, capture or neutralisation must offer military advantages to the other party.

Both criteria under Article 52(2) of Protocol I must be fulfilled 'in the circumstances ruling at the time'.

The above definition is very broad. It certainly encompasses military installations, equipment, and combatants, but does it include anything that may contribute to incapacitating an enemy, e.g. electricity production facilities, telecommunication systems, or radio or TV stations the destruction of which will demoralise an enemy? In this respect it can be said that:

- ■ With regard to dual use objects, i.e. those which can serve both civilian and military purposes, e.g. telecommunication systems and a power plant, the two-pronged test contained in Article 52(2) of Protocol I applies, and therefore even a secondary military use will turn an object into a military objective. However, under the principle of proportionality any attack on such an object may be unlawful if its destruction causes excessive harm to civilians.

---

9   J. Pictet, *Development and Principles of International Humanitarian Law*, Dordrecht/Geneva: Martinus Nijhoff and Henry Dunant Institute, 1985, 62.

10   The *Hostage Case (United States v List) (Judgment)* (19 February 1948) in *Trials of War Criminals before the Nuernberg Military Tribunals*, vol 11, Washington DC: US Government Printing Office, 1950, 1230, 1253, cited by *Y. Dinstein* in *Military Necessity*, Max Planck Encyclopaedia of Public International Law, Oxford, 2008 online edition, [www.mpepil.com] (accessed 11 November 2009), para 1.

- With regard to infrastructure which is particularly useful for the military such as bridges, railway lines, etc., views differ as to whether for example bridges are military objectives *per se* and can be attacked prior to any troop movements, or whether they become military objectives only when ground troops start using them.[11]

- As to objects which are granted special protection, IHL provides that some objects, such as objects necessary for the provision of medical relief and humanitarian relief, works and installations containing dangerous forces, materials and vehicles involved in peacekeeping operations, etc. should not be used for military purposes and thus should never become military objectives. However, if they are actually used for military purposes, they may be attacked only in limited circumstances and subject to precautionary measures taken by the attacker.

- With regard to objects the destruction of which will affect the morale of an enemy, e.g. a TV or a radio station, the prevailing view is that such objects are civilian and therefore should not be attacked.[12] However, during the invasion of Iraq by the US and its allies, the TV station in Bagdad was targeted many times as was the Iraqi Ministry of Information. There were also attacks on a TV station and a radio station in Belgrade by NATO during its intervention in Kosovo. One justification for the Belgrade attacks was that the transmitters of the Belgrade TV station were integrated into the military system and were thus, in fact, military objectives.[13]

- As to objects which are of cultural value, the 1954 Convention for the Protection of Cultural Property in the Event of Armed Conflict imposes a permanent protection regime on such objects. However, in some circumstances it allows military necessity to supervene but this is subject to prior notification to the enemy and the requirement of prior visible identification of certain categories of cultural property.

The two-pronged test for the determination of military objectives is far from being perfect, but, nevertheless, it imposes the following constraints on the exercise of military necessity:

- The advantage must be a 'military' not a political advantage and therefore any attack which is not directed at contributing to the military defeat of the enemy will be unlawful as it is not intended for military purposes.

- The assessment of whether an object constitutes a military objective must be made 'in the circumstances ruling at the time', i.e. taking into account the current situation and not possible future developments, e.g. a toy factory may be in future converted into a weapons factory but at the moment it is a toy factory and therefore not a military objective. Otherwise any object could *in abstracto* become a military objective.

- Only actions which are indispensable to achieving a particular military objective are allowed and the means and methods of undertaking these actions are limited, e.g. military necessity can never justify the inflicting of suffering for the sake of suffering or revenge, or the use of poison or torture of POWs.

- Military necessity cannot justify violations of rules of IHL.

---

11   H.B. Robertson, 'The Principle of the Military Objective in the Law of Armed Conflict' in M.N. Schmitt (ed.), *The Law of Military Operations: Liber Amicorum Professor Jack Grunawalt*, Newport, RI: Naval War College Press, 1998, 197–223, 209.

12   Y. Dinstein, *The Conduct of Hostilities under the Law of International Armed Conflict*, Cambridge: Cambridge University Press, 2004, 116.

13   For more on this topic see M Sassòli, 'Targeting: The Scope and Utility of the Concept of "Military Objectives" for the Protection of Civilians in Contemporary Armed Conflicts' in D. Wippmann and M. Evangelista (eds), *New Wars, New Laws? Applying the Laws of War in 21st Century Conflicts*, New York: Transnational Publishers, 2005, 181–210.

Military objectives may change during the course of a conflict as situations evolve. When some military objectives are destroyed the enemy will adapt other installations for the same purpose, whereupon they will in turn become legitimate military objectives.

IHL includes a number of presumptions that certain actions are unlawful and can only be justified by 'imperative military necessity'. For example Article 54(2) Protocol I, prohibits scorched earth policies. However, Article 54(5) legitimises these if required by 'imperative military necessity'. Thus, even though foodstuffs and agriculture may be indispensable to the survival of civilian population 'imperative military necessity' may prevail.[14] This line of reasoning was probably followed by the ICJ in the *Legality of the Threat or Use of Nuclear Weapons (Advisory Opinion)*, in which it stated that the use of nuclear weapons may be justified when the very survival of the State is seriously threatened (see Chapter 17.3.1.3).

The principle of military necessity allows the taking into account of the practical requirements of a military situation at any given moment, but IHL imposes constraints on its exercise. The assessment of whether requirements of military necessity justify a particular course of action is subject to the requirements of the fundamental principles of IHL, in particular the principles of humanity, proportionality, distinction, and the prohibition of use of weapons of a nature to cause superfluous injury or unnecessary suffering.

17.2.3 The principle of proportionality

The principle of proportionality determines whether the nature and degree of the actions taken are proportionate to the military advantage to be gained. Any kind or degree of force that exceeds what is needed to achieve the military objective is unlawful.

The main function of the principle of proportionality is to strike a balance between the requirements of military necessity and the requirements of humanity. The balancing test takes account, on the one hand, of the concrete and direct military advantage to be gained by a particular action and on the other, of the expected collateral damage that it will cause to civilians and civilian objects. Accordingly some action will be justified by military necessity, but will be unlawful because the method used may cause injury and suffering disproportionate to the military objective sought e.g. a huge loss of civilian life and damage to civilian property might result from an attack on a legitimate military target.

17.2.4 The principle of the prohibition of use of weapons of a nature to cause superfluous injury or unnecessary suffering

Under this principle some weapons have been banned. This topic is examined in depth in Chapter 17.3.1.

17.2.5 The principle of distinction between civilians and combatants

Under the principle of distinction the parties to a conflict must, at all times, distinguish the civilian population from combatants (Article 48 Protocol I). The distinction is vital because civilians should be protected when in the hands of the enemy and against attacks and effects of hostilities. However, civilians lose the protection if they 'directly participate in hostilities'. For that reason, both the concept

---

14 See W.V.O'Brien, *The Meaning of Military Necessity in International Law* (1957) 1 World Polity, 140. He examines the 'Hostage' case in which the Nuremberg Military Tribunal accepted that military necessity justified a scorched earth policy adopted by Germany in Finland to stall a Russian attack.

of 'civilian population' and the concept of 'direct participation in hostilities' are vital for the proper application of IHL. Further, the changing nature of armed conflicts has emphasised the need to clarify the meaning of both concepts. In particular:

■ In modern armed conflicts it is very difficult, and sometimes impossible, to distinguish between battlefields and areas of civilian habitation as sometimes they become one (Gaza City, Grozny or Mogadishu).

■ The military are often outsourcing military functions to civilians. This raises the question whether civilians (e.g. contractors and civilian intelligence services) are civilians or combatants for the purposes of IHL.

■ Combatants often fail to distinguish themselves from the civilian population, despite being required so to do under IHL, with the consequence that civilians are targets of arbitrary attacks.

■ The fight against terrorist organisations such as al-Qaeda entails that IHL should allow a State to attack members of such organisations on the ground of their membership alone, i.e. even when they do not directly participate in hostilities.

In order to respond to the above considerations, the ICRC initiated a study intended to clarify both the notion of 'direct participation' and that of 'civilian population'. In 2009 it published its recommendations in the 'Interpretive Guidance on the Notion of Direct Participation in Hostilities under International Humanitarian Law'.[15] The guidance:

■ Defines civilians as all persons who are not members of State armed forces or of organised armed groups belonging to a party to an armed conflict. The guidance specifies that State armed forces include all organised armed forces, groups or units under a command responsible to a State party to the conflict. With regard to non-international armed conflicts organised armed groups constitute the armed forces of a non-State party to the conflict. Civilians are not regarded as members of State armed forces or organised armed groups unless they assume a 'continuous combat function', i.e. unless they assume continuous function involving their direct participation in hostilities (see Chapter 17.5.1.3).

■ Defines direct participation. This occurs when civilians 'carry out acts, which aim to support one party to the conflict by directly causing harm to another party, either directly inflicting death, injury or destruction, or by directly harming the enemy's military operations or capacity'.[16] This means that they are protected when they indirectly participate in hostilities, e.g. when they provide financial support to the war efforts, or work in a factory producing weapons, but not when they participate directly, e.g. kill military personnel of an enemy or commit acts of sabotage. As it is not easy to decide whether a civilian has directly or indirectly participated in hostilities, the guidance provides that any doubt must be resolved in favour of the person concerned.

When civilians who directly participate in hostilities are captured they have no entitlement to the status of POWs with the consequence that they can be punished for their mere participation in hostilities. Combatants, however, cannot be punished for such participation.

Protocol I prohibits both direct and indiscriminate attacks on the civilian population (Article 51(4)), reprisals (Article 51(6)), attacks against objects indispensable to the survival of civilians (Article 54),

---

15   Geneva: ICRC Publication, 2009, see the official website of the ICRC at www.icrc.org (accessed 9 July 2014).
16   Ibid.

and 'the use of methods or means of warfare which are intended or may be expected to cause . . . damage to the natural environment and thereby to prejudice the health or survival of the population' (Article 55(1)).

Civilians must not be subject to outrages upon personal dignity, tortured, raped, enslaved, used as hostages, or be discriminated against. Also, the parties to an armed conflict must take all feasible precautions in order to minimise deleterious effects of an attack and to prevent damage to civilian property as far as possible. This entails the obligation to warn the civilian population of an attack before it takes place if they are in an area where military objectives are located, and to choose weapons that are least likely to cause incidental loss of civilian life or incidental damage to civilian property. Further, belligerents must not allow children under the age of 15 to participate in hostilities or to be recruited into their armed forces.

Article 56 Protocol I prohibits any attack on works and installations containing dangerous forces even if they are military objectives 'if such attack may cause the release of dangerous forces and consequent severe losses among the civilian population'. Also military objectives located in the vicinity of those works or installations should not be attacked if such attacks will cause severe losses among the civilian population.

The rules examined above are applicable to both international and non-international conflicts (see Chapter 17.5.1). However, there are important differences between Protocols I and II. Some provisions contained in Protocol I are not reproduced in Protocol II, which applies to internal conflicts (e.g. the fundamental principle that means and methods of warfare are not unlimited, the definition of population, the prohibition of perfidy, the protection of civilian objects). This absence is deliberate. Contracting States were reluctant to reinforce the protection of civilian population taking into account that, under Protocol I, wars of liberation were classified as international conflicts. However, nowadays, HRL will fill gaps in IHL to ensure the appropriate protection of individuals in internal conflicts.

17.2.6 The principle of independence of *jus in bello* from *jus ad bellum*

There is a view that the traditional distinction in international law between rules concerning the resort to war (*jus ad bellum*) and rules governing the conduct of war (*jus in bello*) has lost its importance because war which was once considered as the normal way to resolve disputes was outlawed in international law, initially by the 1928 Kellogg-Briand Pact and then by Article 2(4) of the UN Charter.

The above view is, however, incorrect. The separate existence of *jus in bello* is necessary because, on the one hand, unfortunately, humanity has not eliminated armed conflicts and, on the other, only the separate existence of *jus in bello* and *jus ad bellum* ensures that belligerents are treated equally before IHL and that they observe the rules of IHL irrespective of the cause of a conflict.[17] Indeed, if *jus in bello* and *jus ad bellum* were merged it would be inevitable that the question would arise as to which party had breached the prohibition of the use of force enshrined in Article 2(4) of the UN Charter, with the consequence that either party might be tempted not to comply with IHL. For the 'aggressor' this would be because already being a guilty party by having breached Article 2(4) of the UN Charter further breaches of IHL might not weigh too heavily on its conscience. Additionally, as examples of victors being held accountable for breaches of IHL are rare the necessity to win would render very attractive the idea of resorting to prohibited means and methods of warfare. As to the

---

17   On this topic see. D. Bethlehem, *The Relationship between International Humanitarian Law and International Human Rights Law in Situations of Armed Conflict* (2013) 2/2 Cambridge Journal of International and Comparative Law, 180.

victim, there would be a temptation to claim that because it is fighting for a 'just cause' it has more rights and fewer obligations under IHL than the other party. IHL, itself, is not interested in apportioning any blame or in any justification for resort to force. The Preamble to Protocol I states that the Geneva Conventions and this Protocol 'must be fully applied in all circumstances ... without any adverse distinction based on the nature or origin of the armed conflict or on the causes espoused by or attributed to the Parties to the Conflict'.

Additional justifications for the distinction between *jus ad bellum* and *jus in bello* are that:

■ Victims of armed conflicts are not responsible for violations of the prohibition of the use of force by their governments and need protection irrespective of the merits of their side.

■ The practice of the UNSC shows that it is only with extreme reluctance that it determines, under Article 39 of the UN Charter, that an act of aggression has taken place (see Chapter 16.2.2.1). Further, in many cases it is difficult, without extensive investigation, to establish which party is the aggressor.

17.3   The law relating to the conduct of armed conflicts (The Hague law)

The cruelty of warfare in antiquity and in the Middle Ages was rarely limited. The winner had it all – the life and all the possessions of the loser, including his wife and children. Only a handful of military leaders and heads of State imposed a minimum standard of conduct of war upon their soldiers. One example of this is provided by Alexander the Great who in 333 BC ordered his soldiers to spare the civilian population of conquered areas and not to intentionally desecrate religious sites. In 70 BC the Roman commander Titus ensured the safe passage of women and children from Jerusalem when it was under siege. Also between ancient Greek city States some rules limiting the cruelty of wars were developed, e.g. if a city was captured, those who took refuge in a temple were to be spared, and prisoners were to be ransomed or exchanged, or at worst to be enslaved, but not killed (see Chapter.1.2.1.1).

In the Middle Ages there were some attempts to civilise the conduct of war, out of necessity rather than humanity. As captured soldiers were normally killed or enslaved (only knights could be freed upon paying ransom) they fought ferociously and desperately to preserve their life and freedom. In order to avoid making an enemy desperate, some Christian and Muslim leaders imposed limits on savagery in the conduct of wars. Furthermore, the teaching of Christianity and the rules of chivalry influenced some rulers who imposed on their armies certain rules of warfare. In 1386 King Richard II of England published the Ordinance for the Government of the Army that punished by death certain acts, such as violence against women and unarmed priests, the desecration of Churches and the burning of houses. These kinds of rules issued for internal purposes were copied and applied by other nations. Consequently, similar prohibitions can be found in the codes published by Ferdinand of Hungary in 1526, by Emperor Maximilian II in 1570 and by King Gustavus II Adolphus of Sweden in 1570.

In 1625 Hugo Grotius, the father of modern international law, wrote *On the Law of War and Peace*. His work set firm limits on the way in which hostilities should be conducted between belligerents and established the principle of humanitarian treatment of civilians during armed conflicts. It influenced his contemporaries as well as future rulers and leaders.

In the Age of Enlightenment a new perception of wars changed the manner in which they were conducted. Jean Jacques Rousseau in his *Du Contrat Social (Social Contract)* wrote that:

War then is a relation, not between man and man, but between state and state, and individuals are enemies only accidentally, not as men, nor even as citizens, but as soldiers ... The object of the war being the destruction of the hostile state, the other party has a right to kill its defenders while they are bearing arms; but as soon as they lay them down and surrender they become once more merely men, whose life no one has any right to take.[18]

Once the objective of war was identified it became clear that there was no need for unnecessary cruelty and that the civilian population should be protected as it played no role in hostilities. The ideas expressed by J.J. Rousseau and other writers of the Enlightment gained widespread acceptance.

In the next stage, governments started to codify the laws of war for internal use imposing some standards of behaviour on members of their armed forces. During the American civil war, President Abraham Lincoln issued the Lieber Code (Instructions for the Government of Armies of the United States in the Field, General Orders No 100, of 24 April 1863), which was drafted by Professor Francis Lieber and revised by a board of officers. The Code contained provisions relating to 'Protection of persons and especially women, of religion, the arts and sciences. Punishment of crimes against the inhabitants of hostile countries' (Articles 31–47), and provided for the humane treatment of prisoners of war (Articles 49–80). Besides being binding on American soldiers, the Code also influenced the drafting of military regulations of armies of other States. Such rules relating to the customs of war hardened into international customary rules that gradually became incorporated into international conventions.

The first multilateral treaty dealing with the conduct of war was the 1856 Declaration of Paris Respecting Maritime Law. It was followed by the 1864 Geneva Convention for the Amelioration of the Condition of the Wounded in Armies in the Field. Another important codification was the 1868 St Petersburg Declaration Renouncing the Use, in Time of War, of Explosive Projectiles under 400 Grammes Weight, which banned the use of such explosive projectiles. The Declaration, which is still in force, recognised that some weapons or methods of war that are likely to cause unnecessary suffering should be prohibited. This has become one of the fundamental principles of IHL.

In 1874 the government of Russia convened an international conference in Brussels that adopted the International Declaration Concerning the Laws and Customs of War. Although the declaration never entered into force for lack of ratifications it served as a source for the Regulations attached to the 1899 Hague Convention II with Respect to the Laws and Customs of War on Land (amended by the Second International Peace Conference in 1907, it became the Hague Convention IV), which contains in its Preamble the famous Martens clause (see Chapter 17.2.1).

The 1874 conference initiated a series of international conferences which provided a forum for discussions between governments and led to the adoption of numerous international instruments in this area. The First International Peace Conference took place in The Hague in 1899 at the invitation of Russia's Tsar Nicolas. The Conference adopted:

- Hague Convention I for the Pacific Settlement of International Disputes;

- Hague Convention II with Respect to the Laws and Customs of War on Land;

- Hague Convention III for the Adaptation to Maritime Warfare of the Principles of the Geneva Convention of 1864 on the Laws of War;

- Hague Convention IV Prohibiting Launching of Projectiles and Explosives from Balloons;

- Declaration I on the Launching of Projectiles and Explosives from Balloons;

- Declaration II on the Use of Projectiles the Object of Which is the Diffusion of Asphyxiating or Deleterious Gases;

---

18 Du Contract Social ou Principes de Droit Politique, Book 1 Chapter 4 Slavery, 1762 (G.D.H. Cole trans, 1976).

- Declaration III on the Use of Bullets Which Expand or Flatten Easily in the Human Body;

- The Final Act of the International Peace Conference 29 July 1899.

Following the First International Peace Conference States adopted two further conventions:

- The 1904 Convention for the Exemption of Hospital Ships, in Time of War, from Payment of All Dues and Taxes Imposed for the Benefit of the State;

- The 1906 Convention for the Amelioration of the Condition of the Wounded and Sick in Armies in the Field.

A Second Peace Conference took place in The Hague in 1907. The Conference adopted 13 conventions and one declaration. Most of the conventions have been recognised as customary law. The Conference codified the laws of naval warfare and adopted the following conventions:

- Hague Convention I for the Pacific Settlement of International Disputes;

- Hague Convention II on the Limitation of Employment of Force for Recovery of Contract Debts;

- Hague Convention III Relative to the Opening of Hostilities;

- Hague Convention IV Respecting the Laws and Customs of War on Land;

- Hague Convention V Concerning the Rights and Duties of Neutral Powers and Persons in Case of War on Land;

- Hague Convention VI Concerning the Status of Enemy Merchant Ships at the Outbreak of Hostilities;

- Hague Convention VII Concerning the Conversion of Merchant Ships into Warships;

- Hague Convention VIII Concerning the Laying of Automatic Submarine Contact Mines;

- Hague Convention IX Concerning Bombardment by Naval Forces in Time of War;

- Hague Convention X for the Adaptation to Maritime War of the Principles of the Geneva Convention;

- Hague Convention XI Concerning Certain Restrictions with Regard to the Exercise of the Right of Capture in Naval War;

- Hague Convention XII Concerning the Creation of an International Prize Court (which was never ratified);

- Hague Convention XIII Concerning the Rights and Duties of Neutral Powers in Naval War.

The Hague Peace Conferences did not set up any system to deal with violations of the principles established in the above instruments, rather they tried to impose some limitations on the use of force in international relations. In this respect two conventions were adopted: the Convention Respecting the Limitation on the Employment of Force for the Recovery of Contract Debt and The Hague Convention I for the Pacific Settlement of International Disputes 1899 which set up the Permanent Court of Arbitration (see Chapter 14.3.2).

The main contribution of The Hague Peace Conferences to the development of IHL was that they codified customary law on the conduct of warfare. Consequently, The Hague laws are not only binding between the contracting States, but being declaratory of customary international law, they are binding on all States. Some of them have been replaced but some are still in force. For example The Hague Convention IV Concerning the Laws and Customs of War on Land and the annexed Regulations are still applicable. Articles 42–56 of those Regulations constitute the principal text applicable to the government of occupied territory and the treatment of property in occupied territory.

The codification of international customary law clearly established that the means and methods of warfare are not unlimited.

17.3.1 Prohibited weapons

Among the weapons of mass destruction – chemical, biological and nuclear – only chemical and biological weapons are banned under international law. The matter of whether the use of nuclear weapons is prohibited is still unclear. As to conventional weapons only some of them are expressly prohibited.

It is important to note that UNSC Resolution 1540 (2004) adopted under Chapter VII imposes binding obligations on member States, *inter alia*, to refrain from supporting by any means non-State actors developing, acquiring, manufacturing, possessing, transporting, transferring or using nuclear, chemical or biological weapons and their delivery systems. It also requires that member States establish domestic controls to prevent the proliferation of such weapons, and their means of delivery, including by establishing appropriate controls over related materials. In order to supervise the implementation of Resolution 1540 a special '1540 Committee' was established by the UNSC. The consequence of Resolution 1540 is that many obligations imposed under it overlap with obligations under the relevant non-proliferation treaties and thus States which are not contracting parties to the relevant non-proliferation treaties are, under Resolution 1540 obliged to comply with many obligations deriving from these treaties.

17.3.1.1 Chemical weapons

A chemical weapon is a weapon that releases chemicals that kill or disable people. There are a great variety of chemicals: some, such as nerve gas, are lethal, some, such as tear gas, merely irritating. The oldest international agreement limiting the use of chemical weapons is the 1675 Franco-German agreement prohibiting the use of poison bullets. Some provisions of the 1874 Brussels Declaration Concerning the Laws and Customs of War prohibited the employment of poison, or poisoned weapons, and the use of arms, projectiles or material to cause unnecessary suffering. At the first International Peace Conference in The Hague in 1899 an agreement prohibiting the use of projectiles filled with poison gas was signed. Germany interpreted the agreement literally when it used chemical weapons during WWI in that chlorine gas was released from gas cylinders at Ypres but no projectiles were used. In response the Allied Powers also used chemical weapons. The use of chemical weapons during WWI resulted in 91,000 deaths and enormous suffering. This led the international community to ban them.

The 1925 Geneva Protocol for the Prohibition of the Use in War of Asphyxiating, Poisonous or Other Gases and of Bacteriological Methods of Warfare banned the use of chemical weapons but did not prohibit the development, production or possession of such weapons. During WWII chemical weapons were not used by either party. Since then Iraq violated the 1925 Geneva Protocol when it used chemical weapons in the 1980s in the war with Iran, and against the Kurdish population. Chemical weapons were also used against civilians including children on a relatively large scale in the Ghouta area of Damascus, Syria, on 21 August 2013.[19] It has not been established whether the government of

---

19   Report of the UN Mission to Investigate Allegations of the Use of Chemical Weapons in the Syrian Arab Republic, available at www.un.org/disarmament/content/slideshow/Secretary_General_Report_of_CW_Investigation.pdf (accessed 20 October 2014).

Syria, or rebels, used those chemical weapons. However, after chemical attacks in Syria, the Syrian government, under threat from US bombing, agreed to relinquish them (on this topic see Chapter 16.2.7.1). As a result, all chemical weapons declared by the Syrian government were removed and destroyed.[20] On 14 September 2013, Syria became a contracting party to the Chemical Weapon Convention (see below).

After WWII the UN Disarmament Commission (UNDC) put on its agenda the issue of chemical and biological weapons. The UNDC decided to treat these issues separately. In respect of chemical weapons an *ad hoc* working group was set up by the UNDC in 1980 which, after years of deliberations and discussions with representatives of governments and the civil chemical industry, produced an evolving draft convention in 1984. This was elaborated by the draft submitted by Australia in 1992.

On the basis of the above draft, on 3 September 1992 the Conference on Disarmament at Geneva adopted the final text of the Convention on the Prohibition of the Development, Production, Stockpiling and Use of Chemical Weapons and on Their Destruction (CWC). The CWC entered into force on 29 April 1997. As at 31 October 2014, 190 countries had ratified it.

Article II(1) of the CWC defines chemical weapons as all toxic chemicals and their precursors except when intended for purposes not prohibited under the Convention; munitions and devices, specifically designed to cause death or other harm through the toxic properties of those toxic chemicals which would be released as a result of the employment of such munitions and devices; and any equipment specifically designed for use directly in connection with the employment of chemical munitions and devices. Schedules to the CWC enumerate chemical weapons (the list is not exhaustive) which are to be verified under the CWC. Under Article I(1) of the CWC the contracting States undertake never under any circumstances:

(a)   to develop, produce, otherwise acquire, stockpile, or retain chemical weapons, or transfer, directly or indirectly, chemical weapons to anyone;

(b)   to use chemical weapons;

(c)   to engage in any military preparations to use chemical weapons;

(d)   to assist, encourage or induce, in any way, anyone to engage in any activity prohibited to a state party under this Convention.

A contracting State is bound under the CWC not only to destroy all chemical weapons under its jurisdiction but also those abandoned by it on the territory of another State party. The destruction must be done in a safe and environmentally friendly manner within 10 years of the CWC coming into force for the State concerned. The rate of destruction is determined in the CWC. Also facilities used to produce chemical weapons must be destroyed or converted for uses conforming with the CWC.

The Convention set up the Organisation for the Prohibition of Chemical Weapons (OPCW), which has its seat in The Hague, and is charged with the supervision of the implementation of the CWC in contracting States.

The OPCW employs inspectors who, at the request of any contracting party, are entitled to carry out, on short notice and without refusal, 'challenge' inspections at any facility or location which is under the jurisdiction of any other contracting party, to verify the compliance of that contracting party with the provisions of the CWC.

The destruction of chemical weapons and of facilities used to produce them (or their transformation) is also subject to verification by OPCW inspectors.

---

20   See the discussion at UNGA at its 69 session held on 24 October 2014. Available at www.un.org/press/en/2014/gadis3510.doc.htm (30 October 2014).

Under the CWC a contracting State is entitled to request assistance if attacked or threatened with chemical weapons. The Director-General of the OPCW will examine the request and decide on further action. Assistance may consist, *inter alia*, of the supply of detection, protection and decontamination equipment, medical antidotes and treatments, or inspections.

The CWC is the first arms control and non-proliferation treaty which imposes obligations on non-governmental businesses. Even if a contracting State does not manufacture chemical weapons, companies in a contracting State engaged in activities involving certain chemicals may be required to report to the relevant national authority responsible under the CWC for reporting to the OPCW and may be subject to inspections.

17.3.1.2   Biological weapons

Biological weapons are similar to chemical weapons except that they use microorganisms or biologically derived toxins instead of chemicals. Biological weapons have never been used in wars, although Japan did attempt to use them on a few Chinese villages during WWII. The use of biological weapons as a method of warfare was banned by the 1925 Geneva Protocol for the Prohibition of the Use in War of Asphyxiating, Poisonous or Other Gases and of Bacteriological Methods of Warfare.

The main contribution to the total ban on biological weapons came from the US when on 25 November 1969 President Richard Nixon declared that the US unilaterally and unconditionally renounced all methods of biological warfare using microorganisms and that the US's biological programme would be strictly confined to define defence measures such as immunisation. In 1970 the government of the US extended the ban to toxins. The example of the US was followed by Canada, Sweden and the UK. All declared that they had destroyed their existing stock and expressed their intention not to produce anymore. However, unilateral declarations are binding only on the States that make them. For that reason within the framework of the UNDC, negotiations and discussions were conducted in order to produce a binding treaty. Initially, the opposition of Communist countries blocked any progress. The breakthrough came on 30 March 1971 with the submission to the UNDC by the Soviet Union of a draft convention on the prohibition of biological weapons and toxins. This constituted a step towards a global agreement on the matter.

On 16 December 1971 the UNGA approved the Convention on the Prohibition of the Development, Production and Stockpiling of Bacteriological (Biological) and Toxin Weapons and on Their Destruction (BWC) by 110 votes. The Convention entered into force on 26 March 1975. At the time of writing 170 States have ratified the BWC.

Under the Convention contracting parties are bound neither to develop, produce and stockpile or acquire biological agents or toxins 'of types and in quantities that have no justification for prophylactic, protective and other peaceful purposes' nor weapons and means of delivery. All such material had to be destroyed by contracting Parties within nine months of the Convention's entry into force for that party.

The Convention provides for co-operation between contracting States. Review conferences provide a forum for such co-operation. The matter of verification of compliance with the Convention through inspections was discussed at a Special Conference held in September 1994. As a result, an *ad hoc* group was set up. Initially, its work on a Protocol to the BWC was approved by the contracting parties. This occurred mainly as a result of a growing suspicion that at least eight countries had been carrying out active biological programmes in breach of international law and a concern that terrorist organisations might try to acquire and use biological weapons. In 2001 the work on the Protocol was suspended on the grounds that no measure could provide assurances that such programmes were absent and that the Protocol could be abused for non-BWC related objectives.

17.3.1.3 Nuclear weapons

It is estimated that there is a global nuclear stockpile of 22.000 nuclear weapons and that over 2,000 nuclear tests have been conducted to date.[21]

The five declared nuclear weapons States are: China, France, Russia, the UK, and the US. *De facto* nuclear weapons States are: India; Israel; and Pakistan. After the second nuclear test conducted by North Korea on 25 May 2009, there is little doubt that this country has become a nuclear power. Iran is a potential nuclear weapons State. There are 433 nuclear reactors in 44 countries. Any country with a nuclear reactor is considered to have the capacity to produce nuclear weapons.

Nuclear weapons have only been used twice in warfare. That is in the bombings of Hiroshima and Nagasaki in 1945 with disastrous humanitarian effects. In Hiroshima, the blast, heat, fire and radiation killed 90,000 people almost immediately and 145,000 by the end of 1945. In Nagasaki the bomb killed immediately 40,000 and 70,000 by the end of 1945. Thousands died later as a result of radiation.

So far any attempt to ban nuclear weapons has been unsuccessful. Many scholars argue that the use of nuclear weapons is incompatible with the principle of humanity and the principle of the protection of civil populations. Indeed, customary international law starting with the 1868 St Petersburg Declaration prohibits the use of weapons causing unnecessary suffering. Non-tactical nuclear weapons may clearly cause unnecessary suffering and indiscriminately affect combatants and non-combatants.

The UNGA, in Resolution 1653 (XVI) of 21 November 1961 and Resolution 984 of 11 April 1995, unconditionally condemned the use of nuclear weapons.

In 2008, UNS-G Ban Ki-moon submitted a five-points plan to eliminate nuclear weapons by 2020. He considered that this can be achieved, if:

- The contracting parties to the Non-Proliferation of Nuclear Weapons Treaty (NPT) fulfil their obligations deriving from that treaty (see below).

- Permanent members of the UNSC assure non-nuclear weapons States that the latter would not be subjected to the use or threat of use of nuclear weapons.

- Universal membership in multilateral non-proliferation treaties is ensured, in particular, if the Comprehensive Nuclear-Test-Ban Treaty finally enters into force and if the Conference on Disarmament starts immediately negotiations on a fissile material treaty, without preconditions.

- Nuclear power States make public their efforts towards the elimination of nuclear weapons and also expand the amount of information about their nuclear arsenal.

- Other types of WMD are eliminated and new efforts are made to limit production and trade in conventional arms.[22]

The initiative of the UNS-G has been supported by the UNGA,[23] but so far has not brought any concrete achievement.

The matter of the legality of nuclear weapons was examined by the ICJ in the *Legality of the Threat or Use of Nuclear Weapons (Advisory Opinion).*[24]

---

21 See the official website of the UN Office of Disarmament Affairs at www.un.org/disarmament/WMD/Nuclear (accessed 31 October 2014).
22 Ban Ki-moon, *My Plan to Drop the Bomb*, The Washington Times, 6 August 2009.
23 A/Res/63/39 (2008).
24 [1996] ICJ Rep 226.

LEGALITY OF THE THREAT OR USE OF NUCLEAR WEAPONS (ADVISORY OPINION)

Facts:

The ICJ was asked by the World Health Organisation (WHO) to deliver an advisory opinion on the following question:

> *'In view of the health and environmental effects, would the use of nuclear weapons by a state in war or other armed conflict be a breach of its obligations under international law including the WHO Constitution?'*

The WHO being an international organisation is entitled to ask the ICJ for an advisory opinion, but the matter referred must be within the scope of activities of the requesting organisation (see Chapter 14.8). The UNGA, fearing that the question asked by the WHO was not sufficiently connected with the functions of the WHO, decided to ask the ICJ for an advisory opinion on the question: 'Is the threat or use of nuclear weapons in any circumstances permitted under international law?'

Held:

With regard to jurisdiction

In respect of its jurisdiction the ICJ confirmed that the UNGA was entitled to ask for an advisory opinion on the matter, taking into account the broad competence of the UNGA and its long-standing activities relating to disarmament and nuclear weapons. The fact that the question asked was not related to any particular dispute and was expressed in abstract terms did not prevent the ICJ from delivering an advisory opinion. In respect of the WHO, as expected, the ICJ rejected the request for an advisory opinion. The ICJ explained that none of the functions listed in the WHO constitution expressly referred to establishing the legality of any activity related to matters hazardous to health, or depended upon the legality of the situations in which the organisation must act. Under Article 2 of the WHO's constitution its main objective is 'the attainment by all people of the highest possible level of health'. Consequently, the ICJ stated that the WHO's mandate is to deal with effects on health of the use of nuclear weapons, or any other hazardous activity, and to take preventive measures protecting the health of people in a situation where nuclear weapons are used or such activities engaged in. The ICJ found that the request for an advisory opinion was not connected with the effects of the use of nuclear weapons but with the legality of the use of such weapons. It held that 'the legality or illegality of the use of nuclear weapons in no way determines the specific measures, regarding health or otherwise (studies, plans, procedures etc), which could be necessary in order to prevent or cure some of their effects.' Further, it was contrary to the principle of speciality, under which international organisations operate in their clearly established fields of competence, to recognise that the WHO had implied powers to address the question of the legality of the use of nuclear weapons. Consequently, the matter was outside the scope of the mandate of the WHO.

On the merits:

The ICJ held that:

- *There is neither in customary law nor in conventional law any specific authorisation of the threat or use of nuclear weapons (unanimously).*
- *There is neither in customary law nor in conventional law any comprehensive and universal prohibition of the threat or use of nuclear weapons as such (by 11 votes to 3).*
- *A threat of or the use of force by means of nuclear weapons which is in breach of Article 2(4) of the UN Charter and which fails to satisfy the requirements of Article 51 of the UN Charter is unlawful (unanimously).*
- *A threat of or the use of nuclear weapons must be compatible with the requirements of the rules of international humanitarian law. Two principles are fundamental in respect of the conduct of military operations: the prohibition of the use of weapons incapable of distinguishing between combatants and non-combatants; and the principle of humanity which prohibits the use of weapons causing unnecessary suffering. These principles are applicable to any armed conflicts irrespective of whether a particular State has ratified the relevant treaties because they constitute intransgressible principles of international customary law (unanimously).*

The conclusion reached by the ICJ (carried by the President's casting vote) was:

> *It follows from the above-mentioned requirements that the threat or use of nuclear weapons would generally be contrary to the rules of international law applicable to armed conflicts, and in particular the principles and rules of humanitarian law.*
>
> *However, in view of the current state of international law, and of the elements of fact at its disposal, the Court cannot conclude definitely whether the threat or use of nuclear weapons would be lawful or unlawful in an extreme circumstance of self-defence, in which the very survival of a state would be at stake.[25]*

Judge Higgins of the ICJ observed that, on the grounds of uncertainty in the present state of the law and facts, the ICJ pronounced, in fact, a non liquet on the issue of legality of threat or use of nuclear weapons.

The ICJ also held that there is an obligation to negotiate in good faith and to achieve complete nuclear disarmament. This obligation is twofold – it applies to the pursuit of negotiations and to their conclusion.

The above advisory opinion enhances the importance of the 1968 Non-Proliferation Treaty (NPT).[26]

---

25   Ibid, para 105.
26   729 UNTS 161.

A. The 1968 Non-Proliferation Treaty (NPT)

The NPT entered into force on 5 March 1970 and, as at 26 November 2014, had been ratified by 190 States. It creates a framework for preventing the spread of nuclear weapons, weapons technology and weapons expertise while promoting co-operation in the peaceful use of nuclear energy material.

The main objective of the NPT is to limit the number of States possessing nuclear weapons. Under the NPT States which possess nuclear weapons, i.e. those that had manufactured and exploded a nuclear weapon or other nuclear explosive device prior to 1 January 1967 (that is the five permanent members of the UNSC) are obliged not to transfer them, and non-nuclear States, not to acquire and not to manufacture nuclear weapons. The nuclear States are also obliged to negotiate effective measures leading to nuclear disarmament and for general and complete disarmament.

The NPT provides for an inspection body, i.e. the International Atomic Energy Agency (IAEA), a UN agency, based in Vienna. That Agency is charged with inspecting the nuclear power industry in contracting States in order to prevent any spread of nuclear material and any diversion of nuclear energy from peaceful use to nuclear weapons by a contracting State.

Until 1990 no serious attempts had been made by the nuclear powers to meet their obligations under the Treaty. The NPT requires that there be a review and extension conference 25 years after its entry into force. The Review Conference held in 1995 decided to extend the NPT indefinitely and unconditionally, and to take concrete measures to strengthen the non-proliferation regime and to provide assurance of compliance with non-proliferation undertakings. The Conference adopted Principles and Objectives for nuclear non-proliferation and disarmament which were further examined and developed by the NPT Review Conference held in 2000, and which were aimed at ensuring the full implementation of the NPT as well as its universality. The 2005 Review Conference failed to produce any consensus as to the implementation of the NPT as did the 2010 Review Conference.

The main problem with the NPT is that some countries which are in possession of nuclear weapons are not contracting parties. Israel, India, and Pakistan have neither signed the NPT nor the safeguards' agreement with IAEA.

It is to be noted that on 25 April 2014, the Marshall Islands, a non-nuclear weapons State party to the NPT, filed an application before the ICJ against the UK, Pakistan and India for their failure to fulfil their obligations relating to the negotiations in good faith of the cessation of the nuclear arms race at any early date, and to nuclear disarmament. The Marshall Islands submitted that this obligation is based on customary international law with regard to India and Pakistan, and in respect of the UK on customary international law and Article VI of the NPT which requires that all contracting parties pursue in good faith negotiations relating to the cessation of the nuclear arms race and to nuclear disarmament.[27] India, Pakistan and the UK have accepted compulsory jurisdiction of the ICJ under Article 36(2) of the Statute of the ICJ (see Chapter 14.7.3.4). The ICJ will have the first hearing on whether it has jurisdiction to adjudicate the cases in early 2015.

At the time of writing North Korea is of concern to the international community.The UNSC has imposed severe sanction on it for continuous development of its nuclear programmes and for carrying out nuclear tests. However, Iran, another country of concern, by signing a Joint Plan with six nations (the UK, the US, Russia, China, Germany and France) in November 2013, agreed to freeze its nuclear programme in exchange for temporary relief from UN and EU sanctions. The Plan came into force on 20 January 2014.

---

27   For the latest news see the official website of the ICJ.

B. Nuclear tests.

Closely related to non-proliferation is the matter of nuclear tests. The ICJ had an opportunity to deliver a judgment on the legality of nuclear weapons tests in the *Nuclear Tests Case (New Zealand v France) (Judgment)*,[28] but decided that the action of New Zealand was without object because of the undertaking submitted by France not to carry out further atmospheric nuclear tests. Paragraph 63 of the judgment stated that:

> Once the Court has found that a state has entered into a commitment concerning its future conduct it is not the Court's function to contemplate that it will not comply with it. However, the Court observes that if the basis of this Judgment were to be affected, the Applicant could request an examination of the situation in accordance with the provisions of the Statute.

On the basis of para 63 of the above judgment New Zealand brought proceedings against France in the Request for an Examination of the Situation in Accordance with Paragraph 63 of the Court's Judgment of 20 December 1974 in the *Nuclear Tests (New Zealand v France)(Order)*.[29]

REQUEST FOR AN EXAMINATION OF THE SITUATION IN ACCORDANCE WITH PARAGRAPH 63 OF THE COURT'S JUDGMENT OF 20 DECEMBER 1974 IN THE *NUCLEAR TESTS* (NEW ZEALAND *V* FRANCE) (ORDER)

Facts:

When France announced in 1995 its intention to conduct a final series of eight nuclear weapons tests in the South Pacific, New Zealand, on the basis of paragraph 63 of the 1974 judgment, requested the ICJ to resume the 1974 case. Australia, Samoa, the Solomon Islands, the Marshall Islands and the Federated States of Micronesia filed an application for permission to intervene. New Zealand also requested provisional measures. The ICJ restricted the issue it was willing to examine to the following question:

> *Do the Requests submitted to the Court by the Government of New Zealand on 21 August 1995 fall within the provisions of paragraph 63 of the Judgment of the Court of 20 December 1974 in the case concerning Nuclear Tests?*

Held:

The ICJ dismissed the request submitted by New Zealand and the application to intervene submitted by other States. The Court found that the procedure specified in paragraph 63 was applicable only if circumstances were to arise which affected the basis of the 1974 judgment. This was not the case, taking into account that the 1974 ICJ judgment concerned atmospheric nuclear tests while the new tests announced by France were related to a series of underground tests.

Comment:

France resumed its nuclear tests in 1996 under the fragile coral atoll of Mururoa in the South Pacific but due to international pressure aborted the test series at the sixth test. However,

---

28   [1974] ICJ Rep 457.
29   [1995] ICJ Rep 288.

> *the damage to the region inflicted by the French nuclear tests has been enormous. Global action consisting,* inter alia, *of the boycotting of French wine and cheese contributed to the termination of the French nuclear tests.*

The first attempt to prohibit nuclear tests had been the adoption of the 1963 Moscow Treaty Banning Nuclear Weapon Tests in the Atmosphere, in Outer Space and under Water. The Treaty was a failure for two reasons:

- it provided only a partial ban as underground testing was still allowed provided that radioactive debris from underground explosions was kept within the national territories; and

- many States, including two nuclear powers (France and China), did not ratify the Treaty.

In 1974 Russia and the US agreed to limit underground tests to a maximum explosive power of 150 kilotonnes from 31 March 1976, but nuclear tests for peaceful purposes were not included. They were the subject of a 1976 Russia-US Agreement. In 1992 the US Congress declared a moratorium on testing which was later extended by President Clinton. However, some States have continued nuclear tests. Nuclear explosions carried out by India and Pakistan were unanimously condemned by Resolution 1172 (1998) of the UNSC. Both States declared a moratorium on further testing.

A major step in banning nuclear tests was achieved by the UNGA when it adopted on 24 September 1996 the Comprehensive Nuclear-Test-Ban Treaty (CTBT). As at October 2014, 183 States had signed the Treaty and 163 had ratified it. As a prerequisite of its entry into force 44 States believed to have the capacity to build nuclear weapons, however crude, must ratify the Treaty. Nine States of those 44: China, the Democratic Peoples' Republic of Korea, Egypt, India, Indonesia, Iran, Israel, Pakistan and the US have not, as at the time of writing, ratified the Treaty. As a result, the Treaty is not in force. In accordance with Paragraph 2 of Article XIV of the CTBT States which have ratified the Convention upon the request of a majority of those States, may ask the UNS-G, the depository of the CTBT, to convene a Conference if the Treaty has not entered into force 3 years after the date of the anniversary of its opening for signature. Eight such Conferences took place.

If the CTBT ever comes into force it will prohibit any nuclear explosion whether for military or peaceful purposes and establish an organisation to supervise its implementation. It includes a Protocol which provides for an international monitoring system, on-site inspections and confidence-building measures.

C. Nuclear-Weapon-Free-Zones (NWFZ)

Another way leading to the elimination of all nuclear weapons is the establishment of internationally recognised NWFZ. The UNDC, at its 1999 session, unanimously adopted guidelines on the establishment of NWFZ on the basis of arrangements freely arrived at by the States of the region concerned.[30] The UNGA in Resolution 3472 B (1975) defined NWFZ as:

> any zone recognized as such by the General Assembly of the United Nations, which any group of States, in the free exercises of their sovereignty, has established by virtue of a treaty or convention whereby:

---

30   UN Doc A/54/42.

(a) The statute of total absence of nuclear weapons to which the zone shall be subject, including the procedure for the delimitation of the zone, is defined;

(b) An international system of verification and control is established to guarantee compliance with the obligations deriving from that statute.

So far the following arrangements creating NWFZ have been established:

■ The 1967 Thalelolco Treaty signed between 21 Latin American States which has made Latin America a NWFZ. It came into force on 22 April 1968. The Latin American States set up an Agency for the Prohibition of Nuclear Weapons in Latin America in order to ensure compliance of the contracting parties with the Treaty.

■ The 1985 Rarotonga Treaty which came into force on 11 December 1986 which established the South Pacific Nuclear-Weapon-Free Zone. The Treaty set up a Commission to oversee its implementation.

■ The 1995 Bangkok Treaty which created a NWFZ in South Asia. The contracting States are all the States in South East Asia, i.e. Brunei, Darussalam, Cambodia, Indonesia, Malaysia, Myanmar, the Philippines, Singapore, Thailand, Viet Nam, and their respective continental shelves and exclusive economic zones. A commission was also established to ensure compliance with its provision.

■ The 1996 Pelindaba Treaty, which entered into force on 15 July 2009, when Burundi deposited its instrument of ratification, established a NWFZ in Africa. The Treaty required 28 ratifications for its entry into force, Burundi was the 28th State. All 53 African States have signed the Treaty. Under the Treaty an African Commission on Nuclear Energy will be established to ensure that contracting States comply with the treaty provisions.

■ The treaty creating a NWFZ in Central Asia which entered into force on 21 March 2009. Five countries – Kazakhstan, Kyrgyzstan, Tajikistan, Turkmenistan and Uzbekistan – are parties to the Treaty. It is the first NWFZ treaty to require each party to comply with the CTBT, and to conclude and bring into force a Safeguards Agreement and Additional Protocol with IAEA within 18 months after the treaty's entry into force.

■ Mongolia has declared itself to be a nuclear free zone and this was recognised by the UNGA in its Resolution 55/33S on 'Mongolia's International Security and Nuclear Weapon Free Status'.

Under NWFZ Treaties the contracting States are encouraged to develop the research, production and use of nuclear energy for peaceful purposes. A protocol is annexed to treaties establishing a NWFZ which provides for nuclear power States to signify their co-operation in respecting the treaties. All nuclear power States have done so in respect of all the above-mentioned treaties.

Some States have unilaterally renounced the possibility of becoming nuclear powers although they have the potential to make nuclear weapons: Japan and Germany are among them.

D. Other areas free of nuclear weapons

On the basis of the following treaties certain areas are free of nuclear weapons:

■ The 1966 Treaty on Principles Governing the Activities of States in the Exploration and Use of Outer Space which prohibits the orbiting, installing and stationing of nuclear or other weapons of mass destruction anywhere in space. Celestial bodies must remain free from all military activities (in force since October 1967).

■ The 1959 Antarctic Treaty which 'denuclearised' the Antarctic (see Chapter 7.6.2).

■ The 1971 Seabed Treaty which prohibits the placing of weapons of mass destruction, or structures for storing, testing or launching such weapons, on the seabed and ocean floor or in their subsoil. It is more limited than the outer space treaty as it neither prohibits nuclear-armed submarines resting on the seabed nor the placement of military installations within territorial waters.

■ The 1979 Agreement Governing the Activities of States on the Moon and Other Celestial Bodies adopted by the UNGA in Resolution 34/68 which prohibits placing in orbit around the moon any nuclear and other weapons and prohibits any nuclear weapons on its surface. The Treaty entered into force in June 1984.

17.3.1.4 Conventional weapons

Use of some conventional weapons has been prohibited as being excessively inhumane. The following international instruments specifically ban some conventional weapons:

■ The 1868 St Petersburg Declaration Renouncing the Use, in Time of War, of Explosive Projectiles under 400 Grammes Weight. The Declaration was adopted by a conference convened by the Russian government. Its aim was to ban rifle bullets which exploded on impact with a human body, although explosive artillery shells remained lawful.

■ The 1899 Hague Declaration III, which prohibits the use of expanding bullets, was aimed at banning 'dum-dum' bullets as excessively cruel weapons.

■ Article 23(e) of the Regulations annexed to the 1907 Hague IV Convention Respecting the Laws and Customs of War on Land contains a general prohibition of the use of arms, projectiles or material calculated to cause unnecessary suffering.

■ The 1980 Convention on Prohibitions or Restrictions on the Use of Certain Conventional Weapons Which May be Deemed to be Excessively Injurious or to Have Indiscriminate Effects (CCW), also referred to as the Inhumane Weapons Convention entered into force on 2 December 1983. As at November 2014 it had been ratified by 118 States.

■ The 1997 Ottawa Convention on the Prohibition of the Use, Stockpiling, Production and Transfer of Anti-personnel Mines and on Their Destruction. It entered into force on 1 March 1999. As at November 2014, it is in force in 162 States.

■ The 2008 Convention on Cluster Munitions (CCM) which entered into force on 1 August 2010. As at 1 November 2014 it had been ratified by 88 States.

A. The 1980 Convention on Prohibitions or Restrictions on the Use of Certain Conventional Weapons Which May be Deemed to be Excessively Injurious or to Have Indiscriminate Effects (CCW)
The CCW contains only general provisions. In itself it does not prohibit or restrict the use of specific conventional weapons or weapons systems. It is, in effect, an umbrella covering protocols which set out prohibitions or restrictions. Under Article 1, the CCW applies to both international and non-international armed conflicts. Initially, the CCW included three protocols (Protocols I-III see below) which entered into force at the same time as the CCW. With time, CCW Review Conferences, which take place every 5 years, have adopted new protocols so expanding the CCW's scope of application. Each protocol is a separate treaty.

Under the CCW the following Protocols have been adopted:

- Protocol I on Non-Detectable Fragments. This prohibits any weapon the primary effect of which is to cause injury by fragments which in the human body escape detection by X-rays;

- Protocol II on Prohibitions or Restrictions on the Use of Mines, Booby Traps and Other Devices (this Protocol was amended by the First Review Conference). Protocol II prohibits indiscriminate use of landmines, booby traps and other devices and, in all circumstances, their deployment against civilians, but does not ban them for military purposes. Protocol II also requires the recording of the location of minefields and their removal after the termination of hostilities. Shortcomings of Protocol II were that it did not apply to civil war and it did not impose restrictions on the production and transfer of landmines, booby traps and other similar devices. For these reasons the Review Conference amended Protocol II. In its amended version it applies to both international and internal wars;

- Protocol III on Prohibitions or Restrictions on the Use of Incendiary Weapons;

- Protocol IV which was added in 1995 on Blinding Laser Weapons;

- Protocol V on Explosive Remnants of War (ERW).

The CCW was criticised for not providing a complete codification of customary rules relating to the use of dangerous weapons, and so failing to be applicable to a wide range of conventional weapons. However, the majority of States did not want to impose such comprehensive limitations. Accordingly, the Protocols apply only to certain weapons while permitting continued use of others, which are similarly harmful.

B. The 1997 Ottawa Convention on the Prohibition of the Use, Stockpiling, Production and
Transfer of Anti-personnel Mines and on Their Destruction

Antipersonnel mines are cheap and easy to use but expensive to find and disarm (about US $1,000 per mine). They attracted particular attention because of their use in Angola, Afghanistan, Cambodia and Bosnia. They were used by irregular armed forces and were left without being disarmed. Thus, they are still killing civilians long after the wars have ended.

In view of the shortcomings of amended Protocol II to the CCW, and taking into account the suffering that landmines cause to civilians, in particular the fact that one-third of the victims are children, public opinion and NGOs put a lot of pressure on governments to ban the use of landmines. This resulted in the adoption of the Convention on the Prohibition of the Use, Stockpiling, Production and Transfer of Anti-personnel Mines and on Their Destruction, which was signed in Ottawa in 1997.

Under the Ottawa Convention contracting parties are required never to use antipersonnel mines, and to abstain from developing, producing, acquiring, stockpiling, retaining or transferring landmines. The existing stockpiles must be destroyed within 4 years of the entry into force of the Convention for a contracting State. Further, each contracting State shall become a mine-free area within 10 years of the ratification of the Convention. It is obliged, until landmine clearance is completed, to take all necessary measures to protect civilians from landmines. Contracting parties are committed to offer assistance to each other and to take national measures to ensure the proper implementation of the Convention. Also, assistance must be provided to victims in terms of care, rehabilitation, and social and economic reintegration.

C. The 2008 Oslo Convention on Cluster Munitions (CCM)

Cluster weapons are those which disperse sub-munitions or small bombs over a wide area. They may be air-dropped or ground-launched and may explode or ignite after a delay, or fail to explode until touched by a person – most often a child. Article 2(2)of the CCM defines a cluster munition as 'a conventional munition that is designed to disperse or release explosive submunitions each weighing less than 20 kilograms, and includes those explosive submunitions'.

The Convention prohibits the use, stockpiling, production and transfer of cluster munitions. Each contracting State is required to clear areas contaminated with unexploded submunitions within 10 years of the Convention's entry into force for that State. It also agrees to destroy its cluster munitions stockpiles within 8 years. The Convention requires that contracting States provide assistance to cluster munitions victims including medical care, rehabilitation, psychological support, and social and economic inclusion measures.

Contracting States are obliged to take national measures to implement the Convention and submit mandatory and detailed reports including an annual report on all aspects of implementation of their obligations deriving from the Convention.

D. Non proliferation of conventional arms

Non-proliferation of conventional arms is a very important issue taking into account that such arms are acquired for use in internal repression or international aggression or for terrorist purposes. At international level, the Protocol against the Illicit Manufacturing of and Trafficking in Firearms, Their Parts and Components and Ammunition supplementing the UN Convention against Transnational Organized Crime (UNGA Resolution 55/255) provides a legal framework for controlling the proliferation of small arms. As at November 2014, the Protocol had been ratified by 111 States.

On the political level the relevant instrument is the Programme of Action to Prevent, Combat and Eradicate the Illicit Trade in Small Arms and Light Weapons in All Its aspects adopted by an International Conference organised by the UN in 2001 in New York.[31] The Programme of Action contains a wide range of political undertakings at national, regional and global levels. According to the UNS-G, progress in its implementation has been made but there are still obstacles to its full implementation.[32]

17.3.2 Prohibited conduct

Article 23 of the Regulations Respecting the Laws and Customs of War on Land (which Regulations are annexed to the 1907 Hague Convention IV Respecting the Laws and Customs of War on Land) prohibits the following:

(a) to employ poison or poisoned weapons;

(b) to kill or wound treacherously individuals belonging to the hostile nation or army;

(c) to kill or wound an enemy who, having laid down his arms, or having no longer means of defence, has surrendered at discretion;

(d) to declare that no quarter will be given;

(e) to employ arms, projectiles, or material calculated to cause unnecessary suffering;

(f) to make improper use of a flag of truce, of the national flag or of the military insignia and uniform of the enemy, as well as the distinctive badges of the Geneva Convention;

---

31   See Report of the United Nations Conference on the Illicit Trade in Small Arms and Light Weapons in All Its Aspects, New York, 9–20 July 2001 (A/CONF.192/15), chap IV, para 24.

32   See the UNS-G's report submitted to the UNSC in 2011 (S/2011/255).

(g) to destroy or seize the enemy's property, unless such destruction or seizure be imperatively demanded by the necessities of war;

(h) to declare abolished, suspended, or inadmissible in a court of law the rights and actions of the nationals of the hostile party. A belligerent is likewise forbidden to compel the nationals of the hostile party to take part in the operations of war directed against their own country, even if they were in the belligerent's service before the commencement of the war.

The above provision was complemented by Protocol I to the 1949 Geneva Conventions. The Protocol affirms the principle that the right of the parties to armed conflicts to choose methods or means of warfare is not unlimited (Article 35). It also clarifies and expands some provisions of Article 23 of the Regulations as follows:

- In respect of Article 23(d) on quarter, Article 40 Protocol I specifies that it is prohibited 'to order that there shall be no survivors, to threaten an adversary therewith or to conduct hostilities on this basis'.

- Article 37 Protocol I replaced the term 'treachery' by 'perfidy' and defined perfidy in the following terms:

  It is prohibited to kill, injure or capture an adversary by resort to perfidy. Acts inviting the confidence of an adversary to lead him to believe that he is entitled to, or is obliged to be accorded, protection under the rules of international law applicable in armed conflict, with intent to betray that confidence, shall constitute perfidy. The following acts are examples of perfidy:
  (a) the feigning of an intent to negotiate under a flag of truce or of a surrender;
  (b) the feigning of an incapacitation by wounds or sickness;
  (c) the feigning of civilian, non-combatant status; and
  (d) the feigning of protected status by the use of signs, emblems or uniforms of the United Nations or of neutral or other states not parties to the conflict.

- The use of ruses of war, as opposed to perfidy, has always been lawful. Article 37(2) Protocol I defines ruses as acts intended to mislead the other party or induce him to act recklessly, but which neither are perfidious because they do not invite the confidence of an adversary with respect to protection under the rules of international law applicable to armed conflicts nor constitute infringements of that law. Misinformation and the use of decoys or camouflage are 'ruses of war'.

- Under Article 42 it is prohibited to attack, during their descent, persons parachuting from an aircraft in distress. Once they touch the ground they must be given an opportunity to surrender before being attacked, unless such persons are engaged in a hostile act. However, airborne troops are not protected by this article.

- The Protocol prohibits improper use of distinctive emblems (Article 38) such as the emblem of the UN, the red cross, the red crescent or the red crystal provided for by the Geneva Conventions and their Protocol I and Protocol III. It also prohibits deliberate misuse of internationally recognised protective emblems, signs and signals such as the flag of truce and the protective emblem of cultural property covered by the 1954 Hague Convention.

- Protocol I extends its protection to cultural objects and places of worship (Article 53), to the natural environment (Article 55) and to works and installations containing dangerous forces such as dams, dykes and nuclear electrical generating stations (Article 56).

17.3.2.1 Targeted killings as a method of warfare

In recent years the issue of whether IHL allows targeted killings and the use of armed drones for carrying out such killings has raised many controversies,[33] in particular in the light of numerous targeted killings of terrorists carried out by the US using armed drones. In this respect it is important to note that the use of armed drones is not an issue under IHL. This is because armed drones fire conventional missiles and therefore are not different from other conventional weapons such as helicopters, or submarines. Thus the main issue is whether the IHL allows targeted killings, as a method of warfare, whether they are carried out by special forces of a State, e.g. the killing of Osama bin Laden by US special forces in 2011 in Pakistan (see Chapter 15.45.3), or effected by armed drones, e.g. the killing of Hakimullah Mehsud, the leader of the Pakistani Taliban in Pakistan in November 2013.

Targeted killings are not something new invented by the US and its allies. They were used during WWII by Soviet Russia and Germany, by Israel in the never ending Middle East conflict, and by the Viet Cong during the Vietnam war.

The lawfulness or otherwise of targeted killings was subject to a judgment of the Israeli Supreme Court in which it stated that targeted killings against non-State actors, although an exceptional method of warfare, are lawful provided they are carried out in compliance with stringent requirements. It held first that terrorists may be targeted when they are taking direct part in hostilities (see Chapter 17.5.1.3), and thus targeted killings may only be carried out at such a time, second, that the principle of proportionality must be respected, and third that:

> Each case should be examined prospectively by the military authorities and retrospectively in an independent investigation, and the findings should be based on the merits of the specific case. These findings will be subject to the scrutiny of the court.[34]

The judgment of the Supreme Court of Israel is in conformity with IHL. Under IHL targeted killings against non State actors are lawful if they comply with the fundamental principles of IHL law: the principle of military necessity, the principle of proportionality, and the principle of distinction between combatants and civilians. (see Chapter 17.2.5).

It is important to note that whether the campaign of targeted killings by the US in Afghanistan, Somalia, Yemen, Libya, Pakistan, etc., against al-Qaeda and their regional affiliates is within the scope of IHL, i.e. whether the conflict between the US and non-State actors can be classified as an international or non-international conflict within the meaning of the IHL, is a highly contested matter (see Chapter 17.5.1.3).

It is also important to note that IHL is neither concerned about lawfulness or otherwise of the use of force by either party to a conflict nor about the matter of whether targeted killings are in breach, or otherwise, of HRL.

17.4 The law relating to the protection of victims of armed conflicts (the Geneva law) – its origin and development

The Battle of Solferino between the Austro-Hungarian army and the Franco-Sardinian forces which took place on 24 June 1859 is considered as marking the beginning of IHL. A Swiss businessman,

---

33   See Report of the Special Rapporteur on Extrajudicial, Summary or Arbitrary Executions, P. Allston on 'Study on Targeted Killings', submitted to the UNHRC on 28 May 2010, (A/HRC/14/24/Add 6).

34   See The *Targeted Killing Case* before the Israeli Supreme Court sitting as the High Court of Justice, HCJ 769/02 *Public Committee Against Torture v Government of Israel* (2006) 2 Israel Law Reports (2006) 459–529 at 460.

Henri Dunant, happened to be in the vicinity of the battle. He was appalled by the large number of wounded being left to die because of the lack of medical attention. Together with some local women Henri Dunant organised some medical relief for the wounded, collected them from the battlefield, dressed their wounds, fed them and washed them. He could not forget what he saw. In 1862 he published an account of his experience under the title *Memory of Solferino* in which he made proposals:

- for the establishment of a voluntary relief society for the aid of those wounded in battlefields; and

- for the conclusion of an international agreement on the basis of which such voluntary societies might provide relief for the sick and injured in wartime.

Dunant's proposals led to the creation of the International Committee of the Red Cross (ICRC) which met for the first time on 17 February 1863 and the adoption on 22 August 1864 of the first Geneva Convention for the Amelioration of the Condition of the Wounded in Armies in the Field. By the end of the year the Convention had been ratified by France, Switzerland, Belgium, The Netherlands, Italy, Spain, Sweden, Norway, Denmark and the Grand Duchy of Baden. In 1882 the US became a contracting party to the Convention.

The 1864 Convention was limited in scope as it applied only to the sick and wounded in land battles. It did, however, establish the fundamental principles of IHL, such as the neutrality and impartiality of humanitarian aid to the sick and wounded and the protection of military medical personnel. The distinctive emblem of the red cross was recognised as an international protective symbol. Some countries, however, objected to the use of the red cross and adopted different emblems: the red crescent, the red lion and sun (Iran) and *de facto* not *de jure* the red star of David. (Israel). It is important to note that under Protocol III only three emblems are recognised by the ICRC: the red cross, the red crescent and the red crystal.

The 1864 Convention was tested during the Franco-Prussian War in 1870. During that war the ICRC set up the first information agency for families of wounded and captured soldiers. The Prussians and their allies understood and applied the Convention. This was not the case with the French. After the termination of hostilities all parties agreed that a better system should be put in place and, as a result, the Convention was substantially revised in 1906 and 1907. The revised version was applied during WWI. Despite some propaganda claims the 1907 Geneva Convention was well observed by all participants in WWI.

The idea of adopting a Convention protecting the sick, wounded and shipwrecked in naval battles was first proposed in 1868, after the naval victory of the Austro-Hungarians over the Italians at Lissa in 1868, which emphasised the need for the extension of the Geneva regime to naval warfare. The proposal was not successful at that time but was re-examined later by the First Hague Peace Conference and became the 1899 Hague Convention III for the Adaptation to Maritime Warfare of the Principles of the 1864 Geneva Convention on the Laws of War. The Hague Convention was revised in 1907 and, together with the 1909 London Declaration on the Rules of Naval Warfare, was applied during WWI.

After the sick and wounded in land and naval battles, the next category of persons upon whom the protection of humanitarian law was conferred was prisoners of war. The main provisions applicable to them were contained in an annex to the 1899 Hague Convention II with Respect to the Laws and Customs of War, revised by the second Hague Peace Conference. These provisions were applied during WWI and worked reasonably well. However, some gaps were discovered, in particular in respect of repatriation of POWs after the termination of hostilities. Their revision was urged by the ICRC. On the basis of a draft convention on the treatment of prisoners of war submitted by the ICRC the Geneva Convention on Treatment of Prisoners of War was adopted in 1929. The Convention divorced the treatment of POWs from the Hague law and set out fundamental principles in respect of POWs: they should be treated humanely at all times and be protected, in particular against violence and public curiosity, any reprisals against them are prohibited, they need only provide limited information when questioned etc. The 1929 Geneva Convention was the first to introduce a control mechanism verifying compliance of contracting States with its provisions.

The 1929 Geneva Convention was applied during WWII. There were some serious violations of the Convention on both sides, but in general it was, more or less, observed by the contracting parties. The main problem was with non-contracting parties. Before the outbreak of WWII 46 States, including Germany, the UK, France and the US, had ratified the 1929 Convention. However, the Soviet Union had not ratified it. Germany refused to apply the Convention to Soviet prisoners of war. It is believed that of 5.3 million Soviet prisoners of war 3.3 million died. They were treated inhumanely, often sent to concentration camps, and denied food and medical care. The treatment of German prisoners of war by the Soviet Union was similar, although in the case of the Soviet Union this was more a lack of care than a deliberate effort to impose inhumane treatment. It is estimated that one million German POWs died in captivity. Long after the end of WWII, German POWs were still kept in Russia. Their repatriation was settled in 1955. It took so long because their work in labour camps in Russia was very important for the reconstruction of the Soviet Union.

Before WWII the idea of protecting civilians during hostilities was not popular among governments. In 1934 at the International Red Cross Conference in Tokyo the ICRC submitted a proposal in this respect. An international conference to consider the matter was to be called in 1940. Unfortunately WWII interrupted any work in this area.

IHL as tested by WWII proved inadequate. It clearly needed a major revision and in any event required adjustment to accord with the Universal Declaration of Human Rights adopted by the UNGA on 10 December 1948 which recognised the importance of human rights in both peacetime and wartime (see Chapter 11.2.1). Indeed, this recognition of HRL has given a new impetus to the development of IHL. Most serious violations of IHL are also violations of HRL. However, with the creation of the UN, and the role of the UNSC as a guardian of peace and stability, the UN was not very keen on leading the revision of IHL. As a result, the ICRC, not the UN, prepared new conventions and the Swiss government convened an international conference with a view to their adoption. The conference took place in Geneva in 1949 and resulted in the adoption of four Conventions. They were not considered highly relevant, although they were of some importance in wars in Korea and Indochina in the early 1950s.

A new impetus was given to the Geneva Conventions by the UN in 1968. With new conflicts erupting in the 1960s, such as the war in Vietnam, the civil war in Biafra, the conflict between Israel and the Arab States, and the wars of national liberation in Africa, the relevance of IHL became obvious. From 1968 the UNGA adopted a number of resolutions calling for the application of the Geneva Conventions to wars of national liberation, regarding them as international armed conflicts. These resolutions paved the way for the adoption of Additional Protocols I and II which were drafted by the ICRC. They were adopted in 1977.

Since the end of the Cold War the relationship between IHL and HRL has become even closer because most armed conflicts have occurred internally.[35] During the Cold War internal conflicts, whether religious, ethnic or political, were kept under control by totalitarian regimes or external threats. With

---

35   L. Doswald-Becks and S. Vite, *International Humanitarian Law and Human Rights Law* (1993) 33 Intl Rev Red Cross, 94 and A. Okakhelashvili, *The Interaction between Human Rights and Humanitarian Law: Fragmentation, Conflict, Parallelism, or Convergence?* (2008) 19 EJIL, 161.

the collapse of totalitarian States such conflicts have continued to occur, but in the absence of former restraints they have become impossible to tame. It has become clear that only the international community can resolve them. Some attempts at resolving internal conflicts by the UN have been satisfactory, others have failed. The UN was successful, *inter alia*, in sending observer missions and peacekeeping forces to El Salvador, Cambodia and Mozambique. These operations were based on the consent of the parties involved in the conflicts. However, in some conflicts such operations were impossible or inadequate, i.e. in the former Yugoslavia, Somalia, Rwanda and Sierra Leone. In these conflicts however, the role of the international community was more effective at the post-conflict stage in ensuring the criminal justice process was brought to bear (see Chapter 5.12.2.2).

17.5   The scope of application and content of IHL

The main body of IHL is contained in the four 1949 Geneva Conventions and the 1977 (GC I-IV) Additional Protocols I and II. The G-C I-IV were signed in the Alabama Room at Geneva's town hall on 12 August 1949. As at 1 November 2014 they had been ratified by 196 States (including the 2014 ratification by the State of Palestine), virtually all States, i.e. by a greater number of States than are members of the UN.

These Conventions are as follows:

■ GC I for the Amelioration of the Condition of the Wounded and Sick in Armed Forces in the Field;

■ G-C II for the Amelioration of the Condition of Wounded, Sick and Shipwrecked Members of the Armed Forces at Sea;

■ G-C III Relative to the Treatment of Prisoners of War;

■ GC IV Relative to the Protection of Civilian Persons in Times of War.

The necessity of adapting IHL to changing circumstances, both in terms of technological developments, and the kind of conflicts that occurred after WWII, prompted the ICRC to propose the adoption of supplementary rules to G-C I-IV. In 1974 the Swiss government convened an international conference with a view to reaffirming and developing IHL. The Conference held four sessions. The ICRC invited certain national liberation movements to fully participate in the work of the Conference although they were not entitled to vote. At its final session on 8 June 1977 the Conference adopted two protocols:

■ Protocol I to G-C I-IV Relating to the Protection of Victims of International Armed Conflicts (Protocol I). As at 1 November 2014 it had been ratified by 174 States. Article 90 of Protocol I provides for establishment of an International Fact-Finding Commission with competence, *inter alia*, to enquire into facts alleged to be a grave breach or other serious violation of the Conventions. The contracting parties may declare, at any time, but normally at the time of signing, ratifying or acceding to Protocol I that they recognize the competence of the Commission in relation to any other Party accepting the same obligation. As at 1 November 2014, 76 States had made such declarations.

■ Protocol II to G-C I-IV Relating to the Protection of Victims of Non-International Armed Conflicts (Protocol II). As at 1 November 2014 it had achieved 1167 ratifications.

The latest addition to the Geneva Conventions regime is the adoption in 2005 of Protocol III which establishes an additional emblem – the red crystal – for use by the contracting parties and the International

Red Cross and Red Crescent Movement. The red crystal can be used by those countries which do not wish to use the red cross, or the red crescent emblems. Protocol III entered into force on 14 January 2007 and, at 1 November 2014, had been ratified by 68 States.

17.5.1 The types of conflict covered by IHL

IHL makes a distinction between international and non-international or internal conflicts. To international conflicts all provisions of IHL apply. To non-international conflicts, at the least Article 3 common to G-C I-IV applies and, in a situation where a party to a conflict controls part of a territory both Article 3 and Protocol II apply. Although *de lege ferenda* it might be thought that the protection of victims of non-international conflicts should be the same as that of victims of international conflicts, however, under IHL it differs. This is because States have been unwilling to treat conflicts between States (including conflicts where people are fighting against colonial domination, and alien occupation, and against racist regimes in the exercise of their right of self-determination) which are international conflicts, and conflicts which occur within State boundaries (between various groups fighting each other or the government) which are-non-international conflicts, in the same manner. However, the distinction between international and non-international armed conflicts has become problematic with the emergence of a new type of armed conflict, i.e. the global fight against terrorists.

17.5.1.1 International conflicts

The four Geneva Conventions together with Protocol I apply to international conflicts. Article 2, common to G-C I-IV, defines international conflicts as arising between two or more contracting States, even if a state of war is not recognised by one of them. Indeed, even if both contracting parties refuse to recognise a state of war the Conventions apply.

In order to ensure the largest possible application of IHL it applies in all cases of total or partial military occupation even if the occupation meets no armed resistance.[36]

If one of the parties to a conflict is not a contracting party to the Conventions, those Conventions, nevertheless, apply between the remaining contracting parties. Also if a non-contracting party in practice accepts and applies the Conventions all contracting parties involved are bound to observe them in relation to that party.

G-C I-IV were recently applied, for example, to conflicts in Afghanistan (2001–2002), in the Iraq war (2003–2004) and during the conflict between Russia and Georgia (2008).

The consequences of non-application of G-C I-IV to a non-contracting party who does not accept their *de facto* application have been attenuated taking into account that most rules of G-C I-IV are now regarded as customary international law and therefore are binding irrespective of their ratification by a State.

Article 1(3) Protocol I applies to conflicts defined by Article 1(4) of that Protocol, i.e. it applies to 'armed conflicts in which people are fighting against colonial domination and alien occupation and against racist regimes in the exercise of their right of self-determination'. This provision restricts the application of Protocol I to wars against colonial domination which is now mostly a thing of the past. It is uncertain whether Protocol I applies to armed conflicts in the context of self-determination outside colonial and neo-colonial conflicts.

---

36   Article 2(2) GC IV.

17.5.1.2 Non-international conflicts

According to the ICRC non-international armed conflicts:

> are protracted armed confrontations occurring between governmental armed forces and the forces of one or more armed groups, or between such groups arising on the territory of a State [party to the Geneva Conventions]. The armed confrontation must reach a minimum level of intensity and the parties involved in the conflict must show a minimum of organisation.[37]

The above definition requires that for a non-international conflict to be within the scope of IHL two criteria must be satisfied:

First, the armed confrontation must reach a minimum level of intensity. This is determined in the light of factual circumstances such as the duration and gravity of the armed clashes, the types of weaponry used, the number of casualties, the extent of destruction. Accordingly, there can be difficulty in determining the exact level of intensity and duration that a conflict must reach to go beyond 'internal disturbance and tensions', and became a non-international conflict within the meaning of IHL. Views differ on this issue. The ICTY in *Tadić*[38] held that the application of IHL is triggered when there is 'protracted armed violence'. The Report of the International Commission of Inquiry on Darfur to the UNS-G presented in January 2005 fully endorsed the judgment in *Tadić*.[39]

Second, the armed groups involved must show a minimum degree of organisation. According to the 2008 ICRC's Opinion: 'This means for example that these forces have to be under a certain command structure and have the capacity to sustain military operations'.

The above two criteria are applied to distinguish non-international conflicts from internal disturbances, such as riots, isolated and sporadic acts of violence and similar acts. Internal disturbances are regulated by domestic law enforcement rules, HRL and other applicable law.

Two sets of rules, in addition to customary international law, apply to non-international conflicts:

- Article 3 common to G-C I-IV. Its definition of non-international conflict is that it is an 'armed conflict of a non-international character occurring in the territory of one of the High Contracting parties'. Such a conflict may occur between governmental forces and non-governmental armed groups and between non-governmental armed groups. Until the adoption of Protocol II this was the only provision ensuring protection of victims of non-international conflicts.

- Protocol II. It contains a more restrictive definition of a non-international conflict because first, it states that it applies only to a conflict between governmental forces and rebel forces, and second, it requires that rebels 'must exercise such territorial control as to enable them to carry out sustained and concerted military operations and to implement this Protocol'.

The 2008 ICRC Opinion explains that the conditions for the application of Protocol II do not affect the conditions for the application of Article 3 common to G-C I-IV. This is because Protocol II develops and supplements Article 3 without modifying its condition of application. This means that Article 3 applies to all non-international conflicts which satisfy the criteria relating to the threshold of intensity of violence, and a minimum degree of organisation of an armed group, while Protocol II applies to

---

37   ICRC Opinion Paper March 2008 entitled 'How is the Term "Armed Conflict" defined in International Humanitarian Law'. Hereafter referred to as 2008 ICRC Opinion, available at www.icrc.org/eng/assets/files/other/opinion-paper-armed-conflict.pdf (accessed 7 June 2014).

38   It-94-1-AR72, ICTY Appeals Chamber, 2 October 1995, (Jurisdiction) para 70.

39   Available at www.un.org/News/dh/sudan/com_inq_darfur.pdf, paras 74–76 (accessed 26 August 2009).

conflicts which not only satisfy the condition for the application of Article 3, but also those which satisfy its own condition for application, i.e. the condition of territorial command.

When rebels or irregular groups are recognised as belligerents by their own State the internal conflict becomes, in law, international and is thus governed by the rules applicable to international conflicts. However, Protocol II states that its provisions cannot be invoked to alter the status of the parties. Therefore, the Protocol does not erode State sovereignty in that the Protocol's application does not imply recognition of belligerent status to irregular armed groups. As to third States they are free to decide whether they wish to recognise belligerency. If they do, they will retain a position of neutrality with regard to the parties to a conflict (there are some exceptions to this rule). In some circumstances, e.g. where parties are conducting hostilities on the high seas, recognition may be wise given that when an entity is recognised as a belligerent, it becomes a subject of international law and therefore may be held responsible for wrongful acts, by any State that has recognised it.

IHL on non-international conflicts makes no provision for a status of combatant or POW. This is because, in the context of internal violence, disturbance or civil war, no State will accept that the opposition might have some privileges which are granted exclusively to combatants in international conflicts. Whether, after termination of an internal conflict, a State decides to punish its opposition is a matter for that State to decide, but Article 6(5) of Protocol II states that if rebel forces comply with IHL the authority in power should consider, at the end of the conflict, the possibility of granting them the broadest possible amnesty.

The determination of what constitutes a non-international conflict has raised many controversies in the context of the global conflict between the US and al-Qaeda and its affiliates (see Chapter 17.5.1.3).

A. The protection granted under Article 3 common to G-C I-IV

Article 3 common to G-C I-IV provides:

> In the case of armed conflict not of an international character occurring in the territory of one of the High Contracting Parties, each Party to the conflict shall be bound to apply, as a minimum, the following provisions:
>
> (1) Persons taking no active part in the hostilities, including members of armed forces who have laid down their arms and those placed *hors de combat* by sickness, wounds, detention, or any other cause, shall in all circumstances be treated humanely, without any adverse distinction founded on race, colour, religion or faith, sex, birth or wealth, or any other similar criteria. To this end, the following acts are and shall remain prohibited at any time and in any place whatsoever with respect to the above-mentioned persons:
>
>   (a) violence to life and person, in particular murder of all kinds, mutilation, cruel treatment and torture;
>
>   (b) taking of hostages;
>
>   (c) outrages upon personal dignity, in particular humiliating and degrading treatment;
>
>   (d) the passing of sentences and the carrying out of execution without previous judgment pronounced by a regularly constituted court affording all the judicial guarantees which are recognised as indispensable by civilised peoples.
>
> (2) The wounded and sick shall be collected and cared for. An impartial humanitarian body, such as the International Committee of the Red Cross, may offer its services to the Parties to the conflict. The Parties to the conflict should further endeavour to bring into force, by means of special agreements, all or part of the other provisions of the present Convention. The application of the preceding provisions shall not affect the legal status of the parties to the conflict.

The minimum 'safety net' regime set out in Article 3 common to G-C I-IV is often considered as a 'mini treaty' ensuring the lowest level of protection applicable to non-international conflicts.

B. The protection granted under Protocol II

Protocol II is the first-ever international treaty which is devoted exclusively to victims of non-international conflicts. It considerably extends the minimum 'safety net' regime set out in Article 3 common to G-C I-IV in that:

■ It specifies in Articles 4 and 5 the content of fundamental humane treatment.

■ In specifies in Article 6 judicial guarantees in respect of prosecution and punishment of criminal offences related to an armed conflict.

■ It requires humane and non-discriminatory treatment of the wounded, sick and shipwrecked (Articles 7 and 8), and requires the parties to a conflict to search for and collect such persons from the opposing side as well as search for the missing and dead.

■ It contains specific rules relating to the protection of children (Article 4(3)) and medical and religious personal (Articles 9–10).

■ It imposes rules of conduct of hostilities ensuring: the protection of the civilian population against attacks (Article 13); the protection of objects indispensible for the survival of the civilian population (Article 14), the protection of works and installations containing dangerous forces (Article 15) and the protection of cultural objects (Article 16).

■ It prohibits forced movement of civilians (Article 17).

■ It provides that medical units and transports shall be respected and protected at all times and shall not be the object of attack (Article 11).

The material scope of application of Protocol II is disappointing. However, it must be noted that the limited protection granted to the parties is nowadays compensated by the application of HRL to internal conflicts.[40]

17.5.1.3 Is the 'war on terror' (under President Obama's administration referred to as the Overseas Contingency Operations (OCO)) an international or a non-international conflict?

The expression 'war on terror' coined by ex-US President George W. Bush is a misnomer. International law outlawed wars in Article 2(4) of the UN Charter and IHL replaced the term war with the word 'armed conflict'. The expression 'war on terror' was used by ex-US President George W. Bush for propaganda purposes, while his successor US President Obama is not very keen on this expression. Indeed, in March 2009 the Defence Department officially changed the name of relevant operations from 'Global War on Terror' to 'Overseas Contingency Operations'.[41]

For the purposes of the application of IHL it is important to determine whether the OCO should be classified as an international conflict or a non-international conflict or neither.

---

40 See R. Provost, *International Human Rights and Humanitarian Law*, Cambridge: Cambridge University Press, 2002.

41 S.Wilson and A. Kamen, *Global War On Terror' Is Given New Name, The Washington Post*, 25 March 2009, p A04.

The distinction between international and non-international conflicts is problematic in so far as new types of conflict are concerned, e.g. the conflict in the FRY where it was unclear whether the conflict was international, non-international or a mixture of both or an OCO. There is no doubt, in particular in the context of Isis and al-Qaeda, that non-State entities may be as powerful as States in their capacity to engage in violence or aggression and thus the use of 'the State' as a decisive trigger for the application of IHL is problematic. The global conflict between the US and al-Qaeda and its associates has many stages and aspects.

- With regard to the conflict in Afghanistan, the US had ratified G-C I-IV on 2 August 1955 and Afghanistan had done this on 26 September 1956. Consequently, at least from 7 October 2001 (if not from the 9/11 attacks) when the US started bombing Afghanistan, G-C I-IV were applicable. The fact that the Taliban was not recognised as the *de jure* government of Afghanistan by the US has no bearing either on the applicability of G-C I-IV or on the classification of the conflict as being international in nature.

- With regard to Iraq, both Iraq and the US are contracting parties to G-C I-IV and the US government has made many public statements recognising the applicability of international humanitarian law, in particular G-C III and IV, to 'Operation Iraqi Freedom' regarding the invasion of Iraq. Also, UNSC Resolution 1483 (2003) called upon all States to observe their obligations arising from G-C I-IV and the Hague Regulations of 1907 with regard to the conflict in Iraq.

- With regards to terrorists attacks on the US and its allies around the globe (e.g. the 7 July 2005 London bombings) the opinion of the UK Director of Public Prosecutions and head of the Crown Prosecution Service, at the time of the attack, Ken McDonald, highlighted the view that terrorist acts, irrespective of whether these crimes are collective or individual, are ordinary crimes. He stated that those responsible for acts of terror such as the 7 July 2005 London bombings are not 'soldiers' in a war, but 'inadequates' who should be dealt with by the criminal justice system.[42]

The position taken by the US Supreme Court in *Hamdan v Rumsfeld*[43] rendered in 2006 was that the 'war on terror' was not an international conflict within the meaning of Article 2 common to G-C I-IV and that any conflict which is not international must be covered by Article 3 common to G-C I-IV. This judgment seems to suggest, and many commentators agree, that the Court has classified the conflict as non-international.[44] However, the classification of the conflict as non-international raises many issues as explained below.

First, Article 3 common to G-C I-IV states that it applies to conflicts 'not of an international character' which occur 'in the territory of a High Contracting Party' One interpretation of this provision is that a conflict must be confined to the territory of one State. If any conflict spreads outside that territory it is international in nature. However, as international armed conflicts can only occur between States, a conflict which extends beyond the territory of one State against non-State actors is neither international nor non-international within the meaning of IHL but constitutes a new type of conflict, a hybrid conflict.[45] This interpretation raises the issue of what rules should apply to such a conflict?

42　*There is no War on Terror in the UK, says DPP*, The Times, 24 January 2007, p 12.

43　548 US 557 (2006).

44　See M. Sassòli, *Use and Abuse of the Laws of War in the 'War on Terrorism'* (2004) 22 Law and Inequality, 201, and S. Sivakumaran, *The Law of Non-international Armed Conflict*, Oxford: Oxford University Press, 2012, 229.

45　See D. Akande, 'Classification of Armed Conflicts: Relevant Legal Concepts' in E. Wilmshurst (ed.), *International Law and the Classification of Conflicts*, Oxford: Oxford University Press, 2012, Chapter 3.

Another interpretation is that the application of Article 3 is not confined to the territory of one State because the G-C I-IV have been universally ratified, and thus the phrase 'in the territory of one of the High Contracting Parties' has lost its significance. Literal interpretation of Article 3 entails that every armed conflict today takes place 'in the territory of one of the High Contracting Parties'.[46] This interpretation in favour of the geographical expansion of the scope of Article 3 is supported by the judgment of the ICTY in *Tadić*, and confirmed in subsequent judgments.[47] The ICTY held that a non-international armed conflict is not limited to the area of hostility but applies 'in the whole territory under the control of a party, irrespective of whether actual combat takes place there'.[48] Finally, the restrictive interpretation of the geographical scope of Article 3 is contrary to its object and purpose. To summarise, although it is uncertain whether the extraterritorial application of Article 3 is a rule of customary international law, State practice and views of many commentators indicate that IHL does not preclude the application of Article 3 to hostilities when non-State actors cross national borders.

Second, if Article 3 common to G-C I-IV applies to the global conflict between the US and al-Qaeda, does al-Qaeda satisfy the criteria set out in Article 3 in terms of a command structure and the capacity to sustain military operations?

These are factual matters, but it is submitted that al-Queda is sufficiently organised to satisfy the requirement of a command structure, and is certainly capable of sustaining military operations as evidenced by the 9/11 attacks. As to whether there is a sufficient link between al-Qaeda and its affiliates, such as Al-Qaeda in the Arabian Peninsula (AQAP), Al-Qaeda in the Islamic Maghreb, Al Shabaab in Sudan, and Al Qaeda in Iraq, to form a single party to a conflict, (a matter which is relevant to the determination of whether hostilities have reached a sufficient level to trigger the application of Article 3), uncertainty persists. Regrettably, IHL does not provide any guidance on how to identify parts of a group.[49]

Third, civilians, unless they take direct part in hostilities must be protected from any attacks. If non-State actors are refused the status of combatant they become civilians, and accordingly can only be attacked when they directly participate in hostilities. In this context it is of a great importance to determine the meaning of 'direct participation'. The ICCR in its 2009 *Interpretive Guidance on Direct Participation in Hostilities* (see Chapter.17.2.5) endorsed the 'continuous combat function' as a criterion under which membership of an organised armed group is not determined by having a membership card, but by 'whether a person assumes a continuous function for the group involving his or her direct participation in hostilities'.[50] Only persons who assume a continuous combat function can be members of an organised armed group for the purposes of IHL while those whose function is not combat, e.g. administration, or it is in a non-continuous manner (e.g. spontaneous or sporadic), are not. According to the ICCR Guidance the continuous combat function may be expressed through the carrying of uniforms or other signs, or through conduct, e.g. repeated direct participation in hostilities. Members of an organised armed group who perform a continuous combat function are military targets for the entire period during which they have that function irrespective of whether they exercise it or not. The Guidance specifies that persons whose function consists of purchasing, smuggling, manufacturing or maintaining weapons outside military operations or collect intelligence other than that of a tactical nature do not

---

46 Supra note 37, 2008 ICRC's Opinion. See also S. Vité, *Typology of Armed Conflicts in International Humanitarian Law: Legal Concepts and Actual Situations*, (2009) 91International Review of the Red Cross, 90.

47 *Prosecutor v Blaškić (Judgment)* ICTY-95–14-T (3 March 2000) para 64 (*Blaškić; Prosecutor v Delalić (Judgment)* ICTY-96–21-T (16 November 1998) para 209.

48 *Prosecutor v Tadić (Jurisdiction)* ICTY-94–1-AR72 (2 October 1995), para 70.

49 On this topic see: J. Pejic, *Terrorist Acts and Groups: A Role for International Law?* (2004) 75 BYIL, 86, 87.

50 Supra note 15, 33.

exercise a 'combat function' and thus should not be targets of attacks. This interpretation of IHL was highly contested during the preparation of the Guidance.[51] First, it creates a fundamental asymmetry in the protection offered by IHL in that soldiers, whatever their hierarchy in the army, e.g. cooks, can be attacked at any time while non-State actors are immune from attacks unless they perform 'continuous combat function'. Second, the concept of 'continuous combat function' is very difficult, if not impossible, to apply.[52] Indeed, a State would need to infiltrate the relevant organisation to make a distinction between those members of a group who perform a 'continuous combat function' and therefore may be attacked at any time, and those who do not and therefore are immune from such attacks. For the US all members of al-Qaeda and its affiliates can be attacked any time as long as they are members of that organisation irrespective of whether or not they perform continuous combat functions.

In the light of all the above it is uncertain whether the armed conflict between the US and Al-Qaeda and its affiliates can be classified as a non-international conflict triggering the application of Article 3. IHL needs to clarify the rules applicable to non-State actors in a situation where non-State actors act against a State across multiple borders.

The classification of a conflict has important consequences for the parties to it, as exemplified by the approach of the US Administration under President George W. Bush to the determination of the status of suspected terrorists captured by the US during the 'war on terror', and detained at Guantanamo Bay, Bagram and other detention facilities (see Chapter 17.5.4.1.A).

17.5.2   G-C I

G-C I provides detailed rules concerning the protection of the sick and wounded on land. It represents a revised and expanded version of the 1929 Geneva Convention.

G-C I establishes a fundamental rule that the sick and wounded, if they refrain from any act of hostility, become 'protected persons', i.e. beneficiaries of protection granted by the Convention.[53] They should be respected and protected in all circumstances. They should be treated humanely and cared for without any distinction based on sex, religion, nationality, political opinions and similar criteria.[54] The wounded and sick of a belligerent party who fulfil the requirements for combatant status should be considered as POWs and the provisions of international instruments concerning POWs should apply to them.

In addition to the sick and wounded, medical and religious personnel and administrative support staff are protected under G-C I.[55] Medical and religious personnel may in no circumstances be attacked, and should at all times be respected and protected by the parties to the conflict.[56] If captured, medical and religious personnel should not be regarded as POWs, but released, unless they are needed to provide care for POWs.[57] A contracting party is bound to ensure that medical establishments and units are, as far as possible, not situated within the vicinity of military objectives.[58]

---

51   see W.H. Park, *Part IX of the ICRC 'Direct Participation in Hostilities' Study: No Mandate, No Expertise, and Legally Incorrect*, 42 NYU Journal of International Law and Politics (2010) 769, at 805.

52   See M. Hlarkova, *Reconstructing the Civilian/Combatant Divide: A Fresh Look at Targeting in Non-international Armed Conflict* (2014) 19/2 Journal of Conflict and Security Law, 251. *Public Committee Against Torture v Government of Israel* (2006) 2 *Israel Law Reports* (2006) 459–529 at 460.

53   Protected persons are defined in Article 13 of GC-I and Article 13 of GC-II.

54   Article 12 GC I and Article 12 GC II.

55   Article 24 and 25 GC I and Articles 36 and 37 GC II.

56   Articles 24–27 GC I and Articles 36 and 37 of GC II, Articles 15–20 Protocol I and Article 9 Protocol II.

57   Articles 28 and 30 GC I, Article 37 GC II and 33 GC III.

58   Article 3 of Annex I to GC I.

17.5.3 G-C II

G-C II contains detailed rules applicable to the sick, wounded and shipwrecked of armed forces at sea. It replaces the 1907 Hague Convention X and the 1899 Hague Convention III. G-C II embodies principles similar to those set out in G-C I.

In respect of hospital ships Article 22 provides that they may in no circumstances be attacked or captured, and at all times should be protected and respected. This being on condition that their names and descriptions have been notified to the parties to the conflict at least ten days before being employed.

17.5.4 G-C III

G-C III concerns the treatment of prisoners of war. It has been complemented by Protocol I which extends the category of persons entitled to the status of 'combatant' and, if they fall into the hands of the enemy, to the status of 'prisoner of war' (POW) and provides some fundamental guarantees in respect of the treatment of persons in the power of a party to the conflict (Article 75).

In respect of the status of prisoners of war the most important distinction is between combatants and non-combatants. Only combatants, when captured by an enemy, can claim the status of POW. Article 4 G-C III defines prisoners of war as persons belonging to one of the following categories:

(1) Members of the armed forces of a Party to the conflict, as well as members of militias or volunteer corps forming part of such armed forces.

(2) Members of other militias and members of other volunteer corps, including those of organised resistance movements, belonging to a Party to the conflict and operating in or outside their own territory, even if this territory is occupied, provided that such militias or volunteer corps, including such organised resistance movements, fulfil the following conditions:

    (a)   that of being commanded by a person responsible for his subordinates;

    (b)   that of having a fixed distinctive sign recognisable at a distance;

    (c)   that of carrying arms openly;

    (d)   that of conducting their operations in accordance with the laws and customs of war.

The requirement that combatants must distinguish themselves from the civilian population is intended to protect civilians against the effects of hostilities. Regular armed forces wear uniforms when directly involved in hostilities. Members, of organised resistance movements belonging to a party to an armed conflict, whether or not recognised by the other party, are exempted from wearing uniforms but have a fundamental duty to distinguish themselves from civilians in the manner described above.

Article 4 G-C III also applies to:

(3) Members of regular armed forces who profess allegiance to a government or an authority not recognised by the Detaining Power.

(4) Persons who accompany the armed forces without actually being members thereof, such as civilian members of military aircraft crews, war correspondents, supply contractors, members of labour units or of services responsible for the welfare of the armed forces, provided that they have received authorisation, from the armed forces which they accompany, who shall provide them for that purpose with an identity card similar to the annexed model.

(5) Members of crews, including masters, pilots and apprentices, of the merchant marine and the crews of civil aircraft of the Parties to the conflict, who do not benefit by more favourable treatment under any other provisions of international law.

(6) Inhabitants of a non-occupied territory, who on the approach of the enemy spontaneously take up arms to resist the invading forces, without having had time to form themselves into regular armed units, provided they carry arms openly and respect the laws and customs of war.

However, there are situations in occupied territories and in wars of national liberation where a combatant cannot distinguish himself in the manner described above without risking being immediately captured. For that reason, Protocol I provides an exception to the above rules, allowing a combatant who cannot distinguish himself from the civilian population to retain his status as a combatant if he carries his arms openly:

■ during each military engagement; and

■ during such time as he is visible to the adversary while he is engaged in a military deployment preceding the launching of an attack in which he is to participate (Article 44(3) Protocol I).

Combatants cannot be punished for the mere fact of fighting, while non-combatants taking part in hostilities are subject to penal consequences as they cannot claim the status of POWs when captured. Thus, a soldier who shoots an enemy soldier cannot be punished, while a civilian who shoots an enemy soldier may be liable for murder. As a rule, combatants when captured may not be punished for the acts they committed during the fighting unless the detaining power would have punished its own soldiers for those acts. For the above reasons for a person captured by enemy forces during an armed conflict it is sometimes a matter of life and death to be recognised as being a POW.

Under G-C III a person is either a combatant or a civilian. The commentary published by the ICRC confirms this view as it states that:

Every person in enemy hands must have some status under international law: he is either a prisoner of war and, as such, covered by the Third Convention, a civilian covered by the Fourth Convention, or again, a member of the medical personnel of the armed forces who is covered by the First Convention. There is no intermediate status; nobody in enemy hands can be outside the law. We feel that that is a satisfactory solution – not only satisfying to the mind, but also, and above all, satisfactory from the humanitarian point of view.[59]

17.5.4.1 'Unlawful combatants' and their treatment

The US administration under ex-President George W. Bush argued that there is a third category of combatants – 'unlawful combatants' – individuals who participate in hostilities without being authorised by governmental authority or under international law. His view was that they may be attacked until killed or captured and when captured may be detained indefinitely without any judicial decision. In brief, when detained neither IHL, nor HRL nor domestic criminal law applies to them. They are in legal limbo.

The argument submitted by the US administration was that the concept of unlawful combatant was recognised under customary law, confirmed by the US Supreme Court in *Ex Parte Quirin*[60] used by an Israeli Military Court in *Military Prosecutor v Omar Mahmud Kassem et al Israel*[61] and by the

---

59   O.M. Uhler (ed.), 'Geneva Convention Relative to the Protection of Civilian Persons in Time of War' in J. Pictet (ed.), *The Geneva Conventions of 12 August 1949: Commentary*, Geneva: ICRC, vol 3, 1958, 51.

60   *Ex parte Quirin, US Supreme Court* (31 July 1942) 317 US 1.

61   Military Court (Ramallah 13 April 1969) (1971) 42 ILR 470–483.

Privy Council in *Osman bin Haji Mohamed Ali and Another v The Public Prosecutor*[62] although the Privy Council did not address the question of the application of G-C III. The counter argument was that the *Quirin* case was decided before the adoption of the G-C III and applied to spies operating in the territory of the US during WWII. The Obama administration repudiated the term 'unlawful combatant'.[63]

A. Treatment of 'unlawful combatants' during the Presidency of George W. Bush

The submission of former President George W. Bush that unlawful combatants are neither protected under IHL, nor under HRL nor under domestic law of the US, was challenged by the US judiciary in particular the US Supreme Court. It rendered, *inter alia*, the following judgments.

In *Rasul v Bush*,[64] the US Supreme Court held that the right to *habeas corpus* was not dependent on US citizenship. The Court found that US courts have jurisdiction over *habeas corpus* petitions by 'unlawful combatants', unless US Congress legislates otherwise. It also held that while Guantanamo Bay, Cuba, was not a part of the US, it was under the sovereign control of the US and therefore, subject to congressional statutes laying out the rules for *habeas corpus* review.

In *Hamdi v Rumsfeld*,[65] the US Supreme Court ruled that individuals held as 'enemy combatants' were entitled to a fair trial. The Court found that, although the US Congress had authorised the detention, the Fifth Amendment of the US Constitution guarantees the right to challenge that detention before a neutral decision-maker.

In *Hamdan v Rumsfeld*,[66] the US Supreme Court invalidated military commissions established by President Bush[67] as inconsistent with the authorisation of Congress. Justice Breyer explained that 'the Court's conclusion ultimately rests upon a single ground: Congress has not issued the Executive a "blank check"'.[68] In the absence of express provisions, the commissions had to comply with the ordinary law of the US and the laws of war. As they did not, they were unconstitutional. Further, their procedures were in breach of Article 3 common to Geneva Conventions I-IV.

In *Boumediene v Bush*[69] the US Supreme Court held that Congress lacked the power to divest federal courts of jurisdiction to entertain *habeas corpus* petitions from Guantanamo detainees who were not US citizens.

---

62   [1969] 1 AC 430.
63   *U.S. Retires 'Enemy Combatant,' Keeps Broad Right to Detain,* The Washington Post, 14 March 2009.
64   542 US 466 (2004).
65   542 US 507 (2004).
66   548 US 557 (2006).
67   After the 9/11 terrorist attacks on the US, President Bush, in his Order of 13 November 2001 stated that the authority to determine which individuals suspected of being members of Al-Qaeda should be transferred to Guantanamo Bay and which should be tried lay with him as President. The order authorised the establishment of military commissions competent to try terrorist suspects. The broad powers exercised by the US President were based on a joint resolution enacted by US Congress on 18 September 2001 entitled 'The Authorisation for Use of Force against Terrorists' which granted the US President the authority to use all 'necessary and appropriate force' against those whom he determined 'planned, authorised, committed or aided' the 9/11 attack or who harboured said groups (Pub L10740, 115 Stat 224.). The rules and regulations to be applied by commissions at Guantanamo were created by the US Military Department of Defence, without the benefit of the existing US military federal codes, regulations or case law, and in breach of international standards for a fair trial On this topic see J. Bravin, *The Terror Courts: Rough Justice at Guantanamo Bay,* Yale: Yale University Press, 2013.
68   548 US 557 (2006), Concurring Opinion Justice Breyer, 1163.
69   553 US 723 (2008).

Additionally, the US District Court for DC in *Al Maqaleh v Gates*[70] held that *habeas corpus* rights apply to persons detained by the US in places outside US territory other than Guantanamo Bay, in this case in the Bagram detention facility situated in the US Air Base in Afghanistan.

B.   Treatment of suspected terrorists under the presidency of Barack Obama

President Barack Obama, who, on 20 January 2009, became the 44th President of the US, the first African American to hold the office, on the second day of his presidency, ordered the closure of Guantanamo Bay detention facility by January 2010,[71] banned the use of torture by US personnel and ordered the Central Intelligence Agency to shut down its secret overseas prisons detaining suspected terrorists.

Despite efforts made by President Obama, Guantanamo Bay has not been closed. As at 1 September 2014 there were 149 detainees. Seventy-nine have been considered as representing a low risk in terms of their threat to US national security. They have been recommended for transfer, normally to their State of nationality, if security conditions imposed by US Congress are met. Most of States of nationality of detainees do not meet those conditions, e.g. Yemen. The remaining 70 detainees, who represent high risk to US national security have been recommended for transfer to prisons inside the US. So far, US Congress has refused to lift the ban on their transfer.[72]

With the official withdrawal of US armed forces from Iraq and Afghanistan the control of all detention facilities located there was transferred to the relevant national authority.

17.5.4.2   The application of G-C III to mercenaries and spies

Some combatants are denied POW status under the Geneva regime. Protocol I expressly provides that mercenaries are not entitled to the status of POW. Article 47 of Additional Protocol I provides a definition of a mercenary. A mercenary is any person who:

■ is recruited abroad to fight in an armed conflict;

■ is directly and actually participating in hostilities;

■ is motivated by 'the desire for private gain, in fact, is promised, by or on behalf of a party to the conflict, material compensation substantially in excess of that promised or paid to combatants of similar ranks and functions in the armed forces of that party';

■ is neither a national of a party to the conflict, nor a resident of territory controlled by a party to the conflict;

■ is neither a member of the armed forces of a party to the conflict nor has been sent by a State which is not a party to the conflict on official duty as a member of its armed forces.

Mercenaries have been used for centuries. However, their use and employment changed in the 1960s when highly trained ex-members of special forces of the UK, the US and other European countries were recruited to fight for money in Africa. They were employed by governments to act ruthlessly and

---

70   *Al Maqaleh v Gates* 604 Γ. 3d 84 (DC Cir, 2010).

71   Exec Order No 13,492, 74 Fed Reg 4,897 (22 Janauary 2009), available at www.whitehouse.gov/the_press_office/
       ClosureOfGuantanamoDetentionFacilities (accessed 21 August 2009).

72   C. Savage, *Decaying Gunatanamo Defies Closing Plans*, International New York Times, 1 September 2014, avail-
       able at www.nytimes.com/2014/09/01/us/politics/decaying-guantanamo-defies-closing-plans.html?_r=0 (accessed
       2 November 2014).

fought in a manner devoid of any humanitarian concern. Following the instructions of their employers they violated international law while their employers denied any connection with them. The atrocities committed by Colonel 'Mad Mike' Hoare and his five commando units in Zaire on behalf of the breakaway regime of Moise Tshombe, or those of Colonel Bob Denard who appointed himself a military governor of Grande Comore, are examples of conduct which appalled the international community and prompted African countries to introduce Article 47 of Protocol I.

The problem regarding mercenaries has also been dealt with outside the Geneva regime at international level by the 1989 Convention against Recruitment, Use, Financing and Training of Mercenaries and at regional level by the 1977 African Mercenary Convention.

It is to be noted that Article 75 of Protocol I containing fundamental guarantees which are applicable to all persons, covers captured mercenaries and spies.

Spies, defined in Article 46 of Protocol I as persons who clandestinely (not wearing the uniform of their armed forces), or under false pretences, gather information in territory controlled by an adverse party, are not considered as combatants. However, a spy, who after rejoining his own or allied armed forces, having completed his mission is subsequently captured is entitled to the status of a prisoner of war, and must not be punished for his previous acts of espionage (Article 46(4)).

17.5.4.3   The treatment of POWs under G-C III.

POWs are considered as prisoners of a State, i.e. the detaining power, not of the individuals or units that captured them. The fundamental principle of IHL is that POWs cannot be punished for direct participation in hostilities. If they have violated IHL prior to their capture they must be punished, subject to safeguards set out in Article 85 G-C III, but still retain their status of POWs under the Convention. The detaining power is responsible for their treatment in international law.

The Geneva regime sets out fundamental rules for the treatment of prisoners of war. They must not be treated inhumanely or dishonourably, and they must not be discriminated against on grounds of race, nationality, religious belief or political opinions, or similar criteria. Any measures of reprisal against them are prohibited. They must be protected at all times, in particular against acts of violence or intimidation and against insults and public curiosity. The public display of POWs is prohibited.[73]

The detaining power must maintain prisoners of war adequately and free of charges. G-C III contains detailed provisions concerning the conditions of internment of POWs, their labour, financial resources during captivity, relations with the outside world, relations with the military authorities in whose power they are and the termination of captivity.

With regard to G-C III the role of a protecting power is particularly important. A protecting power, which must be a neutral State, should be appointed, at the outbreak of an armed conflict, by each party to that conflict, to safeguard its interests.[74] The system of protecting powers was introduced to ensure that parties to an armed conflict comply with the Geneva regime. The main task of the protecting power is to visit prisoners of war and to question them without witnesses. There should be no limitations on the representatives of the protecting power in so far as time or place of visit is concerned. However, a detaining power may impose a restriction only as a temporary and exceptional measure justified by imperative military reasons. If judicial procedures are commenced against a POW[75] the detaining power

---

73   Articles 12–81 GC III.
74   Articles 8 and 126 GC III and Article 5 Protocol I. On this topic see H.S. Levie, *Prisoners of War and the Protecting Power*, (1961) 55 AJIL, 374.
75   Articles 82–108 GC III set out rules relating to penal and disciplinary proceedings while Articles 91–94 impose limits to punishment for escape, or an attempt to escape, or repetitive attempts to escape.

is obliged to inform the protecting power not less than three weeks before the beginning of the trial. The protecting power, in general, looks after the interests of nationals of the party by which it was appointed, who are under adverse control. The protecting power may participate in the settlement of disputes.

The main weakness of the system of protecting powers is that the appointment of protecting powers must be mutually accepted by the parties to an armed conflict. As a result, the system has rarely been used. One example of use is in the Falklands war, during which Switzerland acted as the protecting power for the UK and Brazil did likewise for Argentina. No protecting powers were appointed in the Korean war, in the Viet Nam war or in the conflict between Iraq and Iran.

If the parties to a conflict cannot reach an agreement on protecting powers, the ICRC, or any other humanitarian organisation, may step in, either to act as a protecting power, or to assume humanitarian tasks normally carried out by a protecting power. However, the first possibility is subject to request and the second subject to approval by the detaining power.[76]

The ICRC has a special position. Whether or not a protecting power has been appointed, the ICRC, with the consent of the detaining power, is permitted to work for the protection and relief of prisoners of war.[77]

17.5.5 G-C IV.

G-C IV was the first international instrument focusing exclusively on the protection of civilians in the time of war. It contains detailed provisions relating to the treatment of civilians who, at a given moment and in any manner whatsoever, find themselves, whether in occupied territory or in internment, in the hands of a party to a conflict of which they themselves are not nationals. It also deals, in a limited manner, with the protection of civilians from the effects of hostilities. This Convention has been extensively supplemented by Protocol I.

G-C IV contains special and detailed rules concerning the protection of civilians in occupied territories. Such civilians have no obligations toward the occupying power apart from that consisting of not participating directly in hostilities. IHL neither allows them to violently resist occupation nor to make attempts at liberating the occupied territory by violent means apart from the '*levée en masse*' against the approaching enemy (Article 4(A)(6) GC III) in which case, if captured, they assume the status of combatants. If they resist they may be tried by the occupying power under laws enacted by that power.

The occupying power must ensure the proper functioning of the occupied territory in terms of public health, medical supplies, and the maintenance of law and order. Local law remains in force although the occupying power is allowed to introduce laws ensuring the security of its armed forces. Local courts remain competent. The local population must not be deported and the occupying power may not transfer its own population into the occupied territory.

The issue of the application of G-C IV was examined by the ICJ in the *Legal Consequences of the Construction of a Wall by Israel in the Occupied Palestinian Territory (Advisory Opinion).*[78]

---

76   Articles 8 and 126(3) GC III.
77   Articles 9 and 126(4) GC III and Articles 5(3) and (4) Protocol I.
78   (2004) 43 ILM 1009.

THE LEGAL CONSEQUENCES OF THE CONSTRUCTION OF A WALL BY ISRAEL IN THE OCCUPIED PALESTINIAN TERRITORY (ADVISORY OPINION).FOR DETAILED FACTS SEE CHAPTER 13.5.2.

Facts:

From the 1967 'six days war' Israel has continuously occupied, inter alia, East Jerusalem, the West Bank, and the Gaza Strip territories which subsequent to the 1949 Armistice between Israel and neighbouring Arab States, were considered by the international community as belonging to Palestine. Prior to the 1967 conflict, the Gaza Strip was controlled by Egypt, and the West Bank was annexed to Jordan, but Israel has always regarded both as part of Israel. For that reason, since 1967 Israel has denied the de jure application of G-C IV to the Occupied Palestinian Territory. On 22 October 1967 the Israeli Minister of Justice stated that Israel would not regard itself as an occupying power in the territories which its forces had liberated from foreigners. He emphasised that these territories were, 20 centuries earlier, Jewish. The main legal argument submitted by Israel for non-application of G-C IV was, however, based on the lack of Jordanian or Egyptian sovereignty over the West Bank and Gaza Strip prior to their annexation by Israel in 1967. Both Jordan and Egypt are contracting parties to G-C I-IV. According to Israel G-C IV did not apply, because the territory was not taken over from the territory of a contracting party which would need to be the situation in order to fall within the scope of Article 2 G-C IV. Article 2 provides that:

> *'The Convention shall apply to all cases of partial or total occupation of the territory of a High Contracting Party.'*

Israel's refusal to apply G-C IV to the Occupied Palestinian Territory has been condemned by the international community as illustrated, inter alia, by numerous UNSC Resolutions (see for example Resolution 799 (1992) the UNSC which states that the UNSC 'reaffirms the applicability of the Geneva Convention IV of 12 August 1949 to all Palestinian territories occupied by Israel since 1967, including Jerusalem').

Held:

The ICJ confirmed the de jure application of the Fourth Hague Convention of 1907, to which The Hague Regulations are annexed, to the Occupied Palestinian Territory, despite the fact that Israel has never ratified it. The ICJ based this confirmation on, first, the fact that the Hague Regulations have become part of customary international law and, second, that Israel as a contracting party to G-C IV is bound by its Article 154 which provides that G-C IV is supplementary to ss II and III of the Hague Regulations. The Court found that s III of those Regulations concerning 'military authority over the territory of the hostile state' was of particular relevance to the situation in the Occupied Palestinian Territory.

The ICJ confirmed the de jure application of G-C IV to the Occupied Palestinian Territory. The ICJ interpreted both paragraphs of Article 2 G-C IV. The Court stated that Article 2(1) G-C IV sets out two conditions necessary for the application of the Convention: first that there exists an armed conflict and second, that the conflict has arisen between two contracting States. It held that both conditions were satisfied in respect of the Occupied Palestinian Territory, including East Jerusalem, as there was an armed conflict between

Israel and Jordan, and both Israel and Jordan were contracting parties at the start of the 1967 war. The ICJ noted that the purpose of Article 2(2) G-C IV, which refers to 'occupation of the territory of a High Contracting Party', is to ensure that, even if occupation effected during a conflict meets no armed resistance, G-C IV will still apply and the scope of its application will not be restricted, as determined in Article 2(1). The ICJ emphasised that this interpretation was confirmed by the Convention's travaux preparatoires, by the contracting parties to G-C IV at their conference on 15 July 1999, by the ICRC, by the UNGA, by the UNSC and by Israel's Supreme Court in its judgment of 30 May 2004 in Beit Sourik Village Council v the Government of Israel.[79]

Having established the applicability of G-C IV to the Occupied Palestinian Territory the ICJ examined whether Israel could rely on the 'military exigencies' exception provided for in Article 49(1), which states that the prohibition of forcible transfers of population and deportations may be lifted when the security of the population or imperative military reasons so demand. The ICJ held that the exception does not apply to Article 49(6) which prohibits not only deportations or forced transfers of population, such as those carried out during WWII, but also any measures taken by an occupying power in order to organise or encourage transfers of parts of its own population into an occupied territory.

Therefore, the establishment of Jewish settlements in the Occupied Palestinian Territory, the ICJ emphasised, was in breach of Article 49(6) G-C IV. Additionally, the ICJ stated that, on the facts, Israel could not, in building the wall, rely upon the exception embodied in Article 53 G-C IV concerning the destruction of personal property 'where such destruction is rendered absolutely necessary by military operations'.

In the *Case concerning Armed Activities on the Territory of the Congo (Democratic Republic of the Congo v Uganda)*,[80] the ICJ had to determine whether Uganda had been an occupying power in parts of the Democratic Republic of the Congo (DRC). The ICJ held that in order to be regarded as an occupying power, mere presence of Ugandan armed forces on the territory was not sufficient. More was required, i.e. that Ugandan armed forces substitute their own authority for that of the Congolese Government. This occurred in the Ituri district but not in other parts of the DRC. Rather, these parts were controlled by rebel movements which were not under the control of Uganda. Therefore, Uganda's duty of vigilance in preventing violations of human rights and international humanitarian law by non-State actors only extended to the Ituri district. This position was criticised by Judge Kooijmans in his separate opinion.[81] He stated that the ICJ's narrow interpretation of the concept of belligerent occupation was out of date because the prohibition of the use of force has resulted in many occupants not introducing any kind of direct administration, but seeking arrangements where authority is said to be exercised by local entities, or simply refraining from establishing an administrative system. He therefore argued that elimination of the DRC's authority so putting Uganda in a position to substitute its own authority for that of the DRC was sufficient to make Uganda an occupying power.

---

79   (2004) 43 ILM, 1099.
80   [2006] 45 ILM, 271–395.
81   Ibid, paras 36–50.

17.5.6   Protocol I to G-C I-IV

Protocol I is intended to ensure the widest possible protection of victims of international armed conflicts. It contains provisions concerning the protection of the wounded and sick, the methods and means of warfare, and the protection of civilian population and civilian objects from the effects of hostilities. The main innovations of Protocol I have been discussed above but they can be summarised as follows:

■ The introduction and consolidation of rules concerning the protection of civilian population against effects of hostilities which rules oblige the parties to the conflict to make a distinction between civilian objectives and military objectives, to prohibit reprisals against civilians, and to ensure protection of refugees and stateless persons, etc.

■ The application of Protocol I to colonial wars. Article 96(3) provides that an authority representing a people engaged in a struggle for self-determination against a contracting State to Protocol I may undertake to apply the full Geneva regime by means of a unilateral declaration. During the Algerian War of Independence the Algerian National Liberation Front (FLN), which was recognised as a provisional government exercising a right of self-determination against the historical colonial aggression of France, made such a declaration. As a result France, as well as the FLN, was bound to apply the G-C I-IV to the conflict.

■ Protocol I extended the categories of combatants by adding members of guerilla movements provided they satisfy certain requirements but denied the status of 'combatant' to mercenaries and spies.

17.5.7   Protocol II

See Chapter 17.5.1.2.B.

17.6   Breaches of IHL

Breaches of the rules and customs of war and of conventions relating to IHL constitute an international tort and impose a duty of reparation on the tortfeasor.

Grave breaches are defined in Article 50 G-C I, Article 51 G-C II, Article 130 G-C III; Article 147 G-C IV and Articles 11(4), 85 and 86 of Protocol I. The list of such breaches is too long to be detailed here but, as an example, Article 50 G-C I is reproduced below. It states that the following acts, if committed against persons and property protected under its provisions are regarded as grave breaches:

> wilful killing, torture, inhumane treatment including biological experiments, wilfully causing great suffering or serious injury to body or health, and extensive destruction and appropriation of property, not justified by military necessity and carried out unlawfully and wantonly.

With regard to Protocol II no grave breaches of its provisions are listed. It is presumed that domestic penal law is sufficient to punish the offenders. Article 6 Protocol II offers an additional guarantee by restating the general rules on the prosecution and punishment of criminal offences related to armed conflicts.

Both States and individuals are capable of committing grave breaches of IHL. In the case of a State the rules of State responsibility apply (see Chapter 11). In the case of an individual grave breaches are always criminal offences punishable through penal proceedings. Breaches that are not considered as grave under the Geneva regime are punished through disciplinary procedures.

In is important to note that G-C I-IV and Protocols exclude any possibility of a contracting party derogating from them or of protected persons contracting out of them. Nothing, however, prevents a contracting party from providing rights greater than those established by the Geneva regime.

17.6.1 Implementation of the Geneva regime at national level

G-C I-IV did not establish an international body empowered to search and try persons alleged to have committed grave breaches of humanitarian law. Instead they imposed on the contracting parties the obligation to enact national legislation providing for effective penal sanctions for persons responsible for grave breaches of the Geneva regime, and the obligation to enforce such legislation in national courts. For that reason G-C I-IV do not specify the punishment for grave breaches of their provisions.

Each contracting party undertakes to search for persons accused of committing grave breaches of any of Geneva Conventions and to try them, regardless of their nationality, or to hand them over for trial to another contracting party provided that the latter has made out a *prima facie* case against the person to be tried. Anyone who is suspected of committing, or ordering to be committed, any grave breaches anywhere in the world can be tried in any contracting State. The handing over of such persons to another contracting State is normally done through the extradition procedure.

What happens in practice is that a contracting State assumes jurisdiction over members of enemy forces and civilians who fall into its power, and are suspected of committing grave breaches of G-C I-IV. The accused, including spies and mercenaries, are entitled to a fair trial. This is provided for, *inter alia*, in Articles 5 and 146(3) G-C IV. The Geneva Conventions prohibit any barbarous form of punishment. Under the Geneva Conventions a contracting State is also bound to punish its own nationals accused of committing, or ordering to be committed, grave breaches of their provisions. In practice it is rare for a contracting party to do this, and in the event it does, the punishment is more symbolic than real. One example is provided by the trial of Lieutenant Calley and Captain Medina accused of a massacre of civilians in the Vietnamese village of My Lai. The inhabitants were murdered in cold blood, women were raped, mutilated and killed, children and babies were stabbed with bayonets, even corpses were beheaded. Both Calley and Medina were simple soldiers. The matter of who gave the orders was never established. As a result of a mass-murder enquiry several officers, superiors of Calley, were charged with dereliction of duty and other soldiers were charged with murder.

Only one person was convicted: Lieutenant Calley. On 29 March 1971 he was sentenced to hard labour for life. Three days later, he was released from prison on the specific instruction of President Nixon and allowed to appeal against his sentence. He spent the next 3 years under house arrest in his own apartment in Georgia. On 9 November 1974 he was paroled a free man.

A more recent example of breaches of international humanitarian law is provided by the ill treatment of Iraqi detainees by the US Coalition Forces, in particular in Abu Ghraib prison in Baghdad.

Subsequent to complaints from Iraqi citizens, from various international human rights organisations and from the ICRC, on 19 January 2004 Lieutenant General Ricardo Sanchez, the senior US Commander in Iraq, requested US Central Command to investigate the matter. Major General Antonio M. Taguba, who was appointed to conduct the investigation, completed his report on 26 February 2004. The Taguba Report found evidence of systematic and illegal 'sadistic, blatant, and wanton criminal abuses ... inflicted on several detainees' in Abu Ghraib prison. Those abuses consisted, *inter alia*, of physical abuses, the videotaping and photographing of naked male and female detainees, posing detainees in various sexually explicit positions for photographing, forcing detainees to remove their clothing and remain naked for several hours at a time, a male military police guard having sex with a female detainee, and intimidating and frightening of detainees using military working dogs, etc.[82] The Report was not made public until graphic pictures depicting US soldiers abusing Iraqi prisoners were aired by the US TV Channel CBS on '60 Minutes II' on 28 April 2004.

---

82   Taguba Report, Part One, Findings of Fact, Para 5, available at www. news.findlaw.com/hdocs/docs/iraq/tagubarpt. html (accessed 2 September 2009).

While the US government has refused to apply G-C III to detainees held at Guantanamo Bay who were captured during 'Operation Enduring Freedom' in Afghanistan, it has never challenged the applicability of IHL, in particular G-C III and IV, to 'Operation Iraqi Freedom' regarding the invasion of Iraq.

Many procedural and substantive requirements of IHL were breached by the manner of arrest of Iraqi citizens, and their subsequent treatment and detention in Abu Ghraib prison in Bagdad. Fundamental provisions of G-C III were violated in respect of Iraqi POWs. The provisions require the humane treatment of POWs at all times (Article 13), prohibit the application of physical and moral coercion against protected persons, in particular to obtain information from them and from third parties (Article 31), and prohibit murder, torture, corporal punishment and any other measures of brutality, whether applied by civilian or military agents (Article 32). Among the detainees in Abu Ghraib prison were civilians. G-C IV requires that a distinction must be made between civilians, and POWs, and that civilians must be treated with dignity and respect (Articles 5, 27, 31 and 32. In addition to the violations of G-C III and IV the US was in breach of customary HRL and many HRs conventions to which the US is a contracting party, such as the ICCPR and the CAT. The US government did not take any measures as a result of the ICRC or the Taguba reports. It was only when the abuses in Abu Ghraib were made public by the media that the US government decided to act. At the time of writing, only a few low-ranking US soldiers have been sentenced to prison for atrocities committed at Abu Ghraib. Some high ranking officials were reprimanded, or demoted.[83]

17.6.2 The enforcement of IHL at international level

Substantial progress has been made in the enforcement of IHL at the international level. This is mainly due to the end of the Cold War since when there has been a new spirit of co-operation between States in the development and enforcement of HRL and IHL. On the one hand, States respecting IHL and HRL are willing to prosecute grave breaches of IHL committed abroad if there is any link which allows national courts to assume jurisdiction (see Chapter 9.6), and on the other, many international tribunals have been established to bring to justice the most notorious abusers of both IHL and HRL. In particular the establishment of the International Criminal Court (ICC) ensures that 'no ruler, no junta and no army anywhere can abuse human rights with impunity'.[84]

The ICC, the first international permanent criminal court, was established on the basis of the Rome Statute of the ICC which entered into force on 1 July 2002. As at 1 September 2014 the number of contracting parties to the ICC was 122.

Unlike other international or internationalised (see below) criminal courts and tribunals, the ICC's jurisdiction is based, by virtue of Article 17 of the Rome Statute, on the principle of complementarity under which the ICC has jurisdiction only if the competent national authorities are 'unwilling or unable genuinely to carry out investigation or prosecution'. The principle that the perpetrators of core international crimes should be brought before national courts has long been recognised by the international community. However, the punishment by national courts of genocide, war crimes and similar serious violations of human rights, whether committed in internal or international conflicts, may be obstructed. In particular, national courts are often unable to try offenders because governments are reluctant to punish their nationals, or because this may jeopardise the existence of fragile democratic structures of a new government of national reconciliation. In some cases national institutions collapse, as in the case of Rwanda and Cambodia, and there are no appropriate courts.

---

83   See The Editorial Board, *Abu Ghraib, 10 Years Later*, International New York Times, 22 April 2014, available at: www.nytimes.com/2014/04/23/opinion/abu-ghraib-10-years-later.html?_r=0 (accessed 19 September 2014).

84   Kofi Annan, UNS-G: see www.un.org/law/icc/general/overview.htm (accessed 24 October 2004).

Article 17 strikes a right balance between the respect for a State's sovereignty in that it ensures that a State, not the ICC, has the primary jurisdiction to prosecute and punish the core international crimes, and on the other, ensures that suspected perpetrators are brought to justice.[85] If a State refuses to co-operate with the ICC, or in a situation where a State is not a party to the Rome Statute, by virtue of Articles 13 (b) of the Statute, the UNSC may, acting under Chapter VII, refer to the ICC situations in which crimes within the jurisdiction *ratione materiae* of the ICC appear to have been committed (see Chapters 1.4 and 5.12.2.3). So far the UNSCl has referred the situation in Darfur, Sudan in 2005, and in Libya in 2011- all non-States Parties to the ICC. However, the referral of the situation in Syria was vetoed by Russia and China in May 2014, while the UK and US have always staunchly opposed the UNSC even considering a referral of the situation in the Occupied Palestinian Territories to the ICC Prosecutor. This shows that the UNSC, on many occasions, has failed victims and undermined international justice efforts.

The contribution of the predecessors of the ICC, i.e. the four international criminal courts (the International Military Tribunal (IMT) at Nuremberg (See Chapter 5.12.2.1) the International Military Tribunal for the Far East (IMTFE), the International Criminal Tribunal for the Former Yugoslavia (ICTY) and the International Criminal Tribunal for Rwanda (ICTR) (see Chapter 5.12.2.2)), to the enforcement of IHL and HRL is substantial. Each of those four courts was created on an *ad hoc* basis in response to a sense of outrage felt by the international community over atrocities committed by a particular group of people in a particular place. The jurisdiction of each court was subject to limits in terms of time and place.

In addition to these above mentioned truly international criminal tribunals, there are, at the time of writing, hybrid or mixed or internationalised criminal tribunals in Sierra Leone, East Timor, Kosovo and Cambodia[86] seated in the States where the crimes were committed. They have both local and international judges and prosecutors and apply substantive and procedural rules of national and international criminal law.

17.7 The role of the International Committee of the Red Cross (ICRC)

The proposals submitted by Henri Dunant in his book entitled *A Memory of Solferino* attracted the attention of Gustave Moynier, who was a Swiss lawyer and the chairman of a local charity (the Geneva Public Welfare Society). At his initiative a five-member committee was set up to further examine Dunant's proposals. This was the beginning of the International Committee of the Red Cross which initially was called the International Committee for Relief of the Wounded. The first meeting of the organisation took place on 17 February 1863.

The ICRC is a private Swiss organisation made up entirely of Swiss nationals. More than 12,000 people work for it. The ICRC is independent from any government, including the Swiss government, and from any international organisation. It is detached from all political issues relating to conflicts. Its mission is to bring relief and assistance to the victims of armed conflicts and internal violence.[87] Its independence, impartiality and Swiss identity (which ensures its neutrality) are the guarantees of the ICRC's acceptability to all parties involved in armed conflicts or internal disturbances.

---

85   J.K. Kleffner, *The Impact of Complementarity on National Implementation of Substantive International Criminal Law* (2003) 1 JICJ, 86.

86   C. Romano, A. Nollkaemper and J. Kleffner (eds), *Internationalized Criminal Courts and Tribunals: Sierra Leone, East Timor, Kosovo, and Cambodia*, Oxford: Oxford University Press, 2004.

87   F. Bugnion, *The International Committee of the Red Cross and the Protection of War Victims*, Geneva/Oxford: ICRC/Macmillan, 2003.

The four Geneva Conventions and Protocols recognise the special status of the ICRC, and allocate special tasks to it. In particular, the ICRC may offer its services as a protecting power if no agreement can be reached between warring parties as to the appointment of a protecting power. The system of protecting powers has rarely worked (see Chapter 17.5.4.3). As a result, in fact, the ICRC has assumed, in many international conflicts, the humanitarian functions of a protecting power.[88] Under the Geneva Conventions the ICRC has been granted a general right of intervention in connection with humanitarian matters which it exercises irrespective of whether or not a protecting power has been appointed[89] Delegates of the ICRC visit prisoners of war, detainees and occupied territories.[90] They interview the POWs and detainees without witnesses in order to ensure that they are being treated humanely. The ICRC makes confidential reports to the authority concerned and if abuses have been discovered urges it to rectify the situation.

Since its inception the ICRC has been a driving force behind the development of international humanitarian law. At its initiative the first Geneva Convention for the Amelioration of the Condition of the Wounded in Armies in the Field was adopted in 1864. Since then the ICRC has been active in drafting, negotiating and amending international humanitarian law. On the basis of the ICRC's experience gained on battlefields it has made proposals aimed at improving existing conventions. This resulted in major revisions of international humanitarian law in 1906, 1929, 1949 and 1977. The ICRC is very much involved in the development of IHL and is constantly assessing it in order to ensure that IHL is attuned to the reality of armed conflicts and internal disturbances.

Another important function of the ICRC is carried out through its Central Tracing Agency (CTA) which maintains records of persons captured, detained, interned, killed and injured.[91] At the request of relatives the CTA provides such information as is in its possession, *via* the local Red Cross, about missing members of their families. The task of the CTA also consists of exchanging messages between family members, separated by hostilities, who are unable to get in touch because the normal communication channels have broken down or because such persons are detained.

The ICRC acts as a neutral intermediary between all parties involved in a conflict urging them to comply with humanitarian law and, if asked, facilitates political negotiations and thus contributes to the restoration of peace and stability.

The ICRC provides medical assistance to the sick and wounded. Its medical activities encompass not only the supply of medical equipment, but also of medical personnel when local hospitals are unable to cope with the influx of wounded or when there are no medical personnel. The ICRC also takes measures to prevent local populations from becoming sick as a result of poor hygiene. The ICRC technical personnel repair water-supply systems destroyed or damaged by conflicts, and set up safe water-distribution and waste-disposal systems in camps, and other settlements, in order to prevent the outbreak of epidemics.

The most generally recognised task of the ICRC is the supply of relief aid to POWs, refugees, displaced persons and people in occupied territories in the form of the famous 'Red Cross Parcels'. The ICRC is especially concerned with internally displaced persons. However, the distribution of food is a temporary measure. Relief programmes of the ICRC, as far as possible, encompass rehabilitation allowing people to stay on their land and start life anew. Agricultural tools and seeds, livestock vaccines, etc, when appropriate, are distributed together with food parcels.

---

88   Article 10(3) common to GC I, II and III, Article 11(3) GC IV and Article 5(4) Protocol I.
89   Articles 9 and 126(4) GC III and Article 5(3) and (4) Protocol I.
90   Article 126(5) GC III and Article 143(5) Protocol I.
91   Article 16(2) GC I; Article 123 GC III; Article 140 of GC IV and Article 33(3) Protocol I.

Another important task of the ICRC is its work for the understanding and dissemination of knowledge of international humanitarian law. The ICRC is very persistent in encouraging governments to ratify the Geneva Conventions and Additional Protocols and to implement them. Through its own delegates, national societies, the Swiss government, international organisations and any other available means the ICRC puts this subject on national agendas, and uses all reasonable means to convince reluctant governments to become parties to the 1949 Conventions and 1977 Protocols. Its reward is that almost all countries in the world are now bound by the Geneva Conventions plus the fact that ratifications of Protocols have increased in recent years.

In fulfilling its task the ICRC is not alone. The ICRC is the founder of the International Red Cross and Red Crescent Movement, which is the largest humanitarian network in the world and comprises the following:

- the ICRC which directs and co-ordinates the international work of the components of the movement in connection with armed conflicts and internal violence;

- the National Red Cross and Red Crescent societies which are considered as 'auxiliary to public authorities' in their respective countries in the humanitarian field. Each society must be approved by the ICRC. They basically work in their own country. In peacetime they provide relief in the case of disasters, and fulfil humanitarian tasks such as caring for the old, sick, poor, etc. In wartime their first-aid personnel become part of the national army medical services. National societies play an important role in disseminating international humanitarian law through conferences, workshops, etc. There are, at the time of writing, 186 national societies of the Red Cross and Red Crescent all over the world;

- the International Federation of Red Cross and Red Crescent Societies, which brings together the national societies. The Federation co-ordinates international assistance from national societies to victims of natural and man-made disasters with the exception of those occurring in conflict areas. Its objectives are described in Article 2 of its Constitution according to which the Federation is 'to inspire, encourage, facilitate and promote at all times all forms of humanitarian activities by the member society with a view to preventing and alleviating human suffering and thereby contributing to the maintenance and the promotion of peace in the world'.

On 12 August 1999, at the 50th anniversary of the signing of the four Geneva Conventions, international figures, including UNS-G Kofi Annan and Prince Hassan of Jordan, gathered in the same room in Geneva's town hall to sign the appeal calling on all nations to eradicate war. Until this occurs the ICRC's presence and exemplary work will continue to be needed.

RECOMMENDED READING

Books

Booth, W., *Weapons and the Law of Armed Conflicts*, Oxford: Oxford University Press, 2009.

Bravin, J., *The Terror Courts: Rough Justice at Guantanamo Bay*, New Haven, CT: Yale University Press, 2013.

Dinstein, Y., *The Conduct of Hostilities under the Law of International Armed Conflict*, Cambridge: Cambridge University Press, 2004.

Forsythe, D.P., *The Humanitarians: The International Committee of the Red Cross*, Cambridge: Cambridge University Press, 2005.

ICRC and IFRC (eds), *Handbook of the International Red Cross and Red Crescent Movement*, 14th edn, Geneva: ICRC, 2008.

Joyner, D.H., *International Law and the Proliferation of Weapons of Mass Destruction*, Oxford: Oxford University Press, 2009.

Mujezinović Larsen, K., Guldahl Cooper, C. and Nystuen, G. (eds), *Searching for a 'Principle of Humanity' in International Humanitarian Law*, Cambridge: Cambridge University Press, 2013.

Rodley, M., *The Treatment of Prisoners under International Law*, Oxford: Oxford University Press, 2009.

Sivakumaran, S., *The Law of Non-international Armed Conflict*, Oxford: Oxford University Press, 2012.

Wilmshurst, E. (ed.), *International Law and the Classification of Conflicts*, Oxford: Oxford University Press, 2012.

Articles

Bethlehem, D., *The Relationship between International Humanitarian Law and International Human Rights Law in Situations of Armed Conflict* (2013) 2/2 Cambridge Journal of International and Comparative Law, 180.

Cassese, A., *The Martens Clause: Half a Loaf or Simply Pie in the Sky* (2000) 11 EJIL, 187.

Dinstein, Y., *Unlawful Combatancy* (2002) 32 Israel YB Hum Rts 247.

Gross, A.M., *Human Proportions: Are Human Rights the Emperor's New Clothes of the International Law of Occupation?* (2007) 18 EJIL, 1.

Hlarkova, M., *Reconstructing the Civilian/Combatant Divide: A Fresh Look at Targeting in Non-international Armed Conflict* (2014) 19/2 Journal of Conflict and Security Law, 251.

Mallette-Piasecki, M., *Missing the Target: Where the Geneva Conventions Fall Short in the Context of Targeted Killing* (2013) 76/1 Albany Law Review, 263.

Okakhelashvili, A., *The Interaction between Human Rights and Humanitarian Law: Fragmentation, Conflict, Parallelism, or Convergence?* (2008) 19 EJIL, 161.

Sassòli, M., 'Targeting: The Scope and Utility of the Concept of "Military Objectives" for the Protection of Civilians in Contemporary Armed Conflicts' in D. Wippmann and M. Evangelista (eds), *New Wars, New Laws? Applying the Laws of War in Twenty-First Century Conflicts*, New York: Transnational Publishers, 2005, 181–210.

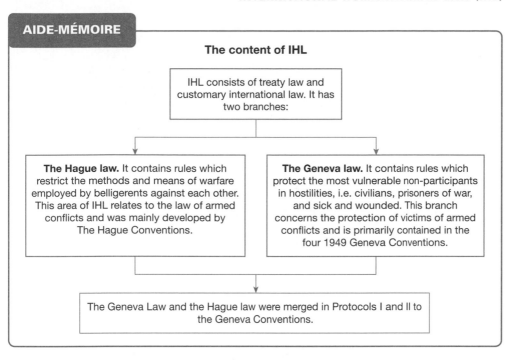

AIDE-MÉMOIRE

The content of IHL

IHL consists of treaty law and customary international law. It has two branches:

The Hague law. It contains rules which restrict the methods and means of warfare employed by belligerents against each other. This area of IHL relates to the law of armed conflicts and was mainly developed by The Hague Conventions.

The Geneva law. It contains rules which protect the most vulnerable non-participants in hostilities, i.e. civilians, prisoners of war, and sick and wounded. This branch concerns the protection of victims of armed conflicts and is primarily contained in the four 1949 Geneva Conventions.

The Geneva Law and the Hague law were merged in Protocols I and II to the Geneva Conventions.

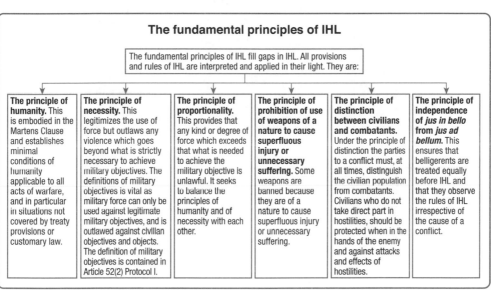

The fundamental principles of IHL

The fundamental principles of IHL fill gaps in IHL. All provisions and rules of IHL are interpreted and applied in their light. They are:

The principle of humanity. This is embodied in the Martens Clause and establishes minimal conditions of humanity applicable to all acts of warfare, and in particular in situations not covered by treaty provisions or customary law.

The principle of necessity. This legitimizes the use of force but outlaws any violence which goes beyond what is strictly necessary to achieve military objectives. The definitions of military objectives is vital as military force can only be used against legitimate military objectives, and is outlawed against civilian objectives and objects. The definition of military objectives is contained in Article 52(2) Protocol I.

The principle of proportionality. This provides that any kind or degree of force which exceeds that what is needed to achieve the military objective is unlawful. It seeks to balance the principles of humanity and of necessity with each other.

The principle of prohibition of use of weapons of a nature to cause superfluous injury or unnecessary suffering. Some weapons are banned because they are of a nature to cause superfluous injury or unnecessary suffering.

The principle of distinction between civilians and combatants. Under the principle of distinction the parties to a conflict must, at all times, distinguish the civilian population from combatants. Civilians who do not take direct part in hostilities, should be protected when in the hands of the enemy and against attacks and effects of hostilities.

The principle of independence of *jus in bello* from *jus ad bellum*. This ensures that belligerents are treated equally before IHL and that they observe the rules of IHL irrespective of the cause of a conflict.

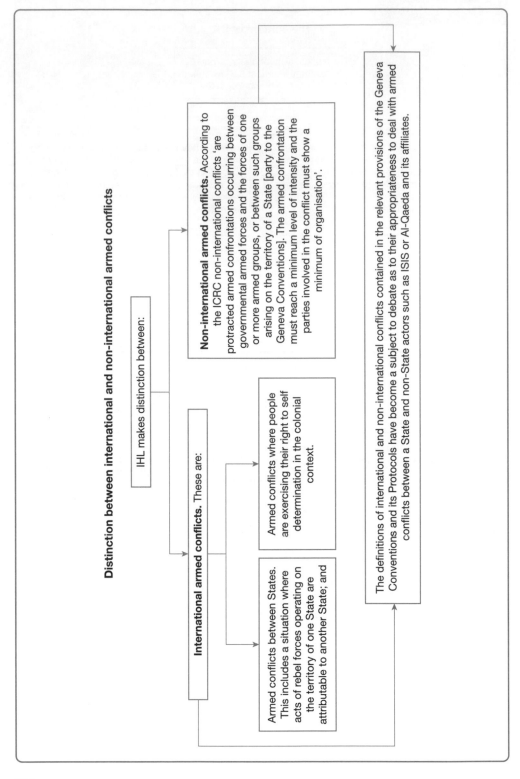

Distinction between international and non-international armed conflicts

IHL makes distinction between:

International armed conflicts. These are:

Armed conflicts between States. This includes a situation where acts of rebel forces operating on the territory of one State are attributable to another State; and

Armed conflicts where people are exercising their right to self determination in the colonial context.

Non-international armed conflicts. According to the ICRC non-international conflicts 'are protracted armed confrontations occurring between governmental armed forces and the forces of one or more armed groups, or between such groups arising on the territory of a State [party to the Geneva Conventions]. The armed confrontation must reach a minimum level of intensity and the parties involved in the conflict must show a minimum of organisation'.

The definitions of international and non-international conflicts contained in the relevant provisions of the Geneva Conventions and its Protocols have become a subject to debate as to their appropriateness to deal with armed conflicts between a State and non-State actors such as ISIS or Al-Qaeda and its affiliates.

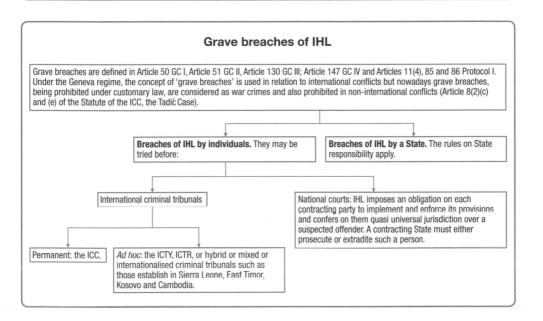

The distinction between combatants and civilians

The distinction between combatants and civilians. This applies to **international conflicts** only. This concept is not recognized with regard to the non-international conflicts. **Combatants**:

| **Have the right to directly participate in an armed conflict.** When actively participating in hostilities can be attacked and killed but, even when fighting, are protected against some means and methods of warfare (Article 35 or Protocol I). | When captured by the enemy become **POWs**. | When POWs **cannot be punished for their direct participation in hostilities**, but may be punished if they violate IHL although they remain POWs (even if convicted of war crimes). | When captured are normally interned. Their internment is not to punish them but to prevent them from direct participation in hostilities or to protect them. While in internment they should be **treated humanely in accordance with the Geneva Convention III**. | **After termination of the conflict should be repatriated**, but HRL prohibits forcible reputation in some situations, i.e. if the person concerned is a refugee within the meaning of Article 1A of the 1951 Geneva Convention on the Status of Refugees, or is in danger of being subjected to torture if repatriated contrary to Article 3 CAT. |

Grave breaches of IHL

Grave breaches are defined in Article 50 GC I, Article 51 GC II, Article 130 GC III; Article 147 GC IV and Articles 11(4), 85 and 86 Protocol I. Under the Geneva regime, the concept of 'grave breaches' is used in relation to international conflicts but nowadays grave breaches, being prohibited under customary law, are considered as war crimes and also prohibited in non-international conflicts (Article 8(2)(c) and (e) of the Statute of the ICC, the Tadić Case).

Breaches of IHL by individuals. They may be tried before:

Breaches of IHL by a State. The rules on State responsibility apply.

International criminal tribunals

National courts: IHL imposes an obligation on each contracting party to implement and enforce its provisions and confers on them quasi universal jurisdiction over a suspected offender. A contracting State must either prosecute or extradite such a person.

Permanent: the ICC.

Ad hoc: the ICTY, ICTR, or hybrid or mixed or internationalised criminal tribunals such as those establish in Sierra Leone, East Timor, Kosovo and Cambodia.

INDEX